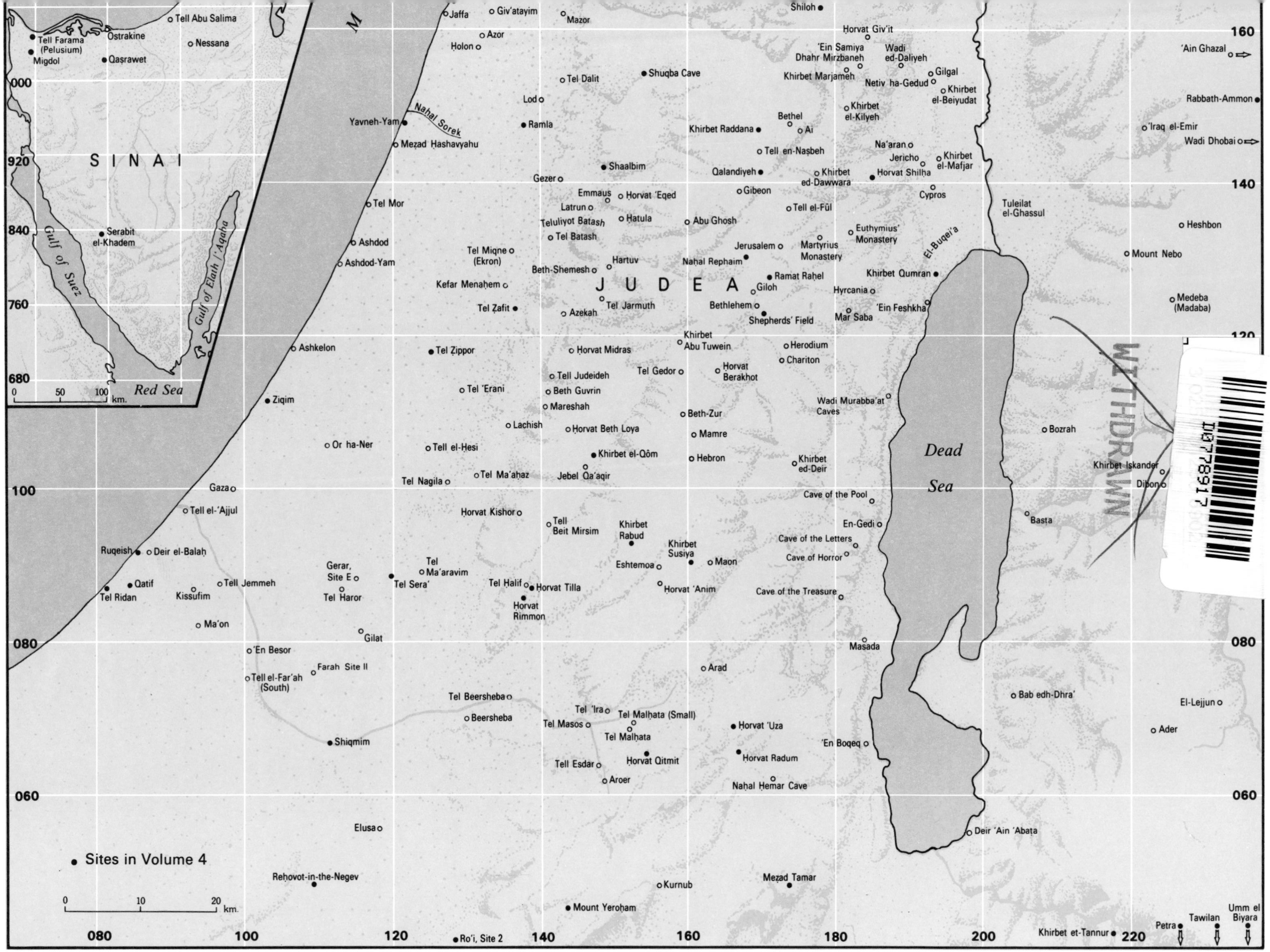

Sites in Volume 4
SINAI
Gulf of Suez
Gulf of Elath / 'Aqaba
Red Sea
JUDEA
Dead Sea
Tell Farama (Pelusium)
Migdol
Ostrakine
Qasrawet
Tell Abu Salima
Nessana
Serabit el-Khadem
Jaffa
Giv'atayim
Mazor
Azor
Holon
Tel Dalit
Shuqba Cave
Lod
Ramla
Yavneh-Yam
Nahal Sorek
Mezad Hashavyahu
Tel Mor
Ashdod
Ashdod-Yam
Gezer
Shaalbim
Emmaus
Latrun
Horvat 'Eqed
Hatula
Teluliyot Batash
Tel Batash
Tel Miqne (Ekron)
Kefar Menahem
Beth-Shemesh
Hartuv
Tel Zafit
Azekah
Tel Jarmuth
Ashkelon
Tel Zippor
Horvat Midras
Tell Judeideh
Beth Guvrin
Mareshah
Tel 'Erani
Lachish
Horvat Beth Loya
Ziqim
Or ha-Ner
Tell el-Hesi
Khirbet el-Qôm
Jebel Qa'aqir
Tel Ma'ahaz
Tel Nagila
Gaza
Tell el-'Ajjul
Horvat Kishor
Tell Beit Mirsim
Khirbet Rabud
Ruqeish
Deir el-Balah
Qatif
Tel Ridan
Kissufim
Tell Jemmeh
Ma'on
Gerar, Site E
Tel Haror
Tel Ma'aravim
Tel Sera'
Tel Halif
Horvat Tilla
Horvat Rimmon
Gilat
'En Besor
Tell el-Far'ah (South)
Farah Site II
Tel Beersheba
Beersheba
Shiqmim
Elusa
Rehovot-in-the-Negev
Ro'i, Site 2
Mount Yeroham
Kurnub
Mezad Tamar
Tel 'Ira
Tel Malhata (Small)
Tel Malhata
Tel Masos
Tel Esdar
Aroer
Horvat Qitmit
Horvat 'Uza
Horvat Radum
Nahal Hemar Cave
'En Boqeq
Arad
Eshtemoa
Khirbet Susiya
Maon
Horvat 'Anim
Shiloh
Horvat Giv'it
'Ein Samiya
Dhahr Mirzbaneh
Khirbet Marjameh
Wadi ed-Daliyeh
Netiv ha-Gedud
Gilgal
Khirbet el-Beiyudat
Khirbet el-Kiliyeh
Bethel
Ai
Khirbet Raddana
Tell en-Nasbeh
Na'aran
Jericho
Khirbet el-Mafjar
Horvat Shilha
Qalandiyeh
Khirbet ed-Dawwara
Gibeon
Tell el-Fûl
Cypros
Abu Ghosh
Euthymius' Monastery
Martyrius Monastery
Jerusalem
Nahal Rephaim
Ramat Rahel
Giloh
El-Buqei'a
Khirbet Qumran
Hyrcania
Bethlehem
Shepherds' Field
Mar Saba
'Ein Feshkha
Khirbet Abu Tuwein
Herodium
Chariton
Tel Gedor
Horvat Berakhot
Wadi Murabba'at Caves
Beth-Zur
Mamre
Hebron
Khirbet ed-Deir
Cave of the Pool
En-Gedi
Cave of the Letters
Cave of Horror
Cave of the Treasure
Masada
Deir 'Ain 'Abata
Tuleilat el-Ghassul
'Ain Ghazal
Rabbath-Ammon
'Iraq el-Emir
Wadi Dhobai
Heshbon
Mount Nebo
Medeba (Madaba)
Bozrah
Khirbet Iskander
Dibon
Basta
Bab edh-Dhra'
El-Lejjun
Ader
Khirbet et-Tannur
Petra
Tawilan
Umm el Biyara
000
920
840
760
680
0
50
100 km.
0
10
20 km.
160
140
120
100
080
060
080
100
120
140
160
180
200
220

THE NEW ENCYCLOPEDIA OF ARCHAEOLOGICAL EXCAVATIONS IN THE HOLY LAND

THE NEW ENCYCLOPEDIA OF ARCHAEOLOGICAL EXCAVATIONS IN THE HOLY LAND

EPHRAIM STERN, Editor
Hebrew University of Jerusalem

AYELET LEWINSON-GILBOA, Assistant Editor
Hebrew University of Jerusalem

JOSEPH AVIRAM, Editorial Director
Israel Exploration Society

Volume 4

THE ISRAEL EXPLORATION SOCIETY & CARTA, JERUSALEM

SIMON & SCHUSTER
A Paramount Communications Company

New York London Toronto Sydney Tokyo Singapore

Printing Number 6 5 4 3 2 1

Printed in Israel

Library of Congress Cataloging-in-Publication Data

The New encyclopedia of archaeological excavations in the Holy Land / editor, Ephraim Stern.
p. cm.
Includes bibliographical references.
ISBN 0-13-276288-9 (set)
ISBN 0-13-276320-6 (v.4)
1. Palestine–Antiquities–Encyclopedias. 2. Bible–Antiquities–Encyclopedias. 3. Excavations (Archaeology)–Palestine–Encyclopedias. I. Stern, Ephraim, 1934-
DS111.A2N488 1992
933'.003–dc20

92-17712
CIP

ABBREVIATIONS

a. acre
AH *anno Hegirae*, in the year of the Hegira
Am. Amos
'Arakh. *'Arakhin*
Avot *Pirkei Avot*
A.Z. *'Avodah Zarah*
b. born
B.B. *Bava Batra*
BCE before the common era
Beits. *Beitsah*
Bekh. *Bekhorot*
Ber. *Berakhot*
Bik. *Bikkurim*
B.M. *Bava Metsi'a*
BP before the present
B.Q. *Bava Qamma*
B.T. Babylonian Talmud
c. *circa*, about, approximately
cat. catalogue
CE of the common era
cent. century
cf. *confer*, compare
1 Chr. 1 Chronicles
2 Chr. 2 Chronicles
cm centimeter
Col. Colossians
comp. compiler (pl., comps.)
1 Cor. 1 Corinthians
2 Cor. 2 Corinthians
cu cubic
d. died
Dan. Daniel
Dem. *Dem'ai*
diss. dissertation
div. division
dm decimeter
Dt. Deuteronomy
EB Early Bronze
Eccles. Ecclesiastes
ed. editor (pl., eds.); edition; edited by
'Eduy. *'Eduyyot*
e.g. *exempli gratia*, for example
Eph. Ephesians
'Eruv. *'Eruvin*
ESR Electro Spin Resonance
et al. *et alii*, and others
etc. *et cetera*, and so forth
Ex. Exodus
Ezek. Ezekiel
f. and following (pl., ff.)
fig. figure (pl., figs.)
g gram
Gal. Galatians
Gen. Genesis
Git. *Gittin*
Hab. Habakkuk
Ḥag. *Ḥagigah*
Ḥal. *Ḥallah*
Heb. Hebrews
Hg. Haggai
Hor. *Horayot*
Hos. Hosea
Ḥul. *Ḥullin*
ibid. *ibidem*, in the same place
id. *idem*, the same
in. inch
in prep. in preparation
Iron Iron Age
Is. Isaiah
Jas. James
Jer. Jeremiah
Jg. Judges
Jn. John
Jon. Jonah
Jos. Joshua
J.T. Jerusalem Talmud
Kel. *Kelim*
Ker. *Keritot*
Ket. *Ketubbot*
kg kilogram
1 Kg. 1 Kings
2 Kg. 2 Kings
Kil. *Kil'ayim*
km kilometer
l. locus
Lam. Lamentations
LB Late Bronze
lb. pound
Lev. Leviticus
Lk. Luke
loc. cit. the place cited
m meter
Mal. Malachi
1 Macc. 1 Maccabees
2 Macc. 2 Maccabees
Mak. *Makkot*
Makh. *Makhshirin*
MB Middle Bronze
Meg. *Megillah*
Me'il. *Me'ilah*
Men. *Menaḥot*
mi. mile
Mi. Micah
Mid. *Middot*
mill. millennium
Miq. *Miqva'ot*
Mk. Mark
ml milliliter
mm millimeter
Mo'ed Q. *Mo'ed Qatan*
Mt. Matthew
MT Masoretic text
n. note
Nah. Nahum
Naz. *Nazir*
n.d. no date
Ned. *Nedarim*
Neg. *Nega'im*
Neh. Nehemiah
Nid. *Niddah*
no. number (pl., nos.)
n.p. no place
n.s. new series
Num. Numbers
Ob. Obadiah
Ohal. *Ohalot*
op. cit. *opere citato*, in the work cited
Par. *Parah*
PEF Palestine Exploration Fund
Pes. *Pesaḥim*
Ph.D. Doctor of Philosophy
Phil. Philippians
Philem. Philemon
pl. plate (pl., pls.)
PPN Pre-Pottery Neolithic
PPNA Pre-Pottery Neolithic A
PPNB Pre-Pottery Neolithic B
PPNC Pre-Pottery Neolithic C
Proc. Proceedings
Prov. Proverbs
Ps. Psalms
P.T. Palestinian Talmud
pt. part
1 Pt. 1 Peter
2 Pt. 2 Peter
Qid. *Qiddushin*
Qin. *Qinnim*
q.v. *quod vide*, which see
r. reigned; ruled
Rab. *Rabbah*
rev. revised
Rev. Revelation
Rom. Romans
1 Sam. 1 Samuel
2 Sam. 2 Samuel
San. *Sanhedrin*
sect. section
Shab. *Shabbat*
Shev. *Shevu'ot*
Sheq. *Sheqalim*
Song Song of Solomon
Sot. *Sotah*
sq square
St. Saint (pl., SS.)
Suk. *Sukkah*
Ta'an. *Ta'anit*
Tam. *Tamid*
Tem. *Temurah*
Ter. *Terumot*
1 Thes. 1 Thessalonians
2 Thes. 2 Thessalonians
1 Tim. 1 Timothy
2 Tim. 2 Timothy
TL Thermoluminescence
Toh. *Tohorot*
tr. translator; translated by
Trans. Transactions
Univ. University
UTM Universal Transverse Mercator
Zech. Zechariah
Zeph. Zephaniah

BOOKS/WORKS

Abel, *GP* F. M. Abel, *Géographie de la Palestine* 1–2, Paris 1933–1938
AE *L'Année Épigraphique* (quoted by year and inscription no.)
Aharoni, *LB* Y. Aharoni, *The Land of the Bible: A Historical Geography*, London 1966, 1967 (2d ed.)
Akkadica Supplementum 7–8 (1989) *Archaeology of Jordan* 2/1–12, Field Reports, Surveys and Sites (Akkadica Supplementum 7–8, eds. D. Homes-Fredericq and J. B. Hennessy), Leuven 1989
Alt, *GIPT* A. Alt, *Die Griechischen Inschriften der Palästina Tertia Westlich der Araba*, Berlin and Leipzig 1921 (quoted by inscription no.)
Alt, *KSch.* A. Alt, *Kleine Schriften zur Geschichte des Volkes Israel* 1–3, Munich 1953–1959
American Archaeology in the Mideast *American Archaeology in the Mideast: A History of the ASOR* (ed. P. T. King), Philadelphia 1983
ANET *Ancient Near Eastern Texts Relating to the Old Testament* (ed. J. B. Pritchard), Princeton 1950
ASOR Symposia *Symposia Celebrating the Seventy-fifth Anniversary of the Founding of the American Schools of Oriental Research (1900–1975)* (ed. F. M. Cross, Jr.), Cambridge, Mass. 1979
ASR *Ancient Synagogues Revealed* (ed. L. I. Levine), Jerusalem 1981
Avi-Yonah, *HL* M. Avi-Yonah, *The Holy Land*, Grand Rapids 1966
Baldi D. Baldi, *Enchiridion Locorum Sanctorum*, Jerusalem 1935 (quoted by text no.)
BAR/IS *British Archaeological Reports*, International Series, Oxford
Benoit et al., *Discoveries* 2 P. Benoit, J. T. Milik, and R. de Vaux, *Discoveries in the Judaean Desert* 2 (*Les Grottes de Murabba'at*), Oxford 1961
Bliss–Macalister, *Excavations* F. J. Bliss and R. A. S. Macalister, *Excavations in Palestine during the Years 1898–1900*, London 1902
Brünnow–Domaszewski, *Die Provincia Arabia* R. E. Brünnow and A. V. Domaszewski, *Die Provincia Arabia* 1–3, Strassbourg 1904–1909
CCSL *Corpus Christianorum, Series Latina*, Turnhout
Chron. J. Malalas, *Chronicon* (ed. L. Dindorf)
CIG *Corpus Inscriptionum Graecarum* (ed. A. Boeck), Berlin 1828–1877
CIJ *Corpus Inscriptionum Judaicarum* 1–2 (ed. J.-B. Frey), Rome 1936–1952 (see also Frey, *Corpus* 2)
Clermont-Ganneau, *ARP* C. Clermont-Ganneau, *Archaeological Researches in Palestine* 1–2, London 1896–1899
Clermont-Ganneau, *RAO* C. Clermont-Ganneau, *Recueil d'Archéologie Orientale* 1–8, Paris 1888 ss.
Conder, *SEP* C. R. Conder, *The Survey of Eastern Palestine*, Memoirs 1, London 1889.
Conder–Kitchener, *SWP* C. R. Conder and H. H. Kitchener, *Survey of Western Palestine*, Memoirs 1–3, London 1881–1883
Crowfoot, *Early Churches* J. W. Crowfoot, *Early Churches in Palestine*, London 1941
DACL *Dictionnaire d'Archéologie Chrétienne et de Liturgie*, Paris
Epiph., *Haer.* Epiphanius Constantiniensis Episcopus, *Panarion seu Adversus LXXX Haereses* (ed. K. Holl), Leipzig 1915–1931 (*GCS* 25, 31, 37; also in *PG* 41–42)
Eus., *Onom.* Eusebius, *Das Onomastikon der biblischen Ortsnamen* (ed. E. Klostermann), Leipzig 1904
Fest. Festschrift (in honor of . . .)
Frey, *Corpus* 2 J.-B. Frey, *Corpus Inscriptionum Judaicarum*, Rome 1952
GCS *Die Griechischen Christlichen Schriftsteller der Ersten Jahrhunderte*, Leipzig
Goodenough, *Jewish Symbols* E. R. Goodenough, *Jewish Symbols in the Greco-Roman Period* 1–12, New York 1953–1968
Guérin, *Galilée* V. Guérin, *Description Géographique, Historique et Archéologique de la Palestine, Galilée* 1–2, Paris 1868–1880
Guérin, *Judée* V. Guérin, *Description Géographique, Historique et Archéologique de la Palestine, Judée* 1–3, Paris 1868–1869
Guérin, *Samarie* V. Guérin, *Description Géographique, Historique et Archéologique de la Palestine, Samarie* 1–2, Paris 1874
Harbour Archaeology, 1985 *Harbour Archaeology—Proceedings, 1st International Workshop on Ancient Mediterranean Harbours, Caesarea Maritima 24–28.6.83* (*BAR*/IS 257, ed. A. Raban), Oxford 1985
HE (various authors) *Historia Ecclesiastica*
Hill, *BMC* G. F. Hill, *Catalogue of the Greek Coins in the British Museum, Palestine*, London 1914
Hüttenmeister–Reeg, *Antiken Synagogen* F. Hüttenmeister and G. Reeg, *Die antiken Synagogen* 1–2, Wiesbaden 1977

IGLS *Inscriptiones Grècques et Latines de la Syries* (eds. L. Jalabert and R. Mouder), Paris 1927–

IG Rom. *Inscriptiones Graecae ad res Romanas pertinentes* 1–4 (ed. R. Cagnat), Paris 1911–1927

Itin. Burdig. *Itinerarium Burdigalense*

Josephus, *Antiq.* Josephus Flavius, *Antiquities*

Josephus, *War* Josephus Flavius, *The Jewish War*

Khouri, *Antiquities* R. C. Khouri, *The Antiquities of the Jordan Rift Valley*, 'Amman 1988

Klein, *Corpus* S. Klein, *Jüdisch-palästinisches Corpus Inscriptionum*, Vienna 1920

Kohl–Watzinger, *Synagogen* H. Kohl and C. Watzinger, *Antike Synagogen in Galilaea*, Leipzig 1916

Lidzbarski, *Ephemeris* M. Lidzbarski, *Ephemeris für Semitische Epigraphik* 1–3, Giessen 1902–1915

Musil, *Arabia Petraea* A. Musil, *Arabia Petraea* 1–3, Vienna 1907–1908

Naveh J. Naveh, *On Stone and Mosaic: The Aramaic and Hebrew Inscriptions from Ancient Synagogues*, Tel Aviv 1978 (Hebrew; quoted by inscription no.)

NEAT *Near Eastern Archaeology in the Twentieth Century: Essays in Honor of Nelson Glueck* (ed. J. A. Sanders), Garden City, N.Y. 1970

P Edgar, P Cairo, P Nessana, P Zen. Various collections of papyri

Perrot–Ladiray, *Tombes et Ossuaires* J. Perrot and D. Ladiray, *Tombes et Ossuaires de la région côtière Palestinienne au IVème millénaire avant l'ère Chrétienne* (Mémoires et Travaux du Centre de Recherches Préhistoriques Française de Jérusalem, 1), Paris 1980

PG *Patrologia Graeca* (ed. Migne), Paris

PL *Patrologia Latina* (ed. Migne), Paris

Pliny, *NH* Pliny, *Naturalis Historia*

PPTS The Library of the Palestine Pilgrims' Text Society, London 1897 (quoted by text no.)

Ptol., *Geog.* *Claudii Ptolomei Geographia* (ed. C. S. A. Nobbe), Hildesheim 1966

Recherches Archéologiques en Israël *Recherches Archéologiques en Israël. Publications jubilaire des Amis Belges de l'Université Hébraïque de Jérusalem à l'Occasion de vingt-cinquième ans de l'Institut d'Archéologie. Reine Élisabeth de Belgique*, Leuven 1984

Reeg, *Ortsnamen* G. Reeg, *Die Ortsnamen Israels nach der Rabbinischen Literatur*, Wiesbaden 1989

Robinson, *Biblical Researches* E. Robinson, *Biblical Researches in Palestine* 1–3, London 1841

Saller–Bagatti, *Town of Nebo* S. J. Saller and B. Bagatti, *The Town of Nebo*, Jerusalem 1949

Schürer, *GJV* 2 E. Schürer, *Geschichte des jüdischen Volkes im Zeitalter Jesu Christi* 2, Leipzig 1907

Schürer, *HJP* E. Schürer, *A History of the Jewish People in the Age of Jesus Christ* 1–3 (new rev. ed.), Edinburgh 1973–1986

SEG *Supplementum Epigraphicum Graecum* (quoted by volume and inscription no.)

Society and Economy *Society and Economy in the Eastern Mediterranean, c. 1500–1000 B.C.* (eds. M. Heltzer and E. Lipinski) (Orientalia Lovaniensia Analecta 23), Leuven 1988

Stern, *GLA* M. Stern, *Greek and Latin Authors on Jews and Judaism* 1–3, Jerusalem 1974–1984 (quoted by text no.)

Stern, *Material Culture* E. Stern, *Material Culture of the Land of the Bible in the Persian Period 538–332 B.C.*, Warminster 1982

Strabo *The Geography of Strabo* (ed. H. L. Jones), London 1949–1969

Sukenik, *Ancient Synagogues* E. L. Sukenik, *Ancient Synagogues in Palestine and Greece*, London 1934

Vincent–Abel, *Jérusalem Nouvelle* L. H. Vincent and F. M. Abel, *Jérusalem Nouvelle* 1–4, Paris 1912–1926

Vincent–Stève, *Jérusalem* L. H. Vincent and A. M. Stève, *Jérusalem de l'Ancien Testament* 1–4, Paris 1954–1956

Waddington W. H. Waddington and P. Le Bas, *Voyage Archéologiques en Grèce et Asie Mineure: Inscriptions et Applications*, 3, Paris 1870

Warren–Conder, *SWP—Jerusalem* C. Warren and C. R. Conder, *The Survey of Western Palestine—Jerusalem*, London 1884

Watzinger, *DP* K. Watzinger, *Denkmäler Palästinas* 1–2, Leipzig 1933–1935

Weippert 1988 H. Weippert, *Palästina in Vorhellenistischer Zeit* (Handbuch der Archäologie-Vorderasien 2/1), Munich 1988. Includes Ortsregister

Woolley–Lawrence, *PEFA* 3 C. L. Woolley and T. E. Lawrence, *The Wilderness of Zin* (PEFA 3), London 1915

JOURNALS

AAA Annals of Archaeology and Anthropology
AASOR Annual of the American Schools of Oriental Research
ADAJ Annual of the Department of Antiquities of Jordan
AJA American Journal of Archaeology
AJSLL American Journal of Semitic Languages and Literature
'Alon Bulletin of the Israel Department of Antiquities (Hebrew)
APEF (see *PEFA*)
'Atiqot Journal of the Israel Antiquities Authority
AUSS Andrews University Seminary Studies
AWA Advances in World Archaeology
BA Biblical Archaeologist
BAIAS Bulletin of the Anglo-Israel Archaeology Society
BAR Biblical Archaeology Review
BASOR Bulletin of the American Schools of Oriental Research
BBSAJ Bulletin of the British School of Archaeology in Jerusalem
BIAL Bulletin of the Institute of Archaeology, London
BIES Bulletin of the Israel Exploration Society (Hebrew)
BJPES Bulletin of the Jewish Palestine Exploration Society
BMB Bulletin du Musée de Beyrouth
BS Bibliotheca Sacra
BTS Bible et Terre Sainte
BZ Biblische Zeitschrift
CNI Christian News from Israel
CRAIBL Comptes-rendus, Académie des Inscriptions et Belles-Lettres
EI Eretz-Israel
ESI Excavations and Surveys in Israel
HUCA Hebrew Union College Annual
HUCMS Haifa University Center for Maritime Studies
IEJ Israel Exploration Journal
IJNA The International Journal of Nautical Archaeology and Underwater Exploration
ILN The Illustrated London News
JAOS Journal of the American Oriental Society
JBL Journal of Biblical Literature
JCS Journal of Cuneiform Studies
JEA Journal of Egyptian Archaeology
JFA Journal of Field Archaeology
JNES Journal of Near Eastern Studies
JPOS Journal of the Palestine Oriental Society
JRAI Journal of the Royal Anthropological Institute
JRAS Journal of the Royal Asiatic Society
JRS Journal of Roman Studies
LA Studii Biblici Franciscani Liber Annuus
MdB Le Monde de la Bible
MDOG Mitteilungen der Deutschen Orientalischen Gesellschaft
MUSJ Mélanges de l'Université Saint Joseph de Beyrouth
OLZ Orientalische Literaturzeitung
PEFA Annual of the Palestine Exploration Fund
PEQ Palestine Exploration Quarterly
PJB Palästina Jahrbuch
PMB Palestine Museum Bulletin
QDAP Quarterly of the Department of Antiquities in Palestine
RAr Revue Archéologique
RB Revue Biblique
RHR Revue de l'Histoire des Religions
SHAJ Studies in the History and Archaeology of Jordan
TA Tel Aviv
TLZ Theologische Literaturzeitung
VT Vetus Testamentum
ZAW Zeitschrift für die Alttestamentliche Wissenschaft
ZDPV Zeitschrift des Deutschen Palästina-Vereins

TRANSLITERATION OF HEBREW

Letter	*Name*	*Transliteration*
א	aleph	'
ב	bheth	v
בּ	beth	b
ג	gimel	g
ד	daleth	d
ה	he	h
ו	vav	v, w
ז	zayin	z
ח	cheth	ḥ
ט	tet	ṭ
י	yod	y
כ, ך	khaph	kh
כּ, ךּ	kaph	k
ל	lamed	l
מ, ם	mem	m
נ, ן	nun	n
ס	samekh	s
ע	'ayin	'
פ, ף	phe	f
פּ	pe	p
צ, ץ	tzadhe, ṣadhe	ẓ, ṣ
ק	koph	q
ר	resh	r
שׁ	shin	sh, š
שׂ	sin	s
ת	tav	t

TRANSLITERATION OF GREEK

Letter	*Name*	*Transliteration*
Α α	alpha	a
Β β	beta	b
Γ γ	gamma	g
Δ δ	delta	d
Ε ε	epsilon	e
Ζ ζ	zeta	z
Η η	eta	ē
Θ θ	theta	th
Ι ι	iota	i
Κ κ	kappa	k
Λ λ	lambda	l
Μ μ	mu	m
Ν ν	nu	n
Ξ ξ	xi	z
Ο ο	omicron	o
Π π	pi	p
Ρ ρ	rho	r
Σ σ, ς	sigma	s
Τ τ	tau	t
Υ υ	upsilon	y, u
Φ φ	phi	ph
Χ χ	chi	kh
Ψ ψ	psi	ps
Ω ω	omega	ō

THE NEW ENCYCLOPEDIA OF ARCHAEOLOGICAL EXCAVATIONS IN THE HOLY LAND

P

(CONTINUED)

PETRA

IDENTIFICATION

Petra (Πέτρα, "rock"), the capital of the Nabatean kingdom in Edom, is situated about 80 km (47.5 mi.) south of the Dead Sea (map reference 192.971). A "rock" in conjunction with the Nabateans is mentioned for the first time by Diodorus of Sicily (XIX, 95–98), not as the name of a settlement but as a term meaning "a certain rock"—where the Nabateans sought refuge for themselves, their goods, and their chattels when they were attacked by the diadoch Antigonus I in 312 BCE, and where they safeguarded their elders, women, and children on the occasion of their annual gatherings. The identification of Petra with the biblical Selah in Edom derives from the Septuagint and was accepted by Eusebius, who also identified Selah Jokteel with Petra (*Onom.* 36, 13; 142, 7; 144, 7). Josephus (*Antiq.* IV, 161), when speaking of the five Midianite kings who were defeated by the Israelites on their way to Canaan (Num. 31:8), identifies Rekem, the town named after its founder, with Petra, the capital of Arabia. This identification has been confirmed by a Nabatean inscription, apparently from the first century CE, discovered at Petra, that mentions Raqmu, the town's Semitic name.

HISTORY

Petra was apparently not settled prior to the Hellenistic period, as is evidenced by the archaeological finds. In all of the sections of the town where excavations have been conducted, no pottery or coins prior to the fourth century BCE have been discovered thus far. The same has been true of the excavations at other Nabatean sites (see Elusa, Nessana, Oboda).

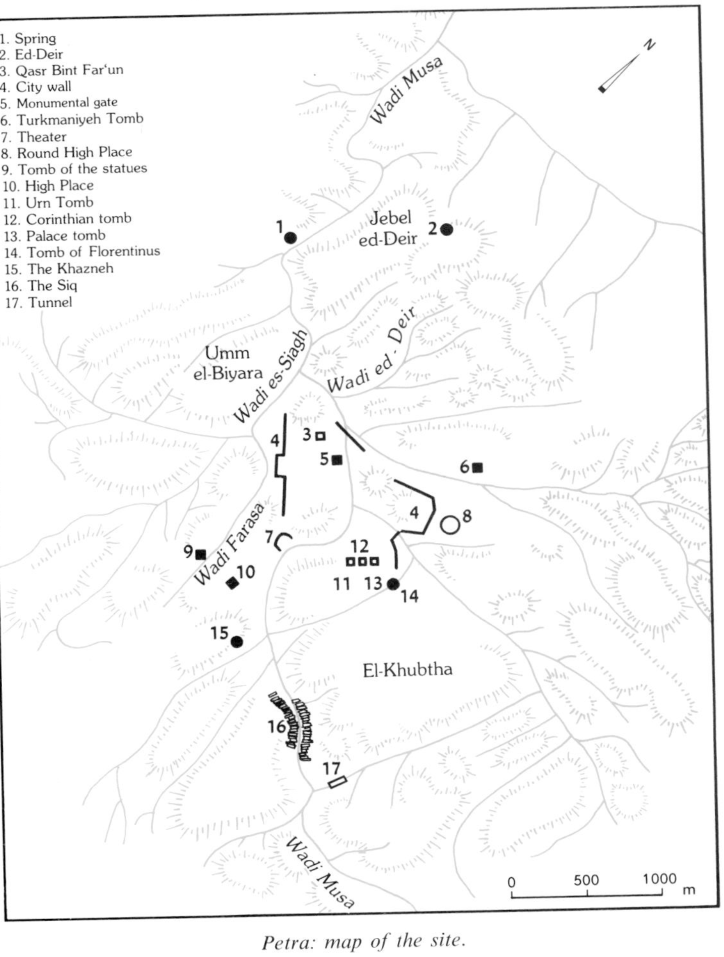

Petra: map of the site.

Aretas I, the first known Nabatean ruler, is mentioned in 2 Maccabees 5:8. He is the Arabian prince from whom the deposed High Priest Jason requested asylum in 168 BCE. He may be the Aretas, king of the Arabs, mentioned in a Nabatean inscription from Elusa. The Nabatean royal dynasty at Petra may have been founded by Erotimus (Justin, *Historiarum Philippicarum*, XXXIX, 5, 5–6), probably the Greek name of Aretas II, who reigned at about the end of the second century BCE. Most of the Nabatean kings who reigned in Petra from that date until the abolishment of the Nabatean kingdom in 106 CE are known. An important event in the history of the Nabatean kingdom was the conquest of southern Syria, including Damascus, in the reign of Aretas III Philellenos or Philhellen (c. 87–62 BCE). The first attempt was made to crush Nabatean independence then as well. The first Roman governor of Syria, Marcus Aemilius Scaurus, marched on Petra after Aretas III's intervention in Judea in support of Hyrcanus against Aristobulus, his brother. The Nabateans were forced to pay tribute to Rome and their kingdom became a client state. During the reigns of Obodas II (or III) (30–9 BCE) and Aretas IV (9 BCE–40 CE), Petra enjoyed a period of prosperity. At the beginning of the reign of Obodas II, the Romans began a struggle for control of the caravan trade, the consequences of which were not felt, however, until the second half of the first century CE.

The history of Petra during the reign of the last two Nabatean kings, Malichus II (40–70 CE) and Rabbel II (70–106)—the latter called the Restorer and Savior of his people—is not known in detail. On the death of Rabbel II in 106 CE, the emperor Trajan annexed the Nabatean kingdom, which became the Province of Arabia, with its capital at Petra, and appointed Cornelius Palma governor. In 131 CE, the emperor Hadrian visited Petra and granted it the name Ἁδριανὴ Πέτρα (Hadriane Petra). However, the diversion of the caravan trade to new routes brought about the rise of Palmyra and the decline of Petra. In the Late Roman period, Petra served mainly as a religious center for towns in Transjordan and southern Syria. In 363, the town was slightly damaged by a severe earthquake.

In the fourth century, the Province of Arabia was divided into two parts. The southern part, the province of Palaestina Tertia, included the town of Petra, which became its capital. The northern part, the Province of Arabia, had Bostra as its capital. In the fifth century, Christianity found its way to Petra, and in the fifth and sixth centuries, it was the see of a bishopric. A Greek inscription in the internal chamber of the Urn Tomb indicates that it was converted into a church in 446–447. The Nabatean temple called ed-Deir was also used by a Christian cult in the Byzantine period, as indicated by crosses incised in its rear wall. There is no information about the history of Petra in the first centuries of the Arab period. At the beginning of the twelfth century, in 1127, the town was occupied by Baldwin I, king of Jerusalem. The Crusaders

City coin from the time of Hadrian.

Petra: city plan.

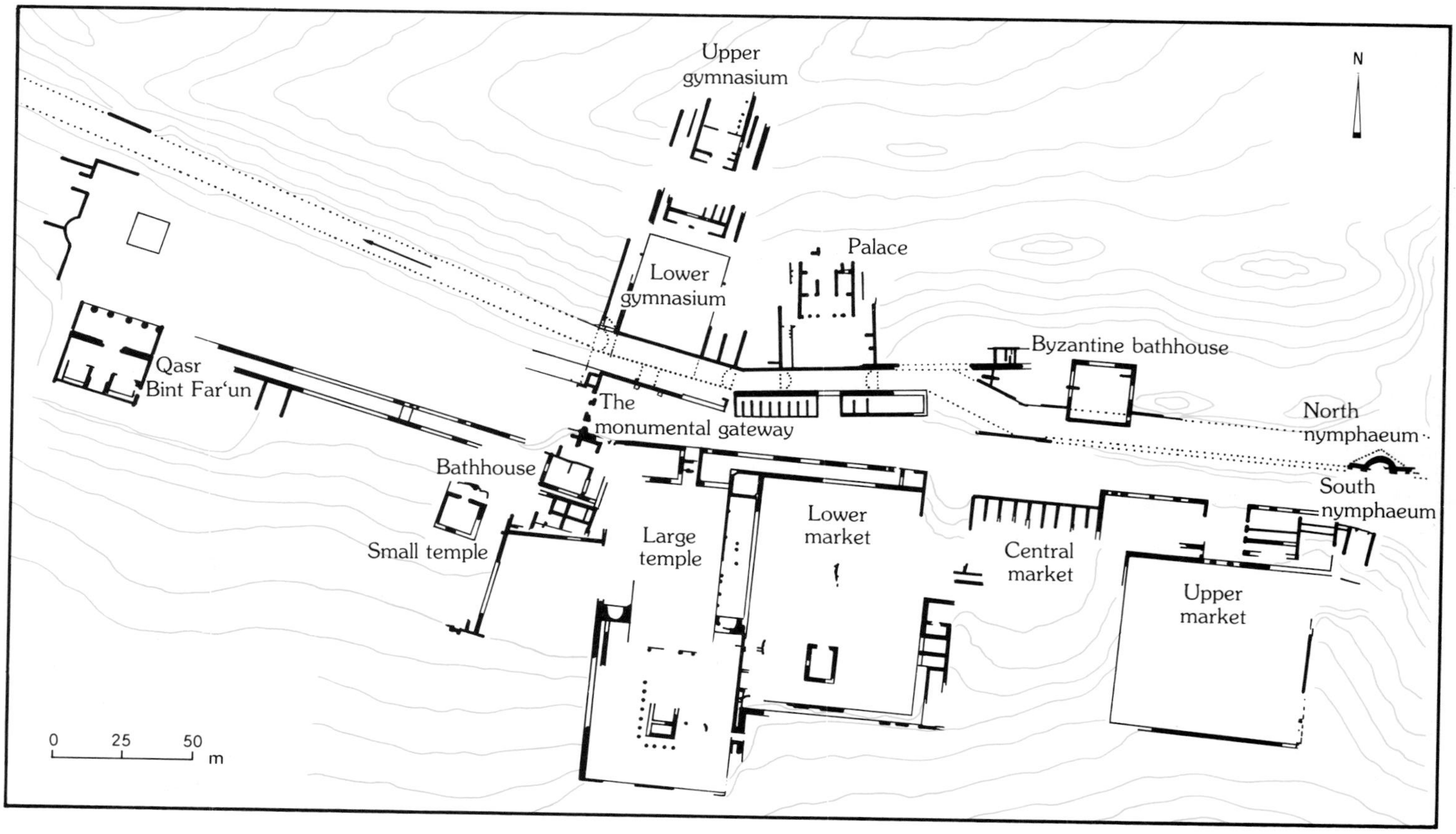

Wadi es-Siq: the aqueduct.

Umm el-Biyara cliff and the tombs at its foot.

gave it the name Li Vaux Moyse (the valley of Moses) and built small forts on the mountaintops. Petra is mentioned in the sources for the last time under the name of al-Aswit, in connection with the visit of Sultan Baybars in 1276; he passed through on his way from Cairo to Kerak, as narrated by his biographer, Numeiri.

EXPLORATION

Although U. J. Seetzen was the first European traveler to reach Petra (in 1807), he had no idea what it was. It was only identified in 1812, by J. L. Burckhardt, who is consequently considered its discoverer. During the nineteenth century, numerous travelers visited Petra. Toward the close of the century, the Dominican fathers at the École Biblique et Archéologique Française in Jerusalem explored Petra; they published their first results in 1896. Of special importance here is the work of R. E. Brünnow and A. von Domaszewski who, in 1897–1898, explored tombs and buildings. Before World War I, G. Dalman examined the necropolis and especially the places of worship, on behalf of the German Evangelic Institute for Exploration of the Antiquities of the Holy Land in Jerusalem. H. Kohl explored the Qaṣr Bint Far'un building on behalf of the German Society for Oriental Research. During World War I, the Committee for the Preservation of Monuments of the German-Turkish army staff worked at Petra under the direction of W. Bachmann, C. Watzinger, and T. Wiegand, mainly investigating the remains of the Nabatean town of the Early Roman period.

The first excavations at Petra were conducted in 1929 by A. Conway-Horsfield and G. Horsfield, sponsored by the Melchett Exploration Fund, on behalf of the Mandatory Department of Antiquities. Work was concentrated in the town dumps, at several sections of the town wall, and in a few tombs. In 1934, another season of excavations was carried out by W. F. Albright for the American School of Oriental Research in Jerusalem and in 1937, by M. Murray and J. C. Ellis, for the British School of Archaeology in Egypt. In 1954, excavations were renewed by the Jordanian government (represented by M. M. Khadija, F. Zayadine, and N. Khairy), in cooperation with the British School of Archaeology, under the direction of P. J. Parr, and various American institutions. D. Kirkbride cleared several sections of the colonnaded street in 1955–1956; the monumental gate, the town dumps, and other sites were excavated in order to establish the chronology of the Nabatean pottery. In 1960, G. R. H. Wright studied and restored the Khazneh (Khaznet Far'un, or "Pharaoh's Treasury"). In 1962–1963, P. C. Hammond uncovered the large so-called Roman theater on behalf of the Princeton Theological Seminary and the Jordan Department of Antiquities. Since 1973, the Nuremberg Prehistoric Society, under the direction of M. Lindner, in cooperation with the Jordan Department of Antiquities, has carried out surveys and excavations at various locations at Petra and its surroundings. In 1982, a Nabatean potter's workshop was excavated by F. Zayadine, on behalf of the Jordan Department of Antiquities. Since 1973, Hammond has conducted excavations in the Temple of Winged Lions.

TOPOGRAPHY

Petra is situated in a valley (Wadi Musa) surrounded by mountain ridges and bisected by deep river gorges into whose steep walls the Nabateans dug monumental tombs. The Nabateans were attracted to Petra because of its unusual layout, which offered safety and protection. The valley is about 1.5 km (0.9 mi.) long from north to south, and 400 m to 1 km wide. On the east and west, the steep mountain slopes rise to a height of 300 m above the surface of the valley. Above the western part of the valley rises the rock massif el-Ḥabis. On the east, the mountain ridge is bisected by the narrow gorge es-Siq, which forms the best approach to Petra.

EXCAVATIONS

PREHISTORIC PERIOD. Remains of the Upper Paleolithic and Neolithic periods have been found at Petra and its surroundings, especially in Wadi Beidha (q.v.), where excavations have been conducted.

IRON AGE. Various surveys, particularly of the Umm el-Biyara mountain west of the valley, have yielded pottery identified by G. Horsfield, N. Glueck, and others as Edomite ware.

EARLY NABATEAN (HELLENISTIC) PERIOD. The literary sources and the numerous small finds from the Hellenistic period discovered at Petra, especially in the town dumps and on the surface, attest to the site's having been occcupied in the third century BCE, although there is no definite proof that the inhabitants were Nabateans. The same picture emerges from excavations at the Nabatean sites of Nessana and Oboda in the Negev desert. In the British School's excavations, trial soundings were made in the town to establish the site's stratigraphy. In the lowest layer, on virgin soil, remains of buildings were discovered. Their foundations and walls were built of rubble and pounded earth and their floors were clay. On the basis of the pottery—especially the lamps and black-glazed ware—and coin finds (Phoenician, Ptolemaic, and Seleucid), the excavators dated the construction of the buildings to the second half of the third century BCE. The buildings continued in use, with numerous repairs, until the end of the second century BCE. Due to the restricted area of excavation, it was impossible to ascertain the plan of the buildings. To the same occupation level also belong small incense altars and small stone figurines in the form of human faces. In later occupation levels (Parr's phases V and VII), coins of Aretas II (c. 110–96 BCE) were found. The beginning of the production of painted Nabatean pottery is ascribed to this period. Should this be accurate, Nabatean painted pottery appears at Petra about half a century earlier than in the Negev. To this period also belongs the earliest Nabatean inscription found at Petra. It is engraved on a triclinium at the entrance to the gorge, the Bab es-Siq, and is dated to the first regnal year of Obodas I (96–95 BCE).

MIDDLE NABATEAN PERIOD (ROMAN I). Most of the architectural remains at Petra belong to the last quarter of the first century BCE to about the middle of the first century CE.

Houses. Thus far, few remains of private buildings have been encountered in the town. It seems that Petra in this period was not a city in the ordinary sense of the word. Although it is believed that it was the seat of the royal house, and certainly of the national shrines and national necropolis and their attendants, its citizens dwelled either at neighboring Gaia, east of Petra, which has a more favorable climate, or in tents, as had their immediate predecessors. At the end of the first century BCE, probably in the reign of Aretas IV, buildings began to be erected of ashlar instead of rubble and clay. To prepare the rocky basin for the construction of a town, a fill (15 m wide) was poured on the northern bank of the valley crossing the town; the main thoroughfare, which ran east–west through the town, was built on the fill. Between this road and the valley, buildings of well-dressed stone were erected. Here, too, the excavators were unable to establish the plans of the houses due to the limited excavation area. Typical Nabatean pottery, both painted and plain ware, was discovered under the floors of these buildings.

In the Katute dump, south of the valley, a house the excavators ascribed to the first century CE was cleared. Because it had been covered by the debris of the Roman II town, its walls were preserved to a height of 3 m. The house is built of ashlars, and its outer face displays characteristic oblique Nabatean dressing. The inner face of the walls is roughly hewn because it was plastered and ornamented with reliefs, remains of which have survived. The building was in continuous use for many years, and its plan was altered several times. In its final stage, it consisted of a long, narrow courtyard (30 m long) that was entered from the town side (on the south). The short sides of the courtyard led into a series of small chambers. The southern side of the courtyard had neither windows nor doorways, and in the excavator's opinion, the house was incorporated into the fortification wall of the town. It was roofed with stone slabs resting on arches, as was common in that period in the Negev and the Nabatean Hauran. The discovery of Early Roman pottery in the foundation of the building led the excavator to attribute its construction to the end of the first quarter of the first century CE. The building continued in use up to the Roman conquest of Petra. It is not certain whether it was a private dwelling.

The houses of the Nabatean town were built not only in the area of the valley, but also on the slopes, where they were supported by terraces. Horsfield examined several such houses, some of which were cut into the rock, as well others built in front of the rock wall. The number of houses discovered to date is small and provides no hint about where the population of a town of the magnitude of Petra was lodged.

The Theater. The road descending to the town from the Siq first reaches the theater, which is situated above the southern bank of Wadi Musa, at the point where it widens. The seats were cut into the Nubian sandstone cliff, destroying several undecorated tomb facades, apparently from the second half of the first century BCE. The upper two tiers of seats were visible to modern visitors to Petra; the third tier was cleared by Hammond. His excavations showed that the cavea was divided by flights of stairs into six wedge-shaped groups of seats (cunei). Two roofed passages were discovered in the wings of the stage. The stage itself was not a building proper, but a decorated *scaena frons* with three entrances, the central one being a large, circular niche. The excavator distinguished three stages of construction in the theater; the last was the type customary in the Imperial period. In the opinion of the excavator, the theater was built in the reign of Aretas IV. Typically Nabatean capitals, mason's marks, and pottery belong to the initial phase. The theater continued in use in Rabbel II's time, and its final phase was in the Late Roman period. It was built following a Vitruvian plan, with some local modifications. According to the excavator, the theater was a place of assembly and entertainment, but this seems doubtful. It is situated in the midst of the huge, main necropolis at Petra, at a considerable distance from the center of the city. This writer has therefore suggested that this theater, like others in the Nabatean kingdom, had a cultic function, in the performance of funerary rites. It was apparently erected by Aretas IV, also the probable builder of the Khazneh, for the performance of these rites after his own death. In any case, it is unthinkable to have had a theater, in the Greco-Roman sense, in Petra's climate and in the midst of a necropolis. The destruction of the theater is ascribed to the earthquake of 363 CE.

THE COLONNADED STREET. A colonnaded street was the main thoroughfare which bisected the town. It also ran along the southern bank of Wadi Musa. To its south the ground rises steeply, and on the slope, three terraces were built that held dwellings. The colonnade is separated from the lowest terrace by its retaining wall, which is preserved to a height of 5 m. The wall extends along the length of the colonnade and joins the southern pier of a tripartite gate (see below).

The colonnade-lined street is 6 m wide and its slope increases 25 cm every

The large High Place.

The theater.

3 m. The pedestals of the columns were found in situ, in a 65-m-long section of the street. On the sides of the street, the stone sidewalks were two steps above the level of the road itself. The date of its construction is not known exactly, but the excavators suggest either 106 CE, when the Nabatean kingdom was annexed to the Province of Arabia, or later, in the reign of the Antonines, a period of extensive building activity in the East. The first date is supported by a Greek inscription from 114 CE found in the debris near the colonnade (*SEG* XXXII, no. 1550). However, judging from what is known of Nabatean history, both dates seem much too late. Like most of the monuments at Petra, the street probably belongs to the beginning of the reign of Rabbel II, as indicated by the latest coin found in Parr's Trench III, although it could also have been used in subsequent periods.

According to Bachmann, Watzinger, and Wiegand, there was a nymphaeum at the center of the city and a small shrine at the eastern end of the colonnaded street. To its south, three markets were identified—upper, middle, and lower—that were followed by a great temple to their west. To the north, the excavators located a royal palace and a gymnasium. Very little has been found to substantiate their reconstruction, however.

The Monumental Gateway. At its western extremity, the street terminates in a tripartite gateway. Excavation has revealed that the gateway was built after the street—part of the street's paving was removed during the gate's construction. The paving was subsequently repaired and enlarged to form a small square. The gateway itself consists of four piers (the inner one measuring 3 by 3 m and the two outer ones 2.2 by 3 m) that form three openings. The central opening is 3.5 m wide and the two lateral ones are 2 m each. Both the inside and the outside of the gateway are built of dressed Nubian sandstone, bound by a thin layer of mortar. Because the mortar cannot be seen from the outside, the construction seems to be dry, or mortarless. The core of the walls is rubble, also laid in courses and leveled with sandstone fragments. In front of the western side of the gateway, four columns stood on high pedestals, a column in front of each pier. The entryways were framed by alternating panels of busts of deities and floral reliefs; the columns were crowned by capitals like those used for the Khazneh. The east side of the gate is adorned with engaged half columns, set on half pedestals, that also are attached to the wall. The columns are crowned with classic Nabatean half capitals. An arch, whose upper parts are not preserved, crowned the gateway. The gate is flanked by towers, now in ruins. Towers of this type were also observed at the entrance to the second temenos court at Seeia in the Hauran. The towers may very well have been typical Nabatean staircase towers, furnishing access to galleries above the colonnades that lined the section of the *via sacra* leading to the temple.

On the basis of its plan, the excavators ascribed the gateway to the time of the Antonines, or even to the beginning of the third century CE. Gateways with three openings—especially those with freestanding columns in front of their piers—are known in the Roman world as early as the beginning of the first century BCE, and thus the dating of this monument appears to be much too late. Wiegand believed that the gateway formed the western entrance to the town. The most recent excavations proved, however, that it was the entrance to the area at whose edge stood the Qaṣr Bint Far'un, Petra's main temple—confirming Domaszewski's opinion. Thus, the construction of the triple gate should be connected to the construction of the temple—that is, to the period from Obodas II to Aretas IV. This dating finds more support at present.

The colonnaded street.

Qaṣr Bint Far'un: plan of the precinct.

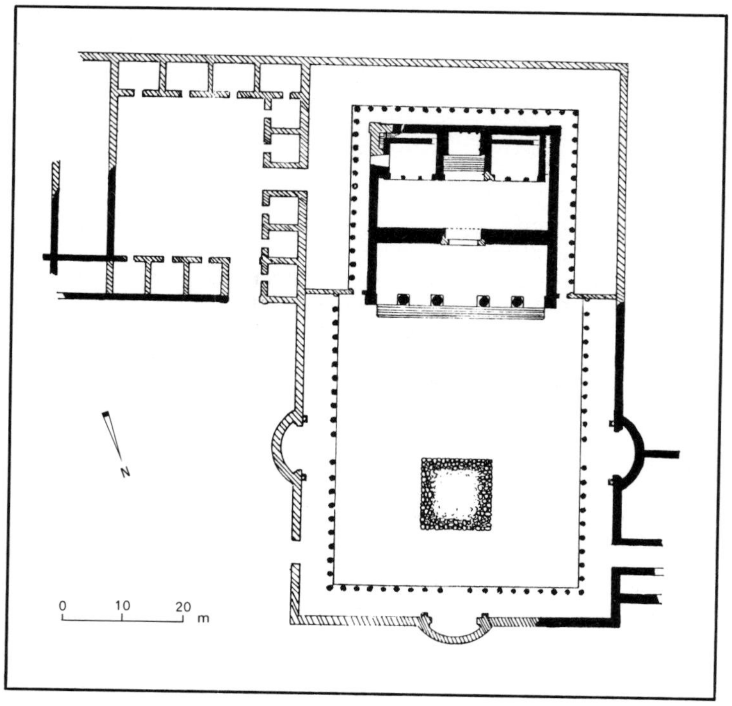

The Bathhouse. Just south of the gateway is a large bathhouse, another important element paralleled in the sacred compound at Seeia. It was identified by Bachmann, Watzinger, and Wiegand, and partially excavated, but not published, by Khadija in 1967–1968. From the temenos a vestibule leads into a columned hall, possibly an apodyterium. West of the hall are at least three rooms belonging to the thermae. One of them is circular and covered by a cupola. The walls are decorated with engaged pilasters and niches, all of which are plastered and painted in red and yellow panels. The pilasters are crowned with a type of Corinthian capital, a variant of the capitals at the Khazneh. This room is identified either as a caldarium or a frigidarium, and a cultic use is ascribed to them. Close to the baths is a small hexastyle temple, as yet unexplored.

Qaṣr Bint Far'un. The temple is situated west of the tripartite gateway, at the edge of a large square (c. 150 m long). The square is partly surrounded by a colonnade, with benches along it, leading from the gateway to the temple. The square ends at the altar court, which is at the foot of the steps that lead to the temple. The altar court is a large rectangle of masonry (13.4 by 11.8 m and 2.75 m high). It was approached by a wide flight of steps and may have been covered with marble. The building—which has been described in detail by Domaszewski, Wiegand, and Kohl—is preserved to a height of 23 m, up to its roof. In the latest excavations, conducted by the British School of Archaeology in Jerusalem, several additional soundings were made in the building. It stands on a high podium (36 by 36 m) and is completely faced with marble in a unique manner: marble orthostats are revetted to the wall at fixed intervals with regular wall construction between them. Nine steps ascend from the road to a narrow platform in front of the building, and from there four more steps lead up to the pronaos (28.8 by 11.2 m). The facade of the pronaos contains four columns between antae. From here an entrance 6.25 m wide and as high as the pronaos itself leads into the naos (28.8 by 8.4 m). Twelve steps lead from the naos to the adyton, in the southern part of the building, which consists of a central cell and two flanking ones. A pair of columns between antae decorate the front of the lateral cells. The outer walls of the adyton are double, and in the space between them spiral stairways lead to the building's flat roof and to the exedra above the lateral cells. The walls of the temple, like those of the tripartite gate, have a rubble core set in clay mortar and sandstone slabs that level the courses; the walls were faced on both sides with dressed stones. In addition, wooden beams laid inside the inner and the outer sides of the walls increased the building's stability in an earthquake. This system is found in other buildings in the Nabatean realm. An early date for the Qaṣr Bint Far'un may be indicated by the location of the tripartite gateway.

In 1964, in other soundings in the temple compound, Parr discovered an inscription of Aretas IV engraved on a bench in the *theatron*, a forecourt surrounded on three sides by porticoes with benches. The inscription, found in situ, attests to the date the porticoes were constructed and indicates that the temple could have been contemporary with the *theatron*, or even earlier—from the time of Obodas II. Greek and Latin inscriptions suggest that the

Qaṣr Bint Far'un: south wall.

Qaṣr Bint Far'un: temple plan and a cross section of the holy of holies.

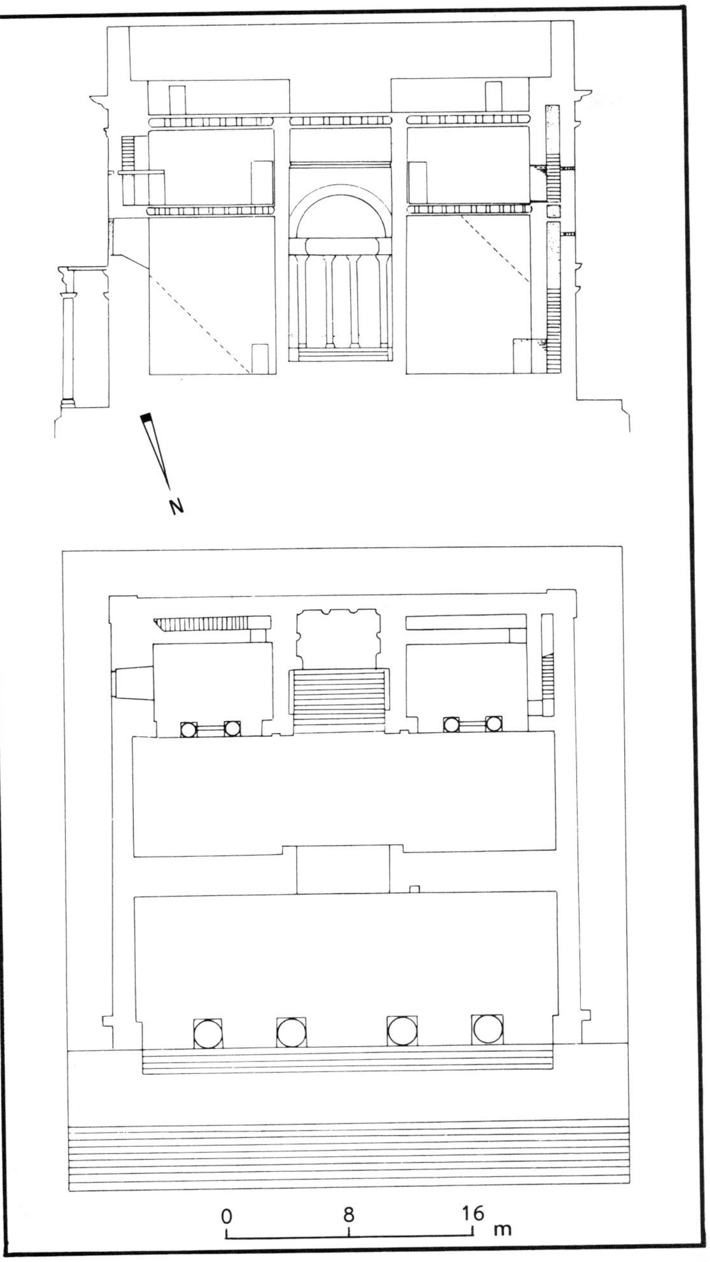

temple was also in use in the reigns of Trajan and Hadrian. It was apparently abandoned after the earthquake of 363 CE.

The Temple of the Winged Lions (the Northern Temple, the Temple of al-Uzza). The Temple of the Winged Lions was discovered and excavated in 1974 by Hammond. The site had been identified in 1921 by Bachmann, Watzinger, and Wiegand as the gymnasium. It is north of the *via sacra*, in the shadow of the isolated peak known as el-Ḥabis, opposite the Qaṣr Bint Far'un. From the *via sacra*, in the vicinity of the triple gate, a road 100 m long leads to the temple. The temple (17.42 by 17.42 m) was built above cryptlike, vaulted halls that acted like a podium. It stands within a temenos, which apparently was once surrounded by colonnades. The building is oriented to the north. At the south, two narrow openings lead to a pronaos. A single wide door in the middle of the northern wall of the hall leads into the naos. The walls of the naos are decorated with engaged half columns; two rows of freestanding columns run along the eastern and western walls. The adyton is behind the naos, which is also surrounded by columns. In its first stage of existence, the temple's columns were covered with plaster and were painted; in its second stage, they were revetted with white and brown marble. In its debris were numerous fragments of statues of human, animal, and mythological creatures, in marble, sandstone, bronze, and clay. Lavishly decorated floral Nabatean capitals also were found. The excavator dates the construction of the temple to the first century CE and believes that it was in use well after the formation of the Province of Arabia.

Nabatean temples follow two distinct plans. Temples in northern Arabia, southern Edom (see er-Ram), northern Edom (Petra itself and Khirbet et-Tannur), and the Hauran and the Ledja (Seeia, Ṣaḥir, and Ṣur) had an encased outer temple, an inner temple, and an adyton—a plan erroneously ascribed to an Iranian origin, but in fact a Nabatean adaptation to specific cultural needs. Each of these temples had a *theatron*. The temple at Sur had a theater in addition to the *theatron*. An altar in the court completed the building's components. Temples of this type were constructed in the reigns of Obodas II and Aretas IV.

The Qaṣr Bint Far'un belongs to the second type of temple, common in the Nabatean district of Moab and in the Negev (q.v. Oboda). Here the traditional Bronze Age–Iron Age plan was preserved with a tripartite division of pronaos, naos, and adyton placed on a longitudinal axis. The benches along the walls of the court, the altar in its center, and the staircases—either in the double back walls of the Qaṣr Bint Far'un or in staircase towers on the side of the facade, as in other temples in Moab—facilitated the Nabatean religious ritual, which most likely included a solemn procession, libations, burning incense on the roof of the temple, animal sacrifice, and a festive meal (partaken in the *theatron*). There is apparently no chronological difference between the two types of temples, only a regional one.

THE LATE NABATEAN PERIOD. This writer is of the opinion that, except perhaps for a handful of funerary monuments, it is unlikely that any of the structures here belong to the Late Nabatean period. It was a period of decline for Petra, during which, at most, there might have been a reuse of some monuments (in the second and third centuries CE). However, the evidence even for this is only slight.

The Necropolis. Two types of tombs were discovered at Petra. The first were shaft tombs cut into horizontal rock platforms. Horsfield excavated some of them in 1929. Because all of them had been plundered, the excavator could only estimate that their dates ranged from the second century BCE to the first century CE. These tombs appear in several forms: a shaft leading to a single burial chamber that has several pits cut into its rock floor; a shaft leading to two burial chambers on either side of it; or a shaft leading to a small, vaulted chamber that has loculi cut into three of its walls.

The second type is represented by tombs dug into the vertical rock walls of the canyons surrounding the wadis, or dry riverbeds, in the valley. To construct these tombs, the canyon walls were first made smooth and then the facades of the tombs were carved—some with ornamentation. Most of the tombs in the necroplis at Petra belong to this type. At the end of the nineteenth century, Domaszewski classified the tomb facades according to style. He also

Obelisk tomb.

The necropolis: (left) stepped tomb; (right) pylon tomb.

The necropolis: triclinium tomb.

attempted to arrive at a chronological classification for them, using topographic and stylistic criteria. He distinguished seven types: (1) pylon, (2) stepped, (3) proto-Hegra, (4) Hegra (the last two take their names from the Nabatean necropolis at Madayin Saliḥ el-Hegr-Egra in northern Arabia, where they were first observed), (5) arched, (6) gabled, and (7) Roman temple.

1. PYLON TOMBS. The simplest, or pylon, tomb, was subdivided by Domaszewski into several groups, according to the decoration on the facade and entrance. The upper part of the facade has one or two rows of crenellations (like those on a city wall), and the entrance is either plain or has a simple cornice; more developed forms have a pediment. The entrance doorposts are either smooth or decorated with pillars, some of which have capitals. On some facades the capitals are typically Nabatean.

2. STEPPED TOMBS. The facade of the stepped tomb is not crenellated but is distinguished by two large, facing steps that lead to its center. The steps are set above an Egyptian cornice. The entrance is decorated only with an architrave or pediment.

3. PROTO-HEGR TOMBS. The proto-Hegr tombs were so named because of their similarity to the tombs at Madayin Saliḥ. Domaszewski saw in their type signs of the beginning of a Greek influence at Petra. At the top of this tomb's facade, two steps are set above an Egyptian cornice. Two engaged pilasters with Nabatean capitals, set at the corners of the facade, support the cornice. The entrance is similar to that of pylon and stepped tombs.

4. THE HEGR TOMB. More developed than the preceding types, the Hegr tomb differs from the proto-Hegr type in the addition of an attic and an extended architrave. As a rule, the architrave rests on corner pillars crowned with Nabatean capitals. Above the architrave is an attic with an additional architrave terminating in a pediment; above this are a cornice and steps. Only a few entrances to these tombs were left undecorated. In some cases, they had one entrance set within another. In the more elaborately decorated facades, for example, small columns can be found in the attic, two engaged half columns on the facade, and pillars with quarter columns attached to the corner pillars.

5. ARCHED TOMBS. In some tombs, the upper part of the facade is constructed in the form of an arch. Sometimes, a libation bowl (*patera*) is placed within the arch above the entrance as a decoration. The entrance itself is either undecorated or has columns supporting an architrave.

6. GABLED TOMBS. The decoration of the twelve gabled tombs at Petra resembles the more developed Hegr model, except for its Egyptian cornice and the two steps crowning the facade, which are replaced here by a pediment. These monuments are larger by far than the other five types.

7. ROMAN TEMPLE-TYPE TOMBS. Domaszewski noted twenty-two Roman templelike tombs, most of them concentrated in Wadi al-Farasa and in the northeastern wall of the Wadi Musa. These monuments differ greatly from one another, and each is a separate type. On the facades of the less ornate ones, two engaged columns support an architrave between two engaged corner pilasters. The columns and pillars have typical Nabatean capitals. In some cases, the frieze is decorated with metopes and triglyphs. More frequently, the pediment-crowned facade has corner pillars with engaged quarter columns and Nabatean capitals that support an architrave and a pediment decorated with acroteria. The opening in the facade is decorated with pillars topped with capitals; the pillars bear simple or double architraves, and the frieze displays metopes and triglyphs. The tympanum of the main pediment is decorated in some cases with a Medusa or with a mask from which coiled serpents emerge. The only tomb at Petra that can be dated with much certainty is that of Sextus Florentinus, the Roman governor of the Province of Arabia in about 127 CE. However, this date seems to be valid only for his burial; the monument might well have been erected about a century earlier. This tomb, situated in the northeastern rock wall, belongs to the class of tombs with a pediment but is more elaborate. Two engaged half columns flank the entrance in its facade, and two corner pillars with engaged quarter columns support an architrave, decorated with flat pilasters. Above this architrave an attic, also decorated with flat pilasters, forms the continuation of the pilasters of the architrave. A semicircular arch, with an eagle at the top, occupies most of the area of the attic. Four short pilasters with Nabatean capitals, which form the continuation of the attic's pilasters, support an extended architrave, above which the urn-crowned pediment rises. This monument, like many others at Petra, indicates how little the architectural decorative art has in common with actual architecture.

Outstanding in their splendor are the tomb of ed-Deir, the Palace tomb, the Corinthian tomb, and the Khaznet Far'un. All these monuments are carved like facades of buildings with two stories or more.

The Khaznet Far'un. The Khaznet Far'un is the most magnificent monument at Petra. Its facade is two-storied. The lower story has six columns: two freestanding, two partly freestanding, and two quarter-engaged Corinthian

Ed-Deir.

The Khazneh.

Siq al-Barid: rock-cut structure.

columns. The lower story is detached from the rock from which it was cut, to form a temple portico the six columns support. The two extreme columns, and the parts of the pediment they support, project from the facade, to give an impression of depth. There are three entrances in the porticio: one leads to the main hall, and the side entrances lead to the lateral halls. The frieze on the lower story is decorated with pairs of griffins flanking a vase with plant tendrils. The pediment, which rests only on the four interior columns, is decorated with plant designs. The symbol of the goddess Isis is an acroterium, which opens the nature of the building to various interpretations. In the upper order, which also is Corinthian, the attic above the pediment of the lower story serves as a base for the upper complex. At its center is a tholos, apparently enclosed by six columns; on its sides are two pavilions with two columns on each side, each pavilion bearing a broken pediment. On top of the tholos, a Corinthian capital is surmounted by an urn. In the space between the columns of the two orders are remains of reliefs that probably represent female figures. Their significance has raised considerable controversy. In general, opinion is divided as to whether the Khaznet Far'un is a tomb or a temple, although scholars are more inclined to consider it a tomb.

Ed-Deir. The facade of the ed-Deir tomb is two-storied. The lower story has six engaged half columns, three on each side of the entrance, and two corner pillars with engaged quarter columns. All the columns and pillars are crowned with Nabatean capitals. The entrance is decorated with an architrave and a pediment. The main pillars and columns support an architrave, above which is the second story. It also is decorated with six columns and two pillars. In the center of its pediment, which is broken, is a tholos, crowned by an urn on a Nabatean capital. Niches between the columns are topped in the lower story by a flat arch and in the upper story by a pediment.

Chronology and Significance of the Tomb Facades. In the tomb facades at Petra, only a single inscription has been preserved that can assist in their dating, and then of only one type. When Domaszewski dated these tombs, he assumed that the Nabateans had first settled in Petra in the sixth century BCE; he therefore ascribed types 1 through 4 to the period from the sixth or fifth century BCE to the first century CE. Dalman attempted to establish the dates of the last type, distinguishing the three following facade types: (1) tombs in the Nabatean-Oriental style, (2) tombs in the Hellenistic style, and (3) tombs in the Roman style. In Dalman's opinion, the first style is to be dated from the third to the second centuries BCE; the second style from the first century BCE to the first century CE; and the last style from the Roman conquest onward. Attempts to arrive at a conclusion on the basis of the numerous inscriptions appearing on the tomb facades at Madayin Saliḥ (Hegra) proved unsuccessful. At that site, tombs belong to the first four of Domaszewski's classifications. Their construction began in the year 1 BCE. The last tomb is dated to 76 CE. Thus, the four types at Madayin Saliḥ were nearly contemporaneous. Scholars accordingly assumed that, at the new provincial center of Madayin Saliḥ, the facades were patterned on the tombs at Petra, where they had passed through all their stages of development. As for the absence of Roman temple tombs at Madayin Saliḥ, two explanations were offered—either the tombs at Petra were cut after the year 76, or the type was too expensive for a provincial center. As far as is known, the material culture of the Nabateans did not attain its zenith until the second half of the first century BCE—or even later, at the beginning of the reign of Obodas III (30–9 BCE), and probably not until the time of Aretas IV (9 BCE–40 CE). During that period most of the magnificent temples in the Hauran, the Negev, and in the southern part of the kingdom were built; in those days Nabatean pottery also reached its peak. It can therefore be assumed that the undecorated tombs, which do not contain any features typical of Hellenistic art, were not hewn before the middle of the first century BCE. In the second half of the century, the tombs belonging to the pylon, stepped, proto-Hegr, and Hegr types (1–4) made their successive appearances. The decoration on the facades was generally Eastern (with Persian and Egyptian elements); Greek elements were always secondary. The development of relations with the Roman Empire and the Hellenized East created an interest in Greek-Roman elements—in the pediment, Ionic and Doric architraves, and Corinthian capitals. Temple plans also probably changed during this period. While the temples from the time of Obodas II and Aretas IV were Oriental in plan, the Qaṣr Bint Far'un followed a Greek-Syrian plan. At any rate, the year 106 CE, when the Nabatean kingdom became the Roman Provincia Arabia, was not a time of transition from one style to another. Hellenistic-Roman elements had already appeared at Petra; typical Nabatean-Oriental elements continued to be used in facades undoubtedly hewn in the second century CE.

In a recent study, this writer has suggested that the differences in style reflect not a chronological, but rather a social division in Nabatean society. This conclusion is based on a study of seventy monuments at Egra, thirty of which bear detailed funerary inscriptions stating ownership, rank, and date, for example. It was seen that the simpler pylons and stepped tombs were made by women, by partnerships of women from different families, by a man and a woman who each represented a different family, or by men who presented the monument to their mothers. It is only in the proto-Hegr tombs that men of some distinction appear among the owners: a daughter of a strategus, a centurion, a Jew (merchant?). The cream of Egraean society built the most developed Hegr tombs; and among the owners were strategi, hipparchs, a doctor, a teller of omens, and rich caravaneers. At Egra, proto-Hegr and Hegr monuments constituted more than 50 percent of the total, a situation befitting an important commercial and military center such as Egra. At Petra, the division of types is entirely different: pylons and stepped tombs constitute 63.7 percent, and the addition of arched tombs, also a simple form, brings them 69.7 percent; proto-Hegr 12.3 percent; Hegr, 11 percent; gabled, 2.3 percent; and temple tombs, 4 percent. This reflects a more normal division in society in the part of Edom of which Petra was the center. The middle class was at the base of Petraean society; 23.3 percent of the monuments were built by the higher administrative, sacerdotal, military, and mercantile classes. We are thus left with 6.3 percent of the monuments for which there are no parallels at Egra. This writer attributes these monuments to the royal house, to members of the government, and to the owners of large commercial corporations—all of them absent from Egra, a provincial capital. Furthermore, three of the Roman-temple tombs are of outstanding design and workmanship: the Khazneh, the Corinthian tomb, and ed-Deir. Common to these is the arrangement of the two superimposed orders: the temple facade in the lower and the tholos in pavillions in the upper. Whereas the latter two monuments contain a mixture of Nabatean and Greek elements in their decoration, the Khazneh is purely Greek. This writer considers that this indicates a relatively early date and attributes its construction to Aretas IV, who would have invited Alexandrian sculptors to erect the monument in about 25 CE. The tomb was a masterpiece and influenced the other monuments at Petra. Accordingly, the Corinthian tomb, situated in the midst of very elaborate tombs in the necropolis, is ascribed to Malichus II, possibly in about 60 CE, and ed-Deir, to Rabbel, who may have constructed it, the latest funerary monument at Petra, in about 100 CE. The rise, development, and decline of Nabatean art is thus compressed into the course of one century. This phenomenon is in complete accordance with the development of Nabatean pottery, for which an Alexandrian origin is also sought.

There has been considerable controversy regarding the significance of the tomb facades. Some scholars believe that their decoration had no precedent in existing architecture but was merely decorative, and that facades such as on the Khaznet Far'un were patterned after wall paintings, like those at Pompeii. In the opinion of other scholars, however, the tomb facades were copies of contemporary buildings. They contend that the pylon tombs and the stepped tombs were imitations of structures in which the Nabateans had lived. No evidence has been found to support this opinion. It should be noted that tombs with similar crenellations and steps have been discovered in Syria and Phoenicia, and also in Roman incense altars. This controversy was especially sharp concerning the tomb facade on the Khaznet Far'un, ed-Deir, and similar ones. Even those scholars who considered the facades copies of real buildings were compelled to consider the paintings at Pompeii, which in their opinion depicted buildings existing at that time. Other scholars held that the Khaznet Far'un tomb was patterned on buildings in Alexandria that have not been preserved. According to this interpretation, the lower story of the Khaznet Far'un facade represents a magnificent entrance to a temple area, and the tholos is a circular building within an exedra behind the entrance. According

Siq al-Barid: Nabatean wall painting.

to another explanation, the tholos represents a tower on the roof of the house, used for relaxation, or a tower containing a staircase leading up to a roof garden.

Such combinations of architectural elements are common in this part of the Near East. Thus, for example, in Jerusalem an Egyptian pyramid is found on an Ionic cubic structure in the "Tomb of Zechariah," and a tholos on top of a Doric frieze adorns the "Tomb of Absalom," an Ionic cubic building. Both of these tombs are contemporary or slightly earlier than the Khaznet Far'un. The closest examples, which may have inspired the somewhat later Petra monuments, are the Herodian buildings at Masada, especially those at the northwestern extremity of the rock. For structural reasons, the elements of the Khaznet Far'un tomb were built in inverse order: the main building is at the upper edge of the rock, the tholos is in the center, and the open exedra is at the foot of the rock; Nabatean-style staircases unite the three elements. It can, therefore, probably be assumed that the facade on the Khaznet Far'un tomb is a perspectival representation of an analogous group of buildings at Masada, adapted to the rock wall in the Bab es-Siq.

Main publications: G. Dalman, *Petra und seine Felsheiligtümer*, Leipzig 1908; id., *APEF* 1 (1911), 95–107; id., *Neue Petra Forschungen*, Leipzig 1912; Musil, *Arabia Petraea* 2, *Edom*, 41–150; H. Kohl, *Kasr Firaun*, Leipzig 1910; E. Cowley, *PEFA* 3 (1914–1915), 145–147; T. Wiegand et al., *Petra*, Leipzig 1921; A. B. W. Kennedy, *Petra: Its History and Monuments*, London 1925; A. Kammerer, *Petra et la Nabatène*, Paris 1929; M. A. Murray and J. C. Ellis, *A Street in Petra*, London 1940; J. Starcky, *Petra et la Nabatène* (Supplement au Dictionnaire de la Bible 7), Paris 1966, 886–1018; P. C. Hammond, *The Excavations of the Main Theater at Petra 1961–1962*, London 1975; id., *American Expedition to Petra 1983 Season*, Salt Lake City 1984; ibid. *1986: Preliminary Report*, Salt Lake City 1986; M. Lindner, *Petra: Der Führer durch die antike Stadt*, Fürth 1985; *Petra: Neue Ausgrabungen und Entdeckungen* (ed. M. Lindner), Munich 1986; Khairieh 'Amr, *The Pottery from Petra: A Neutron Activation Analysis Study* (*BAR*/IS 324), Oxford 1987; I. B. Browning, *Petra*, London 1989; *Petra und das Königreich der Nabatäer* (ed. M. Lindner), 5th ed., Munich 1989; N. I. Khairy, *The 1981 Petra Excavations* (Abhandlungen des Deutschen Palästinavereins 13), Wiesbaden 1990; J. S. McKenzie, *The Architecture of Petra* (British Academy Monographs in Archaeology 1), Oxford 1990.

Other studies: J. L Burckhardt, *Travels in Syria and the Holy Land*, London 1822; Brünnow–Domaszewski, *Die Provincia Arabia* 1; D. Nielsen, *JPOS* 11 (1931), 222–240; 13 (1933), 185–208; W. F. Albright, *BASOR* 57 (1935), 18–26; E. S. G. Robinson, *Numismatic Chronicle* Series 5/16 (1936), 288–291; 6/8 (1948), 131–133; G. Horsfield and A. Horsfield, *QDAP* 7 (1938), 1–42; 8 (1939), 87–115; 9 (1942), 105–204; R. L. Cleveland, *AASOR* 34–35 (1954–1956), 53–97; J. Starcky, *BA* 18 (1955), 84–106; id., *ADAJ* 10 (1965), 43–49; id., *BTS* 73 (1965), 4–22; 74 (1965), 2–17; id., *RB* 72 (1965), 95–97; (with J. Strugnell) 73 (1966), 236–247; id., *Syria* 45 (1968), 41–66; 62 (1985), 348–351; P. J. Parr, *PEQ* 89 (1957), 5–16; 91 (1959), 106–108; 92 (1960), 124–135; 100 (1968), 5–15; id., *RB* 67 (1960), 239–242; 69 (1962), 64–79; 74 (1967), 45–49; 76 (1969), 393–394; id. (with J. Starcky), *ADAJ* 6–7 (1962), 13–20; 12–13 (1967–1968), 5–19; 20 (1975), 31–45; id., *ILN* (Nov. 10, 1962), 746–749; (Nov. 17, 1962), 789–791; id., *Jaarbericht Ex Oriente Lux* 19 (1965–1967), 550–557; id. (et al.), *Syria* 45 (1968), 1–66; id., *NEAT*, 348–381; id., *Proceedings of the Symposium on Bilad al-Sham during the Byzantine Period* 2 (eds. M. A. Bakhit and M. Asfour), Amman 1986, 192–205; P. C. Hammond, *PEQ* 90 (1958), 12–15; 105 (1973), 27–49; 119 (1987), 129–141; id., *BA* 23 (1960), 29–32; id., *BASOR* 159 (1960), 26–31; 174 (1964), 59–66; 192 (1968), 16–21; 214 (1974), 39–41; 226 (1977), 47–51; 238 (1980), 65–67; 263 (1986), 77–80; id., *ILN* (May 25, 1963), 804–805; (July 1978), 64–65; id., *The Nabataeans*, Göthenburg 1973; id., *ADAJ* 20 (1975), 5–30; 22 (1977–1978), 81–101; 32 (1988), 189–194; id., *Bonner Jahrbücher* 180 (1980), 265–269; id., *Archaeology* 34/2 (1981), 27–34; 39/1 (1986), 19–25; id., *BAR* 7/2 (1981), 22–43; id., *AJA* 86 (1982), 268; 88 (1984), 247; id., *LA* 32 (1982), 482–489; 36 (1986), 346–348; id., *SHAJ* 1 (1982), 231–238; id., *Archiv für Orientforschung* 29–30 (1983–1984), 251–252; 33 (1986), 180–183; id., *American Journal of Arabic Studies* 1, n.d., 1–29; D. Kirkbride, *RB* 67 (1960), 235–238; id., *ADAJ* 4–5 (1960), 117–122; id., *SHAJ* 2 (1985), 117–124; G. R. H. Wright, *PEQ* 93 (1961), 8–37, 124–135; 101 (1969), 113–116; 102 (1970), 111–115; 105 (1973), 83–90; id., *ADAJ* 6–7 (1962), 24–54; 12–13 (1967–1968), 20–29; id., RB 73 (1966), 404–419; id., *Syria* 45 (1968), 25–40; id., *ZDPV* 88 (1972), 182–184; id., *MDAI Damaszener Mitteilungen* 2 (1985), 321–325; 3 (1988), 417–425; C.-M. Bennett, *Archaeology* 15 (1962), 277–279; id., *BTS* 84 (1966), 6–16; id., *RB* 73 (1966), 372–403; id., *Levant* 5 (1973), 131–133; (with D. L. Kennedy) 10 (1978), 163–165; id., *Art International* 26 (1983), 2–38; Y. Yadin, *Jaarbericht Ex Oriente Lux* 17 (1963), 227–231; *Syria* 45 (1968); *Die Nabatäer* (ed. H. J. Kellner), Munich 1970; K. Schmitt-Korte, *ADAJ* 14 (1971), 47–60; id., *Die Bemalte nabataäische Keramik* (ed. M. Lindner 1983), 174–197; id., *Studies in the History of Arabia: Proceedings of the Second International Symposium on Studies in the History of Arabia*, Riyadh 1987, 7–40; id. (and M. Cowell), *Numismatic Chronicle* 149 (1989), 33–58; A. Negev, *RB* 79 (1972), 381–389; 80 (1973), 364–383; 83 (1976), 203–236; id., *The Nabataean Potter's Workshop at Oboda*, Bonn 1974; id., *Aufstieg und Niedergang der römischen Welt* 2/8 (eds. W. Haase and H. Temporini), Berlin 1977, 520–686; id., *Antike Welt Sondern.* 7 (1976); id., *Nabatean Archaeology Today*, New York 1986; id., *BAR* 14/6 (1988), 32–35; I. B. Browning, *Petra*, London 1973 (Reviews), *PEQ* 107 (1975), 80–81. — *BASOR* 229 (1978), 75–76; F. Zayadine, *ADAJ* 18 (1973), 81–82; 19 (1974), 135–150; (with P. Hottier) 21 (1976), 93–104; 23 (1979), 185–197; 26 (1982), 365–393; 29 (1985), 239–250, 295–296; (with Z. T. Fiema) 30 (1986), 199–206; (with S. Farajat) 35 (1991), 275–311; id., *RB* 86 (1979), 133–136; id., *Bonner Jahrbücher* 180 (1980), 237–252; id., *SHAJ* 2 (1985), 159–173; 3 (1987), 131–142; id., *The Archaeology of Jordan and Other Studies* (S. H. Horn Fest.), Berrien Springs, Mich. 1986, 465–474; id., *Archiv für Orientforschung* 33 (1986), 177–180; id., *Der Königsweg: 9000 Jahre Kunst und Kultur in Jordanien* (eds. S. Mittmann et al.), Mainz 1987, 193–211; M. Lyttelton, *Baroque Architecture in Classical Antiquity*, London 1974 (index); J. T. Milik and J. Starcky, *ADAJ* 20 (1975), 111–130; J. T. Milik, ibid. 21 (1976), 143–152; J. A. Sauer, *BA* 42 (1979), 134; *Bonner Jahrbücher* 180 (1980), 231–272; *MdB* 14 (1980); J. Hornblower, *Hieronymus of Cardia*, Oxford 1981, 145–146, 148, 184; N. I. Khairy, *ADAJ* 28 (1984), 315–320; id., *ZDPV* 101 (1985), 32–42; id., *PEQ* 118 (1986), 101–108; id., *Levant* 19 (1987), 167–181; M. Lindner et al., *ADAJ* 28 (1984), 163–181; 31 (1987), 175–185; id., *LA* 37 (1987), 389–393; id., *SHAJ* 3 (1987), 291–294; id., *ZDPV* 104 (1988), 84–91; 106 (1990), 144–155; P. Mayerson, *Zeitschrift für Papyrologie und Epigraphik* 56 (1984), 223–230; 69 (1987), 251–260; J. S. McKenzie (with A. Phippen), *ADAJ* 27 (1983), 209–212; id., *Levant* 17 (1985), 157–170; (with A. Phippen) 19 (1987), 145–165, 217–218; id., *SHAJ* 3 (1987), 295–305; id., *PEQ* 120 (1988), 81–107; id., *Syria* 62/1–2 (1985); Z. T. Fiema, *ADAJ* 30 (1986), 329–332; S. Hart, *PEQ* 118 (1986), 91–95; R. G. Khouri, *Petra: A Guide to the Capital of the Nabateans*, London 1986; id., *Petra: A Brief Guide to the Antiquities* (Al Kutba Jordan Guides), Amman 1988; *Petra: Neue Ausgrabungen und Entdeckungen* (ed. M. Lindner) (Reviews), *LA* 37 (1987), 421–423. — *PEQ* 120 (1988), 153–154; D. Tarrier, *RB* 93 (1986), 254–256; P. Bienkowski, *BAIAS* 6 (1986–1987), 60–63; Khairieh 'Amr, ibid. (Review), *LA* 37 (1987), 423–424; M.-J. Roche, *Syria* 64 (1987), 217–222; 67 (1990), 377–395; A. Schmidt-Colinet, *SHAJ* 3 (1987), 143–150; H. Stierlin, *Stadte in der Wüste* (*Antike Kunst im Vorderen Orient*), Zurich 1987; R. Wenning, *Die Nabataäer: Denkmaäler und Geschichte* (Novum Testamentum et Orbis Antiquus 3), Freiburg 1987, 197–304; K. Matthiae, *ZDPV* 104 (1988), 74–83; *Akkadica Supplementum*, 7–8 (1989), 442–457; R. N. Jones, *BASOR* 275 (1989), 41–46; *Petra und das Königreich der Nabatäer* (Review), *Die Welt des Orients* 22 (1991), 155–158; T. F. C. Blagg, *Levant* 22 (1990), 131–137; L. Marino et al., *Marmor* 28 (1990), I–XIII; J. Naveh, *BASOR* 280 (1990), 89; J. Patrich, *The Formation of Nabatean Art*, Jerusalem 1990; R. A. Stucky et al., *ADAJ* 34 (1990), 249–283; 35 (1991), 251–273; K. S. Freyberger, *Damaszener Mitteilungen* 5 (1991), 1–8.

AVRAHAM NEGEV

POLEG, NAḤAL

IDENTIFICATION

Naḥal Poleg (in Arabic, Nahr el-Faliq) drains a large area in the *ḥamra* ridges of the Sharon, between the Yarkon and Alexander rivers. Until the beginning of the twentieth century, the area was one large swamp. Along the edges of the Naḥal Poleg basin are three sites, all of which have been excavated: Tel Poleg, 'Ein Zureiqiyye, and Tel 'Ashir. The results clearly demonstrate that the swamps prevented a fully developed and continuous settlement in the region.

TEL POLEG. Tel Poleg is situated on a *kurkar* spur (map reference 1550.1849) about 6 km (4 mi.) south of Netanya and 1.2 km (1 mi.) inland from the Mediterranean Sea. South of the mound, the old course of the stream cuts across the ridge; in the north, the ridge was breached, by design, in antiquity; the breach is now approximately 10 m wide.

Salvage excavations were carried out at the site in 1959 by R. Gophna, P. Beck, and J. Naveh, on behalf of the Israel Department of Antiquities and Museums; the site was reexamined by Gophna in 1964, after most of it had been destroyed by quarrying. The excavations indicate that the site was occupied in the Middle Bronze Age I and IIA, the Late Bronze Age, the Iron Age, and the Persian, Hellenistic, and Roman periods. The finds indicate that there were large settlements here only in the Middle Bronze Age IIA, the Iron Age, and the Persian period; the occupational remains from the other periods consisted only of sherds.

The Middle Bronze Age IIA remains are from three segments of a well-fortified structure (probably a fortress), enclosing an area of some 3 a. These segments are preserved in the eastern, southwestern, and northwestern parts of the site. The destruction due to quarrying made it impossible to determine the relationships among them. The fortification in the eastern part of the site (area A) was a brick wall (2.7 m thick) built on the steep declivity of the *kurkar* ridge. The surviving fortification in the southwest (area C) was a large brick tower (c. 8.5 m thick). Running up to this tower was a brick wall (c. 5 m thick), built along the western edge of the site

Tel Poleg: fish-shaped pottery vessel, MB II.

Tel Poleg: map of the mound and excavation areas.

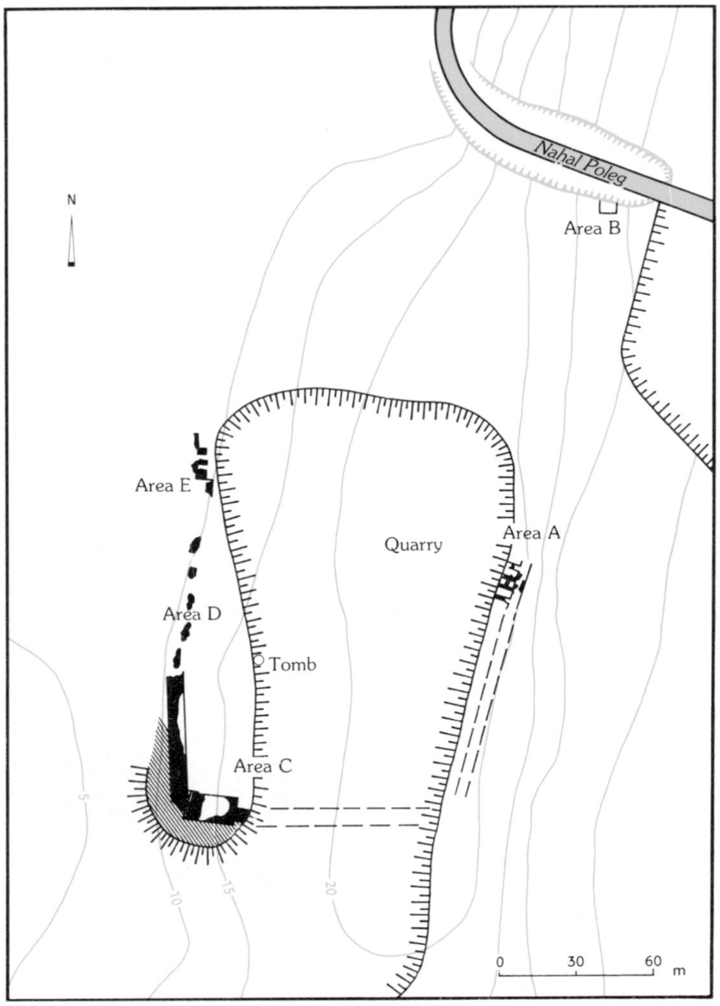

'Ein Zureiqiyye: map of the site and excavation areas.

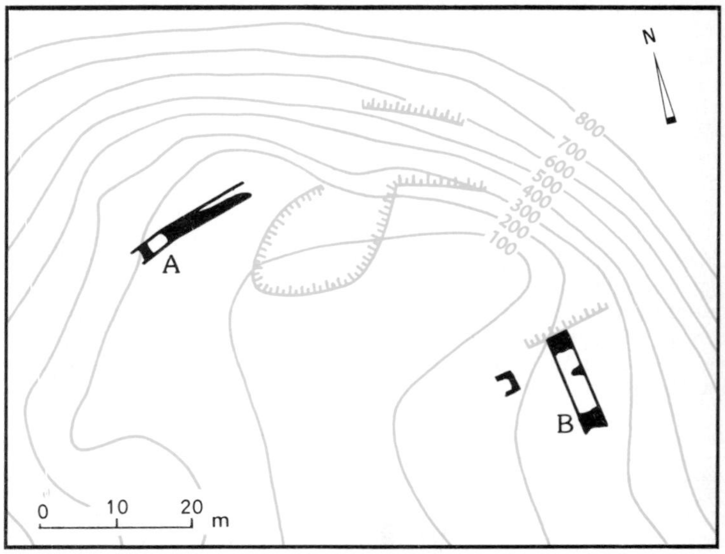

(area D). Unlike the eastern wall, in area A, the tower and western wall were built on slightly sloping ground and reinforced by a rampart built of layers of *kurkar* gravel. Among the remains of the brick fortifications in the northwestern part of the site (area E) was the right side of a gate, probably of the indirect-access type. The excavators also cleared the shaft of a burial cave from the Middle Bronze Age IIA; it had been destroyed by quarrying and its contents robbed (area D). All the Middle Bronze Age II pottery excavated at Tel Poleg in the vicinity of the fortifications and in the burial cave, as well as that found in the debris on the destroyed mound, was assigned to the Middle Bronze Age IIA.

In the Iron Age IIA, Tel Poleg was occupied by an unfortified settlement that extended over most of the site; its remains were almost totally destroyed by the quarry. A few rubbish pits, cut into the remains of the Bronze Age fortifications, were uncovered in area A. They were full of ash and sherds from the Iron Age IIA (fragments of bowls, cooking pots, and storage jars). Overlying the ruins of the Bronze Age fortress in area C sections of walls were found, built of stone and mud brick, from the Iron Age. On the basis of the pottery in these two areas, the Iron Age IIA settlement at Tel Poleg is dated to the second half of the tenth century BCE. Similar pottery has been discovered at other sites on the Coastal Plain and in the Jezreel Valley (Tell Qasile, Tel Michal, Tel Mevorakh, Tell Abu Hawam, Tell Keisan, Megiddo, and Tel 'Amal).

'EIN ZUREIQIYYE. 'Ein Zureiqiyye is a small site on the southern bank of Naḥal Poleg, approximately 3.5 km (2 mi.) southeast of Tel Poleg (map reference 1382.1833). It was excavated in 1978–1979 by R. Gophna and E. Ayalon, under the auspices of the Israel Department of Antiquities and Museums and Tel Aviv University. The excavations revealed two sections of a wall and parts of structures from a fortress dated to the Middle Bronze Age IIA, about one acre in area.

In the northern part of the site, the stone foundations of a wall (3.2 m thick) were exposed for a length of 18 m. Another part of this wall was found running for 16 m along the eastern part of the site, and there, too, it is 3.2 m thick. The eastern segment of the wall also revealed some of its brick superstructure, preserved to a height of 0.6 m. Also uncovered were parts of structures testifying to two phases

Tel Poleg: section through the tower in area C, MB II.

Tel 'Ashir: rounded stones and maṣṣebot *in the center of the excavation area, looking north.*

in the fortress. All the pottery discovered near the wall and inside the structures was assigned to the Middle Bronze Age IIA. Isolated sherds from the Late Bronze Age may indicate that the site was also occupied in that period.

TEL 'ASHIR. Tel 'Ashir is a small mound on a hill above the southern bank of Naḥal Poleg. It is not far from the river's outlet to the sea, in the precincts of the Wingate Institute (map reference 1347.1856). The site was excavated in 1981–1982 by R. Gophna and E. Ayalon, on behalf of the Israel Department of Antiquities and Museums and Tel Aviv University. No structures were found. The finds were a dozen large *kurkar* stones and installations. The stones are rounded, flat, and thick (diameter, 0.5–1.6 m) and surrounded by smaller stones. Almost all the stones were found arranged in one row, and beside them, driven into the ground, were flat pieces of limestone, apparently *maṣṣebot*. The limestone was brought to the site from the Samaria Hills to the east. The round *kurkar* stones and limestone *maṣṣebot* were found in a thick layer of ashes, including sherds and fragments of copper artifacts, all from the Middle Bronze Age I. It is assumed that the site was then an open cultic shrine.

Tel Poleg: R. Gophna, *Museum Ha'aretz Bulletin* 11 (1969), 43–46; id., *TA* 5 (1978), 136–147; (with E. Ayalon) 7 (1980), 147–151; I. Mozel, ibid. 5 (1978), 152–158; M. Kochavi et al., *ZDPV* 95 (1979), 121–165; Weippert 1988, 207, 216, 224; L. Singer-Avitz, *Excavations at Tel Michal, Israel* (eds. Z. Herzog et al.), Minneapolis 1989, 375–380.

'Ein Zureiqiyye: R. Gophna and E. Ayalon, *TA* 9 (1982), 69–78.

RAM GOPHNA

Q

QAFZEH CAVE

IDENTIFICATION

The Qafzeh Cave is located on the left bank of Wadi el-Haj, which descends from Nazareth to the Jezreel Valley. The cave is situated about 220 m above sea level and about 7 m above the wadi channel. The cave was formed in Cenomanian limestone and consists of one major chamber with a few side alcoves and a chimney. The main chamber is about 21 by 17 m; its main opening faces the southwest. In front of its entrance, the prehistoric deposits form a terrace.

EXCAVATIONS

The cave was first excavated by R. Neuville and M. Stekelis (1933–1935), who identified the remains of medieval and Byzantine occupations in its uppermost layers. Below were layers from the Upper Paleolithic period that, among other finds, contained two fragmentary human skulls, as yet unpublished. The Mousterian layers, excavated in more than half of the chamber's area to bedrock, provided many artifacts. However, it was only in the entrance area, where the bedrock slopes toward the wadi, and in an oval-shaped test pit dug on the terrace that a few Mousterian human relics were recovered. The lithic industries from the 1933–1935 excavations were briefly reported by Neuville, who attributed them to the Levalloiso-Mousterian culture.

A new series of excavations began in 1965, carried out by B. Vandermeersch until 1979. He was joined by O. Bar-Yosef in 1978. The main digging efforts were addressed to the "terrace" area where a surface of about 12 sq m was excavated, finally joining Neuville's test pit. Inside the cave, the stratigraphy of the historical, Neolithic, and Upper Paleolithic layers (7–1) was clarified in a small-scale excavated area. These deposits overlay the heavily leached Mousterian layers (12–13). Most of the artifacts in the latter were slightly abraded, indicating that they had been redeposited when the main chamber was flooded. There is a clear stratigraphic break between these layers and the overlying colluvial deposit of terra rossa soil (Mediterranean red earth) with angular limestone fragments, which contains an Upper Paleolithic blade industry.

The excavations on the terrace exposed a sequence of layers, numbered in Roman numerals. Layers III–XV were excavated in a relatively small area and were all brecciated. From layer V downward they contain rich Mousterian assemblages (although the samples from V–VIII are minimal), with numerous animal bones, many broken by humans. The brecciated zone in this section, where the exact identification of the layers is uncertain, was marked XVI.

Layers XVII–XXIV are relatively poor in large animal remains. On the other hand, these layers provided abundant microvertebrate bones. This indicates that at least part of the terrace was shadowed by the cave's roof, where barn owls, the main agent of introducing micromammals to the site, probably nested. This part of the cave's roof has since disappeared.

The lithic assemblages from the lower layers are relatively poor but are identified as Mousterian, with a high incidence of Levallois radial-preparation core-reduction technique. All the human remains were uncovered in this part of the site's stratigraphy. A series of thermoluminescence dates, averaged as 92,000 BP (with a range of 80,000–100,000 years), supported an earlier contention based on paleoclimatic interpretation and correlations between microvertebrate assemblages from the Tabun and Hayonim caves. The possibility that this part of the terrace was under a limestone roof would increase the thermoluminescence dates to about 110,000–120,000 years, thus placing it in the Last Interglacial.

The faunal remains from the site, first studied by J. Bouchud, indicate the presence of numerous deer and wild cattle bones in layers XV–XI and a rapid increase in gazelle bones in the layers above. Among the other animal remains are ibex, wild boar, horse, rhinoceros, and wild camel.

The rodent assemblages, studied in detail by E. Tchernov, are mainly

Qafzeh Cave: general view.

Qafzeh Cave: Mousterian scrapers.

Homo sapiens skull.

derived from layers XVIII–XXIV, with a small collection from the lower part of layer XV. The significance of the rodent community at Qafzeh is in the presence of two archaic forms: *Muridae Mastomys batei*, a commensal African rat that resembles the Levantine house mouse, and *Arvicanthis ectos*, another African rat. These species were also found in the Tabun Cave, in layers E and F.

The main discoveries from Qafzeh are undoubtedly the human remains. The cave entrance served for a long time as a burial ground. The skeletal remains uncovered by Neuville and Stekelis include Homo 4, 5, and 6. The first two were located in the test sounding on the terrace; the excavation of these burials was completed in 1979. Additional skeletal remains, including well-delineated burials, were uncovered after 1965.

Homo 8 was not well preserved, but it appeared to be a semiflexed burial with the head facing east. Homo 9 was a special burial of a male twenty to twenty-one years old, buried in a semiflexed position, with a child burial at his feet. This is the only double burial known from the Middle Paleolithic period. Homo 11 is a child with the antlers of a fallow deer buried across its chest. Homo 12, 13, 14, and 15 are the remains of children, all very fragmentary. In addition, numerous isolated teeth were collected in these layers.

The study of the skeletal remains (the adults by Vandermeersch and the juveniles by A. M. Tillier) indicates that this population was different from the Southwestern Asian Neanderthals, which include the Shanidar group (Iraq), the woman from the Tabun Cave and the groups from the ʿAmud and Kebara caves. The Qafzeh group is closer morphologically to the hominids from the Skhul Cave, known in the literature as Proto-Cro-Magnons.

The layers in which the various burials and isolated human remains were exposed also contained a lump of red ocher that bears signs of scraping, numerous fragments of ostrich eggshells, and a few *Glycemeris* shells brought from the shores of the Mediterranean. The same shells were observed at Skhul, which is closer to the shoreline; neither these nor other species of shells appear at Mousterian sites.

The Upper Paleolithic industry at Qafzeh is characterized by blade and bladelet production, numerous el-Wad points, end scrapers, and burins. The industry is attributed to the Ahmarian tradition, but its exact age is unknown. The presence of an Emireh point may indicate an early age (c. 42,000–38,000 BP), which would be in accordance with an early assay of amino-racemization dating.

The uppermost layers at Qafzeh indicate that this cave was only used ephemerally until the Byzantine period. The washed-in colluvium terra rossa with angular gravels filled most of the upper portion of the main chamber.

Main publication: B. Vandermeersch, *Les Hommes Fossiles de Qafzeh (Israël)* (Cahiers de Paléontologie), Paris 1981.

Other studies: M. R. Neuville, *QDAP* 3 (1934), 175; 4 (1935), 202; 5 (1936), 199; id., *Le Paléolithique et le Mésolithique du Désert de Judée*, Paris 1951, 179–184; B. Vandermeersch, *IEJ* 15 (1965), 247–248; 16 (1966), 267–269; 17 (1967), 264–267; 20 (1970), 115–117; id., *Compte Rendue de l'Académie des Sciences de Paris* 262 (1966), 1434–1436; 268 (1969), 2562–2565; id., *RB* 74 (1967), 60–63; 75 (1968), 258–261; 77 (1970), 561–564; id., *Bulletin de la Société Préhistorique* 66 (1969), 157–158; id., *Archéologia* 45 (1972), 6–15; id., *The Origin of Homo Sapiens* (ed. F. Bordes), *Proceedings of the Paris Symposium, 2–5 Sept. 1969*, Paris 1972, 49–54; id., *Histoire et Archéologie* 100 (1985), 57; id., *Archéologie, Art et Histoire de la Palestine*, (Colloque du Centenaire de la Section des Sciences Religieuses, Ecole Pratique des Hautes Etudes, Sept. 1986, ed. E. -M. Laperrousaz) Paris 1988, 18–22; id. (with O. Bar-Yosef), *Paléorient* 14/2 (1988), 115–117; B. Arensburg and H. Nathan, *L'Anthropologie* 76 (1972), 301–208; B. Arensburg and A.-M. Tillier, *Bulletins et Mémoires de la Société d'Anthropologie de Paris* 10 (1983), 61–69; G. Haas, *Palaeovertebrata* 5 (1972), 261–270; A. Ronen and B. Vandermeersch, *Quaternaria* 16 (1972), 189–202; H. V. Vallois and B. Vandermeersch, *L'Anthropologie* 76 (1972), 71–96; J. Bouchud, *Paléorient* 2 (1974), 87–102; A.-M. Tillier (and B. Vandermeersch), *Compte Rendue de l'Academie des Sciences de Paris*, Série D/282 (1976), 1097–1100; id., *Paléorient* 5 (1979), 17–66; 10 (1984), 7–48; 14/2 (1988), 130–136; id. (and P. Tassy), *Bulletins et Mémoires de la Sociéte d'Anthropologie de Paris*, Série XIV/4 (1987), 297f; id., *Investigations in South Levantine Prehistory: Préhistoire du Sud-Levant* (*BAR*/IS 497, eds. O. Bar-Yosef and B. Vandermeersch,), Oxford 1989, 343–350; O. Bar-Yosef and B. Vandermeersch, *Prehistoire du Levant* (*CNRS Colloque* 598, eds. J. Cauvin and P. Sanlaville), Paris 1981, 281–286; J. Dastugue, *Paléorient* 7/1 (1981), 135–140; H. P. Schwarcz et al., *Journal of Human Evolution* 17 (1988), 733–737; Weippert 1988, 79; B. Boutie, *Investigations in South Levantine Prehistory* (op. cit.), Oxford 1989, 213–229; Y. Rak, *American Journal of Physical Anthropology* 81 (1990), 323–332.

OFER BAR-YOSEF, BERNARD VANDERMEERSCH

QALANDIYEH

IDENTIFICATION

The site is about 8 km (5 mi.) northwest of Jerusalem, at the edge of the Arab village of Qalandiyeh, near the ʿAtarot Airport (map reference 1419.1698). A farm from the Second Temple period was discovered here with buildings, winepresses, and tombs, as well as a quarry, apparently from the same period. The site was excavated in 1978 and 1981 by I. Magen, on behalf of the staff officer for archaeology in Judea and Samaria.

EXCAVATIONS

The farm complex consists of four units: the industrial area in the center (area P); the northern compound, comprising a main building (F) and a storehouse (G); building M, adjoining building F; and the main building in the south (building C), which was severely damaged when the area was cleared of stones and whose plan resembles building F's. Several tombs and winepresses outside the farm were also excavated.

INDUSTRIAL AREA (AREA P). Six winepresses for treading grapes and an installation operating on the beam-and-weights principle used for extracting juice from the grape skins, and possibly for the preparation of perfumes, were found here. Another extraction apparatus was unearthed east of building F. Weights and nails found lying on its floor belonged to the burned beam of a press. In light of the absence of installations for crushing olives—a vat and a pressbeam—it can be assumed that all the extraction installations found here were used in wine production. In Talmudic literature (J.T. *Ter.* 3:7) this type of system is known as "the press room." East of the farm a unique winepress (A) was uncovered. It was unusually large and consisted of two treading floors—an upper and a lower one. In the center of the lower floor is a square hole through which the peels and refuse passed for additional pressing. The press was apparently plastered.

NORTHERN COMPOUND. Two main structures were excavated in the northern compound.

Building F. Building F (30 by 40 m) is composed of a central courtyard (17 by 20 m) surrounded by dwellings, workrooms, and storerooms. The building is constructed of large field stones; but the thresholds and doorjambs are extremely well dressed.

The western wing of the building (area S) consists of six long rooms, with entrances facing the central courtyard. The pottery and tools found in the rooms indicate that they were probably used for storage. This wing extends southward to the industrial area. At its southern end is a rock-cut plastered mikveh (ritual bath) that was entered from the west. An enclosure wall ran to the north.

The eastern and southern wings were the buildings's main wings. The eastern wing contains square rooms, several of them divided into smaller units, probably to facilitate their roofing. In one of the rooms the weights of an extraction installation were found that had been used as a base to support the roof. The main entrance (F13), blocked in the building's final phase, was on this side. The many coins found testify to commercial activity here. The northern part of the eastern wing was damaged when stones were removed.

The southern wing is built on two rock terraces. The upper terrace (area K) includes a staircase leading up to it and built dwelling rooms adjoining area P. The rooms contained numerous basalt pounding and grinding tools. Between the two terraces, a solid wall of large field stones was erected either in the site's last phase, or after its destruction. The lower terrace includes rooms—both built and rock-hewn—and, at its center, a cistern (F39) covered with flat stone slabs. The cistern received its water by means of a gutter whose lower part was hewn out of the bedrock. A roller for smoothing roof plaster was also found in this wing, which indicates that the structure's roofs were made of branches and clay.

Near the cistern is a rock-cut plastered ritual bath. Its upper part was vault-shaped and built of field stones. Despite the proximity of the ritual bath's stepped pool and the cistern, no connection was found between them; the pool apparently received its water from another source. In the southern wing's facade are two small plastered pools (50 by 70 cm) that were used for washing; they are similar to the ones found in building C (see below). Pools like these have also been found at other Hellenistic sites.

In its last phase, building F was used as a pen for sheep and cattle, as is attested by the large boulders placed at the entrances to the rooms. In this phase the ritual bath and industrial area P fell into disuse.

Building G. Building G (13 by 14 m), at the northeastern end of building F, was also damaged when stones were removed in later periods, at least on its eastern side. It contains nine square rooms. Its plan is not typical of a dwelling; it may have been used as a storehouse, as indicated by the many amphorae found here. In several rooms remains of various rock-cut installations from the farm's first building phase were found. The numismatic evidence shows that building G was erected after buildings F and C; it went out of use when the growing of grapes and wine production ceased.

BUILDING M. Building M is a square building (10 by 10 m); it adjoins the eastern outer wall of building F. It differs in plan from building G, but resembles buildings F and C: it has a central courtyard surrounded by rooms—four in the west, three in the north, and two or three in the south—and an enclosure wall in the east. The rooms' entrances all face a square courtyard (F45). The rooms and courtyard were paved with coarse stone slabs. The finds—grinding tools, a cooking pot, small vessels, and many stone vessels—indicate that building M was used as a dwelling.

The building was erected above an ancient extraction installation that had fallen into disuse; stone weights from the installation were found in the courtyard. When building M was erected, the main entrance (F13) was blocked. The finds indicate that building F's eastern complex of rooms was incorporated in building M and used as dwellings; the other parts of the building were converted into a stable. Building G, on the other hand, fell into disuse when building M was erected.

Building M was apparently constructed in the early first century CE, when building F was turned into a pen for sheep or cattle. Building M probably housed those tending the flocks or herds.

SOUTHERN BUILDING (C). Although building C was mostly destroyed during the clearing of stones in the area, it could be established that its plan and dimensions (30 by 40 m) resembled those of building F. The building's western wall extends southward, as shown by the remains beyond the heaps of removed stones. As in building F, several building phases can be distinguished. The earliest phase is that of the agricultural installations—some incorporated in later buildings and others abandoned.

Building C was erected in the second phase; it consists of a square courtyard surrounded by dwelling rooms and storerooms. The western wing resembles

Qalandiyeh: plan of the site.

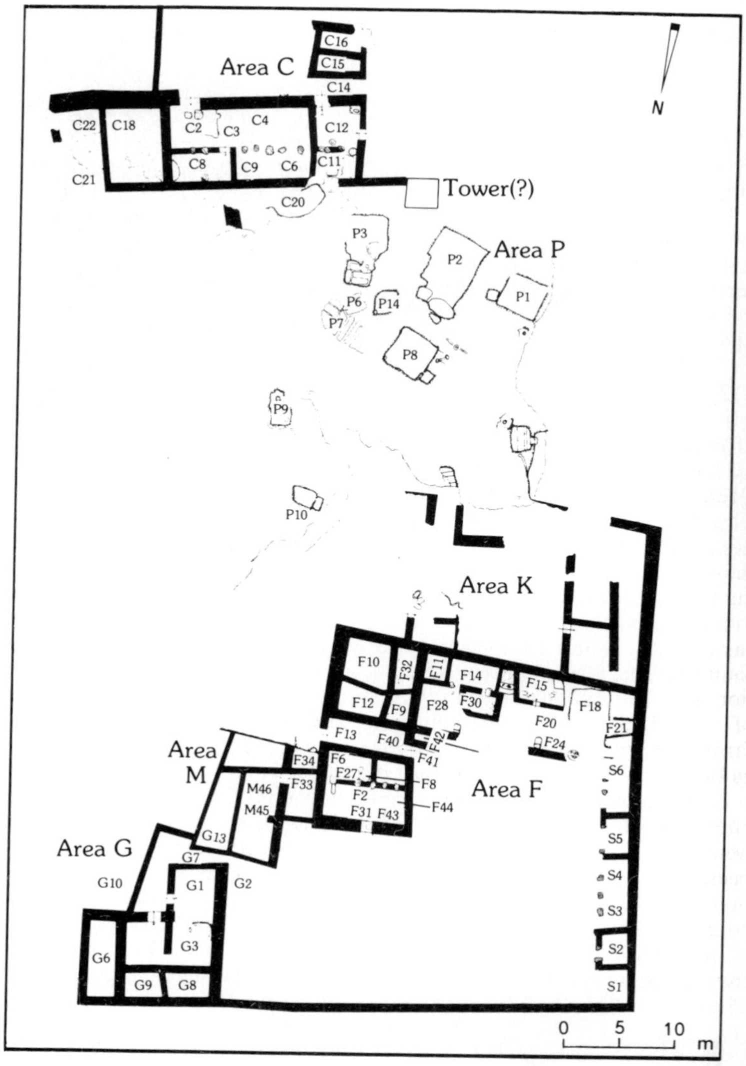

Large winepress east of the site: a treading floor with a square depression in the center for collecting the refuse; (foreground) two pits for collecting the must.

Southern building: the stable area.

that of building F. It is composed of a series of rooms (C11, C12, C15, and C16), with an entrance to the courtyard (C14) reminiscent of that in building F (F13), both in shape and location. The southern and eastern wings are not preserved.

The northern wing has two entrances. One entrance, with a rock-cut threshold and doorjambs, is in the northeastern corner and faces the central courtyard. The other entrance, which survives up to its lintel, is in the western wall and leads to room C12. This wing was composed of a series of rooms (C6, C7, C8, and C9) connected by a long room. In the west are two other rooms (C11 and C12). The entrance to room C12 faces a cave in which amphorae had been stored. Two small pools, similar to those found in the courtyard of building F, were uncovered in the corner of room C12 and in the room next to the eastern gate. In room C12 weights were found belonging to an ancient extraction installation that, over the course of time, had been scattered in the farm's various rooms. They were used as bases for the wooden beams supporting the roof.

In the second phase of building C, the character of the northern wing was altered, as in building F: the walls were reinforced and large stone columns were set along the length of the center of the wing. Some of the columns had been quarried in the industrial area, and others had been removed from the building's eastern wing. Troughs for animals were installed between the columns, thus turning the entire wing into a stable.

In the building's last phase, the northern wing housed families; refugees from the First Jewish Revolt against the Romans may have found refuge here. The western entrance was completely blocked, and the troughs were used as the base for partition walls in the rooms. A small tower may have been erected at the edge of building C in this phase. The sherds, coins of the revolt, and remains of a suit of armor found here should be attributed to this phase.

In the opinion of the excavator, buildings F and C were contemporaneous and had the same plan: a central courtyard, a double wing, a main wing, a series of storerooms, and an enclosure wall on the fourth side. This type of building is reminiscent of the courtyard buildings from the Persian period.

BURIALS. Many tombs were found in the area of the modern village and to the east of the farm. Noteworthy among them is tomb A, east of the farm. It consists of a rock-cut central courtyard (5.5 by 6 m), from which two stepped

Tomb A: facade and entrances, Hellenistic-Roman period.

entrances lead to two burial chambers that can be blocked. Three burial troughs (3 by 3.4 m) were found in a square cistern at the entrance to the main burial chamber. To the right of the main entrance another entrance leads to a tomb (2.4 by 2.7 m) with two loculi. Tomb A may reflect two burial traditions: the troughs were cut in the Hellenistic period, and the loculi in the first century CE.

QUARRIES. The entire southwestern part of the site is dotted with a large number of quarries. These may have been used by the builders of Jerusalem in the Second Temple period. The farm would have been used as a pen and a place for raising the animals that transported the building stones.

SUMMARY

Diverse and rich finds were unearthed at the site, including hundreds of coins and stone and clay vessels, mostly amphorae. The wealth of the finds is in sharp contrast to the farm's simple construction. The ceramic and numismatic finds indicate that the farm at Qalandiyeh was founded in the time of the Ptolemies (third century BCE). This was a period in which Palestine enjoyed economic prosperity as a result of trade with Egypt and other parts of the Ptolemaic empire and from the introduction of new farming methods. In the second century BCE, agricultural activity on the farm reached its peak. In the first century CE, agriculture here ceased, and the farm may have been inhabited by workers, who, with the help of their animals, quarried building stones for the magnificent buildings being constructed in Jerusalem.

D. C. Baramki, *QDAP* 2 (1933), 105–109; A. K. Dajani, *ADAJ* 2 (1953), 75–77.

ITZHAK MAGEN

QASHISH, TEL

IDENTIFICATION

Tel Qashish (Tell Qasis) is located on the northern bank of Naḥal Kishon, at the place where a bend in the stream encloses the site on two sides (map reference 160.232). Tel Qashish thus enjoyed an excellent strategic position on one of the Kishon fords and close proximity to Jokneam, a neighboring city, only some 2 km (1 mi.) away. The elongated mound (c. 270 by 160 m) covers an area of about 2.5 a. The western half is about 5 m higher than the eastern half. The mound slopes steeply on all sides except the northeast, where the approach road was probably located. Y. Aharoni suggested that the site should be identified with Helkath, number 112 on the list of Thutmose III. The excavators propose identifying it with Dabbesheth (Jos. 19:11).

EXPLORATION

Excavations at the site began in 1978. The eight seasons of excavations conducted since then have been under the auspices of the Hebrew University of Jerusalem and the Israel Exploration Society, directed by A. Ben-Tor; they were part of the Jokneam Regional Project (q.v. Jokneam). A survey made before the excavations showed that it was relatively easy to reach Late Bronze and Iron Age strata in the higher part of the site; that Middle Bronze Age strata lay close to the surface in the center of the site; and that throughout the lower part of the site Early Bronze Age strata were closest to the surface.

EXCAVATION RESULTS

The excavations at Tel Qashish have revealed the following stratification:

Period	*Stratum/Finds*
Arab	Sherds
Hellenistic	Sherds; coin
Persian	I
Persian/Iron III	II A–B
Iron III/Iron II	III A–C
Iron I	IV
LB IIB	V
LB IIA	VI
LB I	VII A–B
MB IIC	VIII
MB IIB	IX A–C
MB IIA	X
EB III (MBII?)	XI
EB II–III	XII A–E
EB I	XIII–XV
Chalcolithic	Sherds
Neolithic	Flints

EARLY BRONZE AGE: STRATA XV TO XII (XI?). With the exception of some flint artifacts, including microliths and arrowheads, associated with the Neolithic period, and some Chalcolithic sherds, discovered in the initial survey and on bedrock, the earliest settlement remains at Tel Qashish date to the Early Bronze Age I. Massive, well-built houses from that period were founded directly on bedrock. However, this occupation phase has been identified only in a very limited area. It is, therefore, impossible to trace a coherent plan for the settlement or even for individual buildings. One structure is of special interest, however. Its corners are rounded on the outside and rectilinear on the inside, a phenomenon common in buildings of the period. Three architectural phases could be discerned. Pottery from this period was recovered from an extensive area, extending well beyond the limits of the mound, suggesting that the settlement at that time extended over a large area. The ceramic assemblage includes many pithoi with bow rims, hole-mouth jars, pots with bent spouts, band-slip decoration, and gray-burnished ware. The plant remains from this period included olive pits, wheat grains, and vetch seeds. Of special importance among the finds was a cylinder seal impression depicting a row of animals, similar to a seal impression found recently at Tel Shadud in the Jezreel Valley and to one from Megiddo stage V.

In the next occupation phase, the site was enclosed by a fortification wall built directly on top of the Early Bronze Age I remains. The city wall, of which a stretch of some 20 m was exposed in the northeastern corner of the site, had a 2.5- to 3-m-wide stone foundation laid in a herringbone pattern and preserved to a height of more than one meter. Almost all the brick superstructure has disappeared, but here and there remains of the bottom course of bricks were found. Another wall (c. 1 m thick), some 10 m of which have been exposed, runs outside the city wall and parallel to it. At its southern end, the wall makes a right-angle turn to join the city wall. This may represent an outer wall, or a retaining wall to reinforce the main city wall at a vulnerable point. Several changes and additions to the fortification system were identified in the excavations. At the northern end of the excavated area, the city wall had been

Tel Qashish: plan of the mound and excavation areas.

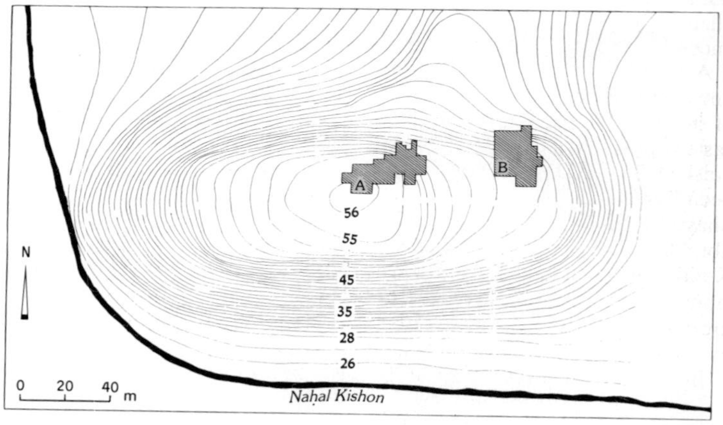

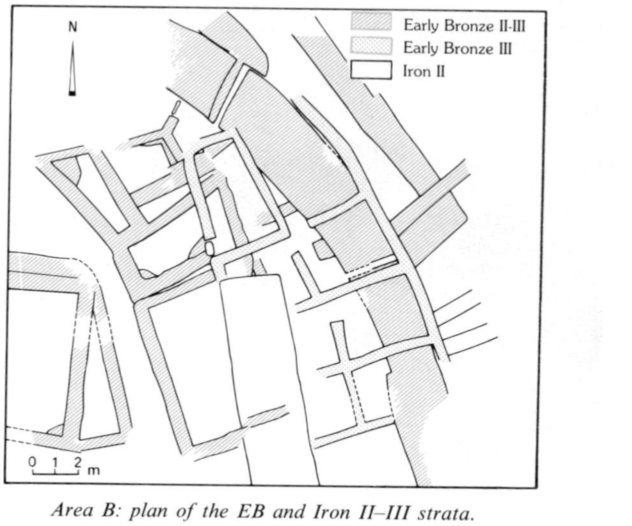

Area B: plan of the EB and Iron II–III strata.

Overview of a street and buildings from the EB.

completely eroded, and probably the gate as well, which must have been located here.

Several of the well-built houses have corners reinforced on the inside by a stone revetment. In area B three clearly defined building phases can be identified in these structures. A stretch of street or alley (c. 1.5 m wide) was uncovered that ran parallel to the city wall.

A short stretch of the city wall and Early Bronze Age buildings were uncovered in area A, in the northern and eastern part of the higher part of the mound. The houses in this area were more solidly built than in the eastern part of the site (area B); here five building phases could be distinguished. The relationship between the two stratigraphic complexes has not been finally clarified, but based on the ceramic evidence, the five building phases in this area should be attributed to the Early Bronze Age II–III. The abundance of various kinds of metallic ware and the absence of Khirbet Kerak ware are noteworthy. A considerable number of cylinder seal impressions were found, generally on metallic-ware jars. Most of these impressions are of the geometric type, but one bears a cult scene depicting a man disguised as an animal, and an animal near a building that is probably a shrine.

In the last phase of the Early Bronze Age settlement, but still in Early Bronze Age III, the fortification system went out of use and houses were built on top of the line of the city wall. However, the houses, mostly uncovered along the edges of the mound, were built close to each other, so that their outer walls formed a kind of defensive line. The standard of construction in this phase is inferior to that in earlier phases; the walls were thin and built of small field stones. The floor level in these houses was lower than the street level, with steps leading to each house. Their floor plan indicates that these were fore-courtyard houses: a courtyard containing various installations is located in front of the living quarters. This settlement appears to have been abandoned, not destroyed.

MIDDLE BRONZE AGE II: STRATA X TO VIII. Remains from the Middle Bronze Age II were found only on the higher part of the site, where they were built on top of the Early Bronze Age walls. There was no accumulation of debris between the strata from the two periods, and since remains of Early Bronze Age walls were probably still visible on the surface, in some cases the Middle Bronze Age walls were founded directly on top of earlier walls.

The architectural remains include part of a planned settlement and a fortification system from the early part of the Middle Bronze Age IIB or from the transition between the Middle Bronze Age IIA and IIB. An even

Pottery vessels, EB I.

Cylinder seal impression, EB III.

EB II–III city wall and (left) EB III walls of houses above it.

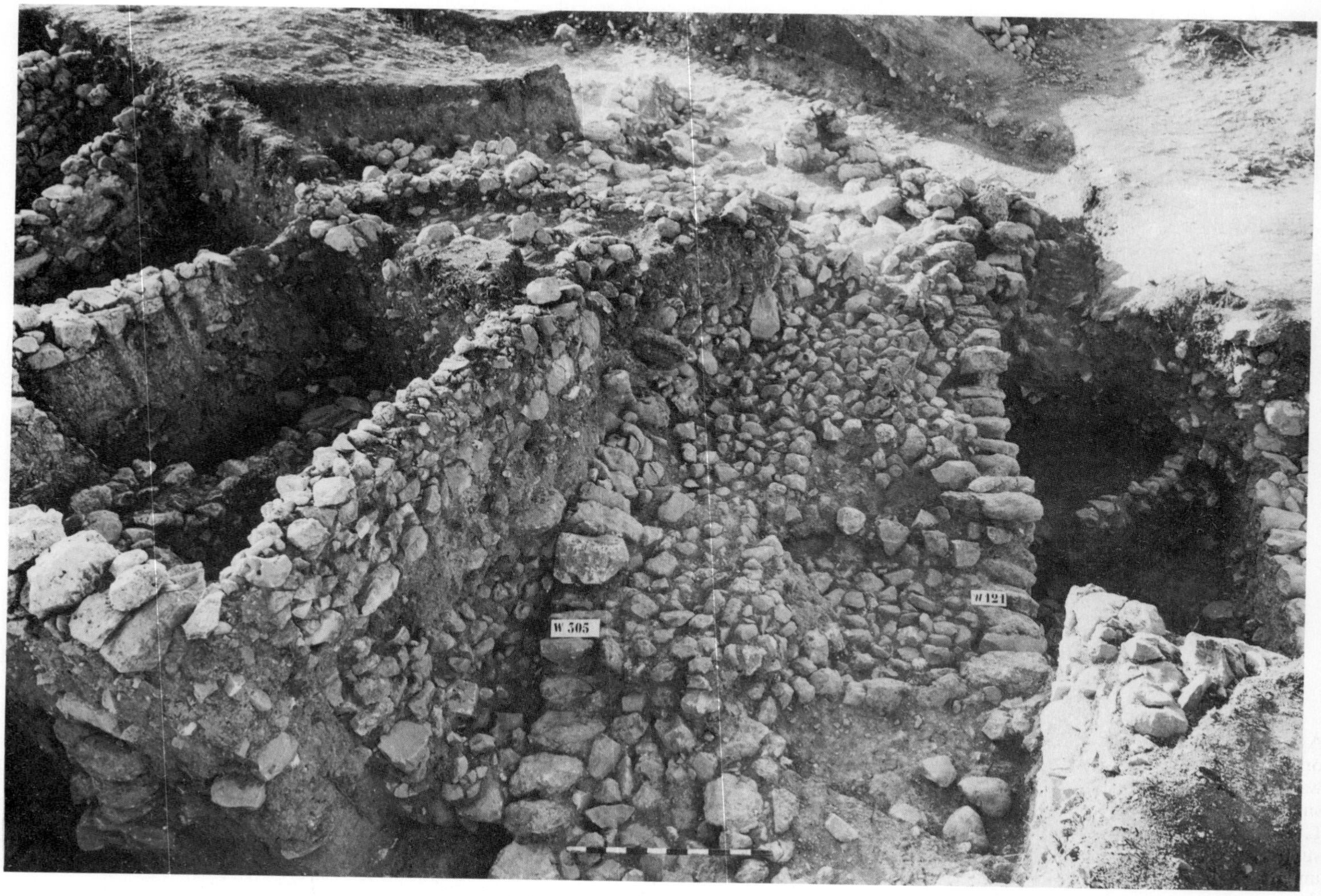

earlier Middle Bronze Age II occupation may have existed on the site, as indicated by floor fragments and some pottery vessels uncovered under the foundations of the fortifications. However, so far, no building remains of this earlier phase have come to light.

Isometric reconstruction of the city wall, the tower, and the structure adjoining the fortifications, MB IIB.

The fortification system is composed of a city wall (c. 2 m thick), with a rectangular tower attached to its inner face at the point where the wall takes a sharp turn to the south. A small glacis built against the outer face of the wall consists mainly of earth and stone chips.

A complex of rooms and a courtyard were exposed inside the city wall. These are associated on one side with the fortifications and on the other with a paved alley or street running east–west, parallel to the line of the city wall. This town plan is typical of Middle Bronze Age settlements, such as at Taanach, Shechem, Shiloh, the City of David in Jerusalem, and Gezer. This stratum had three subphases, all lasting for only a short period of time. Two jar burials were found under the floors of the rooms, a phenomenon known from many other contemporary sites and nearby Jokneam. The finds consisted mostly of pottery; of special interest is a group of eleven large storage jars found in the courtyard of the house.

The nature of the transition from the Middle Bronze Age to the Late Bronze

Pottery krater, end of the MB II.

LB storage jar with a palm-and-ibex design.

Age is not completely clear. In this building phase, exposed in a limited area only, several stone-paved areas were uncovered that are not associated with the walls of buildings. Traces of a fierce fire were found everywhere. Storage jars similar to those from the earlier phase can be attributed to this phase.

LATE BRONZE AGE: STRATA VII TO V. Three main strata and several substrata from this period (sixteenth–thirteenth centuries BCE) have been uncovered. The settlement seems to have been destroyed by fire twice during this period—first in the fourteenth century BCE and again (the final destruction) at the end of the Late Bronze Age. At that time, the settlement was unfortified, although the edge of a massive building with walls some 2 m thick, located near the corner of the mound, may represent part of an isolated tower erected in the last phases of the Late Bronze Age.

The earliest Late Bronze Age buildings follow the orientation of the buildings in the preceding period. However, in the transition to the Late Bronze Age II, the orientation changed. Because only small areas with remains of the period were uncovered, no overall settlement plan could be established. Pebble floors and cooking facilities were uncovered in some of the courtyards. The ceramic assemblage included primarily local wares, with only a few imported Cypriot and Mycenean vessels. Among the local wares, painted decoration was common, including a jar bearing a painted palm-and-ibex design and several sherds of bichrome and chocolate-on-white wares.

Traces of the fierce destruction by fire of the Late Bronze Age settlement (layers of ash, brick rubble, and an abundance of pottery) are evident wherever remains of the period have been uncovered.

IRON AGE: STRATA IV TO IIB. Most of the Iron Age remains were exposed on the higher part of the mound, suggesting that the settlement in that period was located there. Only scattered traces of human activity in the Iron Age were discovered on the lower part of the site.

The architectural remains clearly belong to several phases. The earliest remains are dated to the Iron Age I, including collared-rim jars and some Philistine sherds. Of special interest is a stone-built agricultural installation paved with stone slabs that drained into a krater that was found in situ. A similar installation was found at nearby Jokneam, where it is also attributed to the same, or a slightly later, period. The installations are connected with agricultural production, probably of oil.

The Iron Age II is represented at Tel Qashish by building remains on both the high and the low parts of the site. Of special interest is a pit in which several vessels were placed, among them a globular jug decorated in the black-on-red style and two bowls, one with lugs and the other a kernos. These were special vessels, not intended for daily use. The Iron Age III settlement is represented by isolated building remains and contemporary pottery. No evidence of destruction at the end of the period was found.

PERSIAN PERIOD: STRATUM IIA–I. The last clearly defined occupation strata on the site date to the Persian period. The most impressive building for this period—probably a (fortified?) farmhouse, with thick walls of very large stones—was uncovered on the lower part of the mound. These remains lay directly on the surface, so that only a few patches of floors were preserved. This building probably already existed in an earlier period, because Iron Age sherds were found on the lower floor fragments associated with the same walls.

The latest evidence of human activity at the site is a few sherds, some glass fragments, coins, and other finds from the Hellenistic period and some remains from the Early Arab period.

J. Garstang, *BBSAJ* 2 (1922), 16–17; A. Ben-Tor, *BAR* 6/2 (1980), 30–44; A. Ben-Tor (et al.), *IEJ* 31 (1981), 137–164; id., *ESI* 6 (1987–1988), 106–109; Y. Portugali, *TA* 9 (1982), 170–188; M. L. Hunt, "The Iron Age Pottery of the Yoqneam Regional Project" (Ph.D. diss., Univ. of Calif., Berkeley 1985); Weippert 1988 (Ortsregister); E. Braun, *PEQ* 121 (1989), 1–43.

AMNON BEN-TOR

Tel Qashish: group of pottery vessels from the early 10th century BCE.

QASILE, TELL

IDENTIFICATION

Tell Qasile lies within the borders of Tel Aviv, on the north bank of the Yarkon River, at a distance of about 150 m from the river and about 1.75 km (1 mi.) east of its estuary (map reference 1309.1678). The economic life of the settlement on the site was based to a great extent on the river. Its waters were used for irrigation, which allowed the development of a diversified agriculture. It is very likely that in various periods the settlement was an inland port, and ships sailed upstream through the Yarkon River estuary and anchored near the mound. This is also borne out by the discovery here of imported pottery. The role of this settlement as an inland port is also reflected in the biblical account of the shipment of cedars for the building of the Temple in the time of Solomon (2 Chr. 2:16) and of Zerubbabel (Ezra 3:7). Trees were apparently floated up the Yarkon and unloaded at one of the settlements on its banks, probably at Tell Kudadi or Tell Qasile.

EXCAVATIONS

Three consecutive seasons of excavations were conducted at Tell Qasile from 1948 to 1950, on behalf of the Israel Exploration Society, under the direction of B. Mazar, and with the participation of T. Dothan, I. Dunayevsky, and J. Kaplan. The excavations were concentrated on the southern part of the mound, over an area of about 1,200 sq m (area A); in 1949 and 1950, excavations on a smaller scale were also conducted on the northwest slope. The boundaries of the mound were traced, and its area established: it is 150 m long from north to south and 100 to 110 m wide from east to west. The overall area of the ancient settlement was thus some 4 a. The buildings situated on the boundaries of the settlement on the south and west slopes of the mound were eroded. Scant remains survived of the fortifications from the end of the twelfth to the beginning of the tenth centuries BCE (strata XI–X; see below).

The excavations at Tell Qasile were resumed between 1971 and 1974, and short seasons were conducted between 1982 and 1989. The excavations were directed by A. Mazar, on behalf of the Eretz Israel Museum (formerly Haaretz Museum), the Institute of Archaeology at the Hebrew University of Jerusalem, and the Israel Exploration Society. The recent excavations were concentrated in area C in the central-eastern part of the mound; an area of 1,300 sq m was excavated. The major find in this area was the sacred precinct of the Philistine city.

Except for a few sherds from a short-lived settlement in the Middle Bronze Age I, the earliest remains on the mound date to the beginning of the Iron Age.

EXCAVATIONS IN AREA A

Large sections of the southern part of the mound were cleared down to virgin soil and twelve main strata were distinguished. They range in date from the Iron Age IB to the Arab period.

STRATUM XII. The buildings in stratum XII were constructed on the *kurkar* rock; few remains survived. The best-preserved building was found in the southern sector of the excavations. It was built of mud brick and consisted of two adjoining structures, the length of whose common front measures 12 m. Depressions and pits cut into the *kurkar* in this stratum were encountered all over the excavation area. In the center of the area were remains of brick walls. In the area of the fortifications, a pavement of large stone slabs running beneath the brick wall of stratum XI and continuing westward is attributed to stratum XII. It appears that the inhabited area in stratum XII was more extensive here than in strata XI–X. The pavement was eroded at its western end. It probably reached the city wall, which was also washed down the slope. The architectural remains in stratum XII appear to belong to large buildings that were razed when the city was destroyed by a conflagration, and by building activities in later periods. This was especially true in stratum X, where the foundations of the structures penetrated almost to bedrock.

STRATUM XI. Stratum XI was completely cleared in the southern part of the mound, where a large building, built mostly of *kurkar* stones, was found. The structure's plan was not fully traced. East of it was a large square, and nearby were two clay crucibles containing remains of smelted copper. In the northern sector of the mound, the buildings in this stratum were destroyed down to their foundations when the stratum X buildings were erected. The nature of the ruins indicates that the settlement was destroyed by an earthquake.

The fortifications on the west include a massive brick wall (c. 5 m thick) in stratum XI. No architectural continuity was noted between strata XII and XI. The latter was laid out on a different plan and a new wall was added.

It was possible to distinguish clearly between the different Iron Age I strata (XII–X) at Tell Qasile; thus, separate and well-defined pottery assemblages could be established. Changes and developments can be traced in the ordinary local pottery, in which the Canaanite pottery tradition continues, as well as in the Philistine ware.

The stratum XII Philistine pottery includes the main types: bowls, kraters, jugs with strainer spouts, and stirrup jars. The pottery contains several distinctive features that date it to the early phase of its appearance in Israel: thick white slip; bichrome decoration on some of the vessels with narrow, close-set lines, similar to the Mycenean "close style"; and the bird motif, limited here to stratum XII (only one example was found in stratum XI). The ceramic assemblage of stratum XI is similar to that of stratum XII. However, a change is discernible in the Philistine pottery: there is a deterioration in ornamentation, and monochrome decorations become more frequent.

Other finds in this stratum include bronze arrowheads, a bone graver, spindle whorls, flint sickle blades, numerous loom weights, and various stone objects, such as grindstones and mortars. Iron objects were not found in area A in strata XII and XI. The ceramic finds from these strata parallel those of Megiddo VIIA–VIB, Tell Beit Mirsim B3, and Beth-Shemesh III.

STRATUM X. Because stratum X buildings were encountered throughout the excavated area, it was possible to establish the plans of individual buildings and of an entire quarter. The houses in this stratum were built following an almost uniform plan: a square courtyard in one corner and two adjoining long and narrow rooms meeting at an angle. This plan may be the archetype of the

Tell Qasile: general view of area A.

Tell Qasile: map of the excavation areas and city plan in stratum X.

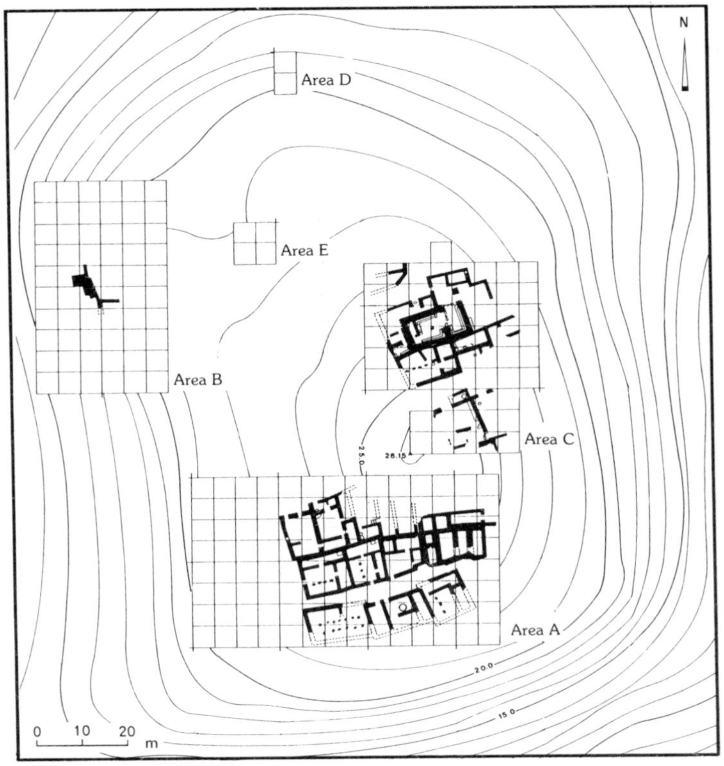

four-room house, widespread in the Iron Age II. Some of the houses had a narrow paved strip along the outer wall of the courtyard and a row of pillars bounding it on the inner side, indicating that the courtyard was roofed. Of special interest is a house in the northwest corner of the excavation. It contained a large courtyard with two wide doorways opening onto the street. Some of the rooms in the buildings were used as storerooms; others, which contained numerous finds, were dwelling rooms and workshops. The buildings in the northern part of the excavated area formed a complete residential quarter. They were surrounded on three sides by streets and comprised two rows of attached houses accessible only from the street.

To the south of this quarter, part of a second block of buildings was cleared that differed from the first. The western building—a large room with two column bases along its length—was not an ordinary dwelling but was probably used for industrial purposes, like the building in stratum XI. These quarters were planned anew in stratum X, and only in a very few places (in the southern area) is there continuity between the buildings of strata XI and X. The city was destroyed by a conflagration. The city wall in stratum XI (see above) was reconstructed by the stratum X inhabitants of the city and continued in use until the final destruction of this city.

A great many finds were uncovered in the ruins, especially in the storerooms, which shed light on the stratum's rich material culture.

New forms and styles were added to the pottery repertoire, with Phoenician-type pottery and Egyptian imported ware appearing here for the first time. The most striking change, however, occurs in the forms and decoration of the Philistine pottery. The white slip and bichrome ornamentation disappear and are replaced by a red slip, usually with an irregular burnish, and brown-painted decoration. Some of the Philistine types of vessels vanish, and new types appear—created through a fusion of Philistine and Canaanite elements and others, new traits that become common in Israelite pottery. The blending of these three elements is especially evident in a group of kraters. The Philistine elements are represented in the horizontal handles and the degenerated spiral pattern; the local tradition is seen in the shape of the kraters and in some of the decorations; and the new feature is the burnished red slip. Parallels to the stratum X ceramic finds are found in stratum IV at Tell Abu Hawam, stratum VIA at Megiddo, and at Tell Jerishe.

In stratum X, iron objects—knives and the blade of a sword—appear for the first time with various bronze implements. Among the finds is a conical seal engraved with the figure of an animal, above which is the figure of a man with outstretched hands.

STRATUM IX2. The Israelite settlement (stratum IX2) arose on the ruins of the stratum X city. The changes in the organization of the new city are evident mainly in the fortifications. It appears that the strong brick wall of the Philistine city (strata XI–X) went out of use with the destruction of stratum X. In the area of the fortifications a row of attached buildings was discovered from the Israelite period; their outer face, toward the slope, was eroded. The city wall probably stood to the west of these buildings and was also washed away. In the center of the mound major changes also took place in the transition from stratum X to stratum IX2. The northern row of buildings in the block of houses in stratum X appears to have been totally razed, and several silos were dug in the open area. The southern row of buildings in this block continued to exist in stratum IX2, however, with only their interiors undergoing alterations. The major change was the addition of a wall dividing the courtyard, thus creating the type of dwelling known as the four-room house. Another innovation was the change in direction of the row of houses—they were now entered from the north, from the area of the silos. It is not known whether buildings also stood to the south of the quarter and were destroyed by erosion, or whether the area of the city was reduced.

STRATUM IX1. In the eastern part of the excavated area a public building (12 by 14 m) was found that had been erected in stratum IX1. Its construction was the main innovation in this stratum. In the northeast part of the building, an entrance hall contained the lower part of a flight of stairs leading to an upper story. South of the entrance hall was a row of four long, narrow rooms, one of which was divided into two parts. These rooms were probably accessible from the upper story through openings in the ceiling. Evidently a public building, this structure indicates that the site was an administrative center in the period. The stratum IX2 dwellings continued in use in stratum IX1 with almost no changes. The walls dividing the courtyards in stratum IX2 were, however, replaced by rows of columns.

This stratum was poor in ceramic and small finds. In addition to the local pottery, which generally had a red slip and an irregular burnish, there is also Cypro-Phoenician ware—white-painted I–II and black-on-red I–II. The pottery, for the most part, parallels that in stratum VA–IVB at Megiddo, stratum III at Tell Abu Hawam, stratum IIA at Beth-Shemesh, and stratum B3 at Tell Beit Mirsim. Some bronze and iron implements were also found in this stratum.

STRATUM VIII. The public building and the block of buildings continued in

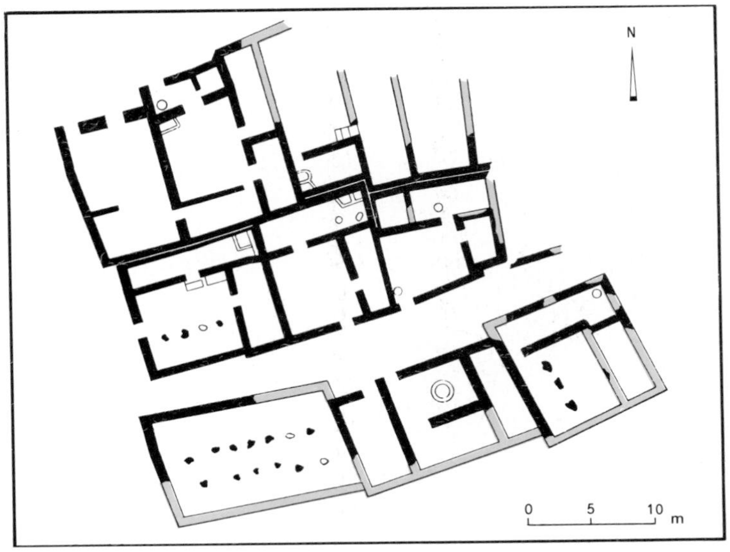

Area A: plan of the residential quarter, stratum X.

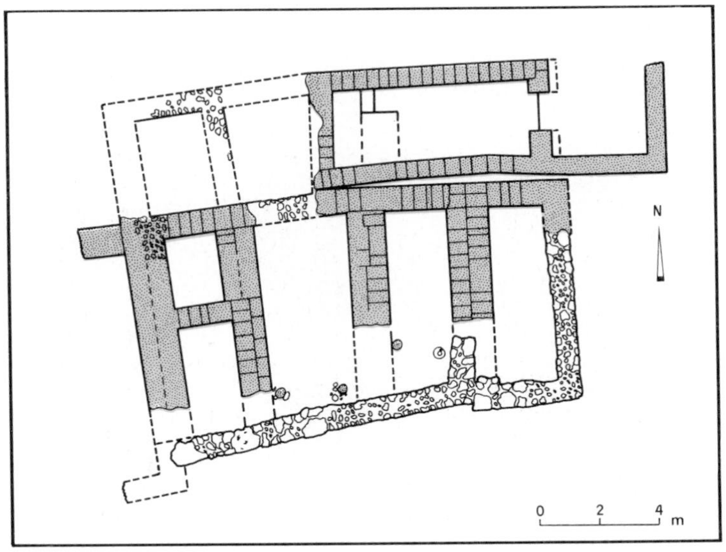

Area A: plan of the public building in stratum VIII, Iron II.

Scaraboid seal from stratum VIII.

Area A: plan of the public building in stratum VI, Persian period.

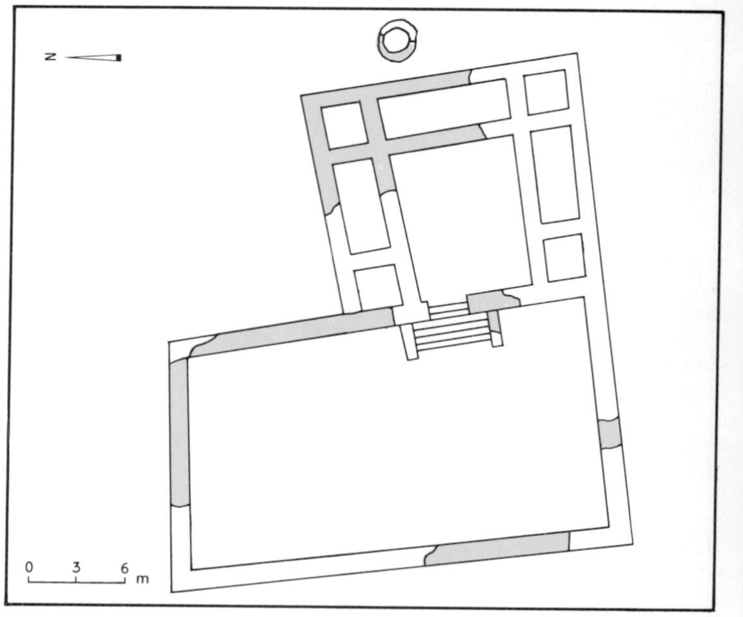

use in stratum VIII. They underwent a certain change of plan with the disappearance of the rows of columns of stratum IX1.

STRATUM VII. In stratum VII, the continuity noted among the buildings of strata X–VIII is no longer apparent. The large stratum VIII public building ceased to exist and was replaced by an ordinary house. Few building remains can be attributed to stratum VII, most of them having been destroyed by building activity in the Persian period (stratum VI). No remains of city walls were discovered in strata VIII–VII, as in strata IX2–IX1, but it can be assumed that a city wall did exist and was washed down the slope. The Israelite town was probably destroyed in 732 BCE, when Tiglath-pileser III invaded the Israelite kingdom and razed numerous towns. This destruction brought the settlement at Tell Qasile to an end, and the site was not resettled until the Persian period.

In the pottery found in strata VIII–VII, the red slip with regular burnish predominates. The bowls and deep bowls show wheel-made concentric burnishing for the first time. Some Samaria ware bowls were also found, in both ivory color and red. Shallow cooking pots occur, as well as those with narrow, grooved mouths from which two handles extend to the shoulder. One large jar resembles Cypro-Phoenician ware in both shape and workmanship. Its slip is various shades of red and is well burnished. The front of the jar is decorated with a drawing of a galloping horse. On the whole, the pottery in strata VIII–VII belongs to ninth- and eighth-century BCE types common in the Israelite kingdom. Other finds include an Astarte pillar figurine, two scarab seals, stone weights, and copper and iron implements.

HEBREW INSCRIPTIONS. Before the excavations began, two ostraca had been found on the surface of the mound. Ceramic and paleographic analysis date them to the Late Iron Age.

Ostracon No. 1. The inscription is deeply carved on the inside of the ring base of a vessel with reddish slip. The script is the cursive Hebrew common in Israel and Judah in the eighth century BCE. The ostracon is damaged only on the edges. It reads: למלך, אל[ף] שמן ומאה̇, [ח̇]יהו (For the king, one thousand /and one hundred [*log* of] oil/ Ḥiyahu). This apparently was a receipt or a record of a quantity of oil sent by an official, whose name was Ḥiyahu, through the port of Tell Qasile. The liquid measure (*log*) is either broken away or not mentioned, but was probably intended.

Ostracon No. 2. The inscription is carved on the sherd of a large vessel, with points separating the words. It reads: [ז]הב. אפר. לבית. חרן. י (Gold of Ophir to Beth-Horon . . . /thirty shekels). The term "gold of Ophir" in the Bible refers to gold of a special, superior quality, named after its country of origin, Ophir. The quantity of gold is given in the second line, in the single letter ש (*shin*), an abbreviation of the word "shekel." Three parallel horizontal lines represent the number of shekels (thirty), following the accepted system of writing numerals in Phoenician inscriptions. This was evidently an official document certifying the dispatch of a consignment of thirty shekels (half a talent) of gold of Ophir to Beth-Horon.

STRATUM VI. Building remains from stratum VI (Persian period) are scattered over the entire western part of the excavated area; all of them belong to a large public building. To construct this building, a large area was leveled, including all building remains from the last Israelite stratum (VII). Although most of the building was demolished when later buildings were erected, it was possible to reconstruct its plan. It was square, with a courtyard surrounded by rooms on three of its sides. On the west side was a large rectangular courtyard. The difference in floor levels between the courtyard and the building indicates

Seal: "'Ashanyahu, servant of the King," Persian period.

*Ostracon inscribed "For the king, one thousand and one hundred (*log *of) oil . . . Ḥiyahu," 8th century BCE.*

that a staircase connected the two. East of the building was a leveled square with a circular silo; north of it a ditch was found containing a considerable quantity of objects and pottery from the Persian period.

The stratum VI pottery includes characteristic types from the Persian period: jars with flat, angular shoulders or with high basket handles and heavy mortaria with ribbed bodies and flat or ring bases. A small quantity of Attic pottery from the fifth and fourth centuries BCE was found, including a fragment showing a dancer in the black-figure technique. A Hebrew seal, found prior to the excavations, may also belong to this period. It is a flat limestone plaque carved with a human figure; along its edges the Hebrew inscription reads: "'Ashanyahu, servant of the King."

STRATUM V. The few remains from stratum V (Hellenistic period) found scattered over the mound do not form an identifiable pattern. It was also difficult to establish a connection between this stratum and the following stratum, IV.

STRATUM IV. The remains of a large building survived from stratum IV (Herodian period) in the eastern part of the excavations. It is difficult to reconstruct its plan, but its foundations penetrated to a considerable depth, pointing to a massive structure. The foundations are of unhewn stones; a single course of well-dressed ashlars survived above the foundations in only one section. This building resembles Herodian buildings at Samaria, both in plan and construction technique. The same date is also indicated by the pottery found on the surviving floors of the building. Fragments of terra sigillata ware were uncovered, one of which bears the potter's mark XAPIC, from the time of Augustus.

STRATUM III. A large bulding that was probably a market belongs to stratum III (Late Roman period, third and fourth centuries CE). It extended over the whole of the eastern part of the excavations. The part of the market unearthed consists of three long, narrow rooms; a wide hall containing two rows of columns to the west; and a section of a similar hall on the east. The market was probably entered from the west, from a street running along its western facade. East of this street was a row of buildings from the same period. Rooms and courtyards were excavated, but it proved impossible to attribute them to clearly defined buildings. The large building can be compared with a nearly contemporary structure discovered in Tiberias. A pottery kiln, found at the southern end of the mound, may also belong to this stratum.

From stratum II (Byzantine period) and stratum I (Arab period) only a few remains scattered over the whole area were preserved.

TRUDE DOTHAN, IMANUEL DUNAYEVSKY

EXCAVATIONS IN AREA C

STRATUM XII. Two phases were discerned in stratum XII. The earlier phase (stratum XIIB) included several floor fragments and parts of poorly built structures constructed on bedrock. Only a few sherds were found on the floors, including Philistine-style pottery. Above these poor remains the first of a series of temples (stratum XIIA, building 319) was constructed. Its external dimensions were 6.4 by 6.6 m. Its brick walls lacked foundations and rested directly on the *kurkar*. The entrance to the building was in the center of the eastern wall, where a large *kurkar* slab was used for a threshold. The temple consisted of a single room with mud-brick benches along the walls and a beaten-earth floor mixed with lime. The holy of holies, in the center of the structure, was a raised platform with a frontal stepped projection. The platform was well plastered and may have had a hollow cavity in the back as a storage space for the temple's treasures, as in the later temples. In a layer of fallen brick debris on the floor a group of pottery vessels was found that included a unique Philistine vessel—a jug flask—decorated with a stylized lotus motif.

To the east and north of the temple was a spacious courtyard that extended beyond the excavated area. Its earth and lime floor had been raised several times. Between the floors were alternate layers of gray and black ashes containing sherds and animal bones. This is evidence that organic material had been gathered in the courtyard and burned for sacrificial and other cultic rites. Noteworthy among the finds recovered from the courtyard was an anthropomorphic juglet and a scarab engraved with a chariot scene. Also found was an ivory knife handle, with its iron blade still held in place by bronze rivets, of a type known from contemporary sites in Cyprus. On the north side of the courtyard was a long, narrow rectangular room, probably an auxiliary room in the sacred precinct. The temple complex was separated from the buildings to the south by a brick wall that was exposed along the entire length of the excavated area (25 m). The wall was repaired in later strata, a fact that implies an architectural continuity from stratum XII onward.

A public building with brick walls founded on bedrock was uncovered southeast of the temple. The structure had been built in stratum XII and, with minor changes to its peripheral rooms, probably continued to be used in stratum XI. The central part of the building consisted of a large hall with an entrance on the west and plastered brick benches lining the inner walls. The walls were covered with a thick layer of fine plaster and the floor was of beaten earth and lime. Inside the hall was a hearth built on an elevated, elliptical brick platform. Part of the platform was paved with broken sherds

General view of the stratum XII temple, looking northwest. Visible above it are the stone walls of the strata XI–X temples.

*Area C: plan of the temples in strata XII–X. **(A)** building 319, stratum XII; **(B)** building 200, stratum XI; **(C)** building 131, stratum X; **(D)** building 300, strata XI–X.*

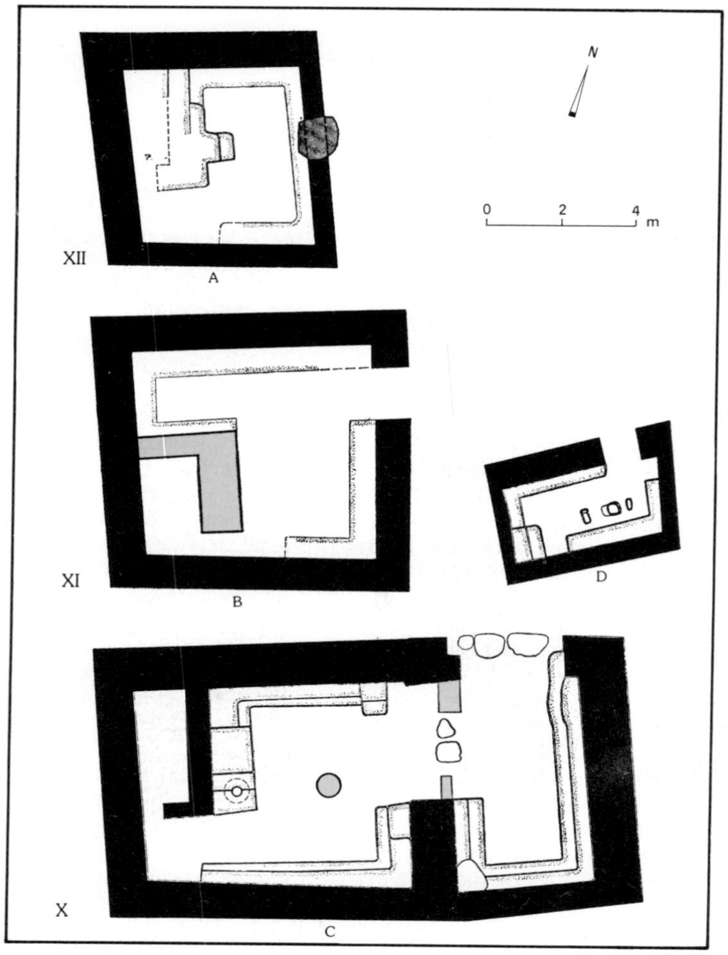

Hearth in the public building southeast of the temple, strata XII–XI.

and in it was a round pit used as a hearth. With the exception of Philistine Ekron (Tel Miqne), no parallels to this hearth have yet been found in this country. However, there are parallels in the Aegean world, in Anatolia, and in Cyprus. It is possible to view this as a foreign architectural element introduced by the Philistines. The building had additional rooms, including a large broadroom that opened onto the eastern side of the main hall. It seems that this was a public building belonging to the city's administrative complex adjacent to the temple area.

STRATUM XI. The stratum XI temple (building 200) was built directly above the earlier brick temple that by now was no longer in use. The walls of the new building were aligned along those of the previous one, while being slightly enlarged to the north and east. It now measured 7.75 by 8.5 m. The walls (1 m thick) were built of *kurkar* stones. A 1.4-m-wide entrance was located in the northeast corner of the building, facing east. The structure consisted of a single large hall and a small corner cubicle (1.5 by 2.8 m) formed by two brick walls in the southwest corner. The preserved height of these walls is not enough to determine whether they formed a proper room or were the foundations of a raised platform used as a holy of holies. Inside the corner space created by the partition, an assemblage of votive offerings and cult objects was found: an anthropomorphic mask, an ivory bird-shaped cosmetic bowl, a triton conch shell used as a horn, several clay figurines, numerous beads, and pottery vessels, including votive bowls. The temple's main hall was lined with brick benches. These extended into a niche opposite the entrance, north of the corner space. In the niche were found the remains of red- and blue-painted plaster(?) and several stirrup jars decorated in the Philistine style. It is possible that this niche was the temple's holy of holies.

A spacious courtyard to the east and north of the temple was also found in this stratum. In several places its floor level had been raised three times. On the north side of the courtyard, a pit for cultic offerings (*favissa*) was found. It yielded a rich assemblage of pottery vessels and cult objects: an anthropomorphic vessel of a female figure (possibly a fertility goddess), whose breasts served as spouts for pouring liquid; a lion-shaped goblet decorated with Philistine motifs; fragments of zoomorphic masks; and pottery vessels bearing typical Philistine decoration, including an unusual horn-shaped vessel. Bottles and bowls with red slip and black decoration were also found here. A layer of animal bones was uncovered in the upper part of the pit. It appears that the pit was dug toward the end of stratum XI and was used to deposit the cult objects no longer in use. The rectangular room in the northern part of the courtyard from the previous stratum was partly restored in this phase. Another rectangular room was now attached to it, built of brick walls without stone foundations.

A small shrine (building 300) was erected to the west of the temple, in stratum XI. The brick structure, without stone foundations, measures

General view of the small temple 300 from strata XI–X, looking west.

Female-shaped cult vessel, stratum XI.

Cylindrical cult stands, strata XI–X.

3.5 by 5.6 m. It consists of an antechamber and a main room with a side entrance in its northeast corner. The walls were lined with benches and in the southwest corner was a raised platform with two plastered steps. Three cylindrical clay cult stands were found leaning against the platform. Clay bowls had been placed on two of the stands and a third bowl was found in the antechamber. Two of the bowls were decorated with bird heads. A group of pottery vessels, including globular decorated goblets, was also found here.

Remains of other large buildings were uncovered south of the temple. The buildings were for the most part a continuation of those from stratum XII, with such minor alterations as the addition of internal partitions and raised floors. The most notable of these was the public building that contained the hearth. This building remained in use in stratum XI in its main area. To its west part of another building was uncovered that contained several rooms built around a central area. The two buildings were at acute angles to one another, apparently due to the absence of a centralized plan for blocks of buildings. Such a plan was implemented in the following stratum.

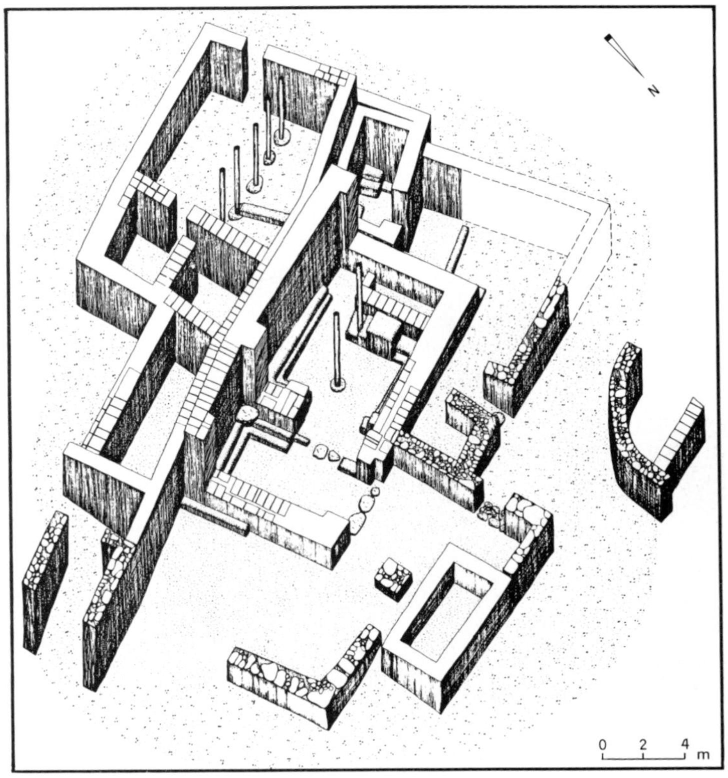

Area C: isometric reconstruction of the temple area in stratum X.

From the abundance of stratum XI finds, several aspects of pottery development could be noted. The white slip common in stratum XII gradually disappeared, and in stratum XI a red slip and black decoration are found on vessels for the first time. Irregular hand burnishing is rare. Many of the vessels are decorated with Philistine motifs, including the distinctive bird design.

STRATUM X. The stratum X temple (building 131) was an enlarged and rebuilt version of the previous stratum's temple. The east wall of the earlier temple was replaced with a new antechamber that formed a side entrance to the building. The new building measured 8 by 14.5 m. Its entrance (2.9 m wide) was situated in the north wall of the antechamber; tiered benches were built along the room's walls. A wide opening in the antechamber led to the cella, whose internal dimensions were 5.65 by 7.2 m. The walls of the earlier temple were reused in the cella: the north wall was widened and new brick construction was set on stone foundations. The floor was raised by an artificial fill, into which round stone bases were set to hold two columns of cedar wood that supported the ceiling. Around the walls were tiered benches similar to those in the antechamber. On the west side of the cella was a brick partition wall. A brick platform was built against the east face of the partition. The platform was raised 0.9 m above the floor and was approached by steps from both sides. The southern steps were built around the wooden column after it was set on its stone base (the column imprint remained in the step).

The raised platform was built north of the building's longitudinal axis, along which the wooden columns were placed. This allowed a direct line of vision between the cella's entrance and the platform. However, because the building itself is of the bent-axis type, it was impossible to look directly into the cell from the outside courtyard. A long, narrow storage chamber was located in the western part of the building, beyond the partition wall.

The temple was destroyed in a fierce conflagration. Many objects were discovered on the floor, particularly near the raised platform and in the storage chamber behind it. Noteworthy among the cult objects found in the temple were a clay plaque in the form of a building's facade (a temple?), with two figures depicted in a frontal stance (only their legs remain); a cylindrical cult stand, whose windows were fashioned with four figures engaged in a ritual dance; another cylindrical cult stand, whose upper part bears two lionesses(?) carrying a bowl; an offering bowl decorated with a

General view of the stratum X temple, looking west.

bird, with a tang for setting it on a cylindrical stand; a conical jar with a composite neck with five openings, red slip, and black floral decoration (this vessel may have contained a holy plant displayed in the temple); and various libation vessels, including a kernos bowl, a libation vessel shaped like a cluster of fruit(?), and a zoomorphic vessel in the shape of a hippopotamus(?) with a small inner tube. Also found were two pomegranate-shaped clay vessels and a large quantity of pottery typical of stratum X: vessels with red slip, irregular hand burnishing, and black decoration; Phoenician bichrome ware; and pottery decorated in typical Philistine style. The latter were found primarily in the storage chamber at the rear of the building, possibly indicating that they were no longer used in the temple's final days. Two metal objects were also discovered in the temple: a bronze double ax, of a type found in Cyprus and in the Aegean world, and an iron bracelet.

To the north and east of the temple was a courtyard enclosed by solid stone walls. The courtyard was entered from a street running northwest of the temple. The courtyard incorporates a rectangular brick room that was erected in the previous stratum and continued unchanged also in stratum X. A square stone foundation (1.5 by 1.3 m), apparently the base of a sacrificial altar, was found in the courtyard, north of the temple entrance.

Another courtyard lay northwest and west of the temple. It was entered

Decorated cult vessel, possibly used to hold sacred plants, stratum X.

Bird-shaped cult bowl, stratum X.

Pottery vessels decorated in the Philistine style.

from the street through a separate entrance. A room erected north of the temple opened onto the courtyard; it contained cooking installations, apparently serving as a kitchen used in connection with the cultic rites performed in the temple. The courtyard led to the small shrine erected in the previous stratum, which continued unchanged in stratum X.

Part of a residential quarter was uncovered south of the temple complex. It was bordered on the south by a wide street paved with *kurkar* paving stones. This street was partly built on top of the public building from strata XII–XI that went out of use. One of the houses (building 225), which was completely cleared, measured 8.5 by 13.5 m and included a spacious courtyard, divided into open and roofed areas by a row of five wooden columns set on flat stone slabs. The house also included two square rooms, one of which was used as a storeroom and contained about eighty storage jars. The other room, the living quarters, yielded five stirrup jars decorated with Philistine motifs and fragments of a decorated kernos. This structure was also destroyed by a violent conflagration. Noteworthy among the finds were two Egyptian storage jars.

The largest residential building on Tell Qasile was uncovered south of the street. The walls (1.4 m thick) were built of *kurkar* stones. The part of the building excavated so far includes an open courtyard paved with layers of *kurkar*. Its western side was a covered area whose roof was supported by a row of three wooden columns set on flat stone slabs. Among the finds uncovered here were two collared-rim jars, kraters decorated with spirals, a multihandled krater, about sixty clay loom weights, and the only fragment from Tell Qasile of an Ashdoda female figurine, which is characteristic of Philistine culture at other sites.

The line of the walls and streets in area C runs parallel to that of the residential area in the southern part of the mound (area A). It thus follows that the stratum X city was carefully planned, with an orthogonal network of streets and well-defined blocks of buildings. The basis of this city plan already existed in the earlier levels, as shown by the long wall crossing area C from east to west that continued in use through all three strata (XII–X).

STRATA IX–VIII. Upon renewed examination of the ceramic finds and the stratigraphy, A. Mazar realized that the chronology of the Iron Age II strata as designated in the first seasons of excavation (see above) would have to be corrected. According to this revision, strata IX–VIII should be dated to the tenth century BCE. Stratum VII is not an independent level, as previously published. However, evidence has been uncovered of a sparse settlement from the end of the Iron Age (late seventh century BCE), now labeled stratum VII. There seems to have been a gap in settlement from the end of the tenth century (after Shishak's campaign) until the seventh century BCE.

Above the destruction level of the temples and courtyards of stratum X, evidence was found of the area's partial reconstruction in strata IX–VIII (tenth century BCE). The remains were extremely meager, as they were found close to the surface. In stratum IX, the temple walls were rebuilt (only a very small portion of which has survived). The floor of a large open area surrounding the temple on the north, east, and west was exposed. This floor was composed of a thick layer of lime that was repaired at least once. A round stone installation found near the previous level's altar may have served as the altar in stratum IX. In stratum VIII, the temple's eastern wall was rebuilt of stone (only one course was preserved). The courtyard's floor was repaired again in this stratum and new buildings were erected northwest of the temple. Despite the paucity of remains, it appears that the temple and its courtyards continued in use in the tenth century BCE.

The change in town planning in the tenth century BCE is most apparent in the southern part of area C, where the street and large house of stratum X were no longer in use. This quarter was turned into an open area, with beaten earth floors that were repaired a number of times over the course of the century. Thus, the remains from areas A and C show that after the violent destruction of stratum X, the city was only partly restored. In strata IX–VIII, the city was sparsely populated and had many open areas, where various buildings had previously stood.

STRATUM "VII." Following the destruction of stratum VIII (probably during Shishak's campaign), the site was abandoned for many years. Close to the surface and covering a substantial portion of area C was a layer of earth containing sherds from the end of the Iron Age (seventh century BCE). The sherds included vessels typical of the Judean kingdom, such as high-based lamps and coastal (late "Philistine") forms. A group of pottery vessels from this period was found in two hewn pits at the foot of the mound.

STRATUM VI. Several pits containing remains from the Persian period were found in various parts of area C. Among the finds was a jar handle bearing a stamped impression in Hebrew letters: ענב (*'nb*). One pit also contained a coin of Alexander the Great. While digging the foundations for the main building of the Eretz Israel Museum, a square shaft (2 by 2 m and 12 m deep) was discovered hewn into the bedrock at the northeastern foot of the mound. The bottom of the shaft is 1.8 m above sea level and undoubtedly had been used as a well. Pottery from the Persian period was found inside the shaft. Remains of human skeletons were also found, possibly thrown into the shaft during Alexander the Great's conquest of the coastal area.

Pottery assemblage from the Tell Qasile temples.

STRATA V–I. Only a few remains were recovered from strata IV–III. A pit, dug in area C and containing Herodian sherds, can be attributed to stratum IV. The remains of a building uncovered in the western part of area C date to the early phase of the Byzantine period (stratum II2). The remains of a bathhouse constructed above this building can be attributed to the later phase of the Byzantine period (stratum II1). The caldarium consisted of a main room with side chambers. The main room terminated in an apse at its east end. The hypocaust was built on a series of arches and columns made of fired bricks. The finds in and around the bathhouse included a coin of Chosroe II, the Persian ruler who conquered Palestine in 614 CE.

A caravanserai(?) from the Early Arab period (stratum I2) was discovered on the mound's summit (the southern part of area C). The structure consisted of a central courtyard surrounded by rooms. Along at least two sides of the courtyard exedrae rested on a row of columns. A well from an earlier phase of this period was incorporated into the northeast corner of the building. The well was connected to well-plastered channels that probably led to a nearby irrigation system. The building was destroyed by fire.

In the Middle Ages (Crusader period or the beginning of the Mameluke period, stratum I1), sugar-producing installations were constructed in this area. A new well was dug in the northern part of the area, partly damaging the Philistine temple walls.

SUMMARY

The sacred precinct at Tell Qasile is an important archaeological source for investigating Philistine temple architecture in the Iron Age I. The great variation between the different temples, built one above the other in a relatively short period of time, points to the absence of a definite tradition of sacred architecture among this population. Although these temples do not have any exact parallels, it is possible to find similarities with several Canaanite temples (the Fosse Temple at Lachish, the temple at Tel Mevorakh, the temples at Beth-Shean), as well as with contemporary temples at Kition in Cyprus and at a few sites in Greece (Mycenae and Melos). Although the cult objects from Tell Qasile reflect Canaanite traditions, they do not manifest a crystallized tradition. It is significant that at Tell Qasile only one Philistine figurine was discovered of the type that continues the Mycenean tradition, such as were found at Ashdod, Aphek, and elsewhere.

The possibility has been raised of a connection between the name Beth-Horon and the temple uncovered here. This was the name mentioned on the Hebrew ostracon found on the mound's surface ("gold of Ophir to Beth-Horon"). The god Horon was venerated by the people of Yavneh as late as the Hellenistic period, and it is possible that the temple here was dedicated to him. However, there is a gap between the date of the ostracon and the date of the last temple (late tenth century BCE).

AMIHAI MAZAR

STRATIGRAPHY AT TELL QASILE, ACCORDING TO THE EXCAVATORS

Stratum	*B. Mazar/T. Dothan*	*A. Mazar*
I1–2	Early Arab period, until the Mameluke period	
II	Byzantine period (4th–6th cent. CE)	
III	Late Roman period (3rd–4th cent. CE)	
IV	Herodian period (1st cent. CE)	
V	Hellenistic period (3rd–2nd cent. BCE)	
VI	Persian period (5th–4th cent. BCE)	
		"VII": 7th cent. BCE
VII	Iron IIC (8th cent. to 732 BCE)	
VIII	Iron IIB (9th cent. BCE)	10th cent. BCE
IX1–2	Iron IIA (10th cent. BCE)	10th cent. BCE
X	Iron IB (late 11th and early 10th cent. BCE)	
XI–XII	Iron IB (late 12th and early 11th cent. BCE)	

Main publications: B. Maisler (Mazar), *IEJ* 1 (1950–1951), 61–76, 125–140, 194–218; A. Mazar, *Excavations at Tell Qasile* 1–2: *The Philistine Sanctuary* (*Qedem* 12; 20), Jerusalem 1980–1985; id., *IEJ* 36 (1986), 1–15.

Other studies: B. Maisler (Mazar), *JNES* 10 (1951), 265–267; A. Mazar, *BA* 36 (1973), 42J–48; 40 (1977), 82–87; id., *IEJ* 23 (1973), 65–71; 25 (1975), 77–88; id., *RB* 80 (1973), 412–415; 82 (1975), 263–268; id., *Temples and High Places in Biblical Times*, Jerusalem 1977, 18–19; ibid., Jerusalem 1981, 105–107; id., *Qedem* 12, 20 (Reviews), *BAR* 7/5 (1980), 8–9. — *Phoenix* 28/1 (1982), 39–41. — *Syria* 59 (1982), 348–349. — *AJA* 87 (1983), 402–403. — *BASOR* 271 (1988), 82–85. — *JQR* 80 (1990), 411–414; id., *ESI* 3 (1984), 90–92; 4 (1985), 89–90; 7–8 (1988–1989), 147–148; (with S. Harpaz) 9 (1989–1990), 52–53; id., *BAR* 10/3 (1984), 54–59; id., *Society and Economy*, 251–260; A. Lemaire, *Inscriptions Hebraïques* 1: *Les Ostraca*, Paris 1977, 251–255; H. Ritter-Kaplan, *IEJ* 28 (1978), 199–200; id., *RB* 85 (1978), 415–416; id., *ESI* 1 (1982), 109; id., *'Atiqot* 17 (1985), 195–200; Y. Tsafrir *IEJ* 31 (1981), 223–226; A. Catastini, *Egitto e Vicino Oriente* 7 (1984), 119–123; id., *Henoch* 6 (1984), 129–138; R. Macuch, *IEJ* 35 (1985), 183–185; M. Burdajewiez, *RB* 93 (1986), 222–235; id., *The Aegean Sea Peoples and Religious Architecture in the Eastern Mediterranean at the Close of the Late Bronze Age* (*BAR*/IS 558), Oxford 1990, 46–54; A. Miller Rosen, *Cities of Clay: The Geoarcheology of Tells* (Prehistoric Archaeology and Ecology), Chicago 1986, 89–91, 99–105; A. Ovadiah, *IEJ* 37 (1987), 36–39; O. Negbi, *Annual of the British School at Athens* 83 (1988), 339–357; Weippert 1988 (Ortsregister); S. Bunimovitz, *TA* 17 (1990), 210–222; J. S. Holladay, Jr., *BASOR* 277–278 (1990), 23–70; W. Zwickel, *ZDPV* 106 (1990), 57–62.

QAṢRAWET

IDENTIFICATION

The site of Qaṣrawet is located in the area of high dunes in northwestern Sinai, about 8 km (5 mi.) southeast of Qatya, a large oasis (map reference 955.035). J. Strugnell and J. L. Starcky suggested that the Arabic name Qaṣrawet may be a corrupted form of the name Qaṣr (fortress) and *'wytw*, mentioned in a Nabatean lintel inscription from the eastern Delta and perhaps also on a miniature alabaster altar discovered in the western temple of Qaṣrawet (see below). They suggested that the ancient place name was Castrum(?) Awiti. These inscriptions refer to Kutba, the Nabatean goddess of writing and wisdom, whose temples stood in these places. Y. Tsafrir has proposed identifying the site of Qaṣrawet with Castrum Autaei, based on Pliny's description of the various caravan routes in northern Sinai; this name may also be recorded on the ostracon uncovered in the excavations at Qaṣrawet in the 1970s.

EXPLORATION

Excavations at Qaṣrawet were first carried out in 1911 by J. Clédat, who uncovered the remains of a temple and several tombs nearby. In 1975–1976, a regional survey and systematic excavations were conducted at Qaṣrawet and adjacent sites by the North Sinai Expedition, on behalf of Ben-Gurion University of the Negev, headed by E. D. Oren. The excavations of the temple quarter were directed by E. Netzer.

EXCAVATION RESULTS

The settlement remains at Qaṣrawet extend over an area of 50 to 75 a. in a large depression surrounded by high mobile sand dunes. A few stone-lined wells were located at a nearby oasis, Hod es-Saqiyya. Other satellite settlements and cemeteries were explored east and north of the central site (D-50 on the survey map). Excavations by the North Sinai Expedition uncovered temples, storehouses, and a necropolis of the Nabatean settlement at Qaṣrawet, as well as an extensive fortified settlement from the Late Roman period.

TEMPLE QUARTER. A splendid complex of monumental Nabatean temples was uncovered at the northwestern corner of the site. The temples were built of gypsum slabs brought from the Bardawil lagoon or even from as far away as the city of Suez. The numerous Hellenistic sherds that were found embedded in the mortar of the walls indicate the existence of an earlier settlement in the vicinity. The temple complex includes a small rectangular temple in the west and a square, larger, temple in the center, in front of which are colonnades and a spacious plaza, ending in a pavilion or kiosk. Both temples are oriented east–west, with entrances in the eastern wall.

Western Temple. Two building phases can be distinguished in the western temple. The earlier building included a rectangular hall (4.4 by 6.5 m) that was entered from the east through an opening flanked by columns and square pilasters. Engaged columns and a stone altar were constructed against its rear wall, together with deep niches, in which crude stone slabs, serving as cultic stelae, or betyls, were set in mortar above the altar. Similar stelae are known from Nabatean cult sites in Transjordan and Syria. In the later stage a square room (cella) with an Egyptian-style entrance was added in the east. A plat-

Qaṣrawet: plan of the temple quarter.

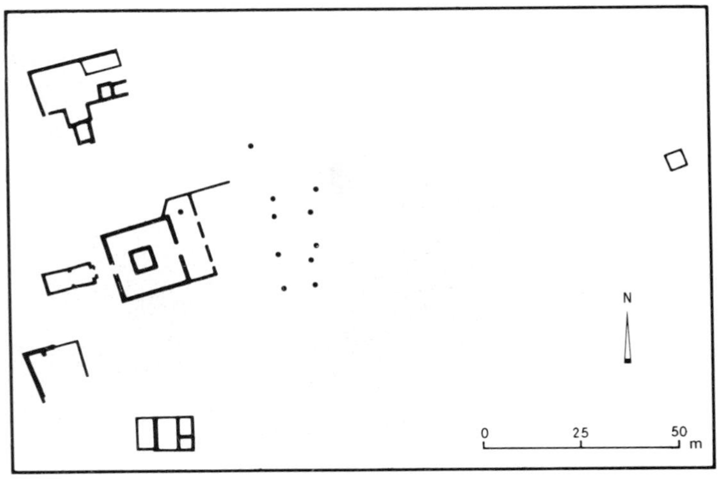

Overview of the temenos, looking east.

Altar and cultic stelae in the western temple.

Central temple, looking west.

form built of baked brick, probably an altar, was uncovered in front of the entrance. On the floor were many broken oil lamps and faience bowls, fragments of a decorated bronze lamp, and a coin of the First Jewish Revolt against Rome, with the inscription שנה ג׳ חרות ציון (Year Three. Freedom of Zion). A fragment of a miniature alabaster altar, uncovered in Clédat's excavations of the western temple, bears a fragmentary Nabatean inscription *hwyrw br grm l' lktb'*, attesting, according to some scholars, to the cult of the goddess Kutba, the Nabatean goddess of writing and wisdom. Beneath the floor of the main hall, an earlier floor was revealed, with finds datable to the Early Roman period. The temple was thus probably first built in the first century BCE and the cella added in the first century CE. The temple continued in use until its abandonment in the late second or early third century CE.

Central Temple. The central temple, the most elaborate at Qaṣrawet (19 by 19 m), consists of two square structures, one encased by the other. The entrance was on the east, through an elaborate system of facades and doorways with Egyptian-style lintels. The outer building's walls are decorated with semicircular pilasters, between which are small windows with stepped cornices. Above the main entrance is a wall or pylon (9.7 m high), topped by an Egyptian cornice and a series of mushroomlike stelae.

At a later stage, a forecourt was added to the central temple; it included an elaborate entrance with three doorways bearing Egyptian-style lintels. The inner building (7.4 by 7.4 m) was decorated with engaged columns crowned by squarish capitals. A heavy wooden beam set above the capitals supported a concave Egyptian-style cornice. Large openings in the eastern and western walls formed porticos between pilasters, while the other walls had six low openings topped by wooden beams. The numerous openings gave the inner unit the appearance of an open structure resting only on columns.

The architecture of the inner structure is unique. A thick wooden "belt" was set above the capitals of the inner walls. Accentuated stone profiles were built above it, as well as a gable with dentils inside a broken pediment. This is an extremely rare decorative style for the interior of buildings; in Hellenistic-Roman architecture such ornamentation is usually reserved for the exterior facades of temples and other public buildings.

The ceiling of the inner building and the space between the two structures were covered with tamarisk and cypress beams, carved into modeled profiles. The excavations of the inner structure revealed that its center contained a structure—perhaps an altar—decorated with delicate dentils. Nearby was a small bronze base for a statuette.

In front of the temple were two colonnades with round columns. The columns probably carried statues or cult symbols; in front of them was a wide open plaza, about one acre in size, which terminated in a pavilion, or kiosk. The structure (5 by 10.5 m) includes an Egyptian cornice on a wooden beam and a colonnade with heart-shaped corner columns.

Building Style and Date of the Temples. Architectural analysis of the temples points to an integration of different styles—Hellenistic, Roman, Egyptian, and Nabatean. Of particular interest is the imitation, in stone, of Egyptian brick construction as well as the use of a wooden frame in stone structures. The western temple is characteristically Egyptian both in ground plan and in architectural details. Similar temples from the Hellenistic-Roman period have been recorded at Karanis, Edfu, Kom Ombo, Philae, and at Dendera in Nubia. At Qaṣrawet, the Nabateans first built a single-chambered temple and later added a cella, an altar, and characteristic Nabatean cult stelae set in the niches. The central temple nearby, on roughly the same axis and orientation, was built when the settlement became more established and flourished economically.

The central temple is completely different from the western one. Its basic plan—two square buildings, one within the other—is typical of Nabatean temple architecture in Transjordan and Syria. However, numerous architectural details in the central temple imply that Egyptian building styles had been adapted, perhaps by Egyptian architects. Judging from the finds and building styles, it seems that the western temple was built in the first century BCE, while the central temple and the western temple's cella were built in the first century CE. The temples continued in use until the late second or third century CE.

The sacred precinct also included auxiliary buildings, built of mud bricks, that served as living quarters (possibly for the temples' priests or servants), and service buildings with large courtyards and various installations. Many pottery vessels, glass objects, decorated Nabatean vessels, oil lamps, and coins were uncovered in the buildings.

NABATEAN SETTLEMENTS. In the survey of the Qaṣrawet area, satellite settlements or suburbs surrounding the town at a radius of 3 km (2 mi.) were examined. The earliest Hellenistic site, about one acre in size, dates to the second century BCE. It contained various installations—including hearths—and numerous stone tools, fragments of hundreds of imported Greek amphorae, "Megarian" bowls, and oil lamps. It seems that the early Nabatean settlement was a campsite consisting of huts and tents. The great number of amphorae imported from Rhodes, Cos, and Cnidos testifies to the commercial ties of the early inhabitants of Qaṣrawet with the coastal and Egyptian Delta regions.

The remains of a large settlement with public and domestic buildings and a large cemetery were investigated a short distance southeast of the main site. One of the central buildings at this site had spacious rooms and courtyards, as well as cooking and baking installations; the finds here include a decorated bronze lamp and Nabatean pottery. Another building was excavated nearby; in one of its rooms was a rounded niche containing a stone stela. Excavations in the building yielded a lamp bearing a relief of a dolphin—a characteristic Nabatean symbol—and a bronze medallion bearing the head of Hermes. *Favissae*—which contained large quantities of ash and clay, and faience and glass vessels, including decorated Nabatean pottery—were found outside the building. This was apparently the site of a small Nabatean shrine, serving the suburb's inhabitants in the Roman period.

CEMETERIES. Three cemeteries belonging to the Nabatean settlement were examined in the course of the Ben-Gurion University excavations. The most common type of tombs was cist tombs built of sandstone slabs and designed for single burials. Above some of the graves were square, pillar-shaped tombstones, whose base may have served as a shelf for offerings. Pockets of ash, hearth remains, and broken pottery vessels found around the tombs were probably related to some funerary ritual or the mourners' meals. The cemeteries at Qaṣrawet are also represented by scores of elaborate family tombs, built of stone in a method reminiscent of brick construction. The tombs have characteristic Egyptian-style entrances and often contain a barrel-vaulted tunnel with steps leading to an underground burial chamber. In some instances the entrances to the tombs were found partially blocked with stones

Inner wall of the central Nabatean temple.

Nabatean tomb: (left) tunnel leading to an underground burial chamber; (right) nefesh *monument and burial troughs.*

and sealed with mortar; stone hearths and various offerings were found nearby.

The underground burial chambers were cube-shaped, with a stone-domed ceiling, a plastered floor, and stone sarcophagi built against the walls. The tombs contained many glass and pottery offering vessels and gold jewelry. Most of the tombs had been disturbed in antiquity; however, the custom of bone gathering (*ossilegium*) was clearly indicated in one of the intact tombs: the skulls were in the corner of the tomb and nearby was an orderly pile of gathered bones and cooking pots. Usually, another room with a separate entrance was built above the underground chamber; it also contained stone sarcophagi. Similar burial customs are known from other Nabatean sites, such as Petra and Kurnub.

The impressive number of finds indicates that Qaṣrawet was the main commercial and cult center for the Nabateans in northern Sinai and perhaps in the entire peninsula between the second century BCE and the second century CE. Its location at the periphery of the Nile Delta provides evidence for a Nabatean trade network along the caravan routes in the Sinai desert and as far away as the Delta region, particularly Pelusium.

LATE ROMAN SETTLEMENT. In the Late Roman period, a fortified settlement was built over the remains of the Nabatean settlement south of the temple quarter. This new settlement, carefully planned, covered an area of approximately 7.5 a. The houses and their contents are unusually well preserved, sometimes as high as roof level. The mud-brick defensive wall is more than 2.5 m thick and its course has been traced for 120 m, along which watchtowers are set at 40-m intervals. The settlement is characterized by clusters of buildings, partly abutting the city wall, with lanes in between them leading to open squares. The houses are well built, with mud-brick walls and stone lintels. The walls are plastered and covered with whitewash, and some are even decorated with frescoes. Colored frescoes depicting caravans of camels and fowl are preserved on the walls of one of the rooms. The theme of these paintings is known from petroglyphs scattered in the Negev and Sinai. The walls of another room were decorated with depictions

Gold earrings from one of the built Nabatean tombs.

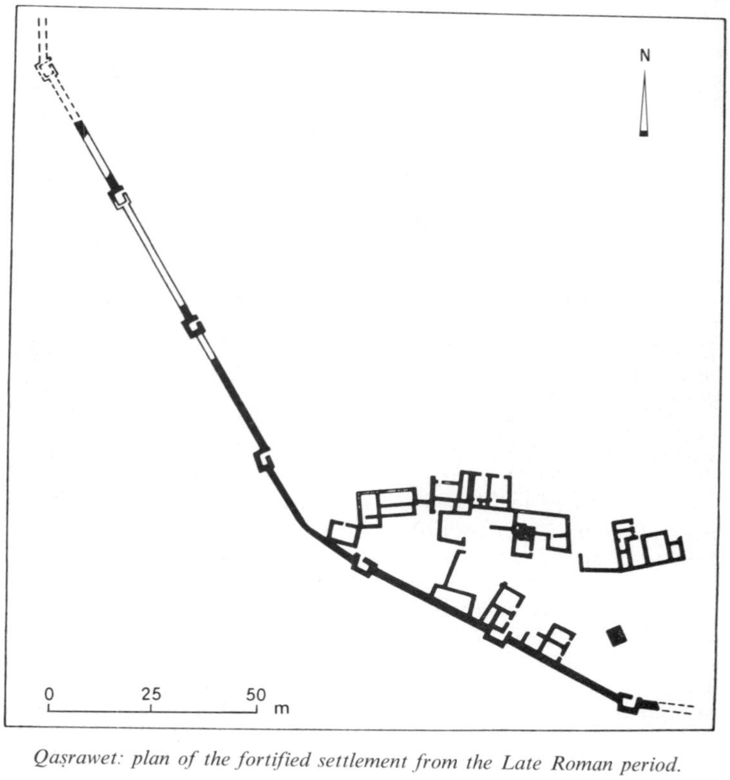

Qaṣrawet: plan of the fortified settlement from the Late Roman period.

Structure buried in a sand dune, Late Roman period.

Room from the Late Roman period with installations and storage jars in situ.

Part of the city wall and one of the towers from the Late Roman period.

***Above and below:** pottery lamps decorated with crosses, from the Late Roman period settlement.*

of groups of date palms laden with fruit and a caravan of camels led by a man wearing a tall hat, surrounded by human figures, dogs, and gazelles. Cooking and baking installations, as well as various storage facilities, were built in the corners of rooms and in the courtyards. The roofs, which collapsed onto the floors after the settlement was abandoned, were made of a frame of branches covered with a thick layer of clay. All the houses show two clear stages of construction that included repairs and floor raisings.

The wealth of the finds in the buildings is surprising. The cooking installations still had pots and pans on them. Intact wine and water jars were still standing in the corners of the rooms. Lamps, glassware, ivory objects, and a great number of coins were found on the floors and in the wall cupboards and niches. A Greek ostracon inscribed with five lines is particularly noteworthy; it describes one of the desert roads along the Egyptian border. A group of oil lamps was decorated with a relief of a seven-branched menorah with a shofar, lulab, and ethrog next to it. Alongside this group were lamps decorated with reliefs of crosses. The coins and the rest of the finds attest to the settlement's existence in the fourth century CE. It was abandoned hurriedly at the end of that century, although there is no evidence of a violent destruction.

It seems that the fortified settlement at Qaṣrawet was partly settled by discharged veterans (*limitani*) of Jewish and Christian origin, who performed paramilitary duties such as escorting caravans. The fortified settlement is undoubtedly part of the defense system (*limes*) erected by the emperor Diocletian at the edge of the Egyptian desert, in order to prevent nomadic tribes from raiding the caravan routes and the settlements along the Egyptian border.

J. Starcky, *Bulletin of the School of Oriental and African Studies* 16 (1954), 211–246; J. Strugnell, id. 156 (1959), 29–36; E. D. Oren, *IEJ* 32 (1982), 203–211; id., *MdB* 24 (1982), 28–35; Y. Tsafrir, *IEJ* 32 (1982), 212–214; D. Rokeah, ibid. 33 (1988), 93–96.

ELIEZER D. OREN

Pottery lamp decorated with the figure of Eros playing the cymbals, from one of the built Nabatean tombs.

Pottery lamp decorated with a seven-branched menorah, ethrog, lulab, and shofar, 4th century CE.

QAṢRIN

IDENTIFICATION

The ancient site of Qaṣrin is in the central Golan, about 1 km (0.6 mi.) southeast of modern Qaẓrin, on a low hill with moderate northern and western slopes (map reference 2161.2661). At the edge of the site is a small spring; a winter stream (locally known as Masil Sheikh Musa), with two small underground springs in its bed, runs north of it. Rock-cut burial caves with *kokhim* (loculi) were found in the hill's cliffs north of the stream. The site is surrounded by extensive fields, and it appears that the ancient inhabitants cultivated fields and olive orchards; two oil presses were found to the west and south of the site.

Tombstone found in the survey: "Rabbi Abun, may he rest in honor."

EXPLORATION

Qaṣrin was discovered by G. Schumacher in 1884 and visited by him again in 1913. The synagogue at Qaṣrin was discovered by S. Gutman in 1967 and surveyed several times by D. Urman from 1969 to 1971. The surveys revealed the synagogue's portal in situ, many architectural remains, and inscriptions, one of which, in Hebrew, was found on a tombstone: רבי אבון משכבו בכבוד (Rabbi Abun, may he rest in honor). In 1971–1972, the synagogue was partly excavated by Urman, on behalf of the archaeology staff officer; in 1975–1976, the excavation of the prayer hall and the adjacent rooms was completed by M. Ben-Ari and S. Barlev. In 1978, a stratigraphic probe was conducted under the synagogue floor by Barlev and Z. Ma'oz. A new series of excavations was carried out in the synagogue from 1982 to 1984, on behalf of the Israel Department of Antiquities and Museums, under the direction of Ma'oz, R. Hachlili, and A. Killebrew. Excavations in the village were begun in 1983, directed by Killebrew. An area of about 1,250 sq m was cleared in the northern part of the village, including the synagogue and domestic buildings.

STRATIGRAPHY

The determination of the site's stratigraphy is based on the structural remains, the building phases in the synagogue, and the ceramic finds.

Stratum I (late nineteenth century–present): cemeteries; reuse of early structures, new structures.

Strata IIA–C (Mameluke period, thirteenth–fifteenth centuries): reuse of Byzantine structures; a mosque (building C) in the northern half of the synagogue; houses.

Stratum III (Early Arab period, mid-eighth century CE): renewed, short-lived squatters, occupation of the village.

Qaṣrin: overview of the synagogue.

Stratum IVB (Late Byzantine and Early Arab periods, seventh–eighth centuries CE): extensive repairs to the synagogue; a new plastered floor; floor raising in the houses.

Stratum IVA (Middle Byzantine period, sixth century CE): erection of the second synagogue (building B); mosaic floor; houses.

Stratum V (Late Roman and Early Byzantine periods, late fourth–fifth centuries CE): erection of the first synagogue (building A).

Stratum VI (Late Roman period, third–fourth centuries CE): building remains; ceramic and numismatic finds.

Stratum VII (Hellenistic period, second–first centuries BCE): ceramic finds only.

Stratum VIII (Iron Age II): hearths, wall fragments and ceramic finds.

Stratum IX (Middle Bronze Age IIB): ceramic finds only.

THE SYNAGOGUE

The synagogue is relatively well preserved, particularly its northern half, where a corner is 2.8 m high and the main gate, with its lintel, is 3.4 m high. The external walls—on the north, west, and partly on the east—are built of well-dressed ashlars; the southern and eastern walls are built of large, solid stones. The latter are adjoined from the outside by rooms. The excavations conducted from 1978 to 1983 revealed three buildings (A–C) here, erected one above the other, in which four architectural phases and five floors (nos. 0–4) could be distinguished. The second synagogue (building B) is the best preserved of the three structures.

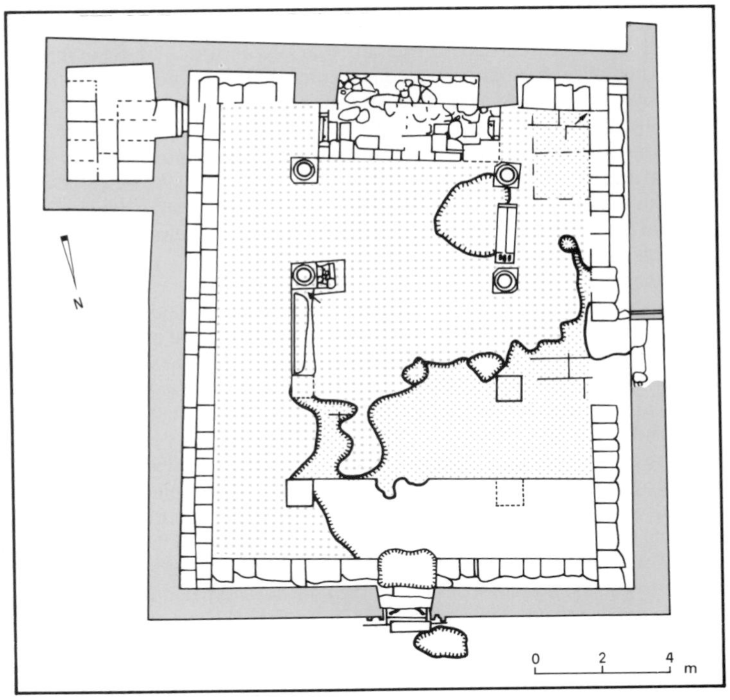

Plan of the synagogue.

Facade of the synagogue.

SECOND SYNAGOGUE—BUILDING B (STRATA IVA–IVB). The second synagogue is a trapezoidal structure, oriented north–south, with unequal sides (external dimensions: on the north, 15.4 m; south, 14.95 m; east, 17.95 m; and west, 17.4 m) and corners set at acute angles. The outer faces of the walls (0.9–1.1 m thick) are well-dressed basalt stone, very precisely laid without the use of mortar. The inner faces were built of solid stone courses, laid unevenly with a fill of small stones and earth. On the inner, plastered, and whitewashed walls, segments of plaster are painted with red bands. The main entrance, which is completely preserved, is in the middle of the synagogue's northern wall—the building's facade. The doorway frame (1.43 m wide and 2.43 high) is composed of sculpted bands with a flat architrave, a convex frieze, and a cornice with an egg-and-dart design. At the foot of the jambs two Attic pilaster bases project from the wall. The lintel bears a relief of a wreath tied in a Hercules knot, flanked by two pomegranates and two amphorae; holes for an iron grill can be discerned in the top-side of the lintel. A relieving arch, ornamented with an architrave and a cornice with egg-and-dart motifs, was built above the doorway. The facade also included one stone cut in a triangular shape, indicating a gable; a fragmentary relief of a serpent was found on it. Other architectural fragments from the facade belong to the cornices and arched windows. Traces of another entrance were found in the western wall. Its lintel bears a double meander relief (swastika). A geometric relief of rhomboids and triangles with a rosette in the center probably belonged to a window above this entrance.

The prayer hall (inner dimensions, 13.25 by 16 m), is divided into a nave (6.1 m wide) and two aisles (western aisle, 3.65 m wide; eastern aisle, 3.45 m wide) by two rows of four columns each and a pair of square engaged pilasters attached to the southern wall. The column capitals are particularly notable, as they are a unique variant of the Ionic capitals characteristic of the Golan. Similar capitals were found at Sussita (Hippos), and identical ones were found among the synagogue ruins near Qaṣrin, such as at 'Assaliyye and Yahudiyye (q.v. Golan, Synagogues). In the building debris parts of windows decorated with engaged half columns (diameter, 0.22 m), with simple bases and Ionic capitals, were also found. These windows were apparently placed in the clerestory walls above the rows of columns (see below). The building's roof was made of tiles laid over a network of wooden beams; a large quantity of tile fragments was found in the debris. In the southeast corner of the hall a door (0.85 m wide) led to an annex room (2.55 by 3.65 m). The room had a plastered floor carved with grooves, imitating stone slabs, as in floor 1 (see below).

In front of the hall's southern wall, oriented toward Jerusalem, was a pair of ashlar-built steps that extended across the width of the nave; the steps led to a raised, solid stone platform (c. 1.2 by 3.15 m), whose edges have not survived. A wooden Ark of the Law apparently stood on it. Behind the platform, at the floor level of the hall, was a long, narrow, stone-paved chamber (0.8 by 4.15 m), probably used as a storage space or genizah. The access to it was through two doorways whose thresholds flanked the ark. It seems that the Ark of the Law and the doors to the chamber behind it were incorporated in a large wooden structure (2 by 5.35 m) built against the hall's southern wall. A pair of small stone-carved pilasters with schematic Ionic capitals may also have belonged to the front of the ark; one of them was found in secondary use in a wall from stratum IVB.

The hall was lined on all sides by a two-tiered bench, built of ashlars. The floor of building B in stratum IVA (floor 2) apparently had been paved with a colored mosaic. Two mosaic sections are preserved between the columns under the walls added in stratum IVB, as are isolated rows of mosaics found near the bottom bench in the hall's northeast corner. Sections of plaster are preserved on the lower parts of the walls; several stones in the debris bore traces of plaster and whitewash, as well as bands of red paint.

Two fragments of an Aramaic inscription, probably belonging to synagogue B, were found in secondary use in the wall of building C from stratum II. The inscription fragments read "['U]zi made this square" and "... gave their share." It was apparently a dedicatory inscription by the building's benefactors.

Basalt stone with the Aramaic inscription "['U]zi made this square," found in secondary use in a wall in a Mameluke building.

Ashlar construction in the northwest corner of the synagogue.

Building B in stratum IV has been assigned to the early sixth century CE, based on a hoard of 180 coins found in the fill between the the hall's bottom bench and wall, along the entire northern side. The coins were apparently buried here during construction work under the upper bench. Sixty-four of the coins have been identified: the later ones were minted in the fifth century CE; the latest is from the reign of Emperor Anastasius I (491–518).

In stratum IVB, the last phase in which building B served as a synagogue, several changes and additions were made in the prayer hall. A new floor (no. 3) of hard white plaster was laid directly above floor 1 (see below). It seems that the wall stubs found between the columns were part of retaining walls for an upper part of the building that had been de-stabilized, thus supporting the theory that building B included a clerestory above the nave but lacked galleries, which were customary at other synagogues of the Galilee and Golan. A clerestory above the nave is characteristic of late synagogue architecture in Palestine, such as at Beth Alpha and Gaza. Z. Yeivin has also proposed a clerestory reconstruction for the synagogue of Chorazin, the closest one in style to those found in the Golan.

The date of floor 3 was based on a hoard of eighty-two coins found under the floor, next to the step leading to the Ark of the Law. The coins were apparently buried here during repair work and the laying of the new floor. All of the coins date to the sixth century, the majority from the century's latter half. The three latest coins are from the reign of Emperor Phocas (607 CE). Judging from the coins, the repairs in stratum IVB were made in the early seventh century CE. On the floor of the building sherds were found from the sixth to seventh centuries CE, along with some sherds from the eighth century. It thus appears that the synagogue at Qaṣrin was still in existence in the seventh and early eighth centuries and was probably destroyed in the earthquake of 749. The finds uncovered in the domestic buildings of the village east of the cemetery (see below) have also helped in dating the final use of the stratum IVB building.

FIRST SYNAGOGUE—BUILDING A (STRATUM V). Another floor (no. 1) of hard plaster was found beneath floors 2 and 3. A system of shallow grooves was carved on it that resemble joints of stone-slab paving. The floor's stone chips and mortar make-up (10 cm thick) was laid on a 20-cm-thick layer of beaten earth, laid above a floor level of beaten earth or brittle plaster (floor 0). The latter (0.2–2 cm thick), covering only part of the building, passes under the benches to the walls. The nature of the floor suggests that it was used as a work surface during the building's construction.

Floor 1, building A's original floor, extends over three-quarters of the prayer hall area of building B and terminates in a straight line at the northern pair of columns. At the center of the northern edge of the floor were traces of an ancient doorway, opposite the main entrance to building B. Floor 1 terminates in a line of stones that were used as a foundation for the bench, behind which were the foundations of an earlier northern wall. The line of building A's northern wall runs 2.8 m south and parallel to that of building B. Floor 1 abuts the bases of the six southern columns and is cut through by the platform for the Ark of the Law in building B. Building A, which predates building B, is an almost square structure (15.2 by 15.3 m) with six columns in two rows; the eastern and western walls were used as foundations for building B. The imprecise way in which the columns of building B were set on their foundation blocks indicates that these footings also came from building A. It seems, too, that the benches in the synagogue were already in use in the earlier building. Various architectural remains found in the adjacent village may have come from building A. These include a doorjamb bearing a relief of a seven-branched menorah and a peacock pecking at a cluster of grapes, as well as a fragment of a cornice with an egg-and-dart motif, on which the inscription דמבר (*dmbr*) was carved.

Doorjamb with a five-branched menorah and a peacock pecking grapes carved in relief, from synagogue A.

The date of floor 1 and of the construction of building A is indicated by the finds sealed between floors 1 and 0 (where a coin from 218–219 CE was recovered), particularly by a large concentration of sherds, mostly of Galilean bowls from the third to fourth centuries CE. It thus appears that building A was erected at the end of the fourth or in the fifth century CE.

THE MOSQUE—BUILDING C (STRATUM II). After a settlement gap of several hundred years in the village, a mosque (8.1 by 15.5 m) was erected in the northern part of synagogue B. At that time, the synagogue's walls and main gate probably stood to a considerable height, as the builders of the mosque only needed to add a new southern wall and to repair the other ancient walls. Architectural elements from the synagogue were reused. A semicircular niche (miḥrab) was cut into the new southern wall, near its center. The ceiling was then supported by crudely constructed square piers. Among the mosque's collapsed ruins, found in piles on the floor, were sherds from the Mameluke period (thirteenth–fifteenth centuries). The site of the mosque was already a sacred place in stratum II, and especially in stratum I. This is attested by the preservation nearby of two Tabor oaks, hundreds of years old, and a sheikh's tomb.

SUMMARY

In the fifth century CE, the synagogue as Qaṣrin was a square structure, with six columns, a pair of benches, and a main entrance in the north. At the beginning of the sixth century, a larger synagogue was built in its place that included eight columns bearing an upper clerestory with windows. The entrance was rebuilt in the north and a large Ark of the Law on a raised stone platform was added in the south. The hall's floor was paved with colored mosaics and the inner walls were probably decorated with panels in red on a white background. The high quality masonry and ornamentation in the second synagogue attests to a period of economic prosperity for the village in the first half of the sixth century. It seems that the building style of the Qaṣrin synagogue was a combination of Galilean and Hauranian architectural traditions (the stone carvings, columns, and walls) and of late Palestinian synagogue construction techniques (entrance in the north, oriented away from Jerusalem; a large Ark of the Law; and a mosaic floor)—a deviation from other synagogues known from the Golan.

The structure's deterioration at the end of the sixth century, apparently as a result of faulty foundations, seems to have caused cracks in the upper story, necessitating the construction of retaining walls between the columns. Therefore, a new floor was also laid, replacing the mosaic. These repairs, dating to the seventh century, testify to a decline in the settlement's economic resources. Still, unlike other Jewish villages excavated in the Golan (Kanaf, Dabiyye, and 'Ein Nashuṭ), whose settlement ended in the early seventh century, it seems that the Jewish village of Qaṣrin and the use of its synagogue continued even after the Arab conquest, at least until the mid-eighth century. The building was probably destroyed in the earthquake of 749, at the end of the Umayyad Dynasty. In the thirteenth century, following a gap in settlement at the site, a mosque was erected on top of the synagogue's ruins that continued in use until the fifteenth century. In the late nineteenth century, after another gap in settlement, the site was resettled by Bedouin of the ed-Diab tribe, who guarded the ruins of the synagogue and mosque, as worthy of a sacred place.

ZVI URI MA'OZ

THE VILLAGE

Between 1983 and 1990, excavations were conducted to the east of the synagogue in a residential area that measures about 45 m (north–south) by 35 m (east–west)—approximately 10 percent of the site.

PRE-SYNAGOGUE OCCUPATION STRATA (STRATA IX–VI). In several probes that reached bedrock, artifacts dating to the Middle Bronze IIB, Iron II, Hellenistic, and Late Roman (second and third centuries CE) periods

Overview of the village: (background) buildings A and B after reconstruction; (foreground) building C and the spring.

Qaṣrin: plan of the village.

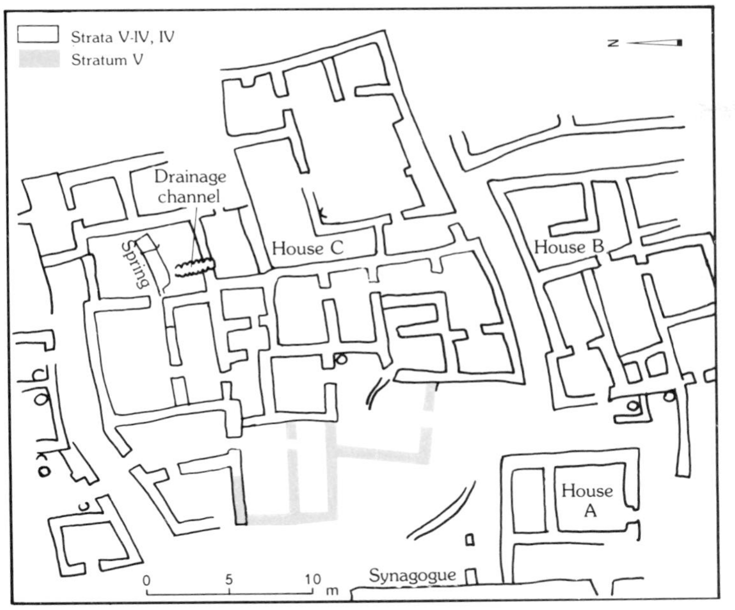

were recovered. The Middle Bronze Age II and Hellenistic periods were represented by pottery sherds only. The Iron Age II and Late Roman occupation included fragmentary architectural remains and large quantities of pottery under the house floors of stratum V (fourth–fifth centuries).

BYZANTINE AND EARLY ARAB PERIODS (STRATA V–IV). In contrast to the synagogue, which has three stratigraphically definable construction phases, the village developed much more "organically," reflecting the needs of individual families. The excavation of each house, and in some cases each room, required a separate stratigraphic phasing sequence.

Parts of three domestic complexes have been uncovered to the east of the synagogue. The basic nuclear family domestic unit consists of a large multipurpose room, or triclinium: a storage room separated from the larger multipurpose room by a wall with a series of large windows (referred to as a window wall, q.v. Golan), an upper story, or sleeping loft above the storage room, and an outdoor courtyard. Sometimes small storage spaces or indoor kitchens were also added to the basic domestic unit.

Additional household units were joined to the single family unit, constructed according to the needs of each extended family. The result was family complexes, or insulae; these sometimes consisted of more than a dozen rooms, housing several generations of the same extended family. By the seventh to eighth centuries, the village was made up of crowded insulae separated from each other by narrow paths.

Stratum V (Fourth–Fifth Centuries CE). The earliest structures uncovered in the village are contemporary with the use of synagogue A. Most of the houses built in this phase continued in use until the mid-eighth century CE, undergoing numerous architectural changes.

The masonry style of the earliest phase of the Byzantine village is the most complex. One face is constructed of large, unworked rounded boulders laid in roughly horizontal courses; numerous chips and small basalt fragments were packed between courses. The second wall face is constructed of smaller field stones.

A few rooms, which were in use only in stratum V, were discovered under the unpaved public square and street of stratum IV, to the east of the synagogue. A multipurpose room, the remains of a window wall, and a storage room were completely excavated. On this floor, and on other contemporary floors, numerous restorable vessels, including cooking pots and storage jars, were recovered. The kitchen ware and storage jars are identical to ceramic assemblages known from the northern Golan and from the potters' workshop site at Ḥawarit, on the slopes of Mount Hermon.

Six coin hoards were found associated with the stratum V houses. Several of these hoards, consisting of up to several hundred bronze coins, were found under the floors, usually in a corner of the room or under the threshold. One

Hoard of 9,000 copper coins discovered under building C, 4th century CE.

coin hoard was deposited in a wall. Because these coins have low monetary value, it is unlikely that they were hidden and meant to be retrieved at a later date. Coin hoards discovered in the excavation of synagogue B at Qaṣrin and in contemporary buildings at other sites indicate that this may have been a custom connected with the construction of a house or public structure.

The largest coin hoard, some nine thousand bronze coins, was found under the beaten-earth floor of the large courtyard in complex C. It includes numerous coins of Julian the Apostate (361–363), and was thus dated to the mid-fourth century. This was a period of high inflation, during which the coin currency lost most of its value. Nine thousand bronze coins were exchangeable for only a few gold coins (solidi).

Stratum IV (Sixth–Mid-Eighth Centuries). In the sixth to mid-eighth centuries, most of the original domestic structures were still in use except for the rooms adjacent to the northeast corner of the synagogue. Following the reconstruction and expansion of the synagogue to the north in the early sixth century, this area along the northern section of the eastern wall became an open public area with a street and a drain. Most of the other domestic structures remained in use. They underwent constant additions and remodeling, which resulted in large family complexes with narrow paths separating the different domestic structures. Most additions to the original houses were built of roughly hewn basalt blocks, square to rectangular in shape; only a few chips were inserted between the courses of these blocks. The floors in the living quarters of the houses were paved in some cases with roughly cut, well-laid basalt blocks; in others, they were paved with field stones and pebbles.

Three houses have been partially excavated. House A, located just outside the southeast corner of the synagogue, against the eastern wall of its annex room, is one of the best-preserved structures excavated thus far. It was built shortly after synagogue A, and it was continuously inhabited through the Early Arab period. There was then a gap in occupation, until it was rebuilt in the Mameluke period (thirteenth–fifteenth centuries CE), which partly explains its well-preserved condition. The house was reoccupied in the twentieth century.

House A consists of two chambers: one 4.4 by 4.2 m, and the other, to the north, 4.2 by 2 m. These were divided by a window wall formed by basalt slabs set on their edges at intervals. Long basalt beams, which formed the ceiling of the small room, were found in situ. They rest on basalt corbels that crown the two sides of its walls, thus creating an upper story that may have been used as a sleeping loft. This plan—consisting of a multipurpose room, storage space, and sleeping loft—formed the basic family unit in the large family complexes of houses B and C.

House B was the last addition to a large, unexcavated family complex continuing to the south. It includes a large multipurpose room (8 by 2.7 m), separated from the storage space (4.4 by 2.6 m) by a window wall, and a second-story sleeping loft above the storage space. An indoor kitchen was the last room added to this unit. To the east of these rooms, at a higher level, is an unpaved courtyard. A low, L-shaped wall divides the courtyard into different activity areas, including an outdoor kitchen with two ovens and a small paved space.

House C is actually several structures that were eventually joined. This complex, which covers an area approximately 25 m (north–south) by 20 m (east–west), continues to the east (outside the boundaries of the current excavations). Several of the rooms were first constructed in the fourth century on top of the architectural remains of stratum VI (second to third centuries CE). Some of the rooms to the west were covered by a street and public area at the close of stratum V. Others continued in use, with remodeling and additions, through the mid-eighth century. At this time, the complex was destabilized, probably by an earthquake, and its inhabitants fled. Shortly thereafter, it was occupied temporarily by squatters.

The northeast corner of house complex C is constructed next to a natural spring, the village's main water source. A room with a plastered floor was directly connected to the spring basin by a narrow channel that led to a small plastered vat. The function of this room is not entirely clear, but it has been suggested that the vat held wine. The finds, which include numerous fragments of storage jars and relatively large amounts of slag, suggest a nondomestic, probably public or industrial, function for the room.

MAMELUKE PERIOD (STRATUM II). The Mameluke village of stratum II, founded approximately 20 to 70 cm above the floors of stratum IV, was in a very disturbed state because of Bedouin and other modern activities at the site. Enough of the Mameluke structures have survived, however, to establish the plan of several rooms and buildings. This village plan differs almost completely from the plan of the Byzantine village. In a few cases, the thirteenth-century inhabitants reused parts of the standing Byzantine structures and built on top of Byzantine wall stubs. In most cases, however, the earlier walls were shaved down and often incorporated into stone-paved floors. The Mameluke builders usually constructed their walls from field stones, reusing the basalt blocks from the Byzantine period as it suited them.

The stratum II floors yielded large quantities of pottery, including complete vessels, as well as other artifacts, such as a richly decorated bronze bowl

bearing an Arabic inscription. Numerous refuse pits, containing many animal bones, were also found in this stratum throughout the excavated area.
TWENTIETH CENTURY (STRATUM I). A small Bedouin settlement was established on top of the Byzantine and Mameluke remains. Several single-room stone houses are visible today and date to the last period of habitation at the site.
THE SPRING. The spring, which supplied water for the village, consisted of a basin, hewn into the basalt bedrock. A channel, also constructed of basalt, brought water from an adjacent underground spring into the hewn basin. This spring was the main water source for the inhabitants of the site throughout its periods of occupation. In stratum V, the entrance to the spring was from the main alley, north of it, which led to the synagogue. As the street level rose, a series of retaining walls was constructed to the north of the spring basin. By the Mameluke period, the living surface had risen approximately 1.5 m; well-constructed stone steps then led down to the spring. In the twentieth century (stratum I), the spring basin was protected by an additional series of retaining walls, and the water was reached by a flight of steep, crudely constructed steps.

ANN KILLEBREW

G. Schumacher, *The Jaulan*, London 1888, 194; Z. Ma'oz, *ASR*, 103–105; id., *Jewish Art in the Golan* (Reuben and Edith Hecht Museum Cat. 3), Haifa 1987; id. (and A. Killebrew), *ESI* 4 (1985), 90–94; id., *IEJ* 35 (1985), 289–293; id., *BA* 51/1 (1988), 5–19; A. LeBorgne and M. Nothmann, *MdB* 53 (1988), 56; D. Chen, *LA* 38 (1988), 247–248; A. Killebrew (and S. Fine), *BAR* 17/3 (1991), 44–56; id., ibid. 17/5 (1991), 20, 22.

QATIF
(THE NEOLITHIC SITE)

IDENTIFICATION
The Late Neolithic site of Qatif is about 400 m northeast of Tel Qatif (map reference 08423.09005), on the eastern edge of the coastal road between Khan Yunis and Deir el-Balaḥ. In the course of road construction work, ashy layers rich in pottery, flint artifacts, and bones were exposed. The site is embedded within a silty layer, capping a *kurkar* ridge, 11 m above sea level and some 100 m from the coastline. The area excavated (250 sq m) lies at the edge of the site, most of which was destroyed in the course of the construction work.

EXPLORATION
Qatif was excavated in 1973 by an expedition directed by A. Biran, on behalf of the Israel Department of Antiquities and Museums, and was excavated by C. Epstein. The site was further surveyed by the North Sinai Expedition (site Y3 on the survey map), headed by E. D. Oren. Excavations were resumed in 1979, 1980, and 1983, under the direction of I. Gilead, on behalf of Ben-Gurion University of the Negev.

EXCAVATION RESULTS
The stratigraphy of the site, which was examined to a maximum depth of 1.4 m, is complex because the sequence was disturbed in the later periods; it consists of at least two occupation levels. The uppermost part of the stratigraphic sequence was principally created as a result of disturbances caused by cultivation of the area, rodent activity, and natural sand deposition.

The main occupation level is 0.1 to 0.4 m below surface level. It is grayish black and consists of packed, oily ashes, in which sherds, flint artifacts, and clay lumps bearing impressions of seeds and twigs are frequent. The 0.2- to 0.3-m thick layer, although discontinuous, is discernible throughout the site. It seems that this occupation level represents small activity zones, in which lumps of fired clay and *kurkar* were found adjacent to reddish ash concentrations, probably the remains of hearths. Between the hearths are yellow packed-sand levels, containing varying quantities of calcareous concretions. No architectural remains were unearthed and only a few small shallow pits were found. An unusual find recovered from the occupation level is a burial jar containing the skeleton of a baby, about one month old, in a flexed position, with no burial offerings.

Under the main occupation level is a yellowish-gray layer, rich in calcareous concretions. On the northeast side of the site, this layer was excavated to a depth of 0.8 m below the main occupation level; its lowermost part was completely sterile. In the center of the site, in a limited area (2 by 2 m), another grayish-black level, containing finds similar to those recovered from the main occupation level, was uncovered below the yellowish-gray layer. This level seems to represent the earliest stage in the site's occupational sequence.

THE FINDS
FLINT IMPLEMENTS. Flint items were recovered from all areas and levels. Flakes constitute the main component of the waste, but many items are not classifiable, as they were burned and broken. Technologically, there is no standardization here, as is evident in the mostly amorphic cores. Flint nodules with no clear striking platforms, from which a few flakes (or blades) had been struck from various directions, are also frequent.

Some of the tools are made of higher-quality flint than that constituting the waste; it is possible that these were made elsewhere and then brought to the site. The most common tool type is the sickle blade—about 30 percent of all the tools recovered. The common sickle blade is rectangular, relatively broad and flat, with a finely retouched working edge. The opposite edge is semi-abruptly retouched and the ends are truncated. A few tabular flint fan scrapers were found whose bulb of percussion had been removed. The few arrowheads are small and shaped by pressure flaking. Axes (some of them polished), burins, borers, notches, denticulates, and retouched blades/bladelets were found, as well.

POTTERY. In the course of the three seasons of excavations by Gilead, more than seven hundred handles, rims, bases, and decorated clay items were collected. Most of the vessels were made of coarse, crumbly clay and were poorly fired. Sherd sections reveal grayish-black cores beneath the reddish-brown surfaces. The clay is rich in materials designed to reduce its oiliness, particularly straw, sand grains, and broken shells.

The variety of vessel shapes is not yet sufficiently known, due to difficulties in restoring the recovered sherds. Examination of the rims shows that flared-rim jars, hole-mouth jars, and a few bowls are the most common items in the assemblage. Of the thousands of sherds recovered, only fifty-six items are decorated, fifteen of which bear plastic decoration—projecting lugs that form a sort of chain made by finger impressions. The other sherds are decorated with red paint. The majority of the decorated items consist of rims and thin-bodied sherds, mostly of bowls. Of the assemblage's characteristic vessels, seven crude fragments retained traces of paint. No decorative pattern was discerned on the painted items, and it appears that the vessels were painted inside and out. Small lumps of red ocher were also recovered.

OTHER FINDS. Many grinding slabs and grinding stones were found scattered over the site—all of them of beach rock or sandstone. The exceedingly brittle beach rock found at the present water line differs from the material of the grinding tools. They were probably made from an ancient beach rock, now under the sea. This may indicate that when the site was occupied, the sea level was lower and the coastline extended farther west than at present. Several fragments of limestone bowls were also recovered. A few bone tools—massive as well as small bone points—were found. A few small pottery beads with holes bored in their center, as well as a few stone and pottery weights, were also found.

FAUNAL REMAINS. In the last three seasons, 404 bones, most (95 percent) of domesticated animals, were recovered. Of the few specimens of wild animals, an antelope (*Alcelaphus sp.*), a lion, and a donkey are noteworthy. The distribution of domesticated animal bones is as follows: goat/sheep (37 percent), cattle (31 percent), and pig (32 percent). The frequency of pig bones implies that the occupation at the site was permanent and that humidity was higher than at present. Despite the site's proximity to the sea, few fish bones were found. It is unlikely that the ancient coastline was so distant as to render fishing unprofitable; it is more probable that the site's economy relied on domesticated animals and that hunting and fishing had minor significance.

SUMMARY
Qatif is among the latest Neolithic sites in Israel. A sample of charred bones yielded a carbon-14 date of 4090 ± 180 BCE (Pta 2968). Several major flint tool types recovered from the site are characteristic of the second half of the fifth millennium. The finely retouched sickle blades are characteristic of the Late Neolithic at Byblos and differ from the earlier, deeply serrated sickle blades common at most of the Late Neolithic sites on the Coastal Plain (Niẓẓanim, Giv'at ha-Parsa, and Herzliya). The presence of fan scrapers is also characteristic of the end of the Neolithic period.

It is difficult to assign the pottery vessels to any particular stage of the terminal Neolithic. The bow-rim jars characteristic of Jericho VIII and of the Wadi Rabah assemblages are absent from this site, as are the various decorative patterns characteristic of those assemblages. The few painted items, made of strawless clay, were fired differently from the more common vessels. These may be imported items, but as it is difficult to determine whether they came from the northern part of the country or from Egypt, they cannot be regarded as chronological indicators.

Pottery vessels closely resembling those from Qatif were found at sites D and M at Naḥal Besor near Tell el-Far'ah (South). These were found with sherds from the Chalcolithic period; they seem to represent Neolithic sites destroyed by later settlements. Occupation remains from the Chalcolithic period were also found in the Qatif region, on a hill next to Tel Qatif, some 300 m from the Neolithic site. The terminal Neolithic site near Tel Qatif and the remains of other similar sites in the Tell el-Far'ah (South) region suggest the existence of an agricultural-pastoral culture in the southern part of the country, shortly before the expansion of the Chalcolithic (Ghassulian) occupation there. A certain resemblance in subsistence modes and in the character of the occupation between these two cultural phases may indicate that the later culture was of local origin.

A. Biran, *IEJ* 24 (1974), 141–142; C. Epstein, *IEJ* 34 (1984), 209–219; I. Gilead and Y. Goren, *BASOR* 275 (1989), 5–14; I. Gilead, *Levant* 22 (1990), 47–63; T. E. Levy, *The Nile Delta in Transition, 4th–3rd Millennium B.C.: Abstracts* (ed. M. Azmi), Cairo 1990, n.p.

ISAAC GILEAD

QEDUMIM

IDENTIFICATION

The site is located in the center of the modern settlement of Qedumim, about 10 km (6 mi.) west of Shechem, on the Shechem–Qalqilya road (map reference 1650.1793). The site was a former Samaritan settlement. Many of the Arab villages in its vicinity preserve the names of Samaritan settlements: Ḥajja—Qiryat Ḥaga; Khirbet Bazzin—Beth Bazzin; Jit—Gath; and Khirbet 'Asafa—'Aẓafa.

EXCAVATIONS

Excavations were conducted at the site from 1979 to 1982, under the direction of I. Magen, on behalf of the archaeology staff officer of Judea and Samaria.

BRONZE AND IRON AGES. Few remains from the Early Bronze Age I were encountered here. Sherds of pottery and metal vessels were discovered that had originally belonged to Middle Bronze Age II tombs. These tombs had been cleared in the Roman period, during the construction of the Samaritan settlement and their contents emptied into cisterns from the Persian-Hellenistic period. There were very few finds from the Iron Age, a period when the site apparently was abandoned.

PERSIAN-HELLENISTIC PERIOD. No settlement remains from the Persian-Hellenistic period have been found so far; all the finds here come from cisterns. Cistern A, a bell-shaped installation coated with a thick layer of rose-tinted plaster, contained hundreds of potsherds, copper needles, and loom weights from the Persian period. The pottery included imported vessels from Greece and a unique, large hole-mouth jar, decorated with faunal and floral designs and an Aramaic inscription: מתרא (*mtr'*). Persian-Hellenistic vessels were also found in a cistern at the center of the site (cistern B). Sparse remains (a ritual bath and a tomb) were found from the first century CE. Judging from the finds, the site was occupied from the Persian period to the first century CE and was completely destroyed in the course of the construction of the second-century CE settlement.

ROMAN-BYZANTINE PERIOD. The Roman settlement on the site was established in the late second and early third centuries CE. The buildings were of excellent ashlar masonry, in the Roman tradition. This settlement was apparently destroyed during the Samaritan revolts. It was succeeded by a larger settlement, whose building standard was inferior; that settlement existed until the Early Arab period.

Area C. Three buildings from the first occupation phase were uncovered in area C. They were built of stones with drafted margins laid in headers and stretchers on rubble foundations. The cellars in the buildings contained numerous caves used for storage. Large plastered cisterns were found in the courtyards. The buildings were destroyed in a conflagration during one of the Samaritan revolts. At the end of the sixth century CE, an unplanned settlement overlay the ruins of the earlier one. Its houses were built of field stones in combination with reused ashlars.

BUILDING I AND THE OIL PRESS. In area C the ruins of a double oil press were found; the press had operated on the beam-and-weights system. The installation for crushing olives—the vat and pressbeam—was not found, although the apparatus for extracting the oil was preserved in situ. The olive press was installed in the cellar of an ashlar-built house. Its floor was of different-shaped stones and its walls were coated with high-quality plaster. The extraction chamber is about 8 m long and 6.5 m wide. Its northern wall contained two large niches for anchoring the pressbeams. The size of the niches indicates that the beams were especially large and thick. Opposite each niche were two supporting posts. Between the two posts was a stone platform, on which the bales of olive pulp were placed. From this platform the oil flowed to a plastered depression and from there, through a narrow hole, to a square, plastered vat (each side c. 70 cm long). The vat was covered by a stone slab with a round opening in its center. An opening was cut in the middle of the southern wall to connect the two parts of the room. This

Decorated hole-mouth jar with the Aramaic inscription "mtr'," Persian period.

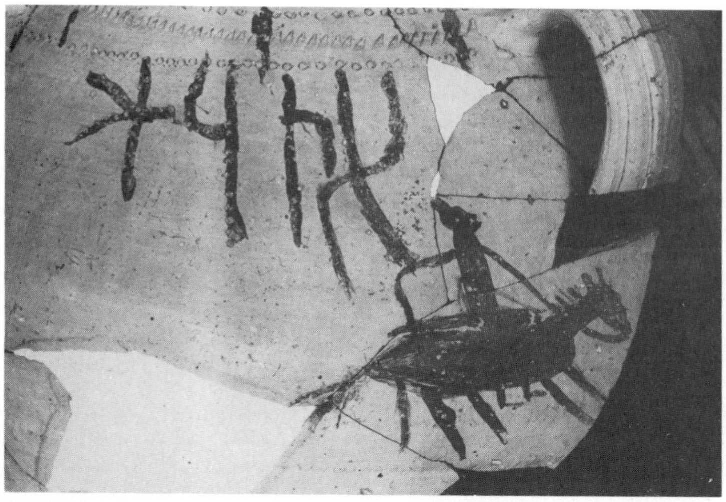

Qedumim: pottery assemblage from one of the cisterns, Persian period.

entrance was blocked in a later building phase. On the floor near the northern wall was a plastered vat, in which the crushed olives were apparently stored before the oil was extracted. Two round pools were hollowed out of the building's eastern wall. A ritual bath (mikveh) was uncovered at the eastern end. The floor of the oil press was covered with a thick layer of ash. The press was apparently destroyed during the Samaritan revolts. Its contents included, inter alia, complete pottery vessels and large bone tools apparently used to scrape the floor clean. Caves for storing the oil were connected to the oil press, which was destroyed by fire and never rebuilt. A structure was later built over it, but it had a different function.

BUILDING II. Rooms C35 and C32 are remnants of an ashlar-built structure that extended from building I to the west. The debris contained many ashlars and fragments of a colored mosaic that had fallen from the second story. An opening in the corner of the room led into cave C34. The building was used in both phases of the settlement.

BUILDING III. Building III belongs to the first phase of settlement. One course of its eastern wall is preserved. It was built of stones with drafted margins laid in headers and stretchers on rubble foundations. Against this wall a later building (C24-C50) was erected that contained sherds attributing it to the Late Byzantine period. The wall is therefore earlier than building C24-C50. The excellent quality of its construction attests that the wall also belongs to the first phase of the settlement. Building III was also apparently destroyed by fire when the site was razed during the Samaritan revolts.

Area M: The Upper Oil Press Complex. Another well-preserved oil press complex was uncovered on a high hill northeast of area C. It comprises a large number of storage rooms as well as a stable for the pack animals that transported the sacks of olives and oil jars. The main room contained the crushing installation, with a vat and pressbeam. The stone base of the screw press, serving as a substitute for the weights, was found in the southern part of an elongated room, west of the main room. In a room to the north of the crushing installation, the oil was extracted from the olives by the beam-and-weights system.

Other rooms were uncovered to the north and east of these rooms. South of the oil press, a pool that was originally a cistern was used as a ritual bath after a partition wall and steps were added. In the upper oil press, the walls, cisterns, and hollowed-out areas can be attributed to the early phase of the settlement. The nature of the building, the method of oil processing, and the potsherds all indicate that the oil press was in use in the seventh century, and part of it in a later period as well.

Area F. Area F is southwest of area C. The building remains uncovered here form the continuation of the Samaritan settlement to the south. Architecturally, this area resembles area C. It contains two spacious square buildings (I and II) with a complete oil press between them. Two building phases can be distinguished here as well. The first phase employed ashlar stone construction, while the second phase is characterized by unplanned, inferior construction. The raising of floors in the second phase attests to a large gap in time between the two building phases. No conflagration layer, as in area C, was discovered here. The ceramic finds were also different: no Roman sherds were unearthed, indicating that construction was begun here in the Early Byzantine period, before the settlement was abandoned, in the wake of the Samaritan revolts.

BUILDING I. So far, building I has yielded a ritual bath at its western end, a well-hewn circular stone, and a small vat belonging to an oil press.

BUILDING II. Building II is square. Its southern wall adjoins the oil press. It is built of well-hewn ashlar stones and apparently belongs to the first building phase. In the second phase, the floors and thresholds were raised. The building was entered from the west, through a lane leading from the north. In the center of the lane, which is paved with different-sized stones, is an opening of a large rock-cut cistern that is covered with a coat of reddish plaster. Other entrances, in the building's southern wall, provided access to the oil press. A door lintel decorated with an incised branch, or possibly a menorah, was found at the eastern end of the lane. The finds in the building included a pyramid-shaped bronze incense vessel with a chain and ring to hold it, a large bronze bowl, and an iron necklace. Various cooking utensils, including a clay funnel for filling oil jars, were also found.

From the paved lane an entrance leads westward down a plastered flight of steps to a ritual bath. The bottom step was unusually high. The ritual bath displayed two types of plaster: the bottom layer is a grayish black, from the first phase; repairs in reddish plaster were made in the second phase. Various pottery vessels lay on the bottom of the pool, including a complete oil lamp from the eighth century CE (Early Arab period).

SOUTHERN OIL PRESS. At the southern end of the lane, another entrance led to a plaza; steps descended from the plaza, through a doorway with a threshold, to an oil press. Discovering another oil press in this area was a surprise, as three large oil presses operating in a small village is a rare occurrence. The oil press was built in the space between buildings I and II, apparently in the period after these spacious buildings had been erected. Evidence of its prolonged use was the discovery of a large, worn vat in the northern room. South of the crushing apparatus was the extraction mechanism that terminated on its western end in a device for the screw press. To its east, at the end of a room

Area M and its oil press.

Oil press in area F.

paved with white tesserae, was a plastered cistern covered by a large stone slab with a hole in its center through which the oil was removed. A channel led to the cistern from the installation on which the olive pulp was placed, which was merely a large stone surrounded by a trench for collecting the oil. Extraction was carried out by a combination of the press beam and the screw press; the screw replaced the weights employed in ancient oil presses—it did not directly press the olive pulp. In the seventh and eighth centuries, the oil press fell into disuse, and the walls of the second phase were built above it.

Ritual Baths. Six ritual baths were discovered at the site. Before excavations began here, ritual baths had been discovered only in Jewish settlements. Here, for the first time, ritual baths were encountered in a Samaritan settlement—evidence that the Samaritans observed laws of ritual purity. Three of the ritual baths are connected with the oil presses. Apparently, the people who produced the oil purified themselves in the baths. It is difficult to assign the other three baths to a specific stratum. They are dated to the period between the first and the seventh to eighth centuries CE.

TOMBS. Three tombs have been excavated so far at the site. They represent three distinct periods in the existence of the settlement. Tomb A, an arcosolia tomb, was entered through a stone door. It consists of a main square chamber with troughs for burial topped by arcosolia along three of its sides. Initially, between six and eight people were buried here; in the second phase of burial, however, apparently in the time of the Samaritan revolts, many more bodies were interred in the main chamber.

Tomb B is a large loculi tomb (c. 7 by 7 m) uncovered on the southeast side of the site. In its center, a square cavity (c. 20 cm deep), is a remnant of the pit tombs of the Second Temple period. Nine loculi were found here: five in the west, three in the east, and one in the south. The tomb is dated to the second and third centuries CE.

Tomb C, another loculi tomb, was uncovered southeast of tomb A. The tomb has a vaulted entrance and a square chamber that is entered through a small vaulted room. Three sides of the square chamber contain rock-cut loculi of various shapes. One loculus in the eastern wall is especially large. The tomb was in use from the Hellenistic period to the first century CE.

I. Magen, *ESI* 1 (1982), 96–100; E. Stern and I. Magen, *BASOR* 253 (1984), 9–27.

ITZHAK MAGEN

Tomb A, Roman-Byzantine period.

QIRI, TEL

IDENTIFICATION

Tel Qiri is a site within Kibbutz ha-Zorea', about 2 km (1 mi.) south of Tel Jokneam, west of the Jokneam–Megiddo road (map reference 161.227).

EXPLORATION AND EXCAVATION

Over the years, numerous archaeological remains have come to light in the kibbutz: tombs, walls, pottery, and other finds, ranging from the Neolithic to the Early Arab periods. At least some of these finds may have come from Tel Qiri, at the western edge of the kibbutz.

The site was excavated from 1975 to 1977, as part of the Jokneam Regional Project (q.v. Jokneam), an archaeological investigation of the western Jezreel Valley. Tel Qiri was the first site to be excavated as part of this project, under the direction of A. Ben-Tor, on behalf of the Institute of Archaeology at the Hebrew University of Jerusalem.

Because of its location within the kibbutz, the site has been damaged by recent construction work. By the time excavations began, only an area of approximately one acre had been unaffected; the original area of the site was probably about 2.5 a. This corresponds to the sizes of other rural sites in the region, such as Tel Qashish and Tel Risim. By 1975, then, nearly half of the site was buried under modern buildings; from 1978 onward, the entire site was gradually covered by construction work. It has now been entirely destroyed.

The site is not an archaeological mound in the conventional sense: the settlement was established at the eastern end of a spur of the Carmel Range, which slopes down steeply to Naḥal Shofet—hence, the sloping sides so characteristic of archaeological mounds are absent. All the various strata of the settlement were built on the slope of the spur. The inhabitants of the settlements drew their water from a spring in the bed of Naḥal Shofet, to the south.

The archaeological remains—stone tools, potsherds, and fragments of glass vessels, and coins—from Tel Qiri represent a very long span of occupation, from the end of the Neolithic to the Ottoman period. The abundance of water, a moderate climate, and fertile soil have always attracted settlers. The excavators assigned stratum numbers only to periods for which masonry remains were discovered; thus, some periods, although represented in the finds (mainly pottery), have not been included in the stratigraphic sequence.

Stratum I	Byzantine period
Stratum II	Roman period
Stratum III	Hellenistic period
Stratum IV	Persian period
Stratum V	Iron Age III
Stratum VI	Iron Age II
Stratum VII	Iron Age II
Stratum VIII	Iron Age I
Stratum IX	Iron Age I
Stratum X	Middle Bronze Age II
Stratum XI	Late Neolithic (or Early Chalcolithic) period

LATE PERIODS (STRATA I–IV). The state of preservation of strata I–IV was extremely fragmentary, especially in the site's western, higher sector; considerable damage was done here by ground leveling in preparation for modern construction. Among the Byzantine remains were a few walls of residential buildings and some sherds. These remains were damaged by a medieval Arab cemetery, whose graves were scattered over the site.

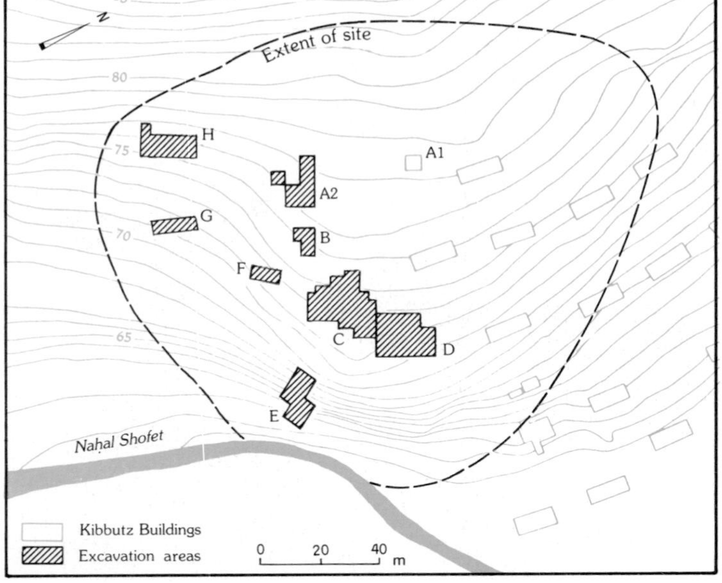

Tel Qiri: plan of the site and excavation areas.

Stratum II is represented by the remains of a building that was in particularly long use: the sherds and glass fragments discovered here, as well as its two building phases, attest to a period of use from the mid-first century BCE to the end of the first century CE. Also dated to this period was a tomb, in which were found, inter alia, a mirror and a bronze spatula.

The principal remains in stratum III consisted of part of a presumably public building, as indicated by its size and the quality of its construction. Only a corner of the building was preserved, as well as part of a stone-paved courtyard. Two coins, one of them silver, from the third century BCE, and a few sherds date the building to the third and second centuries BCE.

Attributable to the Persian period (stratum IV) are a few lengths of wall—which are, however, insufficient to determine the plan of the building—and a cemetery in the western part of the site, with some twenty rock-hewn tombs. The tombs are oriented north–south, and the bodies were placed in them with the heads pointing north. Most of the tombs contained one body each, mostly without funerary offerings. The tombs were sealed with stone slabs. The attribution to the Persian period is based mainly on one of the tombs, which contained offerings of pottery vessels alongside the skeleton. Because of the proximity of the cemetery to the surface, it was disturbed in later periods; this probably accounts for the finds from the Roman and Hellenistic periods discovered in the area, as well as the secondary use of one of the tombs in the Roman period.

IRON AGE (STRATA V–IX). In contrast to the poor finds from the later periods, the fine state of preservation of the Iron Age remains, which constituted the bulk of the finds at the site, is noteworthy. In the main excavated area (c. 500 sq m), in the center of the site, the excavators could identify five Iron Age strata, divided into twelve subphases. These phases formed a continuous sequence; not one of them had been destroyed in a conflagration. Each phase was linked to its predecessor, and some structures remained in use for several periods. Only once during this whole time span was a significant change noticeable in the plan of the settlement—in the transition from stratum VIII to stratum VII (Iron Age I–II). The transition was marked mainly by a change in the alignments of the buildings: entrances previously aligned along an east–west axis were now aligned north–south. This change was not reflected in the method of construction, which remained the same throughout the period. The residential structures of strata V–IX were very similar: the overwhelming majority were broadhouses, their brick walls laid on a stone foundation of standard thickness (60 cm). The bricks (12 by 18 by 55 cm) were thus adapted to the dimensions of the stone foundation; they could be laid alternately as headers—one brick across the width of the wall—or as stretchers—with three bricks laid side by side. As the span of the rooms was at most 2.5 m, there was no need for pillars to support the ceilings. Numerous fragments of these ceilings were found, and the impressions left in the plaster of the ceilings by wooden beams and branches reveal the techniques of ceiling construction.

As already mentioned, these construction characteristics could be distinguished in all the Iron Age levels, probably also indicating continuity in the population. The settlement was an unfortified village, housing a fairly well-to-do population, judging from the quality of the construction. The settlement's rural nature is also implied by the large number of silos discovered in the courtyards of the buildings, most of them lined with stones, with their openings covered by circular stone slabs. An oil press in the courtyard of one building was ascribed to stratum VII. It was made of a large, heavy stone slab, on which the olives were placed; alongside it was a circular installation to receive the oil. The weights were not found. Near the press was a large quantity of olive pits. In all the houses, there was an abundance of basalt grinding and crushing tools. Also found were various kinds of seeds—wheat, pomegranate, peas, and vetch. Prominent among the animal bones found were those of goats and sheep—in roughly equal quantities, constituting some 80 percent of the bone finds—and of cattle—about 15 percent of the bones. Evidence that the inhabitants also hunted for food was provided by bones from wild pigs, gazelle, and roe deer; even a bear tooth was discovered here. The most common items among the flint tools were sickle blades, constituting approximately 45 percent of all tools.

The site's pottery repertoire also indicates uninterrupted occupation: from stratum IX, in the twelfth century BCE, including Philistine ware and collared-rim jars, to stratum V, in the eighth century BCE, including a typical Iron Age III assemblage and an Assyrian-style bottle. Two groups of finds are particularly noteworthy. The first is a group of cooking pots from the tenth century BCE, with incised signs on their rim. Some of these signs are somewhat similar

Part of the Iron Age village.

to letters of the Phoenician alphabet. Cooking pots with similarly incised rims have been discovered at other sites in the region (Megiddo, Tel Qashish, and Jokneam) in contemporary levels. The meaning of the signs and the function of the vessels are as yet unclear. The second group was discovered in a stratum VIII building (end of the Iron Age I, eleventh century BCE). It included an incense burner, a libation vessel, a chalice, a cup and saucer, and a votive bowl. The obvious cultic character of this group, and probably also of the building in which it was discovered, was also indicated by the remains of sacrifices found there: a few dozen right foreleg bones of goats and sheep, undoubtedly remains of the right thigh offering mentioned in the Bible (Lev. 7:32–33) as well as in Canaanite sources.

EARLY PERIODS (STRATA X–XI). Some sherds, discovered out of context in fills in Iron Age levels, were ascribed to the Late Bronze Age. Notable among them were a bichrome sherd, a Cypriot sherd, and a Mycenaean sherd. No architectural elements from this period have survived. It is not yet known whether these sherds reached the site with the fill material, which was brought from the vicinity, or whether there was actually a Late Bronze Age settlement whose remains were completely destroyed by the builders of the Iron Age village.

Some sherds from the Middle Bronze Age II were discovered in most of the excavated areas, but large quantities of such sherds appeared only in a section cut in the eastern slope, together with lengths of wall from that period. These walls, probably of residential structures, did not combine to form any plan. This level, stratum X, although sparse in finds, probably represented the remains of a village (no indications of fortification were found in the section) from the eighteenth to the sixteenth centuries BCE.

Sherds from the Early Bronze Age (mainly from the beginning of the period, including gray burnished and band slip sherds) and from the Chalcolithic period, including fragments of churns and cornets, were discovered out of context in Iron Age levels. The same uncertainty holds here as in regard to the Late Bronze Age pottery (whether the sherds arrived with the fill material from the vicinity or originated in levels completely destroyed by intensive construction in a later period). Of the two possibilities, the excavators favor the second.

One of the excavated areas yielded Late Neolithic remains that included segments of narrow stone walls, a silo, and a rich assemblage of stone tools and pottery. The ceramic finds also included dark-faced burnished ware. These finds should probably be ascribed to the transitional phase between the Neolithic and the Chalcolithic, and dated to the second half of the fifth millennium, perhaps as late as the beginning of the fourth millennium. This is stratum XI, whose remains probably represent the first, earliest agricultural village at the site.

Main publication: A. Ben-Tor et al., *Tell Qiri, A Village in the Jezreel Valley: Report of the Archaeological Excavations 1975–1977 (Qedem* 24), Jerusalem 1987.

Other studies: A. Ben-Tor, *IEJ* 25 (1975), 168–169; 26 (1976), 200–201; id., *RB* 83 (1976), 272–274; id., *BA* 42 (1979), 105–113; id., *BAR* 6/2 (1980), 30–44; id. et al., *Qedem* 24 (Reviews), *VT* 38 (1988), 488–489. — *BIAL* 26 (1989), 237–238. — *JQR* 80 (1989), 179–182. — *Levant* 21 (1989), 203–204; *ASOR Newsletter* Nov. 1976, 10–12; *Buried History* 13/1 (1977), 51–52; 16/2 (1980), 7–8; B. Brandl and A. Schwarzfeld, *IEJ* 28 (1978), 124–125; *RB* 85 (1978), 100–102; M. L. Hunt, "The Iron Age Pottery of the Yoqneam Regional Project" (Ph.D. diss., Univ. of Calif., Berkeley 1985); Weippert 1988 (Ortsregister); J. Briend, *Transeuphratène* 2 (1990), 109–123.

AMNON BEN-TOR

Group of cult vessels, Iron I.

QITMIT, ḤORVAT

IDENTIFICATION AND EXPLORATION

Ḥorvat Qitmit is in the Arad Valley in the Negev desert, on a flat, elongated hill 527 m above sea level (map reference 1564.0660). Extensive areas of the Beersheba and Arad valleys can be seen from the site, as can three neighboring Iron Age settlements—the Arad fortress, Tel Malḥata, and Tel 'Ira.

Ḥorvat Qitmit was discovered in early 1979 by a survey team headed by I. Beit-Arieh. During the survey, remains of buildings with a large quantity of Iron Age II sherds and numerous fragments of clay figurines and reliefs were observed. The site consists of two complexes of rectangular buildings and two circular enclosures. During excavation it became clear that this had been the location of an Edomite shrine from the late seventh and early sixth centuries BCE.

Excavations were conducted from 1984 to 1986, on behalf of the Institute of Archaeology at Tel Aviv University, directed by I. Beit-Arieh. The entire area of this small site was excavated. Because the site was covered by only a very thin layer of sediment, a large portion of the finds had been washed down the slope over the years.

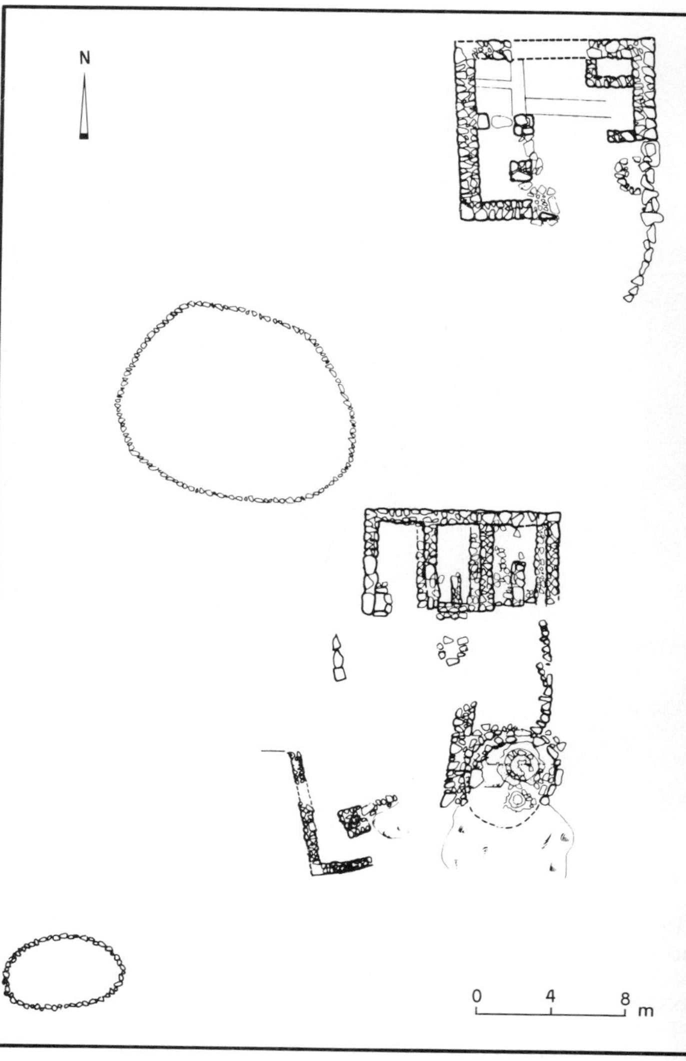

Ḥorvat Qitmit: plan of the site.

EXCAVATION RESULTS

COMPLEX A. A group of structures in the southern part of the site, complex A, was the main cultic area. It consisted of a rectangular building, a platform surrounded by a stone enclosure, and a basin and altar that apparently were also surrounded by an enclosure. The building, 5.5 by 10.5 m (exterior dimensions), is divided into three rooms, each about 2 by 4 m (interior dimensions). The rooms' entrances are 2 m wide. Within each room, at right angles to the entrance, is a short bench (c. 0.6 m high) with a course of flat, broad stones on top of it that may have served as a podium for a statue or an altar. The floors are beaten lime; they were covered with a thick layer of ash (up to 0.4 m), with signs of burning. Two building stages can be distinguished in the structure. Numerous sherds were recovered from the rooms. Except for one complete small Assyrian-type bowl, all of the remaining sherds were discards that were unrestorable. Animal bones and a few figurines were also recovered from the rooms.

In the southern area of the building, on the exposed limestone bedrock, is a low platform (c. 1 by 1.25 m) constructed of medium-sized field stones. The area (6.5 by 7.5 m) around the platform is enclosed by straight walls built of field stones; there is an opening on the north, facing the building's facade. To the east of the enclosure is a basin (diameter, c. 1 m) constructed of unhewn stones and plastered on its inner face and outer edges. Adjoining it are a stone altar and a rock-cut pit. The remains of a curvilinear stone wall on the eastern and western sides imply that the altar and pit were also enclosed.

COMPLEX B. Complex B is in a flat area, some 15 m north of complex A. It is a rectangular enclosure (internal dimensions, 8 by 8.5 m) surrounded by a 1.2-

Ḥorvat Qitmit: aerial view.

General view of the site, looking north.

m-thick wall. Part of it was occupied by buildings, while the rest formed an open courtyard. Along the western wall was a room bounded on its east by two large columns flanked by two openings. There was another entrance in the room's northern wall.

To the east of this room was an open courtyard that contained a circular chamber. A large quantity of sherds and a few faunal remains were recovered from the courtyard floor. Two sherds bearing fragmentary inscriptions were found at the eastern edge of the courtyard.

Anthropomorphic clay figurine, with the lower part in the form of a peg.

At the southern edge of the enclosure, next to the southern wall of the room, a *maṣṣeba* was found in situ, with paving in front of it, indicating that this complex, too, was a sacred area. To the north of the room was another small chamber divided into two cells. Each cell contained a thick layer of ashes with sherds, bones, figurine fragments, and two inscriptions. A cooking pot was found in situ, sunk in a corner of the northern cell.

It is possible that the courtyard was only used in the second stage, while in the first stage another room, walled on the east, existed here. At the northeast corner of the enclosure, abutting its outer wall, was a small cubicle. Only isolated sherds were found on its earth floor. A thick layer of ashes was found between the cubicle and the cells, as well as within the cells themselves. This area was also apparently an open courtyard. It contained a large quantity of sherds, bones, and a single inscription (see below). Above the ash layer in the courtyard, and associated with a later phase, was a row of large rectangular stones about 70 cm high. Apparently related to this phase were additional drums built on the remains of the northern column in the western room. The construction of a wall continuing the line of the enclosure's eastern wall also belongs to this later phase. A small section of this wall above the enclosure wall indicates that the courtyard was in use after the enclosure ceased to function.

POTTERY. Numerous sherds were recovered from the rooms and complexes. The finds were most abundant in complex A. The pottery can be divided into two main groups. The first includes types characteristic of Judea in the seventh and early sixth centuries BCE (at Lachish II, En-Gedi V, Arad VII–VI, Tel 'Ira, Ḥorvat 'Uza, Tel Aroer, and Tel Malḥata). The second group consists of Edomite pottery, in particular flat bowls and bowls of Assyrian type and cooking pots, in addition to vessels painted with geometric designs and those decorated with rows of triangular knobs. Identical pottery is common at Iron Age II sites in Edom (at Bozrah, Tawilan, Umm el-Biyara, and Tell el-Kheleifeh) and, in smaller quantities, at contemporary sites in the eastern Negev (at Tel Malḥata, Tel Aroer, and Tel 'Ira).

CULT OBJECTS AND ICONOGRAPHY. Fragments of tall cylindrical pedestals, including fenestrated and perforated types, were found in complex A, especially in the platform area. These pedestals were used as stands for incense burners. Found with them were scores of anthropomorphic and zoomorphic clay figurines, painted red and black, and various reliefs. There are both hollow and solid figurines; some have attachment surfaces on one side and others have them on their extremities. The figurines were attached to the sides of the pedestals to create reliefs or were placed on protruding "shelves." A few of the anthropoid figurines depict only the upper body; the lower part is in the

Anthropomorphic pedestal.

Upper part of a pedestal bearing a zoomorphic figurine.

form of a peg, which was probably inserted in a pedestal. On the tops of two large reconstructed pedestals were the faces of bearded men and hands grasping daggers. It is likely that these anthropomorphic pedestals represent warriors. Some of their features (hands and noses) are nearly life-sized. A large figurine of a sphinx with the face of a bearded man and the head of a three-horned goddess are especially noteworthy.

Apart from the pedestals, figurines, and reliefs, a large number of fragmentary reliefs and figurines were found on the site and in its surroundings. These included parts of anthropomorphic figurines—eyes, eyebrows, noses, hair curls, hands holding various objects, and legs. Other fragments were depictions of flora and fauna—the horns and limbs of sheep and cattle, heads of birds, pomegranates, and various trees. About five hundred complete or partial figurines and reliefs were collected from the surface and the excavations.

The rich and varied collection of offerings and cult objects is undoubtedly related to the worship of gods in the shrine. Once several of the pedestals, adorned with human and animal images, had been restored, it became clear that these remarkably numerous ritual stands, placed in the open courtyard around the platform, had played a significant part in the shrine ritual.

Important data establishing the shrine's ethnic affiliation were found in the epigraphic material of the fragmentary inscriptions. Six such inscriptions were found, five in complex B and one in complex A. In the center of one is the name קוס (Qos), the principal god of Edom. Two others contain the letters קו (and one of them contained part of the letter ס). Paleographic analysis of the

Head of a three-horned goddess.

Ostrich-shaped figurine.

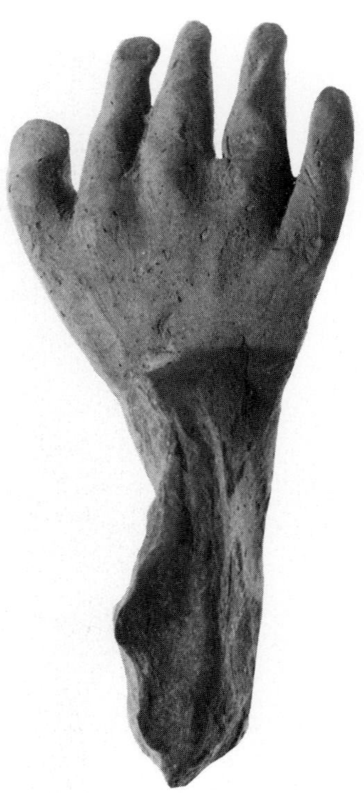

Fragment of a relief/statue in the shape of a human hand.

inscriptions shows that their script is very similar to that used in the same period in the kingdoms of Transjordan; it seems that this is Edomite script.

SUMMARY

Preliminary analysis of the finds has shown that most of the figurines and a variety of other objects are unique to local iconography in the Iron Age. There are no exact parallels to the molded pedestals, even though similar items, made with similar techniques, are known from other sites in the country. It is likely that a few of the objects, such as the sphinx figurine and the anthropomorphic figurines, were influenced by the country's coastal cultures, with origins in Phoenician art. For the other figurines, parallels can be found at contemporary sites in Edom.

The shrine's structure, its open sacred area, and its iconography are foreign to Judah's material culture in general and that of the eastern Negev in particular. In searching for the cultural origins of the shrine, the large amount of Edomite pottery, the figurines of Edomite origin, and the epigraphic material must be taken into account. In light of the data so far obtained, it appears that Qitmit was the site of an Edomite shrine within the Judean kingdom at the end of the First Temple period. Its existence in this region attests to the strengthening of Edomite influence in the eastern Negev then, or even to territorial acquisitions by the Edomites just before or soon after the destruction of the First Temple.

I. Beit-Arieh, *ESI* 3 (1984), 93; 9 (1989–1990), 81; id., *IEJ* 35 (1985), 201–202; id., *XIIe Congress of the International Organization for the Study of the Old Testament: Program and Abstracts*, Jerusalem 1986, 16; id. (and P. Beck), *Edomite Shrine: Discoveries from Qitmit in the Negev* (Israel Museum Cat. 277), Jerusalem 1987; id., *BAR* 14/2 (1988), 28–41; id., *AASOR* 49 (1989), 125–131; id., *TA* 18 (1991), 93–116; Weippert 1988, 623, 625; J. Gunneweg and H. Mommsen, *Archaeometry* 32 (1990), 7–18; P. Beck, *2nd International Congress on Biblical Archaeology, 24 June–4 July 1990: Abstracts*, Jerusalem 1990, 76–77.

ITZHAQ BEIT-ARIEH

QÔM, KHIRBET EL-

IDENTIFICATION

Khirbet el-Qôm (map reference 1465.1045) is located 20 km (12 mi.) west of Hebron, at the juncture of the Shephelah and the foothills of the central ridge, at the inner reaches of Naḥal Lachish. It had been identified with the Saphir of Micah 1:11 by F. M. Abel, on the basis of the Arabic name of the subsidiary wadi nearby, Wadi es-Saffar. More recently, however, D. A. Dorsey has proposed that Khirbet el-Qôm is the Makkedah of Joshua 10 and Eusebius' *Onomasticon*—that is, the inner fortress of the Lachish "trough." In that case it would belong, according to A. F. Rainey, to the third district of the Judean Shephelah, as reflected in Joshua 15. This seems a more plausible identification in the light of Judean toponymy.

EXCAVATIONS

Khirbet el-Qôm was placed on the modern archaeological map in 1967, when the Archaeological Survey of Israel, under M. Kochavi and others, made a quick reconnaissance. Also in the fall of 1967, W. G. Dever surveyed the site in the course of a brief salvage project, noting remnants of an offset-inset cyclopean city wall and quantities of tenth- to seventh-century BCE sherds, including a royal *lamelekh* jar handle stamped with the word *ziph*. The salvage campaign also produced several eighth- to seventh-century BCE Judean bench tombs, several inscribed pottery vessels (a decanter reading "Yahmôl" and a bowl reading "El"), and a group of inscribed shekel weights.

One of the bench tombs (tomb 1) was elaborately laid out and well cut, with

Khirbet el-Qôm: tomb 1, chamber 3, seen from the middle chamber.

Tomb 1: two head niches on a bench in chamber 1.

Inscription in tomb 1: "(belonging) to 'Uzzah daughter of Nethanyahu."

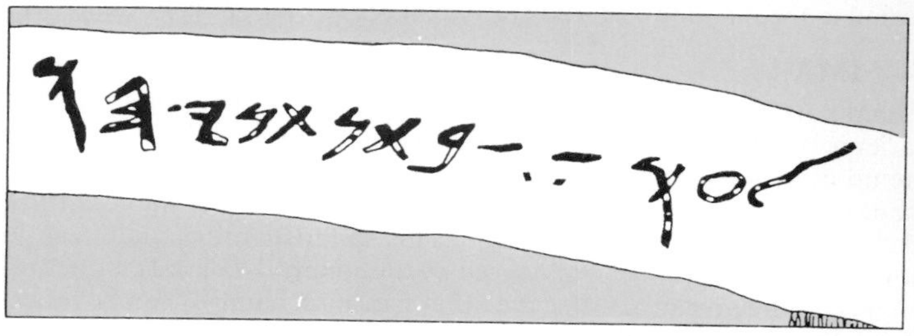

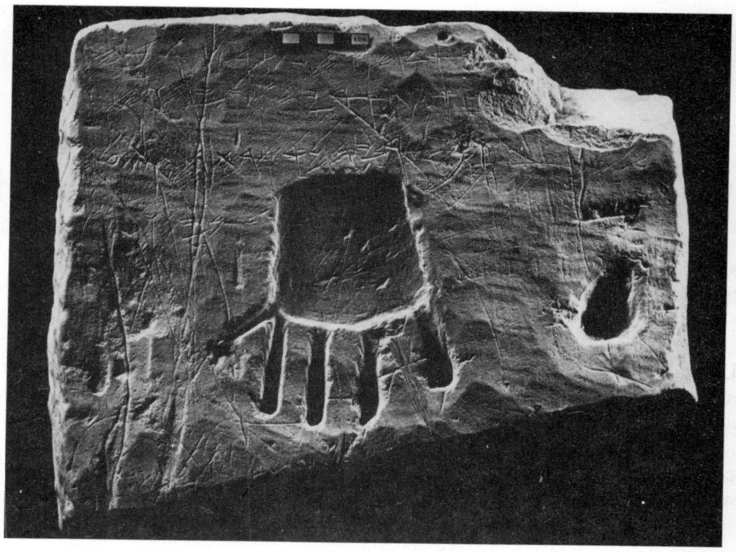

Uriyahu inscription from tomb 2.

three chambers off of a central arcosolium, each of which had three benches with recessed head and foot niches. An inscription (no. 2) over the entrance to the central chamber may be read: "Belonging to 'Uzza, son of Nethanyahu" (or "'Ophah, daughter of Nethanyahu"). To the left was a three-line inscription (no. 1) that read: "Belonging to 'Ophai, son of Nethanyahu; this (is) his tomb-chamber (*ḥeder*)." The name 'Ophai, "swarthy one" (?), occurs in Jeremiah 40:8; and 'Uzza is attested, for instance, in 2 Samuel 6:6–8 and 2 Chronicles 6:14. Another bench tomb, of the "butterfly" type, had a four-line inscription (no. 3) on one of the central pillars that was badly defaced. It read in part:

"Uriyahu the Governor (or 'the singer') wrote it.
May Uriyahu be blessed by Yahweh!"

The third line of the inscription has been interpreted in several ways. J. Naveh read: "My guardian and by his Asherah." A. Lemaire read: "And from his enemies, O Asherata, save him." All authorities except S. Mittmann, however, read *l'šrth*—"Asherah" or "Asherata." The reading is now confirmed by an eighth-century BCE Ḥorvat Teman (Kuntillet 'Ajrud) pithos that has exactly the same expression. It is unclear, however, whether "his (Yahweh's) Asherah" refers simply to a cult symbol, or to a shrine connected with the Canaanite fertility goddess Asherah, or to the goddess herself—in this case understood, at least in popular folk religion, as the consort of Yahweh. The latter would not be surprising, in view of the prophets' well-known proscription against pagan religious cults and practices in the period of the divided monarchy.

In the spring of 1971, J. S. Holladay, J. F. Strange, and L. T. Geraty undertook a brief campaign at Khirbet el-Qôm for the Canada Council that brought to light a two-entryway gate in a stretch of city wall along the south side of the modern Arab village (field III) on the site. Ceramic evidence dates the latest phase to the seventh century BCE, but the foundations of the gate go back to the tenth to ninth centuries BCE. A rock-hewn cistern, more than 8 m deep, was cleared at the northeast corner of the village (field I). It produced a good collection of ninth-century BCE pottery, including red hand-burnished and Cypro-Phoenician ("Ashdod") wares. In addition, a stepped, rock-hewn cellar yielded a collection of seventh- to sixth-century BCE pottery, sealed by destruction debris. Below these levels, a stratified series of Early Bronze Age I–III and Middle Bronze Age I domestic levels was encountered.

Field II, in the threshing floor along the southeastern sector of the village near the modern road, produced several Hellenistic rooms in rebuilt Iron Age II houses abutting the outer portion of the Iron Age defense wall. On the floors were several late fourth- to early third-century BCE ostraca, mostly short dockets. Four were in Aramaic, one was in Greek, and one was an Aramaic-Greek bilingual sherd with nine lines. The latter (no. 3) records a transaction between an Edomite shopkeeper named Qôs-yada and a Greek named Nikeratos, involving the payment of thirty-two drachmas. The ostracon is dated to the 12th of Tammuz, year 6—probably of Ptolemy II Philadelphus, 277 BCE. In field III, in foundation trenches for the initial Hellenistic rebuilding of the Iron Age II gate, two more Aramaic ostraca were found.

Tomb 2, chambers 3 and 4.

W. G. Dever, *HUCA* 40–41 (1969–1970), 139–204; D. Barag, *IEJ* 20 (1970), 216–218; J. S. Holladay, ibid. 21 (1971), 175–177; id., *RB* 78 (1971), 593–595; L. T. Geraty, *BASOR* 220 (1975), 55–61; id., *AUSS* (1981), 137–140; id., *The Word of God Shall Go Forth* (D. N. Freedman Fest., ASOR Special Volume Series 1), Winona Lake, Ind., 1984, 545–548; G. Garbini, *Annali, Istituto Universitario Orientale di Napoli* 38 (1978), 191–193; A. Lemaire, *RB* 84 (1977), 595–608; id., *Maarav* 2 (1982), 159–162; id., *BAR* 10/6 (1984), 42–51; id., *VT* 38 (1988), 220–230; A. Skaist, *IEJ* 28 (1978), 106–108; G. Barkay, ibid., 209–217; J. Naveh, *BASOR* 235 (1979), 27–30; P. A. Dorsey, *TA* 7 (1980), 185–193; S. Mittmann, *ZDPV* 97 (1981), 139–152; K. Jaros, *Biblische Notizen* 19 (1982), 31–42; *Lettre d'Information Archéologique Orientale* 6 (1983), 55–56; A. F. Rainey, *BASOR* 251 (1983), 1–22; S. Schroer, *Ugarit—Forschungen* 15 (1983), 190–199; Z. Zevit, *BASOR* 255 (1984), 39–47; A. Catastini, *Henoch* 6 (1984), 129–138; J. M. Hadley, *VT* 37 (1987), 50–62; Weippert 1988 (Ortsregister); B. Margalit, *VT* 39 (1989), 371–378; W. H. Shea, ibid. 40 (1990), 110–116.

WILLIAM. G. DEVER

QUMRAN, KHIRBET and 'EIN FESHKHA

IDENTIFICATION

Khirbet Qumran is situated on the western shore of the Dead Sea, on a spur of the marl terrace, bounded on the south by Wadi Qumran and on the north and west by ravines. It is probably to be identified with *'Ir ha-Melaḥ* (City of Salt), one of the six cities of Judea listed in Joshua 15:61–62 as situated in the wilderness. The area was inhabited several times, beginning with the Israelite buildings of the City of Salt to the Byzantine hermitage at 'Ein Feshkha.

EXCAVATIONS

During five campaigns of excavation at Khirbet Qumran, a building complex, extending over 80 m from east to west and 100 m from north to south, was completely cleared. Several periods of occupation were clearly distinguished.

The archaeological investigations at Qumran and 'Ein Feshkha are closely connected with the discovery of the Dead Sea Scrolls. The first manuscripts were found by chance in 1947 by Bedouin shepherds in a cave (no. 1) situated near the northwestern shore of the Dead Sea. The cave was excavated in 1949 by a joint expedition from the Jordan Department of Antiquities, the Palestine Archaeological Museum (now the Rockefeller Museum), and the École Biblique et Archéologique Française. The site of Khirbet Qumran, approximately 1 km (0.6 mi.) south of the cave and slightly farther west of the Dead Sea, was excavated under the same auspices in five successive campaigns, from 1951 to 1956. The last campaign surveyed the region situated between Qumran and the source of 'Ein Feshkha, 3 km (2 mi.) to the south. A building complex was excavated near this source in 1958. A second cave containing scrolls, discovered by Bedouin in 1952, prompted the above institutions, together with the American School of Oriental Research in Jerusalem, to explore the entire cliff face dominating Khirbet Qumran. It was during this campaign that cave 3, containing manuscripts and the Copper Scroll, was found. In 1952, Bedouin opened a fourth cave (cave 4) in the marl terrace. When the joint expedition subsequently cleared this cave, it found thousands

Qumran caves: general view.

Khirbet Qumran: aerial view of the main complex.

of fragments belonging to about a hundred manuscripts, as well as a fifth cave on the same terrace. Cave 6, the source of scroll fragments already purchased from Bedouin, was then located at the entrance to Wadi Qumran. In the course of the 1955 expedition at Khirbet Qumran, caves 7 to 10 were discovered at the edge of the plateau overlooking Wadi Qumran, south of Khirbet Qumran. Cave 11, which had been searched by Bedouin in 1956, was cleared by archaeologists during the last season of excavations at Khirbet Qumran.

The investigation results are summarized in three parts: (1) Khirbet Qumran; (2) archaeological remains in the Qumran area; and (3) 'Ein Feshkha. This entry does not deal with the manuscripts themselves nor does it touch upon the problems posed by them, but shows the close connection between the archaeological finds and the texts.

THE IRON AGE. The earliest settlement at Khirbet Qumran dates to the Israelite period. Several walls, reused in later phases, belonged to a rectangular building, in front of which was a courtyard with a large round cistern. Its plan resembles those of Israelite fortresses in the Judean and Negev deserts. The pottery associated with these structures ranges from the eighth century to the beginning of the sixth century BCE. This date is confirmed by a royal *lamelekh* seal impression and by an ostracon with several early Hebrew characters that is attributed to a period shortly before the Babylonian Exile. The settlement was destroyed during the fall of the kingdom of Judah.

THE HELLENISTIC PERIOD. Phase Ia. After several centuries of abandonment, Qumran was resettled. The remnants of the Israelite buildings were reused for the most part, with some additions. Two new cisterns were dug near the large round one. The date of the founding of this new settlement is difficult to fix. The scant pottery uncovered is hardly distinguishable from that of the following period, nor were any coins found. Because the buildings in phase Ib were apparently constructed in the time of John Hyrcanus (134–104 BCE), phase Ia—which was of short duration—may have begun under Hyrcanus himself or, more likely, during the reign of one of his immediate predecessors, his father Simeon (142–134 BCE) or his uncle Jonathan (152–142 BCE).

Phase Ib. In this period, the buildings were further enlarged and took on their more or less final form. They consisted of a main building with a massive tower, a central courtyard, rooms for communal use, a large assembly hall (which also served as a refectory) to the south, and an adjacent pantry, where more than a thousand vessels were found—small jars, jugs, dishes, plates, and bowls. In the southeast was a potter's workshop with a basin for washing the clay, a storage pit, a place for a potter's wheel, and two kilns. Another building, situated to the west, consisted of a courtyard surrounded by storerooms. Between the two buildings were three cisterns from phase Ia and workshops. Other cisterns and two baths were dug nearby. To the north of this complex was a large, walled courtyard and to the south an esplanade that extended to Wadi Qumran. Around the buildings the excavators found animal bones, mostly of sheep and goats, but also of cows and calves, de-

Qaṣrawet: gold earrings from one of the built Nabatean tombs.

Qaṣrawet: interior of the central Nabatean temple, Roman period.

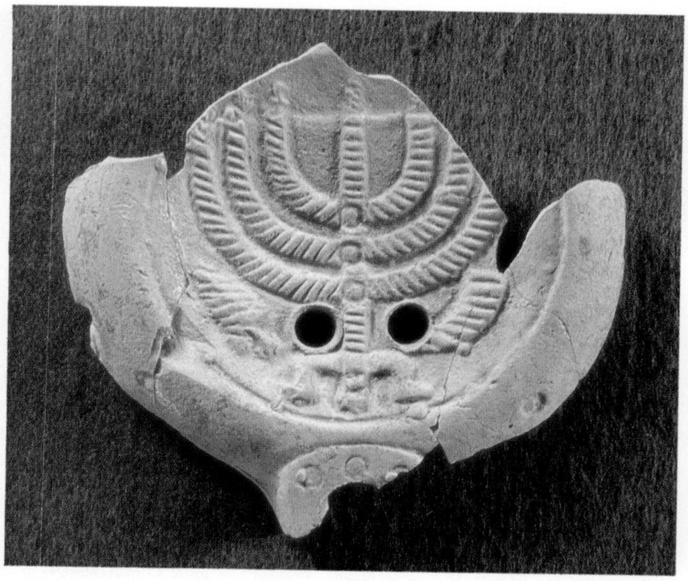

Qaṣrawet: oil lamp decorated with a menorah, ethrog, lulab, and shofar, 4th century CE.

Qaṣrawet: oil lamp decorated with Eros playing the cymbals, from one of the built Nabatean tombs.

Qaṣrawet: overview of a house in the Late Roman settlement, 3rd–4th centuries CE.

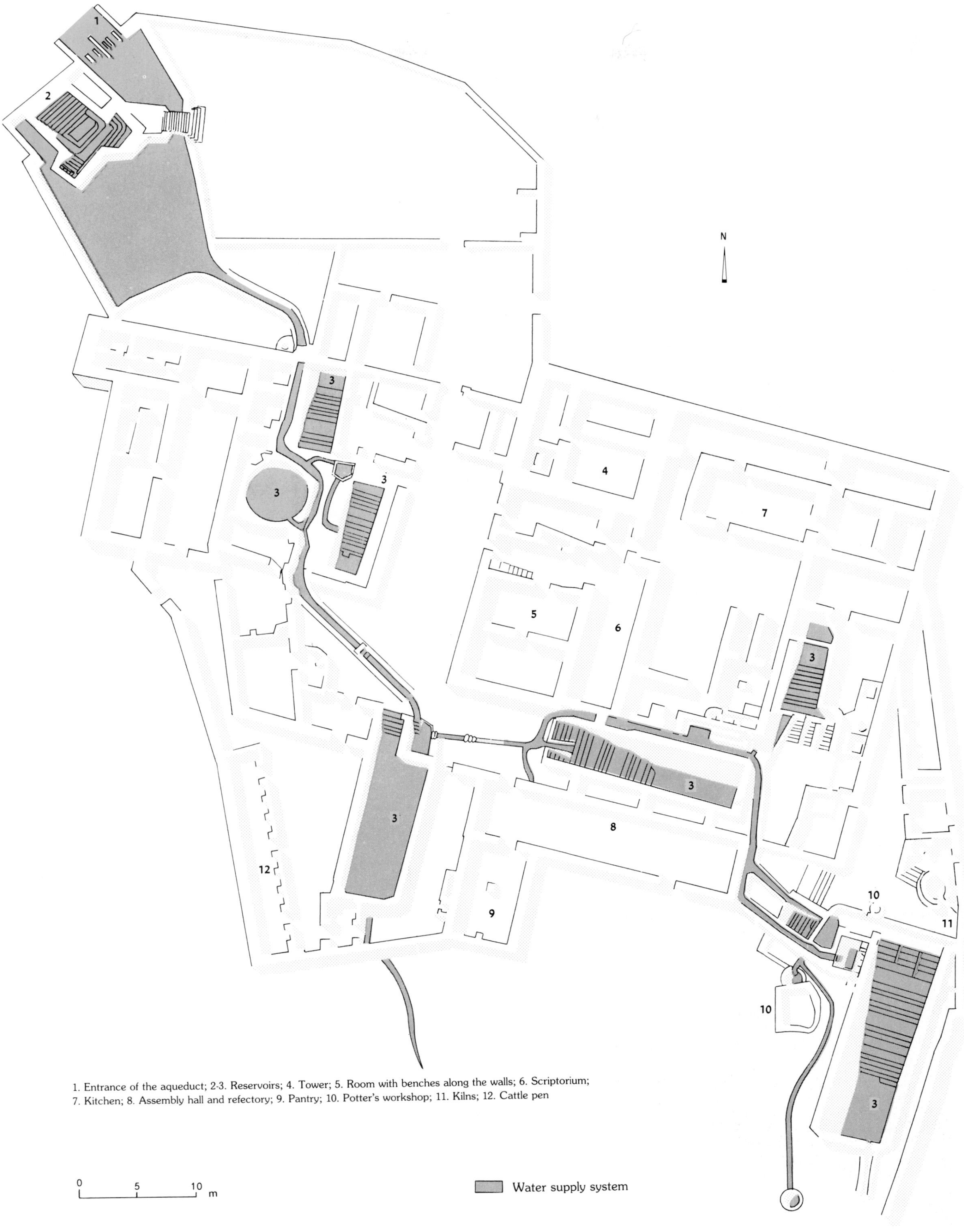

Khirbet Qumran: plan of the phase Ib settlement.

Khirbet Qumran: assembly hall that also served as the refectory.

posited beneath large potsherds or occasionally in covered cooking pots. These were evidently the remains of ritual meals.

The pottery from this phase dates to the end of the Hellenistic period. The coins permit a more precise dating for its beginning, however (see below). It is certain that the buildings were occupied during the reign of Alexander Jannaeus (103 to 76 BCE), and they may have been constructed earlier, under John Hyrcanus. The end of this phase is marked by two catastrophes—an earthquake that damaged two cisterns, the tower of the main building, the pantry of the assembly hall, and a corner of the second building, and a conflagration that left a thick layer of ash in the open areas near the buildings. It is possible that the earthquake affected buildings already burned and in ruins, but this is not supported by any positive evidence. It seems more likely that the earthquake damaged the occupied buildings, which then caught on fire from burning hearths. This is the same earthquake mentioned by Josephus (*Antiq.* XV, 5, 2–122; *War* I, 19, 3–370) as having occurred in 31 BCE, a date corroborated by the coins found in this level.

The site was abandoned at the end of phase Ib. The buildings were not

Bowls in situ in the pantry.

Steps of the reservoir cracked in the earthquake of 31 CE.

Khirbet Qumran: workshop and kiln.

Khirbet Qumran: tables from the scriptorium (reconstructed).

repaired immediately, nor was the water system restored to a usable condition. Sediment soon spread over the ash layer. Repairs made in phase II were discovered above the silt, as well as on virgin soil.

THE ROMAN PERIOD: Phase II. The site was deserted for a brief period and was resettled by the same community that had abandoned it. The general plan and function of the main buildings remained unchanged, and evidence was found that the ritual meals mentioned above continued to be held. Most of the rooms had evidently been cleared of debris, for the rubble was found outside the buildings. Some of the rooms and two of the cisterns went out of use. The most severely damaged structures were strengthened. The new constructions belonging to this period departed from the previous plan only in minor details.

Phase II, the last major period of occupation, provides much instructive information on the function of the buildings. A large room with five fireplaces was apparently the kitchen. The potter's workshop continued in use. Two other workshops between the main buildings are of indeterminate nature. Nearby was a flour mill and a baking oven. In one of the rooms of the main building the remains of three tables were found, one long and two shorter ones made of plastered mud brick. Also found were a low bench along one of the walls and two inkwells, recovered from the debris. All the evidence suggests that this room may well have been a writing room (scriptorium) in which scribes and copyists worked.

A great quantity of pottery was found in phase II. Aside from certain special forms that originated in phase Ib and continued in the following phase as a result of the deep-rooted tradition of the local workshop, the pottery is virtually identical with the pottery dating from the first century CE found in Jewish tombs in Jerusalem and in the excavations at Herodian Jericho. The beginning and end of this phase can be fixed by the coins and the historical sources. Following the earthquake of 31 BCE, the buildings remained unoccupied until the end of Herod's reign (37–4 BCE). Settlement was resumed under Herod Archelaus (4 BCE–6 CE). The termination of this phase can be dated even more precisely. Khirbet Qumran was destroyed during the Jewish Revolt against Rome, probably in June of the year 68 CE, when the Roman army occupied Jericho and Vespasian visited the Dead Sea (Josephus, *War*, IV, 8, 1–48). The coins discovered confirm this proposed history of the site. The latest coins of phase II are four Jewish coins of Year 3 of the Jewish Revolt (in contrast to sixty-eight coins of Year 2). The Year 3, according to the year in which the coins were struck, began in March–April 68 CE, a date verified by the coins discovered in the following stratum. The earliest are Roman coins of Caesarea and Dor minted in 67–68 CE, the same year in which the units that occupied Jericho and probably destroyed Qumran were stationed at Caesarea (Josephus, *War*, IV, 8, 7–443).

Khirbet Qumran: kilns.

Phase III. The above-mentioned coins were not lost during the attack on Qumran, for they were found not in the destruction layer but in the following level: that of the Roman military garrison stationed at the site. This garrison was responsible for the radical changes found in phase III. Only a part of the ruins was restored to use. Some small rooms were built haphazardly over the leveled rubble. Only one of the numerous cisterns was utilized, and the canal system was greatly simplified. A single baking oven was constructed on the rubble of the public buildings and workshops. The pottery, which is scanty, is similar in form to contemporary ware encountered at other first-century CE sites. In this phase, the ceramic types characteristic of Qumran are absent. The coins are less numerous, and the latest, which undoubtedly belong to this occupation, date from the year 72–73 CE. It seems that the garrison at Qumran was withdrawn immediately after the fall of Masada in 73 CE.

The Bar-Kokhba Revolt. The abandoned buildings served as hiding places or centers of resistance by Bar-Kokhba's warriors during the Second Jewish Revolt from 132 to 135. The rebels constructed no new buildings, but they left behind a number of their coins. The rebels represent the final episode in the history of Khirbet Qumran.

The most important periods in the history of Qumran are phases Ib and II, during which the settlement reached its greatest extent. The plan of the setttlement, which was practically unchanged throughout the two periods, had two interesting aspects: the elaborate water-supply system and the communal buildings. The rainwater collected in Wadi Qumran was diverted to the settlement through an aqueduct, which supplied eight cisterns in phase Ib and seven cisterns in phase II. A large settling basin was constructed at the point where the aqueduct entered the walls, and smaller basins were dug before each cistern or group of cisterns. There were two baths, one near the entrance on the northwest, and the other on the southeast. This system was designed to fill the needs of a large community living in an arid region. However, the care taken in constructing these installations suggests that they were intended for the ceremony of ritual immersion. The communal buildings held an important position at Qumran. They included a large kitchen, a large refectory, several assembly halls, storerooms, and workshops. There were few rooms, on the other hand, that might have served as actual living quarters.

An extensive cemetery, comprising some 1,100 graves, was uncovered to the west of the ruins. These are individual graves, dug in rows and oriented on a north–south axis. All the graves excavated in the main part of the cemetery are of men. In an extension to the east, where the graves are placed haphazardly, women and children were also buried. The large number of interments in the cemetery is altogether out of proportion to the small number of living quarters and the length of time the site was occupied. It has therefore been concluded that Khirbet Qumran was the center of a sect, most of whose members lived dispersed throughout the area.

THE QUMRAN AREA

The cliffs dominating Khirbet Qumran are honeycombed with many natural caves. The 1952 survey revealed twenty-six caves or crevices that contained pottery identical to Qumran's. Among these were the caves—numbers 1, 2, 3, and 6—that contained scrolls, to which number 11 was added in 1956. These caves were used by the people of Qumran during phases Ib and II. Some were suitable for living quarters but many served only as storerooms—or as hiding places—for those who lived in nearby tents or huts. In fact, one of these crevices was found to contain a tent pole. The caves in the marl terrace, on the other hand, are not natural and had been dug out to form dwellings (q.v. Judean Desert Caves). Two small cemeteries, in which men, women, and children were buried, were discovered north and south of the Qumran Plateau.

The number of people who lived in or near the caves and who assembled in the buildings at Khirbet Qumran during the village's most populous period probably reached some two hundred. These people earned their livelihood from various occupations—from the workshops, by raising flocks, and by growing a number of crops suitable for the arid soil of this region. An ancient road connecting Qumran and the el-Buqei'a Plain runs above the cliff, along a plateau where various cereals were grown. Between Khirbet Qumran and 'Ein Feshkha, 3 km (2 mi.) to the south, the littoral plain was irrigated by means of small springs, where even today the slightly saline water of the region facilitates the growth of reeds and scrub. Date palms were also cultivated, as is shown by the palm tree fronds, dried dates, and pits found in the ruins and in the caves. Salt and asphalt from the Dead Sea probably provided additional occupations for the local inhabitants.

The region's natural resources were exploited as early as the Iron Age. Remains of a building similar to one found under the ruins of Khirbet Qumran are visible south of Wadi Qumran. The building may date to the ninth century BCE. After a very brief occupation, it was abandoned. The occupants moved to the Qumran Plateau, which boasted a more favorable climate and a better defensive position. The wall bounding the irrigated and cultivated area seems to date from the same period.

Near this Iron Age wall, which continued to be used by the religious community of Qumran, a square structure was discovered that contained pottery contemporary with that at Khirbet Qumran. The structure was eith a watchtower or a building where agricultural works were carried out withi the wall's protective confines. It is very likely that this ancient wall extended 'Ein Feshkha where another wall, although constructed differently, was bui along the same course.

Storage jars from the 1st century CE.

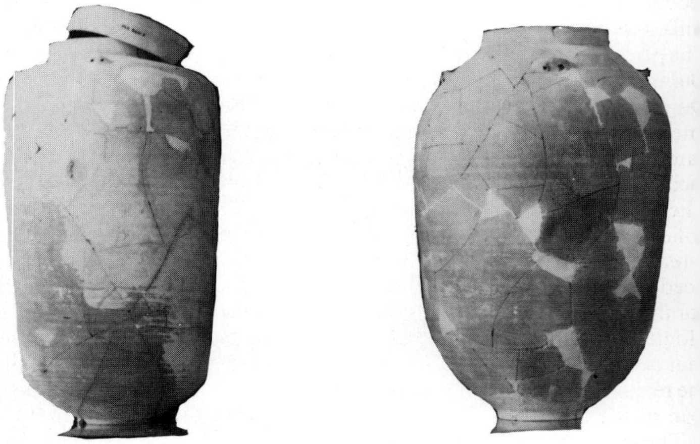

'EIN FESHKHA

An important settlement lay immediately to the north of the large spring 'Ein Feshkha. It contained a large rectangular building with a central cour yard surrounded by rooms. The building was flanked on the south by a enclosure wall with a shed and on the north by a courtyard containing cistern The rooms on the west were used for living quarters or administrative pu poses; the remainder of the building was occupied by storerooms. This buil ing was clearly not a private residence, but was suited to the needs of religious community. As at Khirbet Qumran, here, too, the buildings we mainly public, suggesting that the members of the sect dwelled in the su rounding areas.

The excavators distinguished three occupational phases, whose dates ca be determined by the pottery and coins. Of the first phase there is litt evidence, but the pottery is identical to that from phase Ib at Qumra a date that is also confirmed by the coins, which range from the time Alexander Jannaeus (103–76 BCE) down to Matthias Antigonus (40– BCE). The second phase is undoubtedly contemporary with phase II at Qu ran. The pottery is identical, and the coins range in date from the reign Herod Archelaus (4 BCE–6 CE) until the second year of the First Jewish Revo against Rome. The temporary abandonment of the settlement between ph ses I and II and the widespread destruction that marks the end of phase demonstrate even more clearly that Feshkha and Khirbet Qumran existed the same time.

Phase III was more difficult to date. Only a small portion of the ruins ha been reoccupied. Although it would seem reasonable that, as at Qumran, Roman garrison was stationed at Feshkha, this is not confirmed by t numismatic evidence. At Feshka, unlike Qumran, no Roman coins minte between the years 67–68 and 72–73 CE were found, and there were many coi from the time of Agrippa II (50 to 92–93 CE) and one coin of Domitian (81– CE). It seems then that Feshkha remained abandoned for some time after destruction in 68 CE, and that only toward the end of the first century did small settlement exist on the site. Another parallel in the history of the tw sites appears somewhat later when, as several coins of the Bar-Kokhba Revo indicate, a unit of insurgents passed through Feshkha or remained there f some time. To the south of the building is a cattle pen, which was enlarged phase II. Along its north wall a shed was constructed, one side of whic provided shelter in Byzantine times for the gardener of the monaster as is related by John Moschus (*Pratum spirituale* 158; *PG* 87, col. 3025

In phase II, another enclosure was built on the north side of the building. its eastern half is a system of canals and of reservoirs that are clearly n cisterns, although their function is unknown. According to one theory, the were ponds for breeding fish. Another more plausible theory is that they we vats of a tannery. Such an installation requires large quantities of water. Wh there are positive grounds for this hypothesis, nevertheless its plan does n entirely correspond to that of known Roman tanneries, and the analysis samples extracted from the vats revealed no trace of tannin, essential f processing hides.

In any case, the connection between Feshkha and Qumran is certai Feshkha was the less important settlement. It was based on agriculture a perhaps industry, and served the main community at Qumran.

UMMARY

'he area's most important occupation extended from the second half of the econd century BCE down to the year 68 CE. It left its traces in the caves in the liffs and on the marl terrace and in the buildings at Qumran and Feshkha. 'he people who dwelled in the caves and in the huts near the cliffs assembled at)umran to engage in communal activities. They worked in the workshops at)umran or on the farm at Feshkha, and after their death they were buried in ne of two cemeteries. This was a highly organized sect, as is indicated by the areful planning of the buildings, the water system, the numerous communal acilities, and the arrangement of the graves in the larger of the two cemeteries. 'he special method of burial, the large assembly hall that also served as a ollective dining room, and the remains of meals that were so meticulously aterred, all indicate that this community had a religious character and pracced its own peculiar rites and ceremonies. The scrolls discovered at Qumran onfirm these conclusions and furnish additional information. The archaelogical evidence proves that the scrolls belonged to the religious community nat occupied the caves and the buildings at Qumran. These scrolls represent ne remains of their library, which contained works describing the organizaon of the community and the laws that governed its members.

The archaeological discoveries at Khirbet Qumran and 'Ein Feshkha were nus interpreted in the context of a living community. Some of the scrolls ontain allusions to the history of this sect, which had detached itself from the fficial Judaism in Jerusalem. The sect led a separate existence in the desert, bsorbed in prayer and labor while awaiting the Messiah. The interpretation f these historical references has been the subject of much debate. The arhaeological discoveries cannot be expected to provide a decisive answer. 'hey merely lend credence to the hypotheses that a community flourished n the shore of the Dead Sea from the second half of the second century BCE ntil 68 CE, and that the events described in the manuscripts occurred at)umran during this period.

The religious affiliation of the community has also been the subject of ontroversy. Most scholars, however, consider the community to have been ı some way connected with the Essenes. This is not contradicted by the rchaeological evidence, which indeed provides corroboration. Pliny *VH* V, 73) relates that the Essenes lived in isolation among palm trees a region west of the Dead Sea—at a safe distance from its pestilential alt water. To the south is the region of En-Gedi. There is only one site nat corresponds to this description between En-Gedi and the northern nd of the Dead Sea: the Qumran Plateau. There is only one region where alm trees can grow in quantity and where it is certain they did grow in ancient mes: the region between Khirbet Qumran and Feshkha. The Essenes of 'liny, then, in the opinion of this writer, were the religious community f Qumran-Feshkha.

ROLAND DE VAUX

n the thirty years since de Vaux published his preliminary reports and the 'rench edition of his comprehensive book, a substantial body of literature ealing with problems concerning the archaeology of Qumran has accumuated. In the absence of a final report this discussion relies on preliminary data.

The subject most discussed is the chronological definition of Khirbet)umran's various strata. The general chronological framework suggested y de Vaux enjoys almost universal consensus. However, of the eight dates offered (actually only five, as three coincide), only one can be established with near certainty. This is the end of stratum II—that is, summer 68 CE—the date the Qumran community ceased to exist. Even here, however, the precision of the date is based on interpretation of historical-literary sources.

The subjects most discussed are the nature and duration of the gap between phase Ib and II. Strong arguments, archaeological as well as historical, have been raised against the excavator's assertion that the site was deserted between 31 and 4 BCE. While the date of the beginning of the gap and its cause (an earthquake) seem quite plausible, although by no means certain, there is considerable doubt that the gap lasted longer than a couple of years.

Near Khirbet Qumran are three cemeteries—one large, with about 1,100 graves, and two small, with 100 graves altogether. Only about 50 of these 1,200 graves were excavated. In the large cemetery only skeletons of adult males were found, but in the small cemeteries remains of women and children also were found. The existence of the latter graves in a site presumed to have been occupied by a monastic community naturally raised queries. As there are signs that some of the buried were brought from a distance, the explanation for the presence of the females and minors is that they were related to the regular residents of Qumran, either by kinship or ideological beliefs.

N. Golb, the proponent of a countertheory to the widely accepted view that Qumran was occupied by an Essene monastic community, has suggested that the ruins are, rather, the remains of a fortress. This seems an unlikely explanation, as the site is of inferior strategic value and the flimsy walls of the complex could not have had military value.

Since 1967, several expeditions have conducted surveys, both extensive and intensive, in the neighborhood of Qumran (mainly those led by P. Bar-Adon and J. Patrich). Since 1956, no new manuscripts have been discovered (q.v. Judean Desert Caves).

MAGEN BROSHI

Main publications: R. de Vaux, *L'Archéologie et les manuscrits de la Mer Morte*, London 1961; id., *Archaeology and the Dead Sea Scrolls* (Schweich Lectures of the British Academy), London 1973; J. T. Milik, *Ten Years of Discovery in the Wilderness of Judaea*, London 1959; E.-M. Laperrousaz, *Qoumran: l'Etablissment Essénien des Bord de la Mer Morte, Histoire et Archéologie du Site*, Paris 1976; *Discoveries in the Judaean Desert* 6–7, Oxford 1977–1982.

Other studies: R. de Vaux, *RB* 56 (1949), 234–237, 586–609; 60 (1953), 83–106, 540–561; 61 (1954), 206–236; 63 (1956), 533–577; 66 (1959), 225–255; S. Schulz, *ZDPV* 75 (1960), 50–72; H. Bardtke, *TLZ* 85 (1960), 263–274; J. B. Pool and R. Reed, *PEQ* 93 (1961), 114–123; J. A. Fitzmeyer, *The Dead Sea Scrolls: Major Publications and Tools for Study* (Sources for Biblical Study 8), Missoula, Mont. 1975; H. T. Frank, *BAR* 1/4 (1975), 1, 7–16, 28–30; E.-M. Laperrousaz, *Qoumran* (Review), *BASOR* 231 (1978), 79–80; id., *Revue de Qumran* 46 (1986), 199–212; id., *EI* 20 (1989), 118*–123*; F. M. Cross, Jr., *BAR* 3/1 (1977), 1, 23–32; id., *Bible Review* 1/2 (1985), 12–25; 1/3 (1985), 26–35; J. Murphy-O'Connor, *BA* 40 (1977), 125–129; G. Vermes, *The Dead Sea Scrolls: Qumran in Perspective*, London 1977; id., *BAIAS* 1984–1985, 20–23; *MdB* 4 (1978); J. Licht, *IEJ* 29 (1979), 45–59; M. Sharabani, *RB* 87 (1980), 274–284; P. R. Davies, *Qumran* (Cities of the Biblical World), Guildford, Surrey 1982; id., *BA* 51 (1988), 203–207; *American Archaeology in the Mideast*, 118; J. C. Violette, *Les Esséniens de Qoumrân (Les Portes de l'Étrange)*, Paris 1983; S. Bowman, *Revue de Qumran* 44 (1984), 543–547; N. Golb, *BA* 48 (1985), 68–82; id., *The American Scholar* 58 (1989), 177–207; id., *JNES* 49 (1990), 103–114; M. Weinfeld, *The Organizational Pattern and the Penal Code of the Qumran Sect* (Novum Testamentum et Orbis Antiquus 2), Fribourg 1986; ibid. (Review), *Revue de Qumran* 14/53 (1989), 147–148; B. G. Wood, *BASOR* 256 (1984), 45–60; M. Wise, ibid. 49 (1986), 140–154; *Archéologie, Art et Histoire de la Palestine: Colloque du Centenaire de la Section des Sciences Religieuses, École Pratique des Hautes Études, Sept. 1986* (ed. E.-M. Laperrousaz), Paris 1988, 149–165; G. J. Brooke, *Revue de Qumran* 13/49–52 (1988) 225–237; P. R. Callaway, *The History of the Qumran Community: Investigation* (Journal for the Study of the Pseudepigrapha Supplement Series 3), Sheffield 1988; F. Dionisio, *Bibbia e Oriente*, 156 (1988), 85–110; P. Crocker, *Buried History* 25 (1989), 36–46; E. Lipinski, *EI* 20 (1989), 130*–134*; D. Chen, *10th World Congress of Jewish Studies* B/2, Jerusalem 1990, 9–14; *JNES* 49/2 (1990); L. H. Schiffman, *BA* 53 (1990), 64–73; S. Goranson, ibid. 54 (1991), 110–111.

R

RABAH, WADI

IDENTIFICATION

The ancient site on the southern bank of Wadi Rabah, one of the tributaries of the Yarkon River, is about 1 km (0.6 mi.) east of Tel Aphek. Two Chalcolithic levels and the mixed remains of the two Neolithic phases, contemporary with Jericho IX and the Yarmukian, were identified here.

EXCAVATIONS

In November 1952, J. Kaplan conducted excavations at Wadi Rabah on behalf of the Israel Exploration Society. The first occupation of the site, stratum I, was found to belong to the Ghassulian phase of the Chalcolithic period. Stratum II belonged to an earlier phase, which had already been noted in 1950–1951, in Kaplan's excavations on ha-Bashan Street in Tel Aviv and in 1955 at Teluliyot Batash.

The pottery of stratum II is very similar in form to that of Jericho VIII: carinated bowls, bowl-rim jars, and pithoi with flat, thick tops and small, narrow ledge handles. However, there is a greater amount of slipped and decorated ware at Wadi Rabah than in Jericho VIII. Jars, not only bowls, are red burnished, and black burnish, unknown in Jericho VIII, also appears. Incised decoration is also frequent: a herringbone pattern, chevrons, and parallel lines (sometimes on both faces of the vessel), roller impressions in geometric patterns, and combing in broad bands.

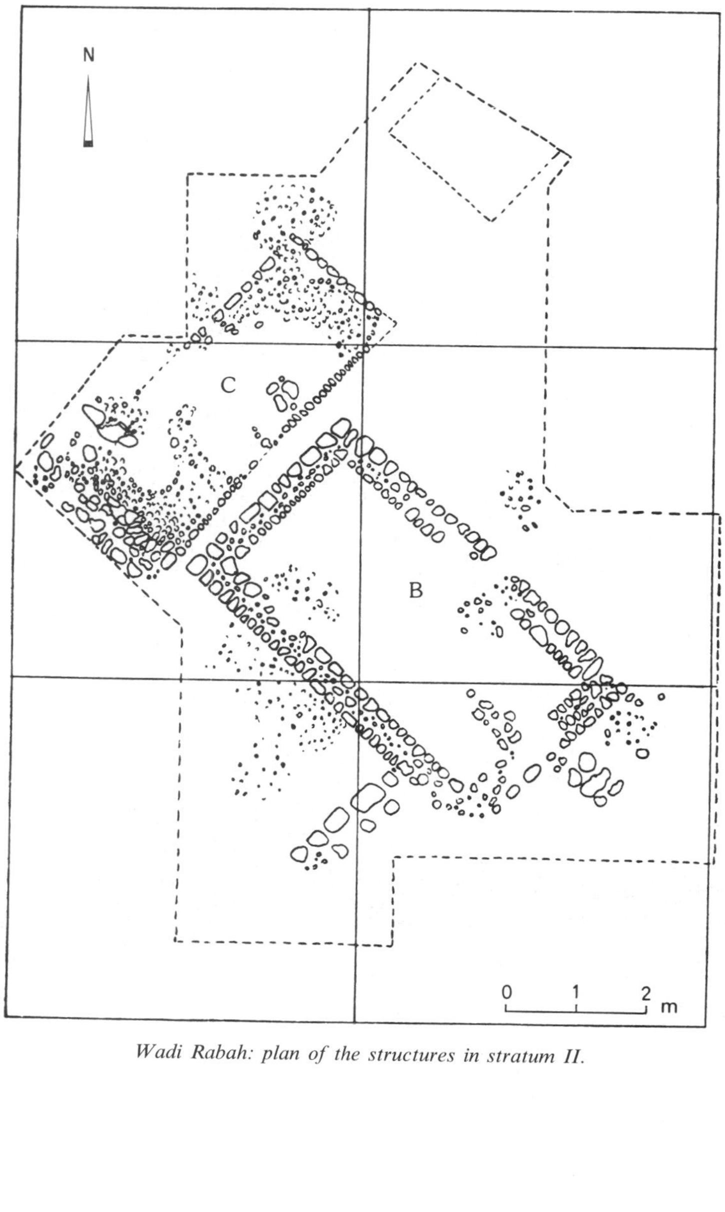

Wadi Rabah: plan of the structures in stratum II.

SUMMARY

The conclusion that the Wadi Rabah finds antedate those in Jericho VIII is illustrated by the fact that most of the pottery is burnished. In Jericho VIII, burnishing appears only on bowls, and at Tuleilat el-Ghassul none at all is found. In all these three phases of the Chalcolithic period, the pottery shows a continuous evolution. A comparison of some of the pottery from these three phases with Halafian ware as a whole, and particularly with Halafian ware and its imitations—which occur in strata XIX–XVI at Mersin, Cilicia—shows a correlation between Mersin's Middle Chalcolithic and the Chalcolithic of Palestine. Because, however, certain shapes and ornamentation characteristic of the Wadi Rabah ware were encountered only in stratum XIX at Mersin, Wadi Rabah can be placed on the same horizon as that stratum—that is, at the beginning of the Middle Chalcolithic period in Syro-Cilicia (as it appeared at Mersin). The Chalcolithic phase at Wadi Rabah has since been discovered in many other parts of Israel and by now some scholars believe that it should be dated earlier, to the Late Neolithic period.

J. Kaplan, *IEJ* 8 (1958), 149–160; id., *BASOR* 159 (1960), 32–36; id., *Museum Haaretz Bulletin* 14 (1972), 23–29, A. Gopher and E. Orrelle, *BASOR* 276 (1989), 67–76.

JACOB KAPLAN

Building B in stratum II, Wadi Rabah culture.

RABBATH-AMMON

IDENTIFICATION

The ancient city that appears in the biblical record as Rabbath-Ammon is unquestionably to be identified with the modern city of 'Amman in Jordan. The identification is based on the strong similarity between the modern name and its ancient predecessor, as well as on archaeological finds and topographical references in numerous historical and epigraphical sources. In the Hellenistic period, the city was known as Philadelphia. However, the old name, Rabbath-Ammon, was still used in the third and second centuries BCE. The city's present name, 'Amman, appears for the first time in Eusebius' *Onomasticon* (16), but it was only after the Arab conquest in 635 CE that this name became generally accepted.

HISTORY

Excavations have shown that the city was inhabited in the Neolithic period. Pottery sherds from the lower city of the citadel, dated to the Neolithic period, display a close similarity with the pottery from the last occupational phase of the Neolithic settlement at 'Ain Ghazal, on the northern outskirts of 'Amman. It is thus highly probable that the inhabitants of the latter site left their village and settled on the citadel. The continuity of settlement in the Amman district throughout the Chalcolithic period and the Early, Middle, and Late Bronze ages is relatively well attested by the archaeological finds: pottery, tombs, fortifications, and a temple. The history of the city in the Iron Age and in the succeeding centuries is also documented in biblical and other historical records.

Deuteronomy 3:11 is the first account in which Rabbath-Ammon is mentioned in association with the Ammonites in their successful war with Og, king of Bashan (twelfth century BCE). In the middle of the eleventh century BCE, the Ammonite king Nahash attacked Jabesh Gilead; the inhabitants of the city asked Saul for help (1 Sam. 11). During the reign of Nahash's son, Hanun, Rabbath-Ammon was captured by King David and his general, Joab. The latter captured only the "royal city" and the "city of waters," while David took the rest of the city later on (2 Sam. 12:26–31; 1 Chr. 20:1–3). Nahash was succeeded by his brother Shobi, and the Ammonite kingdom, with its capital at Rabbath-Ammon, flourished as an independent state until the beginning of the sixth century BCE. In 581 BCE, Rabbath-Ammon was conquered, and probably destroyed, by Nebuchadnezzar II. Information about its later history is very fragmentary. It was probably a period of considerable decline, in which the city became so weak it was destroyed again, this time by "the people of the East" (Ezek. 25:4–5).

At the very end of the sixth century BCE, the city came under Persian rule, under the fifth satrapy. During that period, one of relative prosperity, Rabbath-Ammon was ruled by the local dynasty of Tobiads, who were loyal to the Persians. In the fifth century BCE, they were so strong they hindered the rebuilding of the Temple in Jerusalem. After 259 BCE, Rabbath-Ammon became part of the Ptolemaic realm and subsequently was renamed Phila-

Rabbath-Ammon: plan of the acropolis and the lower city, based on a late 19th-century drawing.

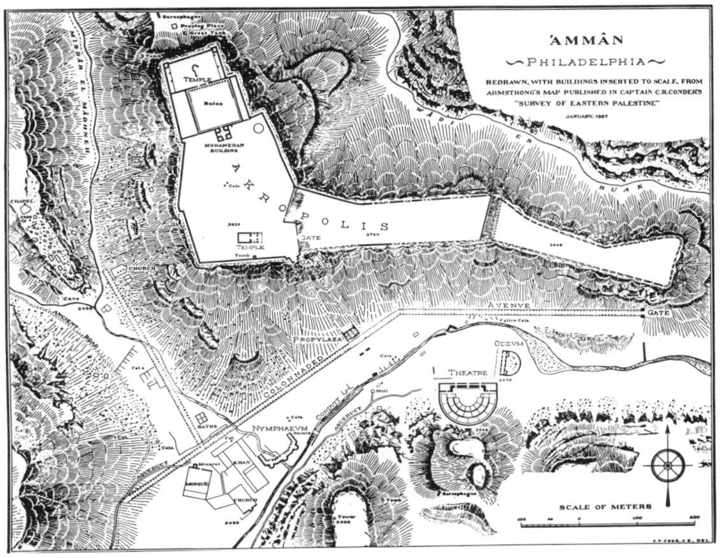

Rabbath-Ammon: general view, looking south from the acropolis; (foreground) the theater.

delphia by Ptolemy II Philadelphus (283–246 BCE). In the Zenon papyri (P Zen. 59.009) the city is described as a *birtha*, "a fortified residence." In 218 BCE, Antiochus III, during his campaign against Ptolemy III Euergetes I (the third Syrian War), forced the garrison in the citadel to surrender after he penetrated the underground passage to the water cistern and cut its water supply (Polybius, *Hist*. V, 71, 9). The Seleucids' control over the city did not last long, and soon, probably in the first decades of the second century BCE, the city slowly came under the political influence of the Nabateans. The local tyrants, like Zenon Cotylas and his son and successor, Theodorus (second half of the second century BCE), were probably Nabatean vassals. The early years of the first century BCE were marked by a strong hostility between Theodorus and the Hasmonean king Alexander Jannaeus, who tried, unsuccessfully, to besiege the city. In 63 BCE, Philadelphia was attached by Pompey to the Roman province of Syria and became one of the cities of the Decapolis. After the annexation of the Nabataean kingdom by the Roman governor of Syria, Cornelius Palma (106 CE), Philadelphia was detached from the *Provincia Syria* and transferred to the newly created *Provincia Arabia*. The city flourished under Roman rule. Heavy international traffic along the *Via Nova Traiana*, a major road passing from the Hejaz and the Red Sea to Damascus via Philadelphia, provided financial resources for ambitious building programs in the city.

In the Byzantine period, Philadelphia was the seat of a bishopric. At least six bishops of Philadelphia are known. Two participated in Councils: Cyrion in Nicaea (325) and Antioch (341), and Eulogios in Chalcedon (451). Three churches were reported in the city at the beginning of the twentieth century: the so-called cathedral, southwest of the nymphaeum; the Church of Saint Elijah, to the west of the acropolis; and the Church of Saint George, to the northwest of the Saint Elijah church, dated by an inscription to the very end of the sixth century. No excavations of these buildings have been undertaken. In 635, the city passed to Arab rule. A magnificent palatial complex built on the citadel indicates that at least in the Umayyad period (661–750) 'Amman continued to prosper. Sources from the succeeding Abbasid (750–969) and Fatimid (969–1071) periods are scarce. The city gradually declined and, in the Mameluke period, was abandoned and fell into ruins. At the end of the nineteenth century (1876), a group of Circassians resettled 'Amman, which very quickly (1921) became the capital, first of the Emirate of Transjordan, and then of the Hashemite kingdom of Jordan.

EXPLORATION

The first descriptions of the city's ancient remains come from the accounts of nineteenth-century travelers. Scientific research in the 'Amman area began with the surveys of C. R. Conder, the Princeton University (New Jersey) expedition directed by H. C. Butler, and R. E. Brünnow and A. von Domaszewski's expedition. They were responsible for the first scholarly descriptions, photographs, plans, and drawings of ancient 'Amman then still visible. The first archaeological excavations, both on the citadel and below it, were conducted in the 1920s and 1930s by the Italian Mission, directed first by G. Guidi and later on by R. Bartoccini. After World War II, accidental discoveries were made and archaeological research was carried out by G. L. Harding (tombs and the citadel), A. Hadidi, and F. Zayadine (tombs, the Roman forum, and the citadel), on behalf of the Jordan Department of Antiquities; by J. B. Hennessy for the British School of Archaeology (the citadel and the 'Amman Airport temple); L. G. Herr for the American Schools of Oriental Research (Airport temple and the citadel); the Spanish Archaeological Mission (excavations and restoration works in the Umayyad palace on the citadel); and the Joint Franco-Jordanian Mission (of the École Biblique et Archéologique Française in Jerusalem and the Jordan Department of Antiquities), directed by J.-B. Humbert and F. Zayadine, in the lower city of the 'Amman citadel (defense systems, an Ammonite palace, and a water reservoir).

TOMBS

The earliest tombs known so far from the 'Amman area are dated to the transitional period of the Early Bronze IV/Middle Bronze I. They are natural caves more or less rectangular or semicircular, roughly cut in the rock, sometimes with a shaft entrance, that resembles a tomb discovered at Jebel el-Taj. The tombs usually have a dome-shaped ceiling cut with a blade. Their contents consist mainly of pottery. An outstanding Early/Middle Bronze Age bilobate tomb cut in the foot of a hill was discovered about 5 km (3 mi.) northwest of 'Amman. The tomb was entered through a short, roughly round shaft. The entrances to both chambers were blocked by two rounded stones. Both chambers have an approximately rectangular plan and a dome-shaped ceiling. Chamber 1 also has a bench, a very rare feature in that period in Transjordan. The finds, apart from human bones, include pottery, four-spouted lamps, a bronze dagger, and a javelin with a hooked tang (chamber 1). The presence of weaponry suggests the burial place of a warrior or other important person (tribal chief?). Another Early Bronze/Middle Bronze Age tomb provided with benches is located at Jebel Jofeh. Two stone benches were situated on the northern and southern sides of a natural, almost rectangular cave (2.8 by 4.3 m) with a dome-shaped ceiling and shaft entrance.

Several Middle Bronze IIB–C/Late Bronze Age tombs have been discovered. One of them, at Jebel Jofeh, is an amorphous hole in the ground. The tomb has been dated by Harding to the Middle Bronze Age II, by B. S. J. Isserlin to the Late Bronze Age I, and by R. H. Dornemann, to the Middle Bronze Age IIB–C. Some of the tombs, like these discovered in the upper city of the citadel, contained Egyptian scarabs and cylinder seals in the Mitannian Common Style as well as pottery.

From the very end of the Late Bronze Age/Early Iron Age I there is a tomb at Jebel Nuzḥa, and there are several Iron Age tombs (mainly from the Iron Age II): at Jebel Jofeh (south of the citadel, tombs A, B, E, and F), on the northern and southern slopes of Jebel Qala (tomb D), at Jebel Qusur (northeast of the citadel, tomb G) and at Jebel 'Amman (southwest of the citadel, tomb C). They are usually natural caves or roughly cut oval or rectangular chambers and contained mainly pottery, although some copper, bronze, and iron artifacts such as jewelry and weaponry have also been recovered. Tomb C yielded a fragmentary pottery figurine of a hermaphrodite that has been interpreted by Harding as a representation of Ashtor-Khemosh, a deity known from the Mesha stela.

Tomb A, discovered at Jebel Jofeh, has a unique T-shaped plan. It consists of a nearly rectangular chamber with two cupboardlike recesses cut in the side walls at the rear, with a bench along the southern wall. The tomb yielded a fragmentary pottery figurine of the horse-and-rider type and about forty vessels generally dated to the eighth century BCE. In the contemporary tomb B nearby, apart from ordinary pottery, a bull-shaped vase was found. The two Roman sarcophagi found indicate that the tomb was reused in later periods.

Of interest also is tomb G, at Jebel Quṣur. It is shaped like a cistern and its entrance was blocked with stones. Inside the burial chamber (5.5 by 4.5 m) five anthropoid clay coffins, pottery, bronze bowls, and a cylinder seal were found. Three of the sarcophagi have lids modeled with human faces and arms at the sides of the body; two others are undecorated. All of the coffins have lug handles on their sides, an unusual feature for this kind of sarcophagus. Each coffin contained more than one skeleton. The tomb has been dated by Dornemann to the tenth century BCE.

Of importance is the so-called Adoni-nur tomb discovered on the southern slope of the citadel. A short corridor leads to a rectangular chamber cut in the rock that contained pottery; a pottery coffin of an Assyrian type; gold, silver,

Anthropoid coffin lid from Rabbath-Ammon.

Clay figurine of a horseman from an Ammonite tomb.

Group of Ammonite limestone statues of deities from Rabbath-Ammon.

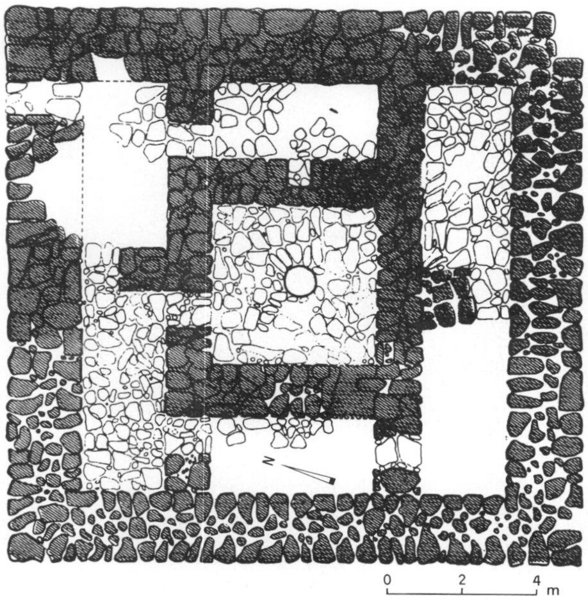

'Amman Airport temple, LB II: ***(left)*** *plan;* ***(below)*** *general view.*

and bronze jewelry; iron knives; bronze and iron arrowheads; beads; and seals. Three of the seals are inscribed. One of them mentions a royal Ammonite official, Adoni-nur (servant of 'Ammi-nadab). The tomb is dated to about 650 BCE, the reign of Amminadab, king of Ammon.

In the Umm Udaina area (west of 'Amman) another tomb was discovered, that, because of its very rich finds, has been interpreted by Hadidi as belonging to one of the Ammonite ruling families. The tomb itself is very typical of the 'Amman district: it is a natural cave adapted for burial use by chiseling the rock to form an almost rectangular chamber (8.5 by 5.5 m); it has a dome-shaped ceiling and a bench running around the walls. At least fifteen skeletons were found in the tomb, which suggests a long period of utilization—according to the excavator, between the mid-eighth century BCE and the early Hellenistic period. The contents of the tomb, apart from the local pottery, include imported Greek ware (black and red Attic types from the sixth and fifth centuries BCE), typical Iron Age II and Hellenistic lamps, an Ammonite inscribed seal, glass and alabaster bottles, silver, bronze, and iron artifacts such as jewelry, vessels, swords, daggers, arrowheads, a caryatid censer from the Achaemenid period, and other ornaments. Most of the finds are dated to the fifth century BCE.

A Nabatean tomb from the first century BCE was discovered at the foot of Jebel 'Amman. This two-chambered family tomb, originally from the Late Bronze Age, had been reused by the Nabateans, who partially cleared it of debris. The finds include two Late Hellenistic and one "Herodian" lamp, an Eastern terra sigillata bowl, eleven glass bottles, and two painted Nabatean bowls.

About 50 m from the Nabatean tomb, a Roman tomb was discovered cut with loculi out of the rock. Three sarcophagi, lamps, and ordinary pottery types were found. The tomb is dated to the second century CE on the evidence of the coins found in it.

At the foot of the southwestern slope of Jebel Jofeh, a Roman tomb (probably from the mid-third century) was built in a natural cave. It consisted of the main hall (8 by 7.2 m) and seven chambers on its northern and eastern sides. The roof had been supported by four pillars; later on, three arches were built to strengthen the roof. In the main hall three sarcophagi were found and eight graves were sunk into the floor. The contents were very rich and included one hundred pottery vessels, lamps, fifty glass vessels, bracelets, rings, thirty-four gold earrings, a silver bracelet and rings, bronze and silver coins, many other bronze objects, some iron items, beads, and even amber and pseudo-jet objects.

From the Roman period, a family tomb was discovered to the north of the 'Amman citadel. It was originally a natural cave adapted as a burial place by chiseling the rock to form a rectangular chamber with two benches on the eastern and southern sides. At the eastern part stood two similar stone sarcophagi whose lids are decorated with garlands and rosettes. The human bones found in the sarcophagi belonged to a man and a woman. The female's sarcophagus also contained some pieces of silver and bronze jewelry. Four lamps and a juglet were found on the floor. The excavator dated the tomb to the second to third centuries. Burials from the third century were also discovered in the lower city of the citadel (see below).

LATE BRONZE AGE TEMPLE

A building discovered by accident in the area of the 'Amman Airport was excavated by Hennessy, and the area around it was examined by Herr. The building is a *Quadratbau* (15 sq m), with walls (2 m thick) built of unhewn stones. Six rectangular rooms surround a square (6.5 by 6.5 m) central room (cella?) or courtyard with two stones (altar or pillar base) in the middle. A narrow entrance was situated in the northeastern corner of the building. About 7 m to the north of the temple, an "incinerator" (4 by 2 m) was found. The very rich contents of the building, mainly from the central cella area, include, apart from the local ware, a large amount of imported pottery (Mycenean IIA–IIIB, Late Cypriot base ring I and II, white slip I and II and Midianite ware), fragments of an Egyptian stone vessel from the Eighteenth to Nineteenth dynasties, as well as gold jewelry, scarabs, bronze, ivory, bone, and stone objects, stabbing swords (among them a *khepesh*, a type of sword), daggers, a bronze lugged axhead, arrowheads, and, both in the building and in the incinerator, several hundred fragments of burned bones, almost exclusively human. The building is dated to the very end of the fourteenth and the beginning of the thirteenth centuries BCE. It is generally considered a temple, probably one in which human sacrifice was performed. Sherds from the Middle Bronze Age II and scarabs from the Thirteenth and Seventeenth dynasties were found in its foundation.

THE CITADEL

The citadel lies in the center of modern 'Amman. It is a high, L-shaped hill that consists of four natural terraces. Two of them—the highest—are oriented

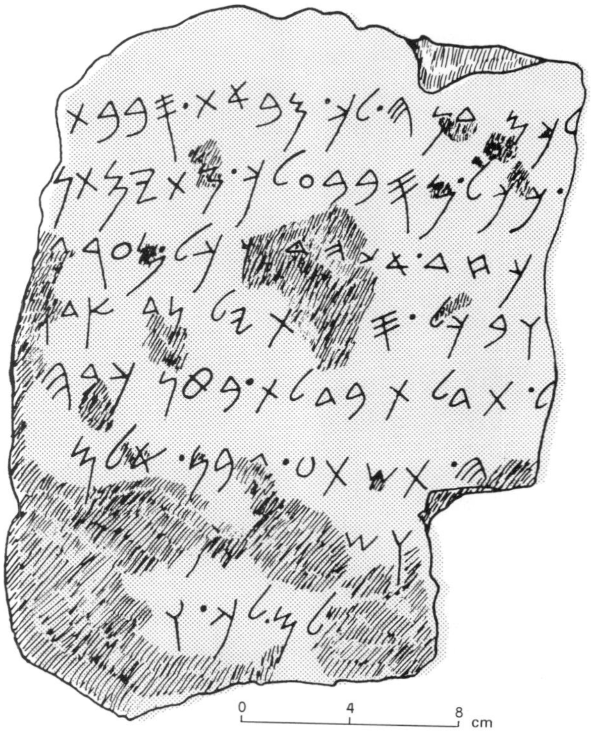

Ammonite building inscription from the acropolis, 9th century BCE.

Limestone figure of a woman used as a window balustrade decoration in the palace of the kings of Rabbath-Ammon.

Round tower at Rujm el-Malfuf.

north–south; they create the so-called acropolis, or upper city (c. 400 by 250 m). The third one, the southern, lower extension of the acropolis to the east, is called the lower city (260 by 80–110 m). The fourth terrace—the easternmost and the lowest—is now completely covered by modern buildings. Fragments of a very badly preserved rampart and pottery sherds from the Iron Age II, the Hellenistic, and the Roman periods found in surface surveys indicate that the fourth terrace was also inhabited.

RESERVOIR. A large underground cistern (c. 16 by 6 m; height, 7 m) with a gabled roof and flanked by two alcoves is cut in the rock at the northern end of the citadel, just below the Roman fortification wall. Two entrances lead to the cistern. The first, located at ground level and vaulted, connected it with the area outside the citadel. The second entrance—a shaft and then a long triple underground passage—gave access to the cistern directly from inside the fortified zone of the citadel. A group of nearby fortification walls, dated to the Middle Bronze Age II and the Iron Age, indicates the periods of utilization of the cistern. If Polybius' account of the siege of the citadel (*Hist.* V, 71, 9), is to be believed, this water system corresponds closely to his description and would have been in use also in the Hellenistic period. The closest example of this kind of installation is found at Gezer.

THE CITADEL'S DEFENSE SYSTEMS. Bronze and Iron I Ages. Remains of fortification walls and a glacis from the Middle Bronze II period were found at the northern part of the citadel, just beneath the Roman wall; a rampart with a sloping glacis and a retaining wall were unearthed along the southern edge of the lower city (area A) and dated to the same period. If the northern and southern parts of the fortifications composed part of the same defense system, the extent of the fortified zone of the Middle Bronze Age II settlement on the citadel was exceptionally large. Although some Late Bronze Age sherds have been found on the citadel, they come from unstratified contexts and cannot be associated with any construction. Therefore, the fortification system in that period is still not understood. The Middle Bronze Age walls may still have been in use. A section of a cyclopean wall more than 2 m thick has been excavated to the west of the Middle Bronze Age rampart. Its preliminary date is the Iron Age I.

Ammonite Iron Age. At the southeastern angle of the lower city (area B), a circular stone wall with a brick superstructure was investigated. According to its excavators, the wall is to be dated to the Ammonite period. Some structures discovered in area A, immediately south of the street lying near the Iron Age palace (see below), probably belong to a fortification wall from the same period. Iron Age II fortifications were also found in the northern part of the citadel, below the Roman wall.

Later Periods. On the southern side of the lower city (area A), a Roman wall (4 m thick) is preserved to a height of 7 m. It was constructed in the fourth century CE, perhaps in connection with the reorganization of the *Limes Arabicus*. Elements of earlier Roman buildings as well as from Bronze and Iron age walls were reused in its construction.

In the southeastern corner of the lower city (area B), remains of a large bastion were found. Several successive construction phases were observed for it. The oldest is represented by parallel walls, oriented east–west, with a sloping revetment. The walls are dated to the end of the Iron Age. Later construction, dated by pottery sherds to the Hellenistic period, is oriented north–south. Slightly to the west, the so-called building 38 has been partially excavated. It is, in fact, a curved casemate wall filled with rubble and earth. Its

Citadel: Ayyubid fortifications.

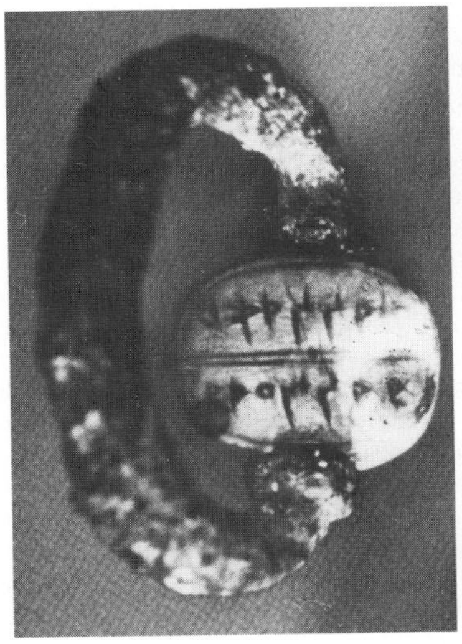

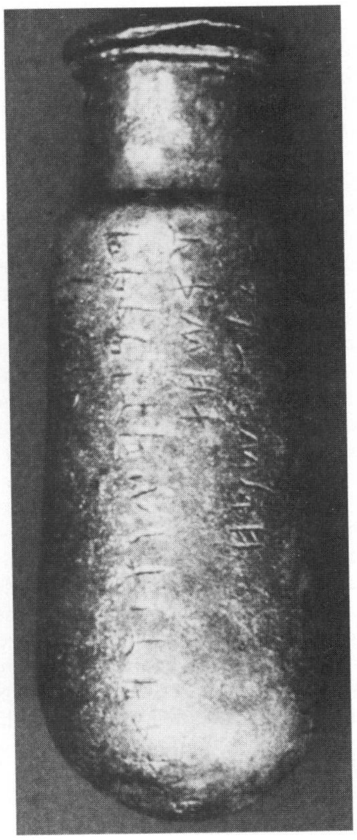

***Above:** seal of "Adoni-nur servant of 'Ammi-nadab" from the Adoni-nur tomb. **Right:** bronze bottle from Tell Siran inscribed with a list of Ammonite kings.*

facade is built of bossed stones in alternating courses of headers and stretchers. This construction has been assigned a preliminary date in the Late Hellenistic period. To the north a fourth-century Roman rampart is oriented north–south. A small gate was found in its northern part. The rampart probably constituted part of the Roman defense system discovered in area A. Roman fortifications were also found in the northern part of the citadel and in various sections along the whole circumference of the upper city. Inside the citadel, a wall dated to the Roman period separated the acropolis from the lower city.

AMMONITE IRON AGE PALACE. Part of a large architectural complex dated to the seventh century BCE was discovered by the Joint Franco–Jordanian Mission in the southern part of the lower city (area A, stratum 7). It consists of a large courtyard about 10 m wide and more than 15 m long (the excavations have not yet reached its eastern and western boundaries). It has a thick (30 cm), polished white-plaster floor of excellent quality. To the south, it is limited by a row of four rectangular rooms with plaster floors. One of the rooms contains a lavatory with a limestone seat. It communicated with another room. In a third room a kind of podium, or dais (1.25 by 1 m; height, 0.5 m, preserved) is attached to the western wall. Its function is not yet clear. To the north, two cellar rooms were found that must have been accessible by ladder from the upper story that existed in this part of the palace. The finds from this area, probably from the upper story, include pottery, a clay mask, Phoenician ivories, blue-glass pendants, a green-glass goblet, fragments of lapis lazuli, more than 120 sheep astragali, and fragments of bitumen from the Dead Sea. Four limestone double-faced Hathor heads discovered nearby in previous excavations probably belong to the palace. Three of them bear inscriptions.

This architectural complex is interpreted by the excavator as an upper-class residence, a palace(?), that shares architectural features with the Neo-Assyrian palatial complexes at Nimrud, Arslan Tash, and Khorsabad, among others. South of these rooms a paved area, probably a street, was discovered, as well as fragments of a fortification wall (see above), farther to the south.

ROMAN TEMENOS. The northern part of the upper city is, in fact, an artificial stepped platform (c. 48 by 104 m) built of rusticated ashlar masonry. There are large buttresses on the northwestern and northeastern corners, suggesting the existence of towers. To the south extends the so-called courtyard (c. 78 by 120–126 m), which projects another 15 m farther to the east. Both were separated by an east–west wall with two gates. The courtyard's superstructures were built of smoothly dressed masonry. Its northern wall was decorated with rectangular podia, square pilasters, and semicircular niches. The courtyard's area was bisected by a street paved with stone slabs, running north–south and giving access to the northern part of the upper city. The courtyard was surrounded by a wall on the east, west, and south; its main entrance was in the southern wall. Both platform and courtyard, evidently contemporary structures, are dated to the Roman period (second–third centuries). It was probably a cultic area with a courtyard, a temenos (in the north), and a temple. The complex was later incorporated into the Umayyad palatial complex.

Roman Temple of Hercules. A large part of the podium of the Roman Temple of Hercules (43.5 by 27.5 m), a fallen column, the bases of three other columns, and several fragments of architectural decoration are preserved. The remains were surveyed by Butler and excavated by Bartoccini and later by Northedge. There are two possible reconstructions of the original plan: as a *tetrastylum in antis* or as a *hexastylum in antis peripterum* (with a row of columns surrounding the cella). The cella itself (c. 20.6 by 13.2 m) faces east. The antae of the pronaos were made of half columns. The outer walls of the temple were probably decorated with a series of pilasters. As indicated by an inscription on a fragmentary architrave found in its vicinity, the building was constructed in the reign of Marcus Aurelius and Lucius Verus (161–169 CE). The temple was situated within a rectangular, terraced temenos (length, 119 m) at the southeastern part of the acropolis. The architectural form of the temenos gate is unusual. It consists of a rectangular interior (with a two-column portico) and a semicircular exterior. The gate is in the southeastern corner of the temenos and leads down to the city, directly to the propylaeum. The temple was probably dedicated to Hercules and his mother. Two larger-than-life marble fragments (an elbow and a hand) were found in the temple area. The temple was built on the site of a sacred rock, the history of whose veneration, as pottery finds may indicate, goes back to the Early Bronze Age (c. 3000 BCE). A fragmentary Ammonite inscription from the ninth century BCE attests to the sanctity of that area and suggests the existence here, in the Iron Age, of an altar and/or a temple dedicated to the Ammonite god Milkom.

DOMESTIC AND OTHER REMAINS. Several trenches and soundings made in the upper city, and recently in the lower city, have shown traces of settlement from as early as the Chalcolithic period. The most important discoveries, however, are related to the later periods. The hitherto existing lack of remains from the early Hellenistic period has been filled by the Franco-Jordanian excavations' discoveries of Hellenistic structures and a contemporary drain-

Marble statue in the Hellenistic style of Icarus, one of a group depicting Icarus and Daedalus.

age channel in area A (stratum IV) in the lower city, above the Iron Age palace (see above). The finds include a bronze coin of Ptolemy II Philadelphus, Rhodian amphora stamped handles from the third to second centuries BCE, Greek black-glazed pottery, and fragments of fresco with a geometric decoration. Other architectural structures attest that the settlement in this area continued through the Roman period.

In stratum III (first century BCE–first century CE) remains of a large, probably public building were discovered. The walls (1.15 m thick; 1.5 m high) are oriented north-south. Their exceptionally deep foundations are built of hewn stones. Several fragments of fresco and stucco decoration, as well as terra sigillata sherds, were found here. The construction of this building appears to correspond to the beginning of the Decapolis.

Several tombs from the third century CE, above the Early Roman (first century) habitation levels were discovered by Zayadine in the middle of the southern part of the lower city. This indicates that at least this part of the site was a cemetery in the Late Roman period (second–third centuries). It was probably a small peripheral cemetery near the residential quarters.

Remains of intensive domestic occupation in the Byzantine period (among them, an oil press) have also been discovered between the temenos of the Temple of Hercules and the Umayyad palace. On the site of the present museum here, a large building complex from the Umayyad period was excavated by Harding in 1949. It consisted of several rooms grouped around a central courtyard. The Byzantine buildings in the upper city underwent an architectural replanning in the Umayyad period, probably in connection with the construction of the palatial complex.

BYZANTINE-UMAYYAD RESIDENTIAL COMPLEX (SIXTH–SEVENTH CENTURIES). This large complex was uncovered in 1987 in the lower city of the citadel, about 100 m west of area A. It consists of several rooms grouped around the main rectangular hall. The hall is decorated with a mosaic floor and an apse (remains of an original Byzantine chapel?) in its eastern wall. The mosaic consists of a circular medallion with a geometric design and a heart-shaped leaf at the center. Farther to the west, another quadrangular medallion depicts an upright man, in the posture of an orante, with two fragments of animals preserved at his sides (a bull and a lion?) and a fragmentary Greek inscription bearing a name, probably of the orante. In one of the nearby rooms (VI), a reused marble block with another Greek inscription has been found. This inscription mentions a Tyche. The block itself must originally

The Byzantine church.

Remains of the Ummayad palace.

have belonged to the base of a statue of this goddess, perhaps the one whose marble head was discovered in 1957 near the Hercules temple. It is probable that there was a temple to a Tyche in the lower city.

BYZANTINE CHURCH. Immediately to the north of the Roman temple is a fifth- to sixth-century church (c. 20.3 by 12.3 m). It has an ordinary basilical plan (slightly trapezoidal): a monoapsidal building with two rows of columns dividing it into the main nave and two lateral aisles. The aisles were paved with stone slabs, while the central nave had a mosaic floor with a pattern of geometric trefoil rosettes and other flowers (probably a sixth-century addition). Two inscriptions have been found here: one, which is very fragmentary, on the mosaic, and the second, originally from the Roman Temple of Hercules, in reuse. The church was first excavated in part by Bartoccini in 1928; the work was completed between 1957 and 1977 by Zayadine.

THE UMAYYAD PALACE. A great palatial complex, probably the residence of a governor and the center of administration, was identified by the Spanish Archaeological Mission at the northern part of the citadel. It was built on the site of the preexisting Roman cultic area, whose remains it incorporated. The palace is trapezoidal and consists of three main parts. The southern part is a large cruciform vestibule, or reception hall. The central area occupies the former courtyard from the Roman period. From the vestibule, the entrance leads to a courtyard with two buildings on its eastern and western sides. A gate in the northern wall led to a colonnaded street running southeast. On either side of the street were two pairs of buildings. All the building complexes in the central part were provided with inner courtyards surrounded by porticoes. The northern part of the complex, entered from the street, was probably the residence of the emir or governor. In front of the main building was a small court that consisted of a large *liwan*-type hall and a central room with a Greek cruciform floor plan. Another small court was situated behind it. This complex was probably surrounded by four buildings with inner porticoed courtyards. The plan of the palatial complex and several architectural details share features with complexes at Mushatta, Khirbet el-Minya, and Medina of Qaṣr el-Hairial Saruqi. A large contemporary cistern (5 m deep; 16 m across) is situated immediately southeast of the vestibule. The palace complex in 'Amman was built between 720 and 750. During the Abbasid and Fatimid periods (750–1071) it fell into disrepair.

MARIUSZ BURDAJEWICZ

ROMAN PHILADELPHIA

The remains of the Roman city of Philadelphia are divided into two principal parts: those in the upper city (citadel, see above) and those in the lower city, scattered along two wadis that form narrow valleys to the south and southwest of the acropolis. As early as the beginning of the nineteenth century, it was reported that the remains on the acropolis were not well preserved, due to the building activity here in the medieval period. In contrast, the remains in the

Remains of the Roman temple on the acropolis.

The agora: southern portico.

lower city were mostly well preserved up to the beginning of the twentieth century, according to evidence recorded by contemporary travelers.

The Roman city was built along two streets: the first ran along the southern and southwestern foot of the acropolis, to the north of Wadi 'Amman, while the second ran past the western foot of the acropolis. Another wadi, which debouches into Wadi 'Amman, crosses the second street about halfway along it. The two wadis formed deep valleys. The wadi to the south of the acropolis was longer and wider, and the center of Roman Philadelphia lay here. All the large public buildings were erected here, first and foremost the agora. From here the ascent to the acropolis, the city's cultic area, passed through the propylaeum. Both the valleys were bounded on their south and southwest by steep hills. The city could thus only be expanded toward the southwest, in the narrow valley of Wadi 'Amman.

THE LOWER CITY. Several major monuments and evidence of the city's plan were found in the lower city.

Propylaeum. At the foot of the acropolis, to the north of the main colonnaded street and to the south of the southern part of the acropolis wall, was a large building described by Conder as a temple or part of an agora. Butler was the first to identify it as a propylaeum. The structure's facade (25 m wide and 2 m thick) includes three square doorways: a high, central entrance flanked by two lower ones. The building was richly decorated. Its pillars were crowned with Corinthian capitals, and above the square doorways were cornices topped by semicircular niches, flanked by flat, engaged pilasters. The central wall was also decorated with engaged pilasters bearing Corinthian capitals. The axis of the propylaeum's central entrance runs north-south, in line with the gate (now completely destroyed) that was in the acropolis's southern wall. Visitors ascended to the city's cultic area on the acropolis from the main street at the foot of the acropolis by passing through the propylaeum and going up a stairway (of which no trace survives).

City coin of Philadelphia.

Colonnaded Streets. Philadelphia's two principal streets were colonnaded on both sides; Conder and Butler saw parts of them and their colonnades still standing. Today, modern 'Amman's two main streets lie over the two ancient streets, which were 8.4 m wide. The columns of the colonnades were set 3 m apart and had Corinthian capitals. The streets were paved with square stone slabs.

Large Theater. The theater was located to the south of Wadi 'Amman, where the valley widens to the south of the acropolis, not far from the eastern end of the city. The seats were built in a depression, partly natural, in the block of hills that bounds the city on the south. The central area of the theater's seating is composed of three horizontal blocks (*ima, media, summa caveae*) hewn out of the hillside; only the sides of the seating are built, supported on a complex of vaults. The seats themselves, unlike those in the theater at Petra, are not hewn from the rock but are built of stone. The *scaena* and *scaenae frons* had already been completely destroyed by the end of the nineteenth century; only their foundations survive. The middle and upper blocks of seating each contained sixteen rows of seats, divided by six scalaria into seven cunei. The lower block of seating had thirteen rows of seats. In the center of the upper seating block an exedra was formed

The large theater: general view.

by a broadhouse with two pillars built against its facade, between two pilasters. In its rear wall a semicircular niche was flanked by square niches.
Small Theater. The small theater was built near the large theater, with its facade facing west. Unlike the larger theater, it was built on a leveled surface. The western facade had five entrances. Its eastern face, the *scaenae frons*, was joined to the western wall by a vault that extended for the width of the facade. Two towers, which stood on either side of the eastern wall, formed the *versurae*. The small theater's cavea was made up of two horizontal blocks: the upper contained seven rows of seats and the lower, eleven.
Agora. Seven meters to the north of the remains of the *scaena* structure is a row of eight columns with Corinthian capitals and an architrave. To the west of the last column in the row is a double column, which was the corner column of another portico; this joined the portico that ran parallel to the *scaena* building of the large theater. The second row of columns does not join the first portico at right angles, but at an angle of 108 degrees. Butler realized that the plaza surrounded by the porticoes was in fact the agora of Roman Philadelphia. From the reconstructed plan of the city it can be seen that the agora was bordered by porticos on its east, south, and west. Confirmation of its identification and of Butler's reconstruction came from an inscription found in the area of the forum during restoration work carried out in the 1960s. The agora lay in the widest open place in the city and was bounded on the north by the colonnade of the main street that ran to the north of the wadi. On the east, west, and south it was bounded by the porticoes whose continuation was found during restoration work carried out in the center of 'Amman.
Nymphaeum. Philadelphia's nymphaeum was in the west of the city, facing north. To its south was Wadi 'Amman. A small wadi that debouches into Wadi 'Amman from the north runs beneath the nymphaeum and joins Wadi 'Amman behind it. The city's main colonnaded street runs to its north. Northwest of the nymphaeum is the northern wadi, in which the second colonnaded street lies.

The nymphaeum consisted of a straight central wall with a large niche. Two diagonal walls adjoined the central wall on either side, with two straight walls joining them at right angles; these combined to form an open, exedralike building decorated with niches (on either side of the large niche were smaller niches in the diagonal walls). The semicircular niches were crowned with halfdomes. Between the large niches were smaller ones, also semicircular, separated by square, engaged pilasters. Opposite the nymphaeum's facade and parallel to it is a pillared portico that carried an architrave topped by Syrian gables above each niche. The facade walls rose two stories high: each story was decorated with statues set in small niches. The facade's two stories were supported on two stories of vaults, which formed the nymphaeum's base. Opposite the large central niche was a stairway that also rested on vaults. The nymphaeum at Philadelphia is one of a group of magnificent nymphaea known from cities in Syria and Asia Minor (Gerasa, Beth-Shean, Side, and Aspendos).
The Vault Over Wadi 'Amman. The vault spanning Wadi 'Amman is one of the most complex engineering projects from the Roman period known in the Middle East. Because of the lack of room to expand the city in the valley to the south of the acropolis, the central part of Wadi 'Amman—probably from the nymphaeum on the west to the agora on the east—was bridged by a broad arch (width, 10.3 m) that rested on a supporting arch (height, 1.5 m) spanning the banks of the wadi. Few traces of the vault survive in situ, but they are sufficient to show the massive Roman method of construction that enabled the structure to withstand floods; not only was the wadi covered by the vault, but its bed was paved with stone slabs in order to control the flow of water. This mighty engineering feat accomplished three aims: it increased the small area available to the city planners, facilitated traffic within the city, and prevented flooding in the rainy season.
City Plan. Philadelphia's town planners were forced to take account of the natural topography. To the south and southwest of the acropolis are two narrow valleys, as mentioned above, that provided the only available level ground for building. The municipal center of Philadelphia was established here, and the city's two main streets extended along the valleys.

There is no way of knowing whether this city plan was laid out in the Hellenistic or Roman period, but all the extant buildings date from the second and third centuries. Roman Philadelphia had no city wall, as the topography did not permit the construction of any practical fortifications; in time of need the inhabitants could seek refuge on the spacious acropolis, which could be defended easily. The stairway that ascended the southern slope of the acropolis hill, between the gate in the southern wall and the propylaeum at the foot of the acropolis, linked the city to the acropolis. In the Roman period, the acropolis was the city's principal sanctuary, as well.

The city's municipal center was to the south of Philadelphia's main street. The valley broadens here to about 200 m. As described above, a vault was built over the wadi that crosses the valley to the south of the main street, in order to expand the limited area in the city's center.

Of the public buildings in the center of Philadelphia, only the large and small theaters (see above) are known. The agora lay between them and the main street; traces of the agora's three porticoes survive. The large theater was built on the side of the steep hill that bounded the valley to the south, while the small theater stood isolated, to the east of the large one. About 180 m to its east, the main street ended in a gate, of which no trace survives.

Philadelphia was a relatively small city: the total area of the two valleys that comprised the heart of it was only 173,000 sq m. If the area of the acropolis, parts of which may have been used for public or private buildings, is added, a total municipal area of 276,000 sq m is reached. The slopes of the hills bounding the two valleys on the south and southwest were probably also used for private residential buildings; the slopes would have been too steep, however, to permit the construction of streets. It is possible that the buildings here were partially built and partially hewn out of the hillside.

ARTHUR SEGAL

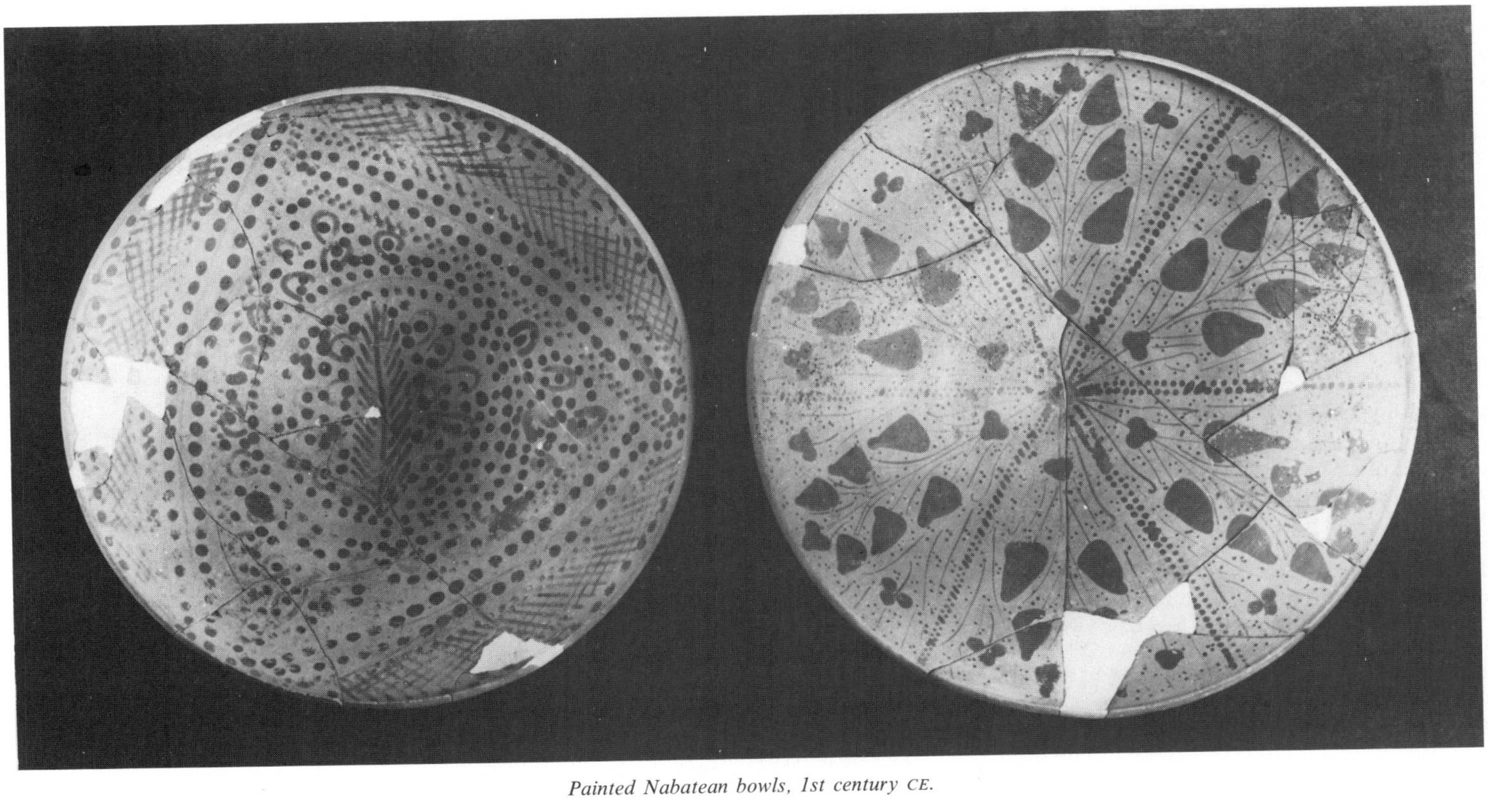

Painted Nabatean bowls, 1st century CE.

Surveys: C. Warren, *PEQ* 2 (1870), 284–306; Conder, *SEP* 1, 19; H. C. Butler, *Syria* (Publications of the Princeton University Archaeological Expedition to Syria: Ancient Architecture, II/A/5), Leiden 1907; Brünnow–Domaszewski, *Die Provincia Arabia*, 208–231; G. L. Harding, *The Antiquities of Jordan*, London 1959, 61–70.

Italian excavations: G. Guidi, *Bolletino dell'Assoziazione Internazionale per gli Studi Mediterranei* 1 (1930), 3, 15ff.; R. Bartoccini, ibid., 3 (1933), 16ff.; 4 (1933–1934), 4–5, 10ff.; id., *Bollettino dell'Arte* (1934), 275–285; id., *Atti del IV Congresso nazionale di Studi romani* 1938, 1–8; id., *Bollettino del R. Istituto di Archeologia e Storia dell'Arte* 9 (1941), 3–5; A. Almagro, *ADAJ* 27 (1983), 607–639.

Early periods: D. Mackenzie, *PEFA* 1 (1911), 1–40; G. L. Harding, *QDAP* 11 (1944), 67–74, 105–106; 12 (1946), 37–40; id., *ADAJ* 1 (1951), 7–16, 37–40; 3 (1956), 80; 4–5 (1960), 114; id., *PEFA* 6 (1953), 14–18, 48–65; G. R. Driver, *QDAP* 11 (1944), 81–82; E. Henschel-Simon, ibid., 75–80; Y. Aharoni, *IEJ* 1 (1950–1951), 219–222; R. D. Barnett, *ADAJ* 1 (1951), 34–36; N. Avigad, *IEJ* 2 (1952), 163–164; R. T. O'Callaghan, *Orientalia* 21 (1952), 184–193; B. S. J. Isserlin, *PEFA* 6 (1953), 19–26; O. Tufnell, ibid., 66–72; P. C. Hammond, *BASOR* 160 (1960), 38–41; G. M. Landes, *BA* 24 (1961), 66–86; R. W. Dajani, *ADAJ* 6–7 (1962), 124–125; 11 (1966), 41–47, 48–52; 12–13 (1967–1968), 65–69; W. A. Ward, ibid. 8–9 (1964), 47–55; 11 (1966), 5–18; J. B. Hennessy, *PEQ* 98 (1966), 155–162; id., *ZAW* 78 (1966), 357–359; G. R. H. Wright, ibid., 350–357; S. H. Horn, *ADAJ* 12–13 (1967–1968), 81–83; id., *BASOR* 193 (1969), 2–13; 205 (1972), 43–45; R. Tournay, *RB* 74 (1967), 248–254; E. F. Campbell and G. E. Wright, *BA* 32 (1969), 104–116; F. M. Cross, Jr., *BASOR* 193 (1969), 13–19; 212 (1973), 12–15; B. Oded, *Rivista degli Studi Orientali* 44 (1969), 187–189; S. K. Tell, *ADAJ* 14 (1969), 28–33; W. F. Albright, *BASOR* 198 (1970), 38–40; R. S. Boraas, *ADAJ* 16 (1971), 31–45; V. Fritz, *ZDPV* 87 (1971), 140–152; M. M. Ibrahim, *ADAJ* 16 (1971), 91–97; K. R. Veenhof, *Phoenix* 18 (1972), 170–179; P. Bordrevil, *ADAJ* 18 (1973), 37–39; E. Puech and A. Rofé, *RB* 80 (1973), 531–546; 92 (1985), 5–24; H. O. Thompson, *Australian Journal of Biblical Archaeology* 2 (1973), 23–38; id. and F. Zayadine, *BASOR* 212 (1973), 5–11; id., *BA* 37 (1974), 13–18; G. Garbini, *Journal of Semitic Studies* 19 (1974), 159–168; V. Hankey, *Levant* 6 (1974), 131–178; F. Zayadine, *Syria* 51 (1974), 129–136; 62 (1985), 152–158; id., *Archaeology in the Levant* (K. M. Kenyon Fest.), Warminster 1978, 59–66; id., *RB* 86 (1979), 120–122; id., *MdB* 4 (1986), 17–20; id. (et al.), *ADAJ* 31 (1987), 299–310; P.-E. Dion, *RB* 82 (1975), 24–33; id., *Archaeology of Jordan: Essays and Reports*, 'Amman 1988, 14–46, 61–64; A. Van Selms, *Bibliotheca Orientalis* 32 (1975), 5–8; K. Yassine, *ADAJ* 20 (1975), 57–68; 27 (1983), 491–494; id., *Archaeology of Jordan*, 'Amman 1988, 33–46; L. G. Herr, *ADAJ* 21 (1976), 109–111; id., *ASOR Newsletter* (1977–1978), 1–4; id., *The Amman Airport Excavations 1976* (AASOR 48), Cambridge, Mass. 1983; id., *BA* 46 (1983), 223–229; W. J. Fulco, *BASOR* 230 (1978), 39–43; id., *JNES* 38 (1979), 37–38; M. Piccirillo, *LA* 28 (1978), 73–86; id., *MdB* 35 (1984), 22–23; V. Sasson, *PEQ* 111 (1979), 117–125; W. H. Shea, ibid., 17–25; 113 (1981), 105–110; A. Hadidi, *ADAJ* 26 (1982), 283–286; id., *Levant* 19 (1987), 101–120; R. H. Dornemann, *The Archaeology of the Transjordan in the Bronze and Iron Ages*, Milwaukee 1983; K. P. Jackson, "The Ammonite Language of the Iron Age" (Ph.D. diss., Chico, Calif. 1983); A. Lemaire, *Syria* 61 (1984), 251–254; S. Abbadi, *ZDPV* 101 (1985), 30–31; M. Abu Taleb, ibid., 21–29; L. A. Khalil, *Levant* 18 (1986), 103–110; *A Cemetery at Queen Alia International Airport* (Yarmouk Univ. Publications Institute of Archaeology and Anthropology Series 1, eds. M. M. Ibrahim and R. L. Gordon), Wiesbaden 1987; E. A. Knauf, *Göttinger Miszellen* 100 (1987), 45–46; A.-J. 'Amr, *PEQ* 120 (1988), 55–63; R. G. Khouri, *Amman: A Brief Guide to the Antiquities* (Al Kutba Jordan Guides), 'Amman 1988; Weippert 1988 (Ortsregister); *Akkadica Supplementum* 7–8 (1989), 167–178; S. Helms, *BASOR* 273 (1989), 17–36; J.-B. Humbert (and F. Zayadine), *Contribution française à l'archéologie jordanienne*, 'Amman 1989, 22–29; id. (et al.), *LA* 39 (1989), 248–253; 41 (1991), 502–506; K. Prag, *PEQ* 121 (1989), 69–70; M. Najjar, *ADAJ* 35 (1991), 105–134; B. Sass, *Levant* 23 (1991), 187–190.

Later periods: W. H. P. Hatch, *AASOR* 7 (1927), 100–104; F. M. Abel, *RB* 45 (1936), 233–235; A. Alt, *ZDPV* 55 (1932), 128–134; id., *PJB* 32 (1936), 110–112; G. L. Harding, *QDAP* 12 (1946), 58–62; 14 (1950), 81–94; id., *ADAJ* 1 (1951), 30–33; J. H. Iliffe, *QDAP* 14 (1950), 95–96; F. Zayadine, *ADAJ* 14 (1969), 34–35; 18 (1973), 17–35; 22 (1977–1978), 20–56; (et al.) 33 (1989), 357–363; id., *MdB* 22 (1982), 20–28; 58 (1989), 52–53; id., *ZDPV* 99 (1983), 184–188; id., *RB* 97 (1990), 68–84; A. Hadidi, *ADAJ* 15 (1970), 11–15; 18 (1973), 51–53, 61–62; 19 (1974), 71–91; id., *Archaeology in the Levant* (K. M. Kenyon Fest.), Warminster 1978, 210–212; D. Schlumberger, *Syria* 48 (1971), 385–389; G. Bisheh, *ADAJ* 17 (1972), 81–83; B. Bagatti, *LA* 23 (1973), 261–285; C.-M. Bennett, *ADAJ* 20 (1975), 131–142; 22 (1977–1978), 172–179; 23 (1979), 151–159, 161–176; id., *Levant* 10 (1978), 1–9; 11 (1979), 1–8; F. el Fakharani, *Archaeologischer Anzeiger* 90 (1975), 377–403; J. A. Sauer, *ASOR Newsletter* (1976–1977), 1–10; id., *BA* 42 (1979), 135; K. Stemmer, *ADAJ* 21 (1976), 33–39; H. Gaube, *ZDPV* 93 (1977), 52–86; A. Northedge, *ADAJ* 22 (1977–1978), 5–13; 27 (1983), 437–460; id., *Levant* 12 (1980), 135–154; id., *PEQ* 114 (1982), 156; E. Olávarri, *RB* 86 (1979), 119–122; id., *El Palacio Omeya de Amman* 1–2, Madrid and Valencia 1983–1985; A. Almagro, *ADAJ* 24 (1980), 111–119; 26 (1982), 277–282; id., *SHAJ* 1 (1982), 305–321; J-P. Rey-Coquais, *ADAJ* 25 (1981), 25–31; E. Suleiman, ibid. 27 (1983), 549–553; M. Piccirillo, *LA* 34 (1984), 329–340; id., *MdB* 65 (1990), 66–67; E. Puech, ibid., 341–346; P-L. Gatier, *Inscriptions de la Jordanie* 2: *Région Centrale* (Bibliothéque Archéologique et Historique 114), Paris 1986, 36–65; id. (and A. -M. Verilhac), *Syria* 66 (1989), 337–348; A. A. Gorbea, *SHAJ* 3 (1987), 181–192; A. Segal, *Town Planning and Architecture in Provincia Arabia* (*BAR*/IS 419), Oxford 1988; *Akkadica Supplementum* 7–8 (1989), 155–166; J. A. Green and A. S. Abu-Dayyah, *AJA* 94 (1990), 311; A. S. Abu-Dayyah et al., *ADAJ* 35 (1991), 361–395; W. H. Shea, *PEQ* 123 (1991), 62–66.

RABUD, KHIRBET

IDENTIFICATION

Khirbet Rabud is a 15-a. mound located on top of a rocky hill surrounded on three sides by the bed of Naḥal Hebron (map reference 1515.0933). This is the only large Late Bronze Age mound in the Hebron Hills. Its water sources (apart from cisterns) are located some 3 km (2 mi.) north of the site, at two wells known as Bir 'Alaqa el-Fauqani and Bir 'Alaqa et-Taḥta (the Upper and Lower Wells of 'Alaqa). Although the upper part of the mound had been denuded down to bedrock, many remains were preserved near the walls on the slopes. The identification of the site with Debir, or Kiriath-Sepher, was first proposed by K. Galling. The excavations provided additional proof for this identification (see below). 1. Biblical Debir (Jos. 15:15; Jg. 1:1 [Kiriath Sepher]; Jos. 15:49 [Kiriath Sannah]) was located south of Hebron in a district that included Anab, Socoh, and Eshtemoa, all of which are within a radius of 5 km (3 mi.) from Khirbet Rabud. 2. There is complete agreement between the archaeological finds and the biblical account of the history of Debir as an important Canaanite city (Jos. 11:21), a Levitical city (Jos. 21:15; 1 Chr. 6:58), and an administrative center in Judah that is not mentioned after the First Temple period. 3. The story of Achsah, daughter of Caleb (Jos. 15:15–19; Jg. 1:11–15), is easily understood in the context of the water-supply system at Rabud, which at the end of summer depends solely on the nearby upper and lower wells. 4. No remains of any other major Canaanite city have yet been found in the hilly area south of Hebron.

EXCAVATIONS

Two short seasons of excavations were carried out at the site in 1968 and 1969, under the direction of M. Kochavi, on behalf of the Institute of Archaeology at Tel Aviv University. Two trenches, A and B, were opened on the western side of the mound and several burial caves were investigated in the 'Ush es-Saqra cemetery, on its eastern flank.

The earliest settlement on the mound dates to the Early Bronze Age I. Sherds from this period were found in both trenches. Some of the tombs were also in use in this period. Middle Bronze Age I sherds were found in trench A and in one of the tombs. The first walled city dates to the Late Bronze Age IIA (fourteenth century BCE). Four strata from this period were revealed in trench A and attributed to the fourteenth and thirteenth centuries BCE. The small wall, which enclosed an area of about 15 a., continued to be employed in all the strata. In the Late Bronze IIA period, burial in the 'Ush es-Saqra caves was at its height. The finds in the tombs include a rich assemblage of imported Cypriot and Mycenean ware, together with local pottery.

Iron Age strata were encountered in both trenches. In trench A, a stratum from the period of the Israelite settlement (twelfth century BCE) lay directly above the last Late Bronze Age level. A rock-cut cistern and a number of tombs were attributed to the tenth century BCE.

A massive wall (W1) was erected in the ninth century BCE (stratum B-III). It was exposed in both trenches, and about 900 m of its course could be traced on the surface of the mound. The wall (c. 4 m thick) enclosed an area of about 12 a. It was constructed in unequal sections (4 to 20 m long); the joints between the sections project about 0.5 m from the line of the wall. The gate was probably erected on the southeastern side, where the village Rabud, which gave its name to the site, now stands. The destruction level (stratum B-II), which was distinguished in all the rooms adjoining the wall, should be attributed to Sennacherib's campaign in 701 BCE. In this stratum, a large amount of pottery was found, including vessels with a jar-handle bearing a *lamelekh* stamp and two jar handles with a "personal" stamp: שלום בן אחא (Shalom son of Aḥa).

The wall was rebuilt in the seventh century BCE, and it was widened in places to 7 m (strata A-II and B-I). An unwalled settlement was also established in this period on a lower terrace northeast of the mound. The city and the unwalled settlement were completely razed with the destruction of the First Temple. Only a few buildings, not enclosed by a wall, could be attributed to the postexilic period (stratum A-I). A Roman watchtower on the summit of the mound is the latest remnant of the ancient occupation of the site.

K. Galling, *ZDPV* 70 (1954), 135–141; H. Donner, ibid. 81 (1965), 24–25; M. Kochavi, *TA* 1 (1974), 1–33; *BAR* 1/1 (1975), 5–7; J. Briend, *BTS* 176 (1975), 4–10; J. M. Miller, *ZDPV* 99 (1983), 121; Weippert 1988, 101, 607, 614.

MOSHE KOCHAVI

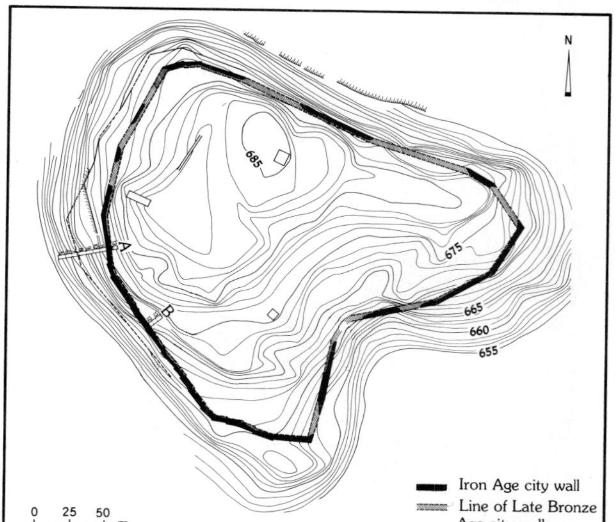

Khirbet Rabud: map of the mound, excavation areas, and fortifications.

Qedumim: hole-mouth jar with Aramaic inscription "mtr'," *Persian period.*

Qedumim: overview of area M and the oil press.

Ḥorvat Qitmit: anthropomorphic cult pedestal, end of Iron II.

Ḥorvat Qitmit: fragmentary cult vessel with pomegranates, end of Iron II.

RADDANA, KHIRBET

IDENTIFICATION

Khirbet Raddana was a small, unfortified village of fewer than 2 a., situated on a hilltop across a deep valley on the northern side of modern Ramallah (map reference 1695.1468). The village was founded at the beginning of the Iron Age I, in about 1200 BCE. It was abandoned before the establishment of the monarchy in Israel, in about 1050 BCE. A few pieces of Early Bronze Age I pottery were found in the crevices of the bedrock underneath the village houses. Fragments of Byzantine pottery lay among the ruins of the houses, but the only evidence of occupation of the site was from the Iron Age I. Y. Aharoni suggested an identification of the site with Ataroth-Addar (Jos. 16:2, 16:5, 18:13) because it was located on the border between Benjamin and Ephraim, between Bethel and Beth-Horon. However, even if this identification is accepted, the village is still obscure, to the point of anonymity. About the same information is available for Ataroth-Addar, the Archites, and the Japhletites as we have of the village at Raddana: they appear suddenly in the period of the settlement, establish an insignificant presence, and then drop from the course of history without having made an appreciable impact.

EXCAVATIONS

A salvage excavation was carried out at the site from June to August 1969, on behalf of the Israel Department of Antiquities and Museums. It was supervised by R. E. Cooley as site R of the Ai excavation project, directed by this writer. Several finds of unusual significance at site R led to the excavation of sites S and T in 1970, 1972, and 1974. Each site consisted of a complex of houses separated from each other by an open space. Each complex was covered by a mound of stones heaped upon the ruins by later owners of the hilltop, who cleared the open spaces for farming or grazing their flocks. Two mounds of stones covering additional house compounds were left unexcavated.

HOUSES AND HOUSING PATTERNS. Each house compound consisted of two or more pier-constructed buildings around a small common area, or court, that seems to have been the focus of family activity. Both sites S and T had three houses each. A possible third house at site R had been removed in 1967 by road builders. Additional structures of various sizes and plans were constructed against the outer walls of the dwellings for storage, workshops, and probable sheepfolds. Thus, each compound seems to have accommodated an extended family with its own independent facilities.

The site S compound may have been larger and more significant than sites R and T. The central pier-type house was larger and boasted taller and better-hewn roof-support pillars, and the storage, workshop, and other structures were more numerous. Evidence of its significance was the bronze slag-encrusted crucibles, tuyeres, and numerous bronze objects found only in this compound.

There was some variation in the way piers for individual houses were constructed. A pattern of four freestanding piers, with an additional pier at each end integrated with the wall construction, seems to have been consistent. However, some piers were squared monoliths, many with the chisel marks still visible; some were stacks of roughly squared stones, from two to four in each pier. In some cases, the interstices between piers were filled with rough walls of small stones that created a long, narrow room space on one side of the piers and a larger room on the other.

A second feature of the houses was a bench constructed along the outer wall of the large room. At site S, the bench was formed by trimming away the bedrock in the center of the room; at site T, the bench was built of field stones. A fireplace in the center of the site S large room suggests that the family lounged informally on the floor around the fire; on formal occasions, however, it is likely that guests sat shoulder to shoulder on the benches. The houses' third feature was a stone-paved platform built in the narrow room. At site S, the platform was constructed against the middle part of the outer wall. However, at site T, the platform was at the end of the room, blocking a doorway that had been used in the house's initial building phase. The function of these platforms is not known, but the discovery of two offering stands at site T suggests a cultic use in some form of family worship. The variations in houses within the overall village layout suggest a kind of social hierarchy within the settlement, with site S having economic preeminence and sites R and T having more religious significance.

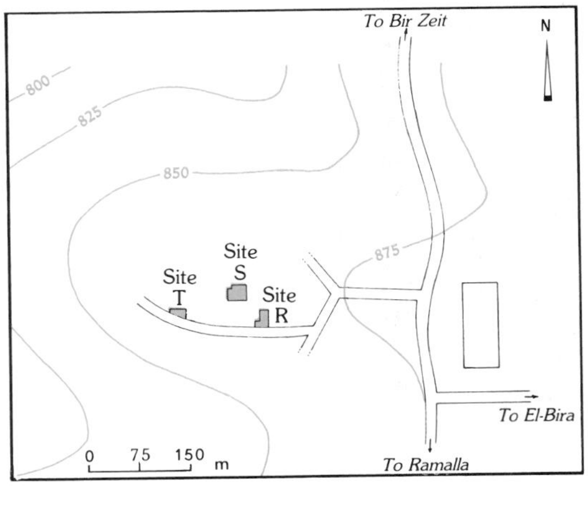

Khirbet Raddana: map of the site and excavation areas.

VILLAGE SUBSISTENCE. Khirbet Raddana was one of almost one hundred new settlements established in the hill country between Hebron and Shechem at the beginning of the Iron Age I. Situated on an unoccupied hilltop that had never before supported a permanent settlement, the villagers wrested a living from the arid hills by employing innovative dry-farming techniques. First, the newcomers conserved water for household use by digging cisterns in the limestone on which the houses were built. Then, the hillsides around the village were terraced on contours to conserve both water and soil for food production.

In order to build houses and terrace the hillsides, a "forest" covering the area had to be cleared. The forest, as in Joshua 17:14–18, probably consisted of scattered shrubs and thickets that yielded reluctantly to the settlers' bronze mattocks and axes. These slopes are very steep and required the construction of very narrow terraces. The terraces converted the hillsides into a staircase of cultivable areas. Numerous stone tools used in processing grain suggest that cereal foods were planted on the terraces, although the area was not broad enough for efficient cultivation.

Meat and dairy foods from the flocks of sheep and goats supplemented the agricultural food products. Bones from these animals were recovered from every house excavated, indicating that a good portion of subsistence was from the flocks that roamed in the region's open areas. However, the basic subsistence was agriculture, evident in the housing patterns and forms, the knowledge of cistern construction for water conservation, the art of terracing hillsides, and a primitive level of metalworking. In fact, the difficulties encountered in surviving on an agricultural base in the arid hill country suggests that the settlers must have fled from a more hospitable region, seeking a refuge and redoubt from more warlike peoples.

MATERIAL CULTURE. Among the initial finds during the 1969 season was a jar handle incised with a personal name. It was read by F. M. Cross, Jr., and D. N. Freedman as *'aḥil*[*ud*] or *'aḥil*[*ay*] or *'aḥl*[*ah*] and dated on the epi-

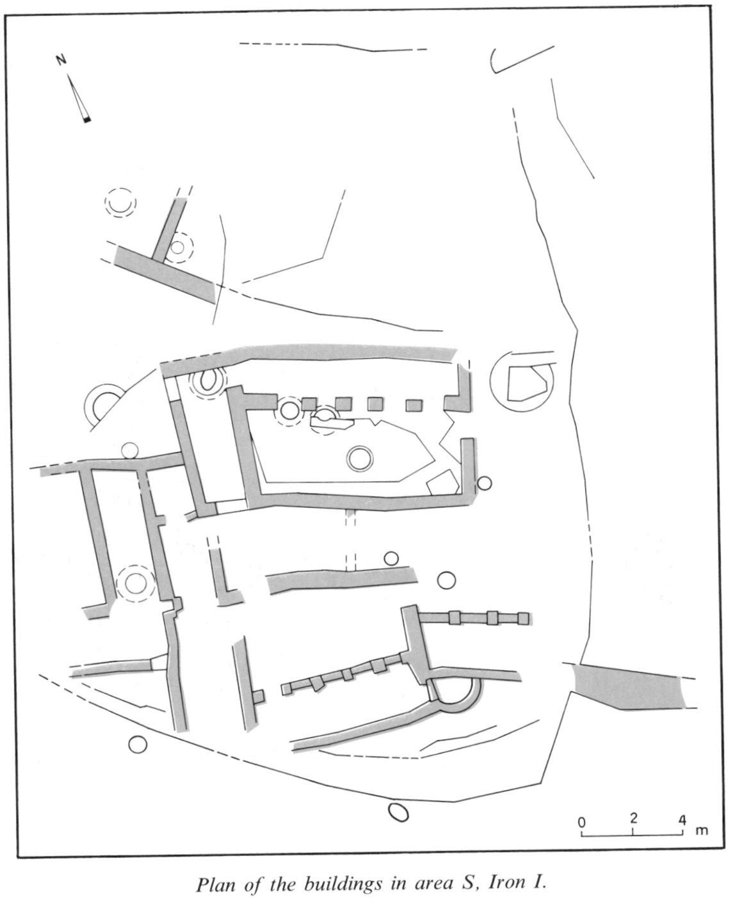

Plan of the buildings in area S, Iron I.

Inscribed jar handle from Khirbet Raddana.

graphical evidence to about 1200 BCE. Aharoni, however, reconstructed the name as *'aḥir*[*am*]—reading *resh* instead of *lamed* for the last character. He dated the inscription to about 1300 BCE, or before the founding of the village, in this writer's opinion. The archaeological context of the inscribed handle was the terminal phase of the village's occupation, a phase dated to about 1125 to 1050 BCE. In view of the context, the epigraphical analyses, based largely on unstratified materials, should probably yield to known stratigraphy in this instance and allow a date not earlier than about 1100 BCE.

Another object of significance almost equal to the inscription's was a multihandled krater, a unique kernos-type bowl with a conduitlike channel built into the upper wall of the vessel. The channel led to twin zoomorphic spouts in the shape of bulls' heads fixed to the inner wall and pointing toward the center of the bowl. This also was found in the destruction debris of the village's last phase. Among the evidence recovered of primitive metalworking were parts of crucibles with bronze slag encrusted on the inside walls, tuyeres of various sizes, and numerous bronze objects. The latter included daggers, leaves from coats-of-mail, needles, javelin points, plow points, a small ax-head, and spearheads.

J. A. Callaway, *IEJ* 19 (1969), 239; 20 (1970), 230–232; id., *BASOR* 201 (1971), 9–19 (with R. E. Cooley); id., *RB* 81 (1974), 91–94; id., *BAR* 9/5 (1983), 42–53; id., *The Answers Lie Below* (L. E. Toombs Fest.), Lanham, Md. 1984, 51–66; Y. Aharoni, *IEJ* 21 (1971), 130–135; F. M. Cross, Jr., and D. N. Freedman, *BASOR* 201 (1971), 19–22; F. M. Cross, Jr., *ASOR Symposia* (ed. F. M. Cross, Jr.), Cambridge, Mass. 1979, 97–111; S. Yeivin, *Museum Ha'aretz Bulletin* 1972, 79–96; R. E. Cooley, *Near East Archaeological Society Bulletin* n.s. 5 (1975), 5–20; *American Archeology in the Mideast*, 186; Weippert 1988, 398–400, 403f, 415; L. E. Stager, *BAR* 15/1 (1989), 51–64.

JAMES A. CALLAWAY

RADUM, ḤORVAT

IDENTIFICATION

Ḥorvat Radum is about 9 km (6 mi.) southwest of Arad, at the edge of a spur overlooking Naḥal Qina, at the point where the wadi turns southeast, some 2 km (1 mi.) south of Ḥorvat 'Uza (map reference 1659.0665). The site was surveyed in the mid-1950s by Y. Aharoni. In 1989 excavations were carried out at the site by I. Beit-Arieh and B. Cresson, on behalf of the Institute of Archaeology at Tel Aviv University and Baylor University, Texas.

EXCAVATIONS

After clearing an area of approximately 250 sq m, the excavators concluded that toward the end of the Iron Age this was the site of a small Judahite fort, probably an advance outpost for the fortress at 'Uza, as it controlled the road along the riverbed. The almost square fort (21 by 25 m) is enclosed by a 2-m-thick wall, preserved to a height of 2 m. Three of the walls were staggered, each consisting of two sections of equal length, one of which projected outward for 0.3 m. The gateway was in the eastern side; it included an opening in the fortress's wall protected by a rectangular structure (2.5 by 5.5 m) outside it, whose walls were about one meter thick. An opening in the structure's north-eastern corner created an indirect entrance to the interior of the fort. The width of both openings, originally about one meter, was reduced to approximately 0.6 m in the last phase of the fort's existence.

Within the courtyard, a network was exposed of rectangular rooms abutting all four walls of the fort. The northwestern room contained three *tabuns* (baking ovens). Next to the gate, against the eastern wall, was a platform (1.5 by 2 m) with three broad steps leading to its top. Another room near the gate contained three benches bearing traces of plaster.

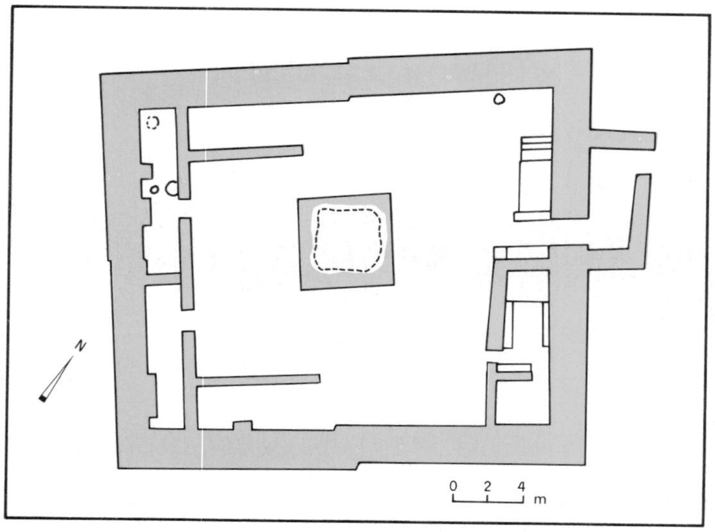

Ḥorvat Radum: plan of the fort.

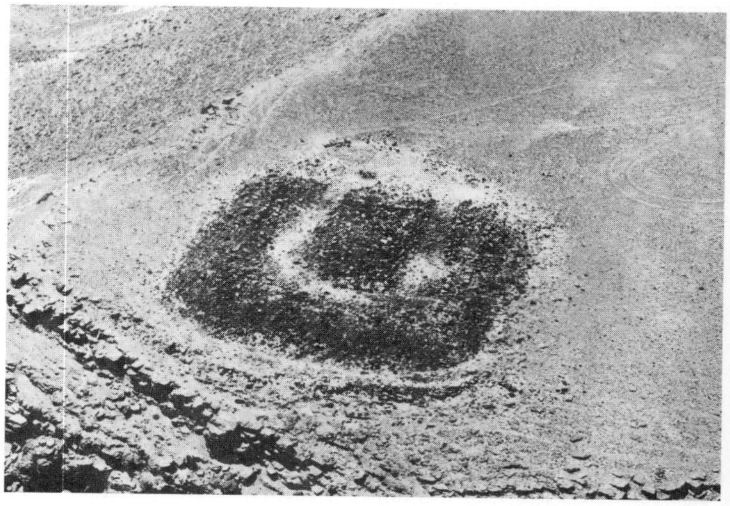

Aerial view of the site before excavation.

General view of the site.

A structure (c. 5 by 5 m) was uncovered in the center of the courtyard. Its nature and function are unclear, as the center of it had been plundered. The base of the structure, which is contemporary with the fort, had apparently been filled with stones and used as a tower. Outside the fort, near the northern wall, were two cisterns, now filled with silt.

A few sherds were found of pottery types characteristic of the end of the Iron Age II in Judah and of cooking pots of the Edomite type. Five Hebrew ostraca were found in various places in the fort.

ITZHAQ BEIT-ARIEH

ER-RAM

IDENTIFICATION

Er-Ram is the site of a Nabatean temple in Jordan, about 40 km (25 mi.) east of 'Aqaba (map reference 190.887). The ancient name of the place is preserved in the Arabic name Jebel er-Ram. In the Nabatean inscriptions (see below) uncovered in the ruins of the temple and in the small shrine of Allat, near the spring of 'Ein esh-Shellaleh at the foot of the mountain, the name of the place appears as "Iram."

EXPLORATION

The shrine of Allat was discovered by G. Horsfield in 1931. About a year later, the site was surveyed by R. Savignac, who found many Nabatean and Greek graffiti. During a survey of Jebel er-Ram in the same year (1932), the remains of a temple were discovered. In 1934, the site was excavated under the direction of Horsfield and Savignac on behalf of the École Biblique et Archéologique Française in Jerusalem and the Jordan Department of Antiquities. In 1959, excavations were undertaken by D. Kirkbride, on behalf of the British School of Archaeology in Jerusalem, in conjunction with the Jordan Department of Antiquities.

Nabatean inscription from er-Ram.

HISTORY

The history of the site is not recorded in any source and is known only from the epigraphic material found here. The dating is based on two Nabatean inscriptions found at the site, one in the ruins of the temple and the other at the spring of 'Ein esh-Shellaleh. The first contains a fragment of a date: "And this is written on the day/ . . . of Ab in the year 40 and . . .," from which one of two alternatives can be inferred: the inscription refers to the forty-first or forty-fifth regnal year of Aretas IV, the only Nabatean king to rule for more than forty years—so that the date of the inscription is 31 or 36 CE; or the date is given according to the era of the *Provincia Arabia*, which would make it the year 147 or 151 CE. The excavators found no mention of Aretas IV's surname (Philodemos) in the inscription and hence were more inclined to accept the second date. The other Nabatean inscription, found in the ruins of the shrine of Allat at 'Ein esh-Shellaleh, has been quite definitely assigned to the reign of Rabbel II (70–106 CE). Because the king's two wives are mentioned, it is assumed that the inscription belongs to the later years of his reign. A third inscription, carved on the base of an altar in the ruins of the temple, is in Latin. It appears to mention the name of Emperor Caracalla (211–217 CE), and belongs not to the temple itself, but to a later period.

It is difficult to accept the opinion of the excavators that the temple was built in the first half of the second century CE. All the Nabatean temples in Hauran (such as the temples at Seeia), in Transjordan (et-Tannur), and in the Negev (Oboda) were built on the same plan either toward the end of the reign of Obodas III or during the reign of Aretas IV, the great period of Nabatean prosperity. It seems, therefore, that the temple at er-Ram, which was erected near the main Nabatean caravan route from Arabia to Transjordan, was also built in the days of Aretas IV, and the date in the inscriptions found in the

Jebel er-Ram: general view of the hill and its environs.

Altar base with a Latin inscription mentioning Caracalla.

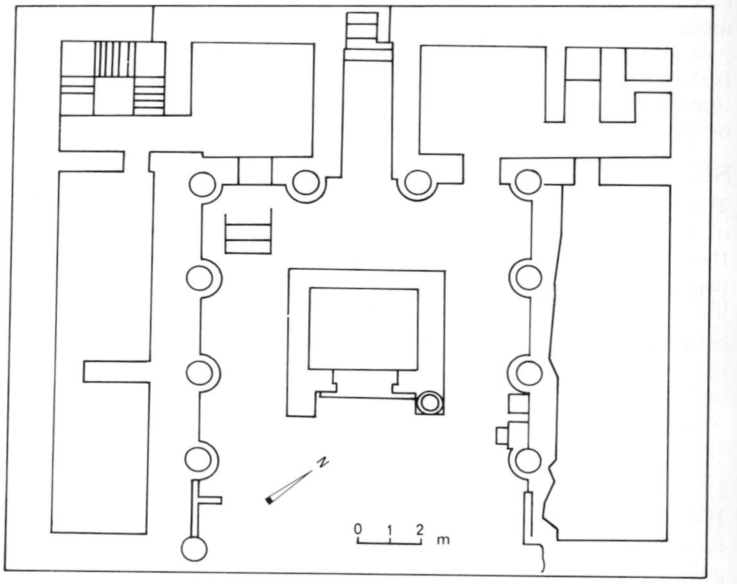

*Er-Ram: plan of the temple, **(above)** after Horsfield and Savignac; **(below)** after Kirkbride.*

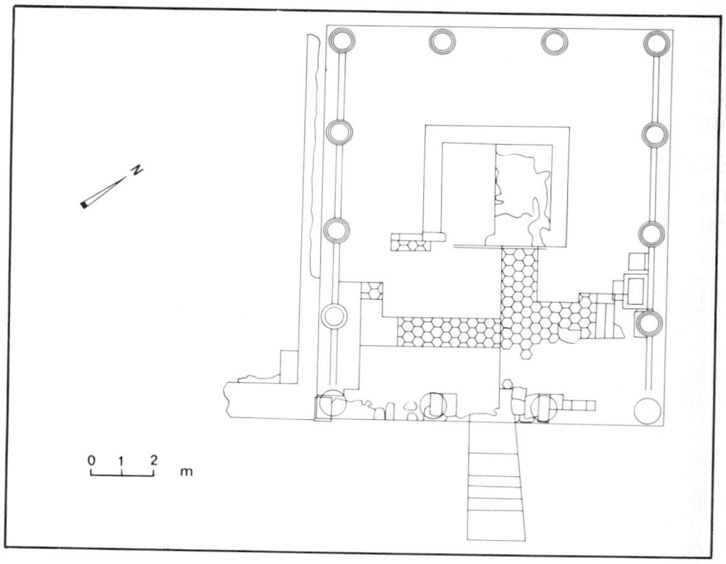

temple is to be interpreted accordingly. This view is corroborated by the typical Nabatean pottery found in the temple area, which at Oboda was assigned to the first half of the first century CE.

In the days of Rabbel II, the water from three or four of the eleven springs near 'Ein esh-Shellaleh was brought through canals to a large reservoir. Excavations at Nabatean Oboda have also yielded information about the water installations constructed in the reign of Rabbel II. A Nabatean military camp apparently was also built in that period near 'Ein esh-Shellaleh.

THE TEMPLE

According to Horsfield's interpretation, the main section of the temple consists of a hall (11 by 13 m) that is entered from the east. The hall contains engaged columns, five on the north and south sides and four on the west. Other rooms were built along its walls. In the center of the hall a small shrine (external measurements, 4.1 by 4.94 m) with stone-faced wooden beams was set in the foundations to protect the building from earthquakes. The floor of the shrine was elevated 0.6 m above the floor of the hall. The entrance to the temple, which also faced east, was flanked by antae with engaged pillars. The walls of the shrine were built of ashlars, and their typically Nabatean oblique dressing served to anchor the plaster. A molded frieze probably decorated the upper part of its walls.

The columns supporting the walls in the hall are well cut. On the drums of the two columns that are still standing in situ were two mason's marks: two Nabatean letters indicating the order of the columns in the hall. The columns were covered with fluted plaster painted red, blue, and yellow. The column bases were molded in torus-scotia-torus. The engaged columns in the hall are completely round and separated by coarsely built partitions, plastered and decorated with colored geometric designs. The inscriptions found on the temple walls record that it was dedicated to Allat, the great goddess of the people of er-Ram. All the artisans, masons, plasterers, and sculptors bear Nabatean names except Anianus, who was in charge of the work. By his name, he was a Syrian or an assimilated Nabatean.

D. Kirkbride disputed the architectonic interpretation advanced by Horsfield. She distinguished three stages in the temple's construction:

1. The first stage was a small temple standing on a podium, which was a tetrastyle, peripteral prostyle. It was probably built, in her opinion, in the reign of Rabbel II.
2. The partitions between the columns were built in the second stage, imparting to the temple a pseudoperipteral form typical of the Nabatean style; the nearly square temple thus stood inside the hall.
3. In the third stage, the walls of the hall were strengthened and additional

Engaged columns in the walls of the hall.

annexes were built around it. The interior plan of the temple underwent no modifications at this stage.

It was correctly pointed out by Kirkbride that this is the only example of a Nabatean peripteral temple erected before 106 CE. From the inscription at 'Ein esh-Shellaleh, she inferred that the temple was built in the reign of Rabbel II.

SUMMARY

The general plan of the temple at er-Ram does not differ essentially from that of the other Nabatean temples erected toward the close of the reign of Obodas III and especially those built in the days of Aretas IV. The plan's distinctive feature is a courtyard surrounded on three sides by porticoes, and a *theatron* like the temples at Seeia, where the shrine stands inside a hall. At er-Ram, a shrine was first erected within porticoes, without a theater, or else the porticoes took the place of the theater; in the second stage, partitions were built between the columns of the porticoes, thus converting them into a closed hall.

The temple at er-Ram is evidently to be assigned to the reign of Aretas IV, whereas the water installations, and perhaps also the military camp near 'Ein esh-Shellaleh, are to be assigned to the reign of Rabbel II.

R. Savignac, *RB* 41 (1932), 581–597; 42 (1933), 405–422; 43 (1934), 572–589; (with G. Horsfield) 44 (1935), 245–278; G. Ryckmans, ibid., 590–591; H. Grimme, ibid. 45 (1936), 90–95; A. S. Kirkbride (and G. L. Harding), *PEQ* 79 (1947), 7–26; D. Kirkbride, *RB* 67 (1960), 65–92; id., *ILN* (Aug. 13, 1960), 262–263; J. Strugnell, *BASOR* 156 (1959), 29–36; J. T. Milik and J. Teixidor, ibid. 163 (1961), 22–25; N. Glueck, *Deities and Dolphins*, New York 1965, passim; J. Patrich, *IEJ* 34 (1984), 39–46; J. A. Bellamy, *JAOS* 108 (1988), 369–378.
Prehistoric site: N. P. S. Price and A. N. Garrard, *ADAJ* 20 (1975), 91–93.

AVRAHAM NEGEV

RAMAT HA-NADIV

IDENTIFICATION

Ramat ha-Nadiv (Arabic, Khirbet Mansur el-'Aqeb) is located at the highest point of the Ramat ha-Nadiv ridge on southern Mount Carmel, 141 m above sea level (map reference 1441.2166). Although the site is not mentioned in early sources, it is possible to identify the ancient name of the ridge on which it is located. The Pilgrim of Bordeaux, who visited Palestine in 330 CE, mentions Mons Syna in his chronicles (*Itin. Burdig.* 586, 1), located 3 Roman miles from Caesarea, where a spring that cures women's barrenness exists. Several scholars have proposed identifying this spring with the Shuni springs south of Ramat ha-Nadiv, at Shuni, and Mons Syna with the ridge on which the site is situated.

EXPLORATION

The site was discovered by a survey expedition from the British Palestine Exploration Fund in 1873. The descriptions by the members of the expedition, C. R. Conder and H. H. Kitchener, were accompanied by a plan and section that included details of the vaulted building on the site (see below) when large portions of it were still standing. Shortly after their visit, the vaults were destroyed, and by the beginning of the twentieth century investigators no longer mentioned them. Three years of excavation at the site were begun in 1984 by Y. Hirschfeld, on behalf of the Institute of Archaeology at the Hebrew University of Jerusalem, during the course of which most of the remains of the site were uncovered.

EXCAVATION RESULTS

Two main strata were distinguished in the excavations: stratum I from the end of the Second Temple period, and stratum II from the Byzantine period. **STRATUM I.** The earlier stratum consists of a large estate with various agricultural installations adjoining it. The estate compound was L shaped, following the site's topography. Its maximum length from north

Aerial view of Ramat ha-Nadiv: the estate from the end of the Second Temple period and the Byzantine villa.

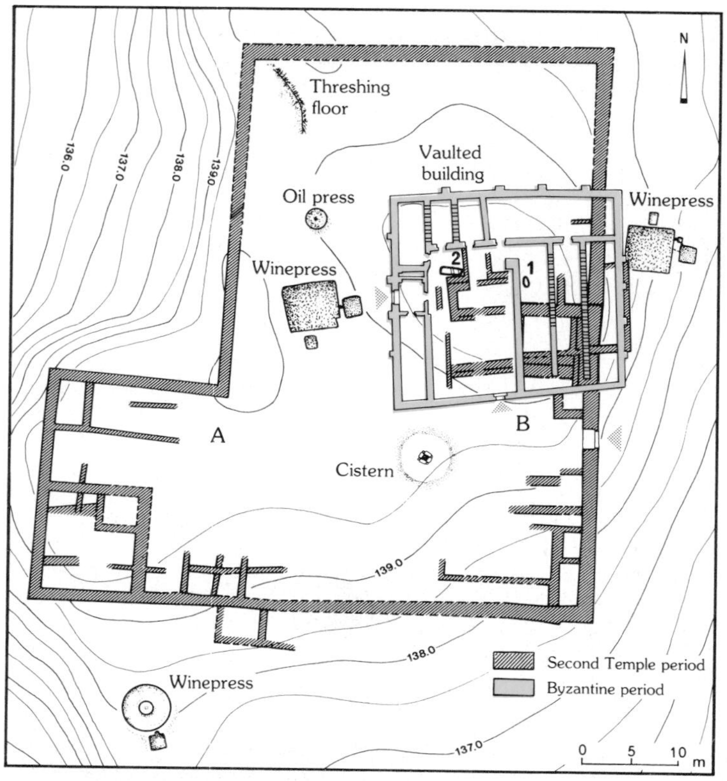

Ramat ha-Nadiv: general plan of the buildings.

Mikveh in the estate, end of the Second Temple period.

to south is 49.4 m and the maximum width from east to west is 58.5 m; the total area is about 0.7 a. The compound is surrounded by a wall (1.2 m thick), whose foundations are built of large, roughly dressed blocks of limestone. The entrance gate (1.5 m wide), is in the eastern side of the enclosure wall. A wide corridor led from the gate to the courtyard in the center of the compound. South of the corridor were storerooms, cattle sheds, and pens; to the north the foundations of a massive building were found, apparently a tower (external dimensions, 9.5 m long and 8 m wide). Other walls belonging to the estate's domestic wing were found nearby, to the north and west. A bathtub with a mikveh (ritual bath) next to it, hewn in bedrock, was found between the walls. The bathtub is oval (0.5 by 1.05 m and c. 0.3 m deep) and coated with grayish plaster. A small seat, for the convenience of the bathers, was carved at its northern end. West of the bathtub is a stepped mikveh (2.3 m long and 0.7 m wide); its maximum depth is 1.7 m, giving it a total capacity of at least 2 cu m. The mikveh was supplied with rainwater through a channel whose remains are preserved in the northeast corner. Its sides are coated with grayish plaster like that used in the other tub. Ritual baths of this type were common at Jewish sites from the end of the second century BCE until the destruction of the Second Temple. Accordingly, it can be assumed that the estate's inhabitants were Jews. Strict observance of the laws of ritual purity was of both halakhic and economic importance: immersion in the ritual bath attested that the wine and oil produced at the site were made solely by Jews and for the use of observant Jews.

Alongside the residential wing of the Second Temple period estate are two winepresses—one to its west and the other outside the building, adjoining the eastern enclosure wall. They have several features in common. In each, a collection vat was cut in the rock east of the treading floor; both are coated with smooth, white plaster; and both are equipped with an identical installation for pressing the grapes. To the north of the western winepress was a round stone pressbeam (diameter, c. 2 m) from an oil press.

The water supply at the site was based on the collection of rainwater. Two cisterns were found: a main cistern dug inside the estate area and another cut into the southern slope. Both were in use in the Byzantine period (see below); it can be assumed, however, that they were dug and first used in the Second Temple period.

The abandonment of the estate, which was the property of a Jewish family, was probably connected either with the First Jewish Revolt against Rome (66–70 CE) or the Bar-Kokhba Revolt (132–135)—but the latter seems the more likely. This conclusion is based on the pottery types uncovered in the Second Temple period stratum, which were in use until the first half of the second century CE. If so, the finds in the excavations attest to the destruction, whether direct or indirect, the Jewish population in the Caesarea region endured as a result of the revolts of the Jews against the Romans.

STRATUM II. Stratum II contains a Byzantine period villa erected in the beginning of the sixth century. It was in use (with some modifications) until the Arab conquest in the seventh century. The villa is square; its external dimensions are 22 by 24 m and its total area is 528 sq m. *Kurkar* stones from the walls of the earlier estate house were reused in the villa, whose walls (0.6–0.8 m thick), are preserved to a height of 2 m. Architectural fragments found in the excavations indicate that the villa originally had two stories. Fragments of tiles were found that had apparently been used to roof parts of the upper story; the various wings of the first story were roofed with vaults of stone and mortar. The vaults were supported by a row of four pilasters built along each of the three enclosure walls in the west, north, and east. Each pilaster was 0.8 m wide and projected 0.25 m from the walls.

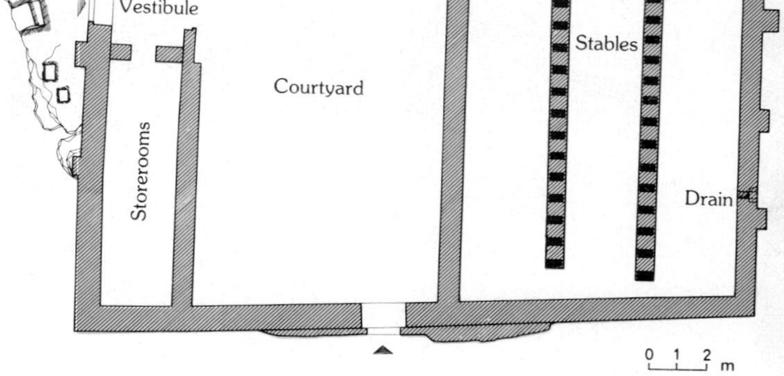

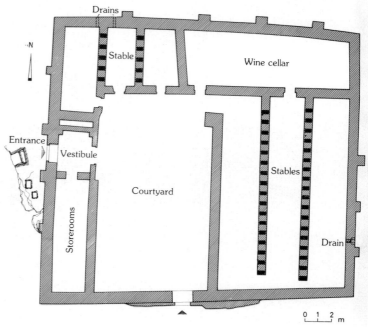

Plan of the Byzantine villa.

Fallen vault in the western wing of the Byzantine villa.

Byzantine winepress.

The Byzantine building complex had two entrances: a southern gate and a western gate. The southern gate was wider (1.4 m), with direct access to the courtyard. This gate was probably used for animals and agricultural equipment, while the narrow (1.2 m wide), western gate was used by people on foot. The gate opened onto a small vestibule (2.4 by 3 m) leading to the estate's inner courtyard (8.5 by 15.6 m). The courtyard was surrounded by wings on the west, north, and east. The western wing contained a very large, long hall (2.4 by 8.8 m) south of the vestibule through which it was entered. A room (2.5 by 6.5 m) north of the vestibule was connected to two rooms, almost identical in size (4.5 m long and 2.2–2.4 m wide), in the northern wing. Each room had a doorway (0.6 m wide) leading to the courtyard. The partition walls between the rooms had six internal windows, about 0.5 m wide. Drains leading to the outside were found on the floors of two of the rooms, suggesting that these rooms were used as stables (for one or two animals). The hall east of the two rooms is rectangular (4 by 12.8 m), with a doorway, (0.7 m wide), opening onto the courtyard. Another doorway in the southern long wall led to the adjoining eastern wing. The eastern wing is 15 m long from north to south and 9.6 m wide from west to east (internal dimensions). Its main entrance (1.4 m wide) opened onto the courtyard.

The spacious eastern wing is roofed by three parallel vaults supported by the inner long walls. Numerous windows were set into these walls, serving as a connection between the three chambers. These features are characteristic of Roman-Byzantine construction in the Hauran region, the Negev, and the Judean Hills. They are rare, however, on the Coastal Plain, and are the first examples of this construction in the region. The windows (c. 0.5 m wide and 0.6 m high), were set at a height of 0.6 m above floor level. According to Conder and Kitchener, another smaller window was set above each. There was room between the windows for wooden troughs with several holes for tying animals to them. These findings and the discovery outside the building of a large drain for conveying liquids indicate that the eastern wing probably was a stable, as well as a storage area for grain, equipment, and jars for the wine produced at the site.

The Byzantine villa was surrounded by gardens, as attested by the layers of red soil brought here for this purpose (which covered all the agricultural installations from the Second Temple period). Water was provided by cisterns. The main cistern, with a capacity of at least 1,200 cu m, is about 5 m south of the building. Another cistern was found on the southern slope, about 50 m southwest of the building. Nearby is a large winepress with a round

Ramat ha-Nadiv: pottery assemblage from the Byzantine villa.

treading floor (4.9 m in diameter) paved with a coarse white mosaic (16 tesserae per sq decimeter). A square depression (0.34 by 0.38 m) cut in the center of the treading floor was used in the pressing of grapes by means of a vertical wooden screw. Next to the treading floor is a collection vat (1.3 by 1.3 m and 1.3 m deep) whose bottom was paved with a coarse white mosaic and with *kurkar* stones; its sides are coated with reddish Byzantine water-resistant plaster.

A few changes were made in the Byzantine villa in its later phase. In the early sixth century, the southern parts of the original structure were damaged and long sections of its walls were rebuilt in a slipshod manner. Dwelling units were built in the inner courtyard, leaving a narrow corridor (3 m wide) that led to the entrance of the eastern wing. The original courtyard was then replaced by a new one south of the building. These changes were probably made to accommodate the needs of an expanding family.

The Byzantine villa was abandoned soon after the Arab conquest in 638. Because there were no signs of violent destruction or fire, it appears that the inhabitants left, in no special haste. After the abandonment, the villa's ruins were used as a temporary shelter; its inhabitants did not build new structures but restored the old ones, including the stone vaults (which, as was noted above, were still standing at the end of the nineteenth century). Judging from the sherds from these later periods, it seems that settlement began here in the tenth century and continued intermittently until the Ottoman period. No signs of destruction were discerned between the different occupations, only abandonment and renewed settlement; the structure was abandoned for the last time in the first half of the nineteenth century.

Y. Hirschfeld and R. Birger, *IEJ* 36 (1986), 275–277; 41 (1991), 81–111; id., *ESI* 4 (1985) 95–97; 7–8 (1988–1989), 152–154; Y. Hirschfeld, ibid. 9 (1989–1990), 34–35; G. Avni, ibid. 7–8 (1988–1989), 53–54.

YIZHAR HIRSCHFELD, RIVKA BIRGER-CALDERON

RAMAT MAṬRED

IDENTIFICATION AND EXPLORATION

Ramat Maṭred (el-Maṭrada), situated about 7 km (4 mi.) southwest of Oboda in the Negev, contains a settlement from the Iron Age. The settlement was discovered in a survey that was part of a study of ancient agriculture in the Negev carried out on behalf of the Hebrew University of Jerusalem, under the direction of M. Evenari. Along the valleys where the soil is suitable for farming, some twenty-five houses were found dispersed over a distance of about 1.5 km (1 mi.), forming two clusters of seven to ten houses each. In addition to the houses and their courtyards, corrals, cisterns, and remains of terraces were found in the valleys. In one of the clusters (settlement 108), the plan was drawn of the adjoining cultivated area covering about 12.5 a. and enclosed by a fence.

EXCAVATIONS

In 1959, excavations were carried out at the site under the direction of Y. Aharoni. Three houses were unearthed, each comprising two or three rooms. In front of the houses were large courtyards with silos and paved areas used for household tasks. Although the walls are built simply and of local stone, the houses are similar in plan to other buildings from the Iron Age. Characteristic features of these houses are the stone pillars built in some of the walls and flanking the entrances. A burned layer on the floors of the rooms attests to the settlements's sudden and total destruction. All the pottery discovered belongs to approximately the tenth century BCE. Two types can be distinguished: wheel-made pottery common in the country in that period, some with a red-burnished slip; and coarse, handmade ware that was very poorly fired (Negbite pottery). The latter includes open cooking pots with flat bases, some with small lug handles. This type of pottery is known only from the Negev—it was probably made for the local population by nomadic potters who used the most primitive methods.

The systematic archaeological survey conducted at Ramat Maṭred and in the vicinity located twenty-seven sites from the Middle Bronze Age I, eighteen sites from the Iron Age (six of which belong to Ramat Maṭred), and five from the Nabatean and the Byzantine periods. Along Naḥal 'Avdat and Naḥal La'ana, east and south of Ramat Maṭred, a line of four Iron Age forts was discovered on the road between Oboda and Be'er Ḥafir. They belong to the network of strongholds along the route to Kadesh-Barnea, the biblical "way

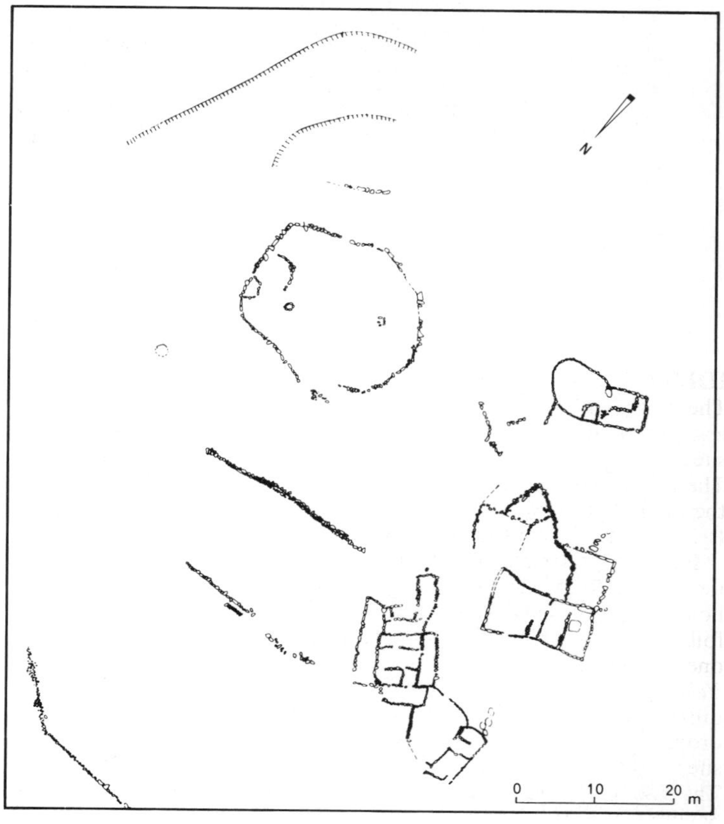

Plan of the Ramat Maṭred site, 10th century BCE.

Ramat Maṭred: plan of a four-room house at site 12, 10th century BCE.

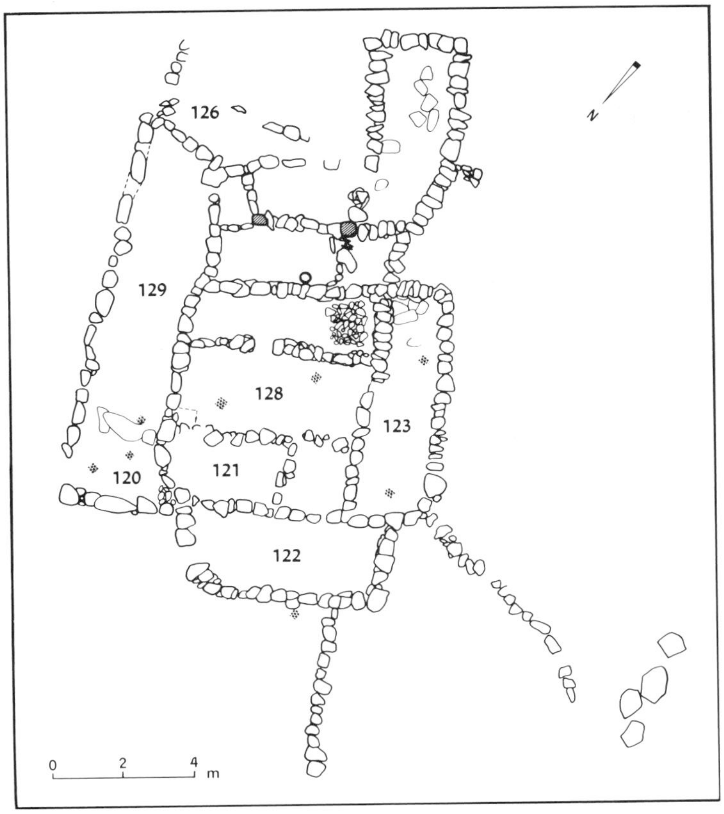

of Atharim" (Num. 21:1). Settlement 108 lies about 3 to 4 km from the nearest fort (142) on this line.

The agricultural settlement at Ramat Maṭred is to be dated to the tenth century BCE. It was apparently established near the Israelite caravan route in the period of the United Monarchy. After a brief period of prosperity, it was completely destroyed, at the end of the tenth century BCE, probably by the armies of the Egyptian pharaoh Shishak, who included in the list of the localities conquered and destroyed by him many settlements and forts in the Negev.

YOHANAN AHARONI

In 1979, as part of the Negev Emergency Survey sponsored by the Israel Department of Antiquities and Museums, excavations were carried out at Ramat Maṭred under the direction of R. Cohen. Another (fourth) building of the four-room house type, measuring 7 by 7 m, was uncovered in the Iron Age settlement. A burned layer was found on the floors of the rooms. The pottery here dates from the tenth century BCE and is similar to that found in the three buildings excavated by Aharoni. Noteworthy among the finds are pendants and a sword.

RUDOLF COHEN

Y. Aharoni et al., *IEJ* 10 (1960), 23–36, 97–111; T. Yizraeli, *PEQ* 99 (1967), 78–85; M. Hopf and G. Zechariae, *IEJ* 21 (1971), 60–64; R. Cohen, ibid. 30 (1980), 231–234; A. N. Goring-Morris and I. Gilead, ibid. 31 (1981), 132–133.

Handmade Negbite cooking pots, 10th century BCE.

RAMAT RAḤEL

IDENTIFICATION AND HISTORY

The mound of Ramat Raḥel is situated on a prominent hill (818 m above sea level) almost midway between the Old City of Jerusalem and Bethlehem. The site is occupied today by Kibbutz Ramat Raḥel (map reference 1708.1275). The ancient name of the site has not been preserved, but about 400 m west of the mound is the well of Bir Qadismu, which preserves the name of the Byzantine Kathisma (Κάθισμα) Church.

Excavations carried out on the mound have established that the first settlement was founded in the ninth or eighth century BCE, when a royal stronghold was constructed surrounded by gardens and farmhouses. This was followed by a fortress with a magnificent palace at its center, erected by one of the later kings of Judah. The many seal impressions stamped *Yehud* (Judah) found on the site indicate that it was an administrative center during the Persian period. At the end of the Second Temple period, an ordinary settlement containing a large number of workshops occupied the site, which shared the fate of Jerusalem when that city was destroyed (70 CE). The Tenth Roman Legion was later stationed here. According to Cyril of Scythopolis (*Vita Theodorii* 1), the Kathisma Church and monastery were built on the site in the middle of the fifth century CE. A poorly constructed Arab settlement here in the eighth century CE was the last before the modern period.

The excavations did not confirm B. Mazar's proposal to identify the site with Netophah since, according to the Bible, that city existed in the days of David (2 Sam. 23:28 and passim), and no remains of so early a period were uncovered there. The results did prompt Y. Aharoni to suggest that the site be identified with Beth-Haccherem, an assumption most scholars share. Beth-Haccherem is first mentioned in a roster of Judean cities in the Bethlehem district that cannot be earlier than the ninth century BCE (addition of the Septuagint to Jos. 15:59a, Καρεμ). In the time of Jeremiah, fire signals to warn Jerusalem were sent up from Beth-Haccherem (Jer. 6:1). In the days of Nehemiah, Beth-Haccherem was a district center (Neh. 3:14). From the Mishnah (*Mid.* 3, 4) and from the Judean Desert scrolls (Genesis Apocryphon XXII, 14; Copper Scroll X, 5), it is learned that Beth-Haccherem and the Valley of Beth-Haccherem were very close to Jerusalem. All these sources are consistent with the conclusions arrived at in the excavations. It can be assumed that the ancient royal citadel was built on the site of the king's vineyards: hence the name Beth-Haccherem ("house of the vineyard"). The later citadel and the palace, which are described in Jeremiah (22:13–19), were

Inner casemate wall.

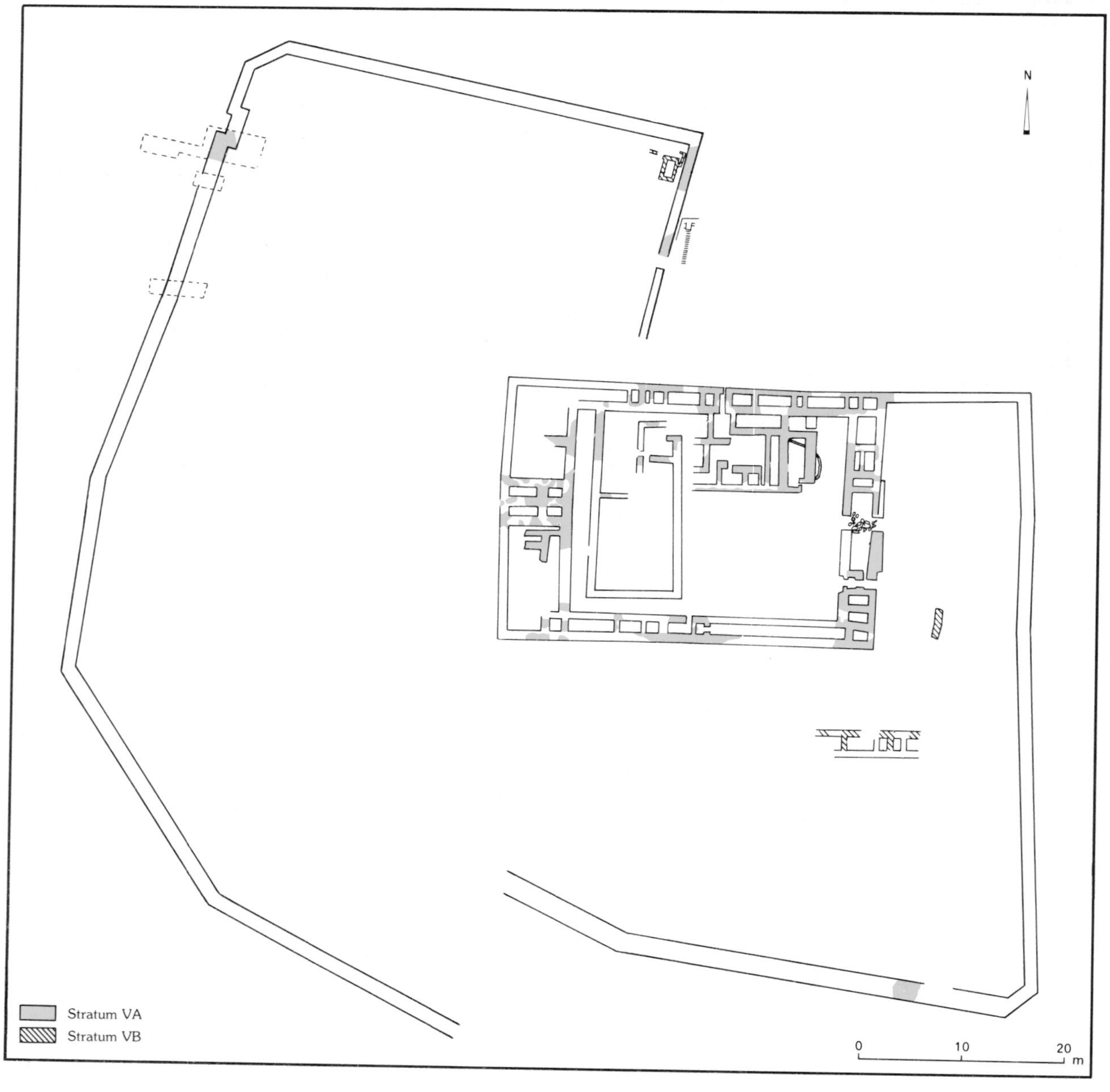

Ramat Raḥel: general plan of the Iron Age remains.

Jar handle stamped "lamelekh Hebron" with the two-winged symbol and next to it another stamp, "(belonging) to Nera (son of) Shebna."

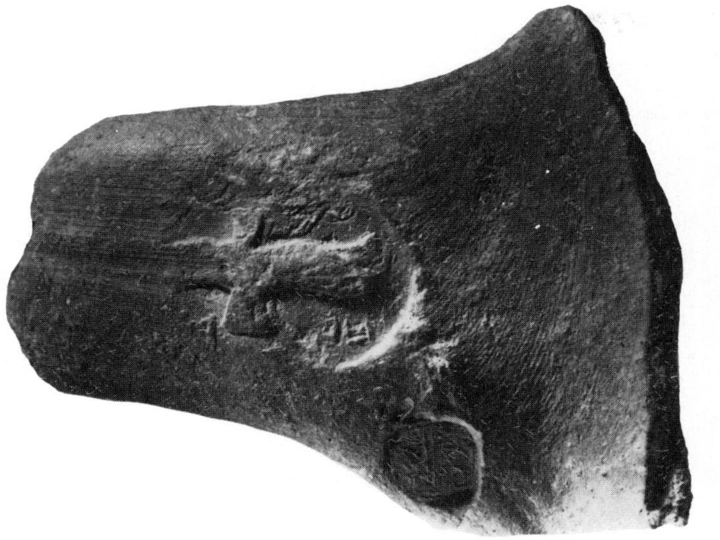

probably built by Jehoiakim, son of Josiah (608–597 BCE). The window balustrades found in the excavations (see below, stratum VA) are apparently those mentioned by Jeremiah 22. Y. Yadin suggested identifying the site with the house Athaliah built for the god Ba'al in Jerusalem (2 Kg. 11:18). The church and the monastery that were built on the site in the Byzantine period were called by the name of Kathisma, "seat," following a Christian tradition, reported in the proto-Evangelion of James (17:2–3), according to which Mary, mother of Jesus, rested here on her way to Bethlehem.

EXCAVATIONS

In 1931, a burial cave dating from the end of the Second Temple period was discovered south of the mound. It was excavated by B. Mazar and M. Stekelis on behalf of the Palestine Exploration Society. Excavations on the mound itself were undertaken in the summer of 1954 under the direction of Y. Aharoni, on behalf of the Israel Department of Antiquities and the Israel Exploration Society. Five seasons of campaigns were conducted at the site. In 1959, the Hebrew University of Jerusalem in conjunction with the above-named institutions, sponsored the excavations; in the years 1960, 1961, and 1962 they were under the joint sponsorship of the three Israeli institutions and the University of Rome.

EXCAVATION RESULTS

After five seasons of excavations, the following main occupation levels were distinguished:

Stratum I	Early Arab period (seventh–eighth centuries CE)
Stratum IIA	Late Byzantine period (sixth–seventh centuries CE)
Stratum IIB	Middle Byzantine period (fifth–sixth centuries CE)
Stratum III	Late Roman and Early Byzantine periods (third–fourth centuries CE)
Stratum IVA	Herodian period (first century BCE–first century CE)
Stratum IVB	Persian-Hellenistic period (fifth–third centuries BCE)
Stratum VA	End of Iron Age (c. 608–597 [587?] BCE)
Stratum VB	Iron Age IIC (eighth–seventh centuries BCE)

STRATUM VB: THE EARLY CITADEL. Only a few remains were uncovered in stratum VB because it had been almost completely destroyed during construction work carried out by the builders of stratum VA. Near the southeast edge of the mound, the excavators uncovered a section of a casemate wall that probably belongs to this stratum. One of its walls, which has been preserved above floor level, is built of ashlar masonry, like the inner wall of the later casemate wall (see below, stratum VA). It is inferred from this that the early casemate wall also belonged to a royal citadel. On the mound's northern slope, the excavators discovered a quarry that supplied the building stones. It was covered by the wall of stratum VA. The early citadel was not large because fewer than 50 m north of the casemate wall there was an agricultural terrace that evidently had been planted with gardens or vineyards. At a distance of 100 m north of the casemate wall were the remains of a house, evidently a private dwelling that had been built at the foot of the royal citadel. It was already in ruins and filled with stones when the wall of stratum VA was erected. Two seal impressions were found in this house bearing the inscription "(belonging) to Shebna (the son of) Shaḥar." The same seal impression is known from Tell en-Naṣbeh and Lachish.

Most of the finds in this stratum came from the fill used to level the ground in constructing stratum VA. The pottery was from the eighth and seventh centuries BCE. One hundred forty-five jar handles with the royal (*lamelekh*) stamp were found, most of them of the two-winged type and some of the four-winged type. More than half came from the rubble fill of stratum VB; it appears that they belonged to this stratum and in all probability went out of use before its end. Seal impressions with names were also found, some identical with stamps discovered at other Judean mounds, such as Tell en-Naṣbeh, Beth-Shemesh, and Lachish. One handle bore two impressions side by side, one *lamelekh*/Hebron with the two-winged symbol and the other a private seal לנרא/שבנא "(belonging) to Nera (son of) Shebna." This was the first instance in which the impressions of royal and private seals were found stamped on the same handle. A Hebrew ostracon was also found bearing two names, חסדיו (Ḥasdiyahu) and אחיו (Aḥiyahu).

STRATUM VA. Near the end of the Iron Age, a new royal citadel arose on the site whose construction must have required a large measure of technical skill and enterprise. Not only were the fortress and its buildings constructed on a completely new plan, with an inner and outer citadel, but all the former buildings seem to have been razed and the terrain of the hill considerably changed.

The Outer Citadel. The outer citadel was surrounded by a massive wall (3–4 m thick), at least partly built with salients and recesses. Although only short sections of the outer wall were uncovered, it was possible to reconstruct its course by following the site's topography. The north and south walls of the outer citadel were approximately 165 m long; those running east and west were 186 m long, enclosing an area of about 5 a.

Near the northwest corner of the wall, a section built in the middle of the slope was uncovered, supporting a layer of artificial fill 2 to 3 m high. The ancient quarry in stratum VB (see above) was uncovered beneath this fill, which also contained sherds similar to those found in the other stratum VA fills and many royal seal impressions. This fill seems to have served to level the area of the outer citadel. The homogeneous composition of these fills indicates that the outer wall must have been built at the same time as the inner fortress. Several trial pits made in the area of the outer citadel failed to reveal any building remains from the Iron Age (except for the scanty remains of stratum VB). Thus, it appears that either the construction of the citadel was for the most part not completed, or its leveled areas were used mainly for mustering troops and chariotry.

The outer wall did not encircle the inner citadel on all sides. It made a right-angle turn and reached the inner citadel in the middle of its northern wall. This section of the outer wall was built of dressed stone laid in headers; one of the gates leading to the outer citadel was probably placed here. An additional gate may have stood in the south, because the terrain reveals a similar depression there in the contour of the slope. Two gates must then have led to the level area on the western side of the outer citadel, which was somewhat lower than the rest of the area. The inner citadel was reached by ascending to an upper terrace encircling the western, southern, and eastern inner walls.

The Inner Citadel. The inner citadel is not large (c. 75 by 50 m), but its excellent construction leaves no doubt that it was the royal palace. It is surrounded by a casemate wall similar in shape and size to other such walls from the Iron Age. In the north and south, its total thickness was 5.2 m: the outer wall (1.6 m), the inner wall (1.1 m), and the space between them (2.5 m). These dimensions apply to the foundations. In several of the sections the upper parts of the walls are not as wide. A well-preserved 50-m-long section of the northern wall displays an upper course laid in headers (c. 1.1 m long) for the depth of the wall. The rooms in the wall were for the most part unfilled and seem to have served mainly as storerooms. It was difficult to determine their original purpose in the northern wall, because most of them had been reused in stratum IVA. It is nevertheless clear that in their original form they were living quarters. A complete section is preserved in the middle of the southern wall, however, where the threshold of a doorway was found. The doorway led from the courtyard to one of the rooms in the wall. From it, narrower doorways, also provided with thresholds, opened onto rooms east of it. The walls and floors of these rooms were coated with a thick, smooth plaster—which suggests they were used as storerooms. Door sockets in the thresholds indicate that the doors were barred from without.

THE GATE. The gate was in the center of the eastern wall. The total thickness of the wall at this point was 7 m, and the outer wall near the gate was more than 2 m thick. The straight double gateway was closed by two doors in a line with two casemate walls. Above floor level, only the southern wall in the outer entrance was preserved. It is built of large, carefully fitted ashlars. The passage between the gate's two openings is paved with massive stone flags that bear signs of a great conflagration. This main gate may have been open only on

Pier of the inner fortress's gate, stratum VA.

festive occasions, such as for the king's passage, while a narrower gate farther to the south was for daily use.

The main gate led into a wide inner courtyard in the inner citadel's southeast quadrangle. The courtyard, uncovered beneath a heap of debris from the adjacent buildings, was paved with a layer of leveled and well-packed limestone.

THE CITADEL'S BUILDINGS. The citadel's buildings ran along the northern and western sides of the inner courtyard. The northern building, which abutted the casemate wall, apparently served storage and domestic needs. In its center was an open courtyard surrounded by rooms, including two long storerooms on the east. One of the northern rooms was a passageway to a postern in the casemate wall. It was an underground corridor, covered with long, dressed-stone blocks, three of which were found in situ. The passage's inner doorway, with its arched stone lintel, is well preserved. Only a narrow, low opening gives access, to the outside. The postern is opposite the outer gate, in the same section of the casemate wall that also serves as an outer wall. It thus led directly from the inner citadel to the outside. In the area of the outer gate an opening to a hewn tunnel was discovered. It may have been connected to the postern.

The main buildings were in the western part of the inner citadel. The construction of the later buildings damaged them greatly and it was impossible to determine their inner plan. The casemate wall's western section is about 14 m wide and evidently was part of the palace.

The few wall fragments preserved above floor level show that the finest building techniques were employed in constructing the buildings and walls. Excellent workmanship can be seen in the gate described above, and in the inner wall of the southern defenses. It was built of smooth ashlars laid in two headers and a stretcher. This wall closely resembles the inner wall at Samaria. On the floor of the inner courtyard three complete proto-Aeolic capitals were found as well as fragments of other capitals. Another complete capital was found reused in the crypt of a columbarium in stratum IVA. Altogether, at least six proto-Aeolic capitals decorated the gates of the citadel and the buildings. These were the first such capitals discovered in Judea. They resemble the capitals found at Samaria and the one found by N. Glueck at Medeibiyeh in Transjordan. A fragment of a smaller proto-Aeolic capital, decorated on both sides, was found on the slope of the mound.

Aside from the capitals, the excavators uncovered other fragments of decorative architectural elements: a stone carved with two triangles; several stones cut in a pyramidal shape which were found in the heap of debris near the northeastern corner of the citadel, probably used as crenellations on top of the city wall or the roofs; and window balustrades consisting of a row of colonnettes decorated with palmettes topped by capitals joined to one another in the proto-Aeolic style. During the Mazar and Stekelis excavations in the burial cave, a stone was found on the surface of the mound that bore, on both faces, a similar decoration of colonettes and linked capitals. A comparison with the motif of "the woman at the window"—common in Phoe-

Proto-Aeolic capital.

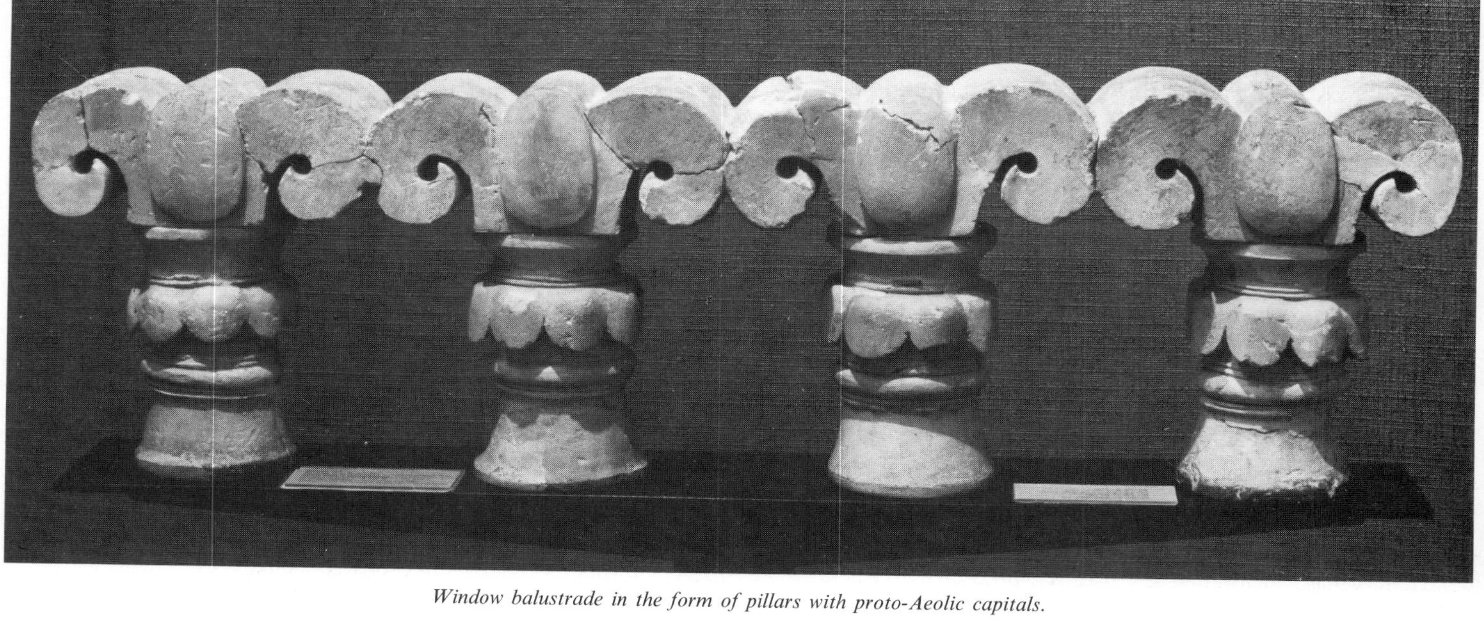

Window balustrade in the form of pillars with proto-Aeolic capitals.

Sherd decorated in the Assyrian style depicting a king seated on a throne.

nician ivory inlays—definitely established that these balustrades adorned the facade of the palace. The colonettes and capitals are limestone and bear remains of red paint. At the top are grooves for inserting a beam, which may have been wood. These windows may have belonged to the house of Jehoiakim described by Jeremiah: "and cuts out windows for it, paneling it with cedar, and painting it with vermilion" (Jer. 22:14). These fragments of window frames were also found in the heap of debris in the northwestern corner of the citadel. It can be assumed that they adorned the upper story of the western facade of the western building, to be seen by whoever ascended from the outer citadel.

The finds in the various rooms were meager because most of the rooms had been destroyed to below floor level when the Byzantine buildings were erected. By far the richest find is from the southern room in the northern building, where there was no Byzantine structure. In it a heap of about two hundred pieces of pottery, mostly burnished bowls, was found. Assyrian palace ware goblets were also found here, as well as sherds of a black and red painted jar depicting a king seated on a throne. Among the various seal impressions found in stratum VA is one bearing the inscription לאליקם נער יוכן (to Eliaqim, steward of Yochin [Jehoiachin]), which is identical with those found at Tell Beit Mirsim and Beth-Shemesh. W. F. Albright ascribed this stamp to an official of King Jehoiachin, the son of Jehoiakim. Stratum VA may thus be attributed to the time of the reign of this king and was probably destroyed when the First Temple was destroyed.

STRATUM IVB: PERSIAN-HELLENISTIC. The fragmentary state of the buildings from the Persian period made it difficult to determine their plan. However, the area of the stratum VA inner citadel was not rebuilt in stratum IVB. A number of strong walls from stratum IVB were uncovered farther south, but because no floors are preserved, their date could not be established. The main finds in stratum IVB were the many stamped jar handles from the Persian period. Most of the stamped handles were found in refuse pits dug into the rubble. Several of the stamps found were identical to stamps from other mounds in Judea: *Yehud* stamps with the letters יהד, יה, and יהד with an additional symbol (which previously was read העיר [the city]); ירשלמ (Jerusalem); an F-shaped symbol; representations of animals, mostly lions; and rosettes. Among the stamps first found at Ramat Raḥel are examples with יהוד written *in pleno*, יה/וד written in two lines, יהוד/חננה (*Yehud/ ḥnnh*) similar to the stamp יהוד/אוריו (*Yehud/'wryw*) found at Jericho, and מצה (*mẓh*) in reverse (mirror writing) and עזבק (בן) צדקיהו (*'zbq* [son of] *ẓdqyhw*). Of special interest are the stamps that bear the word פחוא (*pḥw'*) (if the reading of the third letter is correct), perhaps an Israelite-Aramaic form of the word הפחה (*hpḥh*, district governor), which was discovered recently on a Judean coin of the fourth century BCE. A number of seals are inscribed only יהוד/פחוא, but some also contain a proper name פחוא/ (Yeho'ezer) יהוד/יהועזר (four examples) and פחוא/ (Aḥzai) לאחזי (five examples). The names, previously unknown, may belong to two governors of the Persian province of Judea. F. M. Cross, Jr., on the other hand, suggested that the word be read פחרא (potter). The stamps' exact date cannot be determined because they were found in refuse pits and fills whose contents are mixed. The pottery found with them, however, belongs for the most part to the Late Persian to Early Hellenistic periods. It is likely that most of the stamps are from the fourth century BCE.

Among the 270 seal impressions found, twenty-three bear the stamps ירשלם; twenty-one יהד with an additional symbol, formerly read העיר; two bear the F symbol; sixty-nine יה, forty-nine יהד; twenty-eight יהוד, and ten יה/וד in two lines; fifteen are פחוא (or פחיא) stamps; forty-five bear images of animals and four of rosettes; and four are miscellaneous.

STRATUM IVA: HERODIAN SETTLEMENT. In the area of the stratum VA inner citadel, a number of structures were uncovered—particularly small rooms—as well as various kinds of workshops and cisterns. Vessels dating to the end of the Second Temple period were found on the floors. These installations were scattered throughout the area of the earlier citadel. Not only were ancient stones used in their construction, but here and there rooms from stratum VA had also been reconstructed, especially in the sector of the northern casemate wall, which was evidently partly preserved. It seems that an

Jar handle stamped "(belonging) to Aḥzai/governor(?)," Persian period.

Jar handle stamped "Yehud/Yeho'ezer/governor(?)," Persian period.

ordinary settlement of the poorer classes was established here for the first time in the site's history. The citadel would not have been in existence, having been destroyed and abandoned in the Hellenistic period. There are no further references to a district at Beth ha-Kerem in the Herodian period.

Most of the burial caves uncovered on the slopes of the hill, containing ossuaries, pottery, and glass from the end of the Second Temple period, probably belonged to this settlement. On an ossuary fragment was the inscription [שמעו]ן בר אלעזר (Shim'on bar El'azar, "Simon son of Eleazar"), and on the lid of an ossuary a Greek inscription that reads: "Of Marilla [and] of the small children." A columbarium cave was uncovered next to one of the burial caves. In its center lay an early proto-Aeolic capital being used as an altar. One of its volutes was hollowed out to form a bowl.

One of the burial caves, which had been blocked with its original closing stone, contained a number of lamps from the third century CE, in addition to plain ossuaries and glass vessels. The form of the tomb is typical of Jewish burial caves in the vicinity of Jerusalem. This may be taken as proof of the existence of a Jewish community in Jerusalem or its environs in this late period.

STRATUM III: BUILDINGS OF THE TENTH ROMAN LEGION. After the Second Temple was destroyed in 70 CE, the site was abandoned for about two hundred years. In the second half of the third century CE, buildings were erected here by the Tenth Roman Legion, which was stationed in Jerusalem from the reign of Titus to that of Diocletian. In the northern section of the stratum VA western buildings was a typical Roman villa, whose courtyard had a peristyle and was surrounded by rooms. North of this villa were temporary structures of which only earth-filled foundations remained. A number of burial caves on the rocky slope north of the Roman villa were converted into plastered cisterns during this period.

Above the stratum VA inner gate, a bathhouse was uncovered consisting of a row of rooms with mosaic floors, pools of various shapes, and a hypocaust, all connected by a network of clay pipes and stone channels. The columns of the hypocaust and the floor were made of tiles that bear the stamp of the Tenth Legion. All the Roman buildings continued to be used in the Byzantine period after undergoing repairs; consequently, none of the original floors are preserved.

STRATUM II: THE KATHISMA CHURCH AND MONASTERY. In the Byzantine period, in about the year 455 CE, a church and a monastery were erected on the site by a wealthy matron, the Lady Ikelia. These buildings are known from various sources as the Church of Kathisma. The church occupied the northeastern corner of the stratum VA inner citadel. It was built in the form of a basilica, with an additional row of columns on the western side, where it was adjoined by an annex that appears to have been the narthex. The mosaic floor, whose designs are geometric, is preserved only in the church's southern and western sections. East of the church was a long, paved vestibule and the monastery's rooms, arranged in rows around an additional vestibule. West of the church was a large pool; to its west were two large halls on the foundations of stratum VA's northern building. The bathhouse and the villa, as stated above, continued in use in this stratum, as well; south of them were many other rooms and buildings, including workshops and service rooms. Because two building layers were evident in many of the structures, this stratum was subdivided into stages IIB and IIA. Most of the vessels found on the floors belong to the later stage (IIA). An Arabic name from the end of the seventh century CE was incised on one of the jars, suggesting that the stratum existed until that time.

STRATUM I. Poorly built structures from the Early Arab period were uncovered in stratum I, and with it the history of the settlement on the site came to an end.

SUMMARY

The importance of the excavations conducted at Ramat Raḥel lies chiefly in strata VA–IVB—that is, in the particularly rich finds from the end of the Iron

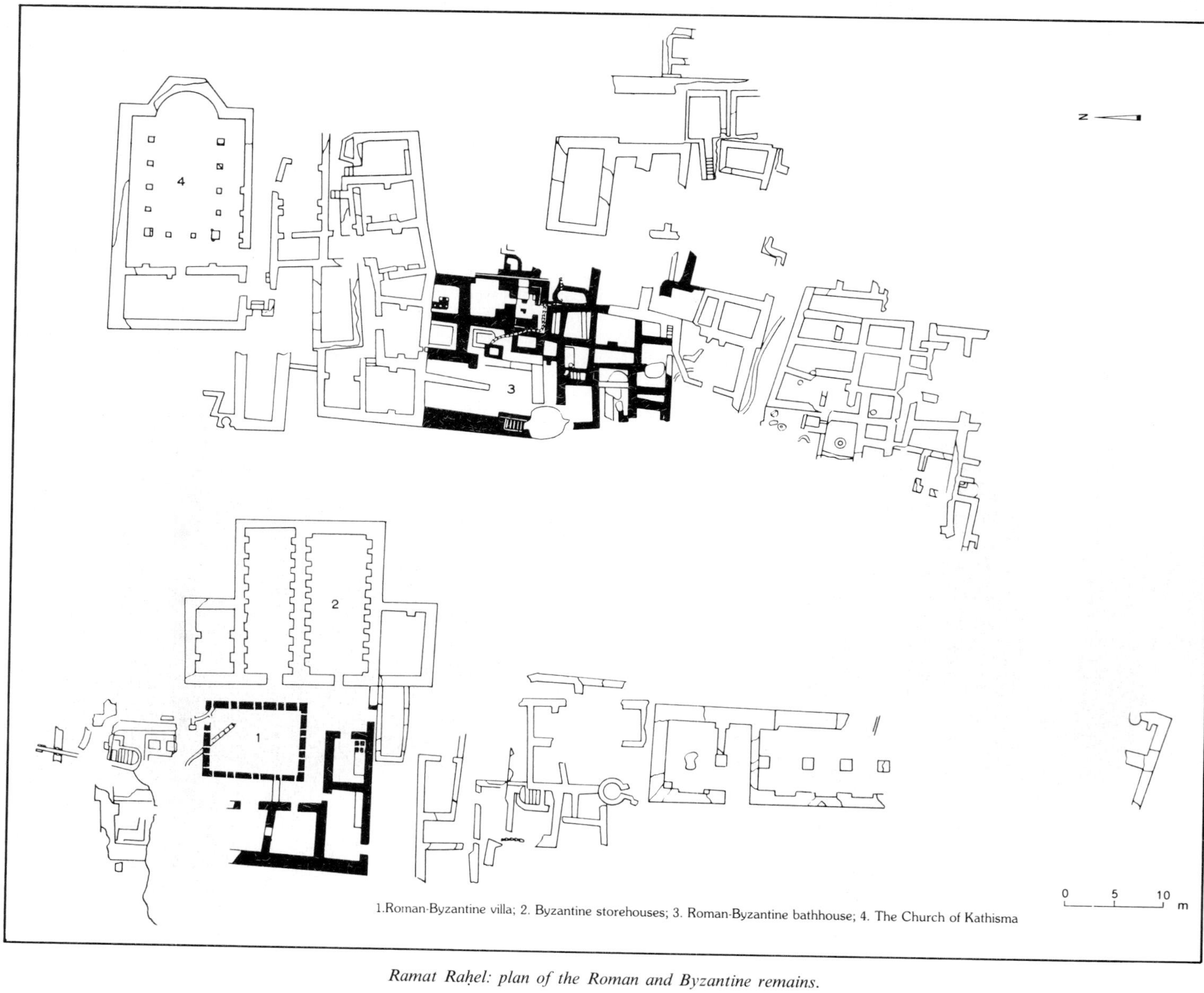

Ramat Raḥel: plan of the Roman and Byzantine remains.

Age and the Persian period. The palace of a Judean king was found here, and here, too, was one of the most complete royal citadels thus far unearthed. This palace was also one of the most instructive examples of Israelite-Phoenician architecture, and its discovery considerably enriched knowledge in this field. The many seal impressions from the Persian period are an important epigraphic addition to the knowledge of the postexilic period.

YOHANAN AHARONI

In 1984, excavations were carried out at Ramat Raḥel under the direction of G. Barkay, on behalf of the Institute of Archaeology at Tel Aviv University, the Israel Exploration Society, and the Institute of Holyland Studies on Mount Zion. The excavations were concentrated in two trenches cut in the northern and the western slopes of the mound. Under the earliest floors of the citadel pottery from the eighth century BCE was found, indicating the period in which, according to the excavator, the first Iron Age buildings were erected. In Barkay's opinion, there was a city here that included a palace built by Hezekiah. He suggests identifying the site with *Mmšt*, one of the four place names mentioned in the *lamelekh* stamps.

EDITORIAL BOARD

Main publications: Y. Aharoni et al., *Excavations at Ramat Rahel* 1: *Seasons 1959 and 1960*, Rome 1962; id., *Excavations at Ramat Rahel* 2: *Seasons 1961 and 1962*, Rome 1964.
Other studies: R. Von Riess, *ZDPV* 12 (1889), 19ff.; A.S. Schneider, *JPOS* 14 (1934), 230ff.; Y. Aharoni, *IEJ* 6 (1956), 102–111, 137–155; 9 (1959), 272–274; 10 (1960), 261–262; 11 (1961), 193–195; id., *RB* 67 (1960), 398–400; 69 (1962), 401–404; 70 (1963), 572–574; id., *BA* 24 (1961), 98–118; id., *BTS* 37 (1961), 4–10; id., *Archaeology* 18 (1965), 15–25; id., *Archaeological Discoveries in the Holy Land*, New York 1967, 77–88; id., *Archaeology and Old Testament Study* (ed. D. W. Thomas), Oxford 1967, 171–184; id., *Archaeology* (Israel Pocket Library), Jerusalem 1974, 179–182; L. Y. Rahmani and U. Ben-Horin, *IEJ* 6 (1956), 155–157; A. F. Rainey, *The Biblical World* (ed. C. F. Pfeiffer), Grand Rapids 1966, 473–477; F. M. Cross, Jr., *EI* 9 (1969), 20*–27*; E. Stern, *BASOR* 202 (1971), 6–16; Y. Shiloh, ibid. 222 (1976), 67–77; A. Lemaire, *Inscriptions Hebraïques* 1, *Les Ostraca*, Paris 1977, 257–258; S. Geva, *IEJ* 31 (1981), 186–189; Weippert 1988 (Ortsregister); E. Lipinski, *Transeuphratène* 1 (1989), 107–109.

RAMLA

IDENTIFICATION

According to scholars, the name Ramla derives from the Arabic word *raml*, meaning "sand," probably referring to the sand dunes on which the city was built, about 4 km (2.5 mi.) south of Lod and 15 km (9 mi.) southeast of Tel Aviv (map reference 138.148). Ramla was founded in the early eighth century (712–715 CE) by the Umayyad caliph Suleiman ibn 'Abd el-Malik (brother of Walid I), the former governor of Jund Filistin (the District of Palestine). It is the only city in Palestine founded by Arabs. Ramla was first made the capital of the newly created province Filistin, which included the regions of Judea and Samaria. According to accounts by Arab geographers, Ramla was built from the ruins of nearby Lod. This destruction was not only expressed in the preferred status granted to Ramla, but also in the reuse in its construction of building materials from the ruins of Lod. To promote its growth, part of the population of Lod was also moved to Ramla.

With the city's founding, many installations and buildings, such as cisterns, a drain channel, the House of Dyers, and the mosque, were erected. Most of the Umayyad city is now covered by later construction. Only in the Umayyad mosque, called the White Mosque (which was later renovated, probably in the Ayyubid period), were several remains of that period preserved. Its minaret, which was rebuilt in the Mameluke period, is the most prominent structure of medieval Ramla.

EXCAVATIONS AT THE WHITE MOSQUE

Excavations at the White Mosque were conducted by J. Kaplan in 1949 on behalf of the Ministry of Religious Affairs and the Israel Department of Antiquities and Museums. The excavations attempted to ascertain which buildings, both above ground and subterranean, belonged to the original mosque enclosure. It was revealed that the mosque enclosure was built in the form of a quadrangle (93 by 84 m), with its walls oriented to the cardinal points. It included the following structures: the mosque itself; two porticoes along the quadrangle's east and west walls; the north wall; the minaret; an unidentified building in the center of the area; and three subterranean cisterns.

The mosque was a broadhouse; the long wall (the *qibla*) faces Mecca, with the miḥrab in the center of the rear wall. The roofed area was divided into two parts by a central row of pillars. The facade was pierced by thirteen openings.

The White Mosque: general view of the remains.

Minaret of the White Mosque.

Ramla: plan and section of the White Mosque.

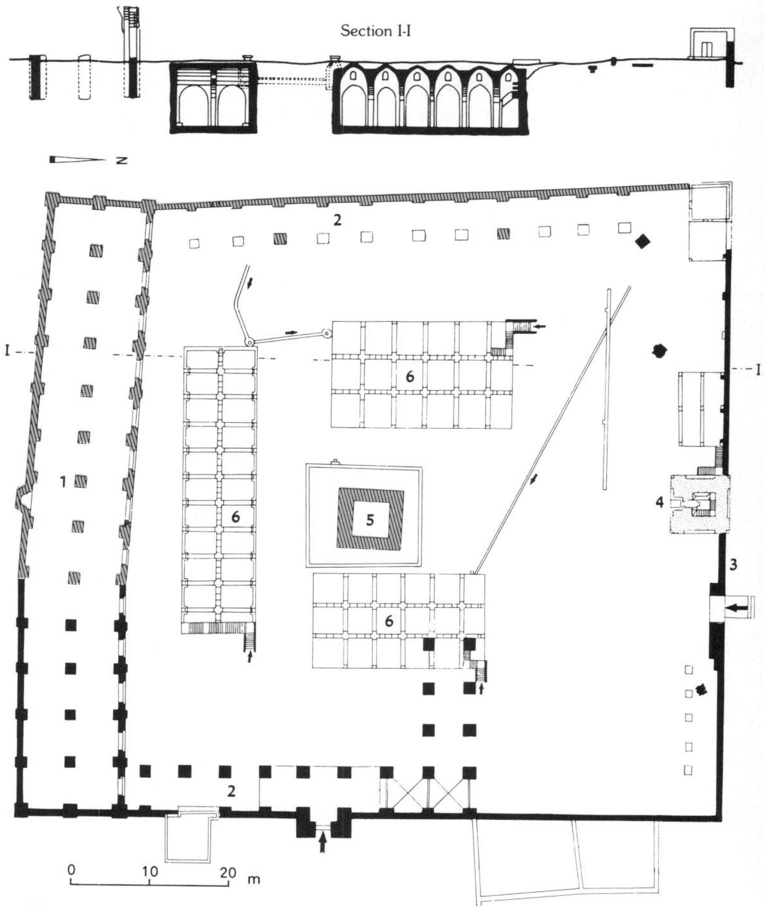

1. The Mosque; 2. Porticos; 3. The North wall; 4. Minaret; 5.Ablution basin(?); 6. Subterranean cisterns.

First stage of building — Second stage of building — Third stage of building

The roof was cross-vaulted and flat on the top. However, the roof apparently belongs to a later phase of renovation, carried out in the Ayyubid period (see above). Excavation disclosed that the right half of the mosque deviates some 6 degrees north of the traditional east–west orientation.

Of the west portico, only the foundations have survived. Of the east portico, a structure remains that includes the main entrance. The north wall of the enclosure is divided in two by the minaret, which stands on the foundations of the wall. In the eastern part of the wall is a pointed arch; a wide mosaic pavement extends along its western part. An Arabic inscription over the entrance to the minaret states that it was built by Sultan Muhammad ibn Qala'un in 1318 CE (although it is known that the minaret was repaired earlier, in the reign of Baybars).

There is an unidentified structure in the center of the enclosure, of which only the foundations remain. It appears to have been a pool for ablutions. The three subterranean cisterns were uniformly constructed of pillars topped by arches that supported barrel-shaped vaults. The southern and western cisterns were supplied by an underground water duct fed by a spring (probably from the vicinity of Gezer); the eastern cistern received the runoff rainwater collected from the mosaic floor near the north wall. Also found in the excavations were two inscriptions that mention repairs made to the mosque. The first inscription relates that Sultan Baybars built a dome over the minaret (see above) and added a door to the mosque. The second inscription states that, in

Building inscription of Muhammad ibn Qala'un, at the entrance to the minaret.

Kufic inscription from Ramla.

Pool of the Arches, Early Arab period.

1408 CE, Seif ed-Din Baighut ez-Zahiri had the walls of the southern cistern coated with plaster.

Both the writings of the Arab geographers and the evidence uncovered in the excavations indicate that the mosque's building complex was constructed in three main stages. The first stage is dated to the period of the Umayyads, when the enclosure was erected in its original form. Of the earliest buildings there remains only the left side of the mosque (oriented east–west), the east wall with the portico, the north wall (aside from the minaret), and the three subterranean cisterns. The construction of the right side of the mosque, the western enclosure wall, and the central ablutions building are attributed to the second phase, in the time of Saladin. The third phase included the minaret, the portico east of the minaret, and two halls attached to the eastern wall, outside the area of the mosque enclosure.

JACOB KAPLAN

The area outside the mosque's northern enclosure wall was excavated by M. Ben-Dov on behalf of the Israel Department of Antiquities and Museums in the winter of 1980. His preliminary report shows that six levels were distinguished. The uppermost level contains a tomb with a human skeleton, which is associated with the Ottoman period. Three earlier strata, all from the Mameluke period, were also uncovered. In the uppermost level was a row of rooms (each 3 by 3 m) containing sherds, under which the mosque's northern enclosure wall, built of ashlars, was exposed. The lowest Mameluke stratum represents the construction phase of the tower built by Sultan en-Nasir Muhammad ibn Qala'un in 1318. The fifth level yielded part of a structure, possibly a public building, according to the excavator, which was found about 6 m north of the enclosure; as no pottery was found, the date of this level cannot be determined. The sixth stratum was found at a depth of 3 m; it contained remains of walls (60 cm high), of typical Umayyad construction, as well as potsherds characteristic of the eighth century.

OTHER EXCAVATIONS

Of the various excavations carried out in different areas of Ramla, the major undertaking was conducted in October 1965 by M. Rosen-Ayalon and A. Eitan, on behalf of the Israel Department of Antiquities and Museums.

Mold for the neck of a jar and a clay neck made from it; a mold for oil lamps and lamps made from it, Early Arab period.

This excavation was concentrated in the southwestern part of the town; however, several trial soundings on a smaller scale were dug simultaneously in an effort to broaden the general picture.

A large number of finds—mainly pottery, but also glass, stone, and metal—was discovered immediately beneath the surface. The material was homogenous in character and could be ascribed to the eighth or beginning of the ninth century CE. Although this suggests a relatively brief period, four levels of settlement were distinguished, the lowest resting directly on virgin soil.

No traces of occupation were found slightly to the southwest of this area, but a trench to the north revealed similar finds. The area must therefore have been the southwestern limit of the town in the Umayyad period. Several trial trenches, dug around the White Mosque and farther to the east, revealed that the border of the early settlement in the Umayyad period continues eastward, where only early finds were uncovered; toward the center, however, later finds (thirteenth and fourteenth centuries) were found above the early Umayyad levels.

Together with the large amount of complete objects and sherds found were a number of installations—including water channels and ovens. There were also numerous wasters and molds, all pointing to the possibility of a potter's workshop having been located in the vicinity. Although only limited quan-

Pottery horse figurine, Early Arab period.

Pottery lantern.

Ramla: interior of the Great Mosque (originally the Church of St. John), 12th century.

tities of the pottery were glazed, the assemblage presents a wide range of shapes, techniques, and decoration, and is of exceptional value for understanding the history of Islamic pottery in Israel, especially its early period.

A salvage excavation was carried out north of this area by A. Druks for the Israel Department of Antiquities and Museums, followed by another undertaken by M. Broshi. In both cases, the pottery finds were very similar to those from the first excavation. This corroborates the assumption that Ramla was an important center of pottery manufacture in the early centuries of Muslim rule. Druks also found some Iron Age sherds.

An extraordinary discovery was made in 1973 in the southeastern part of

Mosaic floor, Early Arab period, 8th century: ***(right)*** *two carpets decorated with guilloches;* ***(below)*** *Kufic inscription within a depiction of a miḥrab.*

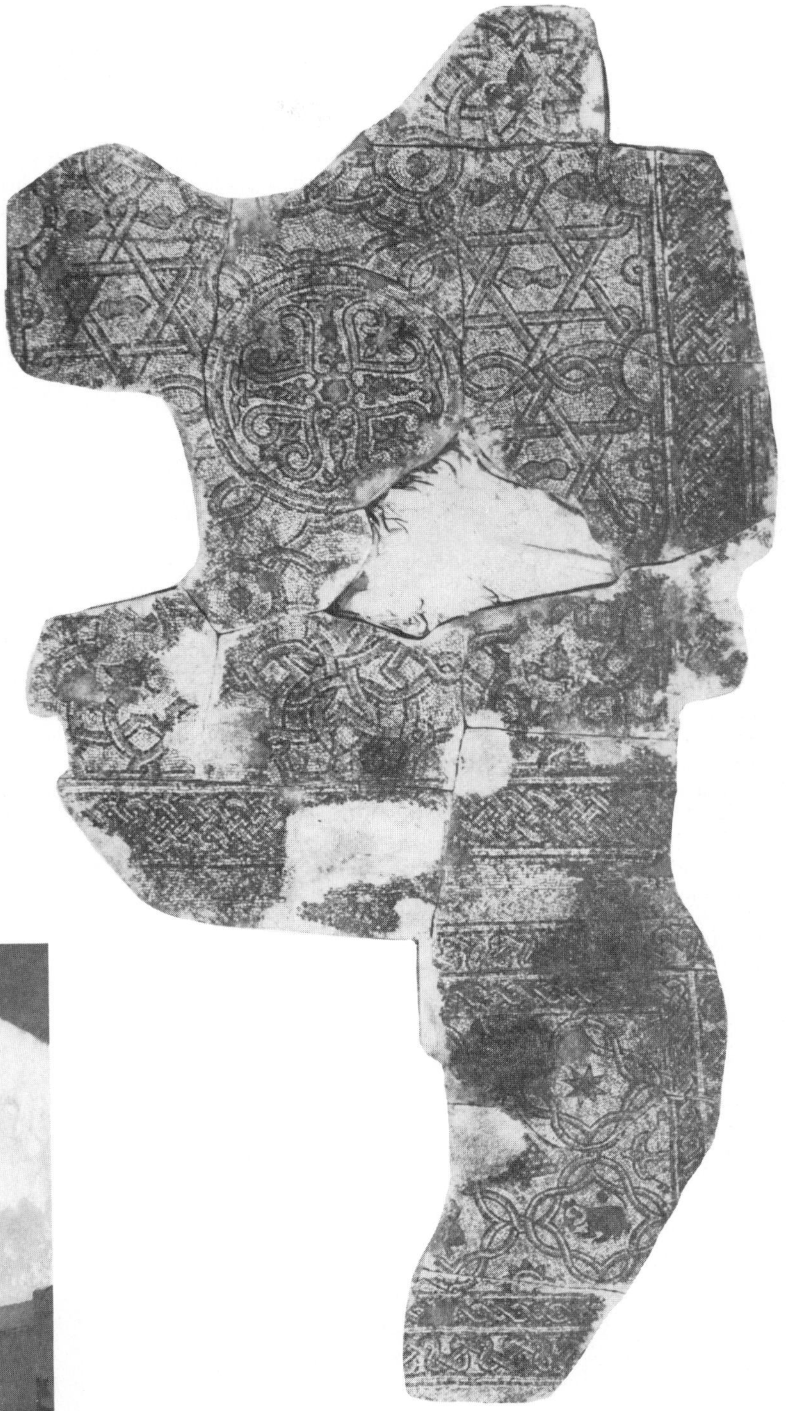

Entrance to the Great Mosque, 12th century.

the town. In the courtyard of one of the private houses in the old quarter, M. Broshi excavated a mosaic pavement, the first found in Ramla. The mosaic comprises three "carpets," two of them with various geometric patterns framing assorted floral, abstract, or geometric motifs. The one exception is the tiny unidentifiable animal in one of the medallions. These designs are thoroughly consistent with many pre-Islamic traditional mosaic decorations, although they do not resemble any known Byzantine pattern. The third mosaic explicitly stamps the whole ensemble with its Islamic character: it bears an inscription in early Kufic script, the only one known in Islamic floor mosaics. The inscription mainly consists of a Koranic quotation, inscribed within an arch supported by two columns. This mosaic find suggests that a kind of private chapel was located in one of Ramla's early Islamic buildings. It is also probably to be dated to the eighth century.

MYRIAM ROSEN-AYALON

Conder–Kitchener *SWP* 2, 271–273; C. Clermont-Ganneau, *ARP* 1, 25; J. Kaplan, *'Atiqot* 2 (1959), 106–115; L. A. Mayer, ibid., 116–117; M. Rosen-Ayalon and A. Eitan, *IEJ* 16 (1966), 148–150; id., *Ramla Excavations* (Israel Museum Cat. 66), Jerusalem 1969; M. Rosen-Ayalon, *IEJ* 26 (1976), 104–119.

REHOB

IDENTIFICATION

Tel Rehob (Tell es-Sarem, in Arabic) is a large mound some 7 km (4 mi.) south of Beth-Shean (map reference 197.207). In the early twentieth century, F. M. Abel identified the site with ancient Rehob, capital of the Beth-Shean Valley during Egyptian rule in Canaan. In the fourth century CE, Eusebius mentioned a settlement called Ro-ob (Ῥοώβ) located 4 Roman miles (6 km) from Beth-Shean (*Onom.* 142, 19). A town called Rihib is mentioned in medieval documents. The name is preserved in the tomb of Sheikh er-Rihab, at the foot of the mound. Surveys conducted here have shown that the mound was occupied from the beginning of the third to the first millennia. The many Roman and Byzantine remains found at the foot of the mound indicate that the settlement moved to this area in those periods.

EXCAVATIONS

In 1968, while preparing an area for agricultural purposes, members of Kibbutz 'En ha-Naẓiv unearthed architectural fragments and other ancient remains about 800 m northeast of the mound, in a place known as Khirbet Farwana (map reference 196.207). Among the remains was a marble chancel screen—carved on one side with a seven-branched menorah within a wreath and on the other with a rosette—and a clay coin box containing twenty-seven gold coins from the sixth and seventh centuries CE. Following these discoveries, five seasons of excavation (1974–1980) were carried out at the site under the direction of F. Vitto, on behalf of the Israel Department of Antiquities and Museums, during which an ancient synagogue was uncovered.

SYNAGOGUE. The synagogue is in the form of a basilica built facing Jerusalem on an almost perfect north–south axis. Three building phases were distinguished:

Phase 1. In phase 1, the building was a prayer hall (11 by 19 m). The walls (0.8 m thick), were built of large field stones with a core of small stones. The building had four entrances: three in the northern wall and a side one in the eastern wall. The hall was divided by two rows of columns into a nave and two aisles. The square column bases were of basalt and stood on a foundation of field stones laid under the floor. The bases probably carried limestone columns with Corinthian capitals, fragments of which were found in secondary use in the building's later phases. A fragment of a limestone lintel, carved with a lion's protome within a medallion, was also found in secondary use. Parts of a decorated mosaic floor were preserved in the aisles. Judging from the architectural remains, coins, and pottery, this synagogue is to be ascribed to the fourth century. It was destroyed in a violent conflagration, as attested by the traces of fire on the mosaic floor and from chunks of charcoal found at the site.

Phase 2. Following the fire, the main part of the building was rebuilt. The walls of this second synagogue were built on the foundations of the earlier one. Two rows of rectangular basalt columns were erected. The new columns were placed directly on the floor, without a base or a stylobate. At the southern end of the nave, facing Jerusalem, a bema was flanked by steps leading up to it. The floor was finely paved with a mosaic decorated with geometric designs. The walls and columns were coated with white plaster, many fragments of which were collected from the debris, enabling a reconstruction of some of the painted decorations and inscriptions. The walls were decorated largely with geometric designs: red stripes, triangles, and stylized flowers. The columns

Fragment of a stone lintel decorated with a medallion and a lion's protome, Late Roman period.

Rehob: general view of the synagogue.

Plan of the synagogue in phase 3.

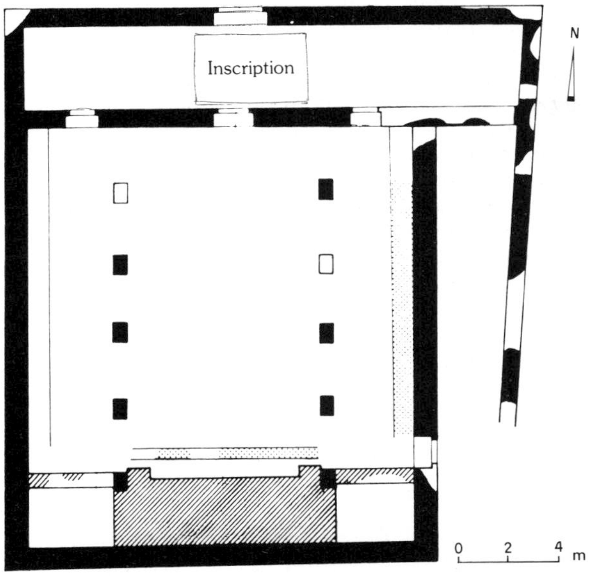

bore large inscriptions in red paint, some of them in a *tabula ansata* and a wreath. The inscriptions, in Hebrew and in Aramaic, included a variety of texts: benedictions, dedications, a list of the priestly courses, and a copy of a letter dealing with the laws of tithes and the Sabbatical year (see below). Judging from the style of the mosaics and the date of the coins and the pottery, the second phase can be attributed to the end of the fifth century.

Phase 3. The building underwent numerous changes between the fifth and seventh centuries, before it was destroyed and abandoned. The modifications were made to the existing structure in stages; they are all included here in the third phase.

The major innovation in phase 3 was the addition of the narthex on the northern side of the prayer hall. The narthex extended along the full width of the hall and 4 m beyond it on the east. Here a narrow corridor with a beaten earth floor was built along the length of the hall and up to its side entrance. The changes introduced in the prayer hall included the widening of the bema and the repositioning of the steps to lead up to it from the front. A low wall was built parallel to the bema, 0.75 m in front of it. Between the wall and the bema another fragment of the chancel screen discovered before the excavations was found, suggesting that the low wall served as the foundation for the chancel screen. Low benches were built along the walls of the aisles. All these additions were constructed over the mosaic floor from the synagogue's second phase. The columns were covered with a new layer of plaster and new inscriptions were made in red and black paint. In this phase the synagogue was lit by candelabra, suspended from the ceiling; they consisted of bronze chains and glass cups, several of which were found on the floor of the prayer hall.

The mosaic floor of the phase 2 synagogue was repaired in phase 3. The artist attempted to copy the original design in some places, although with little success, while in others completely new decorations were introduced. Shortly before the destruction of the synagogue, work was apparently begun on replacing the mosaic pavement in the area of the nave. However, it appears that the artisans had completed only the foundation bed and had started to lay the southern border of the hall when the building was destroyed. Piles of tesserae arranged according to color were uncovered in the area of the nave together with the source material. This indicates that the tesserae were prepared by the artisans inside the building.

INSCRIPTIONS. The narthex was also paved with mosaics in phase 3. The floor was divided into mosaic panels decorated with a simple black geometric design on a white background. Two of the panels bear inscriptions. One of them, a four-line dedicatory inscription, is at the east end of the narthex. The other was located between its outer entrance and the main doorway of the prayer hall. It was positioned in such a way that whoever entered the synagogue could read it and would have to walk on it before entering the prayer hall. It is the longest (2.75 by 4.3 m) inscription uncovered to date on an early mosaic floor. It comprises twenty-nine lines containing 1,807 letters and 365 words. The inscription, in Hebrew, is a halakhic text dealing with the laws of tithes and of the Sabbatical year that were binding on Jews in Palestine. Most of the text is known from Talmudic sources (J.T., *Dem.* 2–22c–d and *Shevi'it* 6–36c) and partly from Tannaitic sources (Tosefta *Shevi'it* 3 and *Sifre Deuteronomy* 51). This synagogue inscription, however, is the earliest extant version of any known rabbinic text.

Section of a mosaic in the eastern aisle of the phase 2 synagogue and the phase 3 repair.

The inscription has eight paragraphs. One of them contains the baraita concerning the "boundaries of Eretz Israel settled by those who returned from Babylon," which defines the regions where the agrictultural precepts were especially binding. Other paragraphs deal with localities where the injunctions were not binding. Regions such as Beth-Shean, Banias, and Caesarea, although situated within the boundaries of the country, were clearly pagan towns and were therefore exempt from fulfilling the commandments binding on the land of Eretz Israel. They are called "the permitted towns." Concerning these towns a detailed list is recorded of fruit that is *dem'ai*—about which a doubt exists whether a tithe is binding because the fruit may have been brought from Jewish localities on which the commandments were binding. Three areas are mentioned—Sussita (Hippos), Naveh, and Tyre—that were considered pagan and therefore outside the boundaries of Eretz Israel. However, because there were towns in these regions in which Jews had settled, they were therefore bound by the commandments. They are called "the forbidden towns."

Aside from minor variants in spelling and in the order of the localities and the fruit, the text of the inscription is similar to that found in the Talmudic and Mishnaic sources. However, the inscription contains two paragraphs that are not known from other sources. The first deals with Beth-Shean, a town only briefly mentioned in the Jerusalem Talmud; here, however, it appears at the top of the list, together with a detailed topographical description of its city gates and surroundings. The second paragraph includes a list of "permitted towns" in the region of Sebaste—some of them mentioned for the first time in such an early source.

Chancel screen decorated with a seven-branched menorah inside a wreath, Byzantine period.

Dedicatory inscription on one of the plastered columns; the inscription was covered with another layer of plaster.

The text of this inscription was reproduced, almost word for word, on a plastered column in the prayer hall (phase 2). Instead of the last paragraph concerning Sebaste, the column inscription ends in blessings to the inhabitants: "Peace upon all the people of the town . . ." It seems that this inscription is a copy of a letter sent to the local community in answer to questions about certain localities in their region—Beth-Shean, for example, which had a mixed population of Jews and pagans. This is indicated by the first word of the inscription (*shalom*, or "peace"), the emphasis on Beth-Shean (the region of the synagogue), and the blessings at the end. This subject was considered of such importance that it was decided at some stage (phase 3) to copy the inscription in the mosaic floor of the narthex and to add the paragraph on Sebaste (but omitting the blessings). The column inscription was then covered with a new coat of plaster.

SETTLEMENT. The synagogue was surrounded by a paved street. Houses containing utensils and tools for domestic use were uncovered on the other side of the street. This indicates that the synagogue was located at the center of a settlement, perhaps the same one that extended to the foot of Tel Rehob.

O. Yogev, *'Atiqot* 17 (1985), 90–113.
The synagogue (and halakhic inscription): D. Bahat, *IEJ* 23 (1973), 181–183; F. Vitto, *Archéologia* 110 (1977), 72; id., *IEJ* 30 (1980), 214–217; id., *ASR*, 90–94; id., *Temples and High Places in Biblical Times*, Jerusalem 1981, 164–167; id., *RB* 88 (1981), 584–586; id., *BAIAS* 1 (1982), 11–14; id., *Jahrbuch der Österreichischen Byzantinistik* 32 (1982), 361–370; Z. Safrai, *Immanuel* 8 (1978), 48–57; A. Demsky, *IEJ* 29 (1979), 182–193; R. Frankel, ibid., 194–196; Y. Liebermann, *Moria* 8/8–9 (1979), 59–68; J. Sussman, *ASR*, 146–153; D. Chen, *LA* 36 (1986), 239–240; G. Foerster, *Actes du XIe Congrés International d'Archéologie Chrétienne* (21–28 Sept. 1986), Rome 1989, 1809–1820.

FANNY VITTO

Rehob: halakhic inscription in the mosaic floor of the narthex, phase 3 of the synagogue.

REḤOVOT-IN-THE-NEGEV

IDENTIFICATION

Reḥovot-in-the-Negev (Khirbet Ruḥeibeh) is one of the large settlements established in the Negev in the Nabatean period that flourished in Byzantine times. The city was built on a flat hill overlooking the bed of Naḥal Shunra (Wadi Ruḥeibeh), a tributary of Naḥal Besor (map reference 108.048). A deep and abundant well was dug in the bed of the brook. Large expanses of the dunes of Ḥaluẓa (Elusa) and Shunra stretch to the north and south. In the valleys around the city, however, are cultivated loess areas. Reḥovot-in-the-Negev lies along the ancient route from Palestine to the Sinai desert via Elusa and Nessana.

Reḥovot-in-the-Negev has not been positively identified. E. Robinson had considered identifying it with Rehoboth, the well of Isaac (Gen. 26:22), on the basis of the similarity of its Arabic name, but in the end he rejected the identification. It was nonetheless accepted by many scholars and even influenced the choice of a Hebrew name for the place. This identification cannot be confirmed by the finds, nor is it likely on geographical grounds. It is possible that the name of the place is to be sought among the settlements mentioned in the Nessana papyrus no. 79, attributed to the beginning of the seventh century CE. This papyrus lists those bringing gifts to the monastery of Saint Sergius in Nessana and mentions their place of residence. Many of these

Reḥovot-in-the-Negev: aerial view, looking north.

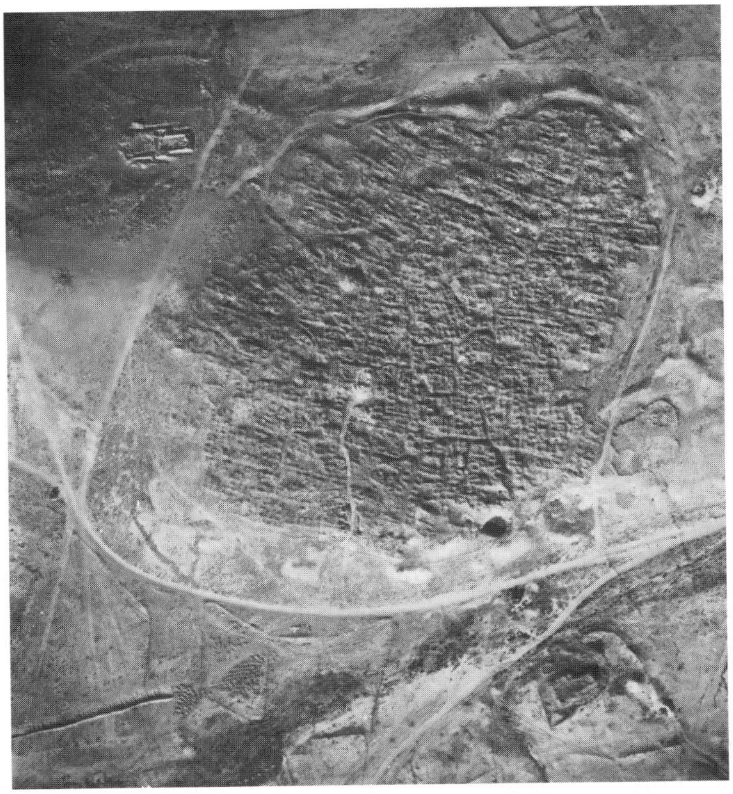

places are known settlements in the region; several others, however, are yet to be identified. It is not likely that the name of Reḥovot, which is located near Nessana, would be missing from this list. Noteworthy among the names are Βηρθείβα (Berteiba), a Hellenized form of the name Beer Tiv, or Beer Tova, and the settlement Βετομόλαχον (Bethomolchon), a Hellenized form of Beth Malchu. The latter settlement is probably to be identified with Reḥovot; like the Greek name that recalls the founder of the Nabatean city of 'Avdat—Oboda—here, too, the name of Malchu or Malichus, the Nabatean king who (according to this opinion) founded the city, is commemorated. This was apparently Malichus I (mid-first century BCE) and not Malichus II (mid-first century CE).

EXPLORATION

Reḥovot-in-the-Negev was first described by U. J. Seetzen in 1807, and in 1838 Robinson described it in detail. The place was subsequently mentioned in the accounts of several travelers, the most important of whom are E. H. Palmer (1870), A. Musil (1902), and E. Huntington (1909). On the eve of World War I, Reḥovot-in-the-Negev was surveyed by C. L. Woolley and T. E. Lawrence; during the war it was examined by T. Wiegand. A complete collection of tombstone inscriptions collected on the site by a number of explorers was published by A. Alt in 1921. The city was later mentioned briefly by various writers. From 1975 to 1979, four seasons of excavations were carried out at the site on behalf of the Institute of Archaeology of the Hebrew University of Jerusalem, under the direction of Y. Tsafrir (the first two seasons were co-directed by R. Rosenthal). In 1986, a fifth season was carried out in conjunction with the University of Maryland (College Park) under the direction of Tsafrir and K. G. Holum. In 1978 and 1990, two short seasons were conducted in the northern cemetery by the same excavators and I. Hershkowitz from Tel Aviv University, focusing on the physical-anthropological investigation of the site's population.

HISTORY

The earliest remains discovered so far on the site are sherds from the Roman period (mainly Eastern terra sigillata ware), and painted Nabataean ware characteristic of the first century BCE and the first century CE. These sherds attest to the establishment of the city by the Nabateans. The extent of the Nabatean settlement at Reḥovot-in-the-Negev is unknown, nor is it clear whether its inhabitants lived in stone buildings, tents, or huts. The settlement was probably originally a way station on a branch of the Nabatean "incense route" to Gaza. This road ran from Elusa (Ḥaluẓa), circumventing a large area of sand dunes, via Reḥovot to Nessana, and from there, via Wadi el-'Arish, to Rhinocorura (el-'Arish), in Egypt. It is possible that the 50-m-deep well found at the site and the reservoir in the south of the city were dug by the Nabateans.

After the annexation of the Nabatean areas to the *Provincia Arabia* (106 CE), the incense route became less important, paralleled by a rise in the prominence of Trajan's Route (*Via Traiana*) in Transjordan and the branch of it passing through Mampsis in the east. In this period (second to fourth centuries CE), the settlement at Reḥovot occupied a limited area. It enjoyed a period of prosperity beginning in the fourth century and reached its peak in the fifth and sixth centuries—the height of Byzantine Christian settlement in the Negev. The city at that time was included in the province of *Palaestina Tertia*. The inhabitants' main source of livelihood was agriculture, based on cultivating the loess in the beds of the valleys, which were irrigated by floodwater. Many agricultural terraces and fences for animals are found in the city's environs. Of special importance was the road leading to Egypt, which was used during this period mainly by the caravans of pilgrims making the ascent to Mount Sinai.

At the height of its expansion, the city covered an area of about 30 a., with an estimated population of four to five thousand. Its stone buildings were spacious, even though the building density was very high. The buildings were roofed with stone slabs resting on arches, and the courtyard of every house contained a cistern. Many of the lintels on the houses were decorated with geometrical and floral designs. A bathhouse built close to the well was apparently destroyed by the Turks at the beginning of the twentieth century; it was, however, described in detail by A. Musil.

Four churches were built on the site, two within the built-up area and two outside it, south of the well and to its north (area E). The city's population was apparently made up of the descendants of the Nabateans and of the ancient settlers of the Negev, intermingled with newcomers from northern Palestine and members of tribes who arrived here from Arabia and took up permanent residence.

The city began to decline after the Arab conquest of Palestine. Although no signs have been found of a violent destruction, it seems that political changes and the undermining of security led to the city's gradual abandonment. Most of its permanent inhabitants had probably left by 700 CE. Nomads took up temporary residence in the deserted buildings, leaving temporary installations, campfire ashes, an occasional coin, and a few Kufic inscriptions behind them.

EXCAVATION RESULTS

HOUSE IN THE SOUTHEASTERN PART OF THE CITY (AREA A). In 1976, a dwelling in the southeast of the city was partially excavated. Excavation did not reveal the building's full plan, but its stratigraphy is clear. This was a large and well constructed building containing a few rooms adjoining a courtyard. The rooms were roofed with arch-supported stone beams. In the fill underneath the floors Byzantine sherds were found, mixed with painted Nabatean sherds and Eastern terra sigillata ware. The large number of early potsherds indicates that the main ancient Nabatean settlement was located here, in the southeast of the city. The building itself was apparently built in the fifth century CE. Most of the room floors, paved with smoothed flagstones, were looted after the building was abandoned, either by the inhabitants of nearby houses or by the nomads who took up temporary residence here.

HOUSES IN THE SOUTHERN PART OF THE CITY (AREA B). In the 1979 and 1986 seasons, dwellings were partially excavated at the the southern end of the city, on the edge of the slope facing the brook. The plan of these houses (like that of the other houses in the city) was centered on a spacious inner courtyard surrounded by rooms on two to four sides. As the courtyard was the center of the house's activities, all the rooms opened onto it. The walls of the rooms are well preserved; a complete door with its lintel was found. In several rooms the collapsed arches of the roof were uncovered, as well as the roofing slabs. The houses had fine spacious entrances; some had locks. The stone walls are well built on their outer face; their inner face is of smaller, less well-fitting stones coated with white plaster. The outer walls of the houses facing the slope were connected to each other by walls, at least at the end of this period. The city may have had several different ap-

Area B: small bronze statuette of an ibex, Byzantine period.

proach roads that were blocked because of the worsening security situation, or to prevent infiltration by tribesmen from the surrounding area.

The finds include mainly local pottery. Painted pottery imported from Egypt, fragments of North African vessels, and glass and metal vessels were also uncovered.

Complete floors were found in several of the rooms, while flagstones had been plundered in others. One room contained thick layers of ashes and sherds separated by thin layers of sand and loess, which may shed light on the process of the building's abandonment. First, the flagstones were looted, and then it was occupied intermittently by squatters, who installed ovens and hearths, heaping the ashes along the walls. Between the periods of temporary settlement, thin layers of sand and loess were built up by the frequent sandstorms that strike the area. Finally, the arches and the roof collapsed. The latest ceramic finds consist of local Byzantine pottery that continued in use into the first decades following the Arab conquest. No typical eighth-century pottery was found, indicating that the site was abandoned no later than the early eighth century CE.

"STABLE" BUILDING (AREA C). Area C, excavated in the 1979 and 1986 seasons, is in the center of the city's built-up area, to the south of the central church. The square building (c. 30 by 30 m) found here consists of rooms on three or four sides of a large central courtyard with a cistern. Two rooms in the western wing have been completely cleared so far, as well as the northwestern wing, which served as a stable, and the main entrance to the house in the north. The plan of the stable building suggests that it was originally built as a wayside inn or caravanserai. Another possibility is that it served as a military barrack or as the residence of one of the city's wealthy inhabitants.

On the bedrock, under the courtyard's living surface, painted Nabatean sherds and Eastern terra sigillata ware were found, dating no later than the first century CE. The building itself was apparently built in the time when Reḥovot belonged to the *Provincia Arabia*, in the second or third century CE. At that time the building was located at the edge of the small settlement. Evidence for this date is provided, inter alia, by a Nabatean capital found in the courtyard and a stone with an inscription in Greek and Nabatean. One of the Greek words is μνήσθε ("remember"), followed by the name of the inscriber. One of the words deciphered from the Nabatean script is *šlm* ("peace"). The stable, with six troughs, is of the type known at Kurnub (Mampsis) from the Late Nabatean period and from the time of the *Provincia Arabia*. The main finds in area C are from the Byzantine period, at which time the stable ceased to serve its original function and was apparently turned into a storeroom or a dwelling. The rooms on the west also contained finds mainly from the Byzantine period, including pottery, glass, wood, bone, and metal artifacts. A room overlying the Byzantine stratum was exposed at the northeast corner of the courtyard. Decorated stones from the central church were reused in its construction. The room was built in the Early Arab period, after the church was abandoned. Aside from the water installations and the modest temporary installations, it is the only substantial structure whose foundation can be dated to this period. At the entrance to the building three clear levels of thresholds were uncovered, representing the building's three phases: the time in which Reḥovot was part of the *Provincia Arabia*, the Byzantine period, and the Early Arab period.

Area C: troughs in the "stable" building, Roman period.

North Church: southern entrance of the crypt; on the floor is a fallen chancel post from the bema.

CENTRAL CHURCH (AREA D). The central church (excavated in the 1979 and 1986 seasons) is located in the heart of the city's built-up area. This was probably the first church erected at the site, and it represents the penetration of Christianity into the city. Only the eastern part of the church has so far been cleared: the apse and the side rooms, as well as parts of the nave and aisles. The church had two building phases. The earlier phase, perhaps the late fourth century, yielded only a few walls on the southern side and the bases of two columns in the nave, under the floor of the later church. The plan and dimensions of the early church cannot be established, but it undoubtedly was smaller and more modest than the church built above it in the second phase. The construction date of the second church is known from the building inscription found on one of the marble flagstones in the nave. The part of the inscription preserved tells of the building of the church by the holy and most revered bishop (whose name is not preserved) and by a person of senior rank by the name of Stephanus, in the year 445 (or 449) of the *Provincia Arabia* (550–551 or 554–555 CE).

The length of the church has not yet been clarified, although it clearly exceeds 20 m. Its external width is 16.3 m. It is built on the slope descending to the east, and its eastern part was therefore built on a foundation rising above ground level. Flanking the apse were two square side rooms erected as a second story over the rooms of the foundation level. They were roofed with arches and stone slabs. The apse had a synthronon. The bema and the nave were paved with marble slabs, only a few of which are preserved, and the aisles were paved with smooth limestone slabs. The bema was elevated above the level of the nave. Depressions in the pavement indicate the location of the altar and of the legs of the ciborium (canopy) covering the altar. Marble columns and the bases and capitals of the ciborium were found in the church, as well as many decorated stones, parts of a marble chancel screen, bronze chandeliers with glass lamps, fragments of wood and metal vessels, and a leather bottle containing remains of dates. A chapel, as yet uncleared, adjoins the church's southern wall.

NORTH CHURCH (AREA E). The North Church (excavated in 1975 and 1986), together with its atrium, is one of the largest church complexes discovered in the Negev. The church was erected northwest of the city's main buildings. The excavators completely cleared the nave and partially cleared the atrium. The church had three apses built inside a rectangular structure (internal dimensions, 24.8 m [80 Byzantine feet] by 13.1 m). In the side apses the bases of tables were found that may have been used in the ritual, or they may have held icons or reliquaries. Most of the central bema had collapsed into the crypt built underneath it. The crypt (4.25 by 3.2 m) had a barrel-vaulted roof, the height of which reached 4.5 m above floor level. The raised apse of the crypt was directly under the altar. At the bottom of the apse was a rectangular alcove in which a reliquary was placed. The crypt was faced with marble. The descent to the crypt was through two stepped corridors, affording convenient access for groups of the devout who could enter and leave the crypt without interrupting the sacred service being conducted in the church. This arrangement, which is typical of pilgrim churches, attests that a relic of special importance was kept in the crypt, attracting large numbers of pilgrims.

Reḥovot-in-the-Negev: aerial view of the North Church, looking east.

North Church: decorated limestone chancel screen from the northern chapel.

A magnificent chapel was built on the northern side of the church. Abutting the church in the south was a stairwell-tower and an additional room containing a fresco with an inscription in ink on the plaster. The eastern side of the atrium was uncovered and found to contain a colonnade that apparently served as an outer narthex. The southern wing contained the entrance gate and a long hall alongside it. This may have been the refectory of the monastery, used by the monks who dwelt in the rooms surrounding the atrium. In the center of the atrium was a large cistern.

The North Church contained numerous Greek inscriptions—mostly funerary, but also dedicatory—on capitals and on stone objects. Most of the funerary inscriptions are dated and correspond to the period between 488 and 555 CE. The earlier date is important because it attests that the church was already in existence in the late fifth century. It also supports the attribution of triapsidal churches to this period. Other inscriptions incised on the paving stones of the atrium contained names written in Greek, including some of local Semitic or Arabic origin; others are of Hellenic-Western origin. The largest group, however, comprises Christian and biblical names. Several of the tombs in the church were examined. The interred bodies (three men and two women) were found to be of southern origin, perhaps of Nabatean descent.

Several Arabic inscriptions in Kufic script were found on the building and paving stones, mainly in the atrium. One of them, according to J. Naveh, mentions a person by the name of Hakim, an official (*maulla*) of ʿAbdallah, son of ʿAmr Ibn el-Aṣ, one of the military commanders during the Arab conquest. This is the only mention of this commander not in a literary text. The inscriptions were probably written by transient occupants of the church (whose permanent inhabitants had abandoned it), no later than the early eighth century.

North Church: funerary inscription of the priest Eliah son of Macedonius from the year 437 (542) from the northern aisle.

Many finds were discovered in the church, including engraved stones and pottery. Especially noteworthy are two small glass bowls (there were apparently originally four), about 6 cm in diameter that depict figures of saints. They may have originally decorated the arms of a cross, the frame of an icon, or a reliquary.

CEMETERY. The cemetery (excavated in 1975–1987 and 1990) extends over several hills north of the city. This is so far the only cemetery to have been located and excavated in the Byzantine Negev. Scores of tombstones from this cemetery, some of them dated to the fifth and sixth centuries CE, had been found at the end of the nineteenth and the beginning of the twentieth centuries. Others were uncovered during the excavations.

The graves were placed very close together. By the 1986 season, more than thirty graves were cleared. These were rectangular pits dug into the earth down to the level of the soft limestone. A narrow pit corresponding to the dimensions of the deceased was dug in the limestone. The body was interred without funerary offerings. The grave was marked by a stone structure, one course high, and a tombstone was placed above the deceased's head. The heads of all the deceased were positioned to the west, with their faces facing east. The tombstone was carved in an anthropomorphic shape with a flat front; a cross was engraved in place of the face, and beside or below it was the name of the deceased. An anthropological examination carried out by I. Hershkowitz of Tel Aviv University indicated that most of the deceased were of local Semitic origin.

Main publication: Y. Tsafrir et al., *Excavations at Rehovot-in-the-Negev* 1, *The Northern Church* (Qedem 25), Jerusalem 1988.

Other studies: Musil, *Arabia Petraea* 2, Edom, 78–83; Robinson, *Biblical Researches*, 196–197; E. H. Palmer, *The Desert of Exodus*, Cambridge 1871, 384; E. Huntington, *Palestine and its Transformation*, Boston 1911, 121; Woolley–Lawrence, *PEFA* 6, 114–116; T. Wiegand, *Sinai*, Berlin 1920, 58–59; E. K. Vogel, *EI* 12 (1975), 1*–17*; Y. Tsafrir (and R. Rosenthal), *Archéologia* 110 (1977), 71; id., *RB* 84 (1977), 422–427; id., *Temples and High Places in Biblical Times*, Jerusalem 1981, 162–163; id., *Recherches Archéologiques en Israël*, 200–205; id. (and K. G. Holum), *ESI* 6 (1987–1988), 89–91; id., *IEJ* 38 (1988), 117–127; id. (et al.), *Qedem* 25 (Reviews), *BAIAS* 8 (1988–1989), 65–68. — *AJA* 95 (1991), 186–188; id., *Christian Archaeology in the Holy Land: New Discoveries* (V. C. Corbo Fest.), Jerusalem 1990, 535–544; R. Cohen, *BASOR* 236 (1979), 61–79; A. Negev, *MdB* 19 (1981), 44; D. Chen, *LA* 35 (1985), 291–296.

YORAM TSAFRIR, KENNETH G. HOLUM

REPHAIM, NAḤAL

IDENTIFICATION

The site of Naḥal Rephaim (map reference 1666.1280) is on an ancient road running east–west along Naḥal Sorek from the Jerusalem Mountains to the Shephelah between Beth-Shemesh and Jerusalem. It is located on the southeastern slopes of a hill, Givʿat Masu'a, near the northern bank of Naḥal Rephaim, at 650–680 m above sea level. Naḥal Manaḥat (Wadi Malḥa) runs between Givʿat Masu'a and the Manaḥat spur, and bounds the site on the east. The site's modern name is derived from its location near the mouth of the Rephaim Valley.

The lower part of the site is on a horizon of the Moẓa formation. The *hawari*

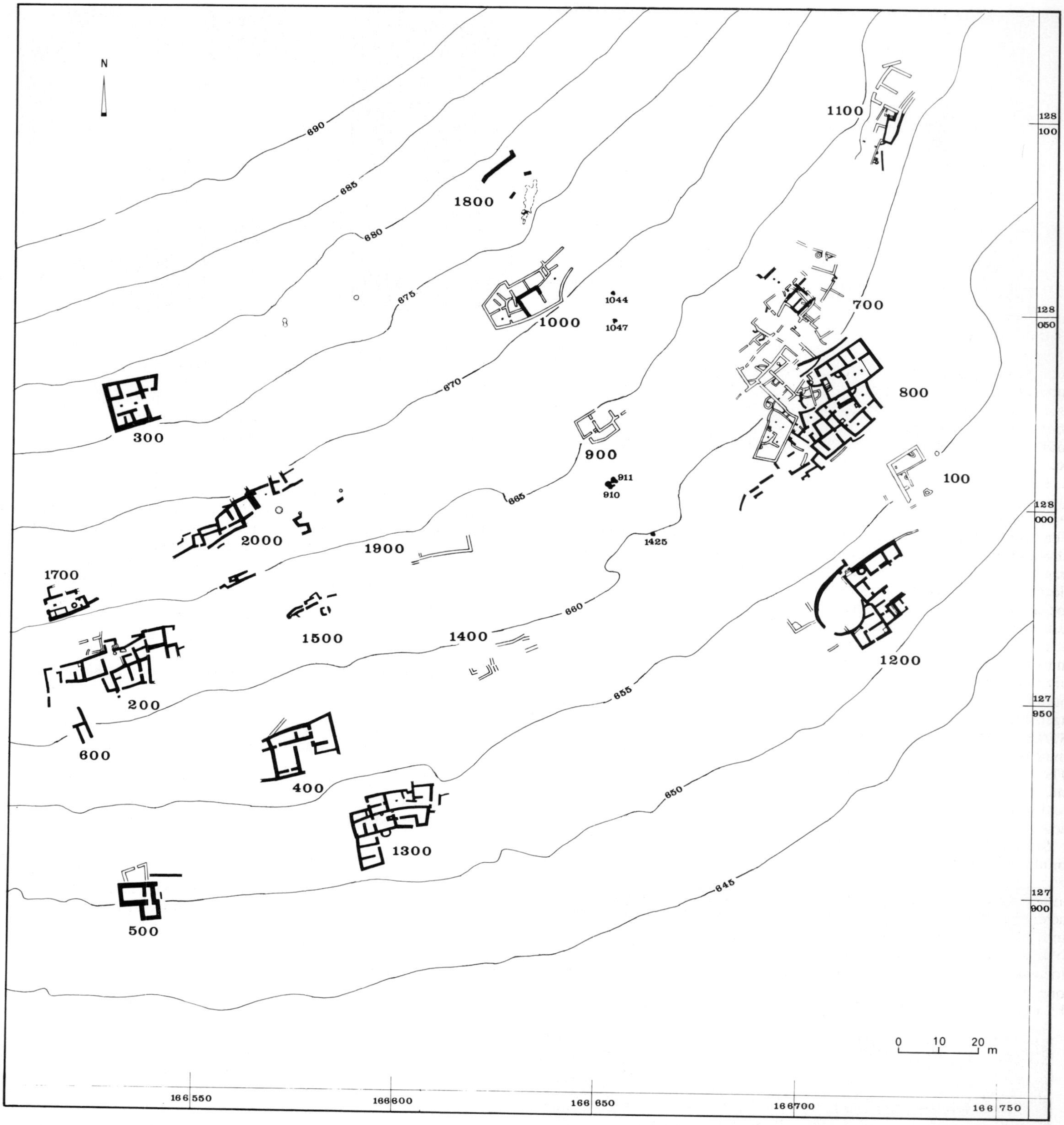

Naḥal Rephaim: general plan of the site.

rock here has been eroded to form a rolling landscape of broad terraces, which led to the choice of the site for settlement in antiquity. Layers of limestone and dolomite from the 'Aminadav formation lie above the Moẓa formation, forming narrower and steeper terraces. The settlement spread out over these terraces. Judging from the ceramic evidence, the site became an agricultural area in the Iron Age II and was cultivated until modern times. The only nearby water source is 'En Ya'el ('Ein Yalu). The spring lies opposite the site, about 300 m away, above the southern bank of Naḥal Rephaim. Until the spring was dammed by the builders of the Roman farm at its source, its waters flowed into Naḥal Rephaim, to the foot of the site.

In 1874, C. Clermont-Ganneau suggested that the biblical settlement of Manahath be identified with the village of Malḥa, about 1.2 km (1 mi.) to the northeast. This suggestion was based on the common change of the letter *n* to *l* in Arabic and on the proximity of Malḥa to Betar in the list in the Septuagint of the eleven cities on Judah's southern border (Jos. 15:59). This identification is generally accepted and now has archaeological support: the excavated evidence indicates that there was a settlement here in the Iron Age II.

The name Manahath can be interpreted as signifying *menuḥa*, "stillness, rest," as in Psalms 23:2, "He leadeth me beside the still waters," perhaps a reference to the spring at 'En Ya'el. In this context, it is possible to identify Manahath not just with the water source, but also with the nearby settlement in Naḥal Rephaim in the Early and Middle Bronze ages. In the wake of the changing geopolitical circumstances in the Iron Age II, the name Manahath was transferred to the settlement established on the top of the hill.

EXPLORATION

The site was discovered by G. Edelstein in 1979, in the course of an emergency survey in Jerusalem, undertaken on behalf of the Israel Department of Antiq-

Plan of stratum III structure in area 1000.

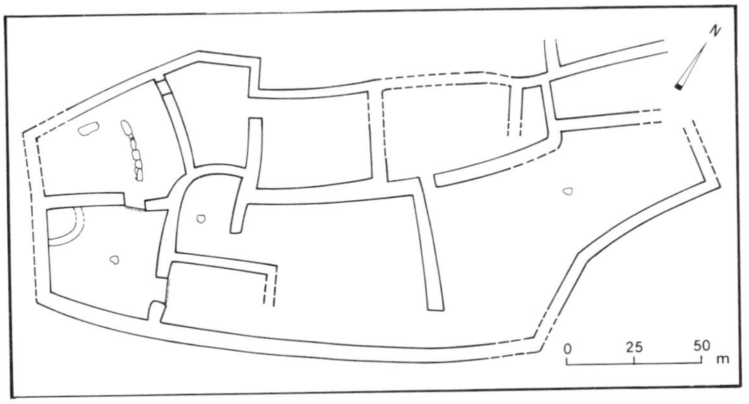

Pottery assemblage from stratum III.

uities and Museums and the Survey of Israel. In a trial excavation Edelstein conducted between 1980 and 1983, the remains of a structure from the Early Bronze Age IV (Middle Bronze Age I) were found. In 1984 and 1985, two excavation seasons were carried out, under the joint direction of G. Edelstein and E. Eisenberg, on the site's eastern side, to establish its size and chronology. At the same time, several caves were excavated in the cemetery found above the site, near the summit of Giv'at Masu'a. From 1987 to 1990, in the course of the work on the new Jerusalem zoo, four large-scale seasons of excavations were undertaken by the Israel Antiquities Authority, directed by E. Eisenberg. These revealed most of the site's ancient buildings.

EXCAVATION RESULTS

The extent of the site (12.5 a.) was determined by a surface survey, aerial photographs, and the preliminary excavation along all the terraces of trial trenches one meter wide. As a result of this method of investigation, it became clear that the site's center had been badly eroded, stripping the deposits down to the natural rock terraces. Greater attention was thus paid to the peripheral excavation areas, which were better preserved.

Twenty-three areas were excavated (including three outside the site), covering 2 a. Three strata were distinguished: stratum III: the mud-brick and stone buildings of an unwalled Middle Bronze Age I settlement; stratum II: stone buildings in an unwalled Middle Bronze Age IIB settlement; and stratum I: agricultural terraces in use from the Iron II period up to modern times.

STRATUM III. The site was first settled in the Middle Bronze Age I, on one of the natural rock terraces. The remains were found in all the excavated areas. The structures were built close together, especially on the eastern side of the site, which was more suitable topographically. A block of adjoining buildings (c. 150 m long) was found here; in certain places it had been damaged by later activity in strata II–I.

Stratum III was characterized by thin-walled structures built of baked mud bricks, laid on stone foundations or directly on bedrock. The floors, most of which were not level, were made of beaten earth over fills of earth and stone and sometimes incorporated the natural rock. The houses contained characteristic elements such as stone mortars sunk in the floors, cupmarks hewn into the rock, and installations for food preparation, storage, cooking, and baking. The plans of the structures vary, having been dictated largely by the local topography. They had a single story and several square rooms, built in one or two rows and at different levels. The roofs were sometimes supported by wooden pillars, judging from the stone bases found on the floors.

Terraced structure in area 700, stratum III.

Three building phases were distinguished in some of the structures, indicating that the settlement lasted for a long time. The structures from the upper two phases of stratum III had been destroyed violently and their contents buried under the debris. No difference in the pottery from the three phases was noted; it belongs to the southern family of pottery from the Middle Bronze Age I, like that from sites in the Judean Hills, the Shephelah, and the Negev.

Cult. Stone *maṣṣebot* were found in situ in three of the dwellings. They were made of slabs of broad, unworked stones fixed in the floor. Two miniature clay zoomorphic figurines were found, probably representing sheep. Because no structure exclusively dedicated to cultic activity was found, this find suggests that religious activities took place in a domestic context.

Economy. Paleobotanical remains (such as cereal grains, lentils, olive pits, and grape seeds) and sickle blades of the Canaanean type indicate that agriculture was an important occupation here. Most of the livestock were sheep (80 percent), with some pigs and cattle. These data reflect a mixed farming economy, which ensured a variety of food and survival even in lean years.

Ceramic Industry. The evidence for the existence of a ceramic industry is indirect because no installations for making or firing pottery have been found. Petrographic studies show that the pottery was made of local clay (Moẓa *ḥawwar*), available in large quantities near the settlement, with dolomitic sand used to temper it. Two unique caves from which this sand was excavated were found. The first, a narrow cave 12 m long with two shafts, is within the site's boundaries, near one of the houses. The second cave, about 300 m north of the settlement, consisted of a broad vertical shaft (c. 9 m deep) with horizontal niches at four levels along its length. An analysis of dolomitic sand from these caves showed that it contained small concentrations of copper and minute traces of silver and gold. In spite of this, it seems that the sand was used only for tempering clay and was not intended for metal extraction.

Burial Customs. The inhabitants of the stratum III settlement buried their dead in caves, which were entered through round, vertical shafts. Surveys revealed two main concentrations of these caves near the site: one on the southwest of the spur running out from the ridge of Manaḥat and the other above the site, near the summit of Giv'at Masu'a. Only one of the five tombs excavated was found intact. In this period, the site itself was also used for burials and five burial caves were found nearby, including three that were undisturbed. These caves were used for individual burials. The corpse was laid in a flexed position accompanied by a few grave goods that included daggers, beads, pottery, and joints of mutton. An unusual feature here is the large dolomitic sand mine (2100) outside the site that was used as a burial cave when it went out of use. The mine was so large it was used for multiple burials, a phenomenon rarely found in southern Canaan in the Middle Bronze Age I.

STRATUM II. The site was resettled in the Middle Bronze Age IIB following a long gap. The new inhabitants often chose to erect their buildings over the earlier ones. The new structures were made of unhewn field stones and large lumps of rock. Mortar was prepared from terra rossa mixed with straw, small stones, and sherds. The settlement was composed of isolated structures and complexes of several buildings with common walls. These probably began as single houses that evolved into a complex to accommodate a growing family. The dwellings had at least three rooms; the larger examples had six or more. Some of the houses had a second story, as indicated by the remains of walls 2 m high, staircases, and stone-slab floors that had collapsed on pottery vessels. The ceilings of the large rooms were supported by pillars, whose bases were found on the floors. There were open courtyards in two areas; particularly interesting was a round courtyard (diameter, 12 m) resembling a threshing floor that adjoined the southeastern complex.

The finds from stratum II were many and varied. The majority were pottery

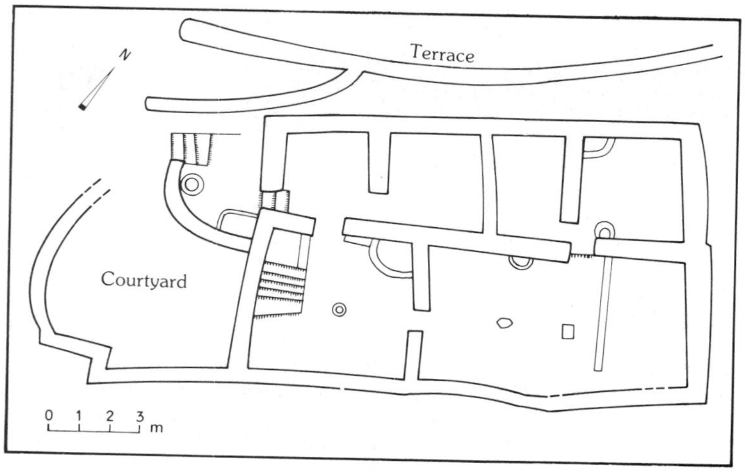

Plan of building 2720 from stratum II.

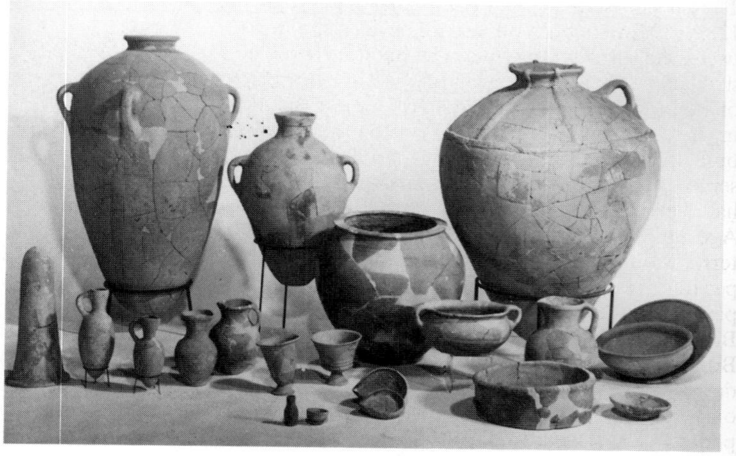
Pottery assemblage from stratum II.

and stone vessels, characteristic of the Middle Bronze Age IIB. Steatite scarabs from the Hyksos period were found. The bronze vessels were mostly tools, such as axes, knives, awls, and needles.

Information about the settlement's end can be gleaned from some of the better-preserved houses: several were empty, while others had collapsed, burying large pottery vessels that would have been difficult to transport. Fragments of these vessels were scattered over several rooms, perhaps as a result of the collapse of the upper stories. These data indicate that the site was abandoned and probably later looted of many of its portable artifacts.

Cult. An isolated building (500) that stood on the southwestern edge of the site has been identified as a temple. It measured 5.7 by 9.6 m and was preserved only up to its foundations. It was built of large blocks of stone and its walls were 1.2 m thick. It was a megaron in plan, divided into two rooms, and faced east. On its facade was a step flanked by two antae, which indicate the location of the entrance. Adjoining the temple was a square room built at a lower level that contained miniature votive vessels, goblets, and bowls. Another building (1700), similar to the temple in plan and dimensions, was uncovered 75 m to its north. It contained installations associated with burning and may also have had a cultic use.

Economy. In spite of the long gap between the Early Bronze Age IV and the Middle Bronze Age IIB, no great changes occurred in the settlement's economy, and the exploitation of the natural resources in the vicinity seems to have been similar. Finds such as flint blades, grinding tools, storage jars, and storage installations yield evidence of agricultural practices. Sheep were still the most important type of livestock, although there was an increase in the number of cattle. Evidence for the use of metal was found in area 200: hidden underneath a floor was a bowl containing pieces of metal, including fragments of vessels and pieces of scrap that were intended for resmelting.

Ceramic Industry. Parts of potters' wheels made of basalt or quartzolite were discovered in four different buildings. A room that opened onto an unroofed courtyard containing a pile of clay and a round, worked stone slab (diameter, 70 cm) may have been a potter's workshop. In another area was a storage jar full of pure dolomitic sand. All these finds are associated with the local ceramic industry. The vessels were made of local Moẓa *ḥawwar*; petrographic studies have shown that sand was the principal temper used in this stratum, too.

Building complex from stratum II in area 800; (center) building 2720.

Burial Customs. The inhabitants of the stratum II settlement were buried in two different ways: burial without grave goods in cist tombs, dug into the soil in the courtyards between the houses, and burial in reused shaft tombs hewn by the inhabitants of stratum III. Two burials of this latter type were uncovered within the settlement. Outside it, the sand mine 2100 was also reused in the Middle Bronze Age IIB for multiple burials, with more than a hundred people interred. Analysis of the human remains shows a marked difference between the people of stratum III and those of stratum II, which indicates that the two populations had different origins.

STRATUM I. Stratum I includes all the finds from the agricultural terraces that covered the remains of the stratum III and stratum II settlements. Most of the terrace walls run parallel to the ancient buildings and are sometimes even founded on them. The terraces were built of large field stones, some of which were taken from the ruins of the ancient buildings. Their inner faces were usually reinforced with smaller stones for support. The terraces were leveled with a soil (terra rossa) fill, brought from the valleys and wadi beds.

The construction of terraces on the mountainsides met the need for new agricultural areas when all the suitable land in the valleys was already in use. The beginning of this process is associated with the expansion of the region's economic basis and population growth from the end of the Judean kingdom onward. It is supported by the small finds and Iron Age II sherds from the terrace walls and the surface of the agricultural fills. A group of pottery vessels found in cave 1806, which was originally hewn in stratum III, and a stone *pym* weight, dating to the Iron Age II, discovered in a stone heap in a stratum II building, are evidence compatible with the contemporary building activity at Manaḥat, the farm at er-Ras, and the tumuli on Giv'at Masu'a.

On the basis of the ceramic evidence, it seems that repairs and rebuilding of the terraces were carried out in the Second Temple period, and they were almost certainly in use until the Early Arab period. In the medieval period, a lime kiln was built in the middle of the site; a pile of slag and ash 16 m across is all that survives of it. Agricultural activity was renewed with the expansion of the village of Malḥa in the nineteenth century.

SUMMARY

In its lack of a wall, the stratum III settlement reflects the situation in the transitional period of the last quarter of the third millennium in Canaan: towns disappeared. The finds from this stratum represent a material culture with its roots in Early Bronze Age urban culture, although its building methods and burial customs are characteristic of Middle Bronze Age I settlements. The few sites parallel to this one in Canaan are all in the densely settled area of the time and in Transjordan. The pottery, in contrast, belongs to the southern culture that extended from the Judean Hills to the Negev.

The stratum II village differed from its predecessor politically, in that it existed in a period of strong urban control. It may well have been within the territory of Jerusalem and under its control. In this framework, the city would have granted the village its protection and served as a refuge, in return for contributions to its economy.

In the excavation at Malḥa (Manaḥat, see below), about 1.5 km (1 mi.) east of the Naḥal Rephaim site, two occupation strata were found, also dating to the Middle Bronze Age I and the Middle Bronze Age IIB. In the area between the two sites, surveys have revealed the remains of several contemporary buildings. The evidence points to extensive settlement along the northern bank of Naḥal Rephaim, a phenomenon of great significance in our understanding of early unwalled settlements.

E. Eisenberg, *ESI* 7–8 (1988–1989), 84–89; 9 (1989–1990), 150–156; id., *Israel Antiquities Authority, Highlights of Recent Excavations*, Jerusalem 1990, 11–13.

EMANUEL EISENBERG

THE MANAḤAT EXCAVATIONS

The ancient settlements of Manaḥat (map reference 1289.1679) were built on a small, leveled lowland between the surrounding hills. The buildings were constructed on bedrock of alternating soft and hard layers of limestone. Some of the soft limestone eroded, forming natural, steplike terraces, on which the houses were built. No indications of ancient buildings were observed in the surface survey conducted at Manaḥat. The few sherds found represented the Late Iron Age and the Roman and Arab periods. The area was covered by agricultural terraces and a few stone mounds. Manaḥat was settled in the Chalcolithic period, as indicated by the flint tools excavated that are characteristic of the period. Three periods are represented in the structural remains: Middle Bronze I, Middle Bronze IIB, Late Bronze II, and Roman. The few Middle Bronze Age I wall remains belonged to a small village whose area could not be determined. The Middle Bronze Age I and II buildings rested on bedrock or on a very thin and sporadic layer of terra rossa. This means that during those phases there was not enough soil to plow, at least not on the hillsides.

In three seasons of excavations (1987–1989) nine areas were opened. Buildings in areas 100, 200, 300, 1000, and 1100 were either completely or partially excavated. Area 400 was an open area, in which three cupmarks were found hewn in the rock. Areas 700, 800, and 1200 included long rooms built around the settlement. Sections excavated on some of the terraces showed that they were part of a Roman farm. A mikveh was found in area 600, 300 m to the south of the site.

MIDDLE BRONZE AGE I VILLAGE. In areas 800 and 1000, wall fragments, pottery, and stone utensils were uncovered. The walls were constructed of only one course of stones with mud bricks on top of it. These Middle Bronze Age I buildings were not found previously because they had either eroded or been completely covered by agricultural terraces.

MIDDLE BRONZE AGE IIB VILLAGE. The Middle Bronze Age IIB settlement was enclosed by a belt of buildings arranged in an orderly fashion, probably to prevent free access from the outside (area 800-8000). The remains revealed a long building tradition. The plans of the Middle Bronze Age II houses and their function reflect the style typical of the era: rooms built around a courtyard. The rooms' interior walls were plastered. These buildings are similar in construction technique, size, and plan to Middle Bronze Age II private buildings at Hazor, Tel Michal, Gezer, and Beth-Shemesh.

Pithoi were installed in the houses for storing commodities for family use. Medium and small storage jars were found in such great quantities it is possible to conclude that they were not only for family use, but also utilized for selling or trading dairy products, oil, wine, grains, and other surplus items. Industries were evidenced by the discovery of hundreds of stone implements: instruments for grinding grain; stone hammers that may have been used in a metal industry; small pestles and mortars, possibly used to crush materials to produce paints or medicinal substances; and crushing stones to prepare the grog for making pottery. Metal needles, pins, punches, and awls represent tools used in such crafts as leather working, carpentry, and basketry.

Several species of plants were cultivated. These included grains, such as wheat and barley, grapes, lentils, and olives. Identifiable cereal phytoliths come from the husk of the cereal grain. Wheat was present in small amounts. Wine and olive oil, as well as dairy products, were produced by the community. Information about the site's environs comes from phytoliths of common reed and a type of sedge. All of these are water-loving plants used in antiquity for roofing, to weave mats, and as windbreaks. It is possible that there was a suitable marshy microenvironment around the site itself. A black sedimentary level of soil found in the vicinity may indicate that in antiquity there was a swamp here.

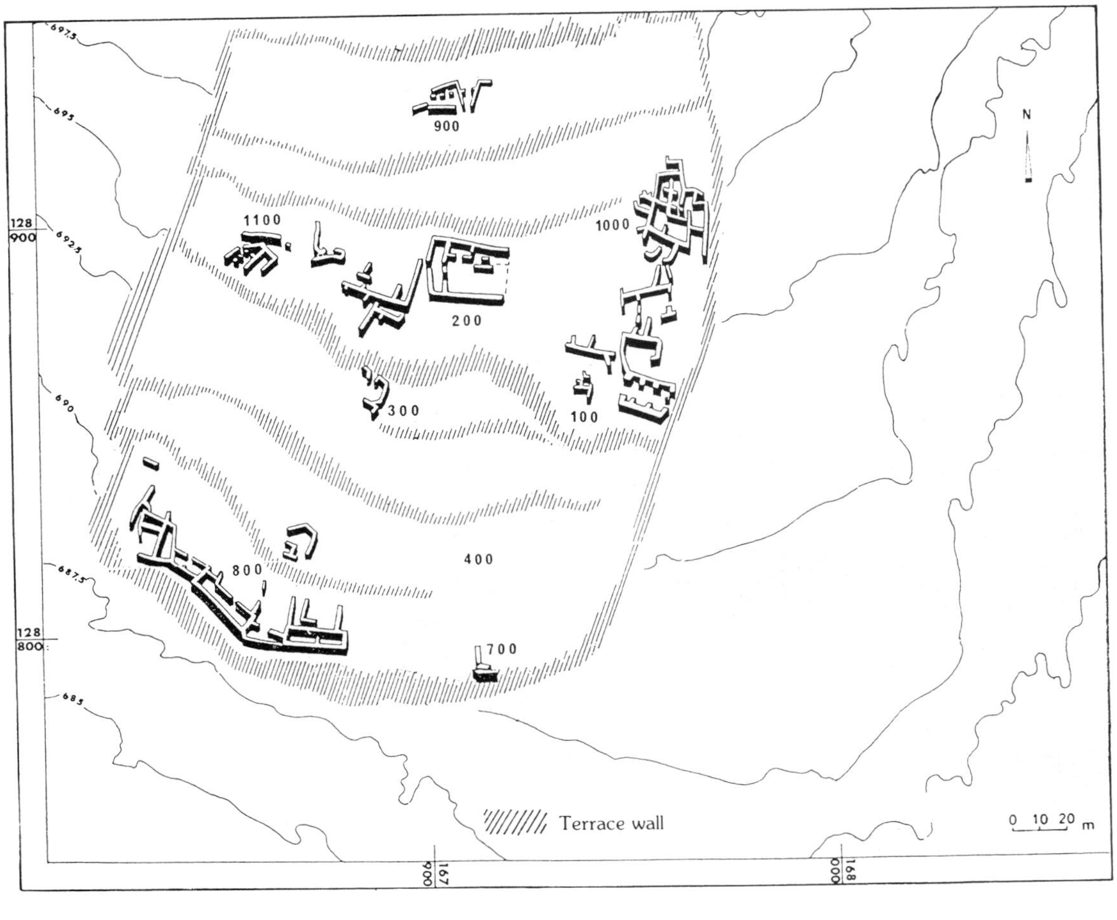

Manaḥat: general plan of the site.

Bronze ax from area 700, MB IIB.

The Middle Bronze Age IIB Manaḥat village was in existence from the eighteenth to sixteenth centuries BCE, with a population of three hundred to five hundred people. A bronze axhead reinforced the chronology fixed by the pottery. This village, along with the material found in the surveys and tombs from the period, revealed that the Jerusalem area had a sizable population at the zenith of the Middle Bronze Age IIB.

Building 106. The plan of building 106—one long rectangular room (12.5 by 7.5 m)—is unique. Its walls were constructed in the manner characteristic of the Manaḥat Middle Bronze Age II buildings, however, utilizing large stones but with small stones to fill gaps. Four internal buttresses were partially preserved on its northern wall and four on its southern wall. They divided the room into six small, cell-like cubicles and a larger central area. The buttresses probably strengthened the walls and supported the roof. The floor of building 106, similar to others at Manaḥat, was composed of a chalky soil a few centimeters thick.

Two standing stones found near the entrance to building 106 may have been stelae. West of building 106 a courtyard, paved with a white floor, may have belonged to the building. In the center of the courtyard were four small rooms. Two interesting clay artifacts in the shape of a bell and a pomegranate were discovered near building 106, in terrace fill. Both were used in cultic worship throughout antiquity and are referred to in the Bible. The peculiar plan of building 106 and the nature of the associated artifacts indicate that it was a cult center or temple. North of building 106 was a large courtyard, 8 m wide and more than 12 m long.

A female burial was found in one of the rooms. Her head faced east and her legs were contracted. The skeleton was buried in the room's occupation level.

Building 215. Building 215 occupied an area of almost 270 sq m (14.5 by 18.5 m). It is rectangular, with one long room, or hall, used as the common entrance for buildings 215 and 251. There were three pillars in the center of the hall. The entrance is on the west and two rooms are in the north around the courtyard. It is possible that more rooms existed around the eastern and southern parts of the courtyard. The courtyard was partially covered with a roof, supported by four pillars. Its floor was finished with a layer of lime and ashes. The complete skeleton of a pregnant sheep was found in a natural pit at the center of the courtyard. In the northwestern corner, a clay *tabun* was lined with large sherds of Middle Bronze Age II storage jars and cooking pots and flat stones. A few changes were made in this building: the southern side of the double entrance was blocked, as were the northern wing of the long room and the entrance to one of the northern rooms which opened into the courtyard. Several Late Bronze Age II jar fragments, of types found in area 1000, appeared in the fill. A Bes figurine, probably dating to the Late Bronze Age II, was also discovered inside the stone mound covering the structure.

Building 8216. Building 8216 had the longest preserved courtyard in the area (13 m long and 8.5 m wide). The floor of one of the rooms seems to have been paved with slabs now preserved in only a few sections. A fairly well-preserved *tabun* was found in the northwestern corner of the courtyard. The area around the *tabun* produced many fragments of Middle Bronze Age IIB jars and cooking pots. On the floor of one of the rooms, a typical Middle Bronze Age IIB bronze ax was found.

The Stone Mound and Building 1028. The walls of building 1028 were found under a mound of stones. The mound was about 12 m long and less than 2 m high from its base. The pottery sherds found between the stones belonged to all periods of settlement at Manaḥat, from the Middle Bronze Age I to modern times. The earlier building 1028 covered an area of about 250 sq m.

The outer walls were constructed of two rows of stones, whereas the partition walls consisted of only one row. Only the southern outer wall was also built of one line of large stones. The entrance to the building was a small passageway, whose side walls were not parallel but narrowed from 2.5 m on the outside to 1.5 m at the actual opening into the building. This type of entrance also can be seen in areas 200, 900, and 800.

Building 1028 contained two courtyards with rooms around them. A row of four pillars divided the courtyards into two parts. The walls of the rooms around the courtyards were plastered with a thick layer of lime and mud. The building appears to have had two stories. Three pillars standing in one of the courtyards supported a lightweight roof. Similar pillars were discovered in other buildings, as well.

In the courtyards, two floor phases were clearly defined. On one of the later floors a Nineteenth Dynasty scarab and Late Bronze Age IIB pottery were found.

It is clear that the new settlers found collapsed walls, on top of which they built new walls with smaller stones. Two entrances were closed in order to create more rooms. Both courtyards continued in existence while the long room was divided into three rooms. At the same time the area between the pillars, in the wall between the courtyards, was filled with stones, leaving space for two doorways connecting them.

A second scarab, bearing a seal of Amenḥotep III, was found under the upper floor. The fact that a Late Bronze Age II scarab was found in a Middle Bronze Age IIB level is not surprising because these tiny objects are easily filtered into the earth.

THE ROMAN FARM. Six terraces oriented east–west covered the Middle Bronze Age IIB settlement at Manaḥat. In most cases, the terrace walls had collapsed and part of the fill had eroded, giving the appearence of a triangular hillock along the former terrace wall.

An external fence was built around the terraced areas, forming a single agricultural unit or farm. A stone fill in the terraces prevented evaporation and allowed water to percolate into the terrace with the excess filtering through the wall into the terrace below. Through this process, the fill prevented the water from accumulating and causing damage to the plant roots. The abundance of stones also helped promote oxygenation of the soil.

A very thin and sporadic layer of terra rossa (between 0.5–0.1 m thick) was found under the floors of the Middle Bronze Age buildings. This is an important piece of information: when the terraces were built, there was no cultivable land on the slopes of the hills. The terraces were clearly constructed not to prevent erosion, but to produce cultivable land. The stones may have come from ancient quarries nearby.

In the terrace fill the most common pottery belonged to the Iron Age II, Middle Bronze Age II, Late Bronze Age II, and Roman period. Because many Roman sherds, glass pieces, and coins were found in the stone fill at the bottom of the terraces, or directly above bedrock, this seems to be the date of the terrace's original construction.

On the rock base of one of the terraces, in area 1000, two coins were found—one from the time of Pontius Pilate and the other possibly dating to Constantius II. Pre-Middle Bronze Age I material appeared only in the terrace fill. Choppers, chopping tools, backed blade sickles (Chalcolithic), and adzes and axes (Neolithic and Chalcolithic) were discovered in topsoil or terrace fill. This is understandable if a Chalcolithic settlement was located near the Middle Bronze Age IIB Manaḥat settlement and some of the fill for the terraces came from there.

STONE MOUNDS. Mounds of stones of various sizes are found in many areas around Jerusalem, including Naḥal Rephaim. During the Manaḥat excavations, two were excavated with Middle Bronze Age II buildings under them (areas 200 and 1000). The mound in area 200 was 15 m long, 12 m wide, and approximately 3.5 m high. Its top and sides consisted of small field stones and its core of larger stones, piled in disarray. A yellowish dust had accumulated between the core stones. Approximately 2 m below the mound's summit, the soil changed to dark brown and Middle Bronze Age II building walls appeared. Mostly Iron Age II and later pottery sherds were found at the top of the mound. Finds from this mound included pottery sherds from all occupation periods at Manaḥat, stone tools, and a figurine of the Egyptian god Bes, which probably dates to the Late Bronze Age II.

SUMMARY

The first settlement at Manaḥat, dating to the Middle Bronze Age I, was built on bedrock. It was abandoned for a long period of time and, due to erosion, most of it was washed away. The buildings in the Middle Bronze Age II village destroyed more of the remains of previous construction. This village was also abandoned; the buildings collapsed and a layer of dark brown soil covered anything erosion had not washed away. In the Roman period, a farm was built on top of the ancient remains. A terrace wall was built alongside the Middle Bronze Age II buildings, and the Roman terrace builders used a layer of light-brown soil to level the terrace for cultivation. Stones from the ancient buildings were used to build fences, and stones and soil were brought for the terrace fill. In turn, these terraces were abandoned for a long period of time. At the end of the process, a stone mound was created, probably over a period of a few hundred years, by farmers plowing what was left of the agricultural land artificially created by the builders of the terraces.

G. Edelstein (and Z. Greenhut), *ESI* 7–8 (1988–1989), 117–123; (and Y. Milevski), 9 (1989–1990), 148–150; id., *RB* 96 (1989), 217–220; L. Kolska Horwitz, *BASOR* 275 (1989), 15–25; id., *PEQ* 121 (1989), 44–54; I. Milevski, *Revista del Istituto de Historia Antiqua Oriental* 7–8 (1991), 201–205.

GERSHON EDELSTEIN

General view of building 1028. Note the pillars (constructed of drums) and the stone pavement of the MB IIB building and the beaten-earth floors of the LB II covering it.

Steatite scarab ring, LB II, 19th Dynasty.

RIDAN, TEL

IDENTIFICATION

Tel Ridan is situated on the Mediterranean coast, 18 km (11 mi.) south of Gaza and 4 km (2.5 mi.) northwest of Khan Yunis (map reference 0822.0882). The mound is 15 m high and about 350 sq m in area. The site consists of two mounds with a cemetery between them, that is located on a low sand dune. Surveys of the site in the 1930s suggested that it had been settled in the Bronze Age. In November 1973, prior to the construction of the coastal highway, a salvage excavation was conducted on the site on behalf of the Israel Department of Antiquities and Museums. F. Vitto directed the excavations on the northern mound and G. Edelstein on the southern mound and in the cemetery.

EXCAVATION

NORTHERN MOUND. Most of the northern part of the settlement had been eroded by the sea and by the removal of sand for construction purposes. An area of 250 sq m was excavated and a complex of rooms from the Middle Bronze Age II was revealed. The walls were built of bricks (51 by 36 by 12 cm) and coated with a 10-cm-thick layer of mud plaster. Two methods of construction were distinguished: bricks laid as stretchers and bricks laid as headers. The walls were preserved to a height of about one meter. Collapsed wall debris was found in most rooms above a layer of about 20 cm of sand, indicating that the site was abandoned and gradually fell into ruin. The thresholds of the entrances were made of brick; one of them had a stone socket. Almost every room had a hearth. One of the rooms had an oven (*tabun*; diameter, 42 cm) built of bricks. Some of the rooms had two superimposed floors mixed with ashes and separated by a layer of sand mixed with sherds (20 cm thick). There were various pottery vessels on the floors—jars, bowls, juglets, and cooking pots from the Middle Bronze Age II.

SOUTHERN MOUND. On the summit of the mound, three brick-lined pits (diameter, c. 1 m) were uncovered, dating to the Byzantine period. They were dug into earlier Bronze Age layers; only a few Byzantine sherds were found in them.

Brick walls and a few sherds belonging to the Late Bronze Age settlement were found on the mound. A cemetery from this period, which was located over the Middle Bronze Age remains, was also found. A brick structure (2 by 5 m) from the Middle Bronze Age II was uncovered next to a pottery kiln. The kiln, also of brick, had a lower chamber, the firebox, and an upper chamber, where the pottery vessels were laid. The two chambers were separated by a perforated floor, through which the heat was conveyed.

Close to the kiln a burial contained the remains of two skeletons laid in an east–west direction. A basalt bowl and a small carinated bowl were found between the two skulls. Three storage jars, covered with small bowls and containing dipper juglets, were found near the feet of the skeletons. A gold signet ring inlaid with a greenstone scarab was also found on a finger bone. The finds included a bronze dagger and sheep and goat bones. The tomb can be dated by the finds to the Middle Bronze Age II.

CEMETERY. Eight cist graves from the Late Bronze Age were uncovered in the cemetery. They were built of *kurkar* slabs and covered with slabs in a gabled fashion. The number of corpses varied in each tomb; the largest (tomb 6) contained four skeletons placed in a north–south direction with two offerings: a complete stirrup jar and a scarab. These offerings are ascribed to the final stage of the tomb's use, in the thirteenth century BCE. Scattered human bones and pottery found in the tomb suggest that earlier burials had been pushed aside to make room for the new ones. The pottery included three storage jars covered by small bowls, an Egyptian-style jug, Cypriot base-ring bowls, "milk bowls," a knife-pared juglet, and a lamp. The early burials should be dated to the fourteenth century BCE. In one of the other burials the deceased wore a glass necklace around its neck. At its side were a jar and a juglet with a gazelle painted on it.

(See also Marine Archaeology: Tel Ridan.)

F. Vitto, *IEJ* 24 (1974), 142; id., RB 82 (1975), 244–245; *HUCMS News* 11–12 (1985), 6.

FANNY VITTO, GERSHON EDELSTEIN

Juglet decorated with a drawing of a gazelle.

Tel Ridan: general view of the mound, looking north.

Southern mound: potter's workshop, MB II.

Southern mound: kiln in potter's workshop.

RIMMON, ḤORVAT

IDENTIFICATION

Ḥorvat Rimmon (Khirbet Umm er-Ramamin) is situated in the southern Judean foothills, about 12 km (7 mi.) south of Tel Ḥalif and about 0.5 km (0.3 mi.) south of Kibbutz Lahav (map reference 137.086). The site lies on a hill 470 m above sea level. To its east is Naḥal Yaval, separating the slopes of the Hebron Hills in the east from the high foothills in the west. Mount Lehavim and the Lahav Hills, reaching about 500 m above sea level, are west of the site, at the southern end of the foothills. The valley's fertile cultivated lands were the main source of livelihood for the ancient settlement.

The remains cover an area of about 25 a. Stone walls, most of them in secondary use, were found on the surface. Numerous caves were cut in the soft limestone, under the *nari* layer. Prior to excavation, a square building (c. 1,000 sq m) could be discerned on the hill's summit. The walls were preserved to a height of 3 m on the north and south; only the upper courses were visible over the mounds of debris and refuse. Many ashlars from ancient buildings were found incorporated in nineteenth- and twentieth-century buildings throughout the site, particularly on the summit. Stones in the ancient walls had been removed down to the foundations, in many cases leaving only "robber trenches."

Commenting on Rimmon in the inheritance of Simeon (Jos. 19:7), Eusebius (*Onom.* 88:17–18) says: "Eremmon (Ἐρεμμών; elsewhere it is called En Rimmon [Ἐν Ῥεμμοῦς], *Onom.* 146:25), a very large Jewish village 16 miles distant from Eleutheropolis [Beth Guvrin]." Jerome in his Latin translation of the text adds the words "towards south in the Daroma," thereby defining its geographical location. The distance provided by Eusebius—16 Roman miles—corresponds to the distance between Beth Guvrin (Eleutheropolis) and Rimmon: 26 km (16 mi.), along the ancient road connecting the two settlements. The ancient name Rimmon (pomegranate) is preserved in the Arabic Khirbet Umm er-Ramamin—"the ruin of the mother of the pomegranates" in diminutive form.

EXCAVATIONS

Three seasons of excavation (1978–1980) were carried out at the site on behalf of the Israel Department of Antiquities and Museums, under the direction of A. Kloner. The excavations were concentrated on the large building at the summit of the hill; only limited soundings were carried out in the settlement's residential area. Remains of four main periods were uncovered.

SECOND TEMPLE PERIOD. Remains of the earliest settlement on the site—floors and walls of buildings—were discovered on bedrock covered by or integrated into later construction. The excavators were therefore unable to establish the complete plan of the dwelling units. The earliest pottery is from the end of the second and the beginning of the first centuries BCE. The settlement existed until the mid-second century CE. No coins or other objects from the time of the Bar-Kokhba Revolt were found. However, it can be

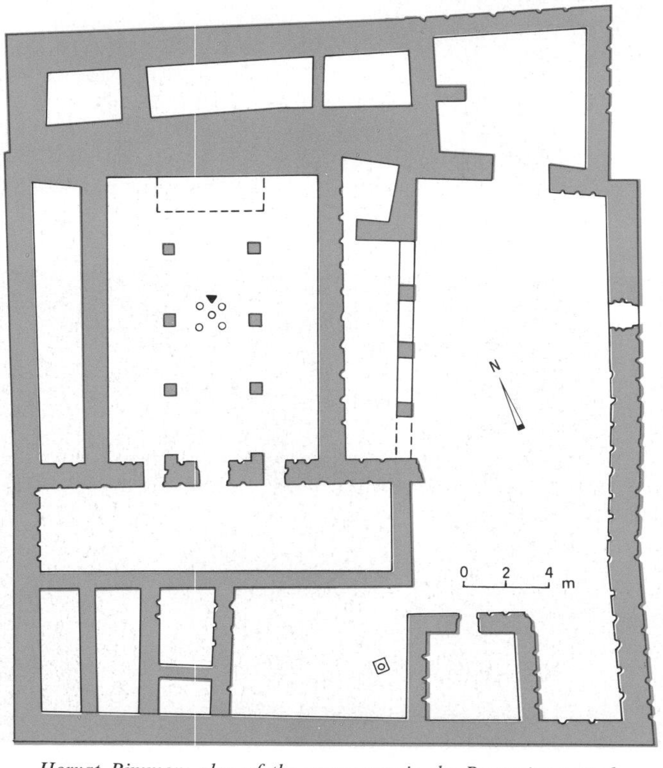

Ḥorvat Rimmon: plan of the synagogue in the Byzantine period.

assumed that the first period of the village's existence did not come to an end until the time of the revolt because caves in the area of the village contain subterranean refuge tunnels from that period. Remains from the Second Temple period were found in most of the excavated areas.

Under the western aisle of the later synagogue (see below), a round oven (*tabun*) was found on bedrock. It was filled with ashes containing fragments of cooking pots from the first and early second centuries CE. The room north of the aisle also had an oven that contained jars, jugs, and small bowls from the first century BCE, as well as sherds from the Late Hellenistic period. An ostracon with a Hebrew inscription שמע(ון) or שמנ(. . .)—Sime(on) or *Šmnn (. . .)*—was found in one of the rooms. A coin from the second year of the First Jewish Revolt against Rome (67/68 CE) was also recovered. A large cave uncovered in the excavations contained a 2-m-high fill of ashes, intact pottery vessels, and sherds from the second and first centuries BCE. Other finds clearly dating to this period are small fragments of painted Nabatean ware. The site was probably also settled in the late second and early third centuries CE, as several coins and a few sherds from the period were found. The major finds, however, are later than the mid-third century CE.

SYNAGOGUE AND SETTLEMENT (THIRD AND FOURTH CENTURIES). A public building stood on the site in the third century. It was assumed to be a synagogue because a synagogue was erected above it. Although the plan has not been fully established, the building is clearly a broadhouse, similar to the somewhat later synagogues at Eshtemoa and Ḥorvat Susiya.

In the eastern part of the building is a stylobate with three pedestals in situ. The northern wall is longer than the walls perpendicular to it on the east and west. In its center, the northeastern corner of a rectangular niche is preserved. This corner was covered with white plaster and decorated with painted red stripes. The niche's ceiling is 2.5 m above the floor of the nave. The niche, which faces Jerusalem, probably served as the Torah ark. Traces of white plaster mixed with sherds were found in other parts of the wall, on the side facing south, toward the nave. Apparently, the inside of the entire building was plastered and its walls partly decorated with colored paint.

The building's western wall stands on a floor from the Second Temple period. It was built of stones from sections of earlier buildings; several plastered stones were dated to the time of the first settlement. The building's southern wall was not found. Its floor was a uniform layer of crushed limestone on a foundation of small stones. The remains discovered under the floor date to the mid-third century CE, and the excavators accordingly attributed the building's construction to the second half of that century.

Many decorated architectural fragments found in the synagogue were reused both in the building and in the fill of the later, sixth-century synagogue. They included fragments of lintels, doorposts, friezes, column bases, and pilasters, as well as various capitals, including Corinthian capitals. The decorative relief bands included various floral motifs, such as vine trellises with clusters of grapes and flower and leaf bands, and motifs from the classical world, such as egg-and-dart, meander, ropelike band, and checkered patterns. In the light of these rich finds, it is assumed that the interior of the early synagogue was ornately decorated.

To the west of and parallel to the hall of the first synagogue was a long, narrow space whose walls rested on floors from the Second Temple period. In its western wall, in a crack between two stones, was a hoard of sixty-four bronze coins from the third, fourth, and early fifth centuries CE. The hoard was a concealed bank into which coins were placed from time to time. Strewn over the floor in this area and in the ash lying on it, another 160 bronze coins from the third to fifth centuries were found.

FIFTH AND SIXTH CENTURIES. There was an additional building stage between the synagogue erected in the third century and the structure that was rebuilt in the sixth century (see below). Its construction and period of use are dated to between the late fourth and mid-sixth centuries. At that time, the area of the synagogues was enclosed by walls to form a large rectangle, 34 m long and 29.5 m wide. The synagogues stood on the northwestern side of the enclosure and rooms were built around them. The walls are preserved to a height of 3 m; some of them were built on bedrock and others on the earlier walls. Architectural fragments from the early synagogue and stones from the Second Temple period houses were reused (mainly in the western wall, that was partly cast).

The elongated space to the west of the synagogue, in whose southern part the hoards of bronze coins were found, was filled with ash and large stones. Many objects were found in this fill, which was 80 cm deep: scores of bronze fragments from vessels and candelabra, such as rings for holding glass oil vessels; shafts for these rings; molded acanthus leaves; beautiful leaf-shaped stands and lids, also molded; a complete bronze oil lamp; various types of chains; and decorated fragments of vessels. Various pieces of metal jewelry, including a pendant that consisted of a silver frame around a greenstone from an earlier period carved in Egyptian style, were also found in the fill, along

Two branches of a bronze menorah, Byzantine period.

with ceramic vessels, bone and ivory handles, a large glass bowl, and numerous iron vessels.

In the upper part of the fill, at the same level, two pottery vessels were found that were placed upside down. Each contained a hoard of gold coins, one with thirty-five coins, and the other with twelve. The hoards had no doubt been intentionally hidden in the fill, after having been meticulously sealed, and then carefully buried in the ashes. Remains of cloth indicate that the coins in one of the hoards had been wrapped before they were hidden. The two hoards date from the reign of Emperor Valentinian I (364–375) to that of Anastasius (491–518).

At this stage, a new synagogue was erected, different in plan from the earlier building. It was a rectangular basilica building (9.5 by 13.5 m) whose long axis ran north–south and whose hall was 130 sq m. The western wall of the third-century synagogue was reused, while new walls were built on the north, east, and south. Two rows of three columns divided the building into a nave and two aisles. Pilasters were attached to the walls at both ends of each of the two rows. Only the column bases, made of square stones, were found in situ; fragments of the columns were found in secondary use in various places on the site. A bema (1.7 by 5 m), was built on the northern side, against the broad wall facing Jerusalem. Although only a few stones from the bema were found in situ, its position was clearly defined by the line of the floor which abutted it.

There were three entrances on the southern side of the synagogue: a middle entrance leading to the nave, and two side entrances leading to the two aisles. Only portions of the original threshold stones from the side entrances are preserved; the middle threshold had been robbed, as were the jambs at the entrances and all the ashlars from the southern wall. A broad entranceway (16 m long and 3.5 m wide), oriented east–west, is south of the synagogue.

SYNAGOGUE AND SETTLEMENT (END OF BYZANTINE PERIOD). At the end of the sixth century, the synagogue was rebuilt. The hall was now paved with tilelike stone slabs laid in straight rows along its entire length from north to south. The stones in the center of the pavement formed a square central carpet (3 m long each side), on which five six-leafed rosettes were carved. The northern side of the carpet was decorated with an incised seven-branched menorah oriented toward Jerusalem. The menorah was probably added later.

The synagogue's floor was very carefully laid on layers of smoothed stones and mortar. The paving stones are slightly worn and some are broken, but the gray mortar in which they were laid was of such excellent quality that the imprint of the missing stones is still visible. Coins from the reigns of Justinian I (527–565) and Tiberius II (578–58) were found in the trenches dug beneath the layer of gray mortar. Judging from the coins, deposited beneath the floor's foundation, the late pavement should be dated to the end of the sixth century. The building seems to have continued in use until the Arab conquest, and perhaps for a short while afterward. A few installations—benches or partitions—found on the floor are dated to the synagogue's last stage, and to the period following its abandonment.

Remains of the last two stages of the synagogue were found in all the excavation areas around it. To the west, in the room where the many objects and two hoards were found, was a beaten-earth floor and an oven. Under the floor was a coin of Heraclius (610–641). This room may have been a kitchen or a workshop in which objects connected with the synagogue were produced. Another oven, built above an earlier one from the Second Temple period, was found in the corner room of the enclosure, north of the synagogue. Two other ovens, one on top of the other and dating to the Byzantine period, were uncovered east of the synagogue. A chimney, consisting of a long narrow jar cut at its lower end, was installed in the lower oven. The area in which the ovens were found contained an abundance of pottery and goblet-shaped glass oil lamps (parts of chandeliers). In the fill covering the floor of one of the rooms north of the "oven room," five sherds were found. Four of them were restored, revealing an engraved adjuration in Aramaic.

Southeast of the synagogue's broad entrance hall (the narthex) was a square, rock-cut cistern, each side of which is 5 m long. Its walls and floor were plastered and its opening was supported by ashlar-built arches. It was filled with runoff water from the roofs and had a second opening for excess water. The cistern was found undamaged; it apparently went out of use at the same time as the synagogue.

OTHER REMAINS. Two limited soundings were conducted outside the main area described above. A large building was found around a central courtyard in the excavations to the northeast of the synagogue. Its stones were looted and reused in later periods, but the building included a drainage system in which water was conveyed into a central cistern. This is additional evidence of the effort devoted to collecting runoff water in cisterns—the large village's main source of water. At the foot of the hill's eastern slope a stone vault (c. 3 m long) connected an above-ground dwelling to the cave beneath it.

Conder–Kitchener *SWP* 3, 392; A. Kloner, *IEJ* 30 (1980), 226–228; 31 (1981), 241–242; id. (and T. Mindel), *Israel Numismatic Journal* 5 (1981), 60–68; id., *RB* 89 (1982), 250–253; id., *Ancient Synagogues in Israel, 3rd–7th Century* CE (*BAR*/IS 499, ed. R. Hachlili), Oxford 1989, 43–47; J. Naveh and S. Shaked, *Amulets and Magic Bowls*, Jerusalem 1985, 84–89; D. Chen, *Judaica* 45 (1989), 57–67.

AMOS KLONER

"Tile" floor of the synagogue, Late Byzantine period.

Seven-branched menorah and rosettes engraved on the synagogue's "tile" floor.

ROGEM HIRI

IDENTIFICATION

Rogem Hiri (Rujm el-Hiri) is a unique megalithic monument in the central Lower Golan, about 16 km (10 mi.) east of the northern shore of the Sea of Galilee (map reference 2254.2573), in the upper valley of Naḥal Daliyyot, 515 m above sea level. Hundreds of dolmens, as well as straight, low stone walls that surround the monument, and petroglyphs on the monuments and in neighboring areas form one of the most impressive megalithic complexes in the southern Levant. There are some important archaeological sites in the immediate vicinity—the Chalcolithic villages of el-Arba'in, 600 m to the north, and 'Ein el-Hariri, about 500 to 600 m to the northeast, and the Early Bronze Age "enclosure" at Sha'baniyyeh, about 1 km (0.6 mi.) to the northeast. The site was discovered in the 1967–1968 Archaeological Survey (and designated as site no. 115).

SITE DESCRIPTION

The monument consists of a central tumulus (or cairn) with four concentric walls around it. The tumulus is made up of three concentric ring walls that form an irregular, oval stone heap 20 to 25 m in diameter and 5 m high. At the foot of the tumulus, several large stones, set side by side, form a ring, probably the base of the tumulus itself.

The concentric walls are numbered 1 to 4, from the inside to the outside. Wall 1 is a semicircle surrounding the tumulus on the northwest (diameter, c. 50 m); its eastern and southern parts are covered by later structures and a large number of fallen stones. It is 1.2 to 1.5 m thick and consists of one or two courses of stones, of various sizes. This wall is connected to the next one (wall 2) by two radial walls. Wall 2 forms an almost complete circle, about 70 m from east to west and 90 m from north to south; it has a pronounced bulge to the south. It is 1.8 to 2 m thick and preserved to a height of more than 1 m. Wall 2 is also connected to wall 3 by several radial walls, some of which are very substantial and were part of the site's original design. Wall 3 is an uninterrupted circle, 105 m from east to west and 115 m from north to south; its overall thickness, 2.6 m, widens in the south to 3 m. It is pierced by several openings or passageways. Wall 4 is the outermost wall of the concentric circles, about 145 m from east to west and 155 m from north to south. It was carefully constructed, and its thickness (3.2–3.3 m) is remarkably consistent on all sides. Its height is preserved in places to more than 2 m, mostly because very large boulders were used—in particular in the eastern section and near the openings that interrupt the line of the wall. The opening, or entryway, in the northeast is 29 m wide and the one in the southeast is 26 m wide. Both are blocked by fallen boulders, some of which are extremely large. They represent the remains of rectangular structures inside the openings that were originally higher than the walls and obstructed the view of the central cairn.

EXPLORATION AND EXCAVATIONS

Three seasons of exploration were conducted at the complex from 1988 to 1990. The research program, which is part of the Land of Geshur Project of the Institute of Archaeology at Tel Aviv University, was directed by Y. Mizrachi and sponsored by the Peabody Museum, Harvard University. Several research programs are represented in the project: an extensive excavation project, a geophysical survey, a study of geometry and astronomy, and a comprehensive aerial and ground survey of the site's environs.

Excavation in the first season (1988) centered on a suspected entrance in the northeast quadrant (area NE 1). A 4-m-wide aperture was unearthed in wall 3 that is part of the monumental northeast entryway in wall 4. This aperture, or gate, led to an inner courtyard (c. 13 by 15 m). The area showed only limited stratigraphic accumulation. A crudely paved floor covered with beaten earth was reached within 10 to 30 cm below the surface. In the earth- and stone-moving operations, a score of Early Bronze and Iron Age potsherds were recovered.

The second excavation season (1990) took place at the southwest quadrant. A small trapezoidal paved cell (c. 3 by 2 m), leaning on wall 2, was excavated

Rogem Hiri: plan of the site.

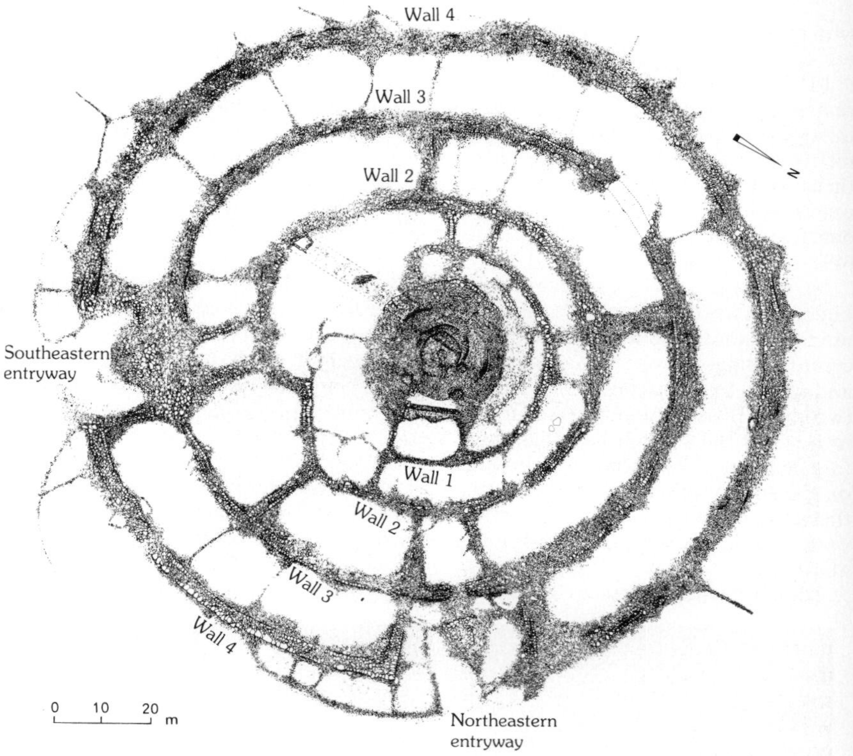

Rogem Hiri: aerial view.

Entrance to the burial chamber in the central tumulus.

underneath collapsed stones originating from this wall. The cell's western wall may have had a small bench in its inner face. It seems that the cell was not structurally integrated into wall 2. Fragmentary remains of large storage vessels, dated to the latter half of the second millennium, were recovered on the crude stone pavement, suggesting that the cell had been used as a storage room.

A series of five excavated squares aimed at establishing a stratigraphic link between concentric wall 2 and the central tumulus. They showed that bedrock is very close to the surface and only fragments of a crude pavement survive. In the northern part, a low, massively constructed wall, which runs parallel to the circular contour of the tumulus, bounds a paved floor stretching to the base of the tumulus. This floor yielded Middle and Late Bronze Age as well as Roman-Byzantine material. A small test pit reached bedrock about 0.7 m below the surface.

A 5-m-wide and 15-m-long section cut through the southern face of the central tumulus continued the line of squares; it runs from its base to the summit, about 4 m above the present surface. It confirmed that the tumulus consists of three terraced stone rings, built in such a way that the outer one leans on the inner one, forming a stepped cone. The outermost terrace was the widest (5 m) and was 2.5 m above the site's general surface. The innermost circular terrace was built around a burial chamber; it is about 7.2 m in diameter on the top and is surrounded by a lower and much narrower intermediate terrace that may be a small embankment or gallery.

On top of the burial chamber, slightly east of the chamber's center point, a pyramidal structure consisting of large basalt slabs was uncovered. Its function and its stratigraphic relationship to the burial chamber below are still unclear. Underneath the superstructure, a circular megalithic chamber (diameter, 1.96 m; height, 1.45 m) was excavated. The roof of the chamber consists of two massive basalt slabs, one of which weighs more than 5.5 tons. Originally, the chamber was paved at the level of the threshold of its entrance, which was made accessible via a 3.44-m-long and 1.1-m-wide passageway in its northeast. The chamber's walls were slanted somewhat inward and built with horizontally-laid stones. The lowest course of its wall does not reach bedrock. A number of medium-sized field stones positioned between the lower course of the chamber wall and the bedrock raise the possibility of an earlier construction phase for the chamber. At the center of the burial chamber, lying on bedrock underneath the floor, an elongated, unworked basalt slab (0.85 by 0.3 by 0.09 m) was found positioned with its long axis, oriented northeast–southwest, pointing to the entrance, indicating some symbolic significance.

The chamber and the passageway were found looted, probably in antiquity. A few gold earrings, bronze arrowheads, and about a dozen carnelian beads, as well as remains of flint blades and ceramic and charcoal samples were recovered from the chamber and, particularly, the passageway. The date for the assemblage appears to be within the second half of the second millennium BCE and raises the question whether this material represents a secondary usage of the burial chamber in the Late Bronze Age—a phenomenon observed at other megalithic structures in the Golan. Either way, the finds indicate the richness of the items placed with the burial.

DATE AND FUNCTION

The most difficult problem posed by Rogem Hiri is its date, because of the near total absence of occupational debris. Material remains collected around the complex and excavated within it cover a time span from the Chalcolithic to the Roman-Byzantine period to the present. The questions that remain are which phases of the presently visible architecture can be associated with each of these periods; and in which of the archaeological periods that are covered in this long time span the site was dominantly used.

Based on the data collected so far, it seems reasonable to suggest that the two dominant utilization phases were the third and late second millennia—the Early Bronze Age and the later phases of the Late Bronze Age. Late Bronze Age remains were dominant not just inside the burial chamber, but also surrounding the central cairn. In fact, well over 95 percent of the ceramics recovered at the site so far (including the 1991 season) consists of Late Bronze Age material.

These data lead to several scenarios. One is that the entire complex was a building project executed at one time by one and the same society in the Early Bronze Age. The second—for the time being the most convincing theory—is that the central cairn and its burial chamber, in their present form, were added to a preexisting Early Bronze Age complex sometime in the Late Bronze Age. A third, however quite unlikely possibility, is that the entire complex dates to the Late Bronze Age.

A systematic study of the astronomical and geometrical aspects of the site is aimed at examining the association between the architecture of the complex and celestial events, physical elements in the landscape and local ecology. Geometrical analysis demonstrates that whoever built the complex had some sense of measured proportions and used care in its design and engineering. There is little doubt that the alignments of the architecture were intentional and meant to manifest notions of religion and cosmology. What is most evident is that proportions of integral lengths seem to be emerging from the data. It is also significant that the site is aligned with the summer solstice sunrise—on a functional basis for the outer northeast entryway and symbolically for the tomb/passage axis (azimuth 61°42'9"). Other putative alignments indicate a sighting point eccentric to the center of the excavated tomb. This could mean that the burial was built within a monumental ceremonial center rather than a monumental ceremonial center built around a burial.

In the opinion of the excavators, Rogem Hiri should be viewed as a multifunctional site, with a distinction between primary and secondary functions within the framework of the region's changing cultural context. This allows a tentative reconstruction of the site's development. The few Chalcolithic remains indicate that some as yet undefined activity—which may not have had any relationship to the later complex—took place here in the fourth millennium. This is not surprising in light of the nearby Chalcolithic sites and extensive Chalcolithic presence in the central Golan. In the third millennium, a large ceremonial center was erected. Traditions associated with the sacredness of the site were preserved up until the late third millennium (the Early Bronze Age IV/Middle Bronze Age I), as is evident from the large dolmen fields of this period that are carefully arranged around it. It was perhaps during this time that the central tumulus was first constructed, although, presently, this suggestion cannot be supported with substantial data. By the late second millennium, the central cairn was extensively used and probably built in its present form. Evidence for construction and the reuse of dolmens in the late second millennium has also been reported at other Golan sites. This may indicate the continuation of earlier religious and cosmological traditions. This idea is supported by the fact that the axis of the supposedly later dromos of the burial chamber is symbolically oriented to the northeast entryway which, according to preliminary data, was built more than a thousand years earlier.

M. Kochavi, *ESI* 7–8 (1988–1989), 112–113; id., *IEJ* 39 (1989), 1–17; 41 (1991), 182–183; M. Zohar, ibid. 39 (1989), 18–31; *Weston Geophysical Corporation, Report of Archaeogeophysical Survey Program, Rujm el-Hiri, Golan Heights, Israel*, Westboro 1990; Y. Mizrachi, "Rujm el-Hiri: Toward an Understanding of a Bronze Age Megalithic Monument in the Levant" (Ph.D. diss., Harvard Univ.; in prep.).

YONATHAN MIZRACHI, MATTANYAH ZOHAR

RO'I, SITE 2

IDENTIFICATION

Ro'i, Site 2 is a Middle Bronze Age I site in the Negev Hills, southeast of the Telalim junction (map reference 1276.0416). It is located on a north–south ridge that tapers sharply to the south and is bounded on the east by a cliff that drops to the bed of Naḥal Be'er Ḥayil. It extends for about 350 m over an area shaped like the neck of a bottle. The site seems to have been established at this location because of its defensibility, its proximity to a water source, and its exposure to western winds. It was discovered in the course of the Negev Emergency Survey, conducted early in 1980. Another site, resembling it in size—Ro'i, Site 1 (Mash'abbe Sade)—is located a short distance to its north (map reference 1298.0432).

EXCAVATIONS

The site was excavated in 1981 by Y. Baumgarten, on behalf of the Israel Department of Antiquities and Museums. It includes scores of structures—probably more than a hundred—built very closely together. The typical structure is oval and 2.5 to 3 m in diameter. On the site's narrow, southern side a structure with an unusual plan was uncovered. It consists of two concentric, semicircular stone walls that form a half-circle surrounding an inner courtyard. The diameters of the outer and inner walls are 33 m and 27 m, respectively. No signs of building, retaining walls, or an inner division could be distinguished between these walls; the entire structure appeared to be an empty space between two arcs. The structure seemed to have openings that faced outward, but this may have been the result of the way in which the remains were preserved. Several segments of the wall are missing from the inner arc. One or more of these gaps may have had openings; the main entrance to the structure, however, must have been located in its northeastern side.

Two trial trenches dug in an area between the arcs failed to uncover any finds. The method of the wall's construction is noteworthy: local field stones were placed on the bare surface with their longitudinal axes facing the center of the courtyard. The northward extension of the structure consists of a block of rooms, of no definite plan, that enclose the courtyard.

Three small circular structures (diameter, 2.5–3 m) were also excavated: two within the circular courtyard and the third outside the block of structures. All the structures are identical: they are ring-shaped in plan. At the center of each is a stone column base. The walls are built of local field stones set on bedrock. The original height of the structures seems to have been somewhat less than the height of a person. Thin stone slabs that may have belonged to the roof were uncovered within the building's ruins.

On the northwestern side, continuous with the space between the semicircles, two oval rooms, built on no definite plan, were uncovered. Their walls, built of local field stones, were preserved to a height of 0.8 m. The collapsed ruins in the rooms also contained thin stone roof slabs. Beneath these remains was a living floor, on which potsherds and traces of fire were apparent. A monolith, more than one meter long, which had been used as a roof support, was found lying on its side in one of the rooms. A relatively large quantity of sherds was recovered from these rooms, whereas the small circular structures and the semicircular structure yielded only a few sherds.

As noted above, the northern part of the structure enclosing the courtyard is not symmetrical and includes rooms that are oval or of no definite shape. Examination of this complex of structures revealed a small circular room built on the earlier collapsed structures, indicating that there were at least two building phases.

On the settlement's northern side and at some distance from the oval structures, on the adjacent ridge and at various distances, rectangular structures (8 to 20 m long and 2 to 5 m wide) were found. They do not belong to the site, but are contemporaneous with it.

SUMMARY

The sherds recovered in the excavations, as well as those collected from the surface of the entire area, date to the Middle Bronze Age I. These sherds, like those recovered at other contemporary sites in the Negev Hills, belong to a single pottery group known as the Southern Group.

While the semicircular structure constitutes an exception to the architecture of the period, the small circular structures are identical to those discovered at other contemporary sites—Ro'i Site 1, Naḥal Reviv, Naḥal Nessana, and Be'er Resisim. All these sites, as well as Mount Yeroḥam and Naḥal Ẓin, are in the Negev Hills—a region that enjoys a greater amount of precipitation than other parts of the Negev. Their distribution, which demonstrates proximity to perennial water sources, indicates that they should be regarded as permanent settlements with a continuous occupation, whose inhabitants were neither nomads nor seminomads.

Y. Baumgarten, *ESI* 1 (1982), 103.

YAACOV BAUMGARTEN

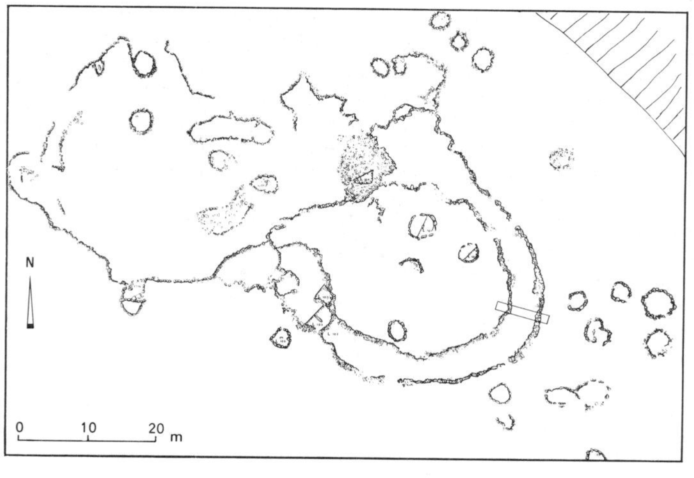

Ro'i 2: plan of the site.

Rounded structure with a stone column base in its center, MB I.

ROSH HA-NIQRA, TEL

IDENTIFICATION AND EXPLORATION

The site is a small mound on the lowest terrace of the Rosh ha-Niqra ridge, on the lands of Kibbutz Rosh ha-Niqra, about 1 km (0.6 mi.) from the Mediterranean Sea and 1.5 km (1 mi.) from the Israel–Lebanon border (map reference 161.276). In Arabic, the site is called Khirbet el-Musheyrife or et-Taba'iq. The mound has clearly defined boundaries on three sides. On the west and south its slopes are quite steep but not very high, and to the east it is bounded by a small valley. On the north, however, the ground rises gradually toward the nearby mountain, and the boundary is indistinguishable.

The proposal by W. M. Thomson and E. Renan to identify el-Musheyrife with Misrephoth-Maim (Jos. 11:8, 13:6) is generally accepted. In the list of settlements drawn up in 1251 by the knight Jean d'Ibelin, the name of the site appears in the form *La Meserefe*. According to Y. Ben-Zvi, the name probably indicates that salt was obtained here from seawater by evaporation in ponds, but, as M. Noth and Y. Yadin pointed out, it is also possible to vocalize the second part of the name to read *mi-yam*—"of the sea" or "western," which would be a simple geographic definition.

In a survey conducted at Tel Rosh ha-Niqra, pottery was found from the Early Bronze and Late Bronze ages, along with a small number of sherds from

Tel Rosh ha-Niqra: general view of the excavation area.

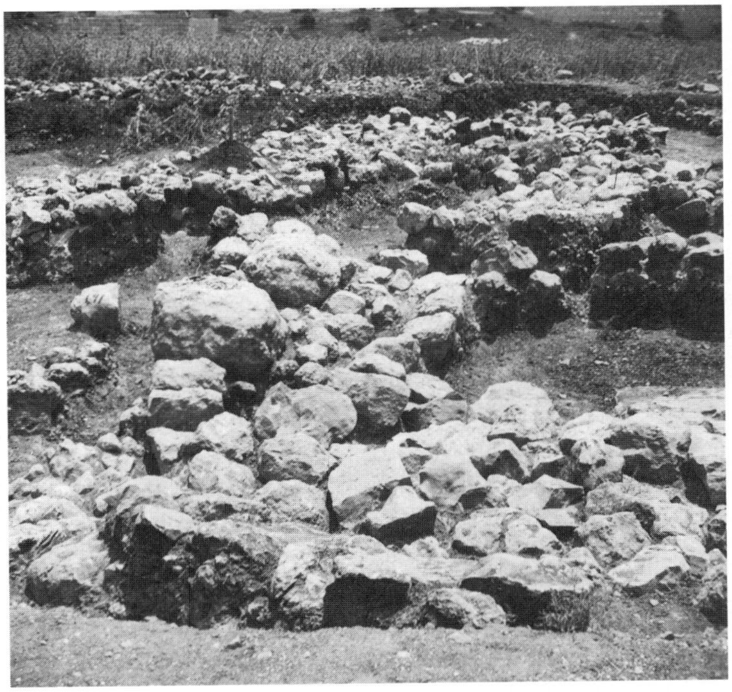

the Iron Age. At the foot of the mound, pottery was uncovered from the Roman, Byzantine, and Early Arab periods. At Minet el-Musheyrife, situated on the shore, Roman and Byzantine pottery were found in abundance. This was probably the site of the port and perhaps also of the salt ponds.

EXCAVATIONS

In 1951–1952, M. Tadmor and M. W. Prausnitz conducted two seasons of excavations on the mound on behalf of the Israel Department of Antiquities and Museums. Three areas on the eastern side of the mound were investigated: area I on the lower part of the mound, to the southeast, and areas II and III on the summit, near the east end.

In area I, buildings were uncovered from the Early Bronze Age I—the earliest occupation on the mound. The inhabitants of this first settlement used the large rock surfaces as floors and enlarged them by adding cobbled terraces. The walls, erected on bedrock and on the floors, were built of courses of stone in their lower part and of mud brick in the upper part. The main finds were coarse storage vessels in the form of hole-mouth jars with broad, flat bases, covered with a red slip and decorated with thumb-indented bands. Decorated lug handles, ledge handles, and loop handles also characterized the Early Bronze Age I pottery. The shape of the adze uncovered is similar to adzes typical of the period.

Buildings from the Early Bronze Age I were also discovered in the foundations of area II. Although it was impossible to determine the complete plan of any of the buildings, rounded walls indicate that they were oval. They were destroyed by fire and the Early Bronze Age II and III (stratum I) buildings were then erected over a layer of ash. The settlement was fortified, and its area was restricted to the summit of the mound.

In area II, a section of the settlement's defenses was cleared. A fortified gateway was apparently placed between walls enclosing the settlement on the north and south. Other walls protected the eastern access, forming a kind of forward entrance. The main building is square (8 by 8 m), possibly the gateway's tower. It is divided by an inner partition wall. The outer walls on the north and south are 3 m thick, and the eastern wall is 2 m thick; the entrance in the gate, paved with stone slabs, some of which reach 1 m in length, is 2.4 m wide; the forward entrance is 2 m wide.

The pottery finds attest that the mound's eastern fortifications were erected in the Early Bronze Age II–III. Some sherds of Khirbet Kerak ware were found on the summit. After the destruction of the fortifications, this area was abandoned and never reoccupied.

In 1950, a rock-hewn tomb from the Roman period was cleared south of the mound. It is rectangular (0.45 by 0.6 by 1.8 m) and was covered with several stone slabs. The tomb contained three skeletons, fragments of three glass vessels, and a glass bowl. In 1953, a grave was accidentally discovered on the slopes of the mountain, northwest of the lands of the kibbutz, to the east of the road leading to Lebanon, in an area of abandoned quarries. The grave consisted of a pit dug in the ground; it contained a large number of bones and pottery from the end of the Early Bronze Age.

M. Prausnitz, *IEJ* 2 (1952), 142; id., *'Atiqot* 1 (1955), 139; M. Tadmor and M. Prausnitz, ibid. 2 (1959), 72–88; Aharoni, *LB*, 21, 48, 90, 171; S. W. Helms, *ZDPV* 92 (1976), 1–9; Weippert 1988 (Ortsregister); E. Braun, *PEQ* 121 (1989), 1–43.

MIRIAM TADMOR

Cylinder seal impression depicting a ritual dance(?), EB III.

Decorated bone handle, EB III.

ROSH ZAYIT, ḤORVAT

IDENTIFICATION

Ḥorvat Rosh Zayit is in the Lower Galilee, about 10 km (6 mi.) east of Acco. It lies on a narrow ridge leading down to the Acco Plain, west of the Saḥnin Valley (map reference 1718.2538). The site overlooks the Coastal Plain to the west and the intermediate hills of Lower Galilee. Remains of stone buildings were discovered there, 3 m above bare bedrock; the central and largest building forms a small mound (30 by 30 m). A terrace built around the site, perhaps the remnant of an enclosure wall, encloses an area of some 6 a. The site has no water source and only rock-cut cisterns were observed. A survey conducted here showed that the site was occupied from the twelfth to eighth centuries BCE. This, together with the site's proximity (1.5 km [1 mi.]) to the Arab village of Kabul, makes it likely that Ḥorvat Rosh Zayit is biblical Cabul (Jos. 19:27).

Excavations at the site were begun in 1983, on behalf of the Israel Department of Antiquities and Museums and the Institute of Archaeology at Haifa University with the collaboration of the Nelson Glueck School of Biblical Archaeology of Hebrew Union College in Jerusalem, under the direction of Z. Gal.

EXCAVATION RESULTS

FORTRESS. A fortress (c. 25 by 25 m) was uncovered on the small mound at the center of the site. Its remains include a 2.3-m-thick perimeter wall with towers; only the southwestern and northwestern corners have been excavated so far. The wall was built of field stones laid on bedrock and preserved to a height of about 3 m, as shown by a section cut in the western side of the mound. At the foot of the wall was a rock-cut cistern that collected rainwater from the area of the fortress. Two occupation phases, both destroyed by fire, can be distinguished here; almost all of the later phase has been excavated.

A single building (12 by 12.5 m) was found within the fortress area. The building was separated from the western wall by a narrow passageway, or

Ḥorvat Rosh Zayit: plan of the fortress.

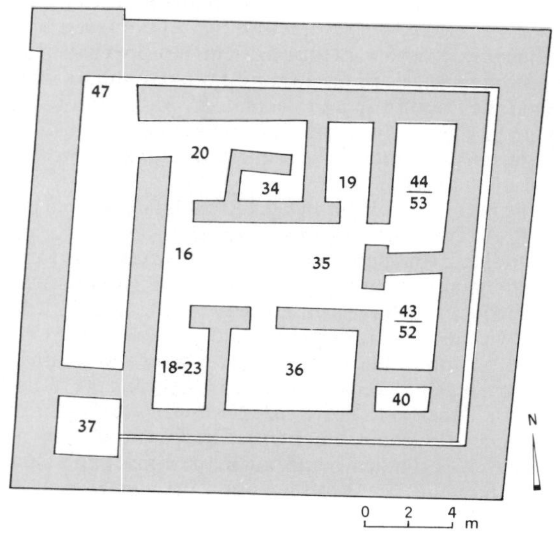

perhaps by a line of casemates; its other sides abutted the wall. The walls are 1.1 m thick; their corners, piers, and jambs are built of fine ashlars laid in headers and stretchers. The building consists of a central hall (3.25 by 9 m) surrounded by rooms. A monolithic column in the center of the hall apparently supported the ceiling. The plan resembles the Assyrian "courtyard" buildings from the Iron Age II. The building's main entrance, in the northwest corner, and the doorways to the rooms were all built with well-dressed jambs and thresholds. The southwestern room and three rooms along the eastern wall were excavated to bedrock; their height (3 m) indicates a two-story building. The level of the upper story was determined by the thresholds, and its floor was apparently made of wooden beams. No opening was found leading to the lower story; it must have been reached from the upper one by a ladder. The southwestern corner of the lower story served as a storage cellar. On its floor dozens of storage jars and clay stoppers were found; some of the stoppers were still in place on the jars. One jar, found sealed, contained wheat grains and charred beans. Other jars were charred inside, evidence of the burning of the olive oil stored in them. Among the finds were Phoenician pottery, including Achzib ware and Samarian bowls. Many iron tools were also found, including plows, sickle blades, axes, and a saw. The floor of the room above the cellar had collapsed into it, and objects from the upper room were found scattered among the debris. This phase of the fortress was destroyed in a violent conflagration, evidence of which was seen in the many clay vessels that had burst open from the heat. The fire also burned the building stones, which were made of soft chalk, turning them into a thick plaster that was found coating the pottery vessels.

The destruction seems to have occurred during a battle in which the defenders blocked the entrance in the northwestern corner with a hastily constructed wall; numerous iron arrowheads were found in a nearby layer of ashes. The intense fire left a layer of melted chalk in three rooms along the eastern wing of the central building. This phenomenon, together with the large number of storage jars found in this wing, indicates that olive oil was stored here.

The building was apparently a Phoenician fortress in its later phase. It seems to have been established in the tenth century BCE and destroyed in the mid-ninth century BCE, based on ceramic analysis of the finds—the most notable of which are Samarian bowls and the complete absence of elongated storage jars ("torpedo" jars).

In situ storage jars on the fortress's floor.

Western wall of the fortress, viewed from the outside.

Bronze decoration with Egyptian motifs that were inlaid with colored precious stones; among the motifs, Horus eyes and an ankh flanked by a pair of falcons.

Ḥorvat Rosh Zayit: assemblage of Cypro-Phoenician juglets from the fortress.

Pottery kernos decorated with pomegranates and animal heads.

The early phase of the fortress was uncovered in three limited excavation areas. The interiors of the northwestern and southwestern towers were cleared to bedrock. Traces of building were discovered here that appear to be casemate walls adjoining the walls of the central building; earth floors covered with a thick layer of ash ran up to them. On the floor of the northwestern tower was a group of pottery vessels, including storage jars, one bichrome, with a tree of life painted on it; black-on-red Phoenician bowls; and a kernos. These finds indicate that the fortress contained a small cultic room in its early phase. The foundations of the early wall were found some 2 m from that of the later phase, in a section cut in the eastern side of the mound. It thus appears that the changes made in the fortress principally affected the line of the walls and not the central building. The finds indicate that the earlier phase was destroyed at the end of the tenth or the beginning of the ninth century BCE and that the fortress was not in use for more than sixty or seventy years.

BUILDING A. About twelve piles of stones were found around the fortress. Traces of walls in several of them suggest that they are the remains of buildings. Excavations began in 1988 of one heap 20 m east of the fortress. They revealed that over the course of time stones had been piled on top of the ruins of an ancient structure, creating a cairn. A few sherds from the Iron Age I and II, as well as from the Byzantine period, were found in the uppermost layer of stones. Under this debris building A (external dimensions: c. 7 by 7 m) was found, which contained two rooms. The northern room (2.5 by 5 m) has a 1-m-wide entrance with ashlar jambs. The two rooms were divided by a row of monolithic columns, each 1.6 m high. The building's floor was the bedrock, in which a cupmark and a basin were carved; clay bowls, a storage jar, and cooking pots were found in situ here. A rock-cut granary was found in the southern room and an olive-press stone was discovered in its eastern corner. The pottery, which included elongated storage jars (torpedo jars), shows that the building was destroyed in the eighth century BCE, about one hundred years after the fortress was destroyed.

OIL PRESS. To the west of the fortress is a large oil press complex, consisting of at least three installations. This, too, existed until the end of the eighth century BCE. After the destruction of the fortress, it appears that a small village was founded on the site, whose inhabitants produced olive oil.

Z. Gal, *ESI* 2 (1983), 90; 9 (1989–1990), 105–106; id., *IEJ* 33 (1983), 257; 39 (1989), 281–283; id., *ASOR Newsletter* 37/1 (1985), 14–15; id., *Hurbat Rosh Zayit: Biblical Cabul* (Reuben and Edith Hecht Museum, Cat. 5), Haifa 1989; id., *BA* 53 (1990), 88–97; id., *Israel Antiquities Authority, Highlights of Recent Excavations*, Jerusalem 1990, 15–16.

ZVI GAL

Building A, 8th century BCE.

RUMEITH, TELL ER-

IDENTIFICATION

Tell er-Rumeith is located in northern Transjordan, near the modern town of Ramtha (map reference 247.212). P. W. Lapp made a sounding at Rumeith in 1962, under the auspices of the American School of Oriental Research in Jerusalem. He directed a six-week excavation there in 1967, sponsored by ASOR and the Pittsburgh Theological Seminary. Excavations did not conclusively prove the site's identification with Ramoth-Gilead, but the continuity of the name, the congruence of occupational history with the literary record, and its geographic location fit such an identification. It is a city in Gilead of the tribe of Gad (Dt. 4:43; Jos. 20:8, 21:38), and one of the seats of Solomon's officials (1 Kg. 4:13). Jehoshaphat and Ahab of Israel inquire of the prophets and go to battle at Ramoth-Gilead (1 Kg. 22). Joram, Ahab's son, is wounded at Ramot-Gilead, and Jehu is anointed there to be the next king (2 Kg. 8:28–9:10). The size of Tell er-Rumeith is the strongest argument against identification with Ramoth-Gilead, but excavation at a larger site in the area with equivalent occupational evidence has not yet been undertaken.

EXCAVATIONS

The stratification at Tell er-Rumeith was exceptionally clear. Rumeith was a small fort whose eastern wall was less than 40 m long. After its complete destruction it was rebuilt following an overall plan. The mound's main stratigraphy represented an occupation of about two centuries, ending with

Tell er-Rumeith: general view, looking west.

Tiglath-pileser III's destructive campaign in about 733 BCE. In the 1962 sounding, Hellenistic, Roman, Byzantine, and Arab material was uncovered east of the main mound. Because there was no substantial architecture, only transient occupation seemed indicated. In the 1967 season, excavation was limited to the mound proper. Surface sherds, pits, dugouts for tents, and graves were the evidence for later occupation. There was a large number of burials from the latest stratum, but few artifacts were associated with them.

In 1967, an effort was made to investigate the four Iron Age strata (VIII–V) further by clearing a quarter or more of the fortress, recovering coherent plans of the strata, and collecting ceramic groups to add precision to the pottery typology of the period. The northeastern quadrant of the tell was excavated to bedrock, or the earliest stratum, and a portion of the southeastern quadrant along the eastern fort wall was also cleared.

STRATUM VIII. If the fort was symmetrical, as the contours of the tell suggest, its dimensions were roughly 37 by 32 m. The northern wall (1.25 m thick) had a recessed gateway with a narrow opening approximately in the middle. The eastern wall (1.5 m thick), almost completely preserved, was founded on a stone socle on bedrock. Presumably, there was a gate in this wall, but it was obliterated by stratum VII operations. In the interior of the fort only a room (c. 3.25 by 2.25 m) in the northeastern corner could be determined with accuracy, due to the frequent rebuilding of the mud-brick structures. The interior walls of the room were about as thick as the exterior walls. In some places, two stratum VIII floors were revealed, each with destruction debris above it. The final stratum VIII destruction produced as much as a half meter of burned debris. Whenever bedrock was reached, a substantial leveling operation prior to construction was indicated. The remains inside the fort indicated that the occupants of Gilead grew grain: stone grinding implements, kraters and bowls, beehive ovens, and bins set in corners and floors. The small ceramic assemblage was adequate to indicate the time of Solomon (tenth century BCE) for stratum VIII.

STRATUM VII. Shortly after the stratum VIII destruction, the stratum VII occupants surrounded the brick fort with a stone defense line more than 1.5 m thick and composed of very large and roughly dressed boulders. The 3.25-m and 1.75-m interstices on the north and east were divided into casemates by thinner walls. The earlier gateways were reused. The eastern entrance, only one meter wide, was protected by a guardroom projecting slightly from the defense line. The gateway was filled with about 2 m of destruction debris that contained a good pottery group. This major destruction was the dominant feature all along the stratum VII defense line and in the rooms in the brick fort reused in stratum VII. The destruction preserved remarkably the stratum VII plan and groups of pots and stone implements. The repertory was distinctly in the Syrian tradition, dating the massive destruction to the ninth century BCE.

STRATUM VI. The stratum VI reconstruction first involved the creation of a platform over the thick burned layer, leveling off the area with debris from the defense walls. The platform consisted of a thick layer of gray clay laid over the entire area defined by the walls of the stratum VII fort. In the southeastern quadrant, the stratum VI plan was well preserved; it indicates that construction was part of an overall plan consistently executed. Walkways between houses were set out in a rectangular grid and had the same width and composition. The houses were alike in character and plan. The walls were only 0.5 m thick; the lower half meter or more was composed of rough, small stones and capped with mud brick. Units consisted typically of two rooms, one with a cobbled floor and the other containing foundations of a stairway to the roof. The floors of the houses were covered with a thick burned layer; several rooms contained significant ceramic groups dating to about 800 BCE.

STRATUM V. Stratum VI and V expanded their occupied area to the north and east, beyond the lines of the fort, but erosion obliterated all evidence of the defenses of these strata. The stratum V walls were generally preserved to 1.5 m in height inside the stratum VII fort lines, and the rooms were filled with destruction debris and artifacts. Stratum VI walkways continued to be resurfaced and the houses were reused after a thick fill raised their floors. A final short phase of stratum V followed the main occupation of houses with mud-brick floors. What seems to be a copper-refining kiln was found above and inside the northern stratum VII defense line.

SUMMARY

It is possible to correlate the Tell er-Rumeith strata and destructions with various incursions from the north. If the stratum VIII brick fort is Solomonic, it may have been destroyed in about 885 BCE, when the area came under the control of the Arameans. The stratum VII fort construction could be related to the conversion of the site into an Aramean border fort. The destruction in the mid-ninth century BCE may be attributed to Jehoshaphat and Ahab, or to

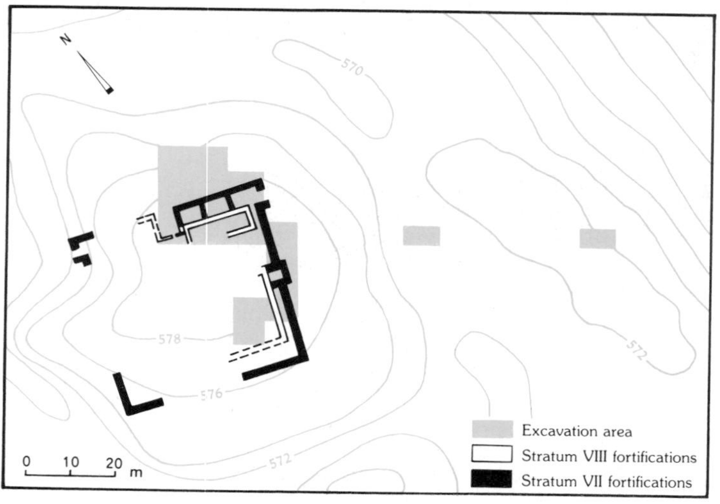

Tell er-Rumeith: plan of the site and excavation areas.

Looking west at the stone stratum VII defenses with the west gate built against the stratum VIII brick wall (on the left).

Ahaziah and Jehoram. The stratum VI occupation could be attributed to the Arameans from the time Hazael extended the borders of Syria to the south of Rumeith until the end of the ninth century, when Joash defeated the Arameans at Aphek. The major stratum V destruction may belong to Tiglath-pileser III's campaign in 733 BCE.

N. Glueck, *BASOR* 92 (1943), 10–16; P. W. Lapp, *RB* 70 (1963), 406–411; 75 (1968), 98–105; id., *The Tale of the Tell*, Pittsburgh 1975, 111–119; *American Archaeology in the Mideast*, 158–159; *Akkadica Supplementum* 7–8 (1989), 495–497.

NANCY L. LAPP

RUQEISH

IDENTIFICATION AND EXPLORATION

The site of Ruqeish is on the Mediterranean coast near Deir el-Balaḥ, about 18 km (11 mi.) southwest of Gaza (map reference 086.091). In 1940 a large cemetery with cremation burials deposited in urns and jars was excavated here by J. Ory, on behalf of the Mandatory Department of Antiquities. In the course of rescue excavations in 1973 by A. Biran, on behalf of the Israel Department of Antiquities and Museums, dozens of similar burials were unearthed, dating to the Late Iron Age (eighth–sixth centuries BCE). Such burials are known from many Phoenician sites in the Mediterranean Basin. From 1982 to 1984, a systematic archaeological survey was conducted in the Raphia–Gaza region by a Ben-Gurion University expedition under the direction of E. D. Oren; it revealed that a continuous strip about 1 km (0.6 mi.) long between the cemetery and Tell 'Aqluq to the north was densely covered with occupation remains from the Iron Age and the Persian period (eighth–fourth centuries BCE). Rescue excavations and probes carried out in this area demonstrated that these remains actually belonged to a single settlement that had been enclosed by a massive fortification system.

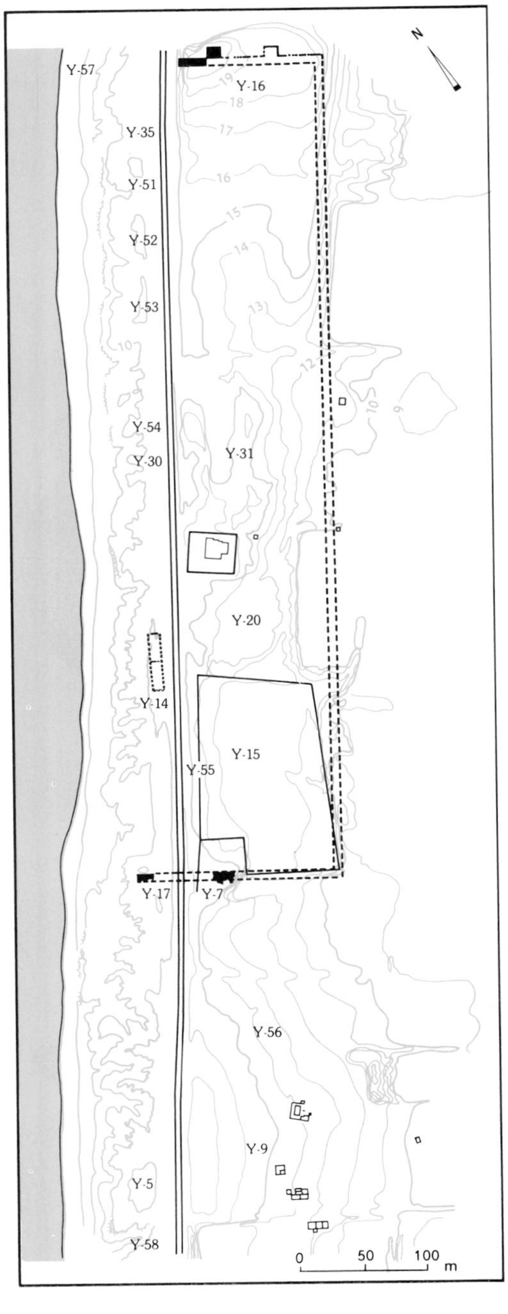

Ruqeish: map of the site; the black lines indicate portions of the wall and towers.

EXCAVATION RESULTS

Excavations at the southern edge of the site (areas Y-7 and Y-17 on the survey map) offer the key to reconstructing the settlement's history and understanding the construction methods employed in building the fortifications. In this area the massive city wall, which bounded the settlement on the south, is about 5.5 m thick and preserved to a height of at least 5 m. The remains of mud-brick buttresses projected out of the wall at intervals of 5 m, and nearby a massive block of mud brick that had formed part of a tower or the city's southern gate was recorded. To the north, the city ends in a prominent mound, Tell 'Aqluq (Y-16), about 2 a. in size, where impressive remains of fortifications, including a massive wall and two huge towers (7.7 by 11.6 m), were found. In this area the city wall is over 6 m thick and stands some 5.5 m high. The settlement site of Ruqeish ends on the east in a steep slope that marks, according to the analysis of aerial photographs and a series of probes, the contour of the eastern city wall. The western edge of the site, along the seashore, was destroyed as a result of the intensive erosion of the coastal cliff, leaving no traces of the city wall. The site measured about 150 by 650 m and covered some 20 to 25 a.; the total length of the defense wall was approximately 1.6 km (1 mi.).

Judging from the evidence uncovered thus far, it appears that the entire area of the site was occupied in the Iron Age and Persian period. The finds from areas Y-7 and Y-17 indicate that, prior to the establishment of the fortified town, the site of Ruqeish was not settled, and the foundation trench for the fortification wall was dug in the sterile sand. The earliest settlement, phase IV, is represented in area Y-17 by structures with thin walls and beaten floors made of brick material, as well as cooking and baking installations. In phase III, the area adjacent to the southern wall was used as a dump for refuse from the settlement. This deposit yielded a rich collection of complete and restorable vessels mixed with *tabun* fragments and animal bones. Phase III was sealed by a thick layer of mud-brick debris (phase II) from the city wall, which went out of use in this period. The accumulation of mud-brick debris in the eastern section of area Y-17 was more than 2 m thick; above it were the remains of the unfortified phase I settlement. The latest stage of the settlement at Ruqeish is represented in area Y-17 by large refuse pits that were dug into the city wall and adjacent structures of phases III and II.

Excavations in the western section of area Y-17 uncovered a continuous, 3-

Segment of the settlement's wall.

Round granary built of bricks, Persian period.

Site Y-59: remains of a quarry on the shore at the foot of the settlement.

m-thick sequence of settlement remains; the earliest (III) are represented by long-halled magazines, around which abundant broken storage jars and wine amphorae were found. To phase I belong extensive remains of an industrial installation with masses of burned mud bricks mixed with thick deposits of ash. The limited excavations at Tell 'Aqluq (area Y-16) revealed a considerable accumulation of settlement debris, about 4 m thick. Analysis of the finds from both areas suggests that the phase IV fortified site was founded in the second half of the eighth century BCE and continued uninterruptedly through phases III and II of the seventh and sixth centuries BCE.

POTTERY. The ceramic repertoire of phases IV–II is characterized by "wide-bellied" and torpedo-shaped storage jars, highly burnished jugs and kraters of "Ruqeish ware," Cypro-Phoenician pottery, Phoenician or "Samarian" bowls, and imported ceramics from Cyprus, Greece, and Egypt. Phase I, from the Persian period (fifth–fourth centuries BCE), is represented by diagnostic pottery, such as thick-walled mortaria, basket-handled storage jars, imported Greek amphorae, numerous examples of imported Athenian black-glazed ware, and Egyptian Bes vessels.

SUMMARY

The large settlement at Ruqeish and its massive defense system, the Phoenician-style cremation burials, and the distinctive Phoenician orientation of its material culture strongly suggest the existence of a flourishing Phoenician settlement at the site in the Late Iron Age and Persian period. The site's coastal location between Gaza and Raphia and its diverse material remains—Phoenician, Cypriot, Greek, and Egyptian—indicate that the town was a center for maritime trade and overland commerce from the international highway connecting Egypt and Asia. This writer has suggested identifying the site of Ruqeish with the "sealed *Karum* of Egypt," mentioned in the Nimrud Prism from the reign of Sargon II, king of Assyria. The "sealed *Karum*" is named as a harbor or commercial headquarters founded on the border with Egypt, at the conclusion of Sargon's second campaign to Philistia in 716 BCE. It was established by Assyria to facilitate and supervise the international trade at the Egyptian border and to control the spice trade or "Arabian trade" network whose administrative headquarters were in Gaza.

The prosperous settlement (phase I) at Ruqeish in the Persian period extended over an area equal to that of the Iron Age town. The fortification system, which went out of use in phase II, was not repaired, and the settlement remained unfortified. The occupational remains, in places more than 2 m high, included public buildings with ashlar masonry in their foundations, domestic buildings, and industrial and storage installations. The site of Ruqeish was evidently an administrative and commercial center in the Persian period, too, as well as the western terminus for the Arabian trade. It is likely that this site should be identified in the Persian period as one of the coastal emporia between Gaza and Yenisos mentioned by Herodotus (III:5).

J. Ory, *QDAP* 10 (1944), 205; C. N. Johns, *PEQ* 80 (1948), 88; W. Culican, *Australian Journal of Biblical Archaeology* 2 (1973), 66–105; A. Biran, *IEJ* 24 (1974), 141–142; R. Hestrin and M. Dayagi-Mendels, *Israel Museum Journal* 2 (1983), 49–57.

ELIEZER D. OREN

"Ruqeish ware": burnished kraters and jugs, 8th century BCE.

S

SA'IDIYEH, TELL ES-

IDENTIFICATION

Tell es-Sa'idiyeh is situated on the south bank of Wadi Kufrinjeh, 1.8 km (1 mi.) east of the Jordan River, about halfway between the Dead Sea and Tiberias. In 1926, W. F. Albright tentatively proposed to identify it with Zaphon, largely on the basis of Judges 12:1. In 1943, N. Glueck suggested the identification Zarethan, on the grounds of biblical references such as Joshua 3:16 and 1 Kings 7:46. The excavations at Tell es-Sa'idiyeh have not as yet produced evidence to support either of these proposals or an alternative.

A surface survey of pottery was made by Glueck in 1942, and in 1953 soundings were carried out by H. de Contenson. In the winter of 1964, the University Museum of the University of Pennsylvania undertook a major excavation on the highest part of the mound, directed by J. B. Pritchard. The initial campaign was followed by two ten-week seasons in the winters of 1965 and 1966 and by a six-week campaign in 1967, with J. E. Huesman as field director. Excavations were resumed in 1985, on behalf of the British Museum, under the direction of J. N. Tubb. As of 1991, five seasons of excavations (1985–1987 and 1989–1990) had been carried out.

Tell es-Sa'idiyeh: map of the mound and excavation areas.

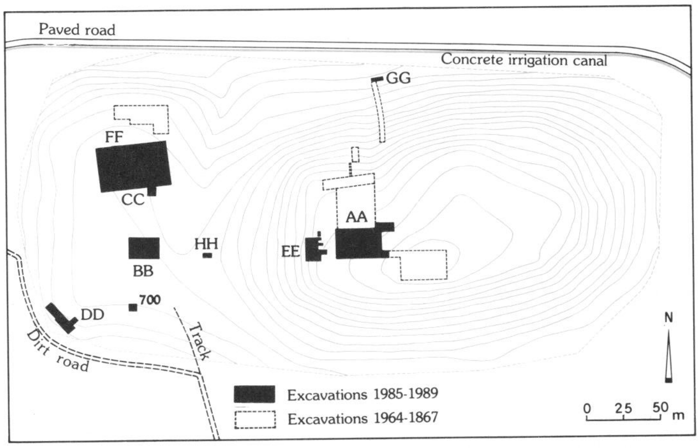

UNIVERSITY OF PENNSYLVANIA EXCAVATIONS

1. LOW BENCH TO THE WEST (EL-GHARBI). A low bench to the west was built up by the debris from the Early Bronze Age occupation. It had been used as a cemetery in the transitional period between the Late Bronze Age and the Iron Age I. In 1964 and 1965, forty-five graves from this period were excavated. The most elaborate was tomb 101, which contained within its mud-brick walls a single skeleton accompanied by a bronze wine set (laver, bowl, strainer, and juglet), a bronze tripod, storage jars, 571 gold and carnelian beads, two electrum pendants with a chain to suspend them, two

Bronze wine set from tomb 101, 13th–12th centuries BCE.

Tell es-Sa'idiyeh: general view, looking south. Staircase leading to the water system in the center.

General view of tomb 101, 13th–12th centuries BCE.

electrum toggle pins, five ivory cosmetic containers, a bronze cauldron, a bronze lamp, and other vessels. In two other tombs, 102 and 117, skeletal material was wrapped in cloth and covered with bitumen. Tomb 102 also contained a bronze sword, a scarab, a piece of ivory, two bronze bowls, and a bronze jug with a handle riveted to its body. In the remainder of the graves the contents were poorer. The ceramic and other evidence points to the last half of the thirteenth through the first half of the twelfth centuries BCE as the span over which the cemetery was in use.

2. NORTH SIDE OF THE MOUND. On the north side of the mound a stairway was found leading from the summit to a water source at the base. In addition to the ninety-five steps actually preserved, there were originally some forty-five more that the erosion of the upper part had destroyed. The 2.25-m space between the stone-built walls of the stairway is divided by a mud-brick wall along its entire length; the wall supported the roof, which camouflaged this means of access to the spring at the foot of the mound from inside the city. The date for the construction and use of this civil-defense installation has not yet been determined with certainty (but see below).

3. NORTHWEST SIDE OF THE MOUND (ESH-SHARQI). By the end of the 1967 season, four main levels of occupation had been distinguished on the northwest side of the mound, in an excavated area of 1,375 sq m. They are summarized in the order of their settlement.

Stratum VII was established on the remains of an occupation that had been destroyed by fire. It contained ten houses built of mud brick laid on stone foundations. The settlement was surrounded by a city wall (c. 3.5 m thick) that was also built of mud brick on a shallow stone foundation. Among the structures is a three-room house with an altar, or table, covered with white plaster. There are two shallow basins in the table, one of which contains a tripod incense burner imbedded in ash and charcoal. It seems that the settlement was not violently destroyed but rather abandoned. It probably dates to 825–790 BCE.

Stratum VI was built according to the same orientation as stratum VII. It consisted of houses and streets erected on the remains of the previous level. It seems that the stratum VII wall continued to be in use. The stratum dates to 790–750 BCE.

In stratum V, twelve houses whose plan is identical and whose sizes are almost identical were constructed as a single unit. Six dwellings opened onto one street and six onto another, parallel street. The houses measure, on the average, 4.83 by 8.37 m. They consisted of a large front room, or court, with a row of mud-brick columns to support the roof, and a smaller room at the back. Half of the larger room was usually paved with rounded stones. This plan has no parallel in contemporary sites on both sides of the Jordan. It seems that the stone foundations of a city wall, uncovered near the mound's northern edge, also belong to this stratum. The settlement was probably destroyed by a conflagration and should be dated to 750–730 BCE.

Plan of the courtyard building on the mound's summit, stratum III, Persian period.

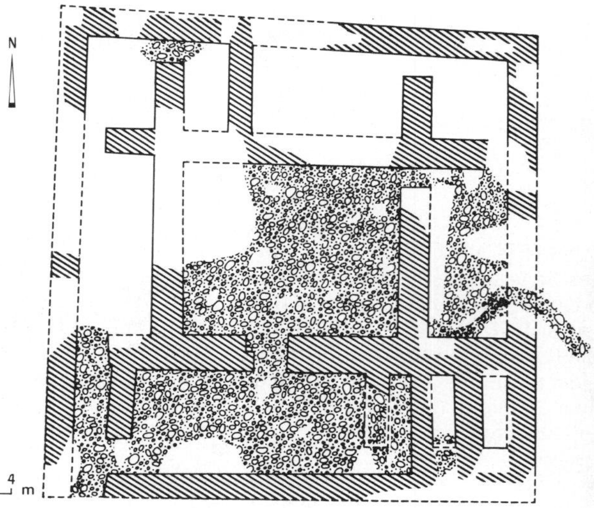

Stratum IV consisted of a smoothed surface in which ninety-seven circular pits and two rectangular bins lined with mud brick had been cut. Remnants of two-row barley and wheat in the crevices of one of the bins suggest that the entire area was a threshing floor in the latest period of occupation. The stratum dates to about 730–600(?) BCE.

4. SOUNDING ON THE "ACROPOLIS." Three layers of occupation extending from the Persian through the Roman periods have thus far been encountered on the highest part of the mound, the "acropolis." However, the stratigraphic sequence there has not yet been correlated with that of the Iron Age layers described above.

Stratum III here contained a palatial building (21.95 by 22.05 m) consisting of seven rooms built around a paved courtyard with a drain and a tower in the southeast corner. A carbon-14 test obtained from a charred roof beam from the palace gave a date of 343 $\pm$ 52 BCE. A limestone incense burner decorated with geometric designs, a horse, and a human figure bore the inscription *lzkwr*, "(belonging) to Zakkur." It seems that the building belongs to the Persian period.

A Hellenistic structure (21.2 by 13.3 m) was built in stratum II. Its mud-brick walls were separated from a stone foundation by a layer of reeds laid crosswise for the length of the wall. The fortresslike building had been roofed with sycamore beams that were covered with reeds and a mud surface.

Stratum I was represented by a Roman building, a watchtower or fortress, and two plastered water reservoirs.

JAMES B. PRITCHARD

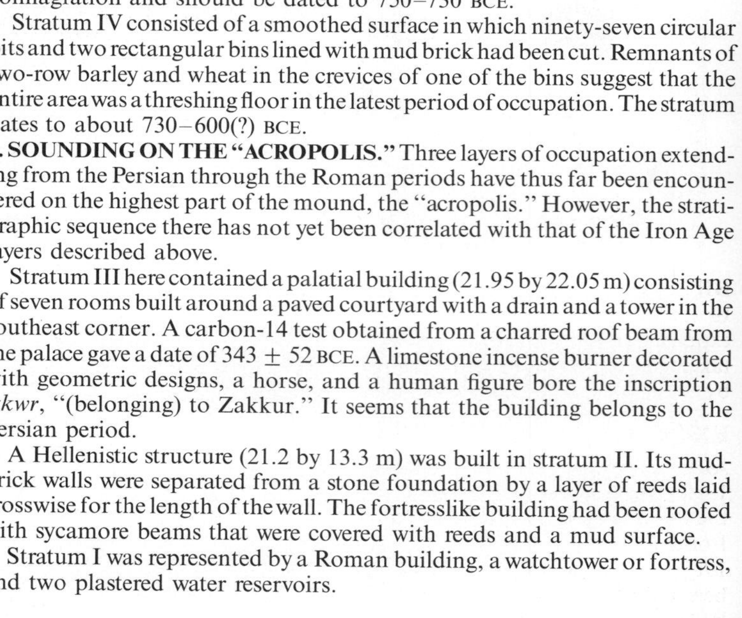

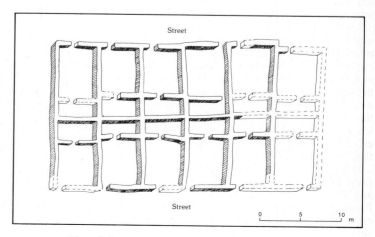

Plan of the structures in stratum V, 8th century BCE.

General view of the structures in stratum V, 8th century BCE.

BRITISH MUSEUM EXCAVATIONS

In 1985, excavations at Tell es-Sa'idiyeh were resumed by a British Museum expedition under the direction of J. N. Tubb. Five seasons of excavations have taken place to date. In the latest two (1989 and 1990), the museum was joined by the Rijksmuseum van Oudheden, Leiden.

EXCAVATIONS ON THE UPPER MOUND

AREA AA. Area AA, in the southern part of Pritchard's large trench from the 1960s, was established to continue the sequence of occupational phases below the lowermost stratum reached by the Pennsylvania team (stratum VII), an Iron Age city level dating to the late ninth to early eighth centuries BCE. In 1985, when area AA was initiated, Pritchard's excavation report had not yet been published, and it was not appreciated that the southern part of his trench had not in fact been excavated down to stratum VII. It had been left in 1967 at some point during the isolation of stratum VI on the eastern side, with deeper soundings into and indeed below stratum VII on the west. Much of the work was initially concerned, therefore, with defining and isolating residual deposits attributable to stratum VI, followed by the complete excavation of stratum VII. As far as stratum VI is concerned, very little can be said; the remains were too eroded to allow anything of value to be added to the plan published by Pritchard for the area to the north. One observation is, however, of interest: stratum VI must have represented a small and quite sparse settlement, nucleated toward the center of the mound's surface. No trace of stratum VI was found on the western side of area AA and, as if to reinforce this point, what was found there was a burial, stratigraphically clearly belonging to stratum VI, and in a context in which it must be seen as having been extramural. The peculiar positions of the two individuals in the burial suggest that they might have been executed rather than routinely interred.

Below the rather miserable remnants of stratum VI, extensive and well-preserved remains of stratum VII were found all over area AA. Substantial architectural features and details have been added to the plan published by Pritchard for the area to the north. A series of houses and courtyards has been excavated, arranged along narrow streets paved with a mixture of pebbles and sherds. Many of the houses contained internal installations, such as mud-brick baths, bins, ovens, and pits. However, one of the main activities, perhaps even on an industrial scale, seems to have been weaving and textile preparation. Many of the rooms contained large numbers of loom weights, often in distinctive alignments suggesting the configuration of the looms. Most of the stratum VII pottery consists of large vessels—kraters, storage jars, pithoi, and cooking pots; only very few fine pieces have been found.

Excavations in area AA have also confirmed Pritchard's subdivision of VII into two subphases, VIIA the later and VIIB the earlier. Again, by virtue of excavating over a wider area, it has been possible to add a further dimension to this purely chronological sequence. It is now clear that VIIB, the original phase, represents a fairly sparse, well-constructed settlement with large rooms and courtyards that was, perhaps, not very extensive. Certainly it did not reach to the edge of the mound. Subphase VIIA, characterized by the use of distinctive orange-colored mud bricks, can now be seen to represent the result of a substantial building program that created extensive additions to the VIIB plan. The VIIA settlement clearly reached the edge of the mound, where in area EE (see below) it was seen to be confined by a perimeter wall associated with a stone-paved walkway. Most of the VIIB rooms showed evidence of having been partitioned, and many of the individual VIIB walls were rebuilt or patched. The homogeneous nature of the VIIA additions suggests a quite rapid process of building, perhaps indicative of a population ingress in the early eighth century BCE. It is possible that this revitalization of the settlement is related to the activities of Jeroboam II, king of Israel, who is known to have reestablished authority over Transjordan as far as the Dead Sea (2 Kg. 14:28).

Below stratum VII, excavations in 1986–1987 on the eastern side of area AA revealed a complicated sequence of earlier occupations. Stratum VIII (ninth century BCE), a non-architectural phase of industrial usage, was characterized by fine ashy deposits, extremely dense in places, emanating from areas in which intense heat had been generated. Those areas had been created by the rough modification of abandoned stratum IX architectural elements. For example, in places stratum IX walls had been reused to form the backs of scooped-out, level platforms; the platforms were then used in some industrial process whose nature is still unknown. Whatever the process was, it created a large volume of ashy waste, which covered the abandoned remains of stratum IX.

Below stratum VIII, and above the large public building of stratum XII

Area AA: part of the "governor's residency" and administrative complex, stratum XII, 12th century BCE.

excavated at the end of the 1987 season, three architectural phases were isolated; the uppermost phase (stratum IX), as mentioned above, having been abandoned. Although stratum IX had suffered considerable damage from weathering and erosion, two phases (IXA and IXB) of a quite large building were found, together with part of its associated, well-constructed, stone-paved courtyard.

Stratum X was also characterized by a well-built stone courtyard, but in this case it was associated with unusual, partially sunken, stone-lined structures interpreted as pens for livestock. The courtyard was found to belong to a massive, stone-constructed building, only one small corner of which was revealed within the excavation area, the remainder lying to the north and west.

A similar, but less massive building clearly occupied the same position in stratum XIA; however, here, to the southeast, and separated from it by a north–south street, a small bipartite building with carefully laid mud-brick floors was found. The building's overall plan, together with various internal details, such as a plastered bench against the rear wall with an inset niche, suggests that it may have been a small temple.

Stratum XIA was built over a dense layer of silting that in turn covered the deep deposit of intensely burnt destruction debris overlying the stratum XII architecture. The excavation of stratum XII in 1987 uncovered the remains of a large public building that, to judge from its Egyptian-style plan and construction method, must be seen as yet another example of a so-called Egyptian governor's residency. The building had clearly been abandoned following its destruction; the depth of silt overlying the collapsed debris suggests that some considerable period of time must have elapsed before the construction of stratum XIA, perhaps as much as a hundred years. The destruction of stratum XII is dated to the mid-twelfth century BCE.

Within two of the rooms in the residency, evidence was found for a phase of squatter or campsite occupation immediately following the destruction. The collapsed debris appeared to have been leveled and rough surfaces had been made within the confines of the still-standing walls. Represented only by hearths and grinding stones, this phase is referred to as stratum XIB.

As mentioned above, the complicated series of rather poor occupation phases between stratum VII and stratum XII were defined in the 1986–1988 seasons on the eastern side of area AA. In the 1989 season, it became clear that, as in the case of stratum VI, these were not extensive settlement phases. None of them appeared to have reached the edge of the mound; stratum XII certainly lies directly below VII on the western side of area AA, a situation paralleled in area EE on the western slope of the upper mound.

AREA EE. Area EE was opened in 1986 to study the site's defenses. Here, beneath some heavily eroded structures attributable to stratum V and the perimeter wall belonging to stratum VII (as defined also by Pritchard on the north side), the dense, heavily burnt destruction debris of stratum XII was found.

Removal of this thick deposit revealed the remains of a 4.5-m-thick city wall and, behind it, a second major public building complex. Again, as in the case of the residency building in area AA, this complex shows purely Egyptian building techniques, with deep brick foundations and no use of stone.

One of the rooms had a finely paved mud-brick floor; to its west were two partially sunken rooms that appear to represent a bath complex. Both rooms were thickly plastered and the slight incurving of the preserved tops of walls suggests that they might have been vaulted. A small tunnel connected the eastern room to the western room, which lay at a lower level and had a clearly defined water channel and an exit conduit at its base. Significantly, in view of

Staircase of the water system.

Lower part of the water system and the entrance to the pool.

the Egyptian nature of the architecture, the lower room contained a clay sealing from a papyrus roll; the texture of the papyrus and the impression of the string tie are clearly visible on the reverse. Elsewhere in the complex, the heavily burnt floor surfaces produced good collections of typical mid-twelfth-century pottery.

One of the rooms had a thickly plastered floor laid on a deliberate slope, facing a diagonally placed *pisée* wall. The floor, which showed evidence of extensive water channeling, was covered with sherds of Egyptian storage jars, perhaps representing as many as fifty or sixty complete vessels. It is possible that this unusual room was used as a sort of water-cooling reservoir, perhaps for wine storage.

AREA GG. One of the major undertakings of the 1987 season was the further examination of Pritchard's staircase on the north slope. The excavation of this structure, which can now also be related to stratum XII, had been left unfinished by the Pennsylvania expedition. In 1987, therefore, the staircase was reexcavated, revealing additional steps. At a depth of some 6 m below the present level of the plain, water was reached, and it was possible to define the structure of an enclosed pool. Pritchard's theory that the staircase was an element of a water system was shown to be correct. It was quite a sophisticated system, with the water issuing through a conduit on the south side and draining through a channel on the north. Although not specifically Egyptian in design, the system is also not Canaanite; its closest parallels are to be found at Mycenae and Tiryns.

STRATIGRAPHY. The stratigraphic sequence on the upper mound, at the end of the 1990 season, can therefore be summarized thus:

Stratum	*Period*
I	Roman (Pritchard)
II	Hellenistic (Pritchard)
III	Persian (Pritchard)
STRATIGRAPHIC DISCONTINUITY	
IV	730–600 BCE (Pritchard)
V	750–730 BCE (Pritchard)
VI	790–750 BCE (Pritchard)
VIIB–A	825–790 BCE (Pritchard)
VIII	860–825 BCE
GAP	
IXB–A	950–900 BCE
X	970–950 BCE
XIA	1040–970 BCE
GAP	
(XIB) XII	destroyed c. 1150 BCE

LATE BRONZE/EARLY IRON AGE CEMETERY ON THE LOWER MOUND

AREA BB. The discovery of Egyptian-style architecture and associated finds in stratum XII suggests that Sa'idiyeh, like Beth-Shean on the other side of the Jordan River, was a center for Egypt's control over Canaan in the very last phase of its New Kingdom empire, under the pharaohs of the Twentieth Dynasty.

Excavations on the lower mound added another important dimension to understanding the nature of stratum XII in area AA by uncovering the extensive and intensively used cemetery contemporary with this settlement. In area BB, which lies toward the center of the lower mound, some 340 graves have so far been excavated. A few of these, perhaps less than 10 percent, belong to the Iron III/Persian period and can be related to the Persian phase of occupation represented by stratum III on the upper mound. The majority of the graves, however, belong to the thirteenth and twelfth centuries BCE—contemporary with stratum XII on the upper mound.

Area BB: part of a well-preserved EB II house, stratum L2.

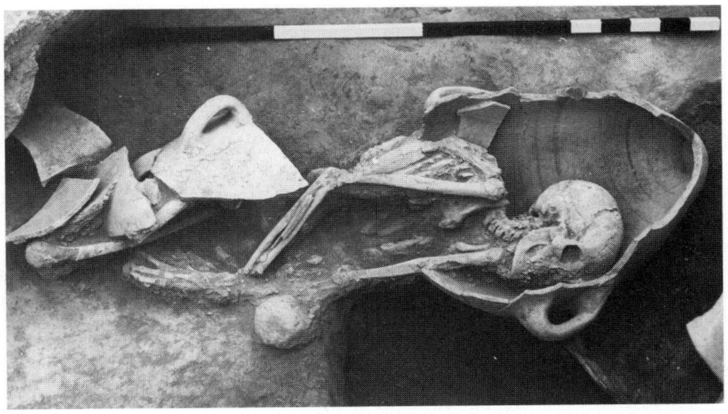

Burial, 12th century BCE: the head has been covered with a storage jar, while the rest of the body has been "shrouded" with large jar sherds.

Many of the graves had been seriously disturbed by intensive reuse of the area, but despite this, it was possible to assemble a substantial corpus of well-preserved burials. They show considerable variation with regard to grave construction, disposition of the deceased, burial practice, and grave goods, which suggests a mixed population. Many of the graves are simple pits, some of which made use of Early Bronze Age architectural elements from the underlying occupation layers—foundation stones, fragments of walling, and even reused structural mud bricks. Several of the graves were more elaborately constructed from mud-brick slabs and were roofed with the same material. Some of these were clearly intended to be partially visible above ground level, being more in the nature of tombs than graves.

One of the most important burial types found at Sa'idiyeh is the so-called double pithos burial, in which the body was contained within a pottery "coffin" composed of two very large storage jars joined shoulder to shoulder. Grave goods were placed both inside and around the outside of the pithoi and, for the most part, were strongly Egyptian in character. This type of burial, which is extremely rare in Canaan, is now well represented in the Sa'idiyeh cemetery, with over twenty examples. Its occurrence may well indicate the presence of a Sea Peoples element in the population; the functional similarity between the double pithos container and the anthropoid clay coffin, known to have been used by the Philistines, seems, in the opinion of this writer, undeniable. A somewhat poorer expression of the same practice has also been found in a number of graves, in which only the head of the deceased was placed inside the storage jar and the rest of the body was covered with large sherds. Small storage jars were frequently used as burial containers for infants, the jar having been cut off at the neck in order to insert the body.

Generally, the burial practice was single and primary. A few examples of double or multiple burials have been found, but quite a common finding is what may be described as a "derived secondary" practice. This should be seen as a function of the extreme intensity of usage of the same cemetery over a period of time. During the digging of graves it must not have been an uncommon event to disturb a previous interment. In such cases, in order to show

Bronze bowl containing an ivory fish-shaped cosmetic box, from grave 232, 12th century BCE.

some degree of respect, the skull, and often a couple of the long bones, was carefully retrieved and placed inside the new grave.

In terms of grave goods, the Sa'idiyeh cemetery is a rich one, arguing for an affluent and sophisticated society. The graves have produced rich assemblages of pottery, metalwork, stone vessels, ivory, and jewelry, many of which show a strong Egyptian influence or are purely Egyptian. Some of the somewhat unusual burial practices are also Egyptian. In several instances a pottery, or more usually a bronze, bowl had been placed over the face of the deceased; examples have also been found in which the genitals were covered with a bowl. Another practice, also with Egyptian parallels, is the ritual "killing" of weapons. Daggers in particular, but also javelins and arrowheads, were bent almost double before being deposited in the grave. This practice was not, however, confined solely to metal weapons: many of the pottery vessels included in the graves had had a tiny piece removed from the rim, again as part of a ritual killing process.

The majority of the bronze objects found in the graves (vessels, weapons, pins, and other jewelry items) were found to be wrapped in textile remains. An examination of these materials demonstrated, in every case so far, that the textiles are Egyptian linen. In some instances the evidence suggests that the objects were wrapped in cloth and deposited separately; in others, however, it is clear that they were incorporated in a tight binding around the body. Even when bronze objects were not included among the grave offerings, the process of binding is often suggested by the deceased's posture. In several cases, the shoulders are tightly drawn up or the arms are drawn across the chest or the feet are crossed. The Egyptian character of these bound burials is evident. Even more remarkable, however, are the traces of a black bituminous material found over the bones in some of the burials. This may even imply an attempt at mummification.

EARLY BRONZE AGE OCCUPATION ON THE LOWER MOUND

The original intention in laying out area BB in 1985 was to provide a good-sized area in which to examine the Early Bronze Age occupation known from Pritchard's excavations below and between the graves of the later cemetery.

AREA DD. Two superimposed architectural phases were isolated; the uppermost one is associated with an extensive and intense destruction. The key to understanding these two poorly preserved phases (strata L2 and L3) was provided by excavations in area DD, at the southwest corner of the mound. Here, between 1985 and 1987, the Early Bronze Age occupation was examined in an area that appeared to lie beyond the limits of the later cemetery.

The uppermost stratum (L2) was badly eroded, but it was nevertheless possible to salvage the plan of a two-roomed building, constructed of mud brick on well-laid stone foundations with carefully prepared white plaster floors. This phase had ended in a destruction. The thick deposit of burnt mud-brick debris and ashes had sealed a rich and varied assemblage of crushed but complete pottery vessels. The examination of the pottery placed stratum L2 and its destruction toward the end of the Early Bronze Age II. Many of the vessels are decorated in a distinctive "ribbon-painted" style, and the repertoire includes many innovative features, such as four-spouted lamps. The brickwork in stratum L2 is peculiar and distinctive, being light grayish-green in color. It has therefore been possible to detect it quite easily in area BB, even in the most fragmentary and disturbed states. There, too, it is associated with an extensive destruction horizon. Combining the evidence from the two areas, it is clear that stratum L2 represents the final phase of habitation on the lower mound.

Below stratum L2 in area DD, excavations have revealed the better-preserved architecture of stratum L3. This phase, which was found to be on the same alignment as L2, was built using bricks of a completely different color: deep orange brown. Again, this distinctive brickwork can be detected in area BB, where it also directly underlies stratum L2. In area DD, it has been possible to recover a coherent plan for stratum L3, showing a rectangular building with an attached courtyard, a pebble-paved street, and part of another building on the other side of the street. The house floors were relatively clean, but enough pottery was recovered to show that this stratum also lies within the Early Bronze Age II. A number of large storage jars had been set into the floors, with stones or sherds as covers. Analysis of the residue on the interior of one of the jars proved it to be olive oil.

There are at least three more Early Bronze Age occupation phases below stratum L3. The first of them, stratum L4, is being examined in area BB. In one of the squares, excavations in 1989 revealed a complicated series of mud-brick-paved platforms and sunken rooms, associated in one part with a thick 20-cm or so horizon of mineralized grape and fig seeds. This finding is fully compatible with what is known of the Early Bronze Age economy, suggesting that wine was produced here, possibly for export to Egypt.

JONATHAN N. TUBB

Main publications: J. B. Pritchard, *The Cemetery at Tell es-Sa'idiyeh, Jordan* (University Museum Monograph 41), Philadelphia 1980; id., *Tell es-Sa'idiyeh: Excavations on the Tell, 1964–1966* (University Museum Monograph 60), Philadelphia 1985.

Other studies: W. F. Albright, *AASOR* 6 (1926), 45–47; N. Glueck, ibid. 25–28 (1951), 290–295; H. de Contenson, *ADAJ* 4–5 (1960), 49–56; 8–9 (1964), 37; J. B. Pritchard, ibid., 95–98; 27 (1983), 645–646; id., *Expedition* 6 (1964), 2–9; 7 (1965), 26–33; 10 (1968), 26–29; 11 (1968), 20–22; id., *ILN* (March 28, 1964), 487–490; id., *Archaeology* 18 (1965), 292–294; 19 (1966), 298–299; id., *BTS* 75 (1965), 6–15; id., *BA* 28 (1965), 10–17, 126–128; id., *RB* 72 (1965), 257–262; 73 (1966), 574–576; id., *Ugaritica* 6, Paris 1969, 427–434; id., *The Role of the Phoenicians* (ed. W. Ward), Beirut 1968, 99–112; id., *Studies on the Ancient Palestinian World* (F. V. Winnett Fest.) Toronto 1971, 3–17; id., *The Cemetery at Tell es-Sa'idiyeh* (Reviews), *ADAJ* 24 (1980), 213. — *PEQ* 113 (1981), 135–136. — *ZDPV* 97 (1981), 116–120; id., *Tell es-Sa'idiyeh: Excavations on the Tell* (Reviews), *ADAJ* 29 (1985), 297. — *JAOS* 108 (1988), 151–152. — *Transeuphratène* 1 (1989), 191–193. — *ZDPV* 105 (1989), 189–195; A. Lemaire, *Rivista di Studi Fenici* 10 (1982), 11–12; Y. Shiloh, *Archaeology and Biblical Interpretation* (D. Glenn Rose Fest.), Atlanta 1987, 225; Khouri, *Antiquities*, 40–46; Weippert 1988 (Ortsregister); *Akkadica Supplementum* 7–8 (1989), 521–542; O. Negbi, *TA* 18 (1991), 205–243.

Preliminary Reports of British Museum Excavations: J. N. Tubb, *ADAJ* 29 (1985), 131–140; 30 (1986), 115–130; 32 (1988), 41–58; 35 (1991), 181–194; id., *Archiv für Orientforschung* 33 (1986), 212–218; id., *Levant* 20 (1988), 23–88; 22 (1990), 21–42; (and P. G. Dorrell), 23 (1991), 67–86; id., *Archaeology and the Bible* (eds. J. N. Tubb and R. L. Chapman), London 1990, 94–110.

SAMARIA (CITY)

IDENTIFICATION AND HISTORY

Samaria, the capital of the kingdom of Israel and center of the region of Samaria, bears the name of the hill of Samaria on which Omri, king of Israel, built his city. The site is identified with the village of Sebastia (c. 10 km northwest of Shechem). The place was renamed Sebaste by Herod when he rebuilt the city. The town lay on a high hill (430 m above sea level), towering over its surroundings. It was situated at a crossroads near the main highway running northward from Shechem, in a fertile agricultural region (map reference 168.187). Its topographic and strategic advantages were probably why the site was chosen for the capital of the kingdom of Israel, even though it lacked an adequate water supply.

The Bible records the foundation of Samaria: "In the thirty-first year of Asa king of Judah, Omri began to reign over Israel, and reigned for twelve years; six years he reigned in Tirzah. He bought the hill of Samaria from Shemer for two talents of silver; and he fortified the hill, and called the name of the city which he built, Samaria, after the name of Shemer, the owner of the hill" (1 Kg. 16:23–24). Even after the fall of Israel, the Assyrians called it the house of Khomry, after Omri, the founder of the dynasty and of Samaria. Omri succeeded in strengthening the kingdom, but because of his failures in his wars with Aram, he was forced to cede to the king of Aram "streets" in Samaria for merchants to set up their bazaars (1 Kg. 20:34).

Ahab, Omri's son, reigned from 873 to 852 BCE. Toward the end of his reign, Samaria was besieged by Ben-hadad II, king of Aram, and his allies (1 Kg. 20:1). Ahab struck back at Ben-hadad, at the gates of Samaria. Later, following a decisive battle at Aphek (1 Kg. 20:26–30), he obtained the return to Israel of the cities previously captured by the Arameans. He also acquired trade concessions in the markets of Damascus (1 Kg. 20:34). In the battle with the Assyrians at Qarqar (853 BCE), Ahab occupied an important position among the twelve members of the coalition. According to Assyrian sources, his army consisted of two thousand cavalry and ten thousand foot soldiers. In the last year of his reign, Ahab and his ally, the Judean king Jehoshaphat, waged war with the Arameans to recapture Ramoth-Gilead for Israel. Before setting out to battle, the two kings sat on the threshing floor at the entrance to the gate at Samaria and asked the prophets to ask God what lay before them (1 Kg. 22:1–10). In the battle of Ramoth-Gilead, Ahab was fatally wounded. His body was brought to Samaria and his chariot was washed of his blood in the pool of Samaria (1 Kg. 22:33–38). With the marriage of Ahab and Jezebel, the daughter of Ethbaal, king of Tyre, the alliance with Tyre was consolidated, and its cultural influence on Israel increased. For his wife, Ahab built a sanctuary to Baal and Astarte in Samaria (1 Kg. 16:32–33; 2 Kg. 10:21) and a temple in the city of Jezreel, thus arousing the wrath of the prophets of Israel, especially Elijah's. The statement in the Bible "Now the rest of the acts of Ahab, and all that he did, and the ivory house which he built, and all the cities that he built. . ." (1 Kg. 22:39) suggests that Ahab was a man of unbounded energy and a zealous builder.

The reign of Joram, the son of Ahab, witnessed a decline in the political and economic position of the kingdom of Israel. Samaria was put under heavy siege by the Aramean king Ben-hadad, and famine spread through the city (2

Kg. 6:24–30). In connection with this great famine, the Bible relates that the "gate of Samaria" was the marketplace for food (2 Kg. 7:1). When Joram renewed the war against Aram for Ramoth-Gilead, Jehu, the commander of his army, who had been anointed king by the prophet Elisha, revolted against Joram. Jehu annihilated Ahab's family and put an end to the cult of Baal in Samaria. He paid tribute to the Assyrians in 841 BCE. His submission is related on the Black Obelisk of Shalmaneser III. On the obelisk Jehu is referred to as the "Son of Omri," that is, king over the land of the House of Omri (which was Israel). Jehu lost large tracts of land east of the Jordan. In the days of the great Israelite king, Jeroboam II (784–748 BCE), Samaria reached the zenith of its prosperity and expansion. Jeroboam conquered Damascus, extending the borders of his kingdom from Hamath to the sea of the Arabah (2 Kg. 14:23–29). In the days of Samaria's greatness, a powerful aristocracy emerged that pursued a life of luxury. Instances of injustice appeared, causing the prophet Amos to protest strongly against the luxuries in the palaces and "ivory houses" in Samaria and against the pomp of the cult at Bethel (Am. 3:9–15, 4:4).

The beginning of the decline and disintegration of the kingdom of Israel followed the death of Jeroboam. Menahem, king of Israel, had to pay heavy tribute to the Assyrians in 783 BCE. Large territories were split from the country during the military expeditions of Tiglath-pileser III in 734 and 733 BCE. Pekah and Hoshea attempted to revolt against the Assyrians, but Shalmaneser V marched against Samaria and held it under siege for three years. In 722 BCE, Sargon II conquered the city and many of its inhabitants were deported to remote districts in the Assyrian empire (2 Kg. 17:5–6, 18:9–10). Samaria became the center of the province of the same name and the seat of the Assyrian, Babylonian, and Persian governors. The Assyrian kings settled colonists there from various countries (2 Kg. 17:24). They mixed

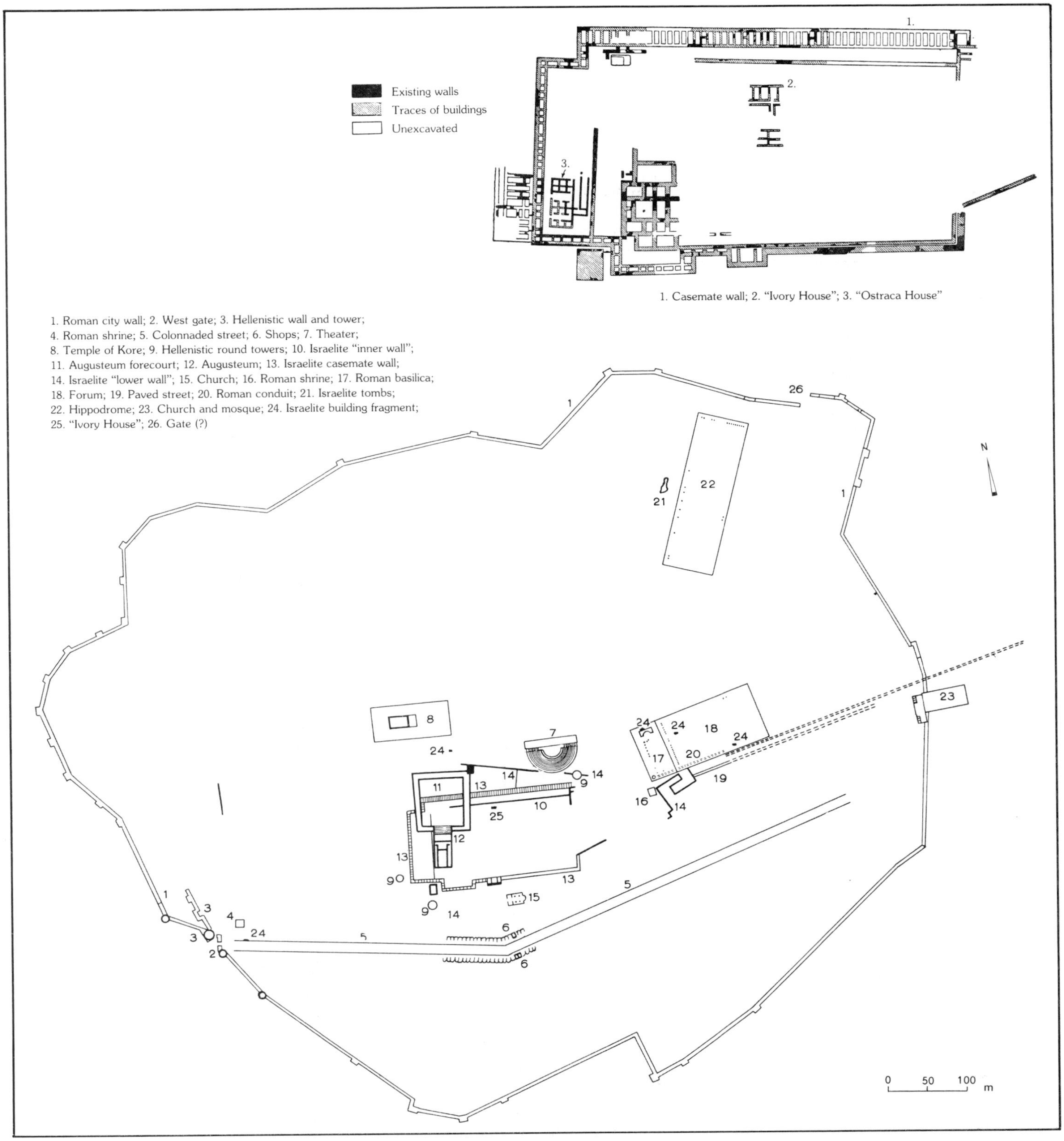

*Samaria: **(below)** general plan of the city and its principal remains; **(above)** plan of the Iron Age acropolis.*

with the local Israelite population, creating an increasing cultural and religious amalgamation. During a period of Assyrian weakness, Josiah, king of Judah (2 Kg. 23:8), raided the towns of Samaria and destroyed the high places (*bamot*) set up by the kings of Israel. This event encouraged those in Samaria who had remained faithful to the Lord, and many of them went on a pilgrimage to Jerusalem after its conquest by Nebuchadnezzar (Jer. 41:5). Nevertheless, in the course of time, a Samaritan community arose in Samaria that broke away from the people of Israel. Sanballat the Horonite, the Persian governor of Samaria, stood at the head of the opposition to the building of the city wall in Jerusalem in the time of Nehemiah.

When the Persian empire fell to Alexander the Great, Samaria too was conquered (332 BCE), and thousands of Macedonian soldiers were settled here. Samaria became a Greek city, differing in its ethnic, cultural, and religious point of view from the provincial cities of the Samaritans, whose religious center was Mount Gerizim. During the reigns of the Hellenistic kings, Samaria experienced a number of wars and conquests, but no destruction so complete as that inflicted upon it by the Hasmoneans under John Hyrcanus in 108 BCE. According to Josephus, Hyrcanus razed the city and sold its inhabitants into slavery.

In the time of Pompey (63 BCE), Samaria was annexed to the Roman province of Syria, and under Gabinius (57 BCE) the city revived. In 30 BCE, the emperor Augustus granted it to King Herod, who rebuilt it, adorned it with buildings, and named it Sebaste, in honor of Augustus (in Greek Sebastos = Augustus) (Josephus, *Antiq.* XV, 246). Herod, too, settled foreign soldiers here, and again the complexion of the city's population changed. During the First Jewish Revolt against Rome, from 66 to 70 CE, the city was once more destroyed. Septimius Severus granted it the status of a Roman colony with all the inherent privileges in 200 CE. Although the city had already begun to decline when Christianity became dominant, in the fourth century CE Sebaste became the seat of a bishop. A popular tradition locating the tomb of John the Baptist here lent the site a certain importance in the eyes of the Christians, who built churches here. After the Arab conquest, various travelers described the many extant ruins.

EXCAVATIONS

Two major archaeological expeditions excavated at Samaria. From 1908 to 1910, an expedition from Harvard University excavated here, first on a small scale, under the direction of G. Schumacher, and later more extensively under G. A. Reisner and C. S. Fisher. This expedition unearthed the western part of the fortress (the acropolis) from the time of the dynasties of Omri and Jehu, including the casemate walls, the royal residence, and the storehouse within its precincts. Especially noteworthy finds are the ostraca (see below). Also uncovered were the ruins of the Hellenistic fortifications of the acropolis, the Roman city wall, the west gate, houses, the temple of Augustus, the forum, the basilica, and the stadium. The second expedition was a consortium of five institutions that worked at the site from 1931 to 1935: Harvard University, the British Palestine Exploration Fund, the British Academy, the British School of Archaeology in Jerusalem, and the Hebrew University of Jerusalem. The director of the excavations was J. W. Crowfoot, with E. L. Sukenik as assistant field director. K. Lake represented Harvard University. K. M. Kenyon and G. M. Crowfoot also participated in the expedition, assuming a major role in the publication of the excavation report, as well as N. Avigad and the architect J. Pinkerfeld. The Joint Expedition extended the area previously excavated by clearing the fortress of the Israelite kings. The finds from the royal quarter included a collection of ivory carvings. A burial cave and a cult place(?) from the Israelite period were also uncovered. Smaller projects included the exploration of the Hellenistic fort, the colonnaded street, the forum, and the stadium. Also discovered were the remains of a temple dedicated to the goddess Kore, a theater, Roman tombs, and a church; the water system of the Roman city was investigated.

Samaria (city): wall in the Israelite palace.

The excavators met with considerable difficulty in distinguishing between the various strata because the town had been destroyed several times. The builders had dismantled previous structures, reused their stones, and deepened foundations down to bedrock. Building foundations from different periods were therefore frequently found side by side, rather than superimposed. Foundation trenches that penetrated several strata of construction disturbed the stratigraphy and the deposits. The conditions on the site forced the excavators to dig according to the strip system: the earth removed from every excavated strip was dumped into the previously excavated strip, a system with numerous disadvantages.

From 1965 to 1967, small-scale excavations were conducted at Samaria under the sponsorship of the Jordan Department of Antiquities, directed by F. Zayadine. These investigations were concentrated mainly in the area of the theater, the colonnaded street, the west gate, and the temple of Augustus. An Iron Age tomb was also uncovered. In 1968, the western sector of the mound was briefly examined by J. B. Hennessy, who exposed several strata from the Hellenistic and Roman periods.

EXCAVATION RESULTS

THE ISRAELITE PERIOD TO THE ASSYRIAN CONQUEST (PERIODS I–VI). Samaria was found to consist of an upper city (acropolis), the royal quarter situated on the summit of the hill, and a lower city extending over the slopes and along the foot of the hill. Very little of the lower city was excavated. Only scattered building remains were found, attesting that the Israelite city stretched from the Roman gate in the west to the middle of the forum in the east—a distance of about 800 m. In Crowfoot's opinion, the area of the walled city did not exceed 18.5 a., and the more distant remains belonged to buildings standing outside the walls. Kenyon, on the other hand, claimed that the Israelite town was equal in size to that of the Roman city.

The Acropolis. The royal quarter was enclosed by walls, and two main systems of fortifications were distinguished. The first wall, which the excavators called the inner wall, encompassed an area on the summit of the hill measuring 178 m east to west and about 89 m north to south. The wall was 1.6 m thick and built of fine ashlar masonry laid in carefully fitted headers and stretchers. Inside the walled area were remains of various buildings, one of which, built against the south wall to the west, consisted of a central courtyard surrounded by rooms (27 by 24 m). This building is considered to be part of the palace of the Israelite kings. North of the northern wall on a lower level, the so-called lower terrace, the remains of another long wall (called the lower wall) were discovered, but its continuation is unknown.

The inner wall, the city's earliest wall, was attributed by the Joint Expedition to Omri. Because the wall was not particularly strong and was probably incapable of defending the royal quarter, a new and much stronger fortification system was built. The summit plateau was enlarged to the north by 16.5 m and to the west by about 30 m and surrounded by a casemate wall (a double wall divided into rooms by partitions). Only part of this wall is preserved, but its rock-cut foundation trenches have survived, so that the course of the wall could be traced. These trenches have also survived in the other structures. The total thickness of the northern casemate wall was 10 m (the outer wall was about 1.8 m thick, the inner wall about 1 m, and the space between them about 7 m). The cross walls formed long, narrow rooms. The western casemate wall was not as wide (5 m), and the casemates were smaller. The western part of the south wall was also of the casemate type. However, in its continuation toward the east, it was built as a single wall against the earlier inner wall, which was erected on the rock terrace. Together the two walls formed a thick and massive defense. The south wall contains several salients and recesses, and near its west end a solid square block (16 by 12 m) was built that was probably a tower. In the opinion of some archaeologists, it may have defended the gate that stood there. In the space between the western casemate wall and the earlier inner wall was a storehouse (25 by 18 m)—the so-called Ostraca House where the inscribed potsherds were found (see below). A pool (10 by 5 m) was built against the casemate wall in the northwest corner of the royal quarter. It has been suggested that this was the pool in which Ahab's chariot was washed when his body was brought from the battle at Ramoth-Gilead.

At a distance of about 17 m from the southeast corner, the wall makes a sharp turn to the northeast and continues in this direction for about 40 m. This oblique turn was probably due to the site's topography, but it is also possible that the royal quarter was entered from this side—that is, from the east. Nearby three proto-Aeolic capitals were found that may have been set at the entrance to the forecourt of the royal quarter.

About 150 m east of the corner of the wall, near the south side of the Roman basilica, extensive remains of Israelite building were discovered. These remains were part of the city's fortifications, and probably included a gate. The walls and the foundation trenches form a kind of meander. Only three courses of the main wall (31.5 m long), running west to east, survive. The stones have drafted margins. At a distance of 4 m from the wall the foundations of a rectangular structure (36 by 21 m) were discovered that the excavators interpreted as a tower. The narrow passage between the wall and the tower probably led to the city gate. This east gate stands on the level of the middle terrace. It is not clear how it connected with the city walls.

Building Technique. The Israelite masonry at Samaria is renowned for its outstanding quality. The foundation stones were laid in rock-cut trenches or on rock-cut steps and set as headers only. The walls were built of courses of headers and stretchers or of two headers alternating with one stretcher. The stones in the lower courses, which are not visible, have drafted margins on two or three sides, with an irregular boss remaining in the center. The stones were dressed on the spot during construction, to ensure an exact fit in the courses. The upper, visible courses were smoothly dressed. All the ashlars were set dry—that is, without mortar—and with outstanding precision. The interior of the walls was also constructed of large regular stones, which considerably increased the stability of the structures. The superstructures of the city walls and of the other walls were probably of brick. It is assumed that the Israelites learned this masonry technique from the Phoenicians.

Stratigraphy. The first expedition distinguished three Israelite building phases: the palace from the time of Omri, the casemate wall and the storehouse from the reign of Ahab, and the buildings west of the casemate wall from the days of Jeroboam II. The Joint Expedition dug a stratigraphic section across the royal quarter. Early Bronze Age I pottery was found on the rock, but the site was not resettled until the Israelite period. Kenyon distinguished eight pre-Hellenistic building and ceramic periods, six of them belonging to the time between the foundation of the city in 876 BCE and its conquest in 721 BCE. This division was based on both architectural and ceramic considerations. According to Kenyon the building periods I–VI coincide with the ceramic periods I–VI, as shown here:

Period I — Omri: construction of the inner wall and the palace.
Period II — Ahab: construction of the casemate wall and probably also of the east gate.
Period III — Jehu and others: repair of the casemate wall, rebuilding of earlier structures, erection of new buildings.
Period IV — Time of Jeroboam II and others: repair of the casemate wall, alterations in existing buildings, and construction of new ones, probably also of the storehouse.
Periods V–VI — Changes and repairs: burned layer attributed to the conquest of Samaria in 721 BCE.

The proposals for the first two periods—decisive for establishing the chronology of the pottery—have been questioned. The disagreement is rooted in the different approaches to archaeological methodology. The pottery from period I was found in the fills of the structures from period I, according to Kenyon's terminology. She attributes this pottery to the construction period of the buildings, claiming that it was brought by the builders in the time of Omri. For the same reason, she ascribes the pottery from period II—which is very similar to the earlier pottery—to building period II.

These conclusions were disputed, however, by W. F. Albright, Y. Aharoni, R. Amiran, G. E. Wright and others, who maintain that the pottery from periods I–II found in the fills of structures I–II predates these buildings. On the grounds of a typological comparison with pottery from other excavations, they date it earlier, to the tenth and beginning of the ninth centuries BCE. In their opinion the pottery attests to the fact that a small settlement existed on the site prior to the foundation of the city of Samaria.

Kenyon did not overlook this problem. Although she noted the discovery of two walls covered by the floors of buildings from period I, when discussing the pottery she stated that there was no trace of occupation from the beginning of the Early Bronze Age until the time of Omri.

Avigad shared the view of those who claim that pottery periods I–II precede building periods I–II and that the pottery of period III—which is richer and more varied than the preceding examples—parallels building periods I–II. Wright has also suggested a correction in the chronology of the walls. In his opinion, Omri, who resided in Samaria for only six years, could not have succeeded in building the first wall and the palace in such a short time. It is difficult as well to assume, according to Wright, that Ahab could have erected a fortification as extensive as the casemate wall during the twenty-two years of his reign. Wright therefore considers that Omri only began the construction of the first wall and that Ahab completed it, whereas Jehu, the founder of the next dynasty, built the casemate wall.

Wright's contentions are not acceptable to this writer. In Avigad's opinion it is highly improbable that Omri would have established his residence in a city that was not walled and in which there were no quarters suitable for a king. In all probability, he began the fortifications of the hill and the building of his palace while still living in his first capital, Tirzah. He would have transferred his capital to Samaria only after the site had been prepared—that is, after the main buildings had been wholly or nearly finished. He could certainly have completed the inner wall, which is a single wall only 1.6 m thick. The building of the casemate wall, on the other hand—for which the summit of the hill had to be widened by an artificial fill—was indeed a major undertaking. It required considerable time and means, as well as the vision of a great builder. It was certainly possible to complete it in the twenty-two years of Ahab's reign. In fact, the work was finished in an even shorter time, because during Ahab's reign Samaria withstood the siege of the Arameans only by virtue of its strong fortifications. (It should be noted that this discussion refers only to the fortifications of the acropolis; in times of emergency, the acropolis could also shelter the inhabitants of the lower city, of whose walls almost nothing is known.) Ahab, who married Jezebel, the daughter of the king of Tyre, certainly received ample assistance from the Phoenicians for this extensive construction project. During his reign, prosperity prevailed in the kingdom of Israel, and the Bible relates that Ahab was a builder of cities and palaces. Archaeological finds from sites other than Samaria also attest that Ahab was a great builder. He erected strong fortifications at Hazor and at Megiddo. At the latter site he probably also built the large stables, an assumption borne out by an Assyrian source recording the considerable number of war chariots that stood at Ahab's disposal. It cannot, therefore, be conceived that in his own capital, Samaria, he would have been satisfied with merely completing the construction of the unpretentious "inner wall" begun by his father.

For these reasons, it is difficult to attribute the construction of the casemate wall to Jehu. Even though Jehu founded a new dynasty, put an end to the cult of Baal, and won the confidence of the prophets, his reign does not seem to have been propitious for such a large building project as this. During his reign, the kingdom of Israel suffered political defeats and lost extensive territory. Jehu was the first Israelite king to pay heavy tribute to the Assyrians. Commercial relations with Tyre were broken off with the killing of Jezebel, and it is hardly likely that the Phoenicians would have nevertheless supplied him with aid to build fortifications. Furthermore, the Bible does not attribute any building activity to Jehu.

Therefore, those archaeologists seem to be correct who have ascribed the building of the casemate wall to Ahab and only its repairs to Jehu and his successors. The following chronological table summarizes the different views on the dating and the correlations between the building and ceramic periods at Samaria, up to its conquest in 722 BCE.

<table>
<tr><th rowspan="2"></th><th colspan="2">Kenyon</th><th colspan="2">Wright</th><th colspan="2">Avigad</th></tr>
<tr><th>Building</th><th>Pottery</th><th>Building</th><th>Pottery</th><th>Building</th><th>Pottery</th></tr>
<tr><td>EB</td><td>—</td><td>+</td><td>—</td><td>+</td><td>—</td><td>+</td></tr>
<tr><td>Property of the Shemer family (10th–early 9th cent. BCE)</td><td>—</td><td>—</td><td>—</td><td>1–2</td><td>0</td><td>1–2</td></tr>
<tr><td>Omri (882–871 BCE)</td><td>I</td><td>1</td><td rowspan="2">I</td><td rowspan="3">3</td><td>I</td><td rowspan="3">3</td></tr>
<tr><td>Ahab (871–852 BCE)</td><td>II</td><td>2</td><td>II</td></tr>
<tr><td>Jehu (842–814 BCE)</td><td>III</td><td>3</td><td>II</td><td>III</td></tr>
<tr><td>Jeroboam II (784–748 BCE)</td><td>IV</td><td>4</td><td>III</td><td>4</td><td>IV</td><td>4</td></tr>
<tr><td>748–722 BCE</td><td>V–VI</td><td>5–6</td><td>IV–VI</td><td>5–6</td><td>V–VI</td><td>5–6</td></tr>
</table>

0 = Remains of walls below building period I.

Samaria ostracon no. 17: "In the tenth year, from Azz/o to Gaddiyau, a jar of fine oil," Iron Age.

Fragment of a monumental Hebrew inscription: ". . . asher . . ."

The Samaria Ostraca and Inscriptions. In the 1910 excavations, sixty-three potsherds with legible Hebrew inscriptions written in black ink were discovered in the northern storerooms of the so-called Ostraca House. Several illegible ostraca were also found. These sherds were records of shipments of oil and wine sent by various settlements in the district of Samaria to the royal household as taxes in kind. These very short inscriptions are of considerable value for the light they shed on the language, script, personal names, taxation system, and organization of the kingdom of Israel and of the topography of the territory of the tribe of Manasseh. Two frequently repeated formulas in the ostraca are בשת התשעת מיצת לאחנעם נבל יין ישן ("In the ninth year, from Yaṣit to Aḥinoam, a jar of old wine") and בשת העשרת מחצרת לגדיו נבל שמן רחץ ("In the tenth year, from Ḥaṣerot to Gaddiyau, a jar of fine oil.") In some of the inscriptions the year is indicated by numerical signs. These inscriptions have been generally interpreted as meaning that, in a certain year of the king's reign, a shipment was dispatched from a certain locality (Yaṣit and Ḥaṣerot, for example) to the court official in charge of taxes (Aḥinoam and Gaddiyau, for example). Y. Yadin rejected this theory. He claimed that the *lamed* prefixed to the personal name is the possessive, and that therefore this name represents the sender and not the tax collector. It should be noted that many of the names are formed with the suffix *yau (yw)* and that the component *ba'al* also appears frequently.

The various suggestions for dating the ostraca are based on paleographic and ceramic evidence, as well as on several numerals that appear in the inscriptions and that are interpreted as 15 or 17(?). The ostraca were consequently attributed to kings who reigned for at least fifteen or seventeen years. Reisner dated them to the reign of Ahab (871–852 BCE); B. Mazar to Jehoahaz (814 to 800 BCE); Albright and others to Jeroboam II (according to their reckoning, 786 to 746 BCE). Yadin, on the other hand, interpreted the sign as representing the numeral 9 and attributed the ostraca to the time of Menahem, who reigned ten years. In the ninth year of his reign (738 BCE), Menahem paid tribute to Pul, king of Assyria (2 Kg. 15:19–20), and for this purpose he imposed a special tax on his subjects—in the ninth and tenth years of his reign. The sherds of the vessels on which the inscriptions were written belong to Samaria's stratum IV or V—that is, to the eighth century BCE.

In addition to this collection of ostraca, some scattered sherds bearing short incised inscriptions in Hebrew, mostly names, were discovered in various areas in the excavations. A fragment of a stone slab was found on which the word *asher* ("which" or "who") was carved in large letters, attesting that stelae with monumental inscriptions were erected in Israel.

The Ivories. The group of ivory objects found in Samaria is the most important collection of miniature art from the Iron Age discovered in Israel. The first ivories were found during the excavations of the Harvard Expedition on the floor of the Ahab courtyard north of the Ostraca House. The largest of these was found together with a fragment of an alabaster jar on which was incised the name of the Egyptian pharaoh Osorkon II (914–874 BCE). This find is of importance for dating the ivories.

The Joint Expedition discovered in various spots in the royal quarter a great number of ivory plaques and hundreds of ivory fragments, most of them difficult to assign to a definite stratum.

The largest concentration of ivories was found in the rubbish deposit of the building ("Ivory House") near the inner wall in the north. Since this debris

Ostracon no. 1 from the excavations of the Joint Expedition. The letters are incised.

Ivory fragments with letters inscribed in Hebrew-Phoenician script.

Samaria: selection of ivories.

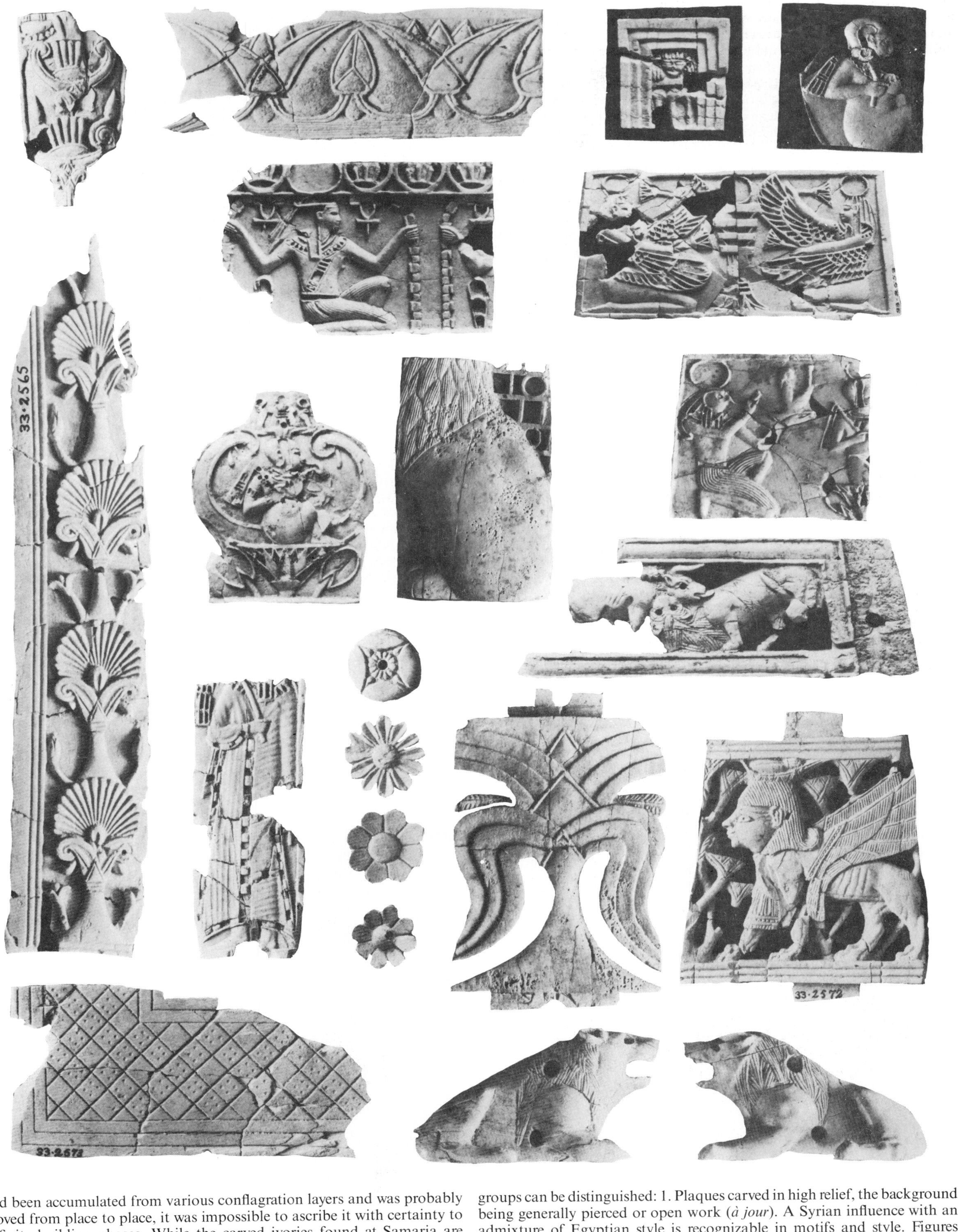

had been accumulated from various conflagration layers and was probably moved from place to place, it was impossible to ascribe it with certainty to definite building phases. While the carved ivories found at Samaria are numerous and diverse in form, decoration, and workmanship, two main groups can be distinguished: 1. Plaques carved in high relief, the background being generally pierced or open work (*à jour*). A Syrian influence with an admixture of Egyptian style is recognizable in motifs and style. Figures frequently represented are winged sphinxes (cherubim), lions grappling with bulls, the "woman at the window," human figures, and so forth. To this group are to be added some ivory objects sculptured in the round. 2. Plaques carved in low relief, that were decorated with insets of precious stones, colored glass, and gold foil. The motifs are taken, as a rule, from Egyptian mythology: the infant Horus seated on a lotus blossom, Isis and Nephthys flanking the *djed* pillar; the god Ra holding the image of Maat, the goddess of truth; the god Hah holding palm branches; and figures of winged creatures, among others.

Many of the ivory plaques bear letters in Hebrew script. The ivories are considered products of Phoenician art, and they were probably used as inlays in the palace furniture of the Israelite kings. The Bible mentions the "ivory house" that Ahab built (1 Kg. 22:39) and the "beds of ivory" that symbolized the life of luxury led in Samaria in Amos's words of reproof (6:4). The excavators attributed all of the ivories to the time of Ahab. Other scholars, however, tend to ascribe to Ahab only those carved in high relief. They show a similarity to ninth-century ivory objects discovered at Arslan Tash (ancient Hadatu) in Syria. The second group, which is very close in style and technique to the ivories from Nimrud, is considered to date to the eighth century BCE. The ivory objects found at these two sites were probably booty taken by the Assyrian kings from Damascus, Phoenicia, and perhaps also from Samaria.

Other Finds. East of the city a trench was discovered that covered an area of 30 by 26 m. It is 4 to 6 m wide and 2 to 5 m deep (E 207 in the Joint Expedition excavation report). This great trench contained an abundance of potsherds and pottery figurines representing humans and animals that date to the eighth century BCE. The installation probably had some cultic purpose. It may have had a connection with one of the cults at Samaria that the prophets so strongly denounced.

A network of rock-cut burial chambers was discovered north of the city, near the Roman stadium. Deep pits sunk into the floors of these chambers contained numerous pottery fragments and other objects from the Israelite period, as well as animal bones. The pits were probably connected with the cult of the dead, widely practiced in Samaria.

The most common finds generally were pottery vessels in all forms and styles. Samaria possessed excellent pottery, attesting to a highly developed pottery craftsmanship in the capital of the kingdom of Israel. Especially outstanding are fine burnished vessels with red slip, which have become known as Samaria ware.

ASSYRIAN, BABYLONIAN, AND PERSIAN RULE (PERIODS VII–VIII). Very few remains have survived from the Assyrian, Babylonian, and Persian periods. Sargon did not destroy Samaria, and its walls continued in use over a long period of time. The Harvard expedition ascribed a wall of the fortress to this period, but in fact it belongs to a later date (see below). The remains of the structures were removed in later building activities. In the Persian period, an extensive area of the summit of the hill was leveled and covered with a layer of brown agricultural soil that may have been brought from elsewhere for planting a garden around the Persian governor's palace. No remains of such a palace have survived, however.

Red-figured Attic krater, Persian period.

Fragment of a Neo-Assyrian stela with a cuneiform inscription, apparently from the time of Sargon II.

Among the small finds—which also were scanty—was pottery showing Assyrian influence (period VII) and Greek pottery from the sixth and fifth centuries BCE. A fragment of a stela with an Assyrian inscription is attributed to Sargon II. Also found was a cylinder seal with an Assyrian inscription and a letter to the local governor, Avi-aḥi, written in Babylonian in the cuneiform script on a tablet. Several Aramean ostraca from the Persian period were also uncovered. In addition, two important chance discoveries are associated with Samaria. One is a hoard of papyri and seals found in the Shinjeh cave in Wadi ed-Daliyeh (q.v.). These were the property of fugitives who had fled from Samaria in the fourth century BCE. The other find, fragments of a bronze throne, probably belonged to the governor of Samaria in the Persian period. Also found was a rich hoard of coins from the Persian period on which the name Samaria is mentioned, as are other proper names, probably of provincial officials.

THE HELLENISTIC PERIOD (PERIOD IX). At the beginning of the Hel-

Round tower built of "headers," Hellenistic period.

Plan of the western gate.

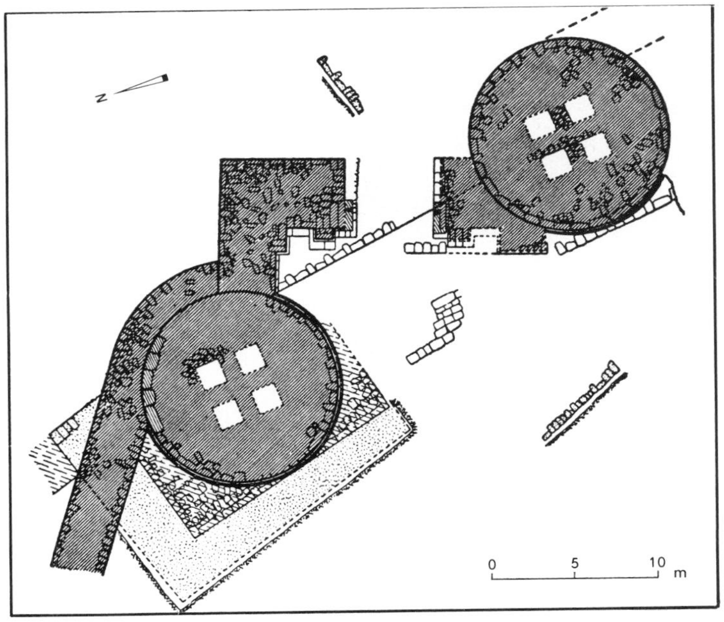

lenistic period, the walls of the Israelite acropolis were still in use, strengthened by a number of round towers. The first expedition had discovered the remains of two such towers near the southwest corner of the fortress and erroneously dated them to the Israelite period. In the northeast, the Joint Expedition unearthed another tower built astride the lower Israelite wall (diameter, 13 m). It still stands, in excellent condition, to a height of 8.5 m. Nineteen well-built courses are preserved, whose stones are laid in headers only. This is one of the most impressive remnants from the Hellenistic period (end of the fourth century BCE) surviving in Israel. Remains of the city wall, dating from the same period, were discovered near the western Roman gate, where the gate of the Hellenistic city probably also stood.

In the Late Hellenistic period, in approximately the second century BCE, the upper city was defended by a very strong fort wall, the thickness of which was 4.2 m at its base. Its lines generally follow the course of the wall of the Israelite acropolis, encompassing an area of about 230 by 120 m and strengthened by square towers. The Harvard expedition dated it erroneously to the neo-Babylonian period. This fort wall was probably destroyed by John Hyrcanus, together with the rest of the city in 108 BCE.

THE ROMAN PERIOD. In the Roman period, the city reached the peak of its greatness and splendor. Its gates and towers, the very impressive colonnaded street, magnificent temples, theater, stadium, and forum all lent it the appearance of a Roman city.

City Plan and Fortifications. The tower-strengthened city wall surrounded an irregular area of about 160 a. The diameter of the city from east to west was 1 km and slightly less from north to south. Only sections of the city wall are still extant—its stones were used to construct the neighboring town of Shechem. The city gate was situated in the west, where it was defended by two round towers, each of which has a diameter of 14 m. Preserved to a height of 8 to 11 m, they stand on square foundations from the Hellenistic period. The towers are attributed to the time of King Herod. The wall of the gate between them is dated to the reign of Septimius Severus (end of the second or beginning of the third century CE). The colonnaded street should also be ascribed to the same period. It started near the west gate, continued eastward, and perhaps terminated near the east gate. Some six hundred columns were erected along the street over a distance of 800 m. Two of the columns still bear Corinthian capitals. Trial soundings were carried out by the Joint Expedition in one section of the street. The width of the roadway was 12.5 m (in its eastern part, the street narrowed somewhat), and monolithic columns (5.5 m high, including their capitals) stood on both sides, supporting a roofed portico along which shops were built. This was a bazaar street.

On the summit of the hill in the western sector, above the Israelite fortress, the remains of a residential quarter were found from the time of Gabinius (57–55 BCE). The plan of the Roman city was found to consist of regularly laid streets and dwellings with a central courtyard (atrium) surrounded by porches and rooms.

Temple of Augustus. Above the remains of these houses, on a height overlooking the entire city, and with a view of the sea, Herod erected a temple in honor of the emperor Augustus. This Augusteum consisted of the temple building proper (35 by 24 m) and a large forecourt, both of which were oriented on a single south–north axis. To build the wide forecourt, a platform (83 by 72 m) was erected, the fill for which was contained by subterranean corridors built around it. The retaining wall on the northern slope,

Plan of the Temple of Augustus enclosure, Herodian period.

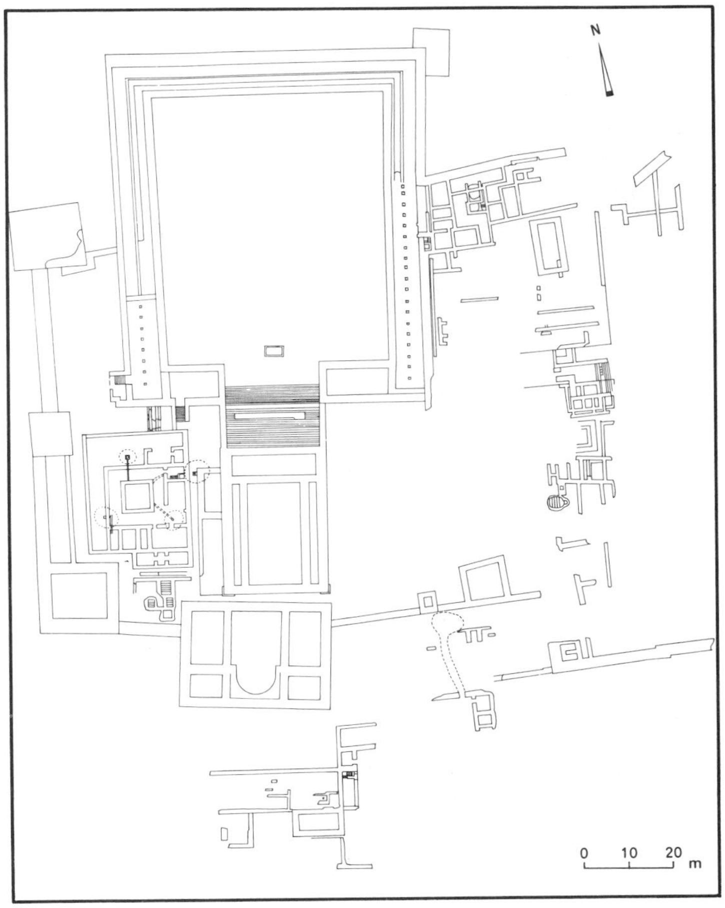

which initially was 15 m high (up to the level of the forecourt), has survived to a height of 7 m. A wide staircase led from the forecourt to the temple, which stood on a base rising 4.4 m above the level of the forecourt. The building's foundations were laid on bedrock at a depth of 9 m. The few ashlars from the remaining walls are dressed with typical Herodian margins. The temple, which was entered through a porch, was divided into a wide nave and two very narrow aisles. During the reign of Septimius Severus (second century), the Augusteum was rebuilt according to its original plan, but slightly longer. The wide stairs visible today and the altar in front of them date from this period. Near the altar the torso of a huge statue was found, probably of the emperor Augustus.

Temple of Kore. North of the Augusteum stood the temple dedicated to the goddess Kore (36 by 15.5 m) in a temenos (84 by 45 m), that may have been surrounded by columns. Only the temple's deep foundations were discovered.

Temple of Augustus: corner tower of the forecourt.

Statue depicting the abduction of Ganymede by Zeus in the form of an eagle.

Relief of a Dioscuri cap, from the temple of Kore.

They were laid on bedrock and built of courses of alternating headers and stretchers. In the building's fill architectural remains were found from an earlier temple that was dated to the third century BCE. It was dedicated mainly to the cult of the goddess Isis, attested by a Greek dedicatory inscription to Serapis-Isis. Two sculptured stones with reliefs of caps wreathed with laurel and crowned with a star—the symbol of the Dioscuri—are attributed to this temple. The temple was probably destroyed by John Hyrcanus. In the Roman period, the temple of Kore was erected on this site, as is evident from an octagonal altar with an engraved dedicatory inscription to her.

The Stadium. Also connected with the cult of Kore was the stadium (230 by 60 m) situated in the northeast sector of the city. Some of its columns were visible prior to its partial excavation. Two building periods were distinguished. The first is from the time of Herod, when the stadium was enclosed by four porticoes with Doric columns and its walls were coated with colored plaster. At about the end of the second century, the stadium was rebuilt, this time in the Corinthian style. In a cistern in the area of the stadium a statue of Kore and a Greek inscription dedicated to her were found. An altar was uncovered bearing an inscription to the Lady Kore by the high priest.

The Theater. At the foot of the northeast end of the acropolis small sections of the remains of a theater were cleared: a section of the foundations of the stage and some architectural details from its facade, a section of the paving in the orchestra, and parts of the first four rows of seats and of the gangway in the middle of the auditorium. The lower block of seats contained fourteen rows and was divided by six flights of steps into seven groups. The theater's external diameter was about 65 m. The facade of the stage was decorated with niches alternately rounded and rectangular. The theater is dated to the first quarter of the third century CE.

The Forum and Basilica. On the plain between the hill of the acropolis and the village of Sebastia lay the forum (128 by 72.5 m). In some places its walls reached bedrock, at a depth of 4 to 6 m, and supported an artificial fill. The forum was enclosed on all sides by roofed porticoes, of which mainly the west portico is extant. Of its twenty-four columns, seven are still standing in situ; of the others, only the bases, resting on a stylobate, have survived. In the middle of the western wall is a door leading to the basilica, which adjoins the forum.

Although the basilica was not completely excavated, all the details of its plan could be ascertained. Its length from north to south is 68 m and its width is 32.6 m. The forum's northern portico continues along the northern side of the basilica. Three rows of columns in the form of an inverted U divide the basilica into a nave and aisles. Some of the columns still stand in situ, while only the bases of others are preserved. The 6-m-high columns are monolithic; two of them are topped by Corinthian capitals. At the northern end of the nave was a bema with a semicircular niche and four benches. Most of the remains visible today are from the second century CE, but various others point to an earlier period of construction, perhaps to the time of Herod or Gabinius. An aqueduct runs beneath the southern end of the forum and the basilica that carried water to the Roman city from springs in hills to the east, near the villages of Naqura and Jinsiniya. (The water supply of the inhabitants of the Israelite city had been limited to rainwater, collected in cisterns).

Tombs. In the southeast corner of the village of Sebastia, a Roman mausoleum was uncovered. Its excavation was begun by the Harvard expedition and was completed in 1937 by the Mandatory Department of Antiquities. The square structure (5.5 by 5.5 m) is built of hewn stones, and its walls are decorated on the outside with pilasters. The tomb consists of one chamber (3.3. by 3.3 m) with arched niches on three of its walls. Two of the niches held stone sarcophagi. Five other sarcophagi were found on the floor of the chamber. The chamber is domed (5 m above the floor) with spherical pendentives—one of the earliest constructions of this kind. At the entrance to the tomb a stone door opens on hinges. Along the building's facade was a portico con-

Burial chamber with a domed roof in the Roman mausoleum, late 2nd–early 3rd centuries CE.

Tomb 220, late 2nd–early 3rd centuries CE.

sisting of two rows of four columns each. Two decorated sarcophagi were found here, one of which is outstanding in its rich reliefs of columns, garlands, masks, and human figures. Near the sarcophagi five stone busts were found. The mausoleum is dated to the second and beginning of the third centuries CE.

East of the city, outside the walls, several rock-cut tombs were discovered. One of them (tomb E 220) consists of a court with two main sepulchral chambers. The court (12.15 by 7.95 m) was cut out of rock and its walls were faced with dressed stones and decorated with pilasters. The two entrances had stone doors that opened on hinges. The two sepulchral chambers (4 by 5 m each) are lined with ashlar masonry, and loculi are cut into their walls. Sarcophagi with gable-shaped lids were found in some of the loculi, and another in the court. The tombs contained numerous objects, including glass vessels, jewelry, and pottery lamps. The tomb was probably built in the second century CE but remained in use into the third century.

Small Finds. The numismatic evidence at Samaria reflects the history of the town and its economy. Most of the coins are Ptolemaic in the third century BCE and Seleucid in the second century BCE. At the end of the century, city coins, especially those of Acre, also appear. Jewish coins are found from the time of the Hasmoneans and of Herod, and in the first century CE coins of the procurators are numerous. In Sebaste itself, coins were minted during the reigns of the emperors Domitian, Commodus, Septimius Severus, Caracalla, and Elagabalus but were not found in great numbers. Byzantine, Arab, and Crusader coins were also found.

The imported pottery—black-glazed ware, "Megarian" bowls, and stamped handles from Rhodian jars—is evidence of commercial relations with foreign countries in the Hellenistic period. During the Roman period much terra sigillata ware was imported. The pagan character of the city of Sebaste is apparent from the statues of Hercules, Dionysus, Apollo, and Kore.

THE LATE PERIODS. A few remains from the Byzantine period are scattered

Decorated sarcophagus from the Roman mausoleum.

City coin of Sebaste-Samaria, 2nd century CE.

Coin of Samaria, 4th century BCE.

over the lower city, but there are none on the summit of the hill. Among the ruins of the Latin cathedral dedicated to John the Baptist (twelfth century), which is in the village, five column capitals from the fifth century CE were found. South of the hill, the Joint Expedition cleared a monastery from the Middle Ages in which, according to tradition, the head of John the Baptist was hidden. The church of this monastery includes remains of an earlier basilican church with an apse.

Main publications: G. A. Reisner, C. S. Fisher, and D. G. Lyon, *Harvard Excavations at Samaria (1908–1910)*, 1–2, Cambridge, Mass. 1924; J. W. Crowfoot and G. M. Crowfoot, *Early Ivories from Samaria* (Samaria-Sebaste 2), London 1938; J. W. Crowfoot, K. M. Kenyon, and E. L. Sukenik, *The Buildings at Samaria* (Samaria-Sebaste 1), London 1942; J. W. Crowfoot, G. M. Crowfoot, and K. M. Kenyon, *The Objects of Samaria* (Samaria-Sebaste 3), London 1957.

Studies and chronology (see also under ostraca below): W. G. Masterman, *PEQ* 57 (1925), 25–30; Y. Aharoni and R. Amiran, *IEJ* 8 (1958), 171–184; W. F. Albright, *BASOR* 150 (1958), 21–25; O. Tufnell, *PEQ* 91 (1959), 90–105; G. E. Wright, *BASOR* 155 (1959), 13–29; K. M. Kenyon, *BIAL* 4 (1964), 143–156; id., *Royal Cities of the Old Testament*, New York 1971; P. R. Ackroyd, *Archaeology and Old Testament Study* (ed. D. W. Thomas), Oxford 1967, 343–354; F. Zayadine, *ADAJ* 12–13 (1967–1968), 77–80; id., *RB* 75 (1968), 562–585; id., *BTS* 121 (1970), 1–15; S. Page, *VT* 19 (1969), 483–484; K. R. Veenhof, *Phoenix* 15 (1969), 221–224; *BTS* 120–121 (1970); 184 (1976); M. Avi-Yonah, *Archaeology* (Israel Pocket Library), Jerusalem 1974, 182–185; Miriam Tadmor, *IEJ* 24 (1974), 37–43; Y. Shiloh, *BASOR* 222 (1976), 67–77; G. Wallis, *VT* 26 (1976), 480–496; R. Giveon, *The Impact of Egypt on Canaan*, Freiburg 1978, 34–44; M. Mallowan, *Archaeology in the Levant* (K. M. Kenyon Fest.), Warminster 1978, 155–163; S. M. Paul, *VT* 28 (1978), 358–359; Y. Yadin, *Archaeology in the Levant*, op. cit., 127–135; M. W. Prausnitz, *Madrider Beiträge* 8 (1982), 31–44; H. Tadmor, *Jerusalem Cathedra* 3 (1983), 1–11; J. Balensi, *MdB* 33 (1984), 53–54; Weippert 1988 (Ortsregister); W. G. Dever, *BASOR* 277–278 (1990), 121–130; I. Finkelstein, ibid., 109–119; N. Na'aman, *Biblica* 71 (1990), 206–225; L. E. Stager, *BASOR* 277–278 (1990), 93–107; J. H. Hayes and J. K. Kuan, *Biblica* 72 (1991), 153–181; B. Becking, *The Fall of Samaria: An Historical and Archaeological Study*, Leiden (in prep.).

The Samaria Ostraca: W. F. Albright, *JPOS* 5 (1925), 38–54; 11 (1931), 241–251; D. Diringer, *Le Inscrizioni*, Florence 1934, 21–68 (with biblio.); B. Maisler (Mazar), *JPOS* 12 (1948), 117–133; S. Moscati, *Epigrafia*, Rome 1951, 27–37; Y. Yadin, *IEJ* 9 (1959), 184–187; 12 (1962), 64–66; 18 (1968), 50–51; id., *Scripta Hierosolymitana* 8 (1960), 1–17; F. M. Cross, Jr., *BASOR* 163 (1961), 12–14; Y. Aharoni, *IEJ* 12 (1962), 67–69; id., *BASOR* 184 (1966), 13–19; A. F. Rainey, *IEJ* 12 (1962), 62–63; id., *PEQ* 99 (1967), 32–41; 102 (1970), 45–51; id., *TA* 6 (1979), 91–95; id., *BASOR* 272 (1988), 69–74; J. Decroix, *BTS* 120 (1970), 15–17; A. Lemaire, *RB* 79 (1972), 565–570; id., *Semitica* 22 (1972), 13–20; id., *Inscriptions Hebraïques* 1: *Les Ostraca*, Paris 1977, 21–81; W. H. Shea, *IEJ* 27 (1977), 16–27; id., *ZDPV* 101 (1985), 9–20; I. T. Kaufman, *BA* 45 (1982), 229–239; B. Rosen, *TA* 13–14 (1986–1987), 39–45; A. J. Poulter and G. I. Davies, *VT* 40 (1990), 237–240.

Late Samaria: L. H. Vincent, *RB* 45 (1936), 221–232; J. W. Crowfoot, *Churches at Bosra and Samaria-Sebaste*, London 1937; R. W. Hamilton, *QDAP* 8 (1938), 64–71; *BTS* 121 (1970); J. B. Hennessy, *Levant* 2 (1970), 1–21; F. Zayadine, *MdB* 17 (1981), 41–45; W. J. Fulco and F. Zayadine, *ADAJ* 25 (1981), 197–225; G. Kühnel, *Wall Paintings in the Latin Kingdom of Jerusalem* (Frankfurter Forschungen zur Kunst 4), Berlin 1988, 193–204; Y. Meshorer and S. Qedar, *The Coinage of Samaria in the 4th Century BCE*, Los Angeles 1991.

NAHMAN AVIGAD

Remains of the cathedral of St. John the Baptist (12th century) and the mosque.

SAMARIA (REGION)

THE PREHISTORIC PERIODS

Information about the settlement in Samaria in prehistoric times is derived from surveys conducted in the 1930s and from a limited number conducted more recently, in the 1970s and 1980s.

LOWER PALEOLITHIC PERIOD. The principal site dated to the Lower Paleolithic in Samaria is that of Sahl el-Ḥussein (map reference 166.168). It is situated on a plateau above a valley separating two elevated areas; the valley connects the Coastal Plain with the Samarian Hills. At the end of the Middle Pleistocene and in the early Upper Pleistocene such valleys in Israel were characterized by permanent or seasonal swamps; the surrounding highlands were commonly the location of sites of the Upper Acheulean culture because, on the one hand, they were close to water sources and, on the other, they dominated, to a certain degree, the routes of potential prey. The lithic material, randomly collected at the site by R. Neuville, was defined as an Upper Acheulean industry. About three-quarters of the implements are hand axes, most of them oval or discoidal. Such an assemblage is characteristic of the Upper Acheulean culture in the mountain region and its margins. Other Lower Paleolithic sites are small find spots, in which several hand axes or other items were collected.

MIDDLE PALEOLITHIC PERIOD. The Shuqba Cave (map reference 154.154) is the only Middle Paleolithic site that was systematically excavated (by D. Garrod in 1928). Layer D at the site yielded a Late Mousterian assemblage, in which most items had been produced in the Levallois technique. About half of the four hundred tools recovered here are side scrapers; the remainder are points, retouched flakes, and a few hand axes and burins in Upper Paleolithic style. The formation of breccia in this layer and the secondary deposition of water-transported Mousterian items in layer C were regarded by Garrod as evidence of a humid climatic phase in the Mousterian period (contrary to the present climate). This assumption was confirmed by the conclusions reached in later research (q.v. Shuqba Cave).

The travertines—spring deposits that testify to a humid climate—traced in Wadi Faṣael, yielded U/TH dates of 136,000 ± 5,000 years BP and 63,000 ± 4,000 years BP. The Mousterian site of Faṣael I seems to be contemporaneous with these travertines.

An in situ Mousterian layer was detected in the section created by the Beqa'ot–Meḥola road (map reference 197.192). There seems to be another small Mousterian site on the southern bank of Wadi Jerusaliya, some 3.5 km (2 mi.) southwest of the Jiftlik junction. The lithic material there comprises mainly Levallois cores for flakes, as well as flakes and a few scrapers—all of them originating in a limited number of cores. The site seems to have been a small campsite.

Flint concentrations dating to the Middle Paleolithic were found in Samaria on mountaintops and slopes. Flint items have often been recovered in proximity to the original site and display little evidence of transportation. Judging from the generally large quantities of debitage relative to those of cores, these seem to be workshop sites.

UPPER PALEOLITHIC TO NEOLITHIC PERIODS. Upper Paleolithic, Epipaleolithic, and Neolithic sites were identified in precise, although limited, surveys in the region of Wadi Faṣael and in Wadi el-Maliḥ. Complementary surveys conducted in the 1980s showed this to be the actual regional picture, rather than a distortion stemming from a paucity of research. The largest concentration of sites was traced in the lowest part of Wadi Faṣael and its tributary, Wadi el-Aḥmar. A total of seventeen sites was detected between the eastern slopes of the Samarian Hills and the alluvial fan within the Jordan Valley. Several of the sites were examined in limited excavations. The geochronological sequence in Wadi Faṣael permits the dating of the depositional and alluvial cycles, as well as the reconstruction of the climatic events that generated them.

Three Upper Paleolithic sites in Wadi Faṣael were found within a colluvium. This period was cold and dry. The faunal assemblages are dominated by gazelle bones (89 percent in Faṣael IX; 72 percent in Faṣael X). Bone tools, Mediterranean seashells, and groundstone utensils (perhaps for pounding ocher, found here in lumps) were recovered as well. The lithic industry in

Survey map of prehistoric sites in Wadi Faṣael (survey boundaries are marked with a dotted line).

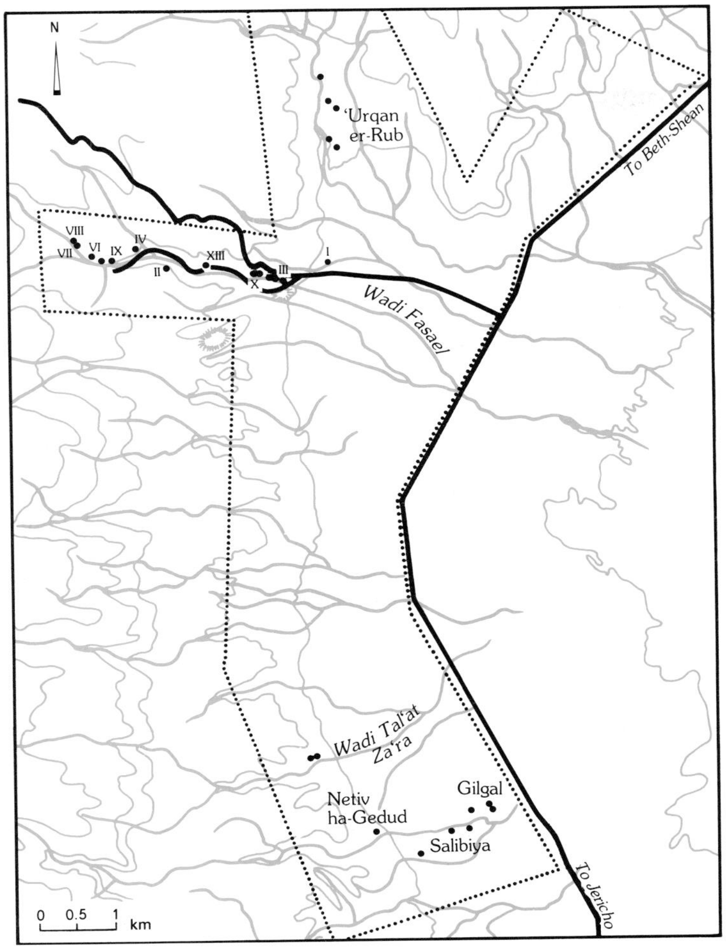

Faṣael IX is flake-oriented, whereas that in Faṣael X–XI is blade/bladelet oriented. This fact lends support to the prevalent tendency to regard the Upper Paleolithic lithic industries as reflecting a branched rather than a linear evolution.

Two Upper Paleolithic sites, transported by water and redeposited, were found in Wadi 'Auja (map reference 1899.1503), damaged by erosion. Kebaran sites (Tal'at Za'ra I and 'Urqan er-Rub II) discovered in the same area in the 1970s are characterized by curved-backed bladelets. The Kebaran sites in Wadi Faṣael display a stratigraphic sequence. The site of Faṣael III, with its various layers, represents the Kebaran culture's inner development. The earliest assemblage (IIIB) is characterized by narrow micropoints; the latest assemblage (IIIA) is dominated by obliquely truncated bladelets and micropoints. Faṣael VII has yielded micro-gravette points, suggesting influences from northern Israel and Transjordan. The sites range in size from about 20 sq m (Faṣael IIID) to 100 sq m (Faṣael IIIA), and they seem to have been located at the juncture between the valley and the foot of the hills. Similar Kebaran sites were traced in Wadi el-Maliḥ.

The wide distribution of Geometric Kebaran sites in the southern Levant has been interpreted as attesting to a more humid climate than in the preceding period. In eastern Samaria, this culture is represented by Tal'at Za'ra II, Urqan er-Rub IV, Wadi el-Aḥmar II, and Faṣael IIIC and VIII. All of them were traced in alluvial layers, on top of wadi terraces. Two similar sites were discovered in Wadi el-Maliḥ.

Two Natufian sites were found in Wadi Faṣael. Faṣael VI, situated within a colluvium on top of a terrace, has no architecture but features cupmarks drilled into the bedrock. The sediment attains a thickness of one meter and the site covers approximately 500 sq m. The lithic assemblage, composed of Helwan lunates, sickle blades, grinding implements, and pestles, is defined as Early Natufian. Faṣael IV is a Late Natufian site with bipolar or abruptly retouched small lunates; a relatively high percentage of sickle blades, indicating intensive harvesting activities; and microliths. Here, too, no architectural remains were detected. Other Natufian sites were traced to the south, in the Salibiya basin, between Moshav Netiv ha-Gedud and Kibbutz Na'aran.

Open-air sites feature prominently in the eastern part of Samaria. Apart from one rock shelter in Wadi el-Maliḥ, no cave sites have as yet been found in this region. The topographic elevation of the sites decreased over time, possibly in accordance with the shrinkage of Lake Lisan and the receding shoreline. Most of the Natufian and Neolithic sites may have been located in the Jordan Valley itself.

In western Samaria, a Late Natufian settlement was exposed by Garrod in her 1928 excavations, in the Shuqba Cave. Layer B yielded lunates and sickle blades, a few of which were Helwan-retouched, as well as single items, using the microburin technique. Several burials were also unearthed in this layer.

Of the Neolithic sites, the settlements in the Jordan Valley itself, situated at the edge of Samaria, are worthy of note: Jericho, Gilgal, and Netiv ha-Gedud (q.v.). Only a few Neolithic sites are known in the hilly region of Samaria, probably because the principal ones were in the stream valleys, in the same places where sites developed in the historical periods. An example of this is Tell el-Far'ah (North), where the finds from the earliest stratum date to the Pre-Pottery Neolithic B period.

D. A. G. Garrod, *PEQ* 60 (1928), 182–185; D. Gilead, "Early Palaeolithic Cultures in Israel and the Near East" (Ph.D. diss., Jerusalem 1970); O. Bar-Yosef et al., *Paléorient* 2 (1974), 415–428; A. N. Goring-Morris, ibid. 6 (1980), 173–191; P. Goldberg, *Préhistoire du Levant* (ed. J. Cauvin and P. Sanlaville), Paris 1981, 55–56; Y. Porath, *ESI* 2 (1983), 31–32; id., *'Atiqot* 17 (1985), 1–19; F. Darmon, *Paléorient* 10/2 (1984), 106–110; R. Gophna and Z. Tsuk, *Mitekufat Ha'even* 20 (1987), 184*–185*; E. Hovers and O. Bar-Yosef, *IEJ* 37 (1987), 77–87.

ERELLA HOVERS

THE MOUNT MANASSEH (NORTHERN SAMARIAN HILLS) SURVEY

THE REGION

The northern Samarian Hills—or, as the area is known in the Bible and in written documents from the Bronze Age, Mount Manasseh or Mount Shechem—are a broad syncline with a southwest–northeast axis. The syncline, which is of Eocene origin, is bounded on the east by the Far'ah anticline and on the west and north by the 'Anabta and the Umm el-Faḥm anticlines. The center of the syncline is characterized by an "inversion of relief"—that is, mountain ranges (the highest, Mount Ebal, rises 940 m above sea level) that are higher than the anticlines flanking it. A network of Neogene faults cuts the syncline in a southeast–northwest direction. Along these faults, wide internal valleys were created within the syncline and wadis on its eastern side (Wadi Far'ah and Wadi el-Maliḥ). On the edges of the syncline, at a junction of impenetrable Senonian limestone and Eocene chalk, the area is dotted with springs, from the bottom of Mount Gerizim on the south to the area north of Jenin.

The six interior valleys of Mount Manasseh, its water sources, and its rich, cultivable land gave the area its unique character and distinguish it from the hill country to its south (the Ephraim and Judean anticlines). The results of the survey (see below) have revealed that the morphological and historical divisions in the central hill country constitute a dividing line between the anticlines of Judea and Ephraim and the syncline of Shechem, and not between Judea and Samaria, as was once thought.

Settlement on Mount Manasseh was concentrated in the Mikhmetat Valley in the south, the Ṭubas (Tevez) and Zababdeh valleys in the east, the Sanur Valley in the center, and the er-Rameh and Dothan valleys in the west and north. West of these valleys extends a hilly region of hard limestone and dolomite, in which vestiges of a natural forest of evergreen oak and Palestinian terebinth can still be found. On the east, extending down to the Jordan Valley, is a broad strip of the desert's fringe. These three landscape units, which are subdivided into smaller, secondary units, decisively influenced the region's history.

EXPLORATION

This region, the site of three of the early capitals of the Israelite kingdom—Shechem, Tirzah, and Samaria—became the object of scholarly interest at the beginning of the twentieth century. E. Sellin excavated at Shechem in 1913–1914 and 1926–1927. In 1908–1910, G. A. Reisner and C. S. Fisher excavated at Samaria-Sebaste; the Palestine Exploration Fund continued that investigation from 1931 to 1935. In another important undertaking, excavations at Shechem were renewed by the Drew-McCormick expedition from 1956 to 1964. Also to be noted is R. de Vaux's work at Tell el-Far'ah (North; Tirzah) from 1946 to 1960. Tel Dothan, which is also in this area, was investigated by J. P. Free between 1953 and 1960, but only partial results of his excavation have been published so far. In spite of all these archaeological projects, however, no systematic survey had been done. Before 1967, two small-scale, limited surveys were fielded—one by German archaeologists, in the vicinity of Sebaste and Wadi Far'ah, and the other by the American Shechem Expedition, under the direction of E. F. Campbell, around Shechem (q.v.). A first glimpse of the history of the settlement and the archaeology of the region was revealed in the wake of an emergency survey conducted by Z. Kallai, R. Gophna and Y. Porath in 1967–1968. In 1978 a comprehensive archaeological survey of the region was undertaken, on behalf of Tel Aviv University, Haifa University, and the Israel Exploration Society, under the direction of A. Zertal.

SURVEY RESULTS

An area of some 1,800 sq km, or about three-quarters of the area of the northern Samarian Hills, was surveyed by the end of 1990. About 821 ancient sites were recorded, 632 of which were previously unknown. The following table presents the number of settlements found from the historical periods (the data for the prehistoric periods are incomplete):

Period	*No. of Settlements*	*Period*	*No. of Settlements*
Chalcolithic	46	Iron II	238
EB I	78	Iron III	95
EB II	37	Persian	247
EB III	2	Hellenistic	140
MB I	55	Early Roman	146
MB IIA	2	Late Roman	179
MB IIB	161	Byzantine	358
LB I	23	Early Arab	169
LB II	21	Medieval	184
LB III	36	Ottoman	77
Iron IA	51		
Iron IB	81		
Iron IC	81		

Settlements in the Chalcolithic period and the Early Bronze Age were concentrated in three areas, in close proximity to water sources: along the "water strip" on the western slope of the syncline, and along Wadi Far'ah and Naḥal Shechem. Large, fortified mounds were found from the Early Bronze Age I: nineteen of the seventy-eight settlements recorded from this period were fortified mounds. Another interesting discovery from this period was the enclosures. Six enclosures were recorded on Mount Manasseh. Their position on mountaintops or at other strategic points indicates that they played a defensive role. At several sites the enclosures did not contain settlements; the inhabitants of nearby sites in the valley probably sought refuge in them in times of danger. Contrary to what was generally believed, the results of the survey revealed that the majority of sites from this period were established at the start of the Early Bronze Age I (beginning of the third millennium) and that a decline in settlement occurred in the second part of the period.

The Middle Bronze Age I was also marked by a sharp increase in settlement. All fifty-five settlements established in this period were concentrated in the eastern valleys and on the desert fringe, without regard for water sources or soil quality. The settlements, which were scattered, were quite large; they yielded a considerable number of potsherds and buildings. The buildings were grouped in clusters, in the center of which was a fortified enclosure and perhaps also a temple. Several unique sites from this period may have been cultic.

The Middle Bronze Age IIA (beginning of the second millennium BCE) witnessed a sharp decline in settlement (although it is also likely that the survey found it difficult to identify the pottery from this period). In the following period (Middle Bronze Age IIB), a large wave of settlement took place in the area (161 sites); its size was unparalleled anywhere else in the country. New cities were founded that were fortified with walls and huge earthen ramparts (Shechem, Tirzah, Dothan, Ibleam, Jenin, Khirbet Najjar, Khirbet Kheibar, Khirbet Qumei, el-Kebara, Shuweiket er-Ras, and Khirbet Qarqaf). At the same time, numerous smaller sites were built on the edges of the valleys, several of which were also defended with ramparts. This was a period of prosperity and growth for Mount Manasseh. In the few contemporary historical sources known (Execration texts), the area is called Mount Shechem or the Land of Shechem. Neither the origins of the settlers of this kingdom of Shechem nor its political and ethnic structure are known.

The survey team suggested that a decrease in precipitation at the end of the sixteenth century BCE may have been one of the causes of the greatly reduced number of settlements in the Late Bronze Age I (23 sites). According to geological and other evidence, the springs on the eastern edge of the syncline that had watered the area in the Middle Bronze Age IIB became dry in this period. This may also have been one of the reasons for the general decline in settlement in this country in the second half of the second millennium BCE (Late Bronze Age), in addition to the destruction caused by the Egyptian Eighteenth Dynasty pharaohs. There is a relatively large amount of historical information about Mount Manasseh for this period. At that time, the absolute ruler of the area was Labaya, prince of Shechem, and his family, whose jurisdiction extended throughout the hill country and over parts of the Jezreel Valley.

The remains of the Iron Age I on Mount Manasseh (the Israelite settlement period) indicate that in this period the area was infiltrated by seminomads who arrived along the historic route that connects the central hill country with Transjordan—Wadi Far'ah. This movement is considered to have taken place in the thirteenth and twelfth centuries BCE. According to pottery experts, three cooking pot types found in the area exhibit the characteristic features of the Israelite settlers' pottery. The earliest settlements arose at that time in the Jordan Valley, Wadi Far'ah, Wadi Maliḥ, and the eastern valleys of Mount Manasseh, where Canaanite settlement was sparse. The sacred center in this period—as many scholars have shown—was at Shechem, and perhaps also at Mount Ebal. There is evidence that the settlement expanded from the eastern to the central and northern valleys (Sanur, er-Rameh, Dothan, and Naḥal Shechem). The settlement pattern was unaltered, and only pottery developments attest to the move. From the biblical sources, it appears that the tribe of Manasseh then included groups or nuclei of other Israelite tribes who migrated from here to the south and north to create Ephraim, Benjamin, Judah, and other, northern tribes. Only at a later stage, due to a lack of cultivable land, was there a move in the direction of the afforested hilly areas on the edge of the syncline and to Mount Ephraim in the south. This view of the settlement process, although incomplete in all details and requiring further study, clarifies some of the inexplicable and contradictory references in the Bible about the beginnings of Israelite settlement on Mount Manasseh.

In the Iron Age II the area reached its peak of settlement (238 sites). All parts of the hill country were cultivated, including parts of the desert fringe. To this period belong the Samaria ostraca (q.v. Samaria), which attest to Mount Manasseh's administrative organization. Based on the results of the survey, a new division has been proposed for the districts of Manasseh (cf. Jos. 17:5). After the conquest of Samaria in 722 BCE and the transformation of the area into an Assyrian, and later a Babylonian, province, fortified farms were built along the desert's edge, between Wadi Far'ah and Wadi el-Maliḥ. The mass deportations of the inhabitants, which are also mentioned in contemporary Assyrian documents, led to a decrease in the number of settlements (95 sites). A unique group of pottery has been distinguished from this period for the first time; it is attributed to Cuthean settlers who were brought to the Samarian Hills from Mesopotamia in the eighth and seventh centuries BCE.

In the Persian period, intensive settlement is again noted (247 sites). The growth in settlement is to be explained by the fact that here it could develop without interference from political instability. A certain symmetry can in fact be distinguished in the development of the settlements in the first millennium BCE in Judah and Israel, although there is a gap of about 150 years between them (corresponding to the gap in time between the conquest of Samaria and the destruction of Jerusalem). Another explanation (proposed by A. Grintz) may be that some of the Babylonian returnees settled in Samaria (and not only in Judah) in the fifth and fourth centuries BCE. The results of the survey strengthen this assumption, as does the wave of settlement in the Dothan Valley and its surroundings. The decline in settlement in the Hellenistic period was due to Samaritan opposition to Alexander the Great's conquest of the country in 332 BCE (the Samaritan revolt). Remains of the Hellenistic period were uncovered in half of the Persian period sites (140 Hellenistic sites). In the Early Roman period there was an upsurge in settlement in the region, and new sites were founded in its northwestern part, in the toparchy connected with Narbata. The Byzantine period represents the peak period of settlement density on Mount Manasseh (358 sites), and from the seventh to fourteenth centuries (the Early Arab and medieval periods), the number of sites again decreased by about half (169 and 184). In the Mameluke period signs of recovery are evident, and new, fortified settlements are recorded. The sharpest decline occurred in the Ottoman period (sixteenth to nineteenth centuries), when settlement in the area decreased to about a quarter of the number of Byzantine settlements.

W. F. Albright, *JPOS* 11 (1931), 241–251, A. Zertal, *ESI* 2 (1983), 43–44; id., *Society and Economy*, 341–352; id., *BASOR* 276 (1989), 77–84; id., *PEQ* 122 (1990), 21–33; id., *Transeuphratène* 3 (1990), 9–30; id., *BAR* 17/5 (1991), 28–49; G. W. Ahlström, *BASOR* 280 (1990), 77–82.

ADAM ZERTAL

THE SOUTHERN SAMARIAN HILLS SURVEY

THE REGION

The southern Samarian Hills—the land of Ephraim—lies in the heart of the central hill country, in an area with very harsh conditions for settlement: it lacks the broad mountain plateaus of Judah and Benjamin and the large valleys of northern Samaria. Its lithological configuration, mainly hard limestone, is extremely difficult to cultivate. Its topography, rock formations and dense vegetation that once covered the area, gave large stretches of the land of Ephraim the characteristics of a frontier region.

The survey of southern Samaria was carried out in 1980–1987, on behalf of the Department of the Land of Israel Studies at Bar-Ilan University, with the assistance of the Archaeological Survey of Israel and the archaeology staff officer for Judea and Samaria, under the direction of I. Finkelstein. The area surveyed—about 1,050 sq km—corresponds to the geographical-historical territory of the land of Ephraim which was bordered in the south by Ma'ale Beth-Horon, Ramallah, and Deir Dibwan; in the north by Naḥal Qanah and the northern tip of the Beit Dajan Valley; in the east by a line beyond the outermost permanent settlements of the desert fringe; and in the west by the so-called Green Line (pre–1967 border). The American Shechem Expedition had investigated several sites in the northern part of the area (q.v. Shechem). The purpose of the 1980–1987 survey was twofold: to investigate the region's history of settlement and the environmental conditions and their influence on settlement dispersal, and to compare early settlements with the modern settlement-economic pattern.

The survey grid was divided into six topographical units, each displaying distinct geographic and economic characteristics.

1. A long, narrow strip of desert fringe in the east: contains tracts of land suitable for grain cultivation and pastoralism, especially sheep raising.

2. Northern central range: contains the small interior valleys, such as the valleys of Shiloh, Lubban esh-Sharqiyye, and Beit Dajan. The economy of the occupants of this area, which had the best conditions for settlement in the land of Ephraim, was based on grain cultivation, especially in the valleys, and, in its eastern part, also on grazing.

3. Southern central range: contains the Bethel plateau, where the cultivation of grain was also possible.

4. Northern mountain slopes: contains moderate ridges and broad wadis but lacks permanent water sources. The principal source of livelihood in this area was based on grain crops and orchards.

5. The dissected southern mountain slopes: contains an area not conducive to human occupation. Its economy was based mainly on orchards.

6. Foothills: contain a moderate terrain, parts of which are rocky. The economy of its inhabitants was based on grain crops and grazing in the rocky areas.

SURVEY RESULTS

About 550 settlements were recorded in the survey of the land of Ephraim, some 350 having been examined for the first time. About 98 percent of the ruins marked on maps and about 92 percent of the 113 Arab villages in the area were surveyed. Most of the sites are relatively small: only a few attain an area of 4 to 5 a. or more. The survey's interim results, as regards the settlement pattern in the area, follow.

The Early Bronze Age is the earliest period in which intensive human occupation of the land of Ephraim can be distinguished. Forty sites from this period were examined, only one of which was a fortified city—Ai. Most of the sites were small settlements, the majority not more than 2.5 a. in area. They were concentrated in the desert fringe, the central range, and the foothills. This period was not marked by intensive occupation in the interior valleys of the central range, and the western slopes were almost entirely devoid of occupation. Most of the land of Ephraim seems still to have been covered with forests, and the settlers primarily inhabited marginal areas.

The main discovery from the Middle Bronze Age I was cemeteries, almost all of them situated in the desert fringe area and the central range. The main burial grounds were around 'Ein Samiya. Their location suggests that the population was engaged in seasonal pastoralism, wandering between the eastern fringe areas in the winter and the central range in summer. Several settlements were also found in the desert fringe area.

In the Middle Bronze Age IIA, settlement in the area was extremely sparse. The first large wave of settlement occurred in the following period (Middle Bronze Age IIB–C) and resembles that encountered in northern Samaria. About eighty-five sites from the Middle Bronze Age IIB–C have been recorded so far, some of which were probably seasonal. They are concentrated in the desert fringe, in the north central range (around the interior valleys), in the northern part of the western slopes, and in the area of the Bethel plateau. Settlement on the southern slopes and the foothills was very sparse in this period. The concentration of sites on the northern slopes, which lacked a permanent water source, indicates that the settlers were not deterred by being far from springs and by the necessity of clearing forested areas. The settlement density in the northern part of the area may be connected to the importance of nearby Shechem. Another concentration of sites was distinguished around Bethel. From the results of the survey and of the excavations at Shiloh, it appears that in the Middle Bronze Age IIB small, unfortified sites were established throughout the region, and that in the Middle Bronze Age IIC there was a sharp decline in settlement: some sites were abandoned, and the population moved to large settlements. Some of the latter were fortified and a few were about 3 to 4 a. in area. These include Bethel, Khirbet Marjama, Shiloh, Sheikh Abu Zarad (biblical Tappuah), and Khirbet el-'Urma (biblical Arumah).

In the Late Bronze Age there was a dramatic decrease in the population of the area (and in the other mountainous regions). Only five sites continued to exist (the five main centers in the previous period), and of these Shiloh was no longer an actual settlement, but only a cultic site. Furthermore, the other four sites still in existence were then probably greatly reduced in area. The population in this period seems to have been largely pastoral.

In the Iron Age I, a second wave of settlement engulfed the area. From this period, 115 sites were recorded. Of these, twenty-six were designated as large villages (one acre or more), thirty-two were small villages (slightly less than one acre), and the remainder were isolated houses or seasonal sites. Settlement was concentrated on the desert fringe and around the small valleys in the north central range, in the Bethel plateau, and in the northern part of the western slopes. The settlement pattern points to a clear preference for areas of grain cultivation and pasturage over horticulture. As far as an internal chronological division can be established, the process of penetration into the western slopes began only in the later part of the period. This penetration involved contending with dense vegetation areas and hard-rock formations, and in some cases being far from permanent water sources. An especially large concentration of sites was noted around Shiloh, the religious and political center of the population in the central hill country in the eleventh century BCE.

The Iron Age II in this area was marked by an unprecedented level of settlement; 190 sites were recorded from this period, most of them inhabited in the eighth century BCE. Of these, about fifteen were large sites (5 a. or more), about fifteen were medium-sized (2.5 a. or more), and the rest were small villages (fewer than 2.5 a.). A dense concentration of settlements was noted throughout the northern part of the area, but settlements were also found on the southern part of the western slopes, in the orchard-growing area. Some sites here contained oil presses that were possibly built by the central government. In contrast to the increase in the number of settlements in all the topographical units in the area in this period, the Bethel plateau showed a decrease in the number of sites. The reason for this decrease may have been the plateau's proximity to the border separating the kingdoms of Judah and Samaria, which was the scene of political upheavals. The intensive settlement activities in the land of Ephraim indicate that at this time almost all the land in this region had been prepared for cultivation.

In the Persian period, there was a sharp decline in the number of settlements in the area. Only about ninety settlements were recorded for this period, and most of them were smaller than those of the Iron Age II. This decline was probably due to the destruction of the kingdoms of Israel and Judah. The

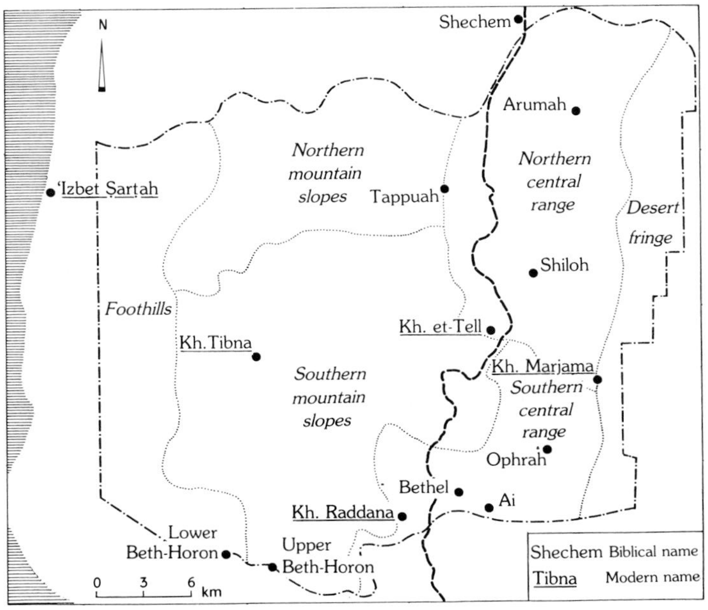

Area of the southern Samarian Hills survey.

bulk of settlement activity then shifted to the western part of the area, probably within the framework of the development taking place on the Coastal Plain.

The Hellenistic period is marked by further development of the area and renewed prosperity. The settlement pattern began to assume the form it embodied in the following centuries.

In the Roman period the number of settlements was about 215. Forty five sites are designated large settlements (2.5 a. or more). They were evenly dispersed throughout the region. The southern part of the area was also marked by increased settlement activity, probably through the influence of Jerusalem to the south. At this time many settlements were established in the most inhospitable area in the land of Ephraim—the southern slopes.

For the Byzantine period, found to have been the peak period of settlement in the land of Ephraim, 267 sites were recorded. The main part of the occupation then moved southward, and settlements in the Shechem area started thinning out, probably in the wake of the policy that suppressed the Samaritans. A concentration of monasteries in the southwestern part of the region is a feature of the Byzantine period. These monasteries probably produced wine and perhaps oil.

In the medieval period, the settlement distribution is again balanced. About 150 sites are known in the land of Ephraim, nearly equally dispersed among the different landscape units. Almost all the sites of modern Arab villages in the area today were already occupied then.

SUMMARY

Settlement in the land of Ephraim was influenced by a number of geographical factors: conditions in the interior valleys in the northern central range and the Bethel plateau were fairly conducive to the establishment of settlements. The land in the dissected southern slopes, on the other hand, did not encourage agricultural activities. The pasturage areas of the desert fringe in the east and the dense vegetation in the west also influenced the settlement pattern. From the historical standpoint, the two important centers in the near vicinity—Shechem in the north and Jerusalem in the south—strongly influenced the area's settlement in various periods, as at times did the Coastal Plain in the west.

W. F. Albright, *BASOR* 35 (1929), 3–7; T. J. Meek, ibid. 61 (1936), 17–19; W. J. Phythian-Adams, *PEQ* 68 (1936), 141–149; I. Finkelstein, *'Izbet Sartah: An Early Iron Age Site Near Rosh Ha'ayin, Israel* (*BAR*/IS 299), Oxford 1986; id., *The Archaeology of the Israelite Settlement*, Jerusalem 1988; id., *BAR* 14/5 (1988), 34–35; id., *TA* 15–16 (1988–1989), 117–183; id., *IEJ* 41 (1991), 19–45; id., *Journal for the Study of the Old Testament* 44 (19890, 43–74; id., *IEJ* 41 (1991), 19–45; B. Mazar, *The Early Biblical Period*, Jerusalem 1986, 173–188; N. Na'aman, *Borders and Districts in Biblical Historiography* (Jerusalem Biblical Studies 4), Jerusalem 1986, 158–166; Z. Kallai, *ZDPV* 102 (1986), 68–74; D. Edelman, *ZDPV* 104 (1988), 44–58; J. Cohen-Finkelstein, "Pottery Distribution, Settlement Patterns and Demographic Oscillations in Southern Samaria in the Islamic Period" (Master's thesis, Hebrew Univ. of Jerusalem, 1991); J. Schwartz and J. Spanier, *RB* 98 (1991), 252–271.

ISRAEL FINKELSTEIN

THE SURVEY OF WESTERN SAMARIA

From 1974 to 1981, the Archaeological Survey of Samaria, focusing on the western part of the region, which had been more heavily populated than the eastern, examined the area from Naḥal 'Iron (Wadi 'Ara) in the north to the streambeds of Nevallat and Nattuf in the south. The survey was directed by S. Dar, assisted by S. Applebaum, Y. Tepper, and A. Siegelmann. Scores of trial soundings were also carried out at the time.

IRON AGE II, PERSIAN, AND HELLENISTIC PERIODS. From the Iron Age II onward, there were clusters of small villages and a large number of farmhouses throughout the area. The villages were small, for the most part seldom exceeding 2.5 a. in area. The four-room house was a common feature in the villages, occasionally occurring also in pairs, as adjoining structures. One of the villages, Khirbet Jama'in (map reference 1569.1752), is located about 1.5 km (1 mi.) southeast of 'Azun. At Khirbet Jama'in about fifteen four-room houses, a defensive wall surrounding the village, a winepress, and a public oil press were found. The pottery there dates to the eighth and seventh centuries BCE. Another village was located at Khirbet Ḥamad (map reference 1596.1661), about 2 km north of Burqin. In the survey of the village, pottery from the Iron Age I to the Byzantine period was found. In the Iron Age II, a storeroom complex had been built in the village, perhaps for storing grain. A large threshing floor, oil presses, and winepresses were found near the village.

Both Jama'in and Ḥamad are situated in hard-rock terrains without perennial water sources. Villagers were, therefore, forced to dig rock-cut cisterns in order to store rainwater and run-off water. Today the same methods of obtaining water characterize the Arab settlements in the region.

Another type of rural village in Samaria in the Iron Age II, in both the north and south, was the farmhouse. Groups of farmhouses were examined in the Umm Riḥan area in northern Samaria and in the foothills between Naḥal Shiloh and Wadi Nattuf. The Qoren Liqrana farm (map reference 1565.1734) is about 2 km east of Kafr Tult. The farm (27.1 by 29.8 m) includes a courtyard, rooms, and towers in the center and on its margins that were used as dwellings and for defense. The pottery found at the farm dates to the Iron Age II and the medieval period. Excavations at the Riḥan farm (map reference 1625.2085) in northern Samaria revealed its plan. The external measurements of the farmhouse are 30.6 by 38 m. A row of small rooms, used as dwellings and as storerooms, extended along the southern wall. The foundations of a small watchtower were uncovered in the corner of the building. The pottery dates to the early Persian and Hellenistic periods; the pottery found in the other farms in the area dates mainly to the Iron Age II.

The dominant branches of agriculture in the villages and farms in the Iron Age II—for which there is archaeological evidence—are vine growing and wine production, olive growing and olive oil production, grain crops and sheep rearing. In the settlements and in the fields there was evidence of efficient agricultural terracing, planting and sowing, well-built rock-cut oil presses, winepresses, threshing floors for grains and legumes, and sheep caves and pens. There were undoubtedly other branches of agriculture and other crops, but no traces of them have yet been found.

ROMAN-BYZANTINE PERIOD. In the Roman-Byzantine period, the small Iron Age II villages grew into medium-sized towns, 5 to 10 a. in area; instead of the four-room house, the typical dwelling was a courtyard house with many rooms. One of these towns—Umm Riḥan in northern Samaria (map reference 163.210)—was examined and the dimensions of its built-up area were measured. The town, covering about 9 to 10 a., included some one hundred well-built courtyard houses. Architecturally, Umm Riḥan was a densely built

Umm Riḥan: plan of the settlement in the Roman-Byzantine period.

Khirbet Jama'in: one of the four-room houses in the settlement.

Umm Riḥan area: field tower.

settlement, but planning and organization are evident in its network of streets, water supply, defenses, and public areas. The buildings at the settlement's edge formed a defensive line reinforced by towers that dominated the entrances to the village. The network of lanes and streets crosses the town along its length and breadth. The lanes were also used as channels for conveying rainwater into rock-cut reservoirs between the houses.

In the public area, remains of a bathhouse and shops were found, as were two mausolea and part of a Latin inscription from a public building. About eight or nine oil presses were uncovered in the town and numerous winepresses and field towers (see below) were found in the surrounding fields. In trial soundings made at Umm Riḥan and in its farmland, there was evidence of human occupation from the Iron Age II to the beginning of the Byzantine period. The city developed in the Persian and Hellenistic periods and reached its apogee in the early centuries CE. On the basis of the numismatic evidence, it seems that the settlement was abandoned at the beginning of the fifth century CE, probably as a result of the Samaritan revolt against the Christians (see below).

Field Towers. More than one hundred field towers were encountered in the vicinity of Umm Riḥan. These were small, very sturdy structures that were common in Samaria where orchards were cultivated. Each tower stood in a specific plot and marked the limits of a farmer's land, on which he had vineyards and orchards. Field towers are scattered throughout Samaria and attest to the existence of planned, sophisticated agriculture from the Hellenistic period onward. It is possible that construction of the towers was initiated by government authorities and was connected with the settlement activities of the Hasmoneans. Judging from the excavations and trial soundings of scores of these field towers, it appears that they were abandoned no later than the second century CE, apparently as a result of political and economic changes in the area.

Farm Estates. In the Roman and Byzantine periods, the early farms were replaced by estates belonging to the wealthy and to those having close connections with the ruling parties. One of the largest and finest of these is Qaṣr el-Lejah in the Umm Riḥan vicinity (map reference 1673.2093). The estate (26.5 by 36 m) was preserved in some parts to a height of 2 to 3 m. The farm consisted of residential and service wings, an oilpress (intact), both an inner and an outer reservoir, an impressive inner tower for the use of the estate owners, and an exterior watchtower a short distance away. A trial sounding revealed pottery from the Late Hellenistic and Early Roman periods. Farms similar to Qaṣr el-Lejah represent the local version of the Roman *villa rustica*; tenant farmers or laborers tilled the soil and tended the

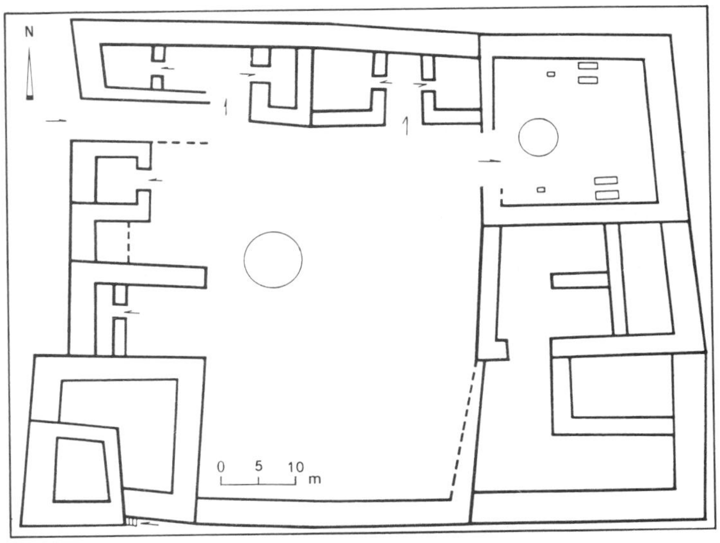

Qaṣr el-Lejah: plan of the farm estate, Roman period.

Ancient road in the area of Qarawet Bani Ḥasan, western Samaria.

orchards of the estate owners, producing large quantities of olive oil and wine for sale.

Road Network. Samaria is crossed by a comprehensive and ramified network of both country and main roads. Every village and town had roads leading to its fields and every settlement was connected by built-up roads to its nearest and most distant neighbors. The length and number of ancient roads compare favorably with the modern road system, indicating that an open economy existed in the region and that the agricultural produce was marketed in centers both near and far.

Settlement began to expand in the Roman and Early Byzantine periods, accompanied by great strides in agriculture in the hill country. The towns showed a considerable increase in population and grand and spacious estates began to appear. The main agricultural enterprises at this time were olive oil and wine produced for export, even though the size of family plots was not particularly large (up to 12.5 a.).

In the Byzantine period, much of the land in Samaria was expropriated by the authorities, and the farmers were forced to become tenant farmers of Christian estate owners. In the fifth and sixth centuries, the Samaritan farmers revolted against their seigneurs, and extensive parts of the area were abandoned until modern times.

Main publication: S. Dar, *Landscape and Pattern: An Archaeological Survey of Samaria, 800 B.C.E.–636 C.E.*, 1–2 (*BAR*/IS 308), Oxford 1986.

Other studies: S. Applebaum, *PEQ* 110 (1978), 91–100; D. Eitam, *TA* 6 (1979), 146–155; S. Dar, *IEJ* 34 (1984), 177–179; id., *BAR* 308 (Reviews), *AJA* 92 (1988), 445–446. — *BIAL* 25 (1988), 112–114; R. Barkay, *BAIAS* 7 (1987–1988) 8–20; D. A. Dorsey, *BASOR* 268 (1987), 57–70.

SHIMON DAR

HELLENISTIC AND ROMAN-BYZANTINE PERIODS

IDENTIFICATION

According to Josephus, "the province of Samaria lies between Galilee and Judaea; beginning [in the north] at the village of Ginae ['En Gannim = Jenin] situated in the Great Plain, it terminates at the toparchy of Acrabattene. Its character differs in no wise from that of Judaea" (*War* III, 48). Samaria extends as far as Jenin and the Gilboa' hills in the north, to the Jordan in the east, and to the toparchy called after its headquarters, Acraba (today 'Aqraba), which was part of Judea, in the southeast. Samaria is bounded in the south by Burj el-Asane and Naḥal Shiloh, and in the west by the Sharon (the territories of Antipatris and Caesarea). To the northwest lies the toparchy of Narbata, which was also inhabited by Jews. In the Roman period, the area of Samaria was divided into two main territories: the territory of Neapolis in the east and that of Sebaste in the west.

The main east–west road crossing Samaria ascends from the Jordan Valley through Wadi Far'ah to the slopes of Mount Ebal, circles the mount on the north, and reaches the Sanur Valley, on to the Dothan Valley and Naḥal 'Iron. Another east–west road approaches Shechem from Naḥal Shechem and descends to the Jordan Valley. Yet another, northern road cuts through Samaria along the Dothan Valley and connects the Jezreel Valley through Naḥal Ḥadera with the Coastal Plain. Samaria's main north–south road runs along the edge of the hilly region, from Jerusalem to Shechem, where it forks into other north–south roads.

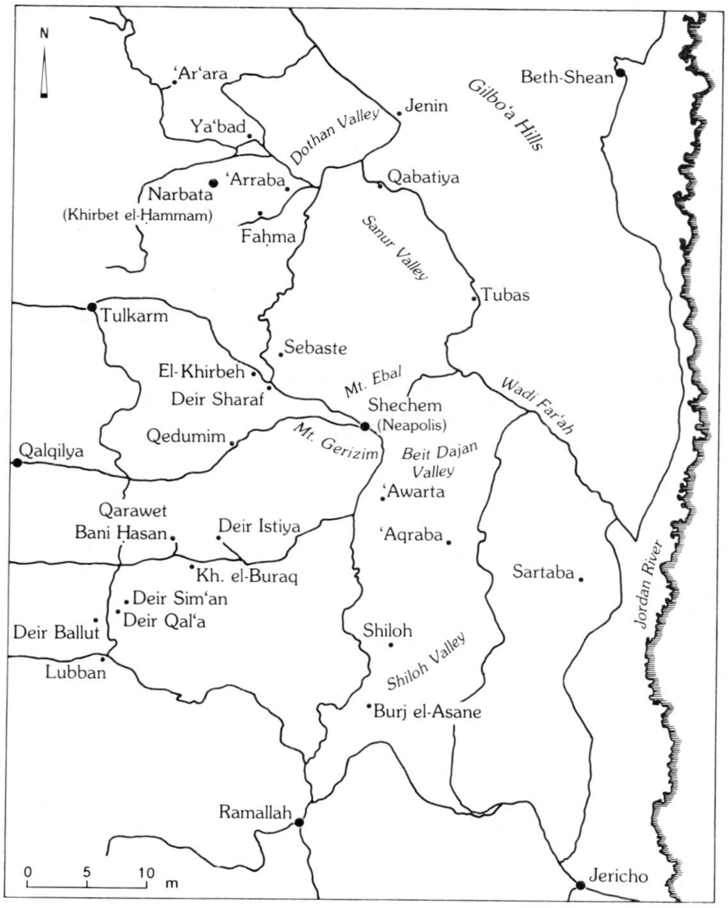

Map of Samaria in the Hellenistic and Roman-Byzantine periods.

HISTORY

When Alexander the Great conquered Samaria in the fourth century BCE, he found a single administrative unit, or satrapy, ruled by the satrap Sanballat (Josephus, *Antiq.* XI, 302, 331) from its capital, the city of Samaria. The city, after having first extended him aid, later rebelled against Alexander, who proceeded to destroy it and build a Macedonian city in its stead (Curtius Rufus, IV, 8, 9–11). Shechem, which lay in ruins for most of the Persian period, was rebuilt at the beginning of the Greek occupation. Like Samaria, it was probably built as a Macedonian city rather than a Samaritan one (contrary to the view of Shechem's excavators). Both Shechem and Samaria were damaged in the wars of the third century BCE (Samaria was laid waste by the Ptolemaic army in 312 and by Demetrius' forces in 296) (Diodorus Siculus, XIX, 93, 7; Eusebius, *Chron.*, Olymp. 121, 1). Early in the second century BCE, when the country was occupied by the Seleucids, the Samaritans built a large city on Mount Gerizim, over an area of some 85 a. Shechem declined in importance and was overshadowed by the city on Mount Gerizim. Both cities survived the Jewish revolt against the Seleucids; in fact, Samaria helped to suppress the revolt (1 Macc. 3:10; Josephus, *Antiq.* XII, 287). When John Hyrcanus conquered the region, however, both cities were destroyed, first the city on Mount Gerizim (Josephus, *Antiq.* XIII, 254–256; *War* I, 63) and then Sebaste (*Antiq.* XIII, 275–281; *War* I, 64–65).

Pompey freed Samaria from Hasmonean rule (63 BCE) and annexed it to the province of Syria. The city of Samaria was restored to its previous inhabitants (*Antiq.* XIV, 75; *War* I, 156), but it is not clear what happened to the Samaritans, whose capital was originally on Mount Gerizim. In any case, the city on Mount Gerizim was never rebuilt, and the Romans apparently did not grant the Samaritans the same privileges they did the Greek inhabitants.

Gabinius built Samaria-Sebaste in 57 BCE (*Antiq.* XIV, 87–88; *War* I, 166). Herod, having received the city from Augustus, also rebuilt Sebaste as a pagan city (*Antiq.* XV, 217, 292, 296). Nothing is known of his treatment of the Samaritans, although he did have a Samaritan wife, and the city on Mount Gerizim and Shechem (Tell Balâtah) both remained in ruins. However, on the northern slope of Mount Gerizim, later the site of the city of Neapolis, a new city began to develop—it was officially founded only after the destruction of the Second Temple. Later, Samaria was included in the Roman province of Judea, established after Archelaus had been deposed in 6 CE.

The Samaritans did not intervene in the dispute over the succession to Herod's throne or take part in the subsequent disturbances in Palestine (*Antiq.* XVII, 319). In the first century CE, the Samaritans were the dominant element in Samaria and in fact harassed the Jews (*Antiq.* XX, 118–136; *War* II, 232–246). As the Samaritan community gained in strength after Herod's death, it attempted to renew its national-religious center on Mount Gerizim. The first attempt was under Pontius Pilate (*Antiq.* XVIII, 85–89) and the second during the First Jewish Revolt (*War* III, 307–315). Immediately after the destruction of Jerusalem, the new city of Neapolis was built on the northern slope of Mount Gerizim (*War* IV, 449; Pliny, *NH* V, 69). Neapolis was built as a pagan city, as the Romans had learned their lesson from the Jewish revolt and from the Samaritans' attempts to rebuild their city on Mount Gerizim. Judging from the dates on coins of Neapolis, which were reckoned from the founding of the city, the Flavian emperors declared Neapolis a city in 73 CE. From that time on, Sebaste and Neapolis, both with a pagan Roman population, were Samaria's two major cities. After the founding of Neapolis, it was granted extensive tracts of land; Samaria was thus divided up between the territories of Sebaste and Neapolis.

At the end of the second century, Neapolis and Sebaste were caught up in the dispute between Pescennius Niger and Septimius Severus over the imperial throne (*Scriptores Historiae Augustae*, Vita Severi 9:5). After Septimius Severus had prevailed, Sebaste, which had sided with him, received the status of *colonia*, in reward for its support, while Neapolis was punished by the removal of its municipal privileges.

Qaṣrin: aerial view of the synagogue, after partial reconstruction.

Reḥovot-in-the-Negev: limestone chancel screen panel from the chapel in the North Church.

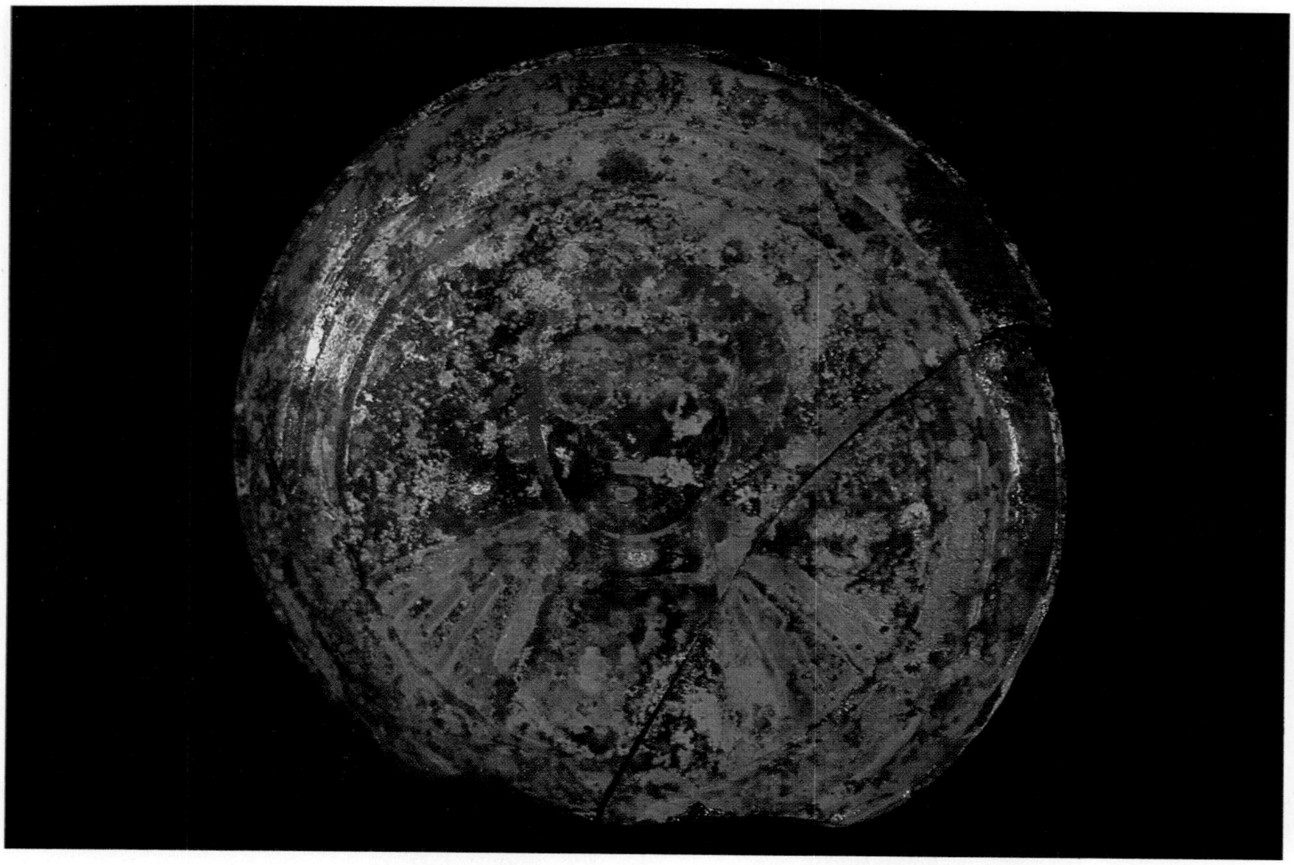

Reḥovot-in-the-Negev: ***(above and below)*** *glass bowls decorated with figures of saints.*

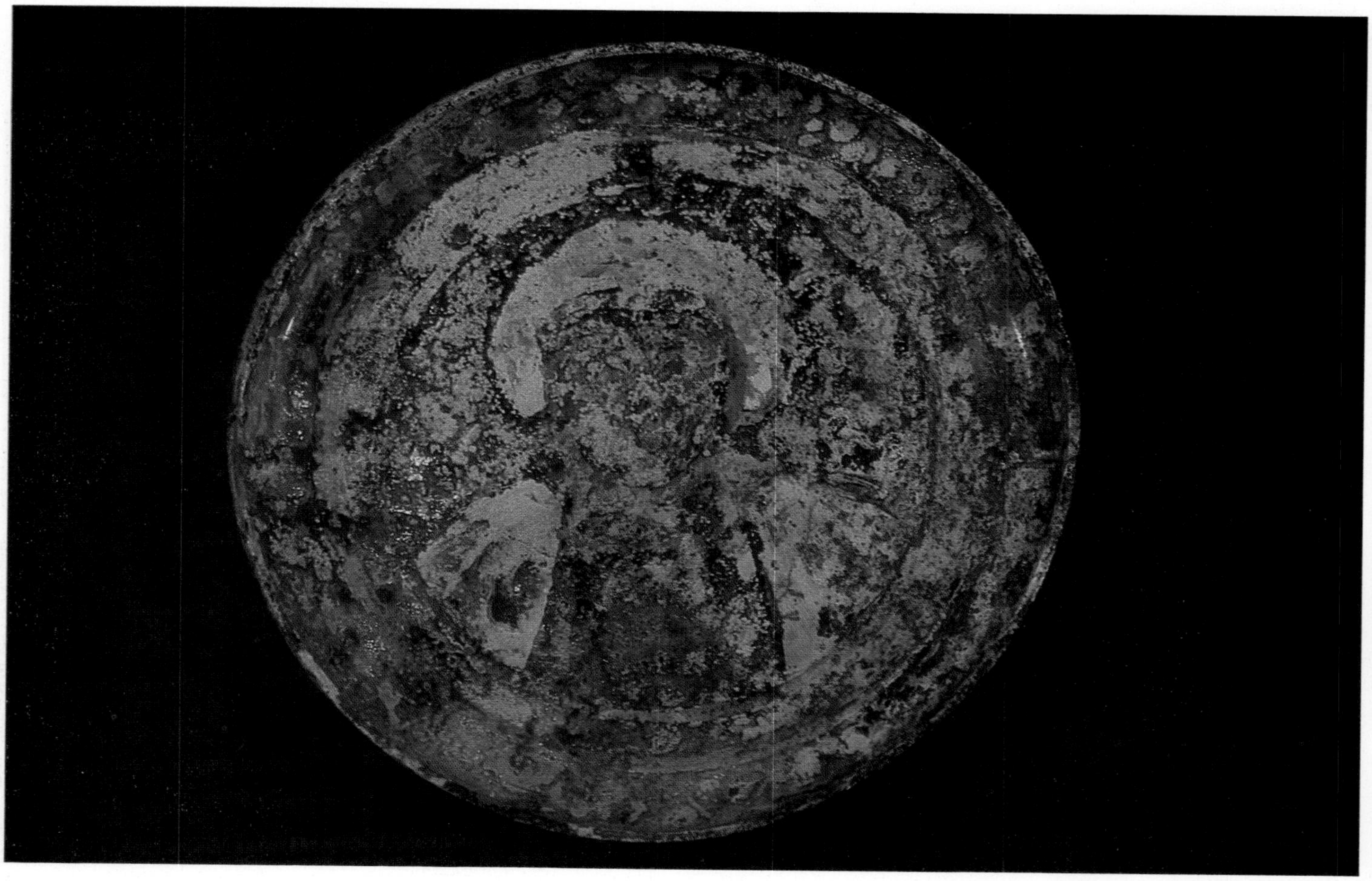

"Samaritan" sarcophagus from the mausoleum of 'Askar in Neapolis (Shechem).

In the mid-third century, Philip the Arab raised Neapolis's status to that of a *colonia*, and during his reign a Roman garrison was probably stationed in the city. In the Byzantine period Sebaste declined, becoming little more than a small village, whereas Neapolis became the scene of a struggle between the Christians and the Samaritans. In 484, the Samaritans rose up against the local Christians. The uprisings lasted intermittently for practically an entire century and extended over the whole of Samaria. It was the Christians' intent, represented particularly by the emperors Zeno and Justinian, to convert the Samaritans to Christianity. As an outcome of the rebellions, the Samaritan community of Samaria was almost wiped out. Neapolis, however, maintained its position as Samaria's principal city.

SETTLEMENT PATTERN

The transition from the Persian period to the Hellenistic period in Samaria involved no destruction. There was, thus, probably no substantial change in the pattern of settlement, although the 1968 archaeological survey revealed a significant decrease in the number of Hellenistic sites as compared with those from the Persian period. Quite possibly, the survey did not reflect the true extent of settlement in the Hellenistic period. Samaria and Shechem were, as mentioned earlier, established at the end of the fourth century as pagan cities and built in the Greek style. At Qedumim (q.v.), archaeological evidence showed that the site was continuously settled from the Persian to the Hellenistic periods.

On the basis of the extensive survey conducted by S. Dar in western Samaria (see above), it would appear that the Hellenistic period, probably the time of the Seleucids, marked the beginning of a considerable expansion of agricultural settlement in Samaria. It is reflected in the construction of terraces, extensive clearing of stones, preparation of ground for cultivation, and building of roads, water reservoirs, and various agricultural installations (wine- and oil presses). The Hasmonean kings encouraged agricultural activities in Samaria in order to judaize the region. Agricultural settlement continued into the Roman period (contrary to the situation elsewhere in the country) and in the Byzantine period. However, the Samaritan uprisings decimated Samaria's rural population, with a subsequent decline in agricultural settlement in the region. At the time, farms were not established in Samaria near water sources but in rocky areas near the cultivated plots. In addition, the traditional settlements, upon which many of the Arab villages were erected much later, continued to exist. There were farms at Umm Riḥan (see above), Qaṣr el-Lejah (see above), and Khirbet en-Najar; a military settlement was established at Qaṣr el-Ḥaramiyye, and there were agricultural settlements at Khirbet Shiḥadeh, Khirbet Bustin, Khirbet Deir Sim'an, Ḥorvat Ḥemed, and Khirbet Kurkush; there were large agricultural settlements at Khirbet el-Buraq and Qarawet Bani Ḥasan. As most of these sites have not been excavated, it is not yet known whether their occupation ceased after the Hellenistic period or continued through the Roman-Byzantine period. One important site that has been excavated in northwestern Samaria is Khirbet el-Ḥammam (q.v.), which is identified by its excavator with Jewish Narbata from the Second Temple period.

The classification of any specific site as a Samaritan, pagan, Jewish, or Christian settlement is difficult and complicated to do. It can only be based on tombs and burials, religious sites, synagogues, churches, or ritual baths. Excavations at Qedumim, a Samaritan site from the Persian period onward, revealed ritual baths dated from the first century CE to the Byzantine period. At el-Khirbeh, near Deir Sharaf, south of Sebaste, a Samaritan synagogue was discovered—its entrance faced Mount Gerizim (see Synagogues, Samaritan Synagogues). Churches have been found at el-Buraq and Bardela. However, unless extensive excavations are carried out, it will not be possible to determine the chronology of the pattern of settlement in this part of the country and the nature of the populations in different periods.

BURIALS AND TOMBS. In contrast to the small number of excavations carried out at settlement sites in Samaria, a great many tombs have been excavated. A large cemetery was excavated at Shechem (q.v.), on the southern slopes of Mount Ebal, where several mausolea were discovered. A large and magnificently appointed mausoleum was discovered at Samaria-Sebaste (q.v.), together with other imposing tombs.

Tombs containing sarcophagi were uncovered in many settlements in Samaria; no ossuaries have yet come to light, however. Hebrew names were

Qarawet Bani Ḥasan: facade of an elaborate tomb.

found incised on some coffins, at Teluza, for example; the deceased were probably Samaritans. In most of the tombs, beginning in the second century CE, peculiarly shaped coffins are found, conventionally known as "Samaritan" coffins. They are about 2 m long and have thin sides decorated with various patterns, such as rosettes and square panels. Some of the decorations are very elaborate; some show a Roman influence—garlands between columns, bulls' heads (bucrania), and eagles. "Samaritan" coffins, some quite early, have been found outside Samaria, at Antipatris (Aphek) and on the Coastal Plain, indicating that they may first have been used by Jews or pagans. In any case, the so-called Samaritan coffin is an imitation of Jewish coffins from the Second Temple period in Jerusalem. However, they are so common in Samaria that they can be considered characteristic of that region and its Samaritan and pagan population.

In addition to the elaborate burial places from the Roman period found at Shechem, Sebaste, and elsewhere, rock-cut tombs have been discovered in western Samaria. Their magnificently carved facades and ornamental friezes on columns (with a courtyard in front), recall the Second Temple tombs in Jerusalem, such as the "Tombs of the Kings." Particularly imposing tombs were discovered at Qarawet Bani Ḥasan, Khirbet 'Abud, Khirbet Kurkush, Ḥorvat Ḥemed, and Khirbet Tibna. The builders probably tried to imitate the Jerusalem tombs. It is not clear when these tombs were constructed, or whether they were hewn by Jews or Samaritans.

SYNAGOGUES. See Synagogues, Samaritan Synagogues.

CHURCHES. As already mentioned, the conversion of Samaria to Christianity occasioned a lengthy and violent struggle with the Samaritans. Unlike inhabitants of other parts of Palestine, the Samaritan population, although quite assimilated and accustomed to Roman culture (toward the end of the Roman period), rejected Christianity. From the sixth century onward, the Byzantine emperors made considerable efforts to convert the Samaritans. One of their most provocative acts in this respect was the construction of the Church of Mary Mother of God (Theotokos) on Mount Gerizim (q.v.), the Samaritans' sacred mountain. It was built in the reign of Zeno (484) and was the cause of Samaritan unrest, which lasted for about one hundred years. The uprising flared under Emperor Justinian particularly, who openly declared his intention of converting the Samaritans. Up to the present, few Byzantine churches have been discovered in Samaria. Two that are known are the Church of Mary Mother of God on Mount Gerizim, mentioned above, and the Church of Jacob's Well, east of Tell Balâtah (ancient Shechem), which commemorates Jesus' conversation with the Samaritan woman (Jn. 4:20–22). Another Byzantine church, discovered at Khirbet el-Buraq, was probably built in a Samaritan settlement destroyed in the uprising. Byzantine churches have also been discovered at Bardela and Shiloh (q.v.). Some place names in Samaria, prefaced by the Arabic *deir*, which means "monastery," may have been sites of monasteries. They may earlier (in the Hellenistic-Roman period) have been farms. Among these sites are Deir Sim'an, Deir Qal'a, and Deir el-Mir.

Conder-Kitchener, *SWP* 2, *Samaria*; B. Bagatti, *Antichi Villaggi Cristiani di Samaria* (Publications of the Studium Biblicum Franciscanum, Collectio Minor 19), Jerusalem 1979.

ITZHAK MAGEN

SARTABA-ALEXANDRIUM

IDENTIFICATION

Sartaba is a fortress situated at the peak of a mountain on an eastern spur of the Samarian Hills in the northern part of the Jericho Valley (map reference 1937.1670).

HISTORY

The ancient Semitic name of the site, Sartaba, is preserved in its modern Arabic name, Qarn el-Sartabeh (the Horn of Sartaba). Sartaba is mentioned in the Mishnah (*Rosh Hashana* 2: 4) and in corresponding references in the Tosefta and the Talmud. In these sources it is referred to as the second station for the transmission of fire signals to announce the new moon on the route from the Mount of Olives in Jerusalem to Babylonia.

Sartaba: general view of the summit, looking north.

In 1866, H. Zschokke identified the remains at the peak of Sartaba with the Alexandrium fortress, mentioned once in the writings of Strabo (XVI, 2, 40). In the writings of Josephus, Alexandrium (Alexandrion in Greek) is mentioned several times as one of the most important of the Hasmonean fortresses. This identification has been accepted by all scholars.

The fortress of Alexandrium is first mentioned together with the fortresses of Hyrcania and Machaerus in the days of Queen Salome Alexandra (Shelomzion [Josephus, *Antiq.* XIII, 417]). It was probably built by her husband, king Alexander Jannaeus (103–76 BCE), after whom the fortress was named. The site became famous as a Judean border fortress when Aristobulus, the son of Jannaeus, based himself there and halted Pompey's siege campaign to Jerusalem in 63 BCE (*Antiq.* XVIV, 48–53; *War*, I, 133–137).

Alexandrium was one of the strongholds of the Hasmoneans in their war against the Roman commander Gabinius (57 BCE), who besieged the fortress and ordered it destroyed (*Antiq.* XIV, 82–91; *War* I, 1160–170). In about 37 BCE, the fortress was seized by Herod, who restored its ruins (*Antiq.* XIV, 419; *War* I, 308). Here, in 15 BCE, he lavishly hosted Marcus Agrippa, the viceroy of Augustus (*Antiq.* XVI, 13). Alexandrium is last mentioned as the burial place of the two sons of Herod by Mariamne (Miriam) the Hasmonean (*Antiq.* XVI, 394). The sons were both charged with conspiracy against their father, who ordered their execution (9–8 BCE). In the same passage Josephus incidentally adds that Alexandrium was the burial site for other members of the Hasmonean dynasty.

The Alexandrium fortress is never mentioned in the context of the First Jewish Revolt against Rome. One possible explanation for this is that the Romans were well aware of the site's strategic importance and held on to it forcibly, preventing its capture by the Zealots.

DESCRIPTION OF THE REMAINS

Walls built of large stones with drafted margins and a coarse, protruding central boss stand on the summit of the site. The stone courses are systematically arranged: a course of headers alternates with a course of stretchers. Both the masonry and the arrangement of stones date the fortress to the time of the Hasmoneans. Judging by the state of the remains, the entire structure was destroyed by an earthquake and slid down toward the east in an enormous collapse. Mostly capitals and architectural remains were uncovered in the stone debris.

The main access to the fortress is from the west, from the direction of Samaria, through a saddle that connects the mountain with its surroundings. The remains of the access path and of the retaining walls are still visible on the slope. A moat was hewn at the bottom of the saddle. The water-supply

Wall of the Hasmonean fortress.

system for the site includes fourteen cisterns hewn into the slope (in addition to those hewn within the built-up area of the fortress), with a capacity of 5,000 cu m. The cisterns were filled by run-off water from the winter rains. At a certain point the main aqueduct, which drains the waters of the nearby plateau (Ras Quneiṭra), crosses a low saddle by means of an inverted siphon, a method typical of the Hellenistic-Hasmonean period.

EXCAVATIONS

From 1981 to 1984, three seasons of excavations were carried out at the site, under the direction of Y. Tsafrir and I. Magen, on behalf of the Hebrew University of Jerusalem and the archaeology officer for Judea and Samaria. The excavations were limited to a relatively small area at the bottom of the main mass of debris on the eastern slope, about 40 meters below the peak. Heart-shaped column drums were visible in the area even before the excavations started, attesting to the existence of a magnificent structure.

The excavations revealed three main occupational strata: (1) elaborate construction dating to the Hasmonean dynasty, (2) a peristyle hall from the Herodian period, and (3) a late occupation in the first century CE. No remains dating later than the first century CE were found. The site was destroyed by an earthquake shortly after its abandonment.

THE HASMONEAN REMAINS. Stone column drums and large Doric capitals, carefully arranged, were found in the fill beneath the floor of the Herodian peristyle. The drums belong to a structure whose plan remains obscure, but that may have been a magnificent stoa or a monumental facade. Several foundations of walls, a small pool covered with a vault, and another small rock-hewn pool—apparently a ritual bath—were also found in this stratum. This elaborate building was apparently destroyed by Gabinius in 57 BCE, as stated by Josephus. Some of its stones were arranged in the fill on which the Herodian peristyle was built.

THE HERODIAN PERISTYLE REMAINS. A peristyle stood on a terrace, the western part of which was hewn out of the rock, and whose eastern side, which faces the slope, lay on a fill of stones, column drums, remains of ancient walls, and earth. The structure was bounded on the south, west, and north by plastered walls. No remains of an eastern wall were uncovered, but it can be assumed there was a low parapet set between columns on that side, to afford an extensive view of the scenery to the east.

The outer length of the sides of the peristyle hall, from north to south, is 19.2 m—the equivalent of 60 Hellenistic feet, measuring 0.32 m per foot. The building was presumably square. An entranceway to the hall was found in the

Heart-shaped corner pillars from the Herodian peristyle.

southern wall. Inside, parallel to the outer walls, four rows of columns were placed in a square whose outer dimensions were 9.6 by 9.6 m, or 30 by 30 Hellenistic feet. The corner piers have heart-shaped cross sections. Colored plaster in black, red, green, and yellow is preserved on some of the columns. The plaster covered an earlier layer of stucco, imitating Doric columns. The walls were covered with colored plaster and decorated with stucco. The columns were crowned with Corinthian capitals. In the center of the peristyle was a mosaic floor. Only parts of the floor's edges, executed in white tesserae, are preserved. Its center, however, was probably decorated with a colored design within a frame, similar to the mosaics found at Jerusalem and at Masada. A cistern with a raised and well-dressed drum was uncovered near the northwest pier. A plastered pool, apparently a small bath, was found in the northern stoa.

How the peristyle was roofed is still an enigma. The hall probably had a raised roof in its center, with windows for light and air installed in the space between the central roof and the roofs of the low stoas situated along the sides. The western wall of the peristyle was particularly thick (about 3 m at its base) and supported a vault that rose to the west, forming a foundation for a raised terrace west of the peristyle level. The terraces probably formed one palace complex, somewhat similar to the Northern Palace at Masada.

The use of a vault to build a foundation, the style of the columns and the capitals, the use of stucco and frescoes, and the general resemblance to some of the Herodian buildings at Masada, Herodium, and Jericho further reinforce the dating of the peristyle to Herod's time. Finds on the floor included a large number of sherds of fine ware, mostly eating and serving vessels, including Eastern terra sigillata ware.

*Sartaba-Alexandrium: two ostraca from the fortress: **(left)** the inscription reads . . . לוי בר (Levy son of. . .).*

LATE OCCUPATION IN THE FIRST CENTURY CE. Shortly after the time of Herod, perhaps when the place was seized by the Roman garrisons, the peristyle no longer served as part of the palace. The soldiers probably lived in the upper part of the fortress, while the other inhabitants, possibly the servants, dwelled in the lower part. The finds from this period include a baking oven (*tabun*) installed in the southwest corner of the peristyle, and layers of ashes rich in sherds of houseware, including cooking vessels. Shelves bearing amphorae for wine were installed in the northern stoa; at a certain stage, the shelves were damaged by fire and reduced to ruins. No remains later than the first century CE were found. It may therefore be assumed that the palace was abandoned in the last years of the century, following the First Jewish Revolt against Rome.

SMALL FINDS. Many sherds were found in the excavations, in addition to the architectural remains described above. A few sherds belong to the period of the Hasmonean dynasty, but most date to the Herodian period and to the first century CE. The earth slide and subsequent collapse of the building damaged and displaced the site's pottery assemblages. In the upper strata, close to ground surface, fragments of a great quantity of storage jars were uncovered that had rolled down from storerooms on a higher terrace. Some of the jars bear inscriptions in Hebrew, Aramaic, and Greek, but only a few are legible. Among these are the names "Pinḥas son of. . ." and "Levy son of. . . ." Alongside the potsherds were fragments of glass, stone and metal ware, coins dating from the Hasmonean period until the time of the Roman garrisons, and a fragment of a stone mold for coins.

THE EARTHQUAKE. The entire building was sealed in a collapse caused by an earthquake and ground slide. The foundations of the peristyle, sills, and lower portion of the walls were found tilted diagonally toward the east, in the direction of the slide. The fact that the lower parts of the walls remained in place and were not completely dismantled indicates that they were already covered with earth when the earthquake began. One possible explanation, albeit difficult to prove, is that the earthquake occurred about two or three centuries after the site had been abandoned, perhaps during the time of the earthquake that destroyed the abandoned buildings at Masada that preserved the Byzantine monastery there. This may also have been the earthquake mentioned in several sources from the time of the emperor Julian (363 CE).

W. J. Moulton, *BASOR* 62 (1936), 14–18; O. Plöger, *ZDPV* 71 (1955), 142–148; J. Briend, *MdB* 17 (1981), 27; Y. Tsafrir, *Jerusalem Cathedra* 2 (1982), 120–145; id., *Recherches Archéologiques en Israël*, 200–205; G. Garbrecht and J. Peleg, *Antike Welt* 20/2 (1989), 2–20; F. Zayadine, *RB* 97 (1990), 70.

YORAM TSAFRIR, ITZHAK MAGEN

SEFUNIM CAVE

IDENTIFICATION

The Sefunim Cave is situated on Mount Carmel, on the southern bank of Naḥal Sefunim, about 1 km (0.6 mi.) east of the stream's debouchment into the Coastal Plain (map reference 1484.2381). As the valley's banks are steep, the cave affords only a restricted view of the twisting channel; unlike other Carmel caves, it overlooks neither the Coastal Plain nor the mountain plateau. These factors were largely responsible for the nature and character of the Sefunim occupation. The cave comprised two roofed chambers and, formerly, a partly overhung terrace, the remains of whose huge, collapsed roof now partly block the entrance.

EXCAVATIONS

The cave's well-lit front chamber measures 17 by 24 m and is 19 m high. Its dark, inner chamber, in which no occupation remains were found, measures 7.5 by 15 by 16 m. The cave was examined by M. Stekelis in 1941, on behalf of the Mandatory Department of Antiquities, and excavated between 1963 and 1970 by A. Ronen of Haifa University.

STRATIGRAPHY. The deposit in the Sefunim Cave comprises two separate geological units: the Pleistocene and the Holocene. The lower part, dating to the Middle and Upper Paleolithic, consists of a reddish-brown, fine material with hardly any stones (except for a few manuports). The upper part, deposited about 7,000 to 5,000 BP, consists of a huge rockfall and is devoid of any fine material.

The earliest assemblage at Sefunim is of the Mousterian culture range (of the Tabun B–C type), the estimated duration of which is between 120,000 and 40,000 BP. Mousterian assemblages were retrieved both from inside the cave (layer 13) and from the terrace (layers VII–VI, which are very rich in calcareous concretions). The Mousterian occupation in the cave is followed by an occupational gap, reflected in layer 11, which is sterile. Occupation in the cave was not resumed until the Aurignacian phase of the Upper Paleolithic. Material dated to the Upper Paleolithic was only recovered from within the cave (layers 8–10).

A small occupation attributed to the Kebaran culture was reported by Stekelis from his excavations near the cave's entrance. Several pits and installations with scanty, uncharacteristic finds, uncovered in the recent excavations (layer 8A), may represent the margins of that occupation. A charcoal sample from this layer yielded a carbon-14 date of 12,250 ± 65 BP.

At this stage, several rock collapses occurred in the cave (layer 7). A rich assemblage attributed mainly to the Pre-Pottery Neolithic B period was recovered from within the rubble. Occupation of the terrace was resumed at that stage or slightly earlier, in the Pre-Pottery Neolithic A (layers V–III). The roof of the cave's entrance collapsed between layers V and IV.

Sefunim Cave: plan of the cave and excavation areas.

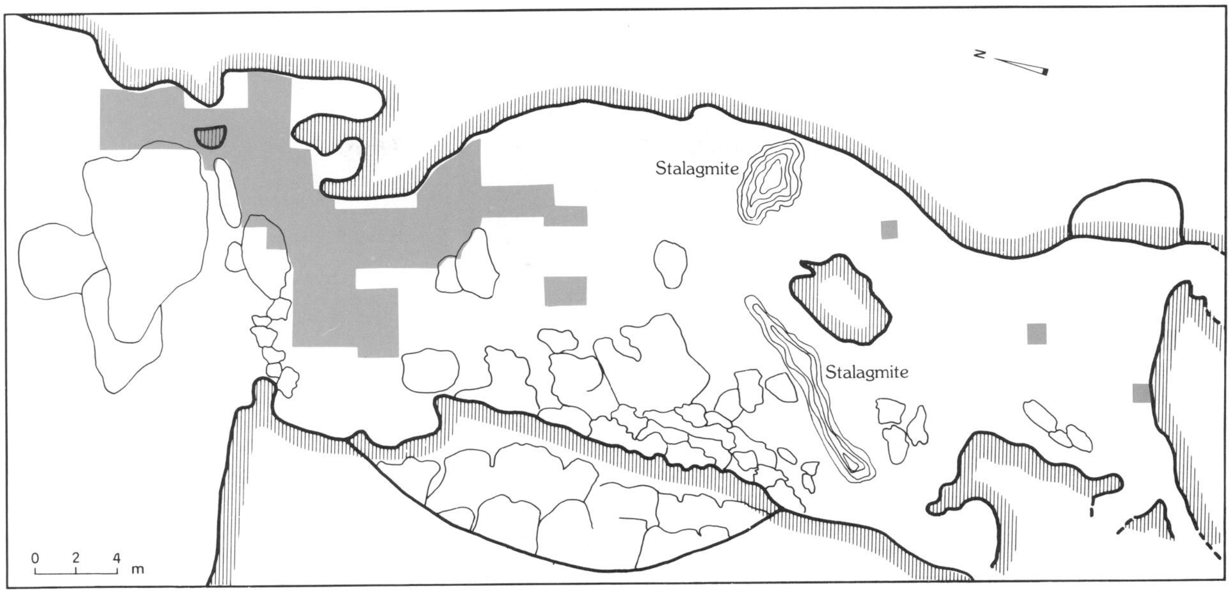

Only a few archaeological remains were found at the site from the end of the Neolithic onward (layers 6–1 inside the cave; layers II–I on the terrace). This attests to short-term encampments in the Chalcolithic period, the Bronze and Iron ages, and the Roman-Byzantine period. The remains from the Early Arab period—a plaster floor and ashy layers covering most of the front chamber—suggest a better-organized occupation.

NATURE OF OCCUPATION. The Mousterian occupation covers a restricted area near the cave's entrance and on the terrace. All the Mousterian assemblages from Sefunim share the following properties: a scant number of items; a limited range of tool types; and a predominance of Levalloisian items—particularly Levallois points. These characteristics indicate that in the Mousterian period, Sefunim did not constitute a residential site but was a hunters' campsite. The hunters who lived in the cave can be assumed to have cooperated with the hunters who occupied the rock shelter located in the valley, west of and within sight of the cave. The occupants of both sites may have blocked the 400-m-long stretch of the valley separating them on both sides, thus turning it into an efficient trap for prey.

According to its tool composition, the small assemblage recovered from layer 12 in the cave is principally Mousterian; however, the technique employed for blade manufacture displays a mixture of traits, some of them typical of the Upper Paleolithic. Above layer 12, which can be taken to represent the latest stage of the Carmel Middle Paleolithic, occupation of the cave ceased (as attested by the sterile layer 11). The Upper Paleolithic assemblages recovered from later layers are characterized by Aurignacian tools, such as carinated and nosed scrapers and various types of burins. These correspond, as a whole, to the Aurignacian tool kit found in other Carmel caves, such as the el-Wad and Kebara caves.

At this stage, the cave seems to have been used for the various activities usual at a hunter-gatherers' residential site. At a certain stage (layer 10), the floor of the dwelling area was paved with uniformly sized stones and a beaten

Sefunim Cave: view of the entrance area.

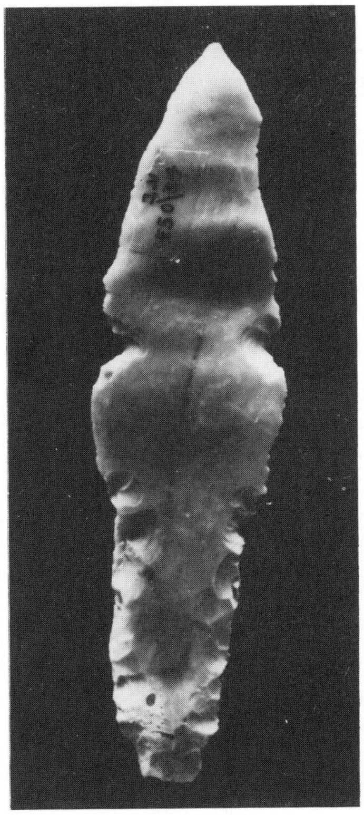

Neolithic flint dagger.

limestone fill. The Upper Paleolithic remains cover an area somewhat larger than that occupied by the Middle Paleolithic remains, although they are still restricted to the area adjacent to the entrance.

Several pits were dug into the Upper Paleolithic layers at a later stage, but no characteristic finds were recovered. A fireplace, possibly from this stage, was dated to 12,250 ± 65 BP, which suggests that this may be the margins of the Kebaran occupation reported by Stekelis. Later rock collapses created a layer of stones over the floor of the entire front chamber and over part of the inner chamber. An assemblage from the Pre-Pottery Neolithic B period, with meager intrusive Chalcolithic and later material, was found among the debris.

Unlike the preceding occupations, in which only a restricted area next to the cave's entrance was used, the Neolithic occupation extended over the entire front chamber. As in the Mousterian period, and in contrast to the Upper Paleolithic, the terrace was also occupied in the Neolithic (layers V–III). The predominance of cores in the Neolithic assemblage, as well as the large number of tools seemingly indicating woodworking—axes, adzes, chisels, and picks—suggest that the Sefunim Cave was a large workshop in the Pre-Pottery Neolithic B period. Its size shows that it was a local center for flint-tool manufacture and woodworking. Large fireplaces unearthed in the Neolithic layers (V–IV) on the terrace may also have formed part of this industrial area. The fireplace in layer V, near which a narrow limestone anvil was found, consists of an elliptical pit (1 by 1.3 m and 30 cm deep) filled with stones and ashes (which gave a carbon-14 date of 9395 ± 130 BP).

Between the Chalcolithic and the Early Arab periods, Sefunim was used only for short-term encampments. Due to the large quantities of organic material accumulated in it in the Late Arab period, it became a center for the production of saltpeter (from which the cave's Arabic name is derived—'Iraq el-Barud).

STRATIGRAPHY OF THE SEFUNIM CAVE

Terrace layer	*Cave layer*	*Assemblage/ period*	*Nature*	*Environmental conditions*
	1	Arab	Saltpeter production workshop	As in modern times
I II	2 3 4 5 6	Iron, Bronze, and Chalcolithic	Temporary encampments	
III IV V	7	Pre-Pottery Neolithic	Flint-tool workshop and woodworking	Rock collapses, humid climate
	8A	Kebaran	Residential	Dry and cold climate
	8 9 10	Upper Paleolithic		
	11	Sterile layer		
VI	12	Transition between Middle and Upper Paleolithic	Hunters' encampment	Humid stage, water activity, enrichment in limestone concentrates
VII	13	Middle Paleolithic		

Main publications: A. Ronen, *Sefunim Prehistoric Sites, Mount Carmel, Israel*, 1–2 (*BAR*/IS 230), Oxford 1984.

Other studies: E. Von Mülinen, *ZDPV* 31 (1908), 81–82; M. Stekelis, *BASOR* 86 (1942), 2–14; id., *Bulletin of the Research Council of Israel* 10 G (1961), 302–320; A. Ronen, *RB* 75 (1968), 261–262; ibid., *Quartär* 19 (1968), 275–288; id., *Archaeology* 26 (1973), 60–62; id., *Sefunim* (Review), *BIAL* 26 (1989), 295–296; Y. Olami, *Prehistoric Carmel*, Jerusalem 1984; Weippert 1988, 76, 79; P. C. Edwards, *Journal of Mediterranean Archaeology* 2 (1989), 5–48.

AVRAHAM RONEN

SENA'IM, MOUNT

IDENTIFICATION

Mount Sena'im is on the Hermon slopes, on a spur 1,146 m above sea level, about 2 km (1 mi.) northwest of Neveh Ativ (map reference 21780.29750). The mount is about 400 m long from west to east and about 150 m wide. Its Arabic name is Ḥafur el-Qurn.

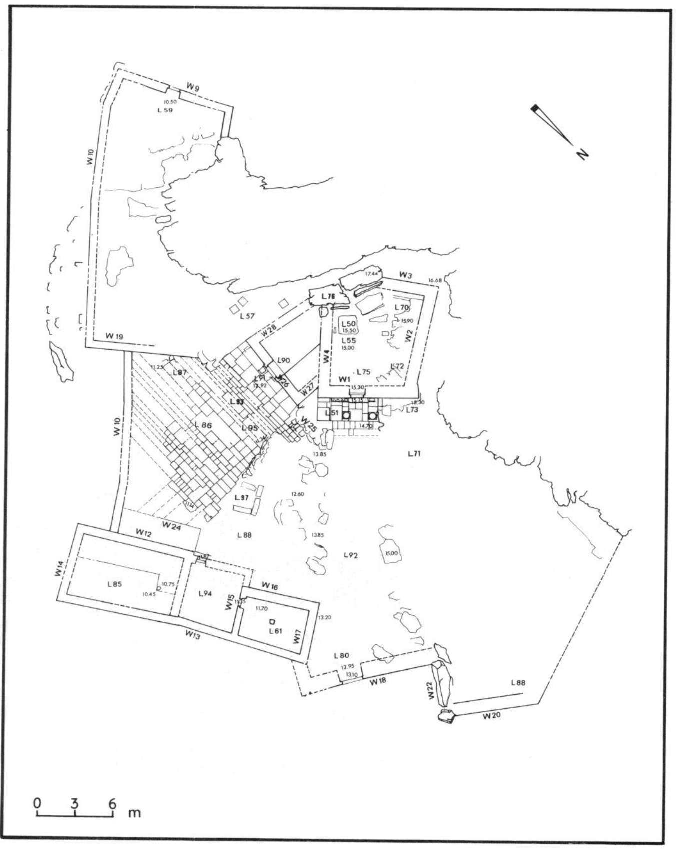

Mount Sena'im: general plan of the site.

EXPLORATION

The site was first surveyed between 1970 and 1972, after remains of an ancient settlement were found on the upper part of the spur and traces of a temple were found southeast of the settlement. From 1983 to 1989 the temple was excavated by S. Dar, on behalf of Bar-Ilan University, and Y. Mintzker of the Israel Department of Antiquities and Museums. A limited sounding was also conducted in the area of the settlement of Sena'im.

EXCAVATION RESULTS

The remains of temples and their temenos were found in a rocky area, surrounded by oak trees and a dense Mediterranean forest. Because the ground is not level, the builders had to build a southern retaining wall. In the temenos and the temples, the walls were partly or entirely cut out of bedrock.

TEMENOS. The temenos area is about 38 by 58 m. The plan is irregular and the unwalled, northwestern part is surrounded by rocks. The temenos walls (0.7–0.8 m thick) are built without mortar; in some places they are preserved to a height of 1.8 m. Entrances were found on the east and west sides of the temenos, and another one probably was located on the south. The main entrance, with its threshold, jambs, and lintel, was found on the east. Its monolithic lintel bears a Greek inscription that had been effaced over time. The door sockets in the gate are made of cast lead; in the northern socket a hinge and a bronze strap were fixed to hold the wooden doorpost.

Three rooms were incorporated in the northeastern and southeastern areas of the temenos; two superimposed floors were found in the smallest of them. On the upper floor a basalt censer or a pillar figure was found and on the lower a cosmetic spoon. The nature of these rooms is not clear; they may have been used as service rooms by the temple servants or to store ritual objects.

Outside the southern wall of the temenos was a fallen stone on which a human face could be discerned. This may have been the statue of a local deity worshiped in the temple's first stage. Two stone basins were also found, one in the temenos and the other outside it.

UPPER TEMPLE. The upper temple stood on the higher portion of the temenos, against the high rocks. Its trapezoidal plan is unusual: it is about 8.4 m wide, 10.4 m long on the southeast, and 9.1 m long on the northwest. The southern part of the temple is built against the retaining wall. The entrance was from the northeast, through a small, well-paved plaza. The facade contained two stone columns whose lower parts were found in situ. All the stones from the entrance—the threshold, jambs, and lintel—were found as they had fallen. The facade was built of extremely large ashlars, while the long walls and the rear one were built of smaller stones not as well dressed. The rear wall extended to a block of karstic rocks that seems to have been incorporated in the interior of the temple. The walls' thickness is not

Mount Sena'im: the temple facade.

uniform: 0.7 m, 0.9 m, and 1 m. No pavement was found inside the temple and the area had not been leveled to a uniform height.

LOWER TEMPLE. In front of the lower temple is a plaza paved with white limestone flagstones. At the edge of this plaza, a flight of seven steps leads to a small square in front of the entrance to the temple. The square contained three depressions, probably used for ritual objects. The lower temple is built at a 45-degree angle from the upper temple and is oriented east–west. It is asymmetrical, with an unpaved interior. The facade is 6.45 m wide and the long axis is 4.75 m. The walls are 0.8 m thick; the interior is very small. The threshold and parts of the entrance's decorated jambs were found. Bronze and lead castings for the doorposts were found in the threshold's sockets. Three stone altars stood next to the southern wall of this temple. On one of them the sun god Helios, who may have represented Jupiter Heliopolitanus at Sena'im, is depicted.

FINDS AND INSCRIPTIONS. A large concentration of modeled architectural items was found on the limestone-paved plaza. The remains include parts of a pediment, cornices, pilasters, three conches, column bases, an egg-and-dart decoration, beams with *tabulae ansatae*, fragments of another magnificent stone altar, the upper part of a basalt altar on which the name Julia in Greek appears to be inscribed, a small metal offering altar, and parts of several eagles made of basalt and limestone.

Basalt altar.

On the fragments of a frieze or stone tablet a Greek inscription extols the activity of the official in charge of Roman military records—a certain Netiras who carried out construction or restoration work in the temple during the rule of the "emperors." The mention of two emperors points to the temple's construction date in the late second or early third century CE, when the practice of coregency was instituted in the Roman Empire. Another Greek inscription memorializes the activity of Galesos and Mobogeos, who erected an altar and other cultic objects at their own expense. Fragments of other Greek inscriptions mention the consecration and construction works in the temple area.

More than a dozen identifiable coins were found in the area of the temenos. The earliest is from the time of Antiochus III (223–187 BCE); the others include a Sidonian coin (first century BCE), a coin of Beirut (first century CE), a coin of Agrippa II (50–100 CE), a Tyrian coin (second century CE), and Roman coins from the third and fourth centuries CE.

Many sherds were recovered in and around the temenos. The material used in making the pottery was either local or regional; some of the pottery is known as Iturean ware (q. v. Golan). A few fragments of Eastern terra sigillata ware were also found. The numismatic and ceramic finds are probably similar in date and indicate the main period in which the temenos and the temple were in use.

THE CULT. In the Hellenistic and Early Roman periods, Mount Hermon was inhabited by Iturean tribes, who established an independent kingdom in the region until it was dismantled by Rome in the mid-first century BCE. Like the Nabateans, the Itureans, tribes of Arab descent, worshiped stones and *maṣṣebot*. Judging from the boulders and rocks in the area, the temenos on Mount Sena'im probably housed the earliest phase of a local Iturean cult place. Its remains were later incorporated in the upper temple erected on the sanctified site. According to the inscriptions, changes and repairs were

Fragments of a basalt eagle.

made in the temples, perhaps in the wake of earthquakes or other natural disasters. The temples appear to have been destroyed in an earthquake in the fourth century CE and never restored. It is also possible, however, that the cult worship continued at the site throughout the fourth and fifth centuries CE.

S. Dar, *ESI* 3 (1984), 39–43; 4 (1985), 75; 5 (1986), 78–80; (with Y. Mintzker) 6 (1987–1988), 84–85; (with Y. Mintzker) 7–8 (1988–1989), 135–136; 9 (1989–1990), 1; id., *PEQ* 120 (1988), 26–44; (with N. Kokkinos) 124 (1991), 9–25; Y. Tepper, *ESI* 3 (1984), 43.

SHIMON DAR, YOHANAN MINTZKER

SEPPHORIS

IDENTIFICATION AND HISTORY

Ancient Sepphoris is clearly identified with the ruined village of Ṣafuriyye, the present-day Moshav Ẓippori. The site overlooks the Beth Netofa Valley in the central Lower Galilee, about 5 km (3 mi.) northwest of Nazareth (map reference 176.239). Sepphoris is first mentioned by Josephus in connection with the reign of Alexander Jannaeus (*Antiq*. XIII, 338), but a few remains from the Iron Age II found here attest to an earlier settlement. In the Hasmonean period, Sepphoris was probably the administrative center of the whole of Galilee. In around 57–55 BCE, the Roman proconsul Gabinius made Sepphoris the capital of the district of Galilee (*Antiq*. XIV, 91; *War* I, 170). Sepphoris submitted to Herod, who attacked the city during a snowstorm in 37 BCE (*Antiq*. XIV, 414; *War* I, 304). After Herod's death, the Romans conquered the city in the "war of Varus" and sold its inhabitants into slavery (*Antiq*. XVII, 289; *War* II, 68). With the partition of Herod's kingdom, Sepphoris was granted to his son Antipas, who resided here until he founded Tiberias and made it the new capital of Galilee. Antipas fortified Sepphoris and changed its name to Autocratoris, according to Josephus (*Antiq*. XVIII, 27). During the First Jewish Revolt against Rome, the inhabitants of Sepphoris sided with Vespasian, surrendered their city to him (*War* III, 30–34), and struck coins in his honor as the "peace maker" (εἰρηνοποίος). After the destruction of the Temple, the priestly family of Jedaiah settled in Sepphoris. During Trajan's reign, coins were minted here by the Jewish local government; the words "Emperor Trajan gave" were stamped on them. During the reign of Hadrian, the "old government" of Sepphoris—the Jewish local city government (Mishnah, *Qid*. 4:5)—was abolished, a gentile administration was appointed, and probably, at the same time, the name of the city was changed to Diocaesarea (Διοκαισαρεία, the city of Zeus and of the emperor). Yet, after Rabbi Judah ha-Nasi and the Sanhedrin established their seat here for seventeen years before the rabbi's death, at the end of the second century (J.T., *Kil*. 9:4, 32b),

Above: *city coin from the time of Trajan.*
Below: *coin from the time of Caracalla, commemorating the "covenant of friendship and mutual aid between the holy council and the senate of the Roman people."*

Sepphoris: general plan of the excavations.

Sepphoris: general view (after the 1986 excavations).

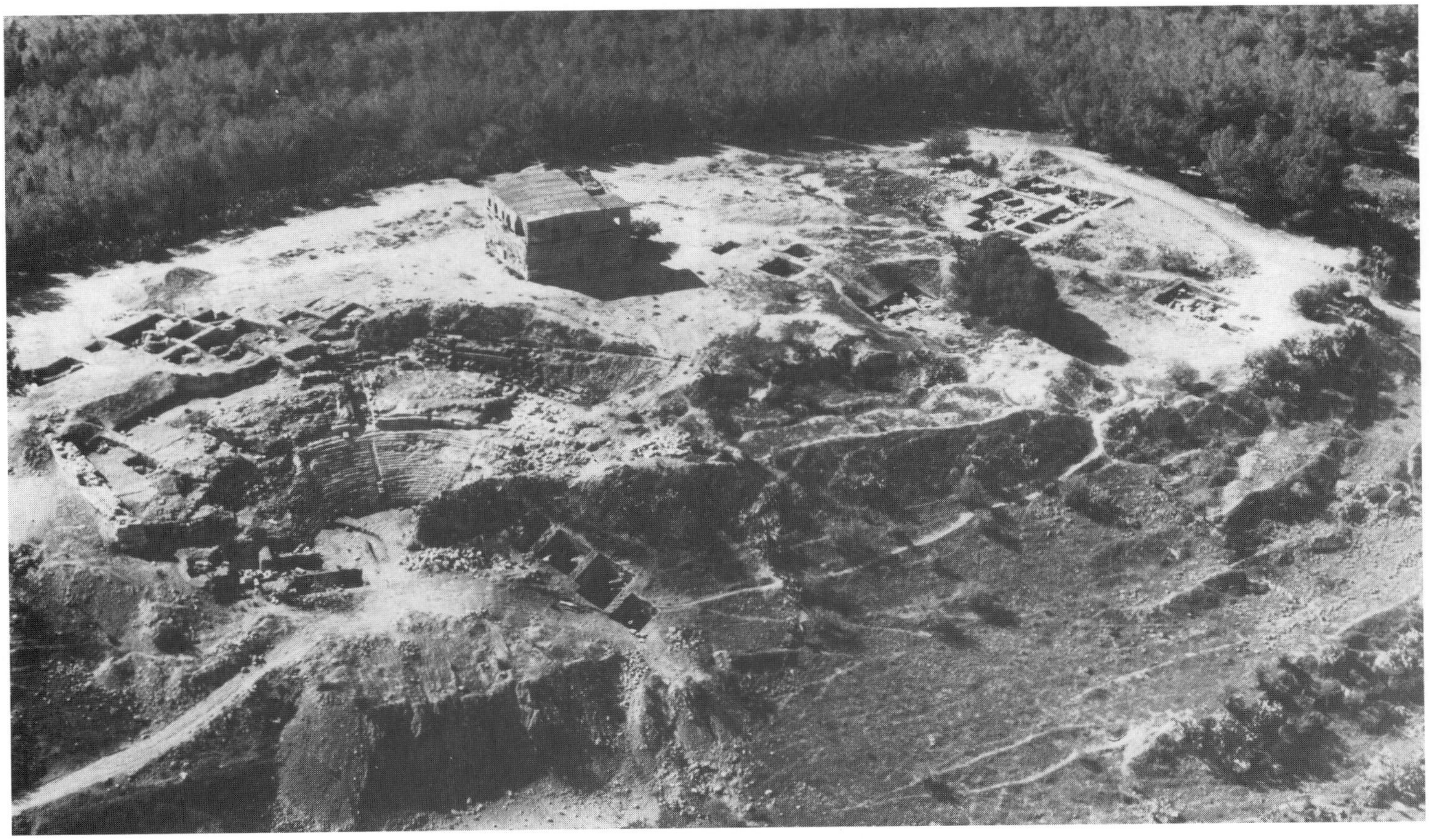

the local government of the city was once more turned over to a Jewish town council. Rabbi Judah ha-Nasi redacted the Mishnah in Sepphoris. At the beginning of the third century, the minting of coins by the Jews was renewed here; the coins were stamped "Covenant of friendship and mutual aid between the holy council and the senate of the Roman people."

Sepphoris is mentioned many times in Talmudic literature and was known throughout its existence as a Jewish city. In the Mishnaic and Talmudic periods many scholars lived here; the best known are rabbis Ḥalafta, Ele'azar ben 'Azariah, and Jose ben Ḥalafta. The seat of the Sanhedrin was also in Sepphoris until it was moved by Rabbi Yoḥanan to Tiberias in the time of Rabbi Judah Nesiah, the grandson of Rabbi Judah ha-Nasi. During the reign of Emperor Constantine, a certain Josephus the Apostate tried in vain to erect a church here (Epiph., *Haer*. 30, 4–12). In the reign of Constantius II, the Jewish revolt against Gallus Caesar, led by Patricius, began in Sepphoris (351 CE). The Roman troops garrisoned in the city were disarmed, and the rebels gained control. The Roman commander Ursicinus succeeded in crushing the revolt, but, in spite of the reports of the Christian sources (Jerome, *Chron*., Olymp. 282; Socrates, *HE* II, 33; Sozomenos, *HE* IV, 7), he failed to level the city. In a letter sent by Cyril, bishop of Jerusalem, mention is made of an earthquake that struck Palestine in 363, making special note of the total destruction of Sepphoris. The town was later partly restored and continued to be a Jewish city until the fifth century; in the sixth century, however, it had a Christian community, headed by a bishop. Bishops of Sepphoris participated in the synods of Jerusalem in 518 and 536. In Crusader times, Sepphoris (Le Sephorie) was a city and fortress in the province of Galilee. Remains of a Crusader church and fortress still stand at the site. In the eighteenth century, the governor of Galilee, Dhahir el-'Amr, refortified it.

EXPLORATION AND EXCAVATION

Excavations were first carried out at Sepphoris in the early 1930s under the direction of L. Waterman of the University of Michigan. Two sections were cut to the east and west of the fortress (see below). About fifty years later, work was resumed by two separate expeditions. The first, begun in 1983 under the direction of J. P. Strange of the University of Tampa, Florida, conducted a survey of the buildings, cisterns, and burial systems across the site. The second expedition, begun in 1985, is a joint project of Duke University, North Carolina, and the Hebrew University of Jerusalem, under the direction of E. M. Meyers, E. Netzer, and C. Meyers, and from 1990, under the direction of Netzer and Z. Weiss from the Hebrew University at Jerusalem. This expedition concentrated on the summit of the site and the area surrounding it. In 1975–1985 a survey of the site's aqueducts was conducted by Z. Zuck; the results were published in a separate report. Since then, a few burial systems have either been excavated or surveyed, along with isolated remains, shedding light on the city's history.

EXCAVATION RESULTS

The main finds uncovered at Sepphoris so far date to the Roman and Byzantine periods. A few sherds from the end of the Iron Age and from the Persian and Early Hellenistic periods were found scattered in several places, but no building remains from these periods have yet appeared. A unique find is a pottery rhyton from the early fourth century BCE that was recovered from the northwestern edge of the mound. This almost complete vessel is shaped like a griffin and has a shiny black-to-brown glaze.

PUBLIC BUILDING AREA. A fortress stood at the summit of the site. It was erected in the Crusader period on top of earlier Roman foundations. The series of rooms cleared to its east may constitute part of the Roman building, or may be a separate fort of unknown plan. This structure, together with the other buildings on the eastern side of the hill, probably formed the city's civic center. In the center of this area, on the hill's northern slope, south of the theater, stands a spacious building (see below). A paved path of beaten limestone on the eastern side of the building led to the plaza between it and the theater. It is possible that another path ran from the western side of the building.

The Theater. The theater apparently was built in the early first century CE, possibly in the reign of Antipas (4 BCE to 39 CE), as part of his building activity at Sepphoris in the beginning of his rule in Galilee. It was constructed in the tradition of Roman theaters; its diameter is 73 m and it had a seating capacity of about 4,500. Three openings in the wall to the cavea gave access to the theater. This wall, ornamented with columns, was built above ancient cisterns, thereby necessitating the incorporation of weight-bearing arches. The exits, or *vomitoria* (each 2.2 m wide), had barrel vaults. Most of the cavea is hewn out of bedrock; only its western and eastern ends were built on stone foundations. The majority of the benches and steps, made of limestone slabs, were looted, leaving only the cuttings in the bedrock on which the benches were laid, along with the steps between them. The orchestra was also rock-hewn and paved with stone slabs. Beneath it were lead drainpipes that channeled rainwater outside the theater. The stage (6 by 31 m) was built of stone and apparently had a wooden floor. Due to the theater's topographical location, the dressing rooms were located beneath the stage—not behind it or to either side. At the two ends of the stage steps led down to the orchestra.

Architectural remains belonging to the wall of the *scaenae frons* were found near the stage. East of the stage was another corridor (parodos), used to enter and leave the stage and orchestra area. The parodos (3.2 m wide) was paved

Roman theater, with the fortress in the background.

Mosaic pavement in the palatial mansion.

with rectangular stone slabs; traces of a red fresco were found on its walls. There may have been another entrance, as yet not cleared, on the western side of the stage. The theater was probably destroyed in the Late Roman or Early Byzantine period.

Palatial Mansion. A spacious building, from the third century CE, oriented northeast–southwest, was partly excavated south of the theater. The building is 23 m wide and, judging from the topographical data, about 30 m long. It was erected partly on bedrock and included a central hall surrounded by rooms on three sides—the east, north, and west. To the south of the central hall porticoes surrounded an open courtyard with a small pool in its center. A row of rooms on the western side of the hall continued southward and adjoined the courtyard on its west. To the east of the hall was a parallel row of rooms including two pools, one of which is stepped. As yet, it is unclear whether the stepped pool was originally part of the building. Two rooms in the east wing had colored mosaic pavements with geometrical designs. The plan of the building south of the courtyard is not clear, as it has not been fully excavated. Its walls, preserved to a height of 2 m and on the average 0.6 m thick, were built mostly of large ashlars coated with white plaster. Fragments of frescoes with red and yellow geometric and floral designs indicate that the walls or ceilings were partly painted. A few rooms were paved with mosaics, whereas others were coated with plaster.

The rooms to the north of the hall were for everyday use. In the middle was a long, open courtyard with a rock-cut cistern on its east. Alongside the courtyard were a few rooms containing water installations. One of the rooms was a latrine, with a Greek inscription ("health") on its floor. West of the central hall is a long corridor that provided access to four rooms in the western part of the building. This side of the building, clearly, had a second story, with a white mosaic floor surrounded by a black border, apparently laid on a wood base.

The central hall (6.9 m wide and 9.25 m long) served as the triclinium, or dining room. Two entrances in the hall's long, east–west walls opened onto the surrounding rooms. Its southern wall included three entrances leading to the courtyard. The hall was decorated with a colored mosaic pavement. The center of the mosaic is a rectangular carpet with a colored mosaic band in the form of an inverted U on one side, and a similar, but larger, band of white tesserae with a thin black mosaic border on the other. In the corners of the white mosaic are black strips resembling the Greek letter gamma (Γ). This mosaic pattern, in which the decorated part is designed in the shape of the letter T, is very common in Roman triclinia. Different-sized tesserae in twenty-eight hues were used in the mosaic.

The pavement's center was decorated with fifteen panels, of which eleven are completely preserved, three destroyed, and one partially preserved. The panels contain Greek inscriptions, intended to be read from the edges of the mosaic, which identify the figures or scenes shown. These depict various events in the life of Dionysius, including a drinking contest between him and Hercules, his victory procession to India, and his marriage to Ariadne. Other depictions represent various aspects of the Dionysian cult—grape treading, shepherds, and scenes of rejoicing and the bringing of gifts.

The central carpet is surrounded by a frame of twenty-two acanthus medallions, extending outward from two centers on the north and south. At the center of the northern side is a depiction of the bust of a beautiful woman, crowned with a laurel garland and wearing earrings. Remnants of a similar figure appear on the southern side of the frame. The acanthus medallions each contain depictions of a hunting scene with two or three nude hunters and animals.

The U-shaped mosaic that borders the central carpet on the south includes depictions of men and women bearing baskets of fruit, animals, garlands, a tripod, and other objects. Depicted in other sections are two men, a child riding on a goat, a woman playing a double flute, and a man leading a donkey. Although only partially preserved, the mosaic appears to have been one continuous scene, beginning at the eastern and western ends of the inverted U and running toward the center of the pavement's southern side. In contrast to the subjects in the central carpet depicting Dionysius and his entourage, the southern band mainly depicts the preparation for the god's earthly cult and related celebrations. The band is surrounded by a geometric frame containing several types of fish, various winged creatures, and masks. This band was partially damaged and a new mosaic section of a different type was laid in its place, integrated into the existing pavement. This section depicts a Nilotic landscape with nude youths hunting fowl and a crocodile.

The palatial mansion underwent various changes in the course of time—mainly the addition of walls and water installations and the blocking of

Overview of the palatial mansion.

Depiction of the head of a woman and a nude hunter; detail of a mosaic pavement in the palatial mansion.

Mikveh in the residential quarter.

entrances. The building's plan—a central triclinium surrounded by rooms—indicates that it was a dwelling. Its location at the eastern end of the acropolis, near the theater, and the pagan content of its mosaics suggests that it housed one of the distinguished gentile citizens of Sepphoris—perhaps the city or district governor. It is, however, possible (though not yet proven) that this was the residence of one of the city's wealthy Jews. The building was apparently destroyed in the earthquake of 363 CE and was never reoccupied.

RESIDENTIAL AREA. The residential area at the summit of the hill is west of the fort. Most of the buildings here are from the Roman period, and some have levels from the end of the Hellenistic period. A street (2.2 m wide) paved with stone slabs running southeast–northwest was repaired at different times, including raising the level of the pavement and resurfacing it with lime plaster. Buildings and courtyards adjoined the street on both sides. The buildings included rooms, storerooms, open courtyards with various installations, and staircases, indicating an upper story. The buildings also had a large number of stepped and plastered pools, some of them used as mikvehs (ritual baths). One building also contained a gutter and a channel that conducted rainwater to the mikveh. Under the buildings were many rock-cut chambers, most of which were cisterns (see below) or storerooms. A large quantity of potsherds and other objects had been deliberately thrown into several of these chambers.

One of the buildings belonging to the residential area was cleared in the 1930s by L. Waterman (trench SII). He called it a Christian basilica. However, M. Avi-Yonah raised objections to this designation, which were confirmed by Strange's excavations. It is now clear that the building's plan is that of a typical Roman house: a central courtyard surrounded by columns and rooms. The rooms were partly cut into the bedrock and were paved with mosaics and lime plaster.

The remains of houses, and perhaps of a public building, were cleared at the western edge of the residential area. These buildings, from the first or second century CE, are mostly in ruins and their plan is unclear. The only traces are hewn in the bedrock, which was the foundation for the looted walls; their floors, plastered pools, and subterranean cisterns were also robbed. The buildings were in use until the fourth century CE. The extent of the built-up area of Sepphoris is still unknown.

WATER SUPPLY. Sepphoris received its water supply from two aqueducts extending from the springs in the villages of er-Reina and Mashhad to the eastern part of the town. The two aqueducts merge into a single conduit and, once close to the city, separate again: the northern one leads to a pool, while the southern one leads to a subterranean reservoir. These aqueducts supplied water to different parts of the city, but the water did not reach the houses on the summit. The summit was supplied by rainwater collected and channeled into the subterranean cisterns cut under each house. Many such cisterns were found in the excavations and in surveys on the summit. Another source of water was the spring of 'En Ẓippori, about 2.4 km (1.4 mi.) south of the city's acropolis. This is an abundant spring, but its low location in Naḥal Ẓippori prevented the city from being regularly supplied with its water. When the city's other water sources were depleted, water was probably brought from the spring in animal skins on donkeys.

BYZANTINE REMAINS. The finds on the summit indicate that a high standard of living was enjoyed in Sepphoris in the Byzantine period and that probably the city was expanded. A number of magnificent buildings were found. However, the number of buildings on the summit was less in the Byzantine period than the Roman period.

A storage building was excavated south of the fortress. In the main hall, which was paved with a white mosaic floor and divided by a row of pillars, large storage jars (pithoi) were found. Smaller rooms, found on both sides of the hall, contained other jars, indicating that the building was used for storage or industry. The building was probably destroyed during the Persian conquest in 614 CE as suggested by the ash found inside.

A narrow street, running north–south and flanked by rooms, was found on the western side of the summit. The street was constructed over the residential section of the Roman city. The remains of a building, including ashlar pillars in secondary use, were excavated on the summit's eastern side. Additional structures with unclear plans were also found here. In this period, the theater was a quarry for stones and raw materials for the lime industry.

East of the summit, a main street, once flanked by colonnades, was found. The street stones bear the marks of wagon wheels. East of the street, a large Byzantine stucture was excavated. Its floors are decorated with multicolored mosaics, except one area that is paved with stone slabs. Most of the floors are adorned with geometric and floral designs, some of exceptional workmanship. The largest room contains a figurative mosaic (6.2 by 6.7 m) depicting the Nile festival and various hunting scenes. The Nile River, flowing from the mouth of a Nilotic beast, is in the center of the mosaic. The flowing water forms the mosaic's upper border, and a secondary stream flows into the hunting scenes. A stork attacking a snake, a bird perched on a lotus, and various fish are shown, representing the Nile's characteristic fauna and flora.

Above the Nile is a nilometer, a rectangular structure with a vaulted opening, facing the river. The nilometer bears the numbers IE, IS, and I2, referring to fifteen, sixteen, and seventeen cubits. Next to it, a man stands on a woman's back as he engraves the number I2 with a hammer and chisel. A reclining man and woman are depicted in the mosaic's upper corners. The female, to the left, personifies Egypt, as indicated by an inscription. Her robe covers her back and leg, leaving her upper body uncovered. Her right arm rests on a basket laden with fruit, and her left hand grasps a fruit-filled cornucopia. To the right, a male personification of the Nile sits on the back of an animal from whose mouth the river flows. His arm is outstretched toward two naked figures bearing gifts who proceed in his direction.

The annual festivities celebrating the rise of the Nile are shown in the mosaic's lower portion. On the right, a column is set on an Attic base, and is surmounted by a Corinthian capital and a statue of a figure holding a spear or a torch. In the middle are two parading horseman. Behind the riders, a youth dressed in a tunic watches them. The horses seem to gallop toward the city of Alexandria, which is represented on the left by a city gate between two towers; an additional tower, also round but significantly higher than the others is also depicted. The fire burning on top of the structure suggests the famous Pharos lighthouse of Alexandria. The area right of the pillar and the bottom section of the mosaic are devoted to various hunting scenes, among them a lion devouring a bull, a bear attacking a boar, and a panther pouncing upon a hind.

Another figurative mosaic floor was found in another room that has not been completely excavated. The mosaic shows a centaur leaping on his hind legs, his forelegs extended forward. He holds an object bearing a Greek inscription. The precise function of the buiding is still unclear and it is unknown whether it was owned by Christians or Jews. The building was destroyed at the end of the Byzantine period.

In the Byzantine period, the Christian community at Sepphoris expanded greatly, although the Jewish community maintained its majority. Two inscriptions from a synagogue were found north of the the Crusader church (see below). To date, no Byzantine church has been uncovered at Sepphoris. In 1959, a Greek inscription was discovered at the site; it is incised on a stone slab and mentions the restoration of a church in the time of Marcellinus (518 CE). This church, whose location is still unknown, was probably built in the fifth century and restored at the beginning of the sixth century. The generally sparse finds from the Byzantine period do not contradict the historical reports that the city had a large population in this period. Rather, the Byzantine buildings may be poorly preserved because of their proximity to the surface.

SYNAGOGUES. In the description of the funeral of Rabbi Judah ha-Nasi, the Talmud (J.T., *Kil.* 9:4, 32b) mentions eighteen synagogues in Sepphoris. However, not a single complete synagogue has yet been found in the city. Part of a mosaic pavement containing a dedicatory inscription in Aramaic, discovered to the north of the Crusader church in the early twentieth century, may indicate the existence of a synagogue. The inscription, framed by a circle, reads: דכיר [לטב] רבי יודן [בר תנ]חום [ב]ר [...ד]יהב חד... (May he be remembered for good, Rabbi Yudan, son of Tanḥum son of . . . who gave one dinar . . .) (Naveh, no. 29). A Greek inscription that may belong to a Byzantine synagogue, was found amid the debris of the Crusader church. It is inscribed on a lintel, and its reading, though uncertain, may be interpreted: "(During the office of) the extolled advocate and Count Gelasius the son of the Count Aetius, (during the time of) Judah the archisynagogus of Sidon . . . Sever-

Crusader church.

ianus Aphrus the extolled archisynagogus of Tyre" (*CIJ*, no. 991).

In the recent excavations, fragments were found of a patterned mosaic pavement that bore an inscription. It is possible to identify a few Hebrew letters, and even the word בר ("son of").

CEMETERIES. The cemeteries at Sepphoris are spread over the hills close to the city. A few burial caves are located on the hill to the southwest. In 1930, E. L. Sukenik, on behalf of the Institute of Archaeology at the Hebrew University of Jerusalem, excavated a burial cave consisting of two chambers connected by a narrow passage. The first room is square and contains thirteen loculi. The southern wall of the passage contains eight loculi, cut in two rows, one above the other. The inner room is round and has fourteen loculi, nine in the bottom row and five in the top. One of the graves had an inscription carved in its plastered wall: ...רב הדין קבורה (ד)רבי יודן ב[ר...] וברה (This is the tomb of Rabbi Yudan, the son of... Rabbi . . . and his son). Two more burial caves were examined nearby; they consisted of several rooms with loculi, arcosolia, and sarcophagi for the interment of the dead. Sukenik deciphered two other inscriptions: רבי י[סא] חיורורה (Rabbi Yissa Ḥiorora) and תיק (קבר) רבי מניסס דניאל (Tomb of Rabbi Manisas Daniel).

Additional rock-cut burial caves containing loculi and arcosolia were found on the hill to the southeast. One of them, excavated by A. Druks in 1980, contained a row of four chambers, with two rows of loculi hewn in the walls. A rock-hewn door sealed the cave's entrance which faces a large courtyard. Caves probably existed on the courtyard's other sides, as well. Among the refuse were marble slabs bearing bilingual funerary inscriptions. One marks the tomb of "Hosea, the son of Tanḥum of Tiberias," and another of "Naḥum and Jacob, the sons of Rabbi Hosochi." There is also a bilingual inscription in red marking the tomb of Crispina. This group of caves is dated to the second and third centuries CE.

A mausoleum northwest of Sepphoris was surveyed by the Sukenik expedition and later excavated and cleaned by N. Avigad. The mausoleum, known as the Tomb of Jacob's Daughters, is partly built of ashlars and partly hewn. It measures 3.4 by 12 m, its walls are 1.8 to 4.4 m thick, and its facade faces south. The entrance lintel and jambs are surrounded by a border carved in earlike projections on either side. A single step descends to the burial chamber. The chamber's interior is built of ashlars without mortar, and its ceiling is barrel vaulted. There are five loculi in each of its long walls, and in the northern wall, opposite the entrance, is a ledge under an arcade. This type of tomb was common in Palestine in the Roman period and should be dated to the second and third centuries CE.

More Byzantine burial caves were surveyed on the spur west of Sepphoris. These are small caves, consisting of a vault or trough tomb intended for the burial of one or two people. A cross is carved on the wall of one tomb.

Also noteworthy are a stone ossuary and a stone door, found in the courtyard of the Crusader church, that came from the town's Jewish cemetery.

FINDS. Large quantities of pottery vessels of different types were found in several pits at the top of the hill, including numerous clay oil lamps. Incense shovels similar to those depicted in Jewish mosaics were also found, as were two bronze figurines, one of the god Pan and the other of Prometheus. In the fill between two floors a lead weight inscribed in Greek on both sides was found. One inscription mentions its weight, a half libra (1,018 g). The inscription is flanked by rows of columns, apparently depicting a colonnaded street or agora. The second inscription states the name of the Jewish agoranomos and his lineage (*SEG* 36, 1342). The two inscriptions were intended to verify the weight's accuracy, under the supervision of the agoranomos. Other small finds of note include bronze bull statuettes and a small bronze altar; molds for casting oil lamps; and several ostraca in Hebrew, Greek, and Syriac.

Lead weight mentioning a Jewish agoranomos from Sepphoris.

Main publications: L. Waterman et al., *Preliminary Report of the University of Michigan Excavations at Sepphoris, Palestine*, 1931, Ann Arbor 1937; S. S. Miller, *Studies in the History and Traditions of Sepphoris* (Studies in Judaism in Late Antiquity 37), Leiden 1984.

Other studies: Clermont-Ganneau, *CRAIBL* (1909), 677–683; M. Avi-Yonah, *QDAP* 3 (1934), 40; id., *IEJ* 11 (1961), 184–187; Frey, *Corpus*, 173–176; H. Seyrig, *Numismatic Chronicle Series* 6/15 (1955), 157–159; F. W. Boelter, *Exploration* 3 (1977), 36–43; Y. Meshorer, *Greek Numismatics and Archaeology* (M. Thompson Fest.), Wetteren 1979, 159–172; C. M. Kraay, *American Numismatic Society Museum Notes* 25 (1980), 56–57; J. F. Strange, *IEJ* 32 (1982), 254–255; 34 (1984), 51–52, 269–270; (with R. W. Longstaff) 37 (1987), 278–280; 38 (1988), 188–190; (et al.) 39 (1989), 104–106; id., *RB* 91 (1984), 239–241; 92 (1985), 429; 93 (1986), 252–254; (et al.) 96 (1989), 240–242; id. (and R. W. Longstaff), *ESI* 4 (1985), 100–102; id. 6 (1987–1988), 97–98; (et al.) 9 (1989–1990), 19–20; Z. Zuck, ibid. 1 (1982), 105–107; 9 (1989–1990), 20; A. Druks, ibid. 3 (1984), 97–98; S. S. Miller (Reviews), *JQR* 76 (1986), 260–262. — *JAOS* 107 (1987), 543–544. — *IEJ* 38 (1988), 283–284; J. McRay, *Near East Archaeological Society Bulletin* 24 (1985), 117–118; E. M. Meyers et al., *IEJ* 35 (1985), 295–299; 37 (1987), 275–278; 40 (1990), 219–222; id., *BA* 49 (1986), 4–19; 50 (1987), 223–231; id., *ESI* 5 (1986), 101–104; 6 (1987–1988), 95–97; 7–8 (1988–1989), 169–173; id., *MdB* 57 (1989), 50–51; id., *Sepphoris*, Winona Lake (in prep.); *Buried History* 23 (1987), 64–76; 24 (1988), 37; R. A. Batey, *JFA* 14 (1987), 1–8; B. Schwank, *Erbe und Auftrag* 63 (1987), 222–225; *BAR* 14/1 (1988), 3–33; C. L. Meyers, *ASOR Newsletter* 39/2 (1988), 1–2; D. Stadler, *The Digging Stick* 5/2 (1988), 3–4; A. Khalbhol, *MdB* 57 (1989), 53–53; A. Adan-Bayewitz and I. Perlman, *IEJ* 40 (1990), 153–172; M. T. Boatwright, *BA* 53 (1990), 190–191; J. Folda, ibid. 54 (1991), 88–96.

ZEEV WEISS

SERA', TEL

IDENTIFICATION

Tel Sera' (Tell esh-Shari'a) is situated in the western Negev desert, on the north bank of Naḥal Gerar (map reference 119.088), approximately 20 km (12.5 mi.) northwest of Beersheba, on the main road from Gaza to the Beersheba Valley and the Dead Sea. Which of the biblical cities in the western Negev should be identified with Tel Sera' has long been disputed by scholars. It has been identified with Hormah (W. F. Albright), Gerar (A. Alt), and Philistine Gath (G. E. Wright). Other scholars, however, following Y. Press, prefer an identification with Ziklag (B. Mazar, Y. Aharoni and Z. Kallai), the city where David found refuge in his flight from Saul. The latter identification seems to be supported by historical and geographical data, as well as by the archaeological evidence.

Tel Sera': plan of the site and excavated areas.

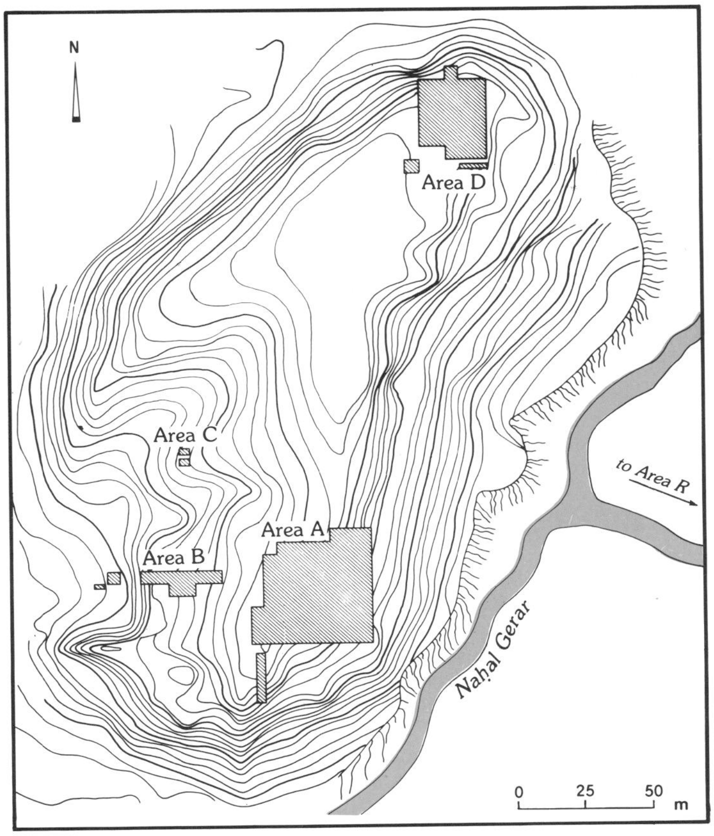

Biblical Ziklag is mentioned in Joshua 15:31 as a city in Judah and in 1 Chronicles 4:30 as a city in the territory of Simeon. The city's population at the beginning of the Iron Age undoubtedly consisted of Philistines and related groups from the Sea Peoples. B. Mazar has suggested that the name Ziklag derives from Sekel/Thekel—one of the Sea Peoples mentioned in Egyptian New Kingdom documents. The Bible preserves evidence of some connection between Ziklag and Philistia—it is referred to as "the country of the Philistines" (1 Sam. 27:7) or "the Negeb of the Cherethites" (1 Sam. 30:14). In Saul's time, Ziklag was included in the territory of Philistine Gath; it was given to David as a refuge by Achish, king of Gath (1 Sam. 27:6). The city functioned as a military and administrative outpost at the southern edge of the kingdom, bordering on territories frequented by nomadic tribes in the Negev and Sinai, which reached as far as Egypt (1 Sam. 27:8). Considered "crown property," it earned the unique designation, "Ziklag has belonged to the kings of Judah to this day" (1 Sam. 27:6). The last biblical reference to Ziklag lists it as one of the cities of Judah during the period of restoration (Neh. 11:28).

THE MOUND

Tel Sera' is shaped like an elongated horseshoe; it rises to a maximum altitude of 168 m above sea level. The area of the mound is 4 to 5 a.; its summit rises 14 m above the surrounding terrain. The earliest settlement was built on a *kurkar* ridge, and the accumulation of occupational debris may be as much as 8 to 10 m thick. With the exception of the western side—probably the site of the city gate—the mound slopes down very steeply on all sides toward Naḥal Gerar. Near the mound, in the bed of the wadi, are several perennial springs.

During nearby railroad construction by the Turks, a broad, deep crater was cut into the western side of the mound. An extensive area (c. 0.5 a.) in the plain south of Naḥal Gerar is scattered with remains of structures from the Roman and Byzantine periods, including a finely built bathhouse, plastered water reservoirs, and other public buildings. Surface finds collected before the excavations indicated that the site had been inhabited periodically from the Chalcolithic period (fourth millennium BCE) to the end of the Byzantine period (sixth century CE).

EXCAVATIONS

Six consecutive seasons of excavations were conducted from 1972 to 1979 by an expedition directed by E. D. Oren. The excavations were sponsored by the Archaeology Division at Ben-Gurion University of the Negev, in cooperation with the Israel Exploration Society. The main areas excavated on the mound were area A in the southeast; area D in the northeast; area C in the west; area B

Tel Sera': aerial view, looking west; (foreground) area A and the residency.

General view of area A: (right) four-room house; (left) structures, 13th century BCE.

in the southwest and the "Turkish crater"; and area R on the southern bank of Naḥal Gerar. Occupation strata from the following periods were identified:

Stratum	Period and location
	Muslim cemetery (areas A, B, C, and D)
	Early Arab and Mameluke periods (area D)
I	Byzantine period, 4th–6th cent. CE (areas D and R)
II	Hellenistic–Roman period, 2nd cent. BCE–2nd cent. CE (areas A, B, D, and R)
III	Persian period, 5th–4th cent. BCE (areas A, B, C, and D)
V–VI	Iron III, 8th–6th cent. BCE (areas A, B, and D)
VII	Iron II, 10th–9th cent. BCE (areas A, B, and D)
VIII	Iron I, 12th–11th cent. BCE (areas A and B)
IX	Iron I–LB III, early 12th cent. BCE (area A)
X	LB III, 13th cent. BCE (area A)
XI	LB II, 14th cent. BCE (area A)
XII	MB III–LB I, 17th–15th cent. BCE (area A)
XIII	Chalcolithic and EB IV period (area A)

CHALCOLITHIC PERIOD AND BRONZE AGE (STRATA XIII–IX).

Stratum XIII. The excavations in the southeastern sector of Tel Sera' (area A) revealed sparse remains of installations and rock-cut pits from the Chalcolithic period and the Early Bronze Age IV (Middle Bronze Age I). Judging from the remains, these were poor settlements of hut and tent dwellers. The Chalcolithic finds are compatible with the dense settlement of the Naḥal Besor basin and Naḥal Gerar in this period. The excavations in area A date the beginning of Canaanite settlement at Tel Sera' to the late Middle Bronze Age (Middle Bronze III or Middle Bronze IIC), in the seventeenth century BCE; it continued uninterrupted until it was destroyed by fire in the mid-twelfth century BCE (stratum IX).

Stratum XII. The earliest phase in stratum XII consisted of the remains of a massive building, probably a palace, built on an artificial platform of large stones and wadi gravel. The fill material was settlement debris from the Chalcolithic and Early Bronze Age IV periods. The building's mud-brick walls, more than 2 m thick, were preserved to a height of 2.5 m and were coated with a thick layer of mud plaster. The parts of this building cleared so far consist of a large rectangular hall enclosed by thick walls, and a group of small rooms on the east. The pottery from the different building phases, including carinated bowls and bichrome and imported Cypriot ware, indicates that the building was in use until the end of the fifteenth century BCE. A trial sounding in area B suggested that the Middle Bronze Age settlement occupied a large area and included public and private buildings and perhaps a defense system. The founding of the Canaanite settlement at Sera' is undoubtedly associated with the intensive urban development in the northern Negev and coastal Philistia during the Late Middle Bronze Age, or Hyksos period.

Stratum XI. Stratum XI (fourteenth century BCE) is represented in area A by a large structure whose walls were built on stone foundations; to its east is a spacious courtyard surrounded by a low stone wall. Within this courtyard were several *favissae* containing animal bones and numerous pottery vessels, including painted chalices, goblets, cylindrical stands, and imported Cypriot ware. Judging from the *favissae* and the pottery types, represented by the stands and chalices, this was the site of a cult building (sanctuary?) whose complete plan is still unknown.

Strata X–IX. Two occupation strata (X–IX) from the thirteenth and early twelfth centuries BCE were exposed over a large area in the southeastern sector of the mound and on its eastern slope (area A). A large structure (building 1118, stratum X) was erected on the ruins of the cultic(?) building from

Egyptian scarab from stratum X, 19th Dynasty.

Area A: plan of the residency (building 906), stratum IX, 12th century BCE.

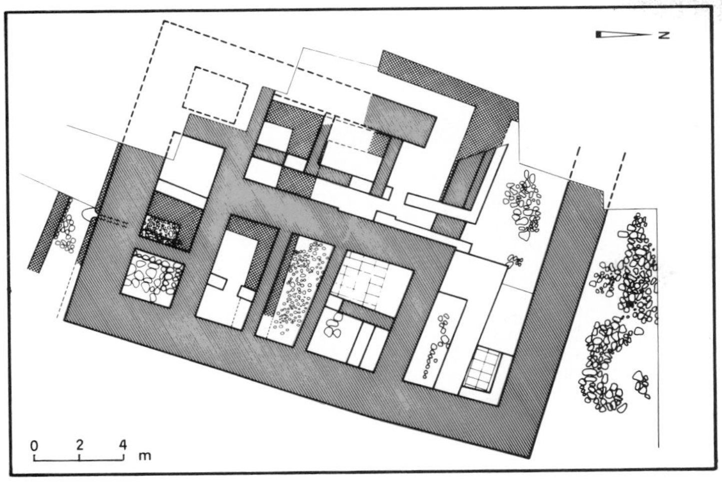

Eastern wing of the residency.

stratum XI, its thick walls founded on brick foundations; near it a circular silo was excavated. Around the walls of the main hall of this building were plastered benches; the center of the hall was occupied by a small brick *bamah*, in front of which was a stone basin coated with thick plaster. On the floor of the hall and in the adjoining rooms large heaps of pottery were mixed with charcoal, ash, and animal bones. Nearby were a few *favissae*, each averaging approximately one meter in diameter. Among the finds were painted clay stands, twin vessels, Egyptian alabaster vases, pomegranate-shaped pottery

Area A: Mycenean pottery from stratum X, 13th century BCE.

Area A: Egyptian-type bowl bearing a hieratic inscription, stratum IX, 12th century BCE.

vessels, ivory inlays, cylindrical seals, scarabs, and a considerable quantity of Mycenean and Cypriot pottery. Building 1118 continued to serve as a cult site in stratum IX, until it was destroyed by fire in the mid-twelfth century BCE.

On the eastern slope of the mound, under strata VIII–VII (Iron Age I–II) a massive building, identified as the residence of the local (Egyptian?) governor (building 906, stratum IX), was uncovered. The structure shows three main building phases, represented by the raising of floor levels and the addition of walls and partitions. The original plan of building 906 was square (25 by 25 m), consisting of a central hall with stone column bases surrounded by small rooms. Remains of the roof beams (made of cedar from Lebanon), brick debris, and layers of charcoal were found on the floors of the rooms, indicating that the Canaanite settlement was destroyed in a massive conflagration. The finds included pottery and metal implements, imported Egyptian vessels and local imitations of these imports, alabaster vases and scarabs of late New Kingdom types, as well as a lump of cobalt blue pigment—the color used in Egypt to decorate pottery and paint stelae and reliefs.

The most important discovery in building 906 was a group of Egyptian-type bowls and ostraca, inscribed in Egyptian hieratic script. The inscriptions refer to large quantities of grain, brought as taxes or tribute to the local temple or the storehouses of the governor's residence. One of the texts mentions the date "year 20 + x," probably referring to the regnal year of Ramses III. Another text is concerned with a certain legal procedure. The inscriptions from Tel Sera', like the similar inscriptions on bowls found at Lachish, are of considerable importance for understanding the Egyptian taxation system in Canaan in the late phases of the empire.

Soundings made beneath the floors of building 906 revealed that it was constructed directly on the foundations of a similar building (2502) in stratum X (thirteenth century BCE). The transition from stratum X to stratum IX did not involve destruction or hiatus; it represents a gradual development of the built-up area. The rich assemblage of finds from stratum IX is typical of the last phase of the Late Bronze Age and the beginning of the Iron Age (first half of the twelfth century BCE). Significantly, stratum IX did not produce imported Mycenean, Cypriot, or characteristic Philistine ware. The excavator therefore concluded that Late Bronze Age Aegean and Cypriot imports ceased altogether at the end of the thirteenth century BCE, while Philistine pottery did not appear until the time of Ramses III's successors, in the mid-twelfth century BCE. Philistine ware indeed makes its earliest appearance at Sera' in stratum VIII, which was built over the ruins of the stratum IX Canaanite settlement. The Canaanite settlement was probably destroyed by the Sea Peoples or by an incursion of nomads (Amalekites?) from the Negev.

IRON AGE (STRATA VIII–IV). Stratum VIII. The Iron Age I is represented at Tel Sera' by three phases of settlement with various installations and sunken silos; they overlay the ruins of the last Canaanite settlement in stratum IX. The pottery repertoire from this stratum includes characteristic Philistine pottery, Ashdod-type ware with geometric decorations painted in black and white on a red background, and irregularly hand-burnished pottery. The stratum VIII architectural remains consisted of characteristic four-room houses. Excavations in area A invariably revealed these houses directly below stratum VII buildings with the same ground plan—hence the conclusion that this class of domestic architecture at Tel Sera' should be considered part of the architectural tradition of the Philistine settlers in the western Negev. It also became clear that the transition from stratum VIII to stratum VII showed no signs of destruction and no gap in occupation. Consequently, because the Israelite settlement in the tenth century BCE must have developed organically from the Philistine habitation, it would seem that the ethnic nucleus at Tel Sera' in the Iron Age I–II was Philistine. This conclusion bears directly on the

Area A: pottery in situ in building 149, stratum VII, 10th–9th centuries BCE.

problematic identification of Tel Sera' with biblical Ziklag.

Stratum VII. Stratum VII (Iron Age II, tenth–ninth centuries BCE) represents the most highly developed stage of the Iron Age settlement. Four phases of construction, repairs, and floor raisings have been assigned to this level. The stratum VII settlement was well planned; its streets and fine buildings are sometimes preserved to a height of 2 m. The buildings' mud-brick walls stood on deep *kurkar*-filled foundation trenches, with alternating courses of mud brick and sand. The last phase of the ninth-century BCE occupation was apparently destroyed by fire.

Area A yielded several examples of four-room houses constructed directly over the remains of similar buildings from the Philistine period in stratum VIII. One of these (building 149) consisted of a rectangular courtyard with small rooms on its eastern side and a long, narrow hall on its south. In the center of the courtyard stood a row of stone pillar bases. The courtyard's western wing, which was probably roofed, was found paved with large pebbles under a layer of crushed chalk. The floor of the courtyard's eastern wing was beaten earth; cooking and baking installations were built into it. In the courtyard and in the rooms were numerous storage jars and clay stoppers, cooking pots, and stone grain pounders and grinders. The small rooms, probably stairwells, and the considerable thickness of the walls indicate that the building had a second story.

Stratum VI. Under the walls of the "Assyrian" citadel in area D (see below) were the impressive remains of a complex of buildings with ashlar masonry. These buildings stood on either side of a wide street leading to the northern end of the settlement. Their mud-brick walls, preserved to a height of some 2 m, were built on ashlar-faced foundation courses. The ashlar blocks were well dressed, with drafted margins and projecting central bosses. The *kurkar* chips found in the foundation trenches indicate that the blocks were drafted and fitted on the spot, while construction was in progress. On the floors of the rooms under the burned debris were large quantities of storage jars, burnished bowls, and hole-mouth jars, ascribed to the eighth century BCE.

The architectural style of the buildings at Tel Sera' is very similar to that of the typical ashlar construction of public buildings—gates and palaces—at such sites as Hazor, Megiddo, Gezer, Samaria, and Ramat Raḥel. However, in contrast to true ashlar masonry, the walls at Tel Sera' are built of mud brick; only the outer facing of the foundation courses is of drafted ashlar masonry. A brick bench abutting the ashlar courses clearly indicates that the marginal drafting was not done entirely for aesthetic reasons.

The construction methods in evidence at Tel Sera'—in particular, incorporating ashlar blocks in the foundation courses of brick walls—represent two distinct architectural traditions: the ashlar masonry typical at Israelite and Phoenician sites in the Iron Age; and orthostat construction, typical of architecture throughout Syria in the Bronze and Iron ages. A close parallel to this style can be found in the brick gate at Ashdod from the tenth to eighth centuries BCE, except that at Ashdod the ashlars were only incorporated in the gate to reinforce the corners—they were not an integral part of the structure.

The walls of the ashlar buildings at Tel Sera' were built directly on the foundations of similarly planned buildings whose foundations were laid—as in the four-room houses in area A—in deep foundation trenches

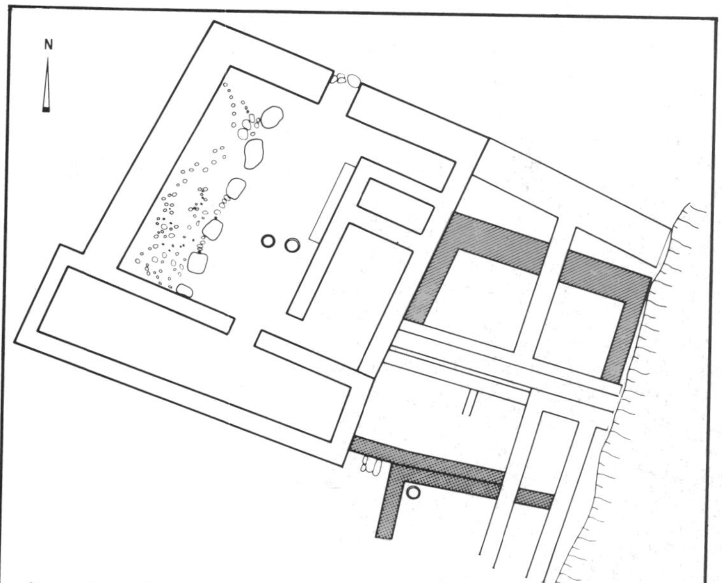

Area A: plan of the four-room house (building 149), stratum VII, 10th–9th centuries BCE.

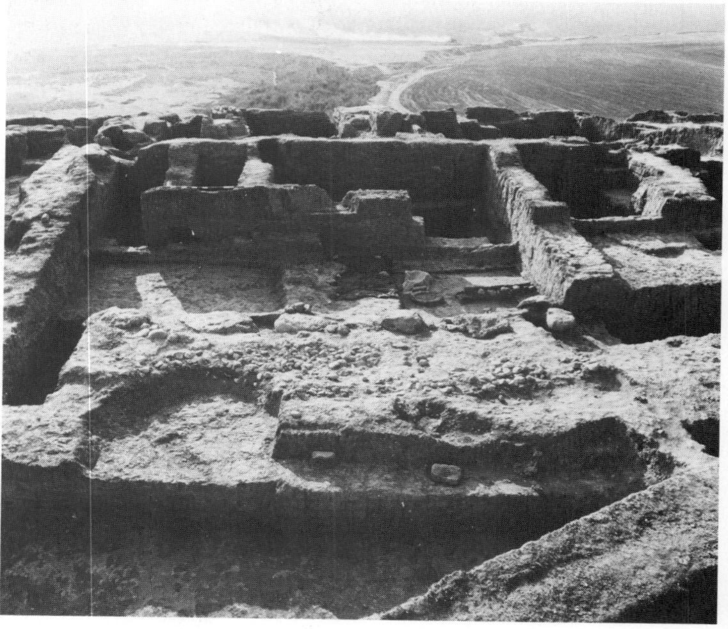

Area A: general view of the four-room house (building 149), stratum VII.

Sepphoris: the Nile festival depicted in a mosaic floor in the Byzantine structure; details ***(above left)*** *of a representation of the city of Alexandria and* ***(above right)*** *of a nilometer;* ***(below)*** *overview.*

Serabit el-Khadem: overview of the stelae on the hill's summit.

Sepphoris: ***(left)*** *a centaur depicted in a mosaic floor in the Byzantine structure, east of the summit;* ***(below)*** *mosaic floor with Dionysian scenes in the palatial mansion, 3rd century* CE.

Pillar figurines, stratum V, 7th century BCE.

filled with *kurkar*. The pottery from this level resembles that from stratum VII in area A, which was dated to the tenth and ninth centuries BCE. In the eighth century BCE, the walls of the buildings were razed and replaced by houses with similar plans; however they were based on ashlar-faced foundation courses. The ashlar buildings in area D were destroyed by a violent conflagration that left great heaps of burned bricks and a layer of ash mixed with sherds and a variety of objects.

It can thus be postulated that ashlar masonry was introduced to this area by the Phoenicians during the period of Assyrian domination.

Strata V–IV. Stratum V (seventh century BCE) represents the last fortified Iron Age settlement at Tel Sera'. Excavations in this stratum in area A revealed remains of a large citadel that defended the southern approaches to the city (its central part was destroyed by a huge silo cut through it in the Persian period). The citadel had long, narrow magazine halls and small rooms, all surrounded by a defensive wall whose thickness reached as much as 5 m. Following the destruction of the citadel, a large number of silos and refuse pits was sunk into its ruins (stratum IV), including one pit 7 m in diameter and approximately 3 m deep. In the pits were spiral-burnished bowls, fragments of Assyrian palace ware and its local imitations, Egyptian-style fertility "pillar figurines," imported East Greek ware, Edomite sherds, and Aramaic and Hebrew ostraca.

Stratum V in area D yielded the impressive remains of a citadel that had defended the northern approaches to the city. This was a rectangular building with very long (up to 14 m) and narrow halls (basements?), surrounded by a wall some 4 m thick. North of the halls was an elevated rectangular area (platform?), to the east of which was a courtyard, or square, paved with pebbles and limestone gravel. Found on the brick-lined floor of the northern hall was a group of metal objects, including a bronze crescent-shaped standard—the symbol of the moon-god Sin—next to which was a bell, perhaps originally attached to the loop in the handle of the standard. The standard probably served ceremonial and cultic functions, like similar standards in contemporary reliefs from Mesopotamia and Syria.

Found nearby was a long iron chain, at whose end was a long pitchforklike prong, that may have been used as a grappeling device for climbing walls. A bronze, Assyrian-type socketed spearhead (c. 60 cm long) was found in the central hall.

Notable among the abundant finds on the floors of the halls and under the rubble of the walls were delicate Assyrian palace ware vessels, a faience statuette of the Egyptian goddess Sekhmet, and an Aramaic ostracon inscribed with a list of North-Arabian names. The pottery assemblage discovered near the citadel wall includes a jug with the Hebrew word לירם (*lyrm*, "belonging to

Bronze standard in the form of a crescent and a bell, in the Assyrian style, from area D, stratum V, 7th century BCE.

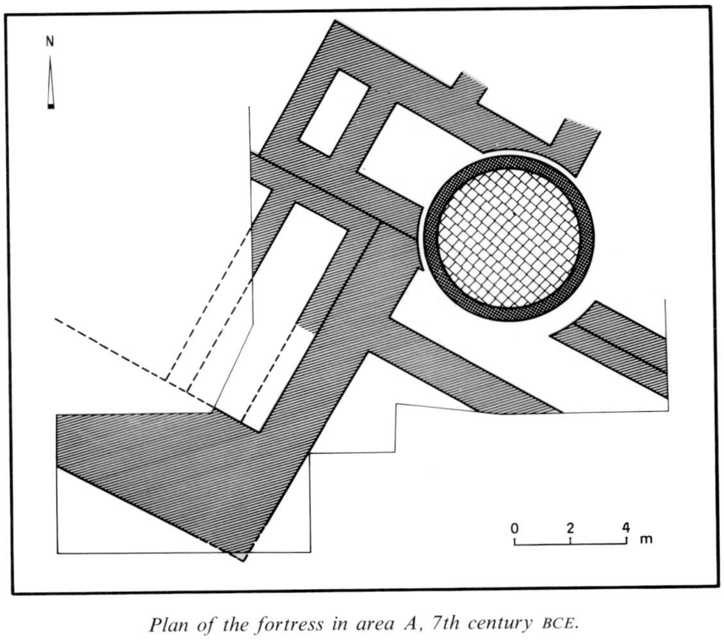

Plan of the fortress in area A, 7th century BCE.

Area D: faience statuette of the Egyptian goddess Sekhmet in the form of a lioness, from the Assyrian fortress, stratum V.

Area A: general view of strata V and IV.

Joram") incised on its shoulder. In the 1978 season, evidence was unearthed in the citadel courtyard of a metal industry, including remains of small furnaces for smelting iron, clay pipes for bellows, and iron slag. One installation was discovered intact: a smithy for forging iron objects, consisting of a depression in the ground surrounded by baked bricks. The sides of the depression were coated with a clayey material, vitrified by the high temperatures in the forge. Clay pipes for bellows were installed in the upper part of the installation. In a shallow hole full of ash and charcoal, in front of the installation, near its opening, the excavators found a spearhead, or chisel, in situ.

Area D: Middle Corinthian aryballos from a pit in stratum IV, early 6th century BCE.

The rooms in the citadel were buried deep under heaps of burned bricks and charred beams, the results of the great conflagration that destroyed the city. The abundant pottery found on the floors—including Assyrian palace ware, thick mortaria bowls, and basket-handled jars—date the citadel to the seventh century BCE and its destruction to the second half of that century. This terminus ad quem is substantiated by pits cut into the rubble of the stratum IV citadel; they contained many broken, burned bricks, thrown there when the ruins were being leveled in preparation for new construction. The pits presumably were dug soon after the destruction of the citadel, perhaps by returning residents. The pottery found in them resembles that on the floor of the stratum V citadel. Imported East Greek ware found in the pits, among them a Middle Corinthian aryballos, confirms the second half of the seventh-century BCE date of the citadel's destruction.

The Assyrian palace ware sherds and bronzes indicate that Tel Sera', like other settlements in the western Negev and southern Philistia, was occupied by an Assyrian military administration. The cause of its destruction, together with both citadels, is unknown. It may be attributable to one of the military expeditions of the Saite dynasty from Egypt to the Palestinian coast. Another possibility is that the city was destroyed during Josiah's attempt to gain control of the Coastal Plain.

PERSIAN PERIOD (STRATUM III). Stratum III (fifth–fourth centuries BCE) is represented at Tel Sera', as at other sites in the southern Shephelah and the northern Negev, by numerous built silos and grain pits. A large, brick-lined granary (diameter, c. 5 m) with a brick floor was excavated in area A. The floor was covered with a thick layer of organic matter, probably remains of cereals, as well as diagnostic pottery of the Persian period. In area D, above the ruins of the "Assyrian" citadel, were the remains of a citadel and courtyard building similar in plan to structures at Ashdod and Tell es-Sa'idiyeh. Stratum III yielded a large collection of imported Attic wares, bronze fibulae, Greek figurines, Aramaic ostraca, and a fine limestone incense altar decorated with incised proto-Aeolic capitals topped with lotus leaves.

HELLENISTIC-ROMAN PERIOD (STRATUM II). Following the Persian period, the site was abandoned and the summit of the mound was built on only sporadically. Poorly constructed walls, associated with Hellenistic "fish plates," attest to the existence of a settlement in the Hellenistic period (second–first centuries BCE, stratum II). The main habitation in the Roman and Byzantine periods was confined to the level area on the southern bank of Naḥal Gerar (area R). Remains of a Roman villa (stratum II) from the first century CE were exposed in area D. The building was partly destroyed when a drainage system was constructed in the Byzantine period and by late Muslim burials in the vicinity. The villa contained a large rectangular hall and a few small rooms; it is surrounded by a stone wall. Overshadowing it was a massive watchtower, built of large stones and pebbles. The foundations of the tower went down to a considerable depth, damaging the Assyrian citadel and one of the ashlar buildings. On the floor of the villa were heaps of fragments of high-quality plaster that had fallen from the walls and ceiling. The plaster was decorated with geometric and floral patterns in a wealth of colors—white, yellow, red, blue, green, and black. This decorated plaster resembles frescoes from the Herodian period discovered in the Jewish Quarter in Jerusalem and at Herodium, Masada, and Jericho. The plaster fragments were found mixed with large quantities of pottery and fragments of stone and glass vessels, including many examples of Arretine and Nabatean pottery, "Herodian" lamps, limestone measuring cups, and numerous sherds of decorated "Jerusalem" bowls.

BYZANTINE (STRATUM I) AND ARAB PERIODS. The remains of a large structure on stone foundations, probably a Byzantine church or monastery (fifth–sixth centuries CE), are visible on the summit of the mound. Fragments of a mosaic pavement decorated with geometric motifs were accidentally discovered here in the early 1950s. To the north, in area D, a drainage system, comprising stone-lined channels and a plastered reservoir, was excavated. In the pool were dozens of ribbed water jars from the fifth and sixth centuries.

In area R, overlooking the steep southern bank of Naḥal Gerar, part of a well-preserved bathhouse was excavated. It consists of a hypocaust with baked brick arches to support the floor of the caldarium, clay pipes built into the walls, and a system of plastered channels supplying and draining water for the baths. Coins and pottery date the latest stage of the bathhouse to the fifth and sixth centuries.

The upper occupation strata at Tel Sera' were badly damaged by hundreds of Muslim burials. Many of the tombs are lined with stone slabs and some contain metal and glass jewelry. The excavations in area D revealed fragmentary walls and floors and *tabun*s and other cooking and storage installations from the Early Arab and Mameluke periods (tenth–fourteenth centuries).

Identification
Alt, *KSch.* 3, 429–450; W. F. Albright, *BASOR* 14 (1925), 6; G. E. Wright, *BA* 29 (1966), 78ff.
Excavations and Finds
Main publication: E. D. Oren, *Tel Sera': A Biblical City on the Edge of the Negev*, Beersheva 1972.
Other studies: E. D. Oren, *IEJ* 22 (1972), 167–169; (with E. Netzer) 23 (1973), 251–254; (with E. Netzer) 24 (1974), 264–266; id., *RB* 80 (1973), 401–405; id., *ILN* 262 (1974), 69–72; id., *BA* 45 (1982), 155–166; id., *Journal of the Society for the Study of Egyptian Antiquities* 14 (1984), 37–56; O. Goldwasser, *TA* 11 (1984), 77–93; J. D. Seger, *BA* 47 (1984), 47–53; S. Wimmer, *Jahrbuch des Deutschen Evangelischen Instituts für Altertumswissenschaft des Heiligen Landes* 1 (1989), 49–50; B. Rothenberg and R. F. Tylecote, *University of London, Institute for Archaeo-Metallurgical Studies Newsletter* 17 (1991), 11–14.

ELIEZER D. OREN

SERABIT EL-KHADEM

IDENTIFICATION

Serabit el-Khadem (Arabic for Columns [or Tunnels] of the Slave), lies high up on a hilly massif in the northwestern part of the southern Sinai Peninsula, in a region of Nubian sandstone. Turquoise deposits in these hills and elsewhere in the vicinity (mainly in Wadi Meghara), some of which are still being exploited by the local Bedouin, have been known since antiquity. The site derives its scientific significance and renown from the Egyptian temple discovered here, the hieroglyphic and Proto-Sinaitic inscriptions in and around the temple, and the ancient turquoise mines for whose workers the temple was built.

EXPLORATION

The first known European visitor to the site was C. Niebuhr, a member of a Danish expedition that explored the Sinai in 1762. Early in 1905, W. M. F. Petrie led an expedition here that explored the temple and its surroundings for more than two months. He prepared and published a detailed plan of the temple and its surroundings, copied most of the inscriptions, and deciphered some of them. He recorded the location of sixteen turquoise mines and discovered about twelve Proto-Sinaitic inscriptions. The Egyptian hieroglyphic inscriptions were fully deciphered and published by A. A. Gardiner, E. T. Peet and J. Černy in the 1950s, after Černy had spent some time at the site in 1935 and examined them. In 1935, too, the turquoise mine M was explored by a Harvard University expedition, resulting in the discovery of some additional Proto-Sinaitic inscriptions and some small artifacts.

Exploration of the site was renewed in 1968 by an expedition under the auspices of the Institute of Archaeology of Tel Aviv University, directed by R. Giveon. The expedition worked at the site intermittently until 1981, reerected some fallen stelae, reexamined the inscriptions, and discovered some hitherto unknown inscriptions and statues. Another expedition, also on behalf of Tel Aviv University, directed by I. Beit-Arieh, conducted further surveys in the vicinity and excavated a Chalcolithic site at the foot of Serabit el-Khadem. In 1977–1978, the same expedition excavated the turquoise mines G and L.

EXCAVATION RESULTS

The earliest evidence for the mining of turquoise at Serabit el-Khadem dates to the Chalcolithic period. A small Chalcolithic site was discovered in Wadi Ḥasif, at the foot of the hilly massif, with pottery indicating an association with the Ghassulian and Beersheba cultures. I. Beit-Arieh, who excavated

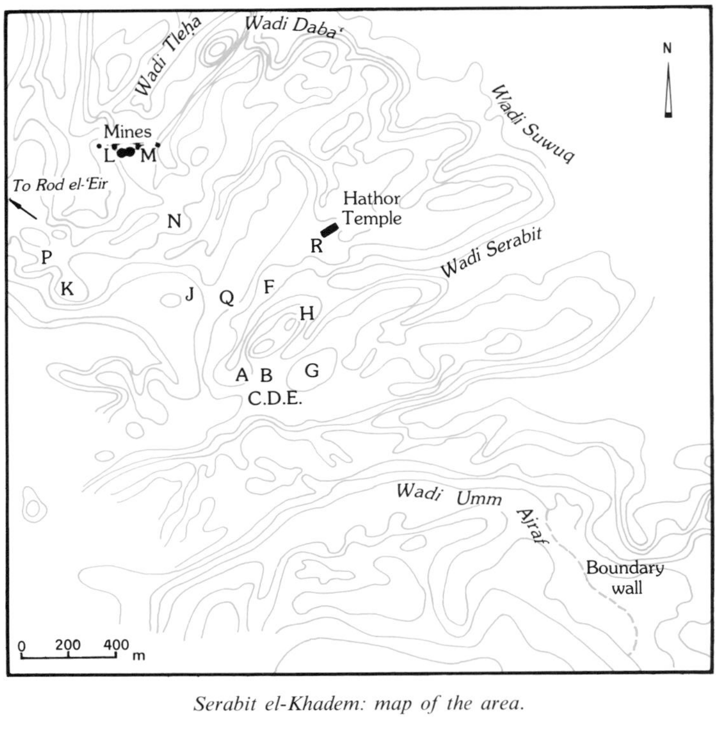

Serabit el-Khadem: map of the area.

Mine L.

General view of the temple, looking northwest.

this site in 1974, unearthed a variety of artifacts indicating that it was a working area for turquoise miners. The finds included unworked turquoise stones; hematite mallets, which were probably used in mining; flint blades with filed points, probably used to pry the turquoise from the rock; and grinding stones for polishing the turquoise. The excavator suggested that the local miners had marketed the polished turquoise in Egypt. In view of the Egyptians' special interest in turquoise—probably because of its unique shades—the Egyptian authorities had begun to exploit the deposits as far back as the Old Kingdom, under the Third Dynasty pharaoh Sekhemkhet. In the Old Kingdom period, the Egyptians mined the deposits in Wadi Meghara, but evidence for their presence in Serabit el-Khadem dates only to the Middle and New Kingdoms.

TEMPLE. Early in the Middle Kingdom, under Pharaoh Amenemḥet I of the Twelfth Dynasty (1991–1962 BCE), the Egyptians built a temple to Hathor,

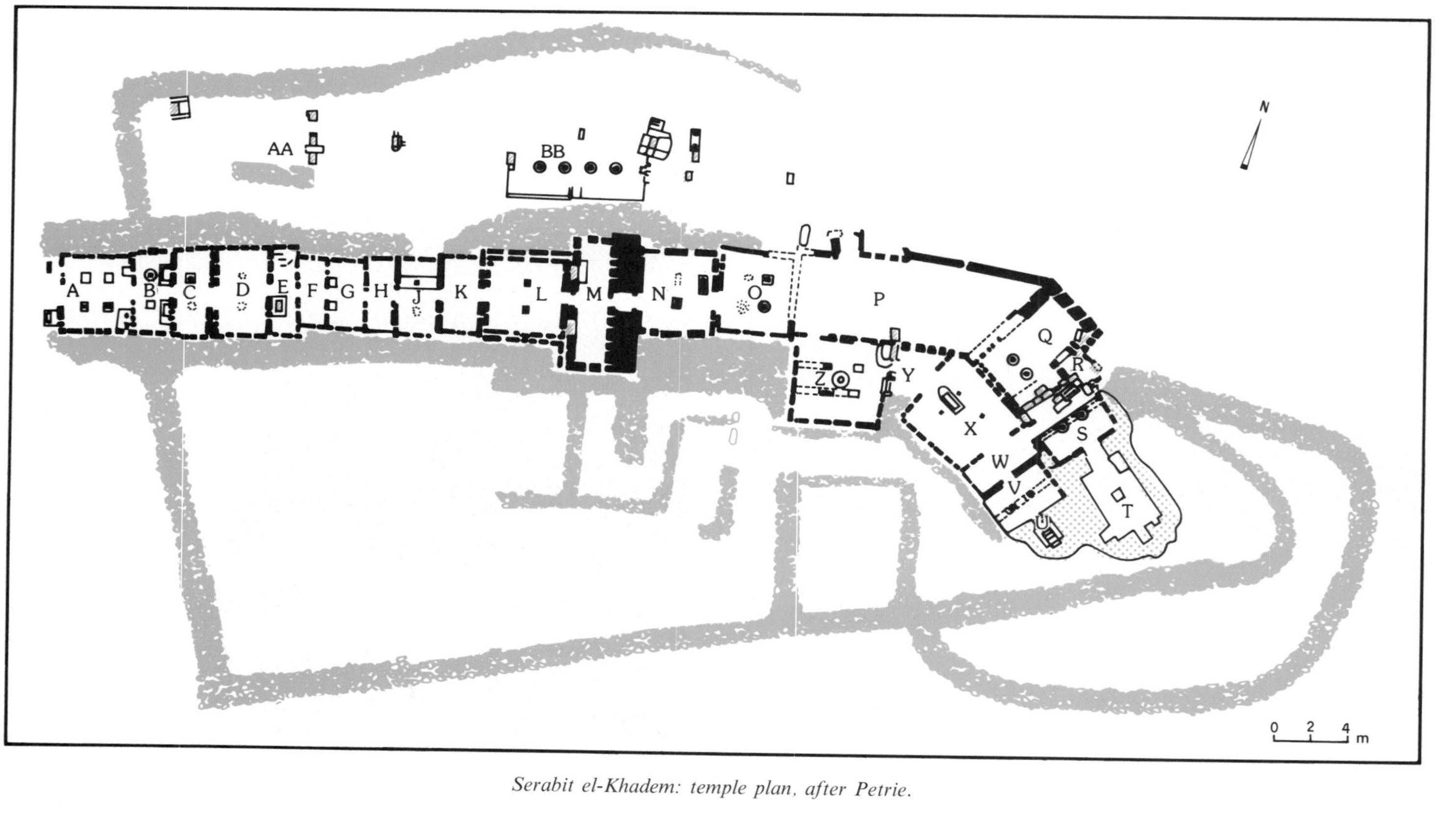

Serabit el-Khadem: temple plan, after Petrie.

"the Lady of Turquoise," here. The temple, first examined and published by Petrie, consists of a series of rooms arranged consecutively in a kind of long chain. Most scholars believe that the core and earliest stage of the temple are to be sought in two caves at its eastern end: the Cave of Hathor and the Cave of Sopdu (U and T in Petrie's plan). According to one hypothesis, first proposed by C. Burckhardt and accepted by Giveon, the Cave of Hathor was originally the burial place of a senior Egyptian official; only later (but still during the Middle Kingdom) did it become the holy of holies of the temple, which had been housed until then in the neighboring cave (Cave of Sopdu). Each of the caves was then extended by the addition of a complex of rooms and courtyards—each, as Petrie conjectured, with its own specific ritual function. The general alignment of the caves is northwest–southeast.

The temple's other rooms, all later additions, were built by various pharaohs: each ruler added one or two rooms. The resulting series of rooms runs east–west, thus altering the temple's previous axis, which was a direct continuation of that of the caves.

At the entrance to the two rooms (N and O) attributed to Thutmose III (1490–1436 BCE) was an imposing gate-tower (pylon). Although it subsequently was absorbed into the row of rooms built by later kings, it clearly forms an architectural unit with rooms M and L, also built by Thutmose III. The last room, at the western end (A) was built by Seti I (1309–1291 BCE) and functioned as the anteroom to the entire temple. The temple contained epigraphic evidence of its existence as late as the reign of Ramses VI (1141–1134 BCE), although there is no doubt that expeditions to the site under Seti I's successors did not add rooms but only renovated the existing chambers and enlarged others. Some expeditions even inscribed their monarchs' names on structural elements built by other kings.

North of this complex of rooms were the remains of masonry dating to the Twelfth Dynasty. They include a building Petrie called the Kings' Sanctuary (BB) and an avenue of stelae (AA) that marked the original entrance to the temple at that time. Part of the Kings' Sanctuary was cut in the rock, while the remainder was built of decorated ashlar blocks. Four column bases found in situ show that the sanctuary was partly roofed.

The temple area was surrounded by a low ashlar-built wall. The quarries from which the building stones and blocks for the stelae were taken can be discerned nearby.

Inscriptions. The more than four hundred hieroglyphic inscriptions discovered in the temple and its immediate surroundings were published by Gardiner, Peet, and Černy. Most were engraved on the stelae standing in the temple, but a few were incised on the natural rock at the entrances to the mines or on stone slabs and statues. Some hitherto unknown inscriptions, as well as reliefs and statues, were discovered by Giveon's expedition. The inscriptions convey detailed information about the organization and personnel of the royal mining expeditions, as well as accounts of the royal officials delegated to join the expeditions—their titles, functions, and status.

Petrie's expedition found about one dozen inscriptions in a script that later became known as Proto-Sinaitic. Some thirty-five Proto-Sinaitic inscriptions have been discovered so far at the site, mostly engraved on stone slabs but some incised on the mine walls. Three other inscriptions were found engraved on the cliffs in nearby Wadi Meghara and Wadi Naṣb. The first was discovered in 1869 by E. H. Palmer in Wadi Meghara. The letters of the script resemble the Proto-Canaanite script of some inscriptions in Canaan (from Gezer, Lachish, and Shechem), which has been dated to the interim between the last phase of the Middle Bronze Age and the end of the Late Bronze Age. Some of the signs resemble Egyptian hieroglyphs. Petrie conjectured that it was an alphabetic script, used by Asiatics working the mines under the Egyptians. Gardiner concurred, adding that the Semitic language of the inscriptions was written in hieroglyphic signs following an acrophonic principle. On this assumption, he identified fifteen of thirty signs and deciphered the word לבעלת (*lb'lt*), the name of a Canaanite goddess, found engraved on a statuette in the temple—a reading now accepted by most scholars. W. F. Albright suggested an identification of all the letters and inscriptions and attempted to compare them with a Northwest-Semitic language; but the reading of both scholars is still only conjectural. For lack of supporting

Proto-Sinaitic inscription from mine L.

Fragment of relief depicting Hathor in the form of a cow.

evidence, the date of the inscriptions is still open to question, with paleographers divided over whether to ascribe them to the time of the Middle Kingdom (Gardiner, R. F. Butin, K. Sethe) or the New Kingdom (Petrie, Albright, J. Leibovitch, F. M. Cross, Jr., J. Naveh). Attempts have been made to adduce evidence from the excavations in mines M, L, and G. The 1935 Harvard University excavations in mine M were of little help, but Beit-Arieh's 1977–1978 excavations in mines L and G unearthed pottery and other evidence indicating a date some time in the New Kingdom. Among the most noteworthy finds were foot-driven bellows and an accumulation of forty-seven stone molds of various shapes, used to cast bronze mining tools. The excavator believes that these were the tools of the metalworkers who accompanied the turquoise miners; their job was to melt down damaged tools on the spot and cast new ones in their stead.

The ancient road to the site climbed up from the southwest to the temple, following a narrow route known as Rod el-'Eir (Asses' Path). The rock walls of this narrow mountain pass are covered with incised inscriptions and drawings from the time of the Middle and New Kingdoms. Depicted in the drawings are animals, boats, axes (symbolizing warriors or miners?), and human figures. The inscriptions were published by Gardiner, Peet, and Černy. Not far from the top of the path, Giveon's expedition discovered the remains of an Egyptian camp.

Main publications: W. M. F. Petrie, *Researches in Sinai*, London 1906; R. F. S. Starr and R. F. Butin, *Excavations and Proto-Sinaitic Inscriptions at Serabit el-Khadem* (Studies and Documents 6), London 1936; A. A. Gardiner et al., *The Inscriptions of Sinai* 1–2, London 1952–1955; W. F. Albright, *The Proto-Sinaitic Inscriptions and Their Decipherment*, Cambridge 1969.

Other studies: R. Weill, *Recueil des Inscriptions Egyptiennes du Sinai*, Paris 1904; K. Lake and R. P. Blake, *Harvard Theological Review* 21 (1928), 1–8; R. F. Butin, ibid. 25 (1932), 182–184; J. Leibovitch, *Les Inscriptions Protosinaitiques*, Cairo 1934; id., *Annales du Service des Antiquités de l'Egypt* 40 (1940), 101–122; R. Giveon, *TA* 1 (1974), 100–108; id., *The Australian Journal of Biblical Archaeology* 2/3 (1974–1975), 29–48; id., *The Impact of Egypt on Canaan*, Freiburg 1978, 61–67; id., *IEJ* 31 (1981), 168–171; 34 (1984), 154–155; I. Beit-Arieh (et al.), *TA* 5 (1978), 170–187; ibid. 7 (1980), 45–64; id., *BA* 45 (1982), 13–18; id., *Levant* 17 (1985), 89–116; 22 (1990), 163; A. F. Rainey, *IEJ* 31 (1981), 92–94; J. Naveh, *Early History of the Alphabet*, Jeruslaem 1982, 23–27; M. Dijkstra, *Ugarit-Forschungen* 15 (1983), 33–38; W. H. Shea, *The Archaeology of Jordan and Other Studies* (S. H. Horn Fest.), Berrien Springs 1986, 449–464; E. A. Knauf, *Ugarit-Forschungen* 20 (1988), 244; R. Ventura, *IEJ* 38 (1988), 128–138; E. Braun, *PEQ* 121 (1989), 1–43; S. Wimmer, *Jahrbuch des Deutschen Evangelischen Instituts für Altertumswissenschaft des Heiligen Landes* 1 (1989), 32–33; id., *Studies in Egyptology Presented to Miriam Lichtheim* (ed. S. Israelit-Groll), Jerusalem 1990, 1065–1106; A. S. Kaufman, *Niv Hamidrashia* (1990), 25–36; P. Simpson, *JEA* 76 (1990), 185–186; G. Pinch, *New Kingdom Votive Offerings to Hathor*, Oxford 1991.

ITZHAQ BEIT-ARIEH

SHAALBIM

IDENTIFICATION

Shaalbim, a city of the tribe of Dan (Jos. 19:42), from which the original Amorite inhabitants were not ejected by the Israelites, was a tribute city of the House of Joseph (Jg. 1:35). Eliahba the Shaalbonite was one of David's "mighty men" (2 Sam. 23:32; 1 Chr. 11:33). In the days of Solomon, it was one of the cities that provided food for the king and his household (1 Kg. 4:9). Jerome mentions the place by the name of Selbi. The site is identified with the Arab village Salbit in the northwestern part of the Ayalon Valley, about 3 km (2 mi.) north of Emmaus (map reference 148.141).

EXCAVATIONS

A fragment of a mosaic pavement bearing a Samaritan inscription was found in the village in 1948. The following summer, E. L. Sukenik and N. Avigad excavated the site on behalf of the Institute of Archaeology of the Hebrew University of Jerusalem. In the course of these excavations, they uncovered the foundations of a rectangular building (8.05 by 15.4 m) whose facade was oriented northeast, in the direction of Mount Gerizim, the holy mountain of the Samaritans. No column bases were encountered, but there seems to be no doubt that the building was a basilica (divided into a nave and two aisles) without an apse. The excavators assumed that there had been a colonnade or a kind of narthex in the southern part of the building (not excavated). Remains of additional rooms were uncovered north and west of the building. In the center of its white mosaic floor was a rectangular panel (6 by 3.2 m) decorated with geometric patterns, with a circular medallion (diameter, 1.45 m) in the center. The southern part of this medallion has been preserved: two seven-branched menorahs flank a stepped design of a mountain, symbolizing, in the opinion of the excavators, Mount Gerizim. Two fragmentary lines of a Greek inscription appear above the menorahs. The northern corner of the rectangle contains the Samaritan version of the verse: "The Lord shall reign for ever and ever" (Ex. 15:18). Smaller fragments of three lines of another Samaritan inscription appear in the southern part of the rectangle. The floor was executed in black and red tesserae; 15 to 28 cm above it three sections were found of a later mosaic floor adorned with geometric and floral designs.

Judging from the building's plan and orientation, the Samaritan inscriptions, and the menorah designs, it can be concluded with a fair degree of certainty that these remains belong to an ancient Samaritan synagogue. Sukenik attributed the construction of the synagogue to the fourth century CE, when the Samaritan settlement flourished, in the days of Baba Rabba. From the style of the mosaic floor, however, it appears more likely that the synagogue was built in the fifth century. The building was probably destroyed during one of the Samaritan revolts against Byzantine rule (484 or 529 CE); the later floor was laid when the building was restored, after the revolt had been crushed.

Abel, *GP* 2, 438; E. L. Sukenik, *Rabinowitz Bulletin* 1 (1949), 15–30; M. N. Tod, ibid. 2 (1951), 27–28; Goodenough, *Jewish Symbols* 1, 262–263; M. Avi-Yonah, *Antiquity and Survival* 2 (1957), 262–272; Centre de Recherche Français de Jérusalem, *Lettre d'Information* 1 (1982), 19.

DAN BARAG

Shaalbim: part of the mosaic floor in the synagogue; a menorah motif and a Greek inscription in the lower floor; (above) a segment of the upper floor.

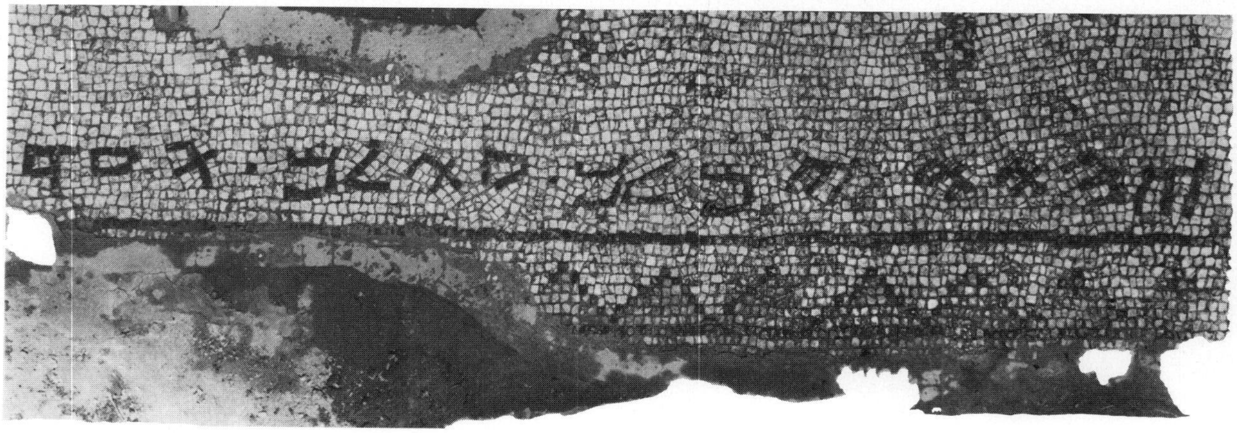

Samaritan inscription in the lower mosaic: "The Lord shall reign forever and ever."

SHA'AR HA-'AMAQIM

IDENTIFICATION AND EXPLORATION

The Hellenistic site of Sha'ar ha-'Amaqim is located to the northwest of the kibbutz of the same name (map reference 1609.2369), at the foot of Qiryat Tiv'on, in the southern Lower Galilee. Only a narrow passage separates the steep slopes of Mount Carmel from the hills over which the site extends, which is clearly strategically advantageous. The site was discovered by chance in 1966. It was surveyed as part of the Survey of Israel and excavated from 1984 to 1991 by a team headed by A. Segal of the Department of Archaeology at Haifa University and Y. Naor of Kibbutz Sha'ar ha-'Amaqim.

As early as the 1930s, B. Mazar proposed identifying the remains of the abandoned Arab village el-Kharitiyye (at present within the bounds of Kibbutz Sha'ar ha-'Amaqim) with ancient Gaba (Geba). The geographical-historical sources that mention Gaba actually refer to several places by this name. The first is Gaba on the Carmel, mentioned by Pliny (*NH* V, 75). This Gaba is not necessarily the "Geba of the cavalry" that Herod built for his veteran cavalrymen (Josephus, *Antiq.* XV, 294; *War* III, 36; *Life*, 115, 117–118). The third city, Gaba of Philippus, is known only from coins and perhaps owed its name to Marcus Philippus, proconsul of Syria in 61–60 BCE, who possibly refounded it. Like other cities restored by the Romans in this period, it may have been a Hellenistic town conquered by the Jews, possibly by Alexander Jannaeus in his campaign to Acco at the beginning of his reign (103–76 BCE). The site in Kibbutz Sha'ar ha-'Amaqim should probably be identified with the Hellenistic Geba. Its strategic location, the style and quality of its building, its subterranean water system, and the nature of the finds here reinforce this identification.

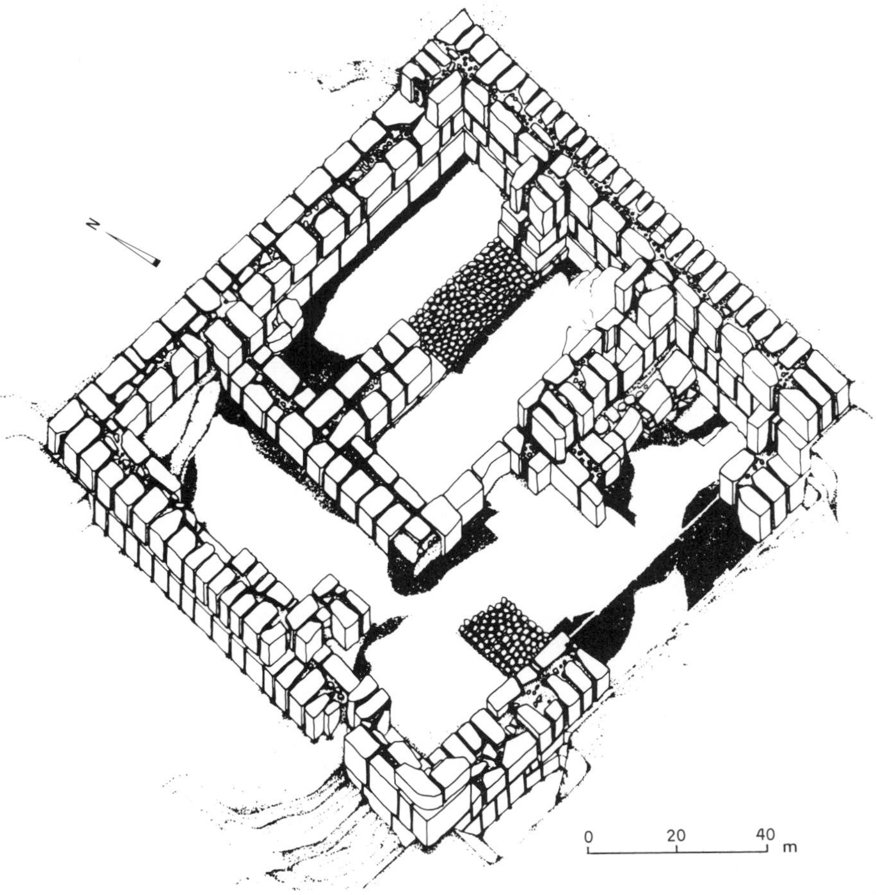

Isometric reconstruction of the central building.

EXCAVATIONS

CENTRAL BUILDING. At the center of the site is an almost square building (12.3 m north–south and 13.2

Sha'ar ha-'Amaqim: general view of the central building, looking east, Hellenistic period.

m east–west) constructed of large ashlars. Preserved to a height of two or three courses, it has been identified as a tower, of which only the foundations survive. Its main walls are built on bedrock; the lower courses are laid in rock-cut foundation trenches. The partition walls, which divide the inner chamber (9.3 by 10.2 m) into smaller rooms, were laid on leveled bedrock or on a foundation of small field stones. All the walls are built of large ashlars, most of them having drafted margins with a central boss. Some courses are laid entirely as headers, while the construction of the others is mixed. This unique construction method has only a few parallels in this country (at Samaria, Dor, and Acco); it is characterized by several courses of headers with drafted margins, with or without a central boss. The lugs are not uniform in shape; in some instances the central boss protrudes and is only slightly dressed, whereas in others it is flat and well dressed. The excavation of the tower uncovered several decorated architectural fragments, all found out of context. They are made of the same limestone as the tower. A fragment of a Corinthian capital and of a pseudo-Doric capital are especially noteworthy. The capitals are among the earliest of their type discovered in this country and should be attributed to the second and first centuries BCE, a date supported by the ceramic and numismatic finds (see below). The tower was surrounded by a low wall (height, 1.5 m) to prevent anyone from undermining it. The wall was parallel to the tower walls at a distance of 4.6 m (except on the eastern side, where the distance was c. 8 m). The system was to prevent the enemy's approach to the tower and to create a killing field favorable to the defenders. The surrounding walls were constructed in characteristically Hellenistic style, with alternating headers and stretchers arranged with remarkable precision.

SUBTERRANEAN WATER SYSTEM. A subterranean water system, consisting of a vertical shaft entrance, a rock-cut tunnel, and a cistern, was uncovered. The vertical shaft is located in the eastern part of wall 105; its upper part is built of large ashlars, while the lower part is hewn on all but its eastern sides. The shaft is rectangular (0.8 by 0.7 m) and about 4 m deep. At its bottom, which can only be reached by ladder, nine rock-cut steps lead to the tunnel.

The tunnel is cut into the bedrock and plastered along its entire length. It has a slightly winding course, gently sloping downward from the shaft to the southwest. It is about 14 m long, one meter wide, and, on the average, 2 m deep. The lower parts of the tunnel walls are parallel and become progressively narrower toward the top. The southwestern end of the tunnel branches off to the north for about 2.5 m, until it reaches the cistern.

The cistern (diameter, c. 6 m) was only partially cleared. A round opening (diameter, 0.8 m) seems to have been cut in its ceiling at a later stage. The cistern's walls, like those of the tunnel, are plastered. The entrance shaft and the tunnel were apparently intended to provide access from within the tower to the underground water source; the cistern was not a collection cistern (otherwise, there would have been no reason for the entrance shaft and tunnel), but rather a pit whose bottom was a water source—a spring or an aquifer. The round opening in the top of the cistern was cut after the pit had become a collection cistern.

NUMISMATIC FINDS. Most of the coins uncovered in the excavations are Seleucid (beginning with Antiochus III, 223–187 BCE, and ending with Antiochus VIII, 125–113 BCE) and were minted in Antiochia, Sidon, Tyre, and Acco. Several Roman coins (second and third centuries CE) were found on the surface. Coins from the first century BCE are noticeably absent.

CERAMIC FINDS. The pottery is divided into two main groups: local and imported ware. The earliest local sherds are from the Persian period (fifth and fourth centuries BCE), but many are characteristic of the third and second centuries BCE. Only a few sherds can be dated to the beginning of the first century BCE or to the first century CE. The imported pottery included Attic sherds from the fourth century BCE, Rhodian handles, and a relative abundance of Hellenistic pottery characteristic of the third and second centuries BCE.

HOARD OF PLOWSHARES. In the center of an area paved with field stones, about 15 m west of the tower, a small ditch was discovered containing a dense concentration of ancient iron plowshares. They apparently were uncovered in their original place of storage, in a superb state of preservation. The ditch contained four plowshares and four rings used to fasten the share to the wooden part of the plow. Each plowshare weighs about 4 kg and has an average length of 0.48 m. Similar ancient plows are known from only two other sites in this country: Shiqmona and Gamala. On the basis of comparative typological analysis and an examination of the ceramic material discovered with the plows, it is possible to date them with considerable certainty to the end of the Hellenistic period (early first century BCE).

CHRONOLOGICAL FRAMEWORK. Based on typological-stylistic analysis of the building methods used in the tower, as well as on a study of the architectural remains, coins, and ceramic finds, it is possible to distinguish three phases in the site's existence.

Phase I (Late Fifth–Fourth Centuries BCE). Although none of the building remains uncovered can be clearly attributed to the Persian period, the large quantity of Persian pottery and Attic ware indicates that it was the time of the earliest settlement here.

Phase II (Late Third–Early Second Centuries BCE). In phase II the tower was erected and the tunnel leading to the subterranean water source was cut. The entrance to the tunnel was through the tower, by means of the vertical shaft. The tower was built at a strategic point that provided an excellent view of the passage from the Jezreel to the Zebulun valleys. The construction of the tower may have been connected with the struggle between the Ptolemies and the Seleucids for the control of the country.

Phase III (Late Second–Early First Centuries BCE). The tower probably fell into disuse in phase III. On the three lower courses a raised platform was created by throwing the original building stones into the spaces between the main and inner walls. In this period the subterranean water system fell into disuse. The entrance shaft and the tunnel were filled with alluvium, and the spring cistern became an ordinary collection cistern fed by trenches draining the area around the tower.

R. Giveon, *BAIAS* (1983–1984), 45–46; B. Mazar, *HUCA* 24 (1952–1953), 75–82; A. Segal and Y. Naor, *The Eastern Frontier of the Roman Empire* (*BAR*/IS 553/2, eds. D. H. French and C. S. Lightfoot), Oxford 1989, 421–435; I. Shatzman, *The Armies of the Hasmonaeans and Herod* (Texte und Studien zum Antiken Judentum 25), Tübingen 1991, 49, 50, 86, 258–259.

ARTHUR SEGAL, YEHUDA NAOR

SHA'AR HA-GOLAN

IDENTIFICATION

Sha'ar ha-Golan is located in the central Jordan Valley, on the western bank of the Yarmuk River (map reference 207.232). The site includes remains of a Pottery Neolithic village from the second half of the sixth millennium and a village from the Middle Bronze Age I (also known as the Early Bronze Age IV or the Intermediate Bronze Age).

The site was discovered by members of Kibbutz Sha'ar ha-Golan during the digging of fish ponds in the early 1940s. M. Stekelis, of the Hebrew University of Jerusalem, was the first to publish finds from the site. Its unique material culture—its pottery, flint tools, and abundant clay and stone art objects—was named Yarmukian, or Sha'ar ha-Golan. A museum on the grounds of the kibbutz houses finds from Sha'ar ha-Golan, as well as objects collected on the surface or in the course of agricultural activity in the vicinity.

EXPLORATION

Four seasons of excavations were carried out at the site by M. Stekelis from 1949 to 1952. In the late 1970s and early 1980s, E. Eisenberg of the Israel Department of Antiquities and Museums conducted a salvage excavation in the Middle Bronze Age I village (see below). In the late 1980s, new excavations were carried out in the Neolithic village by Y. Garfinkel, on behalf of the Institute of Archaeology at the Hebrew University of Jerusalem.

THE NEOLITHIC SITE

THE 1949–1952 EXCAVATIONS. Stekelis, in his four seasons of excavations, uncovered occupation strata containing several round pits (remains of huts?), hearths, a flint-knapping workshop, a tomb, limestone and basalt bowls, and clay and stone art objects. The Neolithic strata were usually found about 1 to 1.5 m below the surface. The deposits above them consisted of layers of river pebbles, coarse sand, and black, marshy earth. Stekelis interpreted this as evidence that an overflow of the Yarmuk River had forced the inhabitants to abandon the site.

The most characteristic tool type was the sickle blade with wide, deep denticulation formed by a series of tiny notches along the edge of the blade. Sometimes both sides of the blade were denticulated. Some of the sickle blades are truncated at both ends and are rectangular; on others the two sides converge, to form a triangle. Other flint tools include polished axes, various scrapers, arrowheads, awls, and burins.

The pottery is one of the novel aspects of Sha'ar ha-Golan's material culture. Stekelis published only a few of the sherds, so the typological aspect of the assemblage is not well known. However, the most typical decoration is in the form of a herringbone pattern within a frame of parallel lines which is a combination of incision and paint.

The assemblage of art objects included various types of figurines and

Anthropomorphic figurines, Pottery Neolithic period.

incised river pebbles. Stekelis associated them with a fertility cult and interpreted the female figurines as images of the "goddess mother" or the "great goddess," who embodied the concept of fertility for humans, animals, and plants.

Stekelis dated Sha'ar ha-Golan to the "Neolithique Ancien" in M. Dunand's excavations at Byblos and with the Pottery Neolithic A in K. M. Kenyon's excavations at Jericho.

THE 1989–1990 EXCAVATIONS. The two seasons of excavations conducted by Garfinkel in 1989 and 1990 were concentrated in an area at the edge of a terrace near the floodplain of the Yarmuk River, 214 m below sea level. A trial trench was dug by mechanical means, revealing a 2-m-thick deposit of Neolithic remains; virgin soil has not yet been reached. An area of about 120 sq m was excavated in the two seasons. The excavation was divided into two squares, separated by a balk 1 m thick.

Western Square. Part of the Neolithic village was exposed in the western square. One structure, consisting of a rectangular room, was completely excavated. The lowest course of its walls, built of medium-sized field stones, was preserved. The room's inner dimensions are 1.6 by 3 m and its area is about 4.8 sq m. The structure has a beaten-earth floor, on which several flat basalt slabs were found that may have been used as anvils.

An open area abutting the room from the north served as the house's courtyard. It was surrounded by "walls" on the east, south, and west. Each wall consists of one haphazardly built course; the general impression is that they were merely rows of stones, placed here as a sign of ownership or perhaps as a support for a fence of perishable materials, rather than as the bases for stone or mud-brick walls. The courtyard floor is comprised of a thin layer of limestones and small pebbles. In four places in the courtyard sections were paved with flat basalt pebbles or large- to medium-sized limestone slabs. In the eastern part of the courtyard a rectangular basalt mortar was sunk in the floor and supported by a circle of stones.

To the west of the room and south of the courtyard, a round basalt mortar was found in an area bounded by two perpendicular walls. The mortar, which was sunk in the ground with small stones carefully placed around it, contained a rectangular basalt pebble, probably used as a pestle.

Eastern Square. The upper stratum uncovered in the eastern square was comprised of a number of thin walls and shallow pits (diameter, 1–1.5 m). The pits contained a concentration of angled stones, sherds, flint, and animal bones. They seem to have been used as refuse pits, at least in their final stage.

A lower stratum contained massive building remains, including a corner of a monumental building of a type never before found at a Neolithic site in this country. The corner is formed by two walls that meet at a 90-degree angle. Each wall is 1 m thick and reaches a maximal height of about 60 cm. The walls, which extend beyond the excavated area, have so far been traced for 8 m along the north–south axis and 6 m from east to west. A rectangular pier adjoins the inner face of one wall, probably to reinforce it. Both walls end at the same height. The stones were carefully and smoothly laid, probably as a base for mud bricks. The enclosure space formed by the walls had remains of two thinner walls, possibly used as partitions. These architectural remains show that there was an impressive amount of construction here—both relatively small dwellings and large, elaborate public buildings. This was hitherto unknown as a characteristic of sixth-millennium material culture.

ART OBJECTS. The site has a large, varied assemblage of art objects: clay, pebble, and zoomorphic figurines; pebbles incised with various geometric designs; and engraved and pierced pendants. The most remarkable of these objects are the anthropomorphic figurines, beautifully modeled in clay, with elongated heads (representing hats?); prominent noses; ears with earrings; slanting, projecting eyes, usually known as cowrie-shell eyes or coffee-bean eyes; and a cord running down the back of the neck from the head (a hairstyle?). The figures, mostly female, are usually robed and seated. Several dozen fragments of these figurines were found at Sha'ar ha-Golan. About one hundred pebble figurines, schematically depicting the same type of figure, were also recovered. The figurines represent different levels of schematization: from depicting facial features and details of dress or body; to depicting the face only, including the eyes, and sometimes the nose and mouth; to completely schematic depictions featuring only the eyes. The large quantity of art and cultic objects found here as well as at Ḥorvat Minḥa (Munḥata), about 10 km (6 mi.) to the south, makes both these sites among the richest known centers of prehistoric art in the Near East.

SUMMARY. It was once believed that the Pottery Neolithic population consisted of nomadic pastoralists who lived in temporary pit dwellings. New excavations at Sha'ar ha-Golan revealed a permanent settlement with rectangular dwellings alongside a massive public building. These excavations also provided new information about the pottery of the period. A rich assemblage was found, including a range of vessel types, both closed and open, and in a variety of sizes: from miniature vessels with a diameter of less than 5 cm to pithoi with a diameter of 70 to 80 cm. The flint assemblage matches in most respects that originally found by Stekelis, although the new excavations uncovered an obsidian bladelet for the first time. Obsidian occurs naturally in Anatolia and Armenia, and the discovery of this material at Sha'ar ha-Golan attests to trade links and the circulation of raw materials over hundreds of kilometers.

The Yarmukian culture is presently known from about ten sites: Sha'ar ha-Golan, Ḥorvat Minḥa, and Ḥamadya in the Jordan Valley; stratum XX at Megiddo in the Jezreel Valley; ha-Bashan Street in Tel Aviv; the Naḥal Qanah Cave in Samaria; and 'Ain Reḥob, 'Ain Ghazal, and Jebel Abu Tawwab in Transjordan. Several radiometric dates obtained from Ḥorvat Minḥa, 'Ain Reḥob, and Naḥal Qanah date the Yarmukian culture to the second half of the sixth millennium (5500–5000 BCE, uncalibrated). The Yarmukian culture is characteristic of the northern and central areas of Palestine and Trans-

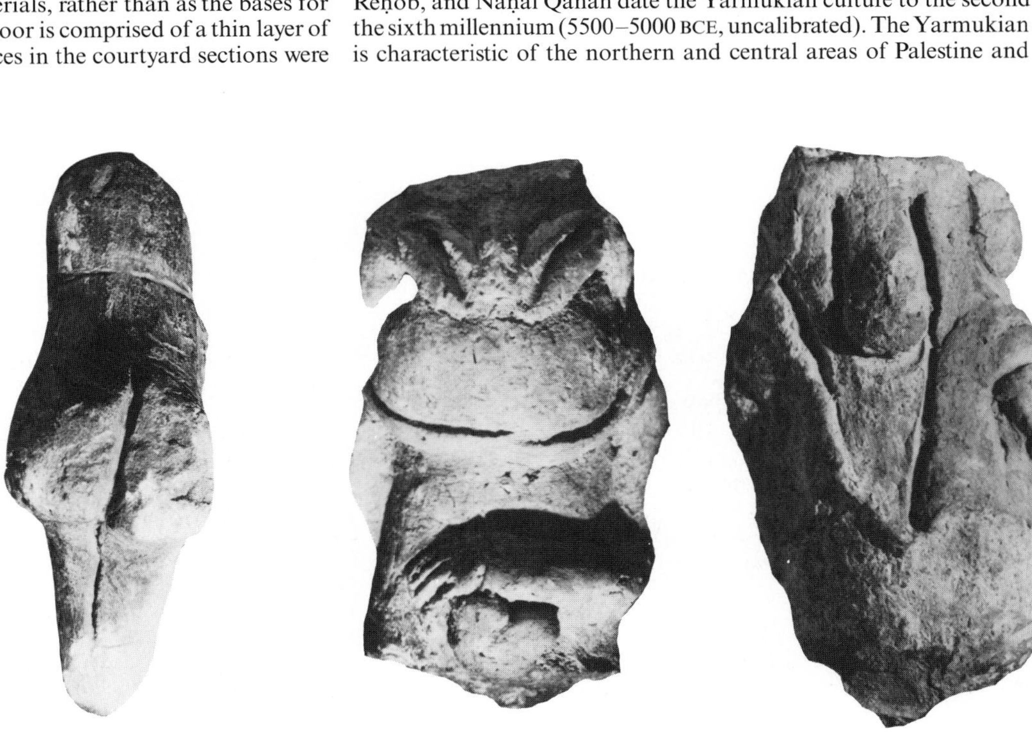

Sha'ar ha-Golan: stone and clay figurines, Pottery Neolithic period.

Sha'ar ha-Golan: schematic plan of the structures in area A, MB I.

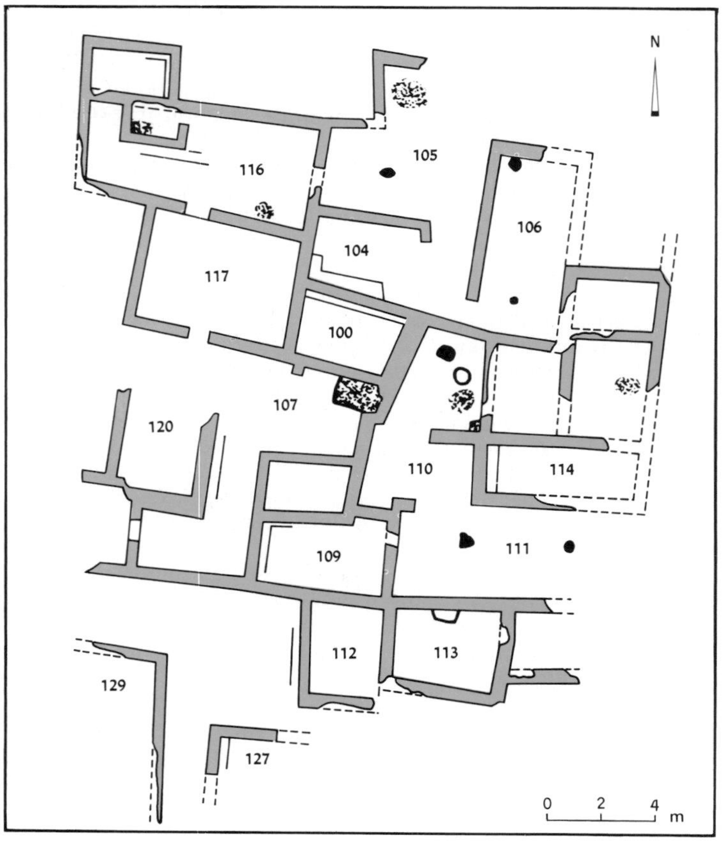

jordan. On the question of the chronological relationship of this culture to other assemblages, the excavators accept Stekelis's view: it is contemporaneous with the "Neolithique Ancien" at Byblos to the north and with the Pottery Neolithic A at Jericho to the south.

YOSEF GARFINKEL

THE MIDDLE BRONZE AGE I SITE

Remains from the Middle Bronze Age I settlement were exposed while work was being done at the bottom of the kibbutz's fish ponds. Stekelis's early excavations, Eisenberg's recent excavations, and a survey of the site confirmed that a large settlement (about 50 a.) existed here in the Middle Bronze Age I. Two areas (A and B) were excavated.

AREA A. Area A is in the southern part of the site, near the old bank of the Yarmuk River. An area of 900 sq m was cleared to a depth of 0.6 m, revealing the remains of a densely built residential quarter. The excavation revealed a central block of buildings, bounded on the north and south by streets, beyond which there were other structural remains. The house foundations (0.35–0.5 m wide) were built of large basalt and limestone boulders, brought from the Yarmuk riverbed and laid in two faces to a height of one to three courses. The foundations were clearly intended to support mud-brick walls, probably destroyed when the fish ponds were built. The bricks had dissolved in the water and Neolithic sherds, gravel, and flint tools were found mixed with finds from the Middle Bronze Age I. The rooms included architectural features, such as flat stone bases to support columns and benches along the walls. The floors, mainly of beaten earth mixed with gravel, sometimes included small surfaces paved with pebbles or stone slabs.

Building 104. Building 104 consists of three rooms and an open courtyard, partly roofed on the western side (the roof was supported by a post); the northeastern part of the building was not preserved. The house may have been entered from the north, through the courtyard. Two rooms are broadrooms and have similar dimensions. They contained numerous pottery vessels, in situ, whose sherds blocked the entrances. A door socket also was found in situ at the entrance between the courtyard and one of the rooms; the southern wall of this room was lined with a bench bearing fragments of storage jars and basalt millstones.

Building 116. Building 116 consists of two large broadrooms and a small room in the northwest. The entrance to the house was in the middle of the southern wall of one of the broadrooms. The other broadroom included a tiny room, paved with basalt stones, on which fragments of two storage jars were found. It seems that this room and the small northwestern one were used for storage. The remains of the wall foundations under the floor of one of the broadrooms indicate that the tiny room described above was a second stage in the structure's internal division.

Other dwelling units adjoin buildings 104 and 116 on the south, but their internal division is not clear. It can be assumed that these structures were enlarged until they eventually abutted buildings 104 and 116. There was an open courtyard in this area; a clay oven stood in its center and next to it a stone-

Area A: general view.

MB I structures.

slab installation affixed to the floor with pebbles. Similar installations were found in some of the rooms and structures in area B. They may have been used as work tables or shelves for vessels.

AREA B. Area B is at the northern edge of the site, about 250 m north of area A. Remains of houses built around large courtyards were uncovered in an area of 0.25 a. The building technique and finds are identical to those in area A. Three buildings surrounded the eastern courtyard.

Building 200. Building 200 was preserved to the height of the floors and foundations. Most of its contents were washed away. This was a spacious dwelling, with rectangular rooms erected around an open courtyard (215). The rooms away from the courtyard were probably added at a later stage.

Building 206. Building 206 consists of a large broadroom and two smaller rooms in the southwest. The entrance to the house was probably in the broadroom's western wall, in which a door socket was found.

Building 209. Building 209 consists of three rooms. The two southern rooms were not well preserved. One room contained a large concentration of pottery vessels lying on a stone platform. In the open area between this structure and building 206, a unique storage jar with applied rope decoration was found. The jar was sunk up to its neck in the earthen floor and may have been used as a water receptacle.

Building 225. A well-preserved broadhouse (225) was uncovered west of open courtyard 215. Its foundations were comprised of two courses and the entrance was in the middle of the southern wall. Next to it, on the south, were two tiny rooms that were built separately and probably used for storage, like the rooms in building 116 in area A.

FINDS. The finds include pottery, stone vessels, flint tools, and animal bones. The pottery is handmade; only the rims were produced with a wheel. The most common vessels include storage jars with folded ledge handles or strap loop handles with fine-combed or band-slip decoration. Globular cooking pots and high, flat bowls, some with a red slip, are also common. The ceramic assemblage from Sha'ar ha-Golan is very similar to the pottery found in shaft tombs in the Jordan Valley.

The stone vessels mainly include basalt grinding stones, basalt mortars fixed in the floor, weights, and jar stoppers made of soft limestone. Most of the flint tools are sickle blades of the Canaanite type, typical of the Early Bronze Age and indicating the practice of agriculture. Analysis of the animal bones revealed that the inhabitants raised sheep but also hunted.

SUMMARY. The recent excavations exposed residential structures dated, on the basis of their contents, to the Middle Bronze Age I. The structures in both excavation areas were only partially preserved due to their proximity to the surface; they represent an unwalled, single-layered settlement, whose economy was based on agriculture, pastoralism, and hunting.

The dwelling units were constructed on the principle of combining broadrooms, but the rooms are not uniform. The crowded character of area A stands out against the more spacious construction in area B, centered on large courtyards. The differences in the nature of the construction in the two areas may be the result of the initial settlement's having developed close to the water source and its subsequent spread northward.

On the one hand, the architecture, pottery, and lithic assemblage at this settlement are linked to the material culture of the urbanization period that preceded it. On the other, it is to be seen as a permanent rural settlement that attests to the radical changes in social structure that occurred after the destruction of the Early Bronze Age cities. This settlement type has so far been excavated at only a few sites, among them Murḥan, Naḥal Rephaim, Naḥal Alexander, and Iktanu.

EMANUEL EISENBERG

Main publication: M. Stekelis, *The Yarmukian Culture of the Neolithic Period*, Jerusalem 1972; Y. Garfinkel, *The Pottery Assemblages of the Sha'ar Hagolan and Rabah Stages of Munhata (Israel)* (Cahiers du Centre de Recherche Français de Jérusalem 6), Paris (in prep.).

Other studies: M. Stekelis, *IEJ* 1 (1950), 1–19; 2 (1952), 216–217; 3 (1953), 132; T. Noy, *Israel Museum News* 3/3 (1968), 22–27; E. E. Wreschner, *Bulletin de la Société Royale Belge d'Anthropologie et de Préhistoire* 87 (1976), 157–165; E. Yeivin and I. Mozel, *TA* 4 (1977), 194–200; Y. Garfinkel, *ESI* 9 (1989–1990, 110–111; R. Maoz, *MdB* 62 (1990), 62–63.

Sha'ar ha-Golan: pottery assemblage, MB I.

SHARON PLAIN

(PREHISTORY)

IDENTIFICATION

The Sharon Plain, bounded by the Yarkon River on the south and by the Carmel Range on the north, has not yet been systematically surveyed; information about its prehistoric sites comes from local surveys and various archaeological excavations. Both the western and eastern parts of the Sharon—the former distinguished from the latter by *kurkar* ridges—are composed of alternating sand or sandstone strata and *ḥamra* soils, in which the prehistoric remains were found. These sediments were mostly transported from the coast and, as far as is presently known, were deposited in the Lower and Middle Pleistocene (c. the last million years).

LOWER PALEOLITHIC PERIOD (ACHEULEAN CULTURE)

The hand axes characteristic of the Acheulean culture found in the Sharon are mostly well made, elongated in shape, and on average 90 mm long. These characteristics suggest a late stage of the Acheulean, although the exact dates of the sites are as yet unknown. It is estimated that the Acheulean sites in the Sharon date to between 300,000 and 150,000 years BP. These sites have only been discovered on the surface, in the eastern part of the Sharon, between the eastern *kurkar* ridge and the foot of the mountains. The strata in the western Sharon were deposited at a later period, and thus covered any Acheulean sites that may have existed here. This notion is supported by evidence from Kibbutz Ma'barot, on the eastern *kurkar* ridge, where an Acheulean assemblage was overlaid by the ridge's upper *kurkar* stratum. The most significant of the Sharon sites, in addition to Ma'barot, are Binyamina, Kefar Glickson, Giv'at Ḥayyim, ha-Ma'pil, Ḥerut, Ramat ha-Kovesh, and Eyal, all of which seem to have been situated near springs, swamps, or ponds.

MIDDLE PALEOLITHIC PERIOD (MOUSTERIAN CULTURE)

The manufacture of hand axes had ceased by the beginning of the Mousterian culture (140,000–40,000 BP); its lithic assemblage consists of flake tools and is

Sharon Plain: hand ax, Lower Paleolithic period.

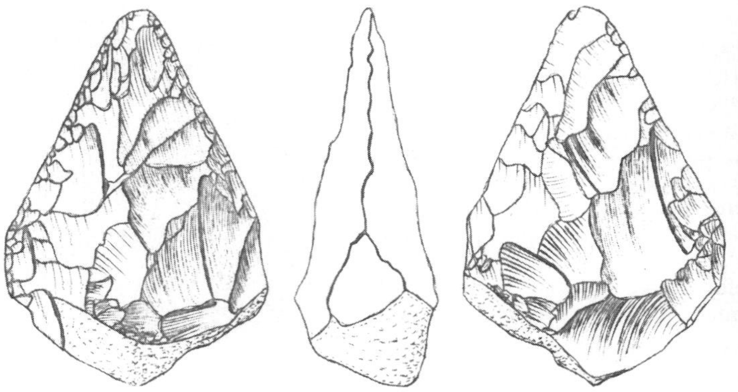

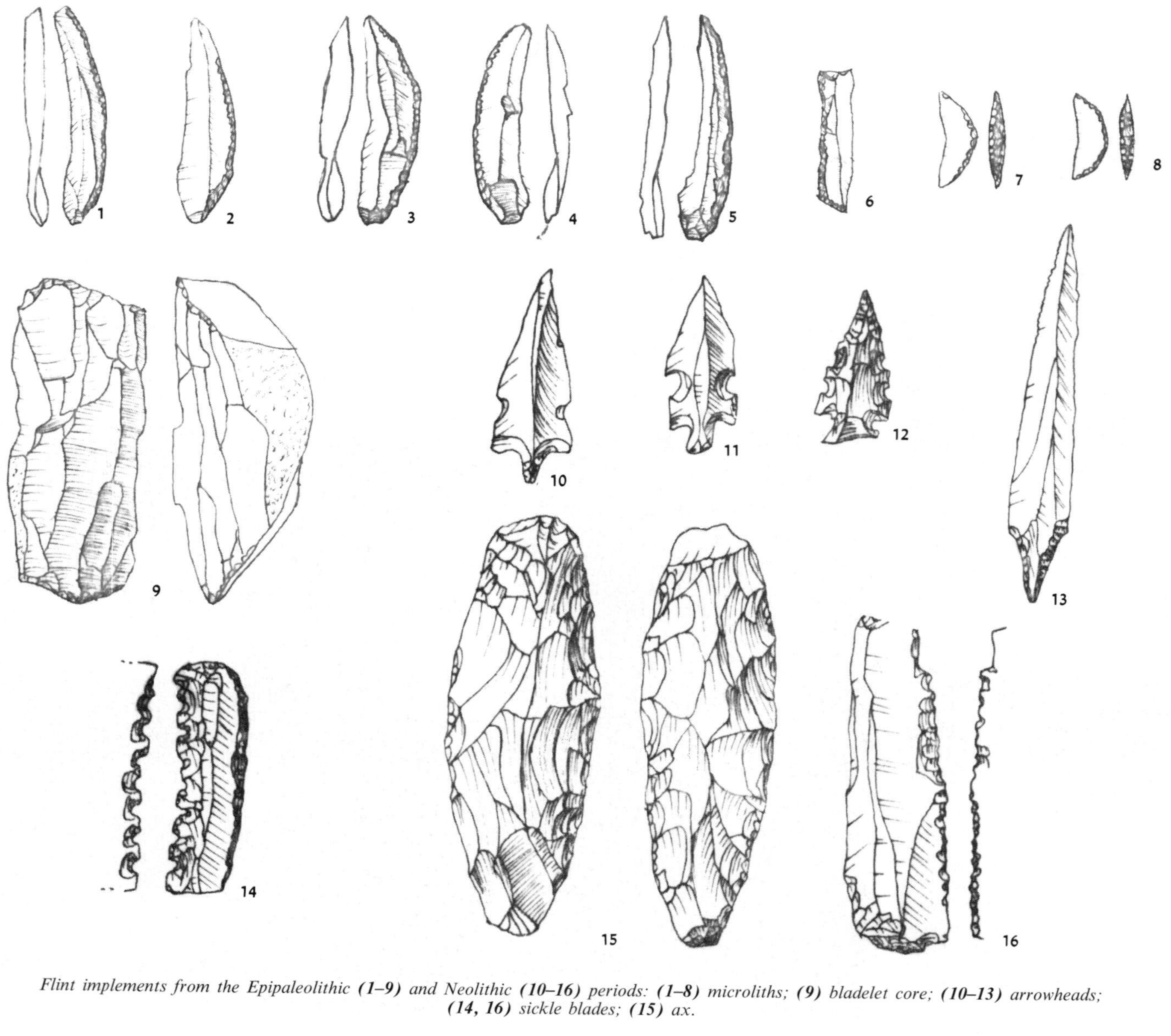

Flint implements from the Epipaleolithic (1–9) and Neolithic (10–16) periods: (1–8) microliths; (9) bladelet core; (10–13) arrowheads; (14, 16) sickle blades; (15) ax.

characterized by side scrapers and Levallois tools. No Mousterian sites have hitherto been found in the eastern Sharon; in the western part, the *ḥamra* layer containing Mousterian sites was overlaid by later strata. Only a single Mousterian site has been discovered, in a quarry, near Kibbutz Yaqum.

UPPER PALEOLITHIC PERIOD

No sites from the Upper Paleolithic (40,000–20,000 BP) are known in the Sharon. According to one hypothesis, several sites assigned to the later Epipaleolithic period may actually date to the Upper Paleolithic.

EPIPALEOLITHIC PERIOD (KEBARAN AND NATUFIAN CULTURES)

The Epipaleolithic period (20,000–10,000 BP) constitutes the final stage of the hunting-gathering economy that characterized humankind from its earliest existence. This stage marks the earliest appearance of domestication, agriculture, and permanent settlements. The earliest of the Epipaleolithic cultures is the Kebaran, to which the earliest mortars so far recovered are attributed. This culture, dated to between 20,000 and 15,000 years BP, is characterized by very small flint tools (microliths). Its later stage, characterized by an increasing number of geometrically shaped microliths (rectangles and triangles) is accordingly named the Geometric Kebaran (15,000–12,000 BP). The Kebaran sites discovered in the Sharon are hunter camps, some of them covering large areas (such as Ḥefẓi Bah—c. 2000 sq m). In the eastern Sharon, the Kebaran sites include Binyamina, Ḥerut, Ẓofit, Kefar Sava, and Ra'ananna; in the western Sharon they include the Ḥadera dunes, Ḥefẓi Bah, Kefar Vitkin, Poleg, Qiryat Arieh, and Gath-Rimmon. The principal game hunted at these sites was gazelle, deer, cattle, and various other species. There is no information regarding plant foods, as no floral remains are preserved.

The Natufian culture that followed the Kebaran is characterized by lunate microliths. It marks the appearance of the earliest permanent settlements, although only a single ephemeral site from this period has been discovered in the Sharon, near Naḥal Poleg.

NEOLITHIC PERIOD

The domestication of several animal species was completed in the Neolithic period, and goat and sheep became the principal sources of food. The cultivation of several species of cereals and various other food plants further developed, too. Nevertheless, hunting and gathering still persisted and fishing was also of significance. The development of agriculture brought about the expansion of permanent settlements.

Arrowheads, sickle blades, and various types of axes are the tools most characteristic of the Neolithic period. The domination of the assemblages from the western Sharon sites (Mikhmoret, Poleg, and Herzliya) by the two former tool types suggests a focus on hunting and gathering there, while in the then-forested eastern Sharon, forest clearing necessitated large numbers of axes.

Prehistory: D. Gilead, *Mitekufat Ha'even* 12 (1974), 32–35.
Ḥadera: A. Ronen and D. Kaufman, *TA* 3 (1976), 16–30; E. C. Saxon et al., *Paléorient* 4 (1978), 253–264.
Ḥefẓi Bah: R. Gophna and E. Yeivin, *IEJ* 19 (1969), 235–236; D. Haker, *Mitekufat Ha'even* 12 (1974), 2–7; A. Ronen et al., *Quartär* 26 (1975), 53–72.
Kefar Vitkin: M. Stekelis, *L'Anthropologie* 72 (1968), 325–336.
Ma'barot: E. Braun, *PEQ* 121 (1989), 1–43; S. Dar, *BAIAS* 9 (1989–1990), 46–52.
Poleg: I. Mozel, *TA* 5 (1978), 152–158.

AVRAHAM RONEN

SHECHEM

TELL BALÂTAH

IDENTIFICATION

Ancient Shechem, located at the hub of a major crossroad in the hill country of Ephraim, 67 km (40 mi.) north of Jerusalem (map reference 177.179) was an important cultic and political center. Biblical and classical references to the site converge to place it between Mount Ebal and Mount Gerizim in the central hill country. Vespasian's foundation of Neapolis, or "new city," in 72 CE, at the western opening to the same pass yielded the Arabic name Nablus, and many have sought the ruins of ancient Shechem there. However, what covers ancient Shechem is the village and mound named Balâtah, at the eastern end of that pass. The slightly elevated 15-a. mound of Balâtah is sited on the lowest flanks of Mount Ebal. It rises some 20 m above the 500 m contour passing through the village at the lowest point of the val-

Aerial view of Shechem (modern Nablus) between Mount Gerizim and Mount Ebal, looking west.

Tell Balâtah, with Mount Gerizim in the background.

ley. Abundant water comes from springs emerging all along the north and east flanks of Mount Gerizim. It looks out upon a fertile plain to the east and south—one of the most pleasant in the central hills and one that constitutes a natural system of ancient settlement. The modern village runs up onto the southern one-third of the ancient mound, but the open two-thirds remains accessible for research.

The road system from Jerusalem on the spine of the hill country divides at Balâtah to circumvent Mount Ebal. Its western arm gives access to the Coastal Plain and north to Samaria/Sebaste and Dothan. The eastern arm gives access to the Jordan River via Wadi Far'ah and north past Tell el-Far'ah (North) to Dothan.

H. Thiersch is credited with finding Tell Balâtah. In 1903, he observed a stretch of exposed fortification wall at the west of the mound and a heavy scattering of sherds. He put that together with the location of the *weli* called Qubr Yusef (Joseph's Tomb) at the eastern edge of the modern village, to confirm the identification. Not much farther east is the traditional location of Jacob's Well, connected with the story in John 4:1–42. Looming over the site is Tell er-Râs, on a forward salient of Mount Gerizim (q.v.), which contains the ruins of a temple dedicated to Zeus Olympus. The Hellenistic remains that constitute the uppermost strata at Tell Balâtah indicate the location of Shechem in Hellenistic times. It remains an open question how the name Sychar in John 4 fits with all of this, especially because there is a modern village called 'Askar on a Hellenistic and Roman ruin just to the north of Balâtah on Mount Ebal. Excavation has established, in any case, that Neapolis (= Nablus) flourished in Roman times (see below), whereas pre-Roman Shechem was at Tell Balâtah.

HISTORY

Prior to excavation, Shechem was known from texts that seem clear enough but require interpretation. Egyptian references in the later set of Execration texts and the Khu-Sebek inscription, both from the nineteenth century BCE, seem to designate both a city and a territory—in short, a city-state—in the Middle Bronze Age IIA. A number of the mid-fourteenth-century BCE Amarna letters point to a city-state center at Shechem ruled by Lab'ayu—a center that had an impact on Megiddo, Jerusalem, Gezer, the Hebron region, and Pella across the river, via the passes to the Jordan Valley. Biblical passages mentioning Shechem relate Abraham (Gen. 12:6), Jacob (Gen. 33:18–20, 35:1–4), Jacob's whole family (Gen. 34), and Joseph (Gen. 37:12–17) to the old city, but these stories are filled with curious ingredients and leave open many questions about the city. The same is true of

Tell Balâtah: map of the mound, excavation areas, and plan of the principal remains.

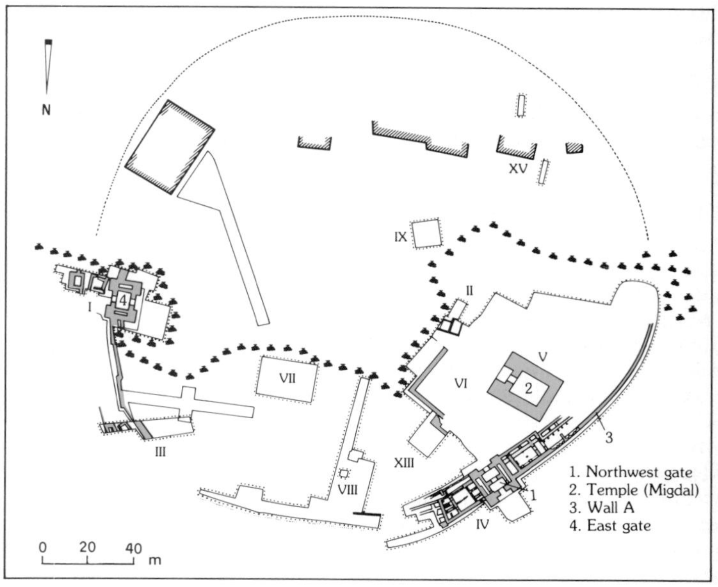

the reference in Genesis 48:22 to "one Shechem" which Israel (= Jacob) is said to have taken by force from the Amorites. Then there are references to the city or its setting in Deuteronomy 27 and in the Deuteronomistic histories in Joshua 8:30–35, Judges 9, Joshua 24:32, Joshua 24:1, and 1 Kings 12. Taken together, these passages make at least some things clear: that in Israelite lore Shechem was a prominent sanctuary center related to Israel's heritage through the patriarchs and hence was a place to return to; that covenant making and renewing were powerful ingredients in the religious significance of Shechem; that Canaanites and Israelites encountered one another here, but the encounter does not seem to have resulted in military conflict—at least at the time of the Joshua "conquest" (cf. Gen. 34); and that Shechem was so prominent that it was the place to go to establish one's right to rule the region (Abimelech in Jg. 9; Rehoboam and Jeroboam in 1 Kg. 12). It is thought to have been the capital of Solomon's first district (1 Kg 4:8) and is named as the city Jeroboam built and occupied (1 Kg. 12:25), the first capital of the Northern Kingdom. Reminiscences of its prominence are found in Hosea 6:9 and Jeremiah 41:5. It was a city of refuge (Jos. 20:7) and as such part of the Levitic allotment (Jos. 21:21), and it is a key marking point on the boundary between

Tell Balâtah: aerial view, looking south.

Ephraim and Manasseh (Jos. 17:7). Mentioned as one of the districts that provisioned Samaria in the Samaria ostraca, presumably from the first half of the eighth century BCE, it appears in a cluster of names in Joshua 17:2 that closely approximate the roster on the ostraca and define Manasseh's allotment. Evidence that Shechem returned to prominence in the Hellenistic period comes from Ecclesiasticus 50:26 and from a critical assessment of Josephus' various references to the city and to Mount Gerizim, most notably in *Antiquities* (XI, 340 ff.), where it is said to be the chief Samaritan city.

EXPLORATION

Because the texts mentioning Shechem speak of the environs as well as the city, there has been an impulse to explore the region around Shechem, as well as the city ruin itself. G. Welter excavated a Middle Bronze Age II structure on the slopes of Gerizim above Balâtah at Tanânîr (1931) and the Church of Mary Mother of God (Theotokos) on the summit of Mount Gerizim (1928). The American Joint Expedition (see below) studied the rock-cut tombs in Shechem's cemetery on the flanks of Mount Ebal, and modern road expansion has revealed others, one of them the cave tomb T-3 excavated by C. Clamer. The number of tombs identified is now about seventy. R. Boling of the American expedition reexcavated Tanânîr in 1968, and R. Bull excavated Tell er-Râs from 1964 to 1968. In 1964, the American Joint Expedition began a more systematic regional survey, intended to examine the Shechem basin as a system. Fifty-four sites were explored in this effort, and 29 more were explored by German and Israeli teams, notably by the Deutsche Evangelische Institut, prior to 1967; by the Israel Survey in 1967–1968; and by I. Finkelstein and A. Zertal since. In addition, a series of chance discoveries in Nablus have been salvaged archaeologically in the past fifteen years, filling out the archaeological history of the pass in Roman times. I. Magen is at work on the major Hellenistic settlement on Mount Gerizim, which spreads south and west from the summit, and various sites in Roman Neapolis (see below), and Zertal has excavated a probable Iron Age sanctuary and altar at el-Burnat on Mount Ebal (q.v.). The result has been to understand Shechem as a regional center, recognizing how the various points of access to the basin were guarded, how secure the population must have been to spread out into villages around the valley's flanks—where military posts and secondary market towns may be located—and what relationship Shechem may have had to such cities as Tappuah, Tirzah, Tubas, and Samaria.

EXCAVATIONS

THE AUSTRO-GERMAN EXPEDITION. E. Sellin began a systematic excavation at Tell Balâtah in the fall of 1913. He returned in the spring of 1914. He focused first on the outcrop of fortification wall that Thiersch had noticed ten years earlier, tracing it northward to the northwest gate and south to where it gave out. He then found a second circumvallation inside the first and traced it to the gate. Sellin used long, 5-m-wide trenches from the mound's edge toward its center, to test the overall stratigraphy. He discerned four major periods in the site's history in the stratified buildings his narrow trenches revealed. He first dated them as Hellenistic, Late Israelite, Early Israelite, and Canaanite. In fact, they turned out to be Hellenistic, Israelite, Middle Bronze, and earlier—the earliest phase being equivalent to what he had found at Jericho, the Early Bronze and Chalcolithic periods.

Sellin returned in 1926 and 1927 for four campaigns. He used his long, narrow trenches to explore the city's interior in the southeast and from the eastern perimeter inward. The former area, trench K, followed up on a remarkable chance discovery made by Balâtah villagers in 1908: bronze weaponry, including a sickle sword. From this trench also came two cuneiform tablets, one a witness list and the other a text W. F. Albright deciphered as a teacher's appeal for remuneration. The other trench, designated L, revealed fortifications on the east side of the city, which were traced to the east gate. Sellin had by now seen that the fortification system was in several phases and would be a complex puzzle to work out.

Much of the rest of Sellin's work was concentrated on the west of the mound, in what would prove to be the acropolis. Just inside the arc of the city wall, he discerned what he called the palace, extending on either side of the northwest gate, and the massive structure of the Migdal Temple and its forecourt, altars, and pillar sockets, enclosed within what he termed the temenos wall (wall 900). Work within the elbow of the temenos wall brought the Germans to the uppermost of a series of courtyard complexes; some soil in the interiors of rooms was scooped out, but work was carried no deeper. Welter was appointed to replace Sellin as director, but only produced some plans, although excellent ones, and explored Mount Gerizim, as noted above. The expedition failed to record find spots carefully, to report stratigraphy in any detail, and to bring the account of the work to a synthetic presentation. Sellin regained the directorship and mounted a final season in 1934. He worked on his final report until 1943. His records and his manuscript, along with many artifacts, were destroyed in Berlin during World War II.

THE AMERICAN EXPEDITION. The Joint Expedition to Shechem began in 1956 as the cooperative effort of Drew University in Madison, New Jersey and McCormick Theological Seminary, in Chicago, under the direction of G. E. Wright and B. W. Anderson. Conceived as a teaching excavation for young American, Canadian, and European scholars, it took into the field teams of as many as thirty researchers, a well-conceived recording system, and a plan to combine the soil deposition technique being perfected by K. M. Kenyon at Jericho with comparative ceramic knowledge based on W. F. Albright's work. A major aim was to recover as much as possible from the materials unearthed by Sellin and Welter and to tie the mound's story together. Methods became more and more sophisticated as the expedition continued and many more institutions became partners. The excavation at Shechem was the first to introduce cross-disciplinary research, including an association with geologist R. Bullard. The expedition, chiefly through its director, G. E. Wright, kept to the task of relating textual evidence to archaeological finds. The expedition entered the field with a reconnaissance season in 1956, and worked in 1957, 1960, 1962, 1964, 1966, and 1968. In the fall of 1968, Boling reexcavated Tanânîr, and in 1969 J. D. Seger tied the acropolis stratigraphy to an area of fine houses just to the north of the acropolis (field XIII). Salvage and clean-up work in 1972 and 1973 were carried out by W. G. Dever, who made several important discoveries in Sellin's "palace" precinct. Work reached bedrock in two locations and identified a total of twenty-four distinct strata, from the Chalcolithic to the Late Hellenistic period. Four major periods of abandonment were interspersed, as shown in the following chart.

Period	*Stratum*	*Dates (BCE)*	*Features*
Hellenistic	I	150–128/107	Eroded; attested by sherds, coins
Hellenistic	II	190–150/128	Refortification on MB II lines; housing, fields I, II, VII, IX
Hellenistic	IIIA–B	250–190	
Hellenistic	IVA–B	331–250	
(ABANDONMENT, c. 475–331)			
Persian	V	600–475	Meager structures, Attic pottery
Iron II	VIA–B	724–600	Residential remains throughout, fortification on MB II lines; rebuilding of wall E, beginning in stratum IX; granary in field V
Iron II	VII	750–724	
Iron II	VIII	810–750	
Iron II	IXA–B	920–810	
Iron II	XA–B	975–920	Recovery; Shishak destruction
(ABANDONMENT, c. 1150/1125–975)			
Iron IA	XI	1200–1150/1125	Reused MB II fortification; new east gate tower; poor housing develops to good; temples 2A and 2B; LB IIA ends in destruction
LB IIB	XII	1350–1200	
LB IIA	XIII	1400–1350	
LB IB	XIV	1450–1400	
(ABANDONMENT, c. 1540–1450)			
MB IIC	XV	1600–1540	Wall B, east gate, temple 1B
MB IIC	XVI	1650–1600	Wall A, northwest gate, temple 1A
MB IIB	XVII	1675–1650	Wall C, earth embankment; courtyard complexes 909–910, 901, 902 in field VI
MB IIB	XVIII	1700–1675	
MB IIB	XIX	1725–1700	
MB IIB	XX	1750–1725	Wall D, courtyard complex 939
MB IIA	XXI	1800–1750	Housing, fields VI and IX
MB IIA	XXII	1900–1800	Platforms 968, 977(?); field VI
(ABANDONMENT, c. 3300–1900)			
EB I	XXIII	3500–3300(?)	Base fields V–VI, sherds in fills
Chalcolithic	XXIV	4000–3500(?)	Base field IX

THE EARLY PERIODS. Probes deep beneath the acropolis buildings, directly under the Migdal Temple and close to the temenos wall, yielded evidence of occupation in the late fourth millennium BCE, the beginning of the Early Bronze Age I. Pottery from this period turns up frequently in fills at Shechem, but there is very little architecture in the small exposures beneath the acropolis. This pottery also occurs in a few places visited by the Regional Survey.

An earlier phase, belonging to the Chalcolithic period, in the first half of the fourth millennium BCE, appeared just above bedrock in field IX, well inside the city and south of the acropolis area. Pebbled surfaces with what may be curved tent floors characterize the settlement. At no place on the mound are Chalcolithic and Early Bronze Age I (strata XXIV and XXIII) stratigraphically superimposed.

There is no stratigraphic evidence of the "Urban" period of the Early Bronze Age at Shechem, and no pottery from the Early Bronze Age II–III. At Khirbet Makhneh el-Fauqa, 4 km (2.5 mi.) south of Balâtah on the southeasternmost flank of Mount Gerizim, however, this pottery abounds; the region's Early Bronze Age town must have been there. Shechem has Middle Bronze Age I sherds in fills, but no occupation layers were found in the several excavation plots that were probed that deep.

MIDDLE BRONZE AGE IIA (STRATA XXII–XXI). The next clear strata belong to the Middle Bronze Age IIA, and the pottery suggests that the site was resettled at a point well into the Middle Bronze Age IIA, in around 1900 BCE. Under the acropolis, this period is represented by two rectangular,

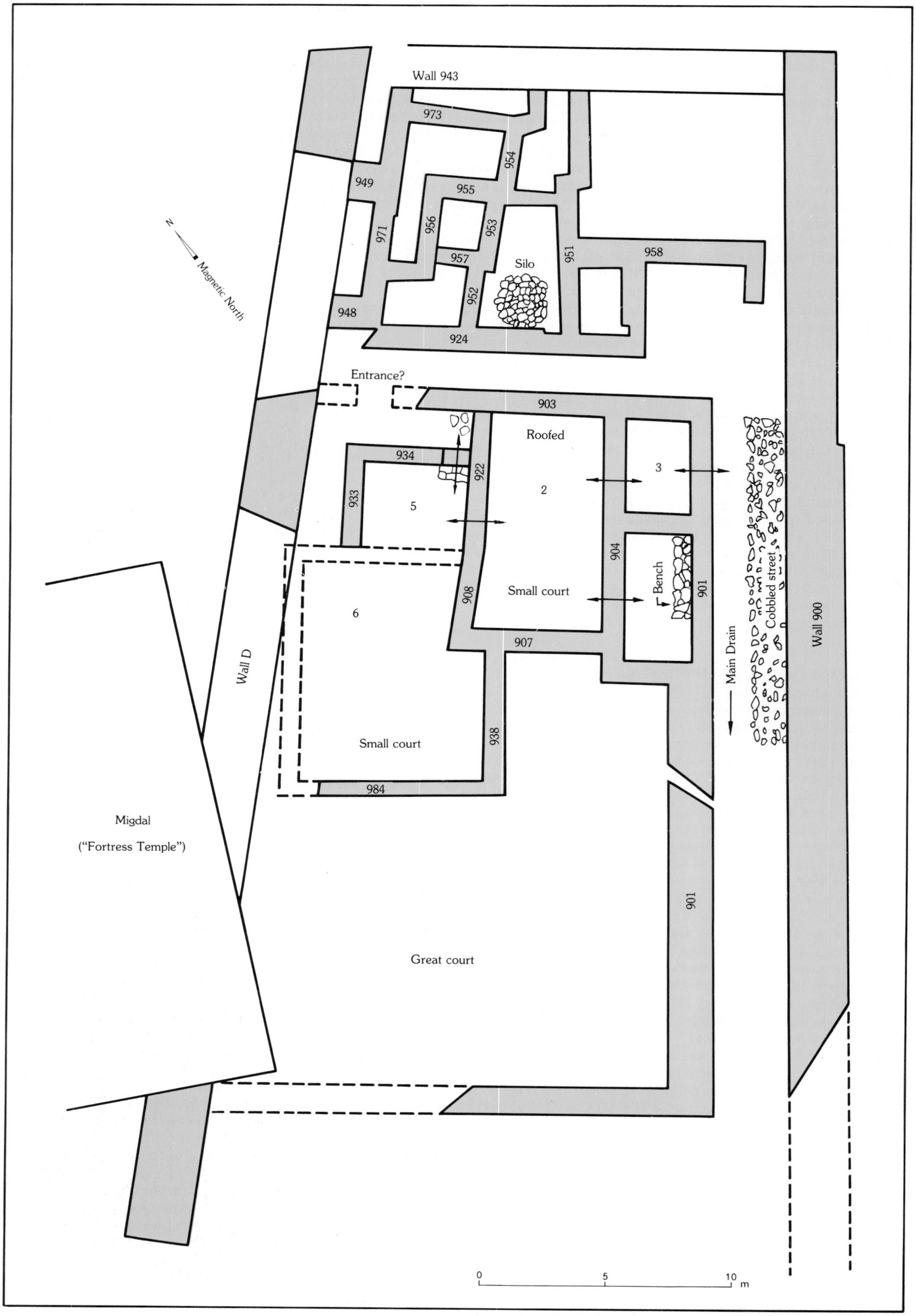

Plan of the MB II courtyard complex in its fourth phase, after Wright.

Dagger, fenestrated ax, and sickle sword, MB IIA.

stone-lined platforms. In a subsequent phase of the Middle Bronze Age IIA, the platforms were built over with typical housewalls, and there are domestic installations outside their line to the west. Thus, the Middle Bronze Age IIA settlement seems to have been unfortified. Domestic layers from this period were also found in field IX, directly above the Chalcolithic. These people built houses on the natural slopes, arranged for drainage, but built no protecting walls.

MIDDLE BRONZE AGE IIB (STRATA XX–XVII). Beginning with stratum XX, the western precinct becomes an acropolis, with the temenos wall (wall 900) separating it from the rest of the city. Its western edge was defined by the earliest known fortification system: first by wall D, a freestanding vertical brick-on-stone construction; then by a huge earthen embankment using wall D as its inner retainer and wall C as its exterior one, making a 37-

(Left) *plan of the* migdal *in phase 1A;* ***(right)*** *phase 1B.*

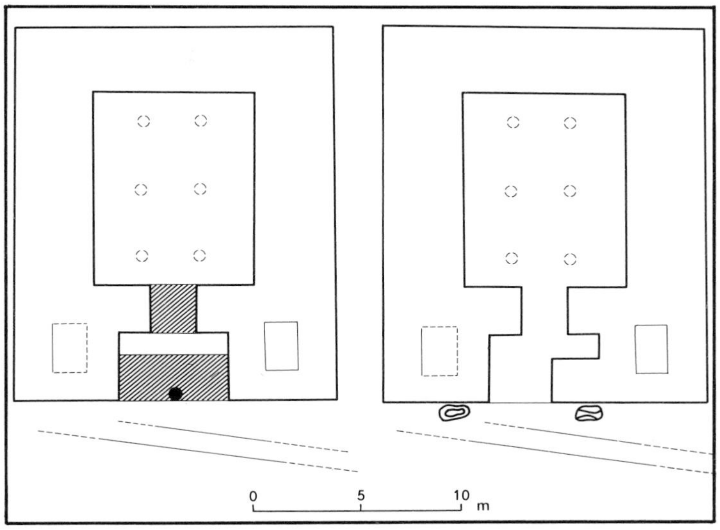

m-thick complex. By an extension of this earthen embankment westward, to the footing of what would later be wall A, a width of 45 m was reached. This development of the fortification system took place during what the excavators designate Middle Bronze Age IIB (c. 1750 to 1650 BCE). Between the fortification walls and wall 900, a succession of four constructions took place, constituting the courtyard complexes that Wright proposed were courtyard temples. While that interpretation has been seriously questioned and is no longer defended in full by the expedition staff, it is likely that a sanctuary room of some sort was part of the complex, along with other buildings. These four phases of development in the acropolis define strata XX–XVII. Field IX, within the city, shows two strata of domestic houses to accompany these four acropolis phases. Middle Bronze Age IIB remains were encountered all around the perimeter of the mound—at the east gate, beneath the northwest gate, in field III at the eastern edge of the mound, and in field XIII north of the acropolis—in the form of the great earthen fortification embankment. Domestic housing from the Middle Bronze Age IIB is attested to in three distinct layers in field IX and in its last stratum by a fine house in field XIII, just inside the earthen embankment.

MIDDLE BRONZE AGE IIC (STRATA XVI–XV). A major change took place in about 1650 BCE; excavation of the site reached this period at virtually every location of digging. The wall A system, consisting of the great battered "Cyclopean wall" Thiersch first saw on the west, now became the fortification, retaining a filled platform out to its top and thus expanding the city's dimensions to their widest. The northwest gate was built. The platform, lying over the courtyard complex on the acropolis, provided the setting for the great fortress temple, or *migdal*. The *migdal* foundation (26.3 by 21 m), with masonry walls 5.1 m thick, held a brick superstructure. In its first phase (1A, stratum XVI), the building had a central-axis access: the entrance was between two towers flanking a front entrance hall (7 m wide and 5 m deep) that led to the cella (13.5 by 11 m), which had interior columns. An altar was located in the forecourt, which was approached by a sloping ramp anchored on the top of the temenos wall, wall 900. The second phase of the *migdal* (1b, stratum XV) had a bent-axis access that passed between two flanking

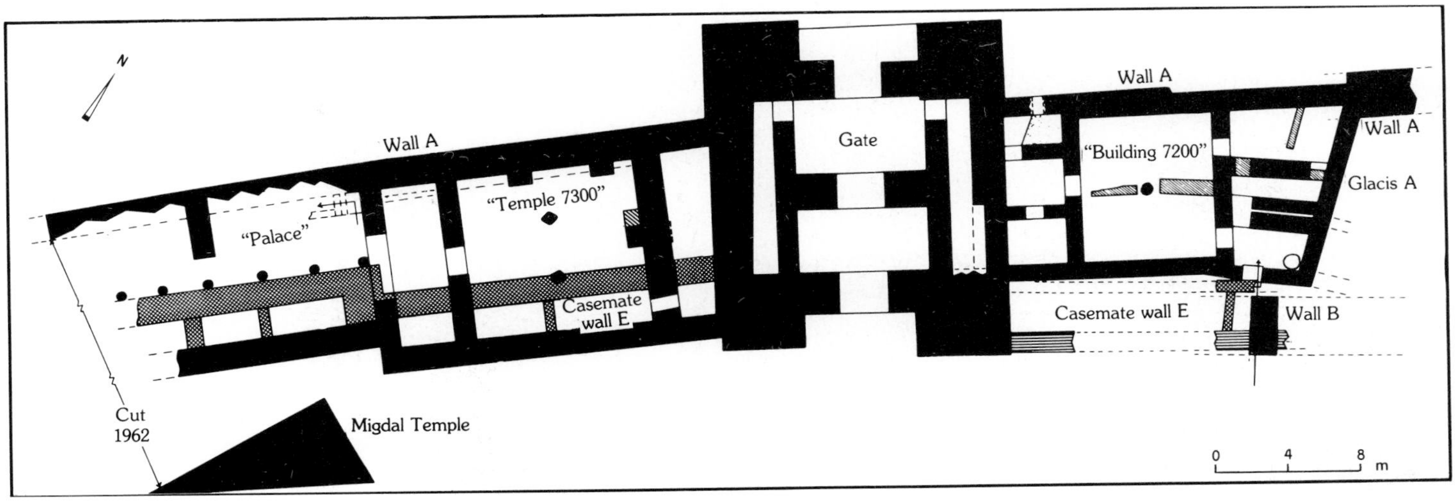

Plan of the northwest gate area.

Sellin's "palace" (foreground) with temple 7300 and the northwest gate, MB IIC.

East gate and steps leading down to the city.

maṣṣebot or stelae; the floor for this phase is 75 cm above that of the first phase. The shift from the first to the second phase of the *migdal* fits with developments in the fortification system, involving the construction of an inner circumvallation, wall B, and the east gate. Strata XVI and XV date to 1650 to 1540 BCE, which the excavators designated the Middle Bronze Age IIC.

Between the *migdal* and fortification wall A lay what Sellin thought was the city palace. In 1973, Dever detected that still another fortification wall, wall E, which overlay the Middle Bronze Age IIC complexes south of the northwest gate, had been built at the very end of the Middle Bronze Age IIC, probably as a desperate defensive effort against attacks accompanying the expulsion of the Hyksos by the Eighteenth Egyptian Dynasty (c. 1540 BCE). It is now clear that the southern wing of Sellin's "palace" was a three-element structure with interior columns and an altar against the interior wall of the central room—a "chapel" sanctuary (7300) contemporary with the *migdal*. Dever also sorted out the architecture in Sellin's northern wing of the "palace" into a system of residences that could have served as guardrooms. Another contemporary sanctuary may be the structure at Tanânîr, first cleared by Welter and reexcavated by Boling in 1969. Its similarity in design to the 'Amman airport temple has been noted, but its function remains debatable; the Tanânîr structure may simply be a domestic estate.

It was during strata XVI and XV that the area north of the acropolis, separated from it by wall 943 (first built in the Middle Bronze Age IIC), was developed as a neighborhood of fine houses. The town's government buildings probably were here. Excavation beneath where Sellin's 1934 (last) campaign had cleared to Iron Age levels, in field XIII, disentangled several phases of two homes, one elegant enough to be proposed as the government residence and the other as a fine patrician house. The finds—including pieces of ivory inlay, several scarabs, a fine dagger blade, and polished goat astragali—point to comparative wealth and status. Fields VII and IX also show Middle Bronze Age IIC houses, as does the platform out to wall A to the east of the city, under the east gate. Everywhere, evidence of destruction, probably in two quickly successive phases, covers the uppermost (stratum XV) Middle

Migdal: *general view, looking southeast. The* maṣṣeba *is in front of the temple. The narrow walls of the LB temple sit on the broad walls of the MB IIC temple.*

The migdal*: the* maṣṣeba *(re-erected).*

Bronze figurine of a Canaanite god, LB IIA.

Bronze phase. Thus ended a two-hundred-year period of prominence as a city-state, covering the centuries from 1750 to 1540 BCE.

LATE BRONZE AGE AND IRON AGE I (STRATA XIV–XI). A gap in occupation of about a century is attested everywhere on the Shechem mound. Cave tomb T-3 on the slopes of Mount Ebal contributed pottery from this gap—the Late Bronze Age IA—and makes it all the more obvious that the mound itself lacks that distinctive pottery. Recovery came in about 1450 BCE. The northwest and east gates were both rebuilt, the latter with a new guard tower inside the position of the Middle Bronze Age IIC towers. The *migdal* was rebuilt, with a broadroom cella in use in two phases (2A–B), and an altar and a huge *maṣṣeba* were placed in the forecourt. A building with what may be an altar and what is certainly a *maṣṣeba* was in use inside the town, in field IX; it remained in use throughout the Late Bronze Age IB–II periods. It was rebuilt in the Iron Age I, but the altar and *maṣṣeba* were buried and covered with a new plaster floor, suggesting its nullification as a shrine.

The houses in field XIII characterize this period in the city's life. Recovery from the Egyptian destruction began with leveling operations and the construction of a brick kiln. The laying out of the first houses in a coherent plan followed. These initiatives represent the Late Bronze Age IB (late fifteenth century BCE). Stratum XIII reflects the zenith of this development: the Amarna Age (fourteenth century BCE). Parts of at least two fine houses fill field XIII, while the corner of an even more impressive structure, conceivably the governor's residence, juts slightly into the field. To stratum XIII belongs a rich and varied collection of complete pottery vessels that had been thrown into an underground chamber and will form the basis of the Late Bronze Age typology for Shechem being prepared by L. E. Toombs and R. S. Boraas; the vast majority of the objects from cave tomb T-3; the above-mentioned shrine in Field IX; a fine bronze figurine of a male deity found in Field VII; the two cuneiform tablets found in 1926 in trench K, along with the small corner of another found in field XIII in 1968; and the buttressed corner of a massive building in field III, at the eastern perimeter of the mound. These finds are evidence of the strength and independence implicit in the Amarna letter portrayal of the ruler Lab'ayu (see above).

A major destruction brought stratum XIII to an end, in about 1350 to 1300 BCE; recovery on simpler lines and suggesting less prosperity followed in stratum XII, which belongs roughly to the thirteenth century BCE. Stratum XII gave way to stratum XI without evidence of destruction, but with the distinct indication of an intervening blanket of fill. Stratum XI then suffered massive destruction in about 1100 BCE; the artifacts representing the end of this stratum are clearly Iron Age I. That is, two significant destructions of Shechem took place—in the fourteenth century and around 1100 BCE—neither of which fits the standard chronological expectations of the time of the Israelite entry into the land, usually fixed in the late thirteenth century. Connecting stratum XI with the story underlying Judges 9 is plausible; the scene underlying Joshua 24 fits conditions on the acropolis in strata XII and XI.

THE MONARCHIC PERIOD (STRATA X–VII). The site lay virtually unpopulated during the eleventh century, and indications from the regional survey are that the whole Shechem basin was sparsely occupied. Residential areas in fields VII and IX reveal the gap and then show recovery in the form of walled working spaces and simple huts. The number of huts in the given space increased as stratum X developed; walls are fairly wide but not well constructed. A destruction ended stratum X, dated by the pottery to the last quarter of the tenth century BCE—presumably in connection with Shishak's raid in about 918 BCE. What he destroyed seems to have been only a modest, unwalled town, representing continuity with the traditional old covenantal site. The stratum IX town, however, may have recovered the line of the last-effort fortification wall, E, from the Middle Bronze Age IIC and rebuilt a circumvallation on it. In stratum IX, the house walls are narrower, but carefully built of selected stones, and foundations for stairs suggest two-story houses. The layout now shows a planned use of space. Stratum IX represents

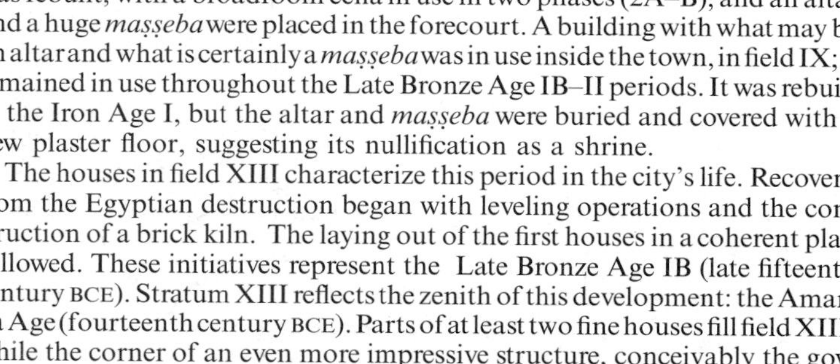

Cylinder seal and impression in the Middle Assyrian style, c. 1200 BCE.

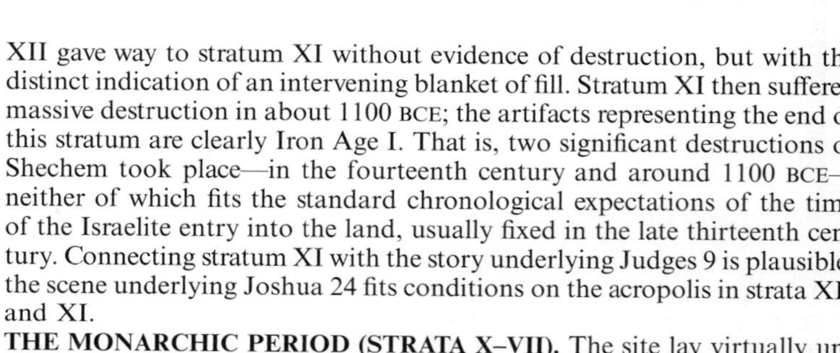

Fruit press or dyeing installation found under the hearth of house 1727, Iron II.

Ruins of the "four-room" house 1727 in field VII, destroyed in 724 BCE; note the large hearth in the central room.

the late tenth and the ninth centuries BCE and becomes the tangible evidence of Jeroboam I's rebuilding (1 Kg. 12:25) and a return to city status.

Strata VIII and VII represent the eighth century BCE. Little remains of stratum VIII, but stratum VII is strikingly well preserved because of the destruction that brought it down. One residence, house 1727 in field VII, is of special interest. It is a fine example from the time of the Assyrian destruction (c. 724 BCE) of the typical "four-room" dwelling around a central room. The entire structure had a second story. A huge hearth in the central room points to a family trade of lime production or something requiring a large fire. The hearth supplanted an earlier vat-and-platter installation with a collecting jar, which suggests another household industry: fruit processing or possibly dyeing. Two rooms were added to this house along its southern edge, suggesting the expansion of the family. The room is adjacent to an open area where food was processed, probably in collaboration with the occupants of another house at the edge of field VII, to its south. A fine adorant seal of Assyrian workmanship, lost by its owner in the debris of the house destruction, confirms the dating.

THE ASSYRIAN OCCUPATION AND THE PERSIAN PERIOD (STRATA VI–V). Stratum VI attests limited occupation of the site in the Assyrian period, covering the seventh century BCE. The remains from the Persian period (stratum V) are also scanty, although the artifacts suggest a cosmopolitan and relatively well-to-do population. Included are 158 sherds of imported Attic black-glazed ware in a variety of forms, incised triangle krater rims, a late sixth-century electrum coin from Thasos, a seal impression of a roaring lion typical of Judean sites in the Persian period, and a Persian seal impression of the king as archer, with Ahura Mazda's seal behind him. Stratum V represents roughly the years 600 to 475 BCE.

THE HELLENISTIC PERIOD (STRATA IV–I). In the late fourth century BCE, Shechem recovered once more. The tops of the old Middle Bronze Age IIC fortifications were exposed, huge quantities of earth were moved to

Assyrian adorant seal found in the ruins of house 1727, and its impression.

Hebrew seal: "(belonging) to mbn*," 7th century BCE.*

Buildings of strata III–II in field II, Hellenistic period; (right) the original room from stratum III.

provide sound foundations, and the town again became a fortified city. The settlers shaped their site by moving earth throughout the city. In field VII, where in the eighth and seventh centuries BCE a succession of three terraces stepped the slope of the mound downward to the southeast, the settlers produced a level area and built sturdy homes on it. The first period of their activity is represented by stratum IV; it involves the initial fortification and preparation of the site, completed by about 300 BCE. Still within stratum IV, the first houses are being built until roughly 250 BCE. In stratum III, the fortifications are strengthened and the quality of the houses improves. All of the coinage related to strata IV and III is Ptolemaic; after the transition to stratum II, Seleucid coins dominate. Stratum III ends then, with the advent of the Seleucids, in about 190 BCE. The best attestation of stratum II at Shechem is a well-preserved house in field II, just at the southeast edge of what a millennium before had been the acropolis. Stratum I is defined mostly by pottery from the late second century BCE and by a few scraps of walls. The numismatic evidence fits well with a final destruction of the city by John Hyrcanus in 107 BCE when Josephus places Hyrcanus' siege of Samaria, rather than in 128, when Josephus reports the destruction of the Gerizim temple and the city of Shechem (*Antiq.* XIII, 254–256, 275–281). In a classic study, Wright established that Shechem must have taken over as the Samaritan center after Alexander took Samaria and gave it to his Macedonian garrison. Its relationship to the Hellenistic city of Lozeh, on Gerizim's summit, remains to be interpreted. The relationship of both to the huge block of masonry on Tell er-Râs, under the Zeus Olympus temple foundations, almost certainly erected in Hellenistic times, and thought by some to be the site of the Samaritan holy place, has still to be clarified as well.

Reports of the Austrian and German expeditions: E. Sellin, *Anzeiger der Kaiserliche Akademie der Wissenschaften in Wien, Philologisch-historische Klasse* 51 (1914), 35–40, 204–207; id., *ZDPV* 49 (1926), 229–236, 304–320; 50 (1927), 205–211, 265–274; 51 (1928), 119–123; E. Sellin and H. Steckeweh, ibid. 64 (1941), 1–20; G. Welter, *Archaeologischer Anzeiger* (1932), 289–314.
Reports of the American expeditions
Main publications: G. E. Wright, *Shechem: The Biography of a Biblical City*, New York 1965; D. P. Cole, *Shechem I: The Middle Bronze IIB Pottery*, Winona Lake, Ind. 1984; E. F. Campbell, *Shechem II: Portrait of a Hill Country Vale*, Atlanta 1991.
Other studies: G. E. Wright et al., *BASOR* 144 (1956), 9–26; 148 (1957), 11–28; L. E. Toombs and G. E. Wright, ibid. 161 (1961), 11–54; 169 (1963), 1–60; L. E. Toombs, *ADAJ* 17 (1972), 99–110; R. J. Bull (et al.), *BASOR* 180 (1965), 7–41; id. (and E. F. Campbell), ibid. 190 (1968), 2–41; E. F. Campbell et al., ibid. 204 (1971), 2–17; J. D. Seger, ibid. 205 (1972), 20–35; G. R. H. Wright, *ZDPV* 89 (1973), 188–196; W. G. Dever, *BASOR* 216 (1974), 31–52; R. Boling, *BASOR* Supplementary Studies 21 (1975), 25–85.
Reports of Israeli excavations: A. Zertal, *TA* 13–14 (1987), 105–165 [el-Burnat].
Ceramic and artifact studies: F. W. Freiherr von Bissing, *Mededelingen der Koniklijke Akademie van Wetenschappen*, Amsterdam, Afd. Letterkunde 62/B (1926), 1–24; H. W. Müller, *Der Waffenfund von Balata-Sichem und die Sichelschwerter*, Munich 1987 [weapon hoard]; F. M. T. Bohl, *ZDPV* 49 (1926) 320–327; W. F. Albright, *BASOR* 86 (1942), 28–31 [cuneiform tablets]; F. M. Cross, Jr., ibid. 167 (1962), 14–15; A. Zeron, *TA* 6 (1979), 156–157 [*lmbn* seal]; S. H. Horn, *JNES* 21 (1962), 1–14; 25 (1966) 48–56; 32 (1973), 281–289 [scarabs]; O. R. Sellers, *BA* 25 (1962), 87–96 [coins]; G. E. Wright, *BASOR* 167 (1962), 5–13 [seals]; G. R. H. Wright, *PEQ* 97 (1965), 66–84; 101 (1969), 34–36 [fluted columns]; V. Kerkhof, *BASOR* 184 (1966), 20–21 [inscribed stone weight]; M. H. Wiencke, *JNES* 35 (1976), 127–130 [clay sealings]; S. Geva, *ZDPV* 96 (1980), 41–47 [tridacna shell]; P. W. Lapp, *BASOR* 172 (1963), 22–35 [stamped jar handles]; id., *Palestinian Ceramic Chronology, 200 BC-AD 70*, New Haven 1961, 41–49 and passim; N. L. Lapp, *BASOR* 175 (1964), 14–26 [Hellenistic pottery]; P. W. Lapp, *Archäologie und Altes Testament* (K. Galling Fest.), Tübingen 1970, 179–197; N. L. Lapp, *BASOR* 257 (1985), 19–43 [Persian pottery]; J. S. Holladay, *Magnalia Dei: The Mighty Acts of God* (G. E. Wright Fest., eds. F. M. Cross, Jr., et al.), Garden City, N.Y. 1976, 253–293 [Iron II pottery]; R. S. Boraas, *The Archaeology of Jordan and Other Studies* (S. H. Horn Fest.), Berrien Springs, Mich. 1986, 249–263 [Iron I pottery]; D. P. Cole, *Shechem I: The Middle Bronze IIB Pottery*, Winona Lake, Ind. 1984; G. R. H. Wright, *Opuscula Atheniensia* 7 (1967), 47–75 [Cypriot and Aegean pottery]; S. H. Horn, *Jaarbericht ex Oriente Lux* 20 (1968), 71–90 [1913–1914 objects]; S. H. Horn and L. G. Moulds, *AUSS* 7 (1969), 2–46 [1913–1914 pottery]; V. Kerkhof, *Oudheidkundige Mededelingen uit het Rijksmuseum van Oudheden te Leiden* 50 (1969), 38–109 [artifacts from the Austro-German expeditions].
Interpretive studies: F. M. T. Bohl, *De Opgraving van Sichem*, Zeist, Netherlands 1927; E. Sellin, *ZAW* 50 (1932), 303–308; R. J. Bull, *BA* 23 (1960), 110–119; R. J. Bull and G. E. Wright, *Harvard Theological Review* 58 (1965), 234–237; E. F. Campbell and J. F. Ross, *BA* 26 (1963), 2–27; E. F. Campbell, *Magnalia Dei: The Mighty Acts of God* (G. E. Wright Fest., eds. F. M. Cross, Jr., et al.), Garden City, N.Y. 1976, 39–54; id., *The Word of the Lord Shall Go Forth* (D. N. Freedman Fest.), Winona Lake, Ind. 1983, 263–271; id., *The Answers Lie Below* (L. E. Toombs Fest.), Lanham, Md. 1984 67–76; S. H. Horn, *Jaarbericht Ex Oriente Lux* 18 (1965), 284–306; G. E. Wright, *Archaeology and Old Testament Study*, London 1967, 355–370; J. F. Ross and L. E. Toombs, *Archaeological Studies in the Holy Land*, New York 1967, 119–127; G. R. H. Wright, *ZDPV* 83 (1967), 199–202; id., *ZAW* 80 (1968), 1–35; 82 (1970), 275–278; 87 (1975) 56–64; id., *PEQ* 103 (1971), 17–32; id., *Zeitschrift für Assyriologie* 74 (1984), 267–289; id., *ZDPV* 101 (1986), 1–8; J. D. Seger, *Levant* 6 (1974), 117–130; id., *EI* 12 (1975), 34*–45*; K. Jaroš, *Sichem*, Göttingen 1976; K. Jaros and B. Deckert, *Studien zür Sichem-Area*, Göttingen 1977; L. E. Toombs, *ASOR Symposia*, 69–83; id., *Put Your Future in Ruins* (R. J. Bull Fest.), Briston, Ind. 1985, 42–60; M. D. Fowler, *PEQ* 115 (1983), 49–53; R. G. Boling and E. F. Campbell, *Archaeology and Biblical Interpretation* (D. Glenn Rose Fest.), Atlanta 1986, 259–272; D. Dorsey *BASOR* 268 (1987), 57–70.

EDWARD F. CAMPBELL

Ptolemaic silver coin from a hoard discovered at Shechem.

NEAPOLIS

Neapolis is surrounded on all sides by extensive, fertile agricultural land and copiously watered by several sources within the city limits. These circumstances, highly favorable for human habitation, coupled with the location of the city at the foot of the sacred Mount Gerizim and at one of the central crossroads in Samaria (see above), have made it the capital of Samaria to this day. The Roman city of Neapolis was built on the northern slope of Mount Gerizim, not around the ancient nucleus of Canaanite-Israelite Shechem. The beginnings of Neapolis probably date to the Hellenistic period, but it did not develop and become a city in the full sense until the Roman period.

The Arabic name Nablus is a corruption of the Greek Neapolis (new city).

Neapolis: general plan of the city.

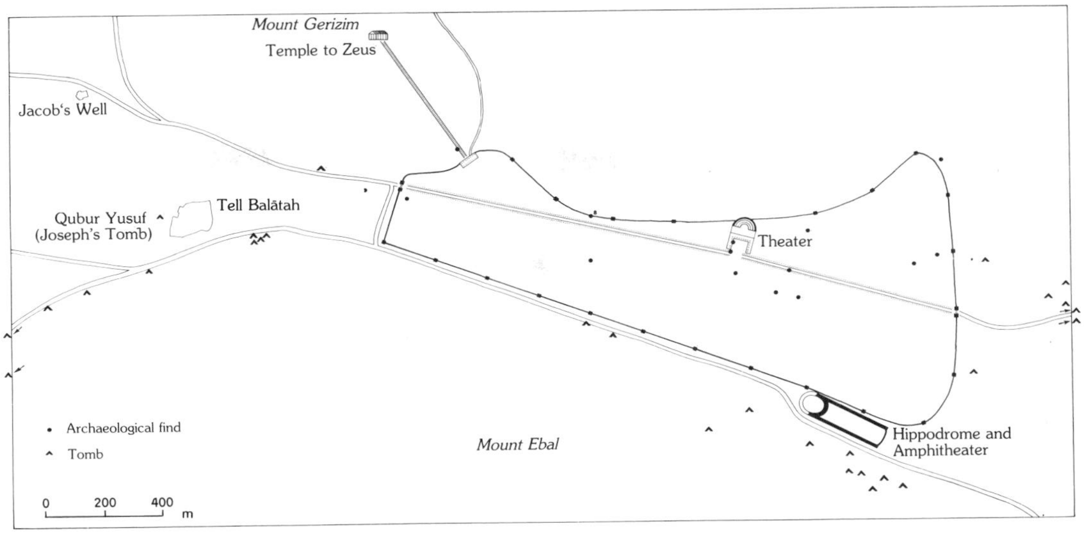

According to Josephus, the local inhabitants used to call Neapolis Mabartha (*War* IV, 8, 1 [449]); Pliny calls it Mamurta (*NH* V, 13).

HISTORY

Neapolis was founded in 72–73 CE by the Flavian emperors, shortly after the destruction of Jerusalem. The evidence for this is the first city coins, issued during the reign of Domitian (81–96 CE), which bear such dates as "year 11" and "year 15" from the city's establishment. Similar conclusions follow from the coins of Marcus Aurelius, who ascended the imperial throne in 161 CE (a typical date is the 89th year since the foundation of Neapolis). The full name of the city on the coins is Flavia Neapolis Samariae, indicating that it was founded by the Flavians, probably in the aftermath of certain events during the First Jewish Revolt; the Samaritans' repeated attempts to resettle on Mount Gerizim (Josephus, *Antiq.* XVIII, 85–89; *War* III, 4, 32) and the fear of another revolt, inspired by the sacred mountain, brought about a decision to build a Roman (pagan) city at Neapolis. After its foundation the city was granted extensive lands, mostly inhabited by Samaritans. The territory of Neapolis bordered on the territories of Sebaste, Scythopolis (Beth-Shean), Pella and Perea (Transjordan) in the east, Jerusalem in the south, and Lydda (Lod), Antipatris, and Caesarea in the west. After the destruction of the Second Temple, the formerly Jewish toparchy of Acrabatene was annexed to Neapolis.

At the beginning of the second century CE work began on several large building projects in Neapolis, among them a hippodrome and a theater, as well as on streets and other public edifices. An inscription from this period (found at Ephesus in Asia Minor), carved in stone in honor of Pompeius Falco, Roman procurator of Judea from 105 to 107 CE, reports that several natives of Neapolis (whose names are Roman) erected a statue in his honor at Ephesus in 123–124 CE. Another inscription, found at Aphrodisias in Caria, also in Asia Minor, and dated to the reign of Marcus Aurelius (165 CE), mentions a person who had won athletic contests in various cities, including Neapolis. At the end of Antoninus Pius' reign, the Roman temple of Zeus on Mount Gerizim (q.v.) was completed, and the event was commemorated with the issue of a coin bearing an illustration of the temple. An inscription on the base of a marble tripod found at Shechem refers to its dedication to the temple of Zeus. It also mentions an Athenian member of the city council who was a Roman citizen.

At the end of the second century CE, Neapolis was drawn into the dispute between Pescennius Niger and Septimius Severus. Neapolis supported Niger, and after the latter was defeated by Severus the city was punished: its civic privileges and the right to mint its own coinage were revoked. Eventually, the emperor pardoned the city, perhaps on the recommendation of his son, Caracalla. During Caracalla's reign the second stage of the Roman temple on Mount Gerizim was built.

In 244 CE, Philip the Arab became emperor and raised Neapolis' status to that of a Roman colony: Colonia Flavia Iulia Sergia Neapolis. Coins minted during his reign are inscribed in Latin and feature all of the hallmarks of a colony, including a depiction of the colony's foundation ceremony at Neapolis. City coins from the second half of the third century CE indicate that units of the Roman army were stationed there at the time. The amphitheater and tombstones of Roman soldiers discovered at Neapolis may well date to this period.

City coin of Neapolis, 3rd century CE.

There is little information about Neapolis during the third and fourth centuries CE. The historian Ammianus Marcellinus, who lived in the fourth century, refers to Neapolis as one of the major Roman cities in Palestine. It is known that the Roman temple on Mount Gerizim was in use even later—until the beginning of the fourth century. It was during that century that Christianity gained rapid acceptance in Neapolis and on Mount Gerizim. In 484 CE, the Church of Mary Mother of God was built on Mount Gerizim, apparently on the site of the Samaritan temple. The erection of the temple caused several wars between the Samaritans and the Byzantine authorities, from Zeno's reign to Justinian's.

EXPLORATION AND EXCAVATIONS

Although various finds had come to light in the area, beginning in the twentieth century, and various studies of the city were made in the ten years following the 1967 Six-Day War, vigorous investigations and systematic excavations of Roman Neapolis only began in 1979. Under the direction of I. Magen, excavations continued until the end of 1988. They revealed a theater, hippodrome, and amphitheater, the city's main street, parts of the wall, water systems and burials.

CITY PLAN AND BUILDINGS. The city of Neapolis is depicted in detail on the Medeba map. F. M. Abel was the first scholar to examine the modern plan of the city and compare it with the one on the map. More modern studies, however, have shown that the area of the Roman city was different and larger than he envisaged.

Neapolis was built on the northern slope of Mount Gerizim. Its estimated length was 1,500 m, its breadth 700 m, and its area approximately 250 a. Its northern border ran along the present-day Faisal Street. Outside the city limits was the main east–west road, linking the eastern and western approaches to Neapolis. North of this road was the main cemetery, which extended over the slopes of Mount Ebal. South of the road a stretch of the city wall and tombstones belonging to Roman soldiers were discovered. A hippodrome and an amphitheater were found in the west; they were apparently built outside the city but very close to the walls. North of the hippodrome was a magnificent tomb. The road seems to have run between it and the hippodrome. The city's southern border is also identifiable. Outside the city limits, a clearly discernible line of quarries extends almost the length of the city. The westernmost point on the southern border of the city is the water system Râs el-'Ayin. From that point, the city wall ran eastward, up to the Roman theater at its southern end. Both the theater and the wall are depicted in the Medeba map.

The wall ran eastward to a gate erected on the site of the propylaeum or colonnade at the beginning of the ascent to Mount Gerizim. From this gate, the wall continued to the main city gate, situated, in the excavator's opinion, on the site presently occupied by the military government headquarters. Here, too, was the city's major spring, 'Ein Dafna. The western border of the city is unclear, particularly as this feature is missing on the Medeba map. The excavator postulates another gate at the western exit from the city. Judging from the positions of the burials in the area, the Roman city extended right up to the edge of the present-day new Samaritan neighborhood and the Muslim cemetery in southwestern Shechem.

General view of the main street of Neapolis, north of the theater.

Plan of the theater.

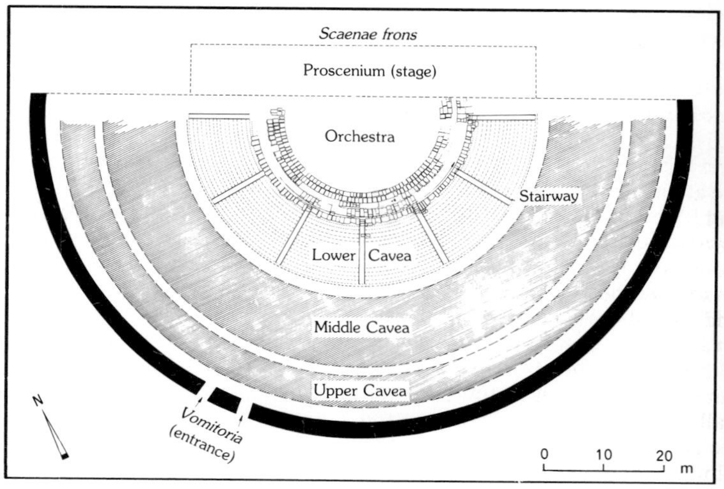

The illustration on the Medeba map shows a central street bisecting the city from east to west. Another street runs south from the middle of the main street, leading to a semicircular structure, which Abel interpreted as a nymphaeum. Excavations at this site, as stated previously, uncovered the Roman theater. Excavations north of the theater revealed the main street, which indeed cut across the city from east to west. It was approximately 11 m wide and paved with fitted flagstones. One column was found in situ on the northern side of the street. Beneath the street ran an aqueduct that probably brought water from 'Ein Dafna within the city walls; it could be reached by a flight of 56 steps, descending to a depth of 12 m. This main street was in use during the Roman-Byzantine and Mameluke periods; during the latter, it was made narrower. Found south of the street were the remains of another street, along which columns stood on bases; the latter were found in situ. The excavator believes that these were parts of the forum, or palaestra.

At the southwestern edge of the city was a large water system, known today as Râs el-'Ayin. It was a large Roman structure, supplying water to the city through a stone channel. In addition, there are several springs in the city, including, in particular, 'Ein Qaryun, in the town center, and 'Ein Dafna, at its eastern edge; some of these, however, are not real springs but outlets of water channels. At the northwestern end of the city the hippodrome was built on an east–west alignment, parallel to the main crosstown street. In the third century CE, an amphitheater was built in the circular part of the hippodrome. A colored mosaic, featuring flora and fauna and human figures, was found in the center of the city and dated to the third century CE.

THE THEATER. The theater was built in the second century CE on the northern slope of Mount Gerizim, on the outskirts of the Roman city. It is surrounded by a massive ashlar masonry wall (2.6 m thick) pierced by the entrances to the theater. The diameter of the theater (c. 110 m) makes it one of the largest Roman theaters discovered in the country to date. Most of its masonry was plundered in the Mameluke period and reused to build the city of Nablus. Examination of the remains brought the excavators to the conclusion that it originally had three sections of seats (cavea). The lower cavea (which was built directly on bedrock) and the middle one were the same size—each contained eighteen tiers of seats—but the upper cavea contained only about twelve tiers. The first tier of the lower cavea contained a total of some 120 seats. The upper and middle cavea are not preserved. Of the lower cavea, one tier of seats, with inscriptions, remains. A concentric gangway ran around the theater, in front of the first row. It was bordered by a latticework partition. The orchestra was paved with marble flagstones of varying hues. The stage and *scenae frons* have not survived. The theater was divided into six sections of seats by seven stairways. Found in the orchestra and the lower gangway were dozens of seats, with their backs carved into the shape of dolphins. These seats were installed at the upper end of the lower cavea, separating it from the upper gangway.

Among the many finds from the theater were architectural elements—marble capitals, columns, fragments of marble slabs that originally adorned the front of the stage, parts of friezes, doorposts, and decorated lintels. Two marble statues of female figures and a statue made of soft limestone were also discovered, along with pottery and hundreds of coins. Eleven inscriptions were found incised in the first row of seats, specifying the names of eleven *phylae*, or tribes. Eight of the *phylae* were named for gods, from Zeus to Dionysus; the central *phyle*, to which twenty-one central seats were assigned, was named for Hercules. The last three *phylae* preserved such names as Phlious, the name of a city in the Peloponnese, the *phyle* of the Antiochs, and another *phyle* whose name has not been preserved. The theater remained

General view of the theater, looking north, 2nd century CE.

in use until the Byzantine period, when the orchestra was turned into a pool and the theater was used for nautical games—a common phenomenon in the Roman world.

THE HIPPODROME. The hippodrome was built at the western approaches to the city, on the slope of Mount Ebal, aligned east–west. The excavator believes it originally stood outside the city limits. Its estimated dimensions were 76 by 320 m. The circular section faced east, and the horses' entrances were in the west. The arena was found covered with stone chips. The remains of the nave—the avenue separating the two parts of the arena—were found at the eastern end. The seats were built on a vaulted substructure (13.65 m wide), made up of rows of rooms (8.35 m long) and an inner lateral aisle (3.5 m wide) separated from the arena by a very massive wall. Numbers in Greek letters were incised on some of the seats. There were eleven entrances for horses—five in the south and six in the north. The center of the hippodrome was marked by a pillar. A great number of cells was hewn in the southern side of the blocks of seats; some of these accommodated horses. The hippodrome was built of well-dressed, but relatively small ashlar blocks, cut from the soft stone of Mount Ebal. The walls rested on foundations of carefully laid field stones. The entrances to the sections of seats were through the cells, by way of staircases, some of which climbed to the upper section. Some entrances led to the lower sections. The inner lateral aisle may also have admitted spectators. The cells in the seat's substructure produced numerous finds—mainly coins, some of which were found on the floors. On the basis of these coins, the construction of the hippodrome is to be dated to the second century CE; it continued in use until the first half of the third century CE.

THE AMPHITHEATER. The amphitheater was superimposed on the circular end of the hippodrome in the third century CE. Its size is estimated at 95 by 76 m. The substructure supporting the seats was 17.5 m wide and consisted of rectangular cells and an inner aisle on the side facing the arena. The central entrance to the amphitheater was built like a corridor, 12.5 m long and 4.5 m wide. The cells adjoining this corridor were used as cages for the animals participating in the events. The cages were entered from the central corridor. Other openings led from the cells to the inner concentric corridor, which opened into the arena. The cells beyond the cages provided access to the spectators' seats. Two cells provided access to the lowest level of seats through a broad staircase; between them was a cell through which the upper seats could be reached.

The amphitheater was built of reused stones, probably obtained by dismantling various buildings around the city. The excavations in fact uncovered many inscriptions in secondary use, some of them incorporated in the amphitheater's walls. Considerable use was made of stones from the hippodrome, particularly from the seats, as the amphitheater was superimposed on part of the now disused hippodrome. In the interests of economy,

Chair with dolphin-shaped arms from the theater.

The entrances to the hippodrome.

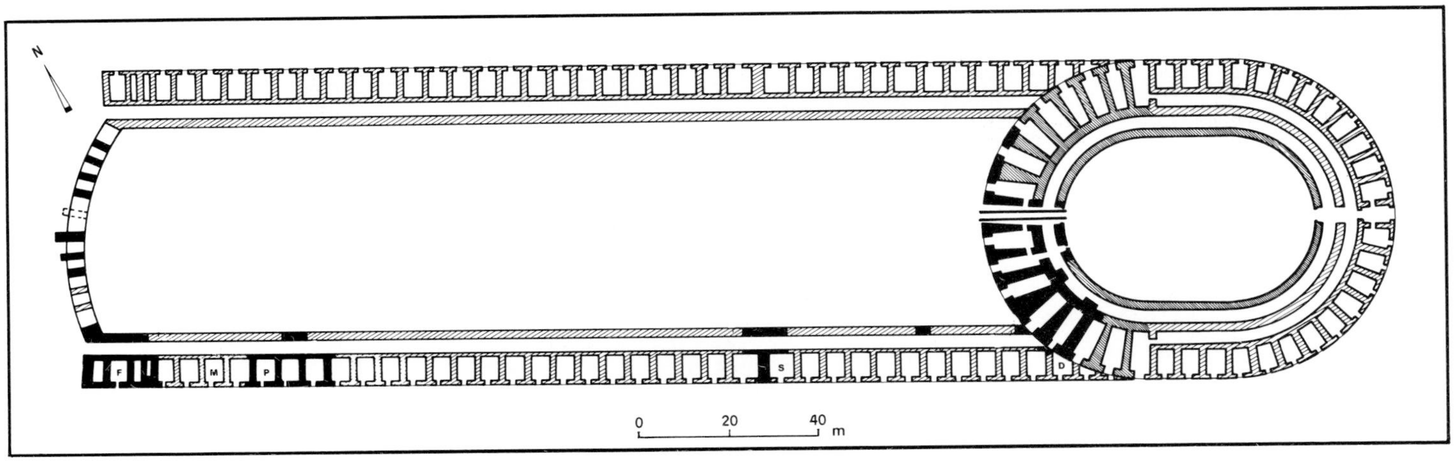

Plan of the hippodrome, 2nd–3rd centuries, and the amphitheater, 3rd century.

General view of the amphitheater.

the builders took advantage of the semicircular section of the hippodrome and simply added on another semicircular structure. A comparison of the pottery and numismatic finds from the hippodrome and the amphitheater indicates that the former went out of use in the middle of the third century CE. The amphitheater was built on the same site not long afterward, when Neapolis was elevated to the status of a Roman colony. The construction of the amphitheater was associated with the Roman army units then stationed at Neapolis.

THE MOSAIC. One of the most beautiful Roman mosaics discovered in this country was uncovered in the center of Shechem, not far from the Roman hippodrome. It comprises three nested designs and a fourth part adjoining the frame on the outside. The border of the mosaic is formed by two dark strips with a continuous spiral pattern between them. The various figures in the mosaic are placed in a system of circles made of acanthus leaves; in each corner of the mosaic a bearded figure looks out of the design, and in the center of each side is the face of a youth. The remaining space is taken up by depictions of various animals. The mosaic's colors and shades are rich and careful attention was given to the uniformity of the size and shape of the designs. It is dated to the third century CE, the time of Emperor Philip the Arab, but it could have been made earlier.

Section of the mosaic discovered in the hippodrome area, Roman period.

BURIALS. Neapolis' main cemetery lay on the southern and eastern slopes of Mount Ebal, stretching from the western approaches of the city to the road leading to Wadi Far'ah (today the Arab village of 'Askar). Mount Ebal had been used for burial since Shechem's earliest days, in the Chalcolithic period, and the cemetery continued in use until the Arab period. As the rock of the mountain is quite soft, it was not possible to carve tomb facades, so most of the more imposing tombs had ashlar-built facades or were mausolea built of stone.

During the Roman period a new site, on the northwestern slope of Mount Gerizim, came into use for burials. This cemetery stretched from the spring of Râs el-'Ayin, along the Muslim cemetery and Samaritan quarter, up to the present-day Rafidiyye neighborhood, not far from the east–west road which ran west from the western gate of the city. More than thirty graves, mostly with sarcopha-

The western mausoleum, Roman period.

gi, have been discovered. Also found here were the tombstones of Roman soldiers who had been buried in the city. Most of the important tombs were discovered on Mount Ebal. A Roman tomb with two stages of burial was uncovered on the upper slope of the mountain, across from Tell Balâtah. The first stage was a loculus tomb, dated by the finds it contained to the first century BCE and the first century CE; in the second stage, sarcophagi were added, without disturbing the earlier burials. It follows that the beginning of the second century CE marked a transition from burial in loculi to burial in coffins. Other tombs from the Roman period were found nearby. Northeast of Tell Balâtah, near the village of 'Askar, a mausoleum (5 by 5 m) built of fine ashlar blocks was found, sealed by a stone door. Its facade is magnificent. Fashioned in the likeness of a Hellenistic-Roman temple, it contained ten sarcophagi, three in arcosolia and seven in the center of the tomb. The arcosolium opposite the entrance contained a particularly ornate sarcophagus, bearing an inscription referring to Justus the founder and his wife. A large Roman mausoleum, partly built and partly cut in the rock, was discovered at the western approaches to the city, on the road to Sebaste, opposite the hippodrome. It contained three rock-cut burial caves. The facade (23.5 m long) of the mausoleum was built of ashlars, with a vault above each entrance. In front of the facade was a court paved with fitted flagstones. Two of the burial caves contained fine sarcophagi; altogether, there were twenty-three large sarcophagi and one small one. Most of them were found in the paved forecourt.

T. Drake, *PEQ* 4 (1872), 190–193; L. Oliphant, ibid. 17 (1885), 94–97; L. H. Vincent, *RB* 29 (1920), 126–135; F. M. Abel, ibid. 31 (1922), 89–99; 32 (1923), 120–132; G. M. Fitzgerald, *PEQ* 61 (1929), 104–110; R. Dajani, *ADAJ* 11 (1966), 103; *The Rosenberger Israel Collection* 3: *Neapolis (City Coins of Palestine)*, Jerusalem 1977; C. M. Dauphin, *IEJ* 29 (1979), 11–33; id., *Archéologia* 186 (1984), 44–53; A. Kindler, *Israel Numismatic Journal* 4 (1980), 56–58; H-D. Neef, *ZDPV* 98 (1982), 163–169; I. Magen, *ESI* 2 (1983), 90–92; K. W. Harl, *American Numismatic Society Museum Notes* 29 (1984), 61–97; J. Margain, *Syria* 61 (1984), 45–47; Y. Meshorer, *Kraay-Morkholm Essays*, Louvain-La-Neuve 1989, 173–177.

ITZHAK MAGEN

SHEMA', KHIRBET

IDENTIFICATION

Khirbet Shema' is located in the Upper Galilee, 760 m above sea level, on a foothill of Mount Meiron, opposite the ancient settlement of Meiron (map reference 1914.2647). It has been known since medieval times as the burial place of Shammai, the contemporary of Hillel the Elder, his opponent. The ruin has been identified with Tekoa of Galilee by S. Klein and M. Avi-Yonah. The expedition that excavated at the site from 1970 to 1972, under the auspices of the American Schools of Oriental Research, directed by E. M. Meyers, found no explicit evidence to support or contradict this theory.

EXCAVATIONS

Excavation of the Great Mausoleum, which is still venerated as a holy place by pious pilgrims, produced no evidence for dating, as its foundations were completely disturbed. Other tombs excavated in its vicinity indicated secondary burial to be the dominant mode of inhumation in a variety of tomb types: loculi, grave-type arcosolia, and variations and mixtures thereof. Coins and pottery indicate the main period of use to have been the fourth century CE, contemporary with the settlement.

The soundings conducted outside the synagogue building and in the public area around it showed that the settlement of Khirbet Shema' existed mainly between the mid-second and early fifth centuries CE. Numerous coins and a few sherds give evidence here of a settlement from the Late Hellenistic period—perhaps connected with the expansion of the Hasmonean kingdom to this part of the Galilee—but the smaller number of finds from the end of the Second Temple period (50 BCE–70 CE) to about 180 CE is more decisive. It is possible that with more extensive soundings at the site, the settlement from that earlier period will come to light. Investigation at adjacent settlements has shown a continuous occupation in this period, rather than a gap, which further study would clarify.

THE SYNAGOGUE

The discovery of the synagogue at Khirbet Shema' is of special importance, both because it is the earliest broadhouse synagogue with internal columniation in the country and because of its two phases, which enable a reconstruction of the changes that were begun in daily life in Upper Galilean villages in the Roman period. The first phase of the synagogue was destroyed in an earthquake in 306 CE; its second phase, constructed shortly afterward, was destroyed together with the rest of the settlement in a more violent earthquake, in 419.

Judging from its two phases, the synagogue seems to be the product of architectural eclecticism. It was not built at the highest point of the settlement, as was the custom; actually, it was necessary to descend a staircase from the street level in order to enter the sanctuary. The proximity of the synagogue to the mausoleum and the caves is especially surprising, considering the traditions of synagogue construction in the Mishnaic period: the building was erected above rock-cut caves, some of which were undoubtedly used for burial. It seems that the primary concern of the synagogue's builders in both phases was to have it face Jerusalem. To overcome the architectural, traditional, and practical problems confronting them, they had to improvise many of the modifications.

The exact dating of the synagogue's two phases was unexpectedly difficult to determine because it stood on an asymetrical rock spur with various ancient installations hewn into it. One of these was a mikveh, set in the synagogue's southeast corner. As the mikveh was not sealed from above, it can only be assumed that it predates the synagogue. It was probably built sometime between 180 and the year in which the synagogue was erected—a period about which very little is known. Other rock-cut installations were found beneath the synagogue's western staircase and in its northwest corner; this area may have been carefully chosen for the synagogue because there was less preliminary work involved in cutting into the bedrock for construction. Another factor making it difficult to determine the dates of the two phases is that the foundations of the earlier structure are in secondary use in the later one. The one date obtained with certainty marks the end of the entire settlement—419 CE. The excavators arrived at that date based on the ceramic and numismatic evidence and on the collapsed condition of the building, which was destroyed in the same earthquake.

Throughout its existence, the synagogue was oriented south, as typifies broadhouse structures. The columns inside the synagogue distinguish it from other broadhouse synagogues—such as those at Susiya and Eshtemoa in the Hebron Hills—which do not have internal columniation. The famous synagogue at Dura Europos, in the Syrian desert, which is considered the earliest broadhouse synagogue, also lacks internal columniation.

The phase 1 synagogue was more elaborate than that in phase 2, built after

Lintel decorated with a menorah, from the synagogue, probably phase 2.

Khirbet Shema': the Great Mausoleum.

Khirbet Shema': general view of the synagogue after its reconstruction, looking southwest.

the earthquake of 306. The well-designed four doorposts of the northern and western gates survived the earthquake and were reused in the phase 2 synagogue. Apart from the addition of the bema in phase 2, the synagogue's general plan, orientation, columns, and dimensions (9 by 18 m) are clearly identical in both phases. Socioeconomic conditions, exacerbated by drought and famine, were probably responsible for the general decline in the quality and workmanship of the later structure. The earthquake of 363 contributed to a worsening condition of the phase 2 synagogue, which was reflected in the repairs made to it following the quake. Several unique features were found in both phases: a monumental staircase in the western wall; a genizah—a cave-like room hewn beneath the staircase; a gallery for additional seating that adjoined the western wall and was entered from the north and west; a frescoed room under the gallery; and a holy ark or Torah shrine.

There are indications that the phase 1 synagogue did not include a bema. First, benches ran along all four sides of the sanctuary, in addition to the bench found underneath the bema in the later synagogue that formed part of its fill. Second, within this fill were several coins, the latest of which—a coin of Constantius (337–341)—was still unused. This coin is evidence that the phase 2 synagogue was completed no later than the fourth century. If so, the bema was, presumably, the last architectural element to have been added to it. Its addition exemplifies the change that was begun in the later synagogue's interior. The four bases of the southern row of columns are also more elaborately decorated in the phase 2 synagogue, in which pedestals were also added—the best preserved of which are the two still standing in front of the bema.

The base of a small column adjoining the southern wall of the phase 1 synagogue may have been part of the Torah shrine. If indeed a holy ark existed in phase 1, it was probably replaced by a bema in phase 2. A wooden Ark of the Law may have stood on the bema of the later synagogue, but no traces of it have so far been found.

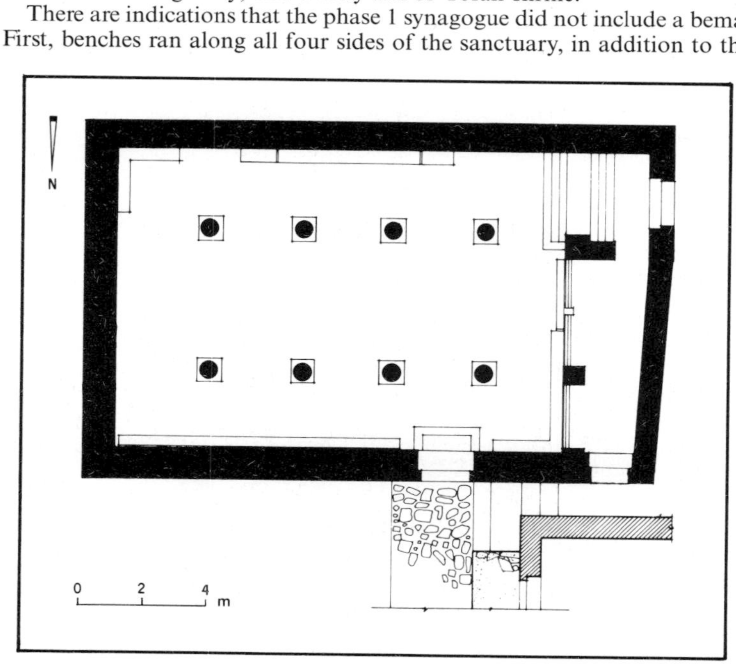

Plan of the synagogue in phase 1.

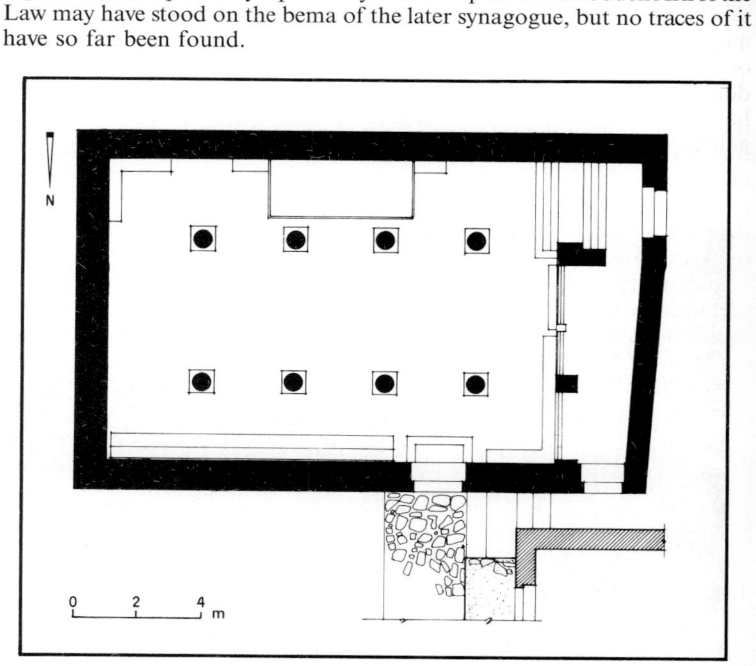

Plan of the synagogue in phase 2.

Isometric reconstruction of the synagogue, with the bema of phase 2.

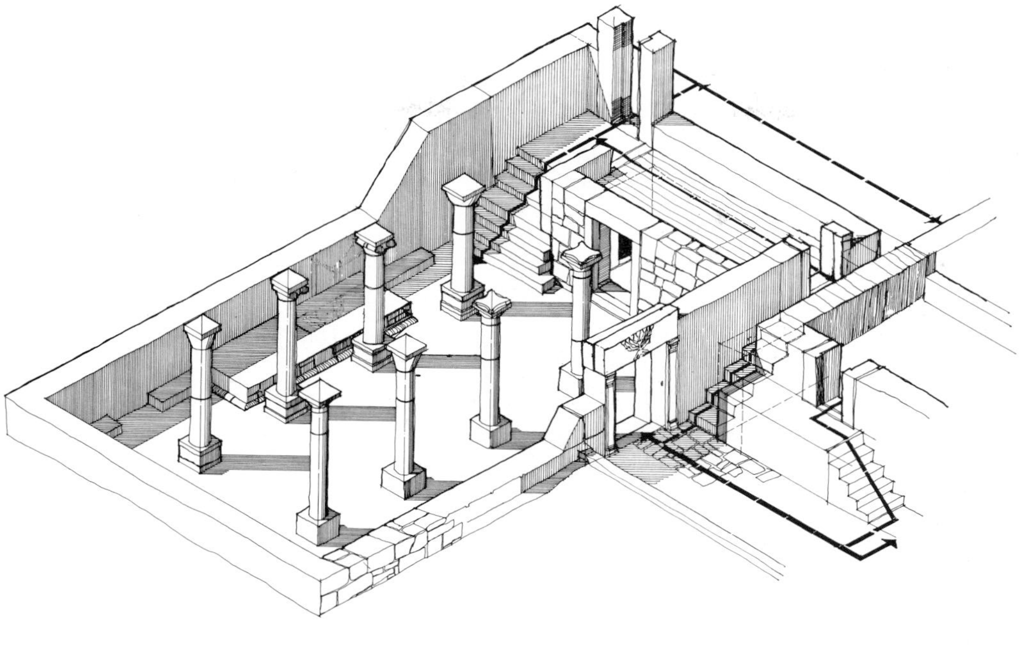

More information is available about the phase 2 synagogue than for its predecessor. The later synagogue had a simple mosaic floor of white and gray tesserae, installed by local artisans. Benches were added along the northern wall, opposite the bema, to accommodate the number of worshipers affected by the missing southern bench—no longer in use because the bema had been built over it. The capitals, columns, and bases of the earlier building were reused in phase 2. A lintel engraved with a menorah may have been among the additions to the synagogue. This ornamental feature, together with an eagle incised with cursive lines on one of the doorposts at the western entrance, was probably the work of local artisans. The doorposts at this entrance are identical to those in the southern entrance, all of which came from the earlier building.

Two other innovations were found in the phase 2 synagogue. One is connected with the frescoed room, hewn under the western staircase and also in use in phase 1. The entrance to it was in the middle of the western wall of the phase 2 synagogue, and its doors were locked from the outside. The walls were painted red and green, in a pattern that cannot be reconstructed. The question remains whether this room was used to store holy manuscripts or other artifacts, such as the utensils used in the ritual washing of hands, an alms box, or the community's documents. The construction of the bema in phase 2 may attest to a change in prayer customs, and thus a change in the room's use.

The second innovation in the phase 2 synagogue was the construction of a new entrance to the gallery above the frescoed room. This entrance led to a stepped alley that separated the synagogue from an adjacent structure that may have been a *beth midrash* or a hospice. The excavators were once of the opinion that the gallery had served as a women's gallery, but this is now doubtful in light of the abundant evidence showing that women and men had practiced joint prayer in the synagogue until the medieval period. The gallery may thus have been used only for additional seating.

Main publication: E. M. Meyers et al., *Ancient Synagogue Excavations at Khirbet Shema', Upper Galilee, Israel, 1970–1972* (AASOR 42), Durham, N.C. 1976.
Other studies: Conder–Kitchener, *SWP* 1, 246–247; Guérin, *Galilée* 2, 433–434; D. G. Dalman, *ZDPV* 29 (1906), 195–199; R. A. S. Macalister, *PEQ* 41 (1909), 195–200; M. Avi-Yonah, *The Macmillan Bible Atlas*, New York 1968, 141, 183; R. J. Bull, *IEJ* 20 (1970), 232–234; id., *AJA* 75 (1971), 196–197; A. T. Kraabel and E. M. Meyers, *RB* 78 (1971), 418–419; 79 (1972), 408–409; 80 (1973), 585–587; E. M. Meyers et al., *BA* 35 (1972), 1–31; id., *IEJ* 22 (1972), 174–176; id., *AASOR* 42 (Reviews), *LA* 28 (1978), 267–276. — *BASOR* 244 (1981), 75–79. — *JNES* 40 (1981), 64–65; E. M. Meyers, *BA* 43 (1980), 97–108; id., *ASR*, 70–74; id., *Archaeology* 35/3 (1982), 51–58; id., *City, Town and Countryside in the Early Byzantine Era* (ed. R. L. Hohlfelder), New York 1982, 115–130; id., *BASOR* 260 (1985), 61–69; id., *The Synagogue in Late Antiquity* (ed. L. I. Levine), Philadelphia 1987, 127–139; *The Times Atlas of the Bible* (ed. J. B. Pritchard), London 1987, 152.

ERIC M. MEYERS

Northern entrance of the synagogue.

Mikveh, looking south.

SHEPHERDS' FIELD

IDENTIFICATION

Shepherds' Field, called Kaniset er-Ru'at (Church of the Shepherds) by the local inhabitants, is located about 1 km (0.6 mi.) east of Bethlehem, within the Arab village of Beit Saḥur (map reference 171.123). According to Christian tradition, this is where the Lord's angel announced the birth of Jesus to the shepherds (Lk. 2:8–20). The results of the excavations at Kaniset er-Ru'at justify the identification of the site with Shepherds' Field, contrary to an earlier identification with the church and monastery at Siyar el-Ghanam, proposed by V. Corbo (q.v. Monasteries: Siyar el-Ghanam).

HISTORY

The earliest sources that mention Shepherds' Field are the Spanish pilgrim Egeria, who visited the site in about 384, and Palladius, a Greek monk who lived in the area from 386 to 388. This part of Egeria's original account is lost, but can be reconstructed from a twelfth-century version by Peter the Deacon. In his account, the sacred site called "At the Shepherds," where the angels announced Jesus' birth, is described as "a splendid cave with an altar" within a walled garden (*De Locis Sanctis* L1; *CCSL* 175, 96). Palladius (*Historia Lausiaca* 36) mentions an ascetic who lived "beyond the Poemenion," the Greek name for Shepherds' Field; it appears that there was a monastery near the church, on the far side of Bethlehem.

Saint Jerome, who resided in the vicinity from 386 to his death in 420, mentions the holy place several times in his Epistles: it was a church visited by many pilgrims (*Ep.* 46, 12; 108, 10), where monks and nuns from the neighborhood came to pray (*Ep.* 147, 6). Jerome was the first to identify Shepherds' Field with the Tower of Eder (Gen. 35:21), where Jacob grazed his flocks (*Ep.* 108, 10). Elsewhere Jerome locates the Tower of Eder at a distance of one Roman mile from Bethlehem (*Onom.* 43, 22–23). He may well be the initiator of this tradition, since Egeria seemingly did not identify the Tower of Eder, where she saw "the foundations of Jacob's house," with Shepherds' Field (*De Locis Sanctis* O2; *CCSL* 175, 98).

At the beginning of the fifth century, the Church of Jerusalem held vigils in the Shepherds' Church on January 5, the eve of the Epiphany, then considered the day of Christmas according to an early fifth-century Armenian lectionary (*Patrologia Orientalis* 36, 211). When Christmas was later transferred to December 25, the church vigil was celebrated a day before, on December 24.

The sixth-century pilgrims did not mention Shepherds' Field—unless it can be identified with the "monastery surrounded by a wall, before Bethlehem," seen by the pilgrim of Piacenze in about 570 (Antoninus Placentinus, *Itinerarium* 29, *CCSL* 175, 144). In 681, Arculf visited the church, where he was shown the tombs of the three shepherds (Adamnanus, *De Locis Sanctis* II, VI, 2; *CCSL* 175, 208). The monk Epiphanius (late seventh or early eighth century) described the Poemenion as a monastery (*Enarratio Syriae*, *PG* 120, col. 264).

EXCAVATIONS

In 1970, the Greek Orthodox Patriarchate of Jerusalem, the owners of the site, made plans to restore the holy place. In the course of clearing the site and digging foundations for new buildings, remains of early construction were uncovered. Excavations were subsequently carried out on behalf of the Israel Department of Antiquities and Museums, under the direction of V. Tzaferis.

The earliest remains are dated to the fourth century CE. These consist of fragments of a colored mosaic floor, one of the earliest Christian mosaics uncovered so far in the country. It is decorated with geometric motifs and black crosses. This mosaic floor, situated under the later buildings, was laid directly on the bedrock, which is 3 m high. The mosaic remains clearly show that a grotto paved with mosaics existed here—perhaps the same one mentioned in early Christian writings.

At a later date, in the early fifth century, the cave was enlarged, mainly on the west and north, and its ceiling was lowered to allow the construction of a large ecclesiastical building. This building, preserved in its entirety, is paved with colored mosaics laid on top of the earlier cave floor.

The new building is a rectangular hall with a vaulted ceiling and a small

Shepherds' Field: general view of the excavation area.

*Shepherds' Field: **(left)** plan of the church in the 4th–6th centuries; **(right)** in the 7th century.*

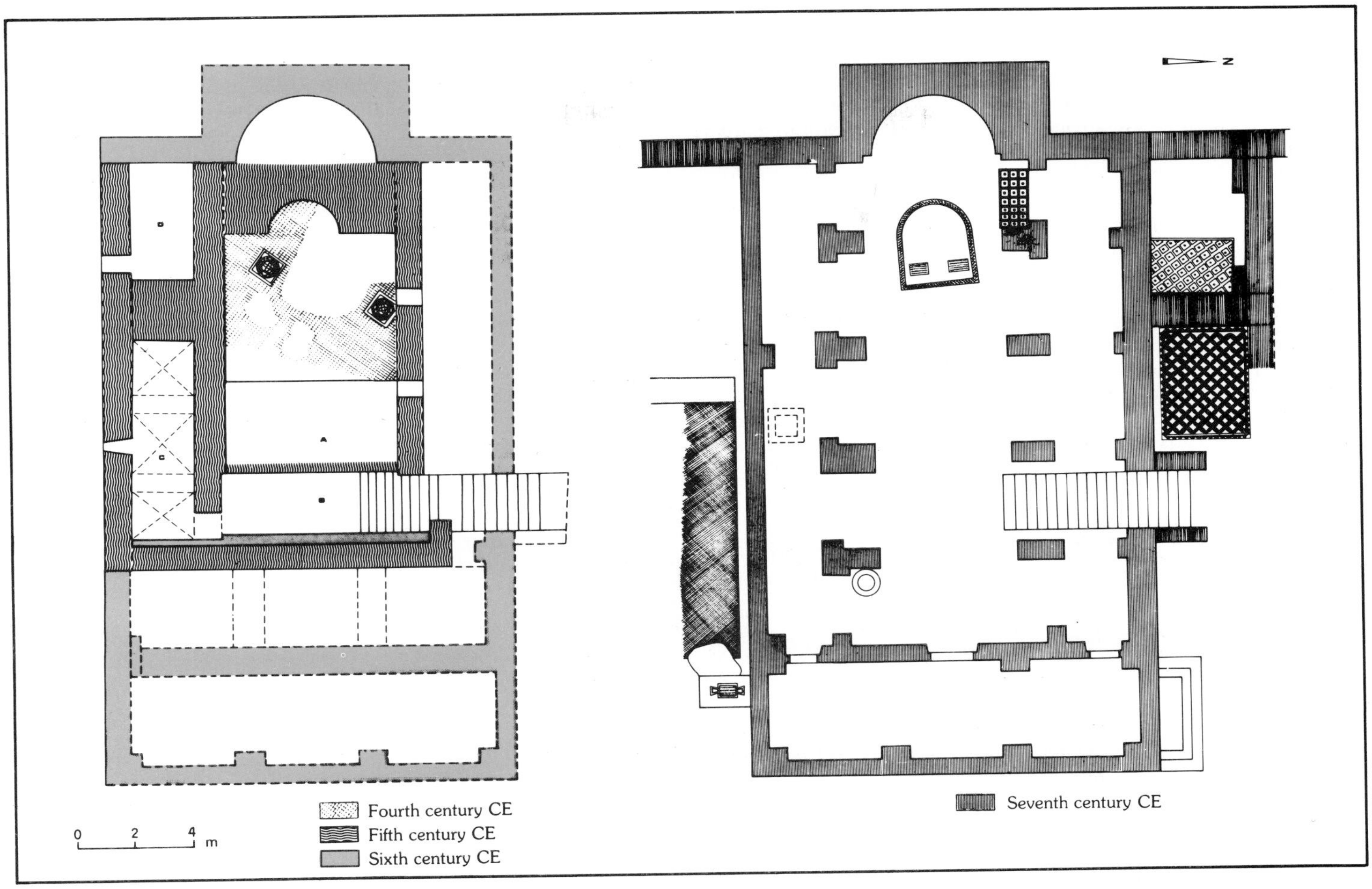

apse at its eastern end. A flight of seventeen steps led to the church's entrance in the south. In this stage, above the church, a small chapel was erected as a kind of memorial. The chapel is paved with colored mosaics decorated with a vine trellis issuing from an amphora. Flanking the amphora are two Greek dedicatory inscriptions listing the names of the donors. The chapel above the church was later removed (in the sixth century) and the surrounding area was leveled for the construction of a large basilica. The fifth-century church then became an underground building that was approached from the southern aisle of the basilica above it. A burial chamber was uncovered under the basilica's northern aisle. It was probably a burial place for the nuns and priests who served in the church. More than one hundred skeletons were found in the vault, as were oil lamps, coins, crosses, and other objects.

The construction of a new and elaborate basilica in the sixth century, while the early church was preserved in its entirety, was undoubtedly due to its importance as a holy site in Palestine and the large number of pilgrims who visited the country in that period. The lectionaries (liturgical books) mentioned above indicate that the basilica in Shepherds' Field was related to the traditional ceremony of Christmas. The Christmas liturgy actually started a day before the holiday, in Shepherds' Church. From there a procession of the faithful, monks, and clergymen left for the Church of the Nativity in Bethlehem.

The basilica was destroyed in the seventh century, possibly as a result of the Persian invasion of 614. Christians erected a new building on its ruins that was architecturally inferior to the previous one. In the Early Arab period, as the living standard of Christians in the Holy Land declined, a wall was built around the precinct with watchtowers in its corners. What used to be a holy site open to all Christians and pilgrims became a cloistered monastery, like those in the Judean Desert. The site was destroyed in the tenth century.

Burial chamber underneath the 6th-century basilica.

C. Guarmani, *Il Migdal e il Santuario dell'Apparizione degli Angeli ai Pastori*, Beirut 1859; B. Meistermann, *Migdal Ader et Siyar el-Ghanem*, Jerusalem 1925; D. Veglio, *La Terra Santa* 21 (1950), 354–358; V. Corbo, *Gli Scavi di Kh. Siyar el-Ghanam e i Monasteri dei Dintorni*, Jerusalem 1955; V. Tzaferis, *CNI* 23 (1973), 248–251; id., *IEJ* 23 (1973), 118–119; id., *RB* 80 (1973), 421–422; id., *LA* 25 (1975), 5–52.

VASSILIOS TZAFERIS

SHILḤA, ḤORVAT

IDENTIFICATION

Ḥorvat Shilḥa is located near the road that runs from the land of Benjamin to Jericho, in the area of Michmash, north of Wadi Qelt (map reference 1818.1408). The site is in a desert region, but near wadis with potentially arable land.

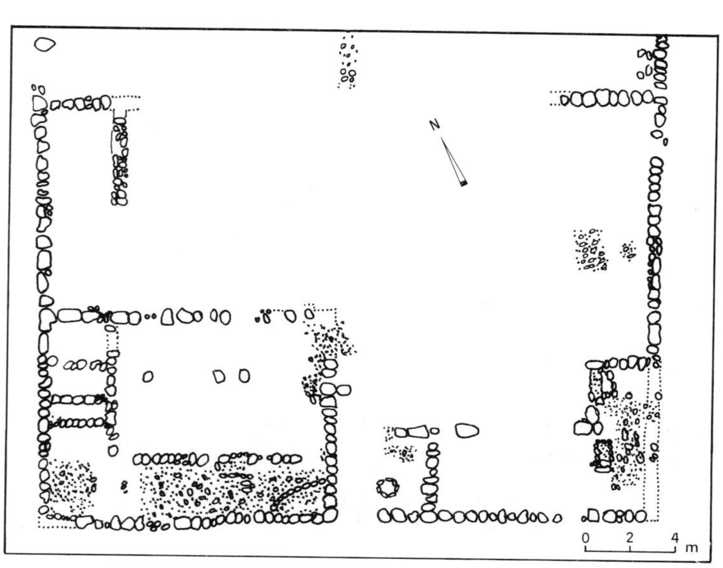

Ḥorvat Shilḥa: general plan.

EXCAVATION

Excavations were carried out at the site in 1981, under the direction of Z. Ilan, A. Mazar, and D. Amit, on behalf of the Hebrew University of Jerusalem and the Kefar Eẓyon Field School, that exposed an isolated structure from the end of the Iron Age. No other remains from this period were found in the vicinity. The building, 27.6 m wide and probably of similar length, had shallow walls about one stone deep (50–60 cm). The entrance was in the south. In the center was a large courtyard, surrounded by rooms arranged along the building's outer walls. A dwelling unit reminiscent of the four-room house that characterizes Iron Age architecture was incorporated in the building's southwestern corner. In this unit, as well as in the building's southeastern corner, rows of stone bases for wooden columns were found. A cistern was uncovered in the corner of the dwelling unit.

The building was only partially preserved. The accumulation on the floors was thin, and the finds were sparse. The sherds uncovered in the excavations are characteristic of the ceramic assemblage in Judah at the end of the Iron Age. The finds include a storage-jar handle with a *lamelekh* seal impression—"(belonging) to the king / Ziph." The building's location seems to have some connection with the route descending from the Samaria Hills to the Jericho Valley. However, it is difficult to determine whether it was a road station, a military post guarding this remote region, or the center of an agricultural estate or isolated farm. In any case, it is one of the only Iron Age sites found in the desert area between the Jordan Valley and the mountains north of Wadi Qelt.

ESI 2 (1983), 94–95.

ZVI ILAN, AMIHAI MAZAR, DAVID AMIT

SHILOH

IDENTIFICATION

The location of Shiloh was already known in the Middle Ages through the investigations of Estori ha-Parḥi and others. In 1838, E. Robinson identified the site with the Arab village of Sailun (map reference 178.162), about 30 km (18.5 mi.) north of Jerusalem, which preserved the ancient name of the site. The Bible contains a very instructive topographical description of the place: "Behold, there is the yearly feast of the Lord at Shiloh, which is north of Bethel, on the east of the highway that goes up from Bethel to Shechem, and south of Lebonah" (Jg. 21:19). The city also appears in later sources. Eusebius notes that Shiloh is 12 mi. from Shechem (*Onom.* 156, 28). It is also mentioned by Jerome (Epistle 108; Commentary on Zephaniah, 1) and noted on the Medeba map. All these sources confirm the accuracy of the identification. The mound is oval in shape and about 7.5 a. in area. It lies north of the village of Turmus 'Aiya. The Roman-Byzantine settlement was built mainly on the southern slope.

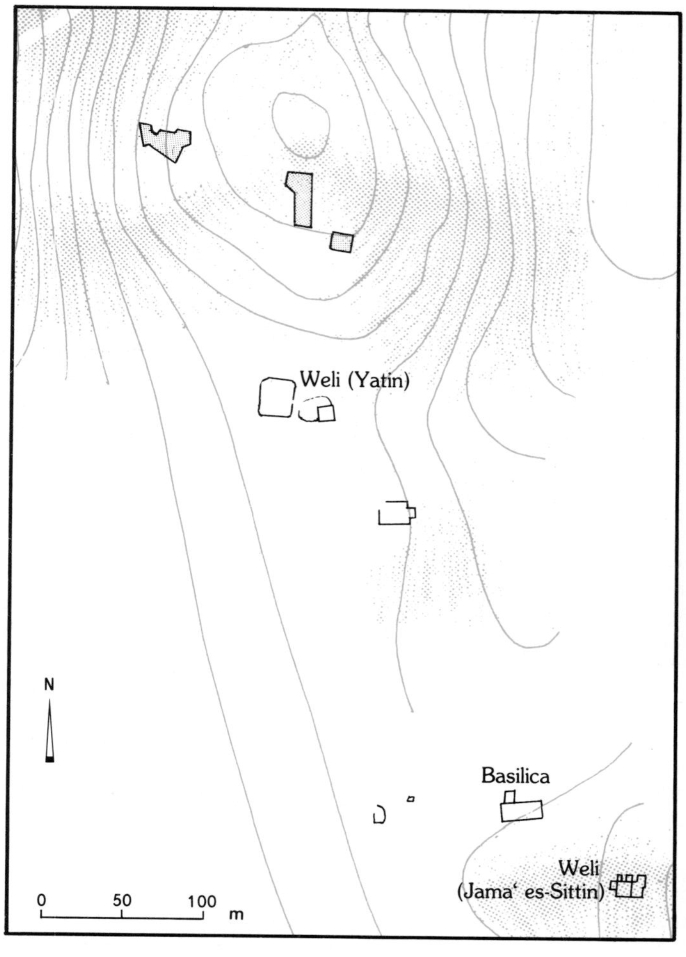

Shiloh: map of the mound and its environs.

HISTORY

According to biblical tradition, Shiloh was the religious capital of the tribes in the period of the Israelite settlement. The tabernacle was set up at Shiloh, and there the land was divided among the tribes and the Levitical cities were distributed (Jos. 18:1, 18:8–10, 21:2). The religious leadership in Shiloh conducted the negotiations between the tribes of Israel when divisiveness in the league threatened (Jos. 22:11–12), and it led a defensive war against a common enemy (1 Sam. 4). Religious festivals were held at Shiloh every year (Jg. 21:19). Two important biblical figures, Eli and Samuel, are connected with Shiloh. The house of Eli led the war against the Philistines. At the battle of Aphek the tribes of Israel suffered a severe defeat, and in consequence the Philistines conquered Shiloh (Jer. 7:12–14; Ps. 78:60). Traces of this destruction were discovered in the excavations.

Even after its ruin, Shiloh was apparently still considered a holy site, and a few inhabitants may have remained here to guard the ancient cult place. Ahijah the Shilonite was known in the days of Jeroboam, and it is evident from Jeremiah that the place was still remembered in his time. After the destruction of the First Temple, the people of Shiloh came to Jerusalem to offer sacrifices (Jer. 41:5).

EXCAVATIONS

The site was excavated by two early expeditions. In the first, in 1915, A. Schmidt conducted trial soundings and dug several test pits. From 1926 to 1932, systematic excavations were carried out under the direction of

Shiloh: map of the mound, excavated areas, and plan of the principal remains.

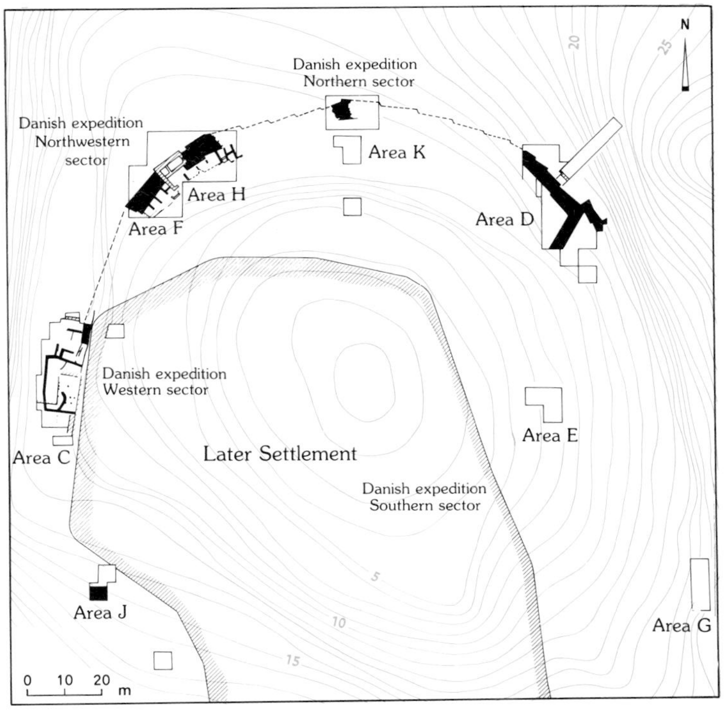

H. Kjaer, with the participation of Schmidt and the architects C. Christensen and S. Beck. The archaeological adviser was W. F. Albright. The second expedition, headed by I. Finkelstein, S. Bunimovitz, and Z. Lederman of Bar-Ilan University, excavated at the site from 1981 to 1984.

EARLY EXCAVATION RESULTS

In the first season of the Danish excavation, the finds were mainly from the later periods. The top stratum was a Crusader settlement apparently destroyed by Saladin; and beneath it were remains from the Hellenistic period. The second season was a longer one, and the excavators, following Albright's suggestion, concentrated their activities along what they called the city wall (found to date to the Roman-Byzantine period and used also in the Early Arab period).

MIDDLE BRONZE TO IRON AGE I. An area (25 by 20 m) was excavated on the western slope of the mound, which was found to consist of two main blocks: house A and room B—its early structures; and houses C and E, rooms H and J, and adjoining buildings—its later structures.

Room B, whose stratigraphy was unclear, contained sherds of juglets, lamps, bowls, and other potsherds that apparently belong to the Middle Bronze Age II. The room may initially have been constructed in that period (however, see below). House A was erected later (Iron Age I) and partially covered room B, perhaps even utilizing the stones from its walls.

House A (4 by 3.1 m) is attributed to the Iron Age I. In its northeast corner was a stone oven. The finds in the house included six collared-rim storage jars. Their presence in the destruction level of house A dates the Philistine conquest of Shiloh to the mid-eleventh century BCE. The "city wall" passes above house A and the adjoining buildings. Although some collared-rim jars were found near the wall, later material from the Iron Age II, Persian, and Hellenistic periods was found, as well. The wall was apparently built at a late date.

IRON AGE II TO ROMAN PERIOD. Potsherds from the Iron Age II and the Persian period indicate that some sort of settlement existed here, although no definite structures were found by the Danish expedition. Building remains from the Hellenistic period were uncovered mainly in the trenches made in 1926, south of the mound. Pottery and coins from this period were also found. Shiloh was reoccupied at the beginning of the Hellenistic period, when it again became a large settlement. Remains of walls and buildings from the Roman period were in continuous use up to the Arab period.

BYZANTINE PERIOD. Two churches from the fifth and sixth centuries CE were exposed at the foot of the mound in the southeast. The excavators called the first church the pilgrims' church and the second, the basilica.

Pilgrims' Church. The plan of the pilgrims' church (c. 11.7 by 25 m) is not entirely clear because it was incorporated into a later building. It seems to have had an internal apse and a bema with a chancel screen raised two steps above the nave. Two rooms north of the nave were identified by the excavator as the prothesis and the diaconicon. Remains of several rooms, probably later ones, were exposed to the west. The church apparently had a narthex and an atrium with a mosaic floor, in the center of which were traces of three columns. North of the atrium was a cistern to which water was conveyed through a channel from a source north of the church. Remains of small rooms (whose plan is unclear) were found near the cistern. They included a burial chamber hewn out of the rock.

The mosaic floor in the apse was decorated with vine leaves and bunches of grapes, and the mosaic in the nave displayed geometric designs. The mosaic floor in the prothesis was the finest and most richly ornamented of the three. It consisted of squares and a central panel, in which a pomegranate tree flanked by two deer is depicted. Behind each deer is the image of a fish. The excavator interpreted the deer as a reference to the passage, "As a hart longs for flowing streams, so longs my soul for thee, O God" (Ps. 42:1). On the floor of the prothesis a five-line Greek dedicatory inscription in a circle is inscribed in a square. It mentions the brothers Profirius and Jacob.

Basilica. The basilica (15.1 by 18 m) is closer to the mound than the pilgrims' church, and apparently also served as a church. It consists of a nave, two aisles, and a narthex on its west side. The nave's mosaic floor is decorated with geometric patterns of intersecting squares and of circles, and with shells, and various floral motifs. It bears a remarkable resemblance to the floor in the crypt of the Church of Elijah at Medeba, and it is very likely that the same artist was responsible for both. The basilica and the pilgrims' church were destroyed during the Arab conquest. Parts of them were dismantled and reused in Arab buildings.

EARLY ARAB PERIOD. The mound also contains numerous remains from the Early Arab period. Most of the houses east of house A also continued in use in this period. In 1926, the expedition discovered an open-air *weli* that, in the opinion of the excavators, represents the place of worship known in Arabic as Jama' es-Sittin (the Mosque of the Sixty), a site that was considered holy prior to the Arab conquest. Several parts of this mosque, which had been abandoned by the time of the excavations, were examined. Among the scanty finds recovered were many Arab lamps from the medieval period. The mosque's columns and capitals had been taken from the Byzantine basilica. The building is square (8.75 m each side) and has a small niche in the southern

Pilgrims' church: mosaic floor in the prothesis, Byzantine period.

wall that probably served as a miḥrab in its latest phase. The building may originally have been a synagogue converted into a mosque, an assumption based on the fact that the niche faces Jerusalem. Remains of a lintel decorated with an amphora and vine leaves were found among the ruins of the mosque.

BURIALS. Two burial caves were excavated. One, with loculi, had its beginnings in the Second Temple period and was later used as a reservoir. The second burial cave—el-Assad—was a cistern that was converted into a burial cave in the Roman period. The excavators noted three layers of burials. The earliest is Roman, the middle Byzantine, and the latest is Early Arab. Many complete pottery vessels, scores of human skeletons, and some animal bones were discovered in the cave from all three periods.

J. Day, *VT Supplement* 30 (1979), 87–94; D. G. Schley, "The Traditions and History of Biblical Shiloh" (Ph.D. diss., Atlanta 1986; Ann Arbor 1987); id., *Shiloh: A Biblical City in Tradition and History* (Journal for the Study of the Old Testament Supplementary Series 63), Sheffield 1989; R. E. Bishop, *Biblical Illustrator* 15/1 (1988), 62–64; A. S. Kaufman, *BAR* 14/6 (1988), 46–52; M. Weinfeld, *VT* 38 (1988), 324–332; Weippert 1988 (Ortsregister).

Danish Excavations

Main publications: M-L. Buhl and S. Holm-Nielsen, *Shiloh: Danish Excavations at Tell Sailun, Palestine, in 1926, 1929, 1932 and 1963*, 1, *The Pre-Hellenistic Remains* (Publications of the National Museum, Archaeological-Historical Series 12), Copenhagen 1969; F. G. Andersen, *Shiloh: The Danish Excavations at Tell Sailun Palestine, in 1926, 1929, 1932 and 1963*, 2: *The Remains from the Hellenistic and Mamluk Periods* (Publications of the National Museum, Archaeological-Historical Series 23), Copenhagen 1985.

Other studies: W. F. Albright, *BASOR* 9 (1923), 10–11; 35 (1929), 4–5; 48 (1932), 14–15; id., *PEQ* 59 (1927), 157–158; 63 (1931), 157–158; A. T. Richardson, ibid. 57 (1925), 162–163; 59 (1927), 85–88; H. Kjaer, ibid., 202–213; 63 (1931), 71–88; id., *JPOS* 10 (1930), 87–174; id., *I det Hellige Land, de Danske udgravninger i Shilo*, Copenhagen 1931; N. Glueck, *AJA* 37 (1933), 166–167; id., *BASOR* 52 (1933), 30–31; id., *QDAP* 3 (1934), 180; J. Starr, *BASOR* 57 (1935), 26–27; O. Eissfeld, *VT* Supplement 4 (1957), 138–147; Buhl–Holm-Nielsen, *Shiloh* 1 (Reviews), *Berytus* 19 (1970), 159–161. — *RB* 77 (1970), 94–96. — *IEJ* 21 (1971), 67–69. — *Qadmoniot* 16 (1971), 137 (Hebrew); *BAR* 1/2 (1975), 3–5.

AHARON KEMPINKSI

RENEWED EXCAVATIONS

Excavations at Shiloh were resumed as part of a regional project that included the survey of the Land of Ephraim (q.v. Samaria [region]). As the summit of the mound and its southern slope are covered by numerous Roman, Byzantine, and medieval remains, the excavators concentrated on the edges of the mound, particularly in its northern sector, which was almost unaffected by erosion or late construction. From 1981 to 1984, full-scale excavations were conducted in three new areas (areas C, D, and F), and trial excavations of a more limited scope in six others.

MIDDLE BRONZE AGE. The earliest occupation on the mound dates to the Middle Bronze Age IIB. The only evidence of its existence is a large quantity of pottery found in the glacis and the earth fills within the mound; these have all been assigned to a slightly later phase of the Middle Bronze Age. The lowest layer of the glacis also produced, in addition to sherds, a fragment of a painted cultic stand, a bone with an incised decoration, and a zoomorphic vessel. Because the fills inside the mound take up all the space between the floors from the Middle Bronze Age IIC (which run up to the city wall), on the one hand, and the bedrock, on the other, it is clear that in this phase the settlement was unwalled.

In the Middle Bronze Age IIC, the site was surrounded by a solid wall and an earthen glacis. These fortifications were found on almost all sides of the site, enabling the excavators to trace the wall's exact course, which enclosed an area of just over 4 a. The wall was founded on bedrock, and its faces were built of large field stones, with a fill of large and medium-sized stones.

Area F: zoomorphic vessel in form of a bull, MB II.

General view of area D: MB II wall, section through the glacis, and Iron I silos.

Area D: section through the glacis, MB II; (foreground) the city wall and the retaining wall of the glacis.

Area F: (left) MB II city wall and (right) the rooms adjoining it.

The wall was 3 to 5.5 m thick. The large section cut through the glacis in area D found the wall preserved to a height of some 8 m; in area F, it survived to a height of 2.3 m above the floors of the rooms built against its inner face. In some places (areas H and J), the constructive "joints" along the core of the wall can be discerned. The wall is not uniform either in thickness or in form: in the north, the 1932 Danish expedition exposed a rectangular solid tower, protruding 0.6 m from either side of the wall; the wall in area D, however, was built in a "sawtooth" technique. A sort of large offset, projecting toward the slope and slightly shallower than the city wall, was also built here. These features should probably be interpreted as technical stages in the building process, rather than chronological stages. The great mass of stones in the wall was an unending source of masonry for secondary construction in all periods and evidence of stone robbing was found in almost all of the wall's exposed parts. A sounding conducted in area H revealed that rooms L and M, originally exposed by the Danish expedition, are later than the city wall and were probably built in the Roman period in a trench created by the looting of the wall's stones.

The glacis was also examined in several places at the edge of the mound, and it too proved not to be uniform in shape. It was particularly impressive in a trench cut in area D, on the steep eastern slope of the mound. Its length there, from the wall to the end of the glacis on the slope, was approximately 25 m and its thickness near the wall was some 6.3 m. Its inclination was 20 to 25 degrees. At a distance of 1.8 m from the wall, another wall (0.9 m thick and 3.2 m high) was discovered within the glacis. Its function was to reinforce the glacis and anchor it to the slope. The glacis rested directly on bedrock. In area D, it consisted of four main layers, from top to bottom: a layer of hard, reddish-brown earth; a friable white layer, also containing small stones—this layer, the dominant constituent of the glacis, also sent "fingers" into the brown overlying layer; a layer consisting of numerous deposits of brown, reddish, and light-colored earth—dumped there in a direction opposite to that of the slope; and a yellowish-gray layer, mainly found up against the wall and the adjoining retaining wall. The three upper layers contained almost no sherds, whereas the lowest layer, as already mentioned, produced a large quantity of Middle Bronze Age IIB pottery. In the white layer, a Hyksos scarab with a geometric design was found. Elsewhere on the mound the construction of the glacis was neither as wide nor as complex.

Analysis of the relationship between the structure of the glacis, the surface, and the construction within the walled area showed that most of the builders' efforts were concentrated on the area where the slope is steepest—where stone fills were found inside the walls, as well. Furthermore, the city wall was almost covered on both sides by stone and earthen fills and by the glacis. It follows that the central concern of the planners of these stone and earthen fortifications was constructional.

All over the northern sector of the mound, Middle Bronze Age remains were found just inside the wall. A row of rooms was found abutting a section of the wall some 115 m long, extending from area F to area M. Fourteen of these rooms were exposed in areas F and H. They were built in the space created between the bedrock—which slopes down toward the edge of the mound—and the inner face of the wall; they must therefore have mainly been cellars. This also explains the excellent state of preservation of their walls, to a height of 2.5 m above the floors. They were bounded on the south by a wall, beyond which (toward the summit of the mound) were earth and stone fills. Fills of a light-colored earth (c. 1 m thick) were also laid between the floors of these rooms and the rock. All these fills produced large quantities of pottery from the earliest occupation—the Middle Bronze Age IIB.

Dozens of vessels and implements, mostly large storage jars, were found in the rooms, implying that they were used as storerooms. On the floor in the corner of one room was a group of bronze weapons and silver jewelry, including flat axes, a unique shaft-hole ax, and a circular silver pendant (diameter, c. 12 cm), engraved with a "Cappadocian symbol." Other finds in the rooms were two cultic stands, votive bowls, and a large zoomorphic vessel shaped like a bull. These finds, combined with the character of the site in the Late Bronze Age, apparently indicate the presence of a cult place in the Middle Bronze Age IIC. No Middle Bronze Age residential building was found. The site was destroyed by a conflagration at the end of the period, in the sixteenth century BCE; two chocolate-on-white sherds were found in the debris of bricks in the rooms in area F.

LATE BRONZE AGE. The Danish expedition unearthed a few finds from the Late Bronze Age, but not in a clear stratigraphic context. The new excavations also proved the existence at Shiloh of activity in the Late Bronze Age. This level was only exposed in area D (wall AA, uncovered by the Danish expedition in the northwest sector of the mound and defined as the Late Bronze Age city wall, was reexamined and found to be a Byzantine terrace); over an area of some 200 sq m inside and above the Middle Bronze Age wall, an accumulation of ash, light-colored material, and stones contained a very large quantity of sherds and bones. The depth of this layer, which could not be associated with any architectural remains, reached 1.5 m. The pottery repertoire found in it—mainly from the Late Bronze Age I—consisted of hundreds of flat bowls, as well as lamps, juglets, chalices, fragments of Cypriot ware, decorated ware, and a few cooking pots. Noteworthy among the small finds were a female figurine, a cylinder seal impression on a handle, and a gold ornament in the shape of a fly. Some of the vessels contained ashes and bones. The material probably represents burials of the remains of votive offerings brought to a cult place. The stratigraphic location of this accumulation, as well as its nature, indicates that the material was dumped onto the slope at a later stage, in the Iron Age I. In view of the fact that the Late Bronze Age stratum was found in area D only, and that it contained no remnants of masonry, it is evident that Shiloh was not actually settled then. Most probably there was only an isolated cult place at the top of the hill; it is not inconceivable that the people of the surrounding region brought offerings to the site of an earlier temple, which may have been rebuilt shortly after it was destroyed.

IRON AGE I. Remains from the Iron Age I were found in almost all the excavated areas: buildings in area C; an installation in area E; stone-lined silos, dumps, and stone-paved areas elsewhere. Lacking a stratigraphic relationship between the different areas, it is difficult to determine whether these remains were contemporary or represented several building stages.

The most impressive Iron Age I remains were found in area C, on the western side of the site. Houses A and B, originally exposed by the Danish expedition (see above), constitute part of these remains. The Middle Bronze Age II pottery found in these buildings originated beneath their floors, which overlay remnants of the glacis. The buildings were erected outside the Middle Bronze Age wall, which had been well preserved and served them as a rear wall. To construct them, the builders had to remove a section of the Middle Bronze Age glacis; the side (north and south) walls were built leaning on the continuation of the glacis. The houses were, in a sense, embedded in the glacis.

Owing to the steep gradient, it was necessary to create two levels of construction, between which was a terrace wall. This wall was built alternately of column drums and fills of small and medium-sized stones. Beyond the wall (toward the summit of the mound) a fill created the foundation for the upper building level. On the upper level were two buildings with columns and a corridor between them; on the lower level there was a large hall.

The southern building on the upper level was divided into four aisles by three rows of column drums. The floor of this building consisted of bedrock, stone slabs, and a few stretches of beaten white material—remnants of the Middle Bronze Age glacis.

The northern building contained two side rooms, carefully paved with stone slabs, and a courtyard with a beaten earth floor, in which there were two installations and a rock-cut cistern that continued in use after the buildings had been destroyed. Between the side rooms and the courtyard were two

*Area C: **(left)** plan; **(right)** isometric reconstruction of the Iron I structures on the mound's western slope.*

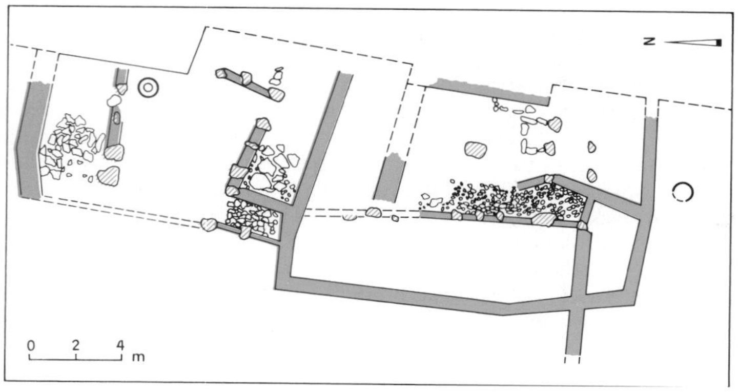

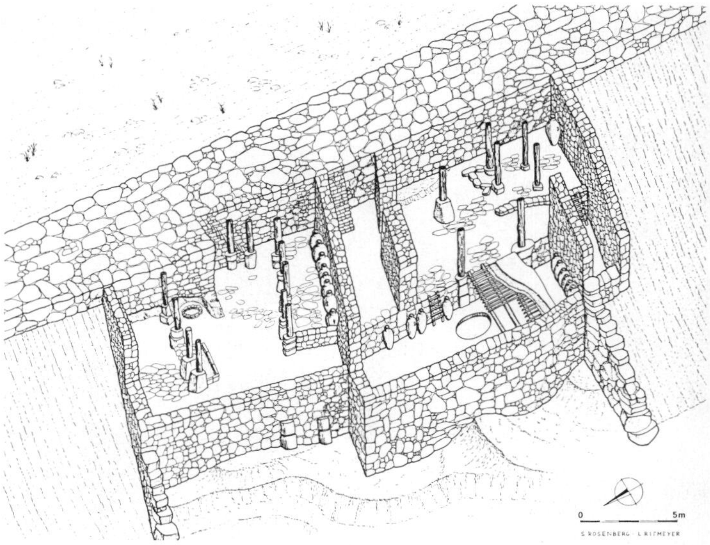

rows of columns with a low partition between the columns. Two additional columns stood between the rows, on the eastern side of the building. The columns survived to a height of one meter and more. On the west, toward the slope, the building terminated in a massive terrace wall, in which constructive columns were incorporated.

The hall on the lower level was paved with beaten earth on gravel; in its center was a refuse pit. This room was probably a kind of cellar for the southern building. It was entered from the corridor, by way of a ladder or steps; because the area was damaged by a furnace built here in the Byzantine period, it is not possible to determine whether there were indeed any steps. The western wall of the hall was also the outer wall of the site toward the western slope. The entrance to this whole complex was probably on the east, from the higher part of the mound. This, too, cannot be ascertained, as part of the eastern side of the buildings was buried under massive late construction.

The buildings in area C yielded a rich assemblage of pottery: the excavations unearthed here a total of more than thirty complete vessels and numerous large fragments of other vessels; the Danish expedition found ten more vessels. The overwhelming majority of the finds consisted of collared-rim jars: six of them found in 1929 in house A—that is, in the southern part of the hall on the lower level—and one found in the southeastern part of the upper building. More jars of this type were found in the hall on the lower level and in other rooms. All the jars were found leaning on the walls, some with their bases stuck into the floors. In addition to collared-rim jars, the finds included other types of jars (one with a handle bearing the impression of a scarab with a geometric design), jugs, and kraters (one with several handles). The ash pit in the hall on the lower level contained cooking pots, as well. A heap of charred raisins was found on one of the floors.

This complex of buildings was destroyed by a violent conflagration whose traces were visible everywhere: charred floors and heaps of fallen bricks, sometimes more than one meter deep (some of the bricks were visibly baked by the fierce fire). Here and there parts of the fallen roof were identifiable. As suggested by Albright following the Danish expedition's excavations, this may be attributable to the Philistine destruction of the site (mid-eleventh century BCE).

Overlying the brick debris of one of the buildings was a dump containing a large quantity of bones and Iron Age I pottery. Among the finds here were a bone seal and fragments of vessels decorated with animals in relief: the rim of a

Aerial view of area C, looking east.

Area C: collared-rim jars in building 335, Iron I.

cooking pot bearing a lioness's head, a bowl handle with a deer's head beneath it, and fragments of a cultic stand with an applied decoration of a horse, a lioness, and a leopard attacking a deer. These objects were probably dumped down the slope in a later period, when the area farther up the mound was being cleared for building purposes.

Area E was excavated over a limited section only; in it a few Iron Age I walls were found resting on the bedrock, as was a hewn installation, inside and beside which was a number of collared-rim jars. In area D, a coarse stone floor was uncovered, running up to the inner face of the Middle Bronze Age wall; a stub of wall, perhaps also dating to this period, was found nearby. The top of the stone part of the Middle Bronze Age wall had been leveled by means of small stones and incorporated as part of the floor. Found on this floor, which may have been in a workshop area, were sherds of collared-rim jars. Another find here was a black stone seal (diameter, 4 cm) bearing two crossed figures of galloping horned animals. About fifteen silos from the same period were also found in area D; each is approximately 1.5 m in diameter. They were cut into the layer of refuse from the Late Bronze Age. Two of the silos contained a large quantity of charred wheat grains. A similar silo was exposed in the southern part of area H, and three more in area K. The last four were cut into the debris of bricks and fills from the Middle Bronze Age. A trench cut in the lower part of area J revealed a dump containing a large quantity of Iron Age I pottery. The depth of this accumulation was some 2 m, and it had been dumped at an angle parallel to the slope. This presumably represents refuse from the buildings standing in the southern sector of the site, thus marking its southern boundary. Among the finds in this material was the rim of a collared-rim jar, bearing three rosette-shaped impressions.

Based on the data from the various areas, the extent of the site in the Iron Age I is estimated at some 2.5 to 3 a. The buildings in area C are pivotal for understanding the plan of the settlement. Considerable effort was expended to construct them on the steep slope, even though the northern part of the mound was empty and readily available for building. The directions in which the walls of these buildings lay indicate that the buildings must have been part of a large complex on the summit. This complex was probably the source of the refuse exposed in area C above the destruction layer. The finds in the buildings in area C suggest that the buildings were not residential; at least some were storehouses.

Area C: restored pottery from building 335, Iron I.

Drawing and photograph of a fragment of a cultic stand from area C, Iron I.

IRON AGE II. After the destruction of Shiloh in the eleventh century BCE, there was a brief gap in occupation until the renewed activity in the Iron Age II. Remains from this period were found in various places on the mound: a few stubs of walls in area E; a structure in area G, badly damaged by erosion down the slope and later activities; an occupational level in room U (whose excavation was begun by the Danish expedition) in area H; and a few remains in area C.

LATE PERIODS. The recent excavations revealed remains from later periods at various places on the site, mainly around the borders of the Roman-Byzantine village that occupied the summit and southern slope. Poor remains of a building from the Hellenistic period were discovered in area G. A floor and the foundations of a building from the Roman (Herodian) period were found in area F. Its walls were founded directly on the walls of the Middle Bronze Age rooms, and its floor was founded on a fill deposited on the brick debris from those rooms. On the floor, among other objects, were some stone vessels. A

*Area C: **(right)** handle of a krater(?) with the head of a ram beneath it; **(left)** the rim of a cooking pot bearing the head of a lioness(?) found in the dump above the northern columned building, Iron I.*

few walls from the Roman period, built on the Middle Bronze Age city wall and the bedrock inside it, were discovered in the upper part of area J. In the lower part of area J a large rectangular retaining structure from the Roman period (length, 19 m; height, 3 m) was found. A square that was excavated up the slope, above area C, produced Roman remains and, above them, the remains of a Byzantine building. A furnace and a long Byzantine terrace wall were found in area C.

I. Finkelstein et al., *IEJ* 32 (1982), 148–150; 33 (1983), 123–126, 267–268; id., *ESI* 2 (1983), 95–100; 3 (1984), 96–97; id., *RB* 91 (1984), 260–267, 404–406; id. (and B. Brandl), *Israel Museum Journal* 4 (1985), 17–26; id. (et al.), *Excavations at Shiloh 1981–1984: Preliminary Report* (TA 12, 123–180), Tel Aviv 1985; id., *BAR* 12/1 (1986), 22–41; id., *The Archaeology of the Israelite Settlement*, Jerusalem 1988; id., S. Bunimovitz, and Z. Lederman, *Shiloh: The Archaeology of a Biblical Site* (Monograph Series of the Institute of Archaeology, Tel Aviv Univ.) (in prep.); *Buried History* 19/2 (1983), 23–27; J. Balensi, *MdB* 33 (1984), 53–54.

ISRAEL FINKELSTEIN

SHIQMIM

IDENTIFICATION

Shiqmim is a large (c. 23.5 a.) Chalcolithic (c. 4500–3700 BCE) village and mortuary center (c. 20 a.) located along the northern bank of Naḥal Beersheba in the Negev desert, some 16 km (10 mi.) downstream from the contemporary sites of Bir Abu Matar, Bir eṣ-Ṣafadi, and Ḥorvat Batar, near Beersheba (map reference 115.067). It is the largest of the Chalcolithic villages in the Beersheba Valley and the only one where a separate cemetery complex has been found. Deep stratigraphy (over 5 m for the Chalcolithic period), settlement planning based on rectilinear architecture, well-preserved subterranean structures, extensive evidence for metalworking, and the location of the site along the semiarid Irano-Turanian and arid Saharo-Arabian climatic zone interface make Shiqmim a key site for studying the emergence of social complexity in one of Israel's marginal environments.

EXCAVATIONS

Shiqmim was first discovered in 1950 by D. Alon in his early survey work in the region. The full significance of the site as a subregional Chalcolithic settlement center emerged from the 1977–1980 systematic survey of the Beersheba Valley and lower Naḥal Besor carried out by T. E. Levy and D. Alon. The survey showed Shiqmim to be a settlement center surrounded by six smaller satellite sites. Systematic excavations were carried out in two phases of field work: phase I in 1979 and 1982 through 1984 by the Israel Department of Antiquities and Museums and the Negev Museum; and phase II from 1987 to 1989 by the Nelson Glueck School of Biblical Archaeology of the Hebrew Union College-Jewish Institute of Religion and the Israel Antiquities Authority. The excavations were co-directed by T. E. Levy and D. Alon and were affiliated with the American Schools of Oriental Research. Excavations in the village covered more than 4,000 sq m and in the cemetery approximately 2,000 sq m. Three main phases of occupation have been distinguished in the village at Shiqmim.

PHASE III (c. 4520–4400 BCE). The earliest occupation phase was dated by averaging eight radiocarbon determinations that span the earliest settlement phases at Shiqmim (average 5626 ± 51 BP). It is contemporary with the beginning of the Badarian culture, the end of the Fayum Early Neolithic, and the Merimda culture. Geomorphological studies at Shiqmim and in its environs show that, in the earliest occupation phase, climatic conditions were more moist than today, and the Beersheba Valley was an active agent. In phase III, human settlement focused along the margins of the Beersheba Valley, away from the present wadi channel, on loessial hilltops and in subterranean houses dug into the hard-packed loessial sediment that characterizes these hills. Like Abu Matar and Bir eṣ-Ṣafadi (q.v. Beersheba), the earliest ("pioneer") settlement at Shiqmim is characterized by subterranean structures connected by networks of tunnels and rooms. In 1989, two separate underground systems were found, one of which was completely excavated.

Subterranean building complex no. 1 contains nine underground rooms and related features. The rooms are oval and vary in size from 2.5 to 4.5 m in diameter, with ceilings more than 2 m high. In five of these rooms, large, stone-built support walls were constructed along the southern sides. The rooms were interconnected by tunnels ranging from 1 to 2 m long, 0.9 wide, and 0.9 high. The entrance to this system was from a tunnel on the site's surface that led 4 m down to a gallery room; two other tunnels connected the other subterranean rooms in the system. A number of bell-shaped storage pits were found cut into the floors of the subterranean rooms. In some cases, hearths were found in them with cooking vessels. A number of ivory objects, including an exquisite vial, was found here.

Phase III was also characterized by extensive quarrying activities that cut

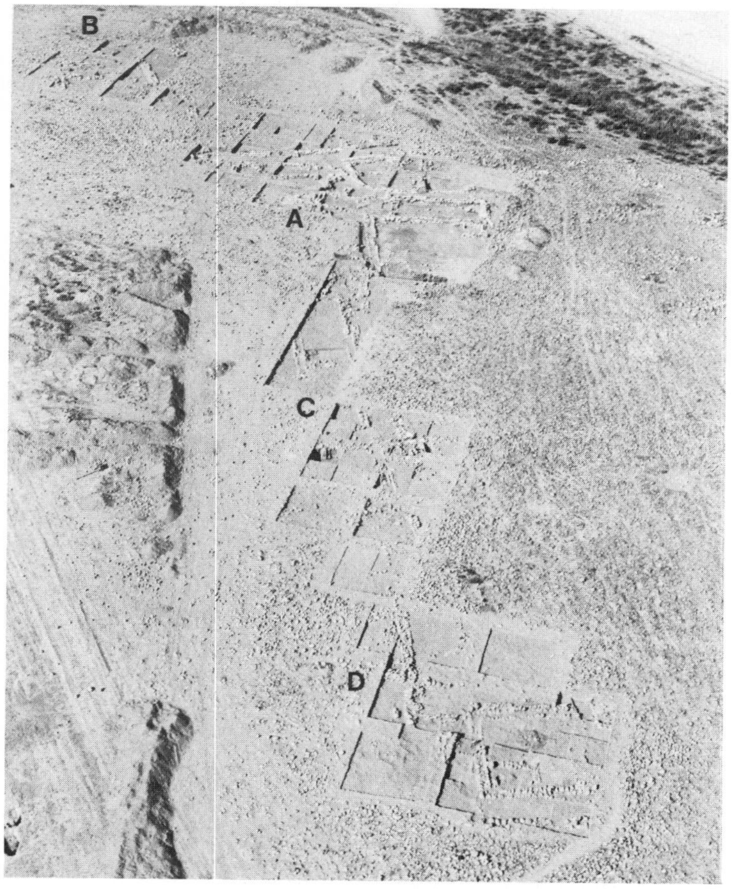

Shiqmim: aerial view.

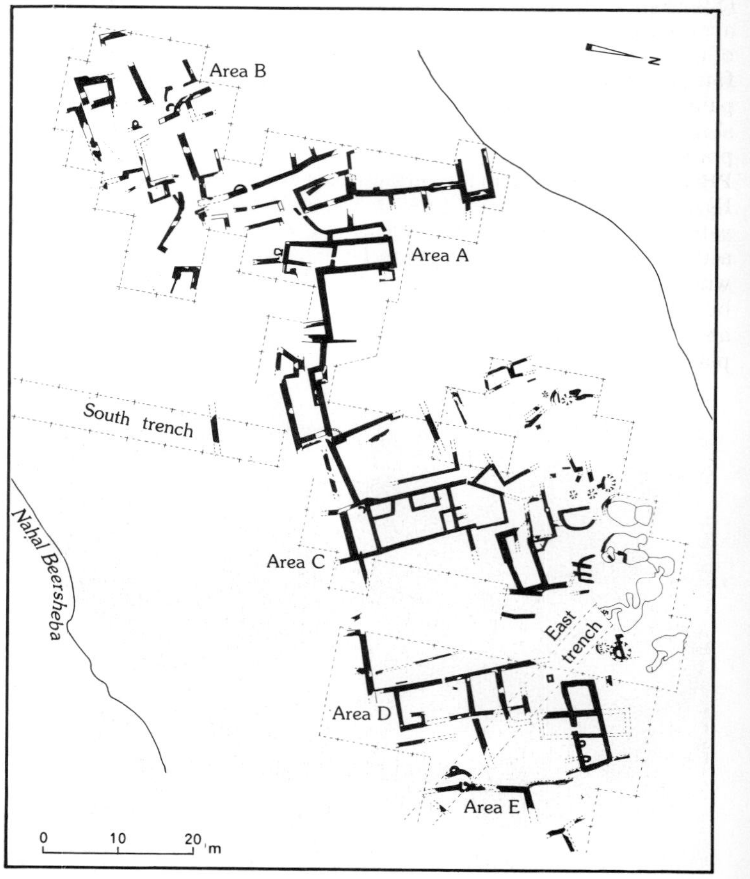

Shiqmim: plan of excavations in western part of the settlement.

Typical cave dwelling.

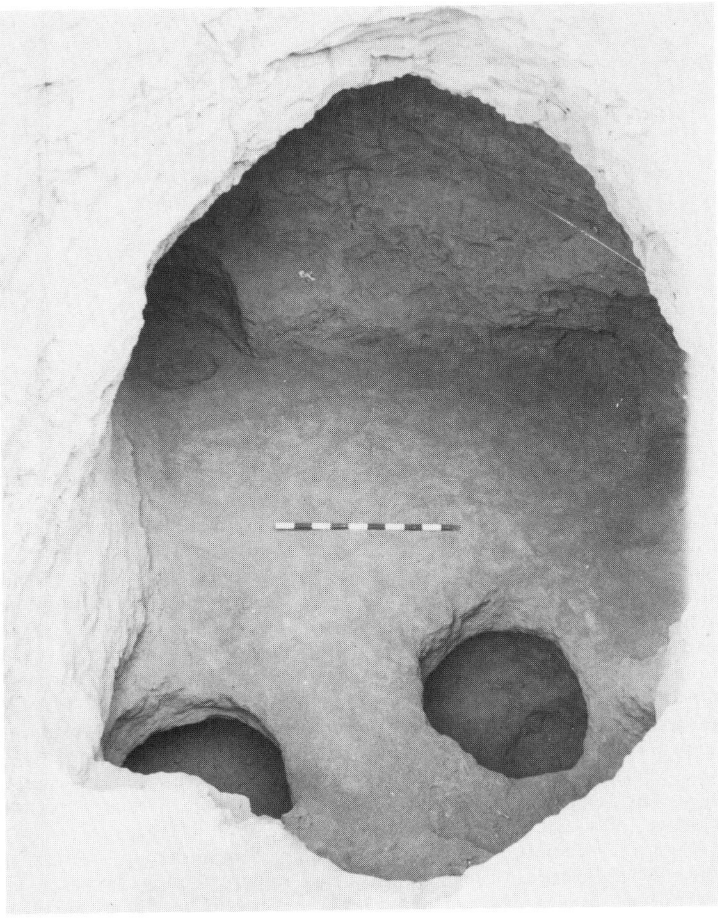

Head of a basalt "Pinocchio" statuette..

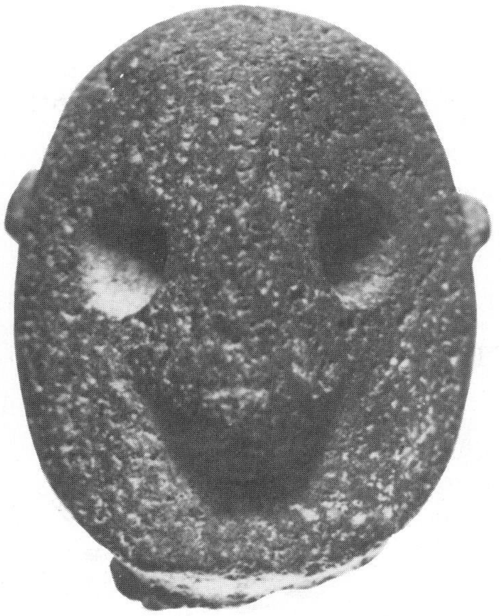

into the loessial hills to create more occupation space away from the wadi. This resulted in the construction of a terrace more than 3 m high and more than 40 m long. The subterranean rooms were dug inside the terrace. Along the terrace face, two large, open-air, semicircular altars were constructed. One of them (5.2 m long, 2.45 m wide, and 2.2 m high) was found with two V-shaped pots and a tabular scraper in the ash on its surface. In the center of the altar, a cache of nine complete pottery vessels and a fenestrated stand had been used as a foundation deposit: a high-neck bottle, a jar with a flared neck and richly painted geometric patterns, two small painted jars, a deep basin, and four V-shaped bowls. These altars reflect communal building activities and ritual practices in the pioneer phase of settlement.

PHASE II (c. 4240–3990 BCE). The date of the main settlement phase (phase II) is based on three determinations from samples from features associated with the planned settlement that reached its zenith in the phase II building activities (average 5280 ± 104 BP). The main occupation is contemporary with the Badarian culture and the Fayum Late Neolithic. The zenith of the building activities was accompanied by a radical shift from a subterranean to an open-air village based on rectilinear architecture. There is evidence for a planned settlement in the distribution of foundation walls made of wadi boulders aligned in the same northwest–southeast orientation. These structures include broadroom domestic houses (c. 3.5 by 4.5 m) associated with enclosed courtyards (c. 5.5 by 10 m); larger broadroom buildings (c. 5 by 10 m) with little evidence of domestic artifacts; storage bins; plazalike open areas; and some subterranean storage facilities. Twenty-nine buildings were excavated from this phase. At the end of the phase II occupation, more than 70 percent of these structures were destroyed and the site was abandoned. While most buildings show evidence of destruction, some structures were abandoned in a pristine state, leaving a full range of domestic items in situ. Many of the architectural features observed in this and the following phase foreshadow Early Bronze Age building styles at Tel Arad and other sites. While some buildings were abandoned, approximately 70 percent of the phase II village was destroyed by fire.

Pottery vessels in situ.

PHASE I (c. 3940–3700 BCE). The dates for the last occupation (phase I) are based on only two determinations, one from a burial in the village and the other from a floor deposit associated with one of the larger buildings (no. 1) at the site (average 5002 ± 63 BP). The last occupation at Shiqmim is contemporary with the beginning of the Naqada I occupation and the early settlement at Maadi. In the final phase, there is little evidence for the utilization of any subsurface structures. Instead, occupation was spread out unevenly over the site in rectilinear buildings of varying size. This phase seems to represent a reoccupation of the village on a much smaller scale than before. Most of the phase I structures also show evidence of destruction. Like other Chalcolithic sites in the Beersheba Valley, Shiqmim was abandoned and most of the valley was not reoccupied until the Iron Age.

METALWORKING. There is extensive evidence for metalworking at Shiqmim associated with the last two occupation phases. On-site production indicators include copper ore (malachite), slags, crucible fragments, and pits where ores were smelted. Trace-element analysis of the copper ores and slags matches that of the cast-copper tools (axes, chisels, adzes, and awl points) found in the village. These studies show that the ore was procured in Transjordan in Wadi Punon and brought to Shiqmim (and the Beersheba sites), where it was smelted and cast into tools.

In addition to tools, copper standards, mace heads, and band fragments point to prestige/cult metalwork at Shiqmim. These objects are similar to the metalwork from the Judean Desert Naḥal Mishmar cave hoard. Technological studies show that the prestige/cult metalwork was done using the lost-wax method and ore with a high arsenic content. No evidence was found for the on-site production of the latter objects. Earlier researchers suggested that the origin of elaborate Chalcolithic metalwork was in Anatolia or Armenia. A petrographic examination of a stone core found inside a copper mace head shows it to be glaconitic chalk from the Arabah Valley opposite Wadi Punon. These findings indicate the local production of prestige/cult metalwork and illustrate the sophisticated level of craft specialization at this time.

POTTERY AND FLINT-TOOL INDUSTRY. More than 3,000 kg of pottery from the village were collected and analyzed. With the exception of a handful of intrusive Byzantine sherds, the entire collection dates to the Chalcolithic period. The 1988 collection is characteristic of the complete assemblage and is discussed here. The minimum number of vessels recovered from the three main occupation phases is 2,458. The most common types, in decreasing order, are V-shaped bowls (48 percent), basins (15 percent), hole-mouth

Shiqmim: tombs, cemetery 1.

jars (14 percent), globular jars (10 percent), bowls (9 percent), churns (2 percent), jars (2 percent), and pithoi (1 percent). Special pottery forms were found in other seasons, but not in significant numbers: fenestrated stands, high-neck bottles, thin cups, and ovoid forms. Unlike sites from neighboring wadis (Besor, Patish, and Gerar), no cornet vessels were found at Shiqmim.

The lithic assemblage is a flake-based industry at Shiqmim. The degree of craft specialization reflected in this industry is open to debate. However, the presence of tabular scrapers may be one indicator of trade with an outside source for non-locally produced tools. The 1987–1989 collections serve as a representative sample and are summarized in the following table:

RELATIVE FREQUENCIES OF LITHIC DEBITAGE FROM SHIQMIM, 1987–1989

Debitage	*% (N=34,996)*	*Tools*	*% (N=3,180)*
Chips	17.33	Notch	3.90
Chunks	29.37	Borer	3.99
Primary flake	10.39	Denticulate	2.48
Flake	33.26	Side scraper	1.23
Blades	4.74	Scrapers	9.40
Bladelet	0.42	Tabular scraper	0.82
Flake core	2.51	Tabular fragments	0.31
Blade core	0.04	Sickles	3.62
Flake core trimming	1.41	Sickle blades	2.39
Blade core trimming	0.24	Celts	2.77
Bladelet trimming	0.08	Choppers	1.92
Bladelet core	0.02	Modified flakes	48.84
Mixed core	0.21	Modified blades	4.72
		Modified bladelets	0.94
		Varia	0.94
		Misc. trimming	11.54
		Canaanite blades	0.19

ORNAMENTS AND FIGURINES. Trapezoidal pendants made of bone, ivory, or shell are the most common ornament found in the village and the cemeteries. Two holes are perforated in the upper portion of the pendant, for hanging on a string. Amorphously shaped pendants made of mother-of-pearl are also found. *Lambis* shell, which originates in the Red Sea, was used to manufacture large arm bracelets. These have been found in both mortuary and village contexts. The bottom half of a female figurine (c. 4 cm long) carved out of animal bone was found. The most important figurine discovered was the head of an anthropomorphic male "Pinocchio" statuette carved out of basalt. It is identical to ivory examples found upstream at Bir eṣ-Ṣafadi and points to a shared iconography in the Beersheba Valley at this time.

CEMETERIES AND BURIAL PRACTICES. Shiqmim is the only Chalcolithic settlement in the northern Negev where a separate cemetery complex was found. The cemetery extends for more than 1 km (0.6 mi.) along an Eocene chalk ridge overlooking the Beersheba Valley. On a series of eight hilltops, clusters of grave circles, cist graves, and burial cairns were found that resemble those at Adeimeh, near Tuleilat el-Ghassul in the Jordan Valley. The grave circles range from 0.9 to 3.5 m in diameter and were filled mostly with secondary human burials. A wide range of offerings was found, including V-shaped bowls, pendants, basins, cups, beads, grinding stones, bracelets, palettes, ossuaries, and a hematite mace head. The clusters of burial monuments range from about ten to twenty-five structures at each hilltop excavation. Twelve cist structures were found on two hilltops; in each case, V-shaped bowls were found on the cist floors but no evidence of human remains. Evidence for social ranking was found in cemetery 1.

Shiqmim: grave circle, cemetery 3.

ECONOMY. As a permanent village settlement, Shiqmim's subsistence base focused on the farming of cereals and a sheep/goat transhumance system. The most important providers of meat were three domestic ungulates: sheep and goat (91 percent) and cattle (9 percent). Kill-off patterns of the sheep/goat bones indicate that these animals were also exploited for their secondary products (milk, hair, and wool). Some animals were hunted, as shown by the bones of foxes, hare, hartebeest, and the single foot bone of a lion. Ostrich eggshells and a single femur indicate that these birds were also exploited. A number of horse bones (*Equus caballus*) indicate that these animals were domesticated. As at other Beersheba Valley sites, no pig bones were found.

The order of relative importance of the crops at Shiqmim is two-rowed, hulled barley (*Hordeum vulgare distichon*), 83 percent; emmer wheat (*Triticum dicoccum*), 11 percent; wheat (*Triticum parvicoccum*), 2.3 percent; lentil (*Lens culinaris*), 2.2 percent; and varia, 1.2 percent. Most of the botanical samples were collected from the later occupation phases at the site. Phytolith studies show that multicelled samples dominate the Shiqmim assemblage, suggesting that wheat and barley were grown under irrigated (as opposed to dry-farming) conditions. Additional evidence for run-off farming are the dozens of Chalcolithic terrace walls found in the vicinity.

SUMMARY

From a social evolutionary perspective, Shiqmim represents a chiefdom society and a type of sociopolitical organization not previously found in the Negev. This reconstruction is based on the two-tier settlement hierarchy of this and other large sites in the Beersheba Valley; the planned architecture in the village; metal production; and the large cemetery complex. Shiqmim served as a center that coordinated social, economic, and ritual activities for the Beersheba Valley culture.

T. E. Levy and D. Alon, *Mitekufat Ha'even* 16 (1979), 109–117; id., *BASOR* 248 (1982), 37–59; id., *ESI* 2 (1983), 100–102; 4 (1985), 99–100; 9 (1989–1990), 167–170; id., *IEJ* 33 (1983), 132–135, 272–274; 35 (1985), 74–76; 38 (1988), 90–92; 39 (1989), 115–117; 40 (1990), 226–228; id., *RB* 91 (1984), 219–226; id., *ASOR Newsletter* 37/1 (1985), 4–5; id., *'Atiqot* 17 (1985), 187–189; id., *BASOR* Supplement 23 (1985), 121–135; 27 (1991), 29–46; T. E. Levy, *BAIAS* 1983–1984, 36–41; id., *Paléorient* 11/1 (1985), 71–83; id., *BA* 49 (1986), 82–108; id. (and A. Holl), *La Recherche* 19/203 (1988), 1166–1174; id., *BAR* 16/6 (1990), 20–31; id. (et al.), *Research and Exploration* 7 (1991), 394–413; C. Gosden, *BAIAS* 1982–1983, 13–14; C. Grigson, ibid. 1984–1985, 36; id., *Mitekufat Ha'even* 22 (1989), 111*–114*; N. Slope, ibid., 37–38; A. Miller Rosen, *Cities of Clay: The Geoarcheology of Tells* (*Prehistoric Archaeology and Ecology*), Chicago 1986, 106–113; id., *Shiqmim I: Studies Concerning Chalcolithic Societies in the Northern Negev Desert, Israel (1982–1984)*, 1–2 (*BAR*/IS 356, ed. T. E. Levy), Oxford 1987; ibid. (Reviews), *Paléorient* 13/2 (1987), 150–152. — *Mitekufat Ha'even* 21 (1988) 138*–164*. — *BAIAS* 8 (1988–1989), 71–76. — *Orientalia Lovaniensia Periodica* 20 (1989), 257–258; P. Goldberg, *BA* 51 (1988), 197–202; Weippert 1988 (Ortsregister); I. Gilead and Y. Goren, *BASOR* 275 (1989), 5–14; B. Rothenberg, *University of London, Institute for Archaeo-Metallurgical Studies Newsletter* 17 (1991), 1–17.

THOMAS E. LEVY, DAVID ALON

SHIQMONA

IDENTIFICATION

Tel Shiqmona (Tell es-Samaq) is on the Mediterranean coast, about 1.3 km (0.8 mi.) southwest of the Carmel Cape (map reference 1462.2478), which is today within the city of Haifa. Its area is more than 2 a. Prior to excavation, it was 12.74 m above sea level at its highest point. The remains of a Byzantine town extend over the flat fields around the mound, at an average altitude of 5 m above sea level. The area of dense ancient remains begins in the north, near the bend in the coastline near the mound, reaching the slopes of Mount Carmel in the east and the beginning of the modern Ẓarfat Road in the south, although isolated remains are found farther south, as well. The maximum extent of the town in Byzantine times was about 55 a. Shiqmona's cemetery is to the east, on the slopes of Mount Carmel; it extends from Elijah's Cave at the cape to the southern boundary of the town. Elijah's Cave is itself part of a sacred precinct that once occupied the Carmel Cape. Although the site has no convenient seaport, there may have been an anchorage farther south, near Kefar Samir, in the sandy coastal belt now known as the Carmel Beach.

EXPLORATION

In 1895, G. Schumacher reported that the cemetery at Shiqmona had been systematically plundered for two years, until the Turkish authorities intervened. A Byzantine monastery, probably outside the town's built-up area, was excavated in 1951 by M. Dothan, on behalf of the Israel Department of Antiquities and Museums (q.v. Monasteries: Sha'ar ha-'Aliyah). In the 1950s, several additional discoveries were made in the area of the town, including a bronze plaque bearing a Hebrew inscription. Systematic excavations at the site began in 1963, under the direction of J. Elgavish, on behalf of the Haifa Municipal Museum of Ancient Art. They continued until 1979, their seventeenth season.

The Persian period strata were examined mainly in the 1963–1964 seasons. The remains of the Byzantine town in the fields surrounding the mound were uncovered mainly in the 1965, 1966, 1978, and 1979 seasons. The cemetery was systematically excavated in 1967–1968. The 1968–1970 seasons concentrated on the Iron Age II strata, and the 1971–1974 seasons on the Iron Age I strata. Late Bronze Age strata were reached in 1975–1977. The grotto popularly known as Elijah's Cave was explored in 1966 by A. Ovadiah, on behalf of the Archaeological Survey of Israel; the inscriptions on the cave walls were cleaned and read at that time. Beginning in 1968, important finds were made by fishermen, on the sea bottom near and south of the mound, up to and including the bathing area known today as Dado's Beach (q.v. Marine Archaeology).

EXCAVATIONS ON THE MOUND

An area of about 800 sq m was cleared on the mound, stretching along the southern edge of the ridge and down the southwestern slope. The limestone bedrock was reached at an altitude of 2.4 m above sea level; the building foundations of the lowest stratum rested on virgin soil, 3.3 m above sea level. The sequence revealed by the excavations follows.

1. The town was established in the Late Bronze Age I and was occupied continuously until the end of the Late Bronze Age II. Two clearly defined strata from this period were discovered, with five levels of settlement between them, some of which can also be considered occupational strata (beneath the Late Bronze Age II stratum only a trial sounding was made).
2. There were three occupational strata from the Iron Age I.
3. There was almost continuous settlement through the Iron Age II, comprising five occupational strata.
4. A Phoenician town existed on the site in the Persian period, comprising two occupational strata.
5. In the Persian, Hellenistic, and Roman periods a series of fortresses stood here.
6. There are two strata of dwellings from the Byzantine period.

Except for a single Middle Bronze Age IIB tomb in the cemetery, no remains earlier than these were found at Tel Shiqmona.

LATE BRONZE AGE I. One complete room and corners of two other rooms from a Late Bronze Age I dwelling were uncovered. Most of the building is buried in the unexcavated area. No other buildings were found in the excavated area. Nine complete jars and a few smaller vessels, including a bichrome juglet, were found standing in the corner of the completely cleared room.

LATE BRONZE AGE II. A public building from the Late Bronze Age II was

Scarab bearing an inscription, from MB II tomb.

Faience goblet, LB II.

Tel Shiqmona: general view, looking northeast; (background) the Carmel Range.

General view of street, houses, and casemates in town A, 10th century BCE.

found whose destruction can be dated to the last third of the thirteenth century BCE or the first quarter of the twelfth century BCE. The part that was excavated consisted of a stretch of a circular megalithic wall; adjoining it were a room, a courtyard, and two silos. The building was quite large, with foundations dug more than 2 m into the ground. Among the more notable finds in the building were various types of pottery vessels, a faience goblet, an ivory implement with the head of the goddess Hathor at one end and a human hand at the other, scarab seals—all Egyptian, a Mycenean zoomorphic vessel representing a porcupine, cylinder seals bearing mythological scenes, and imported Cypriot bowls and juglets.

IRON AGE I. The buildings excavated in the two lowest strata had a simple plan and were not built very well. The late stratum was characterized by small barrel juglets. A house found in the upper stratum was probably destroyed in the eleventh century BCE. It consisted of two square rooms alongside a rectangular courtyard; a Hebrew inscription was found on one of the jars discovered in this room. It was in this stratum that the first appearance was recorded of bowls and juglets decorated with concentric circles, painted in black on a bright red background (Cypro-Phoenician ware).

IRON AGE II. Five consecutive towns occupied the mound in the Iron Age II.

Town A. The destruction of town A can be dated to the tenth century BCE. A stretch of a casemate wall (c. 60 m long) was uncovered near the southern corner of the city wall. Within the town, two streets and four houses were cleared. Two of the houses were identical in plan: two long rooms separated by a wall of stone pillars and an additional room across the width of the house. A third, larger building (11 by 15 m) had an open courtyard, with rows of rooms along three of its sides. The city wall was destroyed in a conflagration. A large quantity of pottery vessels was found in the casemates. Many of the cooking pots were of the type lacking handles, their rims marked with various signs. One storage jar bore an inscription in red ink: *lmlk'l*, "(Belonging) to Malk[i]el." This stratum contained a large proportion of Cypro-Phoenician ware.

Town B. Town B included a large residential building that was probably destroyed in the second half of the ninth century BCE. It was a rectangular structure with an elongated courtyard in the center. Flanking the courtyard were two rectangular rooms, separated from it by rows of pillars. A cache of weapons—arrowheads and spearheads—was discovered in one of the rooms. A jug with a mushroom-shaped rim was found in the same room. This stratum did not contain Cypro-Phoenician ware. Around the far end of the courtyard were four rooms, one of which contained a large group of storage jars. In the center of the courtyard was an oil press, consisting of a silo, a mortar for crushing the olives, and a stone drum for pressing them. A flight of stairs along

Pottery assemblage, 10th century BCE.

Terra-cotta figurine of a woman with a drum, 9th–8th centuries BCE.

House in town B, second half of 9th century BCE.

the wall outside the building led to an upper story and to the dwelling quarters. It is not clear whether the upper story was also built over the courtyard. The ground floor was well preserved: all its walls reached the ceiling; only the lintels that had rested on the pillars did not survive.

Town C. Town C was probably destroyed in the middle of the eighth century BCE. No fortifications were located. Three oil presses were found in the town, all large installations with storerooms containing storage jars and other vessels. The actual presses consisted of a stone mortar, in which the olives were first crushed; a stone drum (diameter, 1.3 m) found nearby in which they were then pressed; and a stone channel, which conveyed the oil to a sunken storage jar. A terra-cotta figurine of a goddess seated on a chair was found in this stratum, as well as a large number of figurines of horsemen and girls holding musical instruments or votive offerings.

Town D. Town D was destroyed in the second half of the eighth century BCE. Several houses were uncovered, but their plans have not been determined. Two had storerooms containing storage jars. One building comprised a room and two courtyards. Hebrew inscriptions were found on two of the jars in this building. Two stone seals portraying a figure worshiping the symbols of the moon god were also found in this stratum.

Town E. Town E was probably destroyed in the seventh century BCE. Few remains were found in this stratum, indicating that it probably does not represent a very densely settled phase. Storage jars with basket handles, used primarily in transporting commodities by sea, made their first appearance here.

PERSIAN PERIOD. A small weaving workshop, dating to the beginning of the Persian period, was destroyed in the second half of the sixth century BCE. Only one room, with a supporting pillar in its center, was discovered. Scattered on the floor were dozens of clay weights in assorted sizes; smaller weights were found stored in jars.

Town (Stratum P). The town of stratum P was built at the end of the sixth century BCE and destroyed in the first third of the fifth century BCE. Its residential quarter was built on the ridge and on a series of terraces along the slope of the mound. The stratum was relatively well preserved. Two stone-paved streets, forming broad steps, intersected at right angles. Three residential units along them were excavated almost in their entirety. Each consisted of a courtyard and three rooms; the entrance from the street was through

Oil press, 9th century BCE.

Pottery and other finds, first phase of the Persian period.

Selection of pottery and stone objects, second phase of the Persian period.

the paved courtyard, which also contained an oven used in the summer. The room adjoining the courtyard served as a kitchen and included an oven (for use in the winter) and a small plastered pool, perhaps a bathtub. One of the rooms, on whose floor fifty-three intact vessels were found, appears to have been either a shop where perfumes and pottery were sold or the storeroom of such a shop.

Fortress (Stratum PB). The remains of only three rooms were found in stratum PB, from the late fourth century BCE. The rooms appear to have belonged to a hastily constructed fortress. From this period onward, the residential quarter was probably situated in the surrounding fields. The fortress, either Tyrian or Persian, was built in about the mid-fourth century BCE and may well have been destroyed in the wars of the Diadochi (Alexander the Great's heirs) to gain control of the region. One of the rooms uncovered was a subterranean storeroom containing scores of vessels of various types, including four storage jars bearing royal Phoenician inscriptions. The remains attest to violent destruction. The place was looted and its pottery was deliberately smashed at the entrance to the underground room. An ostracon assigned to this stratum bore a fragment of a Phoenician alphabet—the letters ל ,כ ,י ,ט ,ח ,ז (*z, ḥ, ṭ, y, k, l*).

HELLENISTIC AND ROMAN PERIODS. Two fortresses from the Hellenistic and Roman periods were discovered.

Hellenistic Fortress (Stratum H). The destruction of stratum H is dated to about 130 BCE. Its remains—the courtyard and three rooms of a building and seven other rooms—were partially cleared. They were destroyed largely by later construction. They may have belonged to a fortress, but there is no conclusive evidence to that effect.

Three of the rooms were large storerooms found full of amphorae and other vessels. Two of the amphorae bear inscriptions in Greek. A locally produced amphora was also found, whose handles bear seal impressions recording the *agoranomos*, and the year 180 of the Seleucid era (132 BCE). The same type of seal impression was found in the excavations at Jaffa.

Roman Fortress (Stratum R). The fortress in stratum R was erected in the second half of the first century, probably in connection with the First Jewish Revolt. It continued to exist until the mid-third century. The date and historical circumstances of its destruction are unknown. Thick, deep-set foundations were found in the area cleared, as well as several adjoining plastered pools. A cistern containing an accumulation of second-century sherds and vessels was also found.

BYZANTINE PERIOD. Part of a large dwelling (9 m long) and several houses, either dwellings or workshops, were uncovered on the slopes of the mound. They came to a sudden and violent end in about the mid-fourth century. The

Wine jar inscribed with the amount and type of wine, as well as its origin (Gat Carmel), 4th century BCE.

Bronze female figurine recovered from the sea near Shiqmona, Hellenistic period.

Zoomorphic vessel in the form of a ram, from a 4th-century tomb.

Byzantine residential quarter south of the mound (after the removal of the mosaics).

structures belonged to the town that extended over the fields around the mound. In the sixth century, a large villa surrounded by a garden stood on the summit. Some 95 sq m of its area, including five rooms, were cleared. It was destroyed at the beginning of the seventh century.

ARAB PERIOD. Overlying the remains of the Byzantine villa were the foundations of an isolated building from the Arab period. The approach road leading to it from the foot of the mound was paved. The date of this structure is unclear.

THE AREA AROUND THE MOUND

In the fields south of the mound, an area of about 0.5 a. of the Byzantine town was thoroughly excavated, adjacent to the seashore. Trial soundings were also carried out in a 0.25-a. area northeast of the mound and in a similar area just east of it. A single stratum was found, most of whose structures were built in the sixth century. Several buildings dated to the fourth century, however, and continued in use with various modifications until the town's final destruction, at the beginning of the seventh century. One of the trial soundings produced Hellenistic remains close to bedrock.

A wealthy residential quarter was excavated south of the mound. Two almost complete dwelling units were cleared, each covering an area of about 170 sq m and consisting of a long corridor, three or four rooms, a kitchen, a large courtyard, and a nymphaeum. Two of the rooms were paved mostly with

One of the mosaic floors in the Byzantine residental quarter south of the mound.

Shiqmona: bronze figurine of a Byzantine empress(?), 6th century CE.

Zoomorphic vessel in the form of a bull, 6th century CE.

mosaics in colorful geometric patterns; the others were paved with flagstones. The walls were plastered and painted. More than forty mosaic floors were uncovered. Scattered on the floors were various household objects—made of pottery, bronze, and ivory—as well as weapons attesting to sudden destruction. Cooking pots were found still standing on stoves. Plaques decorated with menorahs were found, as were bronze crosses. A large industrial building (13 by 24 m) was erected in the fourth century; it consisted of a series of pools of various sizes. It is not clear what industry was involved here, but in the sixth century, the building was adapted for residential use.

The stone-paved streets of the sixth-century town divided the quarter into almost perfect squares. Public cisterns on the streets were fed by a widespread subterranean network of roofed channels carrying rainwater. Sections of this network were examined at various points.

Shops and workshops were situated in the area excavated northeast of the mound. One workshop contained a collection of iron tools. In one of the shops a set of glass and bronze weights was found, from a one-quarter *numisma* to twenty *numismata*. This was undoubtedly the town's commercial quarter, and probably its oldest part. Workshops and stores were located east of the mound, as well, as were many cisterns and cellars hewn in the rock and various installations. The upper stories of these workshops were used as dwellings. On the beach, south of the town's densely built area, parts of a large monastery were uncovered. Marble and mosaic floors, one of them with a dedicatory inscription, were preserved. The monastery continued in use after the town's destruction, but the date of that destruction is unknown.

THE CEMETERY

Within the cemetery, twenty-one tomb caves were cleared, nineteen of them close together inside the area of the modern Histadrut Park. This area was completely excavated down to bedrock. All but one of the tombs dated to the third and fourth centuries, as did most of the finds. Many of the tombs continued in use until the early seventh century. Tombs with typically Jewish and typically Christian symbols were found in close proximity. The tombs are of two types:

1. A square court leading to a hall with arcosolia. These tombs were closed by rolling stones that fitted into a slot and by square stones that sealed the opening above them.
2. A deep shaft with arcosolia on two sides. The shaft of these tombs was closed by rectangular slabs of stone.

One of the tomb caves is dated to the Middle Bronze Age IIB. It contained a shaft 2.5 m deep and two burial chambers. Burial was on rock-cut benches and shelves. A seal was found here bearing the name Ya'aqob-har. A tomb cave with loculi containing clay coffins was found in the nearby 'En ha-Yam neighborhood. It was dated to the second century CE.

Main publication: J. Elgavish, *The Excavations of Shikmona: A Seleucian Garrison Camp from Hasmonean Times*, Haifa 1972.

Other studies: B. Lifshitz, *ZDPV* 78 (1962), 84–85; J. Elgavish, *An Archaeological Trip into the Past of the City through Excavations at Shikmona*, Haifa 1967; id., *RB* 75 (1968), 416–417; 76 (1969), 412–413; 77 (1970), 386–387; 78 (1971), 419–422; 81 (1974), 98–100; 82 (1975), 587–591; 83 (1976), 270–272; 84 (1977), 264–266; 85 (1978), 408–409; 86 (1979), 449–450; 89 (1982), 238–240; id., *IEJ* 19 (1969), 247–248; 20 (1970), 229–230; 22 (1972), 167; 23 (1973), 117–118; 24 (1974), 283–284; 25 (1975), 257–258; 26 (1976), 65–76; 27 (1977), 166–167; 28 (1978), 122–123, 280–281; 30 (1980), 208–209; id., *Raggi* 9 (1969), 1–17; F. M. Cross, Jr., *IEJ* 18 (1968), 226–233; C. Novak, *Antike Welt* 1/3 (1970), 54; A. Spycket, *RB* 81 (1974), 258–259; A. Lemaire, *Semitica* 30 (1980), 17–32; A. Van den Branden, *Bibbia e Oriente* 22 (1980), 219–225; R. Giveon, *Göttinger Miszellen* 44 (1981), 17–20; J. Naveh, *IEJ* 37 (1987), 28–30; N. Karmon and E. Spanier, ibid. 38 (1988), 184–186; Weippert 1988 (Ortsregister); G. Finkielsztejn, *RB* 96 (1989), 224–234.

JOSEPH ELGAVISH

Tomb-cave opening blocked by a rolling stone, 3rd–4th centuries CE.

SHUNAH, TELL ESH-

IDENTIFICATION

Tell esh-Shunah is located on the eastern side of the Jordan Valley, at the foot of the Gilead highlands, opposite Kibbutz Gesher, which is on the valley's western side (map reference 207.224). The mound is about 1 km (0.6 mi.) long and rises about 10 m above its surroundings. Today, there are two villages, Khirbet esh-Shunah and Khirbet Sheikh Ḥussein, on the mound. Probes and limited excavations were carried out here by two teams: one led by J. Mellaart and H. de Contenson (1952–1953), and another directed by C. Gustavson-Gaube (1984–1985).

THE MELLAART/DE CONTENSON EXCAVATIONS

The Mellaart/de Contenson excavations were part of a regional survey undertaken in the Jordan Valley by the Jordan Department of Antiquities, in advance of a development program for the local irrigation systems. Excavations were carried out at Tell Abu Habil and Tell es-Sa'idiyeh et-Taḥta as part of the same survey. At Tell esh-Shunah, de Contenson cut a small trial trench from the surface to bedrock. Mellaart dug another trial trench, but the finds have not been published. The deposits revealed in de Contenson's trench were divided into layers, numbered (with Arabic numerals) from the surface downward. During the examination and analysis of the finds, the sequence of deposits was divided into strata, several of which consisted of several layers. These strata were assigned Roman numerals, running from the bedrock upward, in the opposite direction from the layer numbers. The earliest stratum is thus labeled I, and the latest VI. De Contenson dated the strata as follows:

Stratum I (layers 19–17): Middle Chalcolithic period;
Sterile stratum (layer 16): no finds;
Stratum II (layers 15–14): Late Chalcolithic period;
Stratum III (layers 13–8): Early Bronze Age I;
Stratum IV (layers 7–4): Early Bronze Age II;
Stratum V (surface finds only): Early Bronze Age III;
Stratum VI (layers 3–2): Arab period;
Surface (layer 1): surface stratum.

When the excavation report for the 1952 and 1953 seasons was written in 1955, the terms Wadi Rabah culture, Pottery Neolithic A, and Pottery Neolithic B were not in use; nor had G. E. Wright's work on the division of the Early Bronze Age into stages been published. The excavator regarded Jericho VIII and the early strata at Tuleilat el-Ghassul (strata III–II) as Early Chalcolithic strata. His "Middle Chalcolithic period" included the assemblages from Ghassul IV, the Beersheba sites, the assemblages from Tel Beth-Shean XVIII and the pits beneath them, and the early strata at Tell el-Far'ah (North). His "Late Chalcolithic period" included the "Esdraelon culture," which today, following Wright, is assigned to the Early Bronze Age I.

The following survey of the strata and their dates uses the terminology generally accepted today:

STRATUM I. The earliest settlement at the site included a beaten-earth floor, some hearths, and a pit (1 m deep; diameter, c. 1.5 m). The pottery was handmade from light brown clay; round mat impressions appear on some vessel bases. The shape of the vessels is simple: small bowls, medium-sized deep bowls, hole-mouth jars, and medium-sized storage jars. They have flat loop handles that broaden at their junction with the vessel's body. The vessels were decorated in various ways: a red stripe was painted near the rim, usually on the exterior but sometimes also on the interior (on some the paint dribbled downward in vertical lines to the base); entire vessels were slipped in red; bowls and hole-mouth jars were slipped and burnished; rope decoration, made of clay strips, was appended to some vessels.

The excavator was unsure how to date this stratum, which resembles the finds from stratum XVIII and the pits at Beth-Shean, stratum I at Tell Abu Habil, the finds from Tell es-Sa'idiyeh et-Taḥta, and the Early Chalcolithic finds from R. de Vaux's excavations at Tell el-Far'ah (North). After the excavation at Tell esh-Shunah, de Contenson wrote, at the beginning of the 1960s, about the stratigraphy and terminology of the Pottery Neolithic and the Chalcolithic periods: he suggested that the assemblage from stratum I at Tell esh-Shunah should be regarded as a northern Chalcolithic culture, chronologically parallel to the southern assemblages of Ghassul IV and the Beersheba sites.

STRATUM II. Two occupation levels with traces of buildings were found in this stratum. The pottery is of three types: gray-burnished carinated bowls, known as Esdraelon ware; red-burnished ware, similar to K. M. Kenyon's group A from Jericho; and simple vessels, which the excavator considered parallels to those from stratum XVII at Beth-Shean and from stratum II at Mezer. De Contenson regarded this settlement as a northern variant of the Late Chalcolithic period (the Early Bronze Age I, according to the terminology accepted today by most scholars).

STRATUM III. Stratum III contained pottery decorated with band slip. It was dated to the Early Bronze Age I.

STRATUM IV. Several floors and a wall were found in stratum IV. The pottery is decorated with regular and patterned burnish. De Contenson thought the stratum paralleled strata XIV–XIII at Beth-Shean and dated it to the Early Bronze Age II.

STRATUM V. Stratum V is characterized by Khirbet Kerak ware and was dated to the Early Bronze Age III.

STRATUM VI. Stratum VI, attributed to the Arab (medieval) period, contained glazed and painted pottery.

THE GUSTAVSON-GAUBE EXCAVATIONS

New excavations were carried out in 1984–1985 in the area known as Tell esh-Shunah North by C. Gustavson-Gaube of the University of Tubingen. Three adjoining squares (EI–EIII), each measuring 5 by 5 m, were excavated. Bedrock was reached only in square EI; the deposits were 4.3 m deep. The excavator distinguished 107 separate strata, which were numbered 7 to 114. Three phases were apparent in the ceramic assemblage. The excavator adopted de Contenson's terminology and conclusions entirely, disregarding the many changes and the progress made in the meantime in the research of the periods in question.

EARLY CERAMIC PHASE (STRATA 114–55). The early ceramic stage is divided into three parts: early (strata 114–88/82), middle (strata 81–72), and upper (strata 71–55). The excavator sees this stage as a northern variant, chronologically parallel to the Chalcolithic Ghassulian culture and the Beersheba sites. The pottery from the early part of this stage resembles that of the Pottery Neolithic B at Jericho and, in her opinion, reflects a transitional stage. The pottery is painted red; there are also some isolated slipped and burnished sherds and three sherds painted with a geometric pattern (known from Tel Ẓaf).

MIDDLE CERAMIC PHASE (STRATA 54–23). Gray-burnished ware (Esdraelon culture) is typical of the middle ceramic stage; the excavator attributes it to the Late Chalcolithic period.

LATE CERAMIC PHASE (STRATA 22–7). A new decorative style appears in the late ceramic stage: band slip. The excavator calls this the early phase of the Early Bronze Age I.

In the area excavated by Gustavson-Gaube, only the three earliest stages of the sequence uncovered by de Contenson appear. Following de Contenson, the excavator regards the earliest stage as a local variant paralleling the southern Ghassulian culture, and the Esdraelon culture as a Late Chalcolithic phase. The hundreds of sherds published from the two seasons of excavations were arranged not in stratigraphical order, but according to the excavator's typological criteria. In her detailed ceramic analysis, Gustavson-Gaube emphasizes the characteristics that continue from stage to stage and concludes that the sequence continued throughout the entire fourth millennium. This writer does not agree (see below).

SUMMARY

Tell esh-Shunah's importance lies in the two periods represented on the mound:

1. The Early Bronze Age. A complete Early Bronze Age sequence, in modern terms, was unearthed at the site, as shown in the table.

2. The Pre-Ghassulian Chalcolithic period. This writer believes that stratum I at Tell esh-Shunah and the parallel assemblages from the central Jordan Valley (stratum XVIII and the pits at Tel Beth-Shean; stratum I at Tell Abu Habil; the assemblage from Tell es-Sa'idiyeh et-Taḥta; and the assemblage from Tel Ẓaf) constitute a stage between the Wadi Rabah phase (Pottery Neolithic B) and the Ghassulian Chalcolithic that can be dated to the second half of the fifth millennium BCE. If this is correct, then there is a gap in occupation at Tell esh-Shunah that chronologically parallels the Ghassulian Chalcolithic, in contrast to the conclusions drawn by de Contenson and Gustavson-Gaube.

STRATIGRAPHY OF TELL ESH-SHUNAH

De Contenson Excavations	*Gustavson-Gaube Excavations*	*Period*
Stratum I	Early ceramic stage	Pre-Ghassulian Chalcolithic (2nd half of 5th mill.)
Gap		Ghassulian Chalcolithic
Stratum II	Middle ceramic stage	EB IA
Stratum III	Late ceramic stage	EB IB
Stratum IV		EB II
Stratum V		EB III
Stratum VI		Medieval period

H. de Contenson, *ADAJ* 4–5 (1960), 12–98; 8–9 (1964), 30–34; id., *MUSJ* 37 (1960–1961), 57–77; id., *RB* 68 (1961), 546–556; R. A. Erskine, *ADAJ* 29 (1985), 85–87; C. Gustavson-Gaube, ibid., 43–87; 30 (1986), 69–113; id., *SHAJ* 3, 'Amman 1987, 237–240; D. Baird, *ADAJ* 31 (1987), 461–480.

YOSEF GARFINKEL

SHUNERA DUNES

IDENTIFICATION

The Shunera dunes (Ḥolot Shunera) comprise the smallest and southernmost of the three principal dune fields in the western Negev lowlands, which include Ḥolot Ḥaluẓa and Ḥolot 'Agur. Bounded by Naḥal Lavan and Har Qeren on the west, Mishlat Shivta on the south, Giv'at Ḥayil and Naḥal Besor on the east, and Naḥal Shunera to the north, the Shunera dunes comprise parallel, west–east trending longitudinal dunes with a terminal Pleistocene date overlying earlier, upper Paleolithhic loess sediments.

One of the several systematic surveys and salvage excavations in the western Negev was conducted here in a 10-sq-km area at the southern edge of the dunes under the auspices of the Emergency Archaeological Survey of the Negev under the direction of A. N. Goring-Morris from 1980 onward.

A small northward-flowing *naḥal*, Wadi es-Sid, originates near Mishlat Shivta and cuts through the Eocene bedrock adjacent to Giv'ot Ivḥa at the interface between the dunes and the loess-covered rolling hills. The wadi has incised the bedrock at this point with a small canyon and waterfall, at the base of which is a small *t'mila* (Arabic, water hole) that seasonally fills with water. The wadi originally joined Naḥal Lavan several kilometers farther downstream, although it is today blocked by dunes. The canyon can be dated to the early Holocene; in the terminal Pleistocene, dune incursions from the west blocked the flow of Wadi es-Sid, creating a seasonal playa extending over about 1 sq km; it was subsequently breached when the depression was filled in, sometime in the early Holocene. Such a setting would have enhanced plant growth, which in turn would also have encouraged concentrations of animals and bands of hunter-gatherers. Similar phenomena elsewhere in the western Negev and northern Sinai proved to be attractive localities for prehistoric hunter-gatherers, as witnessed by the clusters of sites on the dunes at such points. Here in the Shunera dunes, a cluster of some thirty late Upper Paleolithic through Late Neolithic temporary campsites was investigated on the sandy terrace adjacent to the wadi, as well as on and in the large dune. The sites range in size from small ephemeral camps about 5 sq m in area to larger camps perhaps reaching 150 sq m. Campsites have been noted elsewhere in the surveyed area, often clustered in prominent locations on the sandy slopes of Giv'ot Ivḥa and Miẓpe Shunera, which enabled monitoring of the landscape.

THE SITES

UPPER PALEOLITHIC. Three of the five late Upper Paleolithic sites discovered have been excavated: Shunera XV, XVI, and XX. All appear to be associated with the beginning of dune accumulation in the area. The site of Shunera XV was associated with a paleosol probably predating dune formation. The lithic industry is similar to that at 'En 'Aqev; both have a flake technology and quantities of carinated items in addition to rare *lamelles Dufour* (Dufour bladelets).

Shunera XVI is the largest and best preserved of the Upper Paleolithic sites and included several hearths associated with flint concentrations or large quantities of ostrich eggshell fragments. The lithic industry included finely and partially retouched bladelets, in addition to carinated flake elements. Of interest are the possibilities of core reconstruction, including massive pieces from a core measuring some 20 by 40 cm. Several tools were smeared with ocher. The lithic industry is reminiscent of that from 'En 'Aqev East. This accords well with most of the dates obtained at Shunera XVI:

	14,150 BCE ± 150 (Pta-3703)	ostrich eggshell
	13,850 BCE ± 160 (Pta-3702)	ostrich eggshell
	14,250 BCE ± 170 (RT-1072N)	charcoal
	102 BP ± 2 (RT-1069N)	charcoal
(paleosol)	20,250 BCE ± 400 (RT-1084)	calcium carbonate

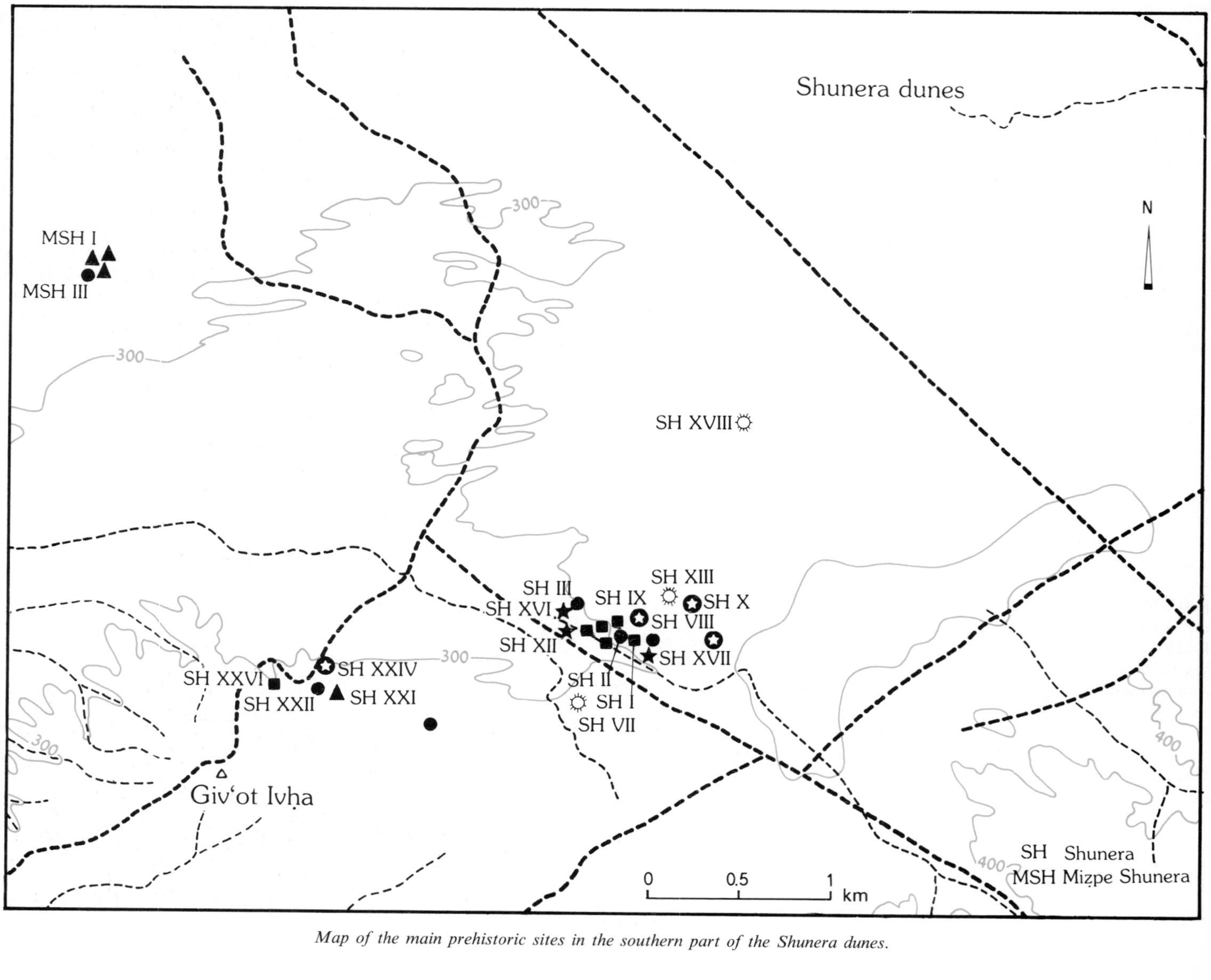

Map of the main prehistoric sites in the southern part of the Shunera dunes.

Southern part of the Shunera dunes: (foreground) Shunera III; (center) Shunera II.

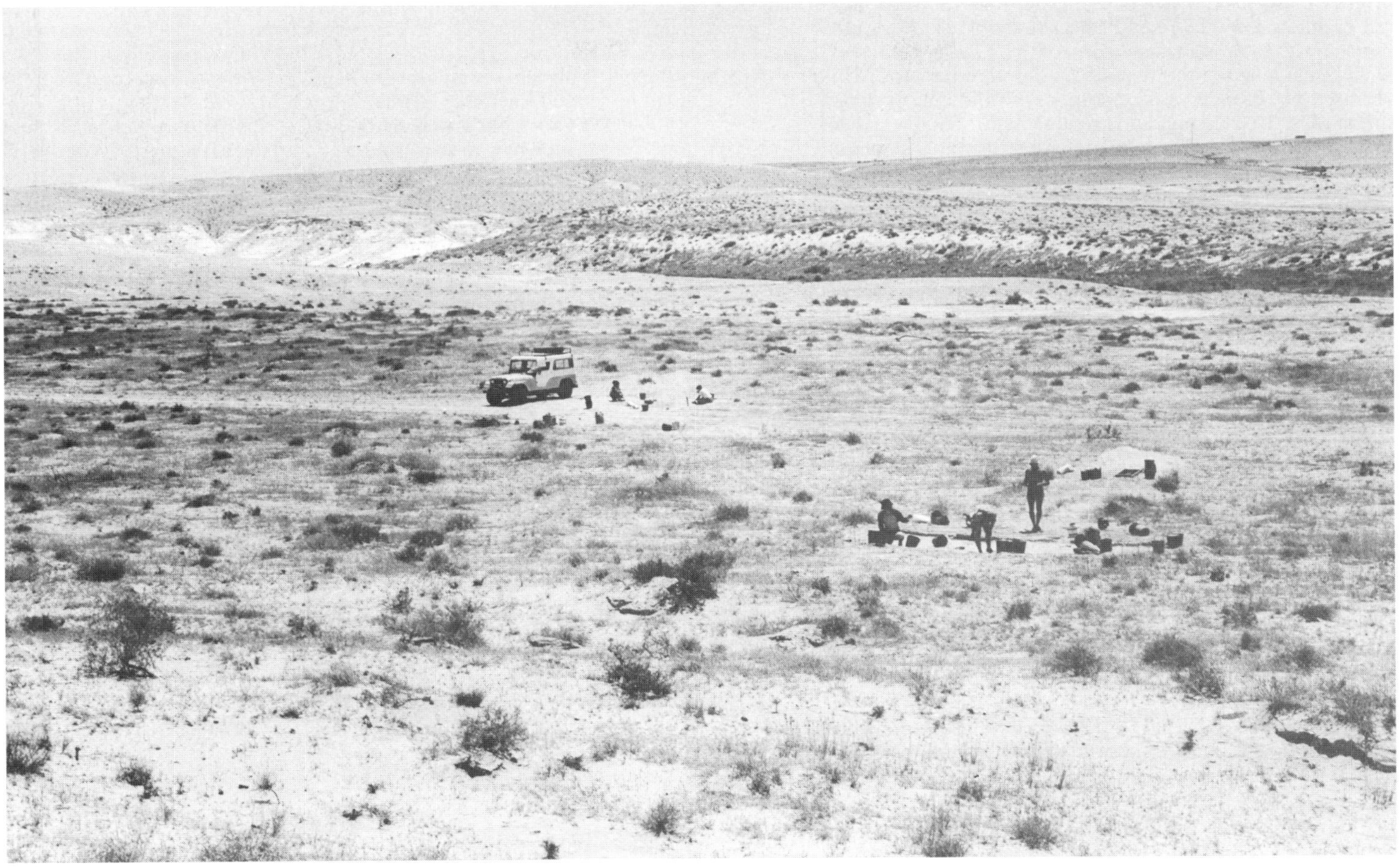

KEBARAN. A single ephemeral Kebaran site was represented by Shunera XVII, which covered just 6 sq m around a hearth, with more than 350 broken microliths, most obliquely truncated backed bladelets, three massive denticulates, and quantities of debitage.

GEOMETRIC KEBARAN. Six Geometric Kebaran occurrences were located, all but one tightly clustered on the right terrace and dune near Wadi es-Sid. Although they have been partially deflated, two major variants can be distinguished: one, characterized by Shunera III, features relatively narrow, elongated rectangles and trapezes; the other—at Shunera I, XII, XIIA, XIIB, and XXV—has wider geometrics. Shunera I also contained quantities of large asymmetric trapezes on flakes, a form previously encountered only in the central Coastal Plain sites of Ḥofit and Qiryat Aryeh I. The size of the Geometric Kebaran sites varies from 20 to 80 sq m; where preserved in situ, they feature a single hearth. It is possible, although unproven, that Shunera I, XII, XIIA, and XIIB represent a single encampment of adjacent family units.

MUSHABIAN. Four sites were provisionally assigned to the Mushabian or similar industries. Thus, Miẓpe Shunera III probably slightly predates the Mushabian in a strict sense and belongs to the later Early Epipaleolithic Niẓẓanan industry. Shunera VIII, however, is clearly Mushabian.

Two other in situ occupations were documented that may be later than the Mushabian. Shunera II was a small site of just 20 sq m with a hearth and accompanying ash dump. Intrasite patterning was marked, with an arc of densely packed debitage adjacent to a worktable to one side of the hearth and a concentration of bladelet blanks, microburins, and broken microliths next to an anvil on the other. Several tools were covered with ocher. Shunera IV is similar. It is the largest and densest of the sites investigated, featuring at least two hearths. Debitage was particularly profuse there. A rich marine mollusc assemblage was also recovered, comprising mostly dentalia beads but also

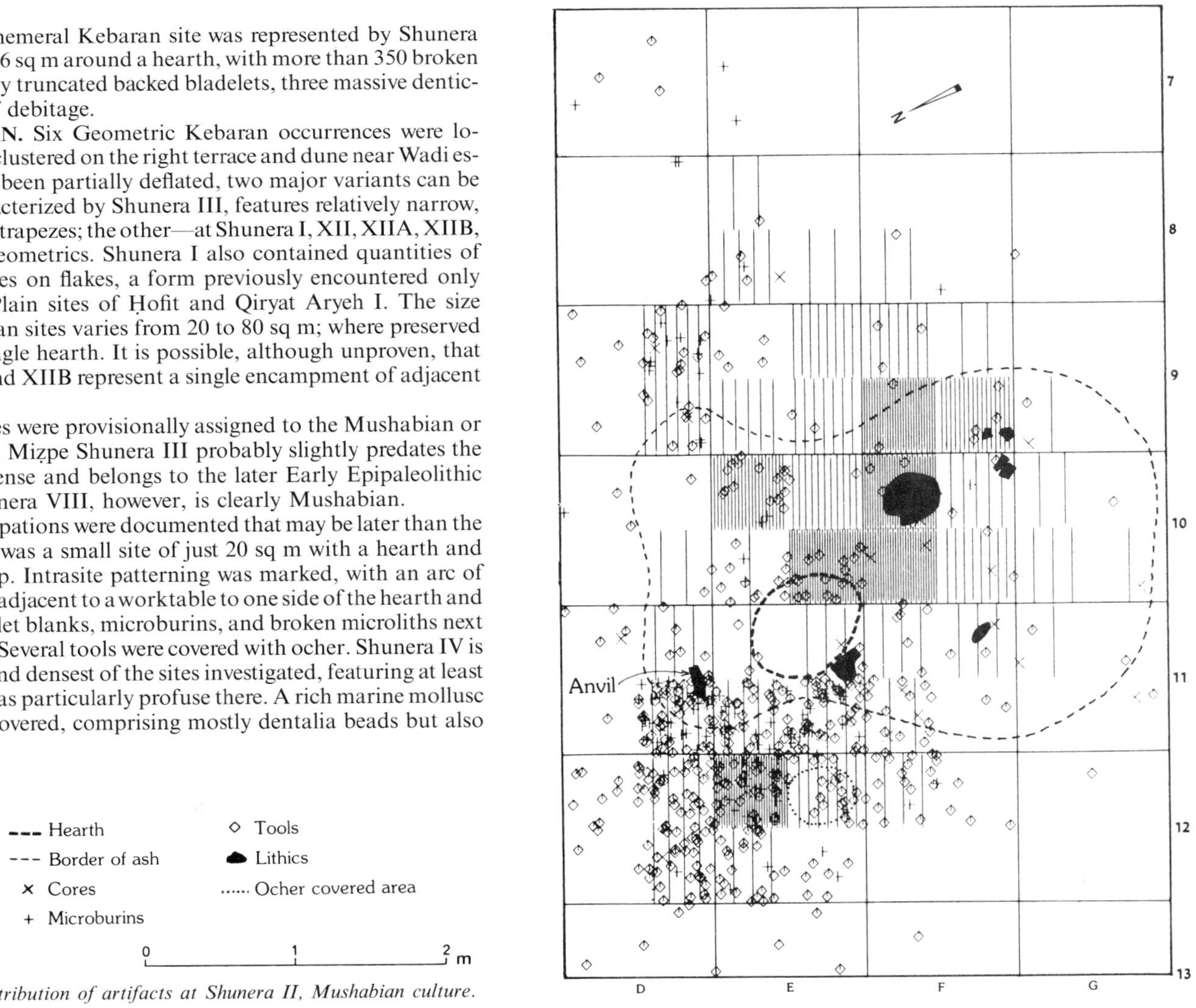

Distribution of artifacts at Shunera II, Mushabian culture.

Anachis miser, an Indo-Erythraean species. The charcoal dating of one of the hearths is at least one thousand years later than for other Mushabian sites. Thus, despite superficial resemblances to the Mushabian, the dates, when combined with other stylistic features of the lithic assemblages, suggest that they represent a later, non-Mushabian industry, perhaps of Sinai or North African origin, broadly contemporary with the Late Natufian.

RAMONIAN. The Ramonian is represented by Shunera XXI and Miẓpe Shunera I, IV, and V, which are located on the sandy slopes of Giv'ot Ivḥa and on a low, but prominent hill 1.5 km (1 mi.) north of the wadi. They were situated to provide maximum monitoring over the surrounding countryside. Only Shunera XXI and Miẓpe Shunera I have been investigated. The in situ, 80-sq-m occurrence of Shunera XXI features at least two hearths, one of which provided a date of 10,150 BCE ± 140 (OxA-2138). The lithic assemblages predominantly comprise characteristic Ramon points made using the microburin technique.

TERMINAL RAMONIAN/EARLY NATUFIAN. Shunera VII was a terminal Ramonian/Early Natufian campsite (c. 120 sq m) on a flat, sandy surface on the left bank of the wadi. It contained the remains of several hearths and at least three distinct clusters of artifacts. Contrary to the preceding assemblages, here the raw material was almost exclusively a fine translucent chalcedony not locally available. In addition to Helwan lunates, the tools include a variant of the Ramon point. Another similar assemblage was collected at Shunera XIII.

LATE NATUFIAN. Late Natufian sites include Shunera XIV and XVIII. The former is notable for its quantities of microburins but very few microliths; the latter, located on a hilltop about 1 km northeast of the wadi, on a sandy hillslope, contained high frequencies of lunates. Both sites are small (15 and 25 sq m, respectively) and probably represent hunting and retooling stands of groups residentially based in the highlands.

HARIFIAN. Harifian sites are relatively common and include Shunera VI, IX, X, and XXIV. These are probably temporary camps of groups residentially based in the highlands. All but Shunera XXIV appear to have been fairly large occurrences of 80 sq m or more, and some may have been repeatedly reoccupied as temporary residential base camps—such as Shunera VI, whose total extent today exceeds 500 sq m. While two appear to be early within the Harifian sequence (Shunera XXIV and IX), the others are apparently slightly later; Shunera VI, for example, includes a few el-Khiam points. Other tools, in addition to the various projectile points, are minute lunates and scrapers. A piece of obsidian at Shunera X proved to have derived from Göllü Dag in central Anatolia.

PRE-POTTERY AND LATE NEOLITHIC. Pre-Pottery Neolithic sites are only represented by two small findspots and occasional stray finds of arrowheads. The Late Neolithic campsite of Shunera V is also limited in extent and featured the remains of a few hearths. In addition to some undiagnostic potsherds, the lithics included a few transverse arrowheads and sickle blades comparable to Herzliya on the Coastal Plain, indicating a date in the fifth millennium.

SUMMARY

The tight cluster of campsites at the edge of the dunes adjacent to Wadi es-Sid, most of them datable to the final Pleistocene and beginning of the Holocene, demonstrates that the occupants chose to locate their sites to maximize access to a mosaic of different resources and ecological zones. Thus, water, plant foods and animals would all have been available in greater densities than elsewhere in the surrounding terrain.

O. Bar-Yosef, "The Epi-Palaeolithic Cultures of Palestine" (Ph.D. diss., Hebrew Univ. of Jerusalem 1970); A. E. Marks, *Prehistory and Paleoenvironments in the Central Negev, Israel* 1: *The Avdat/Aqev Area* 1 (ed. A. E. Marks), Dallas 1976, 227–292; R. Ferring, ibid. 2/2, Dallas 1977, 81–110; A. N. Goring-Morris, "Terminal Pleistocene Hunter-Gatherers in the Negev and Sinai" (Ph.D. diss., Hebrew Univ. of Jerusalem 1985); ibid., *BAR*/IS 361, Oxford 1987; id. (with S. A. Rosen) *Preliminary Safety Analysis Report, Nuclear Power Plant, Shivta Site*, Appendix 2.5E. 9/1, Attachment A, Tel Aviv 1988, 1–81; id., *Proceedings of the 1986 Shell Bead Conference* (Rochester Museum and Science Center Research Records 20, eds. C. F. Hayes III and L. Ceci), Rochester 1989, 175–188; id., *People and Culture in Change* 1 (*BAR*/IS 508/1, ed. I. Hershkowitz), Oxford 1989, 7–28; id., *Paléorient* 14/2 (1990), 231–244; id., *The Natufian Culture of the Southern Levant* (International Monographs in Prehistory, Archaeology Series 1, eds. O. Bar-Yosef and F. R. Valla), Ann Arbor 1991, 173–216; id., *Quaternary International* 5 (1991), 17–216; id., *Palaeoecological Investigations in the Western Negev* 1: *The Shunera Dunes* ('Atiqot), Jerusalem (in prep.).

NIGEL GORING-MORRIS

SHUNI

IDENTIFICATION

Shuni (Miyamas) is located on the eastern slopes of a hill at the southern end of the Carmel Ridge (map reference 1455.2157), near the water sources of the high-level Caesarea aqueduct—the Shuni springs. The bed of Naḥal Tanninim runs along the foot of the site. Shuni has been identified with Kefar Shami (a variant of Shuni) of the mid-third century, a place mentioned in the Jerusalem Talmud (*Ḥal.* 58c); the Bordeaux Pilgrim (333 CE) refers to a mountain called Mons Syna, at the third Roman mile from Caesarea, and a miraculous spring that flowed there and restored fertility to barren women (*Itin. Burdig.* 586, 1).

Shuni: general view of the theater, looking east.

Plan of the theater acccording to the British PEF survey.

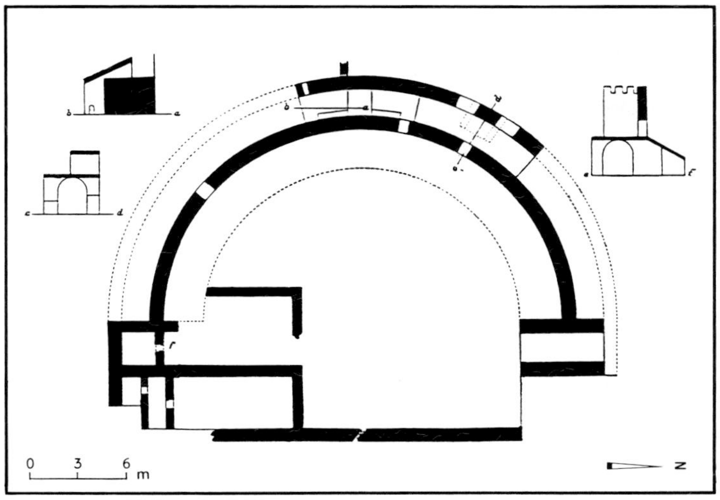

Plan of the orchestra pavement, diazoma, and proscenium wall of the theater.

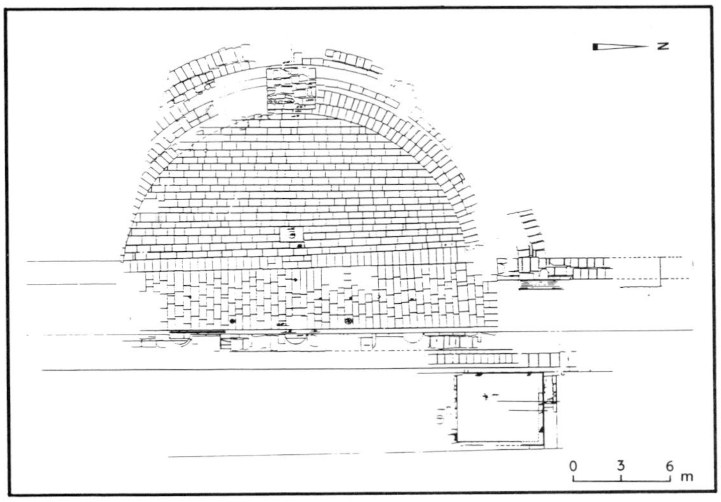

EXPLORATION

In 1870, V. Guérin described the site and called it Khirbet Miyamas (Umm el-Yamas). At the time, it was a pile of ruins being used as a shelter by shepherds and their flocks. The site was surveyed and measured in 1875 by C. R. Conder and H. H. Kitchener of the Palestine Exploration Fund, who established the existence of a theater here. The site was then still called Miyamas. E. von Mülinen visited the site in 1902 and described the new construction erected on top of the theater ruins. At this time the site was known as both Miyamas and Shuni. Two inscriptions were discovered: one, in Latin, mentions the priest Marcus Flavius Agrippa; and the other, in Greek, is a commemorative inscription to which the Hebrew word *Shalom* was appended.

EXCAVATIONS

Excavations were carried out at the site in 1987–1990, on behalf of the Jewish National Fund and the Israel Department of Antiquities and Museums, under the direction of E. Shenhav. The work was concentrated in two main areas: area A (the theater) and area B, to its south.

ROMAN PERIOD. The entire floor of the orchestra and the proscenium wall of the Roman theater were excavated. The floor was paved with smoothed limestones, quarried on Mount Carmel. Ten rows (each 0.3 m wide) of stones were uncovered, followed by a narrower row (0.25 m wide) and ten more broad tiers that ended in two rows of shallow steps—the diazoma—around the orchestra. Incorporated between the paving stones in the center of the orchestra was a smooth marble slab (0.9 by 1.3 m), with a round depression in its center. The slab probably once bore an altar to Dionysus or Asclepius (as was customary in Greek theaters). Two rosette-shaped drain openings, integrated into the pavement as a single unit, were also found. The theater was oriented to the east, so that the audience sat with their backs to the west. In the wall of the proscenium, which was completely excavated, were three niches—one in the center and two lateral ones—with two seatlike rectangular niches in between.

South of the road, near the high-level aqueduct leading to Caesarea (which was excavated by Y. Ne'eman on behalf of the Israel Department of Antiquities and Museums), a marble statue of Asclepius (0.87 m high), depicted as a bearded, naked man attached to a winged serpent, was found. Judging from the artistic style, the statue was probably sculpted in the late second or early third century. The theater was destroyed by an earthquake in the fourth century.

EARLY BYZANTINE PERIOD. Many of the architectural remains from the earlier theater were dismantled and reused in the Early Byzantine period. The orchestra's floor was covered with a fill of sand and *ḥamra*, on which a layer of small, irregular stones was laid. The paving stones (0.35 by 0.7 m) were arranged in a semicircle, forming an orchestra platform one-third larger than the one in the earlier theater. The stones were laid haphazardly—many of them architectural elements from the earlier theater, in secondary use. The orchestra terminates in a wall of only one course that served as a fill between pedestals (comprised of reused architectural remains taken from the frieze of the *scaenae frons*). The pavement east of the wall is uniform, forming a type of *parodos* between the two *versurae* of the original theater.

A system of pools and a local aqueduct uncovered in area B are also ascribed to this period. The aqueduct conveyed water from the spring of Tel Ẓur (Umm el-'Alaq) to a system of stepped pools, until it linked up with the high-level

Marble statue of Aesclepius, god of healing.

Shuni: area of the Byzantine oil press in area A.

aqueduct to Caesarea. The system of pools adjacent to and west of the aqueduct was excavated. The pools' floors were paved with various mosaics, ranging from simple white to a colored mosaic resembling floor tiles to geometric floral designs to a multicolored mosaic with floral motifs and intertwining, braidlike borders. A number of superimposed floors were discerned in several of the pools, indicating continued intensive use. Relatively large and varied quantities of glass vessels were also found.

LATE BYZANTINE AND EARLY ARAB PERIODS. Toward the end of the sixth century, the theater went out of use completely and became an industrial area. The later orchestra was sectioned off by a wall that encompassed an oil press complex. The complex consisted of a crushing installation, including a crushing basin (laver) and a pressbeam. The treading floor was paved with small stones sunk into the beaten earth, to prevent the animals pulling the pressbeam from slipping. On both sides of the crushing installation were installations for pressing the crushed olives, collection vats, and weights. The oil press, of the late Samarian type, operated on the screw-beam method; it was in use from the sixth to eighth centuries.

Guérin, *Samarie*, 340–341; Conder–Kitchener, *SWP* 2, 66–67; F. C. Burkitt, *PEQ* 52 (1920), 47; E. von Mülinen, *ZDPV* 30 (1907), 207; A. Le Borgne and M. Nothmann, *MdB* 53 (1988), 56; E. Shenhav (and Y. Ne'eman), *ESI* 7–8 (1988–1989), 116–168; 9 (1989–1990), 130; id., *MdB* 67 (1990), 58–60; Y. Ne'eman et al., *ESI* 9 (1989–1990), 37.

ELI SHENHAV

SHUQBA CAVE

IDENTIFICATION AND EXPLORATION

The Shuqba Cave lies on the northern bank of Wadi en-Naṭuf (one of the upper effluents of the Yarkon River) in the western part of the Judean Hills, about 14 km (8.5 mi.) northeast of Lod (map reference 154.154). Here were discovered for the first time the remains of the Natufian culture that was named after the wadi.

A. Mallon discovered the Shuqba Cave in 1924. It was briefly excavated by D. Garrod in 1928. The cave opens into a central chamber (diameter, 18 m) with two chimneys in its roof and three side chambers. Blocks of breccia containing Middle Paleolithic flints and bones adhered to the walls of the cave to a height of 2 m. More than half of the central chamber was excavated, and a sounding was made in the middle lateral chamber.

STRATIGRAPHY

The sequence of deposits follows (from the top down):

Layer A: Early Bronze Age to the present;
Layer B: Upper Natufian;
Layer C: redeposited artifacts from layer D;
Layer D: Upper Levallois-Mousterian.

Like many caves, Shuqba was formed by karstic activity. The excavator found that in addition to the two chimneys there is a sinkhole in the rock floor of the chamber to an unknown depth, and the natural floor of the cave was therefore irregular. Water erosion intensified after the deposition of layer D, and flints were redeposited. At this stage, parts of the surface hardened and turned into breccia under the action of water-borne calcium carbonate. Parts not turned into breccia or preserved because of special conditions (such as a band of soft red cave earth or a hearth with gray ashes) suffered damage from the water. For this reason, implements redeposited in the red clay of layer C are abraded, whereas contemporaneous layer D implements are not. In the side chamber, it was found that this redeposition of the material had not occurred at one time. In layer C, there were two beds with abraded implements. In this chamber also, breccia adhered to the vault. A similar phenomenon of water action on Upper Levallois-Mousterian layers was observed in the el-Wad Cave, where Garrod attributed it to the action of a source flowing inside the cave. Garrod regarded this as a generalized process and related it to a period of increased rainfall.

LAYER D. In layer D, some four hundred flint implements were collected, half of them side scrapers. The remainder of the tools are points, retouched flakes, a few disks and hand axes, and a group of typically Upper Paleolithic burins. This industry is strongly reminiscent of the last stage of the Levallois-Mousterian culture of Mount Carmel, where narrow flakes and blades are also found in great numbers. With regard to fauna, a measure of similarity with the el-Wad Cave (q.v.) is claimed by D. Bate, despite the scarcity and poor condition of the remains. Hippopotamus and rhinoceros, the characteristic mammals of the pre-"faunal break" period (placed by Bate between the Lower and the Upper Levallois-Mousterian), are absent.

LAYER B. There is a long gap between layers D and B. Layer B was made up chiefly of black earth with traces of ashes and was classified as Upper Natufian by Garrod. A number of human burials was found, most of them poorly preserved. Seven of them were of children, and one, buried in the typically Natufian contracted position, lay over a large hearth filled with black ashes.

The lithic assemblage recovered by Garrod at layer B was previously unknown in Israel. She therefore named it Natufian, after the wadi in which the cave is situated. Natufian industries have since been discovered at numerous other sites in Israel: the Eẓba', Kebara, Sefunim, and el-Wad caves, the Judean Desert caves, Naḥal Oren, and 'Enan (qq.v.), to mention just a few.

Because the material was examined and published after the report on the Carmel caves, Garrod was able to correlate layer B with the Upper Natufian at the el-Wad Cave (layer B-1). In the flint industry, lunates and sickle blades less frequently display the Helwan-type retouch. Conspicuous by its absence is the microburin technique—a characteristic feature of many Upper Natufian assemblages. Garrod attributes this to the small quantity of tools collected (about 1,350) and the restricted area of excavation. Of the sixty-one bone tools, the majority are points or fragments of points and awls. There are also a few needles and an engraved rib.

FAUNAL REMAINS. The fauna was described by Bate. It is chiefly represented by cattle, deer, wildcat, and abundant gazelle remains.

SUMMARY

In an attempt to reconstruct the process leading to the sequence of deposits in the cave, Garrod pointed out that when human occupation began in Levallois-Mousterian layer D, the pit in the cave floor must have been almost filled. Layer D reached a height of 2 m and filled chamber III. Only later did the water that seeped through the hole in the vault begin its activity, hardening parts of the layer into breccia. Then, due to increased rainfall, parts of layer D were eroded and implements were abraded and redeposited, causing the formation of layer C. Water, again by underground drainage, caused the very deep cavity in the cave's rock floor.

The first Natufian inhabitants found an irregular surface to settle on, but in a short time their occupation filled up the hollows in the ground. At the same time, some subsidence occurred in the pit, and the layer sank in a hollow. After that, rock debris fallen from the roof filled all the hollows, leveling the surface of the deposits.

D. A. E. Garrod, *PEF* 60 (1928), 182ff.; id., *Journal of the Royal Anthropological Institute* 62 (1932), 257–269; id., *Proceedings of the Prehistoric Society* n.s. 8 (1942), 1–20; Y. Olami, *Prehistoric Carmel*, Jerusalem 1984; E. Trinkaus, *Paléorient* 13/1 (1987), 95–100; Weippert 1988, 76, 79, 87f.

OFER BAR-YOSEF

SINAI

PREHISTORIC PERIODS

INTRODUCTION

The beginning of prehistoric research in the Sinai desert, as throughout the Middle East, is linked with reconnaissances conducted in the region by explorers and travelers in the nineteenth and early twentieth centuries. Military officers preparing for World War I or participating in its battles, such as T. Wiegand and van Riet-Loew, also made significant contributions. Between the two World Wars, several exploratory expeditions were conducted on the Sinai peninsula, in which regions in northern Sinai were haphazardly investigated by D. Buzy, R. Neuville, Hussein, and H. Field. Similar limited surveys were also carried out after the Suez Campaign (1956) by E. Anati and B. Rothenberg. After the Six-Day War (1967), a systematic survey was conducted on behalf of the archaeological staff officer of Sinai and Tel Aviv University, by Rothenberg and I. Beit-Arieh along the central routes of northern, western, and particularly southern Sinai. Field research projects, aimed at investigating the Stone Age in Sinai, were conducted in the Kadesh-Barnea region by O. Bar-Yosef and I. Gilead on behalf of the Hebrew University of Jerusalem, at Gebel Maghara in northern Sinai by Bar-Yosef and J. L. Phillips on behalf of the Hebrew University of Jerusalem and the State University of Illinois at Chicago, and in southern Sinai, where Bar-Yosef and other researchers focused on exposing Neolithic sites. A regional research project directed by Phillips has been under way in southern Sinai since the early 1980s, identifying and excavating Upper Paleolithic sites. In spite of all these studies, however, knowledge of the prehistoric remains on the Sinai peninsula, which covers more than 60,000 sq km, is far from comprehensive. The constraints on field work are serious: various important regions can be reached only by foot or with animals, while many others, once used as battle or fortification zones, are still mined.

EARLY AND MIDDLE PALEOLITHIC PERIODS. The scattered remains from the Early and Middle Paleolithic periods do not permit general conclusions to be drawn. Hand axes from the Early Paleolithic period have been found in various places throughout northern Sinai. Most may be attributed to the Upper Acheulean culture (c. 500,000–150,000 BP).

Scatterings of Levallois flakes, a few points, Levallois cores, scrapers, and other items were discerned mainly on the Kadesh-Barnea plateau, forming a direct continuation of the Negev Hills, where sites assigned to the Mousterian culture have been excavated. Scanty finds from this period are known from Gebel Maghara and western Sinai. Mousterian sites have been discerned and investigated west of Sinai—in the Nile Valley and the large basins in western Egypt.

UPPER PALEOLITHIC PERIOD. Of the cultures and traditions identifiable by their lithic remains, the Ahmarian tradition is particularly well known from the Upper Paleolithic period in Sinai. It is characterized by the production of blades, shaped into el-Wad points (probably used as spearheads), knives, and end scrapers. The systematically collected finds from a cluster of excavated sites in Wadi el-Masajid, on Gebel Maghara (in northern Sinai), indicated the existence of small hunter-gatherer groups. The occupants of these sites, termed Lagaman industry for their uniqueness (after Gebel Lagama), apparently used ocher pigments and ostrich egg shells for decoration. The Lagaman industry dates to between about 32,000 and 28,000 BP. At that time the cold, moist climate prevailing in Sinai permitted these groups to roam throughout the peninsula. Contacts between them and their counterparts in Wadi Feiran, where the sites date to 36,000 to 30,000 BP, and the Nile Valley, are apparent in the resemblance between the various lithic industries throughout the area between these regions and the Beersheba Valley. As faunal and

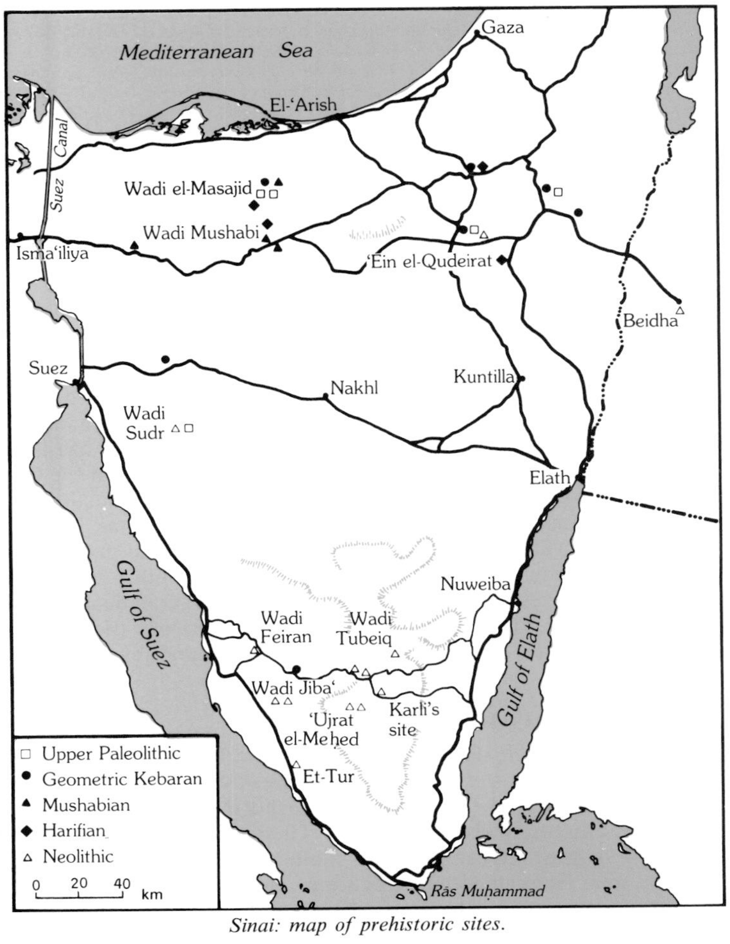

Sinai: map of prehistoric sites.

floral remains are only preserved at the southern Sinai sites, subsistence patterns for the inhabitants of the Negev and Sinai in this period cannot be reconstructed. Judging from site size both in northern Sinai and in Wadi Feiran and its tributaries, the Paleolithic communities seem to have been small. The spread of families or small groups necessitated maintaining links across large geographic expanses.

Another technological tradition represented at several sites, mainly in northern Sinai and at Kadesh-Barnea and Wadi Sudr, is termed the Levantine Aurignacian. Its knapped-tool assemblage mostly features flakes modified into end scrapers, burins, and a few knives. These sites did not yield faunal or botanical remains either. Sinai seems to have formed the boundary of the Aurignacian expansion, and the attribution of finds to this tradition rests on technological considerations only: the most typical elements of the Aurignacian lithic industry (carinated and nosed end scrapers and Aurignacian blades) are either rare at most of the Negev and Sinai sites or absent altogether.

EPIPALEOLITHIC PERIOD. The prehistoric cultural sequence from the Epipaleolithic period suggests two phenomena. One is a change in the region's climate, which occurred in about 13,000 BCE, when the cold, dry conditions prevailing throughout most of the world ended and precipitation began to increase. The second phenomenon—the penetration of populations from the Nile Valley into the Sinai peninsula—is probably linked with these environmental changes. This population expansion established contact between the Geometric Kebaran and Mushabian cultures in northern Sinai and the Negev.

The Geometric Kebaran is defined by the variants of microlithic tools (trapeze rectangles) dominating its assemblages. Its usually small sites (extending over 20–100 sq m), dispersed throughout Sinai, are indicative of the great mobility of small groups (families?) exploiting varied environments, some of them far from water sources. On the basis of carbon-14 dates obtained from organic material from these sites, this culture is dated to about 12,500 to 10,900 BCE.

The Mushabian culture is characterized by high frequencies of arched-backed retouched bladelets, La Mouillah points, and other microlith variants, usually manufactured by the microburin technique. The prevalence of products from this technique (microburins, La Mouillah and triangular points) is interpreted as reflecting the Mushabian's origins in North Africa, where the use of this technique was widespread.

The small Mushabian sites are indicative of the small groups who occupied them. Two Mushabian sites excavated on Gebel Maghara yielded material reflecting seasonal settlement. One site contained a hearth, which had apparently been used to smoke hides. Charred red juniper fruit found here and the direction of the overlying sand deposition suggest that the site was used in early summer. At the other site in the Wadi Mushabi basin, a concentration of hearths was found whose state of preservation suggests repeated use of the encampment. Its location, sheltered by the mountain from the western winds, indicates that it was a winter encampment.

The Mushabian culture evolved in northern Sinai and the Negev. Its later stage, Late Mushabian (or Ramonian) was well adapted to this semiarid region. Flint assemblages from this stage are characterized by the use of the microburin technique for microlith modification. The most common shapes are obliquely truncated retouched bladelets, occasionally with concave retouched backs. Helwan lunates (with bifacial retouch on the convex side) appear in its final stage and indicate a chronological overlap between the terminal Mushabian culture and the Early Natufian culture that developed in Israel and Jordan north of the Beersheba Valley.

No sites from the Late Natufian have yet been discovered in northern Sinai. The presence at isolated sites of backed lunates, of the type characteristic of the Late Natufian, suggests the presence of a contemporary nomadic hunter-gatherer group and this semisedentary culture in the desert region.

The Natufian culture (10,800–8500 BCE) marks the stage preceding the establishment of agricultural settlements on cultivable land. From that time until the emergence of cattle- and sheep-herding societies in the sixth millennium, hunter-gatherer communities continued to live in the desert. The Harifian culture represents the adaptation to environmental conditions in the ninth millennium by the Late Natufian population in the Negev. A complete archaeological representation of this culture has been exposed in the Negev Hills and western Negev. The lithic assemblages from the Harifian sites were defined on the basis of the frequency of Harif points (a rhomboidal quasi-arrowhead, shaped like a microlith) along with lunates, retouched bladelets, a few sickle blades, end scrapers, and other tools. This culture's base camps, discovered on Mount Ḥarif (q.v.), yielded dwelling structures, an abundance of cupmarks, and faunal remains (gazelle, deer, rabbit, and partridge). Small sites (20–100 sq m) assigned to this culture, which were detected in the sandy landscapes of the western Negev and northern Sinai (Gebel Maghara), seem to reflect the population's winter distribution in hunting-gathering encampments; the finds from highland sites suggest summer activities—such as the gathering of plant food (wild barley?, nuts, and acorns), tool knapping, and the exchange of seashells. The seashells, predominantly of Red Sea origin, and pestles made of green metamorphic rock, attest to the links between the Harifians and the desert dwellers.

It seems that as aridity increased, the hunter-gatherer population in Sinai decreased. Its remains, such as those uncovered at Abu Madi I (in southern Sinai), were found in environments where perennial and seasonal water sources were more frequent.

PRE-POTTERY NEOLITHIC A PERIOD. To date, the site of Abu Madi I is the principal representative of the period in about the eighth millennium. In the Negev, too, only scanty remains are attributable to this period, called the Pre-Pottery Neolithic A. The lithic assemblage from Abu Madi I is predominantly microlithic. It is dominated by arrowheads of the el-Khiam point type (with parallel notches in the base); the Abu Madi point (leaf-shaped, sometimes with a short tang); various lunates, including Helwan lunates; pointed, long, and narrow retouched bladelets; awls; end scrapers; and denticulates.

At Abu Madi I, a structure (diameter, c. 4 m) was erected in a depression at the foot of a large granite block. A bell-shaped silo was unearthed at its side. The finds include the burial of a young woman, numerous shells from the Red Sea, and a large quantity of deer, rabbit, and fish bones. This seems to have been a summer occupation by a hunter-gatherer community that lived in southern Sinai; however, the prevalence of el-Khiam points and mushroom-shaped pestles known from the Harifian and Late Natufian cultures indicates links between this population and other contemporary groups in the Levant.

PRE-POTTERY NEOLITHIC B PERIOD. The Neolithic period, which is particularly rich in finds, spans the seventh millennium (according to carbon-14 tests). The evidence from various regions in the Levant indicates climatic amelioration in this period and an increase in precipitation, resulting in the formation of local lakes. The numerous contemporary sites dispersed throughout Sinai are identifiable by common arrowhead types: Jericho points (shouldered or winged), Byblos points (leaf-shaped with a tang), and Amuq points (leaf-shaped), occasionally pressure flaked.

The sites in the dune areas of northern Sinai and the western Negev yielded no architectural remains; it seems that in these regions hut compounds were usual. A large number of burned stones indicates hearths that are not preserved.

The excavations in southern Sinai focused on sites representing marginal zones in this region: the sandy plateau at the foot of the et-Tih escarpments and Gebel Gunna, the highlands and their western margins, bordering the el-Qa Valley. Some of the sites (Wadi Ṭubeiq, and Wadi Jiba' I and II) yielded the remains of structures built of field stones (granite blocks or sandstone slabs) that seem to have been walled huts adapted for winter residence. A great deal of knapping took place at these sites, which are near flint sources. There is also evidence of shell working and the hunting of deer, gazelle, and rabbit. The types of plants these people gathered are not clear, as no charred remains are preserved. By contrast, grinding stones and querns were recovered that were used in the preparation of food from seeds, gathered or acquired through exchange with agricultural communities already established in the Levant.

Sites such as those excavated in the highlands should be regarded as summer occupations. They contain the remains of structures insufficient to shelter their inhabitants from the harsh winter weather in this region, which is about 1,600 m above sea level. One such site ('Ujrat el-Mehed) contained the remains of six structures (in two layers at least) that seem to have been huts with adjacent unroofed courtyards. The remains of both subterranean and above-ground silos were exposed in or near the structures. The rich flint assemblage had been brought from a distance, and very little evidence was found for tool manufacture at the site itself. Secondary burials of males were found inside some of the silos. Animal bones indicate the hunting of ibex, gazelle, and hare. The abundant grinding stones and querns were made of local stone; they also suggest the consumption of plant food. Shells, mostly from the Red Sea and some from the Mediterranean, bone pendants, and a small number of bone tools complete the inventory.

These Neolithic sites were initially thought to represent stations along the migratory routes of hunter-gatherer bands that may have split into smaller groups and reunited later in the course of the year. Shells would have been collected along the Red Sea beaches in the winter, whereas hunting, gathering, and flint-tool knapping would have taken place in the summer and fall. The hunters may have used desert kites (animal traps made of two shallow, elongated, converging stone walls arranged in a kitelike shape) and rounded traps, such as were discovered in southern Sinai.

POTTERY NEOLITHIC PERIOD. Only a few of the sites discovered in Sinai can be dated to the Pottery Neolithic period. A site in the Kadesh-Barnea region has yielded the remains of an undefined structure, small silos built of stone slabs, ovens, and abundant flint artifacts, including axes and a few pressure-flaked arrowheads. The arrowheads from this period are usually small, winged, or leaf-shaped and shaped by pressure flaking. Isolated finds were discerned in the dunes in northern Sinai and Wadi Feiran. In the sixth millennium, settlement patterns in the Middle East as a whole underwent a radical change. Apparently, a similar conclusion can be reached based on the random finds from Sinai. The economy of the Sinai inhabitants was still based on hunting and gathering; it is only in the fifth millennium that evidence is seen of the emergence of pastoral nomad groups.

O. Bar-Yosef (and J. L. Phillips), *Prehistoric Investigations in Gebel Maghara, Northern Sinai* (Qedem 7), Jerusalem 1977; id., *Union International de Ciencias Prehistorica*, Xe Congreso, Mexico 1981, 35–62; id., *BA* 45 (1982), 9–12; id., *Archaeological Survey in the Mediterranean Area* (*BAR*/IS 155, eds. D. R. Keller and D. W. Rupp), Oxford 1983, 369–370; id. (and A. Killebrew), *Paléorient* 10/2 (1984), 95–102; id. (et al.), *IEJ* 36 (1986), 121–167; B. Rothenberg and H. Weyer, *Sinai* 1979; I. Gilead, *Préhistoire du Levant* (eds. J. Cauvin and P. Sanlaville), Paris 1981, 331–342; id., "The Upper Palaeolithic in Sinai and the Negev" (Ph.D. diss., Hebrew Univ. of Jerusalem 1981); id., *Paléorient* 9/1 (1983), 39–54; 10/1 (1984), 135–142; id., *Mitekufat Ha'even* 18 (1985), 67*–69*; id., *Levant* 22 (1990), 47–63; A. Belfer-Cohen and P. Goldberg, *IEJ* 32 (1982), 185–189; U. Baruch and O. Bar-Yosef, *Paléorient* 12/2 (1986), 69–84; T. Dayan et al., *Paléorient* 12/2 (1986), 105–116; A. N. Goring-Morris (and U. Avner), *Mitekufat Ha'even* 19 (1986), 58*–65*; id., *At the Edge: Terminal Pleistocene Hunter-Gatherers in the Negev and Sinai* (*BAR*/IS 361), Oxford 1987; ibid. (Review), *Mitekufat Ha'even* 21 (1988), 49*–86*; id., *Paléorient* 14/2 (1988), 231–244; id., *People and Culture in Change* 1 (*BAR*/IS 508, ed. I. Hershkowitz), Oxford 1989, 7–28; J. L. Phillips, *Paléorient* 14/2 (1988), 183–200; (with B. G. Gladfelter) 15/2 (1989), 113–122; D. O. Henry, *From Foraging to Agriculture: The Levant at the End of the Ice Age*, Philadelphia 1989; B. G. Gladfelter, *Geoarchaeology* 5 (1990), 99–119.

OFER BAR-YOSEF

NORTHERN SINAI

IDENTIFICATION

The Coastal Plain of northern Sinai, between the Suez Canal and the Gaza region, was the principal land bridge connecting Egypt and Asia from predynastic times. Because of its military and economic importance the history of the region has been preserved in the writings of historians, geographers, and church fathers, as well as in travelers' itineraries and on maps. More detailed information is available through sources of the Roman and Byzantine period, such as the historians Strabo, Pliny, and Josephus Flavius, or geographical and administrative records and maps such as *Itinerarium Antonini*, *Notitia Dignitatum*, *Tabula Peutingeriana*, and the Medeba map. The earlier Egyptian sources pertaining to the history of northern Sinai include a brief reference in the itinerary of Thutmose III's expedition to Asia, the series of forts and stations along the "Way of Horus" depicted on the walls of the temple of Amun at Karnak from the first year of Seti I, and the stations along the North Sinai road listed in Papyrus Anastasi I from the reign of Ramses II. The random references in the annals of Assyrian kings and especially Herodotus' report of the Egyptian campaign of Cambyses complete what is known of the inhabitants of northern Sinai.

EXPLORATION

J. Clédat, the pioneer of archaeological research in northern Sinai, investigated from 1910 to 1924 a number of important sites, of which all but one dated to the Hellenistic and Roman periods. More limited archaeological surveys were carried out between 1967 and 1971 by M. Dothan, J. Margovski and A. Berman. From 1972 to 1982, the North Sinai Expedition of Ben-Gurion University, under the direction of E. D. Oren, conducted a systematic survey and excavations along the Mediterranean coast and sand-dune area of northern Sinai—between the Suez Canal and the Gaza region—an area of approximately 2,000 sq km. In the course of the survey, the expedition investigated about thirteen hundred settlement sites, including large towns and villages, forts and road stations, industrial installations, cemeteries and campsites, ranging in date from the Paleolithic to the Ottoman periods. As a result, it is now possible to reconstruct in detail the settlement history of northern Sinai and to assess the pattern of settlements and their material culture, economic subsistence, and cultural interaction with neighboring cultures such as Egypt and Israel.

PRE- AND PROTOHISTORIC PERIODS

The score of prehistoric deposits recorded by the Ben-Gurion University expedition along the coastal strip between Wadi el-'Arish and Wadi Ghazzeh indicate some human activity and settlement in northeastern Sinai as early as the Paleolithic and Epipaleolithic periods. These assemblages, which mark the position of seasonal campsites for hunter-gatherers and perhaps also fishermen, were represented by many stone and flint tools, seashells, and fragments of ostrich eggshells. Carbon-14 determinations made on ostrich eggshells from one of the Epipaleolithic assemblages provided a date of

Map of the North Sinai Survey.

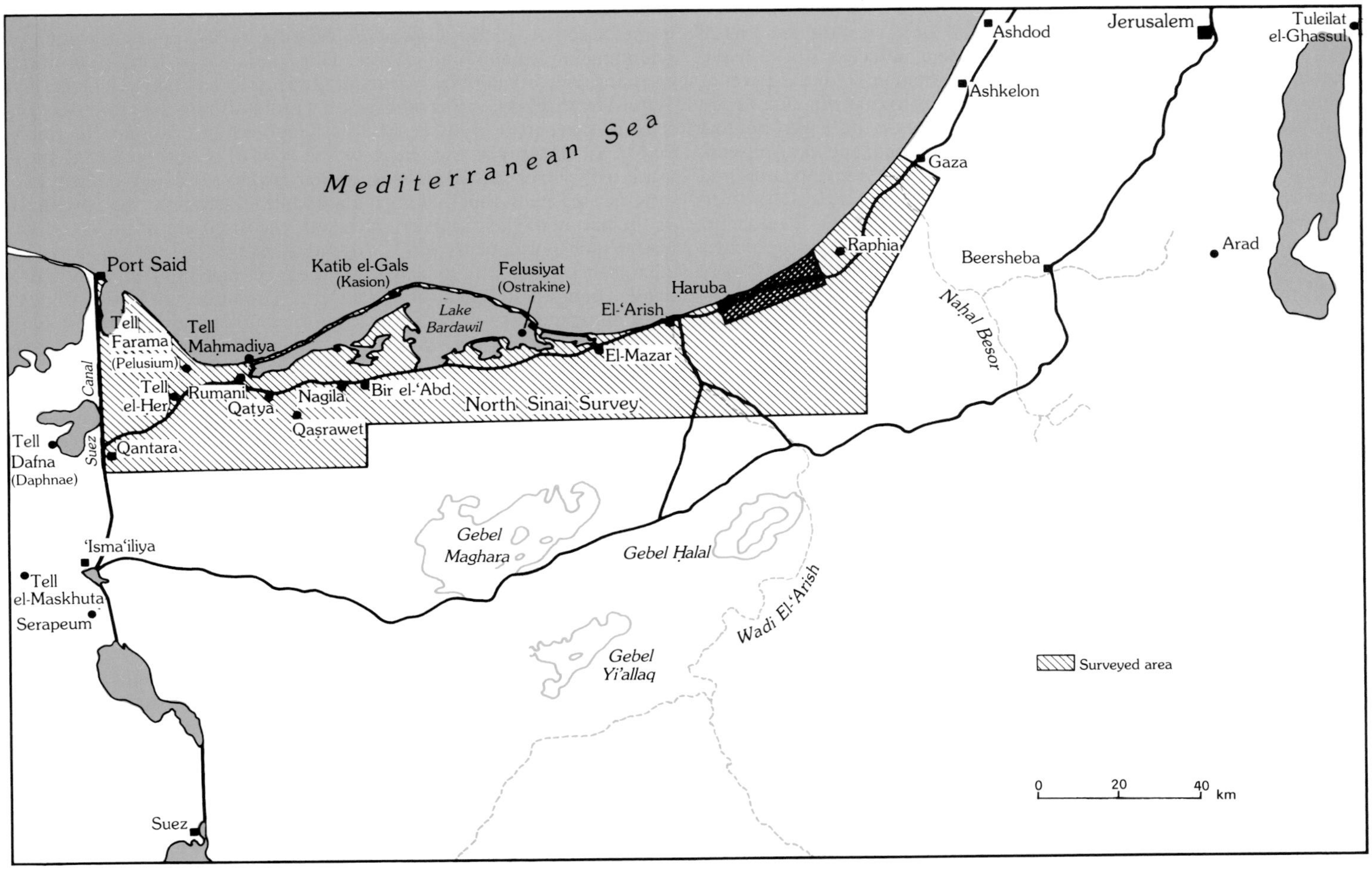

27,000 years BP. The material culture of the sites in northern Sinai is compatible with the prehistoric settlement of the Negev highlands, eastern Sinai, and the anticlinal range of northern Sinai.

Site Y-3, a Pottery Neolithic site near Tel Qatif, south of Gaza, was excavated in the 1970s and 1980s (q.v. Qatif).

About thirty campsites or seasonal encampments of the Chalcolithic period were recorded in the surveyed area, mostly concentrated in northeastern Sinai between el-'Arish and Wadi Ghazzeh; a few were discovered as far away as the edge of the eastern Nile Delta and the southern shore of Lake Bardawil. The sites in northeastern Sinai are located on hard surfaces of inactive sand dunes and grouped in small clusters of four to five sites. The sites produced domestic installations, basalt vessels, flint tools, and large collections of pottery, including sherds of imported Egyptian predynastic wares.

Site R-48. Excavations at one of the sites near (former) Yamit (R-48) unearthed a small settlement with three successive phases of occupation. The upper phase contained the remains of a small rectangular mud-brick structure (3 by 4 m) surrounded by hearths, clay ovens, refuse and ash pits, and a large collection of stone vessels for grinding and pounding. The second and third phases are represented by stone installations and pits. In all three phases many small round depressions containing organic remains which probably mark the location of wooden posts for huts and tents were observed. The rich ceramic assemblage from site R-48, like that of the other Chalcolithic settlements in this region, comprised diagnostic western Negev types such as V-shaped bowls decorated with red bands on the rim, and storage jars and hole-mouth jars equipped with pierced lug handles. The small number of churns and cone-shaped cups is particularly evident. A few imported Egyptian sherds of Naqada I ware and a violin-shaped stone figurine were also found.

Site Y-2. From 1979 to 1983, the North Sinai Expedition conducted extensive excavations at a large Chalcolithic site (Y-2) on the Khan Yunis coast, near the Neolithic settlement Y-3. Three settlement strata were discerned, comprising large open areas with silos, refuse pits, hearths, installations, stone and pottery vessels, and flint tools. The site was evidently occupied for a relatively long period of time by huts and tents with various areas of domestic activity. Unlike the Chalcolithic sites at the Yamit cluster, site Y-2 yielded large quantities of churns and cone-shaped cups. Prominent in the lithic assemblage is a large number of sickle blades, fan scrapers, and axes, as well as numerous microlithic blades of transparent flint and obsidian tools. Special finds included finely worked violin-shaped figurines made of green-veined marble, a seal impression on a lump of clay (jar stopper?), some copper ore, and imported Egyptian pottery. The abundance of sickle blades and stone grinding tools suggests an extensive cultivation of cereals. Analysis of the faunal remains indicates that sheep, goat, and cattle herding, dairy production and fishing were the principal economic base of site Y-2. Among the many fish bones were those of sharks and dolphins.

EARLY BRONZE AGE. The North Sinai Expedition investigated between Qanṭara and Raphia nearly 250 settlement sites with material remains of the Canaanite Early Bronze Age I–II and Egyptian late predynastic and Old Kingdom periods. Large clusters of these sites were particularly dense in the areas immediately south of the Bardawil lagoon and el-'Arish. The settlement pattern in northern Sinai in this period was characterized by clusters of ten to twenty sites that extended over an area of several square kilometers, in

North Sinai: violin-shaped stone figurine, Chalcolithic period.

close proximity to each other. Averaging some 1,000 sq m in size, these localities contained domestic installations, clay ovens, and hearths, as well as a profusion of stone and flint tools. In the large sites the remains of disintegrated mud-brick material of structures were preserved. The distribution pattern of sites and the nature of their material remains indicate a two- or even three-tiered settlement hierarchy of campsites and seasonal encampments of pastoralists alongside permanent settlements in the larger sites that were villages, administrative headquarters, way stations, and caravanserai.

The large ceramic assemblages included both characteristic Canaanite and Egyptian vessels of the Early Bronze Age I–II and the Naqada II–III to "0" to First dynasties. The Egyptian repertoire comprised characteristic transport and domestic vessels best known from settlement and funerary sites such as Giza, Tarkhan, Saqqara, and Abydos. Especially common are the "wavy handled" storage jars, cylindrical "cheese vessels" decorated with net patterns, globular bottles, and baking trays. Several of the sherds bore incised graffiti of animals and *serekhs* surmounted by a double falcon. The Canaanite collection is represented by numerous ledge-handled jars, often decorated with red bands over a white lime wash, jars with arched spouts, high-handled cups and hole-mouth jars, and cooking pots. The sites also produced finely worked stone vessels, a variety of flint tools such as Egyptian-type knives, Canaanean blades, fan scrapers, and transverse arrowheads. Some of the sites near el-'Arish yielded a few kilograms of a sandstone copper ore and a handful of copper objects.

The results of the North Sinai Survey provide important evidence for reconstructing the cultural and economic relations between Egypt and Canaan in the late Egyptian predynastic period, the very beginning of the Canaanite Bronze Age. The complex of sites in northern Sinai represents the eastward extension of the Egyptian sphere of interest into southern Canaan. The influx of Egyptian goods of the Naqada II–III and "0" to First Dynasty horizon in these areas indicates a rapid process of expansion that probably resulted in Egypt's domination and administration of the entire territory of northern Sinai and southwestern Canaan.

The North Sinai Expedition explored more than 280 settlement sites between the Suez Canal and Raphia, which were represented by identifiable Early Bronze IV–Middle Bronze I artifacts. Most of the sites are located in northeastern Sinai, although a few were identified south of the Bardawil lagoon to the fringe of the eastern Nile Delta. The distribution of sites, according to size and number of objects, indicates a distinctive clustering pattern of base sites and smaller campsites nearby. One of the base sites near Salamana occupies 1 to 1.5 a., including some poorly built remains of domestic architecture with large courtyards and animal pens constructed on sandstone foundations. Most sites, however, lack evidence of solid structures, and were seasonal encampments for pastoralists. The homogeneous pottery assemblage is characteristic of the Early Bronze Age IV culture of southern Canaan (Amiran's Group A, Dever's Family S), including features that are clearly of the Early Bronze Age tradition. Significantly, the ceramic repertoire also included late variants of the Egyptian "Maidum ware" which is diagnostic of the late Old Kingdom–early First Intermediate Period. The chronological position of the Early Bronze Age IV settlement in North Sinai is accordingly established in about 2250 to 2150 BCE. Evidently, commercial activity or exchanges between Egypt and Canaan were not important to the economy of the pastoralists of North Sinai. The Early Bronze Age IV population of northern Sinai should be identified with the Anmu groups who, according to Egyptian sources, infiltrated into the Delta and contributed to the anarchy that brought about the collapse of the Egyptian Old Kingdom.

MIDDLE BRONZE AGE. The Middle Bronze Age is represented in the surveyed area by nearly one hundred localities, mostly small campsites, distributed unevenly south of the Bardawil lagoon, between Rumani and Raphia, and clearly away from the coastline. These sites yielded poor remains of domestic activity such as clay *tabuns*, hearths and ash pockets, grinding and pounding implements, and scatters of flint tools and pottery. In contrast, the expedition recorded in the vicinity of the Suez Canal, between Qanṭara and Tell el-Ḥer, five large settlement sites that probably represent the extent of the sedentary occupation in the Middle Kingdom and Second Intermediate Period as far away as the fringe of the desert. The surface of these sites was largely salt encrusted and partially covered by a thick layer of windblown sand and seashells, thus making it impossible to determine their original size or the nature of their remains. However, the discovery of architectural remains, such as fragments of well-dressed granite blocks and patches of eroded mud-brick material, indicates that these belonged to the permanent settlement complex in the eastern Nile Delta. The surface collection of pottery from these sites as well as representative samples from a few test squares yielded some Canaanite Middle Bronze Age IIA–B wares, and particularly a sizable collection of diagnostic Egyptian Middle Kingdom and Second Intermediate Period ceramics of characteristic Nile and desert Marle wares. It should be noted that systematic excavations conducted recently (1988–1992) by M. 'Abd el-Maksoud on behalf of the Egyptian Antiquities Service at one of these sites, Tell Heboua, exposed the stratified remains of a well organized (fortified?) settlement dating from the Middle and Late Bronze ages. Finds included limestone blocks with Middle Kingdom, Second Intermediate, and New Kingdom period inscriptions.

North Sinai: incision on a sherd of an Egyptian vessel, 1st Dynasty.

The ceramic corpus of the Middle Bronze Age campsites in northern Sinai included a variety of Egyptian Middle Kingdom and Second Intermediate Period wares, mainly in the areas of northwestern and north-central Sinai and as far as the eastern edge of the Bardawil lagoon. One of the sites near el-Mazar yielded, alongside typical Middle Bronze Age IIA storage jars and a red-burnished jug with an arched double handle on its shoulder, an impressive collection of late Middle Kingdom pottery vessels such as thick-walled "zirs" and Marle C bag-shaped and beer jars. Canaanite wares are mainly storage jars and a small percentage of serving dishes. The most noticeable feature in the ceramic repertoire of northern Sinai is the crude, straight-sided cooking vessel that was formed by hand on a mat and perforated with holes below the rim. Such vessels are usually associated with the material culture of pastoralists. Significantly, the entire pottery ensemble of North Sinai includes no more than a handful of sherds of Tell el-Yahudiyeh ware. The distribution map of Middle Bronze Age sites in northern Sinai and the nature of their remains, as well as the absence of any road stations or permanent settlements to the east of the Delta plain, imply that the regular commercial contacts and communications between the Egyptian Nile Delta and Canaan were probably via maritime traffic. Salvage excavations in 1973 by F. Vitto and G. Edelstein on behalf of the Israel Department of Antiquities and Museums at the coastal site of Tel Ridan (q.v.), near Khan Yunis, revealed what appears to have been a small harbor site of the Middle Bronze Age IIB, probably the first natural shelter and anchorage facility to be encountered by seagoing vessels that came from the Nile Delta, and the westernmost permanent settlement of the Middle Bronze Age in southwestern Canaan.

LATE BRONZE AGE. The beginning of the Egyptian New Kingdom marked the opening of a new chapter in the history of northern Sinai. The coastal strip became the principal land route for Egyptian military expeditions to Asia, and a vital artery of communication for Egyptian administration of the provinces in Canaan and Syria. A complex network of administrative headquarters, forts, customs and supply stations, complete with water reservoirs and granaries, was established along the "Way of Horus" in northern Sinai. The first campaign of Thutmose III from the border fortress of Seru (Sile in the classical sources, near Qanṭara) to Gaza, about 250 km away, in a record time of nine or ten days, indeed demonstrates the effectiveness of Egyptian organization of the "Way of Horus."

From 1972 to 1982, the Ben-Gurion University expedition explored more than 150 New Kingdom settlement sites along the coastal strip and sand-dune region between Qanṭara and Raphia. The results of that research enable the accurate delineation of the course of the "Way of Horus" and an assessment of the degree of Egyptian involvement along the principal land route between the eastern Delta and southern Canaan. A considerable number of sites was recorded in northwestern Sinai, in the triangle formed by Port Sa'id, Rumani, and Qanṭara. Some of the larger settlements yielded stone and brick building remains, parts of granite columns, and installations that belonged to some public structures. Many of the sites were located in close proximity to the ancient frontier canal which was identified between Pelusium (Tell Farama) and Qanṭara in the early 1980s by a team from the Israel Geological Survey. The occurrence of New Kingdom sites along the canal proves that the construction of this ambitious project was effected in the New Kingdom period, at the latest.

East of the Delta plain and south of the Bardawil lagoon, the New Kingdom settlement sites were recorded in an area roughly parallel to the modern road and railway line between Qanṭara and Raphia. It should be noted that

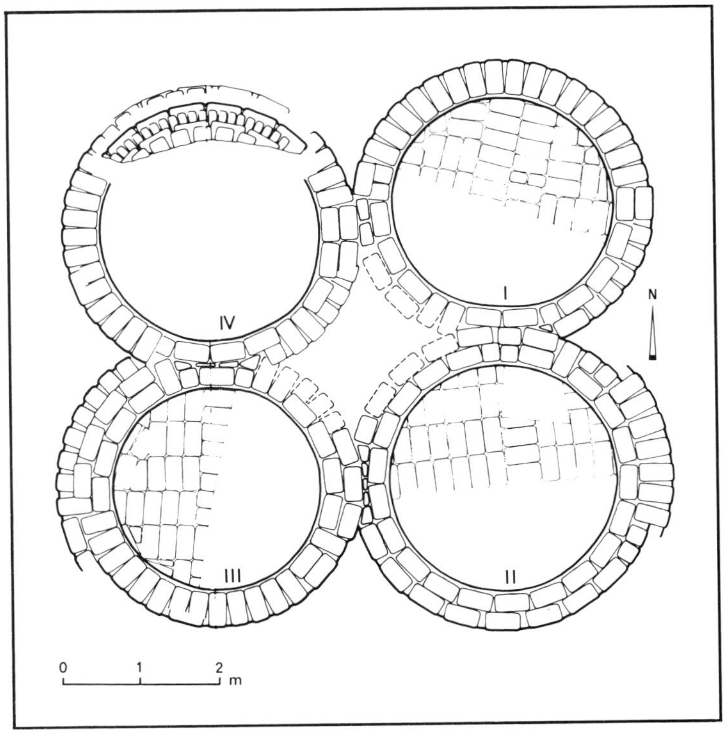

Bir el-'Abd: the silos, 14th–13th centuries BCE. ***Above:*** *general view;* ***(below)*** *plan.*

there were almost no New Kingdom sites on the coastal strip of the Mediterranean, nor on the sandbar enclosing Lake Bardawil to the north, making it highly probable that the New Kingdom settlements were not associated directly with the maritime traffic that operated regularly between the ports of the eastern Nile Delta and the coast of Canaan. The settlement pattern of New Kingdom Sinai was characterized by site clusters in which a base site, usually a fortress or central station, was surrounded by some smaller campsites for transit caravans, and many seasonal encampments of the local Bedouin who were incorporated into the administrative network of the "Way of Horus." At least ten such clusters were identified by the North Sinai Expedition, including the region of the "frontier canal," Rumani, Nagila, Bir el-'Abd, Madba'a, el-Mazar, el-'Arish, and Ḥaruba. Numerous New Kingdom sites were also encountered by the expedition between Raphia and Gaza, and to these may be added the excavation of a Late Bronze Age settlement and burial sites at Tell Abu Salima, Tel Ridan, and Deir el-Balaḥ (qq.v.). The following is a summary of the results of the explorations that the Ben-Gurion University expedition carried out at Bir el-'Abd and Ḥaruba. They represent Egypt's manifold activities—namely, military, administrative, and industrial—along the "Way of Horus."

Bir el-'Abd. The cluster at Bir el-'Abd comprised a central site surrounded by a dense group of about thirty small satellite encampments. The base site (BEA-10) extends over approximately one acre, and is occupied by the remains of a fortress, storage magazines, a granary, and what may have been a water reservoir. The fortress, originally a 1,600-sq-m structure, is represented today by poorly preserved sections of a massive enclosure(?) wall (c. 3 m thick) and various installations in the spacious courtyard area. The patches of floors yielded scores of Egyptian vessels and a considerable deposit of animal and fish bones. South of the fortress, a large magazine building was examined, of which only the foundation courses survive. The mud-brick structure had long narrow halls and was fronted by wide open courtyards. The size of the mud bricks, the method of construction, and the use of brick buttresses for supporting the walls and openings are characteristic features of Egyptian New Kingdom brick architecture and have been observed at other sites in northern Sinai. Noteworthy is the discovery of foundation deposits under walls and floor levels. Nearby, an excellently preserved granary consisting of four cylindrical silos, each about 4 m in diameter, with walls approximately 50 cm thick, was entirely excavated. The entire granary up to the level of the dome (see below) was constructed in a large pit dug below ground level. Two of the silos contained projecting shelves—one brick thick—that may have marked the location of openings. One of the silos still had a few courses of the corbelled dome, which enabled the reconstruction of the entire structure and its building techniques. The floors and walls of the silos were covered with a thick layer of plaster. The granary could have held up to 44,600 liters or about 40 tons of grain or legumes. A layer of organic material, probably grain, was preserved on the silos' floors, buried beneath a large quantity of pottery, alabaster, faience, and animal and fish bones. Judging from the refuse deposits on top of the fallen mud-brick domes, the granary, following the collapse of the domes, became the fort's refuse pit.

About 200 m northwest of the fortress, the remains of an artificial, rectangular depression, measuring nearly 10 by 15 m and bordered by a kind of clay plastered embankment, were recorded. The thick layers of silt that lined the sides and bottom of the depression suggest that it served as a reservoir, designed to collect rainwater for the nearby fortress.

The rich collection of finds from Bir el-'Abd is characteristic of the New Kingdom period and, particularly, of the late Eighteenth and the beginning of the Nineteenth dynasties. The site yielded a large collection of Egyptian pottery, many painted in the "Egyptian blue" style, hundreds of specimens of thumb-indented, thick-based "flower pots," small vessels decorated with heads of gazelles, alabaster and faience vessels, scarabs from the Eighteenth Dynasty as well as a jar handle impressed with the cartouche of Seti I, a prominent figure in the re-establishment of Egyptian domination over the "Way of Horus." The collection of imported ceramics from Bir el-'Abd is represented by very few Canaanite vessels, as well as some Cypriot ware and a few examples of Mycenean pottery.

Bir el-'Abd: Egyptian vessel painted in Egyptian blue, 14th century BCE.

Ḥaruba: typical Egyptian "beer bottle" stamped with the impression of Seti I, early 13th century BCE.

Ḥaruba. From 1979 to 1982, the expedition explored the Ḥaruba (Ḥaruvit) cluster in northeastern Sinai. The twenty-odd sites are grouped in a relatively small area (4–5 sq km) of the active coastal sand dunes, about 12 km east of el-'Arish. These sites are represented by architectural remains, installations, stone tools, as well as Egyptian, Canaanite, and Cypriot ceramics and seal impressions of Thutmose III, Seti I, and Ramses II. The explorations were focused on two particularly impressive sites: A-289, a military fort, and A-345, an administrative center. Both were unusually well preserved and may be considered as models of Egyptian civil and military architecture on the "Way of Horus."

The fort of Ḥaruba is approximately 2,500 sq m in area, comprising a massive enclosure wall (4 m wide), a gatehouse, a wide courtyard, and a complex of compartments, including storage magazines and residential units. Large buttresses on the northern wall and the northeastern corner may have served as watchtowers; a mud-brick structure inside the northeastern corner was apparently the platform for a wooden staircase that led to the top of the walls. The uniform size and bonding pattern of the bricks are typical of New Kingdom public and domestic architecture. The impressive gatehouse in the eastern wing of the fort is 13 by 12 m, with an entryway about 16 m long and 3.7 m wide. It is flanked by two massive buttresses, 8 by 13 m each. Inside the buttresses were two hollow cells that could not be entered from the gateway. These cells were used for storage and were reached from above by wooden scaffoldings and ladders. Approximately one third of the area within the enclosure wall was empty of structures, perhaps to provide room to pitch tents and park chariots. The remaining space was occupied by many rooms that were built against the enclosure wall and were used as dwellings and storerooms for equipment and provisions, or as kitchens. Excavations revealed two clear phases (II–III) of construction and floors as well as an earlier, probably domestic, occupational phase (IV) that preceded the building of the fortress.

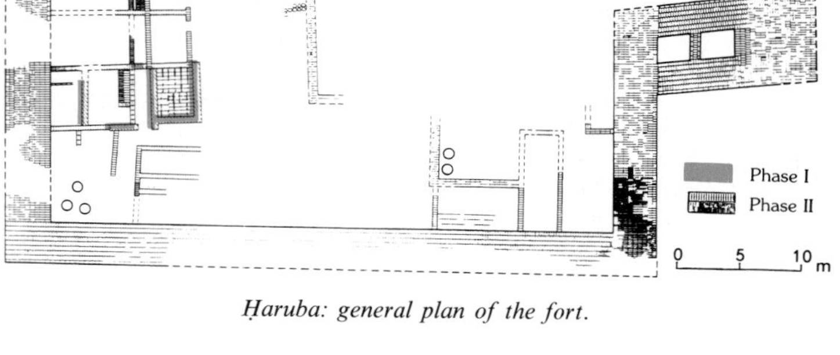

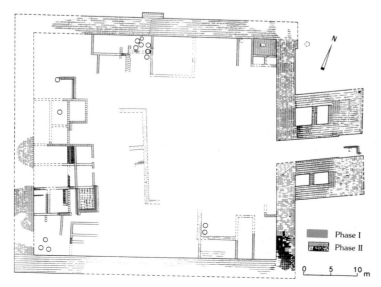

Ḥaruba: general plan of the fort.

Adult and child burials were found in various parts of the fort under floors and under the fallen brick debris. In the casemate of the northern wing of the gatehouse a complete adult male skeleton lying supine on the floor with arms extended above the head was uncovered; the head was covered with a broken storage jar, around which were deposits of ash. A skeleton of a child, oriented north, lying on its back with arms folded on its chest, was uncovered in the gateway and nearby was the flexed burial of an adult. The extremely friable skeletal remains of infants were uncovered in different areas within the fort. Some of the skeletons belonged to phase III, but most of them were assigned to phase II, when the fort was no longer in full operation. One of the rooms in the northeastern corner of the fort contained a huge Egyptian pithos (c. 1 m wide and 1.5 m high), and nearby were fragments of a second pithos. These containers were incised before firing with the cartouches of Seti II. Excavations in the fortress rooms revealed an abundance of finds, including many pottery vessels typical of southern Canaan in the latter part of the Late Bronze Age and beginning of the Iron Age (thirteenth–twelfth centuries BCE) with Egyptian pottery of the Nineteenth and Twentieth dynasties. Mycenean and Cypriot imports, scarabs and seals, terra-cotta uraeus heads, bronze spearheads, alabaster vessels, and a sandstone statue of a lion were also found. Stratified evidence advocates a thirteenth-century BCE date for the building of the fort (phase III), probably as part of the reorganization of the "Way of Horus" by Seti I. Building remains and floors of phase II indicate extensive repairs and reuse of the original structures, although the site evidently ceased to be a fortress. Some of the structures that occupied the western wing of the fort were replaced by a new spacious building that served some public function, perhaps an administrative center. However, judging from the many refuse pits and burials in the dwelling area, it seems that in phase II the fort was in an advanced state of disrepair and had already been partially abandoned. Sections of the enclosure wall had already collapsed and the gatehouse, through neglect, was no longer an effective defense. Following the destruction by fire of phase II in the early or mid-twelfth century BCE, some parts of the fort were reoccupied (phase I), mainly by squatters; refuse pits were cut into the floors of phase II. Characteristic late Philistine wares and hand-burnished pottery suggest a late Iron Age I date, about 1050 to 1000 BCE, for the poor settlement near the fort and overlying its ruins.

About 400 m north of the fort, near the coastline, the North Sinai Expedition explored the symmetrically planned remains of an Egyptian administrative center of the New Kingdom period (site A-345). Three building units were excavated: a complex of magazines in the center of the site, a "casemate-walled" structure in the northwest, and an industrial quarter on the east. The architectural features—the ground plan, building and bonding techniques, and the standard brick size—are purely Egyptian. The magazine unit comprised a series of long, brick-floored halls (10 by 3 m each) that opened onto a central courtyard. The courtyard (20 by 15 m) was enclosed by a wall and divided in the middle by a partition wall. The rooms were found filled with heaps of mud-brick rubble and sections of walls that collapsed onto the floors after the site was abandoned. The floors of the magazines and the courtyard in front were covered with a thick layer of carbonized grain. A variety of rooms and small compartments to the east, south, and west of the magazines probably served as dwellings, offices, and archives. Soundings under the floors yielded evidence of earlier architectural domestic remains as well as storage and refuse installations. The "casemate" structure (c. 25 m long) was built with thin, plastered walls with plastered brick benches. Its interior was partitioned by thin buttressed walls. The "casemate" structure formed the northern border of the settlement, implying that site A-345 was not provided with a defensive wall. Also, the absence of any evidence of violent destruction, coupled with the layer of sand that was naturally deposited under the fallen rubble of the walls, supports the conclusion that the administrative center was abandoned peacefully.

An industrial quarter was located on the eastern edge of the site to avoid the pollution of the settlement and was also separated from the magazine complex by a partition wall. Excavations uncovered a large potter's workshop with installations for storing and preparing the clay, two complete circular pottery kilns, and the remains of a third kiln. The largest kiln was preserved to

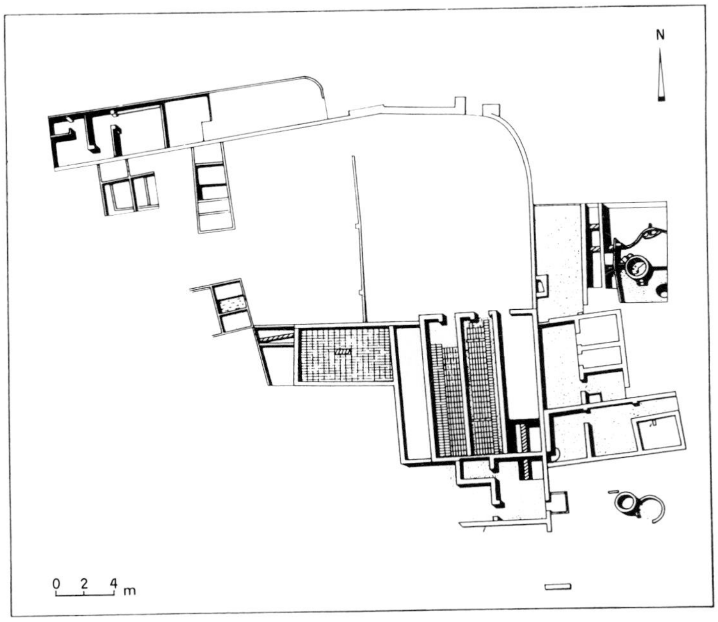

Site A-345, near el-'Arish: Egyptian administrative center, 18th Dynasty (15th–14th centuries BCE*).*
***Above:** plan; **(below)** general view.*

Ḥaruba: potter's kiln, 14th century BCE.

a height of 1.5 m with an outer circumference of 1.8 m. Brick steps gave access to the upper firing chamber and the lower stacking chamber was dug into the sandy soil below. Sections of the brick floor or grating of the upper chamber, provided with a network of holes for the escape of hot air, were preserved in situ. One compartment to the west of the kiln contained large quantities of industrial waste and many fragments of unfired vessels. Evidently, the Ḥaruba workshop manufactured a specific line of Egyptian-type vessels such as bowls and kraters, drop-shaped containers, "flower pots," and offering stands that were distributed to other Egyptian localities in northern Sinai. The corpus of Egyptian pottery, both locally manufactured and imported, is typical of the Eighteenth Dynasty. Here, as in other contemporary sites in northern Sinai, the percentage of Canaanite vessels was small and limited to the storage-jar category. Excavations yielded numerous examples of imported Cypriot ware, but hardly any Mycenean pottery.

The sites surveyed in northern Sinai demonstrate the well planned and organized system of fortresses and road stations that was established to secure and facilitate the principal artery of communication to Canaan and Asia. The abundant finds aid in reconstructing the development of Egyptian military and administrative structures and the "Way of Horus" beginning with Thutmose III and lasting until the late Ramesside period, when Egypt retreated from the region and abandoned the international arena.

THE IRON AGE. In the tenth century BCE, northern Sinai again became an important link between Egypt and Canaan. Egyptian, Assyrian, and biblical sources provide detailed accounts of the military, administrative, and com-

Migdol fortress (site T-21): plan.

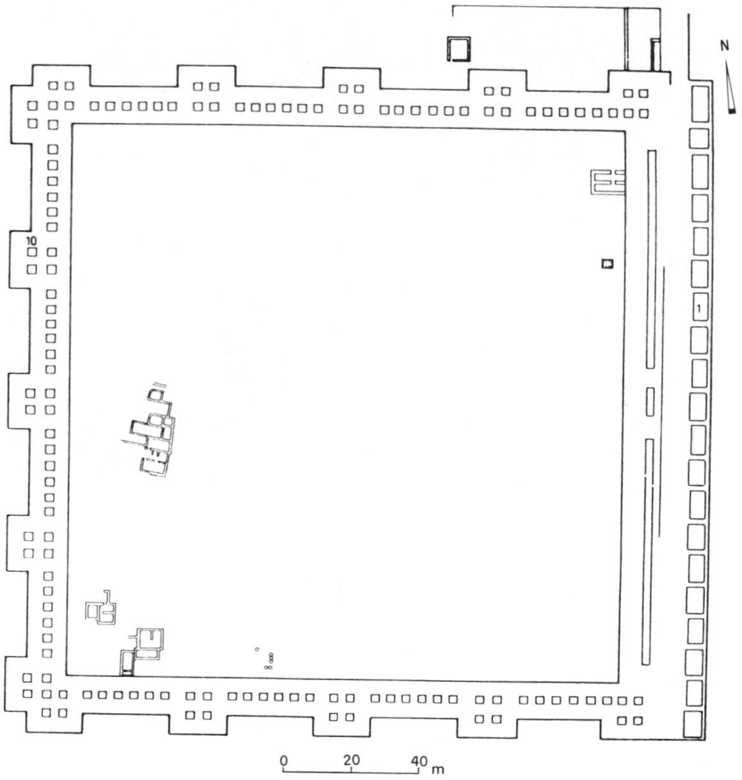

Migdol fortress: wine amphora from Chios, 6th century BCE.

Migdol fortress: amphora from Samos, 6th century BCE.

Migdol fortress: cremation burial, 6th century BCE.

mercial activities along the roads in the Iron Age II–III. More than thirty Iron Age settlement sites between Wadi el-'Arish and Wadi Ghazzeh give evidence of the Assyrian hold on southwestern Philistia in the eighth to seventh centuries BCE. These sites were a springboard for the Assyrian military incursions into Egypt and a buffer zone between Egypt and Assyria. They were also administrative and commercial centers for the international trade, including the Arabian spice trade. One such cluster of Iron Age settlements was investigated recently at Ruqeish near Khan Yunis, yielding new data about Assyria's deployment on the border of Egypt (q.v. Ruqeish). Earlier excavations at Ruqeish uncovered a cemetery with Phoenician-type cremation burials. In the Ben-Gurion University excavations, extensive remains—domestic, public, and industrial—of a well organized town that was enclosed by a massive defense wall were uncovered. The settlement (20–25 a.) at Ruqeish should be considered a major commercial center in southwestern Philistia that also figured prominently in the maritime traffic along the coasts of Phoenicia, Israel, Philistine, and Sinai. In this writer's opinion, the location of Ruqeish along with its size and fortifications support its identification with the new Assyrian commercial headquarters, the "sealed *Karu(m)* of Egypt" where, according to the annals of Sargon II, Assyria coordinated the international trade with Egypt and controlled the spice trade from Arabia. Excavations conducted in 1935 and 1936 by W. M. F. Petrie at Tell Abu Salima (q.v., Sheikh Zuweid) revealed a large building in the Assyrian architectural style. This evidence strengthens the assumption of Assyrian-administered territory in the eighth and seventh centuries BCE as far as the "Brook of Egypt" (Wadi el-'Arish).

In northwestern Sinai, the North Sinai Expedition recorded a dense cluster of sites from the Saite period from the sixth century BCE that yielded evidence, including burial customs, for the settlement of a foreign population. Both written sources and the archaeological record indicate that in this period colonies and border garrisons along the eastern Nile Delta were inhabited by foreign merchants and mercenaries—Greeks, Phoenicians, Arabs, and Jews—merchants who were encouraged to settle there by the pharaohs of the Saite dynasty.

Tell el-Ḥer (Migdol). On the edge of the Delta plain, approximately one kilometer north of Tell el-Ḥer, near the ancient frontier canal, the North Sinai Expedition investigated an extensive site (T-21), about 20 a. in size. At the center of the site is a massive, square mud-brick enclosure (200 by 200 m) with walls 15 to 20 m wide. On three sides, small hollow compartments, 3 by 2 m each, were constructed at fixed intervals inside the walls, and massive buttresses, also with cellular compartments, were appended outside the walls. The widest wall on the east (20 m wide) had rectangular compartments as well as very long and narrow inner corridors. This architectural technique is known from other sites from the Saite period in the Delta, such as Tell Daphnae and Naucratis. The area inside the enclosure wall was primarily occupied by very densely built structures with large courtyards, storage and industrial installations, and stone and metal tools. The pottery assemblage is represented by many Egyptian vessels, Phoenician storage jars, and numerous imported Greek wine amphorae of types similar to the pottery repertoire at Naucratis and Daphnae. Large quantities of copper ore, slag, and complete metal objects, including arrowheads and weights, imply a viable metallurgic industry at the site. The fortified enclosure or garrison should probably be identified with Migdol, which is mentioned in Jeremiah (44:1; 46:14) and Ezekiel (29:10) with Tahpanhes and Noph, as a Jewish garrison with soldiers who served in Egyptian border fortresses. The closely dated pottery corpus points to a late seventh century BCE horizon for the occupation of the fortress. It was subsequently destroyed by fire in the late sixth century BCE, apparently as a direct result of the invasion of Egypt by Cambyses in 525 BCE.

THE PERSIAN PERIOD. The conquest of Egypt in 525 BCE by Cambyses is an important landmark in the history of Sinai. Henceforth, the history of northern Sinai and Egypt was linked to that of the great powers that successively controlled the entire region: the Ptolemies, the Seleucids, the Romans and the Byzantines. The writings of Herodotus contain invaluable data about the demographic map of northern Sinai and the border of Egypt during the Persian period (III:5). In his description of the administrative division of the Fifth Satrapy, the *aber nahara*, Herodotus remarked that "The only entrance into Egypt is through this desert. From Phoenicia to the boundaries of Kadytis [Gaza], the country belongs to the Syrians known as Palestinians. From Kadytis—a town, I should say, not much smaller than Sardis—the emporia [seaports or trade centers] as far as Ienysos, belong to the kings of Arabia: from there as far as Lake Sirbonis near which Mount Casius runs down to the sea, it is once more Syrian territory; and after Lake Sirbonis, where Typhon is supposed to be buried, Egypt begins. The whole area between Ienysos on the one side, and Mount Casius and the lake on the other—and it is of considerable extent, not less than three days' journey—is desert and completely without water." The seaport emporia were apparently the termini of the Arabian trade, and the entire spice trade route in the desert was controlled by the Arabs. Two principal changes occurred in northern Sinai in the Persian period (fifth–fourth centuries BCE). The first was the establishment of a major road along the shore of the Mediterranean and across the sandbar of Lake Bardawil and, consequently, the establishment of a series of permanent settlements, forts and fishing villages on the coastline. The latter became the nuclei for the network of towns and stations that characterized the coast of northern Sinai in the Hellenistic, and particularly the Roman and Byzantine periods.

In the course of the North Sinai Survey, the expedition investigated nearly two hundred settlement sites from the Persian period between the Suez Canal and Gaza, including towns, villages, forts, and cemeteries and numerous seasonal encampments. The settlement map shows large concentrations of sites in northwestern Sinai, on the shores of the Bardawil lagoon and along the coast between el-'Arish and Gaza. Of special consequence is the considerable volume of Greek pottery recorded at almost every site, incontroversible testimony to the major role that Greek trade played in the economy of North Sinai.

At the coastal site of Ruqeish (q.v.), near Deir el-Balaḥ, surveys and excavations recorded impressive remains of a large town, probably an administrative and commercial center and a principal trading station for maritime and land traffic. The location and nature of the rich archaeological remains at Ruqeish in the Persian period support its identification as one of Herodotus' coastal emporia south of Gaza.

Tel Qatif. At Tel Qatif (Y-1), on the coastal ridge about 2 km west of Ruqeish, the remains of a small fort and observation post were excavated. It guarded the traffic in this section of the coastal highway and defended the unfortified town at nearby Ruqeish. Salvage excavations exposed a section of a massive mud-brick structure of the "courtyard fort" type, that was enclosed by a 5-m-wide defensive wall, and a sizable tower overlooking the sea at its northwestern corner. The rich pottery repertoire included Phoenician-type containers, Greek wine amphorae, and quantities of black glazed Attic pottery. Of special interest are Greek-type toggle pins and a fragment from a Greek terra-cotta figurine representing a god or king seated on a decorated throne. On the lower *kurkar* terrace a well-preserved cylindrical mud-brick silo, 2 m in diameter and almost 3 m high, was uncovered. The fort at Tel Qatif belongs to a network of military installations constructed by the Persian administration along the coastal highway of North Sinai, between Gaza and Pelusium (Tell Farama). Remains of similar fortified sites were encountered near Sheikh Zuweid, Mount Casius, Rumani, and Tell el-Ḥer.

Stratified remains of an extensive and well planned settlement of the Persian period were uncovered by Petrie at Tell Abu Salima (q.v.) on the outskirts of Sheikh Zuweid. In 1976, the North Sinai Expedition conducted salvage excavations at a fort site on the coast approximately 3 km north of Sheikh Zuweid (R-54), comprising a massive corner bastion, storerooms, and various cooking and storage installations. Further settlement remains from the Persian period were found in a brief salvage operation in the southeastern

Site T-47: decorated funerary mask, Persian period.

corner of Tell Raphia, where sections of walls, floors, pits, and installations were recorded with quantities of imported Greek pottery. This combined evidence suggests that the Persian period town site at Raphia was rather extensive and probably unfortified. At a distance of about one kilometer west of Tell Raphia, the badly damaged remains of a small cult site (R-26)—perhaps a wayside shrine—that included sections of a small two-room structure with two spacious courtyards and a narrow enclosure wall, were explored. The larger courtyard was occupied by various installations such as a plastered basin for liquids (libations?) and two *favissae* full of ash and charcoal intermixed with animal bones. Many fragmentary terra-cotta and faience figurines of different styles were collected: Greek, Phoenician, Cypriot, and Egyptian. The associated pottery indicates that the site had functioned for a relatively long period, from the seventh to the third centuries BCE, reaching its zenith in the Persian period.

Katib el-Gals. One of the more important stations along the coast of Sinai is located in the center of the Lake Bardawil sandbar near Katib el-Gals, almost universally identified as ancient Kasion. In the classical sources, Kasion is known as an important way station on the coastal road as well as an industrial center that specialized in shipbuilding and for which a particular type of seagoing vessel was named. The prominent ridge nearby, Ras Qaṣrun, is generally considered the location of the temple of Zeus Kasios, the patron god of ships and seafarers. The site of Kasion gained further importance because of the commonly accepted identification of biblical Baal-Zephon with Mount Casius (Ex. 14:2, 14:9). In twenty-two of the forty-three sites that were systematically surveyed in the region of Katib el-Gals, rich occupational evidence of the Persian period, including an abundance of imported Greek pottery, was recorded. Most of the sites were small encampments averaging 0.25 a. Three sites were of particular interest because they were represented by the remains, albeit very deflated, of mud-brick structures and were associated with many storage and cooking installations and stone implements. One of the sites, M-41, was built directly on the *kurkar* ridge that descends to the coastline and may have served as an anchorage for small vessels. The larger site nearby, M-40, may represent the outlying habitation of an extensive settlement, possibly the actual location of Kasion, that is today buried almost entirely under the el-Gals ridge. These sites yielded large quantities of Phoenician pottery, imported Greek ware, fragments of alabaster vessels, and metal objects. The surface collection from M-41 included a fragment of a faience ointment bottle, a silver pin decorated with the head of a cobra, and a round lead die impressed with an Athenian coin from the late fifth or early fourth century BCE. A trial sounding at Ras Qaṣrun, on the northern edge of Katib el-Gals (site M-36), was made to determine the date of the earliest remains at the site, and retrieve data that would shed new light on its traditional identification with Mount Casius and/or Baal-Zephon. Excavations of the trench (c. 10 by 1 m) resulted in the discovery of some scant remains from a brick wall and refuse pits full of ash and fragments of clay *tabun*s positioned directly on the *kurkar* ridge. The small pottery assemblage dates from the Persian period at the earliest to the Late Byzantine period, implying that the site was sanctified to the cult of Zeus Kasios from the Persian period onward.

Tell el-Ḥer: Achaemenid cylinder seal and its impression, Persian period.

The principal concentration of Persian period sites was identified on the edge of the eastern Delta in the region of the Mediterranean terminus of the Pelusian branch of the Nile. In the Persian period, and perhaps even earlier, the Pelusian branch was evidently Egypt's main riverine transportation route, and the city of Pelusium at the estuary of the river became the chief port for Asiatic and Aegean goods. The region was famous for its fine agricultural produce, fish, textile, and glass industries. The new archaeological discoveries corroborate the written sources regarding the density of settlement—towns, garrisons, and trade stations, as well as the prosperity of the region and the varied ethnic composition of its population.

Tell Farama (Pelusium). Limited trial soundings in 1974 and 1976 at the enormous site of Pelusium reached the waterlogged settlement strata from the beginning of the Persian period in the fifth century BCE at a depth of 4 m.

Tell el-Ḥer (Migdol). Explorations at the large site of Tell el-Ḥer, about 10 km south of Pelusium, revealed the excellently preserved remains of three superimposed fortresses, the earliest of which had been constructed in the Persian period on an artificial clay platform about 2 m high. The clay was from the embankment of the nearby eastern canal, which was no longer in use. Beneath the rich Hellenistic and Roman occupational strata and overlying the sterile sand were building remains, installations, and abundant pottery from the Persian period, including a sizable assemblage of imported Greek wares. Two finds from a disturbed deposit in the western section of the site deserve special notice: an Achaemenid cylinder seal made of chalcedony and superbly engraved with a figure of a crowned hero dominating two rampant winged lions; and a miniature limestone incense altar decorated with geometric designs on its sides and rim. Excavations since 1986 at Tell el-Ḥer by a Franco-Egyptian expedition headed by D. Valbelle uncovered a large section of the earliest buttressed fortress and a small shrine with a mud-brick altar in the center. Historical and archaeological considerations suggest that Tell el-Ḥer should be identified with Migdol (Greek Magdolum), which was relocated in the Persian period from the nearby garrison site T-21 (see above) from the Saite period. The archaeological survey of the North Sinai Expedition in the vicinity of Tell el-Ḥer revealed extensive cemeteries from the Persian and Hellenistic–Roman periods. Many badly preserved burials complete with plaster funerary masks were scattered in four of the cemeteries. The masks were decorated in relief and painted with such motifs as wreaths and the Egyptian uraeus and lotus leaves. The burial offerings included Greek pottery, painted plaster figures of sphinxes, lions, Osiris, and Eye of Horus pendants. The masks were fashioned in a mixed Greek, Cypriot, and Egyptian style. The use of Egyptian mythological motifs shows that the population—Greek merchants and mercenaries who settled here at the request of the Persian rulers—assimilated Egyptian funerary customs.

The coastal region between Pelusium and Tell Maḥmadiya, near the western edge of Lake Bardawil, is represented on the Expedition's map by a dense cluster of more than thirty sites from the fifth and fourth centuries BCE that yielded unusually large deposits of imported Greek amphorae and black-glazed Attic ware as well as Phoenician-type transport jars. The westernmost site in this group, S-30, extends over an area of 2.5 a.; its surface is covered by thick deposits of Greek amphorae and Phoenician vessels, stone and clay installations. Apparently, consignments of wine and oil were stored here for redistribution and consumption by the Greek (and Phoenician?) soldiers and merchants in the eastern Nile Delta. The location of site S-30 on the waterfront of the Bardawil lagoon, in a location that provided ideal anchorage and shelter to sea-going vessels, strongly supports this conclusion.

HELLENISTIC-ROMAN PERIOD. In the Hellenistic period, the coastal highway of northern Sinai became a highly organized artery of communication to Palestine, along which were established major towns, military garrisons, way stations, and ports such as Rhinocolura (el-'Arish), Ostrakine (el-Felusiyat), Kasion (el-Gals), Gerrha (Tell Maḥmadiya), Pelusium (Tell Farama), Magdolum (Tell el-Ḥer), and Sile (Tell Abu Seifeh). These centers prospered from commercial activity, collecting customs, and industries such as shipbuilding, textile weaving, glass making, the preservation of fish, salt production, date growing, and quail hunting.

In the course of the North Sinai Survey more than three hundred Hellenistic and principally Roman settlement sites were explored. The distribution map of these sites indicates a drastic change in the settlement pattern and hierarchy; particularly the growth of towns and stations along the coastal road and the expansion of the settlement zone into areas not previously inhabited. The rich finds recorded from these sites demonstrate close commercial ties with markets in North Africa, Egypt, and Palestine on the one hand, and Mediterranean ports in Cyprus, Italy, and Greece on the other.

Northwestern Sinai. The greatest number of sites was studied in northwestern Sinai, in the vicinity of Pelusium, Tell el-Ḥer, and Tell Abu Seifeh. The architectural remains scattered over the surface at Tell Farama reflect the grandeur of this metropolis and the strategic and economic status of the Mediterranean outlet of the Pelusian branch. The size of Pelusium in the Roman period is estimated to have exceeded 3 sq km. Monumental remains of its quays, anchorages, city wall and gates, colonnaded streets, bathhouses, and temple of Zeus Kasios can still be identified on its surface. Recent excavations by the Egypt Antiquities Service (1987–1991) uncovered a well preserved theater, a bathhouse complex, and a large citadel in whose enclosure wall a dedicatory inscription to Marcus Aurelius, chief magistrate of Pelusium, and to Zeus Kasios, the principal god of the city, was incorporated. The architectural remains at Tell el-Ḥer suggest that the Hellenistic-Roman city of Magdolum occupied an area of more than 200 a. The more

Cemetery near Tell el-Ḥer: tombstone, Hellenistic period.

Cemetery on the sandbar of the Bardawil lagoon: Roman tombstone.

Eastern cemetery at Pelusium: Roman tomb.

noticeable remains included a series of fortresses, streets, public and domestic buildings, magazines as well as industrial debris of metal, glass, faience, and pottery. The third city at Tell Abu Seifeh (Sile in the classical sources) reached the same prosperity in the Hellenistic-Roman period; it covered an area of at least 50 a. and was surrounded by a massive city wall.

In the vicinity of these cities were extensive cemeteries exhibiting various burial customs that vividly reflect the population's ethnic variety: brick-lined cist graves, family burials in stone-built loculus tombs, barrel-type clay coffins, cremation urns, and plaster masked burials. The architectural remains of public buildings at Tell Maḥmadiya, with the large cemetery west of the tell, and the extensive settlement of Kasion at the apex of Lake Bardawil's sandbar, are eloquent testimony to the importance of the coastal highway in this period. Although actual building remains of the famous temple of Zeus Kasios have not been discovered, the abundance of fragmentary marble slabs inscribed with Greek letters that perhaps belonged to votive inscriptions indicate the location of the cult site at Katib el-Gals or in its vicinity. Another important commercial center in the Roman period was identified at el-Felusiyat (Ostrakine, q.v.), at the eastern edge of Lake Bardawil and nearby Acregma—the natural outlet of the lagoon to the Mediterranean Sea.

El-ʿArish. The administrative center of northern Sinai in the Roman period and the commercial port for Nabatean trade was evidently el-ʿArish (Rhinocorura or Rhinocolura in the Greco-Roman sources). Rhinocolura was known for its colony of exiled criminals who had been sentenced to hard labor and were severely punished by mutilation of their noses. The North Sinai Expedition identified the extensive ancient ruins in the area west of modern el-ʿArish, in the vicinity of the Turkish fortress. Much of the original area of Rhinocolura is covered today with deep sand dunes as well as a Muslim cemetery. The study of aerial photographs indicated that the lower reaches of Wadi el-ʿArish changed course and shifted eastward as a result of the massive build-up of the coastal sand dunes; thus, it left behind the city of Rhinocolura, which had originally been built on its west bank, and the harbor site at the outlet to the sea. Systematic explorations at ancient el-ʿArish revealed the extensive remains of a carefully planned, fortified city that covered an area of approximately 12.5 a. The city was enclosed by a mud-brick wall (c. 3.5 m thick) with corner towers and buttresses; the streets and alleyways divided it into quarters with specific functions. The residential section shows a high degree of uniformity in the ground plan of the individual houses and architectural details. Surface finds suggest that the settlement was founded in the Hellenistic period. The stratified evidence on the floors belongs to three or four major building phases from the early Roman period to the end of the Byzantine or Early Arab period, in the first to seventh or eighth centuries CE. Of importance are the many Nabatean sherds on the early floor levels. The en-Nebi Yasser Mosque on the coast was apparently built directly on the remains that mark the location of the fishing village and harbor of Roman-Byzantine Rhinocolura.

South of Lake Bardawil, two large Roman period sites were explored, one at Qaṣrawet (q.v.) and the other near Bir Mazar (C-86). The latter is approximately 10 a. in size and has two distinct architectural phases dating to the Early and Late Roman periods. The earliest settlement yielded Nabatean and terra sigillata ware of the first and second centuries. In the fourth century, a new and smaller settlement was established on the eastern part of the site; its buildings closely resembled those at Qaṣrawet. They were also abandoned at the end of the fourth century CE.

The wide distribution of sedentary settlement—towns, villages, trade stations, agricultural farmsteads, and many seasonal encampments—is par-

El-ʿArish: part of the city wall, Roman period.

ticularly significant in the area between el-ʿArish and Raphia. Further, the settlement pattern in this region closely resembles that of Israel's Coastal Plain in the Roman period, namely the location of two related settlements in pairs: the coastal site with its anchorage and fishing facilities, and the central settlement at some distance farther inland. For example, the principal town of Raphia was built at Tell esh-Sheikh Suleiman Rafah (or Tell es-Sultan), and the maritime settlement at Tell Raphia (R-21) on the seashore. Similarly, Tell esh-Sheikh (R-55) was the maritime site for Tell esh-Sheikh Zuweid (R-51) about 5 km (3 mi.) to the southeast.

The commercial significance of the coastal road in northern Sinai was particularly strong in the Roman period, when trade with India and Arabia became a central component of the regional economy; the Nabateans were then the principal intermediaries in the transshipment of luxury goods, primarily spices, from Arabia via Transjordan and the Negev to the ports of Gaza and Rhinocolura. The North Sinai Survey team discovered impressive evidence of the extent of the Nabatean commecial enterprise in northern Sinai, between Pelusium and Gaza. The most important remains—temples, magazines, and cemeteries—were uncovered at Qaṣrawet (q.v.) in northwest Sinai near the large oasis of Qatya. Qaṣrawet was undoubtedly the Nabateans' principal administrative and religious center in the region in the Roman period until its abandonment in the second or third century CE. Nabatean pottery was recorded at dozens of sites in northern Sinai. However, the main network of Nabatean settlement sites and trade stations was found between Wadi Ghazzeh and Wadi el-ʿArish. Some of the key sites were investigated at el-ʿArish and Raphia and in the vicinity of Ḥaruba, Yamit, el-Jorra and Deir el-Balaḥ, yielding caravanserai buildings, warehouses, spacious courtyards, animal pens, and various other installations. Scattered architectural remains of a spacious building, probably a Nabatean temple, were investigated near Raphia. Some of the carved limestone blocks from this building, bearing figures in relief such as an eagle, camels, bull heads, and gazelles, probably belonged to a large altar. Stratigraphic considerations indicate that from the second to first centuries BCE, and prior to the main phase of Nabatean activity (in the first–second centuries CE) and the introduction of solid structures, some of these sites already functioned as caravan stations and encampments that probably represent the early phase of Nabatean commecial enterprise in northern Sinai. The distribution map of Nabatean settlement sites enables a detailed reconstruction of the Nabatean trade network that led from the Negev to the ports of Gaza and el-ʿArish and thence via the Nabatean headquarters of Qaṣrawet to the major markets in the eastern Nile Delta.

BYZANTINE AND ARAB PERIODS. The consolidation of Christianity as the state religion in the fourth century heralded the establishment of Christian centers with monasteries and churches in major towns of northern Sinai, particularly along the coastal road to Egypt. These towns, some of which became episcopal seats, are repeatedly mentioned in pilgrim accounts and in the writings of the church fathers; bishops from North Sinai participated in the church councils at Ephesus and Chalcedon. The list of towns between Rhinocolura and Pelusium on the Medeba map illustrates the importance of these centers in the Byzantine period. The distribution of Byzantine settlement sites in northern Sinai is extensive: to date more than three hundred sites have been recorded, including large towns, trade stations, fishing settlements, cemeteries, industrial installations, and campsites. As in the Roman period, the principal clusters of settlement sites were found along the coastal strip, although many were located south of Lake Bardawil and at a considerable distance from the Mediterranean Sea. Evidently, most of the principal towns and stations that marked the settlement map of the Roman period continued to prosper, or were rebuilt, in the Byzantine period. For example, at Tell Farama major architectural remains such as the city wall and the western citadel were noted, and an impressive triapsidal basilical church was discovered in 1913 by J. Clédat at Tell Makhzan—Pelusium's eastern extension in the Roman-Byzantine period. At Tell el-Ḥer the Franco-Egyptian expedition revealed in 1985–1986 a massive *castellum* from the Byzantine period. The 8,100-sq-m fortress is enclosed by a thick wall, 3.5 m thick, with casemate chambers aligned along its ramparts. Sections of a large public structure, a church or monastery, have been gradually exposed by sea waves on the northern edge of Tell Maḥmadiya, and an extensive burial site was investigated in 1976 by the North Sinai Expedition to the southwest of the tell. The most characteristic tomb types were stone-lined cist graves, and stone-built graves completed with a gabled roof and a niche that was intended to hold an urn of ashes. One of the graves yielded a carved stone cross and an oil lamp decorated with a cross in relief. At the major town site of el-Felusiyat (ancient Ostrakine, q.v.), three basilical churches, a fortified monastery, and a commercial market quarter were uncovered. Evidence of prosperous Byzantine towns with public buildings was revealed at el-ʿArish and Bir Mazar, and the extensive remains of another town, perhaps Sykamazon on the Medeba map, were recently located on the coastal ridge near Deir el-Balaḥ (Y-12). Salvage excavations in 1973 by V. Tzaferis on behalf of the Israel Department of Antiquities and Museums uncovered sections of a well constructed bathhouse and, nearby, a crude mosaic floor of some public (?) building. The survey team of Ben-Gurion University located a major pottery workshop and estimated the town was at least 25 a. in size.

Qalʿat et-Tina: part of the fortress, Early Arab period.

The period between the Arab conquest in 638 and the beginning of the Ottoman period (1516) is represented on the survey map of North Sinai by more than 250 sites, of which approximately 220 were classified as seasonal encampments. The distribution map shows a noticeable difference from the Roman-Byzantine map in a number of ways: the sites are more concentrated in the areas south of the Bardawil lagoon than along the coastal road; many were located more than 10 km farther inland; and settlement hierarchy certainly reflects the increase in the number of seasonal campsites. Evidently, the age-old military highway south of the lagoon regained its importance as the principal caravan road to Egypt.

The dense cluster of sites in northwestern Sinai included many examples of walled settlements and forts, of which the largest (400 by 200 m) was recorded at Tell Farama. A network of smaller fortresses was built over Roman and Byzantine occupational debris, in the swampy plain of et-Tina, including Qalʿat Umm Mefariḥ, Qalʿat et-Tina, Tell el-Fadda, and Tell el-Luli. Excavations by the Ben-Gurion University expedition at Qalʿat et-Tina, near Tell Farama, exposed sections of an exceptionally well-preserved octagonal fortress (diameter, 55 m); the wooden door of the main entrance survived on its hinges. Judging from contemporary historical sources, these forts were part of a complex defensive system designed in the thirteenth to fifteenth centuries by the Mameluke sultans of Egypt to protect the Delta from invading European fleets and prevent nomadic incursions. Farther east, extensive remains of a walled settlement were identified at Tell Maḥmadiya on the edge of the Lake Bardawil sandbar. The largest walled town on the main caravan route was found at the Qatya oasis. The extensive ruins occupy an area of approximately 2 sq km, including sections of a massive wall, large buildings constructed of baked mud bricks, arches, granite columns, and industrial waste of glazed pottery, faience, and glass. At el-ʿArish, the Early Arab settlement was probably confined to the northern section of the extensive Roman-Byzantine site, evidently reflecting the diminishing role of the town in the administration of the North Sinai caravan road.

J. Clédat, *Annales du Service des Antiquités de l'Egypte* 10 (1910), 209–237; 12 (1912), 45–168; 13 (1913), 115–124; 15 (1915), 13–48; 16 (1916), 6–32; id., *Recueil de Travaux* 31 (1915), 115–124; 38 (1922), 22–23; id., *Bulletin de l'Institut Français d'Archéologie Orientale* 21 (1923), 77–79; 160–163; A. H. Gardiner, *JEA* 6 (1920), 99–116; F.-M. Abel, *RB* 48 (1938), 207–236, 530–548; 49 (1940), 55–75, 224–239; J. Ball, *Egypt in the Classical Geographers*, Cairo 1942; M. Dothan, *IEJ* 17 (1967), 279–280; E. D. Oren, *IEJ* 23 (1973), 112–113; 198–205, 215–217; 32 (1982), 303–311; id. (and F. Weinberg), *Metallurgical Society of CIM Annual Volume* (1978), 147–155; id. (et al.), *Metallography* 10 (1979), 305–316; id., *Sinai, Pharaohs, Miners, Pilgrims and Soldiers* (ed. B. Rothenberg), Bern 1979, 181–191; id., *ILN* (Nov. 1981), 76–77 (Dec. 1981), 62–65; id. (and I. Gilead), *TA* 8 (1981), 25–44; id., *MdB* 24 (1982), 3–47; id., *BASOR* 256 (1984), 7–44; id., *Egypt, Israel, Sinai: Archaeological and Historical Relationships in the Biblical Period* (ed. A. F. Rainey), Tel Aviv 1987; 69–119; id., *L'Urbanisation de la Palestine a l'Age du Bronze Ancien* (*BAR*/IS 527 ed. P. de Miroschedji), Oxford 1989, 389–406; T. L. Thompson, *The Settlement of Sinai and the Negev in the Bronze Age*, Wiesbaden 1975; M. Abd el-Maksoud, *Cahiers de Recherches de l'Institut de Papyrologie et d'Egyptologie de Lille* 8 (1986), 15–16; 9 (1987), 13–16; E. Lois and D. Valbelle, ibid. 10 (1988), 61–71.

ELIEZER D. OREN

Tel Sera': Mycenean rhyton, 13th century BCE.

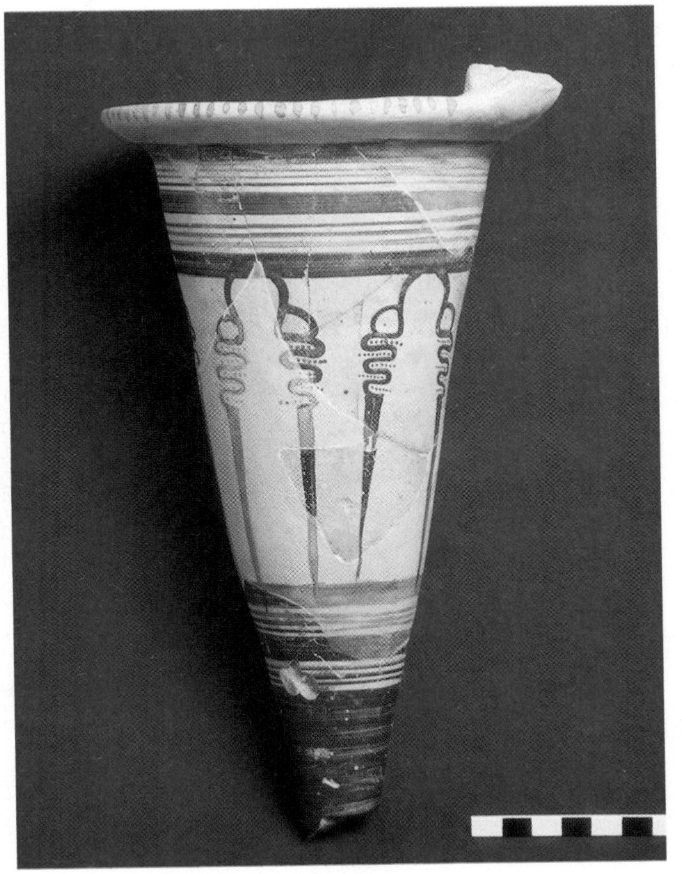

Tel Sera': Mycenean rhyton, 13th century BCE.

Tel Sera': part of the governor's residence, 13th–12th centuries BCE.

Neapolis (Shechem): overview of the theater, 2nd century CE.

Neapolis (Shechem): overview of the amphitheater, 3rd century CE.

SOUTHERN SINAI IN THE EARLY BRONZE AGE

EXPLORATION

Between 1967 and 1982, Israeli researchers conducted extensive archaeological investigations in Sinai, particularly in the peninsula's high southern mountain area. Because of its geographical structure, relatively mild climate, and water sources, generations of continuous human activity there had left their mark on hundreds of mostly single-period sites, many of which are visible to the surveyor's naked eye.

The first excavations in this region were conducted in 1906 by C. T. Currelly, a member of the Petrie expedition, who was working at Serabit el-Khadem at the time. Apart from excavations at *nawamis* in the upper Wadi Naṣb, Currelly excavated at a small site in Wadi Aḥmar, near the copper mine in Wadi Riqiṭiya, and in the "stone circle" in Wadi Umm 'Alawi.

The Sinai Peninsula as a whole was not studied archaeologically until after the 1967 Six Day War. Between 1967 and 1972, a survey of ancient sites was conducted in southern Sinai along the length of the principal wadis by B. Rothenberg's Arabah expedition (q.v. Timna'). This expedition rechecked the Wadi Aḥmar site which had been excavated by Currelly. Other high mountain sites were surveyed and documented by A. Goren.

Between 1971 and 1982, the Ophir expedition, from the Institute of Archaeology at Tel Aviv University, under the direction of I. Beit-Arieh, conducted systematic surveys and excavations in the Sinai area. Eleven of the twenty seasons were dedicated to the high mountain region where, for the first time in the history of research in Sinai, about 50 Early Bronze Age II sites, some with a Canaanite material culture, were found. More than half were defined as dwelling sites and the remainder as campsites. A few pottery sherds and flint tools collected at other contemporary dwelling sites in the high mountains and in the east indicate that at the time those sites were inhabited by a local population.

The Early Bronze Age II sites were established on flat terraces along the banks of wadis, on raised alluvial fans in the wadis and even on the mountains' moderate slopes. Most were near water sources and close to the passes between the cleft granite mountains; however, some sites were built in the high mountains in closed valleys with fertile soil. Two principal concentrations of Early Bronze Age II sites are known: the largest is in the area of the Waṭia pass, the other in the eastern entrance to the Feiran oasis, approximately 60 km (40 mi.) west of the first concentration; isolated sites are located in other areas of the mountain region and on its fringes. The southernmost sites noted were found in the upper third of Wadi Ḥibran and the northernmost at the head of Wadi Birk, approximately 15 km (10 mi.) south of Serabit el-Khadem. Because sites of this type were not found in eastern or western Sinai, or in areas north of the high mountains, it can be concluded that the Canaanite settlements were confined to the high mountains and did not descend to the areas along the Coastal Plain.

THE OPHIR EXPEDITION EXCAVATIONS

The Ophir expedition excavated six Early Bronze Age II sites. The first was excavated in 1971—no. 1049 in the expedition's series—and had been discovered by B. Rothenberg. It is located in Wadi esh-Sheikh, near Nebi Ṣaleḥ. Between 1972 and 1978, three more sites were excavated: Sheikh Mukhsen (no. 1046/7), Wadi Umm Tumur (no. 1014), and Waṭiya Pass (no. 1042). One site was excavated in Wadi Gharaba, near Sheikh 'Awad (no. 1118) and another (no. 1150) near the eastern entrance to the Feiran oasis.

These sites included dwellings built of local granite with a uniform plan: dwelling rooms and smaller adjoining rooms, usually arranged around a large courtyard. Most of the rooms are rectangular broadrooms with rounded corners and an entrance along the long wall that faces the courtyard. Their average dimensions are 3.5 by 5 m. The low entranceways (70 cm high), are

Sheikh 'Awad: one of the dwelling rooms.

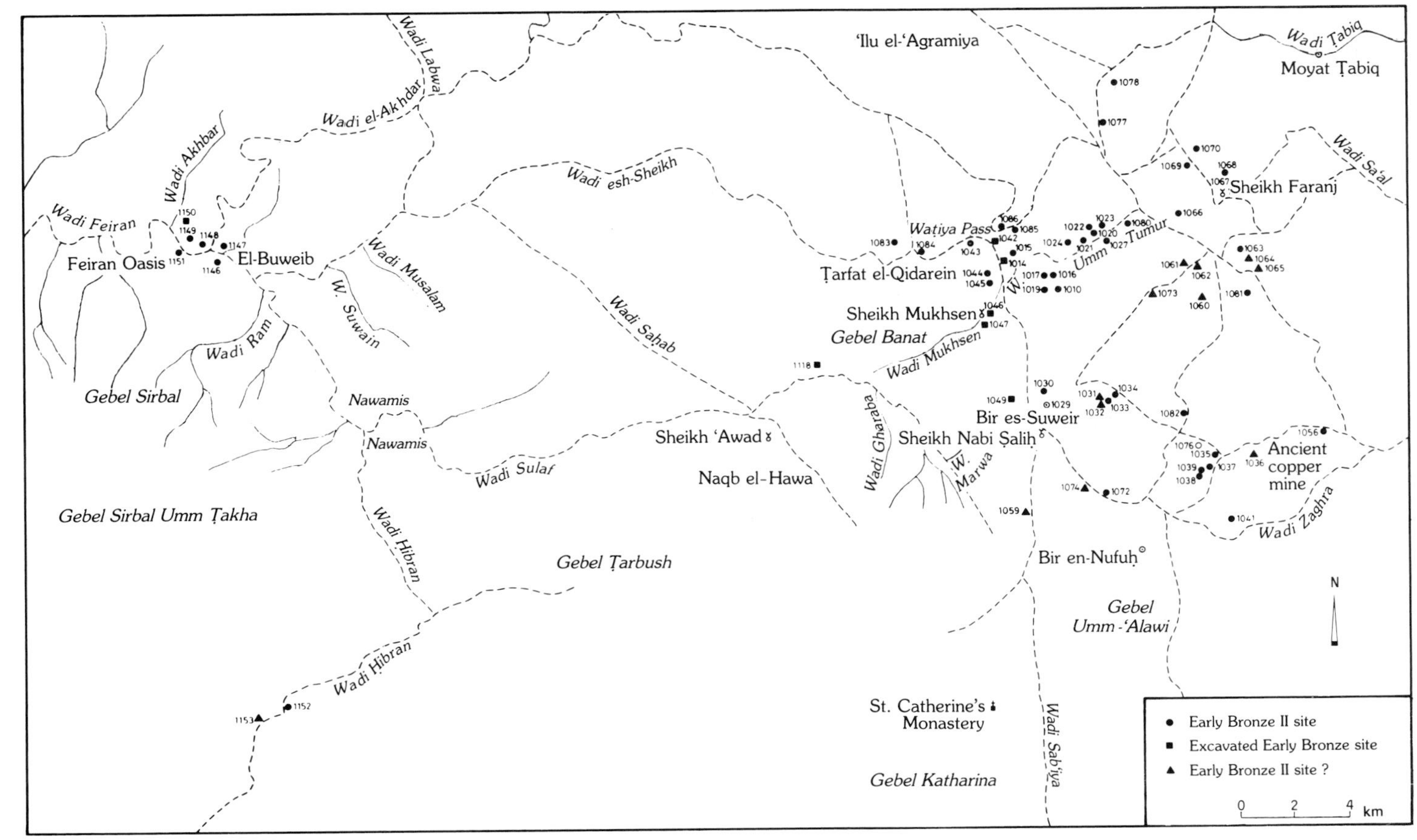

Southern Sinai: map of the EB II sites.

Sheikh 'Awad: plan of complex B.

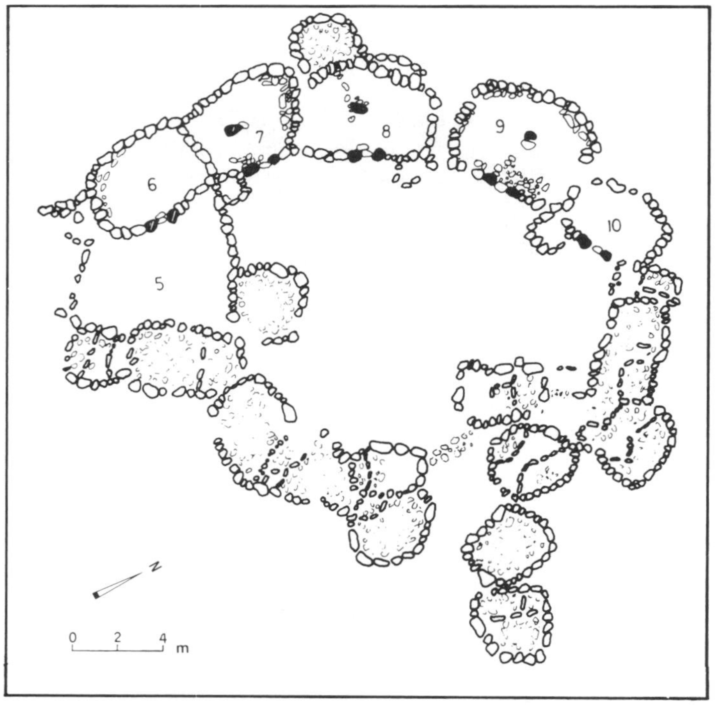

Sheikh 'Awad: plan of complex C.

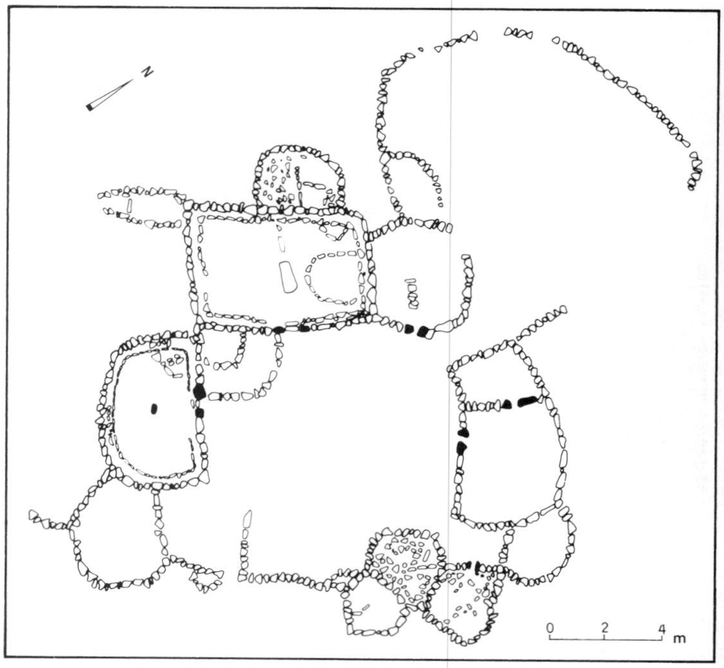

placed between two monolithic columns. In some rooms, door sockets were found near the door post on the left, indicating that the door opened inward on its hinge. Steps led to the level of the rooms' earthen floors which are 20 to 50 cm lower than the immediate surrounding area. Stone benches line the inside of the rooms along the length of the walls, together with ledges and small compartments. In each room there was a hearth, usually on the left, near the doorway. The roof, which was apparently built of light materials, was supported by a stone column (monolithic or composed of drums) or by a wooden beam on a stone foundation. From the architectural data collected during excavation, it appears that in most cases the roof was sloped: the support column for the roof was higher than the tops of the walls. In some rooms there was evidence of repairs and the raising of the floor level, but there were no changes in the overall plan of the dwellings. The compartments, which were smaller than the dwelling rooms, were generally round; most are paved with stone slabs and divided into even smaller compartments. They were built level with the courtyard or higher, were unroofed, and appear to have had low walls. They may have served as workshops or storerooms.

The smaller sites excavated (nos. 1014, 1042, and 1150) contain one dwelling unit, whereas the large ones contain four units of varying sizes: in the smallest there is one room and in the largest there are nine.

THE FINDS

POTTERY. Most of the pottery can be counted among the common Canaanite ceramic forms. There is a wide variety of types and almost all of them have parallels at Arad, strata III through I. These include hole-mouth

Sheikh Mukhsen: general view.

Sheikh Mukhsen: Canaanite storage jar, in situ.

jars, jugs (including Abydos ware), juglets, bowls, bowl-cups, platters, jars, and pithoi. The number of hole-mouth jars is particularly large. Petrographic analysis of identical hole-mouth cooking pots from Sinai and Arad has revealed that their makeup included granite from the Sinai; the small household vessels originated at sites in Canaan, probably at Arad. In these assemblages, a small amount of Egyptian pottery was found, particularly sherds of jars common during the First Dynasty.

FLINT TOOLS. Quantitatively, it appears that these artifacts have an important place among the finds. The dominant group (more than 80 percent) is tabular flint tools—mostly scrapers of various types—whose source is local. The technique in which they were worked is characterized by retouch along most of the circumference of the tool while the outer layer on one side was left untouched, and by percussion bulbs and well formed bases. The number of sickle blades and arrowheads is particularly small. These data are compatible with the evidence regarding the flora and fauna at these sites, confirming the picture of the population's economy. Other than producing copper (see below), that economy was based on herding flocks and minimal hunting.

COPPER TOOLS. Copper tools were discovered in all the sites excavated. Evidence for the various stages of the local production of copper was found, including copper ore, crucibles, molds, and chunks of smelted copper. The copper deposits in this region are in Wadi Riqiṭiya, about 15 km (10 mi.) east of Nebi Ṣaleḥ; chemical tests have shown that the copper was mined there. Near the mine the expedition found three extraction sites with furnaces, ores, slag, and clay tuyeres of bellows.

FLORA AND FAUNA. The remains of wood found in the excavations were

Sheikh Mukhsen: copper ax.

Nebi Ṣaleḥ: mother-of-pearl "buttons," EB II.

primarily of the pistachio tree, although small remains of tamarisk and date palms were also found. Pollen analysis from site no. 1049, near Nebi Ṣaleḥ indicated that a small amount (12 percent) of the sample was cereals.

The faunal remains included large amounts of domesticated goat and some gazelle and mountain goats. Presumably the goats were the dwarf desert goat, common in Sinai today and the economic basis of the Bedouin living there. In the dwellings and adjoining compartments, eighty different species of Red Sea conches were found. Some were used as decoration in their natural form and others were fashioned into beads, such as the diamond-shaped "buttons" made of mother-of-pearl.

SUMMARY

The resemblance between the material culture of southern Sinai and that of Canaanite Arad (strata III–I) shows that they were contemporary. The appearance of certain types of vessels, such as biconical juglets, found at Sheikh Mukhsen, extends the duration of the settlement to the end of the Early Bronze Age II and perhaps longer—to the second half of the twenty-seventh century BCE. This date was also established by carbon-14 tests performed on carbonized wood from Sheikh Mukhsen and Sheikh 'Awad.

The relatively dense, single-period, unfortified "Canaanite" settlements discovered in southern Sinai were built in a uniform plan of closely knit structures around a central courtyard. This plan, which is very suitable for desert conditions, is so characteristic of the "Canaanite" sites in Sinai and at many contemporary sites in the Negev Hills, that it became a chronological criterion. The sunken broadrooms, with their architectural components, were built in a true Aradian style. The portable finds also connect these sites with Canaanite material culture at Arad. The fact that there were few foreign finds strengthens the notion that a population from Arad settled there. This population maintained contact with and dependence on Canaan throughout the settlements' existence.

The fact that copper-extraction sites and metallurgical finds were discovered at the dwelling sites indicates the connection between the "Canaanite" settlement and this ore, which was very valuable at the time. It also explains, to a certain extent, the concentration of sites in southern Sinai. Presumably, the Canaanite hold on southern Sinai was influenced by the dynamics of the population of Canaan, which for the first time since the Neolithic period crossed the border into the Negev hills and the southern Arabah. One of those waves reached southern Sinai and settled in the hills. During this settlement's long existence, new settlements far from the first ones were established, whose economies were not based on copper production. Nonetheless, the connection with southern Canaan and Arad was not lost, and a pattern of city and satellite settlements was maintained: the unfortified Sinai settlements were the satellites under the aegis of the city-state of Arad.

Analysis of the meager Egyptian pottery found suggests sporadic commercial contacts with Egypt along the western coast of the peninsula. Apparently, in the Early Bronze Age II, southern Sinai was not in the Egyptian sphere of influence, and the Egyptians neither took economic advantage of its resources nor settled there.

B. Rothenberg, *PEQ* 102 (1970), 4–29; R. Amiran et al., *IEJ* 23 (1973), 193–197; E. D. Oren, ibid., 198–205; id., *L'Urbanisation de la Palestine à l'Age du Bronze Ancien* (Actes du Colloque d'Emmaüs, 1986; *BAR*/IS 527, ed. P. de Miroschedji), Oxford 1989, 389–405; I. Beit-Arieh, *TA* 1 (1974), 144–156; 8 (1981), 95–127; id., (and R. Gophna), ibid., 128–135; 9 (1982), 146–156; id., *Expedition* 20/4 (1978), 8–11; id., *IEJ* 29 (1979), 256–257; 34 (1984), 20–23; id., *BASOR* 243 (1981), 31–55; 263 (1986), 27–54; id., *Levant* 15 (1983), 39–48; id., *BAR* 10/4 (1984), 26–54; id. *L'Urbanisation de la Palestine à l'Age du Bronze Ancien* (op. cit.), 189–197; T. L. Thompson, *The Settlement of Sinai and the Negev in the Bronze Age* (Beihefte zum Tübinger Atlas des Vorderen Orients B/8), Wiesbaden 1975; W. A. Ward, *BASOR* 281 (1991), 11–26.

ITZHAQ BEIT-ARIEH

INSCRIPTIONS IN SOUTHERN SINAI IN THE HELLENISTIC, ROMAN, AND BYZANTINE PERIODS

IDENTIFICATION AND EXPLORATION

The region of southern Sinai borders the escarpment of the cliffs of et-Tih and Gebel Gunna on the north; on the west, east, and south it is surrounded by the waters of the Gulf of Suez and the Gulf of Elath. At the feet of the cliffs of et-Tih and Gebel Gunna, sandy valleys were formed by the eroded sandstone of the surrounding mountains. In these valleys pilgrims' routes crossed, leading to Gebel Musa and Saint Catherine's Monastery. Inscriptions and drawings engraved by pilgrims have been found on the rocky sandstone walls. South of them rise the lofty central mountains of southern Sinai, in which Gebel Katharina, Gebel Musa, and other ridges are located. Gebel Sirbal is a separate unit, rising above the oasis of Feiran, a mountain, like the others, of granite and porphyry. The large and wide wadis that lead from the north, east, and west to the Feiran oasis and Gebel Sirbal cross between these mountain ridges. On these mountains, especially on the crest of Gebel Sirbal, small concentrations of inscriptions were found.

In 536, the merchant Cosmas Indicopleustes described inscriptions he saw in the Sinai Desert and ascribed them to the Israelites, who, he believed, engraved them during their wanderings in the desert (*Topographia Christiana* 217A). Inscriptions in "Hebrew" letters were noticed also by the pilgrim Egeria in the late fourth century (Peter the Deacon, *CCSL* 175, 102). The in-scriptions were rediscovered with the renewal of Christian pilgrimage in the seventeenth, and especially in the eighteenth centuries. The travelers/researchers A. R. Pococke (1738), J. L. Burckhardt (1821), Leon de Laborde (1828), K. Niebuhr and E. W. Montagu (1866), and others copied many inscriptions. The first attempt at decipherment was made by E. E. F. Beer, who suggested attributing the inscriptions to the Nabateans. Between 1888 and 1900, the French Academy dispatched G. Benedite to Sinai, who copied more than two thousand inscriptions. At about the same time, J. Euting copied six hundred Nabatean inscriptions. In the second volume of *Corpus inscriptionum semiticarum* (1902–1907) 2,743 Nabatean inscriptions were published. After the 1956 war, and especially after the Six-Day War in 1967, extensive research activities were initiated. Numerous inscriptions were photographed by the Arabah Expedition under the direction of B. Rothenberg, by expeditions from the Hebrew University of Jerusalem, by the team of Research and Planning of Southern Sinai (especially by Z. Meshel), and by A. Goren, archaeological staff officer in Sinai. All of these inscriptions were entrusted to A. Negev for documentation and decipherment. In some of the locations at which Nabatean inscriptions were discovered, Hebrew, Aramaic, Greek, Latin, Armenian, and Arabic inscriptions were also found. In 1982, a documentation committee headed by M. Stone was appointed.

HISTORY OF THE REGION AND ITS INSCRIPTIONS

From the description of Diodorus Siculus, it seems that Nabatean or other Arab tribes were already living in Sinai in the Hellenistic period (*Bibliotheca* III, 42). He speaks of an altar to Poseidon Pelagius put up by Ariston, whom Ptolemy I sent to investigate the coast of Arabia. The altar was erected at a place called Poseidion that is identified with Ras Muḥammad. Diodorus reported a famous plantation of palms in the vicinity, and an altar, made of a hard stone, on which characters were inscribed in an unknown language. Strabo (*Geography* XVI, 4, 18) ascribed this information to the geographer Artemidoros (c. 100 BCE), who also mentioned the Gulf of Aila and "the rock of the Nabatean Arabs." Whatever the case, typical Nabatean pottery was found at the oasis of Feiran, at Wadi Ḥaggag (the Valley of the Pilgrims), and at the crest of Gebel Sirbal, among other locations.

Most of what is known about the Nabateans in southern Sinai derives, however, from thousands of rock inscriptions from the second and third centuries. Some are bilingual—Nabatean and Greek. By the end of the third century, an expedition of Egyptian military and civil personnel visited Wadi Ḥaggag (apparently in Diocletian's time), including high-ranking Jewish officials. Inscriptions were found on one of the rocks in Wadi Ḥaggag that had been engraved in Greek by some members of this expedition. With the advent of Christianity, and especially with the foundation of the first monasteries in southern Sinai, pilgrimages were made to Gebel Musa and to Saint Catherine's Monastery, which was built at the site of "the burning bush" associated with the Book of Exodus. The pilgrims came from the Holy Land and Egypt. A few Jews came with the Christians and left behind inscriptions in Hebrew and engravings of the seven-branched menorah.

ROCK INSCRIPTIONS. Large concentrations of inscriptions are found on the banks of Wadi B'ab'a and its tributaries, in the region of Wadi Mukatab–Wadi Feiran (in which Gebel Sirbal and Gebel Moneijah are also located, on whose crests important Nabatean inscriptions were discovered). All these are routes leading from the Gulf of Suez to the oasis of Feiran. Numerous Nabatean inscriptions have also been found along the roads leading to the oasis from the northeast and east, like the road that runs from Wadi Sulaf to Gebel Musa.

There are fewer inscriptions in the eastern part of the peninsula. Small concentrations of inscriptions were found along the eastern route running through Wadi Ḥaggag–Ridhan Eshka–Gebel Gunna. In this region the number of Greek pre-Christian and Christian inscriptions, Jewish inscriptions, and those in other languages exceed the numbers of Nabatean inscriptions. Most of the Nabatean inscriptions in southern Sinai are lists of personal

Rock carvings and drawings by Nabatean pilgrims on the northern road to the Feiran oasis.

Rock carvings made by Nabatean pilgrims on the road to the Feiran oasis.

Nabatean carvings and animal drawings, carved at different times on a rock on the northern road to the Feiran oasis.

names: "such and such son of so and so"; only rarely is a more detailed genealogy made available, such as son, father, and grandfather, and still rarer are the instances in which a fourth generation is mentioned. In a considerable number of inscriptions, two, three, or four brothers are listed. These inscriptions are important in researching the movements of families over the routes in southern Sinai. Names of women rarely appear. At the beginning of numerous inscriptions a sign similar to the letter Y appears that probably symbolizes the cornucopia, or horn of plenty, which the Nabateans used frequently on their coinage.

Numerous inscriptions open with the word שלם (peace), בריך (blessed), or דכיר (be remembered), or with a less common formula, such as דכיר בטב לעלם (be remembered in peace forever) or בטב ושלם קדם אלהא (good and peace in front of the deity). Names of deities are quite rare: דושרא (Dushara); אלבעלי ('Alba'ali); אאלהי ('A'alhy); בובך (*Bwbk*), or כיובך (*Kywbk*); עזיא (the goddess 'Aziya); and תא (T'a). This last-mentioned deity figures six times in Sinaitic inscriptions and may have been a local deity. Except for the inscription that reads: עבדחרתת הפרכא וגרמו עלימה (Hipparchos 'Abdḥaretat and his servant Garmu), no other administrative official titles have been found. However, religious titles occur commonly: כהן אאלהי, priest of 'A'alhy; כהן עזיא, priest of 'Aziya; אפכלא or אכפלא, the priest who is probably in charge of the temple; ביתיא, possibly the priest who is in charge of the management of the "house"; מבקרא, possibly the priest who is in charge of sacrifices; and כתבא, the temple scribe. The last five titles were found in the inscriptions discovered in the sacred compound at Gebel Moneijah, the mountain that rises above the oasis of Feiran.

Most of the Nabatean personal names figuring in inscriptions in southern Sinai are indigenous, but a few can be traced to other regions in the Nabatean realm. Personal names based on geographic locations are rare, and so the personal name אילת (Eilat) in one inscription is remarkable. The appellations אלחגריו (the Hegrite, or one from Egra) and אלזעבליו (the Za'abalite) are more common, while tribal personal names such as מן חתית (of the Hatite tribe) are extremely rare. Babies born during the season of pilgrimage were named חגו (pilgrim) or בחגא (born during pilgrimage).

Unlike the Nabatean inscriptions at Petra, foreign names in inscriptions are rare in southern Sinai; however, סלונס, the Roman name Silvanus, appears, as does the personal name סרפיו, Serapion, which is Greek-Egyptian. One inscription refers to a Jew: חיאל בר שבתי בר אחיו (Ḥiel son of Shabtai son of *'ḥyw*). Numerous personal names contain a theophoric element; some open with the name *'bd* (servant, worshiper), or end with the names *'lhy* (my God), *b'ly* (my Lord or Master), and the like. Numerous personal names refer to physical or spiritual properties. Among the personal names the following are outstanding: פארן (*p'rn*), a geographical name, appears forty-two times and may be the name of babies born at the Feiran oasis and its surroundings; קינו (*qynw*) appears sixty times, and its derivatives mean metal smith or copper smith, which suggests the occupation of many of the Nabateans in southern Sinai, who worked in the copper mines or traded copper and turquoise; and שמרח (*Šmrḥ*), "a cluster laden with palm dates," which may hint at the occupation of the many Nabateans who exploited the date palms at several oases on the peninsula, appears thirty times. A discussion of some of the major concentrations of inscriptions follows:

Gebel el-Moneijah. Gebel el-Moneijah (the Mountain of the Meeting Place) is the name given to a mountain venerated by the Bedouin to this day. Numerous Nabatean invocations are engraved on the rocks along the path leading to its crest, where the Bedouin have erected a roundish enclosure, in which a cult of the fertility of the herds is practiced. Nabatean inscriptions containing the personal names of title holders (see above) were also engraved on many of the stones used to construct the enclosure. One of them dates to 254 CE. The stones originated in a Nabatean sanctuary. It is possible that the sanctuary at Gebel el-Moneijah was a station for pilgrims on their way to the temple built on the higher slope of Gebel Sirbal.

Gebel Sirbal. The earliest inscriptions found at the top of Gebel Sirbal were published in the *Corpus inscriptionum semiticarum*, but new inscriptions have been discovered since 1967. In 1979, limited trial excavations were carried out at the summit by U. Avner, on behalf of the archaeology officer in Sinai. Just below the crest, a courtyard (11 by 24 m) containing a square rock, possibly an altar, was discovered. Two flights of steps lead up to it. In the southwestern part of the building is a hall (2.5 m wide), with a round base, possibly for a statue. The temple consists of an outer shrine (43 by 55 m) and an inner shrine (2.2 by 2.2 m), or *debir*. Among the small finds from the temple are Nabatean painted potsherds, Roman vessels, and a coin of Obodas III (30–9 BCE). This temple belongs to the first century CE, the Middle Nabatean period.

Wadi Ḥaggag and Gebel Gunna. Wadi Ḥaggag and Gebel Gunna are located on the route leading from the Gulf of Elath to the rocky massif in the southern part of the Sinai peninsula. Burckhardt suggested identifying 'Ain Khoudra, which lies below Wadi Ḥaggag, with biblical Hazeroth, the third station of the Israelites after Mount Sinai. The site was later visited by E. Palmer, who

Inscription and drawings on a rock in Wadi Ḥaggag, carved by a Christian pilgim requesting salvation for himself and his family.

copied Nabatean inscriptions and reported on the Greek inscriptions here. Since 1956, numerous inscriptions have been photographed by Rothenberg, Meshel, and others. In 1971, the site was surveyed by A. Negev on behalf of the Hebrew University and some four hundred inscriptions were photographed. There are six groups of inscriptions: Nabatean, Greek pre-Christian, Christian, Jewish, Armenian, and Arabic. Among the Nabatean inscriptions, which are not abundant, are some with personal names not mentioned in other parts of southern Sinai; they appear side by side with names that occur frequently in other regions of the peninsula.

The Greek pre-Christian inscriptions were engraved in the corner of a single rock by a group of Egyptian administrative and military officials (see above). One inscription reads: "One God who helps Valerius son of Antigonus, strategos. Third indiction year." In the upper-right-hand corner are three letters—two in Greek and one in Hebrew—interpreted by Negev as "Highest God. One." Another inscription reads: "By (God's) Grace. Let Theodotos the hipparchos, son of Claudius, be remembered." It seems that these inscriptions are connected with the outbreak of the revolt against Diocletian in Egypt in 297 and with the emperor's visit to Egypt the following year to subdue it.

The hundreds of Christian inscriptions in Greek, Armenian, and other languages were engraved on several rocks by pilgrims who sojourned here from the fifth century onward. The pilgrims rested in the shadow of these rocks, while their guides and camels went down to fetch water at 'Ain Khoudra. From the inscriptions, which include numerous blessing formulae and invocations, it is learned that the pilgrims were escorted by soldiers from fortresses in Transjordan.

The Hebrew-Aramaic Jewish inscriptions are accompanied by engravings of seven-branched menorahs. One of the inscriptions reads: "Let Shmuel son of Hillel be blessed and guarded." Above this inscription the following shortened form is written: שחד, possibly "the Name of God. One," as well as הר אלהים, "the Mountain of God." The Jewish pilgrims may have joined their Christian neighbors on their way to "Mount Sinai."

L. de Laval, *Voyage dans le Peninsula Arabique de Sinai et de l'Egypte Moyenne*, Paris 1855; C. W. Wilson and H. S. Palmer, *Ordnance Survey of the Peninsula of Sinai* 1–2, London 1869; E. H. Palmer, *The Desert of the Exodus* 1, London 1877; J. Euting, *Sinaitische Inschriften*, Berlin 1891; B. Rothenberg, *Corpus Inscriptionum Semiticarum* 2, Paris 1902, 349–357; id., *PEQ* 102 (1970), 4–29; A. Negev, *IEJ* 17 (1967), 250–255; 27 (1977), 219–231; 31 (1981), 66–71; id., *The Inscriptions of Wadi Haggag, Sinai* (Qedem 6), Jerusalem 1977; id., *BA* 44 (1981), 21–25; 45 (1982), 21–26; id., *Tempel, Kirchen und Zisternen*, Stuttgart 1983, 159–167; I. Finkelstein, *IEJ* 31 (1981), 81–91; E. A. Knauf, *ZDPV* 98 (1982), 170–173; P. Mayerson, *IEJ* 32 (1982), 44–57; N. Na'aman, *BA* 45 (1982), 21–25; P. Grossmann, *Annales du Service des Antiquités de l'Egypte* 70 (1984–1985), 75–81; A. Ovadiah, *Dumbarton Oaks Papers* 39 (1985), 77–79; R. Wenning, *Die Nabatäer: Denkmäler und Geschichte*, Göttingen 1987, 188–197; I. Hershkovitz, *IEJ* 38 (1988), 47–58.

See also Monasteries.

AVRAHAM NEGEV

SKHUL CAVE

IDENTIFICATION

The Skhul Cave (Cave of the Kid; in Hebrew, Me'arat ha-Gedi) lies on the southern escarpment of Naḥal Me'arot in the Carmel Range, where it opens into the Coastal Plain, a few kilometers south of 'Atlit (map reference 1471.2307). The escarpment is about 11 m above the level of the valley. The cave opens to the north, and there is a small terrace in front of it.

EXCAVATIONS

In trial soundings carried out in 1929 and 1931–1932 under the direction of D. Garrod, with the assistance of T. D. McCown in the latter seasons, on behalf of the American School of Prehistoric Research, the entire cave and its terrace were cleared. These excavations were carried out in conjunction with those of other caves in the valley. Two layers, B and C, were discovered. This cave, outstanding in its rich finds of human skeletons of the Mousterian culture, was probably a burial place. Fourteen skeletons were uncovered, among them three complete skeletons, two of which were adults; most were in layer B within the cave itself and on the terrace in front of it. The Skhul group has been anatomically defined as modern humans (*Homo sapiens sapiens*). The excavators distinguished the various groups of skeletons according to their location and the degree of bone fossilization. Some of the skeletons were embedded in a hard breccia, so it took the excavators considerable time to extract and prepare them for study and publication. The ESR dating method yielded dates of 101,000 ± 12,000 BP and 81,000 ± 15,000 BP.

Garrod and McCown equated the above layers with layers D–C in the nearby Tabun Cave, but objections have been raised to this hypothesis. E. S. Higgs, for example, considers that the layers in Skhul Cave should be placed between layers B and C in the Tabun Cave.

Layer B is divided into two sublayers. In horizon B1, 1,032 flint implements

Naḥal Me'arot: general view of the southern cliff.

Map of Naḥal Me'arot.

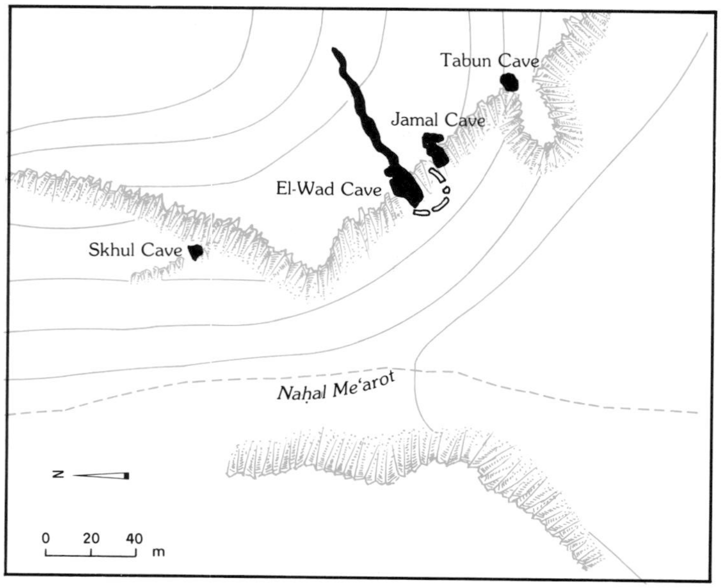

were found, and in B2, 653. In layer C, the flint industry is scanty and the finds mostly broken.

T. McCown, *Bulletin of the American School of Prehistoric Research* 1932, 12–15; 1933, 9–15; T. McCown and A. Keith, *The Stone Age of Mount Carmel* 2, Oxford 1939; D. A. E. Garrod et al., *The Stone Age of Mount Carmel* 1, Oxford 1937; A. Ronen, *Les Sépultures Néandertaliennes* (IXe Congrès de l'UISPP, Colloque XII), Nice 1976, 27–40; Y. Olami, *Prehistoric Carmel*, Jerusalem 1984; A.-M. Tillier et al., *Paléorient* 14/2 (1988), 130–136; B. Vandermeersch, *Archéologie, Art et Histoire de la Palestine: Colloque du Centenaire de la Section des Sciences Religieuses, École Pratique des Hautes Études, Sept. 1986* (ed. E.-M. Laperrousaz), Paris 1988, 15–17; Weippert 1988, 76f., 79; B. Arensburg and A. -M. Tillier, *Bulletins et Mémoires de la Société d'Anthropologie de Paris*, n.s. 1 (1989), 141–143.

TAMAR NOY

SOBATA

IDENTIFICATION

Sobata (Isbeita, or Subeita in Arabic; Shivta in Hebrew), a town in the central Negev desert, is situated about 40 km (25 mi.) southwest of Beersheba (map reference 114.032). It was founded in the Middle Nabatean–Early Roman period and flourished mainly in the Late Nabatean–Late Roman and Byzantine periods. The Arabic name preserves the ancient one. This is known from two Nessana papyri, P79 from the early and P75 from the late seventh century. A faulty reading in Nilus' *Narrationes* (VII, *PG* 79, col. 688), written in the early fifth century, also refers to Sobata; the text was emended by F. M. Abel. The meaning of the name is obscure. Abel considered it a Semitic-Nabatean name. A. Negev looks for the origin of the name in the rare Nabatean personal name Shubitu.

EXPLORATION

The ruins at Sobata were described for the first time in 1870 by E. H. Palmer, and the first general plan of the city, with its most important buildings, was

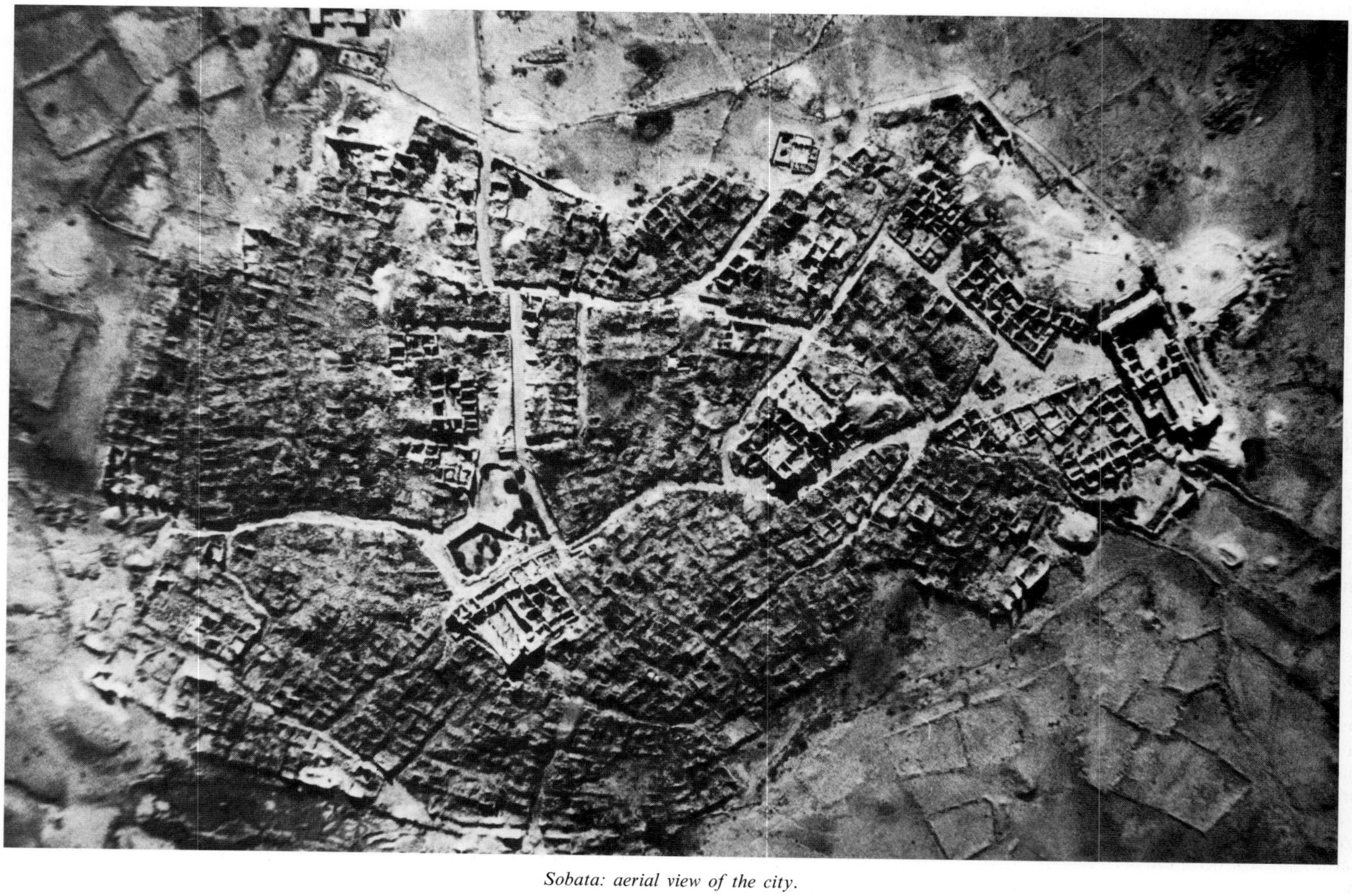

Sobata: aerial view of the city.

Sobata: general plan of the town.

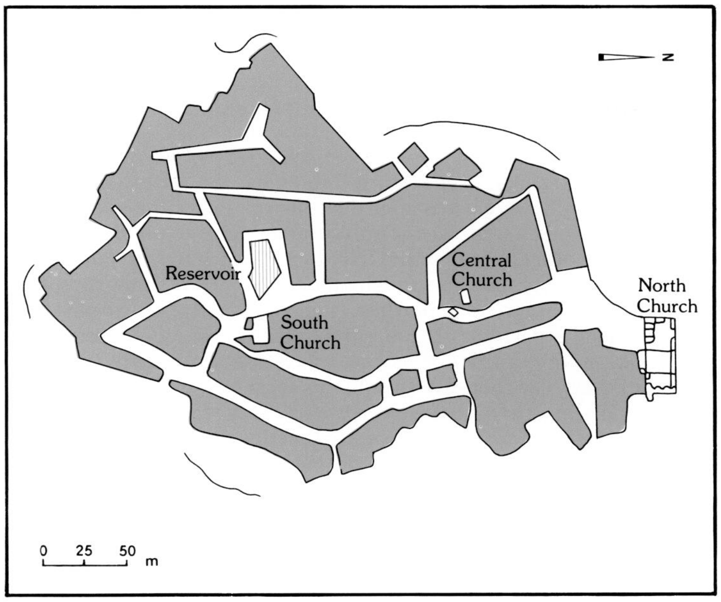

drawn by A. Musil in 1901. Musil's plan, however, is not exact. He failed to notice that the city's streets were slightly curved. In 1905, the site was visited by an expedition from the École Biblique et Archéologique Française in Jerusalem, with the participation of A. Jaussen, R. Savignac, and L. H. Vincent. They located the Byzantine cemetery and several tombstones with inscriptions from the end of the sixth century CE, and found a short Nabatean dedicatory inscription from the time of Aretas IV among the ruins of the city. In 1914, C. L. Woolley and T. E. Lawrence drew more accurate plans of the town, its churches, and several houses. In 1916, the Committee for the Preservation of Monuments of the German-Turkish army sent an expedition to Sobata under the direction of W. Bachmann, C. Watzinger, and T. Wiegand. Its main contribution is the fine aerial photographs they took. From 1934 to 1938, the first large-scale excavations were conducted at Sobata on behalf of New York University and the British Archaeological School in Jerusalem, under the direction of H. D. Colt. The results of these excavations were never published, however. From 1958 to 1960, the buildings and streets were cleared by the Israel National Parks Authority, under the supervision of M. Avi-Yonah.

During several surveys directed by A. Negev from 1970 to 1976, the site and plan of the Nabatean town were studied and a new chronology for the churches and the town evolved. From 1979 to 1982, A. Segal made limited-scale investigations and excavations on behalf of the Ben-Gurion University of the Negev. Sobata's town plan and plans of the central church and four private buildings could then be drawn. Research was resumed in 1985 in the North Church by S. Margalit. Solutions were proposed to some typological–chronological problems pertaining to the churches in the Negev. The city plan of Sobata was again analyzed by J. Shershevski in 1985.

HISTORY

Occupation at Sobata began in the Middle Nabatean period. The settlement was founded on a road that links Oboda, Sobata, and Nessana, by way of a chain of small, as yet unidentified settlements. Nabatean Sobata was established in the early part of the reign of Aretas IV (9 BCE–40 CE), or perhaps even earlier, in the later years of Obodas III (30–9 BCE). During this time, and especially during the reign of Rabbel II (70–106 CE)—that is, in the Late Nabatean period when the Nabateans began to engage in desert agriculture and horse breeding—the city enjoyed a period of prosperity. It was quite large, occupying more than a third of the built-up area of subsequent periods. The history of the city in the third and fourth centuries is not known, but in this writer's opinion, the first churches in the town—the South Church east of the public reservoirs and the North Church on the northern outskirts of the town—were built by the middle of the fourth century. Following the Arab conquest, Sobata, like the other towns in the western central Negev, continued to exist for about another two hundred years. On the basis of the pottery found there—Arab glazed ware and pottery cast in a mold—the site's excavators suggested that the Arab settlement there did not cease until the thirteenth or fourteenth century CE. The earlier date of the eighth to the ninth centuries seems more reasonable, however. At that time settlement also ended at Nessana and Elusa.

EARLY ROMAN PERIOD. In an early survey of the site, a Nabatean dedicatory inscription to the god Dushara was discovered from the time of Aretas IV. The Colt expedition located a Nabatean dump southwest of the city that contained typical Nabatean and Early Roman pottery. This material was published by G. Crowfoot, who erroneously dated it to the second and third centuries CE. The Nabatean settlement founded on the northern bank of Naḥal Zeitan flourished in the Middle and Late Nabatean periods.

LATE ROMAN PERIOD. The history of Sobata in the Late Roman period is not well known. The town may have been resettled at the end of the third century CE when the central Negev was fortified by Diocletian and his successors. They erected fortresses at Oboda and Nessana, and surrounded Mampsis (Kurnub) with a wall, but there is no positive evidence for their activities at Sobata.

BYZANTINE PERIOD. The name Sobata is missing in the Nessana papyrus (P39) that lists the recipient towns of the *annona militaris* in the Negev, which may suggest that the city had no permanent garrison. On the other hand, there is abundant evidence of agriculture in Sobata's immediate surroundings and in the area of Naḥal Lavan, which attests to Sobata's having been an important civil agricultural settlement. Near the city, in Naḥal Lavan, the remains of large plantations and several individual farms were discovered. Additional information about the production and management of those farms is provided by the archaeological finds at Oboda and Nessana and by the Nessana papyri, many of which deal with water rights and land distribution. Sobata also seems to have been an important monastic center in the Byzantine period, as well as the site of regional Christian pilgrimages. Judging by some of the epitaph formulae found in the North Church, and by inscriptions found elsewhere in the town, Sobata enjoyed a high standard of education, notwithstanding the fact that it was situated at the very end of the civilized world. The town, however, should not be understood as having been at the end of the Western world, but at the head of the Semitic-Nabatean-pagan (and later Christian) world.

EARLY ARAB PERIOD. The history of Sobata in the Early Arab period is obscure. At the time of the Arab conquest, the Christian population here, as at Nessana, was not harmed. The Arabs built a mosque near the South Church, taking care not to damage the adjoining baptistery. It seems that the existing Christian community lived side by side in peace with the new Muslim population. The settlement at Sobata probably did not exist longer than that of its neighbor, Nessana. It was apparently abandoned in the eighth or ninth century CE, at the latest.

EXCAVATION RESULTS

A large water cistern from the Nabatean period was found halfway between Miẓpe Shivta (q.v.) and Sobata. Inside the cistern were traces of the characteristic Nabatean technique of stone dressing, and a pilaster with niches symbolizing Dushara and other Nabatean deities. Inside the Nabatean town itself, which occupies the southern and southwestern parts of the site, a large double reservoir was constructed on the northern fringes of the built-up area. Rainwater was collected from the gently sloping terrain by means of an intricate network of channels. Amid the ruins south of the reservoir was a staircase tower, resembling the ones at Nabatean Mampsis. To the southwest, the Colt expedition excavated a building containing a stable from the Late Nabatean period, similar to the stable in building XII at Kurnub (Mampsis), but did not establish its date or function. The stable house was cleared again by Segal and a plan of the house was made. The pottery found on the floors was from the fourth and fifth centuries CE, but this indicates the late use of a house built in the second century CE

PLAN OF THE BYZANTINE TOWN. The Byzantine town covers an area of about 20 a. (according to measurements taken by Segal and later by Shershevski, which differ greatly from previous, much higher, and exaggerated estimates). It measures 430 m from north to south and 330 m east to west and lies on the shoulder of a ridge that slopes gradually to the center of the town and even more steeply to the south, in the direction of Naḥal Shivta. The city was not walled, nor did it have a fortified citadel, but the houses and the walls of their courtyards and gardens were built in continuous lines that terminated at the end of nine streets. There was a gate at the end of each street that could be locked. The houses and their spacious courtyards were not built close together. In the opinion of the excavators, there were gardens inside the city. The streets are quite wide (average width, 4 m). There were three city squares.

Most of Sobata's explorers believed that this town, whose streets turn and twist, was built without a definite plan. However, this writer believes that the layout may have been intentional; the town's builders limited the number of streets that would open into the area outside the town, where their fields and some of the cisterns were located. Inside the built-up area, numerous lanes led to all parts of the town and ended at the doors of the houses at the edge of the town. Water supply being the major problem, the town planners chose to use some of the streets for conveying rainwater to the two large reservoirs in the center of the town and to the numerous cisterns scattered throughout it. The layout of the streets seems to have been adapted to this need, and in this matter the builders of the Byzantine town probably followed Nabatean planning: using the gentle slope to collect rainwater in reservoirs. The Byzantine streets thus ran along the course of the ancient channels, some of which can still be traced in the lower part of their course in the vicinity of the reservoirs. The need to cope with water collection also explains the large number of public squares and the width of the streets.

In this writer's opinion, the construction of the Byzantine town began in the first half of the fourth century CE, with the erection of the South Church. The population must still have lived in the older, Nabatean houses, which, if contemporary Kurnub can serve as an example, required little repair. Irregularities in the plan of the South Church—the absence of a proper atrium and the disharmony between its eastern and western parts—attest to the building's having been squeezed into an already built-up area. The same problem—inserting new buildings into an existing town plan—faced the builders of the two churches at Kurnub. At about the same time, the North Church and monastery were built at the town's northern extremity, beyond the water-catchment area. There they would not interfere with the functioning of the water-supply system. It was only later, possibly from the fifth century onward, that the central and northern quarters were built.

Three different kinds of stone were used to build the houses: hard crystalline stone for the foundations and lower parts of the walls, softer crystalline stone for the lintels and doorposts, and soft and brittle limestone for the upper parts of the walls. The narrow doors have lintels, whereas the wider ones are arched. The rooms are roofed with arches that rest on engaged pilasters that spring directly from the walls and are covered by stone slabs. The inner walls were covered with thick layers of plaster. The walls are 0.6 to 0.7 m wide and were built, Nabatean fashion, with ashlars or hammer-dressed stones on the exterior, coarsely drafted stones on the interior, and a filling of broken stones and mud, which served as insulation. The floors were paved with stone slabs. On the street side, the walls have no windows or only very narrow ones. The wall cupboards were built of stone; only the shelves were wood.

The houses were entered through a small hall that led to a courtyard, from which all the rooms were entered. The opening of the cistern in which the rainwater running off the flat roofs was collected was in the courtyard. This type of house and courtyard is common in the east. Sometimes the cistern was connected to a channel carrying runoff water from the adjoining streets, as well. The stairway leading to the second story was also in the courtyard.

The Reservoirs. The two large Nabatean reservoirs were reused in the Byzantine period. They are the link between the older Nabatean town and the newer central quarter. The reservoirs, irregularly shaped polygons, were interconnected and built of stones set in mortar and coated with waterproof plaster. Steps led to the bottom. The southern reservoir has a capacity of 700 cu m and the northern one about 850 cu m. It was the duty of the citizens to clean the reservoirs and, according to information in Byzantine Greek ostraca, this obligation was fulfilled.

CHURCHES. South Church. From the excavations carried out by the Colt expedition, only the plan of the South Church has thus far been published. Because the church was erected after the construction of the two reservoirs south of it, the builders, for lack of space, were unable to provide it with an atrium, as in the other two churches. It had a narthex, but it did not serve as a vestibule linking the church directly with the outside. The church's entrance is in the southwest corner of the narthex, from which only two entrances lead into the church proper. The church is built on a nearly square plan (17.6 m long and 18.2 m wide) and is divided into a nave and two aisles by two rows of six columns each. The four eastern columns form part of the chancel screen erected on the bema. In front of the northwest corner of the bema is the square base of the ambo. The excavators assumed that this church, like the two other churches at Sobata, was triapsidal. According to Negev, however, this was not the case. The church was originally built as a monoapsidal structure with two rectangular rooms, one on either side of the apse, similar to the plans of the earlier churches at Kurnub, Oboda, Nessana (North Church), and the early stage of the East Church at Elusa. All of these probably date to the second half of the fourth century CE. In a later stage, probably in the early sixth century, the rectangular rooms were blocked and replaced by small lateral apses, with small niches in their curving rear walls. They held the remains of stone-built reliquaries, attesting to a cult of martyrs to which the other churches were dedicated.

The central apse is twice the height of the lateral apses, above which there were chambers, probably entered from the upper story. The three apses were not built on the same axis, and the southern wall of the church deviates slightly southward. The nave is paved with marble slabs and the aisles with limestone slabs. The apses are plastered and decorated with paintings of religious subjects. Woolley and Lawrence identified the scene as the Trans-

Baptistery in the South Church.

Plan of the North Church.

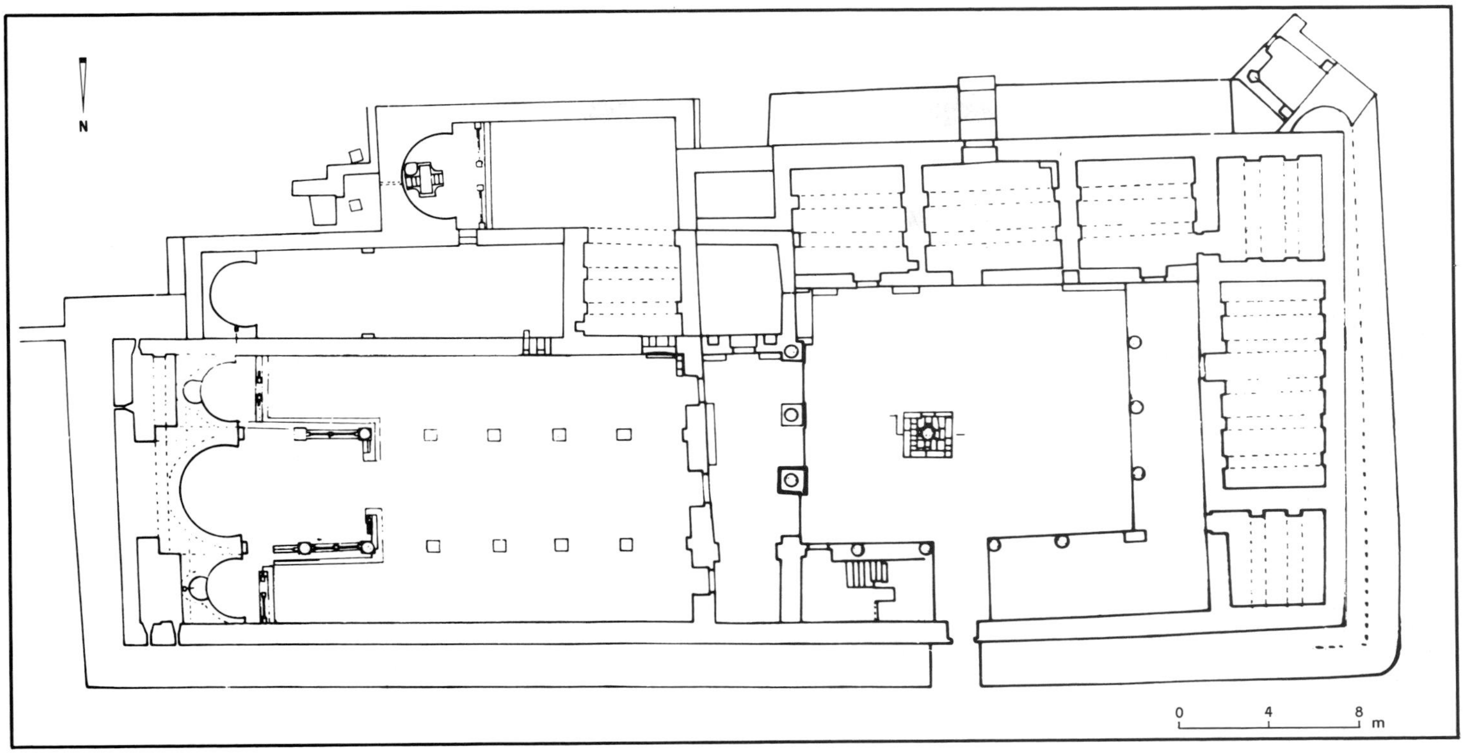

figuration of Jesus (Mt. 17:1–13). Jesus appears crowned by a halo in the center of the scene. Below his feet is the kneeling figure of Peter; John stands to his right. Moses and Elijah also were identified. This same subject is treated in the Monastery of Saint Catherine in the Sinai desert. Only faint traces of the paintings remain.

North of the church stood a chapel and a baptistery. They were entered from a small room north of the narthex, which led to an open square. In front of the square is a small exedra with two columns. A cruciform baptismal font (the length of each arm is 1.5 m) was cut out of a monolith and set inside an ashlar-built apse. Inside the font, at its eastern and western ends, steps lead to its bottom. North of the large baptismal font is a font for infant baptisms, also cut from a monolith. Southeast of the baptistery is a tower, which may have been the bell tower. North of the basilica is an earlier annex, a small courtyard surrounded by rooms. Two inscriptions were found in the church compound. The earlier one was engraved on a lintel and attests to the construction of an annex to the church as early as 415 to 430 CE. The other inscription, in the floor of the southern aisle, states that the pavement was laid in 640 CE.

A mosque was erected to the north of the baptistery. Its miḥrab is built against the north wall of the baptistery, and it seems that the builders of the mosque took special care not to damage the adjoining Christian establishment. The floor of the mosque is laid with limestone slabs.

The Central Church. The Central Church was measured and surveyed by A. Segal. Because of its position in the town plan, this church, facing one of the main streets of the central quarter, has no proper atrium, only a narthex-like corridor. The Central Church has three apses, a type rare in the central Negev. Only the South Church at Nessana (601 CE) and, possibly, the North Church at Reḥovot-in-the-Negev (dated by its excavator to the second half of the fifth century) are triapsidal. The Central Church at Sobata probably dates to the late sixth or early seventh century CE.

The North Church. Because the North Church is on the boundary of the city, its excavators assumed that it was the latest church constructed at Sobata. In Negev's opinion this, however, was not the case. The walls of the church are supported by strong retaining walls, preserved to a considerable height. Although in the opinion of the excavators these walls were meant to strengthen

North Church: view from outside, looking southeast.

North Church: view from the atrium, looking east.

the structure and turn it into a stronghold, such walls also support other buildings in the town. The church complex comprises the church proper, a chapel, a baptistery, a mortuary chapel, and a monastery. The church was entered from a large open square to the south of the atrium, where there is a small exedra supported by three heavy piers. Above the exedra a passage led from the monastery to the church, the only link between them. The atrium (26 by 19 m) was larger than the church proper. It was entered through a single gate in the southern wall. Along three of its walls (west, north, and south) were rooms whose roofs were supported by arches. In the western part of the atrium is a large cistern. In the middle of the atrium the stump of a column is enclosed in a rectangular frame. This was probably a memorial to a stylite who lived there and was later sanctified and venerated in this church, which became a center of pilgrimage. This would account for the unusually large atrium—which has parallels only in the above-mentioned church at Reḥovot-in-the-Negev and the East Church at Elusa—and for the large paved square in front of the church, south of the atrium.

Originally the church was probably entered directly from the atrium, the eastern colonnade of which forms a kind of narthex. Later, the columns were surrounded with wide pilasters, thus forming a true narthex. Three entrances lead into the church from the narthex. The hall (20 by 13 m) is divided into a nave and two aisles by two rows of six columns each, the western columns being attached to the doorposts of the central entrance. In the opinion of the

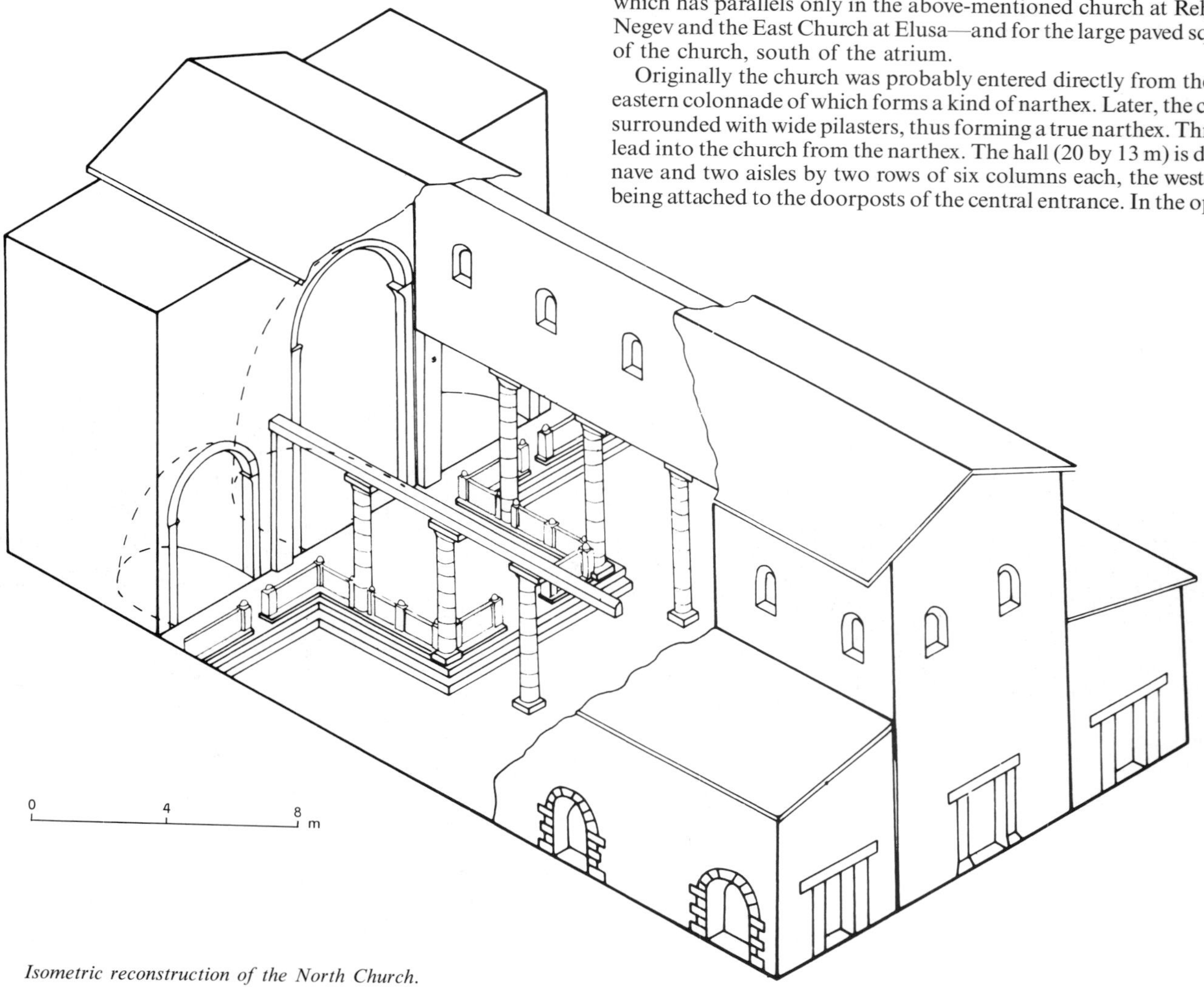

Isometric reconstruction of the North Church.

Sobata: Greek ostraca.

excavators and of subsequent researchers, the church was a triapsidal basilica.

In a study of the typology and chronology of the churches in the central Negev published in 1974, this writer proposed two phases in the history of the North Church: a monoapsidal phase in the second half of the fourth century and a triapsidal phase in the first half of the sixth century. This had been rejected by Rosenthal-Heginbottom, but in 1985, Margalit's excavations in the sanctuary proved the existence of the two phases. He excavated four sectors: the area behind the apses, the two lateral apses, and the area around the bema. These excavations revealed that in the early phase a passage behind the central apse connected the lateral rectangular rooms. Each of these rooms had been roofed by a pair of arches. The floor of the two rooms, made of limestone slabs, was found intact. In the second phase, the side rooms were blocked by small apses. The space between the eastern back wall and the three apses was filled with building stones, supporting the apses. A coin of Justinian (527–565) found in the fill attests to the time of this reconstruction. The excavations in the lateral apses produced two floors, a later floor made of slabs of gray marble and the original floor mentioned above. The same two phases were also observed in the bema. In the early phase, the bema extended one intercolumnium less than in the later phase. The early limestone floor was also discovered here. Found in the fill between the early and late floors were architectural fragments and broken cult implements from the early building. These seem to have been ritually deposited. In the plaster base of the early floor and in the fill between the two floors, coins from the middle of the fourth century were found. The excavators believe that these coins date the construction of the early church. Small niches in the middle of the walls of the small lateral apses apparently housed reliquaries. The church's first excavators distinguished two stages of ornamentation. Initially, the walls were plastered and covered with paintings. Later, they were faced with marble slabs up to half of their height, and the entire floor was paved with marble. A door in the southern aisle leads to a chapel paved with mosaics laid in geometric patterns. A lengthy dedicatory inscription was also laid in the mosaic. A door in the southern wall of the chapel leads into the baptistery. The baptismal font is cut out of a monolith. The western half of the baptismal chapel was a small hypaethral, or roofless, area occupied by a graveyard, in which members of the local clergy were interred from 612 to 679 CE. The only layman was the seven-year-old son of a vicarius. He was buried in 612 CE.

South of the church is a large complex of buildings, consisting of numerous courtyards and dozens of rooms. The excavators believed this complex was a monastery, but others considered it an area of workshops.

A large number of inscriptions was found in the church complex, most of them on gravestones. Laymen were buried in the atrium of the church from 582 to 646 CE. Of great interest is a stone containing a litany that mentions the names Abraham, Isaac, Jacob, Moses, David, Solomon, and Job, each praised for his most characteristic virtue.

Winepresses. In the buildings adjoining the North Church and at two other locations in the town the Colt expedition discovered installations they identified as bathhouses and Wiegand described as tombs. Each installation was in two parts. In the center of a square floor paved with limestone slabs and surrounded by a low wall was the mouth of a channel. The channel ran beneath the floor to the second part of the installation, situated at a lower level. This was a large, round, rock-cut tank, with a small depression in the bottom. The tank was completely coated with waterproof plaster. Comparison with similar installations at Oboda indicates that these doubtless were winepresses. The grapes were crushed in the upper part and the juice ran into the channel and then into the tank, where the skins settled in the tank's depression. There was a difference between the winepress in the northern monastery and the winepresses beyond the limits of the town. The latter have small cells around the treading platform, similar to those around winepresses at Oboda and Elusa. No such cells are found in the monastery's winepress. The other winepresses may have been used by private farmers, who stored baskets of grapes in the cells; the monks, who worked their land in common, would have had no need for such storage facilities.

Sobata: winepress.

Main publications: R. Rosenthal, *Die Kirchen von Sobota und die Dreiapsidenkirchen des Nahen Ostens* (Göttinger Orientforschungen II/7), Wiesbaden 1982; A. Segal, *The Byzantine City of Shivta (Esbeita), Negev Desert, Israel* (*BAR*/IS 179), Oxford 1983; id., *Architectural Decoration in Byzantine Shivta, Negev Desert, Israel* (*BAR*/IS 420), Oxford 1988.

Other studies: E. H. Palmer, *PEQ* 3 (1871), 29–32; A. Jaussen et al., *RB* n.s. 2 (1905), 256–257; Musil, *Arabia Petraea* 2, *Edom*, 36–45; T. Kühtreiber, *ZDPV* 37 (1914), 5f; Woolley–Lawrence, *PEFA* 3, 72–93; T. Wiegand, *Sinai*, Berlin 1920, 62–83; F. M. Abel, *Byzantion* 1 (1924), 57; id., *JPOS* 15 (1935), 7–11; R. Tonneau, *RB* 35 (1926), 583–604; A. Mallon, *JPOS* 10 (1930), 227–229; W. F. Albright, *AJA* 39 (1935), 148; 40 (1936), 160–161; T. J. Colin-Baly, *PEQ* 67 (1935), 171–181; id., *QDAP* 8 (1938), 159; H. D. Colt, *PEQ* 67 (1935), 9–11; id., *QDAP* 4 (1935), 201–202; 5 (1936), 198–199; id., *Archaeology* 1 (1948), 84–91; G. M. Crowfoot, *PEQ* 68 (1936), 14–27; H. C. Youtie, *AJA* 40 (1936), 452–459; G. E. Kirk, *JPOS* 17 (1937), 209–217; J. W. Crowfoot, *Early Churches in Palestine*, London 1941, 70–71; Y. Kedar, *IEJ* 7 (1957), 178–189; C. J. Kraemer, Jr., *Excavations at Nessana* 3, *Non-Literary Papyri*, Princeton 1958, 227–233; P. Mayerson, *BASOR* 153 (1959), 19–31; id., *Proceedings of the American Philosophical Society* 107 (1963), 160–172; A. Negev, *Cities in the Desert*, Tel Aviv 1966; id., *IEJ* 24 (1974), 153–159; id., *RB* 81 (1974), 397–420; 83 (1976), 545–557; id., *MdB* 19 (1981), 16, 37–38; id., *The Greek Inscriptions from the Negev*, Jerusalem 1981, 47–67, 82–97; id., *Antike Welt* 13 (1982), 2–33; id., *Tempel, Kirchen und Cisternen*, Stuttgart 1983, 197–214; id., *BAR* 14/6 (1988), 26–39; id., *LA* 39 (1989), 129–142; A. Negev and S. Margalit, *ESI* 4 (1985), 102; id., *IEJ* 36 (1986), 110–111; id., *RB* 93 (1986), 267–269; N. Glueck, *Rivers in the Desert*, New York 1968, 264–269; M. Evenari et al., *The Negev*, Cambridge, Mass. 1971, 168–171; R. Rosenthal (Heginbottom), "The North Church and the Monastery at Sobota (Shivta)" (Ph.D. diss., Hebrew Univ. of Jerusalem 1974); id., *Das Heilige Land* 108 (1976), 7–30; 109/3 (1977), 5–14; B. Brimer, *IEJ* 31 (1981), 227–229; D. Chen, *LA* 31 (1981), 235–244; N. Kershaw, *Archaeology* 34 (1981), 59; A. Segal, *BAR* 179 (Review), *PEQ* 117 (1985), 154–156; id., *ESI* 3 (1984), 97; id., *Journal of the Society of Architectural Historians* 44 (1985), 317–328; S. Margalit, *PEQ* 119 (1987), 106–121; id., *LA* 39 (1989), 143–164.

AVRAHAM NEGEV

SOREG, TEL

IDENTIFICATION

Tel Soreg (map reference 2145.2424) occupies the top of a limestone hill in the riverbed of Naḥal 'En Gev, about 1 km (0.6 mi.) west of Kibbutz Afiq in the southern Golan. A few springs flow from the slopes to the east, while the streambed to the west becomes quite steep. The site was first discovered and surveyed in 1980. D. Ben-Ami, who discovered the site, suggested that it might be Aphek, the city in the Golan that served Ben-hadad, king of Syria (Aram-Damascus), as an advance outpost and later as a refuge (1 Kg. 20:26–30). Elisha prophesied that Joash, king of Israel, would defeat the Syrians at Aphek (2 Kg. 13:14–17). This identification is based on the preservation of the name at nearby Afiq, and on the fact that Iron Age sherds have been unearthed only at Tel Soreg. The results of the excavation do not corroborate the identification, however: in the ninth century BCE, when the battle of Aphek took place, Tel Soreg was not the site of a large fortified city, but only of a small wayside fort.

EXCAVATIONS

Three seasons of excavations were conducted between 1987 and 1989, as part of the Land of Geshur Project of the Institute of Archaeology at Tel Aviv University, under the direction of M. Kochavi and P. Beck. The field director at Tel Soreg was L. Vinitzky.

The site has an area of just under one acre, but large parts of it were eroded down to bedrock. By the end of the excavations, only one-third of the site remained unexcavated or uneroded. The state of preservation of the remains was not sufficient to yield a clear-cut stratigraphy, although there were traces of human activity from the Intermediate Bronze Age (Middle Bronze Age I) to the Hellenistic period. In the Intermediate Bronze Age, the dwellings rested directly on bedrock and in a natural cave, which was enlarged. The floors were cut in the soft chalk and leveled to prepare them for occupation; basalt mortars are sunk into them. The rich pottery finds include a large quantity of painted ware, in the style of the Jordan Valley and the Gilead, which are distinct from the vessels found in contemporary dolmens in the central and northern Golan. Some sherds from the Middle and Late Bronze ages were found, but they could not be associated with any architectural remains.

A burial cave cut in the northern slope of the mound was first used in the Middle and Late Bronze ages. It was entered through an open, rock-cut corridor. The first few burials in the cave were disturbed by later burials, in the Iron Age II. The mound continued to be occupied in the Iron Age I, from which the remains are a few silo pits and some typical pottery, including a collared-rim jar of the type common then in the Gilead. The majority of the finds are from the Iron Age II. These include private houses, along the southern edge of the mound, containing numerous agricultural implements and installations.

In the ninth and eighth centuries BCE, a small casemate fort was built at the northeastern corner of the mound. Its northern wall was cleared for its entire length (23 m). An abundance of pottery was found amid the debris in the casemate rooms. The site was resettled in the Persian period, when the new occupants dug deep silo pits and lined them with stone. The last occupational level at Tel Soreg dates to the Hellenistic period. A bronze banner, shaped like a jackal—probably the Egyptian god Anubis—found on the surface, may be from that period.

SUMMARY

For two millennia Tel Soreg was a small settlement, inhabited by farmers who cultivated the land in the nearby valleys and used the water from its springs. In the wars between Israel and Syria (Aram), the road through Naḥal 'En Gev gained in importance: a fortified city was built at 'En Gev as an advance outpost for the Syrian armies, and at this time Tel Soreg was fortified—for the only time in its history. It later became a small agricultural village again, but was abandoned when the towns of Aphekah and Hippos developed to its east and west. The unique Egyptian figurine may be explained in terms of the important international route that passed the site.

M. Kochavi, *ESI* 7–8 (1988–1989), 110–113; id., *IEJ* 39 (1989), 1–17; 41 (1991), 180–184.

MOSHE KOCHAVI

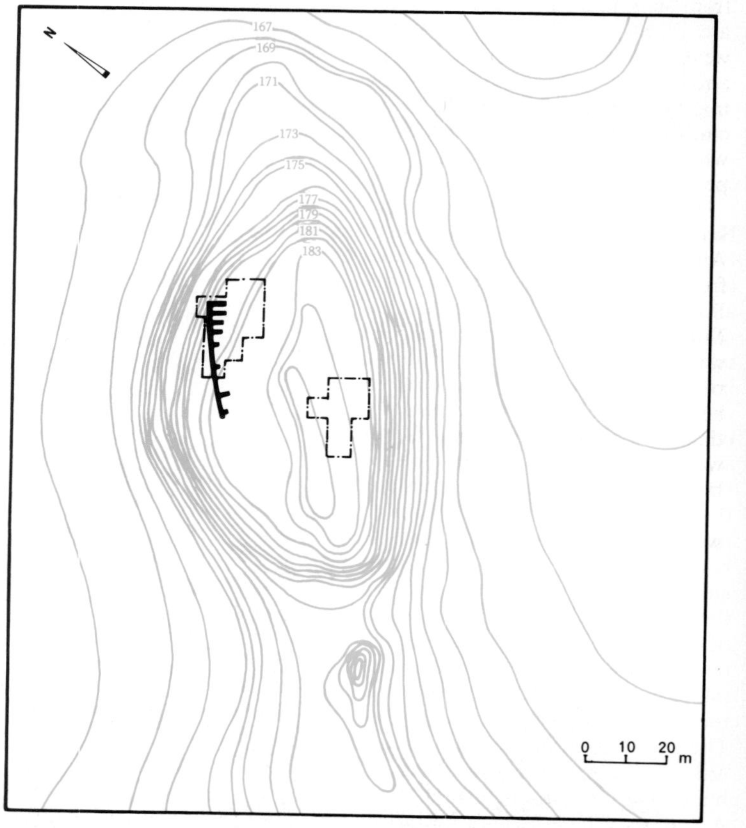

Tel Soreg: general plan.

SOREK, NAḤAL

IDENTIFICATION

Archaeological surveys conducted along the lower course of Naḥal Sorek (Nahr Rubin), between the Jaffa–Gaza road on the east and the Mediterranean coast on the west, have revealed occupation dating from several prehistoric as well as historical periods. In this region, delimited on the north and south by extensive dunes, two large mounds are known to contain remains from both the Bronze and Iron ages: Tel Maḥoz (Tell es-Sultan; map reference 125.147) in the eastern part of the area; and Ḥorvat Yavneh-Yam (Tell Minêt Rubin; map reference 121.148), on the seashore to the west. Additional information about the history of these mounds in the Middle and Late

Map of the main sites in the lower Naḥal Sorek area.

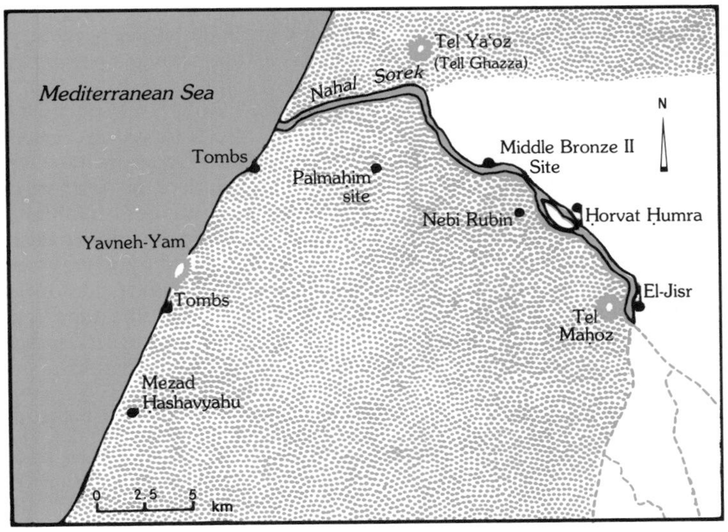

Ḥorvat Ḥumra: bone inlays in human and animal forms, MB IIB.

Bronze Age comes from excavations at the adjacent cemeteries.

VICINITY OF TEL MAḤOZ. Four burial caves cut into the *kurkar* ridge, dating from the Middle Bronze Age I–II, were exposed in the area known as el-Jisr, on the northern bank of Naḥal Sorek, some 200 m north of Tel Maḥoz. One was examined by L. A. Mayer in 1925 and the others were excavated by J. Ory in 1940. Two of the caves (examined by Ory), ascribed to the Middle Bronze Age I, had been destroyed. The third cave (examined by Mayer), ascribed to the Middle Bronze Age IIA, consists of six steps leading to a hall, with two other burial chambers opening off of it. Some forty-five pottery vessels and a single alabaster object were recovered here. The remains from the Middle Bronze Age IIB found in the fourth cave (examined by Ory) are of special interest. Apart from pottery and alabaster vessels, there were weapons, jewelry, scarabs, a basalt pestle and mortar, a complete ostrich egg, and thirty six bone inlays, carved with human and animal figures. Despite a marked Egyptian influence in these inlays (mainly in the men's figures and clothing), they constitute a rare instance of the Canaanite art of carving, which is superior to that on the bone inlays characteristic of the Hyksos period.

In 1942, Ory cleared another burial ground (sixty-three graves), about 1.5 km (1 mi.) northwest of Tel Maḥoz, on a hill known as Ḥorvat Ḥumra (in Arabic, Dhahrat el-Ḥumriyye; map reference 125.149). Most of the graves are from the Middle Bronze Age IIB, and a few are from the Late Bronze Age IIA–B. Apart from one built tomb, all the others are pits dug in the ground. Several Middle Bronze Age graves contained imported Cypriot white-painted IV ware, in addition to numerous other pottery vessels characteristic of the period. The deceased were usually interred in a flexed position, with the head facing east. The goat bones found in three of these graves indicate that the burial of domesticated animals at the head or feet of the deceased was practiced. Among the other finds are alabaster and faience objects, bronze daggers and knives, scarabs, and jewelry.

Four of the graves are ascribed to the Late Bronze Age IIA–B. The deceased were buried in an extended position, with the head facing west. The Cypriot pottery recovered from these graves consists entirely of *bilbil* jugs. Mycenean ware was found only in the one built tomb (cist type) that was exposed in this cemetery. In addition to pottery, the finds from the four graves included faience objects, a glass cosmetic juglet, ivory cosmetic vessels, jewelry, scarabs, and two bronze mirrors.

VICINITY OF YAVNEH-YAM. The remains of a site exposed following quarrying activities, on a *kurkar* ridge some 2 km northeast of Yavneh-Yam, were excavated from 1968 to 1971 by R. Gophna and S. Lifshitz, on behalf of the Israel Department of Antiquities and Museums. They exposed occupation remains from three periods: Chalcolithic, Early Bronze Age I, and Middle Bronze Age I. The cemetery in these settlements was in the northern part of the site. Salvage excavations uncovered ten rock-cut burial caves from the Chalcolithic period. They contained secondary burials in stone and clay ossuaries, accompanied by offerings of pottery, copper artifacts, and stone pendants. Two bird-shaped pottery vessels were found in one of the caves. In almost all these caves, the Chalcolithic burial remains were overlaid by inhumation remains from the Early Bronze Age I, accompanied

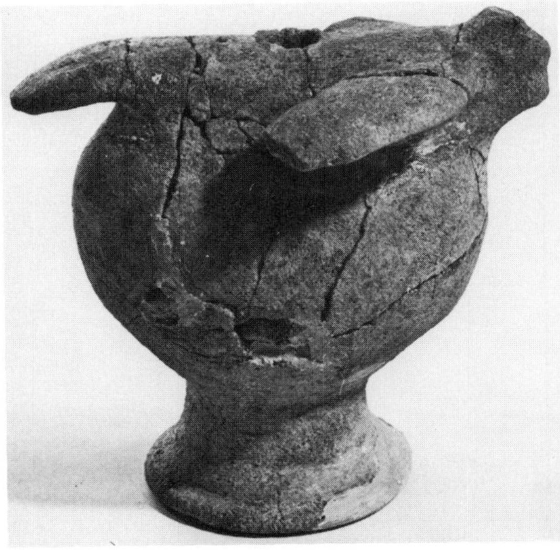

Finds from the burial caves northeast of Yavneh-Yam, Chalcolithic period; ***(left–right)*** *mace head, stone pendants, and a bird-shaped pottery vessel.*

by red-painted ware. A burial from the Middle Bronze Age I was also exposed in one of the caves.

Excavations carried out to the north and south of Yavneh-Yam, under the auspices of the Israel Department of Antiquities and Museums, uncovered two cemeteries from the Late Bronze Age II. The northern cemetery, on the shore near Kibbutz Palmaḥim, contained cist tombs. Two of them were excavated by A. Kempinski and Lifshitz in 1961, while thirteen others were uncovered by Gophna and Lifshitz from 1967 to 1969. The tombs were built of *kurkar* slabs and contained single burials. The majority of the offerings were pottery (much of it Cypriot and Mycenean). The southern cemetery was discovered on a *kurkar* ridge, some 500 m south of Yavneh-Yam. In 1961, two kidney-shaped shaft tombs were exposed there by Kempinski and Lifshitz. In each of the latter, a lamp niche was found to the left of the entrance, as well as Cypriot and Mycenean pottery.

At Yavneh-Yam a Byzantine structure was partly excavated in 1980 by F. Vitto, on behalf of the Israel Department of Antiquities and Museums. One of the rooms contained a colored mosaic with geometric, floral, and faunal designs, including a pomegranate tree in bloom and a bird. A 15-m segment of a Byzantine aqueduct was also uncovered.

VICINITY OF EN-NEBI RUBIN ENCLOSURE. The remains of an unfortified settlement from the Middle Bronze Age IIA were uncovered in excavations conducted in 1981 by Gophna and E. Ayalon, on behalf of the Israel Department of Antiquities and Museums, in the bed of Naḥal Sorek, north of the Nebi Rubin enclosure (map reference 1245.1492). The remains, extending some 100 m in a section of the wadi's northern bank, were overlaid by 2 to 3 m of alluvium. Oval pits containing pottery and the bones of sheep, cattle, pig, and fish were uncovered, as well as segments of stone paving, a pottery kiln, and stone anchors.

TEL YA'OZ (TELL GHAZZA). A mound, about 1 km (0.6 mi.) north of the debouchment of Naḥal Sorek (map reference 1241.1506), was excavated in 1981 by I. Roll, under the joint auspices of the Israel Department of Antiquities and Museums and Tel Aviv University. A length of the northern city wall of a Hellenistic settlement was uncovered. The wall was built of ashlars, as well as fragments of engraved and plastered pillars, originally from a palace or temple. A structure consisting of a courtyard surrounded by several rooms was uncovered on the eastern slope. It was built of ashlars and field stones, in the Phoenician style. The finds here, including pottery from the Persian period and a Phoenician inscription on the shoulder of a storage jar, indicate the settlement's importance in the Persian and Hellenistic periods.

L. A. Mayer, *BPM* 2 (1926), 2–7; J. Ory, *QDAP* 12 (1945), 34–42; 13 (1948), 75–89; M. Dothan, *IEJ* 2 (1952), 104–117; H. J. Kantor, *JNES* 15 (1956), 158; N. Glueck, *BASOR* 153 (1959), 35–38; G. E. Wright, *The Bible and the Ancient Near East*, London 1961, 107, n. 69; A. Kindler, *Israel Numismatic Journal* 1 (1963), 3; R. Amiran, *Israel Museum News* 12 (1977), 65–69; R. Gophna and S. Lifshitz, *'Atiqot* 14 (1980), 1–8; R. Gophna and P. Beck, *TA* 8 (1981), 45–80; R. Gophna, *ESI* 1 (1982), 77–78.

RAM GOPHNA

SUMAQA, ḤORVAT

IDENTIFICATION

Ḥorvat Sumaqa, a Jewish settlement from the Mishnaic and Talmudic periods, is located on Mount Carmel (map reference 1539.2307), 2.5 km (1.5 mi.) south of Daliyyat el-Karmil and 5 km (3 mi.) west of Qeren Karmel (Deir el-Muḥraqa). Its remains extend over a ridge of moderate size, about 200 m long and about 350 m above sea level.

Sumaqa is the Aramaic name of the shrub called in Hebrew *og habursaqa'im* (tanner's sumac), which was in use until modern times as a base for spices, medicines, and in the processing of leather. In Talmudic literature mention is made of several sages who were called Somaq or a derivative thereof: Ḥilfi bar Samqai (*Gen. Rabba* 51:2), Rabbi Tiufi Somaqa (J.T., *Dem.* 3:4), and Rabbi Abba Somaqa (J.T., *Ber.* 9:1). In the opinion of S. Klein, these names may attest their origin from the town of Sumaqa on the Carmel.

EXPLORATION

Ḥorvat Sumaqa was first described by the surveyors from the British Palestine Exploration Fund as an important site containing the remains of numerous buildings, including those of an impressive stone building. They identified the stone building as a synagogue, based on its facade and architectural details

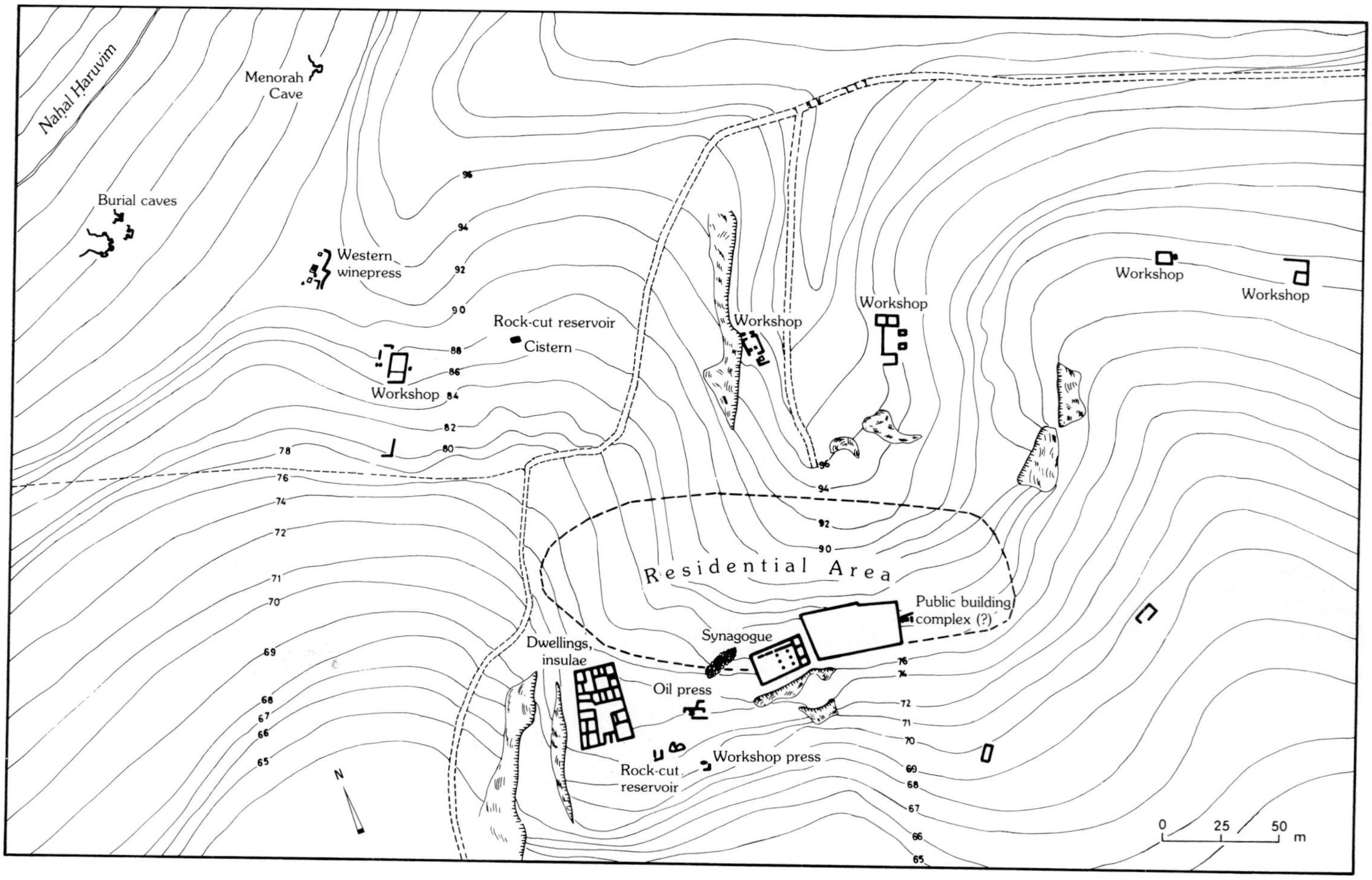

Ḥorvat Sumaqa: general plan.

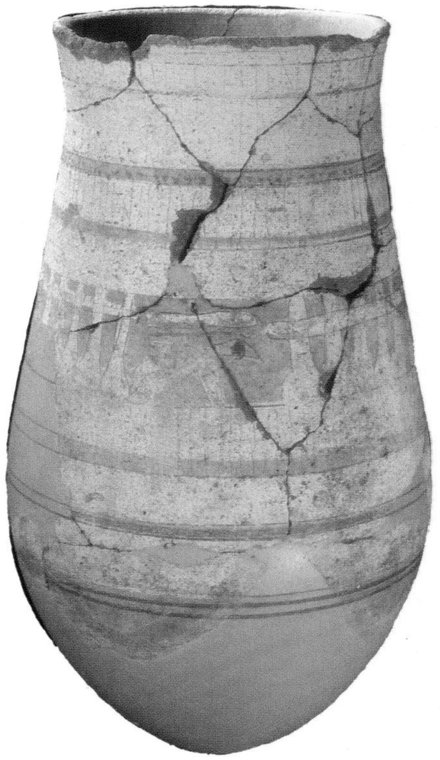

Site T-47 (North Sinai): decorated funerary mask, Persian period.

Bir el-'Abd (North Sinai): ***(left)*** *Egyptian vessel painted in "Egyptian blue," 14th century* BCE; ***(below)*** *overview of the granary, 14th century* BCE.

El-Khirbe: part of the mosaic, depicting a menorah, a shewbread table, a Torah ark, and other objects, in the hall of the Samaritan synagogue.

Khirbet Samara: a cage(?) depicted in the mosaic in the hall of the Samaritan synagogue.

Synagogue facade, looking west.

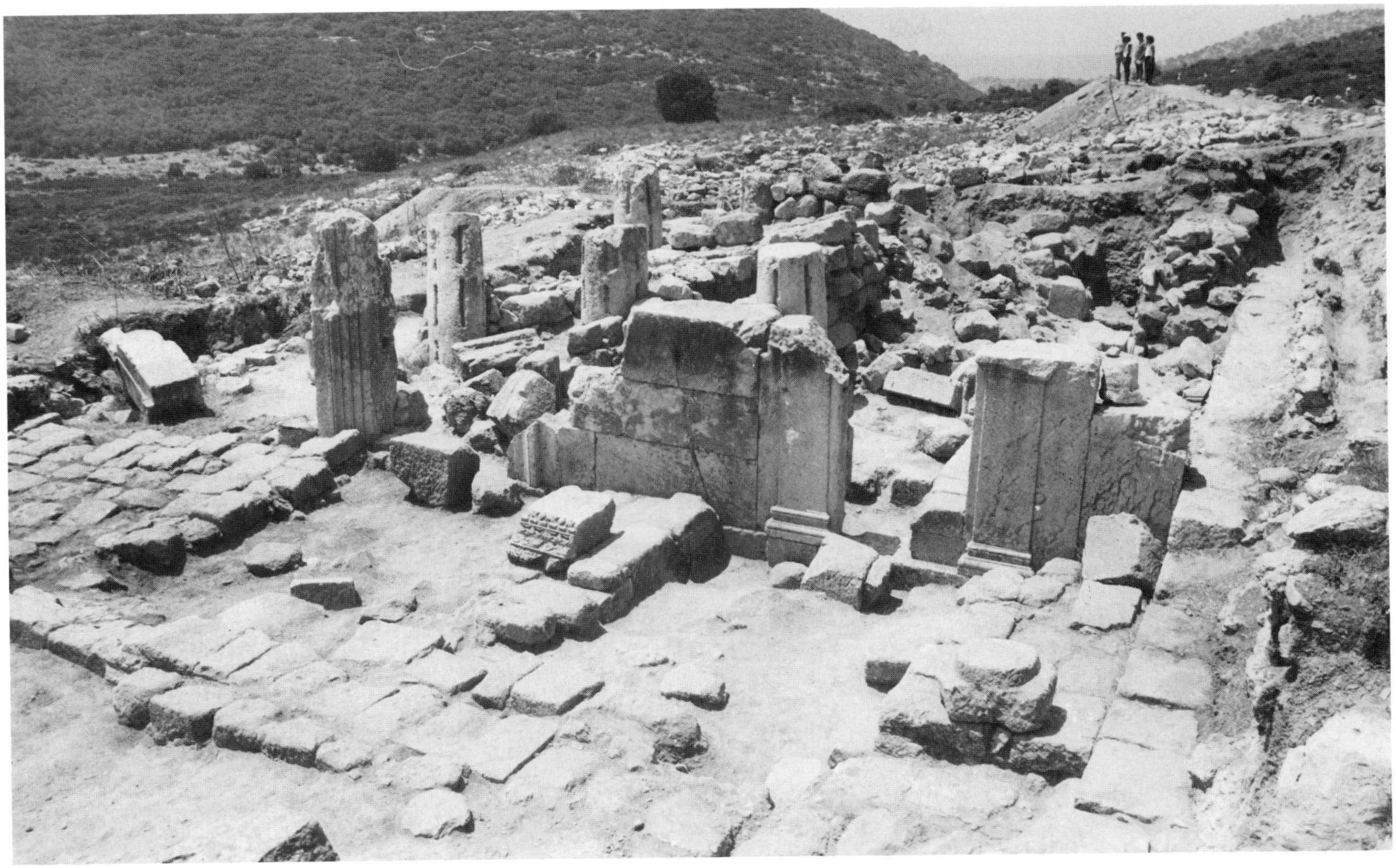

(no longer extant). They believed it was modeled after the synagogues at Bar'am and Meiron. Other surveyors and explorers visited Sumaqa in the late nineteenth and early twentieth centuries, including V. Guérin, L. Oliphant, and E. von Mülinen.

In 1905, the synagogue was excavated by H. Kohl and C. Watzinger, who attempted to reconstruct its plan and dimensions. Their excavations were apparently too limited in size and their reconstruction was based more on a comparison with synagogues in the Galilee than on excavation results.

The Sumaqa area was part of the Archaeological Survey of Israel performed by the northern team, under the direction of Y. Olami. Between 1983 and 1991, excavations were carried out at the site on behalf of Bar-Ilan University, under the direction of S. Dar, with the assistance of A. Siegelmann and Y. Mintzker.

EXCAVATION RESULTS

SYNAGOGUE. The remains of the synagogue were discovered midway up the southern slope of the ridge. Its builders had leveled an extensive area on the chalk hill and laid its foundations and northern wall on bedrock. Most of the eastern facade and the foundations of the original building's other walls have survived. Only the ashlars from the facade are preserved; the synagogue's other stones had been removed, and extensive changes were made inside the building. In the excavations two of the three doorways in the facade were found in situ, while the jambs of the third, southern, entrance were found out of context. The middle entrance is 1.55 m wide and its jambs are 2.46 m high; the northern entrance is 1.07 m wide and the jambs are 1.92 m high. The jambs of the side entrances have Attic bases and capitals decorated with convex and concave moldings. The middle doorway is decorated with three fasciae separated by circular bands decorated with a cyma reversa and with a plaque. In part of the facade three courses of ashlars are preserved. Some of these stones were extremely large (0.6 by 0.6 by 2 m); a small seven-branched menorah was carved on one of them.

East of the synagogue facade is a narthex whose external width is 4.4 m. A stone-built base (1.1 by 1.9 m and 0.3 m high), was found in the northern part of the narthex; it may have been the base of a bema or a wooden ark. In the lane facing the synagogue facade, an 8.6-m-long row of stones forms a bench for those attending the synagogue.

The remains of an impressive, ashlar-built enclosure, whose walls are preserved to a height of three or four courses, were uncovered east of the synagogue. Its western and southern walls, which were partly cleared for a length of about 37 m, may have belonged to the public buildings frequently mentioned by nineteenth-century visitors to Sumaqa and that were dismantled at the beginning of the twentieth century.

The interior of the synagogue was damaged or destroyed a number of times in antiquity and in the medieval period. The building apparently consisted of a basilica-shaped hall that was divided by two rows of columns into a nave and two aisles. Its maximal dimensions were 14.8 by 23.8 m. Many architectural remains of the original building were found in secondary use, as fill for the later walls and foundations. Noteworthy among these are fragments of Ionic capitals; a fragment of the capital of an engaged pilaster of the Corinthian order; four types of column shafts and Attic bases; a fragment of a conch; a large fragment of a cornice; and two types of pedestals. Fragments of statues of eagles and a lion made of local stone were also found. Two fragmentary Hebrew letters were found on a broken *tabula ansata*. The synagogue's hall was covered with strong, light-colored plaster, remains of which were preserved on the eastern wall. Other architectural fragments and many broken tiles indicate that the synagogue was roofed with tiles.

Synagogue Date and Building Phases. The phases of construction and destruction the synagogue underwent make it difficult to establish its precise date. Apart from the strata from the medieval period, the excavations did not uncover any ancient undisturbed loci. Based on the ceramic and numismatic finds and on architectural analysis, three clear phases of existence were distinguished in and around the synagogue:

1. The synagogue was constructed in the second half of the third century. Its design parallels the early Galilean synagogues of the period, such as at Bar'am, Meiron, Khirbet Shema', and Gush Ḥalav. On the site several city coins from the third century, a few fragments of Eastern terra sigillata ware, and the spout of a Herodian lamp were found. They indicate that the synagogue was erected in a settlement that existed in the first and second centuries CE. Phase 1 of the synagogue seems to have been deliberately destroyed in the late fourth or early fifth century.

2. In the second phase, the synagogue's interior was rebuilt. Its eastern facade was left in situ. The northern entrance was narrowed by the base of a wall, and major renovations were carried out in the hall. The original architectural features were incorporated in secondary foundations and walls that altered the building's internal division: in place of the original columns, which stood on fine pedestals, grooved columns, brought from the town's workshops, were installed in the hall. The thick plaster floor, which was found in half the building area, apparently belongs to this phase (late fourth or early fifth century).

3. Still in the second phase further modifications were made in the hall and

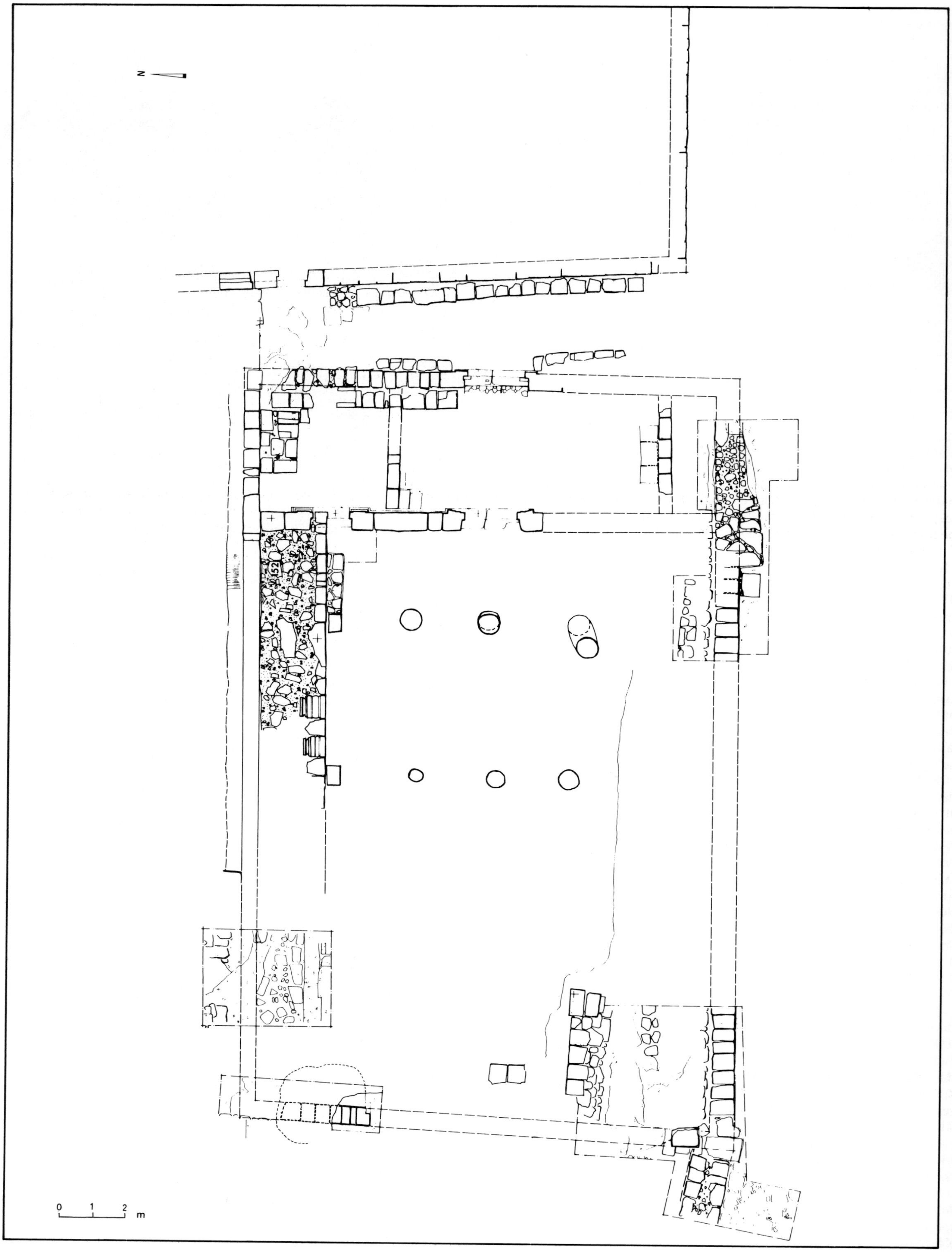

Plan of the synagogue.

in the narthex to its east. A layer of beaten chalk was laid over the previous building, the threshold of the northern entrance was canceled, and stone slabs that had been collected from the vicinity were laid on the new layer of chalk to the east of the facade. A hoard of six coins that were stuck together was uncovered between the paving stones. The earliest coin dates to the time of Justin II (565–578), while the latest is of Heraclius (610–641), and was minted in Nicomedia in 618–619. It can be assumed that the late second building phase is contemporaneous with the hoard.

4. The building's third phase dates to the medieval period (eleventh–fifteenth centuries). At this time the synagogue's hall contained a layer of collapsed debris of earth and stones. Flimsy walls were built on it, dividing it into dwelling units and storerooms. Two cooking ovens, a silo, and a group of kitchen utensils were found in the building of this phase. In addition to the abundant pottery from the medieval period, a contemporary ostracon in Arabic, bearing the name of the owner or artisan of the original vessel, and the impression of a royal Mameluke symbol on a clay vessel were also found.

The Crusader presence in Sumaqa is attested by a coin of Henri de Champagne (1192–1197), minted in Acre. The coin was found in the debris in the synagogue.

From contemporary literary sources it is known that at the end of the thirteenth century the Carmel region passed from the rule of the Crusaders to the Mameluke sultans el-Manṣur (Qala'un) and his son Ṣalaḥ (1283). The medieval stratum in the synagogue appears to reflect this stage of conquest.

SUMMARY

The synagogue at Sumaqa was an elaborate public building in a Jewish townlet in the Late Roman and Early Byzantine periods. Another synagogue on the Carmel was excavated at 'Isfiye (ancient Ḥusifah). The latter synagogue, however, is attributed to the fifth century, whereas that at Sumaqa is earlier; on the basis of its style, it is attributed to the third century, the date generally accepted for the early Galilean synagogues. Sumaqa's proximity to Beth She'arim undoubtedly influenced the settlement's character and the design of its public buildings.

In the late fourth or early fifth century, Sumaqa was destroyed and its synagogue severely damaged. It is possible that this was a local event that left no trace in the written sources. It may have been connected with attacks by fanatic Christians against Jewish and Samaritan synagogues that happened in this period in the eastern provinces of the Byzantine empire, like those launched by Barsauma and his monks, or others that were recorded in the Codex Theodosianus (XVI, 8, 9, 12, 20, 21, 25, 26).

In the Late Byzantine period, parts of the synagogue were rebuilt, but it is doubtful that it was used for worship. The architectural evidence indicates that a Christian population may have settled in Sumaqa then, alongside or in place of the Jewish population: a cross and the image of a saint crowned by a halo appear on two clay vessels, and pig bones were found in several places in the settlement, including the synagogue.

No finds from the Early Arab period were uncovered at Sumaqa; parts of the site were reoccupied only in the Crusader and Mameluke periods. In the Ottoman period there was no permanent settlement in Sumaqa, and until recently the area was pastureland for the local villages.

THE SETTLEMENT. The residential, workshops, and agricultural areas at Sumaqa cover 7 to 9 a. In the 1984–1991 excavations, parts of the residential areas were cleared; five workshops and one oil press were excavated and examined; the rock-cut and plastered reservoirs were cleared; a large winepress and a nearby rock-cut cave used as a winery were excavated; and several rock-cut burial caves, some of them decorated, were examined and surveyed. The dwellings at Sumaqa were built of hewn stone, and the roofs were supported by arches and pilasters. The buildings stood in rows and were separated by courtyards and lanes. One of the dwelling units (23 by 35 m) contained two rows of rooms, a paved entranceway, a central courtyard, and a storeroom and workroom area. The dwellings included a cellar, or ritual bath, which was cut in the bedrock. The residential area yielded iron agricultural tools—a hoe, a chisel, an ax, knives, and cutters. An oil lamp decorated with a seven-branched menorah was also found. Repairs and changes were carried out in the houses, perhaps as required by everyday needs.

Ḥorvat Sumaqa: tomb cave decorated with two seven-branched menorahs.

The entrance to one of the burial caves, when cleared of sediment, revealed a stone door carved to resemble wooden paneling with nailheads, similar to the stone doors of the burial caves at Beth She'arim. Two seven-branched menorahs are carved on the cave's facade.

About two hundred coins were recovered in the excavations at Ḥorvat Sumaqa. Some date to the second and third centuries, but the overwhelming majority are from the fourth century, which is represented by coins of almost all its rulers. Several coins are from the early fifth century, but only three are from the sixth. The small hoard of six coins found in the synagogue (see above) has no chronological connection to the other finds. The ceramic and numismatic finds attest that the settlement at Sumaqa flourished in the third and fourth centuries, but that the damage it suffered in the early fifth century led to an interruption in occupation and to changes in its plan.

Conder–Kitchener, *SWP* 1, 318–320; L. Oliphant, *PEQ* 16 (1894), 41; E. Graf von Mülinen, *ZDPV* 31 (1908), 157–160; Kohl–Watzinger, *Synagogen*, 135–137; Goodenough, *Jewish Symbols* 1, 208; D. Barag, *IEJ* 29 (1979), 197–217; S. Dar, *ESI* 3 (1984), 98–101; 4 (1985), 104–107; 5 (1986), 104–106; 6 (1987–1988), 98–99; 9 (1989–1990), 25–27; id., *IEJ* 34 (1984), 270–271; 35 (1985), 191–193; id., *BAIAS* 8 (1988–1989), 34–48; id. (and J. Mintzker), *Ancient Synagogues in Israel, 3rd–7th Century C.E.* (*BAR*/IS 499, ed. R. Hachlili), Oxford 1989, 17–20; L. Kolska Horwitz et al., *IEJ* 40 (1990), 287–304.

SHIMON DAR

SUSIYA, KHIRBET

IDENTIFICATION AND HISTORY

Khirbet Susiya (map reference 1598.0905) is situated south of Hebron, in the heart of the region bounded by the ancient settlements Carmel (Khirbet Kirmil) and Jutta (Yatta) on the north, and Eshtemoa (es-Samu') on the west. In Jewish sources and in Eusebius' *Onomasticon*, which was compiled when these settlements flourished, this region was called Daroma, meaning "south."

The site's Arabic name, Khirbet Susiya, gives no clue to its identity. *Sus* (in Arabic) are small worms that play an important part in the fermentation of a special kind of cheese that, until recently, was processed in the caves of Khirbet Susiya. A. Negev suggests that Khirbet Susiya is a new name, and that the site is to be identified with southern Carmel, or Khirbet Kurmul, about 2 km (1.2 mi.) northeast of Khirbet Susiya. Carmel is a biblical site, in the territory of Judah (Jos. 15:55), the birthplace of one of David's mighty men (2 Sam. 23:34). In Eusebius' time it was the seat of a military guard (*Onom.* 118:5–7, 177:20–23), a position it held throughout the Byzantine period (*Notitia Dignitatum* 20, 73). Three churches have been discovered at Khirbet Kirmil. In a separate entry Eusebius mentions a Jewish village by the name of Karmelos, that he connects with the biblical narratives. Negev suggests that in Eusebius' time two sites were called Carmel (one of which was changed in later sources to Chermoula): one a pagan Roman and later a Christian town, and the other the Carmel of the Jews, who had been reluctant, or forbidden, to build a synagogue in their original home town. Support for this identification are the references in dedicatory inscriptions found in the synagogue at Khirbet Susiya. In one inscription the dedications were made by members of the *karta* ("the town"), while in the other they were made by a

Susiya: plan of the excavations in the settlement.

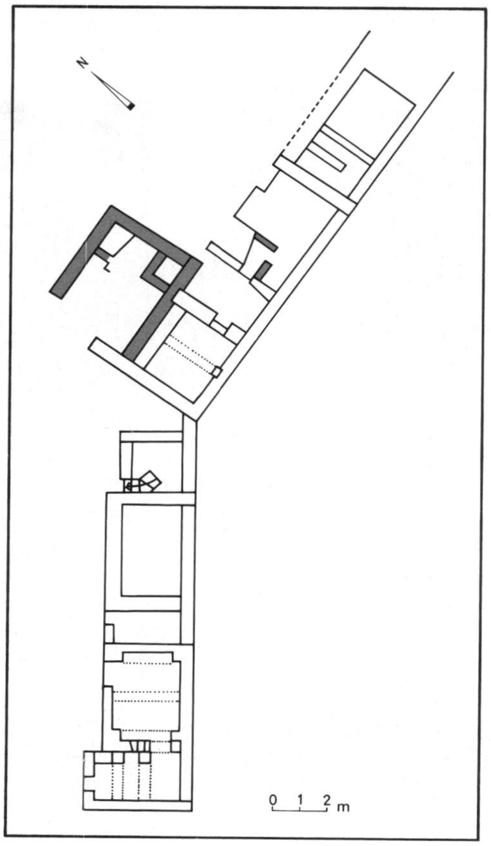

member of *kahala kadisha* ("the holy congregation")—the first was made by inhabitants of Carmel-Khirbet Susiya, and the other by a member of the Jewish congregation that lived in the neighboring Christian town of Chermoula-Khirbet Kirmil. The area between the sites does not exceed the halakhic regulations concerning the distance one may walk on the Sabbath.

EXPLORATION

The extensive ruins at Khirbet Susiya attracted the attention of nineteenth-century researchers; it was described meticulously by V. Guèrin (1869) and by the Survey of Western Palestine team (1874), who were impressed by the size of the ashlars in the ruins. Their attention was drawn to two public buildings, of which one in the eastern part of the town was in a ruinous state. The other was later examined and identified as a synagogue by L. A. Mayer and A. Reifenberg. It was excavated by S. Gutman, Z. Yeivin, and E. Netzer between 1969 and 1972 (see below). A building on the western hill was excavated by Y. Hirschfield in 1978. In 1984 and 1985, Negev, on behalf of the Institute of Archaeology at the Hebrew University of Jerusalem, excavated dwelling caves and some buildings in the eastern part of the town. From 1985 to 1987, Z. Yeivin excavated in the same part of the town, on behalf of the Israel Department of Antiquities and Museums.

1984–1985 EXCAVATIONS

The site is shaped like a horseshoe, open in the north, with its rounded side on the south. It seems that in the first century CE the Jews of neighboring Carmel (Khirbet Kurmul) already had an agricultural hold on the eastern arm of the horseshoe, dominating the hill's terraced fields on the east, north, and west. The settlement's antiquity is indicated by scattered first-century potsherds.

THE TOWER. Apparently after the Bar-Kokhba Revolt was put down, a fortified tower (6 by 11 m), two to three courses of which remain, was constructed at the northern end of the site's eastern arm. Its long northern wall was built of large ashlars, some of which are 1.9 long and 0.8 m wide. Each stone has wide margins and two large, projecting bosses. In order to build the southern wall, a deep trench was excavated in the rock, in which smaller, smooth ashlars were laid in courses of decreasing projection. This seems to be the earliest structure on the site. The view from this tower is of an ancient road, cleared of stones and marked with a border of stones on both sides, and of Khirbet Kirmil to the northeast, to which the road leads. The tower is dated by its pottery to the second and third centuries CE; and the workmanship of the stone cutter is closer to that seen at Beth She'arim rather than to the Herodian mason's art.

THE DEFENSIVE BUILDING. An encircling building, used as a defensive installation, appears to have been used by the local Jews in the place of a wall, which, under the existing political circumstances, they would not have dared to build. The building covered an area of about 15 a. The tower was part of this defensive system, which can be traced along the town's eastern and southern fringes. A 47.5-m-long section of this system was excavated on the southern side of the town. The first part of the building (23.5 m long) is oriented southwest–northeast and consists of three units (1–3). Each of the first two units consists of a small anteroom and another room. In unit 1 the door connecting the anteroom and the room was spanned by a wide arch; traces of roofing arches were found in both. The floor in the room in unit 1 is unleveled bedrock. The presence of an upper floor is indicated by numerous large white tesserae found in the debris. The outer, southern wall in unit 1 was built of finely drafted ashlars with slightly projecting bosses, laid dry, in regular courses. The western wall of the anteroom is unique: it is made of smooth ashlars, some 2 m long but only 0.4 m high. These are not regular building stones; they were taken from a funerary monument (*nefesh*), originally erected above the burial cave, that was discovered only 20 m to the south of the building. In the debris on the northern side of the first two units two lintels were found; one was engraved with two menorahs, and the other with an uninscribed *tabula ansata*. On the right-hand doorpost, a slot for a mezuzah was found. The room (4) in unit 3 occupies a space between the outer walls and the end walls of units 2 and 4. The entrance to this room leads down to a rock-cut ritual bath (mikveh), coated with water-resistant plaster. A cistern and the channel leading to the ritual bath are located just to the north.

Unit 4 is earlier than the other three units. From this point the building is oriented east–west. The western wall of unit 4 is built of extremely large ashlars without margins or bosses. Some of the stones in the lower course were hewn from the unleveled bedrock. The unit's southern wall is built of large, hammer-dressed stones. It is entered from an alley and consists of an anteroom and a room on either side (nos. 5 and 6). The threshold of room 5 is smoothed bedrock. Like the western wall, parts of the southern wall's two lower courses were hewn out of the natural rock. Room 5 was spanned by one arch, and the roof probably consisted of wooden beams. In room 6, the natural bedrock forms the floor. The lower course of the eastern wall is large, smooth ashlars. The excavation of unit 5 (room 7) was not completed. The unit consists of a hall almost 7 m long that seems to have been roofed by a barrel vault. The pottery of the upper levels of all the units was from the twelfth and thirteenth centuries. Some pottery from the Late Roman period was found on the original floors.

To verify the hypothesis that the defensive system encircled the entire settlement, an additional section was excavated at the town's eastern border, along which there is a street from a later period. Several narrow streets (c. 2 m wide) open onto this street. They are provided with gates, thresholds, lintels, and doorposts made of large, well hewn stones that open onto an area that was once the edge of the town. Each of these alleys led to two to four farms, each surrounded by a wall made of hewn stones. Two coins found in this part of town are of Claudius Gothicus (268–270), and of the house of Constantine (324–346). Each farm contained a small stone-built building, part of the enclosing defensive building, that was possibly a store or a storage space but was certainly not a dwelling. The rest of the farmyard was occupied by a cave and at least one cistern.

THE MENORAH CAVE. The Menorah Cave is located just to the west of the synagogue. An L-shaped stepped corridor, cut in the rock, leads down to the cave. The rock of the arm of the corridor, close to the entrance to the cave, was lined with hewn stones and covered by a barrel vault. The lintel and the doorposts of the cave's entrance are hewn in the natural rock. The lintel

Entrance to the Menorah Cave.

General view of the Menorah Cave.

is decorated by a large *tabula ansata* with a raised circle in the middle that is surrounded by a wreath. The circle is decorated with a seven-branched menorah. The doorposts were also lined with hewn stones. The cave (9 by 12 m) is a natural formation but the walls show signs of chiseling. Four additional steps lead from the entrance to the floor of the cave. The cave's eastern side is rounded, while the western side contains an ashlar wall (5.6 m long and 3.2 m high), built of small and medium-sized blocks of stone, some decorated with projecting bosses and flat margins. In the middle of the cave's ceiling a window (diameter, 1 m), cut through the 0.8-m-thick rock, provides light and ventilation. There are additional small windows in the ceiling. At the southern end of the cave is a separate chamber; its hewn entrance has four slots for bolts cut in the rock. Some of the installations built in the large hall are from a later period. The pottery found on the floor is earlier than the synagogue, but this small cave-compartment could have been hewn to serve as the synagogue's treasure room.

THE WINE-CELLAR CAVE. A larger cave is situated south of the Menorah Cave. A sloping, barrel-vaulted corridor cut in the rock leads down to it from the east. The rock-cut entrance is lined with hewn stones. Close to the entrance, on the right, a plastered mikveh is cut in the rock. The cave has an outer and an inner hall. The outer hall (c. 25m long) is divided into two spaces. The outer space, nearer the entrance, is 14 m long. A 4-m-wide narrowing of the outer hall serves as a corridor to the inner space. At the western end of this space another stepped corridor communicates with the terrain outside. These were probably two family units that at some time were joined. At the western end of the inner space an opening 1 m wide, 1.2 m high, and 1.3 m deep leads into the cave's inner space. This part of the cave also consists of two perpendicular halls. The first measures 6.5 by 4.5 m and the inner hall, 10.5 by 6.3 m. The first hall is illuminated by two small circular holes (windows) cut in the 0.8-m-thick rock. A circular stone, with which the window could be blocked, was found in one of the windows. Similar windows, totally blocked, were also observed in the inner hall. Both halls were lined on one side with a wide wall made of hammer-dressed stone blocks, carefully laid in regular courses. Between these walls and the natural rock wall is a 1.5-m-thick fill of field stones and earth. When the western wall of the inner hall was built, an approach to a second mikveh was blocked. The mikveh's excellent state of preservation attests to the fact that its period of use was brief.

At some stage in the history of the cave, a small room (5 by 6 m) was cut to the east of its outer hall. The room was entered by means of a sloping, rock-cut corridor southwest of the cave's main entrance. There is a small cistern on one side of the corridor and a mikveh on the other. A rectangular opening was cut in the ceiling of the room in its northwestern corner. Judging by the frame along the edges of this opening, it may have been closed with wooden planks. Along the walls of the small cave-room are devices for suspending bundles and small niches for lamps.

The living, working, and storage space in the cave is approximately 500 sq m. It seems that the two outer, well-illuminated and ventilated halls were lodgings. It is possible that goats' wool carpets lined the walls, and smaller spaces were created by using similar carpets to separate the living spaces. This writer believes that the inner two halls were wine cellars, where the wine, already processed and poured into jars in the small outer cave, fermented. The full jars were probably passed through the aperture in the western wall of the small cave that communicates with the large outer hall. When the wine cellar was full of the new vintage, the wide opening would have been blocked. The thick inner walls ensured a proper fermentation environment. This cave resembles the one identified as a wine cellar at Oboda in many details. The numerous winepresses found throughout this ancient site attest to the importance of wine production in the local economy.

PRODUCTION OF OLIVE OIL. An olive press was partially excavated to the northeast of the Wine-Cellar Cave. A large round olive-crushing stone was found in an unexplored cave in the vicinity of the synagogue; other olive-pressing devices are scattered throughout the site.

AVRAHAM NEGEV

THE SYNAGOGUE

The synagogue at Khirbet Susiya is situated near the intersection of two streets that passed through the city—one from north to south and the other from east to west. The building includes a courtyard, an exedra, a prayer hall, and another hall adjoining the prayer hall on the south, to form its southern wing. The synagogue is an elongated building, oriented east–west. Its long northern wall faces Jerusalem (which is north of the site). The wall is particularly thick; it probably contained a niche for the Torah ark, flanked by two niches for marble menorahs. The short eastern wall has three entrances that

General view of the synagogue.

lead to the single hall. The building's western wall is preserved to a height of about 3 m. The southern wall was not thick, but there was an additional hall on this side (c. 3.5 m wide), built along the length of the building. The building's gabled roof was apparently supported by the thick wall in the north and by the walls of the southern hall; the building had no inner columns.

The synagogue was entered from the streets through a square courtyard with two openings—one in the northern wall and the other in the eastern wall. Next to the eastern entrance was a large rolling stone (over 2 m in diameter) to seal it. The floor of the courtyard is about one meter lower than that of the exedra and prayer hall, and the street was about 70 cm lower than the courtyard; accordingly, steps led up from the street to the courtyard and on to the exedra.

THE COURTYARD. The courtyard was unroofed and paved with rectangular flagstones. It is bounded on three sides (north, east, and south) by porticoes that were apparently covered with a roof supported by arches on square columns. In the northern and southeastern corners of the porticoes there were small, square rooms. The southern portico was paved with a mosaic with geometric designs. At the

Southern wing of the synagogue.

Plan of the synagogue.

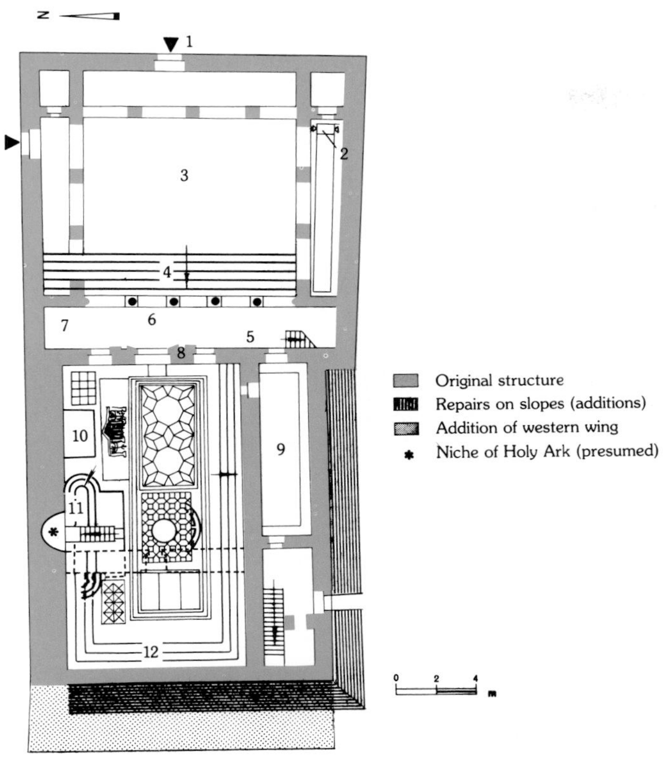

1. Entrance to courtyard; 2. "Feast" inscription; 3. Courtyard; 4. Stairs; 5. Exedra; 6. "Yudan" inscription; 7. "(Mena)ḥumah" inscription; 8. "Four thousand . . ." inscription; 9. Southern hall; 10. Second bema; 11. Central bema; 12. Benches

eastern end of this pavement, close to the southeastern room, a complete Hebrew inscription in a *tabula ansata* was found:

Remembered be for good the sanctity of my master and rabbi,	זכור לטובה קדושת מרי רבי
Isai the priest, the honorable the venerable, who made	איסי הכהן המכובד בירבי שעשה
this mosaic and plastered its walls	הפסיפוס הזה וטח את כותליו
with lime, which he donated at a feast of	בסיד מה שנתנדב במשתה
Rabbi Yoḥanan the priest, the venerable scribe,	רבי יוחנן הכהן הסופר בירבי
his son. Peace on Israel! Amen!	בנו שלום על ישראל אמן

Under a staircase at the western end of the portico was another chamber, that was perhaps used as a storeroom. On the southeastern side of the courtyard, covering a considerable area of the floor, was an opening to a large cistern. The northeastern side contained a wider opening, with rock-cut stairs leading down to a series of caves extending north and east under the courtyard and street and outside about 70 m south of the building.

THE EXEDRA. The exedra was reached from the courtyard by a staircase whose extent was the entire width of the courtyard. In front of the exedra, to the north and south, stood two semicircular pillars with four columns in between. The column bases are square and the style of the capitals is pseudo-Corinthian. The staircase at the southern end of the exedra probably led from the south onto the porticoes. A stone bench was found next to the staircase. The floor of the exedra was paved with a mosaic containing two inscriptions. One, consisting of five lines within a geometric guilloche, is preserved only in part:

זכיר / יושוע יודן / . . . דיהב / . . . / . . .

Remembered be / Yoshu'a Yudan / . . .who gave / . . . / . . .

The mosaic floor in the narthex underwent many repairs, including a depiction of a Torah ark in the northern part. A mosaic inscription at the northern end of the narthex, near the wall, read:

Remembered be for good the Comforter Yeshu'a the witness and the Comforter that (. . .)	(ז)כירן לטב מנחמה ישוע שהדה ומנחמה ש(. . .)

Another word, חומה[. . .] ([Mena]ḥumah), was inserted into the geometric motifs as part of the series of repairs connected with this inscription.

THE PRAYER HALL. The prayer hall is entered from the east through the exedra. The southern and western walls were lined with three rows of stepped benches; the northern wall has benches only along its western part. Slightly west of the center of the wall was an elaborate bema that was probably faced with decorative marble. Flanking the bema were three round decorative steps and in its center, steps leading to the Torah ark niche. To the east of this elaborate bema was a raised ledge, a sort of secondary bema, from which the Scripture would have been read. There were no benches in the area of the two bemas, other than a single bench that filled the space between them.

The floor in the prayer hall, like that in the exedra, was paved with a mosaic, consisting mostly of a large carpet divided into three panels. The largest panel, in the east, depicts a geometric guilloche of squares, lozenges, and octagons, surrounding depictions of fowl, that were damaged. The central panel represented the zodiac, but only a small part of its southern section survives. In a later phase, the main scenes in this carpet were changed: the zodiac was replaced by geometric designs with a large rosette in the center. The western panel seems to have depicted Daniel in the lions' den, as can be deduced from the surviving part of a hand and traces of two lions, as well as from the two letters, אל (*'l*). The mosaic floor east and west of the bemas consists of panels with simple geometric motifs.

The most noteworthy of the mosaic panels is the one opposite the ledge (the secondary bema), from which the Scripture was read. In the middle of this panel, a Torah ark, a structure with a gabled roof and a conch at its center, is depicted on four columns. Flanking the ark, between the columns, are two menorahs, one made of circles and the other plain. Next to the menorahs are the remains of a lulab, ethrog, and a censer, which are characteristic features of the iconography in early synagogues. Flanking the structure are depictions of two rams looking at each other amid a mountain landscape.

A Hebrew inscription of great significance was found in the mosaic pavement opposite the middle entrance It also contains the remains of a date. The left half was destroyed, permitting only a partial reconstruction:

Inscription in the mosaic in the southern portico.

Inscription in the mosaic opposite the central entrance of the prayer hall.

Mosaic pavement opposite the bench; (center) the holy ark and two menorahs.

Remembered be for good . . .	זכורין לטובה ולב. . .
who endeavored and made . . .	שהחזיקו ועשו. . .
the second of the week . . .	הש(ני)ה שלשבוע). . .
four thousand . . .	ארבעת אלפי(ם). . .
when the world was created . . .	שנברה העול(ם). . .
. . .	. . .

THE SOUTHERN HALL. To the south of the prayer hall is a long, narrow hall that was also entered from the east, through the exedra. The hall is divided into two rooms; between its eastern part and the prayer hall there was an open window. The southern and eastern walls in this part of the hall were lined with benches. The hall was paved with long, smooth flagstones. An entrance in the southern wall of the western part of the hall led outside the building. This part of the room was paved with a mosaic executed in large tesserae (each measuring 30 mm). A staircase at the western end of the hall led to the top of the walls.

REPAIRS AND BUILDING PHASES. Many repairs are visible in the synagogue, in the courtyard, at the main bema, and in the mosaic pavement. Five main phases can be distinguished in the building: The original building included a courtyard, an exedra, a prayer hall, and an additional hall in the south. This building was paved with a mosaic, of which small portions in white tesserae were found, primarily under the main bema. It is unclear whether there were bemas and niches in this phase.

In the second phase, the building's outer walls were reinforced with retaining walls; niches were built in the northern wall and in the ledge; and the main bema was installed, probably incorporating the benches, which served as its base. In this phase, the floor was paved with a colored mosaic with the zodiac at its center.

In the third phase, the courtyard was repaired and the floor in the northern portico was paved with a geometric mosaic containing an inscription. The main bema was enlarged and redecorated, as was the adjoining ledge. In a noteworthy repair at this time, the western wall was widened to about 3 m and another staircase was added at the western end of the southern hall. The staircase led to the top of the widened wall that may have been used as the base of an addition to the synagogue in this phase, perhaps a women's gallery.

In the fourth phase, the prayer hall was divided into two unequal parts by a wall that destroyed part of the main bema and part of the mosaic pavement. Retaining walls were also added to the outer walls in several places.

After the fourth phase, the building ceased to be used as a synagogue. The prayer hall and its installations were destroyed. A mosque was erected in the southern half of the courtyard and benches were built in its northern part. The entrance to the mosque was in the building's northern wall, and the miḥrab

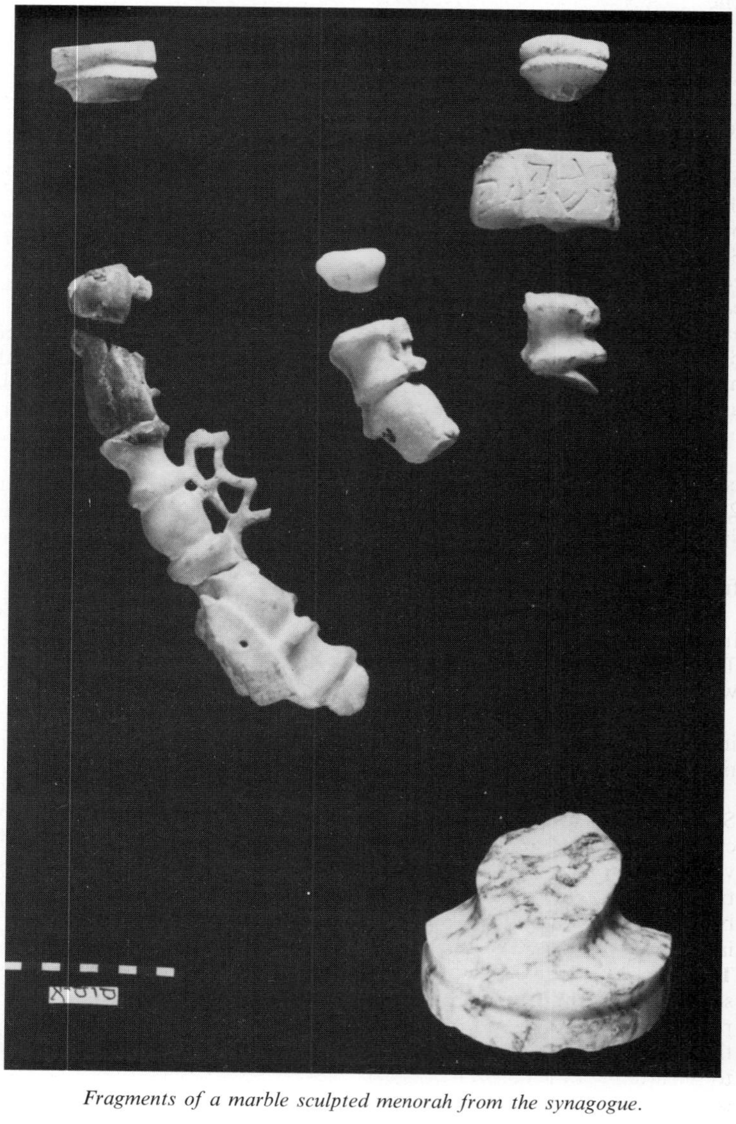

Fragments of a marble sculpted menorah from the synagogue.

was in the southern wall. A large number of Arabic inscriptions were found on plaster fragments that had fallen from the mosque's walls.

The phases of building repairs were accompanied by repairs to the mosaic pavement. More than five phases can be distinguished in the mosaic repairs, which included changes in composition and patching the colorful pavement with white tesserae, without regard for the surrounding patterns or the size of the tesserae.

The many repairs attest to the prolonged use of the synagogue, which was probably founded in the late third or early fourth century CE. The building was used as a synagogue until the eighth or ninth century, when it was abandoned, destroyed, and replaced by a mosque. An Arabic inscription written in ink on a plaster fragment from the mosque testifies to the mosque's existence in the "year 193" of the Hejira (814–815).

The pottery found in the synagogue primarily belongs to four periods: Late Roman and Early Byzantine (fourth–sixth centuries); Byzantine (sixth–seventh centuries); Early Arab (seventh–eighth centuries); and Late Arab (ninth–thirteenth centuries).

Among the ruins of the synagogue were hundreds of white marble fragments, most of them decorated, including parts of chancel screens, marble facings, and chancel posts and panels that apparently decorated the bema, mainly in the synagogue's third phase. Inscriptions in Aramaic and Hebrew, which mentioned various people who donated their energy and money to the synagogue, were found on fourteen of the marble fragments. Among the marble decorations were parts of a sculpted three-dimensional menorah, apparently one of the two that stood in the niches alongside the Torah ark niche.

ZEEV YEIVIN

The synagogue: S. Gutman, *RB* 79 (1972), 421–422; S. Gutman et al., *ASR*, 123–128; Z. Yeivin, *IEJ* 24 (1974), 201–209; id., *Ancient Synagogues in Israel, 3rd–7th Century C.E.* (*BAR*/IS 499, ed. R. Hachlili), Oxford 1989, 93–100; G. Foerster, *Actes du XIe Congrès International d'Archéologie Chrétienne (21–28 Sept. 1986)*, Rome 1989, 1809–1820.
The settlement: D. Barag, *IEJ* 22 (1972), 147–149; A. Negev, ibid. 35 (1985), 231–252; id., *ESI* 3 (1984), 101–102; M. Shashar, *Eretz Magazine* 2/3 (1987), 25–31.

SYNAGOGUES

INTRODUCTION

The synagogue was a revolutionary institution from its inception, embodying dramatic religious and social changes. It appears to have been a uniquely Jewish creation that influenced the subsequent development of the Christian church and the Muslim mosque. As its Greek name—*synagoge*, "place of assembly"—attests, it functioned as a community center, housing the activities of school, court, hostel, charity fund, and meeting place for the local Jewish community. In Second Temple and later sources, the word synagogue often refers to a congregation and not to a building. The focus here is on the latter.

The synagogue differed from the Temple in Jerusalem in four respects: (1) The ritual conducted in it was radically different from anything previously known. Before the emergence of the synagogue, sacrifice was the principal, and possibly exclusive, form of worship; afterward, other patterns of divine worship crystalized: Torah reading, study, prayer, and fasting. (2) The synagogue could be situated anywhere, whereas the Temple could exist only in Jerusalem. (3) Synagogue leadership was open to all, while the Temple's leadership was limited to priestly families. (4) Synagogue congregants sat on benches along the walls of the main hall, witnesses to and participants in the proceedings; in the Temple, worshippers generally were relegated to the outer courts.

SYNAGOGUE ORIGINS. The earliest information about the synagogue comes from Hellenistic Egypt in the third and second centuries BCE. The earliest synagogue remains in Palestine date to the late first century BCE or early first century CE (see below). By the first century CE, the synagogue was a developed central institution throughout the Jewish world. It undoubtedly has a longer history, but the data to determine its earlier stages of development are lacking. Some of the more widely held theories regarding the date for the emergence of the synagogue follow.

1. Seventh century BCE: The abolition of altars (*bamot*) throughout the country by King Josiah and the centralization of the cult in Jerusalem (2 Kg. 23) created the need to fill the ritual vacuum for those who lived far from the Jerusalem Temple.
2. Sixth century BCE: The exiled Jews in Babylonia sought a religious framework to substitute for the destroyed Temple.
3. Fifth century BCE: The impressive ceremony staged by Ezra and Nehemiah when the exiles returned to Jerusalem featured the reading of the Torah (Neh. 8); according to many, this marked the beginning of that custom, which was to play a central role in synagogue liturgy.
4. Third century BCE: The Jewish community in Egypt created a communal institution that was influenced by contemporary religious and social institutions there.
5. The synagogue emerged as part of a gradual process in the course of the Second Temple period. Its roots were in the gathering of the population at the city gate, which, throughout the biblical period, was the location of a wide variety of activities, including those that were strikingly similar to what later transpired in the synagogue. These activities moved from the city gate area to a building (a synagogue) some time in the Hellenistic period, probably in the late second or first century BCE.

THE NATURE OF THE SECOND TEMPLE SYNAGOGUE. The synagogue served first and foremost as a center for all communal needs. From a religious point of view, the reading of the Torah and its ancillary activities (translating the Torah into the vernacular, reciting the haftarah and homily) were central to the liturgy of the Second Temple era. There is no reference in Palestinian sources to the existence of organized communal prayer at that time, with the possible exception of the Qumran community, many of whose ideas and practices were different from those of the rest of society. (In contrast, the Diaspora synagogue, called *proseuche*—in Greek, "place of prayer"—presumably featured the element of prayer, although the reading of the Torah appears to have been central there as well.) Only after the destruction of the Second Temple did the synagogue in Palestine develop and expand as a place of worship.

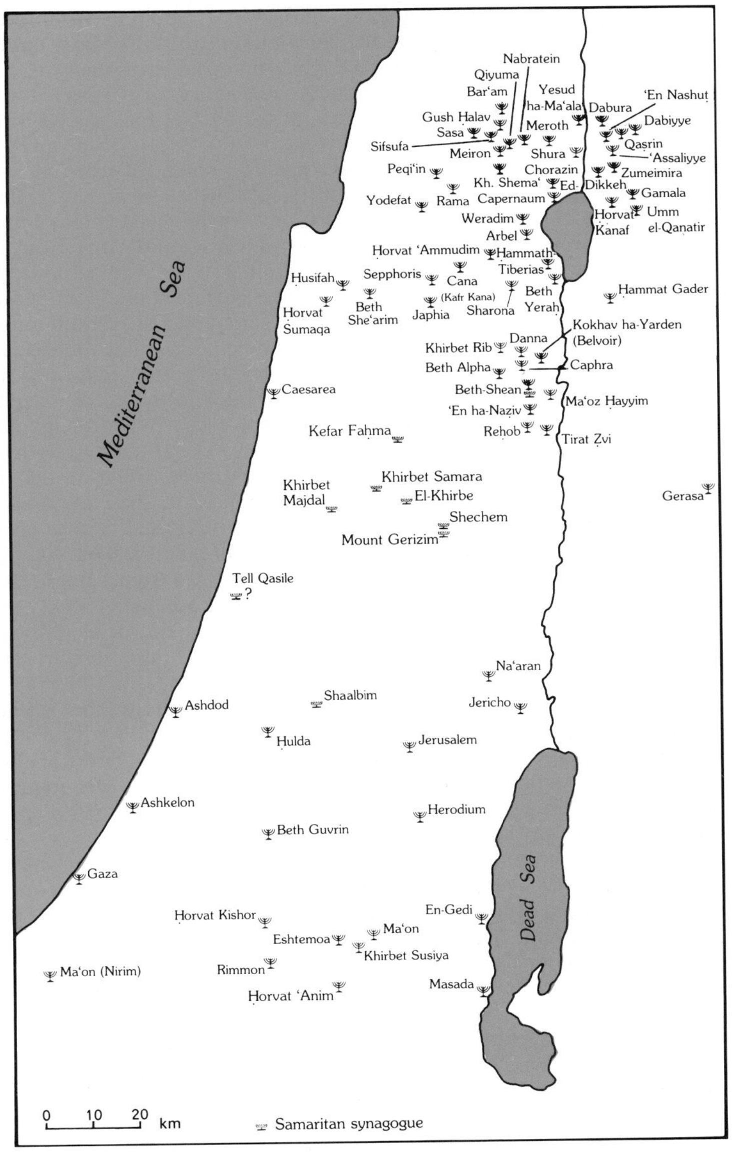

Map of the synagogues in Israel.

EVIDENCE FOR ANCIENT SYNAGOGUES: GEOGRAPHY AND CHRONOLOGY

To date, five Jewish inscriptions are known from Hellenistic Egypt (third century BCE–first century CE) that mention a *proseuche*. The earliest building identified as a synagogue is on the island of Delos (in the Aegean Sea, between Greece and Turkey); it was founded in the first century BCE (some date it to the second century BCE) and functioned as such until the second or third century CE. Literary sources from the first century CE—the writings of Philo, the Acts of the Apostles, and Josephus—also mention synagogues throughout the Diaspora.

The earliest evidence for the existence of synagogues in Palestine dates to the first century CE, in several instances perhaps as early as the late first century BCE. Three buildings (at Gamala, Masada, and Herodium) are dated to the first century CE (Gamala may date from the late first century BCE) as well as the Theodotos inscription from Jerusalem, which specifically mentions a synagogue and its functions (*CIJ*, no. 1404). Also, the writings of Josephus, the Gospels, and rabbinic literature corroborate the existence of numerous synagogues in Palestine at this time. For the era following the destruction of the Temple and down to the end of antiquity, rabbinic literature is the main, and almost exclusive, literary source.

No synagogues have been found in Palestine for the almost two hundred years following the destruction of the Temple; only toward the middle of the third century CE do they begin appearing at a number of sites throughout the country. A great deal is known about synagogue buildings, their furnishings, and their activities from second to fourth-century literary sources. Archaeological remains from many of the sites they mention have yet to be discovered; it is possible that they have been obliterated by later construction or were covered by alterations made in existing buildings in late antiquity.

The timing of the appearance of these later synagogue buildings—in the mid-third century—is noteworthy. This was an era of crisis in the Roman world generally, and it is known to have been a period of political anarchy, runaway inflation, famine, plagues, wars, and general instability. Would such edifices have been erected despite the surrounding turmoil? These monumental buildings would have required great financial investment as well as a degree of social and political stability. A satisfactory correlation between these crises and the possible construction of the synagogues has yet to be made.

From the fourth to seventh centuries, there is evidence of scores of synagogues being built throughout the country. At times these archaeological remains confirm the written sources. The bulk of synagogue remains comes from the Galilee, which was the center of Jewish life in late antiquity (from the Late Roman or Byzantine period to the beginning of the Arab period). To date, more than fifty sites in the Galilee have been securely identified as synagogues. There were no Jewish synagogues at all in Samaria, undoubtedly owing to the longstanding animosity between Samaritans and Jews. Regarding Judea, it was once assumed that in the period following the Bar-Kokhba Revolt the Jewish population relocated in the north (or even left Palestine). However, in light of the discovery of at least twelve synagogues in Judea to date, it is evident that Jewish settlement continued to flourish there. Archaeological remains of synagogues have been found on the periphery of Judea: at Jericho, Na'aran and 'En Gedi to the east; Susiya, Eshtemoa, Maon (in Judea) and 'Anim to the south; and Ma'on (Nirim), Gaza, Ashkelon, Ashdod, and Ḥorvat Rimmon to the west. Surveys and excavations in the Golan before the 1967 war uncovered only a few scattered synagogue remains. However, in the subsequent twenty-five years, remains of at least sixteen buildings, and evidence of eleven others, have been discovered. Almost without exception, these remains date to the Byzantine period (see Golan).

The dating of the remains of most ancient synagogues (the number reaches more than a hundred) has led to a revolution in understanding the Jewish community in Palestine, which flourished until the beginning of the Middle Ages. A salient example of this secure status is the monumental synagogue at Capernaum, completed in the fifth century, which overshadows a more modest church from the Byzantine period located nearby.

These findings contrast sharply with the understanding regnant among scholars for decades, that the Jewish population deteriorated steadily both in number and status following a series of setbacks: the destruction of the Temple in Jerusalem; the failure of the Bar-Kokhba Revolt; anarchy in the third century; and the rise of Christianity and anti-Jewish legislation commencing in the fourth century. The disappearance of the Patriarchate and what appears to have been the hasty editing of the Jerusalem Talmud around the turn of the fifth century were also cited as indications of the onset of a "Dark Ages" for Palestinian Jewry. Today, however, owing to the discovery of scores of synagogues, and the many documents from the Cairo Genizah attesting to a flourishing cultural and spiritual life in Byzantine Palestine, it is apparent that the political, cultural, and economic status of the Jews was far more stable and prosperous than imagined.

SIMILARITIES AND DIFFERENCES AMONG ANCIENT SYNAGOGUES. A close study of synagogues in antiquity reveals a delicate balance between characteristics that were common to all and unique to each. Among the common features are the orientation of the prayer hall toward Jerusalem and the centrality of the Torah shrine in that hall. At an earlier stage, the Torah shrine appears to have been mobile and was brought into the prayer hall only for the Torah-reading ceremony; the shrine in the Byzantine period was permanently placed in the sanctuary, usually in an apse or niche in the wall facing Jerusalem. The status of the synagogue as a holy place was also common to synagogues throughout Roman-Byzantine Palestine.

Alongside these common characteristics were significant differences. There were monumental buildings and modest ones, those located in formerly private homes and those built initially as communal buildings. This diversity is especially striking with regard to art. On the one hand, the synagogues in communities holding a very conservative attitude toward art forms bore no signs of figural representation—neither of humans nor of animals (Jericho, Rehob, Meiron, and Khirbet Shema'). On the other hand, many more-acculturated communities decorated their synagogues figurally (Japhia, Capernaum, and Hammath-Tiberias). Some synagogues featured three-dimensional representations in stone (Chorazin), while others lavishly displayed two-dimensional depictions (Beth Alpha, Hammath-Tiberias, Na'aran, and perhaps Susiya). A more conservative approach toward figural representation is strikingly evident in the synagogue at En-Gedi, where a written list of the zodiac signs is found rather than their figural representation. This community apparently was vigorously opposed to figural representation, especially of humans (birds, however, do appear on the mosaic there).

Differences among synagogues are also apparent regarding the language of inscriptions. Most inscriptions found in Palestine (close to 150, to date) are in Aramaic, Hebrew, or Greek. Greek was especially predominant in the coastal area, in large cities such as Beth-Shean and Tiberias, and in the Lower Galilee. Aramaic and Hebrew were the languages used in the more remote rural regions, such as the Upper Galilee, the Golan, and the Judean hinterland.

A very instructive example of the diversity among synagogues in the Byzantine period is found in the Beth-Shean area. So far, at least five synagogue buildings have been excavated there, all of them operating in the fifth and sixth centuries. One synagogue was 200 m north of the Byzantine city wall; one in the city itself, near its southwestern gate; one at Beth Alpha, to the west; one at Rehob, to the south; and one at Ma'oz Ḥayyim, to the east. The differences among them are striking and fundamental. At one extreme is the very conservative synagogue at Rehob, where there is no figural representation and all the inscriptions are in Hebrew. The longest is a halakhic inscription—in fact, the only one found in any ancient synagogue. At the other extreme are synagogues such as the one at Beth Alpha and the one within Beth-Shean proper, where the inscriptions are in Greek and Aramaic, and there are many depictions of animals. The mosaic floor at Beth Alpha also contains depictions of humans, of Helios, and of the zodiac signs. It is thus clear that the communities in the Beth-Shean area held, at one and the same time, very different and often contrasting positions regarding a number of cultural issues which are reflected in their synagogues.

An important implication emerging from this diversity, and from the archaeological finds of the last quarter century, is that there is little justification for the previously accepted theory that divided ancient synagogues into three categories based on chronological period: the "early" (Galilean) synagogue (second and third centuries CE), the "transitional" (broadhouse) synagogue (third and fourth centuries CE), and the "late" (basilical) synagogue (fifth–seventh centuries CE). The "early" synagogues often featured a lavishly decorated monumental facade, facing Jerusalem, with three entrances, windows, and other architectural features carved in typical Late Roman style. They had three rows of columns dividing the inner space, benches along two or three walls, and a flagstone floor. The distinguishing characteristics of the "transitional" synagogue were its broadhouse orientation, with the bema on the room's long wall. The entrance was usually on the side, and elements of the "early" and "late" models were in evidence as well. The "late" synagogue was patterned after the Christian basilica, with three entrances on the wall opposite Jerusalem, a narthex, a central hall divided into a nave and two side aisles, and an apse at the far end, facing Jerusalem. The decoration was internal, finding expression primarily in mosaic floors.

This theory has been seriously undermined in light of evidence from recent excavations.

1. A number of so-called "early" synagogues are now dated to the fourth, fifth, or sixth century CE (Meroth, Capernaum, and Nabratein).

2. The synagogue at Khirbet Shema', a typical "transitional" type, was, in fact, built in the third century, at exactly the same time as the synagogue at Meiron—a classic "early" type. These two contemporary synagogues are located about 600 m apart.

3. The early stage of the synagogue at Hammath-Tiberias (third century CE) includes elements associated with the so-called "early," "transitional," and "late" types.

4. Synagogues in the Golan, which in some ways resemble the "early" Galilean type and in others resemble the "late" type, were constructed from the fifth to seventh centuries.

Thus, specific types do not belong to specific periods, but rather to different architectural models existing side by side throughout late antiquity. These models were determined by regional factors, social composition and status, as well as by cultural and architectural proclivities and the taste of the community building the synagogue.

GRECO-ROMAN INFLUENCES. A decisive factor in the physical appearance of the Palestinian synagogue was the influence of Hellenistic culture on the region. Aramaic and Greek were regnant in the Near East at the time, and thus it is not surprising that more than 85 percent of all synagogue inscriptions are in those languages. Roman influence can also be seen in regard to synagogue architecture. Many buildings, especially those in the Galilee and Golan, were patterned after some form of Roman civic building; others were patterned on the Christian basilica and featured a central nave, two aisles, an apse (or bema), a narthex (forehall), and an atrium. The latter type of building is found at Beth Alpha, Ma'oz Ḥayyim, Rehob, Ḥammat Gader, Na'aran, Ma'on (Nirim), and elsewhere.

The synagogue adopted many of the prevalent artistic forms of ornamentation of the times. The stone carvings found in many Galilean synagogues are imitations of motifs widespread in late antiquity. The designs in many mosaic floors were drawn from Byzantine models found in churches, palaces, and villas. An example of one such popular mosaic design is of an amphora with extended grape vines forming medallions that encircle depictions of animals, bread baskets, and fruit. Such mosaics are found at Beth-Shean, Ma'on (Nirim), and Gaza.

A similar influence can be detected in the synagogue facade as well—particularly of the Galilean-type synagogue. Such buildings are indistinguishable from contemporary pagan edifices, as their decorations and plans are identical: a main entrance, two side entrances, decorated windows, columns, a semicircular arch above the main entrance, and a gable crowning the facade. One rabbinic source (B.T., *Shab.* 72b) tells of a man who walked along the street and bowed down before a building, thinking it was a synagogue. Only afterward did he realize that the building was, in fact, a pagan temple.

Influence from the outside world also affected the liturgy of the synagogue. In many communities, prayers were conducted in Greek. There is an account of a synagogue in Caesarea in which the congregation read the very basic prayer *Shema' Yisrael* in Greek because it was unable to do so in Hebrew (J.T., *Sot.* 7, 1, 21b). There is no doubt that the translation of the Torah into Greek by Aquilas in the Yavnean period (following the destruction of the Jerusalem Temple in 70 CE) was meant for Greek-speaking communities in Roman Palestine, as well. Finally, the recitation of liturgical poems (*piyyutim*, from the Greek *poetes*) in synagogues began in the Byzantine period, an innovation that may well have developed under the influence of similar practices then spreading throughout the churches of the Byzantine world.

CHANGING JEWISH ATTITUDES TO ART. Several significant developments took place in synagogue art in the course of late antiquity. In the late Second Temple period, starting with the Hasmonean rebellion and until the Bar Kokhba Revolt—a period of some three hundred years—there was a general prohibition among the Jews regarding figural representation. However, from the third century and down to the end of antiquity, figural representations appeared in many synagogues, often depicting human and even pagan motifs. Most striking is the appearance of zodiac signs and of Helios in a number of synagogues throughout the country (Hammath-Tiberias, Beth Alpha, Ḥusifah, Na'aran, and perhaps Susiya). The aniconic policy among the Arabs, and later within the Byzantine Empire, starting in the eighth century, created a similar reaction among the Jews. It resulted in the absence of figural representation (at Jericho and in the last stage of the synagogue at Hammath-Tiberias) and the destruction of already existing images.

A second development in synagogue art in the Byzantine period was the marked increase in the use of Jewish symbols. Remains of buildings from the Second Temple period and from the third century are almost entirely devoid of such symbols; however, beginning in the fourth century, and continuing down to the seventh and eighth centuries, depictions of Jewish ritual objects such as the menorah, shofar, lulab, and ethrog became popular and widespread. They often appear together with a depiction of a Torah shrine (or Temple facade) in a mosaic panel near the bema. In a number of synagogues biblical scenes or figures are found, such as the Binding of Isaac (Beth Alpha), David (Gaza and Meroth [?]), Noah and the ark (Gerasa), and Daniel (Na'aran and Susiya).

THE MYTH OF A WOMEN'S GALLERY. An issue that has drawn scholarly attention of late is whether there was a separate section for women in the ancient synagogue. That women frequented the synagogue throughout antiquity is well known and attested in a wide number of contemporary sources in the first century (for example, see Acts 16:12–13; 17:1–4, 10–12; 1 Cor. 14–34; Tosefta, *Meg.* 3:11; J.T., *Sot.* 1, 4, 16d).

However, there is no mention in rabbinic literature of a special place for women to sit, and no inscription has been found that mentions a women's gallery or hints at any kind of physical separation within the building that might be interpreted as a partition. The tendency to identify evidence for a balcony of a synagogue with a women's gallery is gratuitous. While the balcony is indeed often mentioned in rabbinic literature in connection with a range of functions—study, court proceedings, festive meals, the quarters of the *ḥazzan* (synagogue official)—there is no hint of the gallery as a place for women. Some excavators have identified one room or another with a women's gallery, but, in this writer's opinion, these identifications are purely speculative. Most excavation findings attest to the entire congregation having gathered in one hall. The custom of distinguishing between men and women in a synagogue context apparently evolved in the Middle Ages, possibly under the influence of Christianity or Islam.

THE SAGES AND THE SYNAGOGUE. The sages were a religious elite within Jewish society, but the decisive influence on synagogue-related matters in a particular synagogue and what transpired therein were determined largely by the local community and not by an outside rabbinic authority. An indication of this is that many descriptions of synagogues in rabbinic literature are at odds with archaeological findings. For example, despite the requirement that the entranceways of synagogues always face east (Tosefta, *Meg.* 3:22), very few synagogue entrances do so. The rabbinic directive that when mourning for certain religious leaders people should change their usual seat in the synagogue from the south side to the north and vice versa (B.T., *Mo'ed Q.* 22b) was not translated into synagogue architecture: in almost all synagogues, benches lined the eastern and western walls and in only a few were there benches on the north as well as the south sides. Some dicta in rabbinic literature are reflected in the archaeological record, such as the one requiring the orientation of the worshipers toward Jerusalem; nevertheless, it is difficult to know whether the

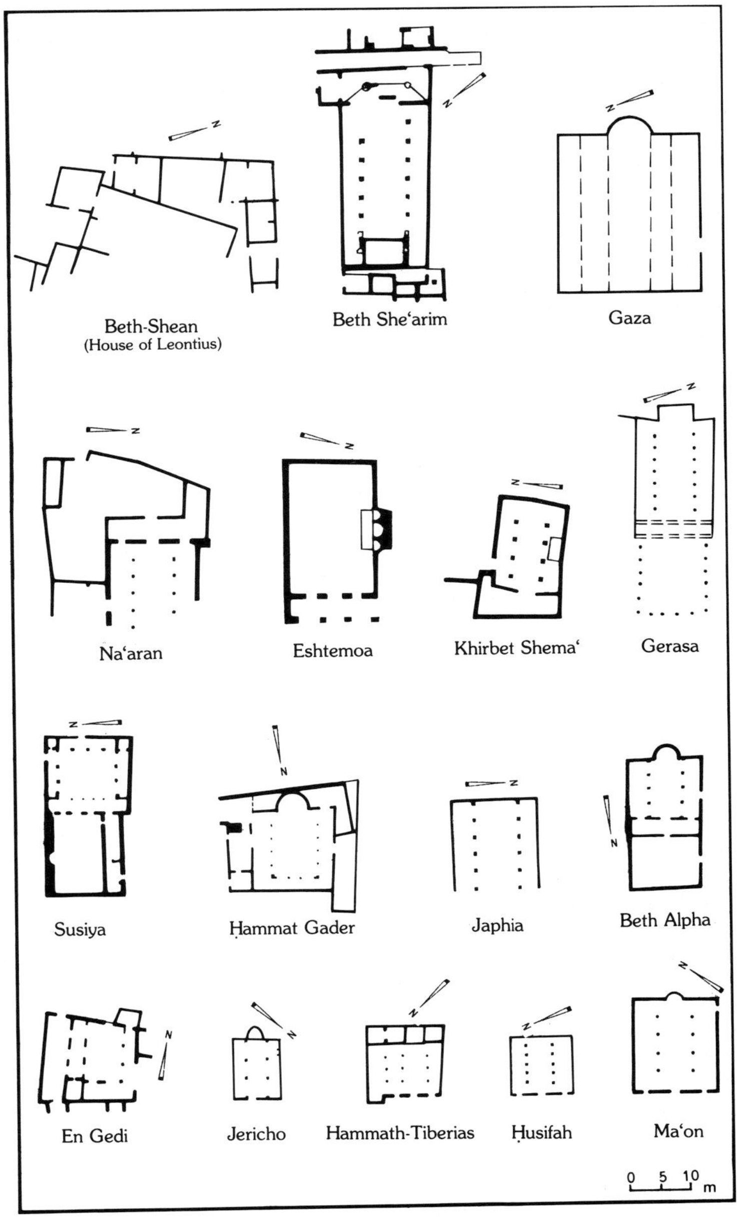

Plans of various synagogues.

rabbis instituted this practice or—which is more likely—it merely reflects a tradition that had already taken root among the people.

In matters of belief and aesthetic taste, it seems that many synagogues were at odds with the views of the rabbis. It is difficult to imagine that the sages would have been at home in a synagogue decorated with images of human beings, and especially of zodiac signs and Helios. The most liberal rabbinic statement on this subject only makes peace with the phenomenon post facto and certainly does not indicate an a priori acceptance of the practice (J.T., *A.Z.* 3, 3 42d). The many Greek inscriptions with Greek names found in synagogues reflect the tastes of the wealthy Jewish aristocracy rather than that of the sages.

THE ANCIENT SYNAGOGUE: FROM A COMMUNITY CENTER TO A "LESSER SANCTUARY"

The synagogue functioned throughout antiquity as a communal center in which most, if not all, the activities of the local community took place. In the early buildings, the synagogue was primarily a place for gathering—a hall surrounded by columns and benches along each wall—as at Gamala and Masada. The focus of the building was the center of the hall and not in the direction of Jerusalem. There were no special decorations or inscriptions hinting at the building's religious function, which took place on Sabbaths and holidays, and when the Torah was read and related activities took place.

Following the destruction of the Temple in 70, Jewish worship underwent major changes. The earliest evidence of such activity—transferring a number of Temple functions to the synagogue—is recorded in rabbinic literature, in the enactments of Rabbi Yoḥanan ben Zakkai (Mishnah, *Rosh Hashana* 4:1–4). Moreover, the Mishnah refers to the synagogue as a holy place; Rabbi Judah hints at a connection between its sanctity and that of the Temple (Mishnah, *Meg.* 3:3; see also Tosefta, *Meg.* 2:18, 3:22).

In the course of the third century there are many more references to the synagogue as a place of religious significance, on a par with that of the Temple. The most pointed statement is from Rabbi Isaac, who called the synagogue a *miqdash me'at*, a "lesser sanctuary" (B.T., *Meg.* 29a). The change in the status of the synagogue by the third century was expressed architecturally, as well, in the building's orientation toward Jerusalem.

This emphasis on the orientation of prayer reached its peak in the Byzantine period, when the Christian basilical model was adopted in many places, with its apse at the far end of the prayer hall—or, alternatively, with its niche or bema in the wall facing Jerusalem. The permanent presence of the Torah scrolls in the prayer hall no doubt significantly influenced the room's interior design. Jewish symbols perhaps intending to recall religious ritual in the Temple (the menorah, shofar, lulab, and ethrog) were now introduced into synagogue art. Their appearance further strengthened the sacred dimension of the building, as did the inscriptions that refer specifically to the synagogue as an *'atra qadisha* in Aramaic, or *hagios topos* in Greek (holy place) and to the congregation as a *qehillah qedoshah* (holy congregation) or *ḥavurta qadisha* (holy association).

It thus appears that, by the end of antiquity, the character of the synagogue had changed significantly. While it continued to serve as a community center, it had achieved a sacred status, fulfilling—even if only partially—the place of the Temple in the life of the people.

See also Ḥorvat 'Ammudim, Ḥorvat 'Anim, Arbel, Ashkelon, Bar'am, Beth Alpha, Beth-Shean, Beth She'arim, Beth Yeraḥ, Caesarea, Capernaum, Chorazin, Dabiyye, En-Gedi, 'En Nashuṭ, Eshtemoa, Galilee, Gamala, Gaza, Gerasa, Golan, Gush Ḥalav, Ḥammat Gader, Hammath-Tiberias, Herodium, Ḥusifah, Japhia, Jericho, Ḥorvat Kanaf, Meiron, Maon (in Judea), Ma'on (Nirim), Ma'oz Ḥayyim, Masada, Meroth, Na'aran, Nabratein, Qaṣrin, Rehob, Ḥorvat Rimmon, Sepphoris, Khirbet Shema', Ḥorvat Sumaqa, Khirbet Susiya, Tiberias, Yesud ha-Ma'ala.

M. Avi-Yonah, *Rabinowitz Bulletin* 3 (1960), 57–60; Wilson–Kitchener, *Special Papers SWP*, 294–305; Kohl–Watzinger, *Synagogen*, 59–79, 107–124, 125–137; Sukenik, *Ancient Synagogues*; id., *JPOS* 15 (1935), 172–174; Watzinger, *DP*, 2, 107–116; Goodenough, *Jewish Symbols* 1, 178–264; UNESCO, *Israel Ancient Mosaics*, New York, (1960), pl. XXVIII (Intro. by M. Shapiro and M. Avi-Yonah); C. Clermont-Ganneau, *PEQ* 33 (1901), 251, 374–389; 34 (1902), 132–134; Conder–Kitchener, *SWP* 1, 318f.; L. Oliphant, *PEQ* 16 (1884), 41; E. G. von Mülinen, *ZDPV* 31 (1908–1909), 158f.; N. Avigad, *Rabinowitz Bulletin* 3 (1960), 62–64; B. Lifshitz, *Cahiers de la Revue Biblique* 7 (1967); S. J. Saller, *A Second Revised Catalogue of the Ancient Synagogues of the Holy Land*, Jerusalem 1972; *Ancient Synagogues: The State of Research* (Brown Judaic Studies 22), Chico, Calif. 1981; V. Corbo, *Cafarnao* I (Publications of the Studium Biblicum Franciscanum 19), Jerusalem 1975; E. M. Meyers, *Ancient Synagogue Excavations at Khirbet Shema', Upper Galilee, Israel, 1970–1972* (AASOR 42), Durham 1976; id., *BA* 43 (1980), 97–108; id., *Archaeology* 35/3 (1982), 51–58; Hüttenmeister–Reeg, *Antiken Synagogen*; D. Chen, *LA* 28 (1978), 193–202; 30 (1980), 255–258; 36 (1986), 235–240; 39 (1989), 199–206; id., *Studia Orientalia Christiana Collectanea* 22 (1989), 43–55; id., *Christian Archaeology in the Holy Land: New Discoveries* (V. C. Corbo Fest.), Jerusalem 1990, 523–534; J. Naveh, *On Stone and Mosaic: The Aramaic and Hebrew Inscriptions from Ancient Synagogues*, Jerusalem 1978; id., *EI 20* (1989), 302–310; M. J. S. Chiat, *Handbook of Synagogue Architecture* (Brown Judaic Studies 29), Chico, Calif. 1982; H. Shanks, *Judaism in Stone: The Archaeology of Ancient Synagogues*, New York 1979; *ASR* (ed. L. I. Levine); M. Dothan, *Recent Archaeology in the Land of Israel* (ed. H. Shanks), Washington, D.C. 1981, 89–96; id., *Hammath Tiberias*, Jerusalem 1983; B. Bagatti, *Studia Hierosolymitana* 3 (1982), 247–253; B. J. Brooten, *Women Leaders in the Ancient Synagogue: Inscriptional Evidence and Background Issues* (Brown Judaic Studies 36), Chico, Calif. 1982; R. and A. Ovadiah, *Mosaic Pavements in Israel* (Bibliotheca Archaeologica 6), Rome 1987; *The Synagogue in Late Antiquity* (ed. L. I. Levine), Philadelphia 1987; F. Vitto, *BAIAS* 7 (1987–1988), 71–74; L. L. Grabbe, *Journal of Theological Studies* 39 (1988), 401–410; D. E. Groh, *BA* 51 (1988), 80–96; R. Hachlili, *Ancient Jewish Art and Archaeology in the Land of Israel* (Handbuch der Orientalistik VII/1/2/B/4), Leiden 1988; ibid. (Review), *BAIAS* 10 (1990–1991), 84–88; R. Jacoby and R. Talgam, *Jerusalem Index of Jewish Art, Ancient Jewish Synagogues, Architectural Glossary* (Moreshet Derech [Hebrew] 25 [1988]), 41ff.; Z. Ma'oz, *BA* 51 (1988), 116–128; H.-P. Stähli, *Antike Synagogenkunst*, Stuttgart 1988; *Ancient Synagogues in Israel, 3rd–7th Century CE: Proceedings of Symposium, University of Haifa, May 1987* (*BAR*/IS 499, ed. R. Hachlili), Oxford 1989; Z. Ilan, *ESI* 7–8 (1988–1989), 5–6; G. Foerster, *ZDPV* 105 (1989), 129–135; id., *Christian Archaeology in the Holy Land: New Discoveries* (V. C. Corbo Fest.), Jerusalem 1990, 545–552; id., *The Galilee in Late Antiquity* (ed. L. I. Levine) (in prep.); *MdB* 57 (1989); L. Y. Rahmani, *IEJ* 40 (1990), 192–214; Z. Safrai, *10th World Congress of Jewish Studies* B/2, Jeruslaem 1990, 23–28; L. Levine, *The Galilee in Late Antiquity* (op. cit.) (in prep.).

Synagogues not discussed in separate articles

Ḥulda: J. Ory, *IEJ* 3 (1953), 133–134; M. Avi-Yonah, *Rabinowitz Bulletin* 3 (1960), 57–60; UNESCO, *Israel Ancient Mosaics*, New York 1960, pl. XXVIII (Intro. by M. Shapiro and M. Avi-Yonah).

Tirat Ẓevi: M. Avi-Yonah, *Antiquity and Survival* 2 (1957), fig. 14 (opp. p. 269).

Cana (Kafr Kanna): C. Clermont-Ganneau, *PEQ* 33 (1901), 251, 374–389; 34 (1902), 132–134; D. H. Müller and E. Sellin, *Die hebräische Mosaikinschrift von Kafr Kanna*, Vienna 1901; S. Klein, *Corpus*, 74–76.

Ḥorvat Shura: G. Foerster, *ESI* 2 (1983), 102–103.

LEE I. LEVINE

SAMARITAN SYNAGOGUES

Research into Samaritan synagogues was initially hampered because of the lack of authentic Samaritan historical and halakhic sources and of archaeological finds. In recent years, however, the remains of a number of Samaritan synagogues have been unearthed in Samaria, thus shedding new light on the subject.

Detailed reports about the existence of synagogues can be found in Samaritan and Christian-Byzantine sources. According to the Samaritan *Chronicles*, the construction of the synagogues is connected with the personality of Baba Rabbah, the Samaritan leader active in the fourth century CE, who built eight synagogues in various locations in Samaria. The *Chronicles* were composed later, so it is not known whether the information they contain is from the Roman-Byzantine period or the Middle Ages.

Stone architectural fragments have been discovered at different sites both in and outside Samaria that bear inscriptions in the Samaritan script containing verses from the Samaritan prayerbook and from the Samaritan version of the Torah. These inscriptions probably belong to synagogue buildings. Three buildings identified as Samaritan synagogues were discovered outside Samaria: at Beth-Shean (q.v.), in Shaalbim (q.v.), and Tel Aviv (q.v.). (The latter has been identified by the excavators as a church.) All three contain inscriptions in the Samaritan script; at Sha'albim a depiction of a menorah was also found. Five Samaritan synagogues discovered in Samaria are reported on here. They shed new light on the subject as well as on Samaritan art in the fourth century.

THE SYNAGOGUE AT KHIRBET SAMARA. A Samaritan synagogue was discovered at Khirbet Samara, one of the largest Roman sites in Samaria, south of the Shechem–Tulkarm road (map reference 1609.1872). The synagogue is situated at the eastern edge of the site, which extends more than 7.5 a. The site was surveyed in the nineteenth century as part of the Survey of Western Palestine, and the synagogue building was described then, albeit as a church. Public buildings constructed with large ashlars were also discovered here, as were tombs, in the hill to the northeast, from the second and third centuries CE.

The synagogue is a long building oriented west–east and facing Mount Gerizim. It comprises a central hall, including an apse in its eastern section; a narthex; a semicircular atrium; a courtyard in the north; and various rooms on the south and on the east.

The Central Hall. The long walls of the central hall (12.7 by 16.4 m) are very thick (more than 2 m) because they supported the synagogue's roof, a barrel-vault spanning 8.4 m. The central entrance (2.2. m wide) is in the west. Its threshold is dressed stone, with recesses to hold the jambs of a wooden door. The lintel above the entrance, which was made of a large stone, was found on the floor of the hall.

The hall itself is flanked by two rows of benches fashioned like theater benches, with a footstool of soft limestone. In the southern row a gap (2.13 m) between the benches forms a niche that is paved with an impressive mosaic carpet containing a depiction of a Torah ark (see below). In the building's second phase, the mosaic was covered by a row of benches. In the middle of the east wall, in the direction of Mount Gerizim, is an apse constructed of ashlars. Technological and historical considerations led the excavators to assume that it was built later than the synagogue. The apse is separated from the hall by a

El-Khirbe: general view of the Samaritan synagogue.

threshold (3.8 m long) with long grooves and two square holes. The Torah ark was apparently installed in the apse in the second building phase.

The synagogue is built over an Early Roman public building that contained a pavement made of close-fitting stone slabs, and over a semicircular courtyard paved with a coarse white mosaic with colored decorations, and a system of large, interconnected cisterns. The synagogue's central hall, built of large ashlars, all in secondary use, was incorporated into the Early Roman building, and the semicircular courtyard became the synagogue's atrium. Other Roman buildings apparently were dismantled and their stones used to construct the synagogue.

East of the apse, a large stone bears a depiction of a Torah ark in relief. In the middle of the ark, a palmlike column is flanked by doors with two square depressions. Above each square is a lozenge, and above it is a conch. The shape of the ark is reminiscent of the depiction of facades of Torah arks discovered at other Samaritan synagogues, such as at Faḥma (see below).

The Mosaics. In the hall are three pavements from three different periods: the stone slabs that preceded the construction of the synagogue; a magnificent mosaic laid in the first phase of the synagogue in a bed of gray-black cement over stone slabs; and the stone slabs that covered the mosaic. The mosaic pavement consisted of small, multicolored tesserae on a black background. Most of it was damaged when the synagogue was later paved with stone slabs. It appears to have been divided into three square carpets, of which only the two eastern ones are preserved (the one closest to the entrance did not survive). The decoration around the whole mosaic includes triangles of dentils and a flowerlike design, followed by a rope decoration in red and gray. The two central squares were surrounded by medallions. The eastern carpet has a guilloche in the center of which a round medallion apparently contained an inscription. In the corners, various leaves issue from amphorae. The second carpet is surrounded by a rope decoration and is divided into four octagons. In the center of the carpet is a Torah ark; its facade has four columns and a gable surmounted by a conch. The ark is covered with a curtain attached to one of the columns.

The medallions around the carpets are configured like palm fronds issuing from a goblet. An additional goblet emerges from the first one, and from it issue fiery torches and a flower. The palm fronds and the goblets are depicted in reddish-brown on a black background. The medallions contain depictions of native flora: olives, dates, pomegranates, grapevines, and what appear to be pine, and perhaps ethrog. Also depicted are various objects such as cages, candelabra, and vessels for pouring wine. Human and animal forms are absent. The mosaic, laid with small tesserae, is probably to be attributed to the fourth century CE.

Between the benches later built on the mosaic, a Torah ark (2.13 by 14.5 m) is depicted in the shape of the facade of a temple with four columns with Ionic capitals. Above the capitals is a conch, and above it, a gable. In the center is a wooden door with a lock in the center. The door is covered with a curtain that hangs from rings on a rod. A rope and dentil decoration surrounds the ark. This is one of the finest Torah ark depictions discovered in the country.

The Narthex. West of the hall is the narthex (3.4 m wide). There is a stylobate in front of it on which three column bases were found in situ; an additional base was found, but not in situ. In the two corners two square piers on pedestals also remained in situ. The pedestals, piers, and column bases were in secondary use. The narthex was paved with a white mosaic of inferior workmanship; it is decorated with flowers in black and red.

The Atrium. The atrium is a semicircle (diameter, 33 m), the only semicircular atrium discovered so far. It was entered from the west, via a staircase. It was probably part of the Roman public building that preceded the synagogue (see above). It was paved in large white tesserae and ornamented in red and black. The edges of the mosaic display a wide band of rope decoration. Near the synagogue's facade the main decoration consists of squares containing a heart- or flower-shaped decoration. The mosaic on the south side of the atrium consists of a pattern of squares.

Dating and Building Phases. Based on the coins found in the building and the mosaic, the synagogue is dated to the fourth century CE. Its establishment seems to have been connected with the activity of the Samaritan leader Baba Rabbah. The apse was built later, probably in the fifth century. The synagogue was destroyed, and possibly damaged by fire, during the Samaritan revolt of 529. At the end of the Byzantine period or the beginning of the Arab period, an attempt was made to restore the synagogue, and the mosaic in the hall was covered with stone slabs.

THE SYNAGOGUE AT EL-KHIRBE NEAR SEBASTE. El-Khirbe is located about 2.5 km (1.5 mi.) southwest of Sebaste, close to the Shechem–Tulkarm road (map reference 1671.1846). The synagogue was built at the edge of an agricultural estate. The area of the estate is about 1.25 a. In antiquity, oil was produced from the olives grown here. Near the site a Roman mausoleum with fine ashlar constuction was found that resembles a temple. The archaeological finds at the site are from the Roman-Byzantine period.

The synagogue is a long building, oriented west–east toward Mount Gerizim, with an entrance on the east, facing the mountain. The building comprises a central hall; a well-built exedra on the north; a courtyard in the south paved with stone slabs; and in front of the facade, an atrium apparently surrounded by columns.

The long walls of the central hall (14 by 12 m), like those in the synagogue at Khirbet Samara, are especially thick (up to 1.8 m) and are preserved to a height of five courses. They are built of very large ashlars laid in two rows, with a fill of undressed stones and poured gray concrete. All the stones are in secondary use, apparently dismantled from Roman buildings on the estate. The walls supported the roof, which was a barrel-vault. The entrance to the hall reused a stone from an olive press for a threshold. Two rows of benches resembling theater seats were built along the inner walls of the hall. The benches encompassed the synagogue, including the areas flanking the entrance.

In the second phase of the synagogue, an additional entrance was constructed in the hall's south wall. Its threshold was paved with a mosaic with an inscription in its center. In that phase, in place of the row of benches along the north wall, a wall the width of the synagogue's long walls was built. The roof of the synagogue had probably collapsed, and it was necessary to build a support wall which reduced the opening of the vault.

The Mosaic in the Hall. The mosaic pavement (9 by 5 m) in the hall of the synagogue was laid with small colored tesserae. Six Greek inscriptions were found in the partially preserved floor. The central mosaic is divided into three carpets and is encompassed by a frame. Each carpet was surrounded by medallions; only a fragment of one is preserved—a branch bearing pomegranates. In the west carpet a figure-8 guilloche is depicted; a medallion in its center contains a Greek inscription: "Good luck to you, Marianus, together with your children." The east carpet, which is barely preserved, may have contained a disclike decoration. Between the two carpets is a rectangular carpet (2.5 m long and 1.0 m wide). To the right is a depiction of a seven-branched menorah whose branches are composed of alternating knobs and flowers. At the end of each branch a lamp faces the center. The central branch is flanked by tongs, and the menorah itself is flanked by trumpets, an incense shovel, and an unidentified object. To the right of the foot of the menorah is a partially preserved inscription; to the left is a showbread table with various objects on it—bowls, goblets, and loaves of bread. Above the table is an incomplete inscription. To the left a Torah ark is depicted whose facade displays four columns topped by a gable with a conchlike ornament. The ark is covered by a curtain draped around one of the columns. These symbols, with the possible exception of the table, are known from Jewish synagogues and appear in the description of the Tabernacle vessels (Ex. 25:10–40, 37:1–24). In their depiction of the menorah, the table, and the Torah ark, the Samaritans attempted to be faithful to the description in the Book of Exodus.

In addition to the above-mentioned inscriptions, two of which begin with the words: "May so-and-so be successful," there are three additional inscriptions beginning with the formula "The One God, help . . ." The three latter inscriptions belong to the second phase of the mosaic. An undecipherable Greek inscription appears on the lintel at the entrance. Following paleographic analysis, the inscriptions were dated to the fourth century.

The courtyard of the synagogue was on the east. It was as wide as the synagogue and the exedra on the north and was paved with large, carefully fitted stone slabs. There was probably a stylobate here with a row of columns. To the south of the building is another courtyard paved with stone slabs.

Date. On the basis of the inscriptions and the coins found in the excavation, the construction of the synagogue is dated to the fourth century. At the end of the fifth or in the sixth century, during the Samaritan revolts, the synagogue was destroyed. It was probably restored at the end of the Byzantine period and used briefly in the Arab period. Its resemblance to the synagogue at Khirbet Samara suggests that its construction followed a model for Samaritan synagogues in the fourth century.

El-Khirbe: mosaic floor of the Samaritan synagogue, decorated with a seven-branched menorah and other symbols.

THE SYNAGOGUE ON MOUNT GERIZIM. Extensive archaeological excavations are being conducted on Mount Gerizim in the area of the Byzantine Church of Mary Mother of God (see Mount Gerizim). Many finds from the Late Roman period have been uncovered, such as coins and Samaritan dedicatory inscriptions in Greek script engraved on stone. A later architectural phase for the gates of the Hellenistic precinct has also been found, which may also be attributed to the late Roman period. The north gate in the east wall of the Hellenistic precinct was rebuilt. Also discovered near the north wall of that precinct is a street paved with carefully fitted stone slabs that leads into the precinct from the north. This building phase preceded the Byzantine period, and was later than the Hellenistic period.

The finds attesting to the existence of a building of a religious-cultic nature in the fourth and fifth centuries CE include dozens of inscriptions carved on stone slabs in Greek script. A few of the stones were incorporated in the Byzantine church. The inscriptions contain dedicatory formulae known from Jewish inscriptions, such as "[He] is One, the One God [who] helps," a formula similar to the one in inscriptions found in the synagogue at el-Khirbe, near Sebaste. This dedicatory formula on building stones was used on Mount Gerizim also in the Hellenistic period. The inscriptions contain dedications by individuals on their own behalf and on behalf of their families. At times they dedicated gold coins to the sacred site. Based on the content of the inscriptions and their paleography, they are to be attributed to the fourth century CE.

Within the boundary of the Byzantine Church of Mary Mother of God precinct and its immediate vicinity, more than eighty coins were found from the Late Roman period (fourth–fifth centuries CE) and from the Byzantine and Arab periods. The earliest are from the reign of Constantine (361–377). These coins were the first to appear after a settlement gap of hundreds of years, following the reigns of John Hyrcanus and Alexander Jannaeus.

The existence of a synagogue on Mount Gerizim is well-documented in the historical sources. The Byzantine author Malalas (*Chron.* 382–383) relates that the Samaritans rebelled in the reign of Zeno (484). Zeno turned their synagogue on Mount Gerizim into the Church of Mary Mother of God (Theotokos). A similar report appears in *Chronicon Paschale* (*PG* 92, cols. 841–844) and in the Samaritan *Chronicles*. Procopius of Caesarea, on the other hand, denied the existence of a Samaritan temple on Mount Gerizim (*Buildings* V, 7). He related that, until the time of Zeno, the Samaritans were free to ascend Mount Gerizim to pray there. Zeno, however, took the mount from them and built a church on the site to Mary. Procopius' attempt to deny the existence of a sacred building on the mount may have been Christian propaganda. There is no doubt though that a sacred structure—a Samaritan synagogue(?)—was built in the Late Roman period and was destroyed at the beginning of the Samaritan revolts, when the Byzantine church was built.

THE ḤAZZAN YA'AQOV SYNAGOGUE AT SHECHEM. There is a synagogue at the northwestern end of the city of Shechem, in the old Samaritan neighborhood near the el-Ḥadra Mosque. A Samaritan tradition identifies this site with the field purchased by Jacob (Gen. 33:18–20). According to Samaritan tradition, the synagogue was built by Akvon the priest, the son of Eleazar the priest, probably in 362 CE, and was confiscated by Zeno in 484. It was returned to the Samaritans at the end of the Byzantine period, but was taken away once again by the Muslim ruler el-Ḥadra.

Excavations were conducted west of the el-Ḥadra Mosque. The mosque is built on early walls of fine ashlars oriented west–east. The minaret seems to be built over the synagogue itself. West of the mosque is an open courtyard (16 m long and 10.20 m wide). It was paved with stone slabs and underwent many changes. To the north and west are square piers of ashlar construction. It is assumed that the courtyard was surrounded by a peristyle of piers, as in the Byzantine church on Mount Gerizim. It was probably used as the synagogue's atrium. The building was entered from the west. On its south side, well-executed mosaic carpets were discovered. The peristyle appears to have been surrounded by rooms partially paved with colorful mosaics. In the center of the building is a square pool, coated with pinkish-white plaster: each side is 4.35 m long. The pool is about 40 cm deep. It may have been connected in some manner with the synagogue ritual. The inner structure is octagonal.

North of the peristyle entrances are rock-cut, round installations that contained remains of animal bones and burned olive branches. These may be the ovens used for roasting the Samaritan paschal lamb, which was eaten within the bounds of the synagogue in those periods when the ascent to Mount Gerizim for this purpose was forbidden to the Samaritans, probably in the Middle Ages. In the vicinity of the synagogue two inscriptions were discovered, in Samaritan script, one of which is incorporated in the mosque.

THE SYNAGOGUE AT ẒUR NATAN (KHIRBET MAJDAL). Khirbet Majdal is located west of Ẓur Natan (map reference 1508.1832). Excavations were conducted here between 1989 and 1991, under the direction of E. Ayalon, on behalf of the Eretz Israel Museum (Tel Aviv). In area B, to the south of the site, a monastery with a central courtyard surrounded by rooms was found from the Byzantine period. Southeast of it a public building was uncovered that its excavators consider to be a Samaritan synagogue. It is oriented west–east and faces Mount Gerizim. It contains a large, square courtyard, or atrium. The edges of the courtyard were paved with a colorful mosaic in geometric patterns. In the center of the atrium are a cistern and a drainage system for rainwater. The synagogue has a narthex paved with a white mosaic. Its central hall (16.5 m long and 15 m wide), has three entrances in the west. In the east is a small apse of fine ashlar construction. Inside the middle door sill a mosaic pavement in a variety of different colors contains geometric and floral patterns, columns, pomegranates, and a medallion with the Greek inscription: "And may the villagers Antasion Theotheokus Julus and . . . be remembered." Architectural elements and a millstone ornamented with a seven-branched menorah were also found. The excavators attribute the construction of the synagogue to the fourth–fifth centuries.

THE SYNAGOGUE AT KEFAR FAḤMA. In Faḥma, a small village in northern Samaria (map reference 167.199), a stone bearing a relief of a Torah ark was found in 1941. This stone, discovered in the courtyard outside a Crusader church, indicates the presence of a synagogue here in antiquity. (It is unlikely that such a heavy stone would have been moved from another location, suggesting that the foundations of the church conceal the remains of the Samaritan synagogue). A Torah ark with two doors, with a conch above them, is depicted on the stone. Each door is divided by prominent borders into five recessed areas: two large areas with a square depression in the middle, and three narrower ones. The opening appears to be flanked by two columns with capitals; in the center is a shape resembling a palm tree.

In addition to the Torah ark, an architectural fragment, probably part of the synagogue's doorjamb, was found. A survey conducted at Kefar Faḥma recovered many architectural fragments, such as columns and bases, suggesting a Samaritan settlement in the village with a synagogue at its center.

See also Beth-Shean, Shaalbim, Tel Aviv.

J. Malalas, *Chronographia* (ed. L. A. Dindorf), Bonn 1831, 382–383; *Chronicon Paschale: 284–628 AD* (ed. L. A. Dindorf), Bonn 1832, 603–604; E. N. Adler and M. Seligson, *Revue des Études Juives* 45 (1902), 90–91; Procopius, *Buildings* V, VII (Procopius 7, tr. H. B. Dewing; Loeb Classical Library), London 1940; E. L. Sukenik, *Bulletin Rabinowitz* 1 (1949), 26–30; B. Lipshitz, *RB* 75 (1968), 368–378; H. G. Kippenberg, *Garizim und Synagoge: Traditionsgeschichtliche Untersuchungen zur Samaritanischen Religion der Aramäischen Periode* (Religionsgeschichtliche Versuche und Vorarbeiten 30), Berlin 1971; ibid., (Review), *IEJ* 22 (1972), 188–190; G. Reeg, *Die Samaritanischen Synagogen* (Hüttenmeister-Reeg, Antiken Synagogen 2), Wiesbaden 1977; id., *Institutum Judaicum der Universität Tübingen im Jahre 1971–1972*, 149–154; Abu'l Fath Ibn Abi'l-Hasan al-Samir, *The Kitab al Tarikh of Abu'l Fath* (tr. P. Stenhouse; Studies in Judaica 1), Sydney 1985, 173–180, 183; R. Pummer, *The Samaritans* (ed. A. Crown). Tübingen 1989, 139–151; L. Di Segni, *Christian Archaeology in the Holy Land: New Discoveries* (V. C. Corbo Fest.), Jerusalem 1990, 343–350.

ITZHAK MAGEN

T

TAANACH

IDENTIFICATION

There has never been any doubt that biblical Taanach is located at Tell Ta'annek (map reference 171.214). It is an impressive 11-a. mound rising more than 40 m above the Jezreel Valley on the southwest flanks of the 'Iron Hills, 8 km (5 mi.) southeast of Megiddo. The maximum north–south limit of this pear-shaped mound is 340 m. Its widest east–west limit is 110 m. Taanach lies between Megiddo and Ibleam on a northwest–southeast route. Unlike them and Jokneam, it does not guard a major pass at the head of the Jezreel Valley. By the tenth century BCE, Taanach was an Israelite administrative and religious center. It may have served the same function during the Bronze Age.

HISTORY

In nonbiblical literary sources, the earliest reference to Taanach is in the fifteenth-century BCE Karnak inscription describing Thutmose III's first military campaign into Asia. To reach the enemy encamped at Megiddo, one of the three routes to the Jezreel Plain was a road along Wadi Abu Nar, past modern Ya'bad, through the Burqin Pass, which debouches into the plain 4 km (2.5 mi.) south of Taanach. Both Thutmose III in 1468 BCE and Shishak I in 918 BCE list Taanach as a city captured by their forces. J. A. Knudtzon's restoration of "Taanach" (Ta-ah-[nu-ka]) in an early fourteenth-century BCE Amarna letter (248:18) is unlikely on both archaeological and paleographic grounds. Eusebius' *Onomasticon* (100, 7–10) indicates that in the third century CE Taanach was a "very large village," 3 Roman miles from Legio-Maximianopolis (near Megiddo).

In biblical tradition, Taanach first achieved eminence as the site of the battle of Israel, mustered by Deborah and Barak, against the Canaanites, led by Sisera (Jg. 5:19). Although the king of Taanach was reported as one of the thirty-one kings defeated by Joshua (Jos. 12:21) and the city was assigned to Issachar and Asher, it was later given to Manasseh (Jos. 17:11, 1 Chr. 7:29) who, however, failed to occupy Taanach because of the strength of the Canaanites (Jg. 1:27). In time, probably not before the tenth century BCE, "When Israel grew strong, they put the Canaanites to forced labor" (Jg. 1:28) and occupied (ruled) the site. In the same century, Taanach seems to have become a Levitical city (Jos. 21:25), as well as the headquarters of Ba'ana, the son of Ahilud. Ahilud was the administrator of Solomon's fifth district, which included all of the Jezreel and the Beth-Shean valleys, to just beyond the Jordan River (1 Kg. 4:12).

EXCAVATIONS

Tell Ta'annek was first excavated between 1902 and 1904 by E. Sellin, then of the University of Vienna. In three campaigns (with a total of four months of actual excavation), he opened long trenches on the mound. He was first assisted by G. Schumacher and later, after the discovery of an archive of Akkadian cuneiform tablets (see below), he was joined by F. Hrozný. Sellin's two major reports were published by 1905, and although they lacked adequate plans and photographs of buildings and pottery, he was nevertheless a perceptive observer and prompt reporter. Two years later, H. Thiersch critically reviewed the results.

The second excavation at the site was the work of a joint American expedition of the American Schools of Oriental Research and the Graduate School of Concordia Seminary, St. Louis, Missouri, directed by P. W. Lapp. In three major seasons, totaling almost six months altogether—in 1963, 1966,

View of Tel Taanach from the Jezreel Valley, looking south.

Plan of the mound and principal remains.

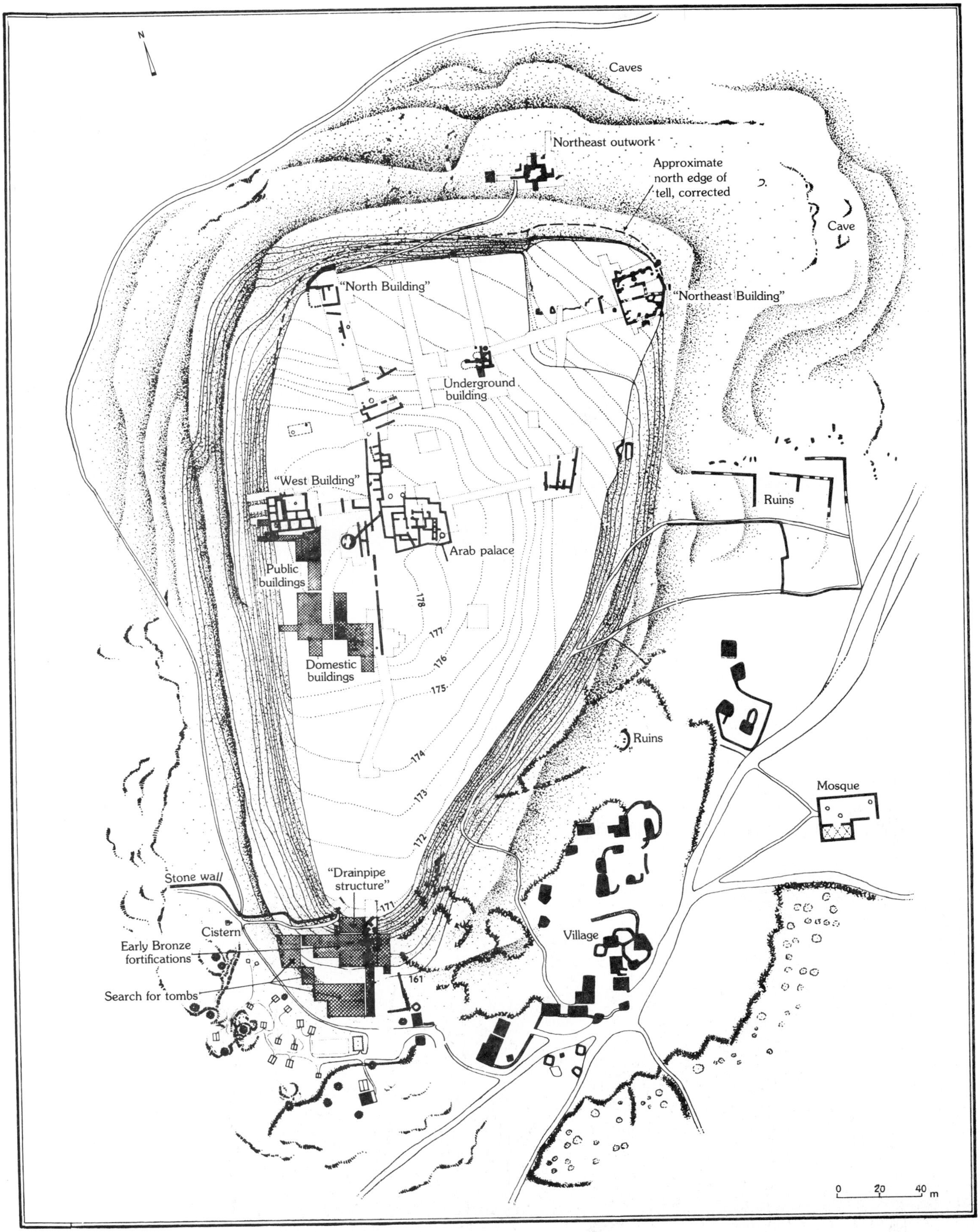

EB fortifications in the southern part of the mound, looking west.

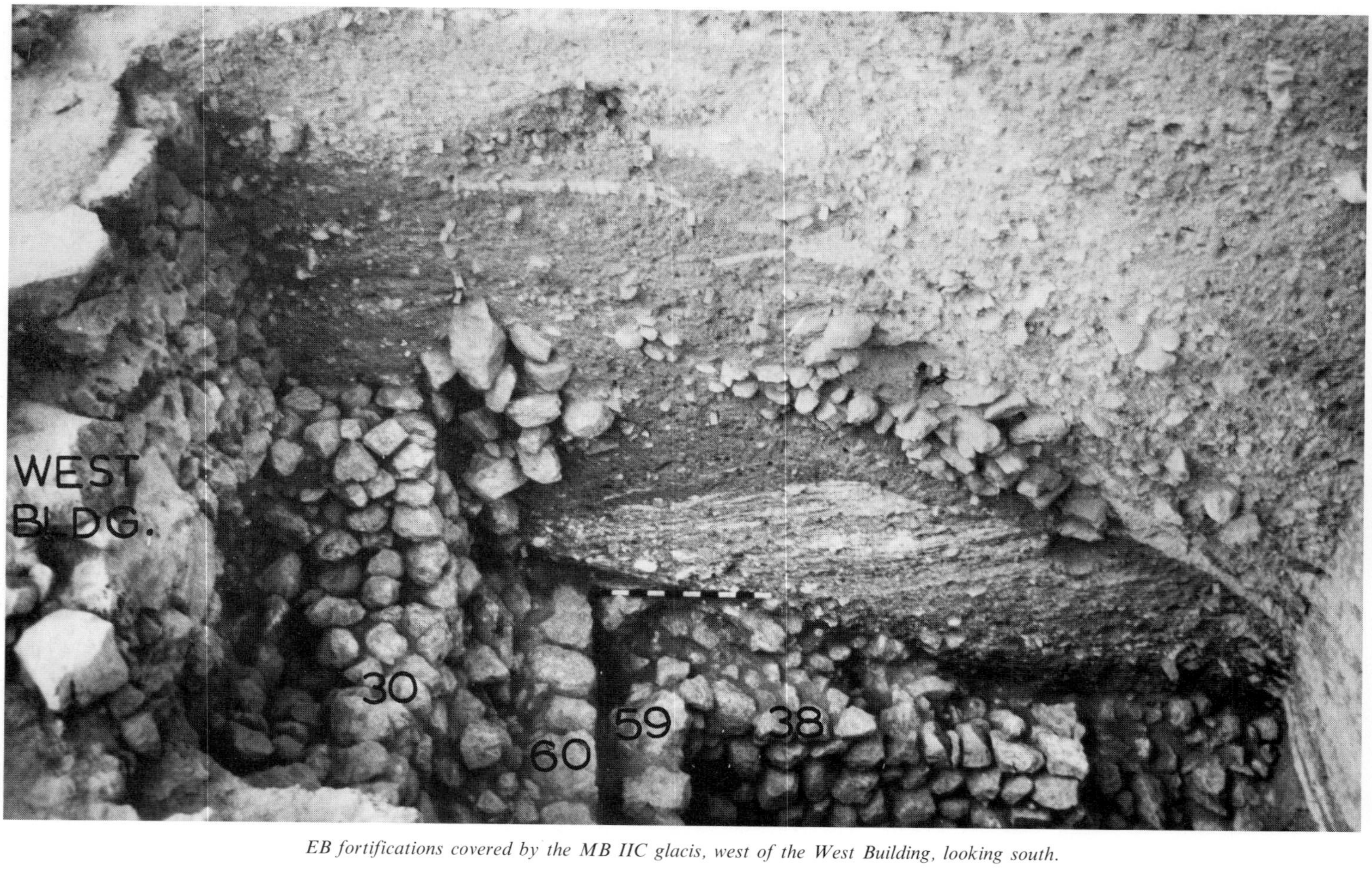

EB fortifications covered by the MB IIC glacis, west of the West Building, looking south.

Cult stand found in Sellin's excavations, 10th century BCE: ***(left)*** *side view (drawing);* ***(right)*** *facade (photograph and drawing).*

and 1968—four areas in the southwest quadrant of the mound were excavated. The aim of the excavations was to clarify the fortifications, domestic and industrial installations, public buildings, and cultic practices.

EXCAVATION RESULTS

SELLIN'S EXCAVATIONS. Sellin's long diagonal trenches were planned to locate the city defenses, as well as any major architecture. By the end of the third season, he was certain that there were no sizable buildings on the mound. In his final report, he included the plans of only five buildings, all of which he designated fortresses. No other structures are described, but he located more than fifteen cisterns.

When Sellin found no defensive city walls, he concluded that the site had been defended by a series of fortresses. The earliest was a modest structure with subterranean rooms, north of the center of the mound, dating to between 1500 and 1350 BCE. W. F. Albright later interpreted the structure as an Early Bronze Age funerary chamber, similar in construction to Third Dynasty Egyptian tombs. According to Sellin, the structure was subsequently reused as a cistern. In the debris above the building's upper level, he discovered an archive of twelve Akkadian cuneiform tablets—eight letters and four name lists. At the southern end of a long central trench, he uncovered fragments of a Canaanite cult stand (incense altar), 90 cm high. It has four tiers of modeled lions on each side of a windowed facade, capped by a basin. On the upper left panel, a youth in relief strangles a serpent. On the front of the lowest panel, there is a tree of life with ibexes on either side. Today, both the tablets and the cult stand are in museums in Istanbul.

Sellin identified four major strata of occupation, each with two subphases. The revised dates from his second report follow: stratum I—fifteenth to fourteenth centuries BCE, including the cuneiform archives, its building, and the subterranean structures, followed by the West Building; stratum II—thirteenth to ninth centuries BCE, including the east fortress, its outbuilding, and most of the burials; stratum III—eighth to sixth centuries BCE, the destruction of the buildings from stratum II, the cult stand. This was the period of Greek influence; and stratum IV—eleventh to twelfth centuries CE, the Arab fortress-palace on the mound's central plateau.

The Cuneiform Tablets. The thirteen Akkadian tablets from Taanach (including the new TT 950 uncovered in Lapp's excavations, see below) are either letters to the local king (eight) or administrative name lists (five). Two of the four legible letters (the other four are fragmentary) are from Amanhatpa, an Egyptian administrator posted in Gaza but probably writing from Megiddo. He requests chariots and men for his garrison and that prisoners of war, as well as tribute, be sent to him. Another correspondent is Ahiyami, who orders a bow, bowstrings, chariot wheels, and a copper javelin. Also, he wishes to be married. A third writer is Ehli-Teshub, who promises to repay fifty shekels of silver, asks for wood and myrrh, and advises that a servant girl be sold or married. Although written in Akkadian, the syntax and morphology of these letters have many West Semitic features. The letters and the five name lists contain some ninety names. About 60 percent are Northwest Semitic and 20 percent are Indo-Aryan or Hurrian-Anatolian. The name of the ruler of Taanach, the addressee, is written RI.WA-shur. The first element may be

Clay tablet in Akkadian cuneiform script, 15th century BCE.

Ugaritic cuneiform tablet, 12th century BCE.

Bronze baboon from a cooking pot filled with weights, 12th century BCE.

Cult stand found in Lapp's excavations, 10th century BCE.

read *ri/e-* or *tal-*, and the second, *wi/e-* or *ya*. Albright took the initial sign to be Egyptian, thus reading the name as Rewashur. According to a later collation, the copies published by Hrozný in the Sellin reports are generally more trustworthy than Albright believed.

LAPP'S EXCAVATIONS. The second excavation, conducted in 1966, clarified and elaborated on many points of Sellin's work. Although mainly limited to the southwest quadrant of the mound, the excavation nevertheless confirmed Sellin's general impression that the city was never extensively occupied by architecture, as were other important sites. However, the discovery of massive defenses on both the south and west showed not only that the site had been protected by city walls in all major periods, but that the earliest city dates to the Early Bronze Age II–III. An Early Bronze Age occupation had already been suggested by Albright on the basis of the pottery Sellin published.

Four phases of the Early Bronze Age defenses were exposed on the south slope by the Concordia expedition. The earliest fortification wall, resting on bedrock, is fronted by a rectangular tower. The east wall of a second tower is fragmentary. In the second phase, the same city wall served as the foundation for a new wall that diverges 19 degrees northwest from its line. In the third phase, this wall is fronted by a stepped revetment almost 4 m wide. Between the city wall and the revetment, a tipped fill provided the base for a ramp or room adjacent to an entrance into the city not yet discovered. In the fourth and final phase, a huge rectangular tower surmounted the wall. A plastered glacis covered all of the earlier walls and towers.

After a long gap in occupation, a campsite from the Middle Bronze Age (from about 1700 BCE) is found on the mound. It is followed by extensive, but poorly constructed, domestic architecture and fortifications. The West Building discovered by Sellin was redated to about 1600 BCE and interpreted as a patrician dwelling that was part of a substantial rebuilding of the Middle Bronze Age IIC city.

The so-called Late Bronze Age I building was found to be a large block of small rooms at the center of the mound, between the west city and a north–south street founded in the early seventeenth century BCE (the "domestic" area). Associated with the later Middle Bronze Age IIC phases, which became the Late Bronze Age I building, was a casemate wall. Below the floors and in the walls of Middle Bronze Age rooms sixty-four burials were found, of which about 90 percent were of children entombed in storage jars. Selective destruction marks the end of the Middle Bronze Age on the site.

Taanach continued to be a substantial city into the Late Bronze Age I, suffering a major catastrophe at the hands of Thutmose III in about 1468 BCE. It was in the modest occupation that followed this destruction that the Akkadian cuneiform tablet TT 950 was found. It is dated to about 1450 BCE, as is the archive Sellin discovered. Although most of the limited quantity of Mycenean pottery dates to the Mycenean IIIA:2 period (fourteenth century BCE), there is no significant occupation between the mid-fifteenth and the late thirteenth centuries BCE. Substantial houses with numerous installations on the south (the "Drainpipe Structure") and west edges of the mound date to the twelfth century BCE and were completely destroyed in about 1125 BCE. Some Iron Age defenses noted on the west were also dated to the twelfth century BCE. North of the center of the southwest quadrant (the "public" area), a Canaanite cuneiform tablet (TT 433) turned up in the early twelfth-century BCE destruction of a large building. The two-line inscription registers the receipt of a shipment of grain.

A slight eleventh-century BCE occupation is followed by a larger tenth-century presence, destroyed by Shishak in about 918 BCE. A structure related to the local cult belongs to this period. A heavy ash layer on the floors contained nine iron knife blades, 140 pig astragali, some eighty restorable vessels, fifty-eight loom weights, many querns, grinding stones, pestles, three small stelae, and a figurine mold. In an adjacent cistern, an elaborate cult stand emerged not far from where Sellin had found the one he called an incense altar. Standing about 50 cm high, the cult stand is built up of four superimposed hollow clay squares topped by a ridged basin. The lion and human faces protruding above animal legs at the corners of the three panels are each accompanied by winged leonine bodies in relief along the side panels. These animals represent demons protecting the deity symbolized in the top panel by the stylized winged sun disk between volutes and above an equid.

Evidence for later occupation is limited to a tower dating to the ninth century BCE (Sellin's Nordostburg, the Northeast Building), located on a terrace below the north end of the mound, and to some fifth-century

Cult structure, 10th century BCE.

Basin in the cult structure, 10th century BCE.

BCE Persian pits and two rooms. In Late Abbasid times, tenth to eleventh centuries CE, an elaborate palace was constructed at the highest point on the mound. A cemetery on the south slope, over the Early Bronze Age defenses, seems to date from the early seventeenth century CE.

Main publications: E. Sellin, *Tell Ta'annek* (Denkschriften der Kaiserlichen Akademie der Wissenschaften, Philosophisch-Historische Klasse 50/4), Vienna 1904; W. E. Rast, *Taanach 1: Studies in the Iron Age Pottery* (ASOR Excavation Reports), Cambridge, Mass. 1978.
Other studies: E. Sellin, *Mitteilungen und Nachrichten des Deutschen Palästina-Vereins* (1902), 13–19, 33–36; (1903), 1–4; (1905), 33–37; id., *PEQ* 34 (1902), 301–304; 35 (1903), 34; 36 (1904), 98, 187, 297, 388–391; 37 (1905), 176, 284; 38 (1906), 115–120; id., *RB* 11 (1902), 596–597; 12 (1903), 646–647; 14 (1905), 114–118, 270–271; 15 (1906), 287–292; id., *Eine Nachlese auf dem Tell Ta'annek in Palästina*, Vienna 1905; H. Thiersch, *Archäologischer Anzeiger, Beiblatt zum Jahrbuch des kaiserlich-Deutschen archäeologischen Institut* 22 (1907), cols. 311–357; L. H. Vincent, *Canaan d'aprés l'Exploration récente*, Paris 1907, 52–63, 181–182; A. E. Mader, *Biblische Zeitschrift* 10 (1912), 351–362; M. Lods, *Revue de l'Histoire des Religions* (1934), 129–147; Y. Aharoni, *LB*, 156–157; P. W. Lapp, *BASOR* 173 (1964), 4–44; 185 (1967), 2–39; 195 (1969), 2–49; id., *BA* 30 (1967), 2–27; id., *RB* 71 (1964), 240–246; 75 (1968), 93–98; 76 (1969), 580–586; id., *The Tale of the Tell*, Pittsburgh 1975, 91–103; A. Biran, *CNI* 20/3–4 (1969), 41–43; A. E. Glock, *BASOR* 219 (1975), 9–28; W. E. Rast, *Taanach* 1 (Review), *PEQ* 113 (1981), 136–137; id., *EI* 20 (1989), 166*–173*; N. Liphschitz and Y. Waisel, *IEJ* 30 (1980), 132–136; T. Stech-Wheeler et al., *AJA* 85 (1981), 245–268, 481; E. Pennels, *BA* 46 (1983), 57–61; M. D. Fowler, *ZDPV* 100 (1984), 30–34; R. Hestrin, *Phoenicia and the East Mediterranean in the First Millennium B.C.* (Studia Phoenicia 5, ed. E. L. Lipinski), Leuven 1987, 61–77; Weippert 1988 (Ortsregister).

Epigraphical finds: A. Gustavs, *ZDPV* 50 (1927), 1–18; 51 (1928), 169–218; W. F. Albright, *BASOR* 94 (1944), 12–27; A. Malamat, *Scripta Hierosolymitana* 8 (1961), 218–227; D. Hillers, *BASOR* 173 (1964), 45–50; M. Weippert, *ZDPV* 83 (1967), 82–83; F. M. Cross, Jr., *BASOR* 190 (1968), 41–46; A. E. Glock, ibid. 204 (1971), 17–30; 219 (1975), 9–28; id., *Berytus* 31 (1983), 57–66; A. F. Rainey, *Israel Oriental Studies* 7 (1977), 33–64; id., *EI* 15 (1981), 61*–66*; P. Der Manuelian, *Studies in the Reign of Amenophis II* (Hildesheimer Ägyptologische Beiträge 26), Hildesheim 1987, 83–90.

ALBERT E. GLOCK

TABUN CAVE

IDENTIFICATION

Tabun Cave (Cave of the Oven) is located on the southern bank of Naḥal Me'arot, at the point of its debouchment into the Coastal Plain, some 20 km (12 mi.) south of Haifa (map reference 1480.2305). It seems originally to have consisted of three chambers. Its outer part is destroyed, but the high, domelike ceiling of the intermediate chamber is still intact. In the interior chamber there is a wide chimney open to the sky, from which the cave's name was derived. The sedimentary fill within the cave has sunk into swallow holes that were formed in the chambers' floors; the layers within the cave are thus tilted at various angles, and none extend over its entire length or width.

Before the excavations, the cave was filled almost to the top with deposits, with only a small opening visible. The depth of the deposit was then about 25 m. The cave was originally excavated by the British archaeologist D. Garrod from 1929 to 1934. She removed about half of its contents and left an almost complete section (20 m high) at the rear of the cave. The cave was subsequently excavated from 1969 to 1971 by A. J. Jellinek of the University of Arizona, who examined the upper part of Garrod's section. Since 1973, the lower part of the fill has been reexamined in a series of excavations, directed by A. Ronen, on behalf of Haifa University.

STRATIGRAPHY

Tabun Cave contains remains from the Lower and Middle Paleolithic periods. Occupation of the cave ceased, according to carbon-14 dates, some fifty thousand to forty thousand years ago (TL and ESR dating methods yielded dates ranging between 100,000 and 120,000 years for the end of the occupation). The date of the start of occupation is unknown and, based on the 1991 excavation, may be estimated at about 500,000 years BP. This is one of the longest archaeological sequences known at any site. However, the sequence is incomplete and displays traces of several erosional periods, in the course of which layers of unknown thickness were washed away from the inside of the cave.

Garrod divided the Paleolithic layers into six units. The excavations since 1973 have distinguished more than one hundred archaeological layers, subsequently integrated into a framework of fourteen principal units (I–XIV). Because a reexamination of the entire section is still in progress, Garrod's stratigraphic terminology is used here and the suggestions made by later researchers are incorporated.

THE LOWER PALEOLITHIC PERIOD. Three assemblages belong to the period:

The Tayacian Assemblage. Garrod named the lithic assemblage from the lowest layer in the cave (layer G) Tayacian. This small assemblage contains a few retouched items, including several hand axes and crude flakes but no faunal remains. This industry is difficult to define with any certainty, but Jellinek regards it as Acheulean. Layer G had been most recently reexamined, and Garrod's observations were generally confirmed.

The Acheulean Assemblage. The industry recovered from layer F is particularly notable for the presence of hand axes and scrapers, as well as for the absence of the Levallois technique.

The Yabrudian and Amudian Assemblages. Two assemblages were recovered from layer E, whose maximum depth was 7 m. The Yabrudian industry is

Map of Naḥal Me'arot.

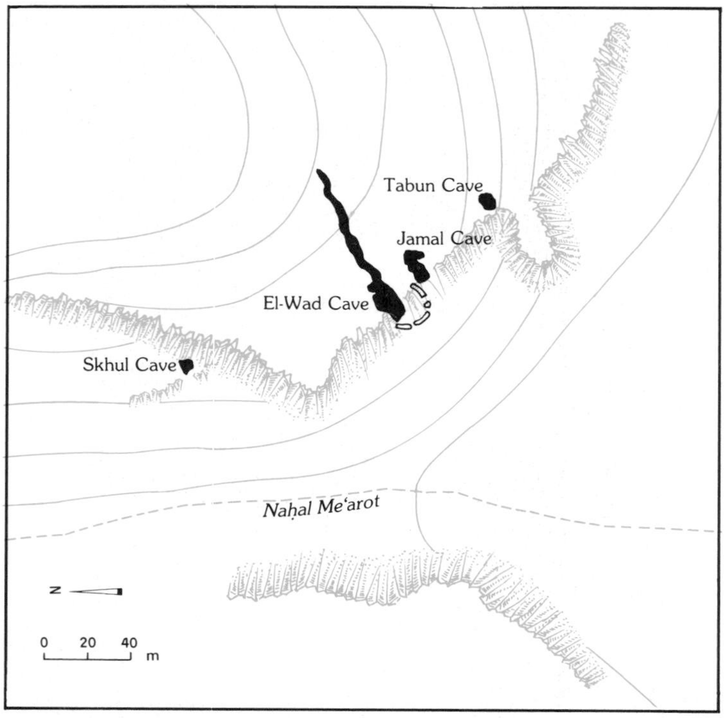

Tabun Cave: cross section of the layers.

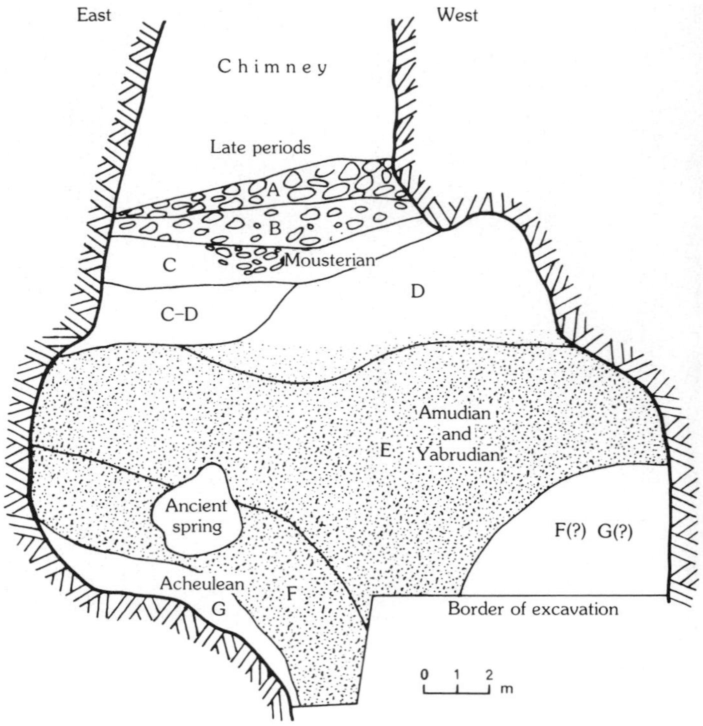

particularly notable for its numerous scrapers, as well as for varying numbers of hand axes. There is no evidence for the use of the Levallois technique. The Amudian is a blade industry, characterized also by typically Upper Paleolithic implements, mainly backed blades. The Amudian assemblage was retrieved from a 1-m-thick level in the upper part of layer E, which was topped by a short continuation of the Yabrudian assemblage, terminating the cave's Lower Paleolithic sequence.

Lately, Jellinek has expressed the view that the entire Lower Paleolithic sequence in the cave actually constitutes a single cultural sequence, which he suggests calling the Mugharan tradition (a term derived from Naḥal Me'arot's Arabic name, Wadi Mughara). Jellinek maintains that the differences betweeen the various assemblages lie in their tool compositions, rather than in the technology employed in their production or in the manner of their manufacture.

General view of Naḥal Me'arot.

General view of the Tabun Cave.

The main difference between the Acheulean and the Yabrudian assemblages lies in the proportions of hand axes and scrapers within each. When the proportion of hand axes is greater, the assemblage is termed Acheulean; when scrapers predominate, the assemblage is termed Yabrudian. Jellinek attributed this to some type of functional difference between the various assemblages. Moreover, he maintains that the functional difference between the Acheulean and the Yabrudian reflects climatic changes: hand axes were predominant when the climate was humid and scrapers in dry periods. According to this view, the Amudian assemblage also reflects some distinct function within the framework of the Mugharan tradition. However, further examination established that the blades within the Amudian were produced using a special technique. It is therefore doubtful whether the Amudian assemblage indeed constitutes part of the Mugharan tradition.

THE MIDDLE PALEOLITHIC PERIOD. The Middle Paleolithic layers exposed in the upper part of the sequence preserved in the cave belong to the Mousterian culture and are characterized by a wide use of the Levallois technique, in contrast to the preceding assemblages. Jellinek, however, maintains that the Levallois technique made its appearance gradually, and that a certain increase in its use is discernible as early as the end of layer E.

The Tabun D, or Abu Sif, Type. The oldest Mousterian assemblage recovered in Israel was found here, in layer D. It is characterized by a large number of Levallois points, including the elongated points called Abu Sif points, after the Judean Desert site. It also contains numerous blades and Upper Paleolithic implements. There are only a few Levallois flakes.

The Tabun C–B Type. Late Mousterian assemblages occurred in the two upper layers, C and B. They consist mostly of many Levallois flakes, scrapers, a small number of short Levallois points, and a few Upper Paleolithic implements. The uppermost layer (A) contained a mixture of Paleolithic flint artifacts and pottery vessels, as well as other, more recent items. Jellinek noted a phenomenon common to all the lithic assemblages from the cave: flakes become increasingly thinner (on average) over time. This phenomenon may be attributed to improved knapping skills, as thin flakes are harder to produce than thick ones. Jellinek proposed interpreting this as evidence of a constant, gradual increase in the mental abilities of the local population. However, flake measurements from other Mousterian sites suggest no such developmental process.

HUMAN REMAINS

A female burial of the Neanderthal type, with a cranial capacity of about 1,300 cu cm, in a semiflexed position, was recovered from a Middle Paleolithic layer. Garrod attributed this burial to layer C, whereas Jellinek proposes assigning it to layer D. A human jaw was exposed a little below this burial, and several isolated human bones were recovered from various other layers in the cave. The date of the woman of Tabun is thus unknown, although by the ESR dates of layer B she is probably older than 120,000 years. She antedates the *Homo sapiens sapiens* type, numerous specimens of which were found in the adjacent Skhul Cave. The latter, with a cranial capacity of 1,500 cu cm, are also ascribed to the Middle Paleolithic. Lately, *Homo sapiens sapiens* remains from the Skhul Cave have yielded a date of about 90,000 years BP, whereas a Neanderthal specimen from the Kebara Cave was found to be more recent—dating to about 60,000 years BP.

PALEOENVIRONMENT

A geological study conducted by W. Farrand and P. Goldberg established that the lowest layers in the cave (F–E) are composed of cross-bedded quartz sand, like the nearby *kurkar* ridges. The researchers agree that the sand in the cave came from the seashore, which was then much closer to the cave than at present. This implies that the sea level was higher then, and that this was a pluvial stage. Thus, during the Lower Paleolithic, the strip of coastal plain in front of the cave was greatly reduced. Recent work revealed that a gley was formed in the base layers of Tabun, indicating that ground water formed a pond. This, in turn, implies a very high sea level of the order of more than 50 m.

In the Middle Paleolithic conditions changed; indeed, in layer D, the proportion of sand decreases while that of silt and clay increases. The upper layers, C and B, contain very little sand, a fact interpreted as reflecting a retreat of the shoreline from the cave's entrance, due to a decline in sea level. The coastal plain in front of the cave expanded beyond its present boundaries, although it is unclear to what extent. This alternation of materials composing the cave's various layers is attributed to alterations of sea level.

The paleovegetation in the cave's vicinity was investigated by analyzing a small number of pollen samples obtained from the various layers. These suggest that at the time of deposition of the sandy layers, dry conditions prevailed in the region: vegetation was predominantly grassy and trees were scant.

The sinkhole.

The decrease in sand in layer D corresponds to an increase in humidity (the predominance of arboreal vegetation over grasses), whereas the composition of layers C and B indicates a gradual decrease in humidity. A comparison between the amounts of the remains of fallow deer (a forest species denoting humid conditions) and gazelle (a steppe species denoting dry conditions) suggests a somewhat different picture. This comparison, made by Garrod, demonstrates that dry conditions prevailed throughout the time span corresponding to layer F and most of layer E. Humidity was greatest during the period corresponding to the upper part of layer E, which was followed by a gradual increase in dryness. However, it should be noted that remains of forest

Lower Paleolithic living surface.

species—such as deer and fallow deer—as well as those of species living in proximity to water sources—such as hippopotamus, rhinoceros, and wild cattle—found throughout the fill, indicate that even in periods defined as dry there were, nevertheless, springs and swamps in the cave's vicinity.

Layer B is exceptional in that it yielded almost exclusively the remains of forest species, particularly fallow deer. This phenomenon had once been interpreted as reflecting a climatic change that brought about an unprecedented expansion of the forest. Today, however, there is general agreement with Jellinek's view that at the period corresponding to the upper part of layer C, the chimney at the rear of the cave opened up, which led to the abandonment of the cave. The opening of the chimney turned the cave into a natural trap and a killing site. The animals that fell or were driven into it naturally belonged to the species inhabiting the upper reaches of the Carmel Range, namely forest species. The hypothesis that the chimney opened up at this stage is supported by the fact that the soil composing layer B is typical terra rossa, probably washed into the cave through the chimney.

WIDTH/LENGTH RATIO OF FLAKES

Layers (Garrod)	*Layers (Jellinek)*	*Average*	*Median*	*Variance*	*Industry*
B, C	I	4.6	4.2	5.0	Late Mousterian
	II	4.5	4.1	5.0	
D	III–VIII	4.3	4.0	3.9	Early Mousterian
	IX	4.2	3.9	3.1	
	X	3.9	3.6	2.8	
	XI	3.4	3.1	2.7	Lower Paleolithic
E	XII	3.5	3.2	2.5	(Mugharan)
	XIII	3.5	3.2	2.3	
F?, G?	XIV	3.2	3.9	1.9	

D. A. E. Garrod and D. M. A. Bate, *The Stone Age of Mount Carmel* 1, Oxford 1937; T. D. McCown and A. Keith, *The Stone Age of Mount Carmel* 2, Oxford 1939; A. J. Jellinek, *IEJ* 19 (1969), 114; id., *International Quaternary Association, 8th Congress*, Paris 1969; id., *RB* 77 (1970), 377–378; id., (et al.), *Paléorient* 1 (1973), 151–183; id., *Problems in Prehistory: North Africa and the Levant* (eds. F. Wendorf and A. E. Marks), Dallas 1975, 297–316; id., *EI* 13 (1977), 87*–96*; id., *Préhistoire du Levant* (CNRS Colloque 598, eds. J. Cauvin and P. Sanlaville), Paris 1981, 265–280; id., *Science* 216 4553 (1982), 1369–1375; id., *The Transition from Early to Middle Palaeolithic and the Origin of Modern Man* (*BAR*/IS 151, ed. A. Ronen), Oxford 1982, 57–101; P. Goldberg, "Sedimentology, Stratigraphy and Palaeoclimatology of et-Tabun Cave, Mount Carmel, Israel" (Ph.D. diss., Univ. of Michigan 1973); id., *Mitekufat Ha'even* 21 (1988), 178*–179*; G. O. Rollefson, "A Quantitative and Qualitative Typological Analysis of Bifaces from the Tabun Excavations 1967–1972" (Ph.D. diss., Univ. of Arizona 1978; Ann Arbor 1981); P. M. Masters, *Transition from Lower to Middle Palaeolithic and the Origin of Modern Man: A Symposium*, Haifa 1980, 1–15; O. Bar-Yosef and N. Goren, *Pre-Acheulean and Acheulean Industries*, Xth UISPP Congress, Mexico City (eds. D. Clark and G. Isaac) 1981, 28–42; O. Bar-Yosef, *Histoire et Archéologie* 100 (1985), 50–54; H. L. Dibble, "Technological Strategies of Stone Tool Production at Tabun Cave (Israel)" (Ph.D. diss., Univ. of Arizona 1981); id., *L'Anthropologie* 91 (1987), 189–196; S. Payne and A. Garrard, *Journal of Archaeological Science* 10 (1983), 243–247; W. Boenigk et al., *Quatär* 35–36 (1985), 113–140; Y. Olami, *Prehistoric Carmel*, Jerusalem 1984; P. A. Bull and P. Goldberg, *Journal of Archaeological Science* 12 (1985), 177–185; A. Ronen, *Histoire et Archéologie* 100 (1985), 53; A.-M. Tillier et al., *Paléorient* 14/2 (1988), 130–136; Weippert 1988 (Ortsregister); M. Lamdan and A. Ronen, *People and Culture in Change* 1 (*BAR*/IS 508, ed. I. Hershkovitz), Oxford 1989, 29–36; R. Grün et al., *Journal of Human Evolution* 20 (1991), 231–248.

AVRAHAM RONEN

TAMAR, MEẒAD

IDENTIFICATION

Meẓad Tamar is a Roman-Byzantine fortress in the northern Negev Hills (map reference 1731.0485). The region was first settled in the Nabatean period, when it was a way station on the road from Moab and the plain of the Jordan River via Kurnub (Mampsis) to Beersheba and onward. A. Alt and many others identified the site, whose Arabic name is Qaṣr Juheiniya el-Fawqa, with Tamara (Θαμάρα), mentioned in such Roman-Byzantine sources as Ptolemy (V, 16, 8), the *Tabula Peutingeriana*, Eusebius' *Onomasticon* (8, 8), and the *Notitia Dignitatum* (XXXIV, 40). Y. Aharoni and M. Avi-Yonah identified Roman Tamara with 'En Ḥaẓeva (map reference 173.024). In the excavations conducted there, however, no finds from the Late Byzantine period were discovered. In this writer's opinion, geographical-historical considerations reinforce the theory that Meẓad Tamar should be identified with the fort of Tamara, as Alt maintained.

HISTORY

Road works and the development of a nearby quarry prevented the excavators from examining a subterranean oblong building, perhaps predating the fort, revealed in an aerial photograph. There is evidence, however, that Meẓad Tamar was already built in the Nabatean period and in 106 CE, when the Romans annexed the Nabatean state, they occupied Tamara along with other buildings and settlements in the area and held it until the time of Hadrian and possibly even later. The fortress was restored by Emperor Aurelian, as part of his reorganization of the Roman administration in the East, from 270 CE onward, in the wake of the revolt at Palmyra. Tamara continued to serve as a fortress until the Arab conquest.

The archaeological evidence attesting to the fort's Nabatean origin consists of unpainted Nabatean vessels found in the lowermost strata, as well as in the upper layers of refuse and ash that were heaped outside the southeastern wall. Large quantities of painted Nabatean sherds were also mixed into the lower layers of refuse and ash but were separated from the upper levels by a layer of sand.

The Roman annexation may have caused the disappearance of the painted Nabatean pottery, while the unpainted pottery remained in use by the new garrison. This attests to a possible continuity of service by Nabateans in the Negev forts. Former Nabatean forces were incorporated into the Roman army as the *cohortes Ulpiae Petraeorum*, an integral part of the Roman *auxilia*, from Trajan's time onward.

Similarly, the accumulation of the lower refuse layers outside the southeastern wall can be interpreted as part of the first "general cleanup" carried out after the Roman occupation in 106 CE; the upper layers of refuse can be understood as the result of the second thorough "house cleaning," during the renovation and restoration of the fortress in the last third of the third century CE. This period saw the erection of the watchtower at nearby Ẓafit (map reference 1683.0504), connected to the system of fortifications around Tamara. Ẓafit was erected in place of the Ef'e fort, which was connected to the

Meẓad Tamar: exterior view of the western wall and northwest tower.

Plan of the fortress, phase 1.

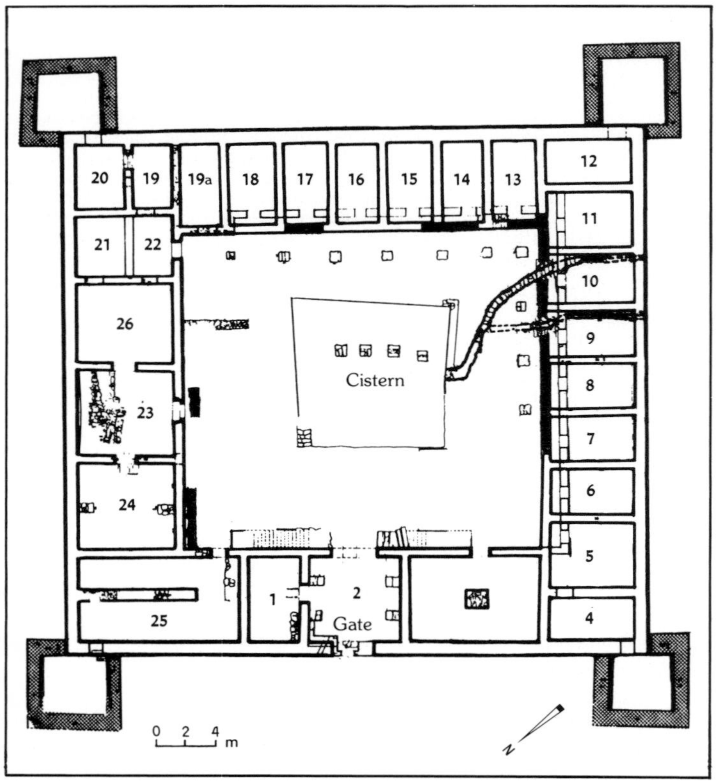

Plan of the fortress, phases 2–3.

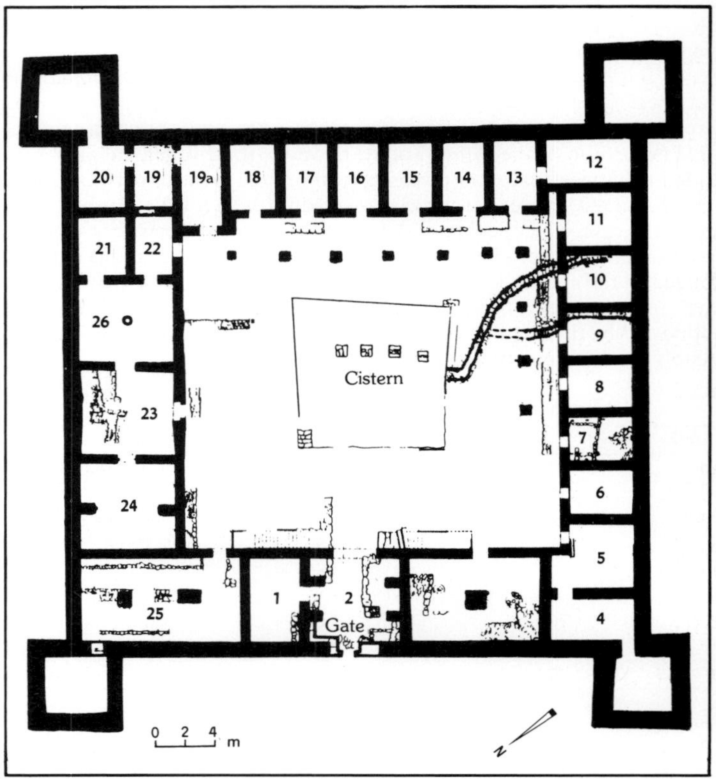

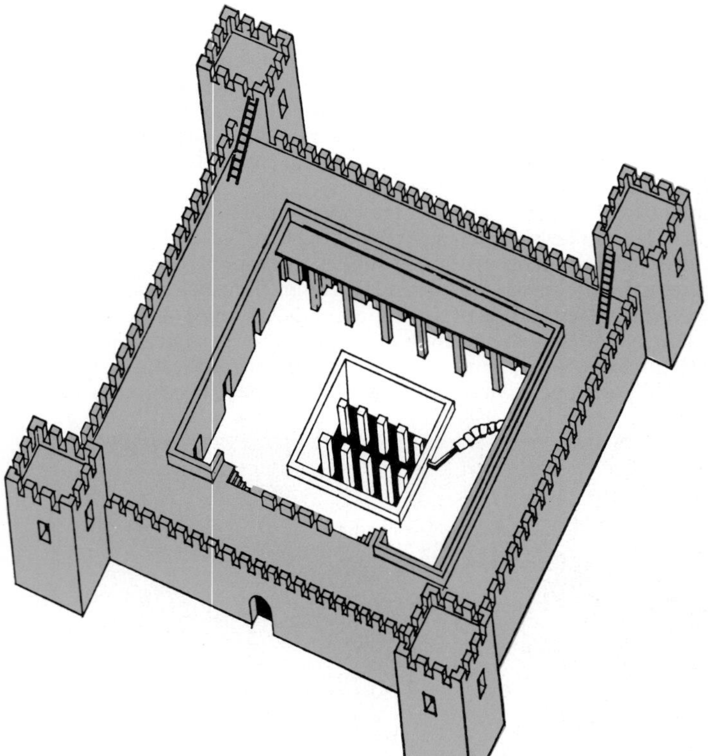

Meẓad Tamar: isometric reconstruction of the fortress. It was also possible to climb the towers from inside. The central cistern's roof does not appear in the drawing.

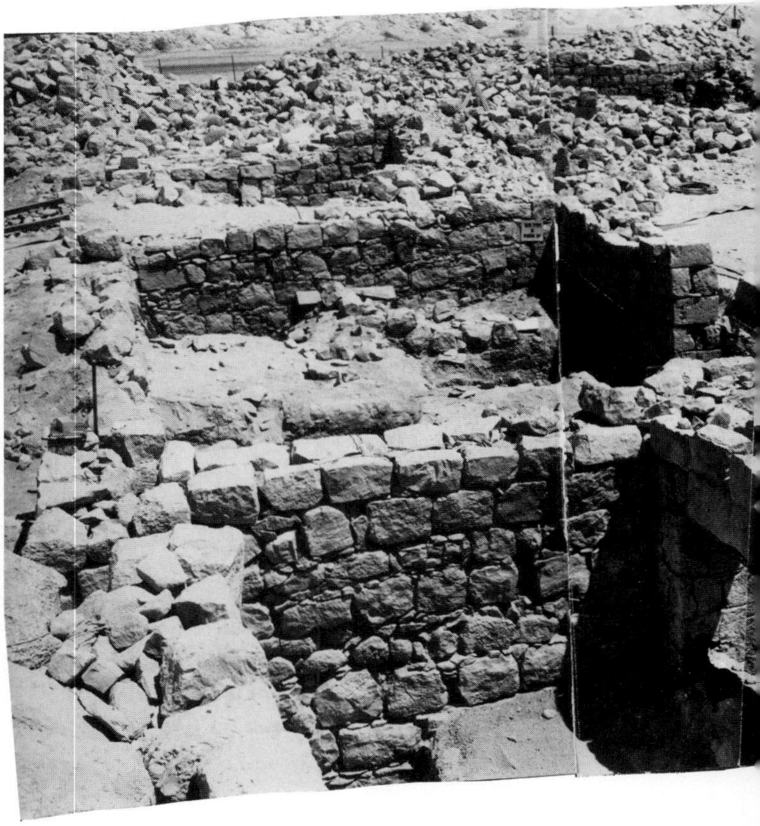

General view from the northwest tower: (right) barrack blocks; (left) officers' quarters; (back) bakery; (center) cistern.

Nabatean system of fortifications and was destroyed in about 106. Tamara was a link in the Late Roman and Byzantine *limes*. Its internal structures were completely rebuilt from the foundations up at least once, possibly in the wake of earthquakes that occasionally struck the area.

According to the list of Roman forces at the end of the fourth century (see above, *Notitia Dignitatum*), the *cohors I*(?) *Palaestinorum* was encamped at Tamara. In the fifth century, the regular forces became a militia (*limitanei*) and the fortress was given additional administrative duties. The fortress was hastily rebuilt to meet the Arab invasion. It was not destroyed after the Arab conquest, but fell into disrepair after the families of the *limitanei* who found shelter here gradually left or died out.

EXPLORATION

The remains of the fortress were first surveyed by F. Frank in 1932 and later examined by G. E. Kirk in 1937. Excavations were begun at the site in 1973, on behalf of Tel Aviv University, under the direction of M. Gichon, and continued from 1974 to 1976 (the last season was directed by M. Fischer).

EXCAVATION RESULTS

Tamara is a typical *tetrapyrgos* (τετραπύργος): a square fort (38 by 38 m), with four protruding corner towers (6 by 6 m), a single entrance, and internal structures built against the walls and arranged around an open central courtyard. In the center of the courtyard is a large cistern (see below). Four main phases can be distinguished:

Phase 1: Nabatean (first century BCE–first century CE) to Hadrianic times (second century CE).

Phase 2: last third of the third century CE to the second half of the fourth century(?) CE. This was the period in which the Nabatean-Early Roman structure was restored.

Phase 3: second half of the fourth century until the Persian conquest (614).

Phase 4: from the reconquest of Heraclius (c. 624) to the Arab conquest (c. 635).

The interior arrangements of the fort (*castellum*) did not change until the eve of the Persian conquest; the rebuilding of the inner structures at the beginning of phase 3 is similar to the plan of the preceding phase (except for minor changes in the buildings' size). On the southwest and southeast sides of the fortress were two barrack blocks (*strigae*). The northeast tract comprised the regimental shrine (*sacellum*) with adjacent side rooms that housed offices, together making up the unit headquarters (*principia*).

In the eastern corner, the commander's private quarters had direct access to the headquarters (*principia*). On the northwest side there was a guardroom adjacent to the gate (possibly only in phase 2). The rest of the space was used as a food storeroom (*horreum*) or an armory (*armamentarium*). Its roof rested on a series of beams supported by two broad pillars. Two partitions in this room, running parallel to the walls, created two long narrow racks, in which spears, javelins, and lances could be placed. West of the gate was a large bakery (*pistrinum*), containing ovens and large basalt millstones. Its roof was also supported by a central pillar. The flat roofs, which extended the rampart walls considerably, were reached by three stone-built staircases, two just inside the gate and one in the southern corner.

The exact number of section rooms (*contubernia*) could not be definitely established. There were probably six such rooms in each barrack. As at other contemporary military bases, the fort was planned so that it contained only the headquarters and housing for part of the full complement of soldiers from the unit stationed there; the rest were stationed in smaller outposts connected to the fortress.

Several of the rooms were plastered. The plaster in the *principia* and the commander's quarters was painted with geometric patterns. The barracks were 3.8 by 5.5 m, allowing each soldier about 2.1 sq m of living space in his *contubernium*, if each section contained ten soldiers.

The barracks in phase 2 were rebuilt on a reduced scale (only 3.8 by 4.5 m), but each was equipped with a *porticus* 3 m wide, built in front, and affording each *contubernium* a shaded space at its entrance. There are various indications that the number of soldiers in a squad decreased in this period, perhaps to only six.

Sometime during phase 3, some of the *contubernia* were converted into workshops or storerooms. The rebuilding carried out in phase 4 was crude. Several rooms in the northeast wing were partitioned into small dwellings. The headquarters' facade collapsed into the courtyard during an earthquake, and the mounds of rubble were not cleared away but stamped into the pavement. When it was rebuilt, the construction was coarser. The outer walls were built of ashlars in two faces, with a rubble core, like many other buildings of the period. The difference in the quality of construction in the various sections of the wall indicates that it was built by several groups of workers of varying skill. Short inscriptions in Greek, as yet undeciphered, were written in red on the stones before they were plastered; these apparently were written by the stonemasons or were instructions from the master builders.

The entire outer face of the wall was coated with a thin layer of shiny white

Interior of the northwest tower and the "seam" formed where it abuts the wall.

Passage from room 4 to room 5 in the officers' quarters along the southeast wall.

plaster. The main purpose of this coating may have been to protect the mud between the joints against erosion by fierce winter winds. The walls are 1.1 m thick, and their minimum height is estimated at 3.8 m, with the towers rising a minimum of 3 m above them. Access to the towers was gained by portable ladders that could be removed when necessary.

It is possible that the towers, which were leaning against the walls and not engaged, were a later addition. If so, the Nabatean structure lacked towers, like the fortress (way station?) at Moa, also in the Negev, and various buildings in Transjordan. The phase marked by their addition is probably the Roman renovation. All the towers are preserved to the height of the ledge (formed by narrowing the wall) that held the wooden beams of the upper story.

The gate also retained its initial plan throughout, but in the third phase, the width of its entrance was reduced from 2.8 m to 1 m. Its plan was that of a straight passage (6 by 6 m) that was narrowed by two pairs of opposing piers protruding about one meter into the gateway. Whether these were merely supports for the roof beams or also served fortification purposes and to check an enemy charge is not clear.

The fortress drew its water from a spring 2 km (1 mi.) away and from a reservoir for runoff water behind a dam in Naḥal Ẓafit (map reference 1698.0493); the reservoir is connected to the fort by a path for pack animals. To ensure a constant supply of water, the fort was erected at the lowest spot in the defile to which the rivulets of winter rains converged. Channels conveyed the water under the walls to the cistern (10 by 10 by 38 m) in the courtyard. The cistern was topped by a grid of wooden beams, on which limestone roof slabs rested, mainly to prevent evaporation. In drought years, the cistern was undoubtedly filled from external water sources. Additional cisterns alongside and outside the walls must have supplied water to the caravans and to guests who took shelter in the fort but who were not permitted to enter the military installation.

The fort, which does not command a good view of its surroundings, was defended by a series of towers built around it. The watchtower on the hilltop south of the fortress is preserved to a height of 3 m and measures 3.8 by 3.8 m. The ceramic evidence, beginning with Late Nabatean pottery, indicates that its history is contemporaneous with that of the fort's. In addition to the ninety builders' inscriptions mentioned above, two Greek inscriptions, engraved on stone slabs found in the debris from the gateway, were uncovered. Both are dedicatory inscriptions to the "Tyche of the Emperors" (Τύχη τῶν δεσπότων) and were written in the fifth or sixth century CE. Coins from all phases of the fort's existence were also found.

Identification: F. Frank, *ZDPV* 57 (1934), 257ff.; A. Alt, ibid. 58 (1935), 34ff.; Abel, *GP* 2, 181; G. E. Kirk, *PEQ* 70 (1938), 221–225; M. Noth, *ZDPV* 67 (1945), 45–71; Y. Aharoni, *IEJ* 13 (1963), 30–42.
Excavations: M. Gichon, *IEJ* 25 (1975), 176–177; 26 (1976), 188–194; id., *RB* 82 (1975), 275–276; id., *Saalburg-Jahrbuch* 33 (1976), 80–94; id., *Tamara (1973–1974), Vorbericht der Grabungen, Limes Studien (Bonner Jahrbücher*, Beiheft), Kevelaer 1976; id., *Studien zu den Militärgrenzen Roms* 2 (1977), 445–452; E. Erdmann, *Saalburg-Jahrbuch* 34 (1977), 96–146.

MORDECHAI GICHON

The phase 3 fortress's gate, looking northwest from the courtyard.

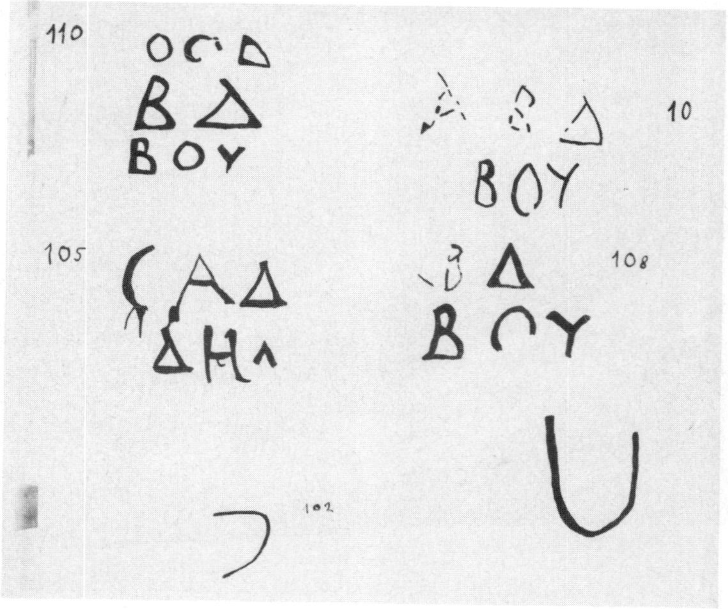

Red-painted inscriptions, on ashlar stones, that probably relate to the drafting or construction process.

TANNUR, KHIRBET ET-

IDENTIFICATION

Khirbet et-Tannur is situated on top of Jebel et-Tannur in Jordan (550 m above sea level, map reference 217.042). It is an isolated mountain between Wadi el-Ḥesa (Zared) and Wadi el-ʿAban. The site is approached from the southeast by a single path with ancient banking that is cut in the rock. It may also have had a flight of steps in its upper part. The top of Jebel et-Tannur is fairly flat. The temple, situated on the east side, is the only building on it.

EXCAVATIONS

In 1937, excavations were carried out at the site by a joint expedition of the American Schools of Oriental Research and the Jordan Department of Antiquities, under the direction of N. Glueck. Several outside rooms and walls remained unexcavated.

THE TEMPLE. An approach cut in the rock leads by way of broad steps to the gateway in the east wall of the temple's outer court. The walls flanking the entrance of the gate were adorned with an engaged column and a pilaster, topped with Nabatean capitals. The east (outer) court is square (15.6 sq m) and on the north and south had porticoes whose columns stood on podiums two steps high. Part of the court's paving on the east and west sides is preserved. Shallow channels leading from the northeast and southeast corners of the court drained the rainwater through apertures in the outer east wall. The floor slopes to the southeast. An altar stood on the court's north side near its east end; there may have been a ritual pool there, in an unpaved area.

The Sanctuary. The sanctuary was oriented to the east. It was approached by four steps that led to a gateway. The steps in the facade are flanked by engaged columns and corner pilasters. On each side of the gateway, between the column and pilaster, was a shallow niche. It was crowned by an architrave, surmounted by a pediment with a denticulated ornament. On the architraves three triglyphs are separated by two rosettes, and the whole is set between two female busts carved in relief. Over the main doorway was a bust of Atargatis, represented as the goddess of foliage and fruit. On her forehead, neck, and bosom are leafy decorations, which, however, do not conceal the features. Two side panels, which together with the centerpiece form a semicircular panel, are decorated with vine, leaf, and fruit (pomegranate and fig) motifs. A relief of a large eagle may have originally been above the head of the goddess. A pediment apparently topped the entire entablature. The walls of the sanctuary, with the exception of the eastern one, had two pilasters between corner pilasters. The engaged columns and pilasters have Attic bases that rest on solid stylobates. Their capitals, which were originally Nabatean, were replaced in a later period with Corinthian capitals. Near the east end of the south wall of the sanctuary was a doorway, probably used by the priests and temple servants.

Aerial view of Jebel et-Tannur and Khirbet et-Tannur at its summit.

The Inner Court. The sanctuary's inner court (10.38 by 9.72 m) was paved, but open to the sky. In its center stood an inner shrine (4 by 3.6 m) oriented almost exactly due east. A staircase on the west side of the shrine led to the presumably flat roof, on which an altar probably stood. The shrine's east facade was ornamented with pilasters with quarter columns. They were built of stone courses, four and possibly five of which were ornamented with busts in relief of Atargatis, either as the dolphin goddess or grain goddess. The bust of the dolphin goddess is carved on a soft white limestone block 36 cm wide, 27.8 cm high, and 34 cm thick. The head and body project from the front of the block. The wavy hair, which is covered with a headcloth, is parted in the middle, clasped on either side by a shell, and falls in two thick braids on either side of the face. Two strands of hair are plastered down each cheek. The groove between the full lips and the sunken areas around the eyeballs show clear traces of red paint. On the headdress two dolphins are realistically portrayed, with their mouths meeting. The entire bust is carved against the background of a shell. At the corners of the shrine's west (back) wall, two square pilasters support a large architrave decorated with rosettes, egg-and-dart motifs, and vine and leaf patterns.

The Inner Shrine. The inner shrine was built on top of an earlier one, which also had steps along its western side, two of which were preserved in situ. The upper four courses of the pilasters on the east facade of this earlier shrine are decorated with rosettes and vine patterns. On the third course of the northern pilaster, this decoration is replaced by a small niche (to hold lamps). The pilasters are set on Attic bases, and their capitals bear the thunderbolt motif. An architrave decorated with rosette designs and niches was set over an arch resting on the jambs of the pilasters. In the shallow niches below the arch, two cult reliefs were apparently set, one of the god Hadad and the other of Atargatis. Hadad was represented sitting. He is carved in almost three-quarter relief on a stone block (c. 1 m long and 45 cm wide). His body, which is disproportionally small (three-quarter length), measures 35 cm. The head, however, is life-size (29 cm long). The hair is waved and curled, and the beard and the ends of the flowing moustache are set in snail curls. The high-girdled chiton is fastened by a brooch at the neck. A fold of it is thrown over the left shoulder. Beneath the lower end of the fold appears the left hand, with the palm turned inward and upward and the fingers turned inward, grasping the right ear of a young bull. The top of the head seems to have been crowned by a low polos (cylindrical headdress). The forehead is low, with two hornlike (?) locks above its center. Around his neck the god wears a torque, the ends of which consist of lions' heads. Attached to the fold of the chiton over the left shoulder is a thunderbolt, which runs from above the left elbow to the palm of

Plan of the Nabatean temple.

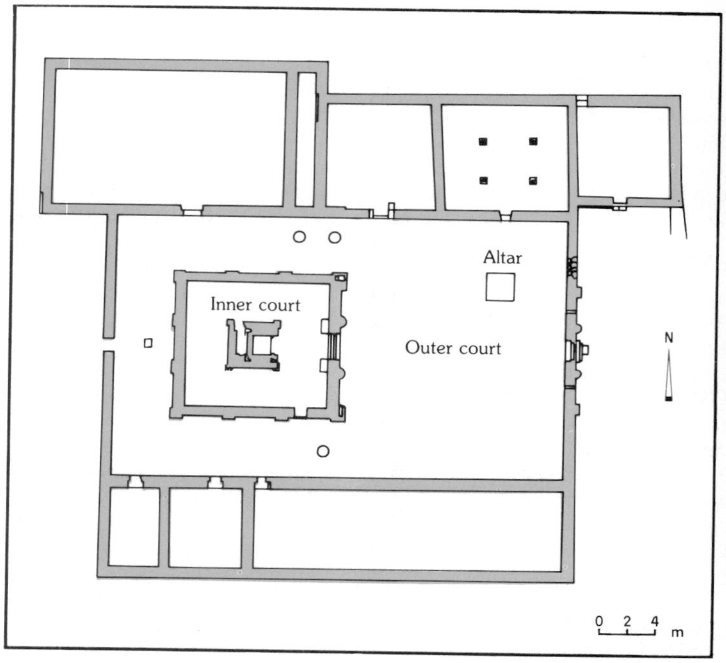

General view of the Nabatean temple.

Relief of Atargatis as a goddess of foliage and fruit.

the hand, its arrowhead pointing toward the head of the young bull. The bull was represented with its two forelegs free of the slab. Its horns are small, and its head realistically portrayed. A small lion's head, part of its body, and a single foot with traces of its mate are indications that a relief of Atargatis was carved beside that of Hadad. On top of the earlier shrine there was also an altar, most of whose remains have been recovered—among them four corner pilasters with tiny female heads ornamenting the tops. It is possible that this altar and the Hadad and Atargatis reliefs were reused in the later shrine.

The Second Shrine. The second shrine was built around a smaller, cruder one, which had been the site's original shrine and the nucleus around which the entire temple complex arose.

In front of the shrine's eastern pilasters are two small subterranean cham-

Relief of Tyche in the center of a zodiac.

bers. They were covered by paving blocks, one of them found in situ, that could be lifted by inserting a finger or a hook in the center of the outside edge of each. A similar concealed chamber was found in the rear of the shrine. These chambers were evidently receptacles for the remains of offerings, for their contents consisted of ashes, charred animal bones, and grains of wheat.

On the north and south sides of the inner temple area and the outer court is a series of well-paved rooms. A high, benchlike platform runs along three sides of each room. The roofs of these chambers were supported by square pillars, each course of which was composed of three triangular stones. The chambers may have served as lodgings and dining rooms for priests and pilgrims. Outside the west wall of the inner temple area, an altar with a thunderbolt motif was found in situ.

The Sculptured Objects. The sculptured objects found during the excavations include a large, crude head of Hadad, revealing Hellenistic-Parthian influence, and a stone water basin, on the front of which a lion is realistically carved in high relief, with its mouth as the waterspout. A winged Victory (Nike), which was found after the excavations and belongs to the zodiac described below, has the right upper arm raised horizontally at shoulder level. The upper part of the left arm is also held horizontally at shoulder level, while the forearm (the right one is missing) is raised perpendicularly above the elbow, with the hand and fingers supporting the zodiac above the goddess's head. In the center of the zodiac is a relief of Tyche. On her head she wears a mural crown covered with a hood. To the right of her head a crescent moon is carved, with a scepterlike symbol to the left. The latter is composed of a torch bound with a wand that ends in a broken crescent moon. Encircling this outer relief is a panel containing the figures of the zodiac, counterclockwise from the top center: Aries, represented by a Minervalike(?) figure; Taurus; Gemini; Cancer; Leo; Virgo carrying a sheaf. Clockwise from the right top to the center are Libra; Scorpio; Sagittarius; Capricorn; Aquarius, with his bucket upside down; and a fragment discovered after the close of the excavations. The order of the signs suggests that one new year began with the spring and another new year began with autumn. Several fragments of a winged Tyche carrying a cornucopia, aloft in each hand, were also found, as was an almost intact incense altar with a relief of Hadad in its central panel and reliefs of winged Victories on the two side panels. On the altar a Greek dedicatory inscription reads: [ΑΛΕΞ] ΑΝΔΡΟΣ ΑΜΡΟΥ.

The Pottery. Pottery found included rouletted ware, sherds of terra sigillata of the Pergamene type, and fine eggshell-like Nabatean sherds. The last are definitely associated with the earlier levels on the site.

SUMMARY

The excavators distinguished three building phases at the site. The first is dated to the first century BCE. The second can apparently be dated by a Nabatean inscription to the second regnal year of Aretas IV (7 BCE). W. F. Albright has suggested, however, that the stone was originally part of a nymphaeum at the source and was later used in building or repairing the temple. The last phase, which includes most of the sculptures, is dated to the beginning of the second century CE. The temple was probably destroyed by an earthquake then, after which the site was abandoned briefly. During the Byzantine period it was occupied sporadically by squatters.

The Art. The art of Khirbet et-Tannur is evidence of the swift development of Nabatean civilization, especially between the second century BCE and the second century CE, when Nabatea was incorporated by Trajan (in 106–107 CE) into his *Provincia Arabia*. The influence of this art is subsequently seen in the Byzantine art of the Negev, in Egypt's Coptic art, and in Umayyad art, as

Hadad-Zeus in the form of an eagle holding a serpent.

Relief of a female head with acanthus leaves.

Two representations of Atargatis: ***(left)*** *as a grain goddess;* ***(center and right)*** *as a dolphin goddess.*

Hadad-Zeus seated on a throne and grasping a young bull.

Male head.

Altar with the name of its donor: Mty''l.

Altar: (right) figure of Zeus-Hadad; (left) winged Victory; (above) a Greek dedicatory inscription.

at Khirbet el-Mafjar in the Jordan Valley and Qaṣr el-Heir in Syria. The art and architecture of the Nabateans were distinctive, but they nevertheless had much in common with their Syrian, Parthian, Arabian, Egyptian, and Mediterranean neighbors. An entire pantheon of Nabatean deities was discovered at et-Tannur, with Atargatis their main deity. She appears as a dolphin goddess, the goddess of vegetation and grain, or as a tutelary divinity. Thunderbolt-carrying Zeus-Hadad was her consort. The deification of the seven planets characterized the Nabateans' theological system. Theirs was a fertility religion whose cultic details they adopted from the Hellenistic civilizations with which they came in contact, but whose essential character was predominantly Semitic.

N. Glueck, *AJA* 41 (1937), 361–376; id., *BASOR* 65 (1937), 15–19; 67 (1937), 6–16; 69 (1938), 7–18; 85 (1942), 3–8; 126 (1952), 5–10; 141 (1956), 22–23; id., *EI* 7 (1964), 40*–43*; 8 (1967), 37*–41*; id., *Deities and Dolphins*, New York 1965; id., *Die Nabataär* (ed. H. J. Kellner), Munich 1970, 31–34; R. Savignac, *RB* 46 (1937), 401–416; id. (and J. Starcky), ibid. 64 (1957), 215–217; P. Thomsen, *Archiv für Orientforschung* 12 (1937–1939), 93, 184–185; M. Avi-Yonah, *QDAP* 10 (1944), 114–118; id., *Oriental Art in Roman Palestine*, Rome 1961, 49–50; J. Starcky, *RB* 75 (1968), 206–235; R. D. Barnett, *NEAT*, 327–330; A. Negev, *PEQ* 106 (1974), 77–78; *American Archaeology in the Mideast*, 98, 107; J. S. McKenzie, *PEQ* 120 (1988), 81–107.

NELSON GLUECK

Khirbet et-Tannur: floral relief.

TAWILAN

IDENTIFICATION AND EXPLORATION

Tawilan is a village in Jordan in the hills to the north of Petra, above 'Ain Musa (map reference 197.971). To the west it overlooks the much larger village of el-Ji, through which visitors pass on their way to Petra. The area is intensely cultivated, even though it is about 1,400 m above sea level. Cultivation is facilitated by Tawilan's proximity to the perennial spring of 'Ain Musa, from which water is piped to the fields and orchards. These form a series of descending terraces to the north and west, down to 'Ain Musa and el-Ji. Jebel Heidan rises above Tawilan to the northeast; it is cut off from the range of hills to the north by Wadi el-Mugr and 'Ain et-Tini. The ancient site is situated on a terrace at the western foot of Jebel Heidan. In every area across the site there is a thick deposit of sterile clay above the very soft friable limestone bedrock.

N. Glueck, in his survey of Transjordan, at first proposed to identify Tawilan with biblical Bozrah, the capital of Edom. Later, though, he changed his mind and accepted the equation of Bozrah with modern Buṣeirah. He then proposed to identify Tawilan with biblical Teman, in his view one of the most important Edomite centers. The excavations by C.-M. Bennett (see below) did nothing to substantiate the equation of Tawilan with biblical Teman. After the excavations had begun, R. de Vaux argued persuasively against the identification, and Bennett accepted his view. Glueck's identification had been based largely on the text of Amos 1:12, which mentions Bozrah and Teman, suggesting the north and south of Edom. Because Bozrah is likely to be modern Buṣeirah in the north, the relative position of Teman is thus indicated in the south. Teman therefore fitted Tawilan. De Vaux showed that in the Amos passage (1:12), Teman is in a position parallel to "Moab" in Amos 2:2. This suggests that Teman does not refer to a town at all but is synonymous with Edom (although in other texts it can sometimes mean a particular region of Edom—the "south"). The ancient name of Tawilan thus remains unknown.

N. Glueck first surveyed Tawilan and suggested it was a very important

Tawilan: general view of the site.

Tawilan: plan of the excavations.

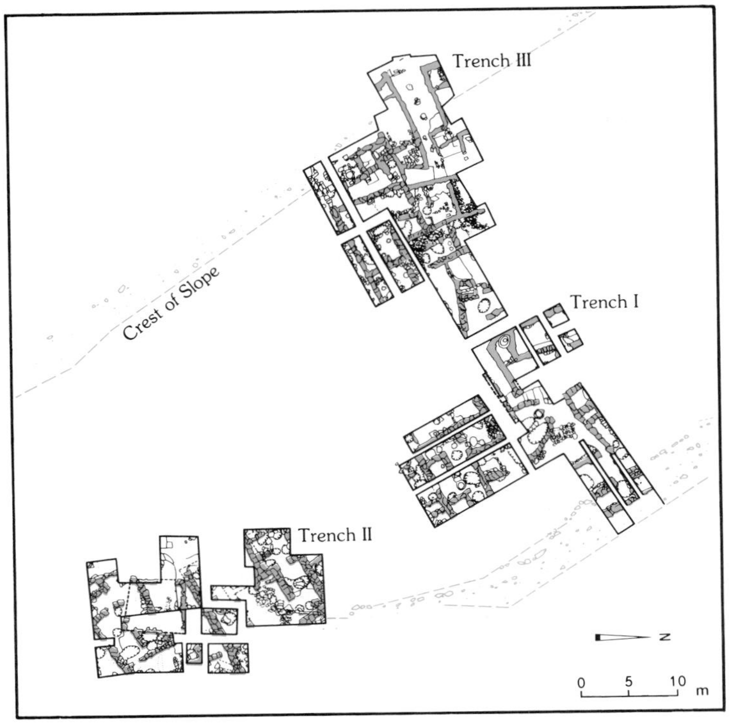

Edomite site in the thirteenth to sixth centuries BCE. He identified a possible outer wall and a "conjectural" inner wall terminating in a northwestern and southern "tower."

EXCAVATIONS

C.-M. Bennett excavated at Tawilan for four seasons from 1968 to 1970 and in 1982, at first on behalf of the British School of Archaeology in Jerusalem and later for the British Institute at 'Amman for Archaeology and History. There were two main reasons why Bennett excavated at Tawilan: Glueck's view that Tawilan was a very important Edomite site and his identification of it as biblical Teman.

The original objective of most of Bennett's trenches was to ascertain the validity of Glueck's identifications. None stood up to scrutiny. Three main areas were excavated, together with three small test trenches. Two of the test trenches were laid across the "outer wall"—area IV in the southeast and area VI in the northwest. Results showed that the wall consisted of one course only, standing within levels containing exclusively Nabatean and Roman sherds from the first and second centuries CE. Clearly, therefore, Glueck's outer wall was a field boundary wall, not earlier than the first century CE, and more likely to be twentieth century.

Area I ran across the highest point of Glueck's conjectural inner rampart. The results of the excavations showed that this was not a defensive wall, but a series of Iron Age house walls and domestic pits. Area V was laid across his so-called north tower. It proved to be an odd feature, clearly nondefensive. It consisted of a large rock outcrop enclosed by two concentric lines of stones. From the associated pottery, it obviously belonged to a period no earlier than medieval. Area II was laid across Glueck's "southern tower." Excavations revealed foundation courses of a square stone structure, but no floor surfaces or installations of any kind. The walls were cut into rubble deposits dating to the Mameluke period, but by how long the building postdated this period it is impossible to judge.

THE EDOMITE TOWN. Bennett's excavations revealed an unfortified Edomite town, essentially agricultural, with the major occupation in the seventh century BCE:

Impression of stamp seal with emblems of the moon god Sin and the goddess Ishtar, Late Iron Age.

Stage 1. A series of pits had been dug into the natural clay in all three main areas (I–III), not associated with any surfaces or dwellings. The pits were probably for extracting clay for pottery or building purposes, such as leveling.
Stage 2. A stone and clay fill was brought in to level the uneven ground for building walls. Rectangular buildings with dry-stone walls were constructed on a northeast–southwest axis in all three main areas; pillars were built in areas II and III.
Stage 3. Minor architectural additions were made—for example, walls were set between the pillars in areas II and III.
Stage 4. Major architectural additions were made—in area III steps were built to higher levels, and in area II a building of inferior construction and no centralized plan was erected.
Stage 5. There is evidence of fire or destruction in all three main areas. Squatters occupied some of area III, but there was collapse and abandonment in the other areas.

Stages 1 to 5 can all be dated within the Iron Age II, probably to the seventh to sixth centuries BCE.
Stage 6. The evidence is of abandonment and accumulation. Area II was reused as a cemetery, possibly in the first and second centuries CE.
Stage 7. A rough field or terrace wall was constructed in area II in the Mameluke period.
Stage 8. A square structure (Glueck's "tower") was built in area II; it is Mameluke or later.

FINDS. A sizable assemblage of painted "Edomite" pottery, dating to the eighth to sixth centuries BCE, was uncovered at Tawilan. Another important find was a seal depicting an altar and a star and crescent (emblems of the moon god Sin and the goddess Ishtar).

The first cuneiform tablet ever found in Jordan was recovered in the 1982 season. It is a legal document concerning the disputed sale of livestock, drawn up in Harran in the accession year of one of the Achaemenid kings named Darius. Also in 1982 Jordan's first large group of gold jewelry was found. It dates to the late sixth and fifth centuries BCE, although some pieces date to the ninth century BCE.

W. J. Phythian-Adams, *PEQ* 66 (1934), 186; N. Glueck, *BASOR* 55 (1934), 3–21; id., *AASOR* 15 (1935), 82–83, 177; C-M. Bennett, *ADAJ* 12–13 (1967–1968), 53–55; id., *RB* 76 (1969), 386–390; 77 (1970), 371–374; id., *Levant* 3 (1971), V–VII; 16 (1984), 1–23; id., *LA* 32 (1982), 482–487; id. (and P. Bienkowski), *Excavations at Tawilan, Southern Jordan* (in prep.); R. de Vaux, *RB* 76 (1969), 379–385; M. F. Oakeshott, *Midian, Moab and Edom* (eds. J. F. A. Sawyer and D. J. A. Clines), Sheffield 1983, 53–63; M. W. Stolper, *JNES* 43 (1984), 299–310; D. Homès-Fredericq and H. J. Franken, *Pottery and Potters, Past and Present: 7000 Years of Ceramic Art in Jordan*, Tübingen 1986, 170; F. Zayadine, *La Voie royale: 9000 ans d'art au royaume de Jordanie*, Paris 1986, 150–151; id., *Der Königsweg: 9000 Jahre Kunst und Kultur in Jordanien und Palästina*, Mainz am Rhein 1987, 178–179; F. Joannès, *Revue d'Assyriologie* 81 (1987), 165–166; P. Bienkowski, *Levant* 22 (1990), 91–109; id., *Aram* 2 (1990), 35–44.

PIOTR BIENKOWSKI

TEL 'AMAL

IDENTIFICATION

The site of Tel 'Amal lies in the Ḥarod Valley, about 3 km (2 mi.) west of Beth-Shean, within the confines of the Gan ha-Shelosha park. The ancient settlement (map reference 193.212) was founded on a low hill, near Naḥal 'Amal (Wadi 'Asi). It covers an area of about 0.75 a. and is divided in two by a depression. The western part, in which soundings were conducted by N. Zori in 1958, covers 0.5 a. and the eastern part 0.25 a. In these excavations five strata were uncovered, dating to the Iron Age II and the Persian, Byzantine and Early Arab periods (two strata from the latter). In 1962, when the Museum for Mediterranean Archaeology was founded on the eastern hill, a salvage excavation lasting for five seasons (1962–1966) was carried out here on behalf of the Israel Department of Antiquities and Museums. The first two seasons were directed by S. Levi and the last three by G. Edelstein with the participation of A. Druks. When the museum was enlarged in 1983, another two seasons of excavations were undertaken, with another in 1985, all directed by N. Feig on behalf of the Israel Department of Antiquities and Museums. Five occupation strata were identified. They had been substantially damaged by graves dug 1 to 2 m into them on the eastern side of the site in the medieval period.

EARLY BRONZE AGE IV: STRATUM V. Some Early Bronze Age IV rock-

Tel 'Amal: general view.

cut cupmarks and tombs were uncovered, including a single shaft tomb, cleared in 1962, containing several storage jars with typical combed decoration. Another burial compound from this period was unearthed in 1983; it consisted of four shaft tombs interconnected by low, narrow passages. Eight more shaft tombs were excavated in 1985. The burial chambers contained the bones of the deceased with many pottery vessels alongside—storage jars, "teapots," jugs, and juglets, some burnished and some white-slipped and decorated with reddish-brown stripes. This decoration is characteristic of the pottery produced in the Beth-Shean Valley.

IRON AGE IIA: STRATA IV–III. The structures dating from the Iron Age IIA (tenth century BCE) were largely destroyed by the medieval tombs and the digging of the museum's foundations, but the preserved parts yielded many finds, including pottery, stone vessels, and iron and bone tools. The remains of the two strata lie close to each other, and in some cases the foundations of the stratum III walls are laid directly above those of stratum IV. Some rooms were used in both phases. The foundations are built of one or two courses of field stones, overlaid by two courses of mud bricks. In some places, walls with four or five courses of bricks were found. The walls are thickly plastered on the inside. Both settlements were destroyed by fire that left a considerable amount of ash on the floors. The pottery vessels were also charred. The walls best preserved were those whose plaster and mud bricks had been hardened by the fire's high temperatures. A long room (3 by 6 or 4 by 8 m) opening onto other, smaller rooms was found in most of the partially excavated structures. Some rooms contained ovens and installations, such as basalt grinding stones on a mud-brick base, which abutted the walls.

Workshops. The long rooms in strata IV–III contained stone and clay installations, clay ovens, and basins, indicating that they were used for weaving and dyeing. Rows of pyriform stone and baked-clay loom weights were found, perforated at the top. Groups of weights of different sizes were found in some of the rooms, indicating that a variety of fabrics was produced by different looms. On the workshop floors many pottery vessels—some whole—including cooking pots, jugs, juglets, and storage jars were found leaning against the walls.

Cultic Structure. In stratum III an almost completely ruined structure (c. 225 sq m in area) was found. It is separated from the workshop to its east by a street made of beaten earth and gravel. The entrance to the structure was on the east and led to a courtyard with a partially preserved stone pavement. In one of the rooms two brick basins filled with ash were found. One contained a stone incense burner topped by a Phoenician-style bowl. A fragment of a similarly decorated stone bowl was also found in the room. Many pottery vessels, including jugs and juglets, both slipped and burnished, as well as chalices and storage jars, were found on the floors. Charred cereal grains were found in one jar. This structure seems to have been a cultic place.

Finds. The pottery from these strata differ in shape and design: those from the earlier stratum (IV) are individually designed, whereas those from the later stratum (III) are uniform in shape and size, indicating mass production. The decorated jugs belong to the Cypro-Phoenician tradition; some of the bowls and juglets were imported from Cyprus. One of the stratum IV storage jars bears three Hebrew letters on the shoulder: נמש. A. Lemaire considers this to be a personal name, similar to that of King Jehu's father, Nimshi.

IRON AGE IIB–C: STRATA II–I. Only isolated remains of foundations and

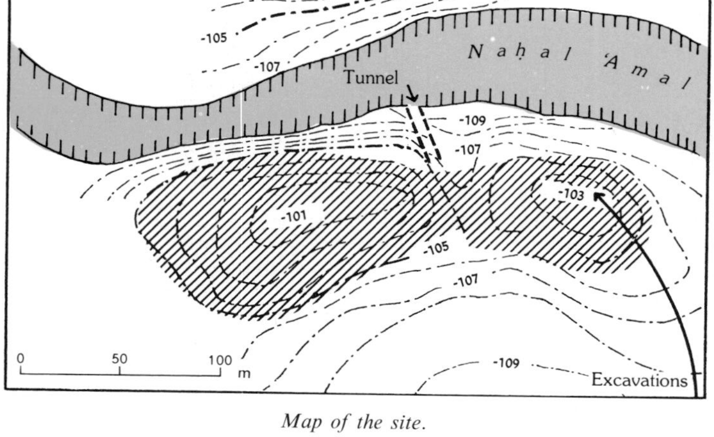

Map of the site.

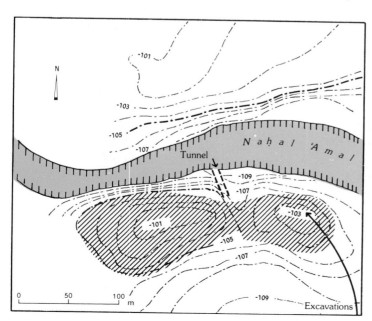

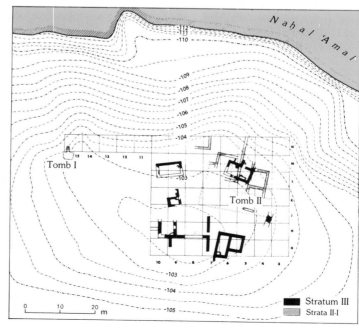

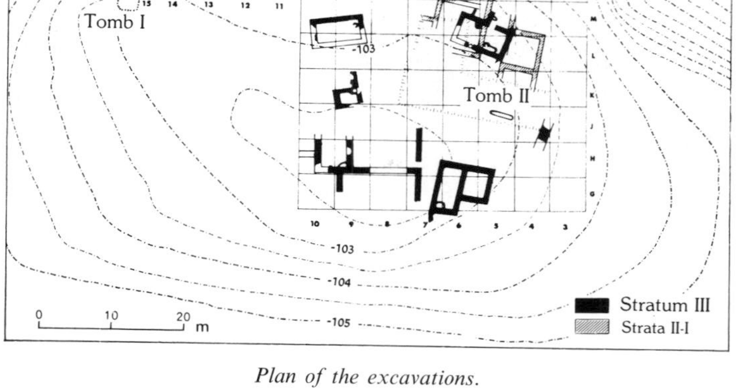

Plan of the excavations.

Pottery vessels from the EB IV tombs.

Chalices and incense burner, Iron IIA.

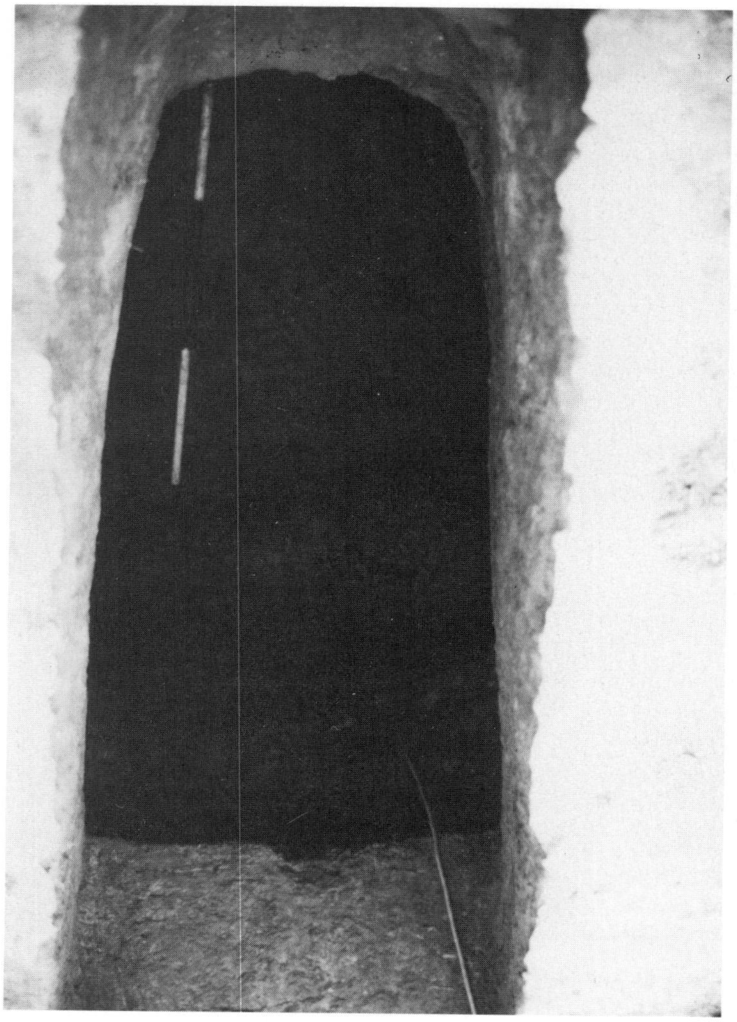

The rolling stone in situ at the entrance to shaft I, EB IV.

Four shaft tombs in the burial compound from the EB IV.

floors with a few sherds were found from the latest strata. A paved area, probably a courtyard, was found in stratum II; it contained two installations—a clay oven and an installation probably used for kneading dough. The sherds found on this floor come from household vessels—storage jars, cooking pots, jugs, and large and small bowls. Judging from the finds, strata II–I should be dated to the eighth and seventh centuries BCE. Between strata II and I lies a sterile layer, indicating a settlement gap. The site may have been used as a cemetery then, as four tombs were found dug into stratum III. A jug, a decanter, and three Assyrian-style *amphoriskoi* were deposited in each of them.

G. Edelstein, *RB* 75 (1968), 395–396; S. Levy and G. Edelstein, ibid. 79 (1972), 325–365; A. Lemaire, ibid. 80 (1973), 559; S. Kunath, *Bericht über Archäologische Oberflachenbeobachtungen und-Funde in Nir David*, n.p. 1978; id., *Biblische Notizen* 38–39 (1987), 50–52; N. Feig, *ESI* 2 (1983), 1; 4 (1985), 3; id., *IEJ* 33 (1983), 264; 36 (1986), 101; id., *'Atiqot* 20 (1991), 119–128; Weippert 1988, 477, 497, 647; Y. Goren, *'Atiqot* 20 (1991), 129–130.

GERSHON EDELSTEIN, NURIT FEIG

Pottery vessels, Iron IIA.

TEL AVIV

IDENTIFICATION AND EXPLORATION

The archaeological survey conducted by J. Kaplan in 1950, in the Yarkon Plain and in the range of hills to its south (today within the city of Tel Aviv), revealed many previously unknown sites. Soon after the completion of the survey, Kaplan began a systematic excavation of these and other sites discovered in Tel Aviv and in the adjoining urban areas of Bene-Berak, Ramat Gan, Giv'atayim, and Bat Yam. Excavations continued for more than thirty-five years, yielding finds dating from the fifth millennium BCE onward.

NEOLITHIC, CHALCOLITHIC, AND EARLY BRONZE AGE SITES

HA-BASHAN STREET. Ha-Bashan Street is located 500 m from the south bank of the Yarkon River, along the rising ground on the eastern part of Bodenheimer Street, between Pinkas (formerly ha-Bashan) and Louis Marshall streets. In three seasons of excavations (1950–1952) three occupation layers were exposed, none with architectural remains. The earliest occupation layer (III), lying above the alluvial virgin soil, belongs to the Neolithic period. Its pottery is identical with that of the Yarmukian culture discovered at Sha'ar ha-Golan (q.v.). The remains of occupation included a thin layer of whitish, ashy soil, as well as pits and depressions in the virgin soil. This occupation layer contained potsherds, animal bones, and flint implements. At the bottom of one of the pits a human burial in a flexed position was covered by a few stones and ringed by a circle of stones and two large Yarmukian sherds. In another pit fragments of a large burnished bowl with small, triangular-shaped ledge handles were found. A pile of stones in a shallow depression showed signs of burning in its upper part; it yielded bones, burned animal horns, fragmentary clay fertility figurines, and polished *kurkar* statuettes. This stone pile was apparently a cultic site. One of the clay figurines—its lower part was missing—had a mask covering the face, similar to figurines found at Sha'ar ha-Golan and Ḥorvat Minḥa (q.v.).

The pottery included all of the types from the Sha'ar ha-Golan repertoire, including vessels decorated with a herringbone design between red-painted incised lines. The zigzag lines of the herringbone decoration surrounded the body of the vessel, and a horizontal band passed round its neck. Alongside typical Yarmukian objects, there was also a number of Pre-Pottery Neolithic flints. It may thus be assumed that long before the arrival of the Yarmukian people, this had been a temporary camp site (Pre-Pottery Neolithic B).

Above layer III was a strip of ashy earth (layer II) containing potsherds, a small number of flints and animal bones, and baked-clay loom weights. The remains belonged to the Chalcolithic period. Its pottery is virtually identical with the pottery uncovered by J. Garstang in stratum VIII at Jericho, except for the black-burnished ware, which is absent there. The same Chalcolithic assemblage was also found in larger quantities on the south bank of Wadi

Map of the main sites in the Tel Aviv area.

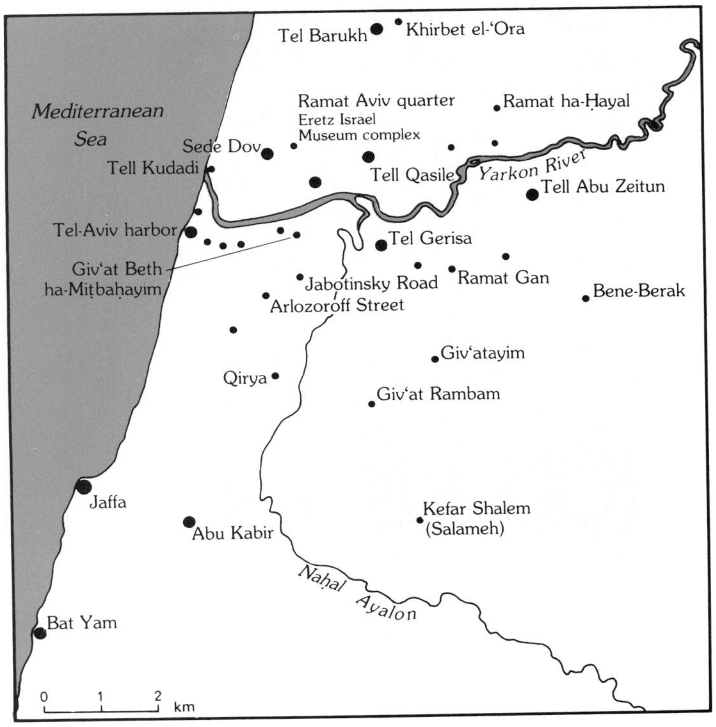

Pinkas Street: shaft tomb, MB I.

Ha-Bashan Street: fertility figurine, Neolithic period.

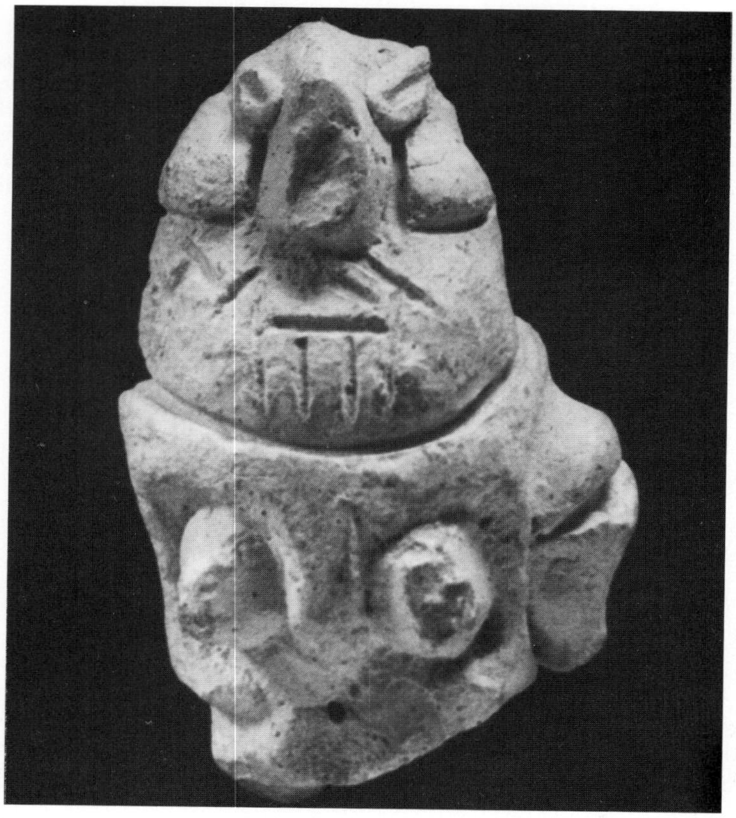

Jabotinsky Street: Chalcolithic churn.

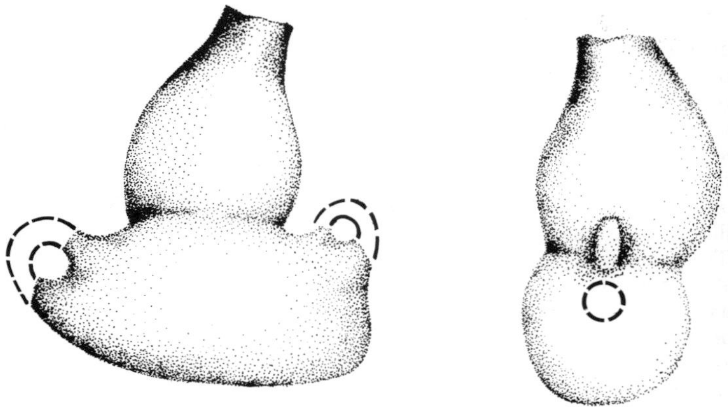

Rabah; it has been named the Wadi Rabah culture by this writer. Layer I (above layer II) dates to the Early Bronze Age IB. Here, too, the finds included numerous potsherds, flint implements, animal bones, and baked-clay loom weights.

Summary. The discovery of the Yarmukian site here implies that the Yarmukian culture was distributed throughout the country. The material from this second site facilitated the identification of the characteristic Yarmukian objects. The most important discovery at ha-Bashan Street, however, was stratigraphic. It placed the Wadi Rabah culture (a kind of prototype of Jericho VIII) later than the Yarmukian.

BODENHEIMER STREET. Excavations were carried out on Bodenheimer Street by H. Ritter-Kaplan from March to June 1979, after the house at number 8 was demolished and the ground cleared for new construction. The excavations revealed that human occupation at the site apparently dated to the Epipaleolithic period, the Proto-Neolithic and Pre-Pottery Neolithic periods (the seventh millennium), the Pottery Neolithic and the Early Bronze Age I. The oldest construction in the area—the stone foundation of a wall—belongs to the Pre-Pottery Neolithic B period. At the northeast corner of the site—in squares 1, 2, and 4—the sequence of the occupation was uncovered; at the southeast corner were a few Early Bronze Age IB remains. The pottery of the Neolithic period is represented by Yarmukian pits, and above them an occupation layer of the Wadi Rabah culture. Among the small number of flints found in the Pre-Pottery Neolithic strata were a few arrowheads. Apart from sickle blades, few flint implements were found. On the other hand, a very large number of rounded, elongated, or elliptical lumps and balls of baked clay were unearthed, in many cases broken and mixed in the rubble of the stratified floors. Many consisted of a stone core covered with a mantle of baked clay. They were generally grooved, sometimes in one direction only, and sometimes cross-hatched. The scarcity of agricultural implements and the numerous bones of wild animals seem to indicate that the inhabitants of the site were mainly hunters and gatherers who had settled in this particular area because of its abundant game. The many "balls" of baked clay (average weight, 500 g) might have been bolas, whose grooves held the thongs or cords to which they were tied. The hunter would twirl and throw the bola at the legs of a fleeing animal, which was stopped in its tracks by the ball-weighted cords that twisted around its legs. The preliminary findings indicate that many bones were of *Bos taurus* and *Sus scrota*, characteristic of swampy areas. Among other bones were those of *Gazella gazella* and of a hippopotamus. It has not been possible to determine whether the sheep and goat bones were wild or domesticated varieties.

JABOTINSKY STREET. The site on Jabotinsky Street is on a commanding *kurkar* hill about 1 km (0.6 mi.) west of Naḥal Ayalon. In 1950–1951 and in 1961, three seasons of excavations were conducted here. Although the major part of the site had been destroyed by *kurkar* quarrying, excavations in the remainder yielded abundant material. On the east side of the quarry, three shelter pits were cleared (the largest was 2 m in diameter and 1.5 m deep); north of them was a beaten clay floor, perhaps of a tent or hut. The pits contained a large quantity of ash, potsherds, flints, and animal bones. One of the pits yielded the second complete example known then of a type of pottery vessel previously found only in a fragmentary state at several Ghassulian sites. In the excavator's view, these vessels were used for churning, and he therefore suggested calling them churns. A number of grinding stones lay face down around the site.

In 1961, excavations were resumed after two shaft pits (diameter, 0.9 m) filled with ash, potsherds, flints, and animal bones were discovered at the western edge of the site. Work in the first pit was stopped at a depth of 11 m, and in the second pit at a depth of 20 m. The finds indicated that the lowest part had probably been a burial cave; due to the cave's great depth, the bottom could not be reached.

Pottery. The pottery from the site is Ghassulian and includes many examples of this ware's rich repertoire of shapes and decorations. The characteristic bowl is shaped like a flowerpot. Also found were hole-mouth jars, jugs, pithoi, horn-shaped beakers, "egg-cups," and perforated and knobbed handles. Decorations are impressed, incised or thumb indentations, nail slashes, short oblique lines, and applied thumb-indented bands. The bases often bear mat impressions. Painted decorations are also present. Rims and occasionally other parts of the vessel are colored red, dark red, or violet.

Other Finds. The flint material included axes, adzes, sickle blades, blades and bladelets, scrapers, and lithic-industry waste. The bone material pointed to sheep and cattle raising. It also included the bones of animals hunted in the Ayalon and Yarkon valleys.

Conclusions. The excavations on Jabotinsky Street indicated that the site had been used as a temporary station by a Ghassulian clan in its seasonal wanderings after grazing its cattle and sheep.

HA-MASGER STREET. The site is located near the west bank of Naḥal Ayalon. During excavations conducted by H. Ritter-Kaplan in 1980, two pits dug in the *kurkar* were exposed. The first was a habitation shelter pit; the diameter of its lower part was 2.5 to 3 m and its depth (below surface level) was about 2.45 m. The second pit was apparently a granary (lowest diameter, c. 2.4 m; depth, c. 2.45 m). The same type of pottery was found in both pits. Most of the sherds are from the Early Bronze Age IA, mixed with some sherds of the Esdraelon culture. In the lower part of the shelter pit some Chalcolithic sherds were also found.

RISHPON 4. Rishpon 4 is located in the southwestern corner of Ḥaviv and Barazani streets in the Ramat Aviv Gimel quarter of Tel Aviv, on the western slopes of the eastern *kurkar* ridge to the east of the Haifa–Tel Aviv highway. The site is about 31 m above sea level. It is an oval-shaped basin (c. 13 by 8 m) dug in the weathered *kurkar* rock; it is 1.5 m deep in the east, and grows deeper from west to east. Rounded niches were cut around its sides. Its floor is concave and has depressions of various sizes: the entrance was apparently from the west, without a step. The excavations conducted by H. Ritter-Kaplan continued intermittently for more than 12 years, beginning in 1978. Throughout the basin were hearths covered by deposits of dark, cohesive, clayey sand and lighter-colored sandy clay sediments formed by seasonal flooding of the site from the east. In the inundation deposits in the basin, thick and thin layers of light gray ash were also found, evidently originating from the hearths. In the southwestern part of the basin, a ceremonial burial of a *Dama mesopotamica* horn was discovered, surrounded by blocks cut from the bedrock but still attached at their bases. Sterile earth, free of sherds and bones, covered the *Dama* horn and the surrounding blocks.

Most of the pottery consisted of hole-mouth jar sherds with brown-to-black slip, thick rims, and ledge handles. The pottery also includes pithoi, small bowls, jars, and juglets; there were relief decorations and incisions on some sherds. Only a very few sherds of Egyptian imitations were found. Among the flints were scrapers, cores, and sickle blades, as well as a large amount of lithic waste. There were no arrowheads. There were also seashells and lumps of various minerals, including mica. These apparently were used to make grits for pottery.

An earthen rampart (c. 33 m long) was discovered near the site, to the east. The top of the rampart was about 1.5 m higher than the rock in which the basin was dug. The rock increases in height to the north and south of the site; the rampart stands to the full height of the rock and coheres with it for about 12 m on either side of the site. The rampart is comprised of different types of soil.

The basin at Rishpon 4 was apparently dug at the edge of a lake, whose maximum depth at this point was about 6 m and that contained plant remains indicative of fresh water. The rampart was designed to protect the site from inundation but was incapable of stopping the more powerful flood waves that covered it and its surroundings with their deposits.

The graffiti incised on some of the sherds make it possible to date Rishpon 4 to the latter part of the predynastic era in Egypt—the end of the Naqada III period. The local ceramic assemblage belongs to the Early Bronze Age IB. From the way the basin was dug, from the concentration of hearths containing *Dama* bones, and from the burial of the horn, it can be concluded that Rishpon 4 was a cultic site. At or near the site, a flint tool industry (as indicated by the lithic waste) and a pottery industry (as attested by the numerous minerals used as grits) were conducted. The stratification of the deposits of clay, sand, and ash testifies to seasonal activity by people who assembled from a distance for the purpose of cultic and other activities at this site, which appears to have been isolated. The absence of arrowheads indicates that the occupants of Rishpon 4 were farmers, not hunters.

Apparently, Bronze Age agriculturalists had migrated to the eastern Nile Delta and there tilled the soil and learned to build earthen ramparts as protection against flooding. In the wake of the political upheaval in Egypt, the uniting of the north and the south, and the assumption of power by Ḥor-aḥa at the beginning of the First Dynasty, the Canaanite migrants either left Egypt or were driven out. At all events, they carried with them the sophisticated engineering know-how for constructing earthen ramparts they had acquired, along with small quantities of Egyptian pottery and other Egyptian artifacts.

GIV'AT BETH HA-MITBAḤAYIM. The mound of the former municipal slaughter house (Giv'at Beth ha-Mitbaḥayim) is located on the bend of the Yarkon River, where it turns northward. The mound overlooks both the Yarkon Valley and the Coastal Plain. Because of its location, it served at various times as a camping and burial site for caravans and armies passing through the country. The sites on the mound are named after the streets on which they are found.

YANNAI STREET. On Yannai Street, Chalcolithic and Early Bronze Age remains were exposed on the eastern margin of Giv'at ha-Mitbaḥayim. The excavations, conducted from 1950 to 1952 and in 1955 by J. Kaplan, on behalf of the Tel Aviv–Jaffa Museum of Antiquities, were concentrated in seven loci. All the caves and pits cut in the *kurkar* belong to the Chalcolithic period. In two caves Chalcolithic burial remains, fragments of clay ossuaries, and human bones were found, as well as a fragment of an ossuary with a relief decoration of two snakes. The other caves were used as shelters or silos.

Only part of cave 1 was excavated. The cave is 5.5 m long, and its ceiling was supported by one or two pillars cut from the solid rock. The cave was linked by short underground passages to smaller caves in the vicinity. The ceiling of the cave had collapsed, burying the occupation remains beneath its debris. Cave 1 revealed the following stratification.

Stratum A (0–0.2 m): humus earth mixed with Persian period and Middle Bronze Age II sherds.

Stratum B (0.2–0.45 m): light-brown earth and Middle Bronze Age II sherds.

Stratum C (0.45–2.65 m): large stones from ceiling debris in the upper part and below them a layer of reddish earth with Early Bronze Age I and a few Chalcolithic sherds.

Stratum D (2.65–2.9 m): powdery gray-black earth and Early Bronze Age I sherds, flints, and animal bones.

Stratum E (2.9–3.3 m): Chalcolithic sherds, flints, and animal bones.

In April 1974, stratum C was examined by H. Ritter-Kaplan, who found that its lower part forms a separate stratum, with pottery dating to the Early Bronze Age I. The collapse of the ceiling occurred at the end of this phase.

93 NORDAU AVENUE. The site on Nordau Avenue is the continuation of the Early Bronze Age I remains found in cave 1 and in the Early Bronze Age I burial cave south of cave 4. The latter was robbed of its contents in 1950; the only object rescued was a juglet with a high loop handle. Although the cave at 93 Nordau Avenue was damaged by a bulldozer, many Early Bronze Age vessels, as well as burned and scorched human bones, were found at its base. A notable find was a cup-and-saucer lamp.

KEFAR SHALEM (SALAMEH). On the bottom of a collapsed burial cave at the corner of ha-Tayasim and Lod streets, pottery vessels and burned human bones were found. The material was dated to the Early Bronze Age I.

Nordau Avenue: oil lamp, EB I.

EXHIBITION GARDENS. The first indication of ancient occupation in the area of the Exhibition Gardens (Ganei ha-Ta'arukha) in Tel Aviv was a few Middle Bronze Age IIA tombs damaged by a bulldozer. In the excavations conducted at the site in 1970 by H. Ritter-Kaplan, several strata dating to the Early Bronze Age I and the beginning of the Early Bronze Age II (stratum 6) were uncovered beneath a layer of black, hard clay (stratum 5, 5A) that occasionally exceeded 1.5 m in thickness. Above this layer, in one place, a thin stratum of encampment occupation (stratum 3A) dating to the Middle Bronze Age I was exposed. Between this occupation and the black clay of stratum 5, a gray quartz sand stratum (stratum 4) appeared. Elsewhere at the site, above stratum 5, 5A, a hard, gray quartz sand level (stratum 3) appeared that continued to accumulate for the entire stratum 3A encampment; finally, with stratum 2, a lighter gray quartz sand covered it to a height of one meter. These two main strata—black clay of stratum 5 and the gray quartz sand of strata 3 and 2—suggest different climatic conditions—one wet, indicating swampy conditions, and the other dry. Pollen analyses confirmed that the clay earth stratum (5) represented a wet period and the gray quartz layers (strata 4, 3, and 2) were barren, indicating a dry climate that caused a vegetation crisis. Because the quartz sand (stratum 4) began to accumulate beneath the encampment, the desiccation crisis apparently began before the Middle Bronze Age I occupation level—at the end of the Early Bronze Age III. The writer believes that evidence from other scientific disciplines supports the thesis that the desiccation crisis caused the collapse of Early Bronze Age cultures throughout the ancient world.

QIRYA QUARTER. A burial cave in the *kurkar* ridge on which the Qirya quarter is located was excavated by H. Ritter-Kaplan in 1979. Much of the eastern part of the cave had long been destroyed, including the southeastern part of the roof. A central rock-cut pillar supported the roof, and the interior was divided into three burial areas. The entrance, part of which was discovered on the eastern slope, had been blocked with stones. Several burial levels, varying in thickness (from 0.5 to 1 m) were found densely placed. Many of the interred were young people, children, and infants.

A number of different burial customs could be observed. The corpse had been laid on the ground with offerings beside it. Offerings were placed on a large flat, *kurkar* slab, on top of which were signs of burning. The large number of charred bones found in some levels indicates that at some stage cremation was practiced. Among the earliest burials in the cave were skulls, some showing evidence of cremation, with offerings placed beside them (one juglet per skull). Burial in cists built of large stones was also found.

Most of the pottery from the burial cave dates to the Early Bronze Age IA; a number of the vessels have good parallels in the early phases of tomb A94 at Jericho. There are indications, including a platter found in one of the upper levels, that the burials continued into the Early Bronze Age II. Also found were a number of squat, round beads of carnelian, crystal, and a greenish semiprecious stone; a faience bead; a quartz pendant drilled in two places; and a few silver rings or earrings.

MIDDLE AND LATE BRONZE AGE

No Middle Bronze Age I occupation remains were discovered in Tel Aviv except for stratum 3A at the Exhibition Gardens, but rock-cut shaft graves from this period have been found, usually as a result of building and road works. These graves are found in groups. Only a few have been excavated. One small graveyard was excavated near the Ramat Aviv petrol station on Haifa Road. Another graveyard is located slightly to the northwest, near the east fence of the Sede Dov Airport, and another is on Pinkas Street, between Yad

Labanim and Shikkun ha-Ẓameret. There apparently was also a graveyard in Ramat ha-Ḥayal, where a grave with a Middle Bronze Age I burial was found beneath a Middle Bronze Age IIA burial. An isolated Middle Bronze Age I grave was found in Yannai Street, north of the Chalcolithic cave 1.

SEDE DOV (MIDDLE BRONZE AGE IIA). A temporary squatters' dwelling of a clan of Amorites (?) was excavated near the Sede Dov Airport. The site, which dates to the Middle Bronze Age IIA, was exposed during building operations. It was excavated in 1969 by H. and J. Kaplan, on behalf of the Tel Aviv–Jaffa Museum of Antiquities. The site is an elliptical hollow (c. 20 by 9 m), dug in the *kurkar*. It was filled with thin layers of drift sand and clayey soil. Between these layers thin occupation strata could be distinguished that contained many potsherds and animal bones—including those of goats, sheep, turtles, and various wild animals—and also the complete skull of a donkey. In a higher section, the remains of ovens and hearths were found. The hollow was probably roofed with a goat-hair tent similar to the Bedouin tents of today. The pottery dates the site to the Middle Bronze Age IIA.

A small graveyard was also exposed in the Exhibition Gardens and seven of its graves were excavated. Individual graves are also known in the Hadar Yosef and Ramat ha-Ḥayal neighborhoods.

EXCAVATIONS NEAR THE TEL AVIV HARBOR. Near the southern fence of the Tel Aviv harbor, approximately 30 m from the shoreline, a small cemetery with eighteen Middle Bronze Age to Late Bronze Age tombs was excavated by J. Kaplan between 1949 and 1951. The tombs are rectangular rock-cut shafts, about 1.6 m deep. The deceased was placed in a vaulted burial niche on the long side of each tomb. The openings of these niches were blocked with clay-sealed stones. In all, the remains of twenty-five adult and infant burials were found. The dead were buried fully clothed, adorned with their jewelry and scarab seals, with their personal belongings placed nearby. The funeral vessels consisted, as a rule, of two large jars, dipper juglets, bowls, carinated bowls, and cosmetic juglets. Among the twenty-four scarab seals found, one is incised with the first name of the Egyptian Queen Hatshepsut (1503–1482 BCE).

Conclusions. There are two dating possibilities for the cemetery: the period ranging between the latter part of stratum D at Tell Beit Mirsim to the end of stratum IX at Megiddo (c. 1550–1480 BCE) and a period of one generation in the reign of Queen Hatshepsut.

HILL SQUARE. In the western part of Hill Square, a pottery kiln and a burial cave, both dating to the Middle Bronze Age IIB, were exposed. On Shimeon Hatarsi Street a cemetery dating from the Middle Bronze Age IIC to the Late Bronze Age I was found. The cemetery was destroyed before excavations could begin.

Tel Aviv harbor: plan of a double burial cave, MB II.

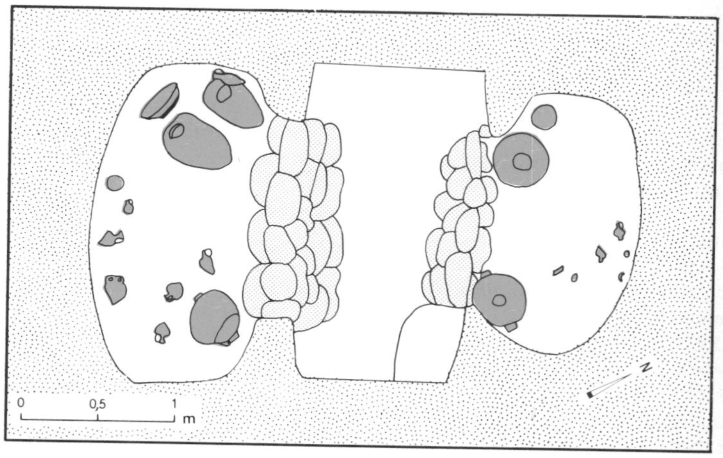

IRON AGE

Iron Age remains in the Tel Aviv area occur mainly at the following mounds: Tell Kudadi, Tell Qasile, Tel Gerisa, Jaffa (q.v.), and Tell Abu Zeitun (q.v. Bene-Berak). Eighth-century BCE remains without buildings, found at Hill Square, Giv'at Beth ha-Mitbaḥayim, and in areas bordering Yehoshua Bin Nun and John Hyrcanus streets, may have belonged to military camps and may be connected with Sennacherib's campaign against Hezekiah in 701 BCE. It is known that on his way to Judah, Sennacherib conquered Jaffa, Beth-Dagon, Azor, and Bene-Berak, all cities of Sidqa, king of Ashkelon, who was Hezekiah's ally. It is therefore possible that, at this strategic position on Giv'at Beth ha-Mitbaḥayim, Hezekiah's allies had a forward camp.

PERSIAN PERIOD

Persian period remains were found at Giv'at Beth ha-Mitbaḥayim. Sections of walls and large quantities of pottery were excavated at various points on the site. The upper part of a faience statuette showing Egyptian influence, found at Hill Square, dates to the Persian period.

HELLENISTIC PERIOD

There are two kinds of Hellenistic sites in the Tel Aviv area: remains of agricultural estates from the time of Ptolemy II (285–246 BCE), and remains

Sede Dov: remains of the MB IIA temporary settlement.

from the Hasmonean period (late second–late first centuries BCE). The remains of buildings and two winepresses belonging to an agricultural estate were excavated on Giv'at Rambam (today within the city limits of Giv'atayim). Similar remains were found at the eastern limit of the Qirya (formerly Sarona), west of Naḥal Ayalon, but those excavations were limited in scope. In addition, such remains were also excavated at the corner of Yehuda ha-Maccabi Street and Haifa Road. Pottery and bronze coins were found at all these sites. At Yehuda ha-Maccabi Street, a military camp of Antiochus III the Great was excavated by Ritter-Kaplan from 1984 to 1986.

In the Hasmonean period, most of the coastal cities in the Yarkon Valley and on the Sharon Plain were conquered and annexed to Judea. Among the Hasmonean remains in Tel Aviv are a winepress dating to the time of Alexander Jannaeus (excavated on Ḥevra Ḥadasha Street), and parts of Jannaeus' defense line.

EXCAVATION OF THE JANNAEUS LINE. In 1949, Hasmonean remains were excavated in Tel Aviv for the first time at two sites in front of the Hilton Hotel on ha-Yarkon Street and at the intersection of Arlosoroff and Bloch streets. The foundations of a rectangular structure (13.5 by 9 m) were exposed at the first site (ha-Yarkon Street), and part of a structure with a hexagonal plan at the second (Arlosoroff Street). The finds include a coin of Alexander Jannaeus (found on ha-Yarkon Street). The three sites are probably part of the fortification line Josephus reports was built by Jannaeus "from the mountainside above Antipatris to the sea coast of Joppa" (*Antiq.* XIII, 390). It is assumed that the main section of this line (its eastern flank) ran from the Rosh ha-'Ayin springs near Tel Aphek (Antipatris) to the mountains in the east; the remaining section (its western flank) was the Yarkon River, which formed a natural defense trench. It appears, therefore, that military camps were erected at regular intervals along the southern bank of the Yarkon and had fortified posts in front of them. The excavated structures may be three such fortified posts and belong to the western sector of the line. In 1961, an additional section of the line was discovered at Pardes Katz, near Bene-Berak (q.v.), where the foundations of another hexagonal structure were exposed. This structure is smaller than the one excavated on Arlosoroff Street. It also dates to the Hellenistic period; here, too, a coin of Jannaeus was found.

RISHPON 1 AND RISHPON 3. In 1964, an archaeological survey was carried out in the northern part of Tel Aviv, which was then still largely untouched by building and road development. The survey was conducted by H. and J. Kaplan within the framework of the Tel Aviv–Jaffa archaeological project begun in 1950. When development of the area began in 1976, a bulldozer penetrated the *kurkar* ridge and exposed four sites: RS-1—a cave with *kokhim*, from the Hellenistic and Roman periods; RS-2—a burial cave from the Middle Bronze Age II; RS-3—a rubbish pit from the Hellenistic period; and RS-4—a rock-cut hollow with Early Bronze Age I material (see above).

RS-1. Cave RS-1 has seven exceptionally large *kokhim* (loculi). Except for *kokh* 1, all the *kokhim* were empty (except for a few sherds and animal bones). The remains are from two phases:

1. Hellenistic (late second–early first centuries BCE). To this phase belong some isolated sherds found on the cave floor, in the *kokhim*. Part of a coffin, built of dressed stones and containing cattle bones, was also found in the cave.

Map showing the route of the Jannaeus line, from the Mediterranean Sea to Antipatris (Aphek).

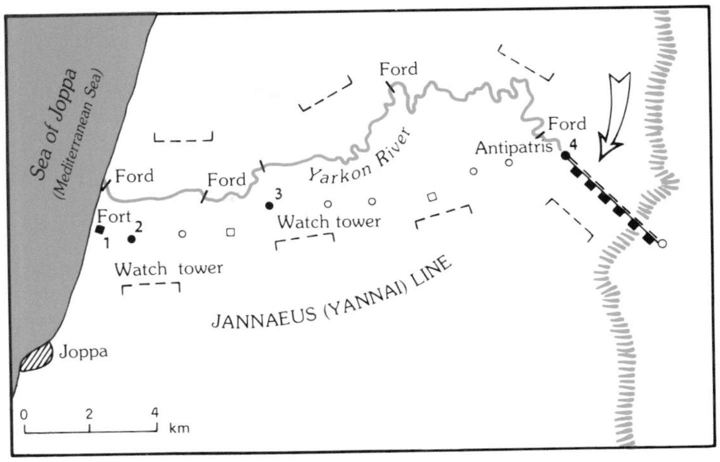

Abu Kabir: a tomb in the Jewish cemetery, Roman period.

2. First century BCE to the early first century CE. To this phase belong the finds originating mostly from *kokh* 1 and the hearth next to it: two large cooking pots, restored from sherds found in *kokh* 1, and fragments of terra sigillata bowls (Augustan period) and of an Arretine plate stamped with the potter's signature—L.ETTI/SAMIA (also from the Augustan period).

RS-3. Cave RS-3 is a rubbish pit (diameter, c. 3 m). Its upper layer of dark earth is mixed with ash that contained small bowl fragments, fish plates, jars, and a Hellenistic lamp—all from the late second to the early first centuries BCE. The pit belongs to the early phase of cave RS-1.

Conclusions. The absence of human bones and of human teeth and the cattle burial found above the floor of the chamber suggest that the cave was hewn specifically for animal burial. After the *kokhim* were filled and blocked off, the stone coffin was installed to provide an additional place for burial. The size of the *kokhim* and the cattle burial in the stone-built coffin also suggest a parallel with Egypt, where mummified animal burials connected with the cult of Serapis are found in such coffins.

Because the burial cave was found empty of its original contents and because the hearth and the pottery in the second phase are dated from the late first century BCE to the early first century CE, it seems that the cave had been cleared and occupied by people looking for shelter. Strabo, following his topographical description of Jaffa, describes "robber" dens on the coast of Sharon(?). In that period, the term robber was also applied to the descendants of the Hasmoneans, sworn enemies of Rome and of King Herod.

Eretz Israel Museum Center: Byzantine winepress.

END OF SECOND TEMPLE PERIOD

Remains from this period include a settlement at Khirbet Hadra, located on a mound across the Yarkon, and a number of tombs, one of which (in Shikkun Dan) contained a limestone ossuary with a rosette decoration. Other tombs from this period were found at the edge of the Herzliya School on Bloch Street. Across the Yarkon, remains of agricultural settlements from this period were found at Khirbet Hadra and Khirbet el-Ora, on the northern municipal boundary, near Tel Barukh. At Yehuda ha-Maccabi Street, a Byzantine military camp of Heraclius was excavated by Ritter-Kaplan above the Hellenistic camp of Antiochus III.

ROMAN-BYZANTINE PERIOD

The principal Roman-Byzantine remains include the Jewish cemetery at Abu Kabir in southern Tel Aviv, extending from Herzl Street to Kibbutz Galuyot Street; the graveyard (near Tel Barukh) west of Khirbet el-Ora in northern Tel Aviv; and the remains in the area of the Eretz Israel Museum (formerly Haaretz Museum), which belong to the settlement at Tell Qasile.

ABU KABIR. In 1872, C. Clermont-Ganneau explored the ancient Jewish cemetery of Jaffa at Abu Kabir, from which about seventy marble tombstones were recovered. Most of them reached various museums in Europe. The funerary inscriptions are mostly in Greek; only a few are in Hebrew or Aramaic. They provide many details on the origin and trades of the Jews of Jaffa in the Roman-Byzantine period. Since 1951, eight burial caves have been excavated by Kaplan. Except for human bones (usually not found in situ), these tombs were empty and had probably been plundered by the local population. However, a tombstone was found near the entrance, in the courtyard in front of two of the caves. Most of the caves have loculi, but several have loculi and arcosolia.

CEMETERY NEAR TEL BARUKH. In 1951–1952, excavations were carried out at a site near Tel Barukh, 1.5 (1 mi.) north of the railway bridge on Rishpon Street. They revealed burial caves dug in the rock and a pit full of animal bones. Each cave had a courtyard with steps and one or two burial chambers (2.5 by 2 m). Often there were benches along the walls of the courtyards and depressions for draining rainwater from the floor. The entrance generally was sealed by a round slab, which fits into a narrow groove on its short side. The cave was opened by rolling the stone aside. Both loculi and arcosolia were cut in the walls of the burial chambers. There were indications that most of the burial chambers and also the floors had been reused several times at various periods.

Numerous offerings were found: glass and pottery vessels, lamps, and bronze, iron, and glass jewelry. There were also iron nails, indicating that the dead had been buried in wooden coffins. In some tombs, bronze coins were found, and in one cave there was a hoard of about one hundred coins, mostly from the fourth century CE. An isolated pit with cattle and sheep bones is noteworthy. This may be early evidence (fifth century CE) of the Jewish custom of burying every firstborn of a ritually clean animal within or near human graves.

ERETZ ISRAEL (HAARETZ) MUSEUM CENTER. Near the main entrance to the museum center, a section of a mosaic pavement was exposed (see below). Excavations showed that the section preserved is about a third of the original, which apparently belonged to a Samaritan church on the site (other scholars have identified this as a Samaritan synagogue). Parts of three pillars from a double row that supported the roof of the church, as well as the rubble-stone foundations of the south wall, were exposed. The building is oriented east–west, with its opening facing east. It had a wide central nave flanked by two narrow aisles. Excavation showed that the church was situated

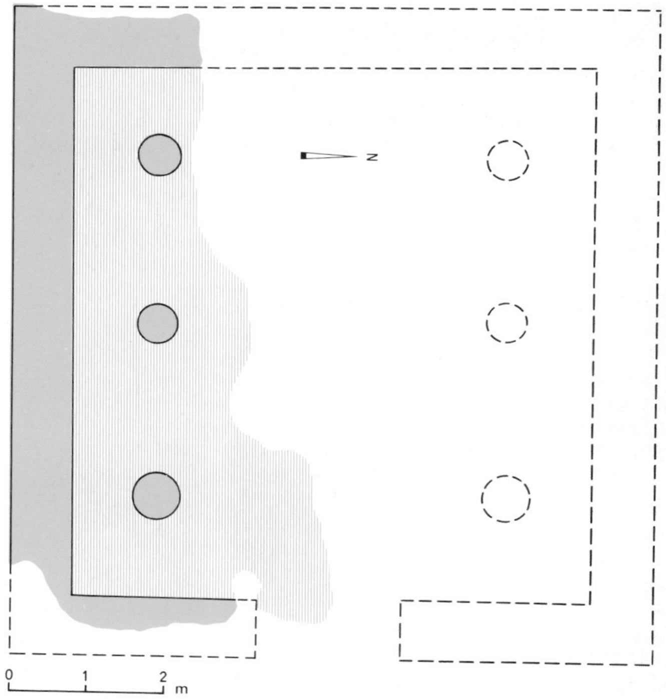

Eretz Israel Museum Center: plan of the Samaritan church.

Eretz Israel Museum Center: mosaic in the Samaritan church. The Greek inscription in the center reads "Blessing and peace on Israel and on this place, Amen."

outside the main settlement at Tell Qasile. It was erected above a large pottery kiln. Such kilns were usually placed outside the city.

The mosaic is beautifully executed in four basic colors and intermediate shades, in a pattern of plant motifs intertwined with geometric designs. The mosaic contains three inscriptions, two in Greek and one in Aramaic in Samaritan script. The latter is definite proof that the building was a Samaritan church. One of the Greek inscriptions reads: "Blessing and peace on Israel and on this place, Amen." The second Greek inscription, placed near the church threshold, lacked half of its right side and two lines at the end. It was apparently the dedicatory inscription of the church builders, who were Christianized Samaritans, as is indicated by the word "baptistery."

The pottery and single bronze coin found in the excavation indicate that the building was erected at the end of the sixth or the beginning of the seventh century CE.

SAMARITAN SETTLEMENTS IN TEL AVIV. From the evidence of two Samaritan amulets—one found in a fourth-century CE tomb near Khirbet Hadra and the other in a grave in the Tel Barukh cemetery—and from the church remains in the area of the Eretz Israel Museum, it can be concluded that these sites were once occupied by Samaritans. These were not, however, the only Samaritan sites in the area; in the Byzantine period there were Samaritan communities at Rishpon (Apollonia) and in the Petaḥ Tikva area.

(See also Tell Kudadi, Tell Qasile, Tel Gerisa, Jaffa.)

S. Tolkovsky, *The Gateway of Palestine*, London 1924, 168–173; Frey, *Corpus* 2; J. Kaplan, *'Atiqot* 1 (1955), 1–12; id., *RB* 62 (1955), 92–99; 78 (1971), 422–423; 80 (1973), 417–418; 82 (1975), 260–263; 84 (1977), 284–285; 85 (1978), 417; id., *IEJ* 8 (1958), 149–160; 16 (1966), 282–283; 17 (1967), 158–160; 20 (1970), 225–226; 24 (1974), 137–138; 25 (1975), 157–159; 28 (1978), 125–126; id., *BASOR* 156 (1959), 15–22; id., *Roman Frontier Studies* 1967 (ed. M. Gichon), Tel Aviv 1971, 201–205; id., *Bulletin Museum Ha'aretz* 11 (1968), 8–9; 12 (1970), 9–15; 13 (1971), 18–22; id., *BA* 35 (1972), 66–95; id., *PEQ* 97 (1975), 144–152; J. Leibovitch, *'Atiqot* 1 (1955), 13–18; H. Ritter-Kaplan and J. Kaplan, *IEJ* 27 (1977), 55; 28 (1978), 125–126; H. Ritter-Kaplan, *Ha'aretz Museum Series* 6 (1979), 1–17; id., *IEJ* 29 (1979), 239–241; 41 (1991), 198–200; id., *RB* 86 (1979), 457–458; id., *ESI* 3 (1984), 44; 9 (1989–1990), 140; id., *ZDPV* 100 (1984), 2–8; P. E. Dion and R. Pummer, *Journal for the Study of Judaism* 11 (1980), 217–222; E. Ayalon, *ESI* 1 (1982), 108; 4 (1985), 107–108; 6 (1987–1988), 100; Weippert 1988 (Ortsregister); Y. Levy, *ESI* 7–8 (1988–1989), 176–177; 9 (1989–1990), 53–54, 173.

JACOB KAPLAN, HAYA RITTER-KAPLAN

TEMAN, ḤORVAT

IDENTIFICATION

Ḥorvat Teman (Kuntillet 'Ajrud) is a small, single-period Iron Age site from the early eighth century BCE. The Arabic name Kuntillet 'Ajrud means "Solitary Hill of Wells." The site is located in northern Sinai (map reference 0940.9560), approximately 50 km (31 mi.) south of Kadesh-Barnea and about 10 km (6.2 mi.) west of Darb el-Ghazza, the road running from Quseima and Kadesh-Barnea to Elath and southern Sinai. The isolated hill is situated in the broad bed of Wadi Quraya, which is a natural east–west route. Several shallow wells dug at the foot of the hill created one of the only permanent water sources in this arid region. The site is at the western edge of the hill's long, narrow summit.

Because of the wells, an important crossroad existed near the site (which can be seen on old maps of the region). One path descended from the north, from the area of Quseima and Kadesh-Barnea, branching off toward Elath and southern Sinai; another path intersected it, passing through the valley of Wadi Quraya. This junction, in addition to the wells, probably determined the site's location.

Ḥorvat Teman was proposed as the modern Hebrew name for the site (whose ancient identification is unknown) because of its southern location and the appearance of the Hebrew word *teman* (south) in several of the inscriptions found here.

EXPLORATION

The site is mentioned in the books of several early explorers, among them E. H. Palmer, who visited the site in 1869 on his way from southern Sinai to Palestine. He conducted a limited probe here, and discovered the site's first written find: the letter *aleph* incised on a potsherd (he thought it was the Greek *alpha*). Palmer, who erred in dating the site, proposed identifying it with the Roman way station Gypsaria on the Elusa–Elath road that appears in the *Tabula Peutingeriana*. The Czech investigator A. Musil arrived at the site in 1902, after hearing rumors of an ancient inscription found here. He describes, in picturesque detail, his violent clash with the local Bedouin, who refused to allow him to climb the hill, claiming it was their holy site. B. Rothenberg visited the site in 1967, and correctly dated it to the Iron Age. Z. Meshel

Ḥorvat Teman: general view of the hill.

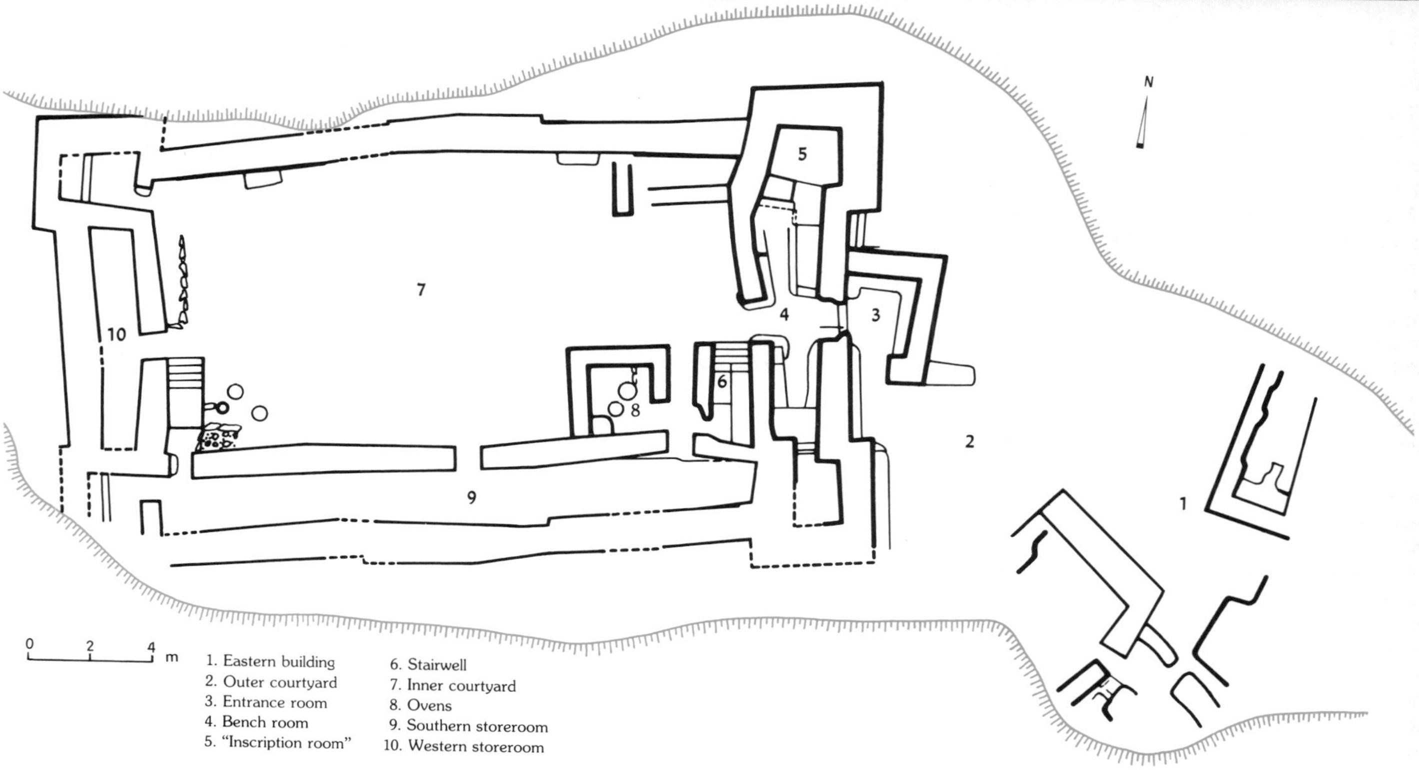

Plan of the site.

Aerial view of the site.

surveyed the site in 1970 and conducted three seasons of excavation (1975–1976) on behalf of Tel Aviv University, the Israel Department of Antiquities, and the Exploring the Land Division of the Kibbutz Movement.

EXCAVATION RESULTS

BUILDINGS. The site contains two single-period buildings: a main building (A) and a secondary building (B) to its east. Building A is the better preserved of the two. The main building's walls are preserved in some places to a height of 1.5 m. It covers the entire western part of the summit in an area of about 15 by 25 m. The structure is rectangular, with four protruding corner rooms and an indirect entrance on the east. The plan is reminiscent of a small fortress and seems like a smaller version of the Israelite tower fortresses found at Kadesh-Barnea, Arad, and Ḥorvat 'Uza. However, the building had no casemate rooms, and certain architectural details, along with the finds, show that it was not a fortress.

As mentioned above, the entrance to building A was from the east, by way of a small outer courtyard surrounded by stone benches. The benches, floor, and walls were plastered with a white, shiny lime plaster. Some of the plaster fragments found on the floor were painted; they depict a female figure seated on a chair and floral motifs. The walls may have been painted above the level to which they were preserved. Stone benches along the walls and white plaster, both decorated and undecorated, characterize the entrance complex, the eastern wing of the main building (A), and the subsidiary building (B).

An opening led from the outer courtyard northward to the white plastered entrance room. No traces of colored decoration were found here. The building's single entrance, which was reached by turning left (west), led to what was termed the bench room: a narrow broadroom that apparently was the most important part of the building. Its entrance divided it into two wings. The plastered stone benches surrounding each wing occupy most of the area, with only a narrow passageway in between. The benches appear to have been the most important element in this room. The way the room is connected with the adjacent corner rooms may also attest to its use: the latter are linked to the bench room by means of raised, windowlike openings, with the side benches as their sills. Probes cut in the benches indicate that they blocked earlier narrow openings. In the excavator's opinion, this represents merely a technical construction stage, as the building existed in only one period and was erected according to a predetermined plan.

Among the fragments of wall plaster in the bench room were two fragmentary inscriptions, written in black ink in Phoenician script. Part of a third inscription was found in situ on the northern jamb of the entrance leading to the inner courtyard. This was the only plaster inscription found in situ; it was placed 1.5 m above floor level, on the jamb to the right of those entering.

Apart from the plaster inscriptions, the majority of unique finds were from the bench room, the corner rooms next to it, and other nearby areas. The finds include two large pithoi decorated with inscriptions and drawings and several large and small stone bowls, four of them bearing the names of their donors incised on the rims. The ceramic assemblage here consists mostly of small vessels, such as juglets, lamps, flasks, bowls, and jugs; storage vessels, such as pithoi and jars, were primarily found in the building's other rooms. Most of the vessels were found in the corner rooms, perhaps used as *favissae*, depositories for the vessels that previously stood on the benches. The room's plan and contents, in particular the inscriptions, attest to its function: to house vessels and objects offered at the site by donors asking for a blessing.

The long narrow room south of and parallel to the courtyard and the room west of the courtyard (whose length equals the courtyard's width) were used as storerooms. The bases of pithoi and storage jars were found in situ, sunk in the beaten earth floor and covered with the fragments of the vessels' upper parts. The shoulders of many of the vessels bore incised names, titles, and marking letters (see below). The storage vessels were set in the floor at very close intervals, making it difficult to understand how it was possible to pass between them. This was especially true in the western storeroom, where large pithoi (1 m high and more than 0.5 m in diameter) completely filled the room. In the eastern part of the southern storeroom, the builders took advantage of the natural rock slope to create a kind of basement. This area yielded a large quantity of vessels and organic objects that had fallen or were thrown in: fragments of wooden vessels, a large sieve made of woven strands, whole pomegranates, and many branches used for roofing. On top of the debris, near the entrance, was a large, heavy stone bowl, bearing the inscription *l'bdyw* (see below). The bowl seems to have been dragged to this spot from the bench room or its vicinity. Fragments of another plaster inscription,

"Bench room," looking south.

probably from the doorjamb, were discovered in the debris at the entrance to the western storeroom. One of the unplastered stones set in the jamb of the central entrance to the southern storeroom bears an indistinct drawing in red, black, and yellow.

The open courtyard was, for the most part, empty of both finds and structures. Only "kitchens" were found, in its two southern corners, at the foot of the staircases that must have led to the roof. The remains of three ovens, built one on top of the other, each relating to a successive floor, were found in each of the kitchens. It is difficult to determine how long each oven was in use, but it is certain that their combined time spans cover the duration of the site's relatively short existence.

Because of the main building's good state of preservation, it was possible to discern a number of architectural details. The walls were built of rough stones that were hewn from the local chalky rock. An intermediate course of tamarisk branches, from the trees along the Wadi Quraya valley bed, was incorporated in the wall at a height of 1.2 m. The branches, laid alternately across the length and width of the walls, reinforced them. The walls and floors in the entrance complex and the bench room were, as mentioned, coated with a white lime plaster; the other walls were covered with a clay plaster mixed with straw. The ceilings were made of branches, many of which were found in the debris in the rooms. The shape of the hill's summit determined the building's dimensions and orientation; the walls are not straight, the width of the rooms varies, and the two wings of the bench room are not identical.

The other structure at the site, the eastern building (B), is about 10 m east of the main building. It was preserved for the most part only up to one course, thus preventing the excavators from clarifying its general plan. However, the white plaster that covered all its surviving parts, as well as the many colored plaster fragments found in the debris, indicate its uniqueness and grandeur. It may have served as a kind of propylaeum to the main building or as the eastern wing of a front courtyard; it is also possible that the two structures did not coexist and that the eastern building was in use before the main building.

In the northern part of building B was a long room that originally reached the summit's edge but has since collapsed. Its floor and wall fragments were coated with white plaster. The entrance was from the west, marked by two pilasters projecting from the wall. Most of the mural fragments were found near this entrance; the shape of several of the fragments indicates that they fell from the jambs and lintel in the entrance.

The southern part of building B contained a few walls, also covered with white plaster, with small stepped areas between them. Their function is not clear.

POTTERY. A large pottery assemblage dating to about 800 BCE was discovered at the site. Three regions provide parallels to this assemblage: Judah; the southern coastal area; and northern Israel and Phoenicia. This is additional evidence for ties between the site and regions to the north. No Negbite ware was found here, and it appears that the desert nomads who produced it did not settle here either.

TEXTILES. A large amount of textiles was recovered: about one hundred cloth fragments, mostly linen, and seven of wool. Several were a mixture of

Pottery vessels in situ in the southern storeroom.

materials; one contained red-dyed woolen threads along with light-blue linen threads. A. Sheffer, who studied them, noted the high quality of the thread and the uniformity of the weave. Loom weights and worked wooden beams attest to local weaving activity. It is noteworthy that the Bible provides an account of the priestly garments made of linen and woven at cultic sites. The discovery of these textiles may provide an insight into the character of this site.

INSCRIPTIONS AND DRAWINGS. The most important finds at Ḥorvat Teman are the inscriptions and drawings. The inscriptions, written in old Hebrew script or in Phoenician, can be divided into several types.

Letters Incised on Pottery Vessels Before Firing. Most of the pithoi (mainly from the storerooms) bore one or two incised letters on their shoulders; these marks are found only on pithoi. The most common letter is א ('), there are a few י (*y*), and the combination קר (*qr*) appears twice. So far, this phenomenon has only appeared at the City of David in Jerusalem, where the letter ט (*ṭ*) is incised on the shoulders of several identical pithoi. This substantiates the excavator's opinion that the letters are abbreviations indicating offerings and tithes, attesting to the antiquity of the tradition. Accordingly, it is possible that *qr* stands for *qorban* (sacrifice), while *y* indicates a tithe, and ' the first or best harvest of the season. In any case, the mark used was decided on before the vessels were fired, and at the place where they were produced. This may mean that the site's inhabitants received offerings and tithes.

Inscriptions Incised on Pottery Vessels After Firing. Inscriptions on the shoulders of storage jars were incised after the jars were fired. The most interesting ones are the four examples of the inscription לשרער (*lšr'r*), which should perhaps be read "(belonging) to a city official." It seems that at least some of the supplies were sent to this official or were registered at the site in his name.

Inscriptions Incised on the Rims of Stone Bowls. The most complete of the four inscriptions incised on the rims of stone bowls reads: לעבדיו בן עדנה בר(ו)ך ה(ו)א ליהו ([belonging] to *'bdyw* son of *'dnh*, blessed be he of YHW[H]). The stone bowls were apparently offered to the site by donors who sought the Lord's blessing.

Ink Inscriptions on Wall Plaster. Fragments of three inscriptions, written in Phoenician script, were found on wall plaster in the bench room; fragments of two other inscriptions, in old Hebrew script, were found in the debris of the entrance to the western storeroom. Only one inscription was discovered in situ, on the doorjamb of the

Pottery from Ḥorvat Teman: the large pithos is of the type that bears inscriptions and drawings.

Stone bowl with the inscription "(belonging) to 'bdyw *son of* 'dnh*, blessed be he of YHW(H)."*

Inscription on plaster: "Your days may be prolonged and you shall be satisfied ... give YHWH of Teman and his ASHERAH favored . . ."

entrance leading from the bench room to the courtyard; it was extremely fragmentary and faded. All the fragments were found among the debris after they fell from the walls, as described above, so that only very small parts of the inscriptions were preserved. One two-line inscription has been reconstructed by the excavators as follows:

. . . your days may be prolonged and you shall be satisfied	[. . .י]ארכ(ו). ימ(י)ם. וישבעו
. . . give YHWH of Teman and his ASHERAH	[. . .] תנו ל[י]הוה [ ] תימן. ול[ ]אשרת
. . .YHWH of Teman and his ASHERAH favored . . .	[. . .]היט(י)ב. יהוה. התי[מן. ואשרתה . . .]

This evidently represents a benediction or prayer directed to the god of Teman and his Asherah.

Another inscription appears to be part of an ancient theophanic poem describing the revelation of God; it is reminiscent of similar descriptions in the Bible, although here God is mentioned together with Ba'al:

. . . and when EL rose up . . .	[/ ובזר(ו)ח. אל. בר]
and hills melted and peaks were pounded . . .	[/ וימס(ו)ן. הר(י)ם / וידו(ו)כ(ו)ן. גבנ(ונ)(י)ם]
	[ושדש. עלי]
bless BA'AL in day of war . . .	[לברך. בעל. בי(ו)ם מלח] מה
. . . the name of EL in day of war . . .	[לשם(.) אל. בי(ו)ם מלח] מה

Ink Inscriptions and Drawings on Pottery Vessels. Two large pithoi bore inscriptions and drawings in red ink; one was found in the bench room, and the other came from the eastern edge of the adjoining courtyard. It can be assumed that the pithoi were originally in the storerooms, as they have incised letters on their shoulders: a ʾ on one and *qr* on the other. Their surface area is wide and seems to have been used as a sort of board for writing and drawing.

Noteworthy among the inscriptions are four repetitions of the alphabet, with the letter פ (*p*) preceding ע (ʿ); a list of names; and a phrase similar to those used in the Bible to designate a righteous man:

. . . Everything he lends he waives and YHWH will grant him all he wishes . . .	כל אשר ישא(י)ל מא(י)ש ח(ו)נן ה(ו)א [ ] ונתן לה יהו(ה) כלבבה

In addition, two inscriptions are reminiscent both of a typical opening formula of a letter and the priestly benediction. The excavators have deciphered the first as follows:

A[shy]o the K[ing] said:	א[שי]ו המ[ ] אמר
tell x, y, and z,	ליהל [ ] וליועשה ול [ ]
may you be blessed by YHWH	ברכת(י) אתכם ליהוה
of Shomron (Samaria) and his ASHERAH	ש(ו)מר(ו)ן ולאשרתה

If this reconstruction is correct, it may be possible to identify Joash (יואש), king of Israel, with א[שי]ו (by switching the place of the theophoric component יו) and thus view him as the one who may have had a part in establishing the site.

The second inscription reads:

Amaryo said: Tell my lord,	אמר אמריו אמר לאד(ו)ני
may you be well	השל(ו)ם את(ה)
and be blessed by YHWH of Teman	ברכתך ליהוה ת(י)מן
and his ASHERAH.	ולאשרתה.
May he bless and keep you	יברכ(ך) וישמרך
and be with you	ויהי עם אד(ו)ני

Inscription and a drawing on a pithos that shows two images of the god Bes, resembling a lyre player and a cow suckling a calf.

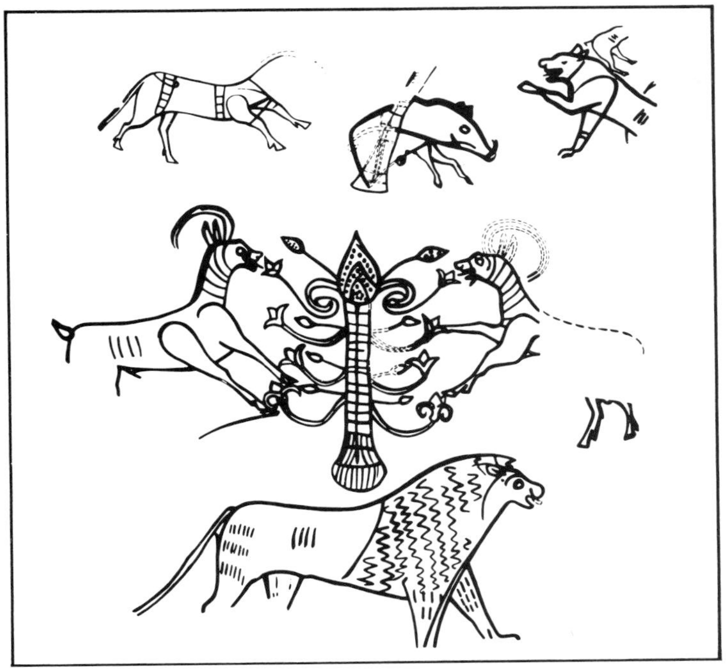

Drawing on a pithos depicting the tree of life flanked by two ibexes and other animals.

Drawing on plaster depicting the heads of two figures at the top of a wall, between towers.

The inscriptions attest to the nature of the site as a religious center but their significance goes far beyond that.

The drawings and decorations found here are unique in Iron Age Israel, both in quantity and in variety. They were drawn on wall plaster, mostly on doorjambs, as well as on pottery vessels—mainly on the two pithoi mentioned above; in one case, they were drawn directly on one of the stones in the jamb of the entrance to the southern storeroom.

Among the drawings on the pithoi, the following scenes are most noteworthy: two figures resembling the Egyptian god Bes, with a lyre player nearby; two ibexes flanking a tree of life; a lion; a procession of animals; a cow licking the tail of a nursing calf; five figures raising their hands in prayer; and an archer shooting a bow. The artistic execution of the drawings is not exceptional, and the majority of motifs are well known from the Syro-Phoenician world; a southern desert influence may also be detected. It appears that the artists were influenced by the style prevalent in the region and were familiar with the iconography of the subjects depicted. The drawings are more examples of folk art than of professional, or "royal art." The traditional character of such folk art is especially valuable, as it sheds light on the various tendencies and trends that existed in the Israelite period. Consequently, the finds from Ḥorvat Teman do not attest to a unique, Israelite artistic style particular to the site. Neither the drawings nor the inscriptions on the pithoi were done at one time or by one hand only. P. Beck has attempted to identify three artists, at least one of whom drew on both pithoi, based on differences in style.

The drawings on the wall plaster—several of which are in black, red, and yellow—differ in subject matter from the depictions on the pithoi and are more decorative. Those found in the debris of the eastern building (B) include a running pattern, which perhaps served as a frame, composed of two rows of lotus flowers and two lines of guilloche; a checkerboard pattern with red and yellow squares; and human figures at the top of a wall with crenellated towers. Plaster fragments found near the main building's entrance (A) were reconstructed to show a large mural in red, black, and yellow, apparently depicting a figure seated on a throne, holding and smelling a lotus flower. Other remains indicate that two superimposed layers of decorated plaster existed in several places. Another drawing of a seated, throned figure was found on a sherd.

It is difficult to determine whether the pithoi and plaster drawings were done by the same artists. The standard of the plaster drawings is higher than for the pithoi scenes, and they depict different subjects; however, the Syro-Phoenician artistic influence is common to both. Most of the parallels belong to the ninth to seventh centuries BCE. If the excavator is correct in dating the site to about 800 BCE, these drawings represent some of the earliest known examples of Phoenician art.

Drawing of praying figures on a pottery vessel.

SUMMARY

The unusual finds at the site, especially the inscriptions and the drawings, attest to its uniqueness. The site differs in both date and character from the Iron Age sites in the Negev known as "Israelite fortresses." The contents of the inscriptions, the mention of various deities, and the vessels dedicated to the site all suggest that it was a religious center. However, the lack of objects related directly to cult, as well as the settlement's secular plan, indicate that the site was not a temple. The excavator suggests that Ḥorvat Teman was a religious center—a kind of wayside shrine that, because of its location, was related to the royal journeys to Elath and Ezion-Geber, and perhaps also to pilgrimages to southern Sinai. These journeys occurred on the road (Darb Ghaza) leaving Kadesh-Barnea, passing near Horvat Teman. This route was the main road to Elath and also marked the kingdom's Negev border. The passersby would stop and leave their offerings dedicated to God in the bench room and receive a blessing in return.

The site reflects a strong northern (Israelite, not Judean) influence, and its construction should be attributed to the kingdom of Israel—perhaps to King Joash, after his defeat of Amaziah, king of Judah, in the conflict which may have been, in part, over shipping rights in the Red Sea, or to one of the Judean kings closely aligned with the Israelite kingdom. This influence can be discerned in various forms: the term "YHWH of Samaria"; the Phoenician writing; the style of the drawings and decorations; the origin of several of the pottery types; the manner in which the personal names are written (the ending *yo* instead of *yahu*); and perhaps also in the mention of several deities, along with the combinations "YHWH of Samaria and his Asherah" and "YHWH of Teman and his Asherah." The site, which was probably occupied for only a few years, was inhabited by a small group of priests, perhaps sent from the kingdom of Israel, and headed by a "*sar*" (officer). They subsisted on tithes

and donations, including supplies, sent mostly from Judah, and provided cultic services for travelers. If some of the inscriptions and drawings are learning exercises, they may reflect one aspect of the priests' duties here.

BAR 2/1 (1976), 32–34; *Buried History* 12 (1976), 157; 14/2 (1978), 1–16; Z. Meshel, BA 39 (1976), 6–10; id., *IEJ* 27 (1977), 52–53; id., *RB* 84 (1977), 270–273; id., *Temples and High Places in Biblical Times*, Jerusalem 1977, 37; ibid., Jerusalem 1981, 161; id., *Expedition* 20/4 (1978), 50–54; id., *Kuntillet 'Ajrud: A Religious Centre from the Time of the Judaean Monarchy on the Border of Sinai* (Israel Museum Cat. 175), Jerusalem 1978; id., *BAR* 5/2 (1979), 24–34; id., *MdB* 10 (1979), 32–36; id., *BAIAS* 1982–1983; 52–55; id., *XIIe Congress of the International Organization for the Study of the Old Testament—Program and Abstracts*, Jerusalem 1986, 92; P. Beck, *TA* 9 (1982), 3–68; A. Catastini, *Annali di Instituto Orientale di Napoli* 42 (1982), 127–134; D. A. Chase, *BASOR* 246 (1982), 63–67; W. G. Dever, *Hebrew Studies* (Univ. of Wisconsin, Madison) 23 (1982), 37–43; id., *BASOR* 255 (1984), 21–37; J. A. Emerton, *ZAW* 94 (1982), 2–20; K. Jeppesen, *VT* 34 (1984), 462–465; A. Lemaire, *BAR* 10/6 (1984), 42–51; id., *Studi Epigrafici e Linguistici* 1 (1984), 131–143; id., *VT* 38 (1988), 220–230; M. Weinfeld, *Studi Epigrafici e Linguistici* 1 (1984), 121–130; J. Gunneweg et al., *IEJ* 35 (1985), 270–283; D. N. Freedman, *BA* 50 (1987), 241–249; J. M. Hadley, *VT* 37 (1987), 180–213; Weippert 1988 (Ortsregister); P. J. King, *EI* 20 (1989), 98*–106*; J. H. Tigay, *IEJ* 40 (1990), 218; R. Hestrin, *BAR* 17/5 (1991), 58; A. Sheffer and A. Tidhar, *'Atiqot* 20 (1991), 1–26.

ZEEV MESHEL

TIBERIAS

IDENTIFICATION

Tiberias was founded between 18 and 20 CE by Herod's son Herod Antipas, who made it the capital of his kingdom; the city was named after the emperor Tiberius. Its location, on the western shore of the Sea of Galilee (map reference 201.242) was then to the south of present-day Tiberias and to the north of the hot springs known as Hammath; the city's western boundary was marked by Mount Berenice, which rises to an altitude of approximately 200 m above the level of the Sea of Galilee.

HISTORY

Josephus states that Tiberias was located "in the best region of Galilee." In order to populate the city as quickly as possible, the king attracted residents "by equipping houses at his own expense and adding new gifts of land" (*Antiq.* XVIII, 36–38). Coins issued in honor of the founding of the city feature the reed plants indigenous to the shores of the Sea of Galilee; later coins, minted toward the end of the Second Temple period, bear a palm tree, symbolizing the city's prosperity.

According to Josephus, the royal palace was a magnificent building, that was decorated with "representations of animals," and whose ceilings were "partly of gold" (*Life* 65–66). The royal treasure houses and archives were also here, at least until 61 CE when Tiberias lost its role as the capital (*Life* 38). Josephus also mentions a synagogue, which was "a huge building, capable of accommodating a large crowd" (*Life* 277). After the death of Herod Antipas' successor, Agrippa I (44 CE), Tiberias came under the authority of the Roman procurators of Judea. The town maintained its position as the capital of Galilee without interruption until 61, when it was annexed to the kingdom of Agrippa II (*Life* 37–38), whose capital was at Caesarea-Philippi (modern Banias). As Agrippa's sister Berenice ruled at his side in Banias, the popular tradition linking her name to the mountain and aqueduct in Tiberias has no historical basis. At the outbreak of the First Jewish Revolt against Rome in 66, Tiberias was fortified with walls that remained standing even after the city had surrendered to the Roman army (*War* II, 572–573; III, 460–461).

Tiberias continued to be part of Agrippa II's kingdom, probably until his death in about 96. Then the town came under direct Roman rule and enjoyed the prosperity characteristic of the Roman Empire. During Hadrian's reign, a temple was built in his honor (the Hadrianeum, "a very great temple" according to Epiphanius, *Haer.* 30, 12). Its four-columned facade is depicted on a series of coins minted at Tiberias in 119. In the mid-second century the city,

previously considered unclean because of the many old graves in it, was purified by Rabbi Simeon Bar Yoḥai (*Gen. Rab.* 79h; J.T., *Shab.* 9, 1–38d).

During the reign of Emperor Elagabalus (218–222), Tiberias was granted the status of a Roman colony, as it appears from coins (B.T., *A.Z.* 10a). It was then that the ruling institutions of the Jewish people were moved from Sepphoris to Tiberias: first (c. 235) the Sanhedrin, with Rabbi Yoḥanan at its head, then the Patriarchate, and the then reigning patriarch, Rabbi Judah II Nesiah (d. c. 270). Yoḥanan established the Great Study House (*beth ha-*

Tiberias: city plan.

City coin of Tiberias, depicting a statue of Zeus in a sanctuary.

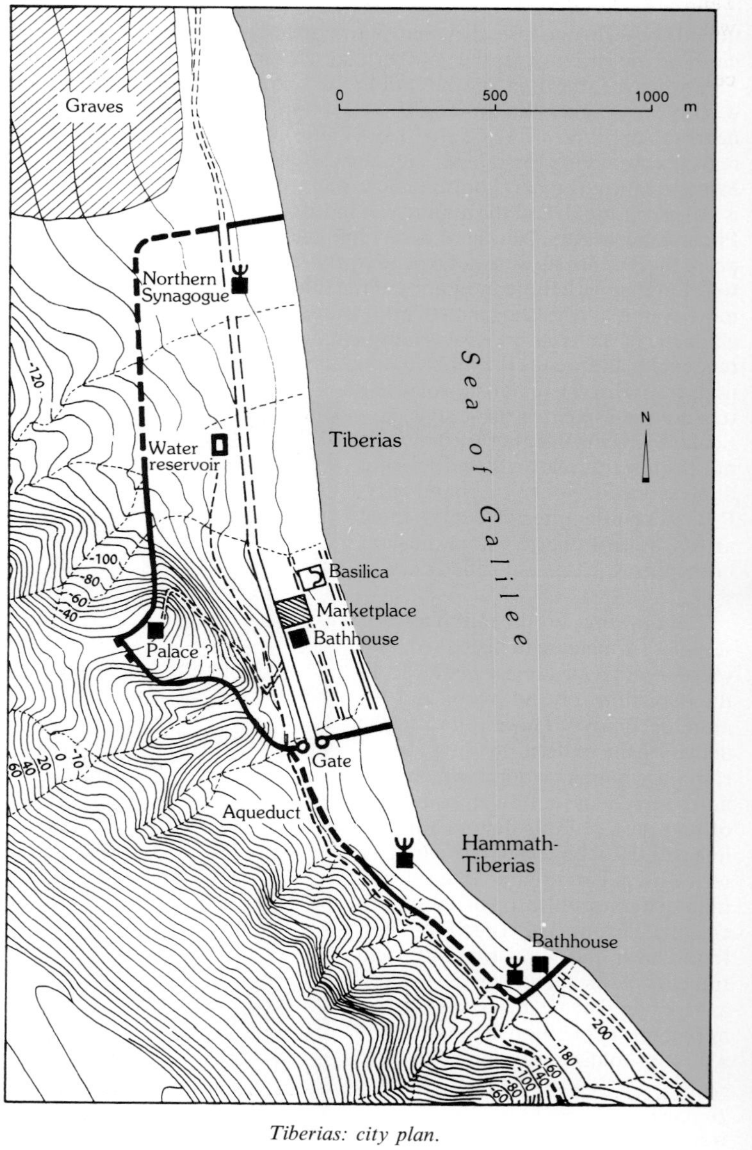

Plan of the main buildings in the city center.

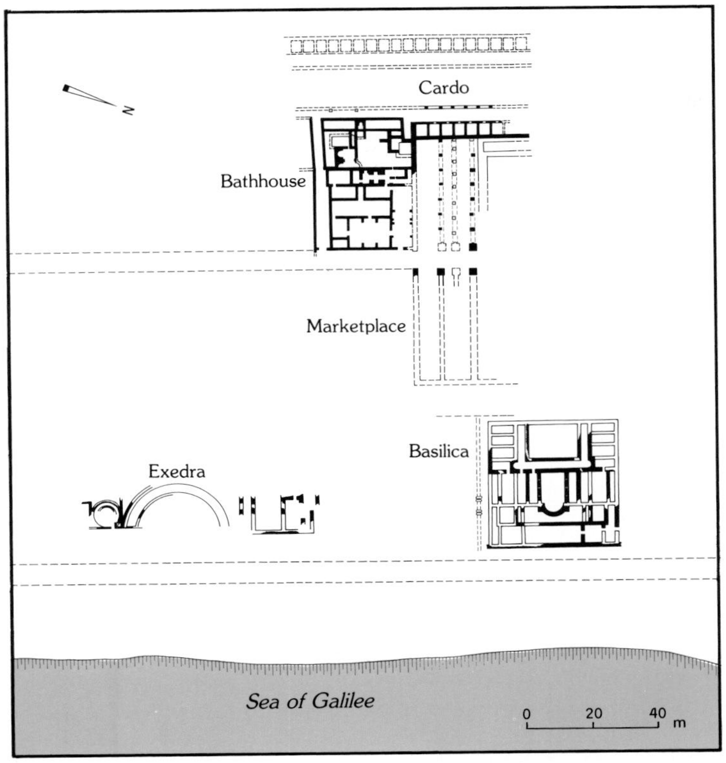

midrash ha-gadol) (see below). In this institution, frequently mentioned in Talmudic literature, the great majority of the Palestinian (Jerusalem) Talmud was written.

After Tiberias became the Jewish capital of Palestine and the Diaspora, it continued to prosper for a considerable time. The sources refer to the city gate and to the fortress, which was probably built on the site of the royal palace from Second Temple times. Mention is also made of the boule (municipal council), various synagogues, study houses, city markets, and a series of public buildings—a stadium, bathhouse, lavatory, and magnificent tombs. Near these were the residential quarters of the city and various industrial areas, which included, inter alia, glassworks and pottery workshops. South of Tiberias, in the vicinity of the hot springs, Hammath-Tiberias (q.v.) developed as a suburb serving the numerous visitors who came from far and near to the medicinal springs.

In the sixth century, the Academy (Yeshiva) of Eretz-Israel, which succeeded the Sanhedrin as the supreme religious institution of the Jewish people, was established in Tiberias. The academy continued its activities here long after the Arab occupation, probably until the tenth century. During that time—the period of the Gaonim—several schools of poets and preachers were active in Tiberias, as were scribes and vocalizers (the Masoretes), whose system of vocalization, still in use today, is known as the Tiberian system.

After the Arab invasion, Tiberias superseded Beth-Shean as the capital of northern Palestine. The city continued to prosper until the ninth century. In the tenth century, however, security in the area began to deteriorate and the population declined. In 1033, Tiberias was destroyed by an earthquake; in the Crusader period, it was moved to the north, to its present location. Since then, most of the area of ancient Tiberias has remained desolate.

EXPLORATION AND EXCAVATION

The remains of ancient Tiberias' walls were first examined by V. Guérin in 1875. A more detailed survey of the walls at the top of Mount Berenice was carried out by G. Schumacher in 1887. A systematic excavation of the southern gate and its vicinity was carried out by G. Foerster in 1973–1974, on behalf of the Israel Department of Antiquities and Museums, the Institute of Archaeology at the Hebrew University of Jerusalem, and the Israel Exploration Society. In addition, a great number of salvage excavations has been carried out. The largest, in both scale and results, was conducted in the center of the municipal area of the ancient city, under the direction of B. Rabani (1954–1956). The excavators cleared a section of the city's central colonnaded street (its *cardo*), as well as a bathhouse and vaulted market. To the east, not far from the lake shore, A. Druks (1964–1968), uncovered the remains of a basilical structure. When the excavations were extended to the south, along the shore,

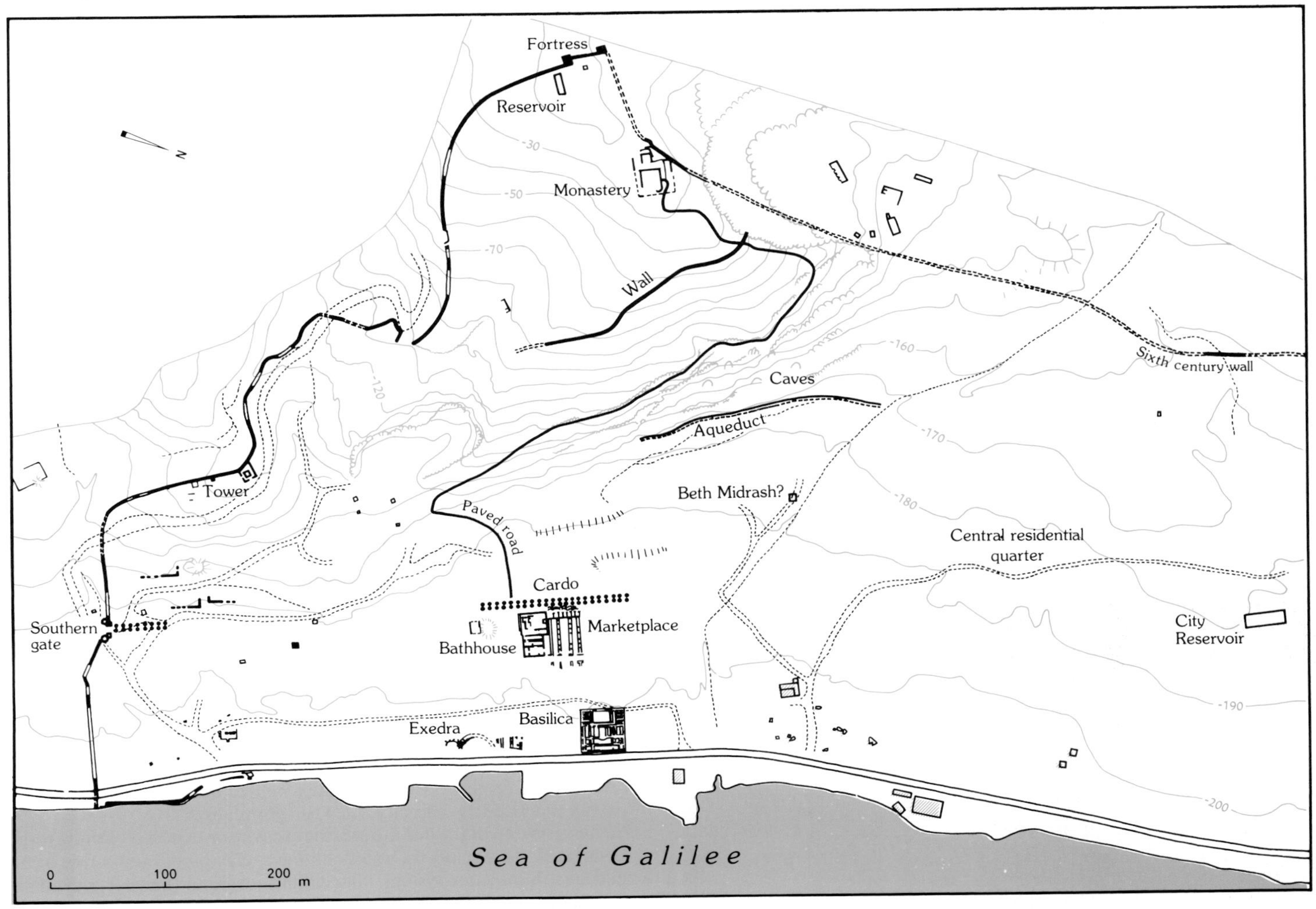

Tiberias: plan of the city and the city wall in the 6th century CE.

the remains of an exedra and various public buildings were revealed. In 1976, F. Vitto excavated a Roman tomb in Tiberias, and in 1989–1990 Y. Hirschfeld's salvage excavation at the foot of Mount Berenice exposed a Roman public building beneath the remains of private houses. Since 1990 Hirschfeld has been directing excavations on the summit of Mount Berenice.

The rapid development of modern Tiberias necessitated several salvage excavations in the southern part of the city. The remains of the Byzantine city wall and a large Crusader church were discovered by A. Harif in 1980, when foundations were dug for the Jordan River Hotel. Farther south, A. Berman, working in 1978–1979, had discovered the remains of a synagogue and private houses from the Byzantine and Early Arab periods.

Other salvage excavations in the area revealed the remains of churches and fortification systems from the Crusader period. Dozens of tombs were discovered in the area to the north and northwest of the Byzantine city wall, mainly on the slopes now occupied by modern Tiberias. The results of these salvage operations provide important data for a reconstruction of the city plan of Roman-Byzantine Tiberias.

EXCAVATION RESULTS

BATHHOUSE. The bathhouse in ancient Tiberias adjoined the *cardo* and the

"Fish mosaic" in the bathhouse.

Hypocaust in the bathhouse, 4th century CE.

marketplace. This location indicates that it was probably the city's central bathhouse, which is frequently referred to in Talmudic literature. The structure, some of whose walls survived to a height of 2.5 m, underwent numerous changes and repairs over its many centuries of existence, but its basic plan remained unchanged. The finds indicate that the bathhouse was built in the fourth century and was used continuously until the city was destroyed in the eleventh century. Its length from east to west was 42 m and its breadth (from north to south) was 31 m, for a total area of approximately 1,300 sq m. It was divided into two main wings: a west wing, including various bathing rooms, and an east wing, containing dressing rooms and halls for social occasions. Bathers entered through the east wing, proceeding into a long, narrow hall (19 by 5.8 m) at the structure's northeast corner. The entrance was in the wall facing the street to the east of the bathhouse. The hall ceiling rested on several basalt arches; the floor was paved with colored mosaics, depicting various animals (elephant, panthers, and asses). Two doors in the hall's southern long wall opened into two additional halls, a larger east hall (12 by 9 m), and a smaller west hall (7 by 3.5 m). Between the two halls was a space whose function is unknown; it may have been a pool. Both the east and west halls also had fine mosaic floors. The mosaic in the west hall was unique for its richness and its state of preservation. The central carpet consisted of multicolored geometric patterns with representations of birds and fish in medallions. A trial sounding beneath the foundations of this floor unearthed sherds dated no later than the fourth century CE.

Some 3 m below the floor level in the west hall was a colonnaded pool that survived almost intact. The ceiling, made of basalt beams, was supported by twenty-four short columns (each 1.4 m long), all of whose sections, including the bases and capitals, were in secondary use. The colonnaded pool received its water from a subterranean channel to the west; excess water was drained through a channel in the pool's southeastern corner. The depth of the water in the pool was stable, approximately one meter above the bottom. A subterranean pool of this type is quite rare in a Roman-Byzantine bathhouse. The efforts invested in its construction may well be connected with the laws of purity as practiced by the city's Jewish population.

In the west wing of the bathhouse, the excavation exposed bathing rooms of various sizes, storage pools, water channels, clay pipes, and a row of rooms heated by a hypocaust system. The caldaria were in the center of the bathhouse, between two pairs of massive basalt pillars that supported the ceiling. Some of the hypocaust colonnettes and the brick arches above them were preserved intact. Adjoining the caldaria were other rooms, equipped with marble-lined bathtubs. Three more pools found to the west were provided with water-heating installations and semicircular niches. A "seam" between the caldaria and the bathing pools indicates a fundamental change in the structure of the bathhouse, which the excavator dated to the sixth century.

MARKETPLACE. In the area north of the bathhouse the excavations revealed a columned structure, extending over a large area. Three rows of column bases have been cleared, over an area of more than 800 sq m. The excavator (Rabani), held that the structure was built in the sixth century and interpreted it as a roofed municipal marketplace. Each row of columns was represented by seven bases, built of a combination of basalt and limestone. Some bases also made use of basalt doors from cave tombs, in secondary use. Each row of columns ended in the east with a square pillar (each side 2.2 m long). These gigantic pillars apparently helped to support the arches, which spanned the adjoining street. The remains of similar pillars were found on the other side of the street. The marketplace was closed off in the north by a solid wall (2.6 m thick), and in the west by the row of shops east of the *cardo*.

CARDO. Part of the main colonnaded street that ran through ancient Tiberias parallel to the lake shore—the *cardo*—was discovered in the area to the west of the bathhouse and the marketplace. The excavator believed that the street was paved, and together with it the street network of the city in general, as early as the second century. The south end of the *cardo* was discovered in the vicinity of the southern gate, approximately 370 m south of the bathhouse (see below, Foerster's excavations). The *cardo* was paved with diagonal basalt slabs and was approximately 12 m wide, which was typical for a city street in the Roman period. Flanking it were colonnades, approximately 5 m wide. In the eastern colonnade, five granite columns that helped to support the ceiling were found in situ. Inside the colonnades were shops, whose openings (1 m wide), faced the street. Six or seven shops of identical size (3.6 by 3 m) have been cleared so far. The *cardo*, including the colonnades and shops on either side, was approximately 33 m wide.

BASILICA. The basilica and its annexes were excavated near the western edge of the modern road to Tiberias, some 80 m northeast of the bathhouse complex. The excavations revealed two stages: a first stage from the Roman period (second century) and a second stage from the Byzantine period (fifth–sixth centuries). The building continued in use until the end of the Early Arab period.

The basilica was part of a large, walled complex that also included adjoining rooms, courtyards, and subterranean drainage systems. The entire complex was square (each side was 38 m long), for a total area of more than 1,400 sq m. It stood between two streets, both parallel to the shoreline: to the west a street separated it from the vaulted market, and to the east a main street, a kind of promenade, overlooked the Sea of Galilee.

The basilica was in the center of the complex; it was a broad, apsidal, colonnaded hall with the semicircular niche at the eastern end. It was entered from an open courtyard on its west. The length of the hall, including the aisles on either side, was 14.5 m; its maximum width, including the apse, was some 12 m. The apse was somewhat oblate. The sherds in the foundations date the building's first stage to the second century. It was a secular building, designed for various functions in the administrative and judicial life of Tiberias. Similar basilicas have been found in other Roman cities, such as Bostra in Transjordan, Samaria–Sebaste, and lately also in Beth-Shean–Scythopolis.

At a later stage, in the Byzantine period, the basilica was apparently converted into a Christian church. The building was repaved with mosaics which the excavator has dated to the fifth and sixth centuries. The eastern apse was also rebuilt, on a plan more in keeping with contemporary churches. The new basilica became a long structure: its length from east to west (including the apse) was 21 m, and its width from north to south (including the aisles) was 15 m. The court on the west continued in use, as did the various service rooms around it.

The remains of a large exedra were uncovered about 100 m south of the basilica. In shape it resembled a gigantic niche equipped with seating facilities, forming part of the promenade that looked out onto the lake and the port. The exedra was built somewhat like a theater. Its outer diameter was about 32 m, thus making it one of the largest exedrae discovered to date in this country. The inner diameter was about 23 m. In the gap between the inner and outer walls were sections of mosaic floors and benches, presumably built for public use.

ROMAN PUBLIC BUILDING. The remains of a Roman public building were excavated at the foot of Mount Berenice, about 250 m west of the lake shore. Bordering on the site was a modern drainage ditch, along which the walls of densely built private homes were found, as well as streets, lanes, and municipal drainage systems. The clearing of the ditch revealed that the residential houses and the streets between them had been built according to a master plan that was adhered to from the Roman period through the end of the Early Arab period.

The remains in the excavated area date to two main periods: the Roman-Byzantine period—from the second century to the earthquake in the mid-eighth century—the Abbasid-Fatimid period. The first occupation level contained part of a large public building paved with a white mosaic. A trial sounding under the mosaic floor revealed a homogeneous collection of sherds from the first and second centuries. These sherds also included fragments of stone vessels, of the type in common use among the country's Jewish population in the Second Temple period, and a bone figurine of a woman.

The public building was made of well-dressed basalt stones. It had a mosaic

Remains of a public building and mosaic pavement from the early 3rd century CE, *looking north.*

Residential building, 9th–11th centuries CE.

floor, in the center of which three black borders surround a pattern of red triangles. A stepped pool (mikveh?), also paved with mosaics, was found on one side of the hall. The hall was roofed and its ceiling rested on columns, as indicated by a basalt base that originally supported the columns. The character of the building was modified in the Byzantine period: the bathing pool went out of use and massive walls reduced the original area. The building's plan in that period is not clear; based on its location—at the foot of Mount Berenice—and the time of its construction, the excavator suggested that this was the Great Study House founded in Tiberias by Rabbi Yoḥanan in the first half of the third century. Following the earthquake of 749, a house was built on top of the ruins of the building that was occupied from the ninth to the eleventh centuries. In its final form, the house had a simple plan that included a courtyard in front.

NORTHERN SYNAGOGUE. Of the "thirteen synagogues" that Tiberias boasted, according to the Talmud, only one has been discovered so far. A salvage excavation west of the Plaza Hotel, in the area of Crusader Tiberias, exposed sparse remains that suggested a synagogue. Judging from the style of its mosaic floor and the inscription in it, the building was probably built in the sixth century (contrary to the view of the excavator, Berman, who dated its construction to

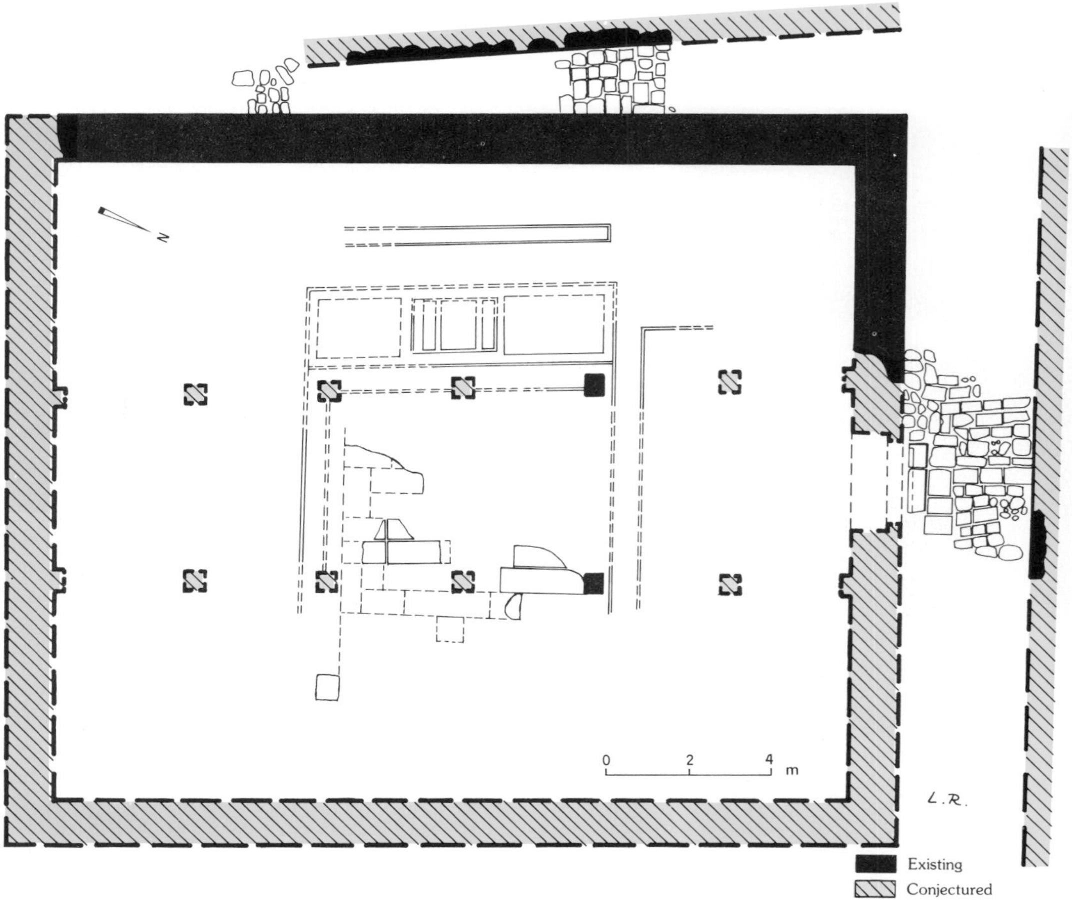

Plan of the northern synagogue, 6th century CE.

Part of the mosaic in the northern synagogue.

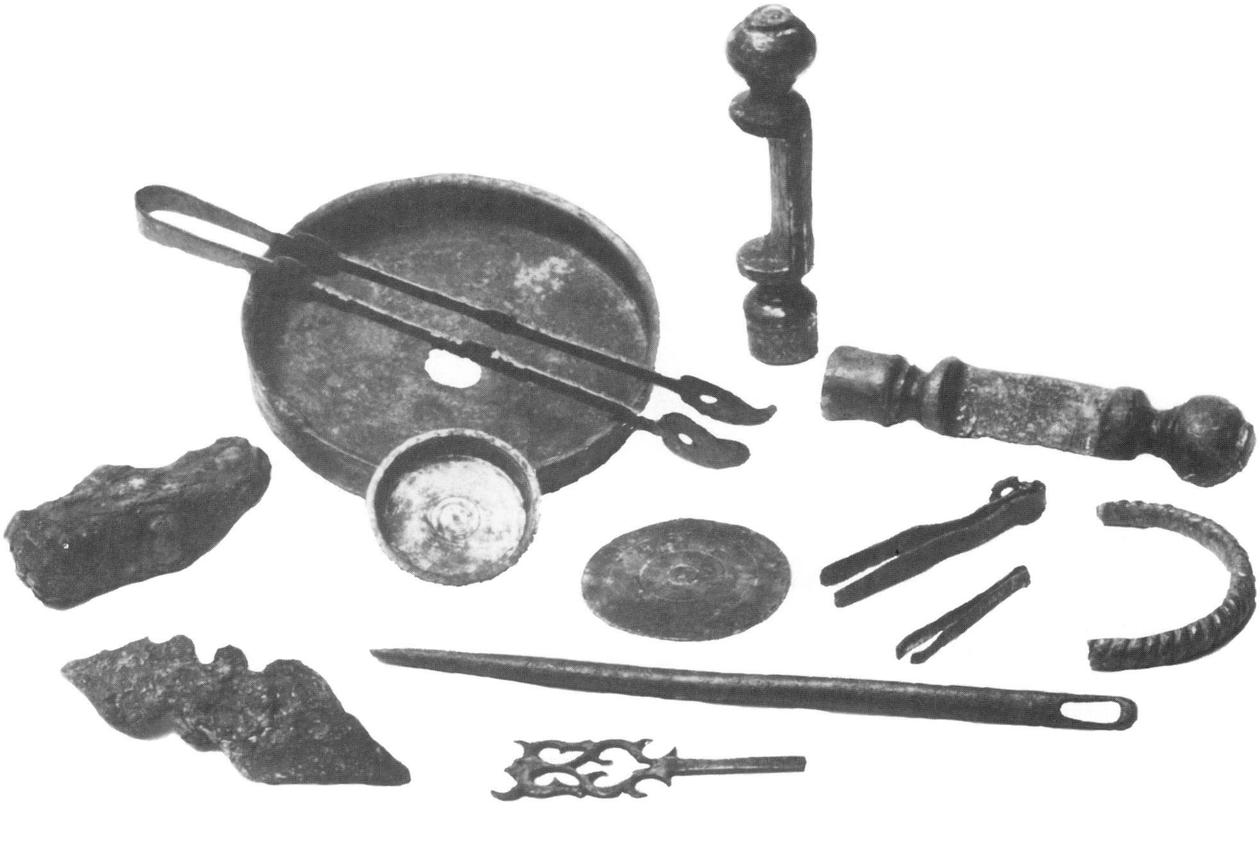

Hoard of bronze vessels, 11th century CE.

the second half of the seventh century). The synagogue continued in use until the end of the Early Arab period, having been completely repaired after the earthquake of 749. In the eleventh century, enormous fortifications were built over the building as part of the Crusader city.

The synagogue was a square building, each side approximately 20 m long. It was aligned along a north–south axis, pointing toward Jerusalem. The only entrance (c. 2 m wide) was in the middle of the northern wall. The prayer hall was divided into three by two rows of columns (two column bases were found in situ). Three colored mosaic carpets were discovered in the western space. The central mosaic included an inscription recording the name either of the mosaic artist or the donor: Procolus son of Crispus. The dedicatory inscription (in Greek) was flanked by typical Jewish symbols—ethrogs and lulabs. In the late phase of the building's existence (after 749), many changes were introduced—mainly the addition of walls and the replacement of the mosaic floor with a stone floor, at least in the central part of the prayer hall. Various finds recovered in the excavations testify to the synagogue's richness and magnificence. Also among the finds were broken tiles, fragments of stucco, and a fragment of a marble plaque decorated with grape and leaf patterns—originally part of the chancel screen marking off the area of the bema and the holy ark.

Near the synagogue a house with a mikveh was found. It was part of the northern residential quarter of Byzantine Tiberias.

BYZANTINE CITY WALL AND CRUSADER CITY. Approximately 100 m north of the synagogue, a section of the Byzantine city wall (c. 50 m long), was excavated. This section was perpendicular to the lake shore—that is, it ran east–west. The wall (2.5 m thick) was faced inside and out with well-dressed ashlars and had a tower (5 by 2.5 m) on its outer (northern) side. The sherds in its foundations date the wall to the end of the Byzantine period, in agreement with Procopius' assertion (*Buildings* V, 9, 24) that the walls of Tiberias were built by the emperor Justinian (527–565). The best-preserved sections of the wall are in the southern part of the city, along a line running west from the lake shore and climbing steeply up the slopes of Mount Berenice. Other sections were found descending from the top of Mount Berenice to the north and the east. The overall length of the city wall was approximately 2.8 km (1.7 mi.), and it enclosed an area of some 185 a.—the extent of Byzantine Tiberias at the zenith of its prosperity.

A large Crusader church was found north of the Byzantine city wall. It was about 30 m long from east to west (including the apse) and 16 m wide from north to south (internal measurements). The entrance was in the middle of the southern wall. The inner space was divided into a nave and two aisles by two rows of solid stone pillars, four to each row. Opposite them were engaged pillars in the walls, which helped to support the vaulted stone ceiling. Similar churches from the Crusader period have been found in Jerusalem (St. Anne's) and at Caesarea. In the northwestern part of the nave, the excavators found a staircase descending to a crypt, which has not yet been fully cleared. In the middle of the nave was a place for a reliquary. Judging from the size and location of this church, it may have been the cathedral of Tiberias in the Crusader period.

YIZHAR HIRSCHFELD

EXCAVATIONS IN THE SOUTH OF THE CITY

Systematic excavations were conducted in the southern part of the modern city of Tiberias in 1973–1974, under G. Foerster's direction. This area, generally identified as the Roman city of Tiberias, stretches along the foot of the mountain range on the west and the shore of the Sea of Galilee on the east, over an area of about 1,200 by 250 m.

The excavations were concentrated in the vicinity of the southern walls (area C) and farther south (areas, A, B, and B1). The area north of the walls was also investigated (areas D1 and D2). In areas A, B, and B1, the remains of a number of spacious, well-built houses were uncovered. They were generally built on virgin soil, some on an earlier cemetery. Two phases of repairs could be distinguished. The walls were constructed of plastered, unhewn stones and were well preserved, in some cases to a height of 2 to 3 m. The buildings yielded a rich variety of pottery, metal and glass objects, and coins, which attest that the area south of the walls enjoyed an era of prosperity between the eighth and the eleventh centuries.

AREA A. Area A is situated near the shore of the Sea of Galilee. Three buildings were partially excavated here, two of them containing staircases leading to a second story. The walls were built of unhewn stones laid without mortar. The corners, strengthened with well-dressed ashlars, were preserved to a height of some 3 m. Traces of plaster have survived on the walls. The floors were generally beaten earth, and the courtyards were paved with basalt slabs or with unhewn stones. One room had a white mosaic pavement. A fine network of drainage and sewage channels, some of them made of clay pipes, was found beneath the rooms.

The buildings had been constructed on rich agricultural soil, which con-

Area C: plan of houses, 6th century CE.

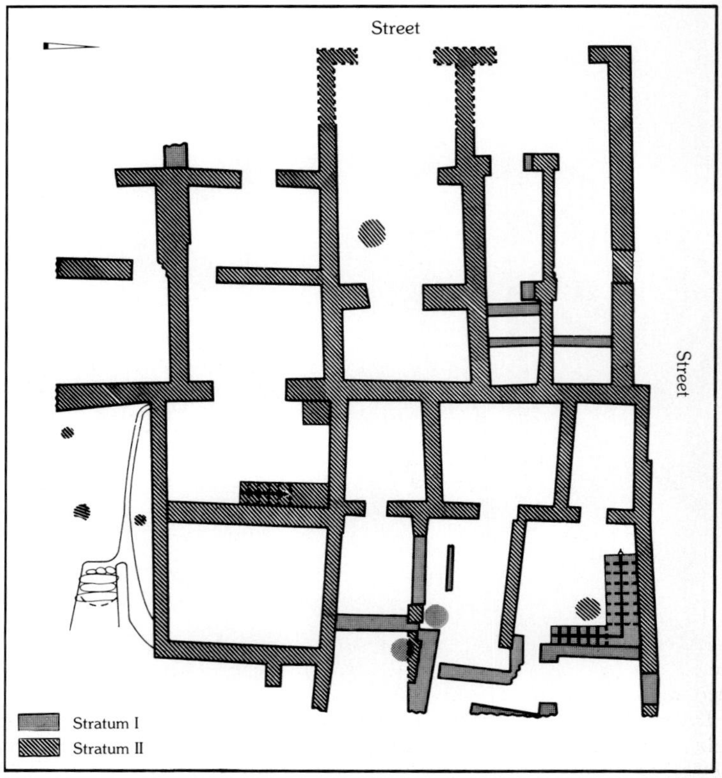

tained sherds from the Roman-Byzantine period, although no building remains from this period were found in the area. Beneath some of the houses were graves attributed, on the basis of the stratigraphy and pottery, to the end of the Byzantine period or beginning of the Early Arab period. No objects were found in the graves.

AREA B. In Area B, which lay some 100 m west of area A, parts of three or four large buildings were excavated. Like the buildings in area A, they had staircases leading to a second story. They were built of unhewn stones, and ashlar masonry was occasionally employed in the corners and the piers. Unbonded walls were discovered in this area (and in other areas as well), a method of construction probably designed to withstand the earthquakes that frequently struck the region. In the western sector of the area a group of rooms of uniform size was found. The rooms were probably used as shops. They faced the road leading from Hammath-Tiberias in the south to the city gate and the *cardo* of Tiberias (see above), farther to the north. One of the rooms contained an interesting assemblage of delicate pottery vessels that may have been used in the spice trade. These buildings were also constructed on virgin soil; beneath them a complex network of drainage and sewage channels was uncovered. The only earlier find in this area was a terra-cotta coffin that apparently came from the cemetery noted both in area A and farther south, near Hammath-Tiberias.

AREA B1. Area B1 was the farthest area investigated in the south. The remains of well-built houses were uncovered, but virgin soil was not reached. The excavations south of the line of the walls and the gate revealed that in the Roman and Byzantine periods the area between the twin cities of Tiberias and Hammath-Tiberias was uninhabited. In the latter city two synagogues and settlements from the Hellenistic, Roman, and Byzantine periods were excavated (see below). It seems that it is this unoccupied area that is referred to in the Talmud where it states that the distance between Tiberias and Hammath-Tiberias was one mile (Tosefta, *Meg.* 4, 3). This source confirms that there was indeed an open area between the two cities, although the distance appears to be exaggerated. In the Byzantine period, some of this area was used for a cemetery. Although it was settled only in the eighth century and abandoned some three centuries later, the two cities were nevertheless considered to be one (J.T., *'Eruv.* 22d).

AREA C: THE CITY GATE. Area C was the main area of excavation. The aim here was to ascertain the nature and date of the series of walls and the gate in the southern part of the city. They had previously been considered Roman, based on some remains visible at surface level and two Roman inscriptions found here in secondary use.

In the center of the area stood the gate and the *cardo* leading from it to the center of the city in the north. The gate, built of well-dressed basalt stones, is the earliest construction in this area. Round towers (diameter, 7 m), projecting to the south, flanked the gate. The lower part of the towers and the gate building were carved with a cyma profile. Two niches flanked the entrance

Area C: plan of the city gate from the Roman period and Early Arab period structures nearby.

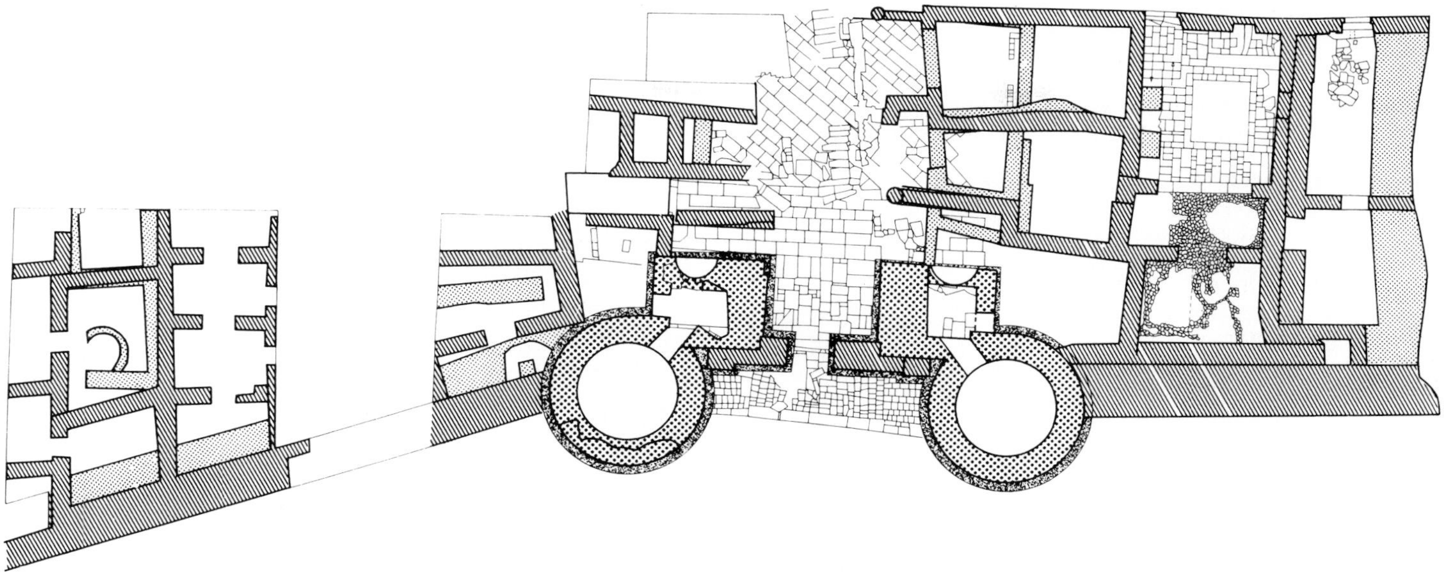

inside the gate building. Two pedestals were set between the round towers and the doorjambs in front of the gate; the pedestals supported columns and were decorated with rhombuses in relief.

The road that ran northward from the gate was paved with square basalt slabs, and the entrance area was paved with rectangular slabs laid parallel to each other. Farther north, the slabs were laid obliquely, as was customary for Roman streets in both the eastern and western parts of the empire. Soundings made at several points revealed that the walls are later than the towers, and thus than the gate itself, which is bonded to the towers. The gate complex was supported by massive foundations composed of small stones and mortar, well suited to the heavy soil on the banks of the Sea of Galilee.

Judging from the stratigraphy and the architectural evidence, the gate was probably built when the city was founded. A sounding made in the street, after several of the heavy basalt slabs were removed, revealed pottery of which the latest sherds were attributed to the first century CE and provide a terminus post quem for the construction of the gate and the street. The plan and ornamentation of the gate point to the same date, probably when the city was founded, in the second decade of the first century. Soundings conducted east and west of the gate area yielded no remains earlier than the sixth or seventh centuries; it can be assumed that in the Roman period the gate and towers stood isolated and served as a kind of outer gate, with no relationship to the walls in that period. Although there is no definite proof that the Roman city was fortified, this possibility should not be dismissed. Allusions to a wall in this period appear in the literary sources, including several Talmudic passages that hint at the existence of a gate outside Tiberias.

The gate complex and the street thus represent the earliest constructions in the excavated area (stratum V). In the Byzantine period, in the sixth or seventh century (stratum IV), a wall (2.7 m wide) was built up to the gate and the towers. Other remains of building activity in this period were found in the gate area and east and west of it; however, because they lay mostly beneath later remains, the plan of the structure adjacent to the wall could not be traced. In the eastern tower a large number of "incendiary bombs" from stratum IV were found. The major building activity east and west of the gate and in the gate itself belongs to the eighth to tenth centuries (strata III–II). To the east of the gate, part of a large structure was uncovered that was built against the wall and above it and caused a narrowing of the wall there. The gate continued to exist

Area C: the city gate and later structures.

Area C: residential building, 11th century CE.

Area C: residential building, 8th–9th centuries CE.

in strata II and I. The floors were raised, but no other significant alterations were made in its plan. The city wall, however, ceased to serve a defensive purpose, as shown by the openings made in it to the south, to accommodate the city's expansion in the eighth and ninth centuries (areas A and B).

To the west of the gate was a very large, well-built structure that had a beautiful, paved courtyard with a small garden in its center. It had two stories, like most of the other buildings uncovered. Doorways led to the gate area at a lower level, where various buildings, mostly shops, were erected. Shops also stood along the side of the *cardo*, considerably narrowing it. Most of the doorways were on the north side of the building, indicating that there was probably a street perpendicular to the *cardo*. In this period, changes were also made in the gate. Openings were pierced in the niches decorating the gate's interior and led to the towers. The narrowing of the street was accompanied by a marked reduction in the width of the entrance, which, in strata II and I, was only 1.5 m wide. Strips of metal and large nails belonging to the doors in the gate's last period of use were uncovered.

The gate's present location in a wadi is probably the result of changes in the course of the wadi, which originally flowed south of the gate—it is hardly conceivable that a gate would be placed in the bed of a wadi. A series of walls was built inside and close to the western tower to protect it from floodwater, but part of it was nevertheless completely destroyed.

AREAS D1 AND D2. Areas D1 and D2 were situated some 200 m north of area

Area D1: hoard of coins and jewelry, 11th century CE.

Two-storied Roman tomb.

C. A workshop from the eighth to the eleventh centuries, possibly for dyeing, was found in area D1. It yielded a hoard of coins and jewelry from the tenth and eleventh centuries. A drainage system from the Early Roman period ran beneath this installation. It contained Early Roman pottery, marble fragments, and coins. No building remains from this period were found here.

In area D2, a series of retaining walls was preserved to a height of about 7 m. The foundations of a very large building were also found, but its nature and date are not yet clear.

SUMMARY. The excavations in the southern part of the city testify to Tiberias' wealth from the eighth to eleventh centuries, when the city was destroyed. Judging from the latest coins and from the ceramic evidence, it appears that the city ceased to prosper in the second half of the eleventh century, and the areas examined were abandoned with the Crusader conquest and never resettled. The city was thereafter confined farther north, within the limits of the modern city of Tiberias, covering a much smaller area than its predecessors.

GIDEON FOERSTER

THE ROMAN TOMB

In 1976, when construction in the Qiryat Shmuel neighborhood was in progress, a Roman tomb was discovered on the site. It was excavated by F. Vitto on behalf of the Israel Department of Antiquities and Museums.

The tomb (8 by 10 m) was built above ground on the mountain slope. It was surrounded by a wall built of basalt ashlars. The entrance faced southeast (downhill) and was approached through a lower courtyard paved with stone slabs, reached via masonry steps. The entrance was sealed by a basalt door (0.85 by 1.3 m), with four carved panels and an iron hinge.

The tomb consisted of two burial chambers: one at the level of the courtyard and another underground. Access to the underground chamber was by way of a narrow passage cut through the floor of the upper chamber. Hewn in the walls of the upper chamber (c. 3.3 by 4 m) were twenty-eight loculi in two rows, one above the other. The openings were built of ashlars, and the interiors of the loculi were lined with white plaster. A bench, also built of ashlars, surrounded the chamber. The underground chamber (1.8 by 2.2 by 4.2 m) was cut under the northwestern loculi of the upper chamber. Its walls and floor were covered with coarse plaster, and its ceiling, which was made of stone beams, was supported by three arches.

Human skeletons were found in most of the loculi in the upper chamber. One loculus contained a limestone ossuary with a gabled lid; in the ossuary were the bones of two skeletons. In the underground chamber thirty-five skeletons were lying on the floor; near them were oil lamps, glass bottles, and cooking pots, all of which date the use of the tomb to the end of the first and beginning of the second centuries CE.

FANNY VITTO

General: M. Avi-Yonah, *IEJ* 1 (1950–1951), 160–169; D. Ussishkin, ibid. 18 (1968), 45–46; B. Lifshitz, *Euphrosyne* n.s. 6 (1973–1974), 23–27; G. Foerster, *RB* 82 (1975), 105–109; id., *Recherches Archéologiques en Israël* 206–209; E. Ballhorn, *Israel—Land and Nature* 1 (1976), 151–153; A. Brunot, *BTS* 192 (1977), 10–20; L. I. Levine, *HUCA* 49 (1978), 143–185; M. Ben-Dov, *ASR*, 157–159; N. Feig, *ESI* 1 (1982), 110; S. Dar, ibid. 2 (1983), 103; id., *IEJ* 33 (1983), 114–115; A. Harif, *PEQ* 116 (1984), 103–109; J-F. Desclaux, *MdB* 38 (1985), 45–47; G. Theissen, *ZDPV* 101 (1985), 43–55; S. Qedar, *Israel Numismatic Journal* 9 (1986–1987), 29–33; H. Dudman and E. Ballhorn, *Tiberias*, Jerusalem 1988; D. Stacey, *BAIAS* 8 (1988–1989), 21–33; A. Cohen, *ESI* 9 (1989–1990), 171; Y. Hirschfeld, ibid., 107–109; id., *BAR* 17/2 (1991), 44–51; id., *MdB* 72 (1991), 21–23; *BA* 54 (1991), 170–171.

The tombs: *BTS* 76 (1965), 16, 79; A. Biran, *CNI* 17/2–3 (1966), 25; V. Tsaferis, *IEJ* 18 (1968), 15–19; A. Ovadiah, ibid. 22 (1972), 229–232; F. Vitto, *Archéologia* 110 (1977), 69–70.

TILLA, ḤORVAT

IDENTIFICATION

Ḥorvat Tilla (Khirbet Khuweilfa) is located east of Tel Ḥalif in the southern Shephelah, about 16 km northeast of Beersheba (map reference 1375.0878). The settlement's cemetery lies to its north, at the foot of the ruin, on the slope of Tel Ḥalif (map reference 1274.0879). Nineteenth-century explorers observed a large ruin with caves, cisterns, walls, and architectural remains. The ruin was used by Bedouin and peasants from Dura (Adoraim) as a seasonal settlement (*mazra'a* in Arabic) in the mid-nineteenth century, and a small permanent year-round settlement existed here between the British Mandatory period and Israel's War of Independence in 1948. The settlement's builders reused ancient building stones found on the surface and in ancient walls. The house of the mukhtar, the head of the village, for example, is built of such stones; similar stones were found in secondary use in other modern buildings.

The site is near the area on which Kibbutz Lahav was established in 1952. In the mid-1970s, when the kibbutz began to extend its houses to the area of the ruin, several soundings were conducted. They made it clear that Ḥorvat Tilla is a low, broad mound adjoining Tel Ḥalif. Its earliest remains belong to the Chalcolithic period and the Early Bronze Age I. The sherds found here also indicate settlement in the Hellenistic, Roman, and Byzantine periods. Only a few structures, mainly field-stone walls, from these periods have been observed. They are insufficient to reconstruct the plan of the settlement or even of individual buildings.

The ancient settlement covered about 20 a. The finds included stone-carved doorposts, as well as fragments of thresholds and lintels, some of them decorated. Many caves, used by the inhabitants in various periods, were found nearby.

The finds from the settlement's cemetery indicate that the settlement was inhabited by Jews. According to Eusebius: "Θαλχά (Thalca), in the territory of Simeon, presently is called Thala, a very large Jewish village about sixteen miles from Beth Guvrin in Daroma" (*Onom.* 98, 26). The distance between the site and Beth Guvrin is indeed about 25 km (16 mi.) as the crow flies; along the ancient road identified in the region, the distance was close to Eusebius' measurement of sixteen miles. The name Tilla clearly indicates the proximity of a mound to the Jewish village. The distance recorded by Eusebius, the name of the ancient village, and the finds from the cemetery all reinforce this identification, which was proposed even before the cemetery was excavated.

CEMETERY FROM THE ROMAN PERIOD

The entrances of tomb caves 3 to 6 were first exposed during the construction of an access road to Kibbutz Lahav and were excavated in 1962, during the widening of the road. Four other caves (1, 2, 7, and 8) were excavated in 1974 by A. Kloner, on behalf of the Israel Department of Antiquities and Museums. The caves, hewn in the slope of the hill, are arranged in a row with their entrances facing north. All have courtyards, most of which were destroyed by the machinery used to build the road.

Cave 1 consists of two rooms and an ashlar-built facade.

Cave 2 contains a single room with a standing pit in its center. In this room nine sarcophagi of the southern Judean type, with gabled lids and acroteria, were found. They are dated to the Late Roman period. The cave also contained pottery and glass vessels from the second and third centuries CE.

Cave 3 is a square room with a standing pit in its center and six loculi (*kokhim*) in its walls.

Cave 4 is also a square room with a standing pit in its center. The walls contain six loculi for primary burial and smaller loculi for collected bones.

Cave 5 was excavated in 1962 and its finds were published by R. Gophna and V. Sussman. The cave consists of two rooms: the first contains a standing pit surrounded by a ledge, on which nineteen sarcophagi were found; five repositories in the walls and the standing pit were also uncovered. The inner room contained a standing pit surrounded by a ledge without loculi. The finds include fragments of a sarcophagus, a lid, and isolated bones. The sarcophagi in cave 5 are the same type and date as those found in cave 2. The cave also contained glass vessels, oil lamps, and pottery vessels that, in the opinion of the excavators, date the use of the cave to the second and third centuries CE. Judging from the glass vessels, the cave was still in use at the beginning of the fourth century.

Cave 6 consists of a square room with a standing pit in its center surrounded by ledges. A large sarcophagus was found in the room.

Caves 3, 4, and 6 were excavated by members of Kibbutz Lahav in 1962, but no orderly records were kept of the locations in which the various objects were found. The finds included glass bottles, oil lamps, and fragments of other pottery vessels, dated to the second and third centuries CE. An oil lamp decorated with clusters of grapes and vine leaves and with the name ΚΑΛΛΙΣΤΟΥ engraved on its base, apparently from Corinth, Greece, was published. Split storage jars from the second to fourth centuries, used as ossuaries, are noteworthy.

Cave 7 is a square room containing eight loculi for primary burial and seven small loculi for collected bones. In its center is a standing pit. About fifty ossuary fragments were found in the cave. The cave's plan, the ossuaries, and some of the sherds indicate that this was one of the earliest caves in the cemetery and was first used in the second half of the first century CE.

Cave 8 is a single hall with sixteen burial benches for primary burial. In its center is a standing pit surrounded by especially wide ledges (1.6–2 m wide). This standing pit is a survival from the architectural tradition originating in earlier burial caves. It exemplifies the conservatism of the tradition, for the quarriers of this tomb cave adhered to the practice of installing a pit with ledges, even though it was possible to stand upright without the pit.

Bench 1 is a single burial bench in an arcosolium; burial benches 2 and 3 are arranged one behind the other in a single arcosolium. Benches 4–13 were arranged in pairs and in groups of three in parallel form, relative to the arcosolium's opening. The form of benches 1 to 13 is common at various sites in the southern Shephelah, such as Ḥorvat Gomer and Ḥorvat Kishor. This burial method is characteristic of the southern part of the country and was used from the third century CE onward, especially in the fourth century.

Judging from the finds, tomb cave 8 was in use at the end of the third and in the fourth centuries. Tomb cave 8 intersects cave 7: the cave's western wall and bench 1 penetrated loculi 5 and 15 of tomb cave 7. Burial cave 8 is the latest of the caves in the cemetery.

Guérin, *Judée* 2, 352; Conder–Kitchener, *SWP* 3, 397; O. Borowski, *BASOR* 227 (1977), 63–65; J. D. Seger, ibid. 252 (1983), 1–23.

AMOS KLONER

Ḥorvat Tilla: plan of the burial system.

TIMNA'

IDENTIFICATION

The Timna' Valley (Wadi Mene'iyeh) lies alongside Naḥal Arabah, some 30 km (18.5 mi.) north of the Gulf of Elath-'Aqaba. It is a large (c. 70 sq km) semicircular erosion formation, open on the east toward the Arabah, containing four wadis that run from the Timna' Cliffs into Naḥal Arabah. Along the foot of the Timna' Cliffs, within white sandstone layers of the Amir-Ḥatira Formation (L. *Cretaceous*), are mainly copper carbonate ore nodules that consist of malachite and chalcocite (up to 55 percent) mixed with azurite, cuprite, paratacamite. A second type of copper ore, of the chrysocolla group (copper silicates), is located in the Timna' Formation of the Lower Cambrian and was therefore more difficult to reach by ancient mining methods. However, both types of ore, the copper carbonates and the copper silicates, were exploited in antiquity. Numerous mine workings, including shafts and galleries, as well as mining tools from various periods, were found in this part of the Timna' Valley.

Eleven camps are located in the center of the valley, west of the Timna' Massif, several containing substantial slag heaps, testimony to the existence of intensive mining activities. These remains belong mainly to the Nineteenth and Twentieth dynasties of the Egyptian New Kingdom (Late Bronze Age–Iron Age I–II). There is only one smelting site in the mining area of the Timna' Valley: Site F2, Early Chalcolithic, perhaps Late Neolithic (Qatifian). All other early (Chalcolithic to Early Bronze IV) smelting sites were located outside the Timna' Valley, along the western fringes of the Arabah. A Chalcolithic copper-smelting installation (Site 39) was excavated east of the mod-

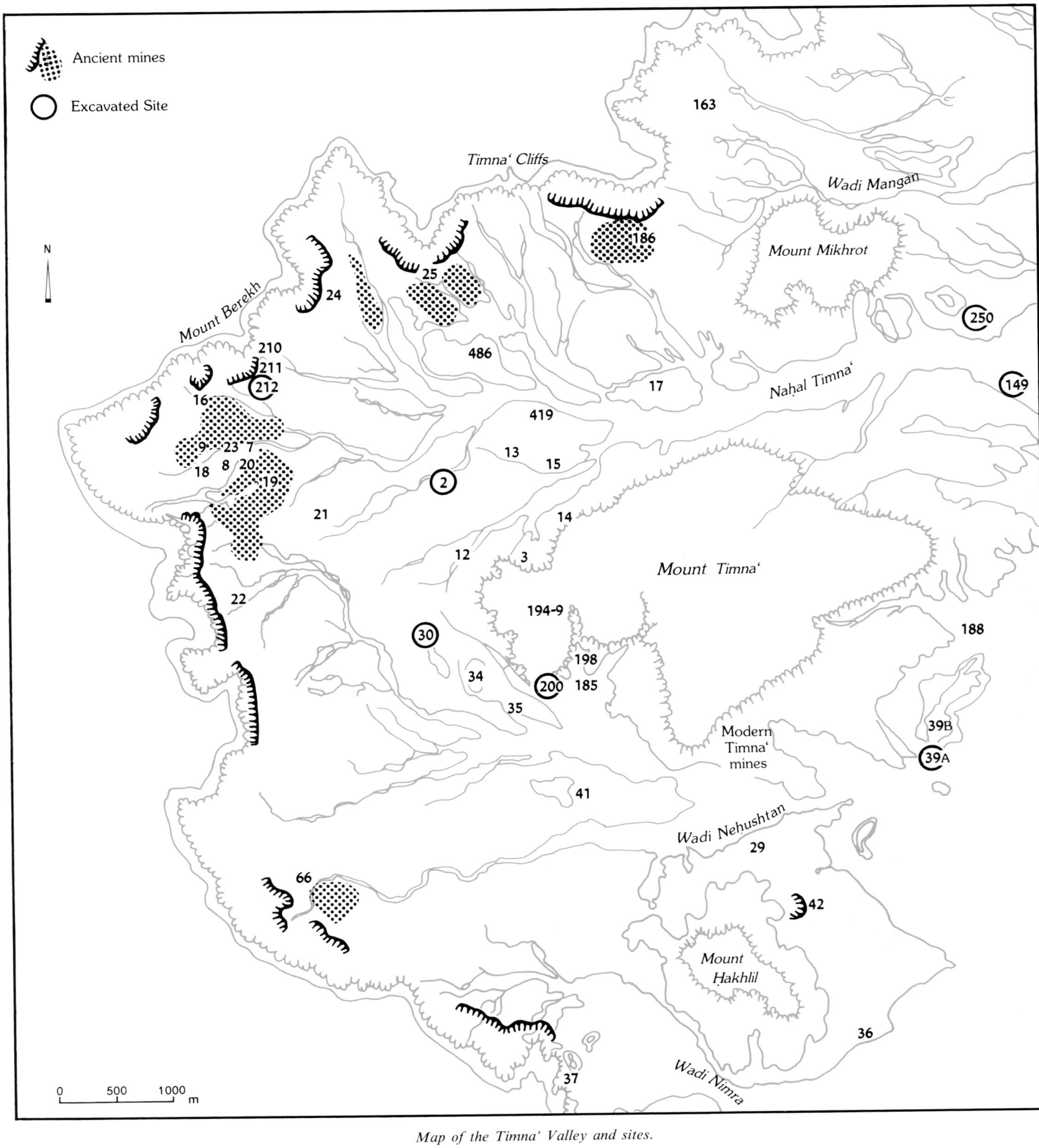

Map of the Timna' Valley and sites.

ern copper works. North of the Timna' Valley, an Early Bronze Age II copper-smelting site (Site 201A) was excavated, as were an Early Bronze Age IV smelting site (Site 149) and mine (Site 250) at the estuary of Wadi Timna'. South of the Timna' Valley, the center of Roman and Early Arab copper smelting in the western Arabah was located at Be'er Ora (Site 28).

HISTORY OF EXPLORATION

In 1845, the British explorer J. Petherick identified copper-smelting slag in Timna' (Wadi el-Maḥait). In 1907, A. Musil found "remains of dwellings" here. F. Frank located seven copper-smelting sites at Timna' in 1934, which N. Glueck also described in 1935. Glueck first dated the pottery found here to the Iron Age I and II; in 1940, he attributed the copper smelting in Timna' to King Solomon, calling the area King Solomon's mines. Between 1959 and 1961, B. Rothenberg explored the Timna' Valley and in 1962 published, with Y. Aharoni and B. H. McLeod, a detailed description of its ancient mines and smelting camps. "King Solomon's mines" were dated to several widely separated periods, from the fourth millennium to Roman times.

EXCAVATIONS

In 1964, Rothenberg founded the Arabah Expedition, an independent research group under the auspices of the Haaretz Museum in Tel Aviv, to excavate at Timna'. A. Lupu, a specialist in extractive metallurgy at the Haifa Technion; R. F. Tylecote, a specialist in metallurgy, then at the University of Newcastle-upon-Tyne and later at the Institute for Archaeo-Metallurgical Studies, University College, London; H. G. Bachmann, a specialist in chemistry and mineralogy at the Institute for Archaeo-Metallurgical Studies, University College, London; and J. W. Goethe University, Frankfurt a/M. (Germany) joined the expedition in the late 1960s. The excavations were directed by Rothenberg. Between 1964 and 1990, the following sites at Timna' were excavated:

1964–1966 and 1981	Site 2, a smelting camp dated to the Ramesside period (19th–20th dynasties).
1965 and 1989	Site 39, a primitive copper-smelting site from the Late Chalcolithic period (fourth millennium).
1969	Site 28 (at Be'er Ora, south of Timna'), a second and seventh-century CE Roman and Early Arab copper-smelting plant.
1969 and 1974	Site 200, a mining sanctuary dedicated to the Egyptian goddess Hathor and dated by inscriptions to the late fourteenth–mid-twelfth centuries BCE.
1974–1976	Site 30, a smelting camp from the Ramesside period and Site F2, probably a Late Neolithic (Qatifian) smelter.

General view of smelting Site 2.

Taanach: cult stand decorated with human and animal figures, 10th century BCE.

Ḥorvat Teman: aerial view of the site.

Site 212: shaft-and-gallery system, LB/Iron I; (left) the upper level. The narrow, shaded section parallel to the gallery is the ventilation shaft.

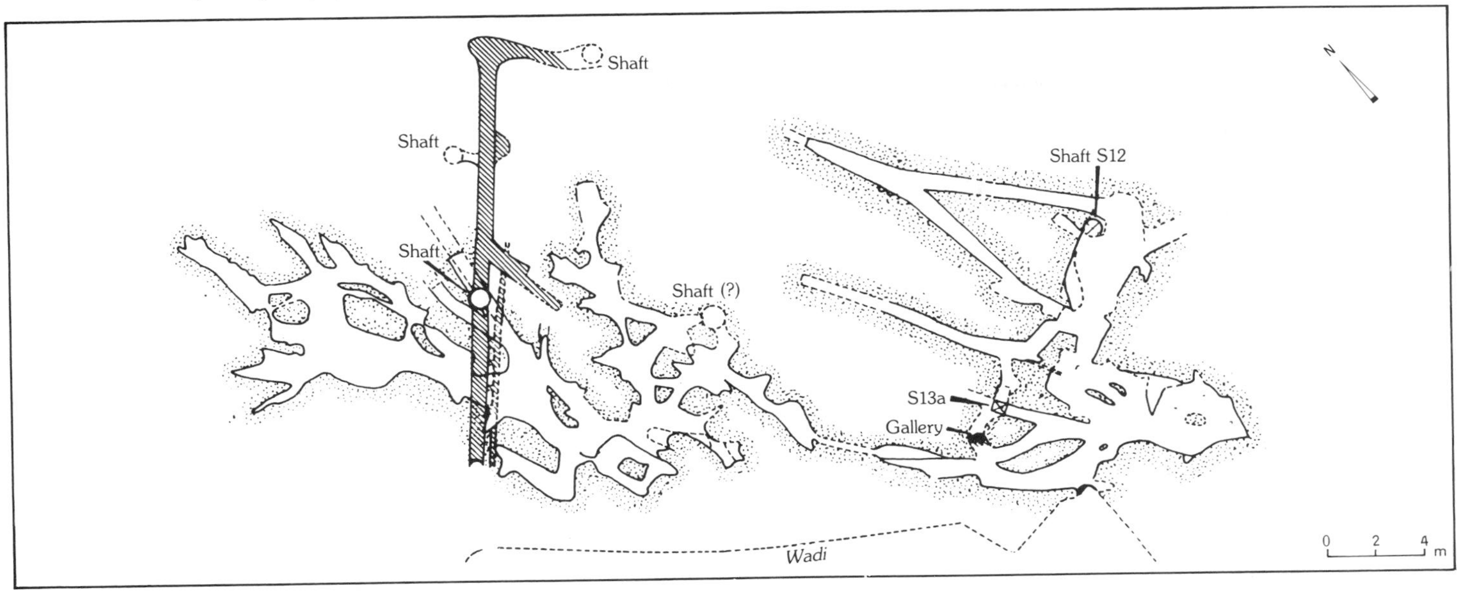

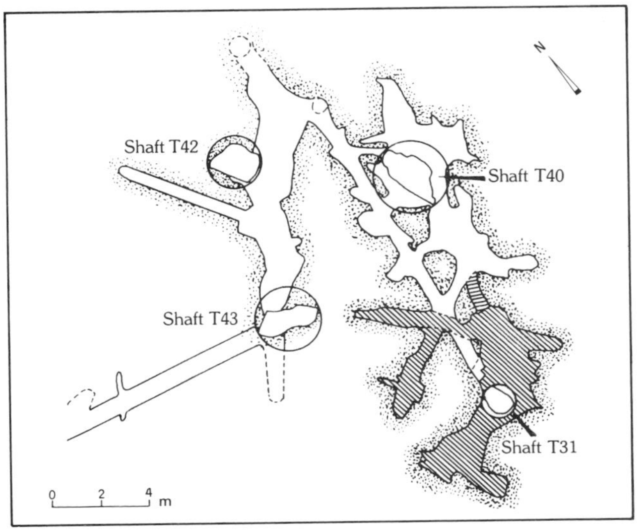

Plan of the Chalcolithic/EB I mine. The shaded section is the upper level. Access was initially gained through shaft T31.

1974–1976	Site 212, an area of shaft and gallery mining, from the Chalcolithic, Early Bronze Age, and, mainly, Ramesside periods.
1977	Site 201A, an Early Bronze Age II smelting site and settlement.
1982	Site 149, an Early Bronze Age IV (Middle Bronze I) copper-smelting plant.
1990	Site 250, a Chalcolithic and Early Bronze Age IV mine.
1990	Site 38, a Roman–Early Arab copper mine in Wadi ‘Amram.

THE MINES—AREA 212

During the survey of the Timna‘ Valley by the Arabah Expedition (1959–1961 and 1967–1982), shafts and galleries were discovered in white sandstone formations at the foot of the 300-m-high Timna‘ Cliffs (map reference 1432.9115). These mine workings were excavated from 1974 to 1976, in collaboration with a specialized team of miners and mining surveyors from the Bergbau Museum in Bochum, Germany. Three different elements of mining technology were revealed in the area investigated.

1. Deep shafts, some more than 35 m deep, sunk vertically into the conglomerate and other rock formations in order to locate areas particularly rich in copper ores in the cupriferous white sandstone layers.

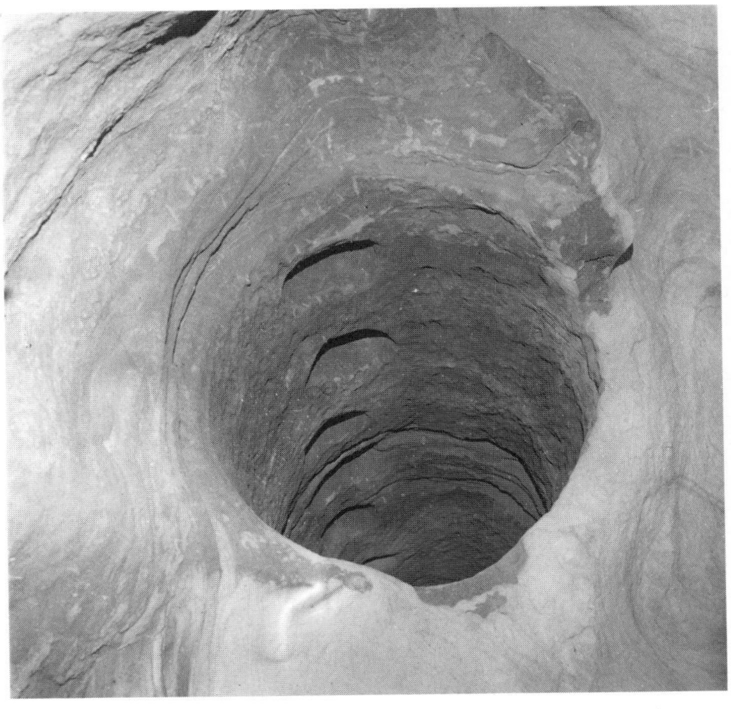

Site 212: a rock-cut shaft with niches for footholds cut into its sides.

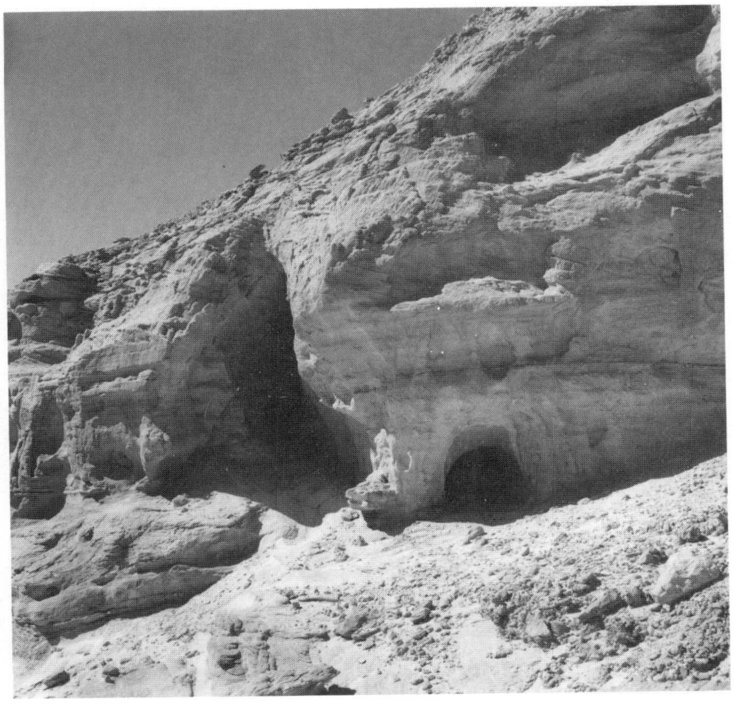

Site 212: the entrance to the LB/Iron I mining system.

2. Narrow galleries (c. 70 cm wide and 1 m high), driven horizontally into the white rock, branched and sometimes widened underground. The entrance to these galleries was through vertical mine shafts. One system of shafts and galleries had two superimposed levels connected by a narrow shaft. In one of the three mining systems cleared in 1974, local wheel-made and Negbite ware were found, confirming the New Kingdom (Late Bronze–Iron Age I) date of these systems. In another, more primitive shaft-and-gallery system, excavated in 1976, shafted mining hammers were found with local Late Chalcolithic/Early Bronze Age I pottery. This is the earliest shaft-and-gallery copper mining technology known so far.

3. On many slopes above the cupriferous white sandstone layer, silt-filled, saucerlike round areas (diameter, 2–6 m) had been noted during the first explorations. They were interpreted as ore-dressing installations, where copper ore, mined nearby, was separated from the unwanted gangue. Investigations in 1975 by a team from the Arabah Expedition established that these "saucers," or plates, were, in fact, silt-filled mining shafts from different periods. They had been dug through the upper conglomerate cover and into the copper-ore-bearing sandstone, either for prospecting or as part of shaft-and-gallery mining systems.

Pottery and stone as well as metal mining tools were recovered on the plate areas and in the mines. They indicate a Chalcolithic/Early Bronze Age phase, major New Kingdom (Late Bronze Age/Iron Age I) mining activities, and Roman and Early Arab small-scale work. The sophisticated technology of the Late Bronze Age/Iron Age I shaft-and-gallery systems at Timna' was previously known only in Roman mines in Europe. These mine workings represented such large-scale, sophisticated enterprises that it called for the revision of the history of mining.

A CHALCOLITHIC AND EARLY BRONZE AGE IV COPPER MINE: SITE 250. A group of mine workings in a low range of hills next to Giv'at Sasgon, in close proximity to Site 149, was the source of blue bisbeeite-chrysocolla ore. Site 250, discovered in 1967, was excavated in 1990. There were essentially two mines—250 and 250A—which were shelterlike "caves" with a thick vein of mineralization, mainly the blue-ore bisbeeite. Many outcrops of the same blue ore were observed on the hills around Giv'at Sasgon and may well have been exploited in ancient times.

Inside mine 250, many fine flint drills were found in shallow, ashy habitation midden, together with tiny bits of platey blue ore. This was a bead manufacturing workshop, dated by sherds to the Chalcolithic period. A small slag heap found on top of this ridge (Site 250B) also contained similar Chalcolithic pottery, providing evidence for Chalcolithic copper smelting also using copper silicate ores.

Mine 250A was a much larger mine, partly destroyed by a huge rockfall. It was essentially also a mineralized, shelterlike cave created by following the mineral vein horizontally. A flat area in front of the mine served as an ore-

Chalcolithic smelting Site 39A. The modern Timna' mines are in the background.

dressing station; a large mineralized boulder brought from inside the mine was found here, together with a number of spherical flint hammer stones. A number of sherds found on the slope outside 250A provided additional dating evidence for Site 250. The importance of Site 250 for the mining history of Timna' is that it provided the first evidence for ancient mining in the southern Arabah of copper silicate ores, the main source of copper in the mines of the northern Arabah, especially around Feinan.

SMELTING CAMPS AND MINING SANCTUARY

The excavations at the mining camps of Timna' not only produced well-dated evidence for the reconstruction of the organization of copper industries from the fourth millennium BCE to the second century CE, but also the actual copper-smelting furnaces, copper ores and fluxes, huge slag heaps, and copper ingots. In the center of the Timna' Valley, a small mining sanctuary was excavated. It contained almost ten thousand small finds, including a large number of metal objects and a small casting installation for votive figurines. The hieroglyphic inscriptions found here provided the evidence for the absolute dating of the Egyptian New Kingdom copper industry at Timna'. The excavations are described below in chronological order.

AN EARLY CHALCOLITHIC (PROBABLY LATE NEOLITHIC [QATIFIAN] COPPER-SMELTING SITE: SITE F2. Site F2 is the only smelting site found within the mining region of the Timna' Valley. It was located next to a pit-mining area (area G); it represents the earliest prehistoric mining technology, which was to dig irregular holes into the conglomerate cover of the rock wadi bed to extract nodules of copper ores. The smelting site F2 consisted of a small quantity (c. 4 kg) of broken, highly viscous slag, with many semimolten ore inclusions, concentrated around two large stone bowls. There was also handmade, chaff-tempered pottery and the stone bowls are typical of the earliest Chalcolithic, probably Qatifian, settlements in the Arabah and Sinai. The site was excavated to bedrock.

Among the slag pieces, fragments of a clay tuyere were found that could be reconstructed. This is the earliest tuyere found so far—evidence for the use of bellows at this early phase of metallurgy in the Arabah. No smelting furnace was preserved, but slagged sand lumps indicated a "hole-in-the-ground" furnace. The slag, although undoubtedly the waste-product of a copper-smelting process, indicated a primitive, incipient copper-smelting technology, the earliest found so far.

A CHALCOLITHIC COPPER-SMELTING SITE: SITE 39. Site 39 is located at the top (39B) and at the foot (39A) of a 30-m-high hill, east of the modern Timna' works and just north of Naḥal Neḥushtan.

Site 39A. The building remains at Site 39A consisted of an oval enclosure of rough field stones and three tumuli. The surface finds indicated that a mixture of ores and fluxes was prepared here, probably the smelting charges for the smelting furnaces on the top of the hill (39B). Chalcolithic flint tools and pottery were also found. In locus 1, a structure (4 by 5 m) with rounded corners was excavated. Inside, small, flat stones formed a roundish "floor" (diameter, c. 80 cm) with a small, ash-filled pit next to it. This arrangement resembles a group of pebbles at Chalcolithic Be'er Abu Matar, near Beersheba, but, unlike it, the Timna' group bore no marks of any kind. Some bone fragments also were found. This structure seems to have been used as a dwelling. In loci 2 to 4 fireplaces built of stone circles and containing ashes were found. Stone hammers and mortars, as well as a quantity of copper ores found here, attest to a connection with copper-smelting site 39B on the hill above.

Site 39B: remains of a Chalcolithic smelting furnace.

Site 39B. Site 39B, on top of the hill, was a copper smelter. Prior to excavation, small pieces of a peculiar rough, viscous slag and some flint implements and sherds had indicated a Chalcolithic smelter. A 3-by-5-m area was excavated. About 10 cm below the surface level, a heavily burned pit was found. This was a primitive, bowl-type copper-smelting furnace that originally had a diameter of 20 cm and was some 60 cm high. A working surface with slag, charcoal, Chalcolithic flint tools, and pottery was found in situ around the furnace. This is the earliest copper-smelting furnace known to date. Its primitive construction represents an early phase of extractive copper metallurgy, although the analysis of the slag indicated the use of iron oxides as flux—a more advanced smelting technology than at Site F2.

AN EARLY BRONZE AGE II SMELTING SITE: SITE 201A. Site 201A is located in the Arabah, about 3 km north of Timna'. It consists of a widely dispersed group of enclosures, one of which was excavated in 1977. It was found to be a habitation and workshop structure, typical of the local population during the Early Bronze Age II in the Arabah and Sinai, and contained pottery and flint implements from the period. A quantity of small crushed slag pieces was also found, but no smelting furnace. The slag resembles the Chalcolithic smelting slag at Site 39, but some pieces show the flow structure of tapping slag. This is the earliest evidence for the tapping of slag found so far and represents an advanced phase of extractive metallurgy.

AN EARLY BRONZE AGE IV COPPER-SMELTING SITE: SITE 149. Site 149 is located on a small, solitary hillock in the middle of the wide estuary of Naḥal Timna'. It was excavated in 1984. There was a workshop area on the lower slope of the hill that had a low wall running right through it, probably as a wind shield. Crushing anvils and mortars and many small stone hammers were found in small groups, as if workers had just left for a short break. Inside some of the mortars were chunks of blue ore and finely crushed blue ore (bisbeeite, of the chrysocolla group of copper silicate ores); malachite ore was found dispersed in the workshop as well. The smelting charge was obviously prepared here. There were also numerous tiny fragments of slag, some looking like typical crucible-melting slag, an indication of secondary refining and casting activities. Fragments of slagged clay crucibles, found on the floor of the workshop, are additional evidence for casting, perhaps of the bar ingots found at contemporary sites in the Negev.

The actual copper smelting took place on the flat top of the hill, which was found covered with a relatively large quantity of tapped slag. This was evidence of a hitherto unknown scale of copper production. This slag was much more solid and homogeneous than the slag at the Chalcolithic and Early Bronze Age II smelting sites. It was mainly low-viscosity, tapped slag. There were several heaps of heavily charred and partly slagged rocks, obviously the debris of stone-built smelting furnaces. These bear witness to a major step forward in the history of extractive metallurgy: the advance from a primitive, indigenous, prehistoric hole-in-the-ground-plus-bellows technology to a quite large-scale industrial production of copper in stone-built furnaces.

A number of sherds of locally made Early Bronze Age IV pottery was found at Site 149, but no other traces of habitation. The site had been set up at a considerable distance from any habitation site of the period as a proper industrial plant. Site 149 exhibits pyrotechnical process details not encountered before in the Arabah; they seem to indicate a "foreign" origin for the technology, or at least a strong outside influence.

A NEW KINGDOM (LATE BRONZE/IRON AGE I) SMELTING CAMP: SITE 2. Site 2 is in a small tributary of Naḥal Timna', where slag heaps indicated smelting activity. The aims of excavation here were to reconstruct how copper was smelted at a large, late second-millennium BCE copper-production plant and to establish a reliable stratigraphy to clarify its chronology. Site 2 was excavated in two seasons, in 1964 and 1966.

Area A. Southeast of the industrial area and higher up on the slope, a tumulus was excavated to bedrock, and two superimposed structures were uncovered. Structure I, a rectangular building (9 by 8 m) was built on bedrock, with its entrance on the east. Flanking the entrance was a low stone bench, probably used for offerings. A large, square, flat-topped monolith stood in the center and may have served as an altar. Around it was a quantity of broken animal bones, ashes, and pottery. On the west side of the building stood a row of five large, roughly dressed *maṣṣebot* (stelae), with a large stone bowl, perhaps for libations, in front of them. A semicircular annex was built next to the entrance and another against the outer northern wall. Much ash and many broken goat bones were found inside both annexes.

Structure I was a small Semitic place of worship, attached to the large smelting site. After its destruction, apparently in an earthquake, it was abandoned and completely covered by wind-blown sand. Structure II (3.5 by 2.5 m) was erected on top of the sand-covered debris, with an

Site 2: LB/Iron I smelting furnace.

Site 2: maṣṣebot *and a stone bowl in the cult site, structure I, area A.*

entrance on the southeast; its walls were 80 cm high. It contained only a few coarse sherds.

Area B. On the eastern side of Site 2, in area B, a large (10 by 7.5 m) installation used to manufacture charcoal from acacia trees was found. An adjacent furnace (40 by 40 cm and 80 cm deep) was uncovered, in which pellets of metallic copper, which had been extracted from the smelting slag, were melted in small crucibles for casting small copper objects. Near this melting installation was a small workshop (5 by 4 m) with a deep, stone-lined ore pit and a stone-paved semicircular crushing platform. Crushing tools and a quantity of finely crushed copper ore were found in situ on this working platform.

Area D–K. In area D–K, at the northern end of Site 2, a large building complex (c. 400 sq m) was uncovered. It comprised a complete working and storage unit. Its walls were dry-built in header-and-stretcher construction. In its center was a courtyard (8 by 11 m), with a very large stone-lined storage pit for ores. Next to it was a stone-paved platform; many crushing and grinding tools and crushed copper ore were found in situ. This courtyard was where the smelting charge was prepared. Two rooms, built against the courtyard's western wall, had stone-lined storage pits along their walls. Attached to the western side of the courtyard, a two-roomed structure was used as a workshop and perhaps living quarters. A small cooking stove was found outside it. At the northern end of area D–K was a casting workshop containing several superimposed working floors of furnaces, together with a large quantity of wood ash, charcoal dust, copper pellets, slag, and slagged crucible fragments. A large storage pit was also found here. The workshop was partially destroyed by an earthquake and subsequently rebuilt.

Area C. In area C, a 10-by-6 m section was excavated, including part of a solid, 50-cm-high heap of heavy circular slag plates (diameter, 35–50 cm). Next to this slag heap two smelting furnaces (Fu III and Fu IV) were found. Furnace IV was very well preserved. The actual smelting hearth was merely a hole in the ground (diameter, 45 cm and 40 cm deep) originally lined with a thick layer of clay mortar that also formed a dome-shaped top. A considerable amount of slag still adhered to the furnace walls. Two flanking stones protected a shallow pit dug in front of the furnace.

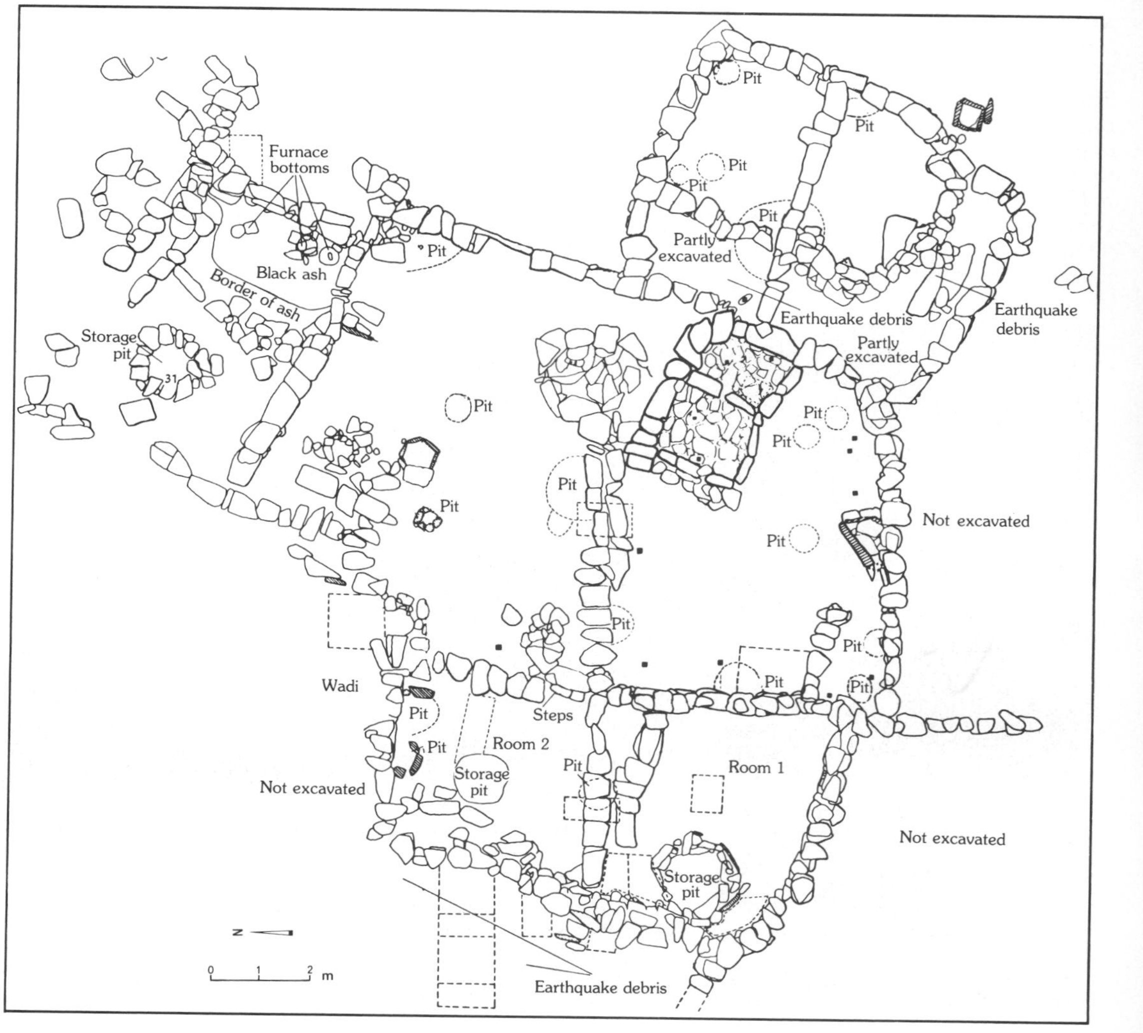

Site 2: plan of the building complex in area D–K.

Site 2: corbel-vaulted tomb in area M containing the remains of two skeletons of African origin.

This was a slag-tapping pit, dug at a lower level to guarantee the swift flow of the hot liquid slag through the tapping hole drilled into the side of the furnace.

A clay tube found in situ, penetrating the furnace wall opposite the tapping hole, must have served as the tuyere for the bellows. Underneath the uppermost stratum, characterized by the large circular slag circles with a hole in the center, there was an earlier stratum of crushed platey slag and small semi-spherical tuyeres; unfortunately, however, no furnaces from this initial period at Site 2 were recovered. Excavations at Site 30 (1974–1976) produced furnaces belonging technologically and stratigraphically to the same phase of New Kingdom Timna' (see below).

In area C, three superimposed working floors were found separated by a thin layer of wind-borne drift sand, attesting to seasonal operations at the site. The pottery found on the floors belonged to the New Kingdom (Late Bronze Age–Iron Age I) and was essentially of three types: Negbite, Midianite, and local wheel-made ware (comprising mainly Egyptian types) found at all the Egyptian smelting camps at Timna'.

Areas E and G. Two smelting furnaces (Fu I and Fu II) were found in these areas next to large slag heaps. They resemble furnace IV described above, except that they are stone built and had no dome-shaped top. They consisted of a semicircular wall of dolomite, with an open side above the tapping pit, which was protected by two flanking stones. The wall and bottom were clay-lined, and a clay tube pierced its back wall. Behind the furnace was a solid working platform of large flat stones. Five superimposed metallurgical working floors, with remains of smelting furnaces and metallurgical waste, were found in area G; the lowest floor rested on bedrock. Many small, bell-shaped pits (20–40 cm deep) were dug in all the floors. In the lowest floor, thirty-six pits were found, some containing date pits and the bones of goats, donkeys, camels, and fish.

Area F. About 70 m west of the actual smelting area, on the summit of a hill, an oval-shaped tumulus (4.8 by 3.1 m and 50 cm high) was excavated and a "floor" of flat stones was exposed, carefully laid on solid rock. An unusually large quantity of sherds was found in clearing area F, including numerous decorated sherds of Midianite ware. Many faience, carnelian, mica schist, stone, and glass beads; several very small copper spatulas and needles; many perforated Red Sea shells and ostrich eggshells; and a quantity of metallurgical debris were also found. On the floor itself were several goat horns, copper rings, two iron armlets, and many beads.

Because of its location, structures and finds, area F has been interpreted as a *bamah*, or "high place," where small copper votive implements, such as were found in the neighboring Hathor sanctuary (see below), were cast. It seems that the small-scale metallurgical operations in area F were an integral part of the actual ritual and that the Midianites were the worshipers.

Area M. Inside a carefully built corbeled vault, a skeleton was found with its

Site 30: LB/Iron I smelting site, surrounded by a wall and towers.

head on a flat stone used as a headrest. There were also remains of a second skeleton. Both were Proto-Boskopoid, of African origin.

The finds at Site 2 included numerous saddle-backed red sandstone querns, flint, granite and sandstone hammer stones, mortars, and pestles. Several copper implements were found, some in an unfinished "as cast" stage. These implements had been made locally.

Date of Site 2. A scarab found in area K belonged to the period of Ramses II (1304–1237 BCE). In all areas, the same three, essentially different kinds of pottery were found: local wheel-made pottery, Negbite ware, and Midianite pottery (see below). Site 2 was dated to the thirteenth to twelfth centuries BCE, a New Kingdom date confirmed in 1969 when the Hathor sanctuary was discovered.

A NEW KINGDOM (LATE BRONZE–IRON AGE I) FORTIFIED SMELTING CAMP: SITE 30. Site 30 is a large smelting camp (40 by 80 m) that was excavated in 1974 and 1976. It is surrounded by a strong defensive wall with two towers guarding its gate. Before excavation, a very large heap of heavy slag "cakes" was found in the center of the camp. The excavation itself provided sound stratigraphic evidence for dating the Egyptian smelting activities at Timna'. Three strata (I–III) were distinguished. Strata III and II consisted of many superimposed working floors, separated by wind- and water-laid sand, dated to the fourteenth to twelfth centuries BCE. The uppermost stratum (I) only appears in part of the site and was a very short-lived operation. It was dated to the tenth century BCE, the time of the Twenty-second Dynasty in Egypt.

In strata III and II, a number of rough enclosures were found that had been used as workshops and contained smelting furnaces. Large heaps of broken platey tapped slag were piled between them. There were also a few more solid rectangular stores, workshops, and perhaps dwellings. Numerous small, mostly stone-lined pits were dug into the working floors of strata III and II. The areas between the workshop enclosures that were not occupied by slag dumps were used to pile up charcoal and clay. Stratum I had only some very rough enclosures and shallow pits next to its smelting installations.

Most of the finds were directly related to the metallurgical character of Site 30: ores, slag, charcoal, and stone implements; however, there were also many goat, donkey, camel, and fish bones, as well as some beads, food remains, textiles, baskets, and ropes. In strata III and II, a large quantity of sherds was found that belong to the same three types—Midianite ware, Negbite ware, and local wheel-made pottery. There was also some imported Egyptian pottery of the Nineteenth to Twentieth dynasties. In stratum I, Late New Kingdom (Twenty-second Dynasty) pottery was uncovered.

In strata III and II, small clay-lined, bowl-shaped smelting furnaces (diameter, 30 cm and c. 50 cm deep) were dug into the ground. There were no tapping pits, but the slag was apparently tapped out of the furnaces onto the ground and was then crushed to extract the metallic copper pellets entrapped in the slag. Many small tuyeres (diameter, c. 10 cm) were found in the slag heaps and next to the furnaces. There were also several melting furnaces, with crucible fragments and melting-casting slag.

In stratum I, a new technology appeared: the furnaces were larger, pear-shaped, and built with slag-tempered clay. There were also much larger tuyeres (diameter, c. 15–20 cm) made of the same slag-tempered clay; the slag was tapped into tapping pits. Stratum I showed a new, highly developed extractive metallurgical technology. Strata III and II correspond with the picture obtained in the excavation of Site 2, with the exception of tapping furnaces Fu I through IV, which represent the final development of Site 2's smelting technology and are different from the stratum I furnaces at Site 30.

THE HATHOR MINING SANCTUARY: SITE 200. Site 200, discovered by Rothenberg in 1966, was a low mound (15 by 15 m and 1.5 m high) leaning against one of "King Solomon's pillars." The pillars are huge, picturesque Nubian sandstone formations at the southwestern end of the Timna' Massif, almost in the center of the ancient mining and smelting area of the Timna' Valley. The site was excavated in 1969 and 1974. The discovery of this mining sanctuary provided absolute dates for the New Kingdom metal industries of Timna' and the Arabah. This is the only Egyptian temple found to date in the center of a copper-mining area.

History of the Hathor Sanctuary. The earliest remains at the site included several shallow rock-cut pits, a few fireplaces, some undefinable building remains, and a number of Chalcolithic rope-decorated sherds and flint implements.

During the reign of Seti I (1318–1304 BCE) of the Nineteenth Dynasty, an Egyptian shrine was erected on top of the Chalcolithic remains. An open court (9 by 7 m) containing a white sandstone naos (2.7 by 1.7 m) was built against the face of one of the pillars, into which a niche almost as high as a person was carved. Two well-dressed, square bases survive. These apparently were the foundations of two square pillars bearing the representation of the

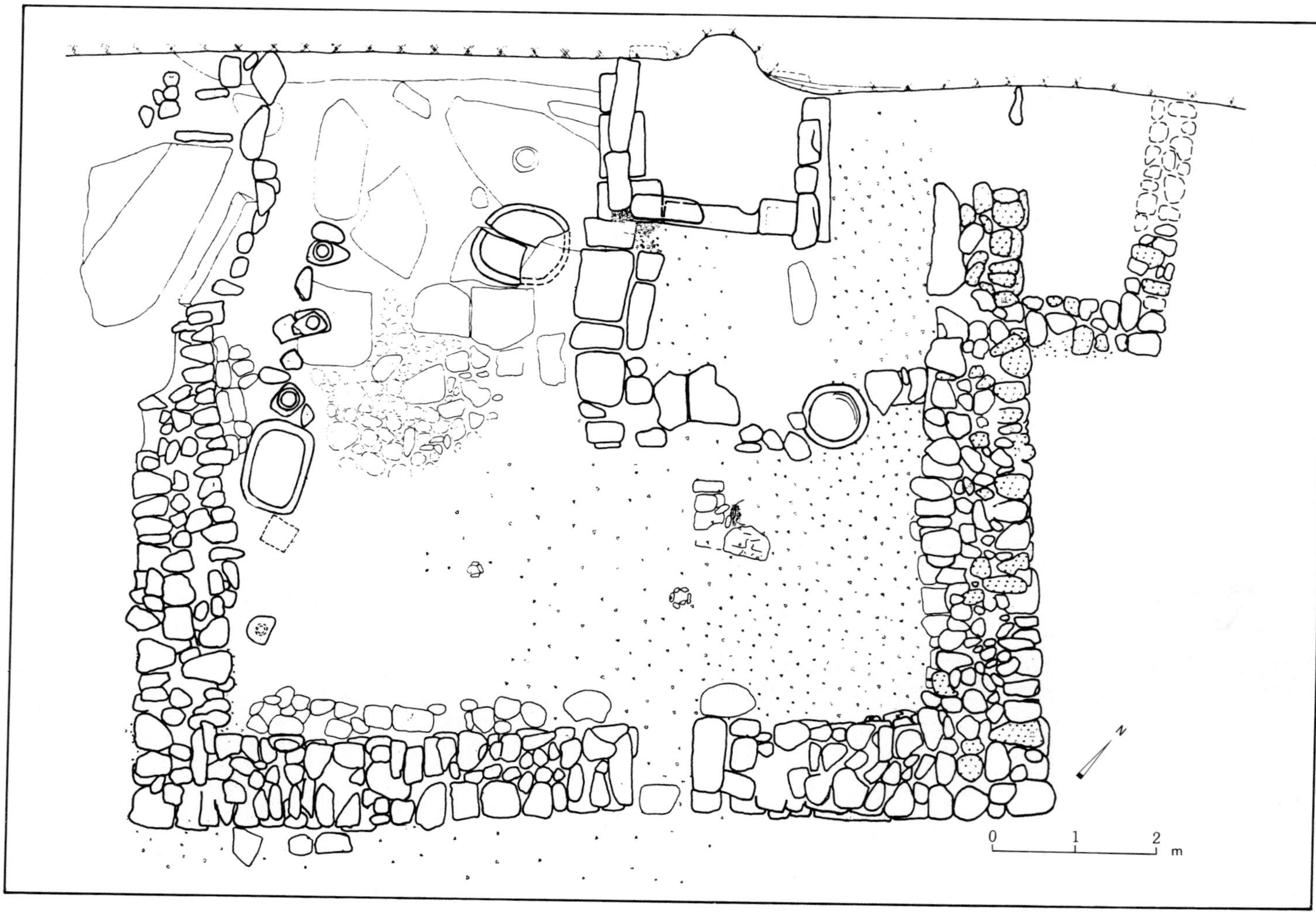

Site 200: plan of the Hathor sanctuary in its last phase.

Site 200: row of stelae in situ, including a Hathor pillar and altars in secondary use, in the last phase of the sanctuary.

Site 200: Hathor pillar; the face of Hathor seems to have been deliberately defaced.

head of Hathor, which were found in the excavation. One end of a large stone architrave had rested on the Hathor pillars, and the other end rested in two niches cut into the rock face. Several square pillars bearing traces of hieroglyphic inscriptions lay around the naos. A number of Egyptian incense altars was found, as well as two flat, rectangular white-sandstone offering tables. The original shrine seems to have been deliberately destroyed, but there is no evidence to indicate by whom.

The shrine was repaired, reusing many pieces of the original structure. A new floor was laid of crushed white stone, perhaps debris from the original shrine. The walls of the court were repaired and expanded to 9 by 9 m. The naos was rebuilt with a lime plaster finish. A vestibule, or pronaos, of large flat stones was built in front of the naos. Inscribed objects found on the floor suggest that the second shrine may have been built by Ramses II (1304–1237 BCE). It was destroyed by an earthquake, and the site was temporarily abandoned.

The shrine was again used for worship after undergoing numerous alterations; an offering bench was built against the interior of the walls flanking the entrance. An additional chamber was built outside the court's east wall, perhaps for use by the priest. Along the west wall a row of stelae was erected, consisting of monoliths and various Egyptian stone fragments in secondary use—such as a Hathor pillar, incense altars, square pillars, and a large basin filled with a large granite boulder.

Along the court's east and west walls a large amount of heavy red and yellow cloth, some with beads woven into it, was uncovered. Evidently, this cloth was part of a tent in the final phase of the sanctuary. There is clear archaeological evidence for attributing this tented sanctuary to the Midianites, who remained at Timna' after the termination of the Egyptian copper-mining expeditions in the middle of the twelfth century BCE. The Midianites, in using Egyptian architectural elements, effaced all the Hathor representations and any visible hieroglyphic inscription. The central niche in the naos was left empty, but close to the naos itself a Midianite copper snake with a gilded head was found. This was the only votive object found in the area of the naos in this period. In the courtyard of the sanctuary a small casting workshop was operated, probably manufacturing votive objects. A melting furnace, crucible fragments, and a hoard of broken copper objects, as well as metallic tin drops, were found on the floor of this workshop. There was also a phallic idol still partly in its mold.

Votive Offerings. The votive offerings found in strata III and II of the shrine are divided into two main groups.

Site 200: the Hathor sanctuary in its last phase.

1. Egyptian-made votive offerings, including pottery, stone and alabaster vessels, faience beads, wands, ring stands, *menats* (amulets), faience bowls, glass, gold ornaments, faience animal figurines, scarabs and seals, and several Hathor figurines and plaques. There was also a small sphinx, perhaps representing Ramses II.

2. Non-Egyptian, probably Midianite, votive offerings, a small cast-copper figure of a phallic idol, a copper sheep figurine, numerous rings, amulets, earrings, armlets, and many copper tools. There were also large numbers of shell beads from the Red Sea and a great deal of beautifully decorated Midianite pottery.

Midianite pottery.

Handmade "Negbite" bowl.

Pottery. The pottery found in the shrine was of the same three types as at Sites 2 and 30: local wheel-made as well as imported Egyptian pottery; handmade, primitive cooking pots and bowls of the type called Negbite ware, found previously in the central Negev and the Arabah; and decorated pottery, whose decorations include large birds, probably ostriches, and many sophisticated geometric designs. This latter pottery, found at Timna' in a stratified context, is identical to pottery found in the Hejaz (northwest Arabia, the biblical Midian) and is therefore called Midianite.

The pottery found at Site 200 is dated by inscribed Egyptian objects found in the same strata. There were many cartouches containing the names of the Nineteenth Dynasty pharaohs: Seti I (1318–1304 BCE), Ramses II (1304–1237 BCE), Merneptah (1236–1223 BCE), Seti II (1216–1210 BCE), and Queen Tewosret (1209–1200 BCE?). The Twentieth Dynasty names included Ramses III (1198–1166 BCE), Ramses IV (1166–1160 BCE), and Ramses V (1160–1156 BCE).

The discovery of an Egyptian mining sanctuary in the center of the copper-production area at Timna', containing numerous absolutely datable inscribed objects, was of decisive importance to the archaeology of the Arabah, northwest Arabia, and Sinai. It is now evident that the Timna' mines of the Late Bronze Age/Iron Age I were run by Egyptian pharaonic mining expeditions in collaboration with the Midianites from across the Red Sea and local inhabitants of the Arabah and the Negev.

Contrary to the hitherto accepted identification of the Arabah copper mines with "King Solomon's mines" (Iron Age II), these New Kingdom (Late Bronze Age/Iron Age I) mines had no connections with Palestine. In fact, throughout the period of the kingdoms of Israel and Judah, with only a short-lived revival in the time of Shishak I of Egypt (Twenty-second Dynasty), the Arabah mines lay deserted. There is no biblical reference to any "King Solomon's mines" and no archaeological evidence for activities by people from Israel or Judah in the mines of the southern Arabah has ever been found.

A ROMAN TO EARLY ARAB AND LATER COPPER MINE IN WADI 'AMRAM: SITE 38. There are two separate mining complexes in Wadi 'Amram. Site 33, about one kilometer from the head of the wadi, resembles the ancient mines at Timna'; Chalcolithic as well as, mainly, New Kingdom pottery and stone tools were also found there. Site 33 has been thoroughly surveyed but has not yet been excavated. Site 38 is near the head of the wadi, next to the formation called the 'Amram Pillars. It was excavated in 1990. Site 38 is a very large mining complex worked by inclined galleries and vertical shafts and later by open-cast methods. Unlike the New Kingdom mines at Timna' and Wadi 'Amram, there are substantial mining waste heaps at Site 38, typical of all mining sites in the southern Arabah, dated by pottery to the Roman to Early Arab periods and later. These indicate ore benefication by hand picking as well as possibly by winnowing and sieving.

In the mine workings at Site 38, numerous sherds were found and dated by M. Gichon to the Roman, Byzantine, Early Arab, Arab (eighth–ninth centuries), and even Mameluke and Ottoman periods, which indicates at least two and most likely three phases of post-Roman workings.

From the main entrance to the mine, high up on the steep slope of the wadi, an incline leads to the complex of works that penetrate underground to below the wadi bottom. It also passes under the mountain ridge and emerges in the adjacent tributary wadi. The Roman galleries have a diameter of about 70 cm and are subcircular. Where concentrations of ore were found, the rock was mined and transported to the surface for ore benefication. In the oldest works of Site 38, dated by pottery to the Roman period, lamp niches were cut into the walls; near the bottom of the mine an almost complete basket, used for carrying ore, was found, indicating the method of transporting the ores to the surface.

Most of the Roman galleries were reworked and cut through by later mining. Very different methods from the Roman shaft-and-gallery system were applied by Arab miners, who worked in large chambers in an irregular pillar-and-stall system. Pillars and walls from the earlier works were extracted for their ore contents, which often led to collapse. It seems that this method was intentionally used as the final exploitation of the mine in the Late Arab period.

A ROMAN AND EARLY ARAB PERIOD COPPER INDUSTRY: SITE 28. Site 28 is located about 1 km (0.6 mi.) north of the well that is today called Be'er Ora (formerly Be'er Hindis). It consisted of two very large and several smaller heaps of circular slag plates (diameter, 60–80 cm) that have a hole cast in the center. Eight areas were excavated.

Area A. A copper-smelting furnace (Fu I) was excavated in area A. This was a pit in the ground (diameter, 55 cm) with a semicircular row of stones around the rim, to support the upper part of the furnace wall that rose above the level of the working surface. The furnace was 70 cm high and its interior was clay-lined. In front of the furnace was a slag-tapping pit.

Area F. A second smelting furnace (Fu IV), similar to Fu I, was unearthed in area F. The original slag pit had been dug in the form of a wide ring, with a hard core left in its center for the casting of the center hole found in most of the Site 28 slag circles.

Site 200: ring stand with a double cartouche of Ramses III.

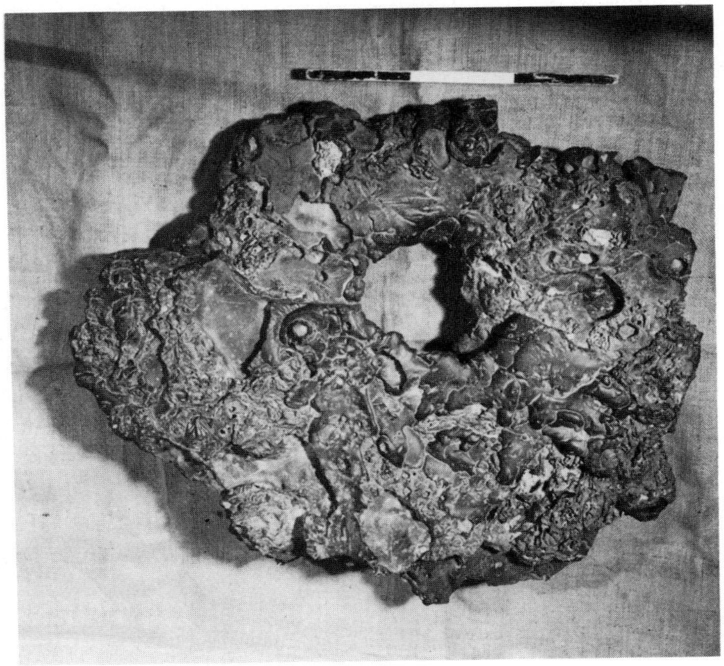

Site 28: circular slag plate with a hole cast in the center.

Site 28: smelting site from the Roman and Early Arab periods near Be'er Ora.

Area E. A shallow, oval-shaped melting-casting hearth (60 by 45 cm and 30 cm deep) was found full of wood ash. A row of small stones plastered with red clay enclosed its rim. A quantity of typical melting slag and casting waste was found here.

In the other areas excavated, storage pits lined with large slag plates, as well as workshops and a workers' kitchen built of slag, were uncovered. Pottery from the Roman period (second century CE) and Early Arab period (seventh and eighth centuries CE) was found in every area. There is reason to assume that Site 28 was the central Roman copper-smelting site in the western Arabah, operated by the Third Legion Cyrenaica. It was also the major smelting site in the southern Arabah in the Early Arab period.

Main publications: B. Rothenberg, *Timna: Valley of the Biblical Copper Mines* (New Aspects of Antiquity), London 1972; id., *The Egyptian Mining Temple at Timna* (Metal in History 2, Researches in the Arabah 1959–1984, 1), London 1988; id. (ed.), *The Ancient Metallurgy of Copper: Archaeology, Experiment, Theory* (Metal in History 3, Researches in the Arabah 1959–1984, 2), London 1990.

Other studies: J. Patherick, *Egypt, The Soudan and Central Africa*, Edinburgh 1861; W. M. F. Petrie, *Researches in Sinai*, London 1906, A. Musil, *Arabia Petraea* 2, 185–187; F. Frank, *ZDPV* 57 (1934), 233–234, 241–242; N. Glueck, *Explorations in Eastern Palestine* 2 (*AASOR* 15), New Haven 1935, 42–45, 139; id., *The Other Side of the Jordan*, New Haven 1940, 77–79, 84; id., *BA* 28 (1965), 70–87; M. Dothan, *Bulletin de la Société d'Anthropologie Série* X/8 (1957), 244–275; B. Rothenberg, *Bilder und Zeiten* (Aug. 15, 1959), no. 187; id., *BTS* 25 (1960), 4–11; 123 (1970), 6–14; id., *God's Wilderness*, London 1961; id., *PEQ* 94 (1962), 5–71; 101 (1969), 57–59; id., *ZDPV* 82 (1966), 125–135; id., *Museum Ha'aretz Bulletin* 7 (1965), 19–28; 8 (1966), 86–93; 9 (1967), 53–70; 10 (1968), 25–35; 12 (1970), 28–35; id., *RB* 74 (1967), 80–85; 79 (1972), 601–602; id., *ILN* (Nov. 15, 1969), 32–33; (Nov. 29, 1969), 28–29; id., *Midianite Timna*, London 1971; id., *Timna* (Reviews), *PEQ* 105 (1973), 174–175. — *Qadmoniot* 23–24 (1973), 131–132 (Hebrew); id., *The New Timna Project* (der Anschnitt), Borhum 1976; id. (with R. F. Tylecote), *Chalcolithic Copper Smelting: Excavations and Experiments* (Archaeo-Metallurgy 1), London 1978, 1–59; id., *Sinai, Pharaohs, Miners, Pilgrims and Soldiers*, Bern 1979; id., *London University Institute for Archaeo-Metallurgical Studies Newsletter* 2ff. (1980 ff.); id., *BAIAS* 1982–1983, 49–51; id., *BASOR* 252 (1983), 69–72; id., *Historical Metallurgy* 17 (1983), 116–119; id. (with J. Glass), *Midian, Moab and Edom* (eds. J. F. A. Sawyer and D. J. A. Clines), Sheffield 1983, 65–124; id. (and A. Lupu), *Furnaces and Smelting Technology in Antiquity* (eds. P. T. Craddock and M. J. Hughes), London 1985, 123–150; id., *Wiener Berichte über Naturwissenschaft in der Kunst* 2/3 (1985–1986), 90–120; id., *Metall* 40/11 (1986), 2–10; id., *The Egyptian Mining Temple at Timna* (Review), *Antiquity* 241 (1989), 858–859; id. (ed.), *The Ancient Metallurgy of Copper* (Review), *Qadmoniot* 93–94 (1991), 62 (Hebrew); B. H. McLeod, *PEQ* 94 (1962), 68–71; A. Lupu and B. Rothenberg, *Archaeologia Austriaca* 47 (1970), 91–130; A. Lupu, *Bulletin of the Historical Metallurgy Group* 4 (1970), 21–23; P. J. Parr et al., *BIAL* 8–9 (1970), 193–242; R. Giveon, *Proceedings of the 5th World Congress of Jewish Studies 1969*, Jerusalem 1971, 50–53; id., *The Impact of Egypt on Canaan*, Freiburg 1978, 61–67; id., *Göttinger Miszellen* 83 (1984), 27–29; O. Lipschitz, *IEJ* 22 (1972), 158; A. Slatkine, *Museum Ha'aretz Yearbook* 15–16 (1972–1973), 107–111; R. Ventura, *TA* 1 (1974), 60–63; *BAR* 1/1 (1975), 1, 10–12, 14, 16; P. Watson, *ILN* (March 1975), 30–40; K. A. Kitchen, *Orientalia* 45 (1976), 262–264; *Buried History* 13 (1977), 47–49; J. F. Merkel, "Neutron Activation Analysis of Copper to Examine Timna as an Ore Source During the Chalcolithic and Early Bronze Ages in Israel" (Ph.D. diss., Univ. of Minnesota 1977); id. (et al.), *AJA* 87 (1983), 245; id., *Ore Beneficiation during the Late Bronze/Early Iron Age at Timna, Israel* (in prep.); S. Singer, *BAR* 4/2 (1978), 16–25; H. G. Conrad and B. Rothenberg, *Antikes Kupfer im Timna-Tal, 4000 Jahr Bergbau und Verhüttung in der Arabah, Israel* (Der Anschnitt, Beiheft 1), Bochum 1980; ibid. (Reviews), *PEQ* 114 (1982), 69–70. — *ZDPV* 99 (1983), 219–224; P. T. Craddock, *Paléorient* 6 (1980), 102–104; U. Avner, *ESI* 3 (1984), 103–104; J. D. Muhly, *Bibliotheca Orientalis* 41 (1984), 275–292; id., *Expedition* 29/2 (1987), 38–47; N. Gale and Z. Stos-Gale, *Discussions in Egyptology* 1 (1985), 7–15; I. M. E. Shaw, *JNES* 44 (1985), 316; M. N. Leese et al., *Wiener Berichte über Naturwissenschaft in der Kunst* 2–3 (1985–1986), 90–120; M. Bamberger et al., *Metall* 40/11 (1986), 2–10; 42/5 (1988), 3–11; Weippert 1988 (Ortsregister); I. Eshel, *ESI* 9 (1989–1990), 81, 171; id., *IEJ* 41 (1991), 293–294; S. Wimmer, *Jahrbuch des Deutschen Evangelischen Instituts für Altertumswissenschaft des Heiligen Landes* 1 (1989), 33–34; id., *Studies in Egyptology Presented to Miriam Lichtheim* (ed. S. Israelit-Groll), Jerusalem 1990, 1065–1106; G. Pinch, *New Kingdom Votive Offerings to Hathor*, Oxford 1991.

BENO ROTHENBERG

U

'UBEIDIYA

IDENTIFICATION

The prehistoric site of 'Ubeidiya is located about 1 km (0.6 mi.) south of Tiberias on the western bank of the Jordan River, on a hill that slopes from 180 to 205 m below sea level (map reference 2024.2328). The site was named after the nearby historical mound, Tell 'Ubeidiya, which lies about 0.5 km (0.3 mi.) eastward from the main area of excavations.

EXPLORATION

The site was discovered in 1959, when a bulldozer scraped the topsoil of the hill and exposed the original layers of the lacustrine-fluviatile complex named by M. Blanckenhorn in 1897. L. Picard had studied the geology of the region, the "Melanopsisstuffe," in the 1920s and 1930s. With the onset of systematic excavating, which followed the discovery of Lower Paleolithic artifacts and bones of extinct mammalian species, the entire sequence was renamed the 'Ubeidiya Formation. The excavations, conducted under the auspices of the Israel Academy of Sciences, were first directed by M. Stekelis (1960–1966) and later by O. Bar-Yosef and E. Tchernov (1967–1974).

EXCAVATIONS

In order to study the site's complex stratification, a series of trenches of various lengths was excavated with heavy machinery. From the exposed sections of the numerous tilted layers, the researchers reconstructed the geological history of the formation and identified the layers—which contained both animal bones and worked-stone artifacts. More than sixty levels were recognized in the trenches, which were located on both sides of the small anticline that characterizes the 'Ubeidiya Formation at this site. Many of these archaeological horizons could have been two parts of the same layer, separated by the erosion that truncated the top of the anticline.

A detailed geological study indicated that the 'Ubeidiya Formation represents the depositional history of the Lower Pleistocene in the central Jordan Valley. At that time, a freshwater lake occupied the area now covered by the Sea of Galilee and expanded southward, at least as far as Gesher. In the lake bottom and on the sides of the shore, clayey, siltic, and sandy layers were deposited when the beaches were covered with gravel (ranging in size from sand to cobbles). The wadis descended from the nearby slopes of the valley, as they do today, carrying soil and gravel. In low-lying areas, marshy deposits accumulated. The climate was Mediterranean, with more winter rain than today; this enabled the oak forests to expand and sometimes to cover the slopes of the valley. The overall exposed sequence at the site indicates that the lake was quite large in its early phase (the Li member). It then partially retreated (the Fi member), expanded again (the Lu member), and then regressed (the Fu member). The final regression was probably caused by the tectonic movement that was responsible for the lake's final disappearance.

The excavations of the implentiferous layers retrieved many artifacts. The common types are defined as core choppers, polyhedrons, spheroids and subspheroids, hand axes, picks, and a wealth of retouched and unretouched flakes. Often 15 to 30 percent of the artifacts exhibit signs of abrasion, caused by their movement, prior to deposition, in the gravelly beach contexts. Assemblages uncovered in clayey layers have the lowest frequencies of abraded items.

Handmade vessels sunk in the gravel surface.

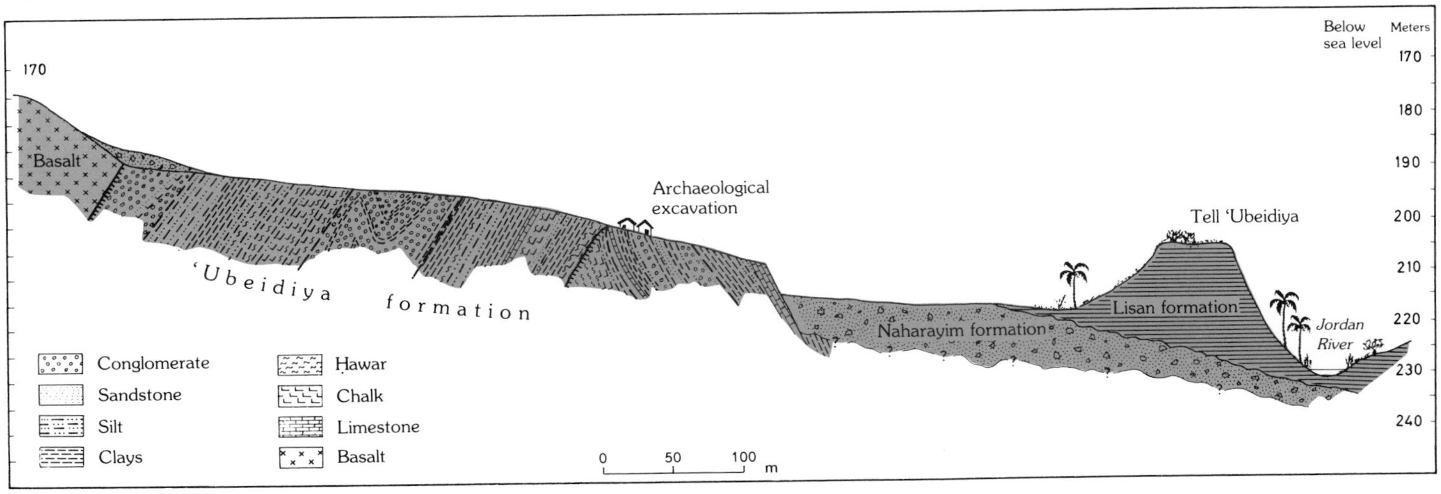

'Ubeidiya: the site and its surroundings, geological cross section.

*Stone artifacts: **(1-2)** limestone spheroids; **(3)** pick; **(4)** flint core chopper; **(5)** hand ax from the living surface.*

'Ubeidiya: wild sheep horns.

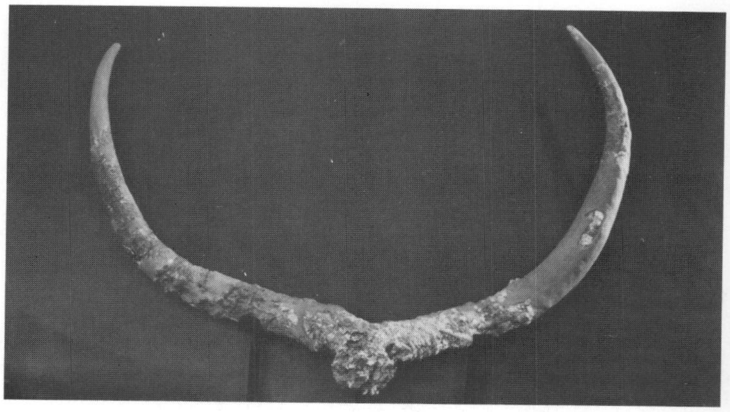

A clear-cut correlation between the main tool groups and raw material exists. Thus, core choppers, polyhedrons, and many flakes are made of flint, spheroids from limestone, and hand axes from basalt, with fewer from limestone and flint. It seems that the size of the desired shape dictated the choice of the raw material. Large flint cobbles are rare, and thus the hand axes were made of basalt. Some of the artifacts were shaped on the beaches; others were made elsewhere and were brought in.

Based on morphological correlations, the lithic assemblages were first classified as variants of the Oldowan (studied and named by L. S. B. and M. D. Leakey in Olduvai Gorge, Tanzania) and a variant of the Abbevillean (the lowermost Acheulean in western Europe). The attribution of the 'Ubeidiya assemblages to the Lower Acheulean is now preferred, although the lowermost layers did not contain hand axes and may therefore be related to the Oldowan.

The dating of 'Ubeidiya is based on faunal correlations and the paleomagnetic reversed position of most of its sequence. The rich faunal collection (more than one hundred species of mammals, reptiles, and birds) includes species such as hedgehog, leopard, wild camel, lemming, bear, fox, rhinoceros, elephant, gazelle, oryx, deer, and hamster. Most of the identified species are Eurasian; only a few are of African origin (the giraffe, a few species of rats, the hippopotamus, the warthog, and a wild sheep). By comparing the more recent species to known assemblages in Europe and Africa, a date of 1 to 1.5 million years BP was suggested. The resemblance between the lithic industries and Olduvai Upper Bed II and the paleomagnetic evidence support this contention.

No human remains were found in situ, but it can be assumed that members of the *Homo erectus* lineage were responsible for making the artifacts. The varied fauna of Lake 'Ubeidiya's immediate environment provided numerous scavenging opportunities, and the Mediterranean vegetation supplied numerous species of plants from which leaves, fruits, and seeds could be gathered.

The archaeological and zoological information from 'Ubeidiya is for the time being the richest of all early Lower Paleolithic sites in Eurasia and constitute the best evidence for the "out of Africa" movement of *Homo erectus*.

Main publications: M. Stekelis, *Archaeological Excavations at 'Ubeidiya, 1960–1963*, Jerusalem 1966; ibid. et al., *1964–1966*, Jerusalem 1969; L. Picard and M. Baida, *Geological Report on the Lower Pleistocene Deposits of the 'Ubeidiya Excavations*, Jerusalem 1966; id., *Stratigraphic Position of the 'Ubeidiya Formation*, Jerusalem 1966; G. Haas, *On the Vertebrata Fauna of the Lower Pleistocene Site 'Ubeidiya*, Jerusalem, 1966–1968; P. V. Tobias, *A Member of the Genus Homo from 'Ubeidiya*, Jerusalem 1966; E. Tchernov, *A Preliminary Investigation of the Birds in the Pleistocene Deposits of 'Ubeidiya*, Jerusalem 1968; id., *The Pleistocene Birds of 'Ubeidiya, Jordan Valley* (Publications of the Israel Academy of Sciences and Humanities, Excavations at 'Ubeidiya), Jerusalem 1980; id., *Les Mammifères du Pleistocène Inférieur de la Vallée du Jourdain à Oubeidiyeh* (Mémoires et Travaux du Centre de Recherche Français de Jérusalem 5), Paris 1986; O. Bar-Yosef and E. Tchernov, *On the Palaeo-Ecological History of the Site of 'Ubeidiya*, Jerusalem 1972; *Mission archéologique et paléontologique d'Oubeidiyeh (Israël): Projet Franco-Israelien* (eds. E. Tchernov et al.), Rapport Préliminaire, Jerusalem 1989.
Other studies: E. Tchernov, *Histoire et Archéologie* 100 (1985), 28–36; id., *L'Anthropologie* 92 (1988), 839–861; id., *Paléorient* 14/2 (1988), 63–64; O. Bar-Yosef and E. Tchernov, *IEJ* 19 (1969), 234–235; 21 (1971), 170–171; 24 (1974), 252–253; id., *RB* 78 (1971), 576–581; 79 (1972), 400–401; 82 (1975), 71–72; id., *ESI* 7–8 (1988–1989), 180–181; 9 (1989–1990), 111; O. Bar-Yosef, *Perspectives in Palaeoanthropology* (D. Sen Fest.), Calcutta 1974, 185–198; id., *After the Australopithecines* (eds. K. W. Butzer and G. L. Isaac), Chicago 1975, 571–604; id., *Archaeology* 28 (1975), 30–37; id., *African Archaeological Review* 5 (1987), 29–38; id., *L'Anthropologie* 92 (1988), 769–795; id., *Investigations in South Levantine Prehistory: Préhistoire du Sud-Levant* (*BAR*/IS 497, eds. O. Bar-Yosef and B. Vandermeersch), Oxford 1989, 101–111; A. Horowitz et al., *Nature* 242 (1973), 186–187; D. Bowman and Y. Giladi, *Israel Journal of Earth Sciences* 28 (1979), 86–93; V. Eisenmann et al., *Geobios* 16 (1983), 629–633; J. J. Jaeger, *Paléorient* 9 (1983), 89–90; N. D. Opkyde et al., *Nature* 304 (1983), 375–376; N. Goren-Inbar, *Histoire et Archéologie* 100 (1985), 34–35; id., "The Lithic Assemblages of the Site of 'Ubeidiya, Jordan Valley" (Ph.D. diss., Hebrew Univ. of Jerusalem 1981); id., *Paléorient* 14/2 (1988), 99–111; Weippert 1988 (Ortsregister); E. Debard et al., *Paléorient* 15/1 (1989), 231–237; P. C. Edwards, *Journal of Mediterranean Archaeology* 2 (1989), 5–48; C. Guerin and M. Faure, *Investigations in South Levantine Prehistory* (op. cit.), Oxford 1989, 19–23; O. Bar-Yosef and N. Goren-Inbar, *The Lithic Assemblages of 'Ubeidiya: A Lower Paleolithic Site in the Jordan Valley* (Qedem 43; in prep).

OFER BAR-YOSEF

UMM EL-BIYARA

IDENTIFICATION

Umm el-Biyara rises 300 m from the Petra basin and is the highest mountain overlooking Petra from the west. It is separated from Petra by Wadi Thugra to the south and Wadi Siyagh to the north. Wadi Thugra, turning east at the foot of Umm el-Biyara, joins Wadi Siyagh, which is a continuation of Wadi Musa. The latter, having run directly east to west across Petra, turns to the northwest and descends toward Wadi Arabah. To the west, Umm el-Biyara is skirted by Wadi Qurei, which also runs toward the Arabah. The summit of Umm el-Biyara is a trapezoidal plateau that slopes steeply from west to east. The total area of the summit is approximately 13 a.

Umm el-Biyara has often been identified with biblical Sela. The Hebrew word *sela'* simply means "rock," or "cleft of rock." There are several references in the Bible to "the rock of Edom." The best-known passage is in 2 Chronicles 25:12, in which Amaziah of Judah (c. 796–781 BCE) took ten thousand Edomites ("men of Seir") prisoner and "threw them down from the top of the rock." Already in the fourth century CE, Eusebius of Caesarea equated Sela with Petra. (In fact, Eusebius did not list the term Sela at all, but identified Petra with Jechthoel/Jechthael/Joktheel. According to 2 Kg. 14:7, Amaziah renamed Sela as Joktheel. The Septuagint translates Sela as Petra.)

C.-M. Bennett's excavations (see below) have shown that there was extensive occupation at Umm el-Biyara in the first half of the seventh century BCE, but no occupation that could be dated to the period of Amaziah (early eighth century BCE). However, the Bible does not mention an actual occupation at Sela under Amaziah. Other references to Sela, particularly Jeremiah 49:16, point more to the north, and are associated with Bozrah, the capital of Edom (and probably modern Buṣeirah). There is a modern Sela near Buṣeirah, an isolated prominence with evidence of Edomite and Nabatean occupation, called "a miniature Petra" by N. Glueck (S. Hart dates the Iron Age pottery from Sela to the seventh and sixth centuries BCE; M. Lindner suggests that there is an Iron Age I occupation there).

EXPLORATION

In 1929, the Petra Exploration Fund Expedition, funded by Lord Melchett, was the first to identify Edomite Iron Age pottery, associated with walls and

Bulla of "Qos-Gabr, King of Edom."

Umm el-Biyara: plan of the settlement.

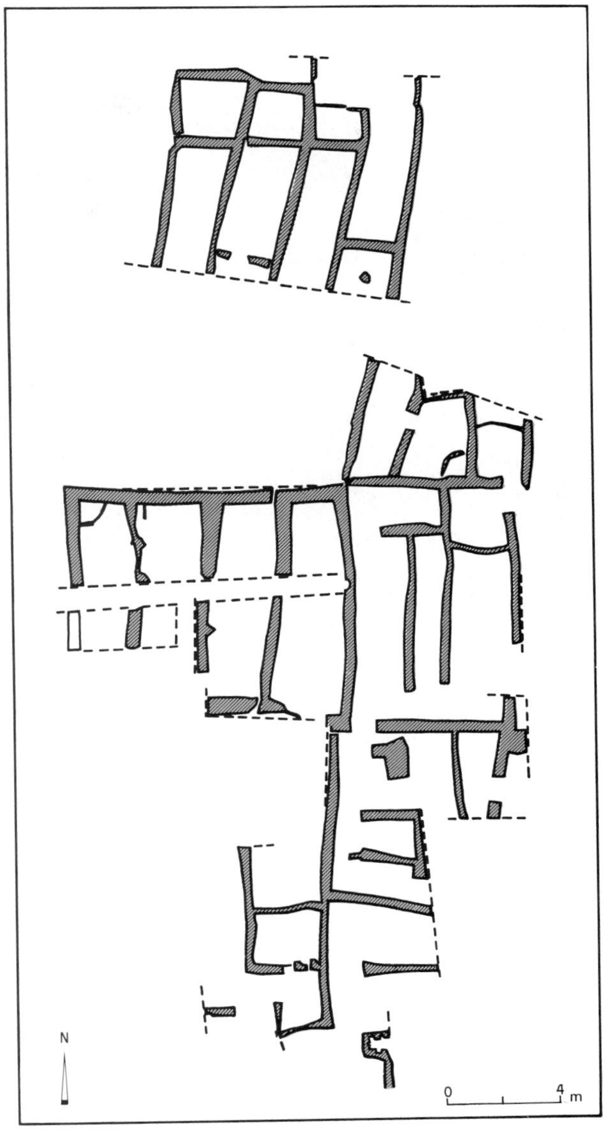

foundations, at Umm el-Biyara. The first small soundings were made by Glueck, in association with G. Horsfield in 1933 and alone in 1934. This work led Glueck to state categorically that Umm el-Biyara was biblical Sela in the time of Amaziah of Judah. The earlier Petra Exploration Fund Expedition had first identified el-Ḥabis as Sela but later accepted the Umm el-Biyara–Sela equation. Further soundings were carried out by W. H. Morton in 1955. Morton found concentrations of Edomite pottery associated with a "jumbled heap of irregular sandstone blocks" but recognized no wall lines.

EXCAVATIONS

Bennett excavated at Umm el-Biyara for three seasons in 1960, 1963, and 1965. The excavations began as an extension of the work of the British School of Archaeology in Jerusalem at Petra, directed by P. J. Parr. Her excavations had two main aims: to confirm or contradict the identification of Umm el-Biyara as biblical Sela and to obtain a corpus of stratified Edomite pottery.

Bennett excavated a total of about 700 sq m, less than one-third of the whole site. She found a group of dry-stone houses with long corridor rooms and small square rooms leading off from them. The occupation was evidently domestic, judging from the quantity of looms and spindle whorls. The main area of the settlement was destroyed by conflagration. In one room a royal seal impression was found, restored convincingly as "Qos-Gabr, King of Edom." Qos-Gabr is mentioned twice in Assyrian inscriptions: on Prism B of Esarhaddon (dated 673/672 BCE) and in a description of the first campaign of Ashurbanipal (667 BCE). Parallels for pottery and small finds also pointed to a seventh-century BCE date.

Umm el-Biyara is essentially a one-period site. The three "phases" of construction noted in the preliminary report are in fact contemporary. In some areas of the site, however, there are indications of two phases of occupation. For example, in trench A.XIIIext., the earliest occupation on bedrock was followed by a destruction and then by a final occupation reusing the same walls. This was overlain by abandonment and collapse, as in other areas. It is unclear whether this final occupation came immediately after the destruction or after a period of abandonment. Bennett implied that the reuse might date to the Hellenistic period, but the pottery throughout A.XIIIext. appears to be homogeneous Iron Age II, except for possible Hellenistic sherds in the post-occupation levels. Umm el-Biyara was used in the Nabatean period as a sanctuary.

SUMMARY

The primary aim of Bennett's excavations—confirmation or contradiction of the identification of Umm el-Biyara with biblical Sela—was not achieved. Results showed that there was extensive occupation in the first half of the

Umm el-Biyara: general view of the settlement.

Cliff of Umm el-Biyara, viewed from the colonnaded street in Petra.

seventh century BCE, but no occupation that could be dated to the period of Amaziah (early eighth century BCE). The seal of Qos-Gabr had verified the dating of the Edomite pottery to the seventh century BCE.

N. Glueck, *BASOR* 51 (1933) 13–14, id., *AASOR* 14 (1934), 77; 15 (1935), 82; G. and A. Horsfield, *QDAP* 7 (1938), 4, n. 1, pl. VI; W. H. Morton, *BA* 19 (1956), 26–36; C.-M. Bennett, *BTS* 84 (1966), 6–16; id., *ILN* 6613 (30.4.66), 29–31; id., *RB* 73 (1966), 372–403; id., *Antiquity* 41 (1967), 197–201; id., *ADAJ* 24 (1980), 209–212; C. P. Wilmart, *Proceedings of the International Congress of Orientalists 1967* (1971), 63–64; W. Culican, *PEQ* 102 (1970), 65–72; id., *Opera Selecta*, Göteborg 1986, 311–315; M. Lindner, *Petra und das Königreich der Nabatäer*, Munich 1989, 271–285; S. Hart, *PEQ* 118 (1986), 91–95; P. Bienkowski, *Levant* 22 (1990), 91–109.

PIOTR BIENKOWSKI

UMM ER-RASAS

IDENTIFICATION AND EXPLORATION

Umm er-Rasas lies in the steppe region of Jordan, 30 km (19 mi.) southeast of Medeba (map reference 237.101). The site is identified with Kastron Mefaa by a mosaic Greek inscription from the Umayyad period. Covering an area of about 7.5 a, the ruins of Umm er-Rasas consist of a walled area that formed a fortified camp and, to the north, an open quarter of roughly the same size. The expedition was headed by M. Piccirillo.

One of the achievements of the excavations at the site (see below) has been the historical identification of the ruins of Umm er-Rasas with Kastron Mefaa, a toponym known in Roman and Arabic sources and in the Bible. Eusebius records a unit of the Roman army stationed on the edge of the desert at Mephaat (*Onom.* 128, 21), a locality he identified with the Levitical city of refuge of Mephaath in the territory of the tribe of Reuben on the Moab Plain (Jos. 13:18, 21:37; Jer. 48:21). The *Notitia Dignitatum* records

Aerial view of Umm er-Rasas: the castrum and the outer quarter.

Church of St. Stephen, as viewed from the northwest corner of the Church of Bishop Sergius.

that *equites promoti indigenae* (auxiliary Roman army troops) were stationed at the camp of Mefaa under the command of the *Dux Arabiae*. The locality's military nature underlined by the name Kastron Mefaa, which is recorded four times in the Greek inscriptions in the Church of Saint Stephen and in the Church of the Lions here. The Arab historian al-Bakry knew Maypha'ah as a village in the Syrian Belqa'.

The name of the ruins was recorded by U. J. Seetzen, the first modern explorer in Jordan, in 1807. It was visited by J. S. Buckingham in 1816. In 1896, S. Vailhé realized that the large square in the city enclosed by thick walls was a Roman camp at the edge of the desert. In 1897, J. Germer-Durand had proposed identifying it with Mephaat in the *Onomasticon*, and, thus, with the biblical city of Mephaath. This identification was rejected by C. Clermont-Ganneau because the ruins lacked the ancient name. Instead, he proposed identifying the Roman-Byzantine and Arabic Mephaat with Khirbet Nefa', a ruin A. Musil had visited 10 km (6 mi.) south of 'Amman. This identification was accepted by all biblical scholars—based also on the conclusion of N. Glueck's 1933 survey, that the ruins at Umm er-Rasas lack any sherds predating the Nabatean-Roman period—until only recently, when it was challenged by scholars who realized that Khirbet Nefa' was in Ammonite territory, at least in the Iron Age II. The archaeological discovery showing that the Roman-Byzantine and Arabic Kastron Mefaa is Umm er-Rasas refutes its identification with Khirbet Nefa'. Moreover, Iron Age sherds (seventh–sixth centuries BCE) were found in a stratigraphic probe inside a small chapel, and a reused basalt pillar base decorated with calyx leaves and dated stylistically to the Iron Age was found near the opening of a water cistern in the Church of Bishop Sergius. These finds are evidence that the locality was inhabited at least from the seventh century BCE until the Umayyad-Abbasid periods.

This new evidence leaves open the possibility of identifying Kastron Mefaa/Umm er-Rasas with biblical Mephaath, as Eusebius proposed. This identification is a better fit with the biblical texts that relate Mephaath with Jahaz, Kedemoth, and Bezer—three cities in the southeastern territory of the tribe of Reuben (Jos. 21:36–37)—and with the Mesha Stela, which records the conquest of Jahaz and Bezer in the plain in the territory between Dibon and Medeba.

Overview of the Church of the Lions.

EXCAVATIONS

Early explorers, such as E. Palmer, H. B. Tristram, and R. E. Brünnow and A. V. Domaszewski, were aware of the settlement's Christian character. In 1948, B. Bagatti tried to establish a schematic plan of the ruins, focusing on the apsidal buildings he identified as churches. In the summer of 1986, the

The sanctuary of the Church of Bishop Sergius.

An Iron Age capital reused in the Church of Bishop Sergius.

Overview of the Church of St. Stephen.

Jordan Department of Antiquities entrusted the archaeological exploration of the site to the Studium Biblicum Franciscanum. Work started at the northeast edge of the ruins, where a large and interconnected liturgical complex with four churches was identified and explored: the two mosaic-paved churches—Bishop Sergius on the north and Saint Stephen on the east—with a paved courtyard between them that was later converted into a church by adding an apse to its western wall (the Church of the Courtyard), and a fourth paved church in the southwest sector (the Church of the Niche). The complex was enclosed by a continuous wall. The main entrances were from the south: a stone-paved courtyard and the Church of Saint Stephen were entered through a double door and a second room on the west side led down to the Courtyard church. A chancel screen separated this church from the Bishop Sergius church. In the latest phase, the double door that led to the Saint Stephen and Courtyard churches was blocked and the adjoining room converted into a chapel with reused materials. The Church of the Niche was in some way isolated from the other three churches and had its own entrance in the southwest corner of the complex. The courtyard with the cistern, north of the Church of the Niche, was reached from the interior of the town through a tunnel that passed below the presbytery of the church.

THE CHURCH OF BISHOP SERGIUS. A dedicatory inscription set in a medallion between two rams in front of the altar in the northern Church of Bishop Sergius records that the church was built and decorated in 586. Iconoclasts destroyed all the other rich figural motifs in the main nave, except for a mosaic of one of the Seasons which was protected by the stone base of the pulpit added later. Originally, the mosaic consisted of a frame featuring acanthus scrolls with hunting, fishing, and vintage scenes. Within the frame, the central carpet included two classical personifications: the Abyss (or Sea) and, at the end, toward the main door, the Earth. Between them were portraits and scenes out of the daily life of the church's benefactors, with their names. Two unusual images in the central carpet were a phoenix with rays emanating from its head and a man carrying a bed on his shoulders. A mosaic-paved area was entered through the two doors on the west wall of the church, it contained the baptistery chapel with a cruciform basin on the north side, and a funeral chapel on the south.

THE CHURCH OF SAINT STEPHEN. The eastern Church of Saint Stephen is one meter higher than the Church of Bishop Sergius. The richness of its inscriptions and the quality of the motifs in its mosaic pavement make it one of the most important archaeological monuments in Jordan. The single-apsed church was built over the corner of a room with white plastered walls, that may be part of an earlier church. The dedicatory inscription along the step of the presbytery provides the ancient name of Umm er-Rasas: Mefaa, or Kastron Mefaa. The church was built in honor of Saint Stephen by the people of Kastron Mefaa and the deacon John, archon or chief of the Mefaonites. It was built at the time of Bishop Sergius II of Medeba in the eighth century, although the date in the inscription, perhaps 785, is not certain. Late Byzantine-Umayyad sherds were collected in the fill below the mosaic floor.

The dedicatory inscription near the altar in the presbytery confirms the dating of the church to the eighth century. It states that the mosaic in the bema (the presbytery) was redone at the time of Bishop Job of Medeba in 756. It also identifies the mosaicist, Staurachios Ezbontinos (from Esbous, Heshbon), the first mosaicist in the region whose place of origin is known. He laid the mosaic with Euremios, his colleague.

The northern room beside the apse was, in its final phase, a small apsed shrine with its own altar built in front of a polygonal niche cut into the wall. The special nature of this shrine was emphasized by a molded arch at the entrance and by the several inscriptions in front of the door.

Unfortunately, in the mosaic in the nave, the portraits of the benefactors and the scenes of hunting, agriculture, and pastoral life were systematically disfigured by iconoclasts and are for the most part unintelligible.

The Geographical Mosaic. The mosaic floor in the Church of Saint Stephen contains a double panel that depicts cities in Palestine, Transjordan, and Egypt. In the intercolumnar spaces in the north row, a series of eight Palestinian cities is depicted: the Holy City of Jerusalem, in which it is possible to identify the aedicule in the Holy Sepulcher according to the iconography attributed to it in the Byzantine period; Neapolis (Shechem), with what may be the facade of the Church of the Theotokos on Mount Gerizim; Sebastis (Sebaste); Caesarea; Diospolis (Lydda); Eleutheropolis (Beth Guvrin); Ascalon; and Gaza. In the intercolumnar spaces in the south row, a series of seven Transjordanian cities is shown, starting with the double plan of Kastron Mefaa–Umm er-Rasas, followed by Philadelphia ('Amman), Medeba, Esbounta (Heshbon), Belemounta (Ma'in), Areopolis (Rabbah), and Charach Mouba (el-Kerak). Two other Transjordanian cities—Limbon and Diblaton—are portrayed, one at the head of each aisle, associated with portraits of benefactors and inscriptions. Another toponym, but without illustration, mentions Mount Nebo-Pisgah and the superior of the monastery of the

Church of St. Stephen: mosaic panel depicting the city of Kastron Mefaa.

Timna': fragment of a mask from the Hathor sanctuary (Site 200).

Timna': overview of the Hathor sanctuary (Site 200), LB/Iron I.

Ḥorvat 'Uza: Edomite ostracon, end of First Temple period.

Ḥorvat 'Uza: aerial view of the fortress and settlement.

Memorial of Moses, who gave an offering to the church. The inner panel, which depicts a river with fish, birds, and water flowers, as well as boats and boys fishing or hunting, also portrays a series of ten cities in the Nile Delta: Alexandria, Kasin, Thenesos, Tamiathis, Panau, Pilousin, Antinau, Heraklion, Kynopolis, and Pseudostomon.

Two barrel-vaulted, multiple tombs in the funeral chapel to the south of the baptistery, which continued east under the presbytery of the Courtyard church, may explain the liturgical purpose of this new church, with its apse oriented to the west. Its funeral character is stressed by the tombs below the floor. Two of them have been excavated.

Developing a chronological sequence for this complicated ecclesiastical building is still premature. In terms of its plan, however, it is clear that the complex was not a monastery. It was more a sanctuary, in which large numbers of people could meet on a variety of occasions. There are only a few rooms in the eastern courtyard that would have been suitable for the daily life of the clergy. These three eastern churches, with their atriums, form a large and interconnected liturgical complex unique in the region. There is also no absolute evidence for the date the ecclesiastical complex of Saint Stephen was finally abandoned, but the ninth century seems likely. It is also possible that the blocked doors indicate a gradual reduction in the use of the interior of the building.

THE TOWER AND THE CHURCH OF THE LIONS. The outstanding monument at Umm er-Rasas is a tower (14 m high) that still stands 1.5 km (1 mi.) north of the ruins. It is in the middle of a square courtyard with a cistern in the north and a small church at its southeast corner. The tower had a domed room at its top and no stairs. The room had one door on its southern side, facing the church, opening at a height of 10 m, and three windows on the other sides. A channel ran from top to bottom on the inside of the tower's western wall. These peculiarities can be explained if it is accepted that this is a stylite tower—a hypothesis proposed by C. Wilson in the nineteenth century. In the church, the eastern end of the northern aisle was turned into a small shrine by adding a small arch. The arch covered a stone reliquary set in the floor. Strangely, both the lid of the stone box and its sides were covered with various kinds of seeds—lentils, chick peas, and corn. The disarticulated bones of an adult had been deposited inside and covered with oil, a Christian practice of veneration for the bones of martyrs. Two coins of the emperor Justinian were found—one inside the reliquary and the other outside, among the seeds.

The excavation of the triapsidal church outside the northeast corner of the castrum uncovered another outstanding artistic work by the mosaicists active in Transjordan in the Byzantine period. Below the fallen stones of the church's central apse, the slabs (*plutei*) from the broken chancel screen were found partly in situ and partly scattered; the slabs could be easily reconstructed. The motifs, partly damaged by the iconoclasts, had been carved into the oil-shale stone.

With the main altar, rebuilt in masonry in a later phase, there were on the north, and still in situ, the base and columns of an offering table. The main discovery, from a liturgical point of view, was the pulpit, on the southern side; it is the best-preserved pulpit found thus far in the churches of Jordan. The priest or deacon had to climb five steps that were protected by a side chancel to reach a polygonal platform; the platform, in turn, was supported by four columns and enclosed by five small, elaborately carved *plutei*. The floor of the church was built in Bishop Sergius' days, possibly in 587. It was paved with well-crafted mosaics whose general composition and figurative details are aesthetically pleasing. In the double frame of the rectangular panel decorating the area in front of the altar, birds alternate with fruits in white medallions on a black background. Of the same high quality are the animals and the fruit-laden trees. In this mosaic, for the first time in a church, two gazelles are depicted as well as two confronting lions (a lion facing a tiger), a motif normally found in synagogues. The iconoclasts dealt with these figures in a peculiar way. They destroyed the two bulls on the side of the altar, one of the two gazelles, the bodies of the two lions, and some birds in the border frame, yet they spared the heads of the two lions, the gazelle on the right, and some birds. They did not spare the human figures of the benefactors in front of the altar or the other figures in the acanthus scrolls in the church's main nave. Only the names of some figures were legible: John the Egyptian, Salamnis son of Sobanu, John son of Saolos, Toemos, and Paul son of Kassianus. Birds and eagles were defaced in the panels decorating the two side apses, where other names of the church's benefactors appear: Pafanon son of Talitha and John son of Soelos.

The Kastron City Plan Mosaic. Of historical and artistic importance is Kastron Mefaa's city plan, which decorates the northern intercolumnar space. Thus, two plans of the city, done within a span of two centuries, can be compared. The plan of Kastron Mefaa in the church of Saint Stephen is more schematic than the second plan, in which the intention of the mosaicists to depict Kastron Mefaa in its urban identity, with the walled castrum and the northern quarter outside the walls, is clear. A church and a smaller, unidentified building are depicted inside the castrum. The outer quarter is also walled, like the town, and united to it by a wall with minor dimensions. Four churches are depicted inside the quarter's perimeter, if the theory that churches are identified with red roofs in the Medeba map is accepted. Once again, as in the first plan, there is an open space with a column raised on a stepped platform. A cross is placed on the capital on the top of the column. It represents a votive column in the middle of the ruins, whose nature is still unknown.

CONCLUSIONS

The evidence collected in the first six campaigns at Umm er-Rasas indicates its outer quarter was occupied in the Iron Age II and again in the Roman-Nabatean period. In the Late Roman period (third–fourth centuries), an official building may have stood here, as attested by a Latin inscription in the eastern courtyard of the Church of Saint Stephen, by some Thamudic inscriptions reused in the eastern wall of the same church, by the ram relief found reused in the apse of the Courtyard church, some coins, and other reused architectural remains from the same period. These archaeological conclusions correspond with the historical data found in the contemporary written sources regarding Kastron Mefaa.

Exploration and identification: S. Vailhé, *Echos de Notre-Dame de France* (1896), 230; J. Jermer-Durand, ibid. (1897), 37ff.; Clermont-Ganneau, *RAO* 4 (1901), 57–60; id., *PEQ* 34 (1902), 260–261; Brünnow-Domaszewski, *Die Provincia Arabia* 2, 63–72; N. Glueck, *AASOR* 14 (1934), 39; S. Saller and B. Bagatti, *The Town of Nebo (Khirbet el-Mekhayyat), with a Brief Survey of Other Ancient Christian Monuments in Transjordan* (Publications of the Studium Biblicum Franciscanum 7), Jerusalem 1949, 245–251; Y. Elitzur, *IEJ* 39 (1989), 267–277.

Excavations: M. Piccirillo (and T. 'Attiyat), *ADAJ* 30 (1986), 341–351; id., *Umm er-Rasas, Kastron Mefaa in Giordania* (Terra Santa Supplement), Jerusalem 1986; id., *LA* 37 (1987), 177–239; 401–403; 39 (1989), 266–268; 40 (1990), 463–466; 41 (1991), 327–364; id., *MdB* 47 (1987), 51–53; id., *Syria* 64 (1987), 302–305; id., *BA* 51 (1988), 203–213; 227–231; id., *Chiese e Mosaici di Giordania*, Jerusalem 1989, 269–308; id., *Biblica* 71 (1990), 527–541; E. Puech, *LA* 39 (1989), 268–270; E. Alliata, ibid. 41 (1991), 365–422.

Inside the castrum: J. Bujard et al., *ADAJ* 32 (1988), 101–113; C. Bonnet et al., *LA* 38 (1988), 459–460.

MICHELE PICCIRILLO

'UVDA VALLEY

THE NEOLITHIC TEMPLE

IDENTIFICATION

The 'Uvda Valley is located in the southern Negev desert, about 40 km (25 mi.) north of Elath. A Neolithic site (site 6) lies in the northern third of the valley, between Naḥal Yitro and Naḥal Re'uel (map reference 146.929), at the mouth of a small gully that descends from the eastern ridge. It is surrounded by dunes of coarse sand that may have covered it for lengthy periods, thus preventing it from total destruction. It was, however, found on the surface.

EXCAVATIONS

The site was excavated in 1980 as part of the large-scale rescue excavations undertaken in the 'Uvda Valley by the Israel Department of Antiquities and Museums, in cooperation with the Survey of Israel. The excavations at site 6 were carried out in two stages, under the direction of O. Yogev. In the first stage (1980) the sanctuary was discovered, and in 1982 the animal representations to its east were uncovered. The isolated position of the site, its unique plan, and the artistic finds nearby show that it was a cultic site, one of the earliest in the country.

THE TEMPLE

The temple is made up of two basic units: a small rectangular room in the west of the area, and a square courtyard adjoining it on the east.

THE CULT ROOM. The cult room is oval, measuring 4 m from north to south and about 1.7 m at its widest point. Its ends are no more than one meter wide. The walls are built of long stone slabs (c. 20 by 60 cm), laid on their long, narrow sides. The walls were preserved to a height of one course (0.75 m), but there is enough debris on both sides of the structure to suggest that they were originally higher. In the middle of the room, above the debris, were some long stone slabs that were probably laid over wooden rafters to form a roof. The

'Uvda Valley: plan of the Neolithic temple.

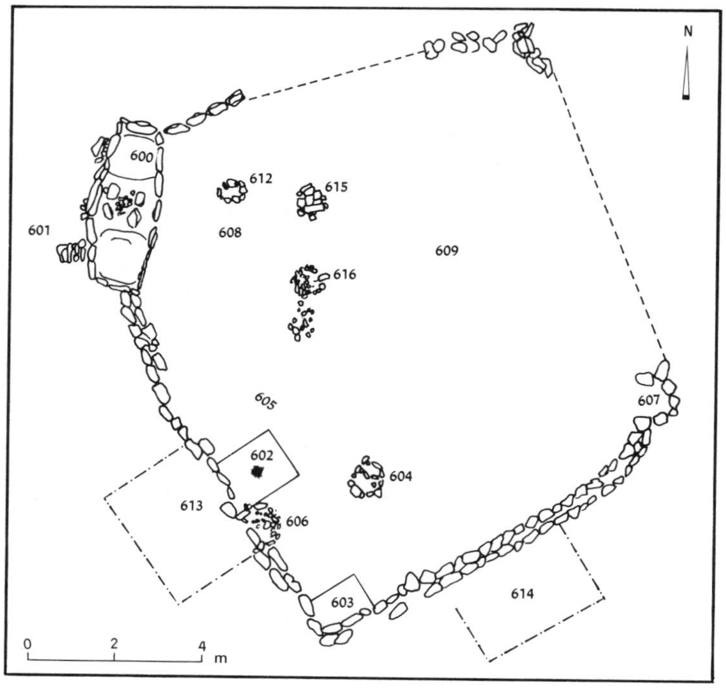

Representations of animals found east of the Neolithic temple.

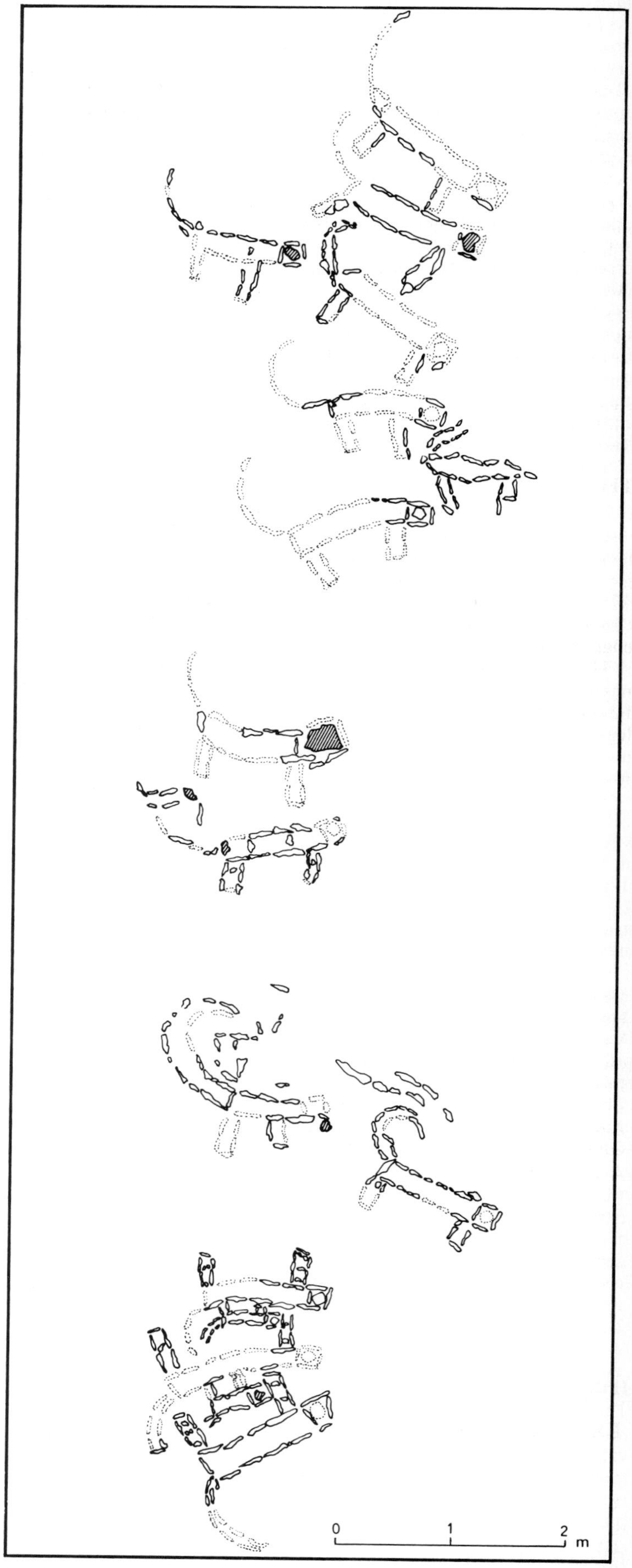

foundation course was unbroken, and its top rose to about half a meter above the level of the courtyard, showing that there was no doorway leading into the chamber.

After the stone debris and the large quantities of sand that had accumulated within the structure had been removed, sixteen field stones were found here, set together in a single block and protruding about 20 to 30 cm above the ground. Most of them were pointed; two, however, had broader ends. These *maṣṣebot*, or stelae, were surrounded by a diamond-shaped frame made of four large stones laid diagonally.

Since the sacred chamber was so small, it was clearly impossible to enter it and find the evidence contained there for the presence of a deity or deities. It may be assumed that an aperture was made in the eastern facade, through which light entered the closed chamber and the *maṣṣebot* could be seen. The *maṣṣebot* chamber was paved with stone.

THE TEMPLE COURTYARD. The courtyard (12 by 11 m) was the less important of the complex's two components. It adjoined the chamber on the east, and its corners were aligned to the cardinal points. It was paved with gravel and was very hard except in one strip of loose earth in the southwest apparently used as a fill to level the courtyard. A test pit excavated in the southern corner of the courtyard confirmed this. Most of the courtyard's installations were built in this southwestern strip (see below).

Only one course of the courtyard's walls was preserved, but it may be assumed that they were no higher than this, since no debris was found along them. The single-course wall probably demarcated the sacred area, to distinguish it from its surroundings. The missing sections of the walls can be easily reconstructed. There may have been an opening in the missing eastern wall, opposite the *maṣṣebot*. The courtyard walls were built of two rows of medium-sized stones. This method of construction is common in structures from the fifth and fourth millennia and is found at such sites as Byblos, Wadi Rabah, and Tuleilat el-Ghassul.

The Courtyard Installations. Six round installations were found at different levels in the loose earth of the courtyard's southwestern strip: three deep, cone-shaped basins and three shallow, paved hearths, built with a single row of stones. Ashes mixed with sand were found in all the installations; the lowest basin also contained pieces of charcoal. The cone-shaped basins were built of stone slabs of varying thickness. Their upper diameters range from 50 to 80 cm, while their lower diameters are about one third the size. The basins were sunk about 50 cm into the floor of the courtyard, up to their tops. The different levels in height show that they were not all set in place at the same time. The top of one basin is 14 cm below the base of another, demonstrating that the two, which were set side by side slightly to the right of the chamber's long axis, were used at different times. The two basins constitute the earliest and latest evidence of the different levels of the courtyard, indicating that the temple was used for a relatively long period.

THE FINDS. Few artifacts were found in the temple, among them two flint scrapers, one coarse and simple and the other oval and finer, made of tabular flint. This tool type, bearing an X-shaped incision, was found near the surface in a section cut outside the courtyard's southwestern wall. Similar scrapers are known from Tuleilat el-Ghassul and Negev and Sinai sites from the fourth and third millennia, although the chronological range of this type is not yet clear.

Apart from the scrapers, only a few fragments of ostrich shell were found. It is known that in early times ostrich eggs were used as containers for liquids, after their original contents had been removed through a hole. The ostrich is depicted in rock drawings near the Chalcolithic sites at Timna', not far from the 'Uvda Valley and, until the beginning of the twentieth century, could still be found in the southern part of the country.

THE DATE OF THE TEMPLE. Two radiocarbon dates were obtained from the charcoal found in one of the basins: 4610 (± 90) BCE and 4450 (± 200) BCE. These dates indicate that the temple was in use in approximately the middle of the fifth millennium, shortly before the end of the Neolithic period in Palestine.

In the light of this date, the question arises about whom the temple served and where they originated. Two Pre-Pottery Neolithic B (seventh millennium) sites were excavated in the 'Uvda Valley, one on the northern bank of Naḥal Re'uel and the other at the mouth of Naḥal 'Isaron. At the latter site, two occupation levels were distinguished, the upper of which had a radiocarbon date identical to that of the temple here. At present, it is still difficult to understand the link between the two sites and between them and the temple. It is also not known whether there was a contemporary settlement nearby. This needs to be clarified.

THE REPRESENTATIONS OF ANIMALS

In the winter of 1982, a strip (c. 15 m long and 6 m wide) was excavated at a distance of about 8 m along the eastern side of the temple courtyard. The remains of sixteen small limestone slabs were found stuck vertically into the ground in a manner suggesting the forms of animals. The slabs (c. 20 cm long, 15 cm wide, and 3 cm thick, on the average) were laid along a predetermined course. This technique seems to have been used as a substitute for rock-face engravings, since no rock faces exist near the temple.

The sixteen representations of animals lie in a roughly straight line, oriented north–south. The animals' heads face east, toward the mountains; their hindquarters face west, toward the temple; their backs face north, and their legs south. Only one group differs from this alignment (see below). All the animals are on the same level and do not overlap, suggesting that they were all made at about the same time. Two types of animals can be distinguished:

1. Carnivores with narrow rectangular bodies, sometimes slightly concave or convex. They are 1.2 m long and 20 cm wide, on the average. All the animals are shown in profile: a square head continuing the outline of the body, with a large eye in its center, two legs, and a tail which curves upward. Dark flints were used for the eyes and sometimes along the body and legs, which gives the depictions some degree of color. This design, which is repeated fifteen times, suggests that they are leopards, which can still be found in the arid parts of the country. The animals' dimensions are close to those of the leopard.

2. An antelope, 1 m long and 25 cm wide. This animal is only depicted once and faces west, unlike the others. Its horns are slightly curved, unlike those of the gazelle, which curve in a broad arc. Careful study of the entire "scene" suggests that it was intended to have a specific meaning. The southern group, for instance, includes five animals: three large ones (females?) with two small ones (cubs?) between them. These five animals are oriented differently from the rest: their backs are turned to the south and their legs to the north, so that they look as though they are standing on the side, taking no part in the scene depicted in the north.

The remains of the northern group of animals show that the antelope's forequarters lie between two leopards, with four other leopards close by. Moreover, despite the distance between the animal depictions and the temple, the antelope lies more or less on the same axis as the *maṣṣebot*. Its sole appearance in the "scene" may imply that it played some special role—perhaps as a sacrifice to the gods; or perhaps it embodies the god himself, who descends from the mountains in order to dwell in the temple. Alternatively, this may be a simple representation of a hunt.

The ancient rock drawings at Qilwe, discovered in the 1930s by N. Glueck and G. Horsfield about 200 km (120 mi.) east of 'Aqaba, show a style parallel to that seen in the animal representations at the 'Uvda temple. According to O. Bar-Yosef, the flint tools collected near Qilwe include types characteristic of the sixth and fifth millennia. It thus seems that the stylistic and chronological evidence from these two sites represents an identical culture of desert dwellers in the Late Neolithic period.

C. F. Graesser, *BA* 35 (1972), 34–63; R. Amiran (et al.), *IEJ* 29 (1979), 256; id. and C. Arnon, *Israel Museum News* 15 (1979), 21–23; U. Avner, *ESI* 1 (1982), 79–82; 2 (1983), 14–17; id., *TA* 11 (1984), 115–131; id., *BA* 53 (1990), 125–141; R. Cohen, *BAR* 9/4 (1983), 16–29; S. A. Rosen, "Lithics in the Bronze and Iron Ages in Israel" (Ph.D. diss., Univ. of Chicago 1983), 138–143; M. Stekelis Museum of Prehistory, *Uvda: Settlements and Temples in an Arid Valley*, Haifa 1988; N. Porat, *L'Urbanisation de la Palestine à l'Age du Bronze Ancien* (Actes du Colloque d'Emmaüs, 1986; *BAR*/IS 527, ed. P. de Miroschedji), Oxford 1989, 169–188.

ORA YOGEV

'UZA, ḤORVAT

IDENTIFICATION

Ḥorvat 'Uza (Khirbet Ghazzeh) is situated at the eastern end of the Arad Valley, some 8 km (5 mi.) southeast of Tel Arad (map reference 1657.0687). It overlooks Naḥal Qina and controls the ancient road linking this region to Edom and the Arabah.

The site consists of a fortress with towers, whose beginnings date to the Iron Age, and near it, at the top of the steep bank of the valley, a small Iron Age settlement. The fortress was first surveyed in the early twentieth century by A. Musil, who described it briefly but made no attempt to date it; A. Alt and M. Avi-Yonah considered it to be a Roman fortress, part of the *limes*. In 1956, a thorough survey was conducted by Y. Aharoni, and the plan of the site was traced. Aharoni ascribed the Iron Age levels mainly to the eighth and seventh centuries BCE, noting a small quantity of pottery from the tenth and ninth centuries BCE. He proposed to identify the site with Ramoth-Negeb, in the territory of Simeon (Jos. 19:8), which is also mentioned in one of the Arad letters (no. 24) as the prospective target of an Edomite attack. According to A. Lemaire, this was the site of biblical Kinah (Jos. 15:22). Based on the excavations so far, chronological considerations favor the identification with Kinah.

EXCAVATIONS

The first season of excavations at the site was carried out in the summer of 1982, by a joint expedition from the Institute of Archaeology at Tel Aviv University and Baylor University (Waco, Texas), headed by I. Beit-Arieh and B. Cresson. Additional seasons were held from 1983 to 1986 and in 1988.

IRON AGE. In the seventh century BCE, a large fortress (51 by 42 m, or c. 120 by 100 cubits) was erected on the site. It was surrounded by a wall (1.5 m thick) with ten square outer towers: four at the corners of the fortress; two in the center of the southern wall; one in the middle of the eastern wall; two flanking the gate in the northern wall of the fortress; and one in the western wall. The fortress is surrounded by a revetment 1.25 m thick. The gateway is 3.7 m wide and 6.5 m long; its left wing consists of two chambers: the first is 1.5 m long

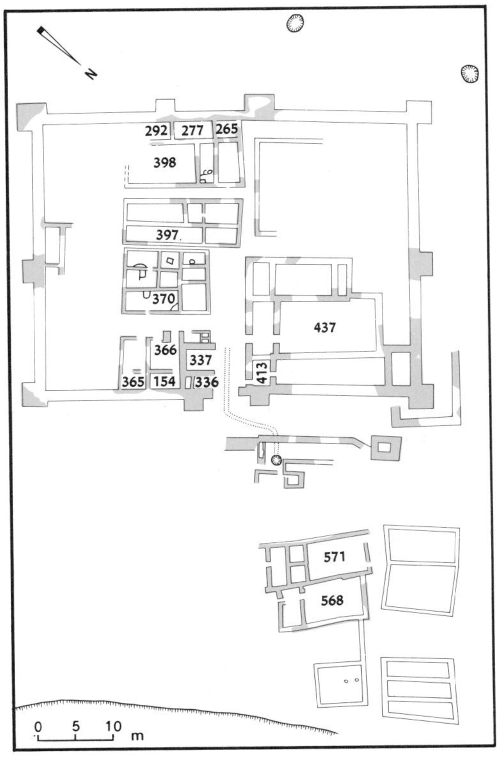

Ḥorvat 'Uza: plan of the fortress and eastern part of the Iron Age settlement.

Ḥorvat 'Uza: aerial view of the fortress and the settlement on the valley's steep bank, looking south.

and the second is 3 m long (interior dimensions). The other wing is quite different in plan; it may not be part of the gate at all, as it is a broadroom, one of a complex of rooms in a massive structure, only part of which has been exposed and whose nature is still unclear.

In the floor of the gateway was a drainage channel covered with stone slabs. Its continuation was found outside the fortress, in the settlement area. Outside the fortress, near the northwest tower, part of the outer gate was discovered—a tower attached to the northern revetment. The excavated parts of the fortress's courtyard revealed rooms abutting the wall (casemates) and a complex of buildings and narrow streets. A platform, perhaps a *bamah* (high place), was found near the gate.

Some of the rooms, particularly in the gate courtyard, contained large accumulations of charred wooden beams and other indications of a violent conflagration. A large quantity of ash mixed with Iron Age sherds—found dumped down the wadi's bank below the site—indicates that the fortress was cleared of debris by its Hellenistic settlers. Depressions in the ground outside the fortress, near the southern wall, attest to the existence of two cisterns.

Edomite ostracon from Ḥorvat 'Uza.

Two building stages have been distinguished in the fortress. The later stage, uncovered in a few places in the courtyard, is 0.6 m higher than the preceding one, but no distinctions could be made between the pottery from the two stages.

In this period (seventh century BCE) a planned settlement (1.7 a. in area) occupied the bank of the wadi, downstream from the fortress. Because of the steep gradient, this settlement's buildings were constructed on terraces, and the walls doubled as retaining walls. A large colonnaded house (6 by 14 m), built at a level 7 m below that of the fortress, was uncovered. The house has two entrances and consists of a paved courtyard and three rooms with plastered floors. The location of the fortress's gate in its northern wall hints at some connection with the settlement, which presumably housed the garrison members' families.

Pottery characteristic of the Negev at the end of the First Temple period was found both in the fortress and in the settlement. Particularly prominent is a rich variety of bowls, including some fine-quality red-slipped and burnished ware, testifying to a sophisticated technique. Among the more important finds are twenty-nine ostraca, most of them from the fortress and two from the settlement, and a jar bearing two inscriptions. Four Hebrew and one Edomite ostraca were found in the first chamber of the gate; the others were found in the rooms. The inscriptions on them are documents of various sorts: a military directive, name lists, the distribution of supplies or inventories, a literary-legal document, and fragmentary lists. The inscriptions on the jar relate to the administration of the fortress. All these documents confirm that 'Uza occupied an important position on the southeastern border of the Judean Negev. The content of the Edomite letter, which includes an order—perhaps meant for the Edomite commander of the fortress at the time—to deliver food supplies to the bearer, furnishes authentic historical evidence to the effect that the fortress fell to the Edomites around the time of the destruction of the First Temple, or perhaps later.

HELLENISTIC PERIOD. The Israelite fortress remained deserted for four hundred years; it was reoccupied in the Hellenistic period, between the late third and late second centuries BCE—the time of the Seleucids. In this period the fortress was part of the fortifications of southern Idumea, its task being to defend commercial routes crossing the Negev toward the port of Gaza.

The excavations revealed that many of the Iron Age rooms, mainly those abutting the fortress wall, were cleared by the Hellenistic settlers (see above) and the debris dumped down the bank of the wadi. The wall was restored and adjoined by new rooms, built approximately one meter wider and on a higher level than the rooms in the Israelite fortress. The fortress area was reduced to

Two chambers in the Iron Age gate; (left) higher wall from the Hellenistic period.

34 by 42 m by the erection of a new wall lined with a row of rooms in the western part of the courtyard. A square tower was built abutting the new wall on the outside. The gate and its towers continued in use, but the gateway itself was narrowed to a width of only 1.75 m. Its floor, about 0.6 m higher than the previous level, was reached by steps. The original chambers in the gate, which by this time no longer existed, were replaced by rooms adjoining the fortress wall. A large stone-faced silo was dug in the courtyard of the fortress. The rooms abutting the wall yielded a rich pottery assemblage, including jars, jugs, juglets, cooking pots, lamps, and bowls characteristic of the second century BCE. An ostracon inscribed in Aramaic was also found.

ROMAN PERIOD. In the Roman period (first to third centuries CE), the fortress was part of the Roman line of fortifications (*limes*). It occupied the same area as the Hellenistic fortress, and its remains were found in almost all the casemates that had been occupied in the Hellenistic period. Some of these rooms were restored and minor changes made in them. Thus, for example, a long Hellenistic room abutting the western wall continued in use in the Roman period as well, but it was divided in two lengthwise by a partition wall with a doorway. Major changes were introduced in the fortress's southwestern corner, opposite the tower: the long, narrow room that was here in the Hellenistic period was now sealed with stones to the ceiling, and broad steps were built north of it, perhaps providing access to the tower. A similar stone fill was found in another room, opposite the middle tower in the western wall; it, too, was apparently connected with the tower. Rooms excavated near the southern wall revealed two building stages from the Herodian period.

Abutting the outer face of the fortress are two solid enclosures built of large stones. These enclosures surround a large area and create the impression of a fortified area. The eastern enclosure had a gate in its eastern wall. A stratigraphic examination of the northern enclosure showed that it overlies the threshold of the Hellenistic gate and should therefore be assigned (together with the eastern enclosure) to the Roman period or later. The pottery from this period included decorated lamps. City coins of Ascalon (Ashkelon), Gaza, and Caesarea, dating from the reigns of Vespasian, Septimius Severus, and Marcus Aurelius, were also among the finds.

I. Beit-Arieh, *IEJ* 32 (1982), 262–263; (with B. Cresson), 33 (1983), 271–272; id., *ESI* 2 (1983), 104–106; 3 (1984), 105; 4 (1985), 108–109; 5 (1986), 110; 7–8 (1988–1989), 181; id. (with B. Cresson), *TA* 12 (1985), 96–101; 13–14 (1986–1987), 32–38; id., *AASOR* 49 (1989), 125–131; id. (with B. Cresson), *BA* 54 (1991), 126–135; A. Lemaire, *VT* 38 (1988), 220–230; Weippert 1988, 579, 614, 616; H. Misgav, *IEJ* 40 (1990), 215–217; L. Tatum, *BA* 54 (1991), 136–145.

ITZHAQ BEIT-ARIEH

W

EL-WAD CAVE

IDENTIFICATION

The el-Wad Cave (Cave of the Valley; in Hebrew, Me'arat ha-Naḥal) is situated on Mount Carmel, on the southern escarpment of Naḥal Me'arot, where it debouches onto the Coastal Plain, about 20 km (12.5 mi.) south of Haifa (map reference 147.230). El-Wad is a karstic cave, located about 44.5 m above sea level and 12 m above the bed of the valley. It is 90 m long and consists of two large chambers (I–II) and a long corridor (chambers III–VI). There is a large terrace in front of the cave.

El-Wad is the largest of the Carmel caves. It was mentioned in the writings of late nineteenth-century travelers and explorers, but did not emerge as a site of archaeological interest until 1928, when the Naḥal Me'arot escarpment was selected as a source of stone for construction works in the Haifa harbor. The discovery of numerous lithics following an initial trial explosion resulted in the cessation of the quarrying and the beginning of the examination of the caves. Test excavations were carried out in the cave and on the terrace in front of it by C. Lambert, on behalf of the Mandatory Department of Antiquities. A Natufian layer was uncovered that contained an abundance of flint artifacts and ground-stone implements. Three human burials, the first discovered on Mount Carmel, were also exposed, as well as a fragment of a bone sickle haft, carved in the shape of an animal's head—the earliest evidence of prehistoric art in the Near East.

The major excavations were carried out in the cave from 1929 to 1933, under the direction of D. Garrod, on behalf of the British School of Archaeology in Jerusalem and the American School of Prehistoric Research. Paleontological analyses were conducted by D. Bate, and the human remains were examined by T. D. McCown and A. Keith. The excavations were concentrated in chambers I–II and on the terrace. Chamber III was partly investigated and in chambers IV and V only test trenches were excavated. Nine layers, dating from the Middle Paleolithic to the historical periods, were uncovered.

EXCAVATION RESULTS

1929–1933 EXCAVATIONS. The layers (from early to late) uncovered in Garrod's excavations follow.

LAYERS G–F. Layers G–F were uncovered in chambers I and II, up to the entrance to chamber III. They filled and covered deep depressions (swallow holes) in the cave's floor. Initially, Garrod believed that layer G belonged to the Upper Mousterian, but she later ascribed both layers to the initial stage of the Upper Paleolithic or to the "transitory industry" between the Middle and Upper Paleolithic in Israel. The tool assemblages included typical Middle Paleolithic components (side scrapers and Levalloisian items) along with Upper Paleolithic tools (end scrapers and burins). Emireh points, characteristic of the transitory industry in Israel, were also found. Most scholars now agree that both layers represent a mixed assemblage, resulting from water activity in the cave at the onset of the Upper Paleolithic. Water had eroded the Mousterian (G) layer's uppermost part, considerably abrading the flints within it, and resulted in a mixture of items from the lowest part of the Upper Paleolithic layer (F) and Mousterian artifacts.

*Southern cliff of Naḥal Me'arot: **(left to right)** el-Wad, el-Jamal, and Tabun caves.*

LAYER E. Layer E, ascribed to the Levantine Aurignacian culture (Upper Paleolithic III, according to Garrod and R. Neuville's division), was uncovered in chambers I–II. The flint industry includes simple, carinated and nosed end scrapers, numerous burins, and large amounts of el-Wad points. Seven bone points were also found.

LAYER D. Layer D, also ascribed to the Levantine Aurignacian culture (Upper Paleolithic IV), was found mainly in chamber II and in the front part of the corridor (chamber III). Two sub-layers were distinguished here, based on the typology of the implements. In sub-layer D2, the percentage of retouched tools is considerably higher and their retouching shows workmanship of high quality. Most of the implements are end scrapers, many of them carinated or nosed. El-Wad points are rare, relative to the number found in the preceding layer.

LAYER C. Layer C, assigned to the late Upper Paleolithic (stage V), was exposed in chambers II and III. Its flint assemblage is characterized by numerous burins and end scrapers, constituting 80 percent of the entire assemblage. Many of the burins are polyhedral and made on tabular flint. Because of these particular characteristics, this assemblage has been given a specific name: the Atlitian. Other Atlitian assemblages dating to the terminal Upper Paleolithic differ typologically, although they all seem to share a flake technology.

LAYER B. Layer B is Natufian and extends over the whole terrace and the two front chambers. The flint assemblage is rich in end scrapers, burins, awls, and sickle blades, along with large quantities of microliths, mainly lunates. Many ground-stone implements, mostly of basalt, were also found. Pestle fragments are the most frequent of the stone tools, which also include grinding implements and fragments of bowls and mortars. In the rich bone-tool assemblage, the most frequent items are points, harpoons, fish hooks, spatulae, and well-made, but mostly broken, sickle hafts. Two sickle blades are still embedded in one of them. Among the art objects are sickle hafts carved at their end with an animal's head, a human head carved in limestone, stone and bone pendants, and beads made of animal bones and of cardium and dentalium shells.

Almost one hundred human skeletons were found—most of them on the terrace, where a large Natufian cemetery was unearthed, and a few in the cave itself. Two main types of inhumation can be distinguished—group and single burials—probably belonging to two phases of the Natufian. In the group burials, the bodies were laid in a tightly flexed position. They wore necklaces of dentalia and bone ornaments, characteristic of the Early Natufian culture. In the single burials, the position of the bodies is only slightly flexed and the skulls bear no ornaments. In some cases, the skeleton was covered with stones. These burials belong to the Late Natufian. Near them, in the center of the terrace, were four basins cut in the rock, one of them with a raised rim. Nearby was a pavement of stone slabs and, to the east, a retaining wall built of large, unhewn stones. It could not be determined with certainty whether these architectural remains were dwellings or were connected with the burials.

Based mainly on the technological features of the lithics and the nature of the burials, the Natufian layer was divided into two stages: an early stage (B2), characterized by extensive use of the Helwan retouch; and a late stage (B1), displaying a decrease in the Helwan retouch and an increase in the use of the microburin technique. The remains from the Early Natufian stage were uncovered both in the cave and on the terrace fronting it, whereas those from the Late Natufian were found only on the terrace.

LAYER A. Layer A contained a mixture of finds from the Neolithic to the late historical periods. They include flint tools, potsherds, fragments of oil lamps,

Natufian burial; the skull is decorated with a necklace of dentalia.

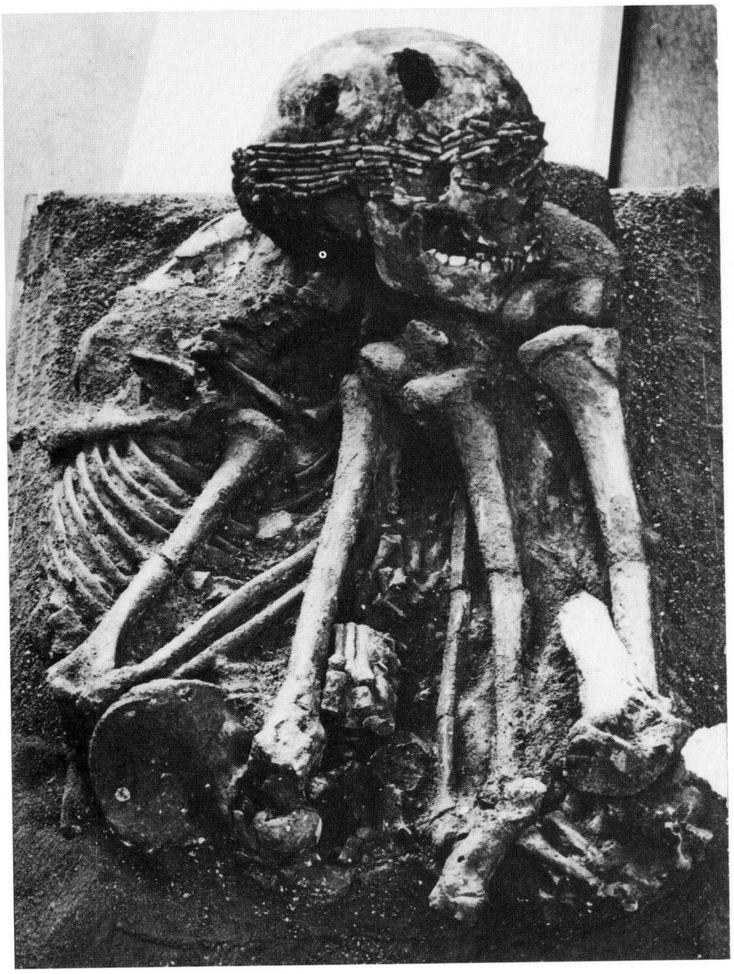

and several art objects, among them a Hellenistic statuette of the goddess Aphrodite. In the medieval period, the cave's eastern entrance was hewn and fitted with a hinged door. The wide main entrance was blocked with a stone wall, still intact when Garrod began her excavations.

1980–1981 EXCAVATIONS. In 1980–1981, limited excavations were conducted in the northern part of the terrace by F. Valla of the French Archaeological Mission in Jerusalem and O. Bar-Yosef of the Hebrew University of Jeru-salem. Their aim was to reexamine the stratigraphy of the Natufian layers as outlined by Garrod. The excavations revealed a final Natufian stratum, which overlaid the Early and Late Natufian layers. The finds include flint artifacts, mostly short lunates, bone tools, and stone implements. Meticulous excavation procedures and the sieving of sediments allowed the recovery of faunal data, which permitted conclusions regarding paleoenvironmental conditions at the site and the Natufians' manner of exploitation of the various biotopes. The faunal material includes remains of mammals, reptiles, birds, and fish, as well as terrestrial snails and marine shells.

1988 EXCAVATION. Excavations were resumed in 1988 in chamber III of the cave, under the direction of M. Weinstein-Evron, on behalf of Haifa University. A Natufian layer was exposed underneath the uppermost deposit containing material from the Neolithic to Byzantine periods. The Natufian layer yielded a wealth of flint and ground-stone implements, as well as faunal remains, ocher, bone tools, and a few art objects. The existence of such a layer in the rather dark, inner part of the cave was hitherto unknown. Various features of the tool assemblage and the art objects, together with carbon-14 dates for the charcoal remains recovered in the cave, indicate that this Natufian assemblage is among the earliest in the region. A Natufian presence at the site persisted for a rather long period of time, from the Early Natufian (12,950 BP), represented in the cave, to the final Natufian (c. 10,300 BP), represented on the terrace. This, however, does not necessarily imply that the cave was permanently occupied; it may have been inhabited for only short periods of time in specific seasons.

FLINT ARTIFACTS. The Natufian flint assemblage from the rear part of the cave is notable for its large number of cores, many of them thoroughly exploited, exhausted, and burned. By contrast, the microliths, particularly the lunates, are markedly scarce. These features set this assemblage apart from the material recovered from the Natufian layers in the front part of the cave and on the terrace. The presence of the finds in the rear part of the cave, the composition of the flint collection, and the numerous fragments of ground-stone implements—particularly the basalt pestles—suggest that the main use of this part of the cave may have been as a dump for waste.

FLORAL AND FAUNAL REMAINS. The analysis of the pollen obtained from the Natufian layers in chamber III reveals that *Olea* and *Tamarix* pollen clusters are amply represented. Such clusters represent whole anthers and indicate that flowering branches—off which these anthers had dropped—had been brought to the site. Due to their high oil content, the easily available young olive branches may have been used as kindling material. The tamarisk branches, extensively represented among the recovered charcoals, were probably gathered on the fringes of coastal marshes and may have been used to feed the fires. Pollen grains and charcoal remains of myrtle attest to the exploitation of this aromatic plant. The floral remains imply that the people who built those fires frequented the site in spring and summer, when olives and myrtle are in bloom.

Ongoing analysis of the faunal remains has still not furnished data pertaining to the season in which the site was inhabited. The majority of the mammal bones found belong to gazelles, as is the case in many other Natufian assemblages. The rest are bones of fallow deer, red deer, wild pig, aurochs, wild capra, fox, hare, mole, rat, and squirrel.

OCHER. Among the finds were numerous remains of ocher in various colors—red, orange, yellow, and brown—resulting from the different concentrations and oxidation levels of iron. Comparisons of natural ocher exposures in the Carmel region with the remains from the cave suggest the exploitation of ocher exposures 1 to 10 km (6 mi.) from the cave. Ocher lumps occasionally found embedded in the sediments of the adjacent wadi may have been used as well. The ocher used by the Natufians, as attested by the remains traced on the pounding tools found in the cave, was of a type composed of the mineral hematite. In the Carmel region goethite is more common. However, as heat transforms goethite into hematite, it is conceivable that the Natufians heat-treated the more easily available goethite to produce the desired hematite.

ART OBJECTS. The art objects found in chamber III include several human figurines and phallic objects. A few stone beads and a fragment of a bone sickle haft, decorated with a typically Natufian pattern of short parallel lines, were also found.

GEOPHYSICAL STUDIES. Seismic refraction analyses, conducted at the site to establish the thickness of the underlying layers, revealed the existence of swallow holes in the centers of chambers III, IV, and V (1.3 m, 2 m, and 3.5 m deep, respectively). The depth of the deposits suggests that remains of even earlier human occupations may still be recoverable from the deepest, darkest parts of the cave.

D. A. E. Garrod, *PEQ* 61 (1929), 220–222; 63 (1931), 99–103; id., *Annual of the British School at Athens* 37 (1936–1937), 123–127; id., *The Natufian Culture* (Proceedings of the British Academy 43), 211–227; id. (et al.), *The Stone Age of Mount Carmel* 1–2, London 1937–1939; D. V. Campana, *JFA* 6 (1979), 237–242; H. Büller, *Traces d'utilization sur les outils Néolithiques du Proche Orient* (Travaux de la Maison de l'Orient 5, ed. M. Cauvin), Lyon 1983, 107–126; Y. Olami, *Prehistoric Carmel*, Jerusalem 1984; F. R. Valla et al., *Paléorient* 12/1 (1986), 21–38; Weippert 1988 (Ortsregister); P. C. Edwards, *Journal of Mediterranean Archaeology* 2 (1989), 5–48; O. Bar-Yosef and A. Belfer-Cohen, *Journal of World Prehistory* 3/4 (1989), 447–498; M. Weinstein-Evron, *ESI* 9 (1989–1990), 109; id. (et al.), *Geoarchaeology* 6 (1991), 355–365; id., *Paléorient* 17/1 (1991), 95–98; D I. Olszewski and C. M. Barton, *Levant* 22 (1990), 43–46.

MINA WEINSTEIN-EVRON

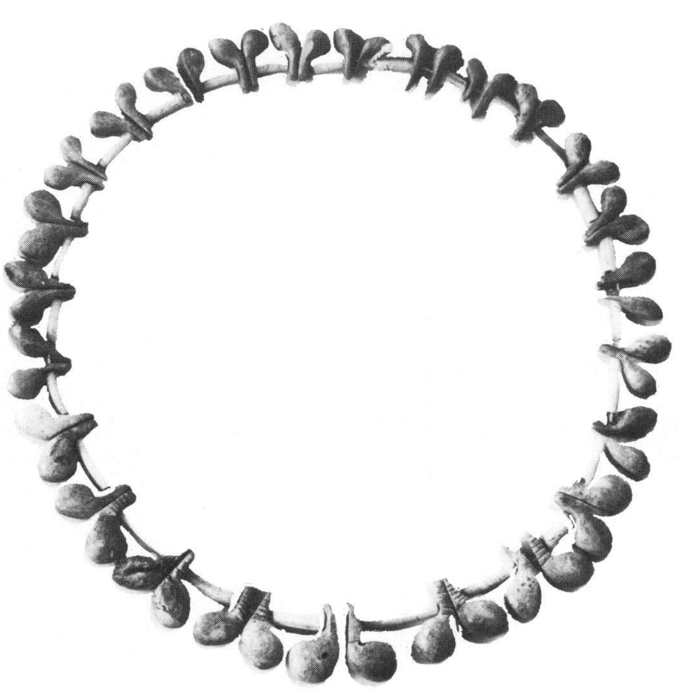

Necklace of dentalium and bone pendants, Natufian culture.

WAWIYAT, TELL EL-

IDENTIFICATION

Tell el-Wawiyat (map reference 178.244) is located in the southwestern quadrant of the Beth Netofa Valley in the Lower Galilee, 12 km (7.5 mi.) north of Nazareth. The site is a roughly circular mound of approximately 1 a., rising 3.75 m above the valley floor. The alluvial soil in the valley is quite rich, and annual rainfall is between 500 and 700 mm. A geomorphological study of the area around the site has shown that a wadi crossed the valley north of the mound, providing an additional source of water in an area in which springs are rare. The size of the site, its buildings, and its material-culture assemblage suggest that in antiquity Wawiyat was a small, unfortified village with the potential for agricultural self-sufficiency.

The biblical identification of Tell el-Wawiyat is uncertain. Biblical tradition ascribes control of the western Lower Galilee, including the Bet Netofa Valley, to the tribe of Zebulun. According to the town lists in Joshua 19:13–14, the border "passes along on the east . . ., and going on to Rimmon it bends toward Neah; then on the north the boundary turns about to Hannathon." In the Late Bronze Age IIA Amarna letters, Hannathon (Ḥinnatuni) was infamous for its unrest, highway robbery, and rebellion against Egypt. It has been identified with Tel Hannathon (Tell el-Badwiyeh), a roughly 12.5-a. mound 4.75 km (3 mi.) west of Wawiyat, and the only other site on the floor of the Bet Netofa Valley. Y. Aharoni identified Rimmon with the Arab village of Rummana, 1 km south of Tell el-Wawiyat. Thus, Wawiyat may have been Neah, as originally suggested by F. M. Abel. Alternately, Neah may be sought at Khirbet Rujma, a site with Iron Age I remains north of Wawiyat, in the foothills of the valley. The modern Arabic name, Tell el-Wawiyat, from which the Hebrew name for the site, Tel Wawit, was derived, offers no clue to the settlement's original identification.

EXPLORATION

Tell el-Wawiyat was mentioned by Abel in the 1930s, and is known from Gal's more exhaustive survey of the Lower Galilee in the 1970s. Excavations at Wawiyat took place in 1986 and 1987, under the direction of B. Alpert Nakhai, J. P. Dessel, and B. L. Wisthoff, on behalf of the University of Arizona, in conjunction with the William F. Albright School of Archaeological Research in Jerusalem and the American Schools of Oriental Research. Principal investigator for the project was W. G. Dever. Thirteen 6-by-6-m squares, twelve of which were in the eastern sector of the site, were excavated. Architectural remains were found within 20 cm of the surface.

EXCAVATION RESULTS

Six strata were found on the mound.

Stratum I: modern. Topsoil and subtopsoil.

Stratum II: Iron Age IB. A poorly preserved squatter settlement, this reoccupation of the site dates to the eleventh century BCE.

Stratum III: Iron Age IA. The main Iron Age settlement at Wawiyat, an agriculturally based village, dates to the late thirteenth to early twelfth centuries BCE.

Stratum IV: Late Bronze Age II. This settlement may have been a way station along the Late Bronze Age trade route across the Lower Galilee.

Stratum V: Late Bronze Age I. This period is represented to date by sherd material only.

Stratum VI: Middle Bronze Age IIB–C. This settlement is known primarily by two child jar burials.

THE MIDDLE BRONZE AGE II. A limited quantity of pottery from stratum VI from the Middle Bronze Age IIB–C has been found. Excluding several Chalcolithic and Early Bronze Age sherds, this is the earliest period represented at the site.

Two Middle Bronze Age IIC child jar burials were found within a thick layer of mud-brick debris. One pithos bore an incised mark and was perforated by two neatly cut holes. Together with a ceramic stopper and a fragment of a flint blade, there were four vessels: a small black-burnished juglet, a black-burnished wide-neck jar, a dipper juglet, and a pitcher. Beneath these lay the poorly preserved body of an infant under six months of age, lying on its left side, in a flexed position. The second burial jar resembled the first but lacked the incision and perforations. Along with a basalt pestle, this pithos contained a Tell el-Yahudiyeh juglet, a dipper juglet, a pyriform juglet with a double handle, and a trefoil cup. The bodies of two children, aged three and five, were found in the jar, along with several animal bones.

Child burial in a storage jar, MB IIC.

THE LATE BRONZE AGE. The limited amount of ceramic material from stratum V, the Late Bronze Age I, reflects the end of the Middle Bronze Age II tradition at Wawiyat. No architectural remains dating to this period have as yet been uncovered.

A very large amount of Late Bronze Age II pottery, encompassing a wide spectrum of local and imported wares, has been found at Wawiyat. The majority of imports are Cypriot white-slip "milk bowls" and vessels in base-ring I, base-ring II, and monochrome wares. A zoomorphic rattle in white-painted ware, found in a small stone bin, resembled one from Enkomi. A limited number of white-shaved juglets, white-painted ware, and

Tell el-Wawiyat: plan of the remains in stratum III, Iron IA.

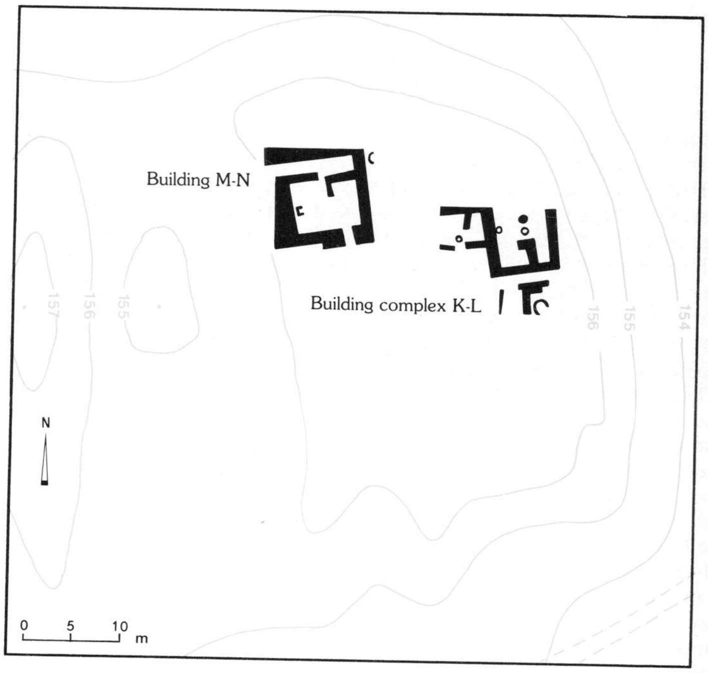

Clay plaque depicting a mother and child, LB II.

Mycenean ware, as well as one Minoan sherd, were also found. Included in the corpus of local, domestic pottery were cooking pots with everted rims, stumpy-based storage jars, and bichrome kraters. The range of imports attests to the site's wealth in this period. The continuation of forms from the Late Bronze Age II into the Iron Age IA is also significant.

To date, the exposure of Late Bronze Age II architecture is limited to a series of surfaces beneath the east side of the stratum III, Iron Age IA, M-N building. It was here that an unusual naturalistic figurine depicting a mother holding her child was found. Late Bronze Age II pottery was found under the floor of the main room in the Iron Age IA K-L building complex. Because the foundation of this building has not yet been reached, further excavation may reveal that the building was originally constructed in the Late Bronze Age II and then used in the Iron Age IA, as well.

The abundance of imported pottery at Tell el-Wawiyat indicates that, as a result of its location, Wawiyat may have played a part in Late Bronze Age trading emporia. Its proximity to several major sites, including Hannathon and the fortified settlement at Tel Qarnei Ḥittin, guarding the descent to the Sea of Galilee east of the Beth Netofa Valley, would have precluded an independent role for the inhabitants of Wawiyat in trade networks across the Lower Galilee. Furthermore, the absence of any defensive structure to offset the site's physical vulnerability would have eliminated the possibility of Wawiyat's functioning as a storage and redistribution center for valuable commodities. Late Bronze Age Wawiyat was likely a way station, under the control of Ḥinnatuni, supplying comestibles and shelter to those traveling east–west across the Lower Galilee.

THE IRON AGE. The Iron Age at Tell el-Wawiyat is represented by stratum III (Iron Age IA, late thirteenth to early twelfth centuries BCE) and stratum II (Iron Age IB, eleventh century BCE). The former is the main occupational period so far excavated at the site, whereas the latter was a rather poor resettlement of the mound. Two stratum III buildings have been excavated.

The M-N Building. A large rectangular building in stratum III, impressive in both its overall dimensions and in the width of its external walls, measured 9.5 m north–south and more than 8.5 m east–west. The exterior walls ranged from 1.25 to 2 m in width. It consisted of two main rooms. The room in the north was long and narrow, while that in the south was further subdivided and included a paved area and some small installations. The western wall of the M-N building was terraced to conform to the slope down into the mound's central depression. Pottery on the surfaces of this building, including storage jars, cooking pots, baking trays, and stands, dates it to the Iron Age IA. Together with the pottery, other artifacts found in the building—flint blades, basalt and limestone mortars, grinding stones and pestles, and worked bone awls and needles—suggest its utilization for domestic activities.

In stratum II, the M-N building was modified by blocking the southern entryway and by constructing new internal walls.

The K-L Building Complex. A multiroomed complex in stratum III stood approximately 10 m southeast of the M-N building. Its most fully excavated room was the rectangular northeastern room, in which a Middle Bronze Age IIB–C geometric Hyksos scarab was found. In the center of the room, providing its focal point, was a circular jar stand, constructed of basalt grinding stones set around a limestone basin. A stone column base stood 0.75 m to its north. A *tabun* (oven) constructed of the inverted upper third of a jar surrounded by two rows of *tabun* ware was set into the floor opposite the jar stand, against the room's western wall. This room contained the only hewn and plastered masonry recovered at the site. In its southwestern corner a small alcove was erected by an L-shaped partition wall. Twenty-four partially articulated bones from a single butchered cow lay on the room's plastered flagstone floor.

The western room of the K-L building complex was subdivided into several smaller chambers. A small circular stone bin was set into the floor near the opening in its southern wall. The floor was primarily of beaten earth, although a poorly preserved cobbling was noted in some areas.

Due to the limits of the excavated area, the southern room is defined only by its northern and western walls. An unusual installation, only partly exposed, filled an area of roughly 3 by 3 m. It consisted of two contiguous east–west walls, met at their western corner by a perpendicular wall running south. These walls formed half of a square, into which a large circular bin was set. Small finds from the debris in this southern room included a complete spearhead, a steatite jewelry mold, a delicate basalt bowl on three legs, part of an Astarte figurine, and a fragment of gold leaf.

In stratum II a series of narrow, curvilinear walls, often built over the earlier walls, was set onto the existing surfaces of the K-L building complex.

SUMMARY. The stratum III Iron Age IA settlement at Tell el-Wawiyat consisted of several large, multiroomed buildings, as well as some spacious open areas. Architectural continuity between the Late Bronze Age II and the Iron Age IA was noted in the K-L building complex, whereas the M-N building was initially constructed in the latter period. The function of the M-N building was primarily domestic, but that of the K-L building complex was specialized, as shown by its elite status markers which may have had cultic functions.

The Iron Age IA site was thus home for an agriculturally based group with complex economic and social activities. The evolution of this community from the local Late Bronze Age Canaanite society is underscored by the transitional nature of the pottery from this stratum, which clearly demonstrates technological and stylistic affinities between the two periods.

The stratum II settlement at Wawiyat, on the other hand, represented an indigent squatters' reuse of the site. It may have been the result of an Israelite reoccupation of a previously abandoned village.

B. Alpert Nakhai et al., *IEJ* 37 (1987), 181–185; id., *ESI* 6 (1987–1988), 100–102; id., *AJA* 92 (1988), 244; id., *RB* 95 (1988), 247–250; J. P. Dessel et al., *ESI* 7–8 (1988–1989), 183–184; id., *IEJ* 39 (1989), 102–104; 40 (1990), 72–73.

BETH ALPERT NAKHAI, J. P. DESSEL, BONNIE L. WISTHOFF

Y

YAQUSH

IDENTIFICATION

Yaqush is located on the rim of the Ghor, facing the Jordan River to its east and backed by the dominating heights of the eastern Lower Galilee to its west (map reference 2024.2244). It overlooks a small wadi, Wadi Kuraiyim, which drains into the Jordan River and runs parallel to the larger Naḥal Tabor, whose mouth is directly west of the site.

Yaqush was first depicted on the 1890 Palestine Exploration Fund map on which it was identified as Tell ez-Zanbakiyeh (Tell of the Lilies). The 1930–1932 British Mandate period map shifted the name Zanbakiyeh to a site 750 m to the southeast, leaving the site now known as Yaqush nameless. The survey of the region conducted by N. Zori described the site as Giv'at ha-Moqshim (Hill of the Mines, site no. 8) because it was heavily mined in 1948, in Israel's War of Independence. The site was cleared of mines and now appears as Ḥorvat Yaqush on modern maps. Yaqush's position near one of the major fords of the Jordan River may explain its settlement in the Early Bronze Age. Directly east of it, across the Jordan River, is the site of esh-Shunah (North), one of the major urban sites in the Early Bronze Age in the central Jordan Valley. A bridge across the Jordan (called Jisr el-Majami') from the Arab period, as well as an earlier, preserved bridge from the Roman period, attests to the importance of this ford. Roman milestones, charted by P. Thomsen in 1917, indicate that the ancient Roman road passed directly by Yaqush. Although Yaqush was essentially abandoned at the end of the third millennium, nearby sites dating to later periods are evidence of the importance of its location astride the major thoroughfare for north–south travel from Syria to Egypt in antiquity.

EXCAVATIONS

Excavations were conducted here in 1989 and 1991 by the Oriental Institute of the University of Chicago, under the direction of D. L. Esse. A total area of 1,055 sq m was cleared in the two seasons. A preliminary estimate indicated that in the Early Bronze Age I, the site comprised approximately 6 a. By the Early Bronze Age III, the area of the village had declined to roughly 1 to 2 a.

EARLY BRONZE AGE I. The Early Bronze Age I is the earliest period reached at Yaqush. Evidence for at least four architectural phases of the Early Bronze Age I was recovered. One of the earlier phases is represented in square P14 by a large building at least 11 m long. Although severely damaged in modern times, at least four courses of a stone wall forming the northern edge of the building were preserved. The stones were laid in a herringbone fashion. Traces of later Early Bronze Age I remains sealed this structure.

The latest phase of the Early Bronze Age I was recovered more extensively on the summit of the mound (square H5) and in a small trench east of the main excavation area at the southeast edge of the site (square T14). Both areas were dominated by evidence of an extremely destructive conflagration. Traces of carbonized roof beams and roof-fall were well enough preserved to indicate that the roofs of the Early Bronze Age I houses were constructed using small wooden beams with brush and twigs placed above them. This framework was then covered and sealed with successive layers of packed clay.

The northern end of one of the structures on the summit was curvilinear. Although not completely excavated, at least two flat stone pillar bases placed along the main axis of the room were recovered, as well as a stone mortar.

Yaqush: plan of the site and excavation areas.

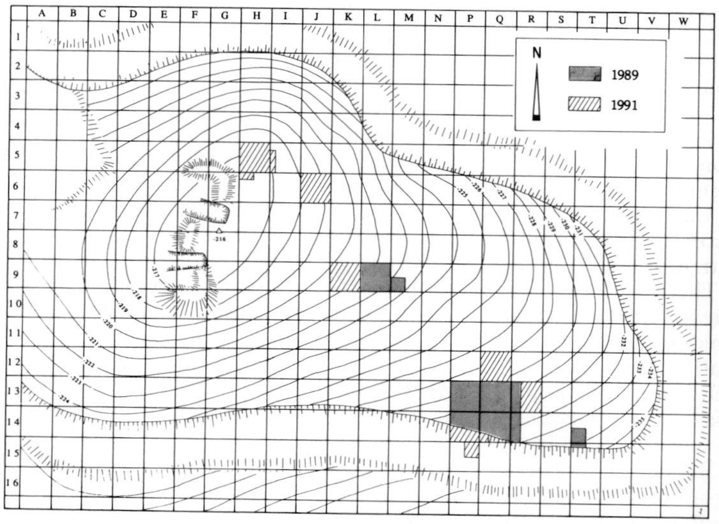

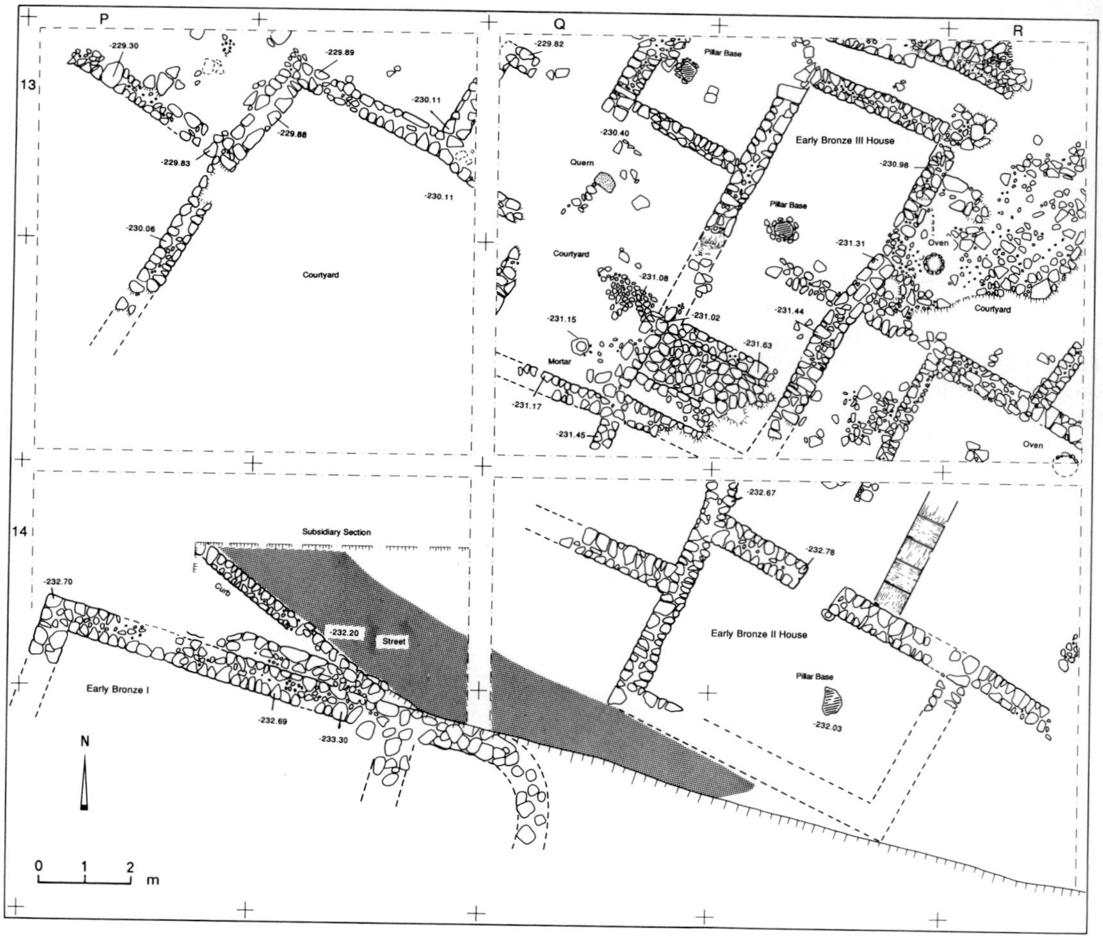

Plan of the main excavation area, 1989 season.

Dozens of smashed pottery vessels, some containing charred grain, were found on the floor. The pottery exhibits a wide array of forms, including large grain-washed storage jars, a grain-washed spouted vat with loop handles, red-burnished jugs, small jugs and juglets, and a bottle. Bone awls, flint knives, and sickle blades were also recovered, as was a perfectly preserved copper ax. Two storage jars were sealed beneath the collapsed roof of a nearby structure: one a common grain-washed jar and the other a fully developed, combed metallic-ware jar. Ceramically, this forces a date at the very end of the Early Bronze Age I.

The small trench along the southeastern edge of the mound also yielded dramatic evidence of a great conflagration. The room's main walls, exposed in this trench, were separated by a doorway and constructed with a stone foundation and a brick superstructure; at least four courses of vitrified brick remained in place. In one of the rooms, a large ceramic silo set on a stone base held a substantial cache of carbonized emmer wheat. Carbon-14 tests on the wheat indicate a date of 3200 BCE. Also found on the floor was the antler of a deer.

Earlier phases of the Early Bronze Age I were recovered at Yaqush. The ceramic repertoire of these stratigraphically earlier phases is not yet clearly defined. Although present, no significant amounts of gray-burnished ware have been recovered in an architectural context. This suggests that the village of Yaqush underwent its greatest development and expansion in the latter part of the Early Bronze Age I and reached its greatest extent at the transition from Early Bronze Age I to II, when the entire village was violently destroyed.

EARLY BRONZE AGE II. Evidence for an Early Bronze Age II occupation was recovered in the main excavation area. A house (7 by 5 m) partially eroded along its southern edge was found. A large stone slab was used as a pillar base to support the roof, and a carved basalt door socket was found just inside and to the left of the doorway. Traces of an adjacent room or building were recovered along the house's eastern wall. A small forecourt opened off the entrance on the north.

The house was apparently destroyed in an earthquake, for the entire structure was sealed with sheets of collapsed mud-brick walls. The bricks remained coursed, indicating a sudden and complete collapse, although at least four courses of mud brick remained intact on the stone foundations. Carbon-14 dates of wood-charcoal samples from the forecourt, the interior of the house itself, and the area just west of the house, clustered around 3100 BCE. The latest date was 2745 BCE; it probably more accurately reflects the destruction date of the house because the samples were wood charcoal and not a short-lived sample like grain.

A street 2.5 m wide ran adjacent to the Early Bronze Age II house. The street was in use over a fairly long period of time, with at least six detectable surfaces and a total buildup of at least 0.4 m over the years. A row of small boulders aligned along the southern, or downslope, side of the street formed a curb that delimited the street through several phases.

The ceramic repertoire was typical of the Early Bronze Age II in northern Canaan. Predominant among the forms and wares was an orange/brown metallic ware, used for small bowls and platters and for large storage jars with combed exteriors. The ceramic finds from Early Bronze Age II Yaqush were identical with those from the Early Bronze Age II levels at Beth Yeraḥ, 10 km (6 mi.) to the north.

EARLY BRONZE AGE III. By the Early Bronze Age III, the village had declined in size to an area of roughly 1 to 2 a. Remains from this period's village were detected in two excavation areas (squares K9/L9 and squares P13, Q12–13, R13). The largest area exposed was located in the main excavation area along the southern edge of the mound. At least three major superimposed architectural phases dating to this period have been revealed.

The earliest and most complete phase yielded a complete house/courtyard complex. The house was composed of at least three rooms, one of which was built perpendicular to the main axis. Two of the rooms had earthen floors, while a third was paved with large, flat stones. Flat stones also served as bases for wooden pillars. The pillars were held in place by a small circle of wedging stones discovered in situ. The house had an entrance on the east and the west. Its western courtyard was partially paved with stone. In it, near a large basalt saddle quern, a basalt mortar was set in the earth. The small eastern courtyard held several clay and stone supports for storage vessels whose bases were recovered in the excavations. Two clay ovens, east of the house, were each constructed with successive layers of clay and with broken storage jar fragments packed into their exteriors to conserve heat. A pebbled path, lined with curbstones on each side, led from the eastern courtyard to the southeastern part of the site. The street was deliberately constricted at the point where it met the courtyard; a door socket located at this junction indicates that a small "garden gate" would have given privacy to the household.

Although only exposed in a limited area in the 1991 season, the plan of the

Overview of the main excavation area, 1989 season; (foreground) EB II house; (background) EB III house/courtyard complex.

Yaqush: votive vessels from the building in square Q12, EB III.

following architectural phase, square Q12, seemed to be unrelated to the earlier house/courtyard complex. A portion of a building was excavated, with its main wall running northeast–southwest and exposed for a distance of at least 7.5 m. The wall was built with stone foundations and at least five courses of its brick superstructure were preserved. The floor of the building was partially paved with large, flat stones. During the life of the building, the floor was raised and a partition wall was added, dividing the building into at least two rooms. The building may have been used as a shrine. Recovered from the earliest floor was a large well-made Khirbet Kerak ware and iron, a complete Khirbet Kerak ware red polished bowl, and a highly polished red-slipped button-base juglet. In the later phase of the building, a cache of ten votive juglets was found in association with two votive bowls, one of which had been used as a lamp.

The latest phase of the Early Bronze Age III in this area saw a reversion to domestic architecture. Just below the mound's surface, a pebbled street and several small domestic structures and rooms were excavated. One house was of the broadroom type, with a large stone mortar and a stone pillar base. Khirbet Kerak ware was ubiquitous, with all types of the standard assemblage represented.

In squares K9 and L9, erosion had damaged the Early Bronze Age III levels, but a portion of one large structure remained, with stone-paved floors and fairly substantial walls. Nearby, a broad street (3 m wide) ran in a north–south direction. The street was composed of packed earth, small pebbles, and pottery sherds, including a large percentage of Khirbet Kerak ware. Running along the western edge were at least two phases of curbing, indicating that at some point the street had been widened. The street was supported on the east by a battered retaining wall constructed of boulders (c. 5 m wide and 1 m high). The width of the street, the effort made to modify the site's topography to support it, and the strong and well-built character of the building with its stone-paved floors suggest a possible public function for this quarter of the village.

The ceramic repertoire of both excavation areas was typical of the Early Bronze Age III in northern Canaan. Red-washed platters with radial burnish, buff storage vessels, and Khirbet Kerak ware were present, resembling the late Early Bronze Age horizon attested at Beth Yeraḥ. The range of Khirbet Kerak ware was complete, with small red and red/black bowls, kraters, stands with corrugated decoration, knobbed lids, and andirons, including one andiron fragment with a human face modeled and incised on it. Two loop-handled lids have their closest parallels at sites with the red/black-burnished ware or "Karaz" ware tradition in central and southern Anatolia.

ECONOMY. The evidence from the excavations suggests that Yaqush was predominantly an agricultural settlement on the major north–south thoroughfare that linked Canaan with Syria. The flint repertoire yielded hundreds of Canaanean-type sickles and knives, in addition to many locally made flake tools. Wheat, barley, and lentils were the main crops. The faunal remains suggest a dependence on sheep, goat, and cattle husbandry. Remains of fallow deer and hartebeest were also recovered.

A stone-lined pit was built into the slope of the retaining wall. The pit yielded sherds from the Middle Bronze–Late Bronze Age transition, the only indication encountered of a post–Early Bronze Age III phase.

P. Thomsen, *ZDPV* 40 (1917), 1–141; N. Zori, *The Beth Shean Valley*, Jerusalem 1962, 138–139; D. Esse, *IEJ* 40 (1990), 222–223.

DOUGLAS L. ESSE

YAVNEH-YAM

IDENTIFICATION

The remains of the ancient coastal city Yavneh-Yam (in Arabic Minet Rubin) are located some 15 km (9 mi.) south of Jaffa, near Kibbutz Palmaḥim (map reference 1212.1479). According to one theory, Yavneh-Yam was the harbor suburb of the city of Yavneh, 8 km (5 mi.) to the southeast; according to another, it was called מחוז, "port" (Mukkazi in Egyptian inscriptions), a name also attributed to Tell es-Sultan, 6 km (3.5 mi.) east of Yavneh-Yam. From the Hellenistic period to the end of the Crusader period, Yavneh-Yam was known by the name 'Ιαμνητῶν. . .λίμηv.

The most impressive remains in this area are those of a square enclosure bounded by freestanding ramparts. More than half of this enclosure has been eroded due to a tectonic line in the sea that runs parallel to the coast. However, the entire east rampart and parts of the north and south ramparts are preserved. The length of the east rampart is approximately 800 m, and it can be reasonably assumed that the entire enclosure measured 800 by 800 m—that is, 158 a. No traces of occupation were uncovered inside the open enclosure, but building remains and graves were found in a strip along part of the inner rampart slope. Occupational remains were also revealed on and around the small mound located on the prominent headland of Yavneh-Yam.

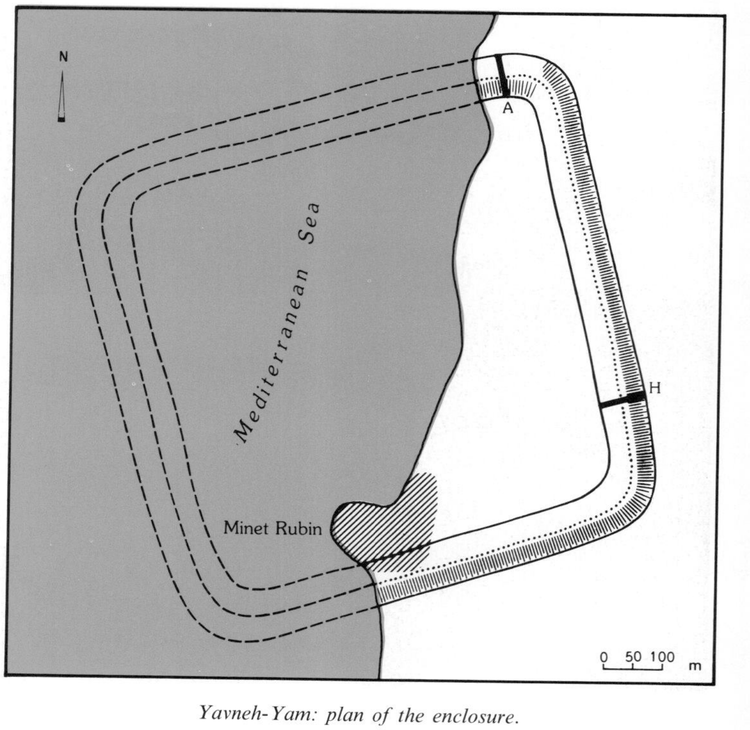

Yavneh-Yam: plan of the enclosure.

EXCAVATIONS

The excavations of the fortifications at Yavneh-Yam were directed by J. Kaplan, with the assistance of H. Kaplan, on behalf of the Tel Aviv–Jaffa Municipal Museum of Antiquities and the Haaretz Museum, and continued for three seasons, from 1967 to 1969. The aim of the excavations was to examine the method of construction of the enclosure and its ramparts. Work was concentrated in two areas: A, in the north rampart, and H, in the southern half of the east rampart.

THE RAMPART. In area A, a vertical cut was made from the top of the

Overview of area H, looking west.

rampart down to its base. The rampart was found to be constructed as follows: first, the whitish sand covering virgin soil was leveled along the rampart's proposed alignment. A layer of *ḥamra* (the red clay soil of the Coastal Plain), 12 cm thick, was then laid as a bedding for the rampart core, constructed of light-brown, pounded earth. In the final stage, the core was encased by a sheath of *ḥamra*, built up from the base on both sides of the core, toward the top. The glacis was in two layers: the lower layer, of heavy clay soil approximately 60–70 cm thick, extends from the top of the rampart down to virgin soil. The second, covering layer, of crushed *kurkar* 50 cm thick, was probably intended to prevent the damp clay soil from desiccating and pulverizing. At a later stage, an additional glacis was laid over the crushed *kurkar* layer. This new glacis was constructed in two parts: the lower, about 3 m high, was in the form of a retaining wall inclined about 45 degrees; from that point, and up to the top, the rampart was paved with stone and raked to approximately a 30-degree angle.

THE GATES. In the survey conducted at the site, a depression was perceived near the southeast corner of the embankment. This specific area was selected for excavation (area H). Three superimposed gates were exposed at this spot, indicating that the enclosure was entered from this same location during each of the periods of its use as a fortified stronghold. A sounding made in the middle of this eastern side of the enclosure indicated an additional system of gates. Thus, there are two systems of gates at Yavneh-Yam on one side (as at el-Mishrefe). The two lower gates in area H (II and III) were built of sun-dried brick and were flanked by towers. The bottom gate (III) contained three pairs of gate piers. The lower part of gate II, with only two pairs of gate piers, is well preserved. One of its defensive towers was of a hitherto unencountered plan. The walls of the right-hand tower were 2.4 m thick, and the narrow space between its walls and its central massive structure apparently had held a staircase leading to the upper story. Both early gates were protected on the outside by thick rubble walls. Above the ruins of gate II, one half of a smaller rubble gate (I) was exposed that dates to the Late Bronze Age I. The remains of this gate included two rooms and an outer stone supporting wall.

OCCUPATION REMAINS. Area A. Nine occupation layers were exposed on the inner rampart slope and in the adjoining enclosure area. The earliest layer (9) contained no building remains and yielded only some Middle Bronze Age IIA sherds. In layers 8–3, sherds and a few vessels dating to the Middle Bronze

MB II gates in area H.

Age IIB–C were found. Layers 2–1 contained Late Bronze Age I sherds, especially of bichrome ware. In a trial pit dug near area A, a circular, rubble structure was found with a bichrome jar filled with pieces of pumice.

Area H. In a small area on virgin soil in front of gate III, the remains of hearths were found. Inside and around them were Middle Bronze Age IIA sherds, fragments of an incense burner, and a number of ivory plaques incised with various designs. Middle Bronze Age IIA sherds were also found on the lowest floor in one of the chambers of the gate towers and in the foundation trench for one of the tower walls.

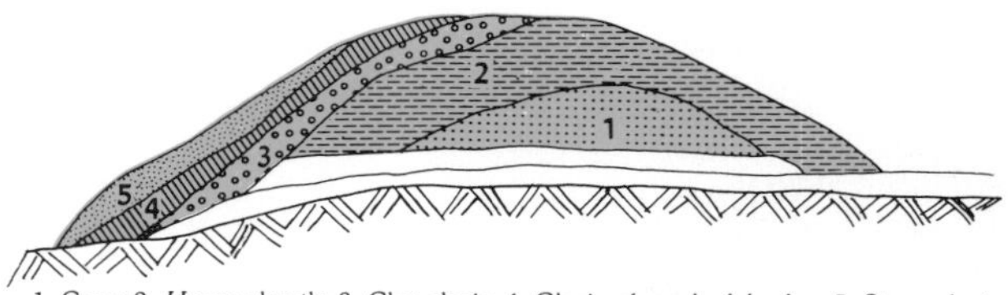

1. Core; 2. *Ḥamra* sheath; 3. Clay glacis; 4. Glacis of crushed *kurkar*; 5. Stone glacis

*Rampart in area A at Yavneh-Yam: **(above)** schematic cross section; **(below)** general view.*

CONCLUSIONS

The Yavneh-Yam excavations have furnished information on the construction method of the *terre pisée* ramparts, glacis, and gate structures of Middle Bronze Age II square enclosures. In the opinion of the excavators, the square enclosure with the three-pier gates made its first appearance in the Middle Bronze Age IIA, between 2000 and 1800 BCE. The pottery found in small quantities in the two excavated areas indicates that the Yavneh-Yam enclosure was used intermittently throughout the Middle Bronze Age II. Only at the beginning of the Late Bronze Age I did the enclosure cease to be used as a fortification (q.v. Marine Archaeology, Yavneh-Yam).

R. Du Mesnil De Buisson, *Syria* 7 (1926), 289–325; 8 (1927), 277–301; M. Dothan, *IEJ* 2 (1952), 104–117; J. Kaplan, *Bulletin of the Museum Ha'aretz* 10 (1968), 4–5; 12 (1970), 13–15; id., *IEJ* 17 (1967), 269; 19 (1969), 120–121; id., *RB* 75 (1968), 402–440; 76 (1969), 567–568; 77 (1970), 388–389; id., *ZDPV* 91 (1975), 1–17; E. Ayalon, *ESI* 2 (1983), 109–110; F. Vitto, *IEJ* 33 (1983), 268–269; id., *RB* 91 (1984), 258–259; I. Eldar and I. Nir, *ESI* 4 (1985), 114–115; *HUCMS News* 11–12 (1985), 6–7; Weippert 1988, 207, 216, 218, 224; Y. Levy, *ESI* 7–8 (1988–1989), 188, 202; B. Isaac, *IEJ* 41 (1991), 132–144.

JACOB KAPLAN

YEROḤAM, MOUNT

IDENTIFICATION

Ancient remains dating to the Intermediate Bronze Age (Middle Bronze Age I) are located in the Negev desert on the northeastern spur of Mount Yeroḥam, above Naḥal Revivim and the Yeroḥam Basin, about 30 km (18.5 mi.) south-southeast of Beersheba (map reference 1385.0434). The site was first discovered and described by B. Rothenberg. It extends over an area of about 5 sq km and includes a narrow ridge of about 1 a. that contains a cluster of densely built structures and several tumuli surrounded by a stone wall. Near this main settlement, on another spur, was a *bamah* (high place), consisting of a rock altar surrounded by a stone wall. About eighty tumuli were observed on another spur. Other tumuli and isolated structures are dispersed throughout the site, mainly on the saddle between the *bamah* and the mountain ridge.

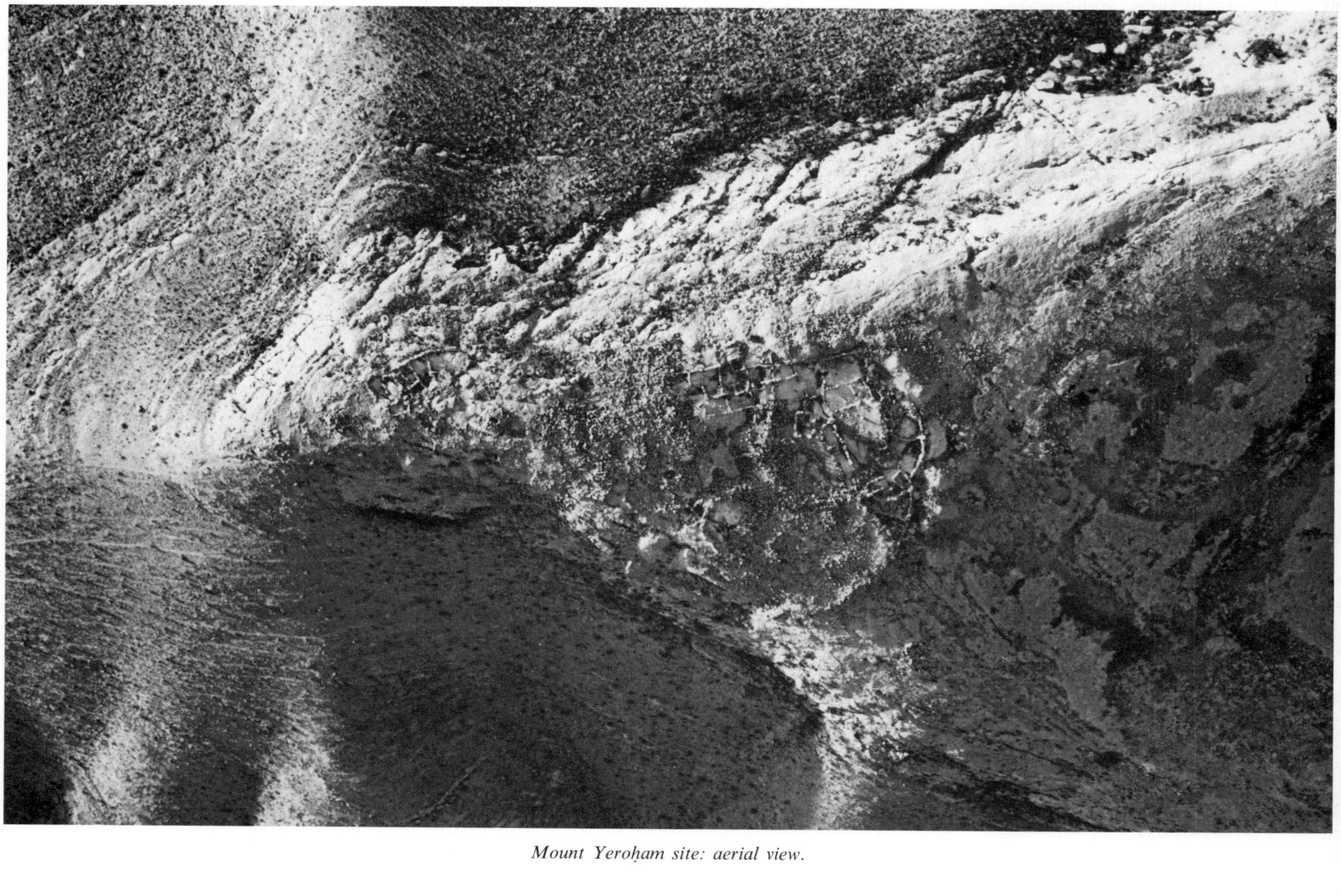

Mount Yeroḥam site: aerial view.

Plan of the Mount Yeroḥam site.

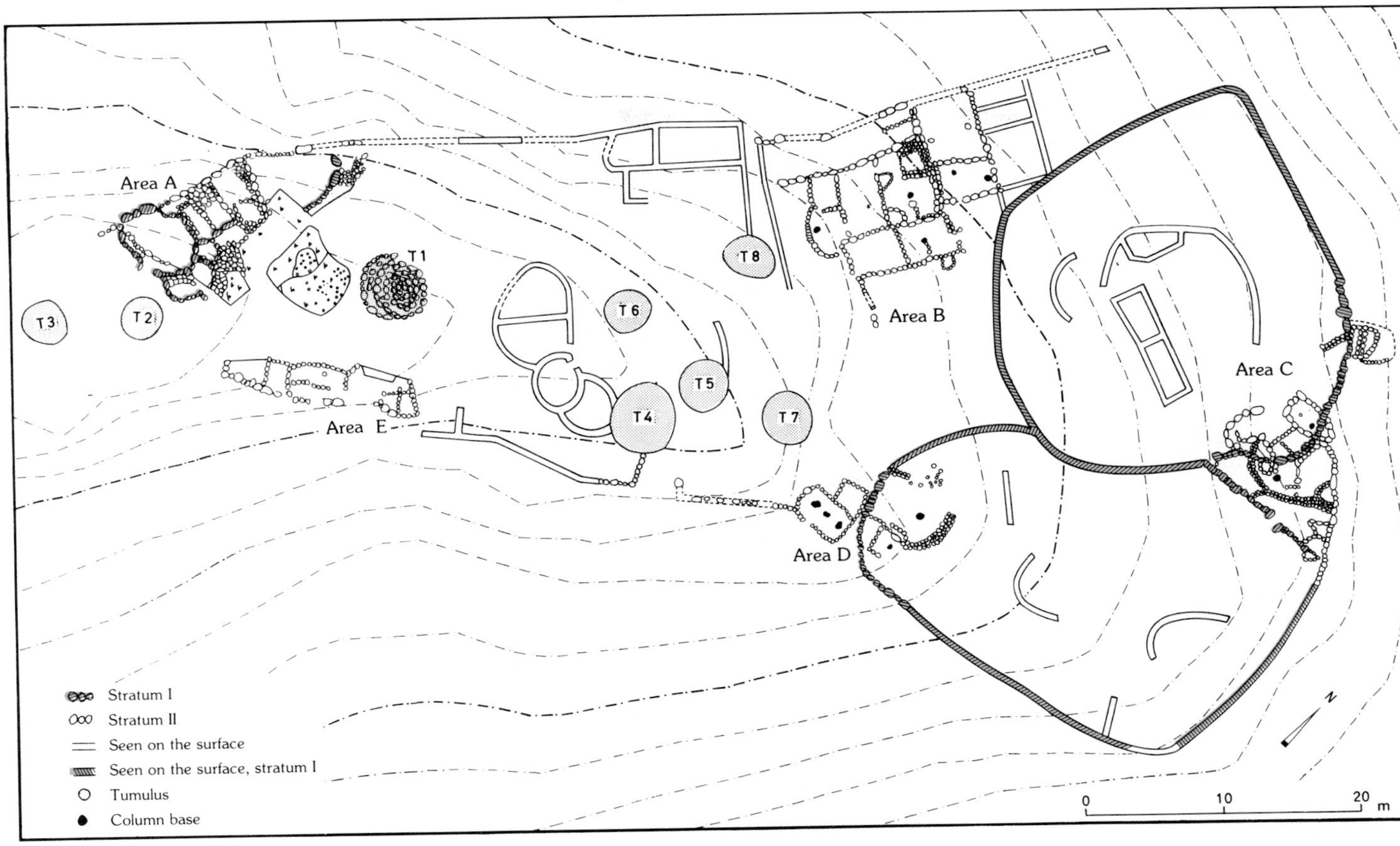

1963 EXCAVATIONS

Excavations were first carried out at the site in 1963 by a joint expedition from the Israel Department of Antiquities and Museums, the Israel Exploration Society, and the Hebrew University, in conjunction with the Fund for the Exploration of Ancient Agriculture in the Negev (headed by M. Evenari of the Hebrew University), the American Institute for Holy Land Studies in Jerusalem, and the Southeastern Baptist Theological Seminary of North Carolina. The expedition was directed by M. Kochavi. The excavations were concentrated in five representative areas of the main settlement, in which two Intermediate Bronze Age levels were distinguished.

LEVEL II. The earlier level (II) contained remains of a densely built settlement with rectangular structures, whose outer walls abutted, or were incorporated in, the stone wall (250 m long) surrounding the entire settlement. More than three-fifths of the wall's length was found in situ. The wall was built of stones much larger than those commonly used in houses, and the structures were erected either parallel (as in areas D and E) or perpendicular (as in areas A and B) to it. The storage installations and workshops (mainly concentrated in area C) were not rectangular but were adapted to their function and to the topography. More than thirty rooms and some thirty different installations were exposed in this level. The structures' roofs were supported by stone pillars built of round drums and erected along the rooms' central axis—in their center or near the end walls. The floor—the leveled bedrock whose hollows were filled—was paved with stones. The vertically cut bedrock sometimes also served as the wall of a structure. Most of the rooms were lined with stone benches. Cupmarks in the rock floor served as mortars, and ash-covered pebble pavements in the corners of rooms were used as hearths. One workshop contained a deposit of stored clay and a pottery kiln that abutted the fence-wall's outer face. Most of the tumuli on the ridge, as well as the *bamah*, should be attributed to this early settlement.

Two types of tumuli were found: the first is 7 to 8 m in diameter, rather low, and filled with stones; the second is only 4 to 5 m in diameter but is at least 1 m high. The tumuli erected above the ruins of level II belong exclusively of the second type, whereas the majority on the ridge belong to the first type. Tumuli of the first type have therefore been attributed to level II and those of the second type to level I. In the ten tumuli excavated, the cist tombs were found to have been built of particularly large stones. The skeletons and funerary offerings were placed on two floors, one above the other. After covering the cist tombs with stone slabs, the tumuli were finished in one of the two styles mentioned above.

The *bamah* is merely a rock cliff, jutting out above the Yeroḥam Basin. At the top of the cliff is a leveled area with twelve cupmarks of various sizes. A stone wall, set a short distance back from the summit, encloses about a quarter of an acre of this area. No structural remains were found in the immediate vicinity of the rock altar. The largest concentration of structures outside the main settlement was found at its foot, on the saddle linking it with the ridge.

LEVEL I. Level I is represented in the main settlement by several round structures, uncovered in area A, as well as by two large animal pens, whose fences pass over the structures of level II in areas C and D. The eight tumuli built above the remains of level II in the main settlement and several other tumuli of the same type, scattered throughout the site, should also be attributed to this level.

POTTERY. The ceramic finds are typical of the Intermediate Bronze Age (Middle Bronze Age I) and for the most part resemble contemporary finds from Lachish, Jebel Qa'aqir, Jericho, and other sites in the southern part of the country. The assemblage is characterized by numerous large storage vessels and hole-mouth jars (used as cooking pots). Several red-slipped sherds suggest a possible connection with Transjordan. The numerous grindstones and querns, flint end scrapers, and sickle blades found on the site indicate that seasonal agriculture was practiced nearby, probably in the adjacent Yeroḥam Basin, which has a high water table. Two animal figurines, unique for this period, one of clay and the other of stone, were found near the pottery kiln. In one of the level I dwellings, a hoard of eighteen copper ingots with low lead content was found. These suggest the existence of a metal industry, which may have provided the means of exchange for trade with other settlements.

SUMMARY. The excavations at Mount Yeroḥam are of particular value because they have brought to light a settlement with clearly defined architectural remains and workshops from a period hitherto known mainly from tombs. The two occupation levels belong to the same period, but differ in character; they appear to represent two separate but consecutive waves of settlement in the Negev. The Intermediate Bronze Age (Middle Bronze Age I) inhabitants of the Negev were apparently seminomads who lived from hunting, grazing, and seasonal agriculture. At a certain stage they even established permanent, though short-lived, settlements, such as that on Mount Yeroḥam. They practiced their religious ceremonies at rock altars and buried their dead in tumuli on mountaintops.

MOSHE KOCHAVI

1973 EXCAVATIONS

In 1973, excavations were resumed at the Mount Yeroḥam site by a joint expedition from the Israel Department of Antiquities and Museums, the Hebrew University, and the Israel Exploration Society, under the direction of R. Cohen. The excavations, which were concentrated in three areas (B, C, and F), were aimed at clarifying the relationship between the two occupation

Overview of area B building.

levels exposed in the previous excavations. They were also intended to investigate the possibility of another occupation level predating the Middle Bronze Age I and the nature of the stone wall surrounding the settlement. Area B of the earlier excavations was extended to the north and northeast, in order to examine whether the northern enclosure wall had indeed damaged any of the rooms not exposed in the earlier excavations.

Ten rooms, covering an area of about 7 by 10 m, were cleared. The rectilinear walls, built of medium-sized field stones laid lengthwise, were preserved to the height of a single course. The rooms' floors were usually the natural bedrock, leveled and smoothed, although its general slope was not leveled. The depressions in the bedrock floor of several rooms were filled with small stones. Two types of rooms could be discerned: large, rectangular rooms (5 by 3.75 m) and small rooms (c. 3 by 2 m). Column drums, although not in situ, were found amid the debris.

Only one occupation level was distinguished in area B; the pottery recovered from the bedrock mainly includes fragments of flat-based storage jars characteristic of the Middle Bronze Age I. In area C, which also was enlarged in the 1973 excavations, two occupation levels could be distinguished. The upper level contains two rooms, each with one rounded corner. The western room (3 by 4 m) is built of large stones and paved with small ones. The smaller, eastern room is 2.5 by 4.5 m.

In the lower level, under the western room's stone floor, the bedrock was

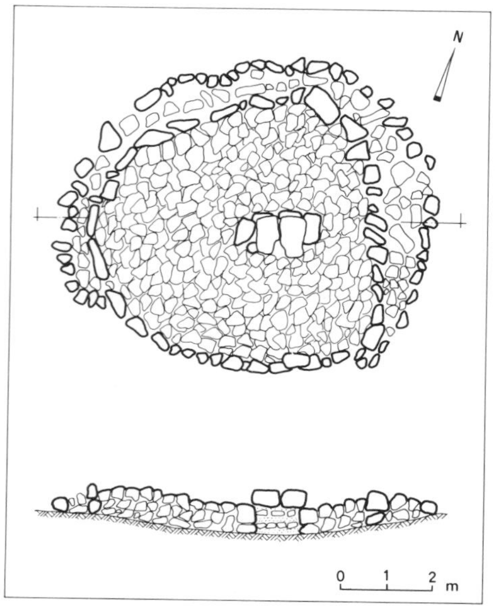

Plan and section of the tumulus.

Tumulus with a rock-cut altar in front.

Structure in area C (Cohen's excavations).

covered with a 10-cm-thick layer of ash containing sherds from the Middle Bronze Age I. The burnt layer also extends beneath this room's eastern wall. A similar burnt layer was observed in the western corner of the eastern room, extending under the wall.

The area where the pottery kiln was found in the earlier excavations was cleared to bedrock, to the kiln's stone foundations. Numerous sherds were found amid the ash layer covering the rock. In area F, between areas B and C, only a single occupation level was traced; it yielded remains of two structures. Building A, situated east of area B's block of rooms, consists of two long, rooms, almost identical in size (2 by 3.5 m) and built of large stones. Between them is a small installation, 1 by 2 m. On the smoothed bedrock floor were pottery sherds characteristic of the Middle Bronze Age I.

Building B, located northwest of building A and north of area B's block of rooms, consists of three rooms. The rectangular southeastern room (4 by 4.5 m) contained two pillars for supporting the roof; only a single drum from each is preserved. Two cupmarks, one of which contained a copper ingot, were observed in the bedrock floor. The long northern room (1.7 by 3.5 m) was built of large stones. Three pillars were found in situ and fragments of two storage jars were uncovered in the southeastern corner. West of the two rooms was a larger room (4 by 6 m), in which a fragment of a copper ingot was found. The two buildings probably shared a courtyard (7 by 13 m), along with the structures in area C.

SUMMARY. The 1973 excavations on Mount Yeroḥam yielded remains no earlier than the Middle Bronze Age I. The rectilinear structures uncovered in areas B, D, E, and F formed the main part of the settlement and seem to represent its last phase of occupation. The structures are built on bedrock and have no overlying architectural remains. The earliest occupational phase was in a clear stratigraphic sequence only in area C, indicating that the settlement may have been confined to the lower, northeastern part of the site. It seems that there was no "stone fence" surrounding the entire settlement. Its unusual and irregular nature, previously commented upon by Kochavi, suggests that the "fence" was actually made up of the outer walls of densely built structures. This would also account for the absence of the stone wall from certain parts of the settlement.

RUDOLF COHEN

N. Glueck, *BASOR* 149 (1958), 10; 152 (1958), 22; 179 (1965), 11; id., *Rivers in the Desert*, Tel Aviv 1960, 78, 81–82; M. Kochavi, *IEJ* 13 (1963), 141–142; R. Cohen, ibid. 24 (1974), 133–134; I. Eldar, *ESI* 1 (1982), 91–93; U. Avner, *TA* 11 (1984), 115–131.

Copper ingots.

Bowl found in the kiln.

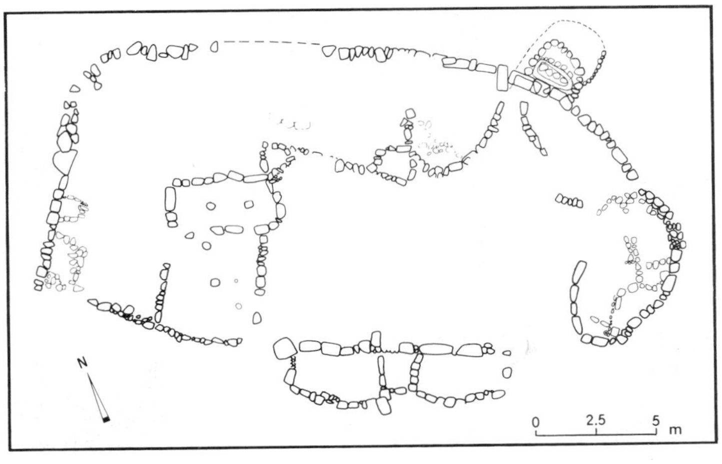

Plan of area F (Cohen's excavations).

YESUD HA-MA'ALA

IDENTIFICATION AND EXPLORATION

Yesud ha-Ma'ala is located in Upper Galilee, about 15 km (9 mi.) northeast of Safed (map reference 207.273). An inscription, capitals, and columns attesting to an ancient synagogue were discovered here in 1883. In the 1970s, two rows of basalt columns were found while the ground was being prepared for cultivation. In 1974, salvage excavations were carried out at the site under the direction of A. Biran and D. Urman, on behalf of the Israel Department of Antiquities and Museums. Two further seasons of excavations, directed by Y. Shoham, were conducted here in 1982 and 1983, on behalf of the Nelson Glueck School of Biblical Archaeology of Hebrew Union College in Jerusalem.

EXCAVATION RESULTS

A hall (15.5 by 21 m) with two rows of four column bases each was excavated (only five columns were preserved). Another column base was uncovered south of the hall. The two rows of columns are about 6 m apart, and the columns in each row are set 2.5 m apart. The column bases stand on a rounded platform of undressed stones on which traces of plaster were found. The building's stone walls (1.5 m wide) as well as stone channels and three plastered pools were uncovered. Two pools (1 by 1.2 m and 0.25 m deep) contain a cylindrical basalt stone in their southwestern corner. The plaster covering the pools' floor also coated the stones. The third pool (0.9 by 1 m and 0.45 m deep) has a stone step in its southeastern corner. The stone channel, uncovered for a length of 5 m, ranges in width from 1.5 m in the south to 0.5 m near the pool.

The sherds and vessels recovered from the building and the pools date to the thirteenth and fourteenth centuries. A thirteenth-century Cypriot Crusader coin was also found. The vessels include flat glazed bowls, many conical bowls with a hole in their base, and several jars with flat bases. Similar vessels are known from various sites in Palestine and Cyprus; they were used as receptacles in the sugar industry. No sherds predating the medieval period have so far been found.

The remains of the columns and bases, and their arrangement in two parallel rows oriented north–south, show that they probably belonged to a synagogue from the third to fifth centuries. The channels, pools, and pottery vessels were installations for the medieval sugar industry.

S. Klein, *ZDPV* 51 (1928), 137; Hüttenmeister–Reeg, *Antiken Synagogen* 1, 514 f.; F. G. Maier, *Report of the Department of Antiquities, Cyprus* 1981, 103f.; A. Biran, *ESI* 2 (1983), 110–111; Y. Shoham, *IEJ* 35 (1985), 189–190.

AVRAHAM BIRAN

Yesud ha-Ma'ala: jar and conical bowls used in the sugar industry, 13th–14th centuries CE.

Yesud ha-Ma'ala: general view of the synagogue remains, looking east.

YIFTAHEL

IDENTIFICATION

The site is situated in Lower Galilee in the alluvial valley of Naḥal Yiftaḥel, southwest of the Beth Netofa Valley, at an elevation of 130 m above sea level (map reference 1719.2401), about 500 m northwest of Kibbutz ha-Solelim and 200 m northeast of Tel Yiftaḥel. A spring close to the site is surrounded by chalk hillocks covered by oak woods and containing raw flint. The site was discovered by A. Berman of the Israel Department of Antiquities and Museums in the course of road construction and was initially investigated in early 1982 by A. Ronen of Haifa University. Three separate excavations were conducted on the site.

EXCAVATION RESULTS

THE LAMDAN-DAVIES EXCAVATIONS: PRE-POTTERY NEOLITHIC B PERIOD. Salvage excavations were carried out at the site in late 1982 and in 1983 by M. Lamdan and M. Davies of the Moshe Stekelis Museum of Prehistory in Haifa. Flint implements were found on the surface over an area of more than 400 m long and at least 100 m wide, extending in a northeast–southwest direction on the eastern bank of the streambed. The general stratification follows: the upper layer (c. 50 cm thick) consists of ploughed, clayey soil containing stones, flint artifacts, and sherds. Below it lies a 1-m-thick, gray, clayey-sandy layer that contained stones and Neolithic flint implements. Above this layer was a settlement from the Early Bronze Age; below it lay an occupation level from the Pottery Neolithic period. Floors from the Pre-Pottery Neolithic period were exposed in the lower part of the above-mentioned gray layer. A few implements were found 5 to 10 cm above the floors. The lowest layer consists of dark, alluvial, clayey soil with occasional lenses of stones without any archaeological finds.

The Early Bronze Age layer was largely destroyed by plowing and is only preserved at the southern edge of the site. It was excavated by E. Braun, on behalf of the Israel Department of Antiquities and Museums (see below).

STRUCTURES. In the northern area, some 100 sq m of the Pre-Pottery Neolithic site were excavated. Fine white plaster floors were exposed that had been plastered in four stages (some showed evidence of repairs). Hollows and pits in the floors attest to the existence of various installations. A plastered step oriented northeast–southwest was uncovered on the main floor. A reused stone bowl fragment was among the stones supporting the step. The lowest stone course of an 80-cm-wide wall was also exposed, as well as a plaster floor running up to it from the west; on the east, the floor is covered by a strip of plaster. A debris of stones and plaster, probably from a collapsed wall, was found at the southern end of the stratum. On the floor lay crumbled brick material, fired at a temperature of over 1,000 degrees C; it had imprints of branches and straw, and was sometimes covered with a thin layer of plaster. These may be the remains of a collapsed roof made of branches covered by a layer of clay mixed with straw and coated with plaster.

FINDS. The finds include thousands of flint implements. About 1,600 retouched items were counted; one-third could be defined as tools and the other two-thirds were retouched blades and flakes. This was an open-air site, which may account for the number of implements, as well as for the widespread use of ad hoc tools in the Neolithic period. The tools include arrowheads (17 percent), sickle blades (21 percent), axes (2 percent), awls and borers (11 percent), and burins (13 percent). The rest (36 percent) are side and end scrapers, notches and denticulates, and bifacial tools.

Only half of the arrowheads can be divided into types (the rest are broken). The most common type is the Jericho point, followed by the Byblos point. One arrowhead each of the Helwan type and the el-Khiam type were also found. The axes are elliptical or elongated; some are polished and some were sharpened by a transversal blow. The sickle blades are finely denticulated, mostly on both sides.

The retouched items constitute only about 5 percent of the flint industry. The cores, half of them naviform blade cores, constitute about 1 percent of the assemblage. Raw materials for producing the tools were noticeably absent from the site. The large nodules may have been broken into fragments close to the source of the flint and then flaked and retouched on the site.

Greenstone beads and votive axes were also found, as well as two broken female figurines, fragments of a "white-ware" vessel, and fragments of basalt grinding stones, probably brought here from Tel Shimron, about 5 km (3 mi.) away. The grinding stones differ from the large millstones common in this period. Many animal bones and seeds (particularly lentil and vetch) were also found.

A skeleton (female?) was found on the floor at the northern part of the excavation. It lay in a flexed position, with the chest downward, the legs folded under it, the left elbow raised, and flint splinters between the fingers.

SUMMARY. Yiftaḥel is a site from the later stage of the Pre-Pottery Neolithic B period. The finds indicate that the inhabitants engaged in flint and stone-tool production, agriculture, and pastoralism. They also had commercial ties with their neighbors. The lentil seeds found in piles above the brick material

Yiftaḥel: map of the site and excavation areas.

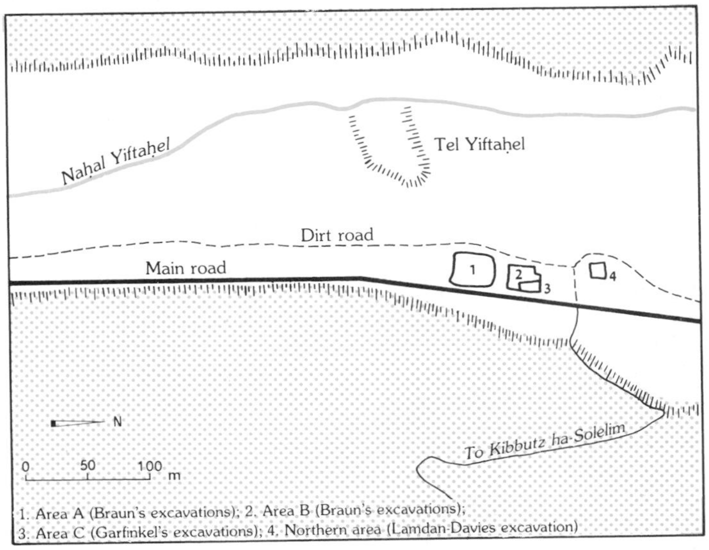

Human skeleton on one of the floors excavated in the Lamdan and Davies excavations, PPNB. The excavator demonstrates the position at the time of burial.

Greenstone beads found in the Lamdan and Davies excavations, PPNB.

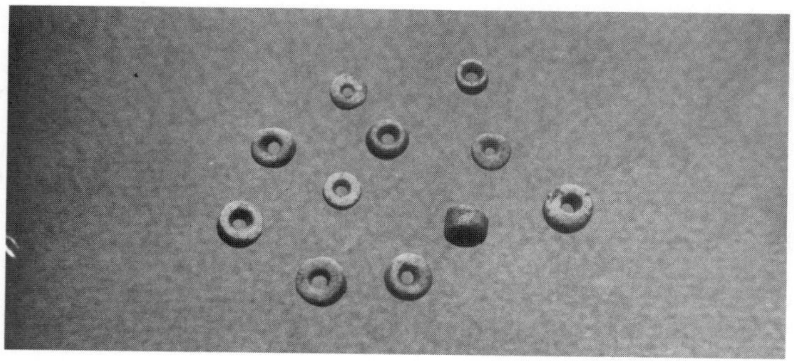

probably indicate that the excavation exposed the site as it functioned in summer, when the seeds were spread on the roof to dry. The absence of grinding stones and bowls may be due to the fact that only seeds of legumes were found which, unlike cereals, need not be ground. In the excavators' opinion, Yiftaḥel is the largest Neolithic site in Israel, with the exception of the sites in the Jordan and Ḥula valleys. It may have been a village like Beisamûn with plastered clay houses.

MORDECHAI LAMDAN, MOSHE DAVIES

GARFINKEL'S EXCAVATIONS: PRE-POTTERY NEOLITHIC B PERIOD. About 50 m south of the area excavated by Lamdan and Davies, another 180 sq m of the Pre-Pottery Neolithic B site (area C) were excavated by Y. Garfinkel in 1983, as part of a salvage project of the Israel Department of Antiquities and Museums (see below). The work focused mainly on the excavation of a rectangular dwelling unit (house 700) with plaster floors.

STRATIGRAPHY. Five stratigraphic units of the Pre-Pottery Neolithic B period were identified in the excavated area, under a 1.5-m-thick layer of alluvium.

UNIT 1. Unit 1 is all the accumulation above unit 2. It consists of a light-gray sediment, 30 cm thick on the average, with large concentrations of flint (including large flint slabs from which cores were produced), animal bones, seashells, and burials dug into the reddish brick debris of unit 2.

UNIT 2. Unit 2 is divided into two phases. The upper phase consists mainly of house 700 and the lower phase, of house 730. The structures contain plaster floors, installations, concentrations of seeds, and hearths.

UNIT 3. Unit 3 is a light gray sediment layer (30 cm thick) similar to unit 1. It lies under the plaster floors of unit 2.

UNIT 4. Unit 4 is a brown clay sediment layer (35 cm thick) reached in two small trial pits. This unit, which contained only a few flints, may represent a settlement gap.

UNIT 5. Unit 5 consists of a 75-cm-thick layer of red-brick material with few flints. A narrow section (0.5 by 2 m) was cut into it (this unit may only be a local phenomenon—not extending throughout the site).

UNIT 6. Unit 6 is a sterile, dark-brown clay sediment, probably virgin soil.

The deposits from the Pre-Pottery Neolithic B period are 2 m thick and the occupation sequence can be divided into two phases: the earlier phase is represented by unit 5; and the later one by units 1, 2, and 3.

HOUSE 700. House 700 consists of three units, 17 m in overall length, on a north–south axis, and 7.5 m wide. The middle unit was the only one preserved in its entirety. If the structure is reconstructed as a symmetrical rectangle, its area would approximate 110 sq m. The floor is baked lime (3–5 cm thick) that is as solid as concrete. About 7 tons of limestone would have been required to plaster the entire structure. Traces of repairs are visible in the floor, as are imprints and the remains of various installations that rested on it or were sunk into it. The edges of the plaster floor merge with the plaster on the walls. The walls were preserved in some places to a height of 60 cm; they were built of bricks laid on field-stone bases.

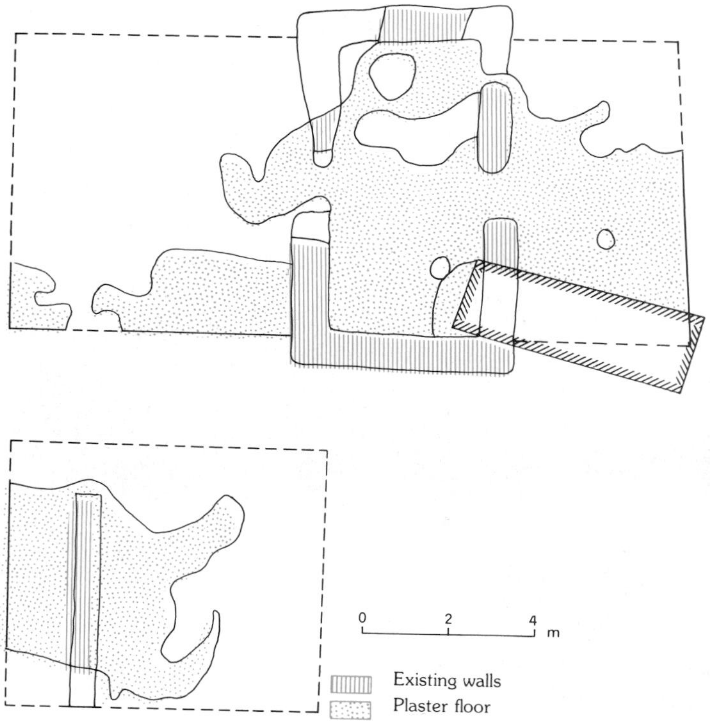

*Plan of house 700: **(above)** upper phase; **(below)** lower phase, PPNB.*

Garfinkel's excavations: general view of the upper phase of house 700.

House 700: corner silo in the upper phase.

A clue to the functions of each of the three units is indicated by the character of the finds. The central unit is a rectangular broadroom (7.5 by 4 m). An opening in the center of each of its long walls leads to the other spaces. A silo, built in the northeastern corner, next to the eastern wall, is preserved to its full height (40 cm). Thousands of broad-bean seeds lay on the silo's floor, and a concentration of 7.3 kg of lentil seeds was found in the western half of the room. The silo, the large quantities of seeds, and the fact that the two kinds of seeds were separated indicate organized storage in a roofed area. The broad-bean seeds at Yiftaḥel are the earliest evidence of the use of this legume as food for humans. The wild plant from which the broad-bean was domesticated has not yet been identified. The find may indicate that Israel is the natural habitat of this wild plant. Six carbon-14 tests performed on the seeds suggest a date of 6840 ± 50 BCE.

The southern unit is a small, plastered, open courtyard (7 by 7 m). The northeastern corner of the floor contained a rounded hollow, next to which were two grinding stones (out of the three recovered in this structure) and what is probably the imprint of a lower millstone. These finds indicate that crushing and grinding activities were carried out in the courtyard, near the seed store.

The northern unit is also a plastered open courtyard (4 by 7.5 m). On its northern side, the floor plaster covered the top of an earlier stone wall, forming a sort of threshold to the house. Remains of round installations sunk into the floor and three large, flat, square stones used as work tables were uncovered in the courtyard, indicating that the area was a workshop.

In an open space north of the structure, a concentration of more than twenty hearths was found. Large concentrations of animal bones (the remains of meals) were also uncovered.

HOUSE 730. House 730 is earlier than house 700. It lay 10 cm below house 700 and was also aligned on a north–south axis. The western part of the structure extended beyond the excavated area; moreover, the area excavated was only poorly preserved. House 730 seems to have had two units: a southern, rectangular, long and narrow space and a northern square space. The partition wall between the two spaces was the northern threshold in the later structure.

FINDS. Approximately 126,000 flint artifacts were collected in the excavations, most of them produced from naviform blade cores typical of the period. The tool assemblage included arrowheads of the Jericho, Byblos, and ʿAmuq types; sickle blades; and bifacial tools, including polished axes. In addition, basalt and limestone artifacts and bone tools were found. Most of the ornaments were made of Mediterranean seashells, but two were made of shells from the Red Sea. Beads of semiprecious stones, such as rosasite (greenstone), serpentine, and agate, were also found. Chunks and chips of greenstone raw material, together with long, narrow flint drills, indicate that beads were produced here.

The picture presented by the site is of spacious rectangular buildings and the extensive use of burnt lime plaster. These buildings and their considerable storage capacity indicate a sedentary occupation.

YOSEF GARFINKEL

BRAUN'S EXCAVATIONS: PRE-POTTERY NEOLITHIC B PERIOD TO THE MIDDLE BRONZE AGE. In 1983, another salvage excavation, directed by E. Braun on behalf of the Israel Department of Antiquities and Museums, was carried out in three areas: A, B, and C, covering a total area of about 2,400 sq m. (For area C, see above, Garfinkel's Excavations.)

AREA A. Soundings were first made in this area and a 1.1-m-thick layer of silt covering it was removed. Five main cultural horizons were uncovered under the silt layer. The remains of the four upper strata in area A are described below:

Stratum I. Remains of a structure more than 20 m long were uncovered; the remains extended north–south across the northern part of the area, continuing beyond its boundaries in both directions. The structure was of stone, one course high, backed on the west by a layer of large and small stones whose width was uneven and whose function is unclear. The date of this stratum could not be determined.

Stratum II. Stratum II is represented by several well-preserved structures of three distinct but related types: rounded structures, oval structures, and sausage-shaped structures with two parallel walls that end in apses. All the walls, except the one connecting two oval structures, are curvilinear. Three structures were paved at one end with large flat stones. In the larger structures (more than 13 m long) these paved areas were separated from the central unit by curvilinear partitions. An earlier occupation phase was attested to by several wall fragments incorporated into the later construction and by the settlement's general layout. Stratum II is dated to an early phase of the Early Bronze Age I.

Stratum III. The buildings in stratum III exhibit an architectural tradition completely different from that of the later strata. The only structure with a complete floor-plan uncovered so far is rectangular and belongs to a known Levantine pier-type structure, with a portico, three rooms, and a passage aligned along its longitudinal axis. Two clear building phases could be dis-

Braun's excavations: general view of area A. The rectangular Levantine pier-type structure in stratum III; to its left (east), the stratum II apsidal building.

Braun's excavations: schematic plan of the buildings in area A.

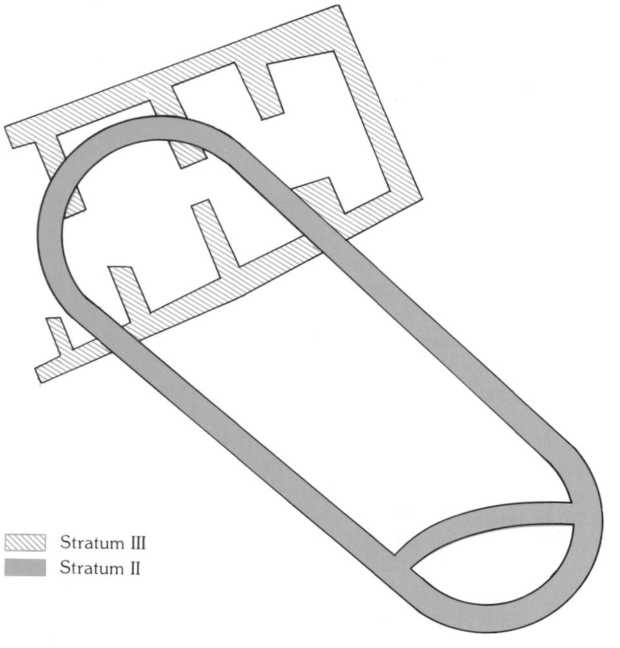

tinguished here. A white plastered floor (or threshold) exposed between the first and second room belongs to the earlier phase. Some bones of a child found under the earthen floor of the back room probably represent the remains of a burial. A secondary burial of two skulls and several long bones, accompanied by a fine sling stone, was found about 2 m east of the structure.

Remains of another rectangular structure, which also has a porch, as well as an appended room and stone-lined bin, indicate the domestic character of the structures. Other contemporary structures, whose complex rectangular forms are only partially preserved, are oriented on a north–south axis, like all the structures in this stratum. This evidence of some degree of planning suggests a somewhat developed social organization in the settlement.

A large number of limestone bowls was found in this stratum; some lay on the floors of the houses and others, broken into fragments, were reused as building material. The small amount of pottery recovered in the fills around the structures apparently belongs to a period of utilization of the site in the Pottery Neolithic period and is not related to these houses. Many aspects of the material culture suggest that this level should probably be dated to the penultimate phase of the Pre-Pottery Neolithic B (or C?) period.

Stratum IV. A series of curvilinear, or meandering, walls was uncovered that are probably remains of large enclosures. If the attribution of the remains of a fragmentary rectangular structure to stratum IV is valid, it stood in the center of one of the enclosures and was associated with it. Several entrances in the enclosure walls were identified. One entrance leads to a pebble-paved surface and the other to a beaten-earth floor, in which an ash-filled pit was uncovered. This stratum, as indicated by the numerous limestone bowls found in it, both in primary and in secondary use, belongs to the same cultural horizon as stratum III.

AREA B. Area B was partially exposed by bulldozers, which resulted in the removal of the upper silt layer and in damage to some of the structures.

Stratum I. Although some of the structures in stratum I are probably not contemporary, they are discussed as one group because they all rest directly on the remains of stratum II. Some of them apparently do form a stratigraphic unit because of their character and location. Stratum I contains two poorly built walls dated by some sherds to the Early Bronze Age IV (Middle Bronze Age I). Two well-built rectangular structures, with several stone-paved rooms, were also exposed but did not yield any datable finds.

Stratum II. A group of curvilinear buildings of the three types found in area A were uncovered under the stratum I structures. Their length varies between 5 and 16 m. Here, as in area A, the curvilinear architectural tradition is evident in all three consecutive, superimposed building phases dating to the beginning of the Early Bronze Age I.

Stratum III. Stratum III, which was exposed in a limited area, yielded only the scanty remains of several rectangular structures; the largest had several rooms and two building phases. A secondary burial of a human skull and some bones was found under the earthen floor in the corner of one of the rooms. A shallow limestone bowl was incorporated into one of the walls. Numerous similar bowls were recovered in strata III and IV in area A, indicating contemporary occupation. Concentrations of Neolithic pottery were found only outside the houses and suggest a limited occupation in that period as in area A.

Braun's excavations in area A: oval structure from stratum II, EB I.

A deep sounding (2 m) was dug in area C into strata earlier than stratum III, in an attempt to correlate the stratigraphy of areas C and B. Large quantities of flint artifacts were found, including cores, tools, and flakes, that can be attributed to the Pre-Pottery Neolithic B period.

A shaft tomb, partially destroyed by road construction, was excavated on the eastern slope of Naḥal Yiftaḥel, close to the site. The single chamber contained numerous pottery vessels, metal artifacts, jewelry, and scarabs dating from the Middle Bronze Age IIA to the Late Bronze Age I.

SUMMARY. Stratum I is a concentration of building remains with common features; the scanty ceramic material can be dated to the Middle Bronze Age I or II, or to both. This scarcity of pottery finds probably indicates sparse occupation in these periods. The rectangular, well-built structures uncovered in area B excavated so far could not be dated, but they may be associated with these periods or even with the Early Bronze Age I.

The stratum II pottery includes carinated bowls with knobs, including gray-burnished "Esdraelon ware" and red-painted bowls; fenestrated pedestaled bowls, storage jars, *amphoriskoi*, and pithoi, many of them with rope decoration, were also found. A preliminary analysis of the pottery indicates that this settlement existed at the beginning of the Early Bronze Age I. This assumption is based on several factors: the only type of gray-burnished bowls that could be identified had knobs projecting from the carinated profile—a type considered to be early in the Esdraelon ware sequence; band-slip decoration is completely absent and red-burnished pottery is scarce—both being typical of the later stages of this period; and there is a certain similarity of form between some of the Yiftaḥel vessels and the storage jars from the late stratum at Tuleilat el-Ghassul.

A date for stratum III late in the Pre-Pottery Neolithic B period is based on the associated flint tool kit. The presence of Pottery Neolithic artifacts may be attributed to either a squatter occupation or a limited use of the site. The large quantities of flint artifacts (tools, cores, and flakes) were found in all the strata, as well as in the silt layer covering the site. These finds cannot, therefore, be used as dating evidence. In addition to the flint artifacts, numerous stone bowls were recovered in stratum III, attesting to the importance of these vessels. It should be noted that stone bowls were also found in stratum IV; however, such bowls are absent from the earlier strata in area C, which undoubtedly belong to the Pre-Pottery Neolithic B period, emphasizing the differences in the material culture between that earlier occupation and the penultimate Pre-Pottery Neolithic B period of stratum III. Very few Neolithic sherds were found. The chronological sequence of the pottery is also difficult to establish. The complete vessels are few in number and parallels suggest affinities with pottery from Jericho IX. However, no Yarmukian ware could be identified in this assemblage; it is possible that the pottery assemblage is mixed and represents several periods.

The stratum IV structures reflect a different settlement pattern from stratum III, but it is possible that rectangular structures were also built. In any case, some continuity between the stratum IV and stratum III settlements is attested to by the stone bowls characteristic of both. There is not much similarity between the settlement of stratum IV and that of the Pre-Pottery Neolithic period, which again emphasizes the difference between the Pre-Pottery Neolithic B period of area C and the later Pre-Pottery phases of areas A and B.

ELIOT BRAUN

M. Lamdan and M. Davies, *L'Anthropologie* 87 (1983), 273–274; id., *ESI* 2 (1983), 111–113; id., *IEJ* 33 (1983), 259; E. L. Braun (and Y. Garfinkel), *ESI* 3 (1984), 111–112; 4 (1985), 116; 5 (1986), 112–113; id., *IEJ* 34 (1984), 191–194; 35 (1985), 58–60; 37 (1987), 185–186; id., *RB* 91 (1984), 400–403; 92 (1985), 389–393; 96 (1989), 210–212; id., *En Shadud* (*BAR*/IS 249), Oxford 1985, 75–76; id., *BAIAS* 1985–1986, 17–

26; id., *PEQ* 121 (1989), 1–43; id., *L'Urbanisation de la Palestine à l'Age du Bronze Ancien* (Actes du Colloque d'Emmaüs 1986; *BAR*/IS 527, ed. P. de Miroschedji), Oxford 1989, 7–27; id., *PEQ* (Jan.–June 1989), 1–45; id., "The Early Northern EBI of Israel and Jordan" (Master's thesis, Hebrew Univ. of Jerusalem 1991); Z. Gal, *ZDPV* 101 (1985), 114–127; Y. Garfinkel, *Mitekufat Ha'even* 18 (1985), 45*–51*; 20 (1987), 79*–90*; id., *IEJ* 37 (1987), 40–42; id., *JFA* 14 (1987), 199–212; id., *Paléorient* 13/1 (1987), 69–76; (with L. Kolska Horwitz), ibid. 14/1 (1988), 73–86; id. (et al.), *Israel Journal of Botany* 37 (1988), 49–51; M. E. Kislev, *ESI* 4 (1985), 121; id., *Science* 228 (1985), 319–320; I. Hershkovitz et al., *Paléorient* 12/1 (1986), 73–81; J. Yellin and Y. Garfinkel, ibid. 12/2 (1986), 99–104; D. Bar-Yosef and J. Heller, ibid. 13/1 (1987), 131–135; L. Kolska Horwitz, *Mitekufat Ha'even* 20 (1987), 181*–182*; B. F. Byrd and E. B. Banning, *Paléorient* 14/1 (1988), 65–72; Weippert 1988, 101, 106, 158; E. B. Banning and B. F. Byrd, *Paléorient* 15/1 (1989), 154–160; A. Miller Rosen, *Mitekufat Ha'even* 22 (1989), 68*–77*; A. Ronen et al., *Paléorient* 17/2 (1991), 149–155.

YIN'AM, TEL

IDENTIFICATION AND EXPLORATION

Tel Yin'am (Tell en-Na'am, map reference 198.235) is situated among the fields of Yavne'el, in the Yavne'el Valley, in the eastern Lower Galilee. Tel Yin'am, identified with biblical Jabneel (Jos. 19:33), a southern border town of the Naphtali tribe, had for many years been associated with Yanoam in Egyptian New Kingdom texts. Although Tel Yin'am yielded a significant Late Bronze Age II occupation and ended in fiery destruction, Yanoam may indeed be located in the Bashan, as suggested by N. Na'aman. In the Jerusalem Talmud (*Meg.* 1, 1, 70a), biblical Jabneel is identified with the nearby site of Khirbet Yamma; however, Khirbet Yamma yielded no evidence of an Iron Age occupation. Tel Yin'am, on the other hand, was occupied in the Neolithic, Chalcolithic, Early Bronze Age IA, Middle Bronze Age IIB, Late Bronze Age II, Iron Age I, Iron Age IIA, Iron Age IIC, Persian, Middle Roman, Late Roman, and Byzantine periods.

The site consists of a small circular mound about 85 m in diameter and a large terrace settlement that extends approximately another 100 m to the north and west and about another 50 m to the south. The mound was once larger than it is today (persistent furrowing and natural erosion reduced its size), and its original extent cannot be determined. The sharply defined mound rises about 7 m above the terrace settlement and about 12 m above the surrounding valley floor.

The site was surveyed in the nineteenth century by the Palestine Exploration Fund, in its survey of Western Palestine. It was later surveyed by A. Saarisalo, who also carried out limited probes at unknown locations on the site. The site was subsequently surveyed by Y. Aharoni and again by R. Amiran. This writer surveyed and conducted a limited probe in 1975, at the inception of the University of Texas excavation of the site.

Small-scale excavations were conducted on the mound in 1976 and 1977 and from 1979 to 1981 and 1983 to 1989; in 1978, a two-week salvage dig was conducted on the terrace settlement 50 m west of the base of the mound.

EXCAVATION RESULTS

Because final stratification has not yet been worked out, cultural horizons are discussed in terms of periods and phases, rather than numbered strata. Three areas (A–C) have been excavated on the mound and one area (D) on the terrace settlement.

NEOLITHIC AND CHALCOLITHIC PERIODS. Neolithic and Chalcolithic sherds, flint blades, and basalt hammers have been found on the surface and in fills on the mound and the terrace settlement. However, no occupational surfaces associated with these periods have been excavated.

EARLY BRONZE AGE I. A surface with associated disturbed walls and a partially preserved circular platform that may be a *bamah* was found in a 10-by-10-m exploratory excavation on the terrace settlement 50 m west of the base of the mound. Neolithic and Chalcolithic sherds were found within the 10-cm-thick surface, which was filled with sherds. However, the surface is dated to the Early Bronze Age IA on the basis of gray-burnished ware and pithoi with painted diagonal and parallel black lines. This surface also yielded a rare terra-cotta bull-head protome.

MIDDLE BRONZE AGE IIB. The Middle Bronze Age is only scantily represented on the mound. Yet, in area B, a small patch of Middle Bronze Age IIB surface, immediately below the earliest phase of a Late Bronze Age II building (building 2), yielded the upper part of a large jar decorated with incised lines and impressed bands. The jar fragment contained a copper/bronze figurine, recalling a type known from Byblos, and a unique, intact electrum figurine of a goddess, recalling aspects of figurines from the temple at Nahariya.

LATE BRONZE AGE II. The mound was abandoned until the latter part of the Late Bronze Age (apparently late in the fourteenth century BCE). Although the central Late Bronze Age building existed throughout the Late Bronze Age occupation, there was evidence for two distinct architectural

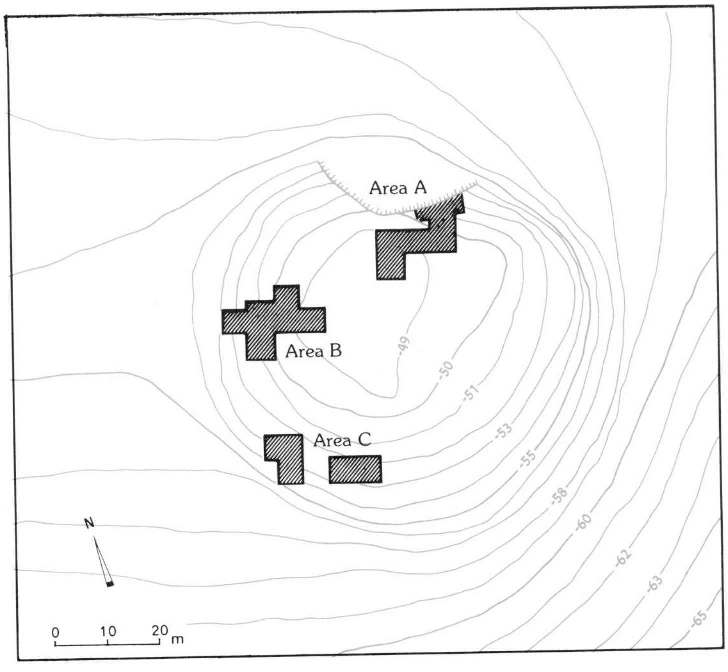

Tel Yin'am: map of the mound and excavation areas.

Bronze plowpoint, LB II.

Decorated jug, LB II.

phases in the subsidiary buildings. The central building, identified as building 1, served as the residence of the local ruler. Eight rooms in this structure were either fully or partially exposed: four storerooms were situated on the west of the building; the area east of the storerooms consisted of a broadroom with a secondary closed room at its western end; and a courtyard with a built-in storage bin in the northwest corner was situated south of the broadroom. The building presumably also had an east wing of rooms.

Storerooms 2–4 contained smashed, restorable storage jars, pithoi, kraters, and small jars, in addition to a well-worked basalt bowl. Room 5, the enclosed area at the western end of the broadroom, had little pottery but yielded a collection of fine objects. Among them were two Mitannian cylinder seals of the Common Style, a stamp seal featuring a crudely carved quadruped, and a necklace consisting of a beautiful chalcedony lion pendant and a broad repertoire of ceramic, faience, and glass beads, including two gray and white barrel-shaped beads and two Egyptian heart amulets. Room 7, the large broadroom, was empty except for a bronze plowpoint, the earliest example known in the Middle East. Room 6, the bin in the northwest corner of the courtyard, yielded an important assemblage of pottery that was found crushed in place within an area of less than a square meter. The restored assemblage included a large four-handled krater, a large two-handled platter, a cooking pot, storage jars, imitation pyxides, a chalice, a goblet, and a lamp. In addition to pottery, the finds included a unique Egyptian blue shallow bowl with a disk base and a single bar-handle, a faience Mitannian cylinder seal, and glass and faience beads. Two sets of upper and lower millstones, storage jars, bowls, and kraters were found fairly close to the west wall of the courtyard, south of the bin.

Room 1 also served as a storeroom, as evidenced by the presence of a 10-cm-thick accumulation of charred wheat in the southeast corner of the room. However, this room was later turned into an industrial installation, at which time a one-row-wide mud-brick cross wall was laid directly on the cobbled floor, and dome-shaped furnaces were built against the walls. Analysis of samples from the 1-m-thick accumulation of industrial debris above the cobbled floor yielded approximately 9 percent iron oxide, no trace of copper or bronze, and spherical iron droplets. This suggests that the furnaces were used, perhaps unsuccessfully, for iron smelting.

If the identification of the industrial installation as an iron smeltery is correct, it is the only evidence for a thirteenth-century BCE iron smeltery in Canaan, and it provides evidence of the period of experimentation and development necessary for the emergence of steel, prior to the beginning of the Iron Age.

Additional thirteenth-century BCE buildings were found burned, against the north wall of the public building. These buildings apparently date to two distinct phases, both of which are contemporary with the period of occupation of the public building. The buildings from the earlier phase are essentially contemporary with the public building's construction, whereas the overlaying buildings (of the later phase) are associated with the public building's later period of occupation.

On the cobbled floor of the storeroom in building 2 of the later phase, a dense concentration of sherds was found, from which unusually large biconical jugs, storage jars, and an unparalleled Mycenean stirrup jar—unusual because of its large size and unique decoration—were restored. The courtyard yielded two ovens, a stone work table and pottery vessels, including an unusual Mycenean vessel, the top of which was shaped like a stirrup jar and the bottom like a pyriform jar. The floor of a building with crudely constructed, meter-wide external walls (building 7), paved with flagstones as much as 1 m in length, was located northwest of building 2.

A large building complex, designated building 5, was found abutting the southern wall of building 1. The clustering of these and other buildings around building 1 indicates that the site was densely built up in the Late Bronze Age II. This thirteenth-century phase of occupation at Tel Yin'am is significant because of the discovery of the iron smelter and the wealth of luxury items—including both locally made objects and imports from Egypt (such as some of the jewelry and the blue bowl) and Mycenean Greece. In the opinion of this writer, the discovery of these objects is further evidence that the generally accepted notion of a decline in the level of material culture in Canaan in the thirteenth century must be modified or abandoned. This phase of occupation, the final Late Bronze Age phase, ended in destruction. An approximately 50-cm-thick deposit of ash, charred wood, fire-cracked rock, and burned and disintegrated mudbrick was found on the floors of the major buildings.

IRON AGE I. A relatively short period separated the destruction of the Late Bronze Age settlement from the rise of the first of a series of Iron Age I settlements. Indeed, in some places the walls of the Late Bronze Age buildings that remained standing were reused and new floors were laid directly above the destruction debris. Occupation of the site was continuous throughout the period of the Judges and into the tenth century. The Iron Age I architectural phases are densely packed, and each is separated from the other by only a few centimeters. The orientation of the buildings in area B remained essentially unchanged from phase to phase. The use of stone socle and mud-brick superstructure continued throughout the Iron I period, in apparent continuity of the architectural tradition from the Late Bronze Age. Floors were still frequently cobbled. Courtyard floors are of beaten earth, and there is no evidence of plastered floors.

While continuity can be observed in some pottery forms, particularly in chalices, new forms appear. There also are marked changes in technology: there is a radical change in the nature of grit inclusions and perhaps even in clays and firing methods. Whereas the Late Bronze Age pottery has approximately an equal percentage of basalt and limestone inclusions, the Iron Age I pottery seems to have a perceptibly higher percentage of limestone.

IRON AGE IIA. The tenth-century BCE level is best represented by two domestic structures in area B. The courtyard of one of these buildings yielded an oil press with stone weights and olive pits. The northern long room of the same buildings yielded forty five loom weights. Some of the most interesting Iron Age objects come from the tenth-century BCE phase. One of them is a rare composite knife consisting of a bone handle, an iron blade and copper rivets, and a black stone, conoidal seal that features two heraldic, long-horned animals with a human figure on the back of each animal.

IRON AGE IIC. Although many Iron Age IIC sherds were found on the mound, there were only two loci with rich assemblages of in situ pottery. Apparently, the Persian period builders destroyed much of the Iron Age IIC stratum. The restored Iron Age IIC pottery from a courtyard includes a homogeneous assemblage of cooking pots, jugs, and storage jars.

PERSIAN PERIOD. Two phases of the Persian period are well represented. The most substantial Persian period structure is a partially excavated building with 1-m-wide walls in area B. North of it is a rectangular structure with a staircase leading up to it from a paved court. A domestic structure with ovens and grain silos was found in area A. The two phases of Persian period occupation yielded a rich local ceramic repertoire, including bowls, jugs, juglets, storage jars, cooking pots, and a large pilgrim flask. The imported assemblage consists of a painted jug from East Greece and Attic sherds.

ROMAN-BYZANTINE PERIOD. The mound seems to have been abandoned throughout the Hellenistic period and was not reoccupied until the Roman period. However, most of the buildings excavated in the upper levels of the mound date to the Late Roman-Byzantine period. With the exception of a large, partially excavated building in area A, on the north side of the mound, the domestic buildings were small and had two rooms each.

A six-stepped, plaster-lined structure in area C is identified as a mikveh. This structure, cut through earlier architectural structures, is the only building on the site for which limestone ashlars were used. Indeed, no ashlars of any type were in evidence elsewhere on the mound. A carbon-14 test conducted on plaster from the mikveh's walls yielded two dates: 505 CE ± 65 and 529 CE ± 65. However, the ceramic evidence suggests that the site was not occupied in the Late Byzantine period. No evidence of a synagogue has been found. The latest structure on the mound, one that partially extends over the mikveh, is a large rectangular enclosure. However, because this structure is just below the surface of the mound, and no surfaces associated with the structure are preserved, its date cannot be determined.

No Arab pottery was found either in the survey or in the excavations. Thus, the mound must have been permanently abandoned at some time before the Arab conquest.

Surveys: Conder-Kitchener, *SWP* 1, London 1881, 417; A. Saarisalo, *The Boundary Between Issachar and Naphtali*, Helsinki 1927, 44–45.

The excavations and other studies: H. Liebowitz, *ASOR Newsletter* (Aug. 1977), 9–10; id., *IEJ* 27 (1977), 53–54; 28 (1978), 193–194; 29 (1979), 229–230; 32 (1982), 64–66; 33 (1983), 115–116; 35 (1985), 190–191; id., *RB* 85 (1978), 409–410; id., *Archaeology* 32/4 (1979), 58–59; id. (and R. L. Folk), *JFA* 7 (1980), 23–42; 11 (1984), 265–280; id., *BASOR* 243 (1981), 79–93; 275 (1989), 63–64; id., *ESI* 1 (1982), 113–114; 4 (1985), 116–117; 5 (1986), 114–115; 6 (1987–1988), 102; 7–8 (1988–1989), 189; 9 (1989–1990), 110; id. (and G. K. Hoops), *JFA* 9 (1982), 455–466; *Archaeological Expedition to Tell Yin'am, Israel: The 1979 Season*, Austin, Tex. n.d.; A. Engle, *The Proto-Sidonians: Glassmakers and Potters* (Readings in Glass History 17), Jerusalem 1983; B. Rothenberg et al., *BASOR* 252 (1983), 69–72; Weippert 1988, 179, 271, 329, 342.

HAROLD LIEBOWITZ

YOTVATA

IDENTIFICATION

Yotvata is the modern name of a small oasis located on the western edge of the southern Arabah on the main road to Elath, about 40 km (25 mi.) north of the city (map reference 155.923). Before the establishment of the state of Israel in 1948, the oasis consisted mainly of a few shallow pits, from which the upper groundwater ran, and a small grove of tamarisks and date palms. In Arabic it was called 'Ein Ghadian, probably after the haloxylon bush (*ghada* in Arabic), commonly found in the surrounding sands. Another possibility is that the Arabic name is derived from ad-Dianam, possibly the site's name in the Roman period (see below). Today Kibbutz Yotvata, a regional center, and a road station stand on the site.

The modern name Yotvata is based on the site's possible identification of the oasis with "Jotbathah, a land with brooks of water" (Dt. 10:7), one of the Israelites' encampments in their desert wanderings, before Ebronah and Ezion-Geber (Num. 33:33–34). There is as yet no proof for this identification; some scholars have suggested the Israelites' route here ran from north to south and have found support for this hypothesis in the Arabic names Sabkhat eṭ-Ṭaba and Bir eṭ-Ṭaba of the Yotvata saline marshes (today bisected by the Israel–Jordan border) and the well on their eastern edge.

The water source and the crossroad here made Yotvata a focus for settlement at different periods, and although there is no mound or multiperiod central site, there are a number of sites in different places. Their remains can be divided into four main groups: remains related to water or agriculture; tombs; remains of settlements or encampments: and remains associated with copper production.

The first group consists mainly of systems of chain-wells, known as *fugara* or *qanat*, some containing pools that reached groundwater ("mother wells"). The open channels, extending from the edge of the underground systems, are now covered with low banks of earth and grass, which also indicate the areas irrigated in the past. According to Y. Porath, who investigated the area after M. Evenari and his team, these systems date to the Early Arab period.

The settlements excavated so far date to the Chalcolithic period, the Early and Middle Bronze Ages, the beginning of the Iron Age, and the Nabatean, Roman, and Early Arab periods. The sites from the last four periods were probably fortresses or way stations.

EXPLORATION

Two of the sites at the oasis were briefly described in the early twentieth century. The large "mother well" (today by the side of the road north of Yotvata) was described by A. Musil, who called it Ḥafriat Ghadian and correlated it with the water supply. T. E. Lawrence described the Roman fortress (but mistakenly dated it to the Byzantine period). In the early 1930s, F. Frank and N. Glueck described the aforementioned Ḥafriat Ghadian, the phenomenon of the chain wells, and the Roman fortress, which Frank correctly identified as a Roman *castellum* and Glueck believed to be a Nabatean khan. Glueck returned to Yotvata in the 1950s and investigated the early Iron Age fortress discovered by kibbutz members. He erroneously identified it as belonging to the series of Negev fortresses "from the time of King Solomon." Y. Aharoni surveyed the site in the 1950s and was the first to describe the Early Arab period site (which he identified as Roman-Byzantine), and Evenari's team carried out the first extensive survey of the chain-wells systems. In the following years, B. Rothenberg surveyed the area as part of his Arabah Survey, but he was unable to establish the exact dates of some of the sites. Partial surveys were later undertaken by U. Avner, Z. Meshel, and Y. Porath. Porath also carried out a short trial excavation at the site which is considered to be the oasis's central settlement in the Roman-Nabatean period (map reference 1543.9214). The main structure here (c. 30 by 35 m) has a central courtyard and parts of it are built of ashlars. Only further excavation will confirm whether this is another fortress in the series found at the oasis or a ritual structure, possibly a temple, which, according to the Roman *Tabula Peutingeriana*, could have stood here.

Since 1974, excavations have been carried out (at the sites described below) on behalf of the Institute of Archaeology at Tel Aviv University, as part of a research project on the history of the Yotvata oasis. The excavations are under the direction of Z. Meshel and co-directed by B. Sass and E. Ayalon.

CHALCOLITHIC PERIOD. The earliest remains discovered at the site are probably from the Chalcolithic period. They extend over the entire hill (on which the early Iron Age fortress was later built; see below), but are found primarily on its eastern part. Also attributed to this phase is a thin layer of ash that was found in several places in pockets in the bedrock beneath the walls and floors of the later fortress's casemate rooms. An unusual find was a deposit of about twenty grinding stones of different sizes, mostly made of granite, that were hidden in a sealed pit under the later fortress wall. At least part of the crushed copper slag scattered over the area of the hill, especially in the east, can be attributed to this period. The site thus joins a series of early sites, possibly Chalcolithic according to Rothenberg, that were found mainly on hilltops in the Arabah and at its perimeters, where copper production was aided by winds that fanned the fires.

EARLY BRONZE AND MIDDLE BRONZE AGE I. Scanty remains of structures, burial cairns, and many sherds, scattered over an area of approximately 2.5 a. (in the vicinity of map reference 1536.9216), belong to the Early Bronze and Middle Bronze Age I. These remains were found on the slope of a scarp at the northern edge of a broad "bay" of the Arabah. The "bay" is protected from the hot north winds that are so oppressive in the summer.

The principal Early Bronze Age remains discovered here so far are the many sherds scattered over the area. Part of an Egyptian alabaster vessel was also found here recently. The excavators date the complex to the Early Bronze Age I, but because the closest sites from this period are southeast of the Dead Sea, dating it to the Early Bronze Age II—to which many sites in the Negev and the 'Uvda Valley have been attributed—cannot be ruled out. It is likely that the

Yotvata: the cliff on which the Early Iron Age fortress was built, looking north.

Yotvata: plan of the Early Iron Age fortress.

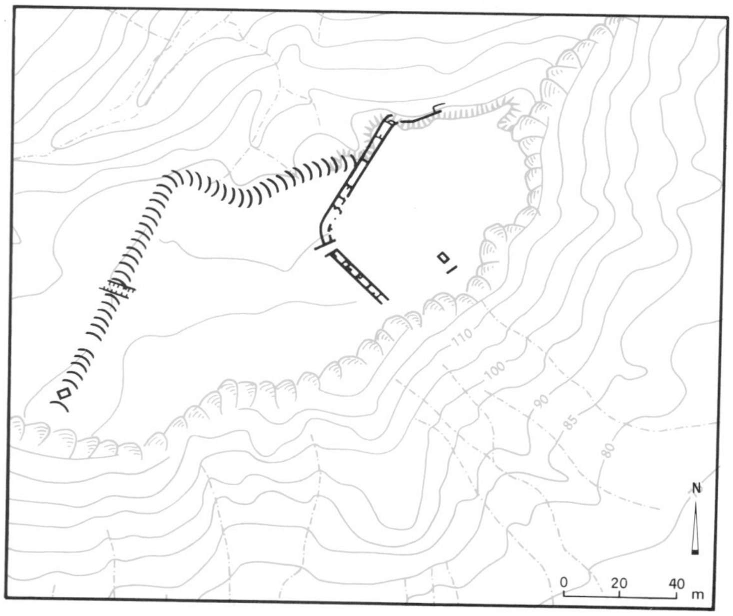

*Fragment of a decorated Midianite bowl: **(a)** exterior; **(b)** interior.*

square-roomed structures built on the slope, and possibly even some of the round structures at the site, were built in the Early Bronze Age. There was probably an encampment here that made use of the site's topographical advantages.

Ten round structures, two of which are linked to each other, and four tumuli are ascribed to the Middle Bronze Age I. The structures (diameter, 2.8–3.8 m) are sunk in an alluvial terrace; the walls survive to a height of 0.6 to 0.9 m. Several of the structures contained layers of ashes beneath earth and stone debris, indicating an occupational level. The characteristic finds included sherds, bones, flint flakes, shells, beads, and pieces of ostrich eggshells. An interesting find was a group of three crude bone spatulas.

All four tumuli that were excavated had a rectangular burial cist in their center, oriented east–west and 1.5 to 2.5 m long. A contracted skeleton was found in one tumulus that had not been completely looted; all that remained in the others were a few sherds, human bone fragments, a few teeth, and stone, shell, ostrich eggshell, and copper beads.

EARLY IRON AGE FORTRESS. An irregular casemate fortress (c. 50 by 76 m), situated south of and above the kibbutz (map reference 1552.9224), is dated to the Early Iron Age. It was built on the flat summit of a high, steep hill that is isolated on three sides. The hill makes up part of the cliff closing off the oasis from the west, and its selection was deliberate. The casemate rooms were built only around the summit's northern and western edges. The hill's steep southern and eastern cliffs made casemate construction unnecessary on those sides. Farther along the summit, 75 m west of the fortress, another fortification was built that looks totally as a beaten-earth heap. Its date is not clear; it may even relate to the Chalcolithic phase. The casemate fortress's plan is reminiscent of the "Negev Israelite fortresses", but the excavators are of the opinion that it predates the latter and was not part of their network.

The casemate rooms are characterized by their irregularity: they are 1.9 to 2.4 m wide and of varying lengths. The walls' foundations are built of rough stones (c. 1 m high) topped by sun-dried mud bricks. The outer wall is 0.8 to 1 m thick, while the inner, thinner wall is 0.5 to 0.7 m thick. Bedrock or a leveled earthen fill comprised the floor. No actual evidence of destruction by fire was found.

The gate and its courtyard in the Early Iron Age fortress; note the maṣṣeba *on the gate floor.*

The ceramic finds include wheel-made vessels, mainly storage jars; crude Negebite vessels, mainly cooking kraters; and several fragments of Midianite pottery. Other important finds, indicating one of the occupation modes of the site's inhabitants and their connections with Timna', are pieces of copper slag, part of a low-quality copper ingot (containing only 75 percent copper), and a small piece of almost pure copper. Both the grinding stones and the flint hammers are probably related to copper production. In sections cut in the fortress's courtyard, a layer of ashes and slag was found against the casemate wall. Remains of date palms and Persian haloxylon; dama, goat, and sheep bones; shells from the Red Sea; and pieces of ostrich eggshells provide evidence of contemporary climatic conditions (which seem to have been similar to those prevalent today).

The only noticeable architectural element in the fortress is the gate, which is actually an open casemate; parallel walls were attached to its front, creating a frontal courtyard. The gate was probably protected by a small tower that apparently stood on a rectangular stone base (which occupied part of the casemate to its south). A stone slab—different in shape and size from the stones found in the walls and debris—was found at the entryway from the courtyard to the gate. It has been interpreted by the excavators as a ritual gate *maṣṣeba*.

The dating of the fortress to the beginning of the Iron Age or, more precisely, to the period of activity at Timna', is based on the resemblance of the finds to those at Timna', especially the Midianite pottery. The finds associated with copper production also point to a connection between the two sites. The excavators believe that the Yotvata oasis and its environs were a major source for water, acacia charcoal, and maybe even for fresh provisions for the people producing the copper at Timna'. The Yotvata fortress overlooks the oasis and the roads leading to it, and it should be attributed to the zenith of copper production at Timna'.

LATE BURIAL STRUCTURES IN AND NEAR THE FORTRESS. A burial structure from the Roman period was discovered at a prominent point on the cliff's edge. The structure consists of two adjoining burial places; it is topped by a square stone structure (3.65 by 3.2 m) that is faced on the outside with white plaster. One burial place contained an empty cedar coffin without a lid; the other held a human skeleton. Sherds found in the soil nearby dated the tomb.

The ruins of another isolated stone structure (1.9 by 2.5 m) were discovered in the southern part of the fortress's courtyard. Its opening faced the Arabah. Both the walls and the floor were coated with white plaster. Few sherds from the Early Arab period were discovered here, but no bones. This structure, too, is clearly visible from all parts of the oasis. The excavators consider that it might have been a *maqam* (sacred place) or a sheikh's tomb.

Cedar coffin from the Roman burial structure.

Plan of the Roman fortress.

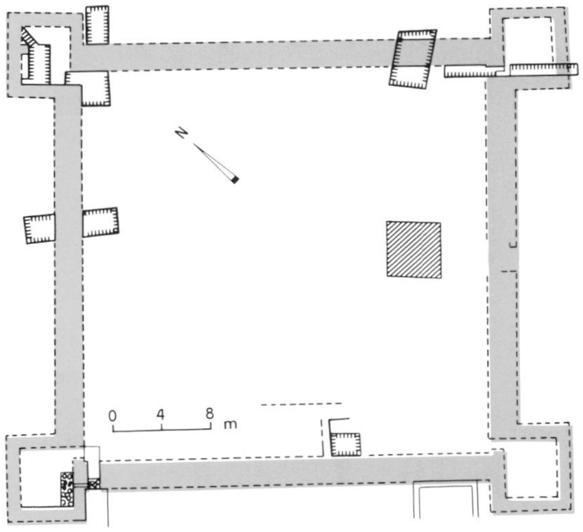

Later tombs, dug in the ruins of the fortress, were found in two of its rooms. Because there were no finds with the skeletons, the date of the tombs could not be established. The main cemetery of the Bedouin who lived in this area until the 1950s was next to the Roman fortress.

ROMAN FORTRESS AND BATH. On the flat area west of the main road to Elath, about 350 m west of 'En Yotvata (map reference 1543.9217), are ruins of a Roman fortress. Its plan was described by the early surveyors of the oasis; it can be clearly seen on the surface as a large square of raised earthen ramparts. A small stone structure still stands on the eastern rampart that served as a police station at the beginning of the British Mandate period.

The site has been identified with ad-Dianam, which appears on the *Tabula Peutingeriana* with the symbol for a temple at the junction of two Roman roads leading to Aelia (Elath). The temple has not yet been located, but the finds from the fortress that defended the oasis and the crossroad support this identification.

Exploratory excavations here uncovered not only the general plan of the fortress, but also a bathhouse next to it. The principal discovery, however, was a royal Roman inscription describing the construction of the fortress in the reign of Diocletian (see below).

Its plan is that of a typical *castellum*: a square enclosure surrounded by a wall, incorporating four corner towers (*quadriburgium*). The external dimensions are 39.4 by 39.7 m, the wall is 2.45 m thick, and the towers are 5.2 by 6.5 m. From its base to an average height of 1.5 m, the wall is built of stones; from that height upward it is constructed of sun-dried mud bricks. The entire structure was plastered with white lime. A row of rooms was built against the wall's inner face, probably on all four sides. The main gate was on the east. In addition, a small entrance adjoining the southwest tower was discovered at the edge of the southern side. The wooden bolt that secured its door was inserted from the tower room. Its socket—an open-ended groove—was found in situ.

Two occupation levels, with a destruction layer in between, were found in the exploratory sections. The abundant coins found in both levels indicate that the periods of occupation were very close to one another—from the last quarter of the third to the mid-fourth centuries CE. More precise evidence of the history of the fortress comes from the Latin imperial inscription that, judging from its findspot, was originally fixed above the gate's lintel. Two and a half lines were intentionally erased in antiquity. I. Roll suggests the inscription be read as follows:

1. Perpetuae paci
2. Diocletianus Augus(tus) et
3. [[Maximianus Augus(tus et)]]
4. Constantius et Maximianus
5. noblissimi Caesar<e>s
6. alam c(um) osti<o> constituerunt
7. per providentia(m) Prisci
8. pr(a)esidis [[[provinciae]]]
9. [[[?Syriae Palaestinae?]]]

Left ear: mul(tis votis) XX (= vicennalibus)
Right ear: mul(tis votis) XL (= quadragennalibus)

The inscription may be translated thus:

1. For perpetual peace,
2. Diocletian Augustus and
3. Maximian Augustus and
4. Constantius and Maximianus
5. the most noble Caesars
6. erected the wing with the gate,
7. by care of Priscus
8. the governor of the province
9. of ? Syria Palaestina?

Left ear: Numerous vows for the twenty-year jubilee.
Right ear: Numerous vows for the forty-year jubilee.

Roman fortress and vicinity; west, among the trees, is the Bedouin cemetery.

Latin imperial inscription from the Roman fortress.

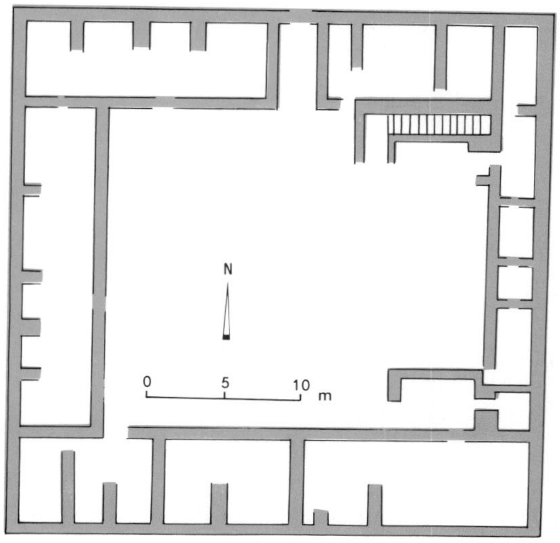

Plan of the main Early Arab structure in its main phase.

The inscription and the finds indicate that the fortress was built by Priscus, probably one of the governors (*praeses*) of the province of Syria Palaestina in the reign of Diocletian and his three partners in the Tetrarchy (293–305). Its construction is no doubt connected to the limes frontier network erected by Diocletian. It was partly destroyed, perhaps in a raid by nomads, in the time of Constantius II (337–362), in whose reign it was also rebuilt. It was finally destroyed in the second half of the fourth century.

About 100 m north of the fortress are the meager remains of a bathhouse whose rooms seem to have been arranged on an east–west axis. The bathhouse is probably related to the fortress; however, it contained no datable finds.

EARLY ARAB SITE. The site from the Early Arab period (map reference 1557.9224) included several structures scattered over an area of about 5 a. When part of the site was surveyed earlier, as mentioned above, it was erroneously dated to the Roman-Byzantine or Nabatean period.

The excavations concentrated on the largest structure, whose main function is still unclear; it may have been part of a center for agricultural activity at the oasis, equipped in this period with about ten systems of chain wells, or it might have been a khan, a way station, a regional administrative center, or all three. The structure is square (c. 33.5 by 35 m); its main part consists of a row of rooms on all four sides of an open courtyard and a wide gate on the south. Almost all the construction was done with sun-dried mud bricks covered with white lime plaster of excellent quality, which in most places also covered the floor.

Three main phases were distinguished in the structure. In the first phase, the rooms, probably on all sides of the courtyard, were relatively narrow (c. 2.6 m wide). In the second, main phase, the outside walls remained in position, but the rooms on three of the sides were enlarged by approximately 2 m and became halls. In order to enable the construction of the roofs, and possibly also to divide them, long piers (1.5–2 m) were built across the width of the rooms; their numbers vary with the length of the rooms. The inner walls in the first phase were leveled almost to the foundations, and new floors were built on top of them, mostly covered with white plaster. The rooms at the southwestern corner probably had a second story, as indicated by a staircase base surrounded by stone walls adjoined to this corner.

The most interesting architectural element is the gate, which was built in the first phase, in the center of the southern side. The gateway is 2.5 m wide and the gate chamber itself is 3.5 m wide. Plastered benches were built on both sides, their ends shaped like arm rests. Partially burned remains of wooden beams (of cedar and pine) were found on the floor of the original entrance. In the second phase, the signs of fire were covered with a beaten-earth floor and the eastern bench was filled in with mud bricks. The walls of the auxiliary structures were probably added in this phase. The separate structures, whose remains were found mainly south and west of the main building, were probably erected then, too. Various finds in the southernmost of these structures suggest that it was a bathhouse.

Most of the finds come from the structure's main phase. Apart from pottery typical of the first part of the Early Arab period, crude handmade pottery (Negbite ware) was found, as well as two finds with chronological significance: a gold coin minted in 164 AH (780 CE), the time of the Abbasid caliph el-Mahdi), found on the plaster floor; and parts of two Arabic inscriptions—probably bills of lading, receipts, or instructions—written in black ink on camel scapulae. In one inscription, ending with the words *Salam Salam*, a few names could be deciphered, such as Aḥmed, Moḥammed, 'Abd el-Malik, and the word *raṭab* (dates). In the second inscription, which is fragmentary and unclear, the word *madin* is repeated three times, probably meaning "two measures."

It seems that the structure was built in the seventh century, during the Umayyad dynasty, and continued in use (certainly in its second phase) through the eighth century. Near the end of that century, the structure was abandoned and some of its rooms were destroyed. It became a sheepfold in the site's third phase, which began shortly after the structure was abandoned. It was probably used then by nomadic Bedouin.

Southwest corner rooms of the Early Arab structure.

Arabic inscription written in ink on a camel scapula, from the Early Arab structure.

Main publications: Z. Meshel, *IEJ* 39 (1989), 228–238; I. Roll, ibid., 239–260; A. Kindler, ibid., 261–266.

Other studies: N. Glueck, *AASOR* 15 (1934–1935), 40–41; 18–19 (1939), 95; id., *BASOR* 145 (1957), 23–24; Z. Meshel and B. Sass, *IEJ* 24 (1974), 273–274; id., *RB* 84 (1977), 266–270; J. Kalsbeek and G. London, *BASOR* 232 (1978), 47–56; G. Avni and U. Dahari, *ESI* 5 (1986), 115; Weippert 1988, 326.

ZEEV MESHEL

Z

ẒAF, TEL

IDENTIFICATION AND EXPLORATION

Tel Ẓaf is located in the Jordan Valley, some 280 m below sea level and some 11 km (7 mi.) southeast of Tel Beth-Shean (map reference 2015.2024), on two low hills separated by a saddle that rises above the western bank of the Jordan River. Chalcolithic flint tools and sherds, as well as Byzantine sherds, were collected here in the 1950s by N. Zori.

EXCAVATIONS

After the partial destruction of the site, salvage excavations were conducted in 1977, 1978, and 1980 by R. Gophna, on behalf of the Israel Department of Antiquities and Museums and the Institute of Archaeology at Tel Aviv University. The excavations, covering an area of about 100 sq m and reaching a depth—to virgin soil—of 2.5 m, yielded occupation remains from two periods, the Pottery Neolithic and the Chalcolithic.

STRATUM II: POTTERY NEOLITHIC PERIOD (sixth millennium). Three shallow pits dug into the marl were exposed in stratum II. They contained pebbles, ashes, several square mud bricks (different from those recovered in stratum I), and a few sherds. The latter have perforated handles and one is decorated with wide red bands. Stratum II represents a Pottery Neolithic culture of the type known elsewhere in the Beth-Shean Valley, such as at Tel Beth-Shean (the pits exposed below stratum XVIII).

STRATUM I: CHALCOLITHIC PERIOD (fifth millennium). Most of the remains uncovered at Tel Ẓaf date to the Chalcolithic period. This stratum, more than 2 m thick, included structures, a wide range of pottery, flint artifacts, an animal figurine, a seal impression, faunal remains, and charred seeds and wood remnants. Lengths of walls built of handmade mud bricks—some plano-convex and the rest square—attest to at least two building phases.

Some of the pottery still shows traces of the dark-faced burnished-ware tradition that originated in the northern Levant as early as the Neolithic period. Some red-burnished ware was also recovered, but the majority of the pottery finds—bowls, *amphoriskoi*, storage jars, pithoi, and occasional hole-mouth jars—are unburnished and characterized by red and black-to-brown painted decoration. Ropelike, thumb-indented plastic decorations are also common, and there are several instances of impressions made by a sharp tool. Most of the handles are strap handles, while others are lug handles.

The Chalcolithic ware from Tel Ẓaf is notable for vessels decorated with black, red, or brown geometric designs painted with a thin brush (up to 0.5 mm) on a yellowish slip. A decorative band encircles the upper part of the vessel, while its lower part is painted red. At least fifteen different combinations of linear geometric designs were found, all of them consisting of several elementary patterns—mainly triangles and lozenges—filled with net or cross-hatch motifs or paint.

Only isolated sherds of decorated ware reminiscent of this delicate Tel Ẓaf pottery have been recovered at other Chalcolithic sites in Israel, such as Beth-Shean (stratum XVIII), Kefar Gil'adi, Ḥorvat 'Uza, Teluliyot Batash, and 'Ein el-Jarba. This pottery seems to belong to one of the regional painted-ware groups that were common in the fifth and fourth millennia in various areas of Syro-Palestine. The potters were influenced by decorative traditions prevalent among the painted wares of the Mesopotamian Halafian and Ubaid cultures. The geometric designs characteristic of the Tel Ẓaf pottery and their characteristic arrangement are also found in the Halafian pottery. Several of these designs are later found on vessels ascribed to the local Ghassulian culture.

Among the remains of domesticated animals recovered at Tel Ẓaf are bones of pig, goat, sheep, and cattle; bones of wild gazelle were also found. Eight arboreal species were identified among the charred wood remnants collected: *Ziziphus lotus*, *Tamarix*, *Populus euphratica*, *Quercus ithaburensis*, *Pistacia lentiscus*, *Pistacia atlantica*, *Acacia albida*, and *Olea europea*. The domesticated plants identified through flotation techniques include naked wheat, emmer, naked barley, six-row hulled barley, lentil, and pea. Charred fig and olive were recovered as well. Palynological analyses indicate that the paleopalynological spectrum, like the range of arboreal species, does not differ from the present one, except for a higher percentage of coniferous trees. Considerable amounts of cereal pollen indicate that in the Chalcolithic period the inhabitants of Tel Ẓaf cultivated cereals nearby.

Charred remains of *Populus euphratica* yielded a calibrated carbon-14 date of 6980 ± 180 years BP (c. 5000 BCE). Further investigations are required to place the Tel Ẓaf occupation more accurately within the framework of the Chalcolithic sequence in Israel. However, there is no doubt that the culture exposed at Tel Ẓaf is merely one of the regional Chalcolithic cultures that existed here throughout the fifth and fourth millennia, such as the Wadi Rabah culture and the different variants of the Ghassulian culture.

R. Gophna and M. Kislev, *RB* 86 (1979), 112–114; R. Gophna and S. Sadeh, *TA* 15–16 (1988–1989), 3–36; A. Gopher, ibid., 37–46; S. Hellwing, ibid., 47–51; A. Horowitz, ibid., 55; N. Liphschitz, ibid., 52–54; S. Sadeh and R. Gophna, *Mitekufat Ha'even* 24 (1991) 135*–148*.

RAM GOPHNA

Tel Ẓaf: fragments of black and red decorated pottery, Chalcolithic period.

ẒAFIT, TEL

IDENTIFICATION

Tel Ẓafit (Tell eṣ-Ṣafi) is located on the southern bank of Wadi Elah, where it enters the Shephelah (map reference 1359.1237). The mound, 232 m above sea level and about 100 m above the valley bed, dominates the road that passes along the foot of Azekah (Tell Zakariyeh) and leads through Wadi Elah into the mountains. It also guards the main north–south route of the Shephelah that runs through the plain, at the foot of the mound to the west, toward Gezer. On the north and east the mound slopes steeply, revealing white limestone cliffs: to the south, the mound slopes gradually and is connected by a saddle to the range behind it. The mound's summit is crescent shaped and slopes moderately to the south, where the acropolis was located in antiquity.

The identification of the site is disputed. J. L. Porter, in 1887, was the first to identify it as Gath, and this was accepted by many scholars—including F. J. Bliss, the mound's excavator. Another suggestion, also widely accepted at the time, located the biblical city of Libnah here. This suggestion was based (aside from various biblical and other sources) on the Arabic name Tell eṣ-Ṣafi, meaning "the white mound," and on the French Crusader name, Blanche Garde, or "white citadel." The recurrence of the word "white" was taken to be a connection with the biblical name Libnah, which also means white. It was suggested that these three interrelated names had their origin in the white cliffs, which are visible from afar. Two primary sources from the Byzantine period contradict this assumption, however. Eusebius states that in his day there was a village named Λοβανά (Lobana, meaning white) in the vicinity of Eleutheropolis (Beth Guvrin) (*Onom.* 120, 25). On the Medeba map, on the other hand, there is a place called CAΦIΘA (Safita), which is identified with Tel Ẓafit. The mound was therefore already known by the name it bears today, and a settlement called Labana was then situated near Beth Guvrin. White cliffs are also found on the slopes of other mounds in the vicinity. In light of these facts, Z. Kallai returned to the early suggestion of C. W. M. Van de Velde and V. Guérin to search for a place in the vicinity with a name like Mizpeh, which could have undergone a change to Safita. W. F. Albright suggested that Tel Ẓafit should be equated with biblical Makkedah (Jos. 10:10). There have been other suggestions as well, but current archaeological research tends to prefer the original proposal identifying it with Gath.

Tel Ẓafit: general plan.

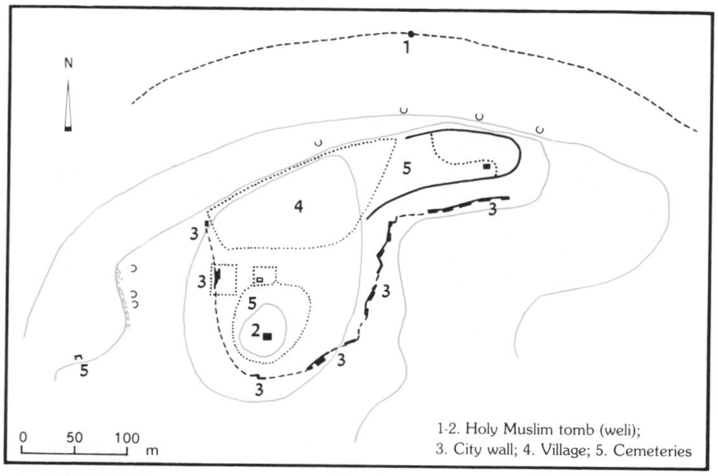

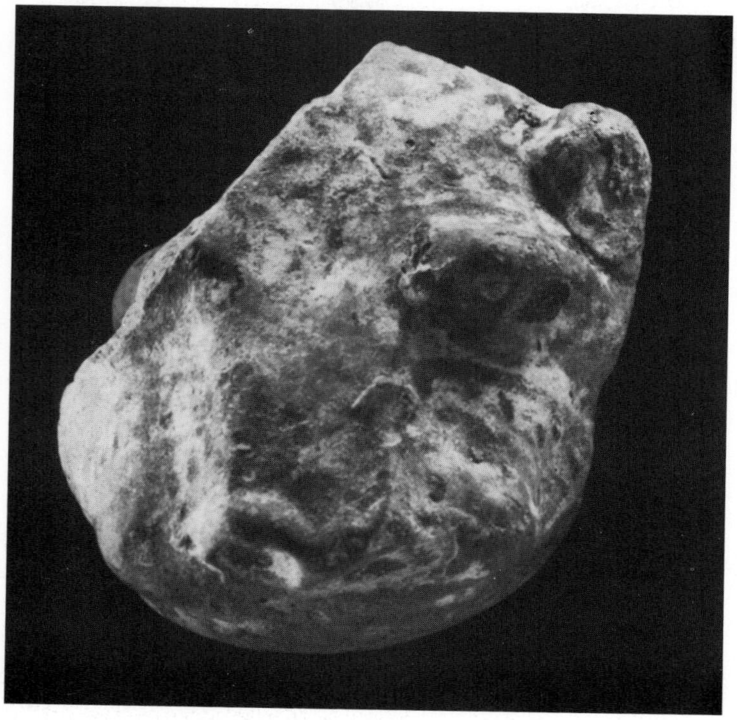

Philistine rhyton in the shape of a lioness's head.

EXCAVATIONS

In 1899, excavations were conducted on the mound sponsored by the British Palestine Exploration Fund, under the direction of Bliss, with the assistance of R. A. S. Macalister. The expedition originally intended to excavate mainly at Tel Ẓafit. However, the license granted by the Ottoman authorites permitted them to excavate an area of 10 sq km, so the expedition also excavated the nearby mounds of Tell Zakariya (Azekah), Tell Judeideh, and Tell Ṣandaḥanna (Mareshah). Tel Ẓafit was excavated for two seasons in 1899. The results of the excavations were published in a comprehensive report in 1902. The account was written by Bliss, and the summary of the findings was compiled by Bliss and Macalister.

When the excavators arrived at the mound, they realized that the areas suitable for excavation were very limited. In the southern part of the summit, the natural place for the acropolis, there was a holy *maqam*, surrounded by a cemetery that it was also impossible to excavate. To the north, on the main part of the mound, were the houses of the Arab village and, behind them on the east, another cemetery that stretched over the remainder of the summit. The excavations were therefore confined to small, noncontiguous sections that were part of five main areas: area A, a narrow strip across the width of the summit between the *maqam* and the village; area B, a second section in the same place, east of area A, toward the center of the mound; area C, the city wall—traced on the south and west slopes; area D, the east side of the mound; and area E, the remains of the Crusader fortress in the southern cemetery.

AREA A. Three soundings were made in a continuous line from east to west. The average depth of the deposit found was 10 m. Another six soundings were sunk farther to the west. The depth of the deposit was found to decrease toward the center of the mound, where it was only 4 m. In all these soundings, three main assemblages of pottery were discovered and designated by the excavators as being from the "Early Pre-Israelite" period, "Late Pre-Israelite" and "Jewish" periods, and the Early Arab period (and see below).

AREA B. In area B, which is closer to the center of the mound, eleven adjoining soundings were made. The stratigraphy here was disturbed, and the pottery was mixed. In one of the soundings, a child burial in a jar was found.

AREA C. Sections of the city wall were visible above surface level in area C. Other sections were exposed elsewhere in the excavations. The maximum thickness of the wall was 4 m. The lower courses were built of roughly squared stones, with a fill of smaller stones between them. In one place, a course of bricks was preserved and many fallen bricks were found near the wall. This led

Decorated Philistine jug.

the excavators to conclude that the upper part of the wall had been built of bricks. Towers (10–11.3 m long) projected from the wall for a distance of 0.6 m. The spaces between them measured 9.3 to 11.6 m. The towers' foundation stones were laid in straight courses, with only the corners built of ashlar masonry. In several places, the face of the wall was plastered with mud and coated with another layer of white plaster—a substance made of white powdery limestone mixed with straw and water. The wall was shaped like a crescent and was parallel to the ridge. From the depth of its foundations in the deposit, the excavators attributed the wall to Rehoboam (928–911 BCE). They found their confirmation in 2 Chronicles 11:8 (as mentioned above, they equated the mound with Gath).

AREA D. A sounding (c. 20 by 27 m) was made on the east side of the mound, in which the average depth of the deposit was 8.5 m. The excavators distinguished four strata of settlement: (1) The lowest stratum contained remains of stone or brick buildings and pottery from the "Early Pre-Israelite" period. (2) Above this stratum a group of rooms was uncovered with walls of rough stones bound with mortar. The pottery in this stratum was "Late Pre-Israelite", with Mycenean sherds. A building with three stone pillars was found in this layer. The excavators interpreted the pillars as a row of *maṣṣebot*, or stelae, and the building as a temple (see below). (3) Above these two strata were several walls whose building technique was similar to that in the second stratum. It was thus difficult for the excavators to distinguish between the buildings in these two strata. This stratum contained pottery from the "Jewish" period. Several vessels bore *lamelekh* stamps. There was also early Greek pottery that the excavators dated to 770 to 550 BCE, Greek black- and red-figure ware dated to 500 to 350 BCE, and isolated sherds of "Seleucid" pottery. (4) Near the surface some large rooms were uncovered whose walls contained a number of stones in the Crusader style. The pottery was local Arab ware.

AREA E. Actual excavations could not be conducted in area E because of the *maqam*. Bliss and Macalister therefore attempted to trace the remains of the Crusader fortress, Blanche Garde, that were visible on the surface. The fortress was built on the southern, elevated sector of the mound, in 1140 CE. It was one of a series of fortresses on the southwest border of the kingdom of Jerusalem, one of whose functions was to encircle Ashkelon, which was held by the Arabs until 1153. In 1191, the fortress was destroyed by Saladin. M. Ray was the first to examine these ruins. He visited here before the *maqam* was built, and so was able to draw a general plan of the fortress. According to his description, the fortress was square (each side was 60 m long), and in two of its corners there were remains of towers. In 1875, when C. R. Conder visited here, the *maqam* had already been built on top of the fortress. He only found cuttings in the rock, which were difficult for him to trace. Bliss and Macalister noted the upper part of a wall built of Crusader-style masonry, near the east wall of the *maqam*. In their opinion, it was a remnant of one of the towers Ray discovered. The second tower had been totally destroyed during the construction of the *maqam*. Additional remains of the fortress, including a gate, were found in area B.

The main finds of the excavations at Tel Ẓafit were discovered not in the stratigraphic excavation, but in an old rubbish dump in the middle of area C, on the mound's southern flank. Among them were sherds from the "Early Pre-Israelite" period, Egyptian beads and ornaments from various periods, part of an Egyptian stela, pottery from the "Jewish" period bearing personal names, *lamelekh* and other stamps, five fragments of an Assyrian limestone stela, early Greek sherds and black- and red-figure ware, fragments of about forty pottery masks, about thirty pottery and stone figurines from the Persian period (see below), and a number of coins—two Ptolemaic, one Roman, one Arab, and two silver Crusader coins.

On the basis of the results of the excavation and of the finds in the dump, the excavators believed that Tel Ẓafit was first settled in the seventeenth century BCE, abandoned in the Seleucid period, and not resettled until Crusader times. Albright examined the pottery published in Bliss and Macalister's report and revised the dating in the following way:

Period	Bliss-Macalister	Albright
"Early Pre-Israelite"	(?) –1500 BCE	3000–1800 BCE
"Late Pre-Israelite"	1500–800 BCE	1800–1000 BCE
"Jewish"	800–300 BCE	1000–587 BCE
"Seleucid"	300– BCE	400–100 BCE

Albright agreed with the excavators about the dates of the later periods. According to him, the first settlement at Tel Ẓafit was a great deal earlier than the excavators had assumed: he ascribed its founding to the beginning of the Early Bronze Age. Albright's revisions were confirmed by potsherds collected by R. Amiran and Y. Aharoni in a survey on the mound in 1955 on behalf of the Department of Antiquities. They attributed the many sherds gathered on the mound's western, southern, and eastern slopes to all phases of the Bronze and Iron ages, as well as later periods—the Roman and medieval. The bulk of the sherds is from the Iron Age, especially the Iron Age II.

Albright claimed that the building Bliss and Macalister considered a temple (area D) was in reality a typical four-room pillared building from the Iron Age that should be dated to between 1000 and 800 BCE. Similar buildings have been found at almost all the sites containing strata from this period.

The excavators dated the city wall to the time of Rehoboam. H. Thiersch attempted to lower the date because of the similarity between the construction of the towers and Assyrian fortifications. C. Watzinger dated it even later, to

Decorated Phoenician jug, 10th century BCE.

Fragment of a small stone relief in Assyrian style.

Tel Ẓafit: limestone head of Heracles, from Cyprus, Persian period.

Tel Ẓafit: clay mask from the Persian period.

the Neo-Babylonian period. However, until additional data become available, A. G. Barrois's assessment is to be taken as correct: the wall's exact date within the Iron Age cannot be fixed.

Among the finds were many Philistine pottery vessels, *lamelekh* stamps, Hebrew stamps with personal names, *nṣf* and shekel weights from the end of the First Temple period, and a group of figurines from the Persian period (fifth–fourth centuries BCE). Similar figurines were found in a temple from the same period at Tel Michal and at nearby Tel Ẓippor, among other sites. In the years following the excavations, several potsherds from the tenth century BCE were discovered by chance; they are being kept in the Israel Museum in Jerusalem.

Main publications: F. J. Bliss and A. S. Macalister, *Excavations in Palestine during the Years 1898–1900*, London 1902.

Other studies: M. Rey, *Études sur les monuments de l'architecture militaire des croisés en Syrie et dans l'Isle de Chypre*, Paris 1877, 173–175; F. J. Bliss, *PEQ* 31 (1899), 188–199, 317–333; 32 (1900), 16–29; A. S. Macalister, ibid., 29–39; W. F. Müller, *OLZ* 3 (1900), 105; W. F. Albright, *AASOR* 2–3 (1921–1922), 7–8; id., *BASOR* 15 (1924), 9; id., *Archaeology and the Religion of Israel* 2, Baltimore 1953, 65–66, 193; id., *The Archaeology of Palestine*, London 1960, 30–31; I. Benzinger, *Hebräische Archaeologie* 3, Leipzig 1927, passim; A. G. Barrois, *Manuel d'Archéologie Biblique* 1, Paris 1939, 142–143; F. M. Cross, Jr., and G. E. Wright, *JBL* 75 (1956), 217–218; R. Giveon, *JEA* 51 (1965), 202–204; Y. Aharoni, *LB*, index; N. Na'aman *BASOR* 214 (1974), 25–38; A. F. Rainey, *EI* 12 (1975), 63*–76*; Weippert 1988, 219.

EPHRAIM STERN

ZEROR, TEL

IDENTIFICATION

Tel Zeror (Khirbet et-Tell Dhurur) is situated in the Sharon Plain, about 0.5 km south of the confluence of Naḥal 'Iron and Naḥal Ḥaviva with Naḥal Ḥadera (map reference 1476.2038). The largest of the chain of mounds on the western fringe of the Sharon, Tel Zeror's main importance in antiquity was its position near the ford of the wadi on the western branch of the Via Maris. The mound is composed of two peaks connected by a saddle: the one on the north is smaller and steeper than the one on the south, which has broad, moderate slopes. B. Mazar and N. Na'aman identified the mound with *d-r-r* in Thutmose III's list (no. 115), and Y. Aharoni identified it with *m-k-t-r* in the same list (no. 71, Migdal-yene in Amenḥotep II's list). Excavation has not confirmed its identification.

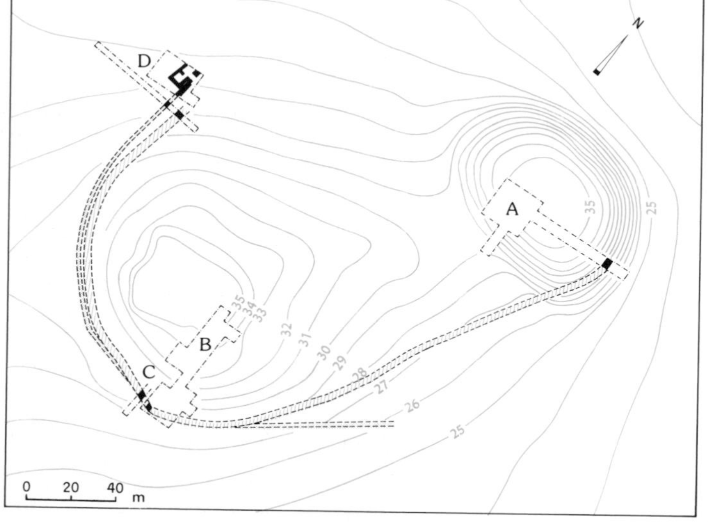

Tel Zeror: map of the mound and excavation areas.

EXCAVATIONS

In 1928, J. Garstang spent a single day digging a trial trench at Tel Zeror. Three seasons of excavations were carried out at the site from 1964 to 1966 by an expedition from the Japanese Society for Near Eastern Research, under the direction of K. Ohata, with M. Kochavi acting as field director. A fourth season was held under the same auspices in 1974, with K. Goto as field director. The excavations were concentrated in the following areas:

Area A, the main excavation area, on the summit of the northern peak and on its southern and eastern slopes, contained remains from the Middle Bronze Age IIA to the Roman period. Areas B and C, on the summit of the southern promontory and on its southern slope, contained remains from the Middle Bronze Age IIA to the end of the Iron Age, as well as from the Mameluke and Arab periods. Areas D and E, on the western slope of the saddle connecting the peaks, contained remains from the Middle Bronze Age IIA urban settlement, as well as installations, pits, and tombs from the other periods represented on the mound. The cemetery, a low *ḥamra* hill, about 150 m west of the mound, was used as a burial ground at the end of the Late Bronze Age, the beginning of the Iron Age, and the Hellenistic period.

MIDDLE BRONZE AGE II. The first settlers at Tel Zeror arrived in the Middle Bronze Age II. The occupation on the mound was limited to the first phase of that period (Middle Bronze Age IIA, 2000–1800 BCE) of which four settlement strata were uncovered. All the areas of excavation, with the exception of the cemetery, yielded remains from this period; the area inhab-

Plan of the tower in area D, MB IIA.

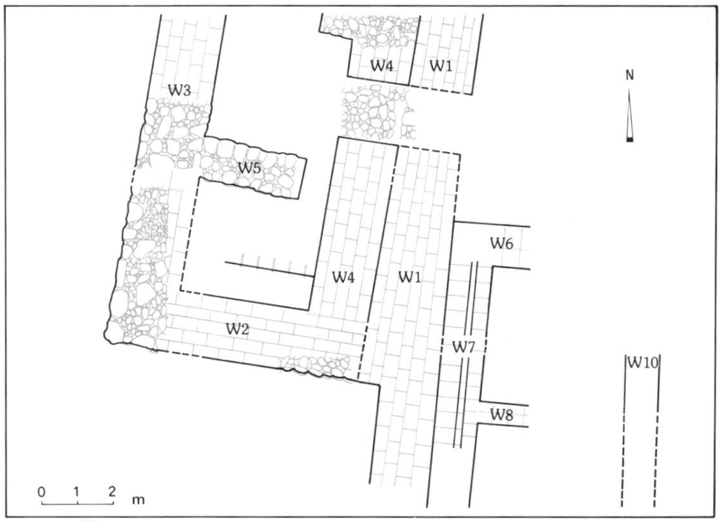

ited is estimated at between 10 and 12.5 a. Two superimposed city walls, up to 4.5 m wide, and built of brick on stone foundations, were excavated. They were constructed on an earthen rampart. A moat was discovered on the western side of the mound. The discovery of the remains of the walls on three sides of the mound made it possible to trace their general course. A two-chambered tower projecting 8 m from the Middle Bronze IIA wall was found on the western side of the mound. It probably formed part of the earlier wall and was also constructed of brick on a very solid foundation of large field stones. The rampart, uncovered in all the excavated areas, consisted of layers of earth laid horizontally and connected by vertical shafts filled with stones and earth.

The sides of the moat were coated with a mixture of *ḥamra* and beaten *kurkar*. The moat was about 10 m wide, but the depth could not be determined because the excavators reached underground water 4.5 m below the surface. It can be assumed that in antiquity water also filled the bottom of the moat.

The ceramic finds in the buildings connected with the walls and in the tower date to the early and middle phases of the period (equivalent to palaces I–II at Aphek) and have close affinities with pottery from other contemporary settlements in the Sharon, such as Tel Poleg and Tel Burga. No signs of destruction are evident from the end of this period, although there is a gap in occupation on the mound from the eighteenth to the beginning of the fifteenth centuries BCE.

LATE BRONZE AGE. No traces of fortifications were found from the Late Bronze Age. The settlers apparently dwelled in an unwalled village. The majority of the Late Bronze remains were uncovered on the summit of the southern peak, in areas B and C. Part of a public building with walls at least one meter thick was cleared. From the small section uncovered, it appears to have been a secular building, perhaps the palace of a local ruler. The building was abandoned at the end of the thirteenth century BCE. Throughout the Late Bronze Age, a coppersmiths' quarter existed on the southern slope of the southern peak, where smelting furnaces, crucibles, clay bellows' pipes, and a quantity of copper slag were found. An unusual amount of Cypriot pottery

Cist tomb, 11th century BCE.

Philistine rhyton in the shape of a lioness.

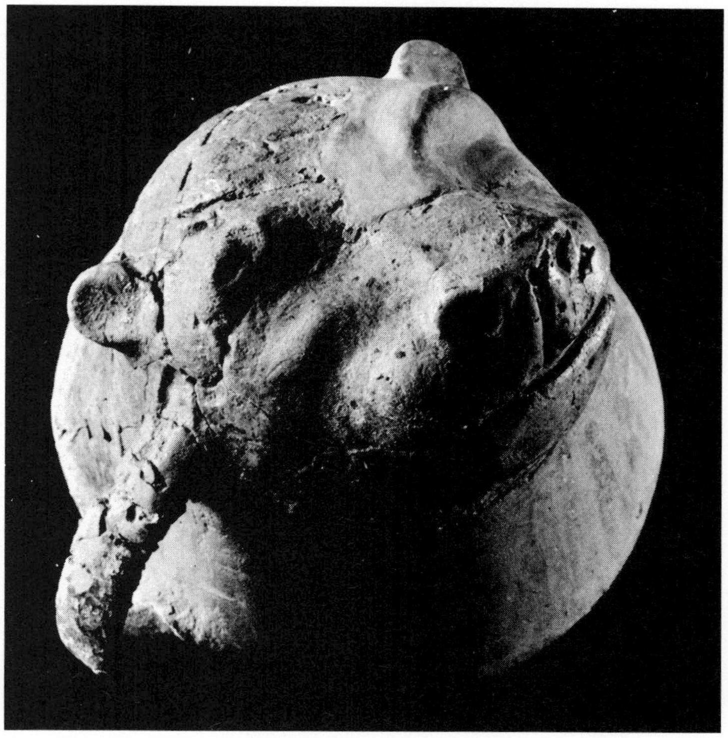

uncovered in this area suggests a connection with Cyprus, the source of copper in the period. Evidence of the Late Bronze Age settlement was also uncovered in the other areas, but fortifications were absent everywhere.

The cemetery was first used for burial in the fourteenth and thirteenth centuries BCE, at which time interment was carried out in simple individual graves cut in the *ḥamra* soil. The body was laid in a supine position, with the funerary offerings beside it and sometimes on the body itself. The graves were oriented east–west with the heads on the west. This cemetery bears a close resemblance to the one excavated at Tell Abu Hawam.

IRON AGE. Pits dug into the ruins of the Late Bronze Age II public building in area B, on the southern peak, represent the beginning of the Iron Age settlement. The pits (diameter, 2 m; depth, 1 m) contained refuse: bones of sheep, goats, and cattle and sherds of bowls, pithoi, and cooking pots typical of the period of the Israelite settlement in the thirteenth and twelfth centuries BCE. About ten graves of children and adults, found in collared-rim pithoi in the cemetery, are ascribed to this period.

In the eleventh century BCE, a citadel with a casemate wall of large bricks was built on the northern peak (area A). In the cemetery a particularly rich assortment of finds is attributed to the eleventh and beginning of the tenth centuries BCE. Nine large cist tombs, built of stone and covered with large stone slabs, were uncovered. The tombs were dug in a southeast–northwest direction, and the bodies were laid in a supine position with the head pointing northwest. These were family tombs. The wealth of funerary offerings included Philistine pottery, bronze hemispheric bowls, and socketed javelin heads. Among the unique pottery finds here were lamps with closed nozzles, a rhyton in the shape of a lioness, and a figurine of a nude goddess (Astarte).

Storehouses containing large numbers of storage jars from the end of the tenth century BCE were found above the ruins of the earlier citadel (area A). In the ninth and eighth centuries BCE, the village also spread to the southern peak (area B), which was left undefended. Typical Iron Age four-room houses on the northern peak (area A) were surrounded by a thin wall (1 m wide) that was strengthened on the interior with piers (0.5 m wide) set at 2-m intervals. During the ninth and eighth centuries BCE, the village suffered a series of destructions in the military campaigns of the Arameans and the Assyrians along the Via Maris. The upper part of a stone-lined cistern uncovered along the foot of the northern slope (area E) in the last season of excavations contained pottery indicating that it was in use up to the end of the Iron Age and it may even have been dug then.

Among the principal finds from this period is an incision on the base of a burnished bowl in a script exhibiting Aramaic influence—. . . בע · לאלסמך (. . . *b'·l'lsmk* [belonging] to 'Elsamakh); a bronze figurine of a deity wearing a high hat and raising its hand (usually identified with the god Reshef); a steatite bowl with the palm of a hand scratched on its base; and a storage jar with the Hebrew letter מ (*m*) incised on its side.

LATER PERIODS. Pottery from the Persian period (fifth century BCE) was found on the northern peak in large pits that penetrated the ruins of buildings

Tel Zeror: pottery assemblage found in the tombs.

Clay Astarte figurine, Iron I.

from the end of the Iron Age. In the third and second centuries BCE, a Hellenistic farmhouse stood on the northern peak, together with a number of agricultural installations. A stepped watchtower was erected there in the Early Roman period. It apparently guarded the road to Caesarea. In the Byzantine period, the settlement was located about 2 km (1.2 mi.) south of the mound. The Arab village Khirbet et-Tell Dhurur on the southern peak dates to the Mameluke period.

Hellenistic graves were found in area E and in the cemetery. Built tombs from the Roman period were uncovered in area D.

SUMMARY

As the first mound to be excavated in the heart of the Sharon Plain, the investigation of Tel Zeror shed light on the history of the entire area. The settlement on the mound reached its greatest period of prosperity at the beginning of the Middle Bronze Age IIA (twentieth–nineteenth centuries BCE), the period of the urbanization of the Sharon and the Coastal plains. It was abandoned in the Middle Bronze Age IIB and at the beginning of the Late Bronze Age, but was resettled with the beginning of Egyptian rule in the country. A community of coppersmiths of Cypriot origin plied its trade on the mound then. At the end of the Bronze Age, the population apparently fled the unwalled settlement and sought refuge in neighboring fortified cities, such as Gath and Yaḥam on the Via Maris. The Israelite tribes arrived in the central Sharon at the start of their settlement period. The village they established on the mound resembles their other settlements, discovered in the survey of the Sharon. The well-built citadel from the eleventh century BCE and the contemporary cemetery may have belonged to the Sikil, one of the Sea Peoples whose capital was at Dor, about 20 km (12.5 mi.) north of Tel Zeror. In the time of King David, the Sharon was restored to Israel's control; the partly fortified Iron Age village continued in existence until the fall of the Israelite kingdom to the Assyrians in 732 or 720 BCE.

Main publications: K. Ohata and M. Kochavi, *Tel Zeror* 1–3, Tokyo 1966–1970.

Other studies: B. Maisler (Mazar), *ZDPV* 58 (1935), 78–84; Y. Aharoni, *IEJ* 9 (1959), 110–122; K. Ohata and M. Kochavi, *IEJ* 14 (1964), 283–284; 16 (1966), 274–276; id., *CNI* 16/3 (1965), 16–17; id., *RB* 72 (1965), 548–551; 74 (1967), 73–76; 75 (1968), 269–272; M. Kochavi, *Ariel* 21 (1967–1968), 65–70; M. Kochavi et al., *ZDPV* 95 (1979), 121–165; A. Biran and R. Gophna, *IEJ* 15 (1965), 253–255; A. Biran, *CNI* 17/2–3 (1966), 22; 18/1–2 (1967), 29–30; K. Goto, *Orient* 5 (1969), 41–53; 9 (1973), 1–30; id., *RB* 82 (1975), 571–573; H. Ogawa, *Orient* 7 (1971), 25–48; 12 (1976), 27–46; 20 (1984), 109–128; Weippert 1988 (Ortsregister).

MOSHE KOCHAVI

ẒIPPOR, TEL

IDENTIFICATION

Tel Ẓippor is a small mound (c. 500 sq m in area and c. 5 m high) on the land of the *moshavim* of Revaḥa and Qomemiyut, on the Coastal Plain, near the main road from Qiryat Gat to Ashkelon. The mound is situated in the center of an area of some 12 a. or more (map reference 125.118), bounded on all sides by dry riverbeds. In the 1950s, M. Bosheri of the Israel Department of Antiquities and Museums found, in a field of deeply plowed soil, a clay vessel containing a hoard of coins from the reign of Alexander the Great. Surveys carried out by R. Gophna, Bosheri, and others turned up numerous clay figurines, stone statuettes, and a fragment of a clay mask, all from the Persian and Hellenistic periods. Philistine sherds and sherds from the Iron Age I, Late Bronze Age, and Middle Bronze Age I were also found. A salvage excavation, comprising three brief seasons, was conducted between 1963 and 1965 by A. Biran and O. Negbi, on behalf of the Israel Department of Antiquities and Museums. The site's ancient name is unknown.

EXCAVATIONS

In the first seasons, four trial soundings were made in the plowed field and a section was cut in the southern side of the mound. The trial soundings produced sherds from the Hellenistic and Persian periods; one sounding also yielded a large quantity of human and animal figurines. The deep plowing had damaged the architectural remains, but it seems probable that the figurines had been deposited in a *favissa* rather than in a building. Sherds from earlier periods were found in burned layers at the bottom of the soundings.

The site was first settled in the Middle Bronze Age I. Sherds from this period were found in an occupation stratum resting on virgin soil in the section (5 by 15 m) cut in the mound. The other occupation strata are from the Late Bronze Age (containing silos, clay ovens, and pottery), and from the Philistine period and the United Monarchy (eleventh–early tenth centuries BCE), which was the last phase of occupation at the site.

In 1964 and 1965, the excavations on the summit of the mound were expanded by some 200 sq m.

STRATUM I. Stratum I was exposed just below the surface. It comprised fragments of floors and brick walls, plastered cisterns, clay ovens, and pottery, some irregularly burnished. Decorated bowls and a flask display typical Philistine features. Other vessels—including a chalice, juglets, flasks, and

Tel Ẓippor: Philistine krater decorated with geometrical patterns, stratum II, 12th–11th centuries BCE.

Decorated chalice, stratum II, 12th–11th centuries BCE.

Bronze figurine of a seated deity, his right hand raised in benediction, stratum III, LB.

storage jars—bear no decoration. Also found in this stratum was a seal with the figure of a man holding an unidentified object in each hand. He wears a short, Egyptian-style tunic. Another find was a scarab with a figure of the god Ptaḥ seated on his throne. Stratum I came to an end at the end of the eleventh

Stone statuette of a seated ruler, stratum III, LB.

or perhaps the beginning of the tenth century BCE. The available material is inadequate to determine whether the settlement at Tel Ẓippor was Israelite with a Philistine influence, or a Philistine outpost whose material culture was in decline.

STRATUM II. Stratum II is represented by brick walls whose stone bases probably supported wooden columns, numerous cisterns, and a plaster floor that slopes down to a shallow plastered cistern. In the cistern was a complete Philistine krater. The fragments of a similar krater, as well as an intact, decorated chalice, were found on the plaster floor near the cistern. Additional sherds of kraters, bowls, a zoomorphic vessel, and other vessels were found on the floor and in the cisterns. Some of the vessels bear typically Philistine geometric decoration; others are undecorated and seem to represent the tradition of the Late Bronze Age.

STRATUM III. Stratum III was found sealed by the plaster floor of stratum II. Stratum IIIB yielded part of a floor, in which an inverted jar and a pit with stones around its mouth were sunk. On a contemporary plaster floor were three lamps, bowls, cooking pots, juglets, imported Mycenaean ware, a bronze figurine, and a stone statuette. The figurine depicts a seated god, his right hand raised in benediction and his left holding a scepter(?). The stone statuette is of an enthroned Canaanite god or king. Although the head is broken, some parts of the coiffure, done in Egyptian style, have survived. The god/king is dressed in a Syrian-style cloak and holds a lotus in his left hand; his right hand rests on his knee. The statuette is probably Canaanite. The stratum III pottery is typical of the last phase of the Late Bronze Age.

SUMMARY

The settlement at Tel Ẓippor was probably quite small at the beginning of the twelfth century BCE (stratum III), and it is not clear how it was destroyed. The next settlement, stratum II, with its abundant pottery, is ascribed to the Philistine period. This was a prosperous settlement (mid-twelfth–mid-eleventh centuries BCE). The transitional period from stratum II to stratum I—the last period in which the site was inhabited—was not marred by any violent events, and there is a clear cultural continuity. In stratum I, however, irregularly burnished vessels appear. The site was abandoned at the end of the eleventh or beginning of the tenth century BCE.

A. Biran and O. Negbi, *IEJ* 14 (1964), 284–285; 15 (1965), 255–256; 16 (1966), 160–173; id., *RB* 71 (1964), 399–400; 72 (1965), 555–556; 74 (1967), 76–77; O. Negbi, *IEJ* 14 (1964), 187–189; id., *'Atiqot* 6 (1966), 1–27; L. Y. Rahmani, *Schweizer Münzblätter* 16 (1966), 129–145; E. Stern, *PEQ* 108 (1976), 112; Weippert 1988 (Ortsregister).

AVRAHAM BIRAN

ZIQIM

IDENTIFICATION

Ziqim is about 7.5 km (4.5 mi.) southwest of Ashkelon. It is located on the bank of Naḥal Shiqma, on the *kurkar* ridge closest to the Mediterranean coast, 25 m above sea level and about 1 km (0.6 mi.) from the sea (map reference 1034.112). The wadi undercut the northern part of the site, eroding the adjacent *kurkar* ridge. Near the shore, where the wadi channel is blocked by sand, there are pools of high groundwater and spots of vegetation. The *kurkar* ridge and the eastern channel are today blocked by the Shiqma Reservoir, whose construction destroyed the southern part of the site. The hill on which the site is situated has a *kurkar* base covered with a 1.5-m-thick layer of *ḥamra*; the thin alluvial layer that overlays the *ḥamra* contains the site. The excavations were conducted on a spur about 20 m long and 5 m wide.

EXPLORATION

Numerous finds from the site and its vicinity were collected by members of Kibbutz Ziqim in the 1950s and 1960s. In 1974 and 1976, two short seasons of excavation were carried out under the direction of T. Noy, on behalf of the Israel Department of Antiquities and Museums, the Israel Museum, and the Israel Exploration Society.

EXCAVATIONS

Unbroken, clear traces of occupation were recovered only in limited areas—particularly those where there had been pits. Various installations, ashes, bones, and implements were found within the occupation level, which was remarkable for its dark color. Two or three short occupation phases could be distinguished: in the earliest phase, shallow pits were dug into the *ḥamra* soil and huts were erected in them. Small stones found in some of them that probably supported the roofing and installations. Various installations built of medium-sized stones were also uncovered. They (diameter, 20–30 cm) contained bases and other fragments of clay storage jars and hole-mouth jars. Piles of refuse—containing, inter alia, bones of fish, birds, cattle, and gazelle—were found in two shallow pits. Several flint tools, possibly from the fifth or fourth millennium, were found on the surface.

The pottery vessels are poorly preserved. They are made of a coarse, reddish clay and are very fragile. The vessels are handmade and rounded. The most common sherds include broad, flat bases of storage jars and hole-mouth jars and several fragments of small red-slipped jars. Lug and pierced handles and a small straight-sided bowl with a plain rim were also found. The poor state of preservation and the small number of artifacts prevent any detailed comparisons, but it can be assumed that the pottery dates to the early stages of the Pottery Neolithic period.

The flint-tool assemblage is covered with the light patina characteristic of sandy regions. The tools were knapped locally, as attested by the presence of cores. The major types are end scrapers, burins, blades, retouched flakes and bladelets, awls, denticulated sickle blades, large and small arrowheads, a knife made of tabular flint, and hammerstones (a perforated implement was also recovered, probably from the Chalcolithic period). Limestone bowls and various seashells were also found.

Judging from the finds in the refuse pits, the site subsisted on a varied economy, based on the hunting of medium-sized animals in the open-woodland region that in antiquity apparently extended up to the site. The inhabitants also hunted fowl and fished in the sea as well as in the freshwater pools in the high groundwater area. The nature of the plant food could not be determined because no grinding stones were found at Ziqim, as they were at various other sites on the Coastal Plain. It is doubtful whether the numerous sickle blades were used for reaping cereals. They may have been used for cutting reeds, later employed in hut building and weaving. The special conditions that prevailed on the western *kurkar* ridge—proximity to the sea and high groundwater—enabled cultivation of the adjacent channels. They may also, however, imply that Ziqim was a seasonal site that the occupants used in the summer when water was scarce elsewhere; near the coast, the groundwater would have been sufficient for drinking and herding.

It is difficult to establish a precise date for the site. Apart from a very thin Chalcolithic stratum, most of the occupation seems to belong to a single period. Based on the simple pottery and the denticulated sickle blades without pressure flaking, the site probably dates to the early stages of the Pottery Neolithic period, like the Yarmukian phase known from the Jordan Valley and from several sites on the Coastal Plain, such as the one on ha-Bashan Street in Tel Aviv.

T. Noy, *IEJ* 26 (1976), 49.

TAMAR NOY

CHRONOLOGICAL TABLES

THE PREHISTORIC-ARCHAEOLOGICAL PERIODS

Period	*Cultures*	*Ice Age in Europe*	*Geological Epoch*	*Approximate dates (BCE)*
Lower Paleolithic	Abbevillean Lower and Middle Acheulean Upper Acheulean	Mindel Mindel-Riss Riss	Middle Pleistocene (Quaternary)	1,000,000–120,000
Middle Paleolithic	Micoquian, "pre-Aurignacian" Yabrudian, Mousterian	Riss-Würm Würm I Würm II	Upper Pleistocene (Quaternary)	120,000–45,000
Upper Paleolithic	Phase I ("Emireh," "Boqer Taḥtit")	Würm III		45,000–35,000
	Phase II (Ahmarian tradition) Phase III–V (Aurignacian tradition)			35,000–18,000
Epipaleolithic (Mesolithic)	Kebaran Geometric Kebaran Natufian	Würm IV		18,000–8,300
Pre-Pottery Neolithic	Phase A Phase B Phase C	Post-glacial	Holocene	8,300–5,500
Pottery Neolithic				5,500–4,500
Chalcolithic	Early phase Ghassulian phase			4,500–3,300

THE HISTORICAL-ARCHAEOLOGICAL PERIODS

Bronze Age (Canaanite Period)

Early Bronze Age	IA–B	3300–3000 BCE
Early Bronze Age	II	3000–2700
Early Bronze Age	III	2700–2200
Middle Bronze Age	I (EB IV–Intermediate Bronze)	2200–2000
Middle Bronze Age	IIA	2000–1750
Middle Bronze Age	IIB	1750–1550
Late Bronze Age	I	1550–1400
Late Bronze Age	IIA	1400–1300
Late Bronze Age	IIB	1300–1200

Iron Age (Israelite Period)

Iron Age	IA	1200–1150
Iron Age	IB	1150–1000
Iron Age	IIA	1000–900
Iron Age	IIB	900–700
Iron Age	IIC	700–586

Babylonian and Persian Periods 586–332

Hellenistic Period

Early Hellenistic period	332–167
Late Hellenistic period	167–37

Roman and Byzantine Periods

Early Roman period	37 BCE–132 CE
(Herodian period, 37 BCE–70 CE)	
Late Roman period	132–324
Byzantine period	324–638

Early Arab to Ottoman Periods

Early Arab period (Umayyad and Abbasid)	638–1099
Crusader and Ayyubid periods	1099–1291
Late Arab period (Fatimid and Mameluke)	1291–1516
Ottoman period	1516–1917

SELECTED LIST OF KINGS

Egypt

"O" Dynasty	**Late 4th mill.**
Early Dynastic Period	
1st Dynasty	**c. 3000–2800 BCE**
2nd Dynasty	**c. 2800–2686**
Old Kingdom	
3rd Dynasty	**c. 2686–2613**
4th Dynasty	**c. 2613–2494**
Snefru, Khufu, Khafre, Menkaure (pyramid builders)	
5th Dynasty	**c. 2494–2345**
6th Dynasty	**c. 2345–2180**
Pepi I; Pepi II	
First Intermediate Period	
7th–8th Dynasties, **9th–10th Dynasties (Heracleopolis)**	**c. 2180–2100**
11th Dynasty (Thebes)	**c. 2180–2133**
Middle Kingdom	
11th Dynasty (all Egypt)	**c. 2133–1991**
12th Dynasty	**c. 1991–1786**
Amenemhet I	1991–1962
Senwosret I	1971–1928
Amenemhet II	1929–1895
Senwosret II	1897–1878
Senwosret III	1878–1843
Amenemhet III	1842–1797
Amenemhet IV	1798–1789
Sebeknefrure	1789–1786
13th–14th Dynasties	
Second Intermediate Period	
15th Dynasty (Hyksos)	**c. 1670–1570**
Salitis (Sheshi)	1670–1650
Khian	1650–1620
Apophis	1620–1580
Khamudi	1580–1570
16th–17th Dynasties	

New Kingdom	High Chronology	Low Chronology
18th Dynasty	**1570–1320**	**1550–1295**
Ahmose	1570–1546	1550–1525
Amenhotep I	1546–1526	1525–1504
Thutmose I	1525–1512	1504–1492
Thutmose II	c. 1512–1504	1492–1479
Hatshepsut	1503–1482	1479–1457
Thutmose III	1504–1450	1479–1425
Amenhotep II	1450–1425	1427–1400
Thutmose IV	1425–1417	1400–1390
Amenhotep III	1417–1379	1390–1352
Amenhotep IV (Akhenaten)	1379–1362	1352–1336
Smenkhkare	1364–1361	1338–1336
Tutankhamun	1361–1352	1336–1327
Aya	1352–1348	1327–1323
Haremhab	1348–1320	1323–1295
19th Dynasty	**1320–1200**	**1295–1186**
Ramses I	1320–1318	1295–1294
Seti I	1318–1304	1294–1279
Ramses II	1304–1237	1279–1213
Merneptah	1236–1223	1213–1203
Seti II	1216–1210	1200–1194
Siptah	1210–1205	1194–1188
Tewosret	1205–1200	1188–1186
20th Dynasty	**1200–1085**	**1186–1070**
Setnakht	1200–1198	1186–1184
Ramses III	1198–1166	1184–1153
Ramses IV–XI	1166–1085	1153–1070

End of New Kingdom

21st Dynasty	**1085–935**	Osorkon II	914–874
22nd Dynasty	**935–730**	**23rd Dynasty**	**817–740**
Shishak I	935–914	**24th Dynasty**	**730–709**

Late Period

25th Dynasty (Nubian or Ethiopian)	**750–656**	Psamtik II	595–589
Shabaka	716–695	Psamtik III	526–525
Taharka	689–664	**27th Dynasty (Persian)**	**525–404**
26th Dynasty	**664–525**	**28th Dynasty**	**404–399**
Psamtik I	664–610	**29th Dynasty**	**399–380**
Necho II	610–595	**30th Dynasty**	**380–343**

Assyria

Shalmaneser I	1274–1245 BCE
Tiglath-pileser I	1115–1077
Ashurnasirpal I	1050–1032
Shalmaneser II	1031–1020
Tiglath-pileser II	967–935
Adadnirari II	911–891
Ashurnasirpal II	883–859
Shalmaneser III	858–824
Adadnirari III	810–783
Shalmaneser IV	782–772
Tiglath-pileser III	744–727
Shalmaneser V	726–722
Sargon II	721–705
Sennacherib	704–681
Esarhaddon	680–669
Ashurbanipal	668–627

Neo-Babylonian Kingdom

Nabopolassar	625–605 BCE
Nebuchadnezzar II	604–562
Amel-Marduk	561–560
Nergal Sarussur	559–556
Nabunaid	555–539

Persia (Achaemenids)

Cyrus II	559–529 BCE
Cambyses II	528–523
Darius I	522–486
Xerxes	485–465
Artaxerxes I	464–424
Darius II	423–405
Artaxerxes II	404–359
Artaxerxes III	358–338
Arses (Xerxes II)	338–335
Darius III	335–331

The Kings of Judah and Israel

THE UNITED MONARCHY

Saul	c. 1020–1004 BCE
David	1004–965
Solomon	965–928

JUDAH

Rehoboam	928–911
Abijam	911–908
Asa	908–867
Jehoshaphat	867–846
Jehoram	846–843
Ahaziah	843–842
Athaliah	842–836
Joash	836–798
Amaziah	798–769
Uzziah	769–733
Jotham	758–743
Ahaz	733–727
Hezekiah	727–698
Manasseh	698–642
Amon	641–640
Josiah	639–609
Jehoahaz	609
Jehoiakim	608–598
Jehoiachin	597
Zedekiah	596–586

ISRAEL

Jeroboam	928–907
Nadab	907–906
Baasha	906–883
Elah	883–882
Zimri	882
Tibni	882–878
Omri	882–871
Ahab	871–852
Ahaziah	852–851
Jehoram	851–842
Jehu	842–814
Jehoahaz	814–800
Jehoash	800–784
Jeroboam	784–748
Zechariah	748/747
Shallum	748/747
Menahem	747–737
Pekahiah	737–735
Pekah	735–733
Hoshea	733–724

Nabatean Kings

Aretas I	c. 168 BCE
Aretas II	c. 110–100
Obodas I	c. 93
Rabbel I	c. 90–85(?)
Aretas III	c. 85–62
Obodas II	62–c. 57
Malichus I	c. 56–28
Obodas III	c. 28–9
Aretas IV	c. 9 BCE–40 CE
Malichus II	40–70
Rabbel II	70/71–106

The Hasmoneans

Jonathan	152–142 BCE
Simeon	142–134
John Hyrcanus	134–104
Aristobulus	104–103
Alexander Jannaeus	103–76
Salome Alexandra	76–67
Aristobulus II	67–63
Hyrcanus II	63–40
Matthias Antigonus	40–37

The Herodians

Herod (the Great)	37–4 BCE
Archelaus	4 BCE–6 CE
Herod Antipas	4 BCE–39 CE
Philip	4 BCE–34 CE
Herod Agrippa I	37–44 CE
Agrippa II	53–100(?)

The Procurators

Coponius	c. 6–9 CE
Marcus Ambibulus	9–12
Annius Rufus	12–15
Valerius Gratus	15–26
Pontius Pilate	26–36
Marcellus	36–37
Cuspius Fadus	44–46
Tiberius Alexander	46–48
Ventidius Cumanus	48–52
Antonius Felix	52–60
Porcius Festus	60–62
Albinus	62–64
Gessius Florus	64–66

The Seleucids

Seleucus I Nicator	311–280 BCE
Antiochus I Soter	280–261
Antiochus II Theos	261–246
Seleucus II Callinicus	246–225
Seleucus III Soter	225–223
Antiochus III Megas (the Great)	223–187
Seleucus IV Philopator	187–175
Antiochus IV Epiphanes	175–164
Antiochus V Eupator	163–162
Demetrius I Soter	162–150
Alexander Balas	150–145
Demetrius II Nicator	145–140
Antiochus VI Epiphanes	145–142
Tryphon	142–138
Antiochus VII Sidetes	138–129
Demetrius II Nicator (restored)	129–125
Alexander Zebinas	128–122
Cleopatra Thea	126
Cleopatra Thea and Antiochus VIII Grypus	125–121
Seleucus V	125
Antiochus VII Grypus	121–113, 111–96
Antiochus IX Cyzicenus	113–95
Seleucus VI Epiphanes Nicator	96–95
Demetrius III Philopator	95–88
Antiochus X Eusebes	95–83
Antiochus XI Philadelphus	94
Philip I Philadelphus	94–83
Antiochus XII Dionysus	87–84
Antiochus XIII Asiaticus	69–64
Philip II	67–65

The Ptolemies

Ptolemy I Soter	304–282 BCE
Ptolemy II Philadelphus	285–246
Ptolemy III Euergetes	246–221
Ptolemy IV Philopator	221–204
Ptolemy V Epiphanes	204–180
Ptolemy VI Philometer	180–145
Ptolemy VII Neos Philopator	145–144
Ptolemy VIII Euergetes II	145–116
Ptolemy IX Soter II (Lathyros)	116–107
Ptolemy X Alexander I	107–88
Ptolemy IX Soter II (restored)	88–81
Ptolemy XI Alexander II	80
Ptolemy XII Neos Dionysos	80–51
Cleopatra VII Philopator	51–30
Ptolemy XIII	51–47
Ptolemy XIV	47–44
Ptolemy XV	44–30

Overlapping dates usually indicate coregencies.

Roman Emperors

Augustus	27 BCE–14 CE
Tiberius	14–37 CE
Gaius (Caligula)	37–41
Claudius	41–54
Nero	54–68
Galba	68–69
Otho	69
Vitellius	69
Vespasian	69–79
Titus	79–81
Domitian	81–96
Nerva	96–98
Trajan	98–117
Hadrian	117–138
Antoninus Pius	138–161
Lucius Verus	161–169
Marcus Aurelius	161–180
Commodus	180–192
Pertinax	193
Didius Julianus	193
Pescennius Niger	193–194
Clodius Albinus	193–197
Septimius Severus	193–211
Geta	211–212
Caracalla	211–217
Macrinus	217–218
Diadumenianus	218
Elagabalus	218–222
Severus Alexander	222–235
Maximinus	235–238
Gordian I–II	238
Pupienus and Balbinus	238
Gordian III	238–244
Philip Senior	244–249
Philip Junior	247–249
Trajanus Decius	249–251
Trebonianus Gallus	251–253
Volusian	251–253
Aemilianus	253
Valerian	253–260
Gallienus	253–268
Claudius Gothicus	268–270
Quintilius	270
Aurelian	270–275
Tacitus	275–276
Annius Florianus	276
Probus	276–282
Carus	282–283

Division between East and West begins in 283.

WEST				EAST	
				Numerianus	283–284
Carinus	283–285			Diocletian	284–305
Maximianus Herculius	286–305			Galerius	305–311
Constantius I Chlorus	305–306				
Severus	306–307			Maximinus II	311–313
[1]Maxentius	306–312				
		[2]Licinius	308–324		
		[3]Constantine the Great	306–337		
		[4]Constantius II	337–361		
[5]Constans	337–350				
Constantine II	337–340				
Magnentius	350–353				
Vetranio	350				
Nepotianus	350	Julian	361–363		
		Jovian	363–364		
Valentinian I	364–375			Valens	364–378
Gratian	367–383				
Valentinian II	375–392			Theodosius I	379–395
[6]Maximus	383–388				
Eugenius	392–394				

1 Part of West (Italy and Africa)
2 Augustus of part of West (Illyricum), then Augustus of East (313–324)
3 Part of West (Spain, France, Britain [306–313]); all of West (313–324); all the empire (324–337)
4 East up until 353, then all the empire
5 Part of West (Italy and Africa); subject to Constantine II until 340, then all of West
6 Spain, France, and Britain

Overlapping dates usually indicate coregencies.

Byzantine Emperors

WEST		EAST	
Honorius	395–423	Arcadius	395–408
Constantius III	421	Theodosius II	408–450
Iohannes	423–425	Marcian	450–457
Valentinian III	425–455	Leo I	457–474
Avitus	455–456	Leo II	474
Majorian	457–461	Zeno	474–491
Livius Severus	461–465	Anastasius I	491–518
Anthemius	467–472	Justin I	518–527
Olybrius	472	Justinian I	527–565
Glycerius	473–474	Justin II	565–578
Julius Nepos	474–475	Tiberius II	578–582
Romulus Augustulus	475–476	Mauricius	582–602
		Phocas	602–610
		Heraclius	610–641
		Constans II	641–668
		Constantine IV	668–685
		Justinian II	685–695
		Leontius	695–698
		Tiberius III	698–705
		Justinian III	705–711

CHRONOLOGICAL CHART OF THE ALPHABET

Upper chart

Proto-Canaanite c. 1500 BCE	South Semitic — Ancient South Arabic 1st mill. BCE	South Semitic — Ethiopian	Proto-Canaanite 13th cent. BCE	Aramaic (?) (Tell Fakhariya) c. 1000 BCE(?)	Greek — Ancient 8th–7th cent. BCE	Greek — Classic	Latin	Phoenician c. 1000 BCE	Phoenician 8th–7th cent. BCE	Phoenician c. 800 BCE	Phoenician 7th–1st cent. BCE	Phoenician — New Punic	Hebrew c. 1000 BCE	Hebrew (Moab.) c. 850 BCE	Hebrew 7th cent. BCE	Hebrew 6th cent. BCE	Hebrew 2nd cent. BCE	Samaritan 13th cent. CE
[aleph forms]	[glyph]	[glyph]	[glyph]	[glyph]	[glyph]	A	A	[glyph]	[glyph]	[glyph]	[glyph]	[glyph]	[glyph]	[glyph]	[glyph]	[glyph]	[glyph]	[glyph]
[beth]	[glyph]	[glyph]	[glyph]	[glyph]	[glyph]	B	B	[glyph]	[glyph]	[glyph]	[glyph]	[glyph]	[glyph]	[glyph]	[glyph]	[glyph]	[glyph]	[glyph]
[gimel]	[glyph]	[glyph]	[glyph]	[glyph]	[glyph] Γ	C G	[glyph]	[glyph]	[glyph]	[glyph]	[glyph]	[glyph]	[glyph]	[glyph]	[glyph]	[glyph]	[glyph]	[glyph]
[daleth]	[glyph]	[glyph]	[glyph]	[glyph]	[glyph] Δ	D	[glyph]	[glyph]	[glyph]	[glyph]	[glyph]	[glyph]	[glyph]	[glyph]	[glyph]	[glyph]	[glyph]	[glyph]
[he]	[glyph]	[glyph]	[glyph]	[glyph]	[glyph] E	E	[glyph]	[glyph]	[glyph]	[glyph]	[glyph]	[glyph]	[glyph]	[glyph]	[glyph]	[glyph]	[glyph]	[glyph]
[waw]	[glyph]	[glyph]	[glyph]	[glyph]	[glyph] Υ	F U V Y W	[glyph]	[glyph]	[glyph]	[glyph]	[glyph]	[glyph]	[glyph]	[glyph]	[glyph]	[glyph]	[glyph]	[glyph]
[zayin]	[glyph]	[glyph]	[glyph]	[glyph]	I	Z	Z	[glyph]	[glyph]	[glyph]	[glyph]	[glyph]	[glyph]	[glyph]	[glyph]	[glyph]	[glyph]	[glyph]
[heth]	[glyph]	[glyph]	[glyph]	[glyph]	H	H	H	[glyph]	[glyph]	[glyph]	[glyph]	[glyph]	[glyph]	[glyph]	[glyph]	[glyph]	[glyph]	[glyph]
[teth]	[glyph]	[glyph]	[glyph]	[glyph]	[glyph] Θ		[glyph]	[glyph]	[glyph]	[glyph]	[glyph]	[glyph]	[glyph]	[glyph]	[glyph]	[glyph]	[glyph]	[glyph]
[yod]	[glyph]	[glyph]	[glyph]	[glyph]	[glyph] I	I J	[glyph]	[glyph]	[glyph]	[glyph]	[glyph]	[glyph]	[glyph]	[glyph]	[glyph]	[glyph]	[glyph]	[glyph]
[kaph]	[glyph]	[glyph]	[glyph]	[glyph]	K	K	[glyph]	[glyph]	[glyph]	[glyph]	[glyph]	[glyph]	[glyph]	[glyph]	[glyph]	[glyph]	[glyph]	[glyph]
[lamed]	[glyph]	[glyph]	[glyph]	[glyph]	Λ	L	[glyph]	[glyph]	[glyph]	[glyph]	[glyph]	[glyph]	[glyph]	[glyph]	[glyph]	[glyph]	[glyph]	[glyph]
[mem]	[glyph]	[glyph]	[glyph]	[glyph]	M	M	[glyph]	[glyph]	[glyph]	[glyph]	[glyph]	[glyph]	[glyph]	[glyph]	[glyph]	[glyph]	[glyph]	[glyph]
[nun]	[glyph]	[glyph]	[glyph]	[glyph]	[glyph]	N	[glyph]	[glyph]	[glyph]	[glyph]	[glyph]	[glyph]	[glyph]	[glyph]	[glyph]	[glyph]	[glyph]	[glyph]
[samekh]	[glyph]	[glyph]	[glyph]	[glyph]	[glyph] Ξ	X	[glyph]	[glyph]	[glyph]	[glyph]	[glyph]	[glyph]	[glyph]	[glyph]	[glyph]	[glyph]	[glyph]	[glyph]
[ayin]	[glyph]	[glyph]	[glyph]	[glyph]	O	O	[glyph]	[glyph]	[glyph]	[glyph]	[glyph]	[glyph]	[glyph]	[glyph]	[glyph]	[glyph]	[glyph]	[glyph]
[pe]	[glyph]	[glyph]	[glyph]	[glyph]	Π	P	[glyph]	[glyph]	[glyph]	[glyph]	[glyph]	[glyph]	[glyph]	[glyph]	[glyph]	[glyph]	[glyph]	[glyph]
[tsade]	[glyph]	[glyph]	[glyph]	[glyph]	M		[glyph]	[glyph]	[glyph]	[glyph]	[glyph]	[glyph]	[glyph]	[glyph]	[glyph]	[glyph]	[glyph]	[glyph]
[qoph]	[glyph]	[glyph]	[glyph]	[glyph]	[glyph] Q	Q	[glyph]	[glyph]	[glyph]	[glyph]	[glyph]	[glyph]	[glyph]	[glyph]	[glyph]	[glyph]	[glyph]	[glyph]
[resh]	[glyph]	[glyph]	[glyph]	[glyph]	[glyph] P	R	[glyph]	[glyph]	[glyph]	[glyph]	[glyph]	[glyph]	[glyph]	[glyph]	[glyph]	[glyph]	[glyph]	[glyph]
[shin]	[glyph]	[glyph] (š)	[glyph]	[glyph]	[glyph] Σ	S	[glyph]	[glyph]	[glyph]	[glyph]	[glyph]	[glyph]	[glyph]	[glyph]	[glyph]	[glyph]	[glyph]	[glyph]
[taw]	[glyph]	[glyph]	[glyph]	[glyph]	T	T	[glyph]	[glyph]	[glyph]	[glyph]	[glyph]	[glyph]	[glyph]	[glyph]	[glyph]	[glyph]	[glyph]	[glyph]

Lower chart

Aramaic (Assyria) 7th cent. BCE	Aramaic (Lapidary) 4th cent. BCE	Aramaic 5th–4th cent. BCE	Aramaic 3rd cent. BCE	"Jewish" c. 100 BCE	"Jewish" "Herodian" 1st cent. BCE	"Jewish" Modern Hebrew	Nabatean c. 100 BCE	Nabatean 1st cent. BCE	Nabatean 1st cent. CE	Classical Arabic	Palmyrene 2nd cent. CE	Syriac 5th cent. CE	Syriac Estrangelo
[glyph]	[glyph]	[glyph]	[glyph]	[glyph]	[glyph]	א	[glyph]	[glyph]	[glyph]	ا	[glyph]	[glyph]	[glyph]
[glyph]	[glyph]	[glyph]	[glyph]	[glyph]	[glyph]	ב	[glyph]	[glyph]	[glyph]	ب ـﺒ	[glyph]	[glyph]	[glyph]
[glyph]	[glyph]	[glyph]	[glyph]	[glyph]	[glyph]	ג	[glyph]	[glyph]	[glyph]	ج ج	[glyph]	[glyph]	[glyph]
[glyph]	[glyph]	[glyph]	[glyph]	[glyph]	[glyph]	ד	[glyph]	[glyph]	[glyph]	د ذ	[glyph]	[glyph]	[glyph]
[glyph]	[glyph]	[glyph]	[glyph]	[glyph]	[glyph]	ה	[glyph]	[glyph]	[glyph]	هـ ه ة	[glyph]	[glyph]	[glyph]
[glyph]	[glyph]	[glyph]	[glyph]	[glyph]	[glyph]	ו	[glyph]	[glyph]	[glyph]	و	[glyph]	[glyph]	[glyph]
[glyph]	[glyph]	[glyph]	[glyph]	[glyph]	[glyph]	ז		[glyph]	[glyph]	ز	[glyph]	[glyph]	[glyph]
[glyph]	[glyph]	[glyph]	[glyph]	[glyph]	[glyph]	ח	[glyph]	[glyph]	[glyph]	ح خ ح	[glyph]	[glyph]	[glyph]
[glyph]	[glyph]	[glyph]	[glyph]	[glyph]	[glyph]	ט	[glyph]	[glyph]	[glyph]	ط ظ	[glyph]	[glyph]	[glyph]
[glyph]	[glyph]	[glyph]	[glyph]	[glyph]	[glyph]	י	[glyph]	[glyph]	[glyph]	ي ـيـ	[glyph]	[glyph]	[glyph]
[glyph]	[glyph]	[glyph]	[glyph]	[glyph]	[glyph]	כך	[glyph]	[glyph]	[glyph]	ك	[glyph]	[glyph]	[glyph]
[glyph]	[glyph]	[glyph]	[glyph]	[glyph]	[glyph]	ל	[glyph]	[glyph]	[glyph]	ل	[glyph]	[glyph]	[glyph]
[glyph]	[glyph]	[glyph]	[glyph]	[glyph]	[glyph]	מם	[glyph]	[glyph]	[glyph]	م م	[glyph]	[glyph]	[glyph]
[glyph]	[glyph]	[glyph]	[glyph]	[glyph]	[glyph]	נן	[glyph]	[glyph]	[glyph]	ن ـنـ	[glyph]	[glyph]	[glyph]
[glyph]	[glyph]	[glyph]	[glyph]	[glyph]	[glyph]	ס	[glyph]	[glyph]	[glyph]		[glyph]	[glyph]	[glyph]
[glyph]	[glyph]	[glyph]	[glyph]	[glyph]	[glyph]	ע	[glyph]	[glyph]	[glyph]	ع ع ع ع	[glyph]	[glyph]	[glyph]
[glyph]	[glyph]	[glyph]	[glyph]	[glyph]	[glyph]	פף	[glyph]	[glyph]	[glyph]	ف ف	[glyph]	[glyph]	[glyph]
[glyph]	[glyph]	[glyph]	[glyph]	[glyph]	[glyph]	צץ	[glyph]	[glyph]	[glyph]	ص ض ص ض	[glyph]	[glyph]	[glyph]
[glyph]	[glyph]	[glyph]	[glyph]	[glyph]	[glyph]	ק	[glyph]	[glyph]	[glyph]	ق ق	[glyph]	[glyph]	[glyph]
[glyph]	[glyph]	[glyph]	[glyph]	[glyph]	[glyph]	ר	[glyph]	[glyph]	[glyph]	ر	[glyph]	[glyph]	[glyph]
[glyph]	[glyph]	[glyph]	[glyph]	[glyph]	[glyph]	ש	[glyph]	[glyph]	[glyph]	س سـ ش شـ	[glyph]	[glyph]	[glyph]
[glyph]	[glyph]	[glyph]	[glyph]	[glyph]	[glyph]	ת	[glyph]	[glyph]	[glyph]	ت ث ت ث	[glyph]	[glyph]	[glyph]

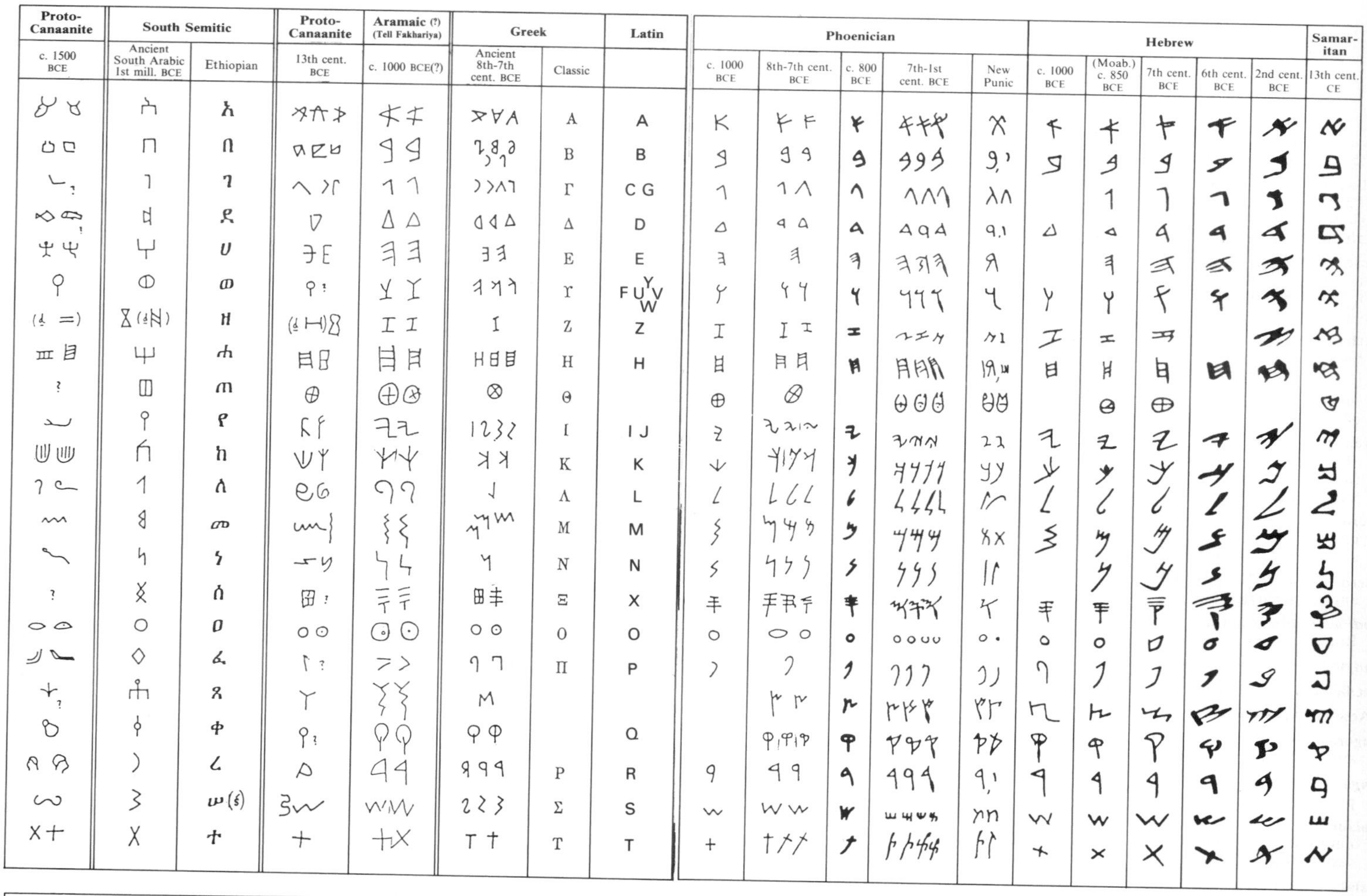

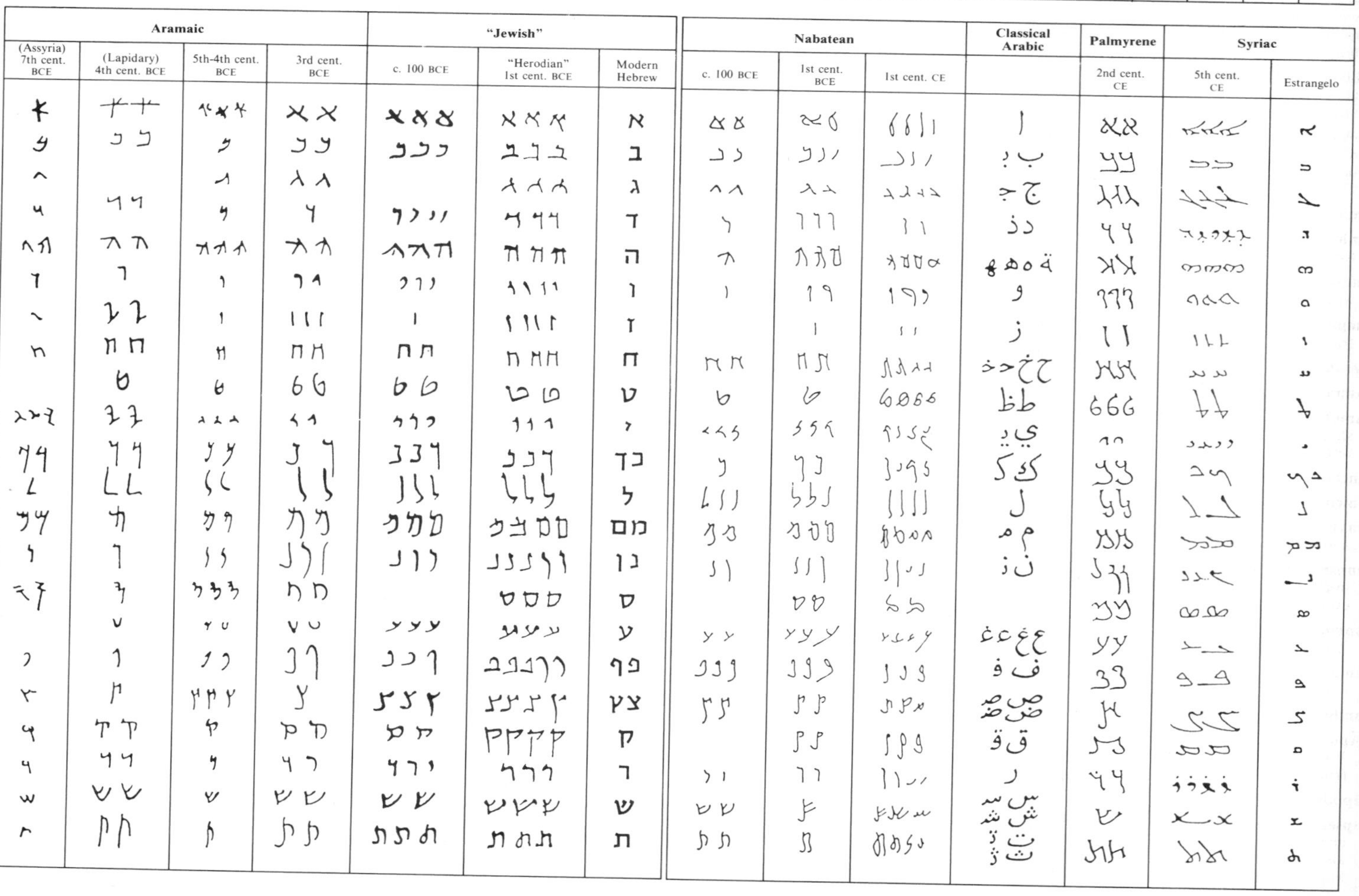

GLOSSARY

abacus seat forming the uppermost member or division of the capital on a column

Abydos ware Early Bronze Age II pottery of Syro-Palestinian origin, mainly "metallic" jugs and jars; red slipped and burnished or painted with geometric motifs; also found in First and Second Dynasty tombs in Egypt

acanthus ornamentation suggesting the leaves of the acanthus, a prickly Mediterranean herb; a common motif in Greco-Roman and Byzantine art and architecture (see Corinthian order)

Achaemenid Persian ruling dynasty from the reign of Cyrus the Great (559 BCE) to the overthrow of Darius III (331 BCE)

Acheulean Lower Paleolithic culture, characterized by bifacial tools such as hand axes and cleavers

Achzib ware part of the Phoenician red slip pottery group of Iron Age II; mainly jugs with trefoil or "mushroom" rims, red slipped and highly burnished; the types spread to many Phoenician colonies in the Mediterranean Basin

acropolis fortified upper part of a city (see also citadel), generally containing the religious, political, and/or administrative center

acroterium(-ia) ornamental finial at the apex or outer angles of a roof

aditus maximus(-i) side entrance to the orchestra in a Roman theater (cf. parodos)

adyton inner sanctuary of a temple

aedicula(-ae) architectural niche; small shrine

Aesclepius (Esclepius) Greek and Roman god of medicine

agora place of assembly, marketplace; a city's economic and civic center (see also forum)

agoranomos Greek magistrate who oversaw the sale of provisions and the weights in the marketplace

alabaster variety of gypsum, usually white or translucent but sometimes other shades, used in antiquity to produce vessels, statues, and other objects

alabastron(-a) elongated bottle, rounded at the bottom, with a flattened lip and a narrow orifice, used in antiquity to hold oils and perfumes, named after Egyptian alabaster bottles of that shape

alluvial soil relatively "young" detrital material that accumulated in the Holocene Age, covering older rocks; any detrital material

el-Amarna letters Akkadian cuneiform clay tablets discovered mainly at el-Amarna in Egypt; correspondence between Amenhotep III and Amenhotep IV and kings in Canaan and other kingdoms in the region (14th cent. BCE)

ambo freestanding pulpit in a church

ambulatory a passageway around the sanctuary, nave, or focal point of a church

amphitheater Roman oval building used for spectacles, with seating facing inward onto a central area (arena)

amphora(-ae) two-handled ceramic jar, usually used to transport liquids or grain

amphoriskos(-oi) small glass or ceramic amphora

Amratian see Naqada

Amuq point Pre-Pottery Neolithic B elongated flint blade, shaped into an oval point partly or completely by pressure retouch

anchorites hermits

aniconic of non-figurative representation or decoration

ankh Egyptian logogram for "life," shaped like a cross with a loop instead of an upper vertical arm

annals lists of officials or of important events arranged in chronological order; in Assyria and Babylon, a list of events arranged in yearly sequence of a king's reign

annona militaris rations, sometimes commuted into money, issued to the Roman army

anta(-ae) quadrangular pilaster engaged at the front end of a lateral wall

anthropomorphic human in form or characteristics

Apocrypha books included in the Septuagint (Greek) and Vulgate (Latin) versions of the Hebrew Bible but excluded from the Jewish and Protestant canons

apodyterium(-ia) changing room in a Roman bath

apse, apsidal semicircular, half-vaulted niche at the narrow end(s) of a basilica or at the eastern end of a church; also used to designate features of similar shape in other buildings

Arabah desert region in the Rift Valley between the Dead Sea and the Gulf of Elath/'Aqaba; in the biblical period, also denoted the valley north of the Dead Sea (Jericho)

Arad house type of broadhouse (Early Bronze Age II), public or private, often with benches along the walls, a stone base for a wooden pillar to support a flat roof, and a door in one of the long walls

Arad letters 7th–6th cent. BCE Hebrew ostraca discovered at Arad, mostly belonging to the archive of Eliashib, commander of the Arad citadel, dealing mainly with food distribution and military matters

Archaic Greek art or architecture of the preclassical period (7th cent.–c. 480 BCE)

architrave stone or timber horizontal beam above an entrance or spanning the interval between two columns or piers

archon city magistrate

arcosolium(-ia) arched recess for burial

Artemis Greek virgin huntress, moon goddess (equivalent of Roman goddess Diana)

artifact any material object altered by human intervention for some purpose: a stone or metal knife, clay formed and fired to a figurine, coin, etc.

aryballos(-oi) small, usually round Greek flask with flattened lip

Ashdoda figurine Philistine schematic figurine consisting of a female body merging into a four-legged throne (only complete example found at Ashdod)

Ashdod ware pottery characteristic of sites in Philistia mainly in the Iron Age II; red slipped, burnished, and decorated with black and sometimes painted lines

Asherah in this work, Canaanite/Phoenician goddess; cultic post at high places (*bamot*)

ashlar square or rectangular hewn stone laid in horizontal courses

assemblage collection of archaeological finds (e.g., pottery, stone implements) found in one stratigraphical context

Astarte Canaanite/Phoenician fertility and love goddess; identified with the Greek goddess Aphrodite (equivalent of biblical Ashtoreth)

astragal a small, convex anklebone tossed like a die

astragalus(-i) narrow, convex molding in the form of beading

atrium forecourt of a Christian church; central court in a Roman house

attic upper horizontal element above a cornice

Attic pottery plain, black lustrous vessels or figurative vessels (cf. black-figure, red-figure); produced in Attica on mainland Greece and exported to the east mainly in the 5th and 4th cent. BCE

auxilia auxiliary troops of non-Roman citizens in the Roman army

awl pointed instrument (of flint, bone, or metal) used to mark surfaces or pierce holes

Ayyubid Muslim dynasty founded in 1171; separate branches flourished in Syria, Palestine, Mesopotamia, and S. Arabia until the 13th cent.

Ba'al a generic term meaning "lord" or "master"; any of numerous Canaanite/Phoenician chief local male deities (e.g., Ba'al Hamon, Ba'al Zaphon)

Ba'alath Canaanite/Phoenician goddess (literally, "mistress")

Babylonian Exile dispersion of the residents of Judah to Babylonia, in Mesopotamia, following the conquest by King Nebuchadnezzar and the destruction of the First Temple in Jerusalem in 586 BCE

Badarian fifth millennium Neolithic culture in the Nile Valley

baetyl stone stela or column thought sacred or worshipped as divine in origin

baldachin domed or pedimental canopy supported on slender columns, usually over the altar table in a church

balk vertical face of the wall of soil left around a trench or between squares in an excavation (usually 0.5–1 m wide)

ballista ancient military engine used to hurl large stone missiles

***bamah(-ot)* (Heb.)** cultic high place; cultic platform within a sanctuary

band slip see grainwash technique

baraita traditional Jewish interpretation of biblical law not included in the Mishnah

barbican outer fortification or tower, often erected over a gate

Bar-Kokhba leader of the Second Jewish Revolt against Rome (132–135 CE)

base-ring ware Late Cypriot I–II handmade pottery, characterized by thin, dark metallic ware with a shiny surface and plastic or painted (white) decoration; mainly carinated bowls, jugs, juglets, and zoomorphic vessels; one of the most frequent exports to the mainland in the Late Bronze Age (cf. *bilbil*)

basilica elongated, rectangular building with double (or more) internal colonnades and often one or two semicircular ends (apses); church with a nave and lateral colonnaded aisles

basilica discoperta unroofed church

bedrock in excavations, solid rock or natural soil underlying the artificial deposits

beer jug Iron Age I (mainly Philistine) ceramic vessel with a perforated spout to filter its liquid contents

bema raised platform in a synagogue or church where the liturgy is performed

beqa' ancient Judean weight, probably half a shekel (cf. shekel weight)

Bes ancient Egyptian dwarf god of music and dancing and the protector of women in childbirth

***beth midrash* (Heb.)** Jewish house of study; often part of early synagogues

bichrome ware (MB IIC/LB I) Middle Bronze Age IIC and Late Bronze Age I pottery group, characterized by geometric and faunal designs in black and red, of both Cypriot and Syro/Canaanite traits and provenance

bichrome ware (Iron Age) Phoenician pottery group in vogue mainly from the 11th–9th cent. BCE; mostly globular flasks, jugs, and bowls, decorated with black, red, and sometimes white concentric circles

biconical vessel vessel in the shape of two cone-shaped pieces that share a base

bifaces stone artifacts flaked on both upper (dorsal) and lower (ventral) surfaces

bilbil jug of Late Cypriot base-ring ware, decorated with painted (white) or plastic decoration and frequently exported

black-figure Greek style of pottery painting in which black silhouette figures are portrayed on the natural orange clay of the vessel and decorated with incisions and added color; produced mainly in Athens at the end of the 7th and the 6th cent. BCE and exported to the Levant in the Persian period (cf. red-figure)

black-on-red ware see Cypro-Phoenician ware

blade flint flake at least twice as long as it is wide

bladelet smaller version of a blade (less than 5 cm long and 1 cm wide)

boss untrimmed projecting face of a stone with drafted or squared margins

boule legislative council in a Greek polis

bouleuterion council building in a Greek polis

BP before present (standardized at 1950 CE)

breccia fossilized cave sediments

broadhouse/broadroom rectangular house or room with an entrance in one of the long walls

bucchero ware mainly jugs with vertically fluted/ribbed bodies, usually black slipped (in this work, referring mainly to Late Cypriot vessels)

bucranium(-ia) ornament consisting of one or more bull heads or skulls

bulla(-ae) seal impression stamped on a lump of clay or other plastic material, used in antiquity to seal documents

burin flint tool used for engraving

burnish polishing the leather-hard surface of a pottery vessel, before firing, with a hard tool to seal the surface or for aesthetic purposes; done by hand (hand burnish or irregular burnish) or on the potter's wheel (wheel burnish, ring burnish), creating a lustrous surface

Byblos point Pre-Pottery Neolithic B point made on a flint blade, with rounded shoulders and a tang only slightly narrower than the main body; shaped partly or completely by pressure retouch

Byzantine Empire Eastern Roman Empire, 4th–7th cent.

caldarium(-ia) hot room in a Roman bath

Canaanean/Canaanite blade Early Bronze Age flint blade

cantharus(-i) Greek deep cup with a high stem and loop-shaped handles that rise above the rim

capital upper member of a column, pier, or pilaster

caravanserai quadrangular inn with inner court where caravans are accommodated (see also khan)

carbon-14 dating technique in which the degree of disintegration of the carbon-14 content (one of the essential elements of all organic matter) is measured to determine the date of an artifact

cardo one of two main streets in a Roman city plan, running north–south and intersecting at right angles with the east–west street (see *decumanus*)

carinated keeled

cartouche oval or oblong ornament with the hieroglyphic names and titles of an Egyptian king

casemate wall double fortification wall with partitioned compartments, sometimes used for storage or dwellings

castellum rectangular fortress of the Roman army

castrum Roman fortified camp

cathedra bishop's official seat in a church

cavea spectators' section in a theater or amphitheater

cella central chamber of a sanctuary or temple.where the image of the deity was often placed

cenobite member of a monastic community

cenotaph empty tomb or monument erected in honor of someone buried elsewhere

chalice drinking or offering cup; eucharistic cup

chiton basic tuniclike garment worn in ancient Greece

chocolate-on-white ware Middle Bronze Age IIC and Late Bronze Age I northern pottery group, characterized mainly by geometric motifs painted in brown on a thick white slip

chopping tools chunks of flint modified by several blows to produce a cutting edge; typical of Lower Paleolithic industries

circus long, narrow arena, curved at one end, for chariot racing, with seating arrangements for the spectators

cist grave boxlike burial chamber lined with stone or brick

citadel fortress commanding a city at its highest point (see also acropolis)

city-state autonomous political unit consisting of a main city, its satellite towns and villages, and the surrounding territory

cleaver bifacial flaked stone artifact with a blunt working edge (see also hand ax)

clerestory upper row of windows lighting the nave of a basilica, above the inner colonnades

codex manuscript volume, especially of the Bible; book of laws in the Byzantine period

coenobium monastery where monks live a communal life

collared-rim jar/pithos large jar of the late Late Bronze Age, mainly Iron Age I (at some sites also early Iron Age II), with ridge under the neck, once thought to be indicative of Israelite settlements only

colluvium rock detritus and soil accumulations at the foot of a slope

colonia status granted to a town outside Roman territory, either inhabited by Roman (or Latin) citizens or by those having special relations with the Roman state; the colonial status had various gradations, each involving different privileges

colonnette small column

columbarium(-ia) cave or structure lined with rows of small triangular niches; generally thought to have been used for storing the ashes of cremated bones, or for breeding doves

comes honorary title, sometimes implying tenure of office in the state administration, in the early Byzantine Empire

corbeil a sculpted basket of fruit or flowers found in architectural decoration

corbel stone bracket projecting from a wall, usually for supporting stone slabs or sculpture

corbeled arch/vault arch or vault constructed with successive horizontal stone courses projecting farther inward as they rise on each side of the opening, until meeting in the middle

cordiform heart-shaped

core in ceramics, central, often dark portion of a sherd in cross section; in stone tools, the original chunk or pebble from which flakes and blades are struck off

Corinthian order most elaborate of the three Greek orders of architecture, characterized by use of bell-shaped capitals decorated with acanthus leaves, stems, and volutes

cornet Chalcolithic V-shaped beaker

cornice upper member of a classical entablature (see also entablature)

corvée forced labor for royal projects

cothon dry dock

course line of laid bricks or stones

cubit biblical measure of length (*ama*), equivalent to c. 18 in. (44.65 cm)

cuneiform script composed of wedge-shaped strokes made with a stylus on soft clay, originating in fourth millennium Mesopotamia; used to write several languages: Sumerian, Akkadian, Hurrian, Urartian, Hittite, Elamite, and Ugaritic

cuneus(-ei) wedge-shaped blocks of seating, divided by radiating passages (*scalaria*) in a theater, amphitheater, or circus

cupmark depression, usually artificial, found in rocks

cursive rapid, handwritten form of a script

cylinder seal cylinder (usually of stone) carved with figures, designs, or writing; when the seal is rolled onto a soft substance, a continuous band of relief is imprinted; a typical Mesopotamian object, usually pierced for suspension

cyma form of decorative, wavy molding

cyma recta double, wavy molding, concave above, convex below

cyma reversa double, wavy molding, convex above, concave below

Cypro-Phoenician ware (black-on-red ware) pottery vessels, mainly bowls, *amphoriskoi*, and juglets, decorated with parallel lines, concentric circles, and occasionally other motifs, painted in black on a bright red polished background, characteristic of mainland and Cypriot sites from Iron Age II; Phoenician, Cypriot, and/or Cilician provenance under debate

dado lower panel of a wall or part of a column pedestal

dark-faced burnished ware dark slipped and burnished pottery typical of the Wadi Rabah culture (Late Neolithic/Chalcolithic periods); also known in Syria

debitage items removed while flaking a stone core; some are waste and others are used as blanks for tools

Decapolis loose confederation of ten commerce-oriented Hellenized cities in N. Transjordan, N. Palestine, and S. Syria, 2nd cent. BCE

decastyle consisting of ten columns

decumanus(-i) one of two main streets in a Roman city plan, running east–west (see also *cardo*)

***deir* (Arab.)** monastery

denarius(-i) silver coin of the Roman Empire

dentils teethlike row of small rectangular blocks under a cornice

diaconicon storage room in Byzantine churches

Diadochi the generals among whom Alexander the Great's conquests were divided

diazoma passage in a Greek theater dividing the upper (*cavea summa*) and lower (*cavea ima*) rows of seats

diglyph block with two grooves set between metopes in a Doric frieze

Dionysus Greek god associated with wine (equivalent of Roman god Bacchus)

Dioscuri in Greek mythology, twin heroes or demigods Castor and Polydeukes (Pollux in Latin), sons of Leda and Zeus, reunited as stars in the sky after Castor's death; patrons of athletes, soldiers, and mariners

distyle consisting of two columns

distyle in antis two columns between two antae (see also anta)

djed ancient Egyptian symbol of stability and endurance, often depicted as a pillar with four capitals

dolmen megalithic monument, usually for burial, consisting of two or more upright stones supporting a horizontal stone slab (from Celtic *dol* [table] and *men* [stone])

domus upper-class Roman residence

domus ecclesia private house transformed into a center for a community's religious needs in early Christianity

donjon in Crusader architecture, strongest part of a fortress; usually an inner, two-storied tower; a keep

Doric order most austere of the three Greek architectural orders, distinguished by its plain capitals and triglyph frieze

draft narrow border along the edge of a stone or across its face, serving as a stone cutter's guide

drafting dressing one or more edges of the face of a stone block to facilitate laying a neat joint

dressed stone trimmed and smoothed stone

dromos horizontal or sloping passage forming the entrance to an underground chamber

drum cylindrical part of a column shaft resembling a drum in shape

duck-bill ax Middle Bronze Age IIA elongated fenestrated axhead

Early Dynastic period period in S. Mesopotamia (c. 2900–2350 BCE) during which Sumerian city-states flourished

Eastern (Byzantine) church communion of dioceses (regional churches) in the East according primacy to the patriarch of Constantinople

Eastern terra sigillata red slipped pottery, mainly bowls and plates, common throughout the eastern Mediterranean region from the 2nd cent. BCE to 2nd cent. CE, manufactured in Cyprus, Asia Minor, and probably other areas of the region

echinus convex molding supporting the abacus of a Doric capital; the molding carved with egg-and-dart under the cushion of an Ionic capital

egg-and-dart ornamental molding of oval elements alternating with downward-pointing darts, originating in Greek architecture

El head of the Canaanite pantheon

electron spin resonance (ESR) dating technique based on measuring the quantity of electrons trapped in the crystal structure of naturally irradiated substances (cf. thermoluminescence dating)

emporium(-ia) trade center

***'en* (Heb.), *'ein/'ain* (Arab.)** spring

engaged order decorative order that projects from and is an integral part of the wall it stands against

entablature collective architectural term applied to the architrave, frieze, and cornice

eparchy district, province; administrative division in Hellenistic and Roman times

epigraphy study of ancient inscriptions (see also paleography)

Esdraelon ware/culture Early Bronze Age I pottery group in northern Israel consisting of gray burnished vessels

ethnarchy country ruled by an ethnarch, the "ruler of the people"

ethrog a lemonlike fruit, one of the "four species" carried by Jews at Succoth, the Feast of Tabernacles

Eucharist Christian celebration of communion with God; the consecrated bread and wine

Eusebius' *Onomasticon* see onomasticon

Execration texts Egyptian texts (20th and 19th cent. BCE) inscribed with the names of rulers of towns and ethnic groups in Palestine and Syria, accompanied by execrations and curses; constitutes an important source concerning these regions in the Middle Bronze Age II

exedra semicircular or rectangular recess; later, a portico in houses

facade front or other face of a building

facies common resemblance among plants, animals, fossils, lithic assemblages, of an epoch or area

faience a glazed ceramic material, usually consisting of a crushed quartz or sandy body with lime and either natron or ash, coated with a glossy glaze; used mainly to produce small vessels, decorations, and jewelry

fascia(-ae) plain horizontal band

Fatimid Shi'ite ruling dynasty in N. Africa, Egypt, Syria, and Palestine from the 10th to 12th cent.

favissa(-ae) repository for discarded cultic objects

fibula(-ae) clasp in the shape of a safety pin or brooch

field a large excavation plot composed of many squares

fill soil, gravel, sand, occupational debris, etc., brought to an area to level or raise a floor or other structure; natural accumulation

First Intermediate period period in Egypt from c. 2180 to 2133 BCE, between the end of the Old Kingdom and beginning of the Middle Kingdom

First Jewish Revolt great revolt by the Jews of Palestine (67–70 CE) against Rome, culminating in the destruction of the Temple in Jerusalem in 70 CE

First Temple period period from the building of the Temple in Jerusalem by King Solomon in the 10th cent. BCE to its destruction by King Nebuchadnezzar of Babylon in 586 BCE

fish plate flat plate with circular depression in center, common in the eastern Mediterranean region from the 4th cent. BCE to the Early Roman period; originally produced in Attica (and only then rarely decorated with fish motifs) and later manufactured throughout the eastern Mediterranean Basin

flake fragment chipped off a stone core

flint tool artifact with intentional shaping of its surfaces or edges, usually by retouch

fluting rounded grooves on a column

forum marketplace of a Roman city, usually its civic center (see also agora)

fosse wide ditch or trench, especially outside a city wall

foundation trench long, narrow trench dug for a wall's founding courses

four-room house characteristic Iron Age structure sometimes attributed to the Israelites, consisting of three rooms or pillared spaces around a rectangular, fourth space, possibly a courtyard open to the sky

fresco decorative painting made with pigments on freshly spread, moist lime plaster

frieze middle member of an entablature, often carved in sculptural relief

frigidarium cold room in a Roman bath

gable triangular, upper end of a building above the cornice

gallery roofed promenade (colonnade) or outdoor balcony

garum fish sauce popular in the Roman period

Gaza ware/jar chocolate-colored clay jar with cylindrical body and rounded, ribbed shoulders, produced from the late 3rd to 6th cent. in Gaza and perhaps Ashkelon; intensively used in maritime trade and found throughout the Roman Empire

geison see cornice

Gemara rabbinic commentary on and interpretation of the Mishnah

genizah repository in a synagogue for discarded sacred books and objects

Gerzean see Naqada

Ghassulian Chalcolithic culture of the fifth and fourth millennia, named after Tuleilat el-Ghassul in the Jordan Valley

glacis diagonal coating of an earthen rampart, slope of a mound, or fortification wall for defensive and constructional purposes; constructed of stone, compact earth, bricks, etc.

graffito(-i) drawing or writing scratched on plaster, pottery, or stone

grainwash (band slip) technique method of jar decoration of the Early Bronze Age I in which painted bands were applied with wide brushes

granulation decoration with tiny (usually gold) balls used in jewelry

griffin Near Eastern and later Greek mythological being, half eagle, half lion; winged lion

guilloche decorative pattern of intersecting bands forming a plait

gutta(-ae) small, droplike motif under the frieze in a Doric entablature

Habiru unsettled people in Late Bronze Age Canaan having no property rights; mentioned in the el-Amarna letters and identified by some scholars with the ancient Hebrews

Ḥalafian N. Mesopotamian and N. Syrian culture (c. 5300–4300 BCE), characterized by first administrative use of stamp seals, tholoi structures, and typical elaborate pottery decorated with monochrome, bichrome, or trichrome geometric and naturalistic designs

half column semicolumn of an engaged order

***ḥamra* (Arab.)** red sandy soil, common mainly on Israel's Sharon Plain

hand ax stone tool bifacially worked with a pointed end, used for cutting

***har* (Heb.)** mountain (cf. *jebel/gebel*)

***ḥaram* (Arab.)** sanctuary

Ḥarifian culture of the Negev and Sinai, contemporary with the Final Natufian and earliest Pre-Pottery Neolithic A cultures of the north; lithic assemblage characterized by the Harif point

Ḥarif point point made on a flint bladelet using microburin technique; retouched on one edge, with triangular or shouldered tang

Hathor ancient Egyptian goddess of joy and love, protectress of women, and sky goddess, often represented as a cow; attributes: sun disk, cow's horns, "Hathor pillar," sistrum

header in masonry, a stone or brick with its narrow end in the face of a wall, usually extending all the way through the wall (cf. stretcher)

Hegira Muhammad's flight from Mecca to Medina in 622 CE, the start of the Muslim era (abbreviated AH)

Helios Greek sun god (equivalent of Greek and Roman god Apollo and Roman god Phoebus)

Helwan point made on a flint blade or bladelet, with bilateral notches and tang; sometimes with shoulders and minute wings or barbs

Hermes Greek messenger of the gods, god of commerce, god of thieves (equivalent of Roman god Mercury)

Herodian lamp Judean wheel-made, plain oil lamp, characterized by a spatula-shaped scraped nozzle, produced from c. 25 BCE to 150 CE; rare outside Judea

Hexapla text edition of the Hebrew Bible compiled in the 3rd cent. by Origen; consists of the Hebrew text, Greek translation, and four Greek versions, including the Septuagint

hexastyle consisting of six columns

hieratic script Egyptian cursive script used mainly for everyday purposes, mostly written on papyri or ostraca

hieroglyphic script (Egyptian) script invented in c. 3000 BCE, composed of phonograms and semograms, used mainly in monumental inscriptions and decorations

himation long, loose outer garment worn in the ancient world by men and women

hipparch cavalry commander in the ancient Greek world

hippodamic plan town plan in which the streets intersect at right angles, sometimes ascribed to Hippodamos of Miletus (5th cent. BCE) but actually not invented by him (see also orthogonal plan)

hole-mouth jar type of jar with a wide mouth and no neck, used for storage and food preparation

holy of holies inner chamber of cultic sanctuary; innermost chamber of a temple

Homo erectus Lower Paleolithic human type found throughout the Old World; cranial capacity 1,000–1,200 cc

Homo sapiens modern human type of Upper Paleolithic origin found throughout the world; earlier appearance in the Levant, c. 100,000 years ago; cranial capacity 1,400 cc

horreum(-ea) storage or granary building

Horus ancient Egyptian sky god; hawk or hawk-headed, often shown wearing the double crown

Horus eye wedjet eye of the hawk-headed Egyptian god Horus, used as a protective charm

***ḥorvah (ḥorvat)* (Heb.)** ruin (cf. *khirbeh*)

Hospitaller knights Crusader religious-military order established in Jerusalem in the 11th cent.; its members were dedicated to healing the sick, aiding the poor, and fighting the Muslims (see also Templar knights)

***ḥuwwar* (Arab.)** white, soft earth composed of a mixture of clayey soil and chalk; after water absorption the soil turns into an aquiclude

hydraulic plaster water-repellent plaster, used mainly for lining water installations

Hyksos 15th Dynasty in Egypt; foreign, Semitic rulers in Lower Egypt; "Hyksos period" used by some scholars to denote Middle Bronze Age IIB–C; "Hyksos fortifications" used to denote massive fortifications of those periods

hyparchy administrative unit in Hellenistic and Roman times

hypocaust hollow space beneath the floor of a caldarium or tepidarium in a Roman bath through which hot air was circulated

iconoclastic of a religious movement opposed to the cult or depiction of images and upholding their destruction or obliteration

iconography imagery or symbolism in art

in antis columns set between two antae (see anta)

indiction fifteen-year cycle inaugurated by Constantine for taxation purposes; a date given by the indiction (e.g., "year 3 of the indiction") is relative and can be reckoned only with the help of additional data

in situ literally, "in place"; refers to undisturbed artifacts and architectural remains

insula(-ae) city block, usually quadrangular, with multiple dwellings

intercolumniation distance between the centers of two adjacent columns

intrados underside of an arch or vault

Ionic order one of the three Greek orders of architecture, characterized by its volute capitals

Isis Egyptian guardian goddess, wife of Osiris, often depicted with her son Horus/Harpocrates

isodomic masonry masonry laid in courses of equal height

Iturea Arab kingdom south of Damascus in Hellenistic and Early Roman times

Jannaeus line fortifications built by Alexander Jannaeus along the Yarkon River in the late 2nd cent. BCE

***jebel/gebel* (Arab.)** mountain (cf. *har*)

Jemdet Nasr culture/period S. Mesopotamian culture (c. 3100–2900 BCE)

Jericho point Pre-Pottery Neolithic B point made on a flint blade, with tang and shoulders graduating from a straight angle to barbs or wings; tang is either elongated, tonguelike, or triangular

juglet small, one-handled container for liquids

karstic rock limestone with sinkholes, underground streams, and caverns

Kebaran Epipaleolithic hunter-gatherer culture, concentrated mainly in northern Israel; lithic assemblage characterized by microliths (Kebara point)

***kerbschnitt* technique** chip carving

kernos(-oi) ceramic vessel consisting of several small vessels and/or figurines joined on a ring or attached to the rim of a vase

khan caravanserai; accommodation for caravans, consisting of a courtyard with a single gate and niches or rooms opening all around

Khiamian Pre-Pottery Neolithic A culture, characterized by el-Khiam points and the first appearance of villages

el-Khiam point Pre-Pottery Neolithic A point made on a small blade or bladelet, with two bilateral notches close to its base that is concave or straight

***khirbeh (khirbet)* (Arab.)** ruin

Khirbet el-Mafjar ware unglazed, white to yellowish pottery comprising basins, bowls, jars, jugs, and juglets, plain or with incised, applied, and stamped decoration; ascribed to the Abbasid period, end of the 8th and especially 9th–10th cent. (a term less frequently used today)

Khirbet Kerak ware Early Bronze Age III pottery named after Khirbet Kerak (Beth Yerah); comprising handmade vessels with hand-burnished red and/or black slip and plastic decorations, possibly inspired by Anatolian pottery; common mainly in N. Israel and in Syria

King's Highway one of the two most important highways that connected Egypt with Mesopotamia, crossing Transjordan from north to south, close to the desert's fringe (see also Way of the Sea)

koine in this work, large international or intercultural area featuring common cultural traits

***kokh(-im)* (Heb.)** Roman period rock-cut burial place (cf. loculus)

krater large bowl; mixing bowl

Kufic script early, angular form of the Arabic alphabet named after the city of Kufa in southern Iraq; used in monumental inscriptions and decorations

kurkar fossilized dune sandstone

kylix wide, shallow, footed drinking cup with two horizontal handles

Lachish letters ostraca inscribed in Hebrew, found at Lachish and dated to the last days of Judah, containing important information about this period

***lamelekh* (Heb.) seal impressions** literally, "(belonging) to the king"; seal impressions on Judahite jar handles of the late 8th cent. BCE depicting a four-winged beetle or a two-winged object and one of four place names: Hebron, Socoh, Ziph, or *Mmšt*; their exact administrative function is under debate

lapidary of stone; lapidary script, script used for monumental inscriptions engraved on stone

lapis lazuli semiprecious blue stone, used mainly for small artifacts and inlays; imported from Afghanistan

larnax(-kes) clay or stone chestlike sarcophagus

Late Assyrian period see Neo-Assyrian period

laura monastery of hermits in the Eastern church; a collection of hermit cells connected by paths around a common church

legatus in the Roman army, lieutenant (deputy) general of a legion; in the Roman administration, the governor of a province directly administered by the emperor

lekane(-ai) Greek basin-shaped vessel

lekythos(-oi) Greek cylindrical, round, or squat vase with one handle, used for oils and ointments

Levalloisian technique prehistoric technological tradition of stone tool manufacture by striking flakes off cores in a preplanned sequence according to the shape of the final product (Late Acheulean and Mousterian cultures)

Levant countries of the eastern Mediterranean: Israel, Jordan, Lebanon, and Syria

levigated clay clay from which impurities have been removed

lime plaster plaster made of ground shells or limestone

limes fortified frontier region in the Roman Empire

limitanei soldiers stationed in the *limes* area

lithic assemblage collection of stone or flint implements

liwan courtyard of a mosque

loculus(-i) rectangular, shelflike burial niche in a tomb (cf. *kokh*)

locus(-i) three-dimensional feature in a stratigraphical excavation: a layer of earth, a wall, a pit, a room, etc., usually one depositional unit; definition varies from excavation to excavation

loess fine, yellowish-gray loam

lost-wax technique technique for casting metal objects consisting of making a wax model on an inner clay core, coating it with clay to form a mold, heating until the wax melts, then pouring the hot metal into the space left vacant

lug handle cylindrical handle, often longitudinally pierced

lulab palm branch carried in the ritual of the Feast of Tabernacles (Succoth) (see also ethrog)

lunate prehistoric microlith shaped like a crescent

machiculation opening between the corbels supporting the parapet of a fortress through which molten lead and projectiles were dropped on attackers; embrasure

madrasa Muslim school, developed by the Mamelukes

Mamelukes military class of former slaves, mostly Turks and Circassians, who ruled Egypt from 1250 to 1517, as well as Syria, Palestine, and parts of Mesopotamia and Asia Minor; constituted a type of military feudal aristocracy, replenishing its ranks by the purchase of new slaves

mansio station where travelers rested and changed horses

Mari documents Akkadian cuneiform letters and administrative records excavated at Mari on the Euphrates, dating to the 18th cent. BCE; some of them mention cities in Canaan

martyrium chapel or church dedicated to a martyr; place where relics of martyrs are preserved

Masoretic accepted text of the Hebrew Bible

***maṣṣeba(-ot)* (Heb.)** ritual standing stone(s)

mausoleum elaborate monumental tomb; named after the tomb erected by Queen Artemisia for her husband, Mausolos, in Halicarnassos in the 4th cent. BCE

***mazra'ah* (Arab.)** literally, "farm"; mainly seasonal agricultural settlement or plot

meander decorative, continuous key pattern originating in Greek art

Medeba (Madaba) map mosaic pavement in a Byzantine church at Medeba, representing a map of the Holy Land, dated to the second half of the 6th cent.

Medusa in Greek mythology, one of three snake-haired sisters (Gorgons), whose glance turned beholders to stone

Megarian bowls mold-made hemispherical relief bowls common throughout the eastern Mediterranean region from the 2nd to 1st cent. BCE, manufactured in Attic, Ionic, and other workshops in the region; decorated with geometric, floral and pictographic motifs

megaron Mycenean three-unit longhouse whose inner room (inner megaron) often contains a hearth surrounded by four columns; basic and simplest architectural form of a Greek temple; also loosely used to describe long and narrow houses and temples with an open porch flanked by two antae and often having columns

menhir single, upright, unworked monolith

menorah seven-branched candelabrum (candlestick) used in Jewish ritual

metope space between two triglyphs, either filled with relief sculpture or left plain

***meẓad* (Heb.)** fort

microburin technique (MBT) knapping technique used in production of microlithic flint tools in most Epipaleolithic cultures

microlith small flint tool usually made on a bladelet, typical of Epipaleolithic cultures

Midianite ware pottery vessels found at several sites in southern Canaan and Transjordan, mainly in 13th- and 12th-cent. BCE contexts; thought to originate in northwestern Arabia; decorated mainly with black and red geometric designs

Middle Assyrian period period in Assyria from c. 1365 to 1000 BCE

miḥrab chamber or niche in a mosque marking the direction of Mecca

mikveh Jewish ritual bath used for purification

milk bowls Cypriot hemispherical bowls with wishbone-shaped handles of the white slip pottery group, Late Cypriot period; brown, latticelike geometric decoration on a thick white slip; a very common import on the mainland in the Late Bronze Age (less frequent in Middle Bronze Age IIC)

minaret tower from which the Muslim call to prayer is made

minbar freestanding pulpit in a mosque

Minoan Bronze Age culture of Crete, c. 3000 to 1100 BCE

Mishnah collection of oral Jewish law and traditions, compiled c. 200 CE; the basic part of the Talmud

Mitanni kingdom dominant in N. Mesopotamia and N. Syria, c. 1500 to mid-14th cent. BCE

Mitannian seals cylinder seals engraved in a style originating in the kingdom of Mitanni in Mesopotamia; frequent in 14th-cent. BCE contexts in Canaan and probably produced locally; made of frit, mainly with animal representations

***mizzi* (Arab.)** hard limestone

***mizzi aḥmar* (Arab.)** red-veined limestone; a hard dolomitic rock

monoapsidal church church with a single apse

monolith pillar or other architectural part composed of a single stone

mortarium(-ia) thick, heavy pottery bowls, mainly from the late Iron Age and Persian period but also Hellenistic and Roman periods

Mousterian Middle Paleolithic culture, characterized by use of the Levallois technique and tools with retouched edges, side scrapers, and points

mural crown crown on a Tyche, the goddess of fortune, in the shape of a city's defensive wall

murex shells mollusk that was the chief source of Phoenician purple dye (mainly *Murex Brandaris* and *Murex Trunculus*)

Mycenean Late Bronze Age culture (Late Helladic, c. 1500–1200 BCE) in Greece and the Aegean islands

Mycenean IIIA–B pottery Mycenean pottery of the 14th–13th cent. BCE; a very frequent import in Syria/Canaan in the Late Bronze Age

Mycenean IIIC pottery Mycenean and Mycenean-derived pottery of the 12th cent. BCE, characterized by regional variations; Mycenean IIIC:1b type was found in Cyprus and on the Levantine coast, mostly produced locally; associated with the arrival of the Sea Peoples

***naḥal* (Heb.)** river, brook, seasonal streambed (cf. wadi)

naos shrine; cella of a (usually Greek) temple

Naqada fourth millennium BCE culture in the Nile Valley (Naqada I also called Amratian and Naqada II, Gerzean)

narthex antechamber, inside or outside, to the nave in a Christian church (from 5th cent.)

Natufian last Epipaleolithic culture, characterized by the onset of sedentarism and the appearance of sickle blades, art objects, cemeteries, and ground stone utensils

nave elongated central hall in a basilica or church

nawamis circular stone burial chambers with corbeled roofs in southern Sinai

Neanderthal human type, adapted to cold, of the European Middle Paleolithic; cranial capacity 1,400 cc; claimed to be present in the Levant at the same time as modern *Homo sapiens*

necropolis Greek for cemetery (literally, "city of the dead"); used mainly to denote large and important cemeteries

***nefesh* (Heb.)** in Semitic cultures, a memorial stela or monument erected above a tomb (literally, "soul")

Negbite pottery rough handmade ware of the late Late Bronze and Iron ages common in the Negev desert and Arabah; thought to have been produced by seminomads

Neo-Assyrian period period of the Assyrian Empire (c. 911–612 BCE)

Neo-Babylonian period period of the Babylonian Empire (625–539 BCE)

neutron activation analysis (NAA) determining an object's chemical profile by analyzing relative quantities of (mainly) trace elements, based on the spectroscopy of gamma rays (in a nuclear reactor); used to identify a stone or clay vessel's provenance

niche hollowed recess in a wall to hold, for example, a Torah ark (in a synagogue), a statue, an interment (in a tomb), or for decorative purposes

Nike (Victory) Greek goddess of victory

nilometer graduated pillar or staircase showing the height to which the Nile rises

Notitia Dignitatum list of military commands and of troops at the commanders' disposal in the provinces of the Byzantine Empire, compiled in the early 5th cent.

nṣf ancient Judean weight, probably 5/6 of a shekel (cf. shekel weight)

nymphaeum(-a) in this work, a public fountain (in Roman architecture); a monumental structure, richly decorated, located in the public areas of Roman cities in the imperial period

obsidian hard, black "volcanic glass," used in making stone tools and jewelry; in the Levant, found only in Anatolia

occupational debris soil mixed with other material characteristic of human occupation: bone, pottery, charcoal, ash, etc.

ocher an earthy, usually red or yellow iron oxide used extensively as a pigment

odeon(-ea) small roofed theater, used mainly for musical performances

officina workshop

onomasticon alphabetical list of place names mentioned in the Bible and identified by the author with contemporary sites; most generally used is the one written (in Greek) by Eusebius, bishop of Caesarea, in the early 4th cent. and translated and annotated (in Latin) by Jerome in the late 4th cent.

opus quadratum Roman ashlar masonry of large, squared stones laid in horizontal courses

opus reticulatum Roman masonry facing consisting of a network of small, pyramidal blocks laid in neat, diagonal lines, their bases facing outward

opus sectile paving of shaped, colored stone or marble tiles

orchestra circular space in front of the stage in a Greek theater or semicircular space in a Roman theater

orthogonal plan city/town plan of parallel streets intersecting at right angles (cf. hippodamic plan)

orthostat upright stone slab, used mainly for lining walls and pilasters, sometimes shaped like an animal or other form

ossilegium custom of gathering bones of a corpse after the flesh has decayed and depositing them in an ossuary

ossuary receptacle for bones after the flesh has decayed (secondary burial)

ostracon(-a) inscribed sherd

ovolo convex molding originating in Greek architecture (see egg-and-dart)

palaestra an open area for sport and training activities; a part of a gymnasium or baths in the Roman imperial period

paleography study of ancient alphabets, writing styles, and inscriptions (see also epigraphy)

paleomagnetism (paleomagnetic stratigraphy) series of past fluctuations in the intensity and direction of the earth's magnetic field (polarity); sequence of polarity changes for the past 5 million years is well known and can be used in dating

Pan Greek god of shepherds and hunters

parapet low, protective wall

parocheth richly ornamented curtain hung in front of the holy ark in a synagogue; curtain used to screen the holy of holies in the Temple in Jerusalem

parodos(-oi) side entrance to the orchestra in a Greek theater (cf. *aditus maximus*)

patera(-ae) shallow bowl for pouring libations

pediment in Greek and Roman architecture, the triangular space below a gabled roof, including the horizontal and raking cornices

pendentive section of masonry forming a curved triangle supporting a dome over a rectangular base

peribolos exterior enclosure around a temple, or the wall bounding such an enclosure

peripteral of a continuous outer ring of columns

peristyle open courtyard surrounded by columns

petroglyph rock carving

Peutinger map see *Tabula Peutingeriana*

Pharisee member of the traditional party of Jews in the Second Temple period noted for their strict observance of the law (cf. Sadducee)

phase stage; subdivision of a stratum (see also stratum); a reuse or rebuilding of a structure or smaller feature, such as a repair of a wall or floor

Philistine pottery pottery characteristic of sites in Philistia in the 12th–early 10th cent. BCE; decorated mainly with geometric, fish, and bird motifs in black and red, often on a white slip, featuring a mixture of Mycenean, Cypriot, Canaanite, and Egyptian traits

pier vertical structural support of roofing, sometimes flanking doors or windows; rectangular in section

pilaster engaged pier projecting only slightly from a wall

pilgrim flask flat, circular (usually ceramic) liquid container

piscina(-ae) pool; literally, a "fish pond"; perforated stone basin near the altar in a church

pisé stiff clay used as a building material

pithos(-oi) large storage jar

plano-convex brick or stone with flat base and convex top

podium platform; high basement of a building

polis Greek city-state

portico colonnade or covered ambulatory at the entrance to a building

postern small opening in a structure or fortification wall

principia headquarters of a Roman military camp

probe small exploratory trench or pit excavated to clarify the nature of the underlying deposits (see also sounding)

pronaos area in front of a temple's sanctuary (space in front of a naos)

propylaeum(-a) gateway to a sanctuary, usually marked by a monumental structure

proscenium stage of a theater

prostyle freestanding columns in front of a portico and across a structure's entire front

prothesis in this work, church area for storing eucharistic elements before consecration

proto-Aeolic capital stone capital decorated with volutes (stylized palmettes) typical mainly of Israelite/Judean monumental architecture

Proto-Canaanite script alphabetic acrophonic script that developed in Canaan in the late Middle Bronze or Late Bronze Age; forerunner of most alphabetic scripts

pym ancient Judean weight, probably 2/3 of a shekel (cf. shekel weight)

pyxis (pyxides) small, usually cylindrical, box or container, usually lidded

***qanatir* (Arab.)** arcade; especially the arched colonnades on the platform of the Dome of the Rock

Qos chief Edomite deity

racloir scraper

Ramonian desertic cultural entity, contemporary with the Late Geometric Kebaran and Early Natufian of the north; typical lithic tools are variants of the northern Kebara point (Ramon point) and the bifacial retouched microlith (Helwan lunate)

rampart raised earth mound or embankment used as a fortification; fortification wall

red-figure Greek style of pottery painting in which the background is black and the figures are left in the natural orange color of the vessel and decorated with diluted paint and some added colors; produced mainly in Athens from the end of the 6th to mid-4th cent. BCE and exported to the Levant in the Persian period (cf. black-figure)

red ware Late Roman-Byzantine pottery, characterized by red oxidation firing and sometimes slipped with the same clay (see terra sigillata)

repository deposit of (valuable) objects; treasury; place in tomb for collecting bones and offerings

repoussé hammering of sheet metal on a mold

Reshef Canaanite/Phoenician deity, smith and craftsman

retouch minute flaking of a flint artifact, to shape and regularize its edge

revetment retaining wall or facing (mainly of fortifications)

rhyton(-a) vessel for liquids; drinking vessel, usually shaped like a funnel, cone, animal, or the head of an animal

robber trench trench dug in antiquity to dismantle walls in order to reuse their stones; indicates the former lines of the walls

***rogem* (Heb.), *rujum* (Arab.)** literally, "stone pile" (cf. tumulus)

rope decoration plastic decoration resembling a rope, common on pottery vessels

rotunda circular structure

Sadducee member of the priestly Jewish aristocracy (2nd cent. BCE to 1st cent. CE); opposed the Pharisees' literal interpretation of the law

Safaitic Arabic dialect and script of the es-Safa region in N. Arabia

salvage excavation emergency excavation, usually carried out before modern construction

Samaria ostraca Sixty-three 9th- or 8th-cent. BCE ostraca uncovered at Samaria, recording dispatches of wine and oil; containing important linguistic, topographical, and economic data relating to the kingdom of Israel

Samaria ware (thin)/Samaria bowls shallow, fine ware bowls of the Iron Age II decorated with highly burnished yellow and red bands; once thought to have been produced in Samaria but probably manufactured in various Phoenican and Israelite centers

Sanhedrin highest court of justice and supreme council of the Jewish people (1st cent. BCE to 6th cent. CE)

sarcophagus(-i) stone coffin

satrapy provincial governorship in the Persian Empire

satyr semidivine being, represented as a man with ears, tail, and hooves of a goat, dweller of woods; often a companion of Dionysus, the god of wine

scaena(-ae) stage building in a Roman theater

scaenae frons facade of a Roman stage building formed by the backdrop of the stage

scalaria staircase in a theater, amphitheater, or circus

scarab beetle-shaped stamp seal, mainly Egyptian

scotia concave molding, usually between the two torus moldings of a column base (cf. torus)

scraper flint flake or blade retouched either on the edges (side scraper) or extremities (end scraper); typical of Middle and Upper Paleolithic industries

scriptorium place where books were written or copied

Sea Peoples collective name for groups of seafarers who invaded the coasts of the eastern Mediterranean toward the end of the Bronze Age (13th cent. BCE), among them the Philistines; associated with the violent overthrow of old political orders in Greece, Asia Minor, and the Levantine coast

Second Intermediate period period in Egypt from c. 1670 to 1570 BCE, between the end of the Middle Kingdom and beginning of the New Kingdom; period of Hyksos rule (cf. Hyksos)

Second Temple period period in Israel beginning with the return of the Babylonian exiles in 536 BCE and ending with the destruction of Jerusalem and the Temple in 70 CE

secondary burial the reburial of bones after the flesh has decomposed (see also ossilegium, ossuary)

section two-dimensional face of a balk; a drawing of a balk

Septuagint pre-Christian (3rd–2nd cent. BCE) Greek translation of the Hebrew Bible, written, according to legend, by 70 scholars in 70 days; the first vernacular translation

***serekh* (Arab.)** literally, "palace facade"; rectangular frame containing the pharaoh's name, surmounted by the hawk of the Egyptian god Horus

shaft tomb a subsurface tomb reached through a vertical shaft

Shasu seminomadic groups in Canaan referred to in Egyptian New Kingdom sources; considered by some scholars to be the biblical Hebrews

shekel a coin used between the 2nd cent. BCE and 2nd cent. CE in Syria-Palestine

shekel weight dome-shaped weight (c. 11.4 g) used in Judah and Philistia in the Iron Age II; rarely found in the north or in Transjordan (cf. *beqa'*, *pym*, *nṣf*)

Shephelah literally, "lowland"; the hilly region between Israel's southern Coastal Plain and the Judean foothills

sherd potsherd; broken piece of pottery

shofar ram's horn sounded in the Jewish New Year ritual

sistrum Egyptian musical instrument, resembling a rattle, sacred to Hathor

skyphos(-oi) Greek drinking cup with handles; chalice

slag waste material formed as a by-product of (mainly) iron or copper smelting

slip mixed clay and water coating on pottery

socle base or pedestal for columns; the lower part of a wall

soffit underside of an architectural member (e.g., architrave)

solidus(-i) Byzantine gold coin weighing 4.54 g (1/72 of a Roman libra [pound]); introduced by Emperor Constantine in the 4th cent., in use in the Near East until the end of the Byzantine Empire (7th cent.)

sounding exploratory excavation (see also probe)

spatula(-ae) small stick with one end wider than the other, used to mix or spread paste (generally cosmetics)

spheroid rounded artifact, usually made of limestone and shaped by battering; typical of Lower Paleolithic industries

stela(-ae) upright slab or pillar, often with inscription or artistic depiction (see also *maṣṣeba*)

stirrup jar/vase small jar with two handles and false spout, common in Mycenean, Minoan, and Philistine pottery

stoa Greek freestanding building, usually one story high, consisting of a long rear wall and a row of columns in front bearing a sloping roof; roofed portico

strategus officer associated with a hipparch as the chief executive in the boule in ancient Greece

stratification superimposed occupational layers as they are uncovered in excavation

stratigraphy process of observation, recording, reconstruction and interpretation of stratification

stratum(-a) the combination of all loci belonging to one construction, habitation, and destruction cycle, representing one historical and cultural period of habitation at a site; usually distinguished from one another by differences in soil makeup, architecture, artifacts, etc.

stretcher in masonry construction, a stone or brick whose long side is in the wall's face (cf. header)

string course horizontal, continuous row in a facade, sometimes ornamental

stucco coating of high-quality plaster or cement, often molded

stylite Christian ascetic who lives on top of a column

stylobate continuous base supporting a row or rows of columns

Sultanian culture from the later phase of the Pre-Pottery Neolithic A; lithic assemblage characterized by bifacial flaking and polished axes with transversal blows; villages with stone and mud-brick structures

surface modern topsoil; ancient topsoil; a floor, courtyard, or other plane on which human activity took place

synthronon bench for clergy within a church's chancel area, usually along the apse wall

Syrian gable gable with an arch in its central lower part, commonly found in Roman architecture of the East (e.g., in synagogues)

tabula ansata representation in a floor or wall of a tablet with triangular handles, intended to carry an inscription

Tabula Peutingeriana road map of the Roman provinces drawn by the Roman cartographer Castorius (c. 365 CE) from an archetype created in the 2nd cent.; preserved in an 11th–12th cent. copy; records main roads, cities, and towns and the distances between them in Roman miles; section X depicts Palestine

***tabun* (Arab.)** clay "beehive" oven, usually with large sherds pressed into its outer surface

talent ancient weight and money unit; heaviest unit of weight system and highest value of monetary system

Talmud interpretation of the Mishnah and the Gemarah (c. 200–500 CE)

Targum any of several Aramaic translations or paraphrases of the Hebrew Bible

tel (Heb.), tell (Arab.) artificial mound

Tell el-Yahudiyeh ware Middle Bronze Age IIB pottery group, mainly jugs, juglets, and zoomorphic vessels decorated with geometric designs created by punctured holes filled with white lime; named after the site of Tell el-Yahudiyeh in the Egyptian Delta region and associated by some scholars with the Hyksos; apparently produced both in Egypt and the Levant

temenos sacred precinct (sanctuary), encircled by a wall

Templar knights 12th cent. military order in Jerusalem established to protect pilgrims and the Church of the Holy Sepulcher (cf. Hospitaller knights)

tepidarium warm room in a Roman bath

terminus ante quem latest datable period to which an event or an object can belong, based on the accompanying dated evidence

terminus post quem earliest datable period to which an event or an object can belong, based on the accompanying dated evidence

terra cotta typically reddish, unglazed ceramic (earthenware) material

terra rossa brown-red, fertile clayey soils formed from hard limestone (see also *ḥamra*)

terra sigillata literally, "stamped earth/clay"; pottery with red, glossy surface, sometimes stamped with potters' marks and decorated with molded decoration; of Italian and Gaulish provenance, produced from the 1st cent. BCE to 2nd cent. CE (cf. Eastern terra sigillata)

terre pisée literally, "beaten earth"

tessera(-ae) small square(s) or cube(s) used to form a mosaic

tête-bêche arrangement of two objects with the head of each one at the foot of the other

tetradrachm coin of four drachms (of different weight, according to the standard)

tetrapylon structure of four piers bearing columns built at the intersection of main streets in a Roman city

tetrarch governor of the fourth part of a country or province within the Roman Empire (instituted by Diocletian in 292 CE)

tetrastyle consisting of four columns

Thamudic Arabic dialect and script used by the Thamudenes of northern Hejaz

Theotokos "Mother of God," epithet of Mary, mother of Jesus

tholos round, domed building

thermoluminescence (TL) dating depends on the fact that electrons become trapped in the crystal structure of naturally irradiated substances; when the substance is heated, the electrons are released along with a quantity of light (TL) directly proportional to the number of trapped electrons; the amount of TL can be used to estimate the time elapsed since an object was last heated (see electron spin resonance)

toparch minor ruler of a small state or district consisting of a few cities or towns

toparchy district governed by a toparch

torus convex molding, usually on a column base (cf. scotia)

Tosefta supplement to the Mishnah

tournette potter's slow wheel

transept space between the nave and the apse of a church, running perpendicular to the longitudinal axis of the building

transhumance seasonal movement of livestock (especially sheep) between mountains and lowland pastures under the care of herders or accompanied by whole populations of owners

tremissis Byzantine gold coin weighing 1.5 g (1/3 of a solidus); see solidus

triclinium(-ia) dining room; derived from the three banqueting couches on which Roman diners reclined

triglyph block with three vertical grooves between metopes on a Doric frieze

tumulus(-i) small mound or stone heap, often covering a tomb (cf. *rogem/rujum*)

tuyere nozzle in a forge or furnace through which air is blown

Tyche "Fortune"; personification of good fortune; protectress of cities, usually wearing a mural crown

tympanum triangular wall above a cornice

typology grouping/taxonomy/classification of artifacts according to a feature or features (form, decoration, surface technique, manufacturing technique, etc.), to achieve various research goals such as dating and location of production centers

Ubeid culture/period Mesopotamian culture of the second half of the 5th and 4th millennia

Umayyad dynasty caliphs who ruled the Muslim Empire from 661 to 750

United Monarchy political unification of the Israelite tribes by David in the 10th cent. BCE until the division between the (northern) Israelite kingdom and the (southern) Judahite kingdom after Solomon's reign, c. 928 BCE

uraeus Egyptian symbol of kingship; a rearing cobra on a king's forehead or crown; also used as architectural decoration

Uruk culture/period Mesopotamian culture of c. 3750–3100 BCE, characterized by urbanization, monumental temples, first cylinder seals, beginning of writing

virgin soil soil undisturbed by human activity

volute spiral scroll (mainly) on an Ionic or Corinthian capital

vomitorium(-ia) entrance to a theater, amphitheater, or circus

voussoir wedge-shaped stone forming one of the units of an arch

Vulgate Latin version of the Bible authorized and used by the Roman Catholic church

wadi (Arab.) dry streambed, flooded during rainy season

waqf (Arab.) Muslim endowment fund and supervisory council

wash unfired, usually thin, light clay coating on pottery that wears off easily

Way of the Sea one of the two most important highways that connected Egypt and Mesopotamia, crossing Canaan/Israel along the Mediterranean coastline and then branching north and northeast; the "Via Maris" of later periods (see also King's Highway)

***weli* (Arab.)** monument dedicated to a Muslim saint or holy man

West Slope ware black-slipped vessels decorated with white and clay-colored paint; produced initially (end of 4th/3rd cent. BCE) in Attica and later (3rd/2nd cent. BCE) in various workshops in the eastern Mediterranean region

white-painted ware (MB and LB) Cypriot pottery group of the very end of the Early Cypriot, Middle Cypriot, and Late Cypriot periods, decorated with linear and geometric motifs in thick, lustrous red paint; several examples were found on the mainland

white-painted ware (Iron Age) Cypriot pottery group of the Cypro-Geometric and Cypro-Archaic periods, decorated with geometric and figurative designs in black or brown on a white background; several examples were found on the mainland

white slip ware Late Cypriot I–II handmade pottery, decorated with geometric patterns in orange or brown on a white slip; the "milk bowls" of the family are one of the hallmarks of the Cypriot exports to the mainland in the Late Bronze Age, starting at the end of Middle Bronze Age II (cf. "milk bowls")

***zawiyah* (Arab.)** small mosque; Muslim religious building

Zenon papyri letters discovered at the site of ancient Philadelphia in Egypt, belonging to the archive of Zenon, a treasury official under Ptolemy II (259 BCE), describing conditions in Palestine at the time and discussing commerce with Egypt

Zeus head of the Greek pantheon; king over humans and the gods (equivalent of Roman god Jupiter)

ziggurat stepped Mesopotamian temple

zoomorphic animal-shaped

INDEX TO PERSONS

INDEX TO PLACES

The index lists only the main references relating to the site.

INDEX TO BIBLICAL REFERENCES

The index lists only references cited in the text.

* In Septuagint

LIST OF COLOR ILLUSTRATIONS

Entry *Facing page*

VOLUME 1

VOLUME 2

VOLUME 3

VOLUME 4

MAIN EXCAVATIONS IN THE HOLY LAND

Additional sites appear on regional and subject maps

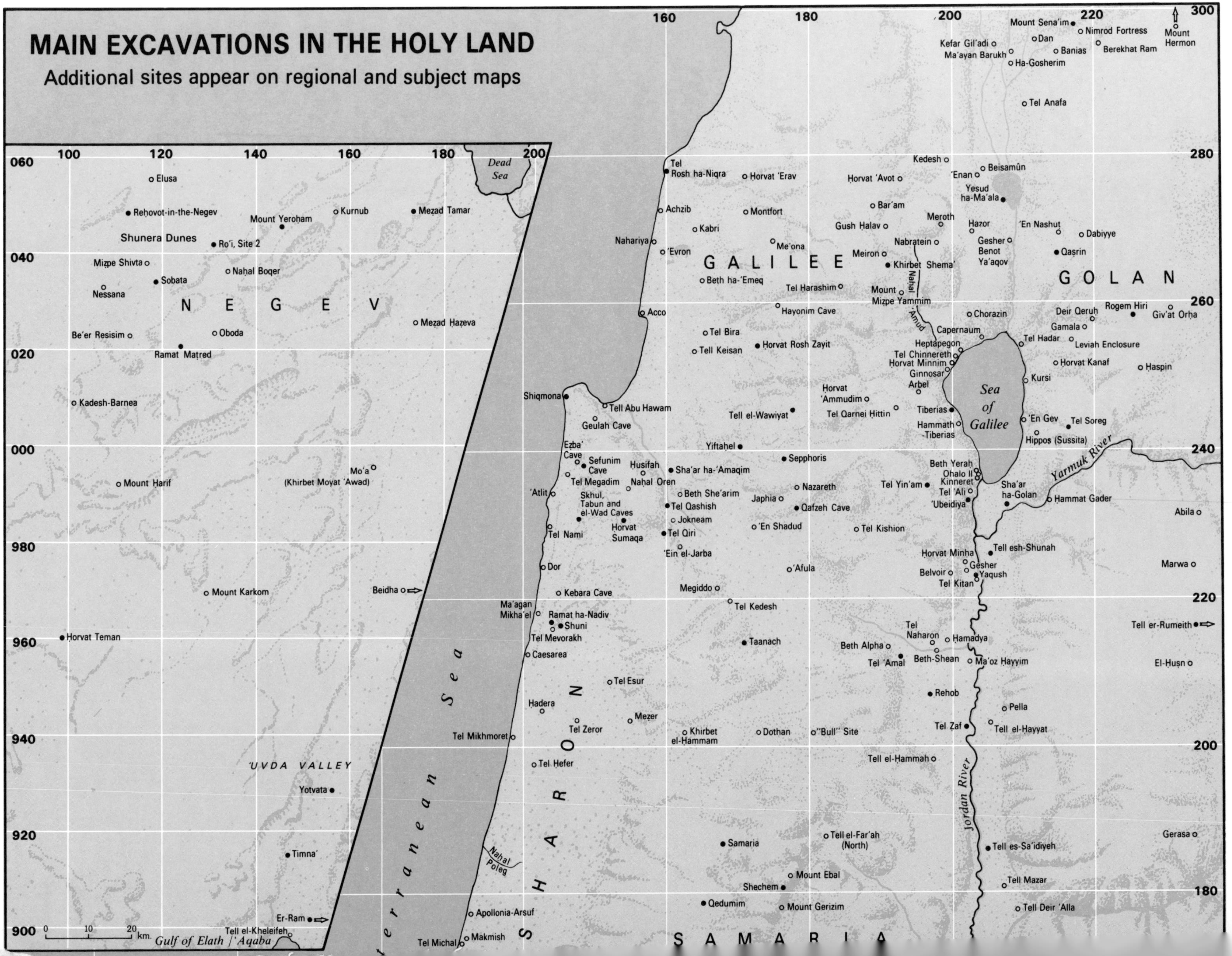